Encyclopedia of

Human Behavior

Volume 2 Cop-I

Editorial Advisory Board

Aaron T. Beck
University of Pennsylvania

David M. Buss
University of Michigan

Antonio R. Damasio
University of Iowa

William G. Iacono
University of Minnesota

Edward E. Jones
Princeton University

Jerome Kagan
Harvard University

ENCYCLOPEDIA OF HUMAN BEHAVIOR

EDITOR-IN-CHIEF
V. S. Ramachandran
University of California, San Diego
La Jolla, California

VOLUME 2 COP-I

ACADEMIC PRESS
San Diego New York Boston London Sydney Tokyo Toronto

WITHDRAWN
Theodore Lownik Library
Illinois Benedictine College
Lisle, IL 60532

150.3
E57
v.2

This book is printed on acid-free paper. ♾

Copyright © 1994 by ACADEMIC PRESS, INC.
All Rights Reserved.
No part of this publication may be reproduced or transmitted in any form or by any means, electronic or mechanical, including photocopy, recording, or any information storage and retrieval system, without permission in writing from the publisher.

Academic Press, Inc.
A Division of Harcourt Brace & Company
525 B Street, Suite 1900, San Diego, California 92101-4495

United Kingdom Edition published by
Academic Press Limited
24–28 Oval Road, London NW1 7DX

Library of Congress Cataloging-in-Publication Data

Encyclopedia of human behavior / edited by V. S. Ramachandran.
p. cm.
Includes index.
ISBN 0-12-226920-9 (set). -- ISBN 0-12-226921-7 (v. 1)
ISBN 0-12-226922-5 (v. 2) -- ISBN 0-12-226923-3 (v. 3)
ISBN 0-12-226924-1 (v. 4).
1. Psychology--Encyclopedias. I. Ramachandran, V. S.
BF31.E5 1994
150'.3--dc20 93-34371
CIP

PRINTED IN THE UNITED STATES OF AMERICA
95 96 97 QW 9 8 7 6 5 4 3 2

CONTENTS

COPING

Edward Zamble and William L. Gekoski
Queen's University, Canada

Glossary

Coping The ways that people respond to and interact with problem situations.

Emotion-focused coping Making oneself feel better about a problematic situation without changing the problem itself or the perception of it.

Palliative coping Engaging in a behavior that reduces the emotional discomfort of a problematic situation by shifting the focus to the palliative behavior (e.g., buying oneself a present).

Primary appraisal The evaluation of a situation as taxing resources and potentially problematic for one's well-being.

Problem-focused coping Changes made by the individual to a situation or to the perception of a situation that render it less or no longer stressful.

Secondary appraisal Generation and evaluation of possible courses of action designed to meet a demand and reduce the threat to well-being.

Stress The psychological and physiological result of an appraisal of a situation by an individual as likely to have harmful effects for him/herself.

COPING refers to the ways that people respond to and interact with problem situations. Life continuously presents us with circumstances that can affect our physical or psychological well-being. The way we deal with these situations can determine whether we surmount them or suffer a variety of undesirable consequences.

I. THE CONCEPT OF COPING

A. Introduction and Definition

There are many aspects to the process of coping and its consequences. Broadly, coping can be seen as involving a great many aspects of human cognitive, emotional, and behavioral processes, and much recent work in the area can be used as exemplary of contemporary psychology's concern with the interaction between the person and the environment.

However, the term "coping" has recently enjoyed some vogue, and it has sometimes been used so promiscuously as to lose any clear meaning. There are some confusions in the scientific literature as well as everyday usage. For example, "coping" sometimes is used to refer to efforts to deal with problems, sometimes the effects of those efforts, and sometimes successful efforts only. In line with the more rigorous definitions by researchers, we shall consider coping to refer to the responses to problem (stressful) situations, regardless of their efficacy. The coping process refers to cognitions, emotions, and behavior, while coping behavior is used in a more restricted sense, referring only to overt actions.

Some other parts of the definition are also implicit, conveyed usually by attributing the notions to contemporary cognitive–behavioral psychology. For example, discussions of coping commonly assume some situational specificity rather than global extensions such as personality traits. Coping behavior is also always subject to conscious control or change, even if coping in frequently recurring situations can become habitual or functionally automatic. Finally, it is usually assumed that the coping process is largely shaped by learning, in line with the arguments of social learning theory, although this learning is undoubtedly determined in part by personality factors, e.g., excitability or arousability, and intelligence. Unfortunately, the literature has not given

Copyright © 1994 by Academic Press, Inc. All rights of reproduction in any form reserved.

the origins of coping in individuals the concerted attention that it deserves.

B. Historical Development

Historically, the concept of coping developed as a topic of interest within two very different traditions in psychology. Animal behaviorists have sometimes used the term to refer to responses animals make to escape from or avoid noxious stimulation. Such responses were seen as either innate or learned according to behaviorist principles.

The more direct route of development to contemporary usage arose with the use of coping as a construct within the psychodynamic tradition. While Freud originally described defense mechanisms as automatic processes triggered by conflict or threat, the later development of "ego psychology," in which defence mechanisms were seen as controllable by ego mechanisms, gave more of a role to conscious—or potentially conscious—processes. Ego psychology was differentiated from alternative psychoanalytic theories in that it gave substantial emphasis to defence mechanisms, referred to as coping devices. Defence mechanisms were defined as traits or dispositions that develop as the individual develops, and are therefore transformed from primitive and immature to more sophisticated and more mature. [*See* DEFENSE MECHANISMS; ID, EGO, AND SUPEREGO.]

Early usage saw coping as less malleable and more uniform across situations for an individual than later conceptualizations, and neither the animal behavioral nor the ego psychology tradition dealt with coping in a manner that acknowledges its richness, complexity, or diversity. Each viewed coping as a largely automatic response to a situation, and neither gave appropriate play to the many and varied emotional and cognitive factors that we now recognize as playing an essential role in the coping process. Still, the early work led to interest in how people deal with threatening situations, and they produced the first empirical investigations of coping. They thus engendered the interest in how people deal with problem situations that led to further work.

C. Coping and Stress

Today the process-oriented approach to coping, first elaborated and advocated by Richard Lazarus and his colleagues, represents the benchmark against which newer developments are evaluated. Lazarus' approach to coping developed out of his earlier attempts to understand stress and how people deal with it. After Selye's pioneering work on stress and its manifestations, there was much interest in the effects of stressful situations. Lazarus began to study stress in laboratory settings by exposing volunteers to unpleasant and presumably stressful experiences, e.g., films of gruesome accidents, and recording their physiological, emotional, cognitive, and behavioral responses. [*See* STRESS.]

Because coping is intimately related to stress, work on coping evolved easily out of this research. Later, in the 1970s, Lazarus developed a variety of written questionnaire measures to assess individual perceptions of stress and attempts to cope with it. These allowed the study of stress and coping to be expanded outside of the laboratory to a wide variety of environments.

The relationship between coping and stress is still quite important, and still somewhat confused. Much of the confusion, perhaps most of it, stems from careless usage of both constructs. Here we will assume that stress is a description of situations perceived by the individual to have harmful effects for him- or herself. Coping describes the response to those situations, and it thus determines what will be the effects of stress.

If one deals with stressful events successfully, then little or no damage will be incurred, while unsuccessful coping leaves one vulnerable. Thus, the coping process necessarily mediates the effects of environmentally stressful events and situations. Although this may conflict with the views in much of the literature on stress, it probably represents the views of the majority of researchers in coping.

II. THEORIES OF COPING

A. Standard Behavioral Theory

Based on his empirical work and that of others, Lazarus has enunciated a theory of stress and coping that is widely accepted as a basis for understanding the processes involved. In many ways appraisal is the cornerstone of Lazarus' theory of stress and coping. The centrality of the appraisal concept becomes clear from Lazarus' definitions of stress (i.e., "A particular relationship between the person and the environment that is appraised by the person as taxing or exceeding his or her resources and endangering his or her well-being") and coping (i.e., "constantly changing cognitive and behavioral efforts to manage specific external and/or internal demands that are appraised as taxing or exceeding the resources of the person'').

As one encounters events or situations, they are evaluated and categorized as irrelevant, benign-positive, or stressful. Primary appraisal entails an individual evaluating a situation as taxing resources and potentially problematic for his or her well-being. If a situation is appraised as stressful in the primary appraisal, then other parts of the coping process are invoked, and secondary appraisal occurs.

In secondary appraisal possible courses of action are generated and assessed as to how effectively they can meet the demand and thereby reduce the threat to well-being; in the process, one or more strategies are selected. It is essential to note here that, despite discussion of secondary appraisal in terms of ''assessment of possible courses of action'' and ''selection of strategies,'' this appraisal process may or may not be carried out consciously. Indeed, all or part of the process may occur outside of conscious awareness. For example, denial of the situation or its gravity are common responses, which, by their nature, involve some minimization of awareness.

The appraisal process is specific to the individual and to the situation in which it occurs. Lazarus outlines a variety of personal and situational factors which influence the process. Two major person factors are commitments and beliefs. Commitments refer to those things that are important to the individual, and thus include such things as values, other people, and activities to which a person may feel committed. Beliefs refer to the expectations the individual has regarding how the world in which he or she lives operates. For example, a belief that action X will lead to outcome Y would influence the appraisal process where X and Y were possibilities under consideration. Beliefs range from mundane preceived contingencies to existential positions. Other situational factors which influence appraisal may include such things as the novelty of the situation for the person, the degree to which the situation is uncertain or unpredictable, temporal factors (e.g., iminence, duration), and ambiguity.

Thus, appraisal for Lazarus represents the process both of ascertaining that a situation is stressful (primary appraisal) and determining what might be done to cope with the situation (secondary appraisal). The appraisal process is seen as very much affected by individual differences, a feature which contributes substantially to the appeal of Lazarus' formulation. Many previous theories of stress and coping have faltered on an inability either to acknowledge the importance of individual differences, or a failure to come to grips with them.

The outcome of the secondary appraisal process is some set of cognitions or behaviors designed to either change or adapt to the stressful situation. In recent discussions, Lazarus has argued that virtually all attempts at coping can be classed as either problem- or emotion-focused.

Problem-focused coping occurs most typically when the individual perceives that it is possible for her to change the situation so that it is less stressful or even to resolve it completely. To some extent it is like problem-solving, but it is seen as broader because it can include strategies that are directed inward (e.g., attempts to change how one conceptualizes the situation) as well as outward to the environment.

Emotion-focused coping is aimed at making oneself feel better about the situation, without changing the problem itself. It involves accepting the situation and trying to survive it as best as possible. There are many situations, e.g., bereavement, where one cannot easily resolve or change the stressful events, but emotion-focused coping allows one to cope successfully nonetheless. Thus, one may sometimes surmount stressful situations only by managing them.

The individual brings to situations requiring coping a set of coping resources. These may include a certain level of health or energy, certain positive beliefs, problem-solving skills, social skills, social support, material resources, etc. Individuals differ of course in the coping resources they possess, and situations vary in the degree to which particular coping resources may be relevant and effective. In addition there are a variety of constraints which may operate to limit utilization of coping resources. Such constraints include personal values and beliefs (e.g., to seek assistance from other people is a sign of weakness), environmental characteristics (e.g., the absence of the appropriate support group in the community), and the level of threat (e.g., a very high level of threat may lead to the adoption of more primitive coping responses, or of emotion-focused rather than problem-focused responses).

Lazarus' conceptualization of coping as an ongoing transaction between the individual and the environment recognizes that coping is part of a dynamic, interactive process by which the individual adapts to an ever changing situation. The individual appraises both the situation creating the demand and the resources she has available to meet the demand as a basis for generating a coping response. Both the coping response itself and other internal and/or external influences are likely to change the situation as perceived, and necessitate some reappraisal. Thus, appraisal, and consequently coping, is not static but rather the product of a continuously changing, interactive recursive process.

The Lazarus theory has a level of sophistication that, unlike many other apporaches, is commensurate with the complexity of the construct. Perhaps for this reason, it has been very widely adopted, and it has become the standard against which other ideas are measured. In addition, it has proven to be a rich source of hypotheses and it has led to a very large body of important empirical work.

B. Other Theoretical Formulations

While the Lazarus model is the most comprehensive and the best articulated overall theory for the coping process, a number of other researchers have dealt with particular parts of the process, sometimes in greater depth than the comprehensive model. Among these are several analyses that stress the importance of problem-solving. In the context of the standard model, this can be seen as part of the appraisal processes, but it can also be considered in isolation. Much work in this area has been done by D'Zurilla, who has been concerned primarily with social problem-solving, which he defines as the process by which individuals identify and implement effective solutions to problems in everyday life. [*See* PROBLEM SOLVING.]

D'Zurilla and Goldfried have analyzed the process into several conceptual stages which are involved in an effective solution to a (social) problem. These stages include: (a) problem orientation, the manner in which the individual approaches problems; (b) problem definition and formulation, the ability to identify the relevant aspects of the situation; (c) generation of alternative solutions, the ability to develop different possible responses to a situation; (d) decision-making, the judgment, comparison and selection from among alternative responses generated; (e) solution implementation and verification, enactment of the response chosen and repetition or modification if the result is ineffective.

Concentrating as it does on the molecular aspects involved in coping with a situation, the social problem-solving model has some advantages over a fully comprehensive model for clinicians attempting to remediate clients' problems. It highlights a set of cognitive and behavioral skills that are amenable to existing clinical techniques and which are applicable in a wide variety of problematic situations. It has been used for a number of specific types of situations, for example the treatment of children with behavior difficulties, interpersonal conflicts within families or in marital disputes, or for the analysis of interpersonal aggression.

A number of other theorists have proposed ideas that contrast with the central theoretical position inspired by Lazarus. Perhaps the most common and most powerful variants are those that hypothesize a major role for some sort of central cognitive state. These cognitions are seen as operating to govern coping in a dispositional fashion. Although they may be seen as simply elaborations of Lazarus' notions regarding the influence of beliefs on problem appraisals, their strong emphases on the major role of certain global cognitions makes them in effect alternative formulations.

Among these, Antonovsky has proposed the notion of Sense of Coherence as a personal disposition that determines the success of coping and adaptation. This global construct is intended to measure an enduring and pervasive feeling of confidence that one's environment is structured and predictable, and that one has both the resources and the motivation to meet the demands it poses. Antonovsky has devised a questionnaire instrument to measure Sense of Coherence, and he has produced some evidence that it relates to measures of adaptation, such as self-appraisals of physical health.

Other theorists have used theoretical constructs that function similarly, although some have discussed them explicitly in terms of coping and others have not overtly made the connection. Coping is a very broad construct, and it is not surprising that there is some difficulty in separating it conceptually from related constructs.

Several constructs are worthy of mention here. Personality hardiness, as proposed and used by Kobasa and Maddi, is a dispositional variable that differentiates individuals who thrive under stress from those who become defeated under challenge from the environment. It is also measured by a questionnaire, and seems to overlap considerably with Antonovsky's construct, even though the rationales for the two mechanisms make them appear quite different on the surface.

Bandura's notion of "self-efficacy" also overlaps with part of the coping process. Essentially, it proposes that an individual's expectation of how well she will be able to accomplish a challenging task is a major determinant—and therefore a good predictor—of subsequent performance. The usefulness of this construct has been confirmed several times in a variety of situations, although the evidence is not unequivocal. As originally proposed, self-efficacy is task specific rather than global, but it seems to be used sometimes as indicative of cognitions that extend broadly across situations, which in effect makes it the equivalent of dispositional mechanisms. Self-efficacy would seem to fit nicely as part of the appraisal process, affecting the coping behaviors that are chosen. In return, the outcomes of coping behavior would likely affect self-efficacy, in the continuous cycle of feedback between cognitions and behavior. [*See* SELF-EFFICACY.]

Personal control is also a very broad construct, that overlaps with coping. It has been conceptualized in several ways by different authors, with some focusing on the beliefs people hold about control (e.g., internal vs external locus of control), and others concerned with behaviors that represent actual attempts at control. There is no doubt that beliefs about (the locus of) control can affect one's appraisals of a situation, as a personal resource or as a constraint in the appraisal process. On the other hand, efforts at achieving control over stress are clearly instances of coping responses. [*See* CONTROL.]

C. Theoretical Issues

A number of unresolved theoretical issues seem quite important in the current literature. Several of these center around the degree of specificity normally involved in the control of coping behavior. For example, considerations of alternative theoretical statements in the preceding section show that one significant unresolved issue is the extent to which global cognitive states govern the coping process. Although each of several positions has some evidence for the generalized influence of cognitions, there has been no concerted attempt to compare or contrast the different hypotheses, or to measure global cognitions at the same time as specific behaviors in order to assess their comparative influences.

A related issue that has plagued theorists for some time is whether coping is best considered to be situation specific or person specific. Use of terms such as "coping style" presupposes some generalized personal disposition to act similarly across situations, but the concrete evidence for such consistency is fairly thin.

Early approaches, arising from the psychoanalytic tradition, generally treated coping as a personality trait or disposition, with the expectation that an individual would cope in the same way across situations. As the influence of the behavioral tradition grew, the view that each individual has a repertoire of coping responses that are deployed as required by different situations became dominant.

It may be quite difficult to distinguish between these hypotheses operationally, because a person may perceive the situations she encounters as similar, and therefore tend to use the same coping response across several situations. Alternatively, some individuals may find a particular coping response especially effective and thus use it extensively across a variety of situations. Thus, in some cases coping responses may appear dispositional even if they are really (in principle) situationally specific.

The issue of whether there are coping styles or only situation specific coping strategies is an important one because it relates both to our ability to predict behavior and our ability to change it. The weight of opinion currently appears to be that the style notion does not buy us very much and that we can account for homogeneity of response without invoking traits or dispositions. However, much more evidence is required, especially from research that contrasts responses across widely different situations in the same individuals, or that compares the coping repertoires of individuals in very different populations. Perhaps our research on coping has not reached the stage of maturity required for detailed choices between closely related theoretical alternatives, but there is much room for some efforts to provide more definitive information on the details of the coping process.

Another important issue in the area of coping is how coping behavior develops and changes over time. Much of the discussion on this topic is unsatisfying because it phrases the question in terms of continuity or change. Within such a formulation the literature, although sparse, indicates that older people have coping repertoires and preferences similar to those of younger people.

Unfortunately there has been little attention paid to this issue from a truly developmental perspective. Clearly one's repertoire of coping responses grows as one develops through childhood, and there are no convincing data to suggest that new responses are not added later in life. However, some have argued that as people age they become more rigid and egocentric such that their coping responses become more immature. Others have argued, invoking a developmental model, that even if no new responses are added to the repertoire, existing responses and their deployment change qualitatively becoming more sophisticated, more highly differentiated, and more complexly related to changing personal resources, constraints, and perceptions of stressful situations as one gains greater experience.

Clearly more data are needed to address the developmental question. However, as Lazarus notes, the issue of developmental change in coping can only be properly addressed in longitudinal studies and there are very few of these available. In conclusion, although little is currently known about the developmental course of coping it is more likely that the appropriate questions have not been asked than that there are no developmental changes.

III. METHODOLOGICAL ISSUES

A. Types of Coping Responses

From its first appearance in the literature, there has been concern with classifying and categorizing coping. In the psychoanalytic perspective of overt behavior as the window into the soul, it was assumed that people could be classified on the basis of the defense mechanisms they chose, and that they would consistently choose the same types of responses across situations.

In contemporary research these assumptions have been abandoned. Although they may be correct in some cases, it is seen as a matter for empirical test rather than necessity. However, the classification of coping according to some descriptive typology is still common practice. One may look at individuals across a wide variety of situations, either to classify and compare them in some fashion or for general information on the consistency and flexibility of coping, or to explore and test theoretical constructs. For these purposes, a variety of investigators have used different schemes, but there has been a considerable amount of overlap among the typologies because they are all based on empirical observations of actions that people actually employ.

Several categories of responses are generally included in classification schemes. The first category includes actions that remove or resolve the problem in question, or at least ameliorate it to some extent. This includes efforts at problem solving, as was described earlier. If all of the elements of a systematic problem-solving approach are not present, as is commonly the case, then a person may be judged to show solution-oriented coping if some of the elements are visible, especially an explicit statement of the problem, and some evidence of planning and evaluation of actions with reference to the problem. In some categorizations, e.g., that of Lazarus and Folkman, most of these elements are largely subsumed into a single category of "problem-oriented" coping, but they can easily be separated into several smaller categories, as D'Zurilla and others have done.

A second set of categories are those usually described as cognitive. Among them are several ways that one can revise the appraisal of a problem situation. For example, one may consciously and deliberately conduct an inner dialogue to challenge the appraisal of an impersonal situation ("It's not that difficult—I've managed harder") or of another person's actions ("He's not out to get me, he's just having a *bad* day"). Another similar technique is that of reducing the perceived threat by distancing oneself from a situation, stoically ("Life's like that"), using humor ("Life's nuts"), or by changing perspective ("This too will pass"). All of these, and other similar thoughts, can cause one to reinterpret the problem situation.

Cognitive techniques can also be used to change or control one's emotional response to a situation, thus affecting its harmful effects. These may be either generalized ("Relax!") or specific ("You're getting tense; unclasp your hands and take a deep breath") and they can employ a variety of ways of achieving or enhancing emotional self-control, from relaxation techniques to continuous self-talk. [*See* RELAXATION.]

Solution of a problem or cognitive control of appraisals or emotional responses is almost always seen as the most effective coping response, but there are several other categories that are very commonly observed. Several of these involve social interactions. When faced with a problem, one may consort with other people for several reasons, including sympathy and solace, information on the problem or possible solutions, or concrete and specific help in dealing with the problem. It is sometimes quite difficult to decide which of these purposes is being served in any given case, and in many cases they are overlapping and inseparable, so some investigators have combined them under a single rubric of "social support." Other observers have maintained some divisions into subcategories. [*See* SOCIAL SUPPORT.]

A fourth broad type of coping response is that of palliation of the emotional discomfort engendered by a situation. A very wide variety of specific behaviors has been described as useful in this regard by individuals, from alcohol use to buying oneself a new item of clothing. Many of the palliatives that people employ are based on the principle of countering discomfort with pleasure, but not all palliatives would be explained this way. For example, simple problem-oriented actions such as writing a letter to a missing loved one are sometimes used effectively to relieve emotional distress, although the acts are not in themselves perceived as pleasurable. It should be noted that palliative coping responses sometimes overlap with social support categories, and they may be difficult to distinguish reliably.

The final conventional set of categories includes actions that remove one from the problem situation. This can take the form of denial, which negates the existence of a situation that is clear to an objective observer, avoidance of the problem either physically or in one's thoughts, or escape from either the physical situation or thoughts about it. Given that these ways of coping will not usually eventuate in the improvement of a problem situation, most commentators have considered them undesirable ways of coping, and they are often considered as evidence of inadequate coping resources. However, as will be considered later, the appropriateness of any particular way of coping depends on the situation to which one is responding, so even denial, escape, or avoidance can be considered legitimate ways of coping at times.

Thus, there are five broad categories that are used in most categorical descriptions of coping. Although these do appear to subsume most of the varieties of responses reported or observed in common problem situations, they are not exhaustive of potential responses. Additional categories are sometimes very useful, especially in describing responses to uncommon situations, or with special populations. For example, the response of becoming emotionally numb and unreactive has been observed in response to catastrophic conditions such as a concentration camp, or particular maladaptive responses, e.g., substance abuse, may be useful in describing a population in which they are extremely common.

B. Effectiveness

It is commonly assumed that there is a hierarchy of goodness of the various categories, with problem-solving the most effective and most desirable and avoidance/escape/denial maladaptive and generally to be eschewed. There is evidence that individuals who are successful use problem-solving and cognitive categories as their preferred means of coping, while those with adaptation difficulties more commonly use avoidance, escape, or denial. Moreover, there is also good evidence that the use of "higher-level" coping categories can be successfully taught in a therapeutic context; such interventions often, although not always, result in improvement in the quality of adaptation.

However, one must consider that the appropriate and effective ways of dealing with a problem are at least in part situationally determined. Some problems are simply not soluble, and others may be so traumatic that they overwhelm even the best and most well-practiced cognitive mechanisms. In such cases, one may find the apparently paradoxical result that persons who employ "inferior" ways of coping will suffer the least damage and survive best.

For example, research has commonly shown that a combination of systematic information-seeking and cognitive strategies, among them distancing or creative distortion, is usually the most successful for dealing with serious episodic or chronic health problems. Individuals who use these strategies to "manage their condition," i.e., to participate actively in making choices regarding their own treatment, are likely to recover more quickly and may even have better chances of survival. On the other hand, some people are not comfortable using these strategies, or are not able to use them well, and the mismatch if they attempt to use them may compound the stress of the illness and lead to a worsened prognosis.

In other cases, the nature of the condition may argue against the use of active strategies. If one has acquired an invariably fatal disease, then persistent and vigorous attempts to resolve the problem may just make the details of one's imminent demise more convincing and more salient. In such a case, for many people the response that best maintains psychological well-being might be that of avoiding or denying the problem for as long as possible. Thus, absolute judgments about the quality of coping methods should be eschewed; instead, we should consider the most appropriate responses for any individual, given his or her capacities and experience, and given the nature of the situation with which he or she must cope.

Similarly, judgments of the effectiveness of coping efforts must take careful note of how well any given type of response is effected. Even though two individuals may use responses in the same basic category, they may differ considerably in how skillfully or how persistently they implement their chosen mode of coping. For example, the literature on problem-solving makes it clear that there is considerable variance in the ability to achieve an effective solution. Most of the common categorizations of coping record simply the presence or the prevalence of responses within modalities, without reference to variations in skill or effectiveness. This omission has undoubtedly limited their explanatory power and it should be remedied in future research.

One must also consider the costs of using any particular coping behavior. Some coping responses require a substantial commitment of time and effort, while others can be done much more economically. Such factors must be included in the assessment of coping, as they are critical in what makes for effective coping. Clearly, merely categorizing coping behavior is not sufficient.

C. Measurement of Coping

Aside from categorization, the assessment of coping is not so simple as it would first seem, because several factors must be taken into account. First, one needs to know how stressful and how difficult is the situation to which a person is responding. Thus, in addition to descriptions of coping, the situation must be clearly described, if possible as seen both by an objective observer and by the subject. If one is interested in overall measures of coping, either across individuals or populations, this requirement can often be met by use of one of a variety of measures of sources of stress, e.g., surveys of major life events. These list and weight a variety of critical or landmark situations that are commonly seen as particularly disruptive or stressful. However, sometimes it is necessary to generate unique surveys of significant problem areas for each individual, in an ipsative fashion.

Although coping with such major events is undoubtedly important, Lazarus has argued that coping with the far more frequent minor stressful events of everyday life may be even more important for well-being. Consequently, he and his colleagues developed the Daily Hassles Scale, and determined that it was a better predictor of symptomatology than were measures of major life stress.

A variety of techniques have been used to measure coping, including interviews, physiological measures, and paper and pencil inventories. Although interviews may get at the complexity and the nuances of coping behavior, scoring can be a problem, as well as the labor-intensive collection of information if numerous individuals are being assessed. Although physiological measures are objective and easily scored, they are intrusive, and the awareness that they are being recorded may change a person's responses. Paper and pencil inventories are easily administered and scored, but like all self-report measures are potentially susceptible to a variety of response biases.

Probably the single most widely used measure of coping is the Ways of Coping Inventory developed by Lazarus and Folkman. On this instrument the respondent is asked to indicate on a four-point scale the degree to which he or she used each of 67 listed ways of coping (e.g., hoped a miracle would happen, tried not to act too hastily, followed my first hunch, got professional help) in a particular stressful situation. The results can be scored several ways, including judgments of the amount of coping effort, or the type of coping responses employed. Although widely used, the Ways of Coping Inventory has also been widely modified, thus limiting the comparability of findings.

Measurement of well-being, presumably the outcome of coping, has also been problematic. Whether the appropriate outcome is related to physical health or mental health, should be measured in the short or the longer term, or should be assessed simply through self-report or from other sources, are just some of the areas of contention. In addition, given the many criteria that might be chosen, there are important issues about the validity and generality of measures across situations and across studies.

D. Other Considerations

A number of other methodological issues in the study of coping have been raised, although not all dealt with satisfactorily. One such issue involves the relative advantages of laboratory versus field or naturalistic research. Typically in laboratory research a subject is placed in a situation designed to be perceived as stressful (e.g., completing a difficult task under severe time pressure) and the manner in which she copes with the situation is monitored. In naturalistic research real life stressful situations are sought, and individuals' responses in these situations are observed.

The latter approach has the advantage of ecological validity: the stress is genuine and coping is not influenced by being the object of study. The former approach has the advantage of experimental control: all subjects are exposed to the same stressor, and the situation is designed so that stress and coping are easily obtained. In the end, neither approach can be considered as inherently preferable. Attempts to find compromise methodologies that combine the advantages of laboratory and field approaches have not been strikingly successful. Rather, each is useful in certain circumstances, and as usual the researcher is well-advised to choose the technique that best fits the question under investigation.

A related issue is the relative desirability of studying individuals intensively—the ipsative approach—versus studying many individuals less intensively—the normative approach. Again, this is an issue where one's choice should depend on what is important for a given study. Ipsative work may be more productive for developing and understanding how potentially relevant variables relate, but normative evidence is necessary in order to insure generalizability.

IV. FURTHER CONSIDERATIONS

Some of the most important issues regarding coping are those relating coping to adaptation. Given that sources of stress are ever present in modern life, the significant determinants (and predictors) of poor adaptation in everyday life should be how well one copes, rather than the amount of stress. Therefore, one would expect that individuals who cope poorly will fall into maladaptation, and, conversely, that people with demonstrated patterns of maladaption likely have inadequate coping resources. The following two sections deal with some of the evidence on these predictions.

A. Coping and Health

One area in which the consequences of coping have been studied extensively is that of health, especially the degree to which coping is related to our health status, both in the short term and over longer periods. Coping has emotional concomitants which ought to be manifested in physiological or biochemical events. Such events, if they are frequent, intense, or of long duration, are seen as having an influence on health. [*See* STRESS AND ILLNESS.]

Although the bulk of research on this issue has focused on exploring the negative effects of poor coping on health, some attention has also been given to demonstrating positive effects. For example, much research has linked coping in patterns characterized as the Type A syndrome with an increased likelihood of developing coronary heart disease. Other research has considered whether certain coping responses result in suppression of some functions of the immune system, thus increasing the likelihood of diseases, especially cancer. Conversely, there are reports of the use of humor and imaging techniques to alter disease processes. [*See* TYPE A–TYPE B PERSONALITIES.]

Research in this domain is considered controversial, both because many claims have been made based upon incomplete evidence and because many people are resistant to the notion that the way we cope can influence our health. There is now a substantial acceptance of the notion that behaviors related to lifestyle, such as smoking or lack of exercise, are responsible, at least in part, for health problems. However, there is much less acceptance of the idea that coping responses such as denial, repression, intellectualization, etc., which may be adaptive in the short run, may also have eventual negative consequences. It should be noted that whether a coping response is effective or not in reducing, eliminating, or otherwise managing a stressful situation is not necessarily related to that response's effect on health over the longer term. Among other things, adrenalin secretion occurs in situations perceived as challenges as part of the flight/fight syndrome, but sustained secretion of adrenalin may be involved in the development of certain disease processes.

Another example of a health-related topic that has generated substantial research interest is that of coping with the stress of caregiving. With increasing numbers of middle-aged adults responsible for providing care for their elderly parents, research in this area is likely to have substantial application. A model often used in this research places coping skills, along with social support and other resources, as mediators between the appraisal of a parent's condition as deteriorating but manageable at home, and the negative physical or health outcomes in the caregiver. Gatz, Bengston, and Blum, among others, have focused on the influence of three types of coping skills on caregiver outcomes: (1) managing the situation, (2) developing an adaptive way of appraising one's position, and (3) managing the stress symptoms that develop in the caregiver.

B. Poor Coping and Maladaptation

There is also some evidence for the link between poor coping and maladaptive consequences. There were several reports in the 1970s that people seeking treatment for clinical problems had inadequate coping skills. For example, deficiencies in problem-solving ability, including consideration and weighing the advantages and disadvantages of response alternatives, were evident in populations of otherwise normal people with complaints including mild depression, loneliness, or anxiety.

Since that time, different investigators have concentrated on the coping patterns in particular populations, and the results are often incorporated into treatment methods. Aaron Beck and his colleagues have shown powerful evidence of the link between distorted processes of primary problem evaluation and depression. Treatments based on remediation, aimed especially at changing patterns of negative global evaluation, have become almost the standard for dealing with depression. Albert Ellis' methods, included under the rubric of "Rational Emotive Training," are quite similar although they were derived entirely independently, and they are also widely employed. [*See* DEPRESSION.]

One may also see coping difficulties in other populations with adjustment problems that are not ordinarily considered clinical in nature. Some studies have shown links with delinquent or criminal behavior. For example, Dodge found that aggressive children are far more likely to interpret ordinary situations as threatening or challenging. Similarly, Guerra and Slaby demonstrated that delinquent youths have a variety of deficiencies in problem-solving abilities that can lead them into aggression. [*See* AGGRESSION.]

An extensive study by Zamble and Porporino was aimed in part at describing coping in prison inmates, and the results show some widespread limitations in coping ability. The problems reported by the prisoners in the study from their lives outside of prison were not unusual, and although they almost always tried to deal with those problems their typical coping behavior was the first response that came to mind, executed inconsistently, and followed by avoidance of the problem and its consequences. Planning or persistence was rarely in evidence. Perhaps the most striking finding was that offenders' coping behavior very frequently exacerbated the objective situation. For example, a worker might choose to deal with pressure from his work supervisor by confronting him; this may reduce the pressure, but it may also lead to physical aggression or dismissal from the job if not done very skillfully, and the offenders seen were rarely skillful.

In all of these aspects, there are substantial differences between offenders and law-abiding comparison populations. The overall pattern of impulsive, uncoordinated, and ineffective coping gives a picture of criminal offenders that is very different from the rational criminal assumed by our legal systems. Moreover, measures of coping taken at the beginning of a prison term were statistically useful in predicting adaptation a year or so later, including both emotional states and institutional misbehavior, and there is some evidence that coping can predict the repetition of criminal behavior after release. Other investigators such as Toch and Adams have given similar descriptions of coping problems in criminal offenders. [*See* CRIMINAL BEHAVIOR.]

Thus, one may argue that deficiencies in various parts of the coping process are determinative of a variety of serious forms of maladjustment, and no doubt many sorts of less serious adjustment problems as well. However, while the predictions of coping theory are supported by the available evidence, that evidence is mostly weak. Far too much of the relevant data are built on the very unreliable bases of concomitant measures or (even worse) clinical postdiction. If we are to assert the strong hypothesis that coping determines the goodness of subsequent adaptation, then we need more longitudinal research that measures coping well in advance of adaptation, or that follows the dynamic interaction and development of the two over periods of several years.

Bibliography

Antonovsky, A. (1979). "Health, Stress, and Coping." Jossey-Bass, San Francisco.

Eckenrode, J. (Ed.) (1991). "The Social Context of Coping." Plenum, New York.

Lazarus, R. S., and Folkman, S. (1984). "Stress, Appraisal and Coping." Springer, New York.

Moos, R. H. (Ed.) (1986). "Coping with the Crises." Plenum, New York.

Selye, H. (1976). "The Stress of Life." McGraw-Hill, New York.

Zamble, E., and Porporino, F. (1988). "Coping, Behavior, and Adaptation in Prison Inmates." Springer, New York.

Creative and Imaginative Thinking

Mark A. Runco
California State University at Fullerton

Glossary

Cognition The operation of the intellect, often portrayed as information processing.

Cognitive structures Clusters of interrelated information which is organized for use.

Divergent thinking Ideational processes including fluency, flexibility, and originality.

Metacognition Strategic thinking, resulting from *procedural knowledge,* or knowledge about how to get something done.

Problem finding The identification and definition of an obstacle which must occur before problem solving. Apparently the quality of a problem determines the quality (and creativity) of solutions.

CREATIVE THINKING can be defined in terms of the cognitive processes that lead to an original and adaptive insight, idea, or solution. That being said, consider the two parts of the definition. The second part of this definition applies to creativity in general; it is widely accepted that all creative achievements are in some way original (e.g., novel, unique, or highly unusual) *and* adaptive (e.g., fitting, useful, or apt).[1] The first part of the definition, focusing on cognitive processes, is a bit more controversial. It has been argued, for example, that thinking is difficult to study and is too far removed from actual creative products, and is thus not fit for scientific study. From the opposite perspective, it has been argued that all creative work requires some cognition: Everything we do requires information processing. This article takes the second view and assumes that cognition underlies all human behavior. Even emotions seem to have cognitive underpinnings. This is a significant point because, as we shall see, creativity is in part emotional and motivational.

Note the terms *insight, idea,* and *solution* in my definition of creative thinking. These are products—the products of thought—though they may be personal and subjective rather than shared and objective. These three terms are included in the definition in part in an attempt to cover all expressions of creative thinking. Some creativity is, for example, problem solving; hence, creativity is expressed as an original solution. Some creativity may be largely independent of problem solving—the arts, for instance, may reflect self-expression more than a clear-cut dilemma or conundrum. Here *idea* or *insight* may be the most appropriate term. [*See* PROBLEM SOLVING.]

With such varied processes and products being concerns, it will come as no surprise that there are various approaches to the study of creative thinking. Some focus on problem solving, others on problem finding or ideas or insights which precede or are otherwise independent of a well-defined obstacle. Similarly, a wide range of methods have been applied to the study of creative thinking, some experimental and some relying on observation with a degree of speculation. Because creativity can be quite personal (and original only for the individual) or it can have worldwide impact, it seems safe to assume

[1] A third critical feature of creativity is aesthetic. In empirical research, creative products have *aesthetic appeal* or are in some way pleasing. The aesthetic dimension is less often used than originality and adaptiveness, but this may reflect the concern for objective studies. Originality and usefulness can be objectively defined; the aesthetic dimension is inherently subjective and personal.

Copyright © 1994 by Academic Press, Inc. All rights of reproduction in any form reserved.

that attention should be given to each of the various approaches. Coincidentally, *attention* is an apt term here because it occurs early in the creative thinking process. This brings us to information processes.

I. INFORMATION PROCESSING

Cognitivists who wish to uncover processes which characterize all humans usually look to three information processes: attention, rehearsal, and retrieval. These three processes can describe most cognition, given that they explain how information is transferred from sensory memory to short-term memory, and retrieved when needed. Attention may be the most critical of the basic processes for those studying creative thinking. Rehearsal and retrieval primarily control existing rather than original information. [*See* MEMORY.]

Humans can attend to only a very small part of their environment, noticing particular salient stimuli. We notice changes in our environment and things which stand out, for instance, along with stimuli which are personally meaningful (e.g., our own names). There is a long-standing controversy about the effort required for attention, and apparently some kinds of information (e.g., some spatial information and frequency of occurrence) can be processed effortlessly, that is, with very little attention. Still, the vast majority of information is processed only with some effort. Attentional resources must be used.

Attention is, then, a limited resource (try to listen to two conversations simultaneously, if you need proof), and it must be invested in particular ways to facilitate creative thinking. Put most simply, creative thinking benefits from *broad attention deployment*. Creative individuals seem to have idiosyncratic attention deployment tendencies which allow them to spread their attention across several pieces of information. This in turn allows the individual to perceive remote and potentially original ideas. In other words, the individual can consider an extended range of possibilities when his or her attention is widely deployed. Interestingly, research has suggested a connection between the deployment of attention and actual cortical processing. There might, then, be a biological explanation for individual differences in attention deployment.

Attention deployment is also relevant in that it facilitates the kinds of associations among ideas which are necessary for creative thinking. A great deal of thought is associative, as suggested when your mind wanders from a sunny day to the beach or golf course and then on to your last vacation. Certain associative tendencies allow an individual to find original and adaptive ideas. Wide attention is helpful in this regard because it allows individuals great freedom as they associate, and as a result many, many ideas are connected with one another. Along the same lines, certain attentional tendencies may actually facilitate analogical thinking, whereby the individual sees similarities or parallels between experiences and can bring insights from one to bear on the other.

II. INTEREST AND KNOWLEDGE

On a more general level attention is important in that it describes an individual's interest; and individuals are not creative unless they are interested. Like wide attention deployment, a special interest, or *intrinsic motivation,* is another of the characteristics common to highly creative individuals. Interest and attention lead to effort, and virtually all famous creations, discoveries, and inventions have required years of effort on the part of the individual. This investment of energy would not have taken place unless that individual was greatly interested. Attention is thus an intellectual prerequisite: Without it, other skills would not be applied to the task, problem, or project.

Attention must also be directed at some endeavor in order for an individual to learn what he or she needs to know about a subject and in order to innovate and be creative. This is an important point because it shows how information (i.e., knowledge) *and* information processing (i.e., attention deployment) are both required for truly creative work. The connection to knowledge further suggests that creative ideas and solutions are not easy to come by. Almost always they depend upon a large knowledge base. Occasionally original insights are viewed as spontaneous bursts of creativity wherein an individual very suddenly comes up with a creative solution to some problem. We now know that insights have developmental histories. Insights seem to only occur when an individual has invested a great deal of their time in an area and is very familiar with that area, having thought long and hard about it. Insights, then, are not sudden and spontaneous—they have histories and require effort.

Why then do insights appear to have that spontaneous, sudden quality? Presumably, this is because some information processing occurs below the level of awareness. Sometimes the mind is inclined toward what is usually called *incubation,* which is simply preconscious information processing. At some point, there may be a breakthrough, and the individual who is open to preconscious processing may seem to suddenly have an idea. At least it may feel sudden, but most likely the individual simply does not know about the preconscious processing which led to the insight. No wonder they often describe insights as sudden and unexpected, often pointing toward intuition and the like. Of course, it is very difficult to study preconscious processes, but their operation can be inferred. Important preconscious processes operate when we find the right word to express ourselves, in slips of the tongue, and when we remember something which we only experienced a long time before.

Attention is, then, not all important. It can help, but processing—preconscious processing—occurs without it. In fact, attention can actually inhibit creative thinking. Apparently, individuals can devote too much attention to a topic or idea, the result being a rigidity of thought. This kind of rigidity precludes creativity. When rigid, individuals only think about things they have experienced before or think only in directions in which others have suggested to them. Rigid thinking keeps an individual on conventional cognitive and associative pathways, and these rarely if ever lead to insight.

A related problem is interpersonal. This occurs when one individual directs his or her attention to some other individual, such as when a child artist depends on the reactions of parents or teachers or an adult artist tries to produce something that will sell. In either case the individual is directing his or her attention outward and away from his or her own insights, feelings, discoveries, and logic. That individual is more concerned with what others think than his or her own information processing. This can distract the potential creator and may lead to a kind of anxiety which can inhibit efficient thought. More often than not, individuals have problems processing information when they are anxious about extrinsic pressures.

Suppose that an individual has devoted his or her attention to a particular subject, is knowledgeable about it, and thinks about it frequently. Suppose also that the individual is curious about some gap or about something that does not seem to fit. Such gaps are often cited when creative individuals are asked why they were drawn to a particular topic or problem. What actually occurs when they incubate? How can the preconscious processes of incubation be described? One description suggests that ideas are generated and compared, and associations are formed among ideas. There are various *associative theories* to describe this activity.

Theories about associative processes go back several hundred years. Early associative theories held that sensory information initiated the process. For creative activity, it is often not sensory in the strict sense, but as suggested above, some sort of gap or curiosity in a specific area or on a specific topic. Whatever the initiation, creative and original ideas are thought to reflect *remote associations.* In other words, individuals tend to find their most creative ideas after they have moved from one idea to the next, to the next, and so on—for quite some time. Obvious ideas are found first, and these tend to be uncreative, or at least unoriginal. The best ideas are relevant (or what I called adaptive) as well as uncommon.

One way of demonstrating this is to think about a very common test of creative thinking called the Remote Associates Test, or RAT. The items on this test contain several key words, and an examinee is asked to find a creative way to associate the words to each other. Here is an example: Think of an associate of Blood, River, and Money. One answer which receives credit on the RAT is "bank." It is associated with all three keywords.

Research using the RAT confirms that remote associations are generally quite original. An important corollary of this is that individuals may need to invest time when thinking creatively or attempting to find an original solution, or they will find only superficial associations. Truly remote associations require time for the individual to move from idea to idea. Once again, then, effort and investment are important for creative thinking.

Why are certain ideas associated with other ideas? Several reasons have been proposed. One looks specifically to the similarity among ideas. Associations might also be functional, as in "car" and "road," or they might be serendipitous. These associations occur when an individual connects one thing with another, apparently by accident. Perhaps the individual was walking by the road when thinking about cars. Associations are often acoustic, occurring when two words sound alike. This of course suggests that the RAT might be verbally biased and represent verbal ability as much as creative ability. Clearly, many, many creative activities are nonverbal. Einstein's insights, for example, seemed to rely very heavily on imagery.

A second model assumes that associations can lead to creative insight, but this model, which focuses on *divergent thinking,* seems to be independent of verbal ability and other biases. Divergent thinking is required whenever an individual is faced with an open-ended task. In the classroom, for example, students can think divergently by being asked to "list all of the things you can think of that are square." Alternatively, they might be given an abstract line drawing and asked to list all of the things the drawing could represent. This would allow imagery to work with divergent thinking. In the natural environment, an individual might have difficulty with an employer, or trouble finding time to exercise. In fact, in the real world, most of our problems are open-ended. When this occurs, various ideas and solutions are usually generated. They may come about via associative thinking, but in the divergent thinking model what is important is that ideas are numerous, varied, and novel. This is another way of saying that a creative individual is fluent, flexible, and original in their thinking.

It may seem that of these, originality would be most closely tied with creative thinking, but in fact, both fluency and flexibility are important for creative thinking. *Ideational fluency* represents productivity with ideas. It is important because it gives an individual ammunition. That is, if an individual is fluent with ideas, he or she has many ideas with which to work and from which to choose the best or most creative. Also, recall what was mentioned above concerning remote associations. Apparently, when an individual is fluent in their thinking and generates many ideas, they may continue until they work through the common ideas and find remote ideas. *Ideational originality* is defined in terms of unusual or unique ideas.

Ideational flexibility is seen in divergent thinking when an individual taps various categories and moves from one domain to another. Consider, for example, the situation in which the individual is asked to list all of the things he or she can think of that are round. One individual might give the following ideas: baseball, soccer ball, basketball, tennis ball, volleyball. Another individual might give these ideas: basketball, the moon, Cheerios, a pencil eraser, and a penny. The first individual gave ideas from one (sports) category. The second individual moved across several categories. This movement is indicative of ideational flexibility. It is helpful because, like wide attention deployment, it allows the individual to consider a wider range of options. It is especially important in creative thinking that is elicited by a problem. This is because ideational flexibility allows the individual to avoid the rigidity mentioned earlier. Often, when solving problems, an individual will get stuck in their own perspective and consider only one type of solution. This may keep them from finding creative and original ideas. An individual who is flexible avoids being stuck in a rut.

III. STRATEGIES AND STRUCTURES

Granted, divergent thinking is partly strategic. Most individuals probably have strategies for solving problems, and some of these can increase the fluency, flexibility, and originality of ideation. Flexibility might, for instance, be increased by intentionally looking for varied solution options. This assumes that the individual knows that flexibility is useful, and further assumes that the individual knows how to find varied ideas. For this reason, strategic thinking is often referred to as *metacognitive,* implying that it is not dependent on ability, but instead is highly dependent upon knowledge and know-how. Of course, it is not entirely independent of ability, because individuals who are highly capable are often also the most strategic. [*See* METACOGNITION.]

It may be best to view strategies as knowledge, but it is *procedural knowledge* rather than *declarative knowledge,* which is knowledge about how things are rather than how to do things. Both kinds of knowledge are very important for creative thinking, for individuals need information and need to know how to use that information. Here again, we must be careful and recognize that more is not always better. Individuals need information, but for creative thinking it should be information which is structured to allow flexible use. Occasionally, knowledge is structured in such a way as to preclude flexible application. This is another example of rigidity. Creative thought requires flexible knowledge structures—structures which allow for new combinations, associations, and possibilities.

Recall here the earlier mention of insight. What exactly is an insight? Apparently, most insights are newly organized information—that is, they are knowledge structures. They suggest relationships among discrete pieces of information and thus give structure to perception and further thought. When an individual has an insight, it sets the tone for the acquisition of new information. It structures how one views the world or at least how one processes information on the topic at hand. This is one of the most important functions of knowledge structures—they lead to predictions and expectations.

Other information structures are called *implicit theories*. These are the views held by individuals about various specific facets of human behavior. Individuals hold, for example, fairly stable implicit theories about what is required for creative thinking, and these can determine the way that person reacts to instances of creativity. Take the parent who thinks that creativity is unconventionality. That parent might expect the creative child to misbehave and rebel, showing only nonconformity and disrespect. This parent might see only those behaviors because he or she expects to see them—because he or she is looking specifically for them. Of course, such expectations might apply to one's self as well as interpersonally. An artist, for example, may have an implicit theory about creativity reflecting rebelliousness and might therefore only value work which reflects rebellion.

This takes us back to the earlier discussion of attention. This is because attention may be one of the most important explanations for differences between judgments about creative products and behaviors. Different individuals attend to different things, and as a result can easily come up with different judgments about their work or behavior. Consider the artist who produces what he or she thinks is his or her best work of art. He or she might enter that in a show, only to have it eliminated at an early stage of judging. That individual may in fact be attending to part of the creative product that the judges are not themselves noticing. In other words, they are judging different things. Similar divergent perspectives might characterize parents or teachers and their children or students. A child might be doing something which he or she considers worthwhile and adaptive in the sense of solving some problem, but the parent will hold an entirely different perspective and might view that same solution (or problem!) as unworthy. It may therefore be the same problem or solution which is being judged, but the perspectives might very well differ, and again, this can very easily lead to two different judgments. Different perspectives can direct attention and can give individuals different knowledge bases. Both can contribute to how we think about and judge creative behavior, our own or that of another.

IV. CONTROVERSIES AND CONCLUSIONS

Various components of the creative thinking process have been identified, including attention, association, incubation, divergent thinking, and judgment. Each of these has been isolated in the empirical research, and each could be targeted in education and training. It is, however, critical to remember that realistically the different components of the creative thinking process are interdependent. It may be useful to view them as stages and as occurring in a particular sequence, but functionally there is interplay among them. For this reason most recent depictions of the creative thinking process include feedback loops and interactions among components.

This is very clear in the case of problem finding. Problem finding is just that—the identification of a problem or obstacle. The distinctiveness of problem finding was first suggested by work with artists, but the problem finding skills of individuals in other domains and those of nonprofessionals, including schoolchildren, have since been identified. Of course, problem finding is a general name, and what probably occurs is that an individual must *identify* a situation as problematic, then *define* it in such a way as to allow work toward a solution, and finally work toward that solution. Problem finding is, then, just a general term for various stages in the creative thinking process. Moreover, there are interactions, such as between the identification of a problem and its definition and solution. Individuals probably start with an ambiguous idea that there is a problem, and then work to clarify it. That is itself a kind of problem solving. After the problem is sufficiently clear, the individual can work toward a final solution.

The recognition of problem finding is in part important because it de-emphasizes problem solving. Not all creativity is problem solving. The concept of problem finding also can be taken as a reminder about the role of affect or emotion in creative cognition. Cognition does not work independently of other aspects of human behavior. Affect seems to be especially important. Recall what was said above about intrinsic motivation. Problem finding is related to intrinsic motivation because when the individual him- or herself has identified a situation as problematic, it guarantees that the individual will view the problem as worth his or her effort. It is not at all like when an individual is presented with a problem which they must solve. And importantly, it has been suggested that the quality of a problem will determine the quality of solutions. Creative solutions may require creative problems. This of course says something about contemporary education, and in particular about the kinds of tasks and opportunities that should be presented to students.

The idea of interactions also applies directly to the divergent thinking model described above. The earliest research with this model attempted to show that divergent thinking was independent of other kinds of thinking. In particular, there was a great interest in showing that divergent thinking was unrelated to convergent thinking, the kind of thinking that is required by most academic and intelligence tests. Convergent thinking occurs when an individual must decide on the correct or one best answer. Unlike divergent thinking tasks, when convergent thinking, there is *always* one correct or conventional answer. The early research succeeded in showing a moderate degree of independence between convergent and divergent thinking, although the most recent research suggests that both are useful for creative thinking. It not only helps that an individual is able to generate possible ideas and think about various possibilities; the individual must also be able to evaluate the utility of the possibilities. The point here is that divergent thinking and convergent thinking must interact for efficient creative thinking.

Before closing, the issues in this area of study should be acknowledged. One of them involves the distribution of creative thinking skills. The question here is whether individuals who are very clearly and unambiguously creative use the same thinking skills as less gifted individuals. Some of the components mentioned above (e.g., attention) are widely distributed, but others (especially the metacognitive ones) are not. Another issue involves the role of problem solving in creative thinking. Some individuals—especially those relying on computers and artificial intelligence to build models of creative thinking—argue that all creative thinking involves problem solving. Most other individuals argue against this. The role of problem finding suggests that problem solving is not all-important for creative thinking, as does art work which is self-expression without a clear target problem. It may be best to conclude that problem solving is only one kind of creative thinking. The third issue involves cognitive representations. There is little certainty about how information is represented and structured. Various representations have been hypothesized, and numerous knowledge structures have been defined, insights and implicit theories being just two examples.

Although much of this area of study is abstract, and many components (especially the knowledge structures) cannot be directly observed, there are concrete applications. Educators, for example, can easily use the divergent thinking model when developing the curriculum. Another practical side of this field is scientific. In fact, it may be that the issues about the distribution of skill and cognitive representations can be resolved using the very models which have been developed so far to describe creative thinking.

Bibliography

Finke, R. A., Ward, T. B., and Smith, S. M. (1992). "Creative Cognition." MIT Press, Cambridge, MA.

Gardner, H. (1983). "Frames of Mind." Basic Books, New York.

Runco, M. A. (Ed.). (1993). "Problem Finding, Problem Solving, and Creativity." Ablex, Norwood, NJ.

Runco, M. A., and Albert, R. S. (Eds.). (1990). "Theories of Creativity." Sage, Newbury Park.

Sternberg, R. J. (Ed.) (1988). "Nature of Creativity." Cambridge University Press, New York.

Vernon, P. E. (Ed.) (1970). "Creativity." Penguin, New York.

Criminal Behavior

Chester L. Britt III
University of Illinois at Urbana-Champaign

Glossary

Crime A behavior proscribed by a governmental body, often involving the use of force or fraud.

Delinquency A behavior proscribed by a governmental body for persons under age 18 (i.e., minors), often involving the use of force or fraud.

Socio-economic status An indicator of a persons' standing in society, relative to that of other persons, on the basis of income, total wealth, and occupational prestige.

CRIME can be defined as a set of behaviors that have been proscribed by some governmental body—local, state, national, or international. Criminal acts generally involve the use of force and/or fraud by one party onto another party. Delinquency refers to criminal acts committed by persons who are still minors—they are under age 18. The only significant difference between crime and delinquency is that there are some behaviors that are illegal for minors, such as possessing and consuming alcohol or truancy, but are not illegal for adults. The distinction of criminal acts by age is arbitrary, and has no bearing on the major correlates of criminal behavior. A vast body of research has investigated the effects of both individual and social factors on the likelihood of crime. This research is summarized below.

I. MEASUREMENT OF CRIMINAL BEHAVIOR

The information we have about crime and its correlates comes from three main sources: official, self-report, and victimization surveys. Each source of data offers a slightly different picture of the nature of crime, but in many ways the general picture is complementary. Official sources of data include the information collected and disseminated by government agencies, such as local police precincts, state departments of public safety, as well as national and international organizations. In the United States, the primary source for official data on crime comes from the Federal Bureau of Investigation's (FBI's) *Uniform Crime Reports* (UCR) which is published annually. Each UCR includes a compilation of thousands of local police precinct reports on crimes that are known to the police (either they have been reported by citizens or the police discovered the crime while on duty) and arrest reports, from which the FBI compiles additional statistics related to the type of crime, the location of the arrest (urban, suburban, or rural), and the demographic characteristics of the offender.

Self-report surveys have most often been conducted with adolescents as respondents. Most self-report delinquency surveys are designed to gauge delinquency rates among youth and to test theories of criminal behavior. One of the main benefits of self-report data is the information obtained on crimes committed by youth that were not discovered by the police. Another benefit to self-report surveys is the detailed information collected on the characteristics of the respondents, which allows for a more thorough examination of the correlates of criminal behavior.

Victimization surveys provide a third source of information on criminal behavior. The logic to this data source is somewhat different, however. The information is not collected from the person who committed the crime, as it is in official and self-report sources, but from the victim of that activity. In the United States, the *National Crime Survey* (NCS) has been conducted annually by the Census Bureau since 1973. Each year, members of approximately 50,000 households are interviewed; each

Copyright © 1994 by Academic Press, Inc. All rights of reproduction in any form reserved.

household selected for the sample is interviewed a total of seven times over a 3-year period. The detailed characteristics of criminal events are obtained when a respondent claims to have been a victim of some crime, and an additional set of questions is asked to gather information about the circumstances of the crime. These questions address the time and location of the crime, the level of physical and property damage, and the perceived characteristics (e.g., age, race, gender) of the offender(s).

II. INDIVIDUAL CORRELATES OF CRIMINAL BEHAVIOR

A. Demographic

The demographic characteristics of individuals—age, race, and gender—represent three of the strongest correlates of criminal behavior. What these characteristics do not represent are causes of crimes. It is not valid to state that a person's age or gender was somehow responsible for the person committing a criminal act. Rather, these demographic characteristics appear to interact with all the other factors (both individual and social) that are related to crime commission, and discussed below.

1. Age

Perhaps the single, strongest correlate of criminal behavior is the age of the offender. In one of the most well-documented relationships in the study of crime, there appears to be a quite consistent pattern of young persons (age <25 years) committing a disproportionate amount of crime. The age distribution of crime generally reveals a rapid increase in the rate of criminal offending through late adolescence, peaking in the late teens or early 20s, and then tapering off gradually across the remaining age groups. Two findings have emerged from recent research on the age distribution of crime. First, the distribution for a single type of crime, such as robbery or burglary, is quite similar over time. In fact, arrest data from the UCR show the age distributions of serious crimes have not changed significantly between 1950 and 1990. Second, the shape of the age distribution does vary by the specific type of crime. Specifically, property and theft crimes (e.g., burglary and auto theft) are more likely to have peak ages of offending in the mid-teen years, while violent crimes (e.g., murder and rape) will tend to peak in the early 20s.

2. Race

The distribution of crime by the race of the offender has also received much research attention in recent years. Apart from any causal analysis, this work points to the need to look at several data sources on crime. According to statistics in the UCR, blacks appear to commit crimes at rates three to four times higher than those of whites. Yet, when self-report data are used, the differences between black and white rates of crime are much less dramatic, although black respondents still report committing crimes at a higher rate. Two explanations have been offered for this pattern. One explanation suggests that blacks are systematically discriminated against by the police and other criminal justice agencies, resulting in a significantly higher arrest rate, but comparable self-report delinquency rate. Much of the research on criminal justice processing published over the last 20 to 30 years has failed to produce findings supportive of this claim, however.

Another explanation suggests that the differences are indeed real. Official data measure more serious forms of crime, while self-report instruments measure more trivial criminal activity and show the difference between races to be negligible. Since there is not widespread acceptance of this view yet, relatively little work has been devoted to explaining what factors are responsible for the different rates of criminal behavior, and we can only hope that future efforts will devote more attention to this issue.

3. Gender

Similar to the effects of age and race, gender is also a consistent indicator of the likelihood of criminal behavior. According to both official and self-report data sources, males commit violent crimes about three to five times as often as females, while the distribution for property offenses is closer to 50–50. Prostitution and runaway (for females under age 18) represent the only two crimes for which females have higher rates of participation.

An interesting trend in female criminal activity in the United States in the 1970s was a significant increase in the rates of female fraud, embezzlement, and serious theft crimes. Several authors attributed this trend to greater female participation in the labor force, which then created greater opportunity for females to commit these kinds of crime. Although increased opportunities for crime may explain part of the increase in female crime rates, it was clearly not the only factor involved. Female involvement in the labor force, especially managerial positions, continued to increase throughout the 1980s, while rates of female crime remained about the same.

B. Criminal Propensity

An issue that is gaining renewed interest in the study of crime is the notion of an underlying, or latent, characteristic of all individuals—aggression, impulsiveness, self-control, or conditionability—that has a direct effect on a person's likelihood of committing criminal acts. The logic to this work runs something like the following. Every person has some measure of a latent trait, such as impulsiveness, which directly influences the chances that each person will commit a crime. In general, the latent trait is assumed to be normally distributed across a population of individuals. For example, those individuals who are more impulsive will be more likely to commit crimes, since impulsive persons will be more likely to act on the spur of the moment, and not think through the consequences of some behavior. Thus, impulsive persons should find the short-term gains associated with many criminal acts to be more attractive than the long-term gains associated with many conventional behaviors. Similar reasoning lies behind the notions of self-control and aggression—that all persons have some level of each of these characteristics, and therefore have some likelihood of committing a criminal act, although some persons will have a much greater likelihood than others. [*See* Control.]

The research bearing on the issue of individual criminal propensity is growing rapidly. Perhaps one of the strongest, and most consistent, individual characteristics related to criminal behavior is IQ. In official and self-report data sources, persons with lower IQs tend to have higher rates of crime and delinquency. The effect of IQ is especially striking in studies of incarcerated samples of offenders, where the mean IQ is often in the range of 93 to 94; at the same time control samples have a mean IQ of approximately 100. There is additional variation by the type of crime a person has committed, where violent offenders, as a group, tend to have even lower average IQs. [*See* Intelligence.]

Recent research from the perspective of behavioral genetics has also helped to establish a biosocial link to criminal behavior. After introducing appropriate controls for social–environmental characteristics, studies of twins (monozygotic and dizygotic) and siblings show a significant influence of the person's genetic background on the likelihood of committing criminal acts. One of the main limitations to this work, however, has been the lack of attention given to measuring characteristics of the latent trait thought to cause criminal behavior, and simply to infer its presence on the basis of a biological effect on crime. Fortunately, several ongoing studies are addressing this problem, and will likely further specify the independent and joint effects of biological and social–environmental characteristics on crime in the next several years. [*See* Behavioral Genetics.]

III. SOCIAL CORRELATES OF CRIMINAL BEHAVIOR

A. Socio-Economic Status (SES)

Historically, socio-economic status has been the key variable for sociological analyses of criminal behavior. The expectation of this work is that persons from lower SES backgrounds will have higher rates of crime. The reason being, persons from lower SES backgrounds do not have the same kinds of legitimate opportunities (e.g., employment with good wages or salary) to subsist and/or to achieve economic success that middle and upper SES persons have. When these opportunities are limited, low SES persons are expected to turn to criminal behavior in order to achieve the same things that middle and upper SES persons achieve through more conventional activities.

The interest in the SES–crime relationship has led to dozens of studies, which have produced a set of findings that are surprisingly consistent. In studies of individuals who have been arrested and convicted (i.e., official statistics), there is a disproportionate representation of persons from lower-class backgrounds. For several decades, this finding was taken as evidence supportive of the expected SES–crime relationship.

The advent of the self-report method in the late-1950s, however, began to alter the picture of the SES–crime relationship. In most large-scale self-report studies of crime and delinquency performed in the 1950s through the 1980s, there has been either a weak, but statistically significant, negative relationship or no relationship between SES and crime. What accounts for the lack of a strong negative correlation between SES and crime in self-report data is a much higher level of criminal activity among middle- and upper-class youth that is not detected in official sources. Similar to the race distribution of crime, the difference in the patterns found in official and self-report data is partially due to the types of crime measured in each data source. In contrast to the race distribution of crime, however, there is evidence supportive of differential handling of crimes by youth in low-income neighborhoods, compared to youth in middle- and upper-income neighborhoods.

B. Family Structure

That the family plays a crucial role in the delinquent behavior of its children is indisputable. At issue, however, are the nature of the family's influence and the theoretical interpretation of these effects. Several decades of research on the relationship between family characteristics and a child's delinquent behavior have focused on five general types of family effect: parental criminality, single-parent household, family size, parental relationship with the child, and parental control–supervision–discipline of the child. Although there is not a uniformity to the findings, some clear patterns emerge from the literature. [*See* FAMILY SYSTEMS.]

One of the more consistent set of findings to emerge from the research on families and delinquency is that delinquent youth are more likely to have parents with criminal records (i.e., an arrest and/or conviction for some crime) than are nodelinquent youth. The significance of this relationship is due to the time when the parent's crime occurred. Specifically, if parental criminality occurred while the child was in the parent's care, there was a greater likelihood of delinquency. Conversely, if the parent's criminal behavior occurred prior to the child's birth or when the child was no longer in the custody of the parent, the effect of parental criminality was greatly reduced.

The effect of single-parent households—often referred to as "broken homes" in the literature—has received a great deal of attention in the delinquency literature. The expectation has been that single-parent households would find it more difficult to supervise and to socialize the child(ren) to conventional values, leading to higher rates of delinquency among children from single-parent families. Much of this research has demonstrated that the effect of having a single parent has little or no significant effect on self-reported delinquency. In contrast, when the measure of delinquency is arrest or juvenile justice processing, there does appear to be a significant relationship between coming from a single-parent household and more extensive contact with the justice system. Additional research has investigated the combined effects of race and family break-up, and the findings are mixed. In one study, young blacks from single-parent households had higher rates of self-reported delinquency compared to young whites with similar family circumstances. However, another study of official rates of violent crime in the United States found the impact of family break-up to be comparable for whites and blacks.

The effect of family size has also been suggested to be an important family characteristic contributing to delinquency. Larger families are expected to produce a disproportionate number of delinquent children, since the parent(s) would be less able to control and/or socialize each child equally well. The research on this issue is limited. In the work that has been published, larger families appear to have a disproportionate number of delinquent children. This relationship can be explained by considering the effect of delinquent siblings, where larger families, simply by chance, will be more likely to have a delinquent child. Then, due to the socializing effect siblings have on each other, the delinquent child may encourage other siblings to commit delinquent acts, too.

The nature of the relationship between the child and the parent is perhaps one of the most important family characteristics to influence the likelihood of delinquency. Those children who feel loved and cared for by their parents (generally referred to as parental attachment) are much less likely to be involved in delinquent activities. Interestingly, the effect of strong parental attachment has no clear effect on the child's delinquency if the parents are engaged in illegal or deviant activities. One study found that while attachment to non-drug-using parents significantly reduced the chances the child would use drugs, attachment to drug-using parents had no relationship with the child's likelihood of using drugs. However, another study found that the drug use of the parent was significant in predicting a child's likelihood of using drugs, regardless of whether there was strong parental attachment.

Research on the issue of parental control–supervision–discipline presents a set of rather complicated and interrelated findings, and also related to many of the issues already raised. Much of the research in this area has clearly established that higher levels of parental control and supervision of their children reduce the chances of delinquency. But the effect of this control is conditioned on whether the parent is consistently able to recognize and to discipline deviance when it occurs. For example, some work has found that adolescents with behavioral disorders are more likely to have parents who are incompetent at recognizing deviance. Once parents learn how to recognize and to correct this behavior, the problem behaviors subside. Relatedly, consistency in discipline is also necessary to prevent future delinquency, so that the child learns what behavior is expected in many different situations as well as how to act accordingly. Finally, while consistent discipline and superivison are necessary to reduce the chances of future delinquency, punishment that is too harsh or physical may increase the chances of problem behaviors. [*See* PARENTING.]

C. Peer Groups

Another established set of research findings on delinquency is the likelihood that adolescents who commit delinquent acts also tend to spend time with other youths who commit delinquent acts. The effect of the peer group to receive the most attention in the literature is simply the relationship between having delinquent friends and committing delinquent acts. Many studies using self-reported delinquency and official arrest data show that young persons with more delinquent friends are more likely to have committed delinquent acts than youth with no or few delinquent friends. Although this is one of the most frequently cited relationships in the delinquency literature, its explanation has been less than satisfactory.

A related issue, which is as important as the effect of delinquent friends, is the group nature of delinquency. Research shows that most delinquent acts are committed in a group context, especially in the case of the use of alcohol and drugs, vandalism, and many theft activities. In addition, there do not appear to be large differences in the group context of delinquency that vary by gender, with the exception that young males are somewhat more likely to shoplift alone than are young females.

The nature of the friendship tie has received surprisingly little attention in the literature, given the apparent importance of having delinquent friends. Several researchers have hypothesized that the friendship ties of adolescents involved in delinquency would be qualitatively different from the friendship ties of adolescents not involved in delinquent behaviors. Some authors have argued that the friendship bonds among delinquents would be reserved and weak, while other authors expected a closely knit peer group that is able to have tremendous influence on each member. In what little research has been published thus far, the friendship bond between persons in delinquent and nondelinquent peer groups appears to be quite similar.

D. Employment

The effects of currently being employed and its relationship to criminal behavior is another issue that has received considerable research attention. Similar to the expected SES–crime relationship, it has been thought that individuals who are unemployed will be more likely to commit criminal acts. Research on unemployment and crime has been less than fully supportive of this link, however. For example, in studies of individual offenders, there tend to be disproportionate numbers of unemployed persons arrested and processed through the criminal justice system, which is consistent with the expected effect of unemployment. Yet, it does not appear that unemployment *per se* is responsible for the crimes committed. In studies examining the effects of jobs programs for adult offenders released from prison, the rearrest rates several months following release were not significantly different for the group of offenders that was given jobs when released from prison compared to a control group of offenders that was simply released from prison. To further complicate the picture of the unemployment–crime relationship, self-report studies of youth often show a positive relationship between employment and rate of delinquency. Contrary to expectations, then, youth who hold jobs commit crimes more often than those who do not, even though the youth without jobs would be expected to have greater motivation to commit crimes.

Aggregate data on crime and unemployment have revealed an additional pair of findings. First, short-term increases in the unemployment rate are most often associated with short-term decreases in property crime rates, while not associated with violent crime rates. However, if an economic downturn lasts for an extended period, then property crime rates tend to increase slightly. The explanation offered for this pattern is that unemployment trends have a direct impact on the number of motivated offenders and the number of suitable targets for victimization. With short-term increases in unemployment, government assistance often provides a way for many persons to meet subsistence needs, but it decreases their ability to buy new consumer goods that are the items most attractive to potential thiefs. In short, the opportunities for crime are decreased, and the property crime rate declines. Conversely, if an economic downturn lasts for an extended period, government assistance may begin to disappear, and it may become increasingly difficult for persons to subsist, thereby increasing the likelihood that they will see criminal activity as a reasonable alternative behavior; in effect, the pool of motivated offenders is increased, and the property crime rate rises.

E. Spatial and Temporal Factors

Urban areas have historically had higher rates of crime, when compared to suburban and rural areas. The reasoning behind this finding is that urban areas tend to have higher levels of other factors that increase the chances of criminal behavior. For example, there are higher rates of family break-up and long-term unemployment in urban areas. Since both of these factors have positive relationships with criminal behavior, it is reasonable to expect that communities which have higher rates of family break-up and unemployment will also have higher rates of crime. Interestingly, as suburban areas across the United States have begun to experience problems traditionally associated with urban areas in the last 10 to 20 years, crime rates have correspondingly increased.

There is also a significant relationship between the time of day and the commission of specific types of crime. For example, many forms of interpersonal violence occur in the early morning hours (e.g., 1 to 2 AM), most auto thefts occur at night, while burglaries are split about 50–50 between daylight and nighttime hours. The key to understanding the time of day and crime relationship is the nature of the criminal act: how the conditions under which it is most likely to occur are time related. For example, interpersonal violence also involves people who tend to know each other and who also tend to have consumed alcohol. Thus, what might have been a simple argument under other circumstances becomes a violent dispute because of the other activities the parties have been engaged (i.e., drinking alcohol) in up to the time of the dispute.

IV. SUMMARY

There is no single theory of criminal behavior that has achieved a consensus in the research literature. However, the set of facts discussed in this chapter are recognized by most researchers, regardless of their theoretical perspective. Individual factors such as age, race, gender, and self-control do have important relationships with criminal behavior. Social factors such as SES, family, peer groups, and employment also are important correlates of crime commission. The goal for future research in this area will be to integrate the individual and social factors in a way that accounts for some of the apparent anomalies discussed above. For example, if we begin with the individual characteristic of impulsiveness as a trait that increases the chances of criminal behavior, then future research might ask under what conditions will the individual's chances of crime be enhanced or mediated? How do institutions such as the family and employment interact with individual characteristics to produce criminal behavior? These are difficult questions, and will likely act as the main focus of much of the research on criminal behavior in the next several decades.

Bibliography

Blumstein, A., Cohen, J., Roth, J., and Visher, C. (1986). "Criminal Careers and 'Career Criminals'," Vol. I. National Academy Press, Washington, DC.

Gottfredson, M., and Hirschi, T. (1990). "A General Theory of Crime." Stanford University Press, Palo Alto, CA.

Jensen, G. F., and Rojek, D. G. (1992). "Delinquency and Youth Crime," 2nd ed. Waveland, Prospect Heights, IL.

Wilson, J. Q., and Herrnstein, R. J. (1985). "Crime and Human Nature." Simon and Schuster, New York.

Crisis Management

Johnny R. Purvis
University of Southern Mississippi

Glossary

Crisis A time of great danger or trouble whose outcome(s) will often determine whether unfavorable consequences will follow. Generally lasts for a short period of time; however, the manner in which the crisis is handled will often have both immediate and long-range implications.

Management Having charge of, directing, or administering a situation, an institution, or an individual(s) in a carefully controlled and tactful manner.

CRISIS MANAGEMENT is the careful and tactful management of a situation in which there is trouble or danger that has the possibility of serious and negative consequences. The possible serious and negative consequences might include litigation, injury to individuals and/or property, death of an individual, disruption of the normal routine, and loss of confidence and trust in an individual or an institution. It is important to note that serious and/or negative consequences associated with a crisis situation can be valid or imagined, depending on the mind-set of the individual directly involved in the crisis or a person totally removed from the event. In either situation, it is extremely important for those assisting in a crisis to be fully aware of this very important aspect and respond in a professional, legal, humane, and ethical manner.

I. INTRODUCTION

Individuals are increasingly being confronted with various crisis situations. Media reports from all across this country inform the public about violence and other crisis situations that occur in our homes, communities, churches, schools, and sites of employment. In many instances, participants have been ill-prepared or totally unprepared for the crisis situation they have encountered. Ill-preparedness or unpreparedness can often contribute to chaotic, difficult, and extremely dangerous situations, along with reinforcing the crisis situation to occur in the future. Thus, if individuals develop, practice, and implement a crisis management plan prior to the occurrence of a crisis situation, the negative impact of an event can often be reduced or in many instances eliminated.

The purpose of this article is to present an overview for developing a crisis management plan for an individual and/or group of individuals at work, play, place of employment, and any other situation in which a crisis might occur. In accordance with this understanding, the reader is encouraged to accept this plan as a model from which specific plans for a person's place of employment, home, school, recreational setting, or a specific crisis situation can be developed. In addition, it is hoped that the reader will accept the assumption that most of the components of a comprehensive crisis management plan, such as the one presented in this article, are applicable to almost any crisis management situation.

The components of a crisis management plan that will be discussed in this document include a definition of crisis management, phases of a crisis, responsibility for safety, events that could create a crisis, and components of a crisis management plan.

II. PHASES OF A CRISIS

The phases of a crisis include pre, interim, and post components. The prephase of a crisis empha-

Encyclopedia of Human Behavior, Volume 2
Copyright © 1994 by Academic Press, Inc. All rights of reproduction in any form reserved.

sizes those conditions and situations within one's place of employment, community, home, and school that may have contributed to the crisis. For example, during a first-period English class a teacher overheard a 15-year-old female tell a 16-year-old female that she will "beat her butt if she dates her boy friend again." On the other hand, there may have been prerequisite behaviors exhibited by the individuals or groups directly or indirectly associated with the crisis. An example of prerequisite behaviors could be illustrated by the same two girls bumping into each other as they left the classroom at the end of the period. These conditions are very important when conducting a postanalysis of a crisis.

The interim phase of a crisis is the actual crisis itself. It is during this phase that the crisis erupts, runs it course, and dissipates. This is, obviously, the most dangerous phase of a crisis. Being sensitive to the prerequisite conditions and/or behaviors associated with the crisis situation along with being well versed in crisis management will often have a significant impact on the final outcome of a crisis.

The postphase of a crisis involves those conditions and experiences existing after the interim phase of the crisis has ceased. This is a very important time for appropriate community agencies and cooperating individuals to examine the conditions prior to the crisis, the events that occurred during the crisis, and the response of those who reacted or did not react to the crisis situation. This information can be utilized in preparing for future crises as well as assisting with developing a more comprehensive understanding of the events, procedures employed, and so forth in the present crisis.

III. RESPONSIBILITY FOR SAFETY

All of us should assume a responsible role in providing for the safety and security of our fellow citizens, be it in a professional setting and/or because of moral and ethical considerations. Whether this assumption is true or false, it is extremely important for those in a service-oriented profession, such as education, to examine state laws, school board policies, and related court cases regarding students' safety and security in an educational setting. On the other hand, each person should demonstrate responsible behaviors for his or her fellow citizen's safety and well-being.

IV. EVENTS THAT COULD CREATE A CRISIS

No matter how trivial an event might first appear, it has the potential to become a major crisis. This certainly is not a paranoid reaction, but a word of caution for an individual's personal well-being and for those who are responsible for others. In accordance with this assumption, the following events serve as a sample of those areas of an individual's life that could become a crisis situation:

1. Home security and safety.
2. Confronted by someone possessing and/or threating to use a weapon (knife, firearm, etc.).
3. Confronted by someone possessing, using, under the influence, and/or distributing an illegal substance.
4. Threatened by a member of a gang or cult.
5. Physical attack by an individual (assault and battery).
6. Psychological intimidation by an individual employing a "stare down."
7. Depending on public transportation for mobility.
8. Threatened by or involved in a natural disaster (earthquake, hurricane, tornado, winter storm, or severe thunderstorms).
9. Confronted with a fire, including false alarms.
10. Threatened by or involved in a technological disaster (train derailment, airplane crash, chemical spill, etc.).
11. Involved in a bomb threat, false reports, and/or explosion.
12. Involved in an automobile accident.
13. Involved in a hostage situation.
14. Confronted with a suicide (friend, family member, employee, etc.).
15. Confronted with death (friend, family member, employee, etc.).
16. Death of a pet.
17. Confronted with an epidemic/health hazard (HIV, AIDS, measles, head lice, chicken pox, etc.).
18. Confronted with an unwanted pregnancy.
19. Confronted with a medical emergency such as choking, laceration, seizure, and child birth.
20. Confronted by child abuse and/or neglect by either a parent/guardian or another adult.
21. Observation of the abduction of a child.
22. Informed of the rape of a friend.

23. Informed of the murder of a member of one's immediate family.
24. Informed by the news media that your child's school bus has just been involved in a serious accident.
25. Sexual harassment by a member of the same or opposite sex.
26. Confrontation of an intruder on one's property.
27. Learning about a vicious and false rumor that has been generated about yourself.
28. Confronted with the issue of an unfaithful spouse or significant other.
29. Attendance school sponsored activities after regular school hours, especially athletic events.
30. Confronted with a riot, sit-in, protest, or march.
31. Confronted with verbal and/or silent psychological abuse.
32. Confronted with domestic violence with a spouse or significant other.

V. COMMITMENT FROM THE LEADERSHIP OF INSTITUTIONS OR ORGANIZATIONS

One of the most important aspects in the development a crisis management plan is the commitment of an individual and/or organization. It is very important that an individual develop a "mind-set" that is oriented toward preventing and managing personal or institutional crisis situations. If it is an organization, the administration, in cooperation with all employees, community, and cooperating agencies, should develop appropriate precedures for implementing a crisis management plan. This is very important for many reasons; one of the most important reasons is that having a plan, even though it may not be the most desirable of plans, gives individuals and organizations a sense of direction in a crisis along with providing a degree of psychological security that comes with knowing at least something about responding to a crisis.

VI. COMPONENTS OF A CRISIS MANAGEMENT PLAN

When a crisis occurs in the home, site of employment, or within the community all those that are directly or indirectly involved should know their roles and responsibilities. In accordance with this assumption, the various components of a crisis management plan are presented to assist those who are developing or have implemented a crisis plan. The following components certainly are not intended to be applicable to every crisis setting or to every type of crisis; however, they do represent common elements of a crisis management plan that most crisis plans share.

A. Determine Goals

To assist those involved in the development and implementation of a crisis management plan it is very important that those committed to crisis prevention and management develop and comprehend the goals of the plan. Goals may be broad or they may be very specific. An example of a broad goal of a crisis management plan might be "to work with all employees, community agencies, groups, and individuals to develop a system for networking all those who may be directly or indirectly involved in the management of a crisis situation."

Conversely, goals for a crisis management plan may be very specific. An illustration of a specific goal might be "to ensure that each employee knows the appropriate procedures and techniques to employ if physically attacked by an intruder." Another example of a specific goal is "to develop a preventative maintenance schedule for a vehicle to reduce the odds of a breakdown while on vacation." It is important to note that this last goal is a preventive goal which is crucial in reducing the odds of an actually having to confront a crisis situation.

B. Conduct a Needs Assessment

After establishing goals for a crisis management system, it is necessary for the individual or group, in cooperation with appropriate community agencies and individuals, to conduct a needs assessment related to aspects of crisis management that are contained within the home, place of employment, school, community, and so forth. With regard to an individual's home, a safety, security, and crisis management audit should be conducted, with an emphasis on risk management. An example of areas or concerns which could be included in this audit would be an audit of the outside lighting system, a check of each exterior door for dead-bolt locks that open from both the inside and outside by the use of a key rather an interior thump bolt, an evaluation of timers on interior lights when no one is at home at night, an evaluation of the burglar alarm system to assure that it is in operating order, an audit of the types of exterior plants that are planted in the yard along with the positioning of each plant to ensure proper distribution of exterior lighting and vision from inside of the house, and an evaluation of the family's evacuation plans in the event of a fire.

It is extremely important that a thorough needs assessment be completed regarding the resources and services that various community members, organizations, and agencies can provide regarding a crisis management plan. It addition to identifying various services, resources, and areas of expertise that the community can provide, it is very important to know the specific kinds or types of contributions the aforementioned community resources can provide. For example, a youth court or family court judge could work with school officials to require both a youngster and his or her parent/guardian to go for counseling if the youngster fights at school. As a general rule, school officials cannot do this, but a judge can and can ensure that the order is enforced. If the order is not enforced, the student's parent/guardian and/or the youngster can be penalized through the court system. School officials certainly do not have the authority to enforce and/or penalize a student's parent/guardian and in most situations breach their own authority in attempting to force a youngster to go to counseling.

C. Examine Other Crisis Management Plans

Prior to the actual planning of a crisis management plan, it is extremely important for the crisis management team of an organization or place of business to examine other crisis management plans. If possible, it is a good idea to secure several crisis plans from similar situations that have needs comparable to the one for which the plan is being developed. In addition, it is very important to obtain crisis management plans from groups that have little in common with the plan being developed. This gives the team a broader vision of the components of a crisis management plan. Finally, by obtaining other management plans, the planning team can compare the collected plans with each other and with the one being developed in an effort to ascertain strengths and weaknesses in the proposed plan.

D. Select Members of the Crisis Management Team

In addition to the crisis management planning team, a crisis response team will need to be selected to handle the actual crisis. This particular component of a crisis management plan is one of the most important components of developing, planning, implementing, evaluating, and revising a crisis plan because it involves human resources. A group, organization, institution, or company can have the very best of material resources along with policies and procedures, but without competent and professional individuals, the crisis plan will be impotent. Thus, it is extremely important to identify those who will be involved in preparing and implementing a crisis management plan along with forming a crisis management committee or team. The group that is preparing and implementing the plan can also serve as the crisis team for the organization, the teams can be totally separate, or the two groups can consist of a combination of members from both groups.

Possible members of the team may include a psychologist, social worker, health professionals, security personnel, law enforcement personnel, lawyer, emergency personnel, fire department personnel, language translator in the event that English is a second language with many individuals in the organization and community, human service personnel, members of the clergy, and any other individual or organization that possesses skills that are important during a crisis situation. Personality characteristics of team members are crucial to ensure that team members are at least compatible, reliable, possess expertise within their specialized area, and are levelheaded, especially when they are under pressure. It addition, it is important to select team members who are willing to commit time and energy to this very important task. Lastly, it is extremely crucial that a record be maintained of each team member's name, address, phone number, and area of expertise.

E. Develop and Implement a Training Program

Once the crisis management response team has been selected, the team needs to pursue extensive staff development activities focused on crisis intervention and management. Manuals that include policies, procedures, techniques, and strategies for the various types of crisis situations that might occur in a setting, such as an office building, should be developed and employed in training the team. Topics to include in the training are similar to those listed under Events That Could Create a Crisis. In addition to preparing the crisis management team, it is crucial to provide extensive crisis prevention and reaction strategies for the crisis team along with all other individuals in the organization.

F. Prepare and Maintain a List of Resources and Support Services

As discussed under Conducting a Needs Assessment, it is very important for the crisis management team to assess both the need for a crisis management plan and the various community and state resources that are available for preventing and handling a crisis situation. In addition to this assessment, other surveys, personal contacts within and outside of the crisis management team, and a list of resources and support services should be developed. This is essential in maintaining communication and soliciting assistance within the organization and the community. This list should be revised regularly, to ensure that all individuals, groups, and agencies that can contribute toward preventing a crisis, as well as provide assistance when one occurs, are included and are kept informed of crisis management needs of the organization. The list of resources and support services is crucial when a crisis occurs and, therefore, both home and office phone numbers and addresses of individuals, groups, or agencies need to be included so that critical time is not wasted. It is interesting to note that the aforementioned is important for obvious purposes, but it is also vital to the mindset and morale of those facing and/or dealing with a crisis situation. In addition, a list of resources and support services can provide a means to pool information, skills, services, materials, equipment, and personnel into a comprehensive plan to prevent, intervene during, and evaluate crisis situations.

G. Establish a Communication Network

Few individuals would dispute the claim that communication is a very vital component of any relationship, organization, agency, or group. Thus, it is crucial that a communication network within the organization and between the crisis response team, employees, and the community be established in regard to group's crisis management plan. This assumption is important in developing a network of individuals and groups within and outside of the organization, instituting and continuing dialogue with employees and their families, accessing telephone and other communication systems, holding meetings with employees, and establishing communication with the print and electronic media.

Probably the best way of communicating during an emergency is verbally. It is vital that individuals with integrity, high visibility, and good communication skills be utilized to formally and informally communicate with employees, families of employees, constituents, members of the crisis team, news media, and the general public. This should be worked out in advance of a crisis along with alternates, if the primary person is not immediately available. Prior to leaving the discussion pertaining to verbal communication, it is extremely important for the individual(s) communicating with those within and outside of the organization be open and honest with those with whom he or she is attempting to communicate. Certainly, the communicator will have to protect the rights of individuals involved in a crisis situation as well as facts that are currently confidential due to the nature and investigative stage of the incident. For example, suppose a member of a high school's teaching staff has just been attacked and stabbed by two students in one of the school's student rest rooms. The initial statement to the general public and press might resemble this, "Yes, one of our faculty members has been attacked and stabbed with an object that we believe is a hunting knife. At this time, we believe that two students confronted the teacher as he entered a rest room and that he was stabbed by one or both of the students. As soon as more information that we are allowed to release to the public becomes available, we will notify you of such information."

In addition to developing and implementing a verbal communication plan, it is important to employ as many methods as possible to communicate with persons and groups who want or need to know about a crisis situation. Meetings with employees, press conferences, internal and external memorandums, letters to constituents, presentations to organizations and groups, and other viable means to openly and honestly share with those individuals who need and desire to be informed about a crisis situation should be used.

If possible, it is generally best to inform employees about a crisis that is developing, on-going, or immediately concluded, prior to informing clients and the general public. For example, once the faculty and staff of an elementary or secondary school are informed about a crisis, a member of the crisis team should be sent to each classroom, to small groups of students, or, if the situation warrants, the teacher can inform students about the crisis situation. Regardless of who informs the students, the more information that teachers and other school officials have, the better they will be able to assist students in understanding and coping with a crisis situation. The school's public address system should *not* be used and in many instances the principal or school officials on the crisis management team should write a memorandum regarding the information to be shared with students. It is very important to inform students in small, typical class size groups, because behaviors of smaller groups are more predictable than larger ones and students can be provided with more individualized attention as they comprehend and cope with the crisis. In addition, the administration should have school psychologists, counselors, social workers, and other similar professionals available to assist students.

The news media must be informed about the crisis situation; this can be a blessing or a curse. Yes, the press can be a nuisance; however, communicating with them can often assist in lessening the negative impact of a crisis. Thus, meeting and communicating with the media in an open and honest manner are extremely vital. A spokesperson from the crisis management team should be designated to speak to the media and all communication with the media should flow through that individual. Comments made to the media should be as brief as possible, factual, and unbiased and presented with a positive attitude and calm demeanor. The spokesperson must remember that the public has a right and a need to know about the crisis. In addition, the spokesperson needs to ignore abrasive personalities or statements generated by members of the press and not argue with reporters.

The spokesperson, along with members of the crisis team, should compile a list of media personnel, their employers, office phone and facsimile machine numbers, home phone numbers, and business addresses. With this information, the public relations spokesperson can mail press releases or, better yet, use a facsimile machine during a crisis situation. In addition, copies of the prepared press releases can be given to members of the media during a regularly scheduled press conference, or when appropriate, on an as needed basis. Regardless of how press releases are handled, do not show favoritism with any members of the press. It is very important that news releases be edited to ensure that they are accurate, do not violate any individual's rights, and are factual and unbiased.

H. Designate a Base of Operation

A base of operations or headquarters should be established in an effort to coordinate crisis management activities and communications from a single location. In addition to the aforementioned, a base of operations should be established at or near the site of the crisis to more effectively coordinate activities of the crisis team. For example, suppose a family's home catches on fire. Fire officials will set-up a temporary site of operation at the site of the fire along with coordinating activities from their home base and the fire department's headquarters.

Each base of operations should have the equipment and materials that allow it to be as efficient as possible to handle the crisis itself along with sufficient equipment to provide communication at the site, at their base of operations, and to network with other agencies or individuals. The type of equipment and materials will vary according to the special services that are provided by the responding crisis team, the type of crisis, and the conditions at the site of the crisis. For example, an elementary or secondary school should have the following equipment: telephones, with at least one unlisted number so that at least one line will be free at all times; at least one computer terminal that can access all personnel and student files; at least one printer for the computer; a typewriter; at least one facsimile machine; writing paper; name tags; pens; pencils; telephone directory; student and employee directories; emergency power; portable (hand-carried) two-way radios and/or cellular phones; at least one rechargeable megaphone; several rechargeable flashlights; names and contact information on all members of the crisis team, administrators in the school district, and all community-school resources that are available in a crisis situation; and other items necessary for a crisis management team.

I. Plan and Conduct Team Meetings

The first meeting of the crisis management planning team should be an organizational meeting. During the first meeting, a tentative site for the base of operation or headquarters should be selected, a record keeper should be appointed, additional meetings should be planned, a review of the organization's management plans should be made, a discussion and evaluation of the institution's crisis management procedures should be held, a reveiw of the organization's current crisis management plan should be conducted, tentative goals for the team should be discussed, tentative team member assignments should be made, a review of the organization and community resources related to crisis management should be held, a date to reconvene the team should be established, and other items related to crisis management should be discussed.

Follow-up meetings should include updates pertaining to various crisis situations and specific plans for preventing or handling crises should be discussed, crisis procedures should be discussed, plans for involving employees or members of an organization should be shared, crisis situations should be rehearsed, and other activities related to the organization's crisis management team. In addition, the overall plan should be reviewed and updated along with a reevaluation each member's responsibilities.

J. Document

Maintaining current and accurate records of all activities related to the crisis management team is extremely important, especially during a crisis situation. The appointed record keeper for the team should prepare a log of all activities, retain a copy of all press releases, maintain a list of all individuals injured, record and document any deaths, maintain a record of all persons involved in a crisis situation along with related circumstances, compile a record of all telephone calls, keep a current list of all members of the crisis team as well as resources within the organization and community, and document all correspondence and telephone conversations.

K. Implement and Evaluate the Plan

A very important component of a crisis management plan is to implement the plan in a mock crisis situation and evaluate the various aspects of the plan during simulation activities. The "real evaluation," of course, will occur when the plan is implemented in an actual crisis situation. After implementing and evaluating either the mock or actual crisis situation, necessary adjustments should be made, following at least one debriefing session with the crisis management team.

L. Revision of the Plan

Regardless of whether a crisis plan is developed for an entire organization, a division or an organization, or for a specific crisis situation, it is never completed. The plan needs to be constantly revised because of changing circumstances and conditions within the organization and society, changes in laws and judicial rulings, changes within the clientele that the organization or institution serves, changes in personnel on the crisis management team, additions and deletions pertaining to community resources and personnel, change in technology and crisis management strategies, personnel changes within the organization, and revisions that are necessary once a crisis plan has been implemented.

VII. SUMMARY

In today's world, leaders of an institution or organization have no choice but to develop a comprehensive crisis management plan that also includes specific plans for specific crisis situations that might occur within the organization. The aforementioned assumption is based on legal issues and associated liability surrounding client and employee safety and security, the diversity of clients and families that the organization serves, and social issues that confront both employees of an organization and the general community. Regardless of the degree to which a crisis plan is developed or the particular crisis situation, all plans share the common components presented in this manuscript. These major components include: (1) determining goals, (2) conducting a needs assessment, (3) examining other institutions' or organizations' crisis management plans, (4) selecting members of the crisis management team, (5) developing and implementing a training program, (6) preparing and maintaining a list of resources and support services, (7) establishing a communication network, (8) designating a base of operation, (9) planning and conducting crisis team meetings, (10) documenting activities, (11) implementing and evaluating the plan, and (12) revising the plan.

Bibliography

Guralnik, D. B. (1984). "Webster's New World Dictionary." Simon and Schuster, New York.

Kelly, D. G., Stimeling, W. F., and Kachur, D. S. (1989). Before worst comes to worst, have your crisis plan ready. *The Executive Educator* **11,** 22–23.

Konet, R. J. (1986). Developing a suicide intervention program in your school. *NASSP* **70,** 51–54.

Nation, C. (1988). Managing crisis. *Streamlined Seminar* **6,** 1–6.

National School Safety Center. (1989). "School Crisis Prevention and Response: National School Safety Center Resource Paper." National School Safety Center, Malibu, CA.

Scottsdale Unified School District #48. (1989). "Course of Action in the Event of a Student's Death." Scottsdale, AZ.

Wisconsin Department of Public Instruction. (1988). "Children at Risk: A Resource and Planning Guide." Madison, WI.

Cross-Cultural Adaptation

Young Yun Kim
University of Oklahoma

Glossary

Acculturation The process of acquiring a new culture's symbols and practices by an individual whose prior cultural learning has taken place elsewhere.

Adaptation The process of internal modification of individuals that makes them become more fit for existence under the conditions of a particular sociocultural environment.

Assimilation The absorption process of foreign-born individuals into the native population by cultural, social, and economic mainstreaming.

Communication The process by which information is exchanged between individuals through the activities of encoding and decoding of verbal and nonverbal symbols, signs, or behavior.

Culture shock Psychological and physiological stress responses to being placed in an unfamiliar cultural environment.

Deculturation The process by which individuals unlearn or lose some of the symbols and practices of their native culture.

CROSS-CULTURAL ADAPTATION refers to the process of internal change in individuals so as to become better able to survive and function in a new and unfamiliar cultural milieu. In this process, many individuals experience culture shock particularly during the initial stages of migration. Yet, they gradually learn to make necessary adjustments in their original cultural habits and become increasingly better able to handle daily challenges in the host environment. This process of adaptive change involves the deculturation of some of the original cultural habits and the acculturation of new ones, both of which occur through continuous and prolonged communication interfaces between the newcomer and the new environment. A long-term cross-cultural adaptation may lead to the newcomer's assimilation into the cultural, social, and economic mainstream of the host society.

I. BACKGROUND

One of the dramatic changes we witness today is the enormous interface of cultures in human affairs—from political and economic to art and leisure activities. At the forefront of this global reality are the countless people who are on the move crossing cultural boundaries. Each year, millions of immigrants and refugees change homes. Finding themselves driven by natural disaster and economic need, or looking for better hopes of freedom, security, or social and economic betterment, people uproot themselves from their familiar homes and embark on the journey of building a new life in an alien, and sometimes hostile, milieu. Along with immigrants and refugees are numerous temporary sojourners. There are diplomats, military personnel, other governmental and inter-governmental agency employees, Peace Corps volunteers, missionaries, journalists, writers, researchers, professors, and exchange students who live for some length of time overseas. Many business employees today are given foreign assignments, while an increasing number of accountants, teachers, construction workers, athletes, artists, and musicians find employment in foreign countries.

A. Long-Term Adaptation

Cross-cultural adaptation studies have been continuous and extensive for the past several decades, par-

Encyclopedia of Human Behavior, Volume 2

Copyright © 1994 by Academic Press, Inc. All rights of reproduction in any form reserved.

ticularly in the United States. These studies have attempted to understand and explain the transitional experiences of individuals and groups in new and unfamiliar cultures. In the 1930s, the Social Science Research Council appointed a Subcommittee on Acculturation and charged it with the task of analyzing and defining the parameters for this new field of inquiry within the domain of cultural anthropology. As the result, acculturation was formally adopted as a legitimate new area of study dealing with those phenomena that result when individuals from one culture come into direct contact with individuals from another culture.

In this anthropological tradition, an assumption underlying studies of cross-cultural adaptation was that a "typical" member of each culture could be described and that the more a stranger could approximate the traits and values of the "ideal type," the more acculturated the stranger was believed to have become. The emphasis in these studies has been placed on assessing the learning and internalization of new personality traits or new values by the group as a replacement for those of their original culture. Such an anthropological focus on a normative or typical cultural personality structure, however, has been less than successful in providing a consistent and concrete picture of a new personality structure that would presumably replace the old one, particularly in the culturally diverse United States where the meaning of "Americanization" is difficult to agree on and gauge precisely.

Since the early anthropological beginning, academic inquiry into cross-cultural adaptation has evolved into a diverse and complex field. Such has been the case due to the application of concepts, definitions, and methodologies peculiar to the different social scientific perspectives of individual researchers. Sociological studies, for example, have approached immigrant adaptation focusing primarily on issues pertaining to social stratification, that is, the hierarchical classification based on the unequal distribution of resources, power, and prestige. Many sociological studies investigated minority–majority relations focusing on the patterns and processes in which minority groups are integrated into the political, social, and economic structure of the new, or host, society. More recent studies in urban sociology and urban anthropology have added the dimension of ethnographic explorations into the dynamics of political, social, and economic patterns played out involving immigrant communities and neighborhoods.

While most of the extensive anthropological and sociological investigations have looked at immigrant adaptation as a group phenomenon, serious examinations of the subjective experiences of individuals have been carried out mainly in the domain of social psychology, sociolinguistics, and communication. Studies have been conducted to assess and explain the patterns of long-term adaptive change in individual immigrants. In this micro-level approach, emphases have been placed on issues pertaining to the psychological acculturation and social integration of individual newcomers into their host sociocultural milieu. Most investigators along this line of inquiry have tended to agree that an individual's adaptive change over time is cumulative and progressive, following a developmental trend toward higher levels of new cultural learning and internalization and of participation in the mainstream sociocultural processes of the host society. This view held by many social scientists indeed reflects the so-called "melting-pot" (or "assimilationist") ideology that has been predominant throughout the history of immigration in the United States.

The linear, progressive conceptualization of an individual's long-term adaptation has been challenged by some following the movements of civil rights and ethnic power in the 1960s and 1970s. With the rise of the ideology of cultural pluralism, academic questions have been often raised against the validity of the cumulative-progressive model of long-term adaptation. More pluralistic conceptualizations of long-term adaptation have been presented by some sociologists and social psychologists, which, in essence, argue that assimilation into the dominant mainstream culture on the part of immigrants does not necessarily need to take place in order for them to be functional in the host society. What has been an important academic concern in this pluralistic approach is the maintenance or strengthening of a positive ethnic or cultural identity.

B. Short-Term Adaptation

Studies of temporary sojourners, on the other hand, have not taken part in this ideological debate on what the long-term adaptive change is or should be like. Studies of sojourners began increasing in number during the 1960s apparently stimulated by the beginning of the Peace Corps movement, the increase in international student exchange programs, and the increase in multinational trade during the post-war reconstruction period. Companies found that their overseas operations were being hampered because their representatives were not effectively coping with unfamiliar social and business practices. Military personnel and experts engaged in technical assistance also experienced similar problems.

Accordingly, short-term adaptation studies of sojourners have been predominantly shaped by practical concerns of "easing" the temporary but difficult transition into a new environment. Extensive literature in this area describes the problems of psychological well-being and social effectiveness in encountering alien environmental demands during one's overseas sojourn. Most researchers have tended to view such experiences as mainly problematic or undesirable, and have justified their studies as scientific efforts to find "answers" to help ease such troublesome experiences. This problematic view of cross-cultural adaptive experience is evident in the many studies that have focused on the concept of "culture shock"—a concept referring to psychological (and sometimes physical) responses of sojourners to an unfamiliar culture. This concept and related terms such as "transition shock," "cultural fatigue," and "self-shock" have been employed to refer to dislocation reactions including irritability, insomnia, and other psychosomatic disorders, an acute sense of loss, loneliness, and "marginality" arising from being uprooted from one's familiar surrounding and significant others, rejection by the natives in the host society, feelings of anxiety, insecurity, and impotence stemming from being unable to competently deal with an unfamiliar environment, and a sense of pain due to the challenge of changing one's cultural or ethnic identity. Recently, the concept of culture shock has been extended to include "reentry shock," the emotional (and sometimes physical) difficulties an individual may experience on returning home from overseas. Implicit in this approach is the assumption that a sojourn in an alien culture brings about changes in the individual, and that the changes and the absence from the original culture introduce psychological problems back home.

While stressing the problematic nature of life in a foreign land, studies of cross-cultural adaptation, both long-term and short-term, have also documented the learning and growth-facilitating aspects of adaptation. Cases have been made to argue, for example, that the cultural shock experience must be viewed in a broader context of profound learning and growth that leads to a higher degree of self-awareness. In some studies, the intensity and directionality of culture shock was found to be unrelated to patterns of psychological adjustment at the end of the first year in an alien culture. Of interest also has been the finding that, in some instances, the magnitude of culture shock was positively associated with the individuals' social and professional effectiveness within the host environment.

From this perspective, culture shock reactions are the core, though not the totality, of the cross-cultural experience. They are fundamental to adaptation in that individuals must somehow confront the physiological, psychological, social, and philosophical discrepancies between their internalized predisposition and that of the local people. Culture shock, accordingly, is a transitional experience reflecting a movement from a state of low self- and cultural awareness to a state of high self- and cultural awareness. The learning and growth-facilitating aspect of a cross-cultural experience is reflected in the extensive research data that show discernible patterns of change in psychological adapation states over time. A variety of sojourner studies have also identified a U-curve of psychological adaptation—depicting the general tendency for sojourners to experience initial optimism and elation, the subsequent emotional dip or "trough," followed by a gradual recovery to higher adaptation levels. This U-curve description has been further extended to the W-curve by adding the "reentry" phase during which the sojourner once again goes through a similar psychological adaptation process upon returning home.

Focusing almost exclusively on the intrapsychic experiences of newcomers, however, the above individual-level studies of cross-cultural adaptation have paid little attention to the macro-level anthropological and sociological concerns. Such has been the case despite the fact that, in reality, the personal experience of adaptation is closely tied to the sociocultural context in which one strives to function, as well as to the sociocultural and other backgrounds and resources that individuals have brought with them. Together, the environmental and predispositional conditions help set the initial parameters within which each individual finds an uniquely personalized passage of cross-cultural adaptation. As such, exclusive focus on individual experiences alone cannot fully explain how and why different individuals experience similar environments differently and similar individuals experience different environments differently. To the extent that the individual and the environment co-influence the individual's adaptation process, a more adequate attention must be given to both environmental and individual factors in order to understand the process of cross-cultural adaptation more fully.

The following discussion, therefore, describes and explains the phenomenon of cross-cultural adaptation as a process of individual transformation that is facilitated or detered by factors both internal and external to a given stranger. An emphasis is given to presenting an account that reflects the salient concepts and concerns in each of the academic approaches that have been briefly reviewed. As such, the following account integrates the psychological (micro-level) and social (macro-level) forces operating on the way cross-cultural adaptation is played out in a stranger's experience of adapting to a new and unfamiliar environment.

II. THE PROCESS OF CROSS-CULTURAL ADAPTATION

Most immigrants and sojourners face some drastic and all-encompassing challenges in having to adapt to the host culture and construct a new life in an unfamiliar milieu at least temporarily. Despite the varied circumstances and differing levels of commitment to the host society, what is common to immigrants and sojourners alike is the fact that they begin their life in the host society more or less as strangers. They realize that many of their previously held beliefs, taken-for-granted assumptions, and routinized behaviors are no longer relevant or appropriate. Faced with things that do not follow their unconscious "script," they must cope with a high level of uncertainty and anxiety about the new environment and the people around them. The gap between the familiar and comfortable surroundings of home and the strange milieu of the host society limits their ability to function effectively. Recognition of verbal and nonverbal codes, behaviors, and interpretations of the hidden assumptions underlying those behaviors are likely to be more difficult. They are between two worlds—the familiar milieu of the original culture and their new locus in the host society.

Adding to the uncertainty stemming from cultural differences and unfamiliarity with them is the experience of the psychological distance between the newcomer as an outsider and the natives as insiders. The intergroup "posturing" expresses an attitude of "us-and-them" based on one's group identity. Intercultural interactants tend to see themselves, as well as their interaction partners, in light of their respective cultural membership. The drawing of invisible lines between people encourages an impersonal perception and treatment of each other as the representative of a group rather than as a unique person. Such intergroup posturing often is accompanied by "ingroup loyalty" and "outgroup discrimination," which are reflected in the tendencies to shy away from getting to know each other and to accentuate differences in perceiving and interpreting each other's actions and attributes.

Cross-cultural challenges such as these—cultural difference, unfamiliarity, and intergroup posturing—naturally and inevitably bring stress to newcomers. Stressful experiences, no matter how miniscule, are inherent in the very nature of crossing cultures. Stress is experienced by individuals whenever their capabilities are not adequate to predict or manage the demands of an environment. Stress is further intensified because of the fact that strangers must learn new ways to think, feel, and behave so as to coordinate their activities with local people—an activity commonly called *acculturation*. In varying degrees, they further go through the process of *deculturation*, or unlearning of some of the childhood cultural patterns—at least in the sense that new responses are adopted in situations that previously would have evoked old ones. The experience of acculturation and deculturation, in turn, inevitably produce forms of temporary psychic disturbance and even "breakdown" in some extreme cases. As parts of their internal organization undergo changes, the strangers are temporarily in a state of disequilibrium manifested in emotional "lows" of confusion and anxiety. This state of internal flux is met by the strangers' tendency to use various "defense" mechanisms such as selective perception, denial, hostility, cynicism, avoidance, and withdrawal—all of which hinder the activities of acculturation and deculturation necessary for adapting to the host milieu. [*See* STRESS.]

Such cross-cultural stress experiences are particularly acute during the initial phase of sojourn or immigration, as indicated by the difficulties and disruptions that have been documented amply in studies of "culture shock" and related social psychological phenomena. Indeed, individuals crossing cultures experience an acute "existential alertness." Numerous people struggle to cope with feelings of inadequacy and frustration in the changed environment. Yet, the stress they experience is at the very heart of the cross-cultural experience, and works as a necessary impetus for new learning. In time, most strangers manage to achieve an increasing level of adaptation to their changed circumstances. Prompted by the cross-cultural challenges they face in the host environment, they work out new ways of handling their daily activities. Willingly or not, to handle the transactions of daily living necessitates that strangers detect similarities and differences between the new surrounding and the home culture—from maintaining basic survival necessities to pursuing life goals. In the on-going relationship with the environment, they gradually modify their cognitive, affective, and behavioral habits, and acquire increasing proficiency in expressing themselves, understanding the host cultural practices, and coordinating their thoughts and actions with those of the local people.

The interplay of stress and adaptation levels to an internal growth—a transformation in the direction of increased functional fitness and psychological health vis-à-vis the host environment. Stress is part and parcel of the strangers' adaptation and growth experiences over time. Together, stress and adaptation define the nature of the strangers' psychological movement forward in the direction of increased chances of success in meeting the demands of the host environment. As such, cross-cultural adaptation plays out not in a smooth, arrow-like linear progression, but in a cyclic and continual "draw-back-to-leap" pattern: Each stressful experience is responded to by strangers with a "draw back" (or temporary disintegration and disengagement), which then activates their adaptive energy to help them reorganize themselves and "leap forward" (temporary integration and engagement). The process is simultaneously disturbing and promising, as it involves continual new cultural learning (acculturation) and the unlearning of some of the old culture (deculturation).

Numerous sojourners and immigrants bear witness to the remarkable human capacity to carry on life when completely estranged from one's familiar home. From them, we learn that crossing cultures provides opportunities for learning and growth beyond the original cultural parameters. Although their tribulations are often staggering, their success stories offer insights into the process in which strangers work through the setbacks and come out "victorious" with an increased capacity to see others, themselves, and situations in a new light and to face new challenges yet to come.

III. COMMUNICATION FACTORS

Given the developmental process of cross-cultural adaptation, we now turn to the phenomenon of differential adaptation rates, or speeds at which different strangers adapt. Even though most strangers in alien cultures have demonstrated an impressive capacity to manage cross-cultural challenges successfully without damaging their overall integrity, some do suffer more from an extreme inability to find ways to overcome the challenges they face in the host environment. Some may strongly resist the idea of having to change their original cultural habits, thereby raising psychological barriers to work against their own adaptive change. Others may be ill-equipped to deal with states of panic causing a prolonged damage to their internal system, leading to a more extreme withdrawal and alienation from the host society or a decision to return to their home country prematurely.

The fact that individual strangers differ in their adaptation rate leads to the question, "Why do some strangers adapt faster than others?" or "Given the same length of time, why do some strangers attain a higher level of adaptation?" To explain differential adaptative changes, we need to focus on the fact that communication—the process of encoding and decoding verbal and nonverbal information—lies at the heart of cross-cultural adaptation. After all, adaptation occurs through the communication interface between the stranger and the host milieu—just as the natives acquire their capacity to function in their social environment through communicative interactions throughout their lives. It is only through communication that strangers can come to learn the significant symbols and practices of the host culture, and thereby to organize their own and others' activities successfully.

A. Personal Communication

Communication activities can be conceptualized into two basic, inseparable dimensions—personal communication and social communication. Personal (or intrapersonal) communication refers to the mental activities by which we organize ourselves in and with our sociocultural milieu, developing ways of seeing, hearing, understanding, and responding to the environment. As such, personal communication can be thought of as the "private symbolization" activities, that is, sensing, making-sense-of, and acting toward the objects and people in one's milieu. It is the process by which the individual informationally fits himself into his environment. In the context of cross-cultural adaptation, personal communication can be considered to be *host communication competence*, that is, the overall internal capacity of a stranger to decode and encode information in accordance with the host cultural practices of communication. For the natives, such communication competence has been acquired from so early in life and has been so internalized into their personal communication system that, by and large, it operates automatically and unconsciously. For strangers, however, such competence has to be acquired and cultivated through trial and error. Until they have acquired a sufficient level of host communication competence, they are handicapped in their ability to relate to the host environment. [*See* Interpersonal Communication; Interpersonal Perception and Communication.]

The many elements of host communication competence—from the knowledge about the host language and social norms to the ability to manage interpersonal relationships and solving impending problems at work—can be grouped into three categories that have been commonly employed in the study of communication competence: cognitive, affective, and operational or behavioral. *Cognitive competence* includes intellectual capacities such as the knowledge of the host language and culture including the history, social institutions, world views, beliefs, laws, regulations, social norms, and rules of interpersonal conduct. The knowledge of the host language not only means the linguistic knowledge such as phonetics, syntax, and vocabulary but also includes the knowledge about the pragmatic uses of the language in everyday life, that is, the many subtle nuances in the way the language is used and interpreted by the natives in various formal and informal contexts of social engagement. Linguistic and cultural knowledge is accompanied by a development of cognitive complexity, that is, the structural differentiation and integration in an individual's information-processing capacity. During the initial phase of adaptation, a stranger's perception of the host culture is relatively simple; gross stereotypes are salient in the perception of the unfamiliar environment. As the stranger learns more about the host culture, however, his or her perception becomes more refined and complex, enabling him or her to participate in the host social processes meaningfully.

Along with cognitive competence, *affective competence* facilitates cross-cultural adaptation by providing an emotional and motivational capacity to deal with the various challenges of living in the host environment. Included in this competence is the strangers' willingness and determination to learn the host language and culture. Also included is their ability to understand and empathize with the emotional and aesthetic sensibilities of the natives, and to participate in the local experiences of joy, excitement, humor, and triumph as well as sadness, anger, and despair. Relatedly, the strangers' affective competence also includes their attitude toward the host society and toward themselves. Strangers who feel positive and respectful toward the host society are likely to maintain less psychological distance from and prejudice against its members, compared with other strangers who may resent or look down on the natives, or who have little genuine interest in understanding them. In addition, strangers lack affective competence when they feel insecure or confused about themselves and their own cultural identity, and thus feel "marginal."

Closely linked with cognitive and affective competence is *operational competence* or the enactment tendencies. The operational competence of strangers refers to their capacity to enact, or express, their cognitive and affective experiences outwardly when communicating with others. The strangers' operational competence, as such, is based on their cognitive and affective competence. As they try to come up with a mental plan for action, they must base the decision on their current knowledge about the host culture and language, the degree of sophistication in their information-processing capacity, as well as their ability and motivation to appreciate, empathize, and participate in the emotions and aesthetic experiences of the natives. As such, the strangers' operational competence enables them to choose a "right" combination of verbal and nonverbal activities to meet the demands of daily activities—from managing face-to-face encounters, initiating and maintaining relationships, seeking appropriate information sources, and solving various problems they may encounter, to finding ways to succeed in accomplishing their goals.

B. Social Communication

Personal communication is linked to social communication when two or more individuals interact with one another, knowingly or not. Social communication is the process underlying "intersubjectivization," a phenomenon that occurs as a consequence of "public symbolization." If the personal communication (or host communication competence) can be compared to the "off-line functions" of computer systems, social communication is the "on-line functions" which interface with the computer environment through input–output transactions of messages.

The strangers' host communication competence is directly and reciprocally connected to their participation in the social communication activities of the host society. On the one hand, their social communication activities are constrained by their capacity to communicate effectively and appropriately in the host cultural context. On the other hand, every social communication event offers them an opportunity to cultivate their communication competence—cognitively, affectively, and behaviorally. In particular interpersonal communication, or direct face-to-face interaction, helps strangers to secure vital information and insight into the mind-sets and behaviors of the local people. In interacting with natives face-to-face, strangers also learn about themselves—how they think, express themselves, and respond to others. As such, the strangers' interpersonal communication activities not only can enable them to carry out their daily tasks but also can provide them with needed emotional support and points of reference for checking and validating their own thoughts and actions.

In addition to interpersonal communication, the strangers' adaptation is facilitated by attending to the mass communication activities of the host society. Mass communication refers to social communication that occurs through various forms of media such as radio, television, newspaper, magazine, movie, art, music, and drama. By engaging in such communication activities, strangers interact with their host milieu without direct involvement in relationships with specific individuals, and thereby expand the scope of their adaptive learning beyond the immediate social context with which they come into contact. In transmitting messages that reflect the aspirations, myths, work and play, and specific issues and events of the host society, the media explicitly or implicitly convey the world views, beliefs, values, mores, and norms of the culture. Of the strangers' various mass communication experiences, exposure to information-oriented mass media messages (such as newspapers, magazines, television news, and other informational programs) has been found to be particularly associated with greater adaptation, when compared to more entertainment-oriented media contents.

The adaptation function of mass communication should be particularly significant during the initial phase of resettlement. During this phase, strangers have not yet developed a level of host communication competence sufficient to develop interpersonal relationships with local people. The communication experiences in direct face-to-face contact with the natives can be intensely frustrating or intimidating to many strangers. They may feel awkward and out of place in relating to others, and the direct negative feedback from another person can be too overwhelming for the strangers to have pleasurable interpersonal encounters with the natives. Under such circumstances, the strangers naturally tend to withdraw from such direct contact, preferring mass media as an alternative, pressure-free channel through which elements of the host culture can be experienced.

IV. ENVIRONMENTAL FACTORS

The adaptation function of the strangers' personal and social (interpersonal, mass) communication cannot be fully understood in isolation from the conditions of the new sociocultural milieu. Societies and communities present different environments for strangers: Strangers may be more successful in adapting to a certain environment than to others. Many of the environmental characteristics can be grouped as (1) host receptivity and conformity pressure, and (2) ethnic group strength. These factors are discussed here as crucial to defining the relative degrees of "push and pull" that a receiving society offers to strangers, thereby influencing their cross-cultural adaptation.

A. Host Receptivity and Conformity Pressure

The receptivity of the host environment refers to the degree to which the environment is open to, welcomes, and accepts strangers into its social communication networks and offers them various forms of informational, technical, material, and emotional support. This term incorporates the meaning of other similar terms such as "interaction potential" or "acquaintance potential" that have been employed to refer to the access that strangers have to the host social communication processes. A given environment can be more receptive toward certain groups of strangers while unwelcoming toward certain others. For example, Canadian visitors arriving in a small town in the United States are likely to find a largely receptive environment. On the other hand, the same town may show less receptivity toward visitors from lesser known and vastly different cultures such as

Turkey or Iran. Such differences in host receptivity extended to strangers can be attributed to a number of plausible reasons including: (1) the nature of the relationship, friendly or hostile, between the host country and the stranger's home country; (2) the degree of cultural and ideological difference and incompatibility between the two cultures; (3) the perceived or actual status or power of the stranger's home country and culture; (4) the perceived or actual economic, social, and political standing (or merit) of the stranger's ethnic group within the host society; (5) the perceived or actual economic, social, and political threat to the host society brought about by the stranger's ethnic group; and (6) the racial/ethnic prejudice predominantly held by the society against strangers in general or the particular group. These and related factors, individually and interactively, help shape the degree of receptivity a particular host environment offers a particular stranger.

Along with receptivity, conformity pressure on the part of the host society influences the social communication activities of strangers. Here, conformity pressure refers to the extent to which the society challenges strangers to adopt the normative patterns of the host culture. Different host environments show different levels of acceptance of strangers and their ethnic characteristics. Heterogeneous and "open" host environments such as the United States generally tend to hold a more pluralistic political ideology concerning ethnic differences and thereby exert less pressure on strangers to change their habitual ways. Even within a country, ethnically more heterogenous metropolitan areas tend to demand that strangers conform less than do small, ethnically homogeneous rural towns. Even within a city, certain neighborhoods may be more homogeneous and thus expect more conformity from strangers. [*See* Obedience and Conformity.]

B. Ethnic Group Strength

Another important aspect of an environment that influences strangers' cross-cultural adaptation is the strength of their ethnic group relative to the host society at large. Ethnic groups differ in their relative status or power within the host society. Ethnic group strength has been conceptualized as following common stages. The first is the stage of the economic adjustment which occurs upon arrival of the group until they become an integral part of the permanent economy. The second stage is community building, or the development of community leadership and institutional resources used to assert the ethnic group's identity and interests. This stage of ethnic community development corresponds to the concept of "institutional completeness." The third stage is the period of political growth and aggressive self-assertion in order to strengthen the collective ethnic identity and common interests of the group as a whole.

In social psychology, the phenomenon of ethnic group strength has been discussed in terms of "ethnolinguistic vitality." In social psychological studies, ethnolinguistic vitality has been explained in terms of three structural variables: (1) the status of a language in a community, (2) the absolute and relative number of its locuters, and (4) the institutional support (e.g., governmental services, schools, mass media) for the ethnic language. Ethnolinguistic vitality as an objective environmental condition has been linked to the "subjective ethnolinguistic vitality" or perceived legitimacy of the position of one's ethnic group. For example, speakers who perceive a subordinate position of their group as legitimate are likely to adapt their communication behaviors and "converge" to those of the dominant outgroup.

These views on ethnic group strength offer implications for the role of ethnic group strength in a stranger's adaptation to the host society. Integrating these views, we can describe the strength of an ethnic group in terms of one or more of the following elements: (1) ethnolinguistic vitality; (2) economic status, (3) institutional completeness, and (4) ethnic political activism. Frequently, these community characteristics are closely associated with the size of the ethnic population and the historical "maturity" of the community in the host society. From this view, the Cuban-Americans in Miami, Florida, for example, have an ethnic community that is stronger than a smaller Russian community in Chicago. Exceptions are seen in a small-size ethnic group such as the Americans who recently began working and living in Czekoslovakia. Even though they are small in size and relatively unorganized, their political and economic status/prestige as Americans renders it a strength as an ethnic group.

Because a stronger ethnic group provides its members with a stronger subculture and offers many of the vital services to its members, it is likely to facilitate the cross-cultural adaptation of strangers during the initial phase. In the long run, however, a strong ethnic community is likely to discourage their adaptation to the host society, as it encourages ethnolinguistic maintenance. A strong ethnic community is further likely to exert a subtle or explicit pressure to conform to the ethnic community norms and thereby discourage an active participation in the host social communication activities. Empirical evidence shows, for example, that, in Australia, the Greek immigrant community is more cohesive and organized than is the Italian, and that Greek-Australian adolescents are reported to place more emphasis than Italian-Australian adolescents on their ethnic identity and maintaining their heritage. In addition, according to the investigators, the Greek-Australian adolescents placed less emphasis on adapting to the dominant Australian culture at large. Similar results were reported in Canada, that an ethnic group's status within the society interacted with its institutional completeness, so that groups high on both status and institutional completeness (French and Jews) had the strongest sense of ethnic identity.

V. BACKGROUND FACTORS

The adaptation of strangers is influenced not only by the environmental condition, but also by the condition of the strangers. Each stranger begins the cross-cultural adaptation process with a different set of pre-existing characteristics. Some may begin with enthusiasm, while others may find themselves "forced" into it by unavoidable circumstances. Some may be young, while others may feel they are too old to make changes in their lifetime habits. The internal conditions with which they begin their life in the host society help set the parameters for their own subsequent adaptive changes. The various ways in which strangers differ in their background conditions can be organized into three categories: (1) preparedness, (2) ethnicity, and (3) personality. Together, these characteristics help define the degree of a stranger's "adaptive potential" or "permeability" into the host environment.

A. Preparedness

Strangers come to their new environment with differing levels of readiness for dealing with that environment. Specifically, preparedness refers to the level of host communication competence prior to moving to the host culture, or the cognitive, affective, and operational abilities to participate in the social communication activities of the host society—from the knowledge of the host culture and language and the attitude toward the host society to the ability to empathize with the local people's emotional and aesthetic experiences and to perform and engage in various social situations appropriately and effectively. Influencing the strangers' readiness is a wide range of formal and informal learning activities they may have had prior to moving to the host society. Included in such activities are the schooling and training in, and the media exposure to, the host language and culture, as well as their prior contacts with members of the host society. In addition, the strangers' preparedness is often influenced by whether their move to the host society is voluntary or involuntary and for how long. Voluntary, long-term immigrants, for example, are likely to enter the host society with a greater readiness and willingness for making necessary changes in themselves compared to the temporary visitors who unwillingly relocate for reasons other than their own volition.

B. Ethnicity

Strangers arrive in a host society with different cultural, racial, and linguistic backgrounds. The term *ethnicity* is used here as an inclusive term to refer to various characteristics of strangers pertaining to their distinctiveness as a people. As such, the Japanese sojourners and immigrants bring to a given host society common physical, linguistic, and cultural features that are different from, say, Mexicans or French. Such ethnic characteristics play a crucial role in the cross-cultural adaptation process. They do so by affecting the ease or difficulty with which the stranger is able to develop the communication competence in a given host society, and to participate in its social communication activities. For instance, many of the Japanese business executives in the United States are likely to face a greater amount of challenge in overcoming their language barrier than are their British counterparts. In particular, the strangers' physical features (such as height, skin color, and facial features) play an important role in their cross-cultural adaptation by influencing the degree to which the natives are psychologically prepared to welcome them into their interpersonal networks. Compared to Columbian visitors, for instance, Caucasian visitors from Ireland would be more readily accepted in the United States.

The ethnicity of a given stranger influences the strangers' adaptation process in two interrelated manners. First, each presents its particular level of linguistic and cultural barrier for the stranger to overcome in order to develop the host communication competence and participate in the host social communication activities. Second, each creates a certain level of psychological distance (or affinity) in the minds of the natives, which, in turn, would affect the natives' receptivity toward the stranger. As such, strangers embark on their cross-cultural adaptation process with certain levels of "advantage" (or "handicap") simply due to their ethnic characteristics.

C. Personality

Along with ethnic backgrounds, strangers enter a host environment with a "personality," or a set of more or less enduring traits of sensibilities. They begin the challenges of the new environment within the context of their existing personality, which serves as the basis upon which they pursue and internalize new experiences with varying degrees of success. Of particular interest to the present theory are those personality resources that would help facilitate the strangers' adaptation by enabling them to endure stressful challenges and to maximize new learning—both of which are essential to their adaptive transformation. [*See* TRAITS.]

Openness is such a personality trait. Openness is defined as an internal posture that is receptive to new information. Openness, like a child's innocence, enables strangers to minimize their resistance and to maximize their willingness to attend to the new and changed circumstances. Openness further enables strangers to perceive and interpret various events and situations in the new environment as they occur with less rigid, ethnocentric judgments. Accordingly, the term, openness incorporates other similar but more specific concepts such as "flexibility" and "tolerance for ambiguity." It further connotes the optimism and affirmative orientation in strangers' basic outlook on life in general, as well as their fundamental "self-trust" in the face of adverse circumstances. As such, openness is a dimension of personality that enables strangers to continually seek to acquire new cultural knowledge, to cultivate greater emotional and aesthetic sensitivity, and to expand the range of their behavioral repertoire—all of which are vital to actively participating in and accommodating the demands of the host milieu.

Strength is an additional personality trait closely related to openness. Along with openness, the present theory identifies personality strength as vital to cross-cultural adaptation. Like openness, the concept of personality strength is a broad concept that represents a range of interrelated personality attributes such as resilience, risk-taking, hardiness, persistence, patience, elasticity, and resourcefulness. As such, personality strength means the inner quality that absorbs "shocks" from the environment and bounces back without being seriously damaged by them. Low levels of personality strength are seen in tendencies to be shy, fearful, and easily distressed by uncertain or stressful situations. On the other hand, individuals with high levels of personality strength tend to be stimulated by new challenges and remain effervescent and confident.

Strength, together with openness, helps define the personality predisposition that serves as the inner resources, based on which strangers "push" themselves in their adaptation process. Strong and open strangers are less likely to give up easily and are more likely to take risks willingly under challenging situations in the host society. They are better equipped to work toward developing host communication competence since they would continually seek new learning and new ways to handle their life activities. In doing so, they would be better able to make necessary adjustments in themselves so as to facilitate their own intercultural transformation and growth. Serious lack of these qualities, on the other hand, would weaken their adaptive capacity, and thereby work as self-imposed psychological barriers against their own cross-cultural adaptation process.

VI. CONCLUSION

In essence, cross-cultural adaptation is about change in individual strangers. As sojourners and immigrants undergo continual communication activities in the host society, they will become more functionally fit and psychologically healthier vis-à-vis the environment. The internal change process is possible because of the stress–adaptation–growth dynamic that strangers experience as they try to cope with and manage the challenges of the unfamiliar milieu. In doing so, strangers acculturate (learn) new cultural patterns, as well as deculturate (unlearn) at least some of the old cultural patterns. All of the learning and unlearning takes place via communication interfaces between the stranger and the host environment. As such, the quantity and quality of communication strangers have with the host environment critically contribute to the different rates of adaptive change they achieve in a given period of time.

Realistically, no stranger's adaptation can ever be complete no matter how long he or she interacts with the host environment. Most of them, nonetheless, do make a workable adaptation given a sufficient amount of time, as they continue to interact with the host environment. Gradually the strangers are transformed so that they become increasingly capable of managing their daily activities. At the heart of interactive adaptation lies the communication process linking the individual strangers to the host sociocultural milieu. The importance of communication to adaptation cannot be overemphasized. Acquisition of communication competence by the stranger is not only instrumental to all other aspects of his or her life activities, but also vital for the host society if it is to effectively accommodate diverse elements and, at the same time, maintain the necessary societal unity and strength. As long as common channels of communication remain, concensus and patterns of concerted action will persist in the society. Communication makes it possible to merge the new arrivals into one social organization of commonly shared ideas and values.

The dimension of personal communication—the cognitive, affective, and operational components of the strangers' host communication competence—serves as the very "engine" which "moves" them along the adaptive journey. Inseparably linked with the host communication competence is the dimension of social communication, through which strangers participate in the on-going social milieu of the host society. As strangers participate in various forms of interpersonal and mass communication activities, they are both encouraged and pressured by the host environment as well as by their ethnic community environment. The three environmental conditions—host receptivity, conformity pressure, and ethnic group strength—help define the relative degree of "push and pull" that a receiving society offers to strangers. An environment offering an optimal influence on the strangers' adaptation is viewed as one in which the native population welcomes and supports the strangers while expecting them to conform to the local norms. At the same time, an optimal environment includes an ethnic community that provides informational, material, and emotional support during the initial transition period, without exerting social pressure on the strangers against their adaptation to the host society at large. In facing such environmental forces, the strangers' own readiness, ethnicity, and personality strength and openness set the initial parameters for the subsequent unfolding of their own cross-cultural experiences.

Should strangers choose to become successfully adapted, they must, above all, be prepared and willing to face the stressful experiences of coping with the uncertainties and anxieties in an unfamiliar milieu. They must concentrate on acquiring new cultural communication practices and putting aside some of the old ones. They must recognize the importance of host communication competence as the fundamental mechanism by which they adapt successfully. Through openness and strength of personality, strangers can better overcome temporary setbacks and embrace cultural differences. They must also maximally participate in the interpersonal and mass communication processes of the host society. Through active participation, the strangers can in turn develop a more realistic understanding of, and appreciation for, the native culture and ways of life.

Few strangers can escape cross-cultural adaptation completely as long as they are engaged in direct and continuous communication interactions with the host environment. Adaptation is a phenomenon that occurs naturally and is desired by most, if not all, strangers. Through communication activities, strangers acquire at least some degree of new cultural learning (acculturation). At the same time, they are bound to lose at least some of the original cultural patterns (deculturation)—regardless of the ideological viewpoint they themselves may have concerning the nature of their relationship with the dominant cultural group in the host society. In this view, the on-going debate between assimilationists (who adhere to the "melting-pot" ideology) and "pluralists" (proponents of conservation and strengthening of ethnic identity) loses its relevance. It is too simplistic to view adaptation and ethnicity maintenance as mutually incompatible or exclusive phenomena and argue that strangers choose one or the other. They are two sides of the same coin. They are interrelated and inseparable. What is important is for both assimilationists and pluralists to acknowledge the fact that at least some adaptive changes do occur in individuals over time and that such changes do accompany a certain degree of loss of ethnicity.

All in all, the cross-cultural adaptation process is a journey of personal transformation in which each stranger cultivates an inroad into the host environment. It is further a joint venture between the stranger and the environment. Out of the dynamic interface arises a fluctuating psychic movement of stress, adaptation, and growth. Gradually and imperceptibly, most strangers advance in the direction of an intercultural realm of personhood, where they are better able to see and manage cultural differences with depth and appreciation. The fact that countless people have gone through this process successfully is a tribute to the ever-present human capacity—the capacity to face challenges, learn from them, and evolve into a greater self-integration.

Bibliography

Adler, P. S. (1987). Culture shock and the cross-cultural learning experience. In "Toward Internationalism" (L. F. Luce and E. C. Smith, Eds.). Newbury, Cambridge, Massachusetts.

Berry, J. W. (1990). Psychology of acculturation: Understanding individuals moving between cultures. In "Applied Cross-Cultural Psychology" (R. W. Brislin, Ed.), pp. 232–253. Sage, Newbury Park, CA.

Furnham, A., and Bochner, S. (1986). "Culture Shock: Psychological Reactions to Unfamiliar Environment." Methuen, London.

Kim, Y. Y. (1988). "Communication and Cross-Cultural Adaptation." Multilingual Matters, Clevedon, England.

Kim, Y. Y., and Gudykunst, W. B. (Eds.) (1988). "Cross-Cultural Adaptation: Current Approaches." Sage, Newbury Park, CA.

Torbiorn, I. (1982). "Living Abroad." Wiley, New York.

Crowding: Effects on Health and Behavior

Stephen J. Lepore
Carnegie Mellon University

Glossary

Community density Number of people in a community area or proportion of people per available dwellings or space in a community.

Crowding A negative psychological state that results from perceiving that there are too many people present in the available space.

Density Number of people in a specified amount of space or proportion of people per available space.

Household density Number of people in a residential dwelling or proportion of people per available rooms or space in a residential dwelling.

CROWDING is a complex of undesirable or negative psychological reactions to highly populated, or high-density, settings. The experience of crowding is almost always aversive. It is the feeling of being cramped, perceiving that others are too close for comfort, or feeling that there is not enough elbow room and breathing space. People who feel crowded for prolonged periods of time can become psychologically demoralized, depressed, and anxious. People who experience crowding often exhibit a pattern of somatic and social reactions in addition to their psychological reactions. The body often responds to the experience of crowding with increased arousal, as indicated by elevated blood pressure and a faster heart rate. Social responses to crowding can include physically withdrawing from interactions with other people. Thus, crowding appears to have adverse effects on interpersonal relations, as well as undesirable effects on psychological and bodily functioning. Crowding, therefore, can be conceived of as a syndrome of psychological, somatic, and social reactions to the stress associated with high density.

I. DISTINCTION BETWEEN DENSITY AND CROWDING

It is important to distinguish between the subjective, psychological experience of crowding and the objective, environmental source of the crowding experience: high population density. Density is a property of the physical environment whereas crowding is primarily a psychological experience. The negative effects of high density on human health and behavior are strongest and most prevalent when individuals are uncomfortable or stressed by the high density. That is, high density might only affect health and behavior when individuals appraise the high-density setting as being crowded. Density is an important antecedent to the experience of crowding but is often not sufficient to explain everyone's feeling of crowding or a particular individual's experience of crowding in different settings or at different times.

Density is typically measured by calculating a ratio score of the number of people to a given amount of space. There are two broad types of density studied by social scientists, *household density* and *community density* (see Table I). Household density can be determined in many ways. For example, one could calculate the number of people per rooms or square footage within a household. According to the U.S. census, households with more than 1.0 persons per room are overpopulated. Absolute number of people in a household in a residence also can be

Copyright © 1994 by Academic Press, Inc. All rights of reproduction in any form reserved.

TABLE I
Different Environmental Sources of Crowding

Types of household density
Number of people per household area[a]
Number of rooms per household
Square footage per household
Number of persons per room in a household
Types of community density
Number of residents per community area[b]
Number of households per community area
Number of commercial buildings per residential community area
Number of multi-unit housing structures per community area
Proportion of households with more than one person per room in a community area
Proportion of households with five or more persons in a community area
Number of persons per 10,000 square feet of residential space in a community area
Number of persons living on a street per 1000 feet

[a] Household areas can be measured in square footage or meters.
[b] Community areas can be measured in acres, square miles, or by census tract.

used as indicators of objective levels of household crowding. Community density measures reflect the amount of space for a given population over a wider space than an individual's residence. Community density can be determined by calculating the number of people per acre, people per square mile, or people per census tract. Occasionally community density will be defined as the ratio of dwellings or buildings to a given area or the total number of dwellings in a community area.

Public health officials, city planners, housing developers, and policy analysts in charge of setting housing standards are particularly interested in understanding the effects of household and community density levels on human health and behavior. In general, ratio measures of density are better predictors of health, especially mental health, than are absolute measures, such as number of persons or number of rooms. In addition, measures of density in a dwelling, such as persons per room, are better predictors of individual health and behavior problems than are community measures of density, such as dwellings per square mile or persons per acre. These latter two findings may be explained by the fact that individuals will tend to have greater difficulty escaping from or avoiding unwanted interactions with other people when they are inside a highly populated dwelling with little available space than when they are in the outside world or in a highly populated dwelling with lots of space. The different behavioral and health effects of density in a dwelling versus density outside of a dwelling are discussed in more detail below.

II. ROLE OF SOCIAL AND PERSONAL CHARACTERISTICS

The correspondence between density and the psychological experience of crowding often depends upon the individual and the social situation. For example, people can be exposed to high levels of density in a bustling city street, a cramped apartment, a sporting event, a concert, a supermarket, or a political rally. Some of these crowded situations are exciting and inviting and some are threatening and foreboding. While many people would concede that the throngs of people cheering at a football stadium contribute to the excitement of the sport, few would agree that the clanging and banging of shopping carts and waiting in long lines to make a purchase in a crowded supermarket are enjoyable experiences.

Why do different situations evoke different experiences of and feelings toward high density? There are, of course, important differences between high density in different settings, like stadiums or supermarkets. For example, in a stadium the cheers and enthusiasm of a crowd can be stimulating and help a spectator to have a good time. In the supermarket, the presence of many people can interfere with or constrain a shopper's movement through the supermarket and his or her ability to finish shopping. When high density thwarts goal-directed behaviors it is more likely to be experienced as stressful and crowded than when it does not block goal-directed behaviors. Interference with goal-directed behaviors can diminish individuals' actual and perceived control over their environment. Lack of control over the environment can cause some people to feel psychologically distressed. The role of control in explaining the negative effects of crowding is discussed in more detail below.

There are also wide differences in peoples' reactions to high density. For example, men and women appear to experience high density quite differently. When men and women are required to interact in small groups, men are more uncomfortable and less social than are women. Thus, men appear to prefer a larger amount of personal space or physical distance between themselves and other people than do women. Different cultural groups also seem to experience density differently. For example, American college students appear to be less tolerant of household crowding than are adult males in India. Many Chinese and Japanese families appear to be relatively unaffected by living in very high-density homes. Among different American ethnic groups, household density tends to have a stronger negative effect on the mental health and social relations of black Americans than white Americans, and only a weak effect on Americans of Hispanic descent.

Why do individuals have unique reactions to similar levels of density? One explanation of the cultural differences is that people who have had long-term exposure to high-density conditions develop methods of coping with the crowding. For example, in crowded Chinese households, it is not uncommon for family members to eat at different times to reduce the amount of crowding during meals. Japanese homes often have movable walls and partitions than can be used to get the maximal function from the limited space and rooms in the homes. In addition, customs regarding appropriate social interaction distances might be developed in particular cultures to make the social environment more predictable and controllable. Gender differences in reaction to high density might be explained by adaptation to different levels of closeness in interpersonal interactions. In comparison with males, females might be socialized to expect and to engage in contact with others in closer physical proximity. As they mature, males might become more accustomed than females to having large interpersonal distances between themselves and others. Thus, experience with high-density settings can diminish the negative psychological experience of crowding because individuals can learn how to cope with the undesirable aspects of high density or they become accustomed to close physical contact with others

III. EFFECTS OF CROWDING ON HEALTH AND BEHAVIOR

There has been a long history of interest in the effects of crowding on human health and behavior. The spread of various diseases and social pathologies is often attributed to the vast numbers of people living in urban areas. High population density is often cited as a reason for the very high rates of mental and physical health problems and various deviant social behaviors found in cities. It is not entirely clear, however, what aspects of high density might cause various social and health problems.

Observations of the negative effects of overpopulation in non-human animal species have fueled some of the concern over the effects of high density and crowding in human populations. Much of what has been learned about density and disease processes has been through experimentation with animals because of ethical limitations in experimenting with humans. However, even in animal populations it is difficult to ascertain the exact causes for the negative effects of density on health and behavior. Take, for example, the observation that high density is associated with higher rates of mortality in many animal species. Many animal species exhibit cycles of population escalation followed by a sudden and tremendous mortality, or a "population crash." Different pathways have been identified that may link density to mortality. For example, food shortages or the rapid spread of disease, as in plagues and other epidemics, could explain population crashes in high-density settings. However, starvation and contagious disease do not fully explain the effects of high population density on mortality. One group of scientists observed that deer living on an island multiplied quite rapidly until their population reached about one deer per acre, then their mortality rate skyrocketed. The deer population crashed, even though the deer had plenty of food and water and showed no signs of contagious disease spread. Examinations of the deer's internal organs, however, revealed signs of stress-related disease processes, which suggested another explanation of why high density can increase mortality: social stress.

Social stress can be caused by uncontrollable, threatening, unwanted, or otherwise negative social contacts and interactions with other organisms in an environment. High density can increase social stress, which can induce fighting between animals, interfere with reproductive behaviors, and cause unhealthy metabolic disturbances. Under high-density conditions, rodents' reproduction rates drop, cannibalism and deviant sexual behavior increase, and other social and biological pathologies all increase. In some animal studies, higher mortality among animals in high-density pens appears to be caused by overactive adrenal glandular systems. Many of the biological pathologies manifest in crowded rodents are similar to those observed in many species of animals after they have been exposed to noxious environmental stimuli, or stressors. Thus, it appears that the stress-related disease processes that might be caused by high population density could contribute to death and illness in different animal species. [*See* STRESS.]

It is tempting to draw analogies between overpopulated animal populations and overpopulation that occurs in human settlements. For example, birth and mortality rates of high-density human communities could be compared to similar outcomes in high-density rat colonies. However, many outcomes, such as criminal behavior in humans versus aggression in rats, are not so directly comparable. In addition, it is more difficult to prove that density is the cause of deviant behaviors in humans than it is to do so in animals. In animal research, scientists can control the effects of external factors other than high density that could influence the behaviors of crowded animals. Researchers studying human crowding can seldom control other factors, such as poverty and noise, that tend to accompany high density and influence humans' health and behaviors independently of density. In social science terms, the uncontrollable factors could cause a "spurious," or illusory, relation between density and human health and behaviors. Some researchers use statistical techniques to attempt to examine the effects of density independent of other social factors. The problem with making such statistical judgments is that researchers never know for certain whether they have identified all possible factors that could influence both density and the outcome of interest. These points should be kept in mind when reading the next section on the evidence relating high density to human health and behaviors.

A. Chronic versus Acute Crowding

The effects of high population density on humans do not appear to be as dramatic as in animals. This is partly due to the sophisticated and complex ways in which humans experience and adapt to noxious environmental stimuli like high density. For example, humans can hoard food supplies or increase food production to avoid starvation under high population conditions. Humans also can modify their environments, perhaps through scheduling or architectural interventions, to minimize social stress in high-density settings. Nevertheless, social research has revealed some relations between density and various health and social problems in humans.

In discussing the effects of crowding on humans, it is important to distinguish between *chronic crowding* and *acute crowding*. Chronic crowding takes place in settings where people tend to spend much of their time, like work places, residential settings, or institutional settings such as dormitories, prisons, and military barracks. Acute crowding takes place in settings where people tend to spend very little time, like stores, elevators, sidewalks, restaurants, theaters, stadiums, and other public places. The effects of acute crowding also have been examined by researchers in laboratory settings modified to represent different levels of density.

1. Effects of Chronic Community Crowding on Social Pathology

Social pathology can be defined as those phenomena that contribute to the demise of a society, typically by reducing its population, but also by disrupting its institutions and social relations. Thus, high rates of crime, mortality, accidents, disease, and divorce are indicators of social pathology. In the minds of many, social pathologies are linked to large cities, where they seem to proliferate and concentrate. Because large cities are both highly populated and full of social pathology, scientists have attempted to determine whether community crowding is at the root of the pathology evident in cities.

Interest in the relation between community density and pathology has been apparent since at least the end of the 19th century. Along with the industrial revolution came a rapid growth in cities throughout the western world. Some social theorists thought that the diversity of people, the personal anonymity, and high levels of individual autonomy existing between people in large cities would lead to psychological distress and anomie. In contrast, people from small towns and agrarian societies were expected to have richer social lives and greater morale because of familiarity and close interaction with similar others. Other social theorists argued that the high density of cities would expose people to overwhelming amounts of stimulation. In response to the stimulus overload, city-people would socially withdraw. Social withdrawal could be a strategy for reducing stimulus overload. By reducing concern for others and by interacting at a superficial level, there would be fewer stimulus inputs to cope with in day-to-day life. However, there would naturally be social costs if everyone acted this way, including apathy, frustration, conflict, and competition.

Contemporary social scientists pursue many of the same questions regarding community crowding and pathology as did their counterparts from a hundred years ago. Typically, crowding researchers investigate whether areas with high levels of community density also have high concentrations of social, psychological, and biological pathologies or problems. Community population density has been studied in relation to rates of death, infant mortality, perinatal mortality, accidental death, suicide, tuberculosis, venereal disease, mental hospitalization, birth, illegitimate birth, juvenile delinquency, imprisonment, crimes, public welfare, admissions to general hospitals, and divorce. The current evidence suggests that there is little or no relation between population density and major indicators of social pathology, such as mortality, crime, and juvenile delinquency. One research group observed that a higher ratio of persons per acre was associated with slightly elevated rates of mortality, fertility, juvenile delinquency, admissions to mental hospitals, and public assistance. However, the researchers also noted that certain ethnic and economic groups were overrepresented in the high-density areas. Thus, factors such as poverty, rather than density, could have caused the higher rates of pathology observed among individuals living in high-density areas. Indeed, when the researchers controlled for the effects of social class and ethnic background on the pathological outcomes, the relations between density and the outcomes disappeared.

On the other hand, it is possible that some community-crowding studies have underestimated the effects of high density on human pathology. Aggregate measures of density, such as persons per square mile, and aggregate measures of pathology, such as number of hospital admissions, do not precisely reveal the exposure to high density or its effects on individuals. For example, a person living in a high-density community might spend most of his or her waking hours at a job in a community that has a low-level of density. Or, a person from a low-density suburb might work all day in a high-density city. The actual exposure of these respective individuals to high density is different than what one would expect based on the density of their communities. In one instance, the negative effects of living in a high-density community could be underestimated. In the other instance, the benefits of living in a low-density community could be overestimated. If there are many of these peculiar cases in a study population, then an aggregate measure of community density will not be a good estimate of exposure to crowding. Nor would such a measure be useful for examining the effects of crowding on human health and behavior. There are also problems with aggregate measures of pathology. The principle problem is that data on social pathology originate from official public records, which can be incomplete and inaccurate.

To make matters more complicated, when analyzing aggregate data researchers can never know whether the relations between density and pathology are overestimated or underestimated. That is, the data errors caused by using aggregate measures could make the effects of density on pathology look stronger or weaker than they are in reality. One way around the problems associated with aggregate data is to study the effects of high density on individuals rather than on whole communities. That is, one could carefully measure individuals' exposure to density and their health and behaviors. This is usually done by surveying individuals about the levels of density in their households and about their health, behavior, and psychological well-being. Findings from this type of research are discussed in the next section.

2. Effects of Chronic Household Crowding on Health and Behavior

Household crowding stems from high density in the residential environment. Residential environments include individuals' homes and apartments, as well as institutional settings such as prisons, dormitories, and military bases. Household density appears to have a wide-range of effects on human health, behavior, and general well-being.

Prisoners in high-density cells, for instance, report more negative moods, discomfort, and illness symptoms than those in single-person cells or relatively low-density cells. Disciplinary problems, psychiatric commitment rates, suicide rates, and death rates also appear to increase in prison populations that grow in size without increases in prison facilities' size. Crowding also is a frequent problem in student populations. This often occurs because of a shortage of desirable housing near colleges or because students often double-up in apartments to save money on rent. In comparison with students in low-density dormitories or off-campus apartments, students in high-density residences feel more crowded, have more unwanted social contact and interactions, have more frequent negative moods, are less happy, and try to avoid interactions by socially withdrawing. In comparison with their uncrowded counterparts, crowded students are less sensitive to others' needs, less willing to help others, and less aware that others are available to provide emotional support or help to them when they need it.

People living in high-density residences can become insensitive to social cues even when they are not in the high-density setting. That is, the social insensitivity cultivated in high-density environments can carry over into low-density settings. College students who are withdrawn and insensitive to social cues in their high-density residences also act this way in low-density laboratory settings. Crowded students exhibit their withdrawn behaviors by sitting far away from others, not initiating conversation, making little eye contact with others, and not being helpful to others in need.

High household density in noninstitutional settings also results in antisocial behaviors and complaints of excessive social interaction. High household density is also related to increased negative mood and symptoms of depression and anxiety among adults. People from high-density households tend to have fewer friends and greater difficulty getting along with their neighbors than do people from relatively low-density homes. Parents tend to interact less with their young when they live in high-density homes than when they live in relatively low-density homes.

Children appear to be more negatively affected by high density than are adults, partly because they have less control over their environment than do adults. In comparison with children from low-density homes, those from high-density homes tend to have more behavioral problems in school, more anxiety, greater distractibility, more conflicts, lower achievement motivation, and poorer verbal abilities. However, caution must be applied when interpreting these results. As discussed above, density often accompanies other environmental conditions that could influence children's behaviors. Noise, for example, is likely to be greater in high-density households than in low-density households; and noise can interfere with children's attention, hearing, and learning abilities. Uncoupling the effects of density from those of noise is nearly impossible in naturalistic settings.

Earlier in this article, it was noted that social factors could influence whether an individual would perceive a particular setting as crowded. The social environment also can have a strong influence on the relation between crowding and psychological distress symptoms. As Figure 1 shows, students living in high-density households who have frequent hassles from roommates are more likely to be psychologically distressed than are students living in high-density households with relatively few hassles. Students living in low-density homes do not appear to be adversely affected by social hassles. People living in high-density households may be particularly distressed by roommate hassles because it is more difficult to avoid or escape from the hassles in a high-density home than in a low-density home. In contrast to the effects of social hassles, positive social relations can counteract the negative psychological effects of high-density living situations. As Figure 2 shows, college students living in high-density households who have supportive roommates are less likely to be distressed than are students living in high-density households with relatively unsupportive roommates or student living in low-density households. However, as mentioned earlier, chronic

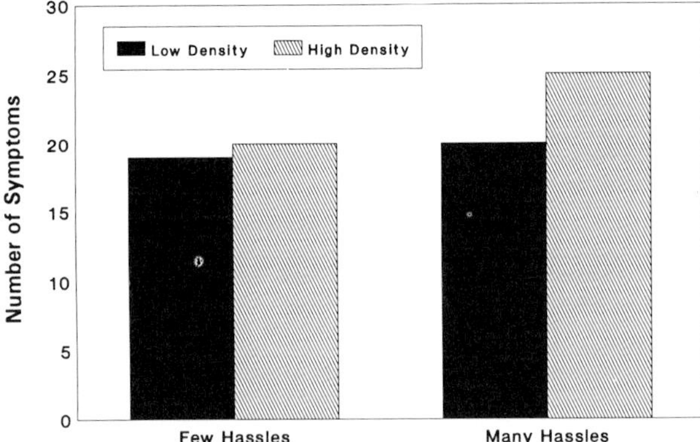

FIGURE 1 Psychological distress symptoms as a function of household density and levels of social hassles from roommates. [Reprinted, with permission, from S. J. Lepore, G. W. Evans, and M. L. Schneider (1992). *Environ. Behav.* **24,** 795–8111. Copyright © Sage Publications.]

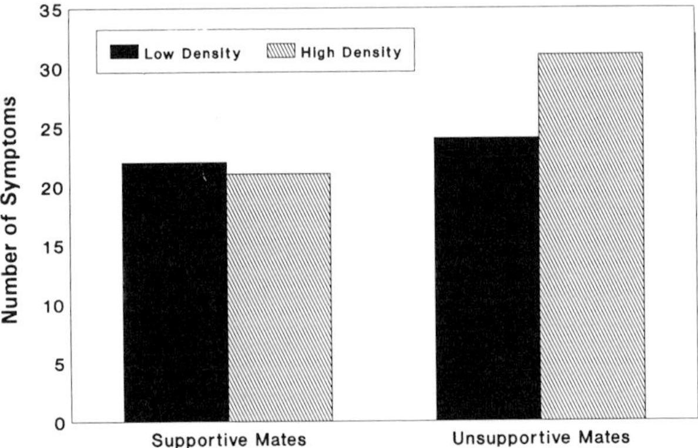

FIGURE 2 Psychological distress symptoms as a function of household density and levels of social support from roommates. [Reprinted, with permission, from S. J. Lepore, G. W. Evans, and M. L. Schneider (1991). *J. Pers. Soc. Psychol.* **61,** 899–909. Copyright © 1991 by the American Psychological Association.]

household crowding can undermine socially supportive relations because people become withdrawn and insensitive to social cues. Thus, although positive social relations may be beneficial to crowded individuals, such relations may be rare in households that are chronically overpopulated.

3. Effects of Acute Crowding on Physiology and Behavior

Acute crowding has been studied in scientific laboratories and in natural settings, like trains and elevators. In the animal studies discussed above, it was noted that many animals living in high-density populations showed biological signs of stress, such as enlarged adrenal glands. Elevated and sustained physiological arousal is another sign of stress that is commonly observed in organisms under stress. In high-density laboratory settings, arousal has been exhibited in human subjects using many different measures. People exposed to acute crowding in laboratories exhibit increased perspiration, skin conductance, and blood pressure. Passengers in crowded commuter trains exhibit increases in blood levels of adrenaline. Interestingly, passengers who board a train when it is already near capacity are more negatively affected by the crowded conditions than passengers who board early, when the train is nearly empty. Even though the latter passengers ride the train longer, they had more choice, or control, over where they could sit on the train than passengers who board the train when it is already loaded with other passengers.

It should be noted that although acute exposure to high-density settings usually increases physiological arousal, it is not clear whether there are negative health consequences of the increased arousal. It is possible that elevated and prolonged arousal can wear down the body's defenses against illness and generate illness itself, such as hypertension or ulcers. However, there is not enough evidence at this point to state unequivocally whether the arousing effects of high-density have health implications. [*See* STRESS AND ILLNESS.]

Impaired task performance is another common side-effect of acute exposure to high density. Mostly, this research has been conducted in laboratory settings that manipulate individuals' exposure to high or low density and then measure performance on problem-solving tasks or assess one's ability to concentrate or persist on a task. Although high density does not seem to interfere with performance on simple tasks, it does diminish complex task performance. It also appears that individuals are more easily distracted and are less persistent at completing challenging tasks under high- versus low-density conditions.

Short-term exposure to high density produces many of the same withdrawal behaviors observed in people chronically exposed to high density. It is not uncommon, for example, for people on crowded subways to read newspapers and books as a way of avoiding interaction with others. In laboratory settings, crowded people are more likely to leave the settings, increase social distance, withdraw from social interactions, increase defensive posturing, and reduce eye contact than uncrowded people. Another way to maintain space from others is to be aggressive and threatening. Several studies have shown increased competition and aggression between individuals in high-density settings. Interestingly, crowding is more likely to evoke aggression in men than in women and when resources in the environment are scarce rather than plentiful. The adaptive value of withdrawal and aggression in high-density settings is not completely understood, but it does appear that these social behaviors may help people to cope with crowding. For example, social withdrawal might be a way of minimizing physiological arousal by avoiding unwanted social interactions and the excessive social stimulation that is common in high-density settings.

IV. EXPLAINING THE NEGATIVE EFFECTS OF CROWDING

Several theoretical explanations of the effects of crowding on human health and behavior have been alluded to throughout this article. Below we discuss three of the more prominent of these theories: behavioral constraint, control, and overload/arousal theories.

A. Behavioral Constraint

According to this theory, high density interferes with individuals' goal obtainment by restricting or inhibiting their movements and behaviors. The diminished freedom makes the high density noxious and undesirable. When people are in high-density settings that do not thwart their goal-directed behaviors, they tend to be less negatively affected by the high density than when their goals are thwarted. Imagine, for instance, two groups of individuals performing a task in a crowded room, but one group has to complete the task while sitting still and the other group has to complete the task while moving around the room. It is more likely that crowding will interfere with the task performance of the moving group than of the still group because the crowded group will be coping with the task and the constraints on their movements caused by the crowding.

Behavioral constraints do not refer only to restrictions in bodily movement. Sometimes high density can create resource shortages, such as food shortages, which constrain behavioral choices. That is, density can restrict access to valued resources. In the case of food shortages, behaviors such as eating might be inhibited. In addition, people in such situations might act aggressively to get valued resources. Finally, it should be noted, that high density often can have negative effects on mood and performance because people perceive that there are behavioral constraints in high-density environments. That is, simply believing that high density can limit one's behaviors or access to valued resources is sufficient to diminish task performance or increase discomfort in high-density settings.

B. Control

Limits to behavioral freedom also can be construed as limits in personal control over the self and the environment. Control models of crowding hypothesize that high density is undesirable and harmful because it renders the environment more unpredictable and exposes individuals to situations over which they have little or no control. A lack of control in high-density settings has been shown to exacerbate the negative effects of density on humans, whereas the availability of control has been shown to reduce the negative effects of density.

One group of researchers tested the control hypothesis by examining the effects of control on people's moods in crowded elevators. Control in the elevator was manipulated by giving some people access to the elevator control panel and other people no access. Those who had panel access, or more control, in the crowded elevators felt less crowded and had more positive moods than those without control. As with behavioral constraint, sometimes it is enough to simply perceive, or believe, that control is available to reduce the negative effects of high density on performance or mood. However, if one's expectations for control in a high-density situation do not match the actual availability of control, then the high density can be more disturbing than if one expected little control in the situation. Thus, it appears that control or beliefs and expectations about control in high-density environments influences how strongly humans are affected by crowding. [*See* CONTROL.]

C. Overload/Arousal

A final theory posits that high density increases pathology because of sensory overload from excessive stimulation. Humans have a limited capacity to process information; in high-density settings the information available in the environment exceeds that capacity. This process is similar to information-overload in a computer system, which can cause a computer to make errors or shut-down operations. In humans, overarousal is often unpleasant, can diminish complex task performance, and could contribute to health problems.

Evidence for the overload/arousal model of crowding is found in studies such as those discussed above that have shown increased sympathetic arousal under high-density situations. Some scholars have suggested that heightened social withdrawal in high-density settings is a method of reducing arousal. At present, however, there is no strong evidence that social withdrawal can actually lower sympathetic arousal in crowded people. In addition, there is no evidence that the levels or duration of arousal people experience in high-density settings is significant enough to compromise health or contribute to disease processes.

V. CONCLUSIONS

Crowding in humans is a syndrome of stress associated with exposure to high-density households, community, or laboratory settings. A distinction exists between the subjective experience of crowding and the objective source of that feeling: high population density. Overpopulation in non-human animals leads to deviant social behaviors and health problems. However, exposure to high density and overpopulation in humans seldom results in extreme social pathologies. Unlike lower animals, humans appear to be able to adapt to and cope with high-density situations with a good deal of tolerance. Humans can adapt by limiting their exposure to high density through many means, including architectural interventions, careful scheduling and planning of space usage, and by engaging in distracting or withdrawal behaviors. Unfortunately, some adaptations to density, such as social withdrawal, can have unintended consequences, such as loneliness or deterioration of interpersonal relations.

The research evidence to date suggests that people do have undesirable psychological, social, and biological responses to crowding. However, it is also clear that crowding is more or less aversive and detrimental to people depending on their personal experiences with and preferences for particular levels of density. In addition, social conditions, such as the presence of supportive others or undesirable social hassles from others, can influence the strength of the relation between density and various outcomes, such as psychological well-being. Thus, density does not necessarily increase social pathology in humans. Indeed, low levels of density can be undesirable at some occasions, such as parties, sporting events, or concerts. It appears that density is most detrimental to human behavior and health when individuals feel a lack of control over their own behaviors or the environment, or when they experience excessive stimulation and arousal from the density.

Bibliography

Baum, A., and Paulus, P. B. (1987). Crowding. In "Handbook of Environmental Psychology" (D. Stokols and I. Altman, eds.). Wiley, New York.

Evans, G. W., and Lepore, S. J. (1992). Conceptual and analytic issues in crowding research. *J. Environ. Psychol.* **12,** 163–173.

Gove, W. M., and Hughes, M. (1983). "Overcrowding in the Household." Academic Press, New York.

Paulus, P. B., and Nagar, D. (1989). Environmental influences on groups. In "Psychology of Group Influence" (P. B. Paulus, ed.), 2nd ed. Erlbaum, Hillsdale, NJ.

Taylor, R. B. (1988). "Human Territorial Functioning." Cambridge University Press, Cambridge.

Crowd Psychology

Erika G. King
Chatham College

Glossary

Collective behavior/collective psychology/mass psychology The study of the actions and/or mentality of people in unorganized, unstructured social groupings such as mobs, crowds, publics, and the mass.

CROWD PSYCHOLOGY is a theory of collective behavior and mass psychology that developed in France and Italy in the late 19th century and achieved widespread popularity in Europe and America prior to World War I. Based initially on theories of hypnotism and suggestibility, it held that members of any human aggregation were subject to group entrancement and would, through a process known as "mental contagion," irresistibly and unconsciously be incorporated into a single "crowd mind." According to crowd psychology, this collective mentality reduced all persons in the crowd to intellectual mediocrity and heightened emotionalism; acts of collective irrationality and irresponsibility were the inevitable outcome. Some crowd psychologists equated all modern collectivities (from street mobs to parliaments and even the publics of modern society) with mentally debased crowds and used crowd psychology to criticize leftist political movements as well as democratic institutions and procedures. Others drew a distinction between physically proximate crowds and dispersed publics, a perspective that provided some of the foundation for advertising and propaganda theories before and during World War I and for mass society theory between the two World Wars.

I. THEORIES OF CROWD PSYCHOLOGY: 1870–1915

A. The French Revolution and the Revolutionary Crowd

The French Revolution raised the specter of the rampaging mob as a potent social and political instrument of modern society. Outbreaks of collective violence in Europe throughout the 19th century also contributed to fears of society's vulnerability to crowd frenzy, and a number of conservative thinkers began to develop theories of society critical of changes that disrupted the traditional social order. In the 1870s, the eminent French historian Hippolyte Taine began a multi-volume work entitled *Origins of Contemporary France*. Seeking to explain France's turbulent historical experiences as analogous to pathological psychological processes, Taine argued that the bloody events of the Revolution could be attributed to a reversion by people in unorganized groupings to the savage natural state. When people were cut loose from the traditional social hierarchy they would experience a loss of reason, their rationality to be replaced by precivilized, brutal, instinctual drives. In such crowds there would suddenly spring forth the "barbarian," the "primitive animal." The psychological mechanism by which this atavistic transformation took place in the crowd was mental contagion, a mutual inflaming of the passions which uniformly affected all assembled, drawing everyone into a destructive blind rage. This infectious emotionalism was spurred on by the lowest elements in the crowd who, in the drunken ecstasy of violence, would lead the crowd down a path of infamy and mental delirium.

Taine's conception of mental contagion was drawn from mid-19th century psychiatry and clinical pathology, where it had been used to explain the transmission of mental illness between two individuals and then among many individuals. It then appeared in the work of such noted French psycholo-

Copyright © 1994 by Academic Press, Inc. All rights of reproduction in any form reserved.

gists as Theodule Ribot, Alfred Binet, and Pierre Janet, who incorporated it in their theories of the unconscious mind's involuntary and automatic control over the individual. Mental contagion was also used in the 1870s by French naturalist Alfred Espinas to explain the contagion of emotion among both humans and animals in a massed state. Taine's highly influential tome gave impetus to other theorists to view historical events from a perspective that equated group dynamics with individual psychopathology. Several writers were shortly to take theories drawn from criminology and social psychology and apply them to the mentality of crowds and present what they firmly believed to be a scientifically grounded theory of collective psychology that would account for the myriad problems of modern society.

B. Collective Suggestibility and the Crowd

The notion of the crowd as an explanation of contemporary social life was elaborated in the early 1890s by Gabriel Tarde, a noted French social theorist, jurist, and criminologist, and Scipio Sighele, and Italian trained in the positive school of criminal anthropology. Reflecting their shared interest in criminal behavior, both Tarde and Sighele initially confined their observations on the crowd to the realm of collective violence. Both viewed it as a social milieu in which even law-abiding citizens were reduced to the level of criminals, "infected" by mental contagion with the passion and delirium of those around them, driven by social suggestion to acts of degradation and even murder. All persons in the crowd, they wrote, possessed a uniform crowd mind which was barbaric and instinctively cruel, frenzied and utterly without restraint, and intellectually debased and illogical. Because of the mutual contagion of sentiments the crowd existed in a state of heightened suggestibility far more intense than that which existed between a hypnotist and a single subject.

This psychological view of the crowd drew upon late 19th century suggestion–imitation theory. Developed in large part by Tarde and also by students of hypnotic theory, this perspective held that all social life was a nonrational process of suggestion–imitation, with suggestion as the mental or cognitive aspect (stimulus) and imitation as the motor outcome (response). Two highly influential schools of hypnotic thought existed in in the late 1800s—the Nancy school, which emphasized everyone's susceptibility to hypnotic suggestions, and the Salpêtrière school, which held that the hypnotic state could be produced only in hysterics. The former perspective won out in suggestion–imitation theory, and theorists like Tarde began to write about the nonrational, uncritical, and automatic process of suggestion-imitation as the basic law of social life. The social process was thus viewed as essentially unconscious and involuntary and social life was presented as analogous to the mental condition of a hypnotized subject. Suggestion–imitation theorists sought to ascertain those causal factors which heightened individual susceptibility to suggestion; one group, which included Tarde and Sighele, turned its attention to the impact of the crowd and singled it out as the major explanation for modern man's suggestive and imitative nature.

Tarde and Sighele quickly moved from studying the criminal crowd to analyzing other forms of crowds as well. And even though they differentiated crowds from other social groupings, they clung to the view that all forms of social aggregates—whether juries, sects, or mobs—displayed qualities which were always morally and intellectually inferior to those of the individuals comprising them. But the best known of the crowd theorists, the French scientific writer and popularizer Gustave Le Bon, viewed all types of modern collectivities as a crowd.

According to Le Bon's international best-seller, *The Crowd,* published in 1895, the modern world was entering the "era of crowds," an age in which the "substitution of the unconscious action of crowds for the conscious activity of individuals is one of the principal characteristics. . . ." Like Tarde and Sighele, Le Bon focused on the psychological characteristics of the crowd, particularly its homogeneous mental condition. The crowd forms a single being, he wrote, and is subjected to the "law of the mental unity of crowds." To qualify as a crowd, a common focus of attention was necessary, and this fixation of attention he likened to a hypnotic trance. And like individuals in a trance, all members of the crowd existed in a state of heightened suggestibility, an undifferentiated mental condition made all the more intense by the psychic interaction of individuals in the crowd.

Because everyone in the crowd was focused on a common object or idea, Le Bon argued, normal faculties of reason and powers of critical observation were inhibited, and all perceptions, thoughts, and sentiments would move in an identical current. Such uniform movement of actions and thoughts was instantaneous, automatic, and involuntary—in an entranced suggestible state, ideas or images were accepted unquestioningly and immediately translated into action, with each member of the crowd automatically and unconsciously imitating whatever was presented to him. A new collective psychological entity was consequently formed which represented not the sum of its parts but an entirely new phenomenon in which reason was diminished but emotions were intensified and spread like a disease by the process of emotional contagion.

At the very end of the 19th century, Tarde departed from his two fellow crowd theorists and drew an important distinction between the physically proximate crowd and the dispersed public. Whereas the former was a collection of psychic connections produced essentially by physical contacts, the latter was a dispersion of individuals whose cohesion was purely mental. The contemporary age, he argued, is not that of crowds but of publics, and these would also be the collectivities of the future. According to Tarde, the public had come into existence only because of recent developments in mass communications, particularly the newspaper, which greatly enlarged the potential size of the aggregation.

Tarde held that members of publics had the potential to be more rational and tolerant than members of crowds, for an individual could be a member of more than one public, each of which presented divergent viewpoints. Such diversity of opinion and outlook was simply not possible in the physically restricted crowd. The reader of a newspaper also had more control over his intellectual freedom than someone swept up in a crowd. But he despairingly noted that even though publics were less extremist, dogmatic, and despotic than crowds, they were not necessarily rational and reasonable. He believed that members of publics were extremely suggestible and that mental contagion was running rampant through the publics of modern society. He was particularly dismayed about the insidious influence of certain journalists and publicists who had proven adept at raising their publics to great heights of collective irrationality, fanaticism, and intolerance.

C. Social Instinct Theory and the Crowd

In 1908 two British scholars published major social psychological works which utilized social instinct theory as an explanatory framework for human behavior. William McDougall, trained in physiology, and Wilfred Trotter, trained in medicine, maintained that certain innate or inherited tendencies accounted for man's collective and individual actions. Both agreed that the gregarious (or herd) instinct was the most important of the social instincts and that it was responsible for man's evolutionary adaptability. Unlike the French and Italian crowd theorists who had emphasized mass contagion and suggestibility while simultaneously affirming individual rationality, the instinct theorists held that human nature was both individually and collectively nonrational. Even the solitary individual was a prisoner of his unconscious and unreflective inborn impulses—collective emotionalism, credulity, and impulsiveness were seen simply as a manifestation (albeit on a massive and intensified scale) of individual innate drives and tendencies. Because social instinct theory had much to say about the psychology of the crowd, McDougall and Trotter are regarded as the two leading exponents of the British school of crowd psychology.

In his best-selling textbook, *Introduction to Social Psychology,* McDougall noted that being drawn to membership in a crowd was a manifestation of man's gregarious nature. Even "cultivated" minds, he claimed, were not immune to the "fascination of the herd," an attraction which increased as the aggregation grew in size. He also noted that in all social groupings there arose a mental unity different from the sum of its parts, a result of reciprocal mental action with other members of the group.

By 1912 McDougall had come to share Le Bon's, Tarde's, and Sighele's perspective that crowd membership degraded individual mentality and behavior and invariably led to heightened states of suggestibility, irresponsibility, and emotionalism. He also maintained that the crowd was an omnipresent entity in the modern world and that this emotionally intensifying milieu created grave social problems such as outbreaks of urban violence. But most unlike the French and Italian theorists, McDougall believed that well-organized groups could overcome the innate irrationalism and selfishness of their members. A true "group mind" could elevate the mentality of its members, whereas the "crowd mind" would only debase them.

For Wilfred Trotter, the crowd was evidence of man's innate gregarious nature. The herd instinct—the need to be one of the group—was the most powerful of the instincts, and man was eternally subject to the pull of the herd, condemned to exist in a condition of receptivity to all suggestions emanating from it. Thus, conformity and suggestibility were hallmarks of man in the mass. The bulk of a person's opinions was therefore a product of herd suggestions rather than reasoned reflection. Such beliefs were more often than not completely irrational and quite uninformed, but because they derived from the group they were held with absolute tenacity, thought to be rational, and defended as such. Anyone holding contrary views would be seen as obviously unreasonable, for another defining characteristic of herd mentality was its extreme intolerance.

D. The Political Dimensions of European Crowd Psychology

European crowd psychology was replete with political implications, and it should be regarded as a psychology of politics as well as a social psychology. All of the crowd psychologists used this perspective to demonstrate that mass psychology and collective behavior were irrevocably at odds with classical liberalism's idealistic conception of human nature. They offered a psychologically based critique of mass democracy and proletarian movements which evolved into an illiberal psychology of leadership and social control. [*See* LEADERSHIP.]

In their initial writings on the crowd Tarde and Sighele were briefly critical of the mentality of the mass electorate and parliament. But both held out some hope for parliamentary democracy as long as the ideas of a small elite were imitated by the crowds of modern society. Le Bon devoted much of *The Crowd* to warning his readers about the dire political consequences of mass sovereignty, or what he termed rule by the "sovereign crowd." The horrifying but logical outcome of crowd rule, he insisted, was socialism. To Le Bon parliaments merely formed small crowds, and their members were thus prey to the debased mental states of all crowds. And members of the electorate, although spatially separated, shared the characteristics of any mob. Even an electorate limited to persons of superior intellect would still be subject to the law of the mental unity of crowds and hence mentally deficient. But he did note that parliamentary democracy was one of the firmly held ideals of modern society and therefore impossible to do away with.

Because rule by the crowd was here to stay, Le Bon advocated elite manipulation of unconscious mass impulses. In a series of volumes written before the outbreak of World War I, he advised would-be crowd leaders to employ such nonrational devices as suggestion, affirmation, repetition, and the appeal to prestige; he also devoted a volume to long-term psychological domination of the crowd through control of the content of the educational system.

In 1910 Le Bon presented what he thought to be the most effective persuasive device for elite management of the crowd: indoctrination of a fervent patriotic sentiment through the use of emotionally laden nationalistic imagery, slogans, and symbols. Under the firm guidance of elite leadership, a patriotic collective mentality would be capable, he claimed, of noble and even heroic (although never independently intelligent) actions.

Sighele's political psychology evolved in directions similar to Le Bon's. By the late 1890s his views of the political implications of the crowd had turned distinctly more pessimistic than at the beginning of the decade. No longer did he believe the superior few could remain immune to crowd mentality, nor was he convinced that crowds would follow the lead of the intellectual elite. He concluded that there really was no remedy to crowd domination since he agreed with Le Bon that the concept of democratic governance was too widely accepted to be discarded.

But like Le Bon, Sighele soon began to formulate a psychology of mass social control that used the concept of nationalism as the theme for captivating the crowd and channeling this immoral and illogical collective entity into the service of the bourgeois state. Instilled with a strong sense of nationalistic zeal and devotion, the crowd would support an aggressive and expansionist foreign policy and the traditional social order. War would provide the perfect outlet for the energy of the crowd and the ideal means for focusing its newly acquired devotion to the nation.

Tarde's conception of democratic governance was less sanguine by 1898 than it had been in the early 1890s. He now warned of the ease with which crowd mentality—via the pens of calculating journalists practiced in the art of mass suggestion—could invade the supposedly more rational public. In none of his writings did he defend the mentality of the democratic electorate or of elected representatives, nor did he ever champion democratic institutions. But he never came to view with approbation the potential for elites to manipulate the collectivities of modern society. He held instead that any involvement of the elite few with the masses was a destructive phenomenon which leveled the social pyramid on which civilized society had to exist.

The British crowd psychologists were also critical of mass sovereignty and embraced elite management of the crowd. According to McDougall, as an unorganized grouping or crowd the mass electorate was incapable of elevated thought or action. Even in a political meeting, when people were drawn together by common political beliefs and sentiments, the resultant crowd would experience only a heightening of emotions, never an intensification of the intellect. And even such partially organized bodies as juries were notoriously likely to reach decisions more defective than those the least intelligent member would have produced alone.

But McDougall did not reject parliamentary democracy. Representative government could exist when disorganized crowds were fused into a well-organized, national "group mind." Under the guidance of an enlightened elite, the crowd could be molded into an organized collective entity whose mental life would elevate the mind and spirit of all its members. But in the absence of proper elite direction, the masses would revert to the mental level of the crowd.

Trotter also equated democracy with rule by the crowd and believed that the only political hope of mankind was the intellectual elite. Since suggestibility and conforming herd behavior were innate human characteristics, only a corps of properly trained social scientists was equal to the mighty task of ensuring that rational suggestions were the only type presented to the masses. The "tyrannous power" of the gregarious herd instinct would have to be controlled and directed through scientific statecraft.

E. The Crowd in American Social Psychological Thought

At the turn of the century the concept of the crowd rapidly made its way into the emerging discipline of American social psychology and figured prominently in the early writings of a number of noted pioneers in the field, including Franklin Giddings, James Mark Baldwin, Boris Sidis, Edward Ross, Charles Cooley, Robert Park, and Michael Davis. Adopting without modification the French and Italian theorists' suggestion–imitation framework, the Americans concurred that crowd mentality was uniformly credulous, suggestible, and irresponsible. But by the beginning of the 20th century most of the American writers had adopted Tarde's distinction between the crowd and the public and argued that the public, the far more important collectivity in the modern world, was a qualitatively different social grouping from the crowd.

Although the Americans all recognized the manipulability of public opinion, their writings were infused with cautious optimism about the ability of public opinion to rise above the mental level of the crowd. In dispersed groups, they argued, people had the luxury to deliberate and reflect; they also could simultaneously be a member of several competing publics. Although mass suggestion did exist in the public, it was more cold and unemotional than in the crowd and it allowed the intellect rather than just the emotions to work.

American crowd psychologists did caution that crowd suggestibility and irrationality were far from over in the modern era of dispersed publics. The potential for public mentality to regress to the debased level of the crowd was always close at hand because the advent of modern communication media, especially the newspaper, enabled mental contagion to operate on a wider scale than ever before. But the American writers were far less pessimistic about the public's rationality than was Tarde.

Most unlike the European crowd psychologists, the Americans never offered a critique of mass democracy nor did they ever move in the direction of an elitist psychology of leadership and social control. They all agreed that mass sovereignty was not rule by an electoral crowd, nor was parliamentary democracy rule by a small crowd. They also saw no need for elite manipulation of the crowd in the political realm. Early 20th century American theorists instead began to apply mass psychology to the emerging fields of advertising, public relations, and marketing, hailing suggestible crowds and publics as the ideal audiences for these new arts of mass persuasion.

Pioneer in the field of advertising psychology Walter Dill Scott used suggestion theory as the basis of commercial persuasion, noting that crowd membership heightened suggestibility. In a 1906 manual on public speaking he counseled orators to create a homogeneous crowd mentality among their audiences as a means of producing unhesitating acceptance of almost any idea. Other scholars of speech education and audience psychology made the equation of audience with crowd in the years before the war. In both academic and popular literature a number of writers also made reference to crowd suggestibility and mental contagion to account for a variety of social phenomena, including the behavior of theater audiences, fads in fashion, the excesses of newspapers, the panic of soldiers in war, and mob outbursts.

F. Criticisms of Crowd Psychology

Even in its heyday between 1895 and the outbreak of World War I, crowd psychology did not win universal acceptance among scholars of collective behavior. The theories of Emile Durkheim, Georges Sorel, Georg Simmel, and Ferdinand Tönnies, among others, offered competing explanations of the actions and mentality of modern collectivities. Some scholars criticized crowd psychology's reduction of social groupings to hypnotized throngs and attacked the notion that collective suggestibility was *the* explanation for social behavior. Others opposed its political overtones. The eminent British political theorist Graham Wallas took crowd psychology to task on both dimensions. Although he initially applauded crowd psychology's emphasis on human irrationality, in his 1914 volume *The Great Society* he noted that physically proximate crowds were no longer a major social phenomenon and that even in dispersed publics mental contagion and heightened suggestibility were "habitually and grossly exaggerated" by the crowd psychologists. He also castigated the crowd psychologists for allowing their illiberal ideological convictions to permeate their supposedly scientific analyses. But Wallas did agree with Le Bon that the essence of 20th century politics entailed "the art of controlling other men's unconscious impulses," an observation shortly to be demonstrated by the wide scale mass manipulation of World War I.

II. CROWD PSYCHOLOGY BETWEEN THE TWO WORLD WARS

In both Europe and America, the First World War saw the establishment of governmental agencies whose purpose was to mobilize mass support for the war effort. As George Creel, head of the U.S. Committee on Public Information (CPI), declared, the purpose was to weld the people into "one white-hot mass instinct." Many of the people who worked for the CPI came from backgrounds in advertising and public relations, fields that had utilized crowd theory's perspectives on mass credulity and suggestibility for over a decade. The success of all of the combatants' war propaganda machinery provided powerful testimony to mass irrationality and manipulability. Although there was widespread criticism of propaganda in the aftermath of the war, the techniques of mass persuasion that had been perfected during the conflict were widely applied to a peacetime society during the interwar years.

A. Interwar European Crowd Psychology

Crowd psychology continued to be a subject of some study in the 1920s and 1930s, although under the intellectual leadership of a new generation of theorists and practitioners. Sigmund Freud incorporated the relationship among crowd members and between the crowd and its leader into his psychoanalytic framework in *Group Psychology and the Analysis of the Ego*, published in 1921. Beginning with a very approving overview of the perspectives of Le Bon and his contemporaries, Freud argued that collective suggestibility, the herd instinct, and the group mind were nonetheless incomplete explanations of collective psychology because they failed adequately to account for the bonds that united the grouping.

Of particular interest to Freud were the intense emotional ties that developed between the members of any social aggregate and its leader. Utilizing libido theory's premise of the sublimated erotic bond between parent and child which resulted in the child's identification with and idealization of the father, Freud maintained that group members would idealize the group leader as a father substitute and unconsciously internalize the leader's standards as their own. In addition, mutual identification with other group members would result from the common idealization of the leader. He also noted that group psychology represented a regression to a primitive form of human society, the "primal horde," in which the group was ruled over despotically by a powerful male. Even in modern society, when the father figure called forth the liberation of repressed instinctual drives, the result could be the destructiveness of the mob, the revolutionary crowd, or war. Freud's profound sense of unease about the regressive nature of group leadership would be realized in the writings and actions of the great practitioners of crowd psychology—Adolph Hitler and Benito Mussolini.

The ideas of the long-lived Gustave Le Bon (who died at the age of 90 in 1931) provided inspiration for Italy's and Germany's fascist leaders in the 1920s. Mussolini expressed his indebtedness to Le Bon's concepts of crowd mentality and crowd manipulation in an interview, noting that he had applied Le Bon's principles of mass persuasion with great success. In his 1924 blueprint for mass manipulation, *Mein Kampf*, Hitler took Le Bon's ideas about crowd suggestibility and the means by which the leader could control and direct the crowd and incorporated them into a treatise on how to mobilize the crowds of modern Germany and forge them into a potent nationalistic entity. Violence and the symbols of violence would energize the crowd; reversion to the brutal, racist, barbarian state was embraced as a means of bending the masses to his will. And the propagandists of the Third Reich, under Goebbels' leadership, translated these ideas into practice as fascism rather than socialism became the political result of rule by the crowd.

B. Interwar American Crowd Psychology

In postwar America, a sense of disillusionment about public mentality set in among a number of writers, some of whom had been willing and active participants in the government's efforts to mobilize wartime mass opinion. Psychologist Boris Sidis vilified the war as the greatest of Western history's "mental epidemics," the product of a "social trance" induced by hypnotizing oratory, parades, and a chauvinist press. In his 1920 book *The Behavior of Crowds*, educator Everett Dean Martin complained that society was becoming a "veritable babel of gibbering crowds." Applying psychoanalytic theory to collective behavior, he warned that the crowd mind was not a mere excess of emotion but a psychopathological condition which, in its release of dangerous repressed impulses, posed a great menace to society. A crowd was a device for "indulging ourselves in a kind of temporary insanity by all going crazy together." This collective delusional state remained omnipresent in modern society because even the dispersed public was forged into a crowd mind by a daily press which operated solely on the level of the "lowest cranial altitude."

The noted journalist Walter Lippmann wrote of the irrationality, emotionalism, and suggestibility of the public in his influential works, *Public Opinion* (1922) and *The Phantom Public* (1925), noting that the most significant revolution of modern times was the "manufacturing of consent" among the governed. Pessimistic about the mental capacity of the democratic electorate, he advocated management of the public by wise and responsible leaders whose use of emotionally laden symbols would engage the masses in "purposeful action," something he thought the inert public incapable of achieving on its own. Other journalists and essayists warned about the insidious role of propaganda, noting that the ease with which the public had been manipulated during the war was continuing unabated in its aftermath. Some authors thought that the public needed to be warned about the pervasiveness of mass manipulation, and a number of articles on how to identify propaganda appeared in popular publications in the 1920s and 1930s. The topic of propaganda and affiliated concepts of mass susceptibility to it also appeared in a number of academic books and articles during this period. Underlying all of these writings was the notion that the public was far from a rational entity and that it could easily be swayed by those schooled in the techniques of modern mass persuasion.

A few writers, the most prominent of whom was Edward L. Bernays, were more sanguine about mass suggestibility and maintained that techniques of mass persuasion could greatly benefit society by inducing the public to accept progressive changes. Bernays, one of the major interwar figures in public relations, had honed his ideas on mass manipulation as a member of the CPI during the war. Essential to any public relations campaign, he believed, was a thorough knowledge of group psychology, for the crowd was a state of mind which "permeates society and its individuals at almost all times." In his numerous writings he used crowd psychology's notions of the public's malleability and receptivity to new stimuli as the theoretical base for p.r. techniques.

C. From Crowd Psychology to Mass Society Theory

In the interwar years, references to crowd psychology still appeared in the academic literature on collective behavior, but new perspectives on mass psychology supplanted crowd theory by the outbreak of World War II. Crowd theory's concept of modern society as the crowd writ large was rejected as overly simplistic, as was the notion of a collective crowd mind. Some scholars viewed the psychology of unorganized collectivities in a positive light, as a potential agent of social progress. The crowd was also given a more restricted definition as scholars drew sharper distinctions among a variety of unorganized social phenomena, particularly the crowd, the public, and the mass.

In their 1921 textbook *Introduction to the Science of Sociology*, sociologists Robert Park and Ernest Burgess included exerpts from Le Bon's writings on the crowd. But Park and Burgess presented the crowd as an agent of social change, a phase in institutional evolution that converted "social unrest" into mass movements and then into new organizations. In this perspective, the crowd provided a milieu in which mental contagion released individuals from traditional loyalties and made them receptive to new ideas and institutions.

In *Social Psychology,* published in 1924, psychologist Floyd Allport rejected crowd psychology's notion of a unitary crowd consciousness, arguing instead that the explanation for collective behavior lay in the interstimulation and reaction among individuals. He limited the crowd to a collection of individuals who are all attending and reacting to some common object. But he agreed with the earlier crowd psychologists that such a grouping would call forth "primitive, unsocialized" responses from its members. The public he defined as a dispersed grouping, an "imagined crowd" in which individual members believe certain opinions, feelings, and overt reactions to be held in common and therefore act in uniform ways. Although the impression of universality could be exploited by the press and propagandists alike, members of the public (unlike crowd members) could be educated to contribute to social progress.

As researchers focused on propaganda in the 1930s, they began to concentrate more on the media used to communicate among dispersed publics. Social psychologists Hadley Cantril and Gordon Allport held that by instantaneously creating an "impression of universality" among many millions, radio was more capable than any other medium of forming a crowd mentality among physically separated individuals. But like most other researchers in the 1930s, they also noted that the radio audience, physically separated from one another and from the speaker, would be less emotional, more critical, more individualistic, and therefore "less crowdish" than people congregated together.

On the eve of the outbreak of World War II, sociologists began to make an important distinction among the crowd, the public, and the mass. Sociologist Herbert Blumer relegated the crowd to physically congregated groupings subject to "milling" and the "contagion" of emotions and concurred that it could be a "potential device" for the emergence of new forms of personality and behavior. But two other types of spontaneous, transient, and unorganized groupings were deemed to be of greater importance in modern society: the public and the mass. The former was defined as a dispersed grouping that is confronted by an issue on which there is disagreement, and which reaches agreement or some collective decision through discussion. The latter was a dispersed multitude that lacked any unity and was composed of detached, anonymous individuals. As atomized units, members of the mass were not part of a uniform collective mentality nor would they develop an emotional rapport. They were instead heterogeneous individuals who independently converged in their actions or thoughts upon the same stimulus or sought the same goals. Lacking traditional identities or loyalties, mass members would turn to influences beyond "local cultures and groups," and were therefore very susceptible to the pull of mass persuasion.

The term "mass society" was used to designate the kind of social system in which mass behavior plays an important role, and crowd psychology was subsumed under mass society theory in the years following the second World War. The psychopathology of the crowd as the explanation for modern collective behavior gave way to a more empirical approach that examined the processes, manifestations, and impacts of a variety of collective phenomena.

III. RECENT APPROACHES AND RESEARCH IN CROWD PSYCHOLOGY

The behavior of unstructured social groupings remains a focus of contemporary social psychological research, although the social contagion perspective of the crowd psychologists from Le Bon to Blumer, which emphasizes the suggestibility and rapidly transmitted mental unity of aggregated individuals, has been largely supplanted by other theories of collective behavior. More recent approaches see a variety of social and psychological forces at work in the crowd and reject the notion that crowd membership reduces everyone to a uniform emotional condition. Early 20th century crowd psychology's sweeping generalizations about the dire social and political implications of the crowd have also disappeared as contemporary scholars focus on defining which social phenomena constitute collective behavior and which research techniques are best for empirically investigating them.

As sociologist David L. Miller notes in *Introduction to Collective Behavior,* three theoretical perspectives have replaced the earlier crowd psychologists' view of collective behavior as aroused emotion: Collective behavior as an adaptive response to new situations, collective behavior as a response to social strain, and collective behavior as social behavior. The first of these new approaches, presented by sociologists Ralph Turner and Lewis Killian in their 1957 text, *Collective Behavior,* defines collective behavior as emergent and transitory social behavior that is an adaptive response to novel and ambiguous social conditions. This emergent norm perspective holds that crowd members exhibit a range of behaviors, reflecting the interaction of individual predispositions with the emergence of new and untried norms (rules and expectations). Thus the group impact is one of normative constraint leading to differential expression rather than contagious mental homogeneity.

The value-added perspective, as developed by sociologist Neil Smelser in his 1962 volume, *Theory of Collective Behavior,* holds that any collective episode is an uninstitutionalized response to stressful social conditions such as economic deprivation, disasters, or inconsistencies between social values and societal norms. Prior evidence of social strain is thus necessary to explain collective events such as riots, panics, or revolutionary movements, all of which are seen in this approach as attempts to restructure values and/or social structures.

The most recent approach to collective behavior is the social behavioral/interactionist perspective, or SBI, elaborated by sociologist Clark McPhail in the 1970s. This approach sees no real difference between collective and other forms of social behavior and conceptualizes collective behavior as the organization of convergent activity. It focuses on empirically observing and recording the processes involved in the assembling and dispersal processes of crowds as well as behavior within these gatherings. Of particular concern are the instructions or cues to conduct that occur in social groupings.

Current research applies these theoretical perspectives to the study of collective behavior both in everyday life (fads and fashion, rumor and communication, mass hysteria, UFO sightings) and in disruptive social situations (migrations, disasters, protests, riots, social movements). Research techniques include the examination of historical materials on crowd episodes such as the French Revolution, surveys of riot participants supplemented by official police statistics, film recordings of aggregated groups, participant observation of groups, direct observation and group interviews, and controlled experiments of collective activities. Whereas the early crowd psychologists were content to generalize on the basis of little empirical evidence, contemporary researchers are concentrating on refining the procedures to identify, observe, and record collective behavior phenomena.

Bibliography

King, E. G. (1990). Reconciling democracy and the crowd in turn-of-the-century social-psychological thought. *J. History Behav. Sci.,* **26,** 334–344.

Leach, E. E. (1986). Mastering the crowd: Collective behavior and mass society in american social thought, 1917–1939. *Am. Studies,* **27,** 99–114.

Leach, E. E. (1992). 'Mental epidemics': Crowd psychology and american culture, 1890–1940. *Am. Studies,* **33,** 5–29.

McClelland, J. S. (1989). "The Crowd and the Public from Plato to Canetti." Unwin Hyman, London.

Miller, D. L. (1985). "Introduction to Collective Behavior." Wadsworth, Belmont, CA.

Van Ginneken, J. (1984). The killing of the father: The background of Freud's group psychology. *Pol. Psychol.* **5,** 391–414.

Van Ginneken, J. (1992). "Crowds, Psychology, and Politics: 1871–1899." Cambridge University Press, Cambridge.

CYBERNETICS

John N. Warfield
George Mason University

Glossary

Constructivism A philosophical doctrine that embodies these beliefs: (a) a universe exists, which includes human beings capable of observing small parts of that universe; (b) observation by the human occurs through sensory perception; (c) the aggregate of all prior and present sensory perception is translated into patterns by each individual observer, this aggregate constituting the "virtual world" of that observer.

Fallibilism in science The doctrine that "every proposition which we can be entitled to make about the real world must be an approximate one" (C. S. Peirce).

Feedback A portion of the information arising at some point B in physical space, which is embodied in some signal Z at that point B, passes through some medium to reach a second point A in physical space where it can be compared and mixed with a second signal Y that is present at point A (i.e., with the signal Y whose presence at A caused the signal Z to arise at point B).

Semiotic The doctrine of "the necessary laws of signs" (C. S. Peirce)

Sysarian A recognized area of study, so characterized only by the interest displayed in that area concerning systems; without regard to other interests possibly exhibited in that area.

Sysiety A professional society, formally organized for educational and scientific purposes, so characterized only by the interest displayed by that society concerning systems; without regard to other interests possibly exhibited by that society.

System "Any portion of the material universe which we choose to separate in thought from the rest of the universe for the purpose of considering and discussing the various changes which may occur within it under various conditions" (J. Willard Gibbs).

THE DEFINITION OF *cybernetics* has evolved (or, some would say, transmuted) over time. The most commonly stated definition is "control and communication in the animal and the machine." In the ancient Greek language it was written as Κυβερνητης. The most frequently stated translations of that term are "steersman" or "helmsman," but the term can also be translated as "governance": a usage that is current in Greece. There is little unanimity among devotees as to how to express its essence, although there is substantial agreement on the constituent ideas that are seen as going across disciplinary boundaries.

I. INTRODUCTION TO CYBERNETICS AND RELATED AREAS

A. Origins and Definitions

The term "cybernetics" was used by Heron of Alexandria a few hundred years after the birth of Christ, and again by André Marie Ampère in the early 1800s. The idea of regulation or control was implemented in water clocks and self-feeding oil lamps several hundred years before the birth of Christ. The concept was introduced in the context of living organisms by Claude Bernard in the 19th century. A very early, if not the earliest, technical paper on regulation was published by J. Wischnegradski in *Civil Ing.* in 1877.

It is probably fair to say that the modern field of cybernetics was an outgrowth of developments taking place in World War II. When Norbert Wiener published his book titled *Cybernetics* in 1948, which

Copyright © 1994 by Academic Press, Inc. All rights of reproduction in any form reserved.

is usually acknowledged to be the inaugural event that triggered the growth of cybernetics, it followed several experiences in his career that stimulated his thinking along cybernetics lines.

Wiener had been involved in four distinct, but related, areas of research that heavily involved mathematics, biology, and physics. These areas were: the study of brain waves in human beings (studied while visiting in Mexico), the study of the extraction of data from signals contaminated by noise or distortion, the study of nonlinear mathematics, and the study of signal representation by Fourier integrals. In observing the field-independent nature of the underlying mathematics, and in noting the phenomena that seemed to be discipline-independent, Wiener developed a synthesis that reflected those and other experiences. He had also been involved in a study group supported by the Josiah Macy Foundation, chaired by Warren McCulloch, that had as its goal the study of "circular causal and feedback mechanisms in biological and social systems." Because of his involvement in this McCulloch-led activity, some observers feel that McCulloch should be credited with originating the United States beginnings of cybernetics. In any event, both McCulloch and Wiener deserve significant credit for initiating this field.

B. Pioneers and Major Contributors

In the formative period of any significant area of study, the initial threads of integration inevitably involve some reference to specific actors: the pioneers and major contributors to the field. As their contributions begin to be integrated, the field tends to evolve to the point where the substantive conceptual material gradually replaces the individual references. Cybernetics has not attained the level of maturity where it can be presented without some reference to the pioneers and major contributors. On the other hand, in several subdomains it is now possible to be sufficiently definitive that it is not necessary to rely on reference to specific individuals in order to characterize the subdomain. Instead it is possible to identify contributions of actors within the broader discussion of the relevant subdomain.

For decades, investigators from Spanish-speaking nations have been leaders in neurophysiology. Ramon e Cahal discovered that neurons were not connected, but that there were gaps among them (now called synapses). Wiener learned elements of neurophysiology from Rosenblueth in Mexico City, while Maturana studied under McCulloch in Cambridge, Massachusetts. In the mid 1980s Varela studied cat brains. Maturana used laboratory studies to posit that the brain is a closed (finite) network of neurons. Nothing goes in or out. Rather the existing behavior of the nervous system is disturbed by patterns on the retina, and other sensing mechanisms. Computations in the nervous system produce signs (see John Poinsot and C. S. Peirce for the origins of the theory of signs) that become part of the individual's reality. The linguistic domain and the experiential domain within the nervous system form the neurophysiological basis for constructivism. They also provide the empirical basis for Peirce's view of fallibilism, and they strike a blow at the fixation of belief through authority, which has significant political implications. Through such findings, cyberneticians become positioned to critique significant parts of philosophy, including ethics.[1]

Compounding the difficulty of discussing cybernetics is, ironically (ironic, in view of the integrative nature of cybernetics), the fragmentation of the areas that fall naturally within the realm of interests of cyberneticians. There are literally dozens of currently active areas that are recognizable in academic or professional society domains, populated by relatively small groups of colleagues, all sharing an interest in some aspects of communication and control in the animal and in the machine.

The development and evolution of these areas of intellectual proximity to cybernetics did not all begin after the onset of cybernetics. Several of them were in place decades before Wiener's publication of *Cybernetics*, while others came along after that publication had appeared.

It is absolutely necessary, from a variety of standpoints, to identify a good many of these "proximity areas," because some significant contributions relevant to cybernetics have evolved from or even been developed within them. To exclude reference to them would not only present a misleading picture of historical developments, but would do an injustice to cybernetics by dramatically warping the context in which cybernetics lies.

In discussing the pioneers and major contributors to cybernetics, the initial focus will be on those individuals who appear to be most closely allied with cybernetics itself; but shortly this roster will be ex-

[1] Contributions to this paragraph came from Dr. Stuart Umpleby, with editing to meet space requirements done by J. Warfield.

panded to recognize individuals not so closely allied with cybernetics, or not even connected with it, who have played major roles in terms of advancing concepts of great interest to cyberneticians.

Among the prominent names associated closely with cybernetics are W. Ross Ashby, Gregory Bateson, Stafford Beer, Barry Clemson, Heinz von Foerster, Ernst von Glaserfeld, Klaus Krippendorff, Humberto Maturana, Warren McCulloch, Gordon Pask, William Powers, Fenton Robb, Stuart Umpleby, Francisco Varela, and the aforementioned Norbert Wiener.

Because the contributions of these pioneers are, for the most part, readily accessible in the literature, and are quite varied, it is impractical to go into detail on the specifics of their contributions. However, reference will be made in subsequent sections to a few of their contributions, in the context of discussions of particular subareas of cybernetics.

C. The Sysarians

There is no common term that describes the collection of proximity areas to cybernetics. Yet any discussion of cybernetics suffers in the absence of appropriate terminology. Unlike many disciplinary areas for which academic nomenclature is associated with academic departments, cybernetics is mostly alien to the standard university lexicon. Moreover, while most of the old-line academic disciplines align themselves with one or more professional societies that reflect the research activities in those disciplines (the disciplines and the societies being heavily coupled through the tenure-granting requirements for publication), the societies that have been formed to discuss and assess research in cybernetics and its proximity disciplines can only be partially aligned with academic disciplines. Where such alignment is close, the proximity discipline tends to be narrowly focused and thus not representative of the metadisciplinary nature of cybernetics.

For this reason, two distinct terms are required to present a proper overview of the field. One of these, "the Sysarians," refers to those proximity areas of cybernetics (and includes cybernetics as well). The other, "the Sysieties," refers to all those professional societies that profess interest in subjects integral to cybernetics. Some of the Sysarians and some of the Sysieties will match up in a one-to-one way with academic disciplines, but some will not. Some individuals will affiliate intellectually with several of the Sysarians, or with several of the Sysieties, while others will restrict their interest to just one.

Table I identifies some of the most prominent Sysarians. This table reflects the existence of a number of academic areas that overlap because they represent some form of shared interest in *systems*. Accordingly, we choose to call these areas the *Sysarians*.

While all Sysarians, by definition, share an interest in systems, the intensity, scope, focus, and other attributes of their interest will vary considerably. Therefore, we will have to be rather systematic in order to make distinctions that will be of value in considering the evaluation of Sysarians and the possibilities of integrating Sysarians. This systematic activity begins with the identification of Sysarians given in Table I.

D. The Sysieties

Just as there are numerous areas of study that have been identified by their members, so there are numerous societies formed to provide a focal point for research reports and sharing of information. Like the Sysarians, these Sysieties are characterized as representing some form of interest in systems. Table II identifies some of these Sysieties, and briefly identifies their interests.

The International Institute for Applied Systems Analysis (IIASA) should be mentioned for completeness. It is headquartered in Laxenburg, Austria, near Vienna. Extant since about 1970, it is a kind of international joint venture to enhance systems analysis and to provide opportunities for analysts to obtain fellowships which allow some interaction with others that share their interests. Since it is primarily a political creation of governments, rather than a society growing out of individual scientific interests, it does not meet the conditions required in order to be listed in Table II.

II. INITIAL AREAS OF FOCUS OF CYBERNETICS

In its initial period, stemming from the publication of Wiener's book bearing the title *Cybernetics*, interest focused primarily in these four areas: (a) automatic control, (b) communications and instrumentation allied with communications, (c) robotics, and (d) organizations.

TABLE I
Sysarians

Title	Typical academic affiliation	Illustrative member persons
Management science	Business schools	G. Huber
Operations research	Business/engineering schools	(early) R. Ackoff, (early) C. W. Churchman,
Systems analysis	Business/engineering schools	E. Quade, C. C. White, A. P. Sage
Systems engineering	Engineering schools	A. D. Hall III, P. Checkland, F. Pichler, P. Gardner, W. Wymore
Information systems	Business/engineering schools	F. Brooks
Systems science	Arts and science college, Engineering/business schools	G. Klir, R. Hirasawa, W. Gasparski, B. H. Banathy
Hierarchical systems	Biology departments	L. Troncale
General systems	None	K. Boulding, W. Gasparski, I. Prigogine, A. Rappoport, L. Von Bertalanffy, M. DeCleris, R. Hirosawa
Cybernetics	None	S. Umpleby, S. Beer, N. Weiner, R. Ashby, W. McCulloch, B. Clemson, H. Von Foerster, E. von Glasersfeld, F. Robb
Systems dynamics	Business/engineering schools	J. Forrester, D. Meadows, P. Gardner, G. Richardson,
Automatic control	Engineering schools	J. G. Truxal
Sociology/social services	Liberal arts colleges	G. DeZeeuw
Anthropology	Liberal arts colleges	M. Mead, G. Bateson
Psychology/psychiatry	Liberal arts colleges	J. G. Miller, K. Hammond
Economics	Arts and science college	G. Soros, E. Herrscher, A. Morales Rivas
Geography	Arts and science colleges	K. Haynes
Astronomy	Arts and science colleges	C. Sagan
Software engineering	Engineering schools	G. Weinberg
Mathematics	Arts and science colleges, Liberal arts colleges, Engineering schools	L. Zadeh, Anatol Rappoport, N. Weiner
Medicine (living systems)	Medical schools/general systems	J. G. Miller
Integrative studies	Liberal arts colleges	J. Kline, P. Caws
Philosophy	Liberal arts colleges	A. N. Whitehead, A. Bahm, I. Laszlo, M. Bunge

A. Automatic Control

Automatic control developed rapidly as a subject of study during World War II, primarily because of the need to develop sophisticated defenses against aircraft bombings and submarine torpedo attacks. Radar, sonar, and infrared systems were developed to track and destroy aircraft and submarines. These systems typically could be described as either passive or active. The passive type merely detected the presence of natural radiation coming from targets; but the active type emitted radiation in the direction of a presumed target, and received return information in the form of reflected signals.

The active type of defense system transmitted a signal and then received a reflected signal from a target, and used this signal to track the target and to guide weaponry toward the target. Computers could be used to compensate for the time delay occurring between the original reflection from the target and the time the reflection was received at the detecting unit. The target being in motion, received signals that no longer carried information as to the current location of a target, but only as to where it was and what its velocity and acceleration were at the time the transmitted signal was reflected from the target.

Two commonly faced difficulties were inherent in such operations. One was the corruption of received signals by a variety of interfering signals from other sources. All such interference could generically be described as "noise." The other was the fact that equipment used to position defensive weapons for firing did not respond proportionately (linearly) to

TABLE II
Sysieties

Title	Acronym	Discussion	Headquarters location
American Society for Cybernetics	ASC	The original American society dealing with cybernetics as it originated	Antioch, Seattle, Washington
Argentina Association for Theory of General Systems and Cybernetics	GESI	A co-located group of dedicated members who meet regularly to discuss topics of mutual interest	Buenos Aires, Argentina
Association for Integrative Studies	AIS	Oriented toward interdisciplinary studies in the humanities, but with an open door to the sciences	Miami, Ohio
Austrian Society for Cybernetics Studies		Broad, but oriented toward artificial intelligence	Vienna, Austria
Club of Rome		Sustaining the original interest in "world problems"	France
College de Systemique de l'AFCET	AFCET	A broad interest in systems, with a tilt toward engineering systems	Paris, France
Cybernetics Society, U. K.		Similar to those of ASC	London, England
Dutch Systems Group		A broad interest in systems, with a tilt toward social systems and information systems	Amsterdam, The Netherlands
Greek Systems Society		A broad interest in systems, with a tilt toward organizations and social systems	Athens, Greece
General Systems Research Group		Unknown	Japan
Institute of Electrical and Electronics Engineers Automatic Control Society	IEEE AC Society	Highly specialized to the mathematical theory of automatic control	New York
Institute of Electrical and Electronics Engineers Society for Systems, Man, and Cybernetics	IEEE SMC Society	Originally with a balanced interest between systems and cybernetics, but more recently placing emphasis on theoretical engineering constructs	New York
International Federation for Systems Research	IFSR	A "holding company" for societies with interests in systems, organized by the Austrian Society for Cybernetics Studies, the Dutch Systems Group, and the Society for General Systems Research (and its successor titles)	Vienna, Austria
International Society for General Systems Research	ISGSR	Name was changed. See "International Society for Systems Sciences"	
International Society for the Systems Sciences	ISSS	The successor to the Society for General Systems Research, now divided into many and varied Special Interest Groups (SIGS)	Louisville, Kentucky
Operations Research Society of America	ORSA	The original American society for sharing technical interests in operations research, with interests tilted toward relatively small-scale systems, and with relatively little direct interest in cybernetics	
Operational Research Society of Canada	ORSC	The original Canadian society for sharing interests in operational research	
Operational Research Society		The United Kindgom society for sharing interests in operational research	
Polish Cybernetical Society		A group that sustains an interest in the science of science, praxiology, and other aspects of interest to the Polish Academy of Sciences	Warsaw, Poland
Society of Management Science and Applied Cybernetics	SMSAC	Maintaining an interest in organizations, societies, and social development	New Delhi, India

(*continues*)

TABLE II (*Continued*)

Title	Acronym	Discussion	Headquarters location
Society for General Systems Research	SGSR	A society founded in the mid-1950s with the aim of correlating across disciplines to discover those features that systems hold in common, whatever their origins	
Spanish Society of General Systems	SESGE	Maintaining the tradition of interest in general systems begun by SGSR	Madrid, Spain
Systems Dynamics Society		Maintaining interest in system dynamics as set forth by J W. Forrester	Cambridge, Massachussetts
The Institute of Management Science	TIMS	Oriented toward theory and applications germane to business decisions	
United Kingdom Systems Society		Maintaining a broad interest in systems theory and applications	
Washington (D. C.) Evolutionary Systems Society	WESS	The theory of evolutionary systems	Washington, D. C.
World Organization of General Systems and Cybernetics	WOGSC	Holding world conferences every few years, with an open-door policy, this organization provides an opportunity for those with common interests in the areas to come together and share experiences and ideas	

control signals, but instead introduced nonlinearities that in turn produced errors in tracking.

The automatic controls that were developed could draw heavily on prior research from the communications field. In the late 1920s and early 1930s developments were published at the Bell Telephone Laboratories in each of these areas. For example, in 1934 H. S. Black of the Bell Telephone Laboratories published information on "stabilized feedback amplifiers" and gained U.S. Patent No. 2,102,671, in which the benefits of feedback in reducing the impact of nonlinearities and noise were prominently described.

The idea of using feedback is possibly the most important single idea introduced in the early days of cybernetics. The basic model of a feedback system presumed the availability of a signal, the "desired" signal, which, in effect, told the control system what it should do. The control system then responded to the desired signal but, unfortunately, imprecisely. Still it was possible to measure with considerable precision the response of the control system to the desired signal. By electronically subtracting the actual response of the system from the desired response (i.e., the control signal,) an *error signal* could be produced. The error signal derived from instrumentation became a key indicator of performance of the control system. As soon as this recognition is attained, one immediately observes that instead of using the desired signal to drive the controller (which only produces imprecise, erroneous response), why not use the error signal to drive the controller. If this were done, several advantages would accrue. First of all, if the error were zero, this would be the indication of perfect performance. Second, if the error were either positive or negative, the direction required to reduce the error would be clearly indicated by the sign of the error, and the intensity of change required would be clearly indicated by the amplitude of the signal. Third, the error signal would normally be much smaller than the desired signal, and this would produce significant improvement in the precision of the control system, because large signals normally are corrupted by nonlinearities in the system, while small signals can normally be amplified with much less distortion.

While all these benefits were possible, the introduction of feedback also introduced a potential hazard of instability in the control system. Instability refers to a condition where the energy made available to the control system from its power source becomes the source of self-excitation within the control system producing possibly disastrous oscillations within that system having nothing to do with the primary application of the system. Fortunately the Bell Telephone Laboratories, as well as various European research organizations in such fields as telephony and radio, had developed significant theoretical backgrounds concerning the analysis of instability, and ways for preventing this from occurring were already being practiced long before 1948. Accordingly, it was possible to develop automatic control systems using newly developed sensors that operated with feedback to provide an adequate response to threats from airplanes and submarines.

B. Communication and Instrumentation

Communication and instrumentation areas provided significant theory to automatic control personnel. As soon as the image of automatic control of weaponry became a visible reality, and the impact could be assessed, earlier visions of control within living organisms came rapidly to the forefront of thinking. About 150 years earlier, Claude Bernard had discussed "the advantages gained by the so-called warm blooded animals in developing a regulator to maintain a constant internal body temperature." He declared that this "stability of the internal milieu" was a "condition of free and independent life." The recognition of advances in theory and instrumentation stimulated a new era of study of the human being as a physiological system involving communication and control.

C. Robotics

The same body of knowledge that was developed during World War II as a response to weaponry clearly could be carried over to a newly emerging field called "robotics." Robotics envisaged creating mechanical devices that would look like and perform like human beings, but without some of the frailties or political behavior of humans. Of special interest was the use of robotics in hazardous environments, such as nuclear environments. With the birth of the atomic bomb in World War II, it became clear that if the so-called peaceful uses of atomic energy were to come to fruition, it would be highly desirable or perhaps absolutely necessary to develop robots capable of processing nuclear materials. While the robots would be radiation-contaminated, they would not develop medical problems of life-threatening nature such as human beings could expect to face if called upon to handle "hot" nuclear materials.

Accordingly many organizations began to develop programmable "automatic arms," i.e., mechanical devices shaped somewhat like the human arm, with vise-like grips at the end of the arm to take hold of materials and move them to positions under the management of an automatic control system with feedback.

The idea of robotic vision led to a new interest in studying human sight, this being made possible with greater precision by the use of instrumentation and feedback, providing the precision to create valuable data having to do with human vision.

D. Organizations

To persons concerned with the viability and performance of organizations, the idea of introducing cybernetic concepts in organizations was highly attractive. One individual in particular was attracted to this area specifically to apply concepts from the automatic control systems directly to organizations. Jay W. Forrester, of the Massachusetts Institute of Technology, promoted the idea of "industrial dynamics," and the use of feedback theory to understand organizational behavior. [*See* ORGANIZATIONAL BEHAVIOR.]

This idea would subsequently be applied by Forrester (with only minor changes) to create "urban dynamics," and later to create "world dynamics."

The escalation of the application of feedback theory first to corporations, then to urban areas, and finally to the entire world attracted great attention and produced both highly positive and highly negative responses.

The early application to corporations could be done with only modest opposition, because issues of corporate finance and production could be dealt with internally at a level of understanding that was much deeper than what could be had concerning urban complexes or the entire world. Success with machinery could be extended fairly well to success with financial and production controls. Success would be much more difficult when the scale of human performance was extended in such areas as urban societies and the world (which, as is now abundantly clear, provide the environment within which industries operate).

Another pioneer in bringing cybernetics to organizations was Stafford Beer. Beer is well known for his work on organization structure, and his on-the-spot involvement in organizations. His "viable systems model" is widely known in Europe, relying far less upon system dynamics than Forrester, and relying far more on the logic of organizational practice.

III. EVOLUTION TO DIVERSITY

Cybernetics evolved significantly in the period extending forward in time from around 1965, with four areas involved in major ways in the diversity that was to march along in parallel with the development of cybernetics. The four areas that can be examined here with respect to this evolution are: (a) computers, and all of the impact and related topics that accompany this exploding field, (b) sociotechnical systems, i.e., the combination of human beings and machines in systems, (c) biological systems, i.e., those self-contained living organisms and their relation with their environments (including family therapy), and (d) general systems of complexity.

A. Cybernetics and Computers

The computer field is still expanding at a rapid pace, the capabilities of the purposeless machine becoming more and more powerful in the hands of purposeful human beings. It is too early to conclude where this field is taking society, but one can say that the impact is already dramatic, and that it promises to be much more so in the future. The most significant conclusion that can be drawn now is that the computer will have more visible (as opposed to intellectual) impact on cybernetics than any development in the history of mankind.

B. Sociotechnical Systems

Sociotechnical systems involve combinations of human beings and machines, operating in many kinds of partitions and combinations. The complexity of such systems is well known, if seldom honored by political practitioners in the means they use to analyze and synthesize in this realm. Because of the rapid and evolutionary growth of communications and computing machinery, the public has the opportunity to know more and more about such systems. This awareness can have very significant impact on the administration and management of sociotechnical systems everywhere. The principles embedded in cybernetics can be taken seriously in the applications, and used to prescribe social steering mechanisms that are acceptable to people.

There is a growing area of activity in family therapy with roots in cybernetics.

C. Biological Systems

More and more research is taking place concerning the biological bases of human reasoning. Discoveries in this area will pose major challenges at the interface between the human being and the larger social environment. Put the power of cybernetic thinking at both the individual and social level, and mix it in with cultures heavily involved in cocaine and other related drugs, and the future of society begins to look like a garden implanted with thousands of questions marks.

D. Systems of Complexity

Complexity, as such, has only begun to be studied seriously (1993 marked the silver anniversary of Warfield's work in studying complexity, which has produced almost 2000 pages on the subject in several books). Earlier it was stated that the Sysarians are joined together by an interest in systems. Ultimately this interest can evolve into an interest in complexity, because that seems to be the predominant attribute of the systems facing the individual in today's environment; and the escalation of complexity can be compared with the growth of world population in terms of its silent impact on the quality of human life.

IV. KEY DISCOVERIES

The key discoveries germane to cybernetics arise from the entire field of Sysarians (partly identified in Table I). Likely to be mentioned in any discussion of such key discoveries are the following: The Law of Requisite Variety, set forth by Ashby; autopoiesis, set forth by Maturana and Varela; the Viable Systems Model of Stafford Beer; the philosophy of constructivism made highly visible by von Foerster, von Glasersfeld, Pask, and Krippendorff; second-order cybernetics, distinguished from first-order cybernetics by Von Foerster; and a class of discoveries relevant to the physical nature of the human brain with contributions coming from McCulloch, Wiener, Maturana, Varela, and others, and with an initial summary platform coming from Patricia Churchland.

One of the less commendable attributes of the Sysarians is their tendency to ascribe discoveries to contemporaries when, in some instances, the literature is clear that the discoveries were made well before most of the Sysarians came into being, with the following discussion offering a particularly striking example.

A particular shortcoming is the failure to recognize the contributions of the man who, according to the contemporary German philosopher Apel, was "America's greatest thinker." Charles Sanders Peirce contributed to so many fields that it is very difficult to conceive how one individual could make so many contributions; and it is even more surprising to learn that much of his work remains unpublished. Indiana University Press anticipates publishing some 30 volumes of his work. The first true biography appeared in 1993, eighty-three years after his death in poverty in Milford, Pennsylvania.

Peirce studied how belief is fixed, and concluded that all belief was fixed by inference. Peirce's pioneering work in semiotics clearly distinguished the observed, the observer, and the mediation between the observed and observer not only stemming from the physical media involved in transmission of signs, but of equal significance, the impact of language and the "deceit of language" which is fundamental to Pask's conversation theory, and to concepts of "linguistic domains" set forth by contemporary cyberneticians. Peirce and Piaget, taken together, can be seen as the modern creators of the foundations of constructivism, and today's advocates should properly take note of this.

In addition to the best-known results mentioned above, other results are narrowly known, but are potentially quite significant. Those to be mentioned have the property that they stem from a combination of theory and empirical results, and they they are founded in the Peirce philosophy of science. (That philosophy incorporates important concepts of fallibilism of the observer, and the need for a community of scholars constantly engaged in reviewing and upgrading scientific products of the past; a philosophy of science that transcends the popular, often-cited philosophy of science of T. S. Kuhn.) These results are found in a newly developed science called the "science of generic design" and these results are stated as "laws of generic design."

Included therein is the law of inherent conflict, which states that no matter what the complex topic and no matter what the group that considers it, there will be significant conflict among the members concerning the relative importance of the factors. This law stems from empirical confirmation of constructivism's most basic idea, and explains why social and political debate on complex issues that does not incorporate systematic provisions for learning ("framebreaking and remodeling," to use a phrase of Argyris) is ill-conceived and unproductive.

Also included in the science of generic design is the law of structural underconceptualization. This law rests in part on the foundation of structural mathematics, which shows that the prototype form of foundational logic structure is a hybrid structure comprising two types of substructure: hierarchy and cycle. Linear thinking, often criticized, presumes a linear hierarchy of logic. But the linear form is a special case of a hierarchy, and the hierarchy is a special case of a hybrid structure. Because there is virtually no way that human beings can construct and interpret more than the most elementary hybrid structures without machine assistance, and because hybrid structures are required to embody the logic of complex systems, most conceptualizations of systems are faulty, illustrating the validity of the Peirce concept of scientific fallibilism, and emphasizing the need for a scientific community to become more fundamental in the way they view systems.

V. OPEN ISSUES IN CYBERNETICS

Today, as has been true since the field came into view, cybernetics must continue to struggle with certain open issues. However, the struggle can be much better informed than in the early period, thanks to the efforts of many scholars.

A. Integration of Knowledge

Perhaps the most important issue facing cybernetics is the integration of knowledge. It has already been demonstrated above that the topics of study of interest to cyberneticians stretch across many areas and involve many professional societies. Virtually all of these areas and societies involve only modest numbers of individuals. If each society continues to make broad claims of its scope and coverage, while dealing in depth with only a few pieces of the whole, continued modest credibility will be one of the fruits; and the absence of effective academic programs dealing with the subjects will belie the expressed aim of many of those involved to see their subject become widely known to students. Under this condition, the best that can be hoped for is that established disciplines will selectively and intelligently incorporate Sysarian elements in their own programs.

B. Cognition

The general area of cognition remains of great social importance. Ideas from cybernetics are highly relevant to this area. The field has an incipient political dimension that needs to be continuously dealt with as new discoveries are made, and at the practical level of public education of children there is already major knowledge that remains unused in the educational systems. Cyberneticians in particular, and Sysarians in general, hold knowledge that could be implemented, but remains fallow. This is an organizational and management issue, in part, and involves the organizational thinking that is a key part of cybernetics.

C. Cyclic Closure of the Domain of Cybernetics

If cybernetics can be construed as a science, then perhaps it can be seen through the Domain of Science model. This model asserts that if a body of information is to deserve the title *"science"* it must have documented, identified, foundations, theory, and methodology; and the methodology and the application areas comprise the *arena* in which that science is tested and applied. The domain of cybernetics includes areas of its application, where science and the arena should (but often do not) overlap through methodology arising from the science. The overlap provides the only significant opportunity for the necessary corrective feedback from applications to reach the science in a timely way. Much contemporary methodology eschews reference to scientific foundations, frustrating the application of cybernetic principles in developing science.

For proper development of any science, a strong feedback component between the arena and the science is required to provide the testing and amendment that is required to upgrade the quality of a science. Closure through feedback ("cyclic closure") of the domain of cybernetics demands that such a linkage be not only established, but made much more visible and given much more emphasis by the Sysieties.

Bibliography[2]

Arbib, M. A. (1989). "The Metaphorical Brain 2: Neural Networks and Beyond." Wiley, New York.

Brent, J. (1993). "Charles Sanders Peirce: A Life," Indiana University Press, Bloomington, IA.

Bryant, J. (1991). "Systems Theory and Scientific Philosophy: An Application of the Cybernetics of W. Ross Ashby to Personal and Social Philosophy, the Philosophy of Mind, and the Problems of Artificial Intelligence," University Press of America, Lanham, MD.

Churchland, P. S. (1986). "Neurophilosophy: Toward a Unified Science of the Mind-Brain," The MIT Press, Cambridge, MA.

Deely, J. (1990). "Basics of Semiotics," Indiana University Press, Bloomington, IN.

Espejo, R., and Harnden, R. (1989). "The Viable Systems Model: Interpretations and Applications of Stafford Beer's Viable System Model," Wiley, New York.

Fidelman, U. (1991). Experimental testing of constructivism and related theories. *Behav. Sci.* **36**(4), 274–297.

François, C. (1992). "Diccionario de Teoria General de Sistemas y Cibernetica," Asociacion Argentina de Teoria General de Sistemas y Cibernetica, Buenos Aires.

Kuhn, A. J. (1986). "Organizational Cybernetics and Business Policy: System Design for Performance Control," Pennsylvania State University Press, University Park, PA.

Maturana, R., and Varela, F. J. (1980). "Autopoesis and Cognition." Reidel, Dordrecht.

Prigogine, I. (1984). "Order out of Chaos," Bantam Books, New York.

Umpleby, S. A., and Sadovskii, V. N. (1991). "A Science of Goal Formulation: American and Soviet Discussions of Cybernetics and Systems Theory," Hemisphere, New York.

von Foerster, H. (1984). "Observing Systems," 2nd ed. with an introduction by F. J. Varela. Intersystems, Salinas, CA.

von Glasersfeld, E., (1984). An introduction to radical constructivism. In "The Invented Reality" (P. Watzlawick, Ed.), pp. 17–40. Norton, New York.

von Glasersfeld, E., and Steffe, L. P. (1991). Conceptual models in educational research and practice. *J. Educational Thought* **25**(2), 91–103.

Warfield, J. N. (1990). "A Science of Generic Design: Managing Complexity through Systems Design," Intersystems, Salinas, CA.

[2] Many of the linguistic challenges associated with the development and evolution of cybernetics require greater attention to the terminology of cybernetics than has been possible in the past. In Argentina, Charles François, a retired Belgian diplomat, has been developing a "dictionary of general systems and cybernetics" for several years. A preliminary Spanish version has been published, but the English version now being developed includes more entries. According to Charles, "my main motivation is to produce a basic user's tool for anyone who should need or want a global view of the field integrated as a whole, or more specific information about some systemic or cybernetic concept or model, as well as some closely related topics."

Decision Making, Individuals

K. J. Radford
University of Waterloo, Canada

Glossary

Decision conference A group of persons meeting to make recommendations regarding a particular situation.

Decision making The process of arriving at a decision after evaluating all relevant alternatives in achieving a decision maker's objective or objectives.

Ill-structured decisions Decisions that appear to the decision maker to be new and unique in one or more respects.

Rationality Choice between alternatives in a manner endowed with reason.

Well-structured decisions Decisions that have become well-understood as a result of many encounters with situations of the same type.

SITUATIONS IN WHICH a decision must be made arise continually in our daily lives, in the organizations in which we work and in the communities in which we live. Decision making is a major part of the work of individuals in modern organizations. A decision is the process of making a judgment regarding what one *ought* to do in a certain situation, after having deliberated on some alternative courses of action. A decision maker is a person who decides among alternative courses of action. This person must decide which course of action will lead to the accomplishment of a desired objective or set of objectives. The essence of decision making, according to these and other authors, is in the formulation of alternative courses of action to meet a situation under consideration and in the choice between these alternatives after an evaluation of their effectiveness in achieving the decision maker's objective or objectives.

I. CATEGORIES OF DECISION SITUATIONS

There are four major factors that must be taken into account in the study of decision situations:

- The nature and the amount of the information that is available to form a basis for an approach to resolution of a problem. If the information is complete, this gives rise to a condition of *certainty;* if the information is incomplete, this causes *uncertainty*.
- Whether costs and benefits of taking a course of action can be described wholly in *quantitative* terms; if not, decisions may have to be made on the basis of *nonquantitative* factors such as preferences.
- Whether those involved in the decision situation have a *single objective* or a set of *multiple objectives*.

Copyright © 1994 by Academic Press, Inc. All rights of reproduction in any form reserved.

TABLE I
Categories of Decision Situations

	Category 1	Category 2	Category 3	Category 4	Category 5
Certainty or uncertainty	Certainty	Certainty or uncertainty	Uncertainty	Certainty or uncertainty	Certainty or uncertainty
Quantitative or nonquantitative measures of benefits and costs	Quantitative	Nonquantitative	Quantitative	Quantitative or nonquantitative	Quantitative or nonquantitative
Single or multiple objectives	Single objective	Single objective	Single objective	Multiple objectives	Single or multiple objectives
Single or more than one participant	Single participant	Single participant	Single participant	Single participant	Many participants
Examples	Optimum use of resources in a production process: optimum distribution from warehouses to retail points: optimal flow through networks	Do I choose 5 apples or 4 oranges: or a chance of obtaining 5 apples or a different chance of obtaining 4 oranges?	Do I choose a 30% chance of a $10,000 profit or 60% chance of a $6000 profit?	Should I buy a new set of golf clubs, go on an ocean cruise, or buy a new suit?	Should we build low-cost housing or develop the land as a recreational facility?

- Whether one or more *participants* have an interest in the resolution of the decision situation.

Combination of the two states of each of these characteristics leads to 16 categories of decision situations. These 16 categories can be condensed into 5, as shown in Table I.

II. "WELL-STRUCTURED" DECISION SITUATIONS

Decisions in Category 1 are said to be "well-structured. These decisions are those that have become well-understood as a result of many encounters with situations of the same type. Choice of a preferred alternative in a well-structured situation is said to be *objectively rational* because it refers to a course of action that can be seen to be uniquely best under conditions of certainty.

Many "well-structured" decision situations that arise in the management of production processes can be analyzed by use of the *linear programming* model. This model provides a method of obtaining a solution to the problem of determining the best allocation of resources in many operational situations.

There are other types of situations that have the characteristic that they may be studied by reference to a series of stages or time periods. Consider, for example, the situation in which customers requiring a certain item are supplied from inventory held by a retailer. This inventory can be replenished from time to time by ordering from a supplier. There are certain set-up (or ordering) costs and delivery costs which make it desirable to replenish the inventory by larger rather than smaller amounts. However, if production or reordering is done in larger quantities, the costs of maintaining the inventory may be greater. The decision maker wishes to minimize the cost of the inventory. The analytical procedure most frequently associated with such decision situations is called *dynamic programming*.

Other types of decision situations that can be studied by these analytical procedures are as follows:

1. *Shortest-route problems,* which are concerned with finding the shortest route between

two geographic points when a number of alternate routes exist.

2. *Assignment problems,* which are concerned with optimal procedures when there are a number of tasks to be undertaken and a number of ways in which each task can be completed.

3. *Critical path,* situations which are typically those in which specific activities necessary to complete a project must be scheduled so as to minimize the time or the costs incurred between the beginning and end of a project.

III. "ILL-STRUCTURED" DECISION SITUATIONS

Ill-structured decisions are those that appear to the decision maker to be new and unique in one or more respects. No complete and well-established mathematical procedure is available for dealing with them because there is no direct experience available from previous encounters with a problem of exactly the same sort. These decision situations often contain a measure of uncertainty because information describing them may be incomplete. It may not be possible to evaluate the results of courses of action in quantitative terms and the decision maker may be required to satisfy more than one objective. In addition it may be necessary to take into account multiple objectives rather than a single objective in coming to a conclusion. Such decision situations fall into Categories 2, 3, and 4 in Table I.

In other ill-structured decision situations, there are two or more participants that may each have a significant effect on the outcome. In such situations, resolution of the situation may take place only after an explicit or implicit process of negotiation between the participants. These situations fall into Category 5 in Table I.

IV. RATIONALITY IN DECISION MAKING

The question of what constitutes rational behavior in the resolution of a decision situation can be linked to the description of the characteristics of various categories of decisions in Table I.

A dictionary definition of the word "rational" is "endowed with reason." We may infer, therefore, that the definition of a rational decision maker is one who, after consideration of the results of alternative courses of action, chooses that which is most in line with his or her objectives. This concept of rationality is straightforward in well-structured situations in which there is complete information, a single objective, the ability to evaluate benefits and costs in quantitative terms, and a single decision maker (Category 1). In these circumstances, all possible alternatives can be envisaged and evaluated. Rational behavior consists of choosing the alternative that is the best (or most preferred) according to criteria determined by the objective.

Some modification of this concept of rationality is clearly needed under the conditions prevailing in ill-structured situations such as those included in Categories 2, 3, and 4 in Table I. In Category 2 for example, no generally accepted quantitative measure of the benefit or cost of selecting a particular course of action may be available. Unless those involved can agree on a measure of effectiveness, they will likely disagree about what is the best outcome, and therefore, about what is the rational choice of outcome. Similarly, in Category 3, where there is incomplete information (and hence considerable uncertainty), any list of the alternatives available to the decision maker is likely to be incomplete. In these circumstances, it is possible that another course of action preferable to that which is considered to be the best might be revealed if more information were available. Under these circumstances, no choice between alternatives can be said unequivocally to be the best and therefore rational. Furthermore, two individuals involved in the same decision might have different information and consequently different perceptions of that situation. In these circumstances, the two individuals might recommend different courses of action for resolution of the same problem, each claiming, however, that he or she decided logically. In Category 4, progress toward achievement of multiple objectives may be measured in different and incompatible terms. Under these circumstances, there may be more than one way of comparing the results of two possible courses of action and there may be no single method of judging which of them is best.

A modification of the concept of rationality is clearly needed in these circumstances. Such a modification can be introduced in the following terms:

- The choice of an alternative that is seen as best under conditions of complete information can be called *objectively rational;* such an objectively rational choice is unique and optimal under the conditions stated.

- Choice between alternatives when measures of performance are not quantitative (Category 2), or when there is uncertainty (Category 3), or when multiple objectives exist (Category 4), can be called *subjectively rational.* A subjectively rational choice is not uniquely best, although it is regarded as best under the conditions in which it is made. Two individuals may reach different conclusions in a situation which they assess differently and each may claim to be subjectively rational in the circumstances as they perceive them.

A further extension of the idea of rationality is necessary when two or more participants are involved in an ill-structured decision situation (Category 5). In these circumstances, the outcome is often reached only after a process of negotiation between the participants. This outcome may be viewed as being *jointly rational.* A jointly rational outcome may not correspond to the outcome most desired by any one of the participants. It is, however, an outcome to which all participants can subscribe, and which is preferred by these participants to continued consideration of the decision situation. Paul Diesing has suggested that rationality could be more related to the *approach* to the decision situation rather than to the actual choice between alternatives. From this point of view, a rational approach is one that, in Diesing's words, ". . . yields adequate decisions for complex situations with some regularity." This more flexible approach to the concept of rationality has many advantages in dealing with the more complex types of decision situations.

V. MEASURES OF BENEFITS AND COST

Decision making was defined earlier in this article as ". . . the choice between alternatives after an evaluation of their effectiveness in achieving the decision makers objective or objectives." The process of evaluation must consist of (i) an assessment of the benefits of each of the alternate courses of action relative to the objective or objectives of the decision maker and (ii) an estimate of the costs of each of the possible courses of action. The decision can then be made on the basis of the greatest benefit for a given cost or the least cost for a particular benefit.

The most commonly used and easily appreciated measure of benefits and costs in modern society is *money*. Money is a good such measure in many situations in the private sector where maximization of profit per dollar invested is a common first objective of many organizations. Increasingly in modern times, however, such organizations have additional objectives, not necessarily as important as the maximization of profit, but nevertheless vital to their perceived role in the community. For example, a company may have an objective of "appearing to be a good corporate citizen" as second in priority to making a profit.

The problem of defining appropriate quantitative measures of benefit and cost exists also in the public sector. Cost can still be measured in dollars for a public sector organization, at least in part. However, the benefits of such activities as providing health care services, educational opportunities, services to the elderly and sick, and programs of support for single mothers are much more difficult to measure in quantitative terms. Similarly, the costs of not providing such services are also most difficult to assess in terms of money or any other quantitative measure.

Two particular types of measurement in common use in practical situations are concerned with *efficiency* and *effectiveness*. In general, efficiency refers to the best use of resources in a process; a course of action that results in the greatest amount of output for a given amount of resources used (or the least amount of resources for a given amount of output) is the most efficient. A measure of efficiency might be concerned, for example, with the greatest amount of flow through a pipeline or the maximum use of space in a building. Measures of effectiveness, on the other hand, relate to the degree to which objectives are achieved. Such a measure might be concerned, for example, with the degree to which a particular course of action contributes to the diversification of the activities of a company, or to the well-being of a particular class of citizens.

VI. DECISION MAKING IN THE PRESENCE OF UNCERTAINTY

The decision-making behavior of individuals in the presence of uncertainty is influenced by their attitude to risk. A conservative person who is very averse to risk would probably concentrate on possible adverse outcomes in the choice between alternatives. A person with a more entrepreneurial attitude might stress the possible beneficial outcomes in a decision situation.

TABLE II
Net Monthly Profit of the Restaurant (thousands of dollars)

	Possible future customer demand		
	Low	Medium	High
Do not expand the restaurant	2	4	5
Build a small extension	13	25	20
Build a large extension	−60	10	80

Consider, for example, the situation of someone who owns a restaurant in the center of town. He has noticed that his establishment seems to be getting full more often recently and he has been forced on an increasing number of occasions to turn patrons away. He concludes that he is faced with the possibility of having to build a small or a large extension of his restaurant or to keep the facility as it is and possibly have his clientele dimish due to disappointment on being turned away.

The choice between these alternatives is influenced by the possible future size of the clientele at the restaurant. Let us suppose, for simplicity, that the possible future demand for seats at the restaurant can be described as low, medium, or high. Let us assume, further, that the owner of the restaurant can estimate his net monthly profit for each of the three possible future states of demand as shown in Table II.

The owner of the restaurant can now argue as follows. The minimum profits for a low state of future customer demand are as shown in Table III.

The alternative of building a small extension provides the maximum of the three minimum net monthly profits shown in Table III. A cautious owner might therefore decide that to build a small extension is the alternative that is most advantageous to the restaurant.

Decision-making behavior in which an individual consciously or unconsciously determines the minimum benefit for each of the alternatives and then selects the alternative that gives the maximum of these minima is called *maximin*. Note that if the decision maker is endeavoring to minimize cost, the approach would require minimization of the maximum cost. This prinicple if called *minimax*. Conceptually, maximin and minimax are the same thing, one referring to benefits and the other to costs.

TABLE III
Minimum Net Monthly Profit for Low Demand

Do not expand the restaurant	2
Build a small extension	13
Build a large extension	−60

Another type of decision-making behavior is closely linked to the concept of opportunity cost, or the cost of lost opportunities. A number of authors have suggested that decision makers are influenced in their choice between alternatives by the difference between the benefits associated with any particular alternative and the maximum benefit that could be expected by the "correct" choice for a particular future state of the world. This type of behavior can be represented by constructing a table showing a quantity called *"regret"* for each of the alternatives available to the decision maker. Regret represents the loss that a decision maker suffers because the exact future state of the world was not known at the time of selection of an alternative. It can be regarded as the cost of lost opportunities.

The regret values for each of the alternatives in each of the future states of customer demand in the restaurant situation are shown in Table IV.

The idea of regret can be combined with that of minimax to obtain a description of decision-making behavior that is called *minimax regret*. Note that the term minimax is used here because we are seeking to minimize the maximum loss of opportunity. In the particular example chosen, the choice on the basis of minimax regret is to build the small extension. The maximum regret that would be experienced in that case is 60 units which is less than that for the other two courses of action.

Probability is often used in practical situations as a quantitative expression of uncertainty. Suppose, for example, that the owner of the restaurant discussed earlier estimates that the probability of low,

TABLE IV
Regret in the Restaurant Expansion Problem (thousands of dollars)

	Possible future customer demand		
	Low	Medium	High
Do not expand the restaurant	11	21	75
Build a small extension	0	0	60
Build a large extension	73	15	0

TABLE V

Expected Value of Net Monthly Profit at the Restaurant (thousands of dollars)

	Possible future customer demand			
	Low	Medium	High	Expected values of monthly profit
Probability of future demand	.25	.25	.50	
Do not expand the restaurant	2	4	5	4.00
Build a small extension	13	25	20	19.50
Build a large extension	−60	10	80	27.50

medium, and high demand for seats at the restaurant at some future time will be 1/4, 1/4, and 1/2, respectively. He could then calculate what is called the *expected value* of his monthly profit for each of his possible extensions of the restaurant by multiplying the profit for each of the extension plans and future demands by his estimates of the probability of the future demands actually occurring. For example, he could calculate the expected value of his monthly profit if he built a small extension as (0.25 × $13,000) + (0.25 × $25,000) + (0.5 × $20,000) which equals $19,500. Calculation of the expected values of monthly profit for all possible circumstances under these assumptions is shown in Table V.

If the owner of the restaurant elected to make the decision between not expanding the facility and building a small or large extension on the basis of maximum expected value, he would choose to build the larger extension and expect to receive $27,500 net monthly profit.

There are, however, some serious reservations with respect to the use of the criterion of maximum expected profit (or minimum expected loss) in this type of decision. The main reservation of this sort is that the use of expected values is appropriate only in decision situations that are repetitive in substantially the same form.

VII. DECISION MAKING IN MULTIPLE-OBJECTIVE SITUATIONS

The methods available to assist decision makers engaged in multiple-objective decision situations are determined by three conditions.

1. Whether quantitative measures of progress toward the achievement of each objective are available.
2. Whether a direct relationship exists between the units in which these measures can be expressed.
3. Whether numeric weighting factors or ordinal preferences exist to express priorities of objectives.

If the answer to these three conditions is yes, weighting methods are available by means of which performance of alternatives can be aggregated into a single objective function. The choice can then be made in terms of the greatest or least value of this objective function.

For example, suppose that a family is in the market for a house and that the choice has been narrowed to four possibilities. The family's objectives (or criteria) can be listed (not in any order of priority) as

- To have at least four bedrooms, a family room, a living room, dining room, and a kitchen.
- To have reasonable access to downtown, schools, and major highways.
- To have a reasonably large back yard.
- To be priced within the family's possible range.

The four possible houses are then assessed against the criteria as shown in Table VI. The relative importance of the criteria in the choice of expressed by allocating arbitrary weightings of 4, 5, 3, and 6, respectively, to the above characteristics of the houses. On the basis of the weighted score, the family would select House D.

This method has several apparent advantages for the decision maker faced with the choice between alternatives in a multiple-objective situation. It is not complex; it is simply applied and it is apparently

TABLE VI

Criteria, Weights, and Scores in the House Selection Problem

		Houses			
Criteria	Numerical weightings	A	B	C	D
Accommodation	4	8	6	7	5
Access	5	7	4	5	6
Back yard	3	6	5	4	7
Price	6	4	7	6	9
Weighted scores		109	101	101	125

logical. The analysis results in what appears to be a basis for unequivocal choice in the form of performance scores for each of the alternatives. However, there are serious reservations about the employment of the method as the sole basis for choice between alternatives in a multiple-objective situation. These reservations concern the assumptions implicit in the use of the method, namely:

1. That the preferences for the three houses with respect to four different characteristics can be assessed on an arbitrary scale of 0 to 10.
2. That the priorities for the four areas of assessment can be expressed in terms of the numerical weightings used.
3. That the weighted score, summing performance in the four areas, represents a valid assessment of the desirability of the four houses in the light of the four criteria.

Those in favor of the weighted score technique would argue that it presents a realistic representation of the views and preferences of the individuals involved in the assessment. They might add that the process of producing the weighted score provides an opportunity for discussion and thought during which individual opinions are formulated and clarified. The danger remains, however, that weighted score methods may be used as a superficial means of comparing alternatives that replaces the more comprehensive considerations required in the treatment of many multiple-objective decisions.

In many practical decision situations, no truly representative quantitative measures of performance can be found with respect to some of the objectives: nor are numeric weightings available in which to express priorities. In these situations, elimination methods offer some capability of placing a number of alternatives in an order of preference. These methods involve the evaluation of the alternatives against a factor related to each objective in turn, starting with that with highest priority. Alternatives not meeting a specified level of performance are eliminated until only one is left that has satisfied all the tests to that point. Ties are resolved by making the levels of performance or the criteria used more discriminating. These methods are known under the general heading of "sequential elimination."

VIII. RISK SHARING

Situations arise in which two or more individuals wish to cooperate in a venture that involves risk. They seek an arrangement by which they can share that risk. By doing so, they hope to divide the rewards to the venture among themselves if the venture is successful. However, they must face the fact that they may have to share the losses if the venture fails. The manner in which the partners share in this risky venture depends upon their individual attitudes toward gain and loss.

The task of finding an appropriate sharing of the venture involves finding a part of that venture for each partner that falls within his or her acceptable region. The division of the risk can be either proportional or nonproportional. In proportional sharings, the partners, each take a fraction of the total gain and the same fraction of the loss. The fractions assumed by the partners must add up to 1. Proportional sharing may not be feasible in many circumstances. If this is the case, the partners may try to find a suitable nonproportional share of the venture. In such a sharing, each individual takes a share of the possible gain which is different from his or her share of the potential loss.

A nonproportional sharing of a venture involves a disproportionate allocation of risk that may be assumed by one or more of the partners for their own reasons. For example, a father may assume a less favorable position in a business venture in order to help his son become established in that business. In other circumstances, one partner might assume a less advantageous part of a venture in return for a favor received from the other partner on another occasion. Every nonproportional sharing of a risk involves a consideration granted by one partner to another. This consideration is called a *side payment*. In cases in which the venture is described entirely in quantitative terms, the value of the side payment can be calculated numerically. In other circumstances where the possible outcomes of a venture can be assessed only partially in quantitative terms, the side payment is assessable only in nonquantitative terms. For example, one partner may accept a somewhat less favorable share of a venture in recognition of the contribution of experience by another. Similarly, valued friendship is often taken into account by partners discussing possible sharing of a venture.

IX. DECISION MAKING IN GROUPS

For the purpose of studying decision making, a group is defined as a number of individuals or subgroups that share a common purpose. Each member of the group has the capability of making a decision alone, but each is committed to joint decision making according to the purpose of the group. There are a number of practical methods of decision making in a group, of which voting is the one most commonly used.

Simple majority rule is often the most readily acceptable method of choice between two alternatives by a group. However, other decision rules such as three-quarters majority are often used in practice. The search for an appropriate decision-making method becomes much more complex when three or more alternatives are available. A procedure often used is *approval voting,* whereby members vote for any number of alternatives, rather than just one as in plurality voting. However, voting procedures such as these may lead to paradoxical outcomes that may not be acceptable to the group.

A theorem developed by Arrow shows that no decision rule can be regarded as uniquely best or more correct for group decision-making over a wide range of circumstances. In practice, a group must construct a rule by which the members can arrive at a decision. It is desirable that the decision rule be determined before an attempt is made to make the choice between alternatives. Sometimes, however, there is no explicit discussion of the rule to be used for this choice. In such cases, the tasks of deciding how to decide and of choosing between alternatives are intermixed.

The group decision-making process consists of several activities which do not necessarily take place in any given order. The first of these activities is an exchange of information among the members of the group. The second activity is a process of interaction among the group members during which some members of the group may try to influence the opinions and preferences of others. Sometimes this interaction results in the emergence of a consensus. In other cases, opinions in the group may polarize and subgroups may form with views that are in conflict with those of others. The amount and nature of this conflict is a major factor in determining how the group will choose between alternatives.

X. COMPLEX DECISION SITUATIONS

Complex decision situations arise with increasing frequency in modern society, particularly in business and industry. These worrisome problems are not like those that have been treated successfully in recent times by the methods of operations research and quantitative analysis. They are not primarily concerned with the efficiency of an operation or with the redesign of a production process for minimum cost or maximum profitability. They are, instead, concerned with questions such as "Do we need another freeway?" "Where should we locate our new factory?" "Can we reach a new working agreement with our labor force?" "How do we cope with the increasing government regulation of our activities?"

Complex decisions involve the interaction of participants who may each be pursuing a number of objectives simultaneously. Some of these objectives may be directly related to a particular situation and some may be indirectly related. The objectives of the various participants in any one situation are generally different. Also one or all of the objectives of one particpant may be in conflict with those of one or more of the others.

Seldom is the information available to the participants sufficient to allow each to formulate a complete description of a complex situation. Different participants may have different sets of incomplete information on which to base their appreciation of the circumstances. Each participant in a complex decision situation may, therefore, have a different appreciation of its nature. On some occasions, the different perceptions may arise from different interpretations of the same information.

Complex decision situations are seldom resolved as a result of a "one-time" approach or study by one or more of the participants. More often, the outcome emerges only after considerable interaction between the participants, which may take place over a period of time. During the course of this interaction, participants' perceptions and preferences for outcomes may be modified.

A model for study and resolution of complex decision situations comprises three stages of activity that can be described briefly as follows:

Stage 1: *Information gathering,* consisting of an examination of the environment of the decision situation and the seeking out of details of the participants and of all of the factors that might bear on or affect the outcome of the situation.

Stage 2: *Analysis,* consisting of two parts: strategic analysis, which is concerned with possible final outcomes of the situation and with the participants' preferences for them, and tactical analysis, which is concerned with the choice of courses of action that a participant might use in order to bring about an outcome that is more preferred.

Stage 3: *Interaction,* consisting of communication between the participants with the purpose of bringing about a final outcome; the objective of each participant in this stage if to persuade or coerce the other participants to agree to an outcome that he or she most prefers.

The process of study and resolution of a complex decision situation does not usually take place by a single journey through the three phases. On the contrary, resolution usually results from may repetitions of the phases over an extended period of time.

A first step for those involved in the resolution of a complex problem is to build up a base of information about the situation and about the environment in which it is situated. The next step is a detailed consideration of possible future outcomes of the situation. A simple model of a complex decision situation that is useful in strategic analysis is shown in Figure 1. In this diagram, the participants are shown in the box at the top. They are involved in the "present situation" which surrounds an issue. The situation is shown unfolding down the page.

Each of the participants in this diagram is engaged in estimating possible final or stable interim outcomes of the decision. Four such outcomes are shown in the diagram as being available at some time in the future as a possible resolution. The estimated preferences of the participants for the outcomes are shown at the bottom of the diagram. Each of the participants must undertake some tactical analysis with the objective of attaining an outcome that is most preferred.

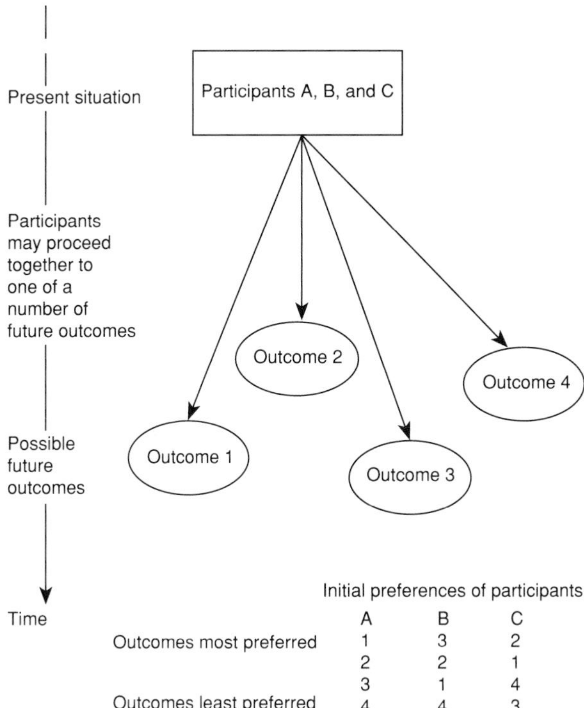

	Initial preferences of participants		
	A	B	C
Outcomes most preferred	1	3	2
	2	2	1
	3	1	4
Outcomes least preferred	4	4	3

FIGURE 1 Strategic analysis of a complex decision situation.

XI. DECISION CONFERENCES AND SANTA

When faced with major decisions about policy and future directions of the enterprise, many successful organizations convene a group of senior managers and charge them with making recommendations about the situation.

Communication between members of such a group can be encouraged and enhanced by including an experienced person in the group, not necessarily as a chairman or an expert in the field under discussion, but as a *facilitator* for the process under way. The prime role for a facilitator in the group is to encourage and improve communications between the members. Under some circumstances, the facilitator has an assistant who records summaries of the proceedings, often using computer and display equipment for this purpose. The whole activity in such a group is called a *decision conference.*

The purpose of a decision conference is to promote understanding of the situation under consideration and to arrive at a commitment to action on the parts of those involved. This is achieved by creating a model of the situation under discussion that incorporates the perceptions of all those taking part and then examining the implications of the model.

An extension of the conferencing idea (code-named SANTA) involves the simulation of the resolution of a problem prior to the actual event. In such a simulation, staff members of an organization involved in a decision situation are brought together in a 2- or 3-day conference prior to the actual resolution of the situation. At the start of this conference, the representatives of the organization are divided into two or three or more teams, each of which is instructed to take the position of one of the participants in the situation under study for the purposes of the exercise. Each of the teams represents only the views of the participant assigned to it, as far as the team understands them.

The interaction takes the form of a "hearing" before an impartial chairperson (usually the facilitator) during which each participant (team) is given 10 or 15 minutes to express its opinion on the situation at hand. These presentations are followed by a 15- to 30-minute free exchange, during which participants are allowed to question or challenge others, subject only to the direction of the chair. At the end of the first interaction, the facilitator adjourns the meeting and calls for a second interaction to take place after the teams have taken time to reconsider their positions. Sometimes direct negotiations between participants are allowed or encouraged between rounds of interaction. These negotiations often provide useful experience for the team members.

The simulation may be allowed to run into two or three interactions (or more), depending on the progress made on the issue. At the end of the last interaction, each team is instruced to retire and to report later to the whole meeting on the following topics: (a) How well did our team do in furthering its participant's cause? (b) How well did the other teams do in this respect? (c) What are the lessions for our organization in real life? (d) What policies and courses of action should our organization adopt in the light of the exercise? The team members then reconvene (now restored to their normal positions in the organization) to discuss these questions and to formulate policies and courses of action for use in the real situations.

One of the most valuable learning experiences in a simulation arises from the rehearsal of situations that may occur in the future. For example, in one practical simulation a group of senior managers from a company considering an acquisition was called together. In strictest secrecy, the managers were briefed on the situation and instructed to simulate the acquisition. The purpose of the exercise was to define and study the methods by which the company could make the acquisition, taking into account the possible actions of the target company and other participants in the situation. Steps toward making the acquisition in the real world took place 3 weeks later. The policies and actions arising from the simulation were implemented in a series of steps that followed closely the interactions studied in the earlier exercise. Perhaps the most beneficial consequence of the simulation was that the managers actually taking part in the acquisition had a sense of having been there before. The experience in the simulation gave them a unique advantage in that possible reactions of the other participants had been studied for some time in advance.

Bibliography

Axelrod, R. M. (1986). "The Evolution of Cooperation." Basic Books, New York.

Cook, Wade D. (1988). Problems with ordinal data and multiple criteria. In "Complex Location Problems: Interdisciplinary Approaches." (B. H. Massam, Ed.), Institute for Social Science Research, York University, North York, Ontario.

Hillier, F. S., and Lieberman, G. H. (1990). "Introduction to Operations Research," 5th ed. McGraw-Hill, New York.

Hipel K. W. (1990). Decision technologies for conflict analysis. *Information and Decision Technologies*, Special Issue on Conflict Analysis: Part I. **16**(3).

Phillips, L. D. (1989). People-centered decision support. In "Knowledge-Based Management Support Systems." (G. I. Doukidis, F. Land and G. Miller, Eds.), Ellis Horwood.

Radford, K. J. (1989). "Individual and Group Decisions." Springer Verlag and Captus University Publications, New York.

Radford, K. J. (1990). The strategic/tactical model for resolution of complex decision situations (SANTA). *Information and Decision Technologies*, Special Issue on Conflict Analysis: Part 2, **16**(4).

Deductive Reasoning

William J. Lyddon and Darlys J. Alford
University of Southern Mississippi

Glossary

Availability A heuristic for judging the frequency of an event. Availability relies primarily on relevant information that is most easily and readily available to the person.

Epistemic style Personality factors based on conceptual, perceptual, and symbolizing cognitive abilities which are believed to account for individual differences in human reasoning and understanding.

Formal logic A theory of deductive reasoning based on rule-governed procedures that, when appropriately applied, produce logically valid conclusions from premises that are true. These formal rules serve as a framework for ideal logical thought and are often used as a basis for evaluating errors and biases in thinking.

Heuristics Quick and intuitively reasonable rule-of-thumb strategies that allow persons to reason and make judgments under conditions of incomplete or unavailable information.

Mathematical rules of logic Rules for evaluating the accuracy of predictions about the likelihood of events occurring. Mathematical rules are based on principles of statistical probability.

Representativeness A heuristic for judging the probability of an event that relies on the resemblance of the event to a category or prototype.

Syllogism A method of deductive reasoning associated with formal logic in which two premises (if true) are combined to produce a valid conclusion.

Syntactic rules of logic Principles of deductive reasoning that rely on word meanings and word order to specify the relations among objects, ideas, or persons in logical problems. Syntactic rules involve the use of words like "all," "some," "none," "and," "or," "if–then," "more," and "less" and may be applied through the use of Venn diagrams and truth trees to evaluate the validity of a logically derived conclusion.

DEDUCTIVE REASONING can be defined as a form of human thinking in which current knowledge and beliefs are combined to produce new conclusions or consequences. In broad terms, the process of deductive reasoning proceeds from the abstract to the particular—from foundational premises to specific predictions. Discussions of deductive reasoning in psychology focus on the validity of the thinker's conclusions by evaluating the more or less systematic nature of the thinking sequence from the initial premises to the inferred consequence. Deductive reasoning is most often compared to inductive reasoning— a generalization or conclusion that follows repeated experience. In contrast to deductive reasoning, inductive reasoning begins with specific facts or cases and concludes with general principles.

I. HISTORICAL AND PHILOSOPHICAL CONTEXTS

The contemporary study of deductive reasoning has its origins in the systems of mathematics and logic of the early Greeks as well as in more recent developments in the philosophy of science. There seems to be little doubt that the invention of mathematics by the Greeks (and to some extent the Egyptians before them) represented the emergence of a system of logic—one which permitted the manipulation of symbols (numbers) according to certain deductive rules. For example, the solution of an algebraic equation starts with the equation (premise) and, through the application of rules,

Copyright © 1994 by Academic Press, Inc. All rights of reproduction in any form reserved.

deduces the necessary values of the unknown variables as a conclusion. Similarly, Euclid's geometry consists of a set of initial *axioms* (premises) from which a set of *theorems* (conclusions) may be deductively derived.

The development of deductive logic as a formal branch of philosophy is usually credited to the Greek philosopher Aristotle. In Aristotle's system all arguments were broken down into three essential propositions, the first and second being the premises, and the third being the conclusion drawn from them. This form of argument is termed a syllogism and serves as a basic model for deduction. The classic example of the syllogism is

All men are mortals.
Socrates is a man.
Therefore, Socrates is a mortal.

Although there are many forms of syllogisms which are less obvious, in all of them the purpose is to determine not the quality of the evidence nor the quality of the conclusion, but rather whether the evidence presented in the premises in fact leads to the conclusion.

One contemporary area in which logical arguments play a central role is in the construction and testing of scientific theories. Philosophers of science traditionally viewed science as an inductive process—that is, a process whereby valid generalizations could be made from making repeated observations. The modern philosopher Karl Popper, however, challenged the inductive view of science by asserting that because inductive inferences can never be valid, it is unsatisfactory for science to be based on this type of logic. For example, the inductive inference

All the swans I have ever seen are white.
Therefore, all swans are white.

can never be shown to be valid because no matter how many white swans one may have seen, there may be some black ones. Popper contended that the purpose of science is not the verification but the *falsification* of theories. Further, he pointed out that falsification involves a deductive process in which (a) a theory is stated, (b) necessary and empirically testable predictions are deduced, (c) the predictions are tested by experiment or observation, and (d) the theory is re-evaluated in light of the experimental results. It is important to note that within a deductive framework, a theory can never be ultimately confirmed as true or valid. The best that can be said about a theory is that it has managed to survive refutation and, as a result, constitutes a viable explanation of phenomena.

In recent years, the cognitive revolution in psychology and the emergence of the interdisciplinary field of cognitive science have contributed to a focal interest in human reasoning and cognitive processes. Although still tethered to its philosophical roots, the study of deductive reasoning and problem solving has become a prominent focus among more empirically minded cognitive psychologists and scientists. We shall now turn to exploring some of the fruits of these efforts.

II. FORMAL LOGIC

Currently, there are two major approaches to understanding deductive reasoning: formal logic and heuristics of judgment. Formal logic is based on the idea that there exists an ideal, perfect, or correct logical formula that must be used to arrive at valid conclusions. The most extreme proponents of the formal logic school claim that humans *cannot* be illogical because the rules of logic are in essence viewed as innate features of the human mind. To support this view, they point out that violations of simple logic forms, for example,

All men are mortals.
Socrates is a man.
Therefore, Socrates is not a mortal.

are easily identified and rejected by virtually all normal adults.

In formal logic models there are normative rules by which each deductive reasoning problem *should* be solved. These rules may be syntactic or mathematical. Syntactic rules rely on the meaning of words such as quantifiers (e.g., *all, some, none*), connectives (e.g., *and, or, if–then*), and comparatives (e.g., *more, less*) which indicate specific and certain relationships between objects, ideas, or persons. Similarly, mathematical rules rely on normative statistical probabilities that are applied to estimate the likelihood of consequences or relationships that are less than certain. [*See* LOGIC.]

As a starting point for understanding syntactic rules, note the following syllogism:

Premise 1: Some taxpayers are foreigners.
Premise 2: No foreigners are citizens.
Conclusion: Therefore, some taxpayers are not citizens.

There are three rules that must be followed in order to arrive at the correct solution to all syllogistic problems. First, all possible meanings of the premises must be considered. Second, all of the possible meanings of the premises must be combined in every conceivable way. And third, a conclusion is *valid* only if it can be applied to every combination of possible meanings of the premises. In courses on formal logic students are instructed in the use of the Venn diagrams and/or truth trees in order to systematically proceed through the stepwise process of evaluating the validity of conclusions. The syllogism above can be represented in the following general form:

Some *A* are *B*.
No *B* are *C*.
Therefore, some *A* are not *C*.

To solve this syllogism, a person first must generate all possible meanings of the premises (see Table I) and second, using Venn diagrams (see Fig. 1), must determine all possible combinations of the premises. Venn diagrams are used to evaluate whether a situation exists in which both premises could be true but the conclusion false, thereby invalidating the syllogism. A truth table may be used in a similar fashion. In a truth table all possible combinations of the premises are listed. Each possible combination is then evaluated in terms of the actual premises stated. When it becomes clear that the conclusion is the only possible one that is valid in relationship to the actual stated premises, the conclusion is determined to be deductively valid. A simple truth table based on the syllogism

TABLE I
Syllogism Example: Possible Meanings and Combinations

Possible meanings	Possible combinations
All *A* are *B*	1, 2
Some *A* are *B*	1, 2, 3, 4
No *A* are *B*	5
Some *A* are not *B*	3, 4, 5

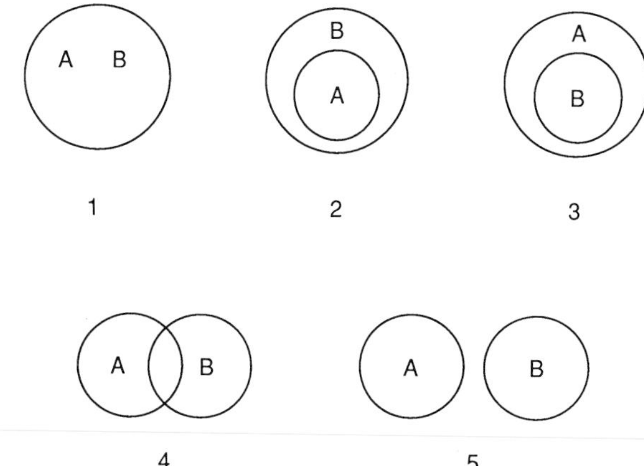

FIGURE 1 Syllogism example: Venn diagrams.

If *p*, then *q*.
Not *p*.
Therefore, not *q*.

appears in Table II.

It is important to note that in formal models of logic, *validity* rather than *truth* of conclusions is what is significant. Conclusions are only evaluated according to their logical relation to the premises. In other words, a conclusion can be valid while quite untrue in every practical sense. Take for instance the following:

If grass is pink, then flamingos quack.
The grass is pink.
Therefore, flamingos quack.

The conclusion that flamingos quack is a valid conclusion even though the premises are quite untrue. This creates a very practical problem with formal models of logic, because in everyday life, persons are probably more concerned with determining the truth of conclusions rather than the form of their reasoning. Therefore, it is common for people to make mistakes in logical reasoning when they are asked to evaluate the validity of arguments that con-

TABLE II
Syllogism Example: Truth Tree

p	*q*	Premise 1	Premise 2	
T	T	True	False	
T	F	False	True	
F	T	False	False	
F	F	True	True	Only valid conclusion

tradict their personal experience as with the quacking flamingos.

Two other common errors in problems based on syntactic logic include atmosphere effect and conversion error. Both of these types of errors demonstrate how the actual words used to structure the premises and conclusions can influence thinking. With the atmosphere effect, words like "no," "some," or "not" are carried over to the conclusion:

Some lawyers are in the legislature.
Some Republicans are in the legislature.
Therefore, some lawyers are Republicans.

Those evaluating this conclusion are often tempted to accept it because they know from experience that actually some lawyers are Republicans even though the conclusion does not follow logically from the premises. The conversion error is another common pitfall in logical reasoning. Here, the premise is "converted" so that its reverse is assumed to also be true. For example, one can easily reverse the premise "All Mississippians are Southerners" and conclude, "All Southerners are Mississippians." Although it is easy to see the folly of this simple example, consider the following:

All Communists wanted the U.S. to stop the war in Vietnam.
Carol wanted to stop the war in Vietnam.
Therefore, Carol is a Communist.

In contrast to syntactic logical problems, estimating the likelihood or mathematical probability of events is also a form of deductive logic. As previously mentioned, mathematical rules represent normative parameters for how predictions *should* be deduced. In such instances, conclusions are valid to the extent that they correspond to normative statistical probabilities of events. However, researchers have demonstrated that the way in which people think every day does not necessarily follow even the most simple normative mathematical rules of logic. One classic experiment involves the following probability rule: Increasing the specificity of an event can only decrease its probability [$P\ (A + B) \leq P\ (A)$]. For example, it is a fact that there are more *bank tellers* than *feminist bank tellers*. Yet, most people (even those knowledgeable about statistics) violate this simple rule. When first given background information about "Linda"—31 years old, single, outspoken, very bright, majored in philosophy, active (during college) in activities related to discrimination, social justice, anti-nuclear energy—most people predict that it is more likely that Linda is a feminist bank teller rather than a bank teller.

III. HEURISTIC MODELS OF REASONING

Everyday decision making and reasoning entail much more than making logical deduction from premises known to be true. People often have to make real life decisions under conditions of uncertainty, that is, on the basis of incomplete or unavailable information. Many cognitive psychologists suggest that under conditions of uncertainty reasoning and judgment tend to involve the use of certain rule-of-thumb strategies, or *heuristics,* that can be applied easily in a wide range of situations. Heuristics are believed to play an important role when one makes inferences about probability. For example, people often employ heuristics when making judgments about how likely it is that a particular person is a member of a certain category or how likely a given outcome is to be explained by a certain set of antecedent conditions. Although judgment heuristics can yield quick and intuitive insights, the time heuristics save can often be offset by significant errors in judgment. Three heuristics that have been extensively studied are those of *representativeness, availability,* and *analogical reasoning.* [*See* DECISION MAKING, INDIVIDUALS.]

Representativeness is a heuristic strategy that involves making judgments on the basis of a few characteristics thought to be representative of the category or outcome rather than on the basis of relevant statistical considerations. For example, when asked to say which sequence of heads and tails is more likely to occur, H–T–H–T–T–H or H–H–H–T–T–T, most persons will choose the former (because "irregularity" is thought to be an essential or representative feature of randomness) even though both series are equally probable. Because representativeness relies on the use of prototypes and stereotypes, new information that resembles these conceptual categories is treated as more relevant than more abstract statistical information. As a result, the prototypes and stereotypes remain resistant to disconfirming data and thus continue to bias decision-making in a stereotype confirming direction. [*See* PREJUDICE AND STEREOTYPES.]

The availability heuristic is a strategy used to estimate the probability of an event or an outcome by the ease with which instances or associations can be retrieved from memory. This heuristic is characterized by the use of the most readily available information or thought as if it were the most relevant and predictive. The availability heuristic is based on two assumptions: (a) that the probability of an event is directly related to the frequency with which it has occurred in the past; and (b) that more frequently occurring events are usually easier to remember than less common ones. Because availability does increase with frequency, this heuristic is often quite accurate. However, availability is also affected by other factors—factors that can produce systematic errors in judgment. Researchers point out that the ease with which information is brought to mind may be a function of such factors as recency, saliency, or stereotypic preconceptions, even though these factors may be irrelevant and may bias prediction and judgments. For example, people will often overestimate the frequency of well-publicized causes of death (e.g., homicide) while underestimating the frequency of less notorious yet significantly more common causes (e.g., death by stroke). Similarly, clinicians often overestimate the probability that a particular depressed patient will commit suicide because they more vividly recall experiences with patients who were depressed and suicidal rather than with patients who were depressed but not suicidal.

Another judgment heuristic which incorporates aspects of both representativeness and availability is analogical reasoning. When faced with a novel situation or problem, persons may recall a similar situation that seems related, evaluate its similarity to the new problem, and use the similar case to make predictions about the novel one. The distinctive feature of analogical reasoning is that the judgment is based on those attributes of the known case that are *functionally* relevant to the new problem or decision. Analogical reasoning is often used in educational settings to facilitate the understanding of new material. For example, when introducing students to the phenomenon of electricity, teachers may draw the analogy between electricity and a hydraulic system—that is, electricity flowing through a conductor is analogous to water flowing through a pipe; batteries act like reservoirs; and resistors act like constrictions in the pipe. The degree to which students solve particular types of novel problems often depends on the degree to which the analogy they have learned generates correct inferences about problems in the new domain. Similar to the biasing potential of the representativeness and availability heuristics, analogical reasoning can lead to a normatively unjustified decision when functionally irrelevant similarities guide the selection of an analogy. [*See* ANALOGICAL REASONING.]

The underlying assumptions of research on cognitive heuristics is that it is theoretically possible to distinguish between an accurate and inaccurate inference. Within this framework, an accurate inference is one that is based on a logical synthesis of all the available and relevant base rate or normative statistical data, whereas an inaccurate inference is one which ignores such information. As pointed out above, researchers suggest that human reasoning is often inaccurate or biased due to the operation of heuristics. One shortcoming of the heuristic approach to human reasoning, however, is that by primarily focusing on the "flawed" cognitive processes of the human subject, adherents to this approach fail to consider the way in which contextual and social factors contribute to definitions of "normative" reasoning. For example, because judgments in social perception and cognition are often situation specific, what is considered logical or true in situation A may be considered illogical or false in situation B. The argument here is that there may be no universal "normative" criterion that is not contextually or culturally bound. Similarly, and relatedly, it is important to note that any criterion for normative reasoning is after all a socially negotiated (or constructed) *standard*—one that may be revised by the sway of a different social consensus. This criticism of the heuristic approach to human reasoning suggests that instead of attempting to isolate universal flaws in human cognition, a situationally specific approach to issues of accuracy may be more viable. Such an approach would continue to define accuracy in terms of the correspondence between a judgment and a criterion but would also acknowledge that any criterion for accuracy cannot be separated from the standard setter's preconceptions and the context of socially shared beliefs and values.

IV. DEVELOPMENTAL CONSIDERATIONS

Human cognitive growth and development are characterized by the emergence of qualitatively different abilities and capacities at different lifespan developmental periods. As a case in point, the development of deductive reasoning is closely related to language development. Researchers suggest that the conceptual understanding of connectives (and, or), quantifiers (some, none), and comparatives (more, less) is common in the early school years. Even "if–then" constructions are mastered by the time children reach Piaget's concrete operational stage (ages 5–7). For example, the simple instruction "if no one is home, then go to Tommy's house," requires the child to reason according to the syllogistic form:

If *p*, then *q*.
p.
Therefore, *q*.

Piaget, however, defined full competence in deductive reasoning as a central feature of the formal stage of cognitive development (ages 12–18). He also noted that because simple logical forms may be understood before formal operations have developed, these logical abilities are limited to familiar, concrete objects and events. To achieve competence in deductive reasoning one must be able to conduct complex analyses of propositional and predicate logic which involves abstract as well as concrete subject matter. To adequately generate all possible meanings of a set of premises, the thinker must understand and be able to generate obvious and subtle meanings of the syntactic form which requires great verbal sophistication. In addition, there are significant demands made on working memory when persons must generate all possible combinations of the premises and evaluate the validity of the conclusion in relation to each combination. Moreover, a competent logical thinker must be able to keep track of his or her own thinking process and decide when all the combinations have been generated, separate the valid and invalid arguments, and evaluate the adequacy of the thinking procedures to estimate the correctness of the answer (or repeat some former step in the process). These skills—thinking about the thinking process—are considered to be *metalogical* and are not expected to develop until the formal operational stage. [*See* COGNITIVE DEVELOPMENT.]

Most researchers agree that all normal adults are capable of systematic logical thinking, but the clear evidence of the use of cognitive heuristics raises questions about when and how effectively adults use formal rules of logic. Even those who have been trained in the use of Venn diagrams or truth trees in logic classes in college rarely use these methods spontaneously to solve problems in everyday life. Researchers who take an information processing approach to cognition have identified conditions under which a person is most likely to engage in "effortful" thinking. Effortful processing involves the kind of systematic processing required for thorough assessment of the validity of an conclusive argument. Persons are more likely to be systematic in their reasoning when they are motivated, the problem is particularly meaningful to them, and they are adequately knowledgeable about the subject matter to feel confident about being successful.

Cognitive–developmental psychologists who study thinking in adulthood suggest that individuals become experts in content-specific areas related to their occupations or career and that "expert" thinking is more likely to have the qualities of formal logic and be guided by metalogical thinking. By way of contrast, when the thinker is a "novice," heuristics are more likely to be employed in content-specific problem-solving situations. In addition, adult thinkers seem to be motivated to solve social problems related to family life when they marry and have children. Social problem solving in family settings poses special problems for adult thinkers because the solution of these problems must involve emotional content and most adults believe that emotions do not follow logical rules.

V. INDIVIDUAL DIFFERENCES IN HUMAN REASONING

In recent years there has been increasing interest in the study of individual differences in human reasoning. One line of research suggests that differences in how people reason are a function of differences in their relative commitments to three basic epistemic styles or approaches to construing the world: rational, empirical, and metaphorical. These epistemic styles are conceptualized as higher order personality factors that are believed (a) to be related to a subhierarchy of component cognitive abilities and (b) to account for individual differences in the way persons test the validity of their beliefs. The *rational* epistemic style relies on conceptual cognitive abilities, entails a proclivity to relating to the world using one's rational and analytic skills, and involves testing the validity of personal beliefs in terms of their logical consistency. Because of its emphasis on the logical analysis of information, a rational style is fundamentally a deductive, theory-driven way of knowing. The *empirical* style of knowing relies on perceptual cognitive abilities, involves a commitment to understanding the world using one's senses, and entails evaluating the validity of personal beliefs in terms of their reliable correspondence to relevant observations. Because of its reliance on sense perception and the cognitive processes involved in empirical observation, the empirical type of knowing is more inductive than deductive. The *metaphorical* style of knowing relies on symbolizing cognitive abilities, involves a commitment to relating to the world through symbolic representation, and involves testing the validity of personal beliefs in terms of their utility across different domains of experience. Because of its focus on symbolic representations and the generalizability of such representations to new life situations, the metaphorical epistemic style is fundamentally analogical rather than deductive or inductive.

Although the three epistemic styles are conceptualized as interdependent to the extent that all human reasoning and understanding involves rational, empirical, and metaphorical component processes, researchers point out that persons tend to exhibit a dominant epistemic style. Empirical support for the epistemic style concept stems largely from research related to the Psycho-Epistemological Profile (PEP), a reliable and valid instrument designed to assess persons' epistemic commitments. Initial research using the PEP examined the dominant epistemic commitments of members of different occupational groups. Rational knowers were found to be dominant among mathematicians and theoretical physicists, empirical knowers dominant among biologists and chemists, and metaphorical knowers dominant among professional musicians and dramatists. A related line of research has explored the relation between epistemic styles and personal interests and values. Particularly noteworthy are the associations between the PEP dimensions and the value dimensions of the Allport–Vernon–Lindzey Study of Values. Positive correlations have been found between rational knowing and theoretical values, between empirical knowing and theoretical, economic, and political values, and between metaphorical knowing and aesthetic, social, and religious values. Negative correlations have been found between empirical knowing and aesthetic, social, and religious values, and between metaphorical knowing and economic and political values. These associations corroborate the characterizations of epistemic styles and suggest that individual differences in human reason may be understood as reflecting qualitatively different cognitive and epistemological foundations.

Bibliography

Byrne, R. M. J. (1989). Human deductive reasoning. *Irish J. Psych.* **10,** 216–231.

Caverni, J., Fabre, J., and Gonzalez, M. (Eds.) (1990). "Cognitive Biases." North-Holland, New York.

Johnson-Laird, P. N., Byrne, R. M. J., and Fabossi, P. (1989). Reasoning by model: The case of multiple quantification. *Psych. Rev.* **96,** 658–673.

Overton, W. F. (1990). "Constraints on Logical Reasoning Development." Erlbaum, Hillsdale, NJ.

Ripps, L. J. (1990). Reasoning. *Annu. Rev. Psychol.* **44,** 321–353.

DEFENSE MECHANISMS

Phebe Cramer
Williams College

Glossary

Anxiety An unpleasant emotional state, often including a feeling of threat, in which the nature of the threat is unknown.

Ego A descriptive term encompassing those aspects of the psyche that are most in touch with external reality, including cognition, perception, reality testing, reasoning, and judgment. Defense mechanisms are also considered to be ego functions.

Fear An intense emotion in response to present or anticipated danger or pain. In contrast to anxiety, the stimulus producing the reaction is known.

Guilt An unpleasant feeling resulting from having violated the principles of one's own conscience, often accompanied by a lessened sense of self-worth.

Id A descriptive term encompassing those aspects of the psyche that are in contact with the inner body but not directly with the external world, including the instinctual drives.

Superego A descriptive term encompassing those aspects of the psyche derived from the moral standards of the parents or of society, including conscience and the ego ideal.

DEFENSE MECHANISMS are mental operations which disguise or otherwise modify the content of the mind and/or the perception of reality. The purpose of these ego functions is to protect the individual from being disturbed by excessively painful feelings, drives, or ideas. The operation of defense mechanisms is generally unconscious—that is, unknown to the individual—for the function of disguise is effective only if the individual is unaware of the deception. Because of the distortions involved, the operation of defense mechanisms may interfere with the veracity of the individual's view of internal or external reality.

I. HISTORY OF THE CONCEPT

In Sigmund Freud's early explorations of psychopathology, he noted that the human mind has the capacity to keep certain painful feelings hidden from consciousness. Prior to 1900, this capacity was thought of as a general mental function, in which one type of mental material was used to screen or conceal other more painful material.

During the period from 1900 to 1923, Freud's interest shifted away from the role of affect and of external reality as factors in determining the use of defenses. Instead, his work focused on the importance of inner, instinctual drives in understanding human behavior. With this new direction, the idea of defense mechanism was also modified. At this time, defense was conceptualized as a kind of counterforce which prevented the open and unchecked discharge of the drives. This idea of a single counterforce, termed repression, was used to replace the several different varieties of defense mechanisms which had been previously identified. However, after 1926, Freud found it useful to reintroduce the idea of multiple defense mechanisms, of which repression was one variety. At this time, Freud had developed his tripartite model of the personality as consisting of id, ego, and superego. The concept of defense mechanism was considered to be one of the ego functions. [*See* ID, EGO, AND SUPEREGO.]

Thus, in the development of the concept of defense mechanism, there were changing ideas about two problematic issues. The first was concerned

Copyright © 1994 by Academic Press, Inc. All rights of reproduction in any form reserved.

with whether defenses were directed against painful affect emanating from experiences with the environment (objective anxiety), or whether the defense was against the pressure of instinctual drives (instinctual anxiety). The second issue involved the question of whether there was one single defense function, or whether there were multiple, qualitatively distinct defense mechanisms. To some degree, these issues remain unsettled today.

II. MOTIVES FOR DEFENSE

The issue of the source of the anxiety—objective or instinctual—was reconciled in the work of Anna Freud, who proposed that defenses against painful feelings and defenses against instinctual drives are based on the same motives—namely, to "ward off" feelings of anxiety and guilt. [*See* ANXIETY AND FEAR; GUILT.]

Early in life, the individual has little capacity to protect against excessive stimulation or excitement resulting from the discharge of instinctual drives; when excessive, this discharge produces a state of anxiety, or, when more extreme, of panic. Later in development, the individual becomes able to anticipate the possible occurrence of this painful stimulation. This anticipation is expressed in the form of an anxiety signal, which instigates the use of a defense mechanism. The motive in this case for the use of defenses is the warding off of instinctual anxiety.

A second motive for defense—the warding off of feelings of guilt—has a different origin. In the course of development, the individual experiences satisfaction and pleasure as a result of the nurturance and benevolent caretaking of an important other. In time, the individual's sense of well-being and security becomes tied to the reception of these narcissistic supplies, either from the external caretaker or, later, from the internal representation of that caretaker—i.e., from the development of conscience which provides a sense of nurturance or disapproval, much as the original caretaker once did. Initially, the infant's continuing existence depends on receiving these narcissistic supplies; in their absence, there is a threat of annihilation. At this stage, the threat of loss of these supplies is experienced as objective anxiety—i.e., as emanating from the environment. Later, with the development of conscience, the loss of self-approval is experienced as superego anxiety, or guilt. In order to protect the self from the ensuing loss of self-esteem which occurs when the dictates of conscience are violated, defense mechanisms may be called into play. [*See* SELF-ESTEEM.]

Defense mechanisms thus function to "ward off" dangers to the ego from two directions. The ego is defended against inner dangers—the discharge of instinctual drives and the related instinctual anxiety. It is also defended against dangers based on external prohibitions and the related objective anxiety, and against dangers emanating from the mental representations of those prohibitions (conscience) that produce feelings of guilt and loss of self-esteem (superego anxiety). These three motives—instinctual anxiety, objective anxiety, and superego anxiety, or guilt—prompt the use of defense mechanisms to protect the ego from being disrupted by instinctual impulses and to protect the self from the loss of self-esteem.

III. VARIETIES OF DEFENSE MECHANISMS

Although Freud originally thought of only a single defense function, in the development of psychoanalytic theory he came to recognize some 17 qualitatively different mental operations that provided a defensive function. Subsequently, there have been several attempts to provide an exhaustive cataloguing of the many varieties of defense, with incomplete agreement across the various listings. As many as 44 different defense mechanisms have been described, although most listings focus on a smaller number of operations. Attempts to provide definitive listings of defenses are complicated by issues such as whether normal developmental processes (such as introjection, or identification) should be included, or whether successful coping mechanisms, such as suppression and humor, should be considered defense mechanisms. Some attempts have been made to classify defenses in terms of cognitive complexity, level of abstraction, developmental maturity/immaturity, and degree of psychopathology, but no single classificatory system has been agreed upon.

Among the most frequently cited defense mechanisms are repression, denial, displacement, projection, reaction formation, undoing, isolation, rationalization, intellectualization, and sublimation. While it is not possible in the present brief essay to provide a comprehensive description of each of these mechanisms, a few examples of certain distinctions and relationships between mechanisms may be given. For example, *repression* is generally thought of as being directed against painful internal thoughts or impulses, while *denial* is directed against disturbing external stimuli, the perception of which would arouse painful feelings. However, this distinction is relative, for repression may be directed against the memory of a painful external event, while denial may play a role in the adherence to inner, wish-fulfilling fantasies. In its prototypical form, the mechanism of denial is cognitively rather simple, involving only the attachment of a negative sign to a perception: for example, "the night is frightening" is changed into "the night is *not* frightening."

In contrast, the mechanisms of *displacement* and *projection* are cognitively more complex. In displacement, thoughts or feelings about one person are transferred or displaced onto another (who is often less powerful, or less important to the individual). Thus the feeling "I am angry at my boss" is displaced and becomes "I am angry at my son." Cognitively, this defense involves a change in the object to whom the emotion is attached, but the subject, or owner of the feeling remains the same. In contrast, in projection, the owner of an unacceptable thought or feeling projects the thought outward and attributes it to some other individual: the unacceptable thought "I hate Tom" becomes "Tom hates me." For both displacement and projection, the object of the unacceptable feeling is changed (anger at boss changed to anger at son; anger at Tom changed to anger at me) but projection involves additionally a change in the subject of the emotion ("I hate" becomes "Tom hates"). Projection is thus cognitively more complex than displacement.

IV. DEFENSE MECHANISMS AND PSYCHOPATHOLOGY

The concept of defense mechanism was originally developed in the exploration of psychopathology. Neurotic symptoms were explained as the manifestation of particular defense mechanisms, and the diagnosis of a particular neurosis was based on the presence of these defenses. For example, use of the defense of repression is associated with a diagnosis of hysteria, while the presence of undoing and rationalization contributes to a diagnosis of obsessive–compulsive neurosis. Within the range of psychosis, excessive use of projection is a diagnostic indicator of paranoia.

From this origin, it was easy to infer that the use of defense mechanisms was necessarily associated with psychopathology. This conception of defenses, however, involves both an overgeneralization and an oversimplification. While the use of defenses may sometimes be pathological, in other instances defenses are adaptive and promote psychological adjustment. Defenses are pathological when they are used in an overly rigid fashion, occur in connection with too many people or situations, significantly distort reality perception, and interfere with other ego functions. Pathological defenses are also inappropriate, in the sense of being out of phase with the developmental level of the individual or maladaptive for the current situation.

However, insofar as defense mechanisms function to reduce anxiety and thus contribute to psychological adjustment, they also have a positive, nonpathological function. Just what the relationship is between defense mechanisms and other mechanisms used for coping or adaptation is not clear. It has been suggested that the same mechanisms may be used either for defense or for coping purposes, depending on the demands of the situation. Alternatively, it may be that one type of mechanism evolves out of the other, or the two may be entirely separate in origin.

V. DEFENSES AND DEVELOPMENT

While defenses may be associated with psychopathology, they are also a necessary part of normal development. Because the child's developing ego is weak, it is the presence of defense mechanisms that prevents painful affects from disrupting its functioning and interfering with its development. This view was early presented by S. Freud and was amplified by A. Freud. Subsequently, attempts have been made to describe the relationship between defenses and development. At the core of this work is the assumption that the choice of defenses changes over time. In this case, it should be possible to specify a developmental continuum showing a chronological ordering of the emergence of the different defenses over the lifespan. In this conception, different defenses are conceived of as age- or stage-related and can be characterized as age appropriate or inappropriate.

A second conception of defense development refers to the idea that individual defenses have a developmental history of their own, with early beginnings in reflex behaviors which are gradually transformed into voluntary motor behavior and then internalized into mental operations. The relative strength of any one defense waxes and wanes over the lifespan, with individual defenses reaching their zenith at different stages of development.

Two different models have been used to characterize the developmental relationships among defense mechanisms. The "horizontal" approach uses a time line as a point of reference; the appearance of different defenses is ordered chronologically along this time line. This approach encompasses both the idea that different defenses emerge at different points in time, or at different developmental stages, and the conception that each defense has its own developmental history. The "vertical" approach orders defenses in terms of a hierarchy, based on some principle of classification, such as degree of complexity or reality distortion. While the vertical approach may use a dimension such as maturity/immaturity to classify defenses, and may arrange a hierarchy based on this dimension, such models are not truly developmental because the levels within the hierarchy are not related to age or developmental stage. Rather, the model describes different levels of defense used by individuals of the same age.

Research evidence from empirical studies supports the horizontal model of defense mechanisms development. Denial, a cognitively simple defense, is used frequently in early childhood; its use decreases across middle and later childhood and adolescence. Projection, somewhat more complex, cognitively, increases in use from early childhood to later childhood and adolescence. The use of identification as a defense is relatively infrequent in childhood but increases during adolescence. These trends may be seen in Figure 1, which is based on the projective test findings of 320 children, ages 3 to 18 years.

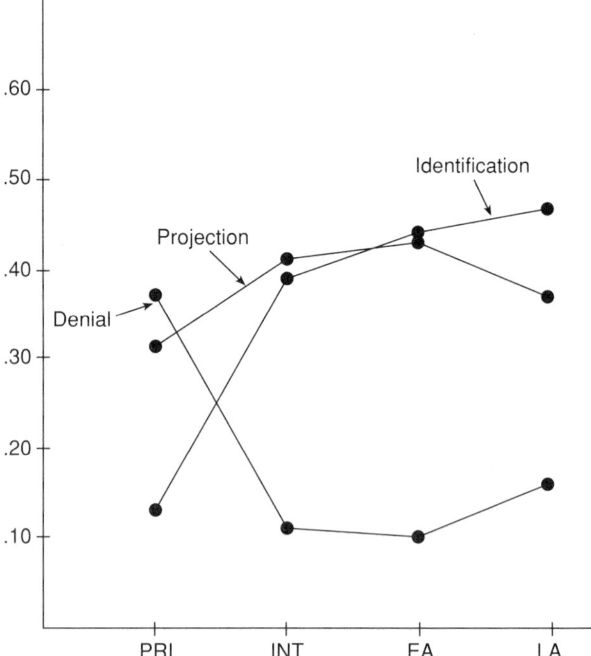

FIGURE 1 The use of defense mechanisms by children and adolescents of four age groups: primary (PRI)—mean age = 5 years, 8 months; intermediate (INT)—mean age = 9 years, 10 months; early adolescent (EA)—mean age = 14 years, 6 months; and late adolescent (LA)—mean age = 16 years.

Similar results have been found for children's *understanding* of the functioning of defense mechanisms. These findings are relevant to the issue of defense mechanisms development since, in order for the disguise function of a defense to be effective, the operation of the mechanism cannot be understood. Once it is understood, the defense is no longer effective. Thus, the use of a defense must precede its understanding, and a developmental progression of defense use, followed by defense understanding, is an expected repetitive pattern. Cognitively simple forms of defense, such as denial, are used by young children until they are figured out or understood. When the defense is understood, it becomes ineffective. At this point, an increase in cognitive capacities allows the child to use a more complex defense, such as displacement, the functioning of which is not yet understood. When this defense becomes understood by the child, it, too, becomes ineffective and is replaced with another more complex defense, such as projection, which is not yet understood.

Other research studies have related the use of different defense mechanisms to different levels of ego development, with results consistent with the age-related findings reported above.

VI. MEASURES OF DEFENSE

One of the most difficult issues in the study of defense mechanisms is the problem of observation and measurement. Since a defense is effective only if the individual is unaware of its occurrence (i.e., it is unconscious) this raises the problem of how the defense may be known or studied. While some attempts to measure defense are based on direct questioning of the individual, this approach clearly runs into a logical dilemma: if the defense is effective, the individual using the defense is unaware of its existence and so cannot report on its use. A solution to this dilemma is to note that, while the person using the defense may not be conscious of the defensive behavior, another observer of the behavior could be aware of its defensive function. These two approaches—direct report and indirect observation—have formed the basis of the some 58 different measures that have been used to study defense mechanisms. Direct report measures include questionnaire items which may bear no obvious relationship to the defense being studied but have been shown empirically to correlate with defense use. Other direct measures ask subjects to self-report on the use of various manifestations of different defenses. While this method may seem to involve the logical contradiction discussed above, supporters of this approach indicate that a person may be capable of reporting on the use of defensive behaviors without realizing that the behavior serves a defensive purpose. While there are clear advantages to using such structured-inquiry, structured-response approaches—they are straightforward, objective, and easily scored without rater bias—there are equally obvious limitations. The information collected is limited to the questions asked and the range of responses allowed by the test format. Further, the request for the individual to comment on his own behavior creates a substantial possibility for reporter bias: the wish to appear in a positive light, and the use of one's customary defenses in reaction to the somewhat stressful situation of reporting on oneself may confound the results obtained.

More indirect measures of defense mechanisms have included story-completion tasks and clinical interviews. Both of these methods involve a structured inquiry, but there is generally more latitude provided for the individual to give responses, which may be relatively open-ended and unstructured. This allows a free-flowing sample of the individual's thought processes to be obtained, in which the actual use of defenses may be manifest. However, the relatively unstructured nature of the response material raises issues of observer bias or subjectivity. Problems stemming from the wish to appear in a socially desireable light are not eliminated, but may be recognized in this format as a manifestation of a defense mechanism.

Other indirect measures of defense mechanisms largely circumvent problems relating to social desirability by using techniques for which there are no clearly desirable responses. These approaches, consisting of projective tests, such as the Thematic Apperception Test, and perceptual defense paradigms, in which stimulus material is presented below the visual threshold level, utilize an unstructured or ambiguous inquiry, and call for an open-ended response. It is the way in which the individual goes about formulating a response that provides the material for judging defensive functioning. Problems of possible observer or rater bias are also present in this approach.

VII. SELECTED CONTEMPORARY RESEARCH

As mentioned above, research with children has shown that cognitively simpler defenses, such as denial, are used more frequently by younger children, while more complex defenses, such as identification, occur more frequently among adolescents and young adults. Long-term studies of adult males have found that the use of defenses continues to change with age. Between late adolescence and adulthood, the use of immature defenses, such as turning against the self, denial, and reaction formation, decreased, while mature defenses, such as sublimation and suppression, increased with age. Further, the use of mature defenses, such as altruism, suppression, and sublimation, was found to be associated with positive psychological adjustment, marital success, happiness, and objective physical health, while the use of immature defenses, such as denial and projection, was associated with psychiatric illness. In addition, within a sample of working-class men, the use of mature, as compared to immature, defenses appeared to causally contribute to the men's upward social mobility.

Self-report measures of defense mechanisms have found systematic differences between men and women in the choice of defense, with men scoring higher on the outwardly directed defenses of projection and turning against the object, and women scoring higher on the inwardly directed defenses of turning against the self and reversal. Defense use has also been found to be related to sexual orientation, regardless of biological gender. Persons with a feminine orientation use defenses more often associated with females, and vice versa.

While the use of immature defenses has been found to be associated with psychopathology, clinical improvement in psychiatric status following on a course of psychotherapy has been shown to be accompanied by a decrease in the use of these defenses. A similar change in defense use has been found during the recovery period of heroin addicts. Other types of intervention, such as experimentally induced failure experiences and naturally occurring trauma, have been shown to increase the use of defense mechanisms, presumably to protect the individual from the negative emotions associated with the experience.

Bibliography

Blum, H. P. (Ed.) (1985). "Defense and Resistance." International Universities Press, New York.

Cramer, P. (1988). The Defense Mechanism Inventory: A review of research and discussion of the scales. *J. Pers. Assess.* **52,** 142–164.

Cramer, P. (1991). "The Development of Defense Mechanisms: Theory, Research, and Assessment." Springer-Verlag, New York.

Dorprat, T. L. (1985). "Denial and Defense in the Therapeutic Situation." Jason Aronson, New York.

Giovacchini, P. L. (1987). "A Narrative Textbook of Psychoanalysis." Aronson, Northvale, N.J.

Ihilevich, D., and Gleser, G. C. (1986). "Defense Mechanisms. Their classification, Correlates, and Measurement with the Defense Mechanisms Inventory." DMI Associates, Owosso, MI.

Lerner, P. M., and Lerner, H. D. (1980). Rorschach assessment of primitive defenses in borderline personality structure. In "Borderline Phenomena and the Rorschach Test" (J. S. Kwawer, H. Lerner, P. Lerner, and A. Sugarman, Eds.), pp. 257–274. International Universities Press, New York.

Perry, J. C., and Cooper, S. H. (1989). An empirical study of defense mechanisms. *Arch. Gen. Psych.* **46,** 444–452.

Sandler, J. (1985). "The Analysis of Defense. The Ego and the Mechanisms of Defense Revisited" (with A. Freud). International Universities Press, New York.

Smith, G. J. W., and Danielsson, A. (1982). "Anxiety and Defense Strategies in Childhood and Adolescence." International Universities Press, New York.

Swanson, G. E. (1988). "Ego Defenses and the Legitimization of Behavior." Cambridge University Press, New York.

Vaillant, G. E. (1986). "Empirical Studies of Ego Mechanisms of Defense." American Psychiatric Press, Inc., Washington, DC.

Vaillant, G. E. (1992). The historical origins and future potential of Sigmund Freud's concept of the mechanisms of defence. *Int. Rev. Psycho-anal.* **19,** 35–50.

Dementia

James T. Becker and Oscar L. Lopez
University of Pittsburgh Medical Center

Glossary

Definite Alzheimer's disease A diagnostic group including those individuals who meet the clinical criteria for Alzheimer's disease, but who also meet specific neuropathological criteria involving the presence of neuritic plaques and neurofibrillary tangles obtained through autopsy or biopsy.

Dementia A syndrome noted for loss of intellectual abilities sufficient to interfere with activities of daily living. It may be static or remitting, depending on the phase of the illness, although it is frequently progressive.

Dementia of the frontal lobe type A syndrome of progressive impairments of the functions of the frontal lobe, with marked focal neuropathological abnormalities noted.

Pick's disease A syndrome of dementia characterized by relatively isolated damage to frontal and/or temporal lobes. May include patients with focal lobar atrophy and semantic dementia.

Possible Alzheimer's disease A syndrome of intellectual loss similar to that seen in probable Alzheimer's disease, but in a context in which the diagnosis of Alzheimer's disease is less clear.

Probable Alzheimer's disease A syndrome of loss of intellectual skills involving more than one area of cognitive function and meeting criteria described by the NINCDS/ARDRA Work Group.

Semantic dementia A syndrome of progressive fluent aphasia with marked anomia. Surface dyslexia may also be present. The syndrome appears to be due to Pick's disease and is in contrast with progressive aphasia without dementia, a nonfluent progressive language disorder.

Vascular dementia A syndrome of dementia associated with the presence of cerebrovascular disease. Diagnosis is complicated in that atherosclerotic changes in the brain may co-occur with Alzheimer's disease and pathological findings.

DEMENTIA and the term "dement" are from the latin "dementare" meaning "to deprive of mind, drive mad," in contrast to the term "encephalopathy," which refers simply to "a disease of the brain." The concept of dementia was noted by Lucretius as "being out of one's mind," and our understanding of dementia during the past 200 years has evolved to where sensitive and specific diagnostic criteria have been developed. However, the concept of dementia, including the symptomatology and presumed etiological factors (e.g., toxins, infections, age), continues to change as a function of medical knowledge and social context.

I. BACKGROUND

The term "dementia" first appeared in English in Pinel's *A Treatise on Insanity* as "a species of insanity characterized by failure or loss of mental power." The syndrome was noted to be progressive: "To cause periodical and curable mania to degenerate into dementia or idiotism." Copland's Dictionary of Medicine (1858) noted that "Maniacs and monomaniacs are carried away . . . by illusions and hallucinations . . . the demented person neither imagines or [*sic*] supposes anything."

In 1778, dementia was noted by the French Encyclopedia to be "difficult to cure as it is probably related to damage of brain fibers or of nervous fluids." Dementia, at that time, was distinguished from

Encyclopedia of Human Behavior, Volume 2

Copyright © 1994 by Academic Press, Inc. All rights of reproduction in any form reserved.

acute confusional states and tended to be chronic, although irreversibility was not considered a core feature of the syndrome. Pinel's writing established the term and concept as "including all states of psychosocial incompetence due to impairment of intellectual function. These could be reversible or irreversible, congenital or acquired, and caused by brain disorder or by insanity."

At the beginning of the 20th century the dementia syndromes of the elderly were classified in part by the presence of psychotic and other "noncognitive" symptoms. After World War I, this changed. Experiences such as hallucinations and delusions, which can be well described by psychotic patients, as in schizophrenia, are difficult to elicit or verify in demented patients. This may have been one of the important reasons that psychiatric symptomatology did not evolve as part of the diagnostic systems or of particular research interest in the dementias. Thus, cognitive or neuropsychological failures became the central feature of the dementia syndromes. While cognition was a very broad concept, memory and the measurement of memory capacity were then topics of much study; and thus Berrios and Freeman state that "memory became, *de facto,* if not *de jure,* the central feature of the state of dementia." This emphasis on requiring a memory disorder to diagnose dementia has persisted to the present day, although as will be seen below, it is not universally accepted. Furthermore, as will be discussed later, this requirement has an impact on the permitted variations of patterns of presentation of the dementia. [*See* MEMORY.]

II. CURRENT CONCEPTS (ca. 1975)

In Victor and Adams's 1981 textbook on neurology, the term dementia was used to denote a syndrome composed of failing memory and loss of other intellectual functions due to a chronic progressive degenerative disease of the brain. However, they emphasized that because there are several states of dementia with multiple etiologies, it was more correct to speak of "the dementias or of the dementing diseases." They classify the disorders into three groups: (1) those with associated signs of medical disease (e.g., hypothyroidism, nutritional deficiency, etc.), (2) those associated with neurologic signs but *not* obvious medical disease (e.g., Huntington's disease, progressive supranuclear palsy, etc.), and (3) those in which the dementia is the *only* evidence of neurologic or medical disease (e.g., Alzheimer's disease, etc.).

In Wells' first volume on the dementing disorders, he presented the psychiatric viewpoint of the mid-1970s. He emphasized that the term dementia was useful to describe "those clinical states resulting from diffuse or disseminated disease of the cerebral hemispheres," and further emphasized the distinction between dementia and diseases resulting in focal neurobehavioral abnormalities (e.g., aphasia, apraxia). The term dementia could refer to a change or *deterioration* of mental status, but irreversibility was not considered a core symptom. Presumably, progression was not considered critical, since the neurobehavioral consequences of carbon monoxide poisoning were called a dementia syndrome. [*See* APHASIA; APRAXIA.]

It is worth noting Wells' description of the patient early in the course of a dementing illness:

> In the incipient phases of cerebral degeneration the individual experiences diminished energy and enthusiasm. He has less interest and concern for vocational, family, and social activities. Lability of affect is common often with considerable increase in overall anxiety level, particularly as the individual becomes aware of his failing powers. He has less interest in goals and achievements, diminished creativity, less incentive to stick to a task, trouble concentrating, and difficulty screening out disturbing environmental stimuli. Failures, frustrations, changes, postponements, and troublesome decisions produce more annoyance and internal upheaval than usual, and it is harder to recover equilibrium after such disturbances. The individual's characteristic defense mechanisms are utilized more frequently and more blatantly, often with less than normal effectiveness.

III. DSM-III AND AFTERWARD

The American Psychological Association defined dementia in 1980 as:

> The essential feature is a loss of intellectual abilities of sufficient severity to interfere with social or occupational functioning.
>
> When the Dementia is the result of some clearly defined episode of neurological disease . . . it may begin quite suddenly, but then

> remain stationary for a long period of time. Primary Degenerative Dementia . . . is usually insidious in onset and slowly, but relentlessly, progresses to death over a period of several years.

According to the Third Edition of the *Diagnostic and Statistical Manual of the American Psychiatric Association* (DSM-III) (1980), the dementias may be treatable and reversible, although with widespread damage to the brain full recovery may not be possible. The differential diagnosis included delirium, schizophrenia, and major depressive disorder. The criteria for diagnosis specify that a memory impairment must exist, as well as impairment in at least one additional area of cognitive function.

By the time of the 1987 revision of DSM-III, the extent of intellectual impairment necessary for a diagnosis of dementia remained the same, but the assumptions about clinical course were now specified:

> In the past, *Dementia* often implied a progressive or irreversible course. The definition of Dementia in this manual . . . carries no connotation concerning prognosis. Dementia may be progressive, static, or remitting. The reversibility of a Dementia is a function of the underlying pathology and of the availability and timely application of effective treatment.

The current DSM-III-R criteria for dementia are shown below:

A. Demonstrable evidence of impairment in short- and long-term memory. Impairment in short-term memory (inability to learn new information) may be indicated by inability to remember three objects after 5 minutes. Long-term memory impairment (inability to remember information that was known in the past) may be indicated by inability to remember past personal information (e.g., what happened yesterday, birthplace, occupation) or facts of common knowledge (e.g., past presidents, well-known dates).

B. At least one of the following:
   1. impairment in abstract thinking, as indicated by inability to find similarities and differences between related words, difficulty in defining words and concepts, and other similar tasks;
   2. impaired judgment, as indicated by inability to make reasonable plans to deal with interpersonal, family, and job-related problems and issues;
   3. other disturbances of higher cortical function, such as aphasia (disorder of language), apraxia (inability to carry out motor activities despite intact comprehension and motor function), agnosia (failure to recognize or identify objects despite intact sensory function), and "constructional difficulty" (e.g., inability to copy three-dimensional figures, assemble blocks, or arrange sticks in specific designs);
   4. personality change, i.e., alteration or accentuation of premorbid traits.

C. The disturbances in A and B significantly interfere with work or usual social activities or relationships with others.

D. Not occurring exclusively during the course of delirium.

E. Either of the following:
   1. there is evidence from the history, physical examination, or laboratory tests of a specific organic factor (or factors) judged to be etiologically related to the disturbance;
   2. in the absence of such evidence, an etiologic organic factor can be presumed if the disturbance cannot be accounted for by any nonorganic mental disorder, e.g., major depression accounting for cognitive impairment.

Of particular note is the requirement that both memory and one other disturbance of higher cortical function must be present. Further, an etiological agent must be either identified or presumed if the dementia cannot be accounted for by another factor (e.g., major depressive disorder). The continued reliance on memory dysfunction as a diagnostic marker is curious if only for the fact that there is increasing evidence of distinct subgroups of AD (Alzheimer's disease) patients, and personality change and other signs or symptoms of neuropsychiatric disorder may be present early in the clinical course without equally abnormal memory function.

In 1984, the report of an NINCDS-ADRDA sponsored Work Group was published to establish clinical criteria for the diagnosis of Alzheimer's disease.

A. The criteria for the clinical diagnosis of *probable* Alzheimer's disease include

1. dementia established by clinical examination and documented by the Mini-Mental Test, Blessed Dementia Scale, or some similar examination, and confirmed by neuropsychological tests;
2. deficits in two or more areas of cognition;
3. progressive worsening of memory and other cognitive functions;
4. no disturbance of consciousness;
5. onset between ages 40 and 90, most often after age 65; and
6. absence of systemic disorders or other brain disease that in and of themselves could account for the progressive deficits in memory and cognition.

B. The diagnosis of *probable* Alzheimer's disease is supported by
1. progressive deteriorations of specific cognitive functions such as language (aphasia), motor skills (apraxia), and perception (agnosia);
2. impaired activities of daily living and altered patterns of behavior;
3. family history of similar disorders, particularly if confirmed neuropathologically; and
4. laboratory results of
   (a) normal lumbar puncture as evaluated by standard techniques,
   (b) normal pattern or nonspecific changes in EEG, such as increased slow-wave activity, and
   (c) evidence of cerebral atrophy on CT with progression documented by serial observation.

C. Clinical diagnosis of *possible* Alzheimer's disease:
1. may be made on the basis of the dementia syndrome, in the absence of other neurologic, psychiatric, or systematic disorders sufficient to cause dementia, and in the presence of variations in the onset, in the presentation, or in the clinical course;
2. may be made in the presence of a second systemic or brain disorder sufficient to produce dementia, which is not considered to be *the* cause of the dementia; and
3. should be used in research studies when a single, gradually progressive severe cognitive deficit is identified in the absence of other identifiable cause.

D. Criteria for diagnosis of *definite* Alzheimer's disease are
1. the clinical criteria for probable Alzheimer's disease and
2. histopathological evidence obtained from a biopsy or autopsy.

The Work Group noted that their criteria were tentative and likely to change as more knowledge was gained about the disease. However, these criteria have been widely adopted, and accuracy (i.e., sensitivity) of diagnosis relative to the neuropathological analysis can usually exceed 90%. These criteria permit a variety of different patterns of cognitive dysfunction to be classified as "probable" AD, since they do *not* require the presence of a memory loss for the diagnosis. Impairments in two or more areas of cognition are all that is required to demonstrate cognitive dysfunction. Delusions and hallucinations and other subjective symptoms of neuropsychiatric disorder are consistent with a diagnosis of dementia, but are not essential features of the syndrome. [*See* ALZHEIMER'S DISEASE.]

IV. CASE DEFINITIONS

In diagnosing or classifying an individual patient, the clinician or researcher must answer two distinct questions—is the patient demented, and what disease is associated with that syndrome? Dementia should be defined in its *broadest* sense, that is, as a decline in intellectual functioning, including both cognitive and behavioral manifestations. Cognition should be broadly defined to subsume all of the major domains including attention, language, perception, spatial abilities, memory, abstract thinking, problem solving, judgment, and others. No assumptions should be made concerning the type or nature of the impairment, or whether it reflects a specific pattern of CNS dysfunction. The only restriction is that more than one domain must be compromised. This formulation allows for marked individual variation in the pattern of cognitive deficits and their progression over time. Single, domain-specific abnormalities would not be classified as dementia unless or until either impairment developed within an additional cognitive domain or there was evidence of significant behavioral disturbances (e.g., delusions, aggression). Behavioral manifestations such as hallucinations, delusions, aggression, and personality change should be considered part of the diagnostic picture of a dementia. These "subjective" symptoms can be reliably elicited from demented patients or their caregivers, although the qualitative features of the symptoms may not be well described.

The second question that must be addressed—what is the disease associated with the dementia—requires a second set of guidelines or criteria. The NINCDS/ADRDA scheme for Alzheimer's disease and the NINDS/AIREN criteria for ischemic vascular dementia adopt the view that the certainty of the diagnosis can be stratified. By classifying a disease or factor as the *probable* or *possible* factor responsible for the dementia, it allows the clinician and researcher to reliably group patients according to standard clinical signs or symptoms. In the case where a specific neuropathological feature may be the defining characteristic of the disease, it may be possible to include a category of *definite* although this will not be discussed here.

One of the major achievements of the past decade was to increase the accuracy of the clinical diagnosis of different types of dementia, especially AD. Recent studies based on strict adherence to clinical criteria with pathological verification confirm the diagnosis of AD in 85 to 95% of cases. An important element in diagnostic accuracy is the differentiation among the dementia syndromes, and the recognition of the variety of specific disorders that may present with declining intellectual function; it is now recognized that there are more than 70 such disorders. However, among adults, AD and ischemic vascular dementia (IVD) are the most frequent, and AD alone accounts for more than half of the cases with dementia.

V. HISTORICAL PERSPECTIVE

When Kraepelin first used the term "Alzheimer's disease" he noted that this dementia syndrome was not exclusively of the elderly, but might occur earlier in the lifespan. Indeed, the reason that this disorder was considered important then—as now—was that it was *not* due to aging alone; neither was it a form of atherosclerotic dementia. It was also recognized by Kraepelin's contemporaries that AD was different from a dementia secondary to vascular based syndrome. However, during the first half of the 20th century medical attention continued to focus on other disease processes that were able to cause dementia (e.g., neurosyphilis). The number of patients with AD or IVD was not overwhelming, and thus medical and community concerns were minimal. This perspective has changed dramatically, however, as life expectancy, which was about 49 years in 1900, will approach 79 years by the year 2000. Life expectancy of those over 60 has also increased, and thus, the number of individuals at risk for AD or IVD has risen. At the same time, the development of potent psychotropic and antibiotic therapeutics has made it possible to treat the most serious behavioral and medical complications of these syndromes, thus lengthening and enhancing patients' lives.

It is now recognized that the major causes of dementia in individuals over 60 are AD and IVD, as well as a combined form of both diseases. It is traditionally accepted that 50% of the dementias are AD and 18% IVD, and that both co-occur in 18% of demented patients. Tomlinson and colleagues examined the accuracy of the clinical diagnosis of dementia and found that individuals diagnosed with "arteriosclerotic dementia" had significant loss of cerebral substance due to infarction; the location and size of the individual lesion were less important than the total mass of tissue affected. The authors stressed the notion that multiple small infarcts were observed in nondemented as well as demented individuals, and that gross cerebrovascular lesions were responsible for the clinical symptomatology in patients with atherosclerotic dementia.

Hachinski and colleagues introduced the term "multi-infarct dementia" to emphasize that atherosclerosis is independent of AD, and rarely causes dementia without clinical stroke. The presence of focal signs and symptoms, abrupt onset, hypertension, and stepwise deterioration seem to reinforce Tomlinson's perspective that one or more strokes in a patient with dementia means the dementia is of vascular etiology. However, Hachinski and colleagues recognized that this term may be limited to a subgroup of patients, and "it is likely that the true incidence will be overestimated clinically [since] Alzheimer-like conditions may co-exist."

Recent observations suggest that a change in the clinical presentation of the dementia syndrome of vascular etiology is occurring. IVD as a consequence of major vascular insults is not as frequent as it was 20 years ago, perhaps consistent with a changing health care environment. Medical and community concern about diseases that can affect the integrity of the cerebral vessels (e.g., hypertension, diabetes mellitus, atherosclerosis) has been heightened and preventive measures have been undertaken. The early detection of risk factors and the implementation of effective medication to treat those diseases may have had an input.

This change in the presentation of IVD complicates clinical classification, especially when clinicians have to identify patients in the "border zone" between AD and IVD. IVD patients can resemble AD in their clinical presentation, but not necessarily show major vascular lesions on neuroradiological studies. Indeed, the vascular lesions seen on neuroimaging studies among these patients can also be seen in neurologically normal individuals. Some demented patients may have focal lesions based on the CT or MRI scans of the brain, but no focal neurological signs can be observed, and no history of stroke can be established. Still other patients can have a history of clinical events which resemble strokes, but there are no focal lesions observed with imaging studies. Among these border-zone patients is one particular group with cerebrovascular disease and dementia classified as having subcortical atherosclerotic encephalopathy or Binswanger disease. Sometimes considered a variant of *l'etat lacunaire*, Binswanger's disease presents a characteristic pattern of white matter abnormalities on CT and MRI scans of the brain. However, it has been very difficult to correlate the image-identified abnormalities with vascular lesions found in brains postmortem.

VI. RECENTLY RECOGNIZED FORMS OF DEMENTIA

As noted above, the clinical presentation of a dementing disorder can evolve over the time, making its clinical diagnosis more difficult depending on when in the natural history of the disease medical care is sought. This issue becomes more complicated as forms of dementia that are neuropathologically distinct from AD, but meet clinical diagnostic criteria for AD (e.g., DSM-III), are described. These new forms of dementia are more common than previously supposed, and they include dementia of the frontal lobe type, lobar atrophy, and diffuse Lewy body dementia. It is evident from recent experience that not all forms of progressive dementia represent AD, and it is probable that new clinical–pathological designations will proliferate. Important progress is being made to characterize these new forms of dementia by specifying the *qualitative* aspects of the clinical syndrome, rather than submerging differences under the weight of numbers generated by standard test batteries.

A careful neuropsychiatric evaluation is critical in the diagnosis of these new forms of dementia. Personality changes, disinhibited behavior, and social breakdown usually precede the onset of the dementia of the frontal lobe type. This pattern of behavior may help clinicians to differentiate frontal lobe dementia from AD. Although disinhibited behavior can be observed in AD, it is rarely noted as the first symptom of the illness. Another important element to define clinically these forms of dementia is provided by modern neuroradiological techniques (e.g., SPECT, PET). Distinct neurological syndromes can now be evaluated in life using functional imaging procedures which are capable of generating topographical cerebral correlates of behavior.

VII. GENETIC FEATURES

The recognition that some forms of dementia occur with an autosomal dominant pattern of inheritance led researchers to seek for disease-related genes. Significant progress has been made in Huntington's disease where the hereditary component is a hallmark in the disease, and abnormalities in chromosome 4 appear to be linked to this form of dementia. The issue becomes more complicated in those dementias that have both sporadic and familial presentations, such as AD.

Amyloid is a generic term for a group of fibrillary proteins that stain with Congo Red because of the beta-pleated structure of proteins. The evidence that amyloid plays an important role in early pathogenesis of AD comes primarily from studies of individuals with Down's syndrome—chromosome 21 trisomy. It has been known for many years that individuals with Down's syndrome develop the characteristic pathological feature of AD, that is neuritic plaques and neurofibrillary tangles, usually at the age of 35–40. Glenner and Wong (1983) were able to purify and sequence the amyloid peptide from the meninges of several patients who had amyloid present in large concentration in their cerebral blood vessels. The amino acid sequence of this peptide was used by researchers to develop complementary DNA probes which enabled them to identify the precursor protein, now known as amyloid precursor protein (APP). The full gene was sequenced along with the adjacent region of the chromosome, the promoter region. The genetic message for APP was found markedly elevated early in the course of the fetal brain development. However, its exact role in the adult brain is unknown.

This relationship between APP and Down's syndrome led researchers to the speculation that chromosome 21 was the locus for familial forms of AD. However, several subsequent studies of DNA recombination events between the locus for the familial form and the gene for APP indicate that this gene was not affected. In some families with autosomal dominant pattern of inheritance, linkage to chromosome 21 markers could not be determined. In addition, it has been found that the APP gene is normal in the vast majority of AD patients.

Genetic studies are very promising in AD, but appear not to be the answer to the problem. Such a mechanism could be possible in the closely related disorder of the Dutch congophilic angiopathy, which is associated with a mutation within the beta-protein domain, and in some familial forms of AD. However, the study of the genetics of AD is critical, not only to understand the most common form of dementia in the adult, but also to understand new forms of dementia where familial forms are predominant, such as motor neuron disease with frontal lobe dementia.

VIII. COMMENT

Dementia is a syndrome of acquired intellectual dysfunction including cognitive and behavioral manifestations. It can be progressive, static, or may remit. It can have a variety of causes, but the underlying supposition is that it is always secondary to an alteration in CNS functions, either permanent or temporary. The diagnosis and classification of any dementia syndrome must proceed in two steps—first, establish that sufficient intellectual change has occurred to warrant a diagnosis of dementia, and second, to establish, with various levels of confidence, the disease(s) or causal factor(s) associated with the development of the dementia. We view this two-step process to be general in that it may be applied to any dementia syndrome. Indeed, in the development of the Cambridge Examination for Mental Disorders of the Elderly (CAMDEX), just such an approach was taken toward classifying the nature of mental status disorders in the elderly.

The present discussion has focused on the clinical presentation and has not addressed the very important issue of the pathophysiology of the dementias, since the central focus was the clinical characteristics of the syndrome(s) and the best way to identify a dementia syndrome. Further, the study of many dementia syndromes has not yet reached the point where they warrant conclusions about proximal causes. In the case of Alzheimer's disease, for example, it is certainly true that the presence of senile plaques and neurofibrillary tangles, in sufficient quantity, warrant a diagnosis of "definite" Alzheimer's disease. Yet as many as 15% of demented elderly patients may not meet these diagnostic criteria, and yet have profound dementia syndromes at the time of death. Further, deposition of amyloid in the cerebrovasculature appears common in Alzheimer's disease and is thought by some to be related to the underlying pathophysiology. Data from *in vivo* studies suggest that plaques and tangles may not, in fact, be related to the dementia syndrome, but are merely correlated with its presence.

Similarly, some patients with IVD do not present major ischemic or hemorrhagic lesions on the brain that explain the cognitive deficits. These observations indicate that the relation between dementia and vascular lesions is not yet completely understood. As noted above similar cerebral vascular lesions can be seen in nondemented individuals. This may suggest that factors other than infarcts are involved in the etiology of IVD. Recent reports appear to favor a multifactorial etiology of IVD, where not only infarcts but also small vessel disease and an autoimmune process may play a critical role.

Thus, there is a great deal more to be learned about the dementia syndromes. Increasing awareness of subgroups within a diagnostic grouping (e.g., AD) and subtle differences between diagnostic groups (e.g., AD vs lobar atrophy) will aid significantly in evaluating treatments and management techniques. The continuing search for proximal causes, and their reversal, by basic neuroscientists will be aided by these refined clinical classifications and by detailed neuroanatomical and neurochemical analyses. With this multifactorial approach, the search for cure and prevention of the dementias will be ultimately successful.

Acknowledgments

The preparation of this manuscript was supported in part by funds from the National Institute of Mental Health to J.T.B. (1RO1-MH-45311), and by the Alzheimer's Disease Research Center at the University of Pittsburgh (PO1-AG05133).

Bibliography

Adams, R. D., and Victor, M. (1990). Dementia and the amnesic (Korsakoff) syndrome. In "Principles of Neurology" (R. D.

Adams and M. Victor, eds.), 4th ed., pp. 334. McGraw–Hill, New York.

Alzheimer, A. (1895). Die arteriosklerotische Atrophie des Gehirns. *Allgemeine Zeitschrift fur Psychiatrie und Psychisch-Gerichtliche Medizin,* **51,** 809–811. Translated by Forsl, H., and Levy, R. (1991). Arteriosclerotic brain atrophy. *Intern J. Geriat. Psychiatry* **16,** 129–130.

American Psychiatric Association (1987). "Diagnostic and Statistical Manual of Mental Disorders," 3rd ed., revised, pp. 103–107. APA, New York.

Berrios, G. E., and Freeman, H. L. (1991). "Alzheimer and the Dementias (Eponymists in Medicine)." Royal Society of Medicine Services, Ltd., London.

Erkinjuntti, T., Haltia, M., Palo, J., Sulkava, R., and Paetau, A. (1988). Accuracy of the clinical diagnosis of vascular dementia: A prospective clinical and post-mortem neuropathological study. *J. Neurol. Neurosurg. Psychiatry* **51,** 1037–1044.

Hachinski, V. C., Lassen, N. A., and Marshall, J. (1974). Multi-infarct dementia: A cause of mental deterioration in the elderly. *Lancet* **2,** 207–210.

Katzman, R., Lasker, B., and Bernstein, N. (1988). Advances in the diagnosis of dementia: Accuracy of diagnosis and consequences of misdiagnosis of disorders causing dementia. In "Aging and the Brain" (R. D. Terry, Ed.), pp. 17–58. Raven Press, New York.

Khachaturian, Z. (1985). Diagnosis of Alzheimer's disease. *Arch. Neurol.* **45,** 251–254.

Lopez, O. L., Swihart, A. A., Becker, J. T., *et al.* Reliability of NINCDS-ADRDA criteria for the diagnosis of Alzheimer's disease. *Neurology* **40,** 1517–1522.

McKhann, G., Drachman, D., Folstein, M., Katzman, R., Price, D., and Stadlan, E. (1984). Clinical diagnosis of Alzheimer's disease: Report of the NINCDS-ADRDA Work Group under the auspices of the Department of Health and Human Services Task Force on Alzheimer's Disease. *Neurology* **34,** 939–944.

Neary, D. (1990). Non Alzheimer's disease forms of cerebral atrophy. *J. Neurol. Neurosurg. Psychiatry* **53,** 929–931.

Roman, G. C., Tatemichi, T. K., Erkinjuntti, T., *et al.* (1993). Vascular dementia: Diagnostic criteria for research studies. Report of the NINDS-AIREN International Work Group. *Neurology* **43,** 250–260.

Tomlinson, B. E., Blessed, G., and Roth, M. (1970). Observation on the brain of demented old people. *J. Neurol. Sci.* **11,** 205–242.

Dependent Personality

Robert F. Bornstein
Gettysburg College

Glossary

Authoritarian parenting A parenting style wherein the primary caretakers impose rigid and inflexible rules and expectations on the child, and the child is expected to conform completely and without question to these rules and expectations.

Dependent personality disorder A psychiatric disorder characterized by long-standing, extreme dependency which causes significant interpersonal and/or occupational impairment for the afflicted individual.

Diathesis Predisposition or risk factor; the term is typically used in psychiatric or medical settings to refer to any form of vulnerability which places an individual at increased risk for physical or psychological illness.

Disease-prone personality A hypothetical construct referring to a set of personality traits, attitudes, and behaviors which place an individual at risk for disease.

Interactionism A framework for conceptualizing personality dynamics wherein behavior is understood as reflecting the interaction of stable personality traits and immediate situational influences.

Oral dependency A psychoanalytic term referring to a set of traits which simultaneously reflect a passive, helpless outlook and a predisposition to cope with stress and anxiety via food- and mouth-related activities (e.g., cigarette smoking).

Self-concept One's mental representation of the self, which is relatively stable and not strongly affected by changes in mood state; the self-concept may have both conscious and unconscious components, and is often associated with a strong affective (i.e., emotional) response.

Suggestibility The degree to which a person's attitudes or opinions are easily swayed by the expressed opinions of others.

THE TERM DEPENDENCY as it is used in personality theory and research refers to a personality orientation (or "style") wherein an individual: (1) perceives him- or herself as helpless, powerless, and ineffectual, and therefore (2) turns to others for support, advice, and reassurance rather than attempting to cope with tasks and challenges in an autonomous, self-directed manner. Individuals who consistently display a passive, help-seeking orientation in a variety of situations and circumstances are described as having a *dependent personality*. During the past several decades there have been hundreds of published studies examining the antecedents, correlates, and consequences of dependent personality traits. These investigations may be grouped into three broad areas: developmental, social, and clinical. Research in each of these areas is discussed in this article.

I. HISTORICAL OVERVIEW OF DEPENDENCY THEORY AND RESEARCH

Although Freud made little mention of the psychodynamics of dependent personality traits, several prominent psychoanalytic theorists (e.g., Karl Abraham, Otto Fenichel, Edward Glover) published papers on the dependent personality during the first few decades of the 20th century. These seminal papers stimulated clinicians' and researchers' interest in the topic of dependency, and not surprisingly, much of the early research on dependency came

Encyclopedia of Human Behavior, Volume 2

Copyright © 1994 by Academic Press, Inc. All rights of reproduction in any form reserved.

from a psychoanalytic perspective. Early psychoanalytic studies tested the hypothesis that a dependent personality orientation in adolescence or adulthood could be traced to events that occurred during the infantile "oral" period (i.e., during the first 1 to 2 years of life).

Specifically, the psychoanalytic model hypothesized that high levels of dependency resulted from overgratification or frustration during breastfeeding and weaning. Infantile experiences of frustration or overgratification were presumed to result in "oral fixation" and an inability to accomplish the developmental tasks associated with the infantile, oral stage (i.e., the development of a stable self-concept, along with feelings of autonomy, self-efficacy, and self-sufficiency). Although later studies indicated that dependency in adulthood was not directly related to infantile feeding or weaning experiences, the psychoanalytic model played a central role in bringing dependency research into mainstream psychology.

During the 1950s and 1960s, social learning models began to influence dependency theory and research, supplanting (to some degree) the classical psychoanalytic model. These social learning models differed in certain respects, although they shared the fundamental hypothesis that high levels of dependency result from the reinforcement of passive, dependent behavior in the context of the infant–caretaker relationship. Social learning models of dependency further hypothesized that—insofar as passive, help-seeking behavior was reinforced by the parents (and other authority figures) during early and middle childhood—the individual would continue to show high levels of dependency later in life.

By the early 1970s, the social learning view of dependency began to give way to ethological (i.e., attachment) theory, which was becoming increasingly influential in a number of domains within psychology. In contrast to the classical psychoanalytic and social learning models of dependency, attachment theory emphasized the innate, biological underpinnings of the infant–mother relationship as a primary factor in the development of dependent personality traits. Attachment models of dependency have not yet achieved the same status and influence as have the psychoanalytic and social learning models. Nonetheless, attachment theory stimulated a great deal of research examining the etiology and development of dependent personality traits, including some noteworthy studies examining infant–mother bonding in infrahuman subjects. Recent research in this area has focused on exploring the similarities and differences between dependency and various forms of attachment behavior (e.g., insecure attachment) in children and adults.

During the 1980s researchers took a more eclectic view of dependent personality traits, combining aspects of the psychoanalytic, social learning, and attachment models in order to arrive at a more integrated, comprehensive perspective on dependency. Thus, relatively few studies during the past decade have focused exclusively on one theoretical framework. Rather, researchers have built upon the strengths of different theoretical models, integrating and synthesizing these models to formulate hypotheses that account for aspects of dependency which are best explained via attention to multiple theoretical perspectives. Recent research on dependency has emphasized the importance of unconscious, unexpressed dependency needs (a concept typically associated with the psychoanalytic model), along with an exploration of the impact of early learning and socialization experiences in the development dependent personality traits (an area of inquiry which originated in social learning theory). During the past decade there have also been increasing efforts to integrate the results of developmental, social, and clinical studies of dependency in order to understand the ways in which findings from these three areas of dependency research complement (and contradict) each other.

II. THE DEVELOPMENT OF DEPENDENCY

Developmental studies of dependency can be divided into three areas: (1) studies of the acquisition of dependent personality traits in infancy and early childhood; (2) investigations of the development of dependency during adolescence and adulthood; and (3) studies of dependency in older adults.

A. Childhood Antecedents of Dependency

The results of numerous studies indicate that overprotective, authoritarian parenting is a primary cause of exaggerated dependency needs during adolescence and adulthood. Prospective and retrospective studies of the parenting style–dependency link have produced highly similar results, allowing strong conclusions to be drawn regarding the etiology of dependent personality traits. Findings in this area confirm that when parents show one of these qualities (i.e., overprotectiveness or authoritarianism), the likelihood that their children will show high levels of dependency increases significantly. When parents show both of these qualities, high levels of dependency in their offspring are particularly likely to result.

It appears that overprotective, authoritarian parenting produces high levels of dependency in children largely because overprotective, authoritarian parents prevent the child from engaging in the kinds of trial-and-error learning that help to provide a sense of mastery, autonomy, and self-sufficiency in children. Consequently, the child of overprotective, authoritarian parents comes to perceive him- or herself as powerless and ineffectual, and continues to rely on others—especially figures of authority—for advice, guidance, and protection. As numerous researchers have noted, the child's inability (or unwillingness) to behave in an assertive, autonomous manner exacerbates the situation, in that behaving in a passive, helpless way encourages figures of authority (e.g., parents, teachers) to continue to perform tasks for the child which the child is actually capable of doing on his or her own. Thus, the child's expressions of dependency come to serve as cues which continue to elicit helping and caretaking behavior on the part of others, further reinforcing the child's passive, dependent behavior and ultimately resulting in even greater levels of helplessness and dependency. Recent research confirms that the overt expression of dependency strivings does in fact serve as a help-eliciting cue in both children and adults. [*See* PARENTING.]

B. Dependency in Adolescence and Adulthood

During adolescence, substantial sex differences in dependency emerge, with girls showing significantly higher levels of dependency than boys. This pattern of results is consistent across different cultures (e.g., American, British, Japanese, Indian, German, Israeli), and across different cultural groups within American society. Moreover, the finding that females show higher levels of dependency than do males has been replicated numerous times. Recent studies further suggest that traditional sex-role socialization practices may be largely responsible for the higher levels of dependency typically found in women relative to men. Insofar as traditional sex-role socialization practices tend to encourage passive, help-seeking behavior in girls to a greater extent than boys, these socialization practices would be expected to produce higher levels of dependency in women than in men. Not surprisingly, empirical studies confirm that—to the extent that a girl grows up in a household which emphasizes traditional sex-role socialization practices—she is likely to show high levels of dependency during adolescence and adulthood. Conversely, to the extent that a boy is exposed to traditional sex-role socialization practices (which emphasize assertive, autonomous behavior in boys), he is likely to show low levels of dependency later in life. [*See* SEX ROLES.]

Not only do sex-role socialization practices play an important role in determining the expression of dependency needs in adolescents, but studies confirm that the object of an individual's dependency strivings (i.e., the person toward whom dependency needs are expressed most readily) changes from childhood to adolescence. Although dependency needs in childhood are typically directed toward the parents and other authority figures (e.g., teachers), during adolescence the dependent individual directs his or her dependency strivings toward members of the peer group rather than toward figures of authority. This shift continues to occur throughout early adulthood, at which point romantic partners become primary outlets for the expression of an individual's dependency needs. In addition, adults often express dependency strivings toward various "pseudo-parental" authority figures (e.g., supervisors, physicians, therapists), and (to a lesser extent) toward peers, parents, and siblings.

C. Dependency in Older Adults

There have been no published studies examining individual differences in level of dependency in older adults. However, research suggests that, in general, older adults tend to exhibit more pronounced dependency needs than do younger adults. To some extent, the higher levels of dependency shown by older adults relative to younger adults reflects the fact that older adults as a group are more dependent on others to carry out tasks associated with daily living (e.g., cooking, shopping, driving). In this context, it is not surprising to learn that those older adults who live in environments which encourage autonomy and independence tend to show lower levels of dependency than do those older adults who live in environments where passivity and dependency are permitted or encouraged. Several investigations have demonstrated that changes in older adults' frequency of dependent behaviors can be traced directly to the contingencies which characterize the environments in which they live: Environments that directly or indirectly encourage the overt expression of dependency needs (e.g., certain nursing home environments and residential treatment facilities) actually appear to cause significant, long-term increases in the dependency levels of older adults.

III. INTERPERSONAL CORRELATES OF DEPENDENCY

In general, studies of the interpersonal correlates of dependency indicate that dependent persons adopt a passive, helpless stance in interpersonal interactions. Specifically, laboratory and field investigations indicate that individuals with a dependent personality orientation show high levels of suggestibility, cooperativeness, compliance, and interpersonal yielding. These results are not surprising when one considers the underlying goals and motivations of the dependent person. Clearly, being helped, nurtured, and protected is very important to the dependent person. In this context, one would expect that the dependent individual would exhibit behaviors that serve to strengthen and reinforce ties to potential nurturers and caretakers. Thus, dependent persons (1) tend to yield to the opinions of others in laboratory conformity experiments; (2) show high levels of suggestibility in both laboratory and field studies; and (3) are cooperative and compliant in social, academic, psychiatric, and medical settings.

Although the dependent person is generally suggestible, cooperative, compliant, and yielding, it is noteworthy that these dependency-related behaviors are even more pronounced when the dependent person is interacting with a figure of authority than when he or she is interacting with a peer. Apparently, figures of authority are perceived by the dependent individual as being particularly good protectors and caretakers. Consequently, the kinds of ingratiation strategies used the dependent person with peers (e.g., compliance and interpersonal yielding) are exhibited even more readily around figures of authority.

Dependent persons in social settings also show high levels of help-seeking behávior. The dependency–help-seeking relationship is found in both men and women, and is consistent across different age groups (i.e., children, adolescents, adults), and across different measures of help-seeking. The dependency–help-seeking relationship found in adults clearly reflects the early developmental experiences of the dependent person: To the extent that help-seeking behavior during childhood was reinforced by the parents and other authority figures, the dependent adolescent or adult will continue to show exaggerated help-seeking behaviors in a variety of situations and settings.

Performance anxiety and fear of negative evaluation might also play a role in encouraging the dependent individual to behave in a help-seeking manner in social situations. Although there have been relatively few studies examining directly the dependency–performance anxiety relationship, studies in this area indicate that (1) dependent persons show higher levels of performance anxiety (and fear of negative evaulation) than do nondependent persons; and (2) there is a positive relationship between the degree to which a dependent person reports high levels of performance anxiety and the degree to which that person show high levels of help-seeking behavior in various situations and settings.

One final set of findings regarding the interpersonal correlates of dependency warrants mention in the present context. In a series of investigations conducted during the 1970s and 1980s, researchers demonstrated that dependent persons exhibit higher levels of interpersonal sensitivity (i.e., sensitivity to subtle verbal and nonverbal cues) than do nondependent persons. In fact, dependent persons are able to infer with surprising accuracy the attitudes and personal beliefs of strangers, roommates, teachers, and therapists. Although at first glance these results seem inconsistent with the oft-reported finding that dependency is associated with passivity and helplessness, findings regarding the dependency–interpersonal sensitivity relationship are actually quite consistent with these other findings. Clearly, to the extent that a dependent person is able to infer accurately the attitudes and personal beliefs of teachers, roommates, and therapists, the dependent person will be better able to develop strong ties to these potential nurturers, protectors, and caretakers.

IV. DEPENDENCY AND PSYCHOPATHOLOGY

Because dependency has typically been conceptualized as a flaw or deficit in functioning, numerous studies have examined the relationship between level of dependency and risk for psychopathology. Studies of the dependency–psychopathology relationship can be divided into four areas: (1) studies of dependency and depression; (2) investigations of the dependency–substance use disorders relationship; (3) studies of dependency, obesity, and eating disorders; and (4) research on dependent personality disorder.

A. Dependency and Depression

Although laboratory and field studies confirm that there is a positive relationship between level of dependency and level of depression in children, adolescents, and adults, the dependency–depression relationship is more complex than early researchers had thought. On the one hand, exaggerated dependency needs do in fact place an individual at increased risk for the subsequent onset of depression. However, it is also the case that the onset of depressive symptoms results in increases in dependent thoughts, feelings, and behaviors in a variety of subject groups. Presumably, the feelings of helplessness, hopelessness, anhedonia, and anergia that are frequently associated with depression can manifest themselves in increases in overt dependent behaviors in depressed subjects. [*See* DEPRESSION.]

The mechanism by which dependent personality traits place an individual at risk for depression is not completely understood, but initial findings suggest that dependency increases risk for depression by causing the dependent person to be particularly upset and threatened by experiences of interpersonal loss. To be sure, interpersonal stressors affect everyone to some degree. However, the dependent person's lifelong tendency to look to others for nurturance, guidance, and protection may cause him or her to become extremely sensitive to the possibility that a potential caretaker will no longer be available to fulfill their protective and nurturing role. In this respect, dependency represents a vulnerability (or diathesis) that—when combined with interpersonal stressors—places the dependent person at increased risk for depression.

B. Dependency and Substance Use Disorders

Dozens of studies have examined the possibility that dependent persons might be at elevated risk for substance use disorders. The results of these investigations have been decidedly mixed. For example, although studies confirm that dependent persons are at increased risk for tobacco addiction, numerous investigations have failed to obtain the hypothesized relationship between dependency and risk for alcoholism. In fact, longitudinal studies of the dependency–alcoholism link indicate that the onset of alcoholism is followed by increases in dependent thoughts, feelings, and behaviors. However, there is no evidence that dependency actually places individuals at increased risk for alcohol abuse or dependence. [*See* SUBSTANCE ABUSE.]

Similar findings have emerged in studies of dependency and other types of substance use disorders. Researchers have examined possible links between dependency and risk of opiate, cocaine, barbituate, marijuana, and poly-drug abuse. The results of these studies have been relatively clear-cut: Dependent individuals do not show elevated risk for these substance use disorders, although—consistent with earlier findings regarding the dependency–alcoholism link—research confirms that the onset of an addictive disorder is often associated with elevations in dependent feelings, thoughts, and behaviors.

C. Dependency, Obesity, and Eating Disorders

The hypothesis that dependent personality traits would be associated with obesity and other eating disorders (i.e., anorexia and bulimia) can be traced to the classical psychoanalytic hypothesis (described earlier) that the etiology of dependency lies in "oral fixation." There have been numerous studies examining the dependency–obesity relationship, and in general these investigations have found only weak relationships between dependency and obesity. Moreover, the dependency–obesity link (when it occurs at all) is somewhat stronger in women than in men. The disappointing results obtained in this area have caused researchers to shift their attention from examining the dependency–obesity relationship to examining the relationship between dependency and eating disorders such as anorexia and bulimia.

Studies of the relationship between dependency and anorexia and bulimia have produced much stronger and more consistent findings than did studies of the dependency–obesity link. Anorexic and bulimic subjects almost invariably show higher levels of dependency than do matched control subjects who do not have these disorders. The dependency–bulimia link appears to be somewhat stronger than the dependency–anorexia link, although additional studies will be needed to confirm and clarify these preliminary results. Studies in this area also suggest that interpersonal stressors (e.g., the breakup of a romantic relationship) might increase the dependent person's risk for anorexia and bulimia in much the same way as they increase the dependent person's risk for depression. Thus, a diathesis–stress conceptualization of the dependency–eating disorders relationship holds considerable promise for future research in this area.

D. Dependent Personality Disorder

Although the vast majority of studies of the dependency–psychopathology relationship have explored possible links between dependency and other forms of psychopathology (e.g., depression), in recent years there has been an increasing emphasis on conceptualizing exaggerated dependency needs as a separate and distinct form of psychological illness. The most prominent framework used to examine the pathological aspects of dependency is the concept of "dependent personality disorder" as this disorder is described in the *Diagnostic and Statistical Manual of Mental Disorders* (DSM). The DSM framework argues that individuals who show exaggerated, inflexible dependency needs which cause social or occupational impairment may be diagnosed as having a dependent personality disorder. Unfortunately, because the diagnostic category of dependent personality disorder was first discussed in 1980, with the publication of the third edition of the DSM series, there has been relatively little research on this disorder. Initial findings regarding the correlates and consequences of dependent personality disorder can be grouped into three areas and summarized simply. [*See* PERSONALITY DISORDERS.]

First, studies confirm that individuals with dependent personality disorder are at increased risk for a wide range of psychopathologies, including depression, anxiety disorders, eating disorders, and somatization disorders. Individuals diagnosed with dependent personality disorder also show elevated risk for certain other personality disorders (e.g., borderline, avoidant, passive–aggressive). To some extent, findings regarding the links between dependent personality disorder and other forms of psychopathology dovetail with findings regarding the dependency–psychopathology relationship in general: As discussed earlier, studies to date suggest that dependent individuals show increased risk for a wide range of psychopathologies.

Second, epidemiological research suggests that the prevalence of dependent personality disorder in community samples is relatively low, with about 5% of community subjects showing clinically significant dependent personality disorder symptoms. As expected, the frequency of dependent personality disorder symptoms and diagnoses in clinical (i.e., psychiatric inpatient or outpatient) samples is somewhat higher, with many studies reporting base rates of this disorder in clinical subjects of about 10–15%. Although dependent personality disorder appears to be somewhat more prevalent in women than in men, the magnitude of the sex difference in dependent personality disorder diagnosis rates is not great.

Third, studies confirm that dependent personality disorder symptoms predict some important aspects of psychological treatment. For example, clinicians report elevated rates of help-seeking behaviors (e.g., requests for emergency sessions, requests for feedback and advice) among dependent personality disorder patients relative to nondependent patients. Along slightly different lines, recent research in this area suggests that dependent personality disorder is associated with cooperativeness and compliance with therapeutic regimens. Finally, several studies indicate that patients diagnosed with dependent personality disorder remain in psychological and medical treatment significantly longer than do nondependent patients, presumably because treatment termination involves giving up a relationship with an important caretaking figure, which the dependent person is reluctant to do.

V. DEPENDENCY AND PHYSICAL DISORDERS

One of the most interesting and noteworthy findings to emerge from recent studies of the dependent personality has to do with risk for physical disorders. Research indicates that dependent persons are at increased risk for a wide variety of physical illnesses, including infectious diseases, ulcers, heart disease, and cancer. Longitudinal (i.e., prospective) studies and archival (retrospective) studies have produced highly consistent findings in this area. The dependency–disease link has been found in men and women, and in both children and adults. Furthermore, the magnitude of the dependency–disease relationship is quite substantial. In fact, a recent direct comparison of the magnitude of the disease risk associated with dependency and the magnitude of the disease risk associated with other "illness-related" personality variables (e.g., hostility, compulsiveness, introversion) revealed that the magnitude of the relationship between dependency and risk for physical illness is actually larger than the personality–illness risk relationship found for all other illness-related personality variables. Clearly, dependency must be regarded as an important component of the "disease-prone personality."

The mechanism by which dependency increases an individual's risk for physical illness parallels closely the mechanism by which dependency increases an individual's risk for depression. Specifically, it appears that dependency acts as a diathesis which—when coupled with experiences of interpersonal stress or loss—increases an individual's risk for various forms of illness. Preliminary findings in this area further suggest that the dependency–interpersonal stress–illness relationship may be mediated by the immune system: Dependent persons who experience significant interpersonal stressors show measurable deficits in immune function. The diminished immunocompetence associated with dependency and interpersonal stress may represent the common pathway through which the dependent individual is placed at increased risk for various forms of illness. However, additional studies will be needed to confirm and extend these initial results. [*See* Stress and Illness.]

Ironically, although the dependent person is at increased risk for physical illness, the personality traits associated with dependency (e.g., cooperativeness, compliance, help-seeking) may actually help the dependent person to respond well to various treatment regimens. Physicians and other health-care professionals consistently report that dependent individuals are compliant, cooperative patients who adhere particularly well to difficult treatment regimens. In addition, the dependent person is inclined to seek the advice and help of a physician relatively quickly when physical symptoms appear. This "medical help-seeking" tendency is certainly consistent with findings regarding the help-seeking behaviors of dependent persons in social settings. In addition, the help-seeking tendencies of the dependent person clearly represent a positive, adaptive quality of dependency: To the extent that the dependent person seeks help relatively quickly when physical symptoms appear, the likelihood of successful treatment should increase.

VI. THE DEPENDENT PERSONALITY: PAST, PRESENT, AND FUTURE

Early research on the dependent personality was concerned primarily with two issues: (1) the exploration of personality traits and behaviors that were hypothesized to be associated with dependency (e.g., passivity, low self-esteem); and (2) the examination of psychoanalytic hypotheses regarding the etiology and dynamics of dependency (i.e., studies of oral fixation and oral dependency). Needless to say, the focus of dependency research has changed considerably during the past several decades. It is worthwhile to review some of these changes in odrder to get a sense of the directions in which dependency research is likely to head during the coming years.

One important shift in this area has occurred with respect to the focus of dependency research. Whereas early studies in this area tended to focus on understanding the antecedents of dependent personality traits, recent studies have instead focused on understanding the consequences of dependency. Many of these recent investigations have examined the interpersonal (i.e., social) consequences of dependency, although other studies have assessed the effects of dependent personality traits on risk for physical or psychological illness.

A second shift characterizing the study of dependency has involved the research methodologies used in this area. Many early investigations of the dependent personality employed correlational designs. Moreover, many of these early studies took place in field settings (e.g., schools) rather than in the laboratory. In contrast, recent research in this area has tended to use experimental (rather than correlational) designs, and most recent investigations of dependency have taken place in laboratory rather than field settings.

A third shift characterizing research in this area has to do with clinicians' and researchers' conceptualization of dependency. For most of this century, dependency has been regarded primarily as a flaw or deficit in functioning. However, in recent years researchers have begun to examine the positive, adaptive qualities of dependency (e.g., compliance with medical regimens, willingness to seek help when symptoms appear). Thus, psychologists have moved from conceptualizing dependency solely in terms of deficit and dysfunction to conceptualizing dependency in a way which recognizes that dependency is associated with both positive and negative qualities.

Fourth, the emphasis in dependency research has shifted from a more-or-less exclusive focus on dependency-related behaviors (e.g., help-seeking), to the study of dependency-related emotions and cognitions. Recent studies in this area have suggested that the disparate behaviors of dependent individuals can be understood more completely (and predicted more accurately) if the dependent individual's cognitive style is assessed directly. As researchers have increasingly emphasized the ways in which the dependent person's self-concept and perceptions of other people mediate his or her behavior, many apparent inconsistencies in previous studies of dependency-related behaviors have been resolved.

Finally, researchers are beginning to examine more closely the interaction of dependent personality traits and aspects of the situation or setting in which behavior is exhibited. Although dependency is often associated with passivity and helplessness, recent studies suggest that situational variables (e.g., the status of the person with whom the dependent individual is interacting, the type of environment in which an interaction occurs) also play a significant role in directing the behavior of the dependent person. In this respect, traditional trait models are beginning to give way to interactionist models of dependency. This shift has already generated some noteworthy findings, and the interactionist perspective on dependency is likely to produce many more important advances in dependency theory and research during the coming years.

Bibliography

Birtchnell, J. (1988). Defining dependence. *Br. J. Med. Psychol.* **61,** 111–123.

Birtchnell, J. (1991). The measurement of dependence by questionnaire. *J. Pers. Disorders* **5,** 281–295.

Blatt, S. J., and Homann, E. (1992). Parent–child interaction in the etiology of dependent and self-critical depression. *Clin. Psychol. Rev.* **12,** 47–91.

Bornstein, R. F. (1992). The dependent personality: Developmental, social and clinical perspectives. *Psychol. Bull.* **112,** 3–23.

Bornstein, R. F. (1993). "The Dependent Personality." Guilford, New York.

Hirschfeld, R. M. A., Shea, M. T., and Weise, R. (1991). Dependent personality disorder: Perspectives for DSM-IV. *J. Pers. Disorders* **5,** 135–149.

Overholser, J. C. (1992). Interpersonal dependency and social loss. *Pers. Individual Diff.* **13,** 17–23.

Zuroff, D. C., Igrega, I., and Mongrain, M. (1990). Dysfunctional attitudes, dependency and self-criticism as predictors of depressive mood states. *Cog. Ther. Res.* **14,** 315–326.

DEPRESSION

Rick E. Ingram
San Diego State University

Glossary

Bipolar disorder An affective disorder that includes both depression and mania. Previously referred to as manic-depression.

Clinical depression A severe form of depression that typically warrants treatment.

Continuity hypothesis Proposes that depression exists on a continuum ranging from normal feelings of depression to clinically significant depression. See discontinuity hypothesis.

Discontinuity hypothesis Proposes that mild and clinically significant depression do not exist on a continuum and are completely different disorders. See continuity hypothesis.

Hypomania A state of lesser excitement than mania.

Learned helplessness A theory proposed by Seligman which suggests that depressed people have learned that their responses to stressful life events do not make any difference.

Mania A dysfunctional state of excitement, frenzied activity, and grandiosity.

Negative cognitive schema An information processing structure proposed by Aaron Beck that filters a depressed person's personal experience in a negative manner.

Subclinical depression A less severe form of depression that does not typically warrant treatment.

Unipolar disorder An affective disorder that does not include any mania.

DEPRESSION is an *affective,* or mood, disorder—a disorder characterized by mood deviations that exceed normal mood fluctuations. Some estimates suggest that one of every five Americans will experience a clinically significant episode of depression in their lives. Other estimates indicate that 10 million Americans will experience depression during any 6-month period. Milder forms of depression will affect virtually everyone and, although perhaps not as great as clinical depression, will also exact a price in unhappiness, disrupted lives and relationships, and a loss of productivity.

I. DEFINITIONS OF DEPRESSION

Because it has so many meanings, the term depression can be confusing. Depression is the term used by many to describe their emotions when feeling sad or a little down, "I'm a little depressed today" or "I just saw a really depressing movie." On the other hand, depression is also a term given to a psychological disorder. At its most extreme, depression can describe a psychotic state where the individual cannot function on his or her own. Researchers have described the terminology problem this way.

> The professional use of the term *depression* has several levels of reference: symptom, syndrome, nosological disorder (Beck, 1967). Depression itself can be a symptom—for example, being sad. As a syndrome, depression is a constellation of signs and symptoms that cluster together (e.g., sadness, negative self-concept, sleep and appetite disturbances). The syndrome of depression is itself a psychological dysfunction but can also be present in secondary ways, in other diagnosed disorders. Finally, for depression to be nosologic, careful diagnostic procedures are required during which other potential diagnostic categories are excluded. The presumption, of course, is that a discrete nosologic entity will ultimately prove to be etiologically distinct from other discrete

Copyright © 1994 by Academic Press, Inc. All rights of reproduction in any form reserved.

entities, with associated differences likely in course, prognosis, and treatment response. Although two individuals might evidence the same manifest symptomatology, with respect to the syndrome of depression, learning that one also showed all the hallmarks of paranoid schizophrenia, while the other did not, would lead us to exclude the first individual from the nosologic category of primary major depressive disorders." (Kendall *et al.*, p. 290)

A. Symptoms of Depression

To help clarify the concept of depression, researchers have generally agreed upon a group of symptoms that are associated with depression. Depression symptoms fall into several clusters that are typically grouped into broad categories based on their similarities. *Mood* symptoms (e.g., sad mood) are the defining feature of affective disorders such as depression. *Motivational* symptoms include those behaviors that refer to goal directedness. Depressed people often suffer a deficit in this area and some may find it extremely difficult to do even the smallest chore. *Somatic* symptoms refer to the physical changes that may accompany depression and include alterations in sleeping patterns, appetite, and sexual interest. Finally, *cognitive* symptoms reflect peoples' ability to concentrate and make decisions, and how they evaluate themselves.

A number of symptoms are commonly observed in a depressive disorder, although not all symptoms always occur. The cardinal or defining symptom that must be observed for depression to be diagnosed is the occurrence of a sad mood that is present most of the day nearly every day for at least 2 weeks. A sad mood alone, however, is not sufficient to indicate depression. A number of symptoms are usually present and the type and pattern of symptoms that occur inform decisions about the kind of depression that is present. Other common symptoms include a diminished interest or pleasure in activities, a decrease or increase in appetite, insomnia or hypersomnia, fatigue or loss of energy nearly every day, feelings of worthlessness or excessive or inappropriate guilt, diminished ability to think or concentrate, and recurrent thoughts of death or recurrent suicidal ideation.

B. Relationship between Depression and Anxiety

Although depression is considered a distinct disorder by many researchers, it is also widely acknowledged that depressive affect is correlated with other affective states. In fact, this correlation is so consistent that some investigators have suggested that depression and anxiety are merely different manifestations of the same underlying disorder. Research has not yet established if this is the case or if depression and anxiety represent different disorders that share some common symptoms. Recent proposals are gaining significant attention among clinical psychologists. It is argued that depression and anxiety share a general distress factor that accounts for much of the overlap between the two states. By and large, this general distress is composed of high levels of negative affect. Beyond this general distress, what distinguishes depression from anxiety is that positive affect is still present in anxiety but not in depression. Anxiety, on the other hand, is characterized by heightened physiological arousal that is not characteristic of depression. Thus, the relative absence of positive affect or the presence of physiological arousal allows researchers to make distinctions about whether the disorder is a depressive disorder or an anxiety disorder. In cases where it is not possible to distinguish these different processes, there is arguement for a mixed depression and anxiety diagnosis. While it too early to determine whether this classificatory scheme will catch on, it has certainly gained the attention of an increasing number of researchers. [*See* ANXIETY DISORDERS.]

II. CLASSIFICATION OF DEPRESSION

There are a number of classification schemes that seek to distinguish what appear to be different kinds of depression. The major distinctions will be reviewed here, although it should be noted that there is some overlap between the different classifications.

A. Normal Depression, Subclinical Depression, and Clinical Depression

At the broadest level, depression can be defined and classified on a continuum ranging from normal depression to subclinical depression to clinical depression. Normal depression refers to the mood swings that every individual experiences and is usually expressed as feelings of sadness. Normal depression is generally synonymous to depression viewed as a symptom. Beyond a sad mood, few if any of the other symptoms of depression are present in normal depression.

Subclinical depression is a more severe form of depression that includes not only a sad mood but also some of the other symptoms of depression. Although any pattern of symptoms can occur, according to DSM-III-R no more than four of the symptoms listed in Table I can occur; if there are more than four, the depression is no longer considered subclinical but is instead considered clinically significant. Although different from typical mood swings, subclinical depression is also considered "normal" depression in that it is not severe enough to receive a diagnosis or in most cases to warrant treatment. Subclinical depression is usually precipitated by significant stresses in the person's life. [*See* STRESS.]

In contrast to normal and subclinical depression, clinical depression refers to depression that is severe enough to warrant treatment or that substantially interferes with an individual's functioning. According to DSM-III-R, clinical depression has at least five of the nine depressive symptoms that persist for at least a 2-week period.

1. The Continuity/Discontinuity Controversy

The discussion of normal versus subclinical versus clinical depression may imply that depression falls on a severity continuum, with different forms of depression representing the same disorder that differs primarily in the severity of the depressive symptoms experienced. This view reflects the *continuity hypothesis*. This hypothesis holds that affective states occur on a continuum from normal to abnormal and that a disorder is an extreme version of a normal mood. Hence, feeling sad is essentially the same process as a disabling case of depression requiring treatment, just on a much less severe scale. The alternative *discontinuity hypothesis*, on the other hand, suggests that these different levels of psychological states represent fundamentally different processes. That is, while some of the characteristics such as sad mood may seem similar, normal feelings of being depressed and clinical depression are two separate and unrelated phenomena. Research has not yet established which of these competing hypotheses comes closest to the truth.

TABLE I

Symptoms of Depression According to the *Diagnostic and Statistical Manual of Mental Disorders* (Revised, Third Edition)

1. Depressed mood most of the day, nearly every day.
2. Markedly diminished interest or pleasure in all, or almost all, activities most of the day.
3. Significant weight loss or weight gain when not dieting, or decrease or increase in appetite nearly every day.
4. Insomnia or hypersomnia.
5. Psychomotor agitation or retardation nearly every day.
6. Fatigue or loss of energy nearly every day.
7. Feelings of worthlessness or excessive or inappropriate guilt.
8. Diminished ability to think or concentrate.
9. Recurrent thoughts of death, recurrent suicidal ideation without a specific plan, or a suicide attempt, or a specific plan for committing suicide.

B. The Unipolar–Bipolar Distinction

One of the most widely agreed upon distinctions is between unipolar and bipolar disorders. "Clinical depression" can consist of either a unipolar depressive disorder or a bipolar depressive disorder. Unipolar disorder refers to the occurrence of only depression while bipolar disorder (sometimes referred to as manic-depression) is usually thought of as a cyclic disorder with manic and depressive phases. In order to be considered to have bipolar disorder, one need only experience a genuine manic episode at some point in life. In fact, many researchers suggest that individuals can be considered to have a bipolar depressive disorder if they have had a manic episode, even if they have *never* had a bout with depression. Another form of bipolar disorder is known as bipolar II; individuals with bipolar II disorder experience occasional periods of depression and hypomania. Hypomania is defined as a milder form of excitement than mania.

When a bipolar disordered individual is depressed, the clinical features of the depression are virtually indistinguishable from unipolar depression. There are, however, several important distinctions between bipolar and unipolar depression. Research indicates, for example, that unipolar depression tends to occur later in life than bipolar disorder. Additionally, studies have found that bipolar disorder is more frequently characterized by hyposomnia (less of a need for sleep) during mania whereas unipolar depressed people are more likely to suffer from insomnia. Relatives of bipolar disordered people are also more likely to suffer from affective disorders than are the relatives of a person with unipolar disorder. This latter finding tends to support genetic and biological explanations of bipolar disorder. Several types of unipolar and bipolar depressive disorders can be described.

1. Unipolar Depressive Disorder: Major Depressive Episode

Unipolar depression is the type of depression that comes to mind when most people think about depression. Accordingly, a major depressive episode is diagnosed according to DSM-III-R criteria when at least five of the nine possible symptoms are continuously present for at least a 2-week period. In addition to the presence of these symptoms, other symptoms must not also be present (e.g., hallucinations in the absence of mood symptoms). If they are, the depression is not considered the primary diagnosis; depression would be secondary to (presumably a result of) some other disorder. This other primary disorder may be psychological in nature or may be a physical illness. Thus, it is important to recognize that depression sometimes does not constitute a primary affective disorder.

Although there are different subcategories of major depressive disorder, one that is particularly noteworthy is seasonal affective disorder (SAD). As the name implies, SAD refers to depression that varies with the seasons. The disorder typically starts between October and November and disappears approximately 60 days later (from mid-February to mid April). Researchers believe that the quantity of light available may trigger certain biological effects in some individuals by shifting cercadin rhythms and melatonin production. Thus, as days become shorter during the winter, these people become progressively more depressed. Not surprisingly, a treatment that had been recognized for SAD is "light therapy." Lewy *et al.* found that their depressed patients improved substantially after 1 week of exposure to bright light in the morning. This improvement was accompanied by an increased onset of melatonin production. Thus, light therapy offers promise for people suffering from SAD and, although more research is needed to confirm its effects, this approach is being increasingly employed in treatment settings.

While SAD, as it is described here, is classified as a unipolar disorder, some recent research suggests that SAD, or at least certain forms of SAD, may represent a bipolar disorder. In cases where all and winter depression are followed by spring hypomania, SAD may be a bipolar II disorder. This form of SAD may be very common.

2. Unipolar Depressive Disorder: Dysthymia

Dysthymia does not include as many depressive symptoms as a major depressive episode and is thus considered a milder form of depression. For example, in addition to sad mood, a diagnosis of dysthymia requires only that two of the following symptoms occur: (1) poor appetite or overeating, (2) insomnia or hypersomnia, (3) low energy or fatigue, (4) low self-esteem, (5) poor concentration or difficulty in making decisions, and (6) feelings of hopelessness. The defining feature of dysthymia, however, is that these symptoms must occur most of the day, more days than not, for at least a 2-year period of time.

In previous diagnostic schemes, dysthymia was sometimes referred to as "neurotic" depression because it was assumed that the depressive symptomatology was an aspect of the individual's personality structure. While this still may be the case, the label neurotic has been dropped because it was not particularly helpful in understanding the disorder. A diagnosis of dysthymia does not rule out a major depressive episode: DSM-III-R notes that both dysthymia and a major depressive episode can coexist. This co-existence of disorders is known as "double depression." When the major depressive episode had subsided, the dysthymia usually continues.

3. Bipolar Depressive Disorder

As previously noted, while major depressive episode and dysthymia are considered unipolar disorders, the other form of clinical depression is bipolar disorder. Although individuals with bipolar disorder typically cycle between depression and mania, there is usually a period of normal functioning in between these episodes. Rapid cycling between episodes is relatively rare.

4. Bipolar Depressive Disorder: Cyclothymia

Cyclothymia is the bipolar analogue of unipolar dysthymia in that it constitutes, according to DSM-III-R, a "chronic mood disturbance, of at least two years' duration . . . involving numerous Hypomanic episodes and numerous periods of depressed mood." Like dysthymia, these hypomanic and depressed periods are not sufficient to meet the criteria for mania or major depression. Much of the clinical significance of cyclothymia lies in the fact that it often leads to major depressive complications.

C. The Reactive–Endogenous Distinction

Another way of distinguishing among different classes of depressive disorders is the reactive–

endogenous distinction. This distinction is based on assumptions about the underlying etiology of depressive disorders. While any kind of depressive disorder has both underlying psychological and biological components, endogenous depression is presumed to be primarily biological in origin. Although controversial, such disorders are thought to be distinguishable by a lack of precipitating life events and a particular cluster of symptoms that include weight loss, terminal insomnia (waking up too early in the morning), guilt, and psychomotor retardation. As such, endogenous depression usually denotes a more severe set of symptoms. Conversely, reactive depressions are thought to be more psychological in nature and are seen as a reaction to negative events in one's life.

D. The Neurotic–Psychotic Distinction

One of the most widely used, and confusing, distinctions is between neurotic and psychotic depressive disorders. In its strictest sense, *psychotic* depression refers to a disorder that is accomplished by hallucinations or delusions while *neurotic* disorders refer to depressions where hallucinations and delusions are absent. What is confusing about this distinction is that these two categories of depression cut across a number of other distinctions. For example, psychotic depression is sometimes seen to be the same as severe or endogenous depression. Neurotic depression, on the other hand, can be seen as anything ranging from reactive depression to mild depression to chronic depression to depression that is secondary to a personality disorder. In fact, there are so many possible meanings for the "neurotic" label that researchers have suggested that it lacks any real clinical usefulness. Not surprisingly, reference to neurosis has been dropped from DSM-III-R.

III. EPIDEMIOLOGY OF DEPRESSION

Epidemiology refers to information about the prevalence of a disorder in the population. Prevalence means not only how widespread is the disorder, but also how it is distributed in different segments of the population as well as what features seem to be systematically associated with the disorder.

In 1978, the National Institute of Mental Health initiated a large-scale epidemiological study to examine the prevalence of a number of mental disorders, including depression. Known as the Epidemiologic Catchment Area (ECA) study, 20,000 people in New Haven, Baltimore, St. Louis, Durham, and Los Angeles were interviewed with the Diagnostic Interview Schedule (DIS). The DIS was used to determine the rates of various mental disorders according to the criteria specified by DSM III.

A. Prevalence of Depression

The ECA study found a 1-year prevalence of 2.7%, meaning that in a given year, it can be estimated that 2.7% of the population will experience a diagnosable major depressive episode. The lifetime rate of depression was 4.9%. Lifetime rates refer to the number of people who will experience the disorder at some point in their lives. Although this is lower than some estimates which have suggested that as much as 20% of the population will experience depression, this figure does not include the large number of people who will experience significant depressive symptoms, but who do not meet enough criteria to receive a formal diagnosis of depression. For example, roughly 30% of the study sample reported experiencing a period of at least 2 weeks where they felt blue or sad. Approximately 25% reported other significant symptoms such as increased or decreased appetite, thoughts of death, or sleep disturbance. Thus, even though the actual lifetime incidence of a diagnosable depressive disorder was only about 5% in this study, the experience of significant depression is much higher.

The ECA study also found that the lifetime dysthymia rate was lower than major depression at 3.2%, and that the rate of bipolar disorder was even lower at .08%. Thus, unipolar major depression is by far the most common of the affective disorders, with bipolar disorder being much less widespread.

B. Sex Differences

A number of studies have found that women are twice as likely as men to receive a diagnosis of unipolar depression. Studies of community samples have continually found that women are significantly more likely to be depressed than men. In a comprehensive study of depression, researchers found consistent evidence of sex differences in over 30 countries. The ECA study bears out these differences; women had a lifetime prevalence rate of 7.0% while men had a rate of 2.6%. No evidence, however, was found for significant sex differences in the incidence of bipolar disorder; the rate for women was .9 while the rate for men was .7.

The reason for sex differences in depression is unknown. Some investigators have suggested that different depression rates are an artifact; men and women actually experience similar rates of depression, but women are more likely to acknowledge their symptoms or clinicians may simply overdiagnose depressive symptoms in women. Other investigators have argued that women are more likely to encounter the stressful factors that lead to depression, while still others have suggested endocrinological differences in men and women that predispose women to depression. Finally, some researchers have suggested differences in cognitive tendencies; women tend to ruminate over negative events while men in turn dampen their cognitive responses and hence their emotional responses as well. Which of these hypotheses, or combination of hypotheses, will ultimately prove to be the most accurate account of sex differences is unclear.

C. Ethnic Differences

There are some ethnic differences in the incidence of depression. For example, whites have a lifetime unipolar depression rate of 5.1 while the rate for hispanics is somewhat lower at 4.4 and is even lower for blacks at 3.1. For bipolar disorder the differences are less; for whites the rate is .8, for hispanics .7 and for blacks 1.0. For dysthymia hispanics have the highest rate at 4.0, followed by whites at 3.3 and blacks at 2.5.

D. Social Correlates

Social correlates refer to factors such as employment status, socioeconomic status, urban versus rural residence, and marital status. Although all of these are important, we will focus here on marital status.

According to the ECA study,

> For bipolar disorders, the adjusted [for age, sex, and race] odds are higher for persons who are cohabitating, have a history of divorce (regardless of current marital status), or who have never married, compared to married or widowed persons without a history of divorce. A similar relationship, but not nearly so strong, holds for major depression. When current marital status regardless of past history or divorce is considered, the separated and divorced men and women have the highest rates of both disorders.

What are the reasons that married people are less likely to experience either a bipolar or unipolar depressive disorder? There are several possible explanations, each of which may be partially true. One possibility is that marriage provides a protective relationship against the stresses and strains that can precipitate depression; having a supportive confidant may help people deal more effectively with the problems in their lives. Alternatively, it may be that the stress of living with a depressed partner may lead to the breakup of a marriage by the nondepressed partner, or the marriage may be dissolved by the depressed partner who blames the distress on the shortcomings of the partner. A final alternative is that people who are prone to depression may lack the internal stability to successfully navigate the inevitable vicissitudes of a marital relationship.

IV. THEORIES OF DEPRESSION

A. Psychological Theories

Perhaps the most currently influential psychological theories of depression are the cognitive theories. While the specifics of these theories differ somewhat, in general, they all propose that depression results in large part from dysfunctional thinking patterns that not only help to cause the depression, but serve to maintain and sometimes worsen the disorder.

1. The Negative Cognitive Schema Theory of Depression

One of the most influential theories of depression has been proposed by Aaron Beck. The cornerstone of Beck's theory is the cognitive schema. Experimental psychologists propose that all individuals possess cognitive schemata (plural of schema) that help them to screen out certain irrelevant information in their environment and let in important information. According to Beck, in addition to these normal adaptive schemata, depressed individuals also possess a negative cognitive *self*-schema that selectively filters out positive information about oneself and lets in negative information. Beck suggests that at some point in childhood, depressed individuals develop such a schema, possibly through excessive criticism by parents or perhaps due to strongly negative life events. Then as an adult, when similar kinds of events occur to individuals vulnerable to these events, the negative schema is activated and begins to screen their personal experience in a negative way.

In addition to selectively filtering information, the negative schema also gives rise to a negative cognitive triad. This triad predisposes individuals to see themselves, their world, and their future in an unrealistically negative light. Thus, depressed people may believe that they are flawed and inferior, that there is nothing worthwhile in their life, and that their future holds nothing but misery. While life is certainly not always rosy, Beck suggests that such a pervasively negative view is surely a distortion of the individual's life. The depressed person therefore continually thinks negative thoughts about him or herself, misinterprets minor stresses as catastrophic, and believes that none of this will ever change.

2. Learned Helplessness Theory

Another influential cognitive theory of depression has been proposed by Seligman and his colleagues. Seligman suggested that depressed people may have learned early on that their responses to stressful situations made little difference in those situations. Thus, when problematic situations arise, rather than seek solutions, people who are prone to depression simply give up and passively take the punishment of an aversive environment; they become depressed. [*See* LEARNED HELPLESSNESS.]

Although researchers have found the learned helplessness theory to have much appeal, conflicting experimental evidence about its validity has led to several major modifications of the theory. For instance, a major modification of helplessness theory was proposed by Abramson et al. This modification has come to be known as the *reformulated helplessness model.* They noted that although everyone experiences negative events that are beyond their control, not everyone becomes depressed. There must, therefore, be factors that either insulate from or predispose individuals to depression in light of these events. Abramson's group proposed that attributions about the event have these predisposing or insulating effects. Attributions are beliefs as to why something happened; an *internal* attribution suggests that the person was responsible for the event while an *external* attribution suggests that somebody or something else was at fault. Attributions regarding the *stability* of the event are relevant to whether the cause of the event will always be present while attributions about *globality* refer to whether the cause of the event is global versus more specific. An attribution for an event can be any combination of the above dimensions.

It was proposed that individuals who are vulnerable to depression are characterized by certain attributional tendencies. In particular, it is suggested that vulnerable individuals evidence a tendency to make internal, stable, and global attributions for negative events and external, unstable, and specific attributions for positive events. In effect, individuals predisposed to depression will make highly self-critical attributions for negative life events, but will not take credit for positive events.

Seligman also proposed a modification of the original learned helplessness theory. In particular, he posited a *helplessness depression* that suggested a specific subtype of depression. Along the same lines but somewhat more broadly, another group of researchers led by Abramson proposed a negative cognition subtype of depression. Recognizing that many investigators believe that depression is not a single disorder but is rather a heterogeneous group of disorders, it is argued that a subset of depressive disorders is characterized by the emergence of a negative cognitive triad and thoughts of hopelessness. These hopelessness thoughts are the result of the pattern of attributions that lead people to feel helpless to deal effectively with the stresses in their lives.

3. Interpersonal Approaches to Depression

Interpersonal approaches to depression focus on the interactions between depressed people and their environments and how these interactions facilitate the maintenance of the disorder. At the heart of the interpersonal approach is the observation that depressed people may use the symptoms of their disorder to elicit certain reactions in others. Interpersonal approach advocates argue that depressed individuals attempt to seek reinforcement from others by behaving in such a way as to place others in a position of care and support. These behaviors, however, may have paradoxical effects. While other people may initially offer support and sympathy, the depressed person's continual attempts to elicit this comfort eventually grow tiresome and lead to an avoidance of the person because he or she is simply depressing to be around. Indeed, some investigators have labeled depression a "contagious" disease because of these effects. As other people begin to withdraw, however, the depressed person intensifies efforts to elicit support and a vicious cycle begins.

4. The Psychodynamic Model of Depression

Freud and Abraham represent the original contributors to the psychodynamic approach to depression. Freud expanded on the work of Abraham (his student) and in his seminal work entitled *Mourning and Melancholia* developed a picture of depression that was characterized by a turning inward of negative emotion. In particular, both Freud and Abraham argued that sadness is precipitated by the loss of a valued person. What differentiates this sadness, or normal grief, from a depressive disorder is anger that is turned against the self. While the healthy individual feels very deep sadness over the loss, the depressed person interprets the loss as rejection and feels resentment and anger. Because the lost person was a source of love and value, however, the depressed person cannot express this anger openly and thus turns it inward instead. Consequently, the person begins to develop a sense of guilt, worthlessness, helplessness, and self-recrimination.

Freud saw the early antecedents of depression in the patient's childhood. All children develop strong emotional bonds with others. For depressed individuals, however, psychodynamic perspectives suggest that the child has experienced either the real or perceived loss of a loved one. This view is interesting in that many years after Freud's proposals, Brown summarized epidemiological data showing that before the age of 11, many subsequently depressed people experienced the death of their mother. According to Freud, this loss is accompanied by a juvenile but extreme anger at being rejected. If the child cannot resolve or replace this loss he or she eventually engages in a process known as *introjection*. Perhaps as a way to negate the loss, introjection allows the child to identify with the lost individual and, in a sense, to psychologically become the lost person. The result of doing this, however, is that the child now becomes the subject or his or her own rage. As a natural consequence of this rage at oneself, the child also begins to blame him or herself for the loss.

Having experienced this sequence of early childhood environmental and psychological events, as an adult the individual is now vulnerable to depression. Thus, instead of encountering the normal grief and eventual resolution following a loss, the juvenile turning inward of anger is again energized, and the person succumbs to a depressive disorder that is characterized by intense sadness but also self-blame and guilt. The person also develops a dependent personality style that relies to a great extent on others for self-esteem and acceptance.

B. Biological Approaches

There is little doubt that biological factors play an important role in affective disorders. In fact, many medical researchers consider affective disorders to be caused primarily by biological, physiological, or genetic phenomena. Sometimes these factors are seen as interacting; for example, genetic explanations may suggest that certain individuals inherit a predisposition to disordered biological processes. Most of the speculation regarding biological approaches to affective disorders has centered on neurotransmitters. Genetic studies have examined the incidence of affective disorders in people who are related and who are thus genetically similar.

1. Genetic Approaches

Genetic approaches suggest that certain people inherit a vulnerability to affective disorders. Whether this vulnerability is ever realized in an affective disorder most likely depends on the interplay between biological, psychological, and social factors. For example, a vulnerable individual who leads a life relatively free of stressful events, or who has learned to effectively cope with stressful events, may never encounter a depressive disorder. On the other hand, an individual who has not learned good psychological coping strategies may be at much higher risk for the disorder because he or she is more likely to interpret a wide range of events as stressful. Thus, even if genetic factors are quite important, the precise relationship is a complicated one that makes research aimed at understanding the relationship exceedingly difficult.

Despite this difficulty, studies have supported the importance of at least a genetic component in affective disorders, particularly with regard to bipolar disorders. This work has tended to employ both family and twin studies. The incidence of affective disorder in first-degree relatives of bipolar disordered patients is significantly higher than the incidence in the population at large. Some data have suggested, for example, that while only about 5% of the population evidence the characteristics of bipolar disorder, roughly 15% of individuals who had a family history of the disorder also are diagnosed with the condition. [*See* BEHAVIORAL GENETICS.]

Twin studies have also generated support for genetic explanations. Several investigators have examined the concordance rate for affective disorders in monozygotic and dizygotic twins. Although studies vary, concordance rates for bipolar disorder in identical twins are around 70% while the figure is only about 15% for fraternal twins. At least for bipolar disorders, then, these data argue strongly for the presence of at least a genetic component to the disorder.

2. Biological Theories

Biological theories focus on the functioning of neurochemical agents in the brain. Two classes of these neurotransmitters have been implicated in affective disorders; catecholamines and indoleamines. In particular, a type of catecholamine, norepinephrine (NE), is thought to be involved in the central nervous system's motivation complex. NE is also related to the secretion of adrenalin, a neurotransmitter partially responsible for the energy of the system. NE has been suggested to be depleted in the case of depression while an excess of NE has been proposed to be responsible for manic episodes. Low levels of an indoleamine neurotransmitter, serotonin (5HT), have also been suggested by some theories to play a role in depression.

It is extremely difficult to directly measure brain levels of NE. For example, although the residuals of these neurotransmitters can be assessed in the blood or urine, these by-products are not the same as the chemicals in the brain. Indirect evidence for the functioning of these neurotransmitters was therefore initially provided by examining the effects of drugs used in the treatment of depression. Animal studies indicated that tricyclics and monoamine (MAO) inhibitors had the effect of increasing both NE and 5HT. Coupled with the fact that these drugs were generally effective for treating depression in humans, researchers argued that this provided compelling evidence for neurotransmitter depletion theories. It is not possible, however, to use these data as direct support of NE or 5HT depletion hypotheses as the causes of affective disorders. Just as the fact that asprin relieves a headache does not suggest that the headache was caused by a depletion of asprin in the system, neither do the effects of pharmacological agents support causal inferences about NE or 5HT. Hence, these chemicals may be only a part of the cause or perhaps secondary to some other causal agent. The difficulty of directly measuring these chemicals has thus made it quite difficult to independently confirm their role in affective disorders.

While neurotransmitters are clearly involved in affective disorders at some level, recent evidence has suggested that the neurotransmitter relationship is much more complex than was originally thought. For example, investigators have reported that tricyclics and MAO inhibitors may be effective in alleviating depression not because of increasing the availability of NE or 5HT, but rather by making receptor sites more sensitive to existing supplies of these neurotransmitters. Thus, affective disorders might be caused by receptor problems rather than by depletion of neurotransmitters. Consequently, research examining receptor sites will likely see a burst of activity in the coming years.

C. Summary of Theories

Which of these theories offers the most accurate account of depression? Although research has supported each of the various approaches to depression, research data have not been able to convincingly demonstrate the superiority of one model over another. While the reasons for this are many, the primary difficulty in depression research is that complexity of the subject. For example, although studies may show a specified variable to operate in depression, this does not suggest that this variable caused the depression. It may be, for example, that the variable showed up after the depression was initiated, thus making it a possible consequence of depression rather than a cause. Until longitudinal research is able to effectively measure key variables before a person is depressed, definitive answers to the problem of depression will not be forthcoming. Until then it seems reasonable to conclude that the various theoretical models of depression most likely all account for some aspect of various forms of depression. Although it would be preferable to have a clear and unambiguous understanding of depression, the current understanding that we do have, while blurred, has led researchers to some important insights.

Bibliography

Abramson, L. Y., Alloy, L. B., and Metalsky, G. I. (1988). The cognitive diathesis-stress theories of depression: Toward an adequate evaluation of the theories' validity. In "Cognitive Processes in Depression" (L. B. Alloy, Ed.), pp. 3–30. Guilford Press, New York.

Abramson, L. Y., Seligman, M. E. P., and Teasdale, J. D. (1978). Learned helplessness in humans: Critique and reformulation. *J. Abnormal Psychol.* **87,** 40–74.

Beck, A. T. (1967). "Depression: Clinical, Experimental, and Theoretical Aspects." Hoeber, New York.

Brown, G. W. (1979). The social etiology of depression—London studies. In "The Psychobiology of the Depressive Disorders:

Implications for the Effects of Stress.'' (R. A. Depue, Ed.), pp. 263–289. Academic Press, New York.
Clark, L. A., and Watson, D. (1991). Tripartite model of depression and anxiety: Psychometric evidence and taxonomic implications. *J. Abnormal Psychol.* **100,** 316–336.
Coppen, A. (1967). The biochemistry of affective disorders. *Br. J. Psych.* **113,** 1237–1264.
Coyne, J. C. (1976). Toward an interactional description of depression. *Psychiatry* **39,** 28–40.
Ingram, R. E., Cruet, D., Johnson, B., and Wisnicki, K. S. (1988). Self-focused attention, gender, gender role, and vulnerability to negative affect. *J. Person. Soc. Psychol.* **55,** 967–978.
Kendall, P. C., Hollon, S. D., Beck, A. T., Hammen, C. L., and Ingram, R. E. (1987). Issues and recommendations regarding use of the Beck Depression Inventory. *Cog. Ther. Res.* **11,** 289–299.
Lewy, A. J., Sack, R. L., Miller, S., and Hoban, T. M. (1987). Antidepressant and circadian phase-shifting effects of light. *Science* **235,** 352–354.
Nolen-Hoeksema, S. (1987). Sex differences in unipolar depression: Evidence and Theory. *Psychol. Bull.* **101,** 259–282.
Robins, L. N., and Regier, D. A. (1991). ''Psychiatric Disorders in America.'' Free Press, New York.
Schildkraut, J. J. (1965). The catecholamine hypothesis of affective disorders. *Am. J. Psych.* **122,** 509–522.
Weissman, M. M., and Klerman, G. L. (1977). Sex differences and the epidemology of depression. *Arch. Gen. Psych.* **39,** 98–111.

Depth Perception

Stanley Coren
University of British Columbia, Canada

Glossary

Accommodation The change in focus of the lens of the eye, which may serve as a depth cue.

Aerial perspective A distance cue in which objects appear hazy, less distinct, and more blue the farther away they are, because of the interaction of light with dust and moisture particles in the air.

Binocular disparity The difference in the monocular views of the two eyes.

Convergence The inward rotation of both eyes toward the nose as a fixated object becomes closer.

Cyclopean eye An imaginary point midway between the eyes thought to be used as a reference point for the straight ahead direction.

Diplopia Double vision.

Dominant eye The eye whose use is preferred in monocular tasks such as looking through a telescope.

Egocentric localization The location of objects in terms of their distance and direction relative to our body.

Height in the (picture) plane A cue for distance referring to where an object is relative to the horizon.

Horopter An imaginary plane in external space used to describe the region of binocularly fused images.

Interposition The depth cue based on the blocking of an bject from view by another closer object.

Linear perspective The apparent convergence of physically parallel lines as they recede into the distance.

Motion parallax The apparent relative motion of objects in the visual field as the observer moves his head or body.

Pictorial depth cues Monocular cues for distance that can be found in photographs and pictures.

Stereomotion A dynamic cue to depth based on the relative rates of motion in the two eyes.

Stereopsis The ability to see depth based solely on the disparity of the two retinal images.

Texture gradient Distance cue based on variations in surface texture as a function of distance from the observer.

DEPTH PERCEPTION refers to our ability to see the world as three-dimensional and to locate objects (and ourselves) in space. It is difficult to imagine how one could survive without the ability to see depth and distance. Without this skill you could not determine how far you need to reach to pick up any object, whether you were stepping off a curb or off a cliff, or how far away an oncoming vehicle was, to mention but a few instances. Perception of depth consists of at least two different aspects. *Egocentric localization* involves the perception of the absolute distance that an object is from you, such as how far away from you is a coffee cup that rests on the table. The second aspect is *object-relative localization*, which involves estimates of the distances between objects. This aspect of depth perception is also involved in the perception of whether an object is flat (as in a two-dimensional picture) or solid (three-dimensional). To perceive an object as solid requires the perception that different parts of it differ in their relative depth.

I. PICTORIAL DEPTH CUES

Photographs and realistic paintings give the illusion of objects at various distances. Your impression of the relative depth in such scenes is based on a set of *pictorial depth cues*. These cues are the result of the geometric rules that control the projection of

Copyright © 1994 by Academic Press, Inc. All rights of reproduction in any form reserved.

light and the way in which light interacts with the environment.

A. Interposition or Occlusion

Since light reflected from distant objects cannot pass through opaque objects that stand between them and the observer, an object that tends to block the view of another is seen as closer. This can be seen in Figure 1 where the man is clearly closer to the viewer than the woman since parts of his body occlude our view of parts of her body.

B. Shading and Shadows

Because light usually travels in straight lines, surfaces facing the light source will be relatively bright while surfaces away from the light source will be in shadow. Particular patterns of shadow can provide information about the relative shape of solid objects. Thus, if light comes from above, the lower part of an in-going dent or "dimple" will catch more of the light while upper part will be in relative shadow. For an out-going protrusion or "pimple," the top part will be bright and the lower part in shadow. Thus, Figure 2 shows a rise or mound of earth, yet if we invert the picture (and hence invert the pattern of light and shadow) it now appears to be a crater.

FIGURE 2 Shading makes it clear that we are looking at a mound of earth. Turning the figure upside-down reverses the pattern of shadows and highlights, and now makes the picture look like a crater.

C. Aerial Perspective

Over long distances light is absorbed or scattered. This causes a blurring or loss of contrast for lines in the retinal image of more distant objects. They also appear to be a bit bluer in color, since short wave lengths of light (seen as blue) are more easily scattered by moisture in the atmosphere.

D. Retinal Size

As an object moves farther away from you, its retinal image size grows smaller. In the absence of any other information, smaller objects appear to be more distant than larger objects. This can be seen as in Figure 3 where the man appears to be more distant than the woman due to his smaller retinal image size.

FIGURE 1 Interposition as a depth cue is illustrated by the fact that the man is seen as closer than the woman since our view of her is partially blocked by our view of him.

FIGURE 3 Because of the relative size cue, the man's smaller size makes him appear to be more distant than the woman.

E. Familiar Size

When objects are known or familiar to us, estimates of distance take into account our knowledge of the size of the object. Thus, Figure 4, is most commonly interpreted as a man mowing a lawn with his house farther away in the background. In this interpretation the man appears closer to us than the house, even though they are both the same retinal heights. This perceptual depth organization involves the use of familiar size. We rely upon our knowledge that houses are normally much larger than people. Actually, there was a similar presumption in Figure 3, where, based upon our knowledge of the size of people, we are more apt to see the man as being farther away than as being a midget at the same distance as the woman.

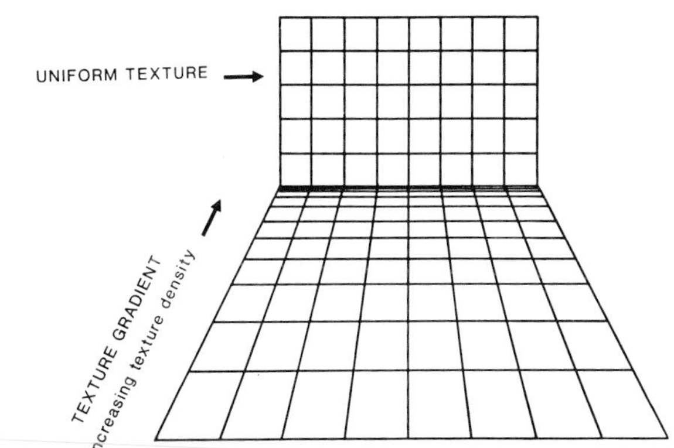

FIGURE 5 The texture gradient is interpreted as a surface receding into the distance, while the uniform texture is interpreted as a wall at a fixed egocentric distance from the observer.

F. Texture Gradients

A visual texture is loosely defined as any collection of objects or features in the visual image. A texture gradient is a region of continuous change in the relative size and compactness of the object elements that make up the texture. The more distant parts of the texture have smaller elements that are more densely packed together. Sudden changes in texture usually signal a change in the direction or distance of a surface. Thus, Figure 5 shows how the texture gradient is perceived as a floor receding in distance from us, while the uniform texture is seen as a wall, with all points relatively the same distance from us.

G. Linear Perspective

This well-known pictorial depth cue may be seen as an extension of the retinal image size and texture gradient cues to distance. The operation of linear perspective was illustrated in a drawing textbook published in 1605, which we have reproduced as Figure 6. As emphasized by the lines added for instructional purposes, you can see that linear perspective involves the convergence of physically parallel lines, such as those defining the paving blocks making up the floor, or contours (or extrapolated dimensions) defining tops and bottoms of objects. Because of this convergence, objects appear to get smaller and smaller in a systematic fashion as their distance from you increases, eventually reaching a *vanishing point*. The term vanishing point was selected because it represents a point where all the perspective lines converge and objects diminish to invisibility. This point is usually at the horizon. There may be many vanishing points, each defining the point of convergence of parallel lines extrapolated from a different angle toward the horizon.

FIGURE 4 This scene appears as a man mowing a lawn near a more distant house. Despite the fact that man and house have the same retinal height, our knowledge of the usual or familiar size of these objects can serve as a cue to relative distance.

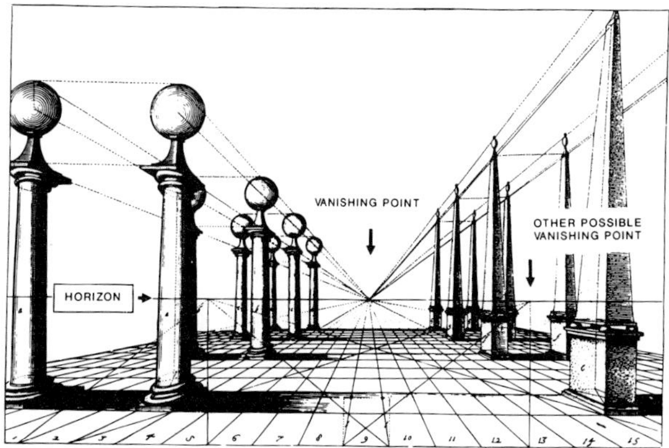

FIGURE 6 The linear perspective cue involves parallel lines (or imputed parallel lines from objects that are the same physical size) which appear to converge to a vanishing point on the horizon.

H. Height in the Plane

This cue, sometimes called *relative height,* refers to where an object is relative to the line depicting the horizon. Generally speaking, the closer the base of an object is to the horizon line, the farther away it appears. As is shown in Figure 7, the cat B appears to be more distant than cat A because its base is closer to the horizon line. Thus, below the horizon, objects that are higher in the picture plane appear farther away. The reverse holds for targets above the horizon. Here the bird marked X appears to be farther away than the bird marked Y since its top is closer to the horizon line with lower targets seen as more distant. Notice that above the horizon objects with their tops lower in the picture plane tend to appear to be more distant.

I. Motion Parallax

All of the pictorial cues to depth can be defined with respect to a single static image such as a photograph or a painting. Adding motion to the scene, particularly motion on the part of the observer, such as head or body movements, provides additional cues for depth perception. Of particular importance is the pattern motion of objects as you travel past them.

The cue of *motion parallax* can easily be observed when you travel in a car or bus. Suppose that you were looking out the window at the scene in Figure 8. If your vehicle were moving from right to left and you were looking at the spot marked "fixation point," all objects closer to you than the fixation point would appear to move in a direction opposite to your movement (here to the right), while objects that are farther away will appear to move in the same direction you are moving (here to the left). The speed of movement also varies with the objects' distance, such that the nearer the object is, the faster will be its motion across the retina relative to other objects, while objects closer to the fixation point would move very slowly. Very distant objects (such as the moon) would appear to exactly match your speed and direction.

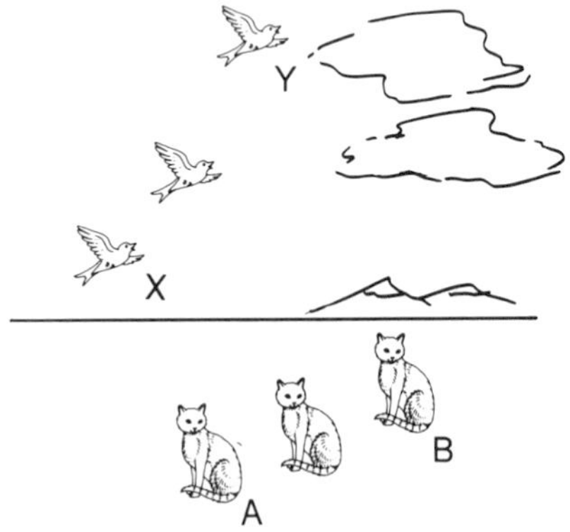

FIGURE 7 The height in the plane distance cue: Below the horizon line Cat B is seen as more distant than Cat A since it is higher in the picture plane, while above the horizon Bird X appears more distant than Bird Y because it is lower in the picture plane.

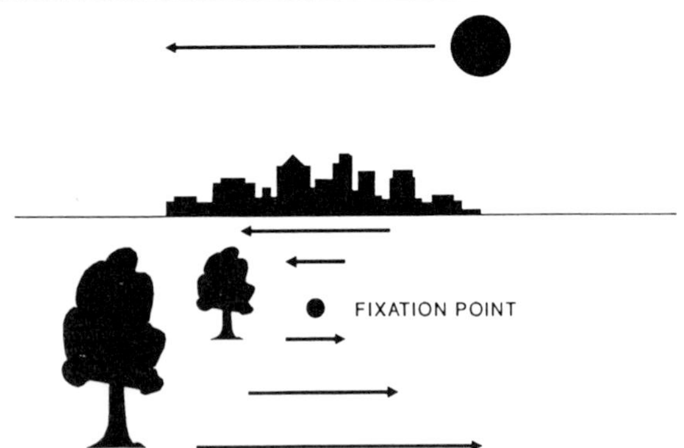

FIGURE 8 Motion parallax as a depth cue illustrated for a scene in which the observer is moving from right to left. The arrows illustrate the direction of movement of the images, while the length of the arrows illustrates the speed of movement, with longer arrows indicating faster passage across the retina.

II. PHYSIOLOGICAL DEPTH CUES

While pictorial depth cues refer to aspects of the retinal image itself, there are other cues for distance that come about because of the way the visual system responds to stimuli, in terms of its muscular responses and adjustments of the eye.

A. Accommodation

Images are focused on the eye by the crystalline lens which must change its curvature in order to keep the retinal image of objects at different distances in clear focus. This process is called *accommodation.* Relaxed accommodation, where the lens is relatively flattened, is necessary if distant objects are to be clearly focused on the retina, whereas a strongly curved lens is needed to image closer objects on the retinal surface. The feedback from the changes in the tension on the ciliary muscles, which control the lens shape, provides us with additional information about the distance of the object we are looking at.

This cue is useful only at close distances (less than 3 m) since beyond that range the lens has already reached fully relaxed accommodation and it cannot flatten out any further.

B. Convergence

The pictorial depth cues and accommodation were *monocular* cues (from the Latin *mon,* meaning "one," and *ocula,* meaning "eye") since they work quite well with only one eye. Convergence is a *binocular* cue (from *bin,* meaning "two together") since it requires both eyes working in conjunction. In order to keep the image of an object on the part of the retina that has the best visual acuity (the *fovea*) the eyes must adjust themselves to reflect the distance of the object. If an object is close to you, you must rotate your eyes inward (toward the nose) in order to focus its image on the fovea (a movement called *convergence*). When a target is farther away, the eyes must move away from each other in an outward rotation (toward the temples). Each target distance, up to about 6 m, is associated with a unique angle between the eyes called the *convergence angle*. For objects beyond about 6 m, the eyes are virtually parallel and no further convergence changes occur. Feedback from the muscular contractions needed to make the convergence eye movements seems to be useful in determining the distances of nearby objects.

III. STEREOPSIS

In many common tasks involving judgments of relative depth, such as threading a needle, inserting items into slots, or even pouring liquid into bottles, people perform up to 30% faster and more accurately when using both eyes than they do with one eye alone. The cues for binocular depth perception (*stereopsis*) in humans arise because the centers of the two eyes are horizontally separated by a distance of up to 6.5 cm. This separation causes each eye to have a different direction of view, which in turn results in a different image of the world. The difference between the images of the two eyes is referred to as *binocular disparity*. Thus, Figure 9A shows the left and right eye views if you were viewing a cube from directly in front of it. Note that the two images are different or *disparate*. *Binocular fusion* refers to the process by which we merge these disparate images into a single unified view. That the fusing

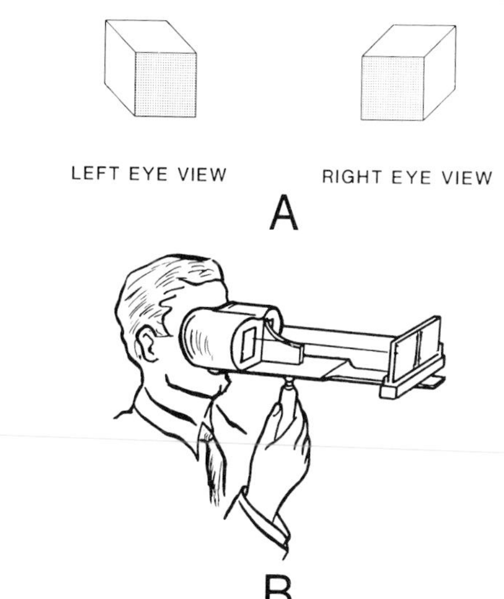

FIGURE 9 (A) An example of binocular disparity: notice how the left and right eye views of a square differ. (B) A simple lens (Brewster) stereoscope. If the views in part A are placed in the stereoscope the observer will fuse them, so that a single, three-dimensional cube is seen.

of the two disparate images results in the perception of a unified three-dimensional view was demonstrated in the 1830s by two physicists, Charles Wheatstone and Sir David Brewster, who independently invented the *stereoscope,* one version of which is seen in Figure 9B. This optical device allows each eye to separately view drawings or photographs containing the usual disparate views seen by the two eyes. The result is the strong perception of depth from the two flat pictures. Thus, if each of the two halves of Figure 9A were placed in front of their appropriate eye in a stereoscope, you would see what appears to be a solid, three-dimensional cube.

There are limits to the degree of disparity between the two monocular views that can be fused. When fusion fails it results in double vision or *diplopia*. This diplopia actually provides an additional cue for the perception of the relative distance of objects. Only the views from items at about the same distance as the target you are converged upon are fused and seen singly. A map of all the points where targets are at about the same convergence or fixation distance in visual space produces an imaginary curved plane called the *horopter*. The narrow region on either side of the horopter which includes all points in visual space that are fused into single images is called *Panum's area* (Fig. 10).

For objects outside of Panum's area we should see double images. Although we are generally not

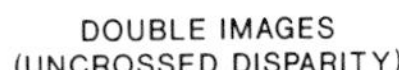

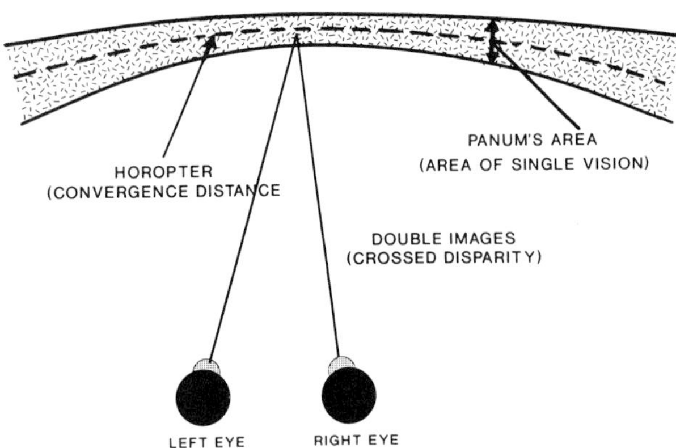

FIGURE 10 All points at the same distance that the eyes are converged upon fall on the horopter. The shaded region around the horopter is Panum's area. The disparate images of targets falling within Panum's area will fuse (seen as single) while targets nearer or farther than this region will be seen as double images.

consciously aware of the existence of these double images we can bring them into view through certain techniques. For example, align your two index fingers directly in front of your nose with one finger upright at about arms length and the other nearer, say about 6 in. from your nose. Look at the distant finger but try to pay attention to the nearer finger. Since the distant finger is at the horopter it appears to be single while the near finger appears to be double. Reverse the process by looking at the near finger and the far finger appears to be double. Depsite the fact that you are usually unaware of these double images, their exact nature provides information as to where an object is located relative to the horopter. Specifically, objects more distant than the point of fixation are seen in *uncrossed disparity* (which means that the double image from the right eye is on the right side while the double image from the left eye is on the left side) while closer objects are seen with *crossed disparity* (with the double image from the right eye on the left and vice versa). Thus, the type of double image tells you whether the object is nearer or farther than the horopter. In addition, the distance between the double images is a cue to how far from the horopter the object is (with smaller distances meaning closer to the horopter).

Our knowledge of the mechanisms that allow steropsis is still incomplete. There is evidence that cells in the primary visual areas of the cerebral cortex are finely tuned to respond to binocular disparity in the form of small horizontal differences in the placement of stimuli in the two eyes. For example, suppose there is no disparity in the images of the two eyes and a particular cell responds maximally to this condition. This particular neuron would represent a spatial position that lies on the horopter, or in the zone of fused images nearby (Panum's area) when mapped in external space. In a like manner, other neurons may be tuned to particular disparities that represent locations in space that lie in front of or behind the horopter.

Unfortunately, it is now clear that the mere existence of disparity-tuned detectors is not enough to explain stereoscopic depth perception. The problem is illustrated by Figure 11, which contains a random-dot stereoscopic display. If viewed in a stereoscope, this pair of stimuli would produce the perception of a textured square floating in front of the background of random dots. This particular perceptual organization comes about because of disparity cues built into the dot patterns. At first consideration, you might suppose that since there is disparity readily available in the random-dot stimulus pair, any neurons tuned for such information should be capable of detecting depth from these arrays. In actuality, it is not quite that simple because the stimulus is composed of identical dot elements rather than discrete and identifiable contours. If stereopsis is based on the action of disparity-tuned detectors, each of which responds to one disparity value (relative horizontal position) in the array, any dot potentially could be combined with any other dot. Each of the many possible combinations would produce a different depth perception. The task of the visual system is find the dots in one eye that correspond to the same dots in the other eye. This is called the *correspondence problem* by visual researchers who use computational, rather than physiological, approaches. To solve the correspondence problem there must be a method of eliminating or avoiding false combination and selecting

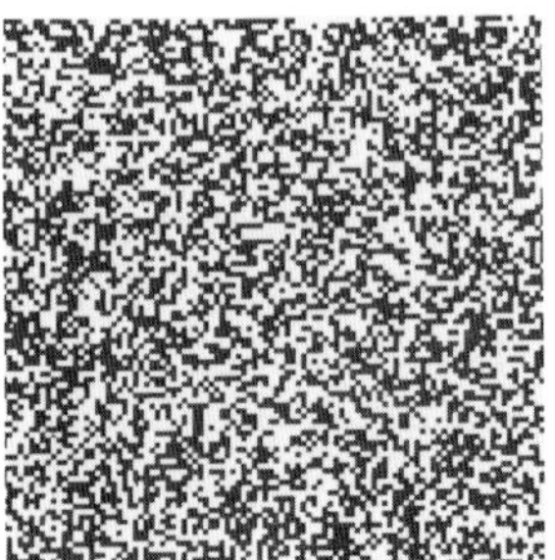

FIGURE 11 A random dot stereogram. When viewed in a stereoscope a textured square will be seen floating in space, nearer to the observer than to the textured background.

only correct disparity pairs. Thus far the best solution that has been suggested involves some pretty sophisticated computational processes. These are based upon the assumption that neurons tuned to the same disparity cooperate, while those tuned to different disparities inhibit each other. Mathematically it can be shown that with a population of detectors working together in this fashion, only one depth solution would be common to this facility–inhibitory process and only one global stereoscopic view would be seen.

Binocular disparity is most effective as a relative depth cue, which indicates whether one target is nearer or farther than another, rather than how close they are to an observer. Geometrically, however, the situation is complicated by the fact that if we keep the relative difference in depth between two targets constant, but move both targets farther away, the amount of disparity (here, the horizontal separation between the double images) grows smaller. This should lead to an underestimation of the distance between the two objects. Despite this theoretically predicted complication, our perception of the relative difference in the depth of target pairs placed at different distances from us remains quite accurate. This phenomenon is sometimes called *stereoscopic depth constancy*. It appears that the accuracy of our object-relative depth judgments is maintained because we use other depth cues (such as the pictorial or physiological cues) to give us an estimate of egocentric distance of the cluster targets, which we then use to recalibrate our interpretation of the magnitude of depth difference signalled by a particular amount of binocular disparity. This is an example of the interaction between various types of depth cues. Such interactions are quite important in improving the accuracy of depth perceptions, as we will see in the next section.

IV. EMERGENT DEPTH CUES

In the natural environment, depth cues do not occur alone. The evidence that your friend Howard is farther away from you than your friend Heather might be derived from their relative placements on a texture gradient in conjunction with their relative height in the plane and the fact that Heather is interposed in front of Howard. While the accuracy of depth perception is often augmented by the use of a combination of cues, the interaction of various types of information can produce new, or *emergent*, properties which can also serve as depth cues.

As an example, consider what happens to the image of your retina as you watch an automobile pass by a house that lies between you and the highway. One cue to the relative depths of these objects is interposition, since the automobile will be only partially visible for some period of time and perhaps entirely occluded for a brief period as it passes behind the building. Another cue is given by motion parallax, since the car will be moving at a faster speed on your retina than the house as you move your head. The combination of these two cues produces the emergent cues called *surface deletion* and *surface accretion*, where deletion refers to the fact that parts of the automobile will disappear as is moves past the house, while accretion refers to the fact that portions of the car's surface will again become visible when it passes the interposed object. This new cue is quite powerful and can even work in random dot displays (for example, either the left or right view of Fig. 11). The stimuli that are deleted or accreted over time are perceived to lie in a plane behind the dots that remain continuously visible.

Another emergent depth cue is *stereomotion*, which results from analysis of the difference in the relative rates of motion in the two eyes. Suppose that a soccer ball is flying toward you on a direct collision course with your head. Under these conditions the edge of the ball that projects onto your left eye will be moving across the retina at exactly the same rate as the edge that projects to your right eye (although in opposite directions on retina, one moving to the left and the other to the right, toward the temples). If, however, the ball is flying toward you at an angle (perhaps for a near miss), then the rate of motion will be faster in one eye than in the other. The comparison of the two rates of motion gives us the cue for the direction of flight. There actually appear to be neurons in the striate cortex of cats and monkeys that are sensitive to leftward motion in one eye at the same time that they are sensitive to rightward motion in the other eye, which would allow for the emergence of stereomotion. It seems that some neurons are even tuned sharply enough to be able to detect the difference between a near miss and a direct hit in the head. [*See* Visual Motion Perception.]

V. PERCEPTION OF DIRECTION

Up to now we have only spoken about one aspect of egocentric depth perception, namely the distance that targets are from the observer. The perception of the location of an object also involves its direction relative to our bodies. Since direction must have a reference point, we usually speak about two types of directional judgments that we combine to give us our sense of up, down, right, and left. *Bodycentric direction* uses the midline of the body (an imaginary line drawn parallel to the spine passing vertically through the naval) as a reference point. *Headcentric direction* uses the midline of the head (an imaginary vertical line running up and down, centered on the nose) as a reference location for right and left. As one might guess, complications in direction perception can arise since bodycentric and headcentric directions are potentially different, such as when you are standing in front of an object but have turned your head to the side.

Researchers have concentrated on one particular aspect of headcentric perception, namely the *visual straight ahead*. Straight ahead, is generally defined as a direction in front of us, oriented around the midline of the head. Actually the reference point is directly between the two eyes, which is often called *visual egocenter*. The use of the egocenter as a reference point is really a simplification of the situation, since it ignores the directions that the eyes themselves are pointing. Some researchers acknowledge that this is a theoretical compromise by speaking about a hypothetical *cyclopean eye* which is used for directional reference. This name is derived from the mythical Greek giant Cyclops who had a single eye in the middle of his forehead, exactly where we locate the visual egocenter.

A. Stimulus Factors

Generally speaking, the more stimuli available, the more stable our directional judgments are. This fact accounts for the observation that our ability to judge direction is much less precise in the dark. It is also the case that certain stimulus configurations can bias our judgments of direction. Thus, if a subject is presented with a square or rectangle that is somewhat to one side of the center of the visual field, there will be a tendency for him to judge the straight ahead direction in terms of the center of this displaced square or rectangle. It is as if the perceptual system confuses what is straight ahead of the observer with what is centered with respect to the other contents in the visual field.

B. Eye Movements

Earlier we noted that eye movements (specifically convergence) could provide cues to the distance of an object. Eye movements also provide information about the direction of objects. There are at least two sources of eye movement information which assist in determining the direction of an object in space. These sources are (1) copies of the movement commands sent to the eye muscles (*efferent information*) and (2) proprioceptive feedback from the eye movement itself (*afferent information*). [*See* EYE MOVEMENTS.]

Obviously, every time we move our eyes, the location of the images of targets moves across our retina, in much the same way that images would move if they had physically shifted their direction relative to our body. One important function of the efferent and afferent feedback systems is to compensate for such movements. Therefore, we continue to see the world as being stationary, and targets as maintaining a fixed position in space, even though our eyes are moving, thus causing the images to slide across our retinas. This process of compensating for eye movements is called *position constancy*, and the fact that objects seem to maintain a fixed position relative to us, despite rotations of both our head and eyes, is called *direction constancy*. We are quite accurate in our ability to distinguish shifts in position caused by target movements from those caused by our own movements.

The afferent contribution to direction constancy comes via feedback information from the six extraocular muscles that control the eye movements. This feedback information, called *proprioceptive* or *position information*, enables the observer to monitor eye position. The proprioceptive information tells the brain that the eyes have moved, and in turn this information allows the brain to interpret shifts in location of stimuli across the retina as being observer-generated rather than object-generated. Because the interpretation of movement is based upon incoming proprioceptive inputs, this is often referred to as an *inflow theory* of direction constance. In support of this theory, evidence exists that there are cells in the superior colliculus and visual cortex of the cat that monitor eye position.

The efferent contribution to direction constancy works in a different manner. When the brain initiates an eye movement, efferent (motor) signals are sent to the muscles that will move the eyes. Copies of these signals are sent back to central regions of the visual system and are used to cancel the movement information coming from the retina as the incoming images slide in the direction opposite the movement of the eyes. Since the interpretation of the origin of movement is based on information from the message sent out from the brain that initiates an eye movement, this is called an *outflow theory*. As in the case of inflow information, there seem to be some cells in the cerebellum and the cortex of monkeys that contain information about eye position. Since these cells respond before the actual movement takes place, they could represent the source of outflow information registering the *intention to move*, rather than the movements themselves.

To see how outflow information might compensate for eye movements, try this little experiment suggested by Helmholtz. Cover one eye. Now gently tap or push the side of your other (uncovered) eye toward your nose very gently with your fingertip. This rotates the eye in a movement similar to one that could be initiated by the brain. However, in this case the brain has not sent a signal to move the eye. When the eye is rotated in this passive fashion, the objects in the visual field will be seen to shift their location in the direction opposite to the movements of the eye. Thus, the stability of visual direction holds only for eye movements initiated by signals from the brain, and cannot compensate for other forces that might shift the direction of the eye.

C. Eye Dominance

In the previous discussion we considered eye movements of the right and left eye to be interchangeable. This is not fully true, since there are data which suggest that one eye may be more important than the other in determining visual direction. There are a number of tasks that we habitually do with one eye. In sighting tasks where only one eye can be used at a time (such as in looking through a telescope) 70% of all observers consistently use their right eye, while the remainder consistently use their left. The preferred eye for such tasks is usually called the *dominant eye*. You can determine which is your dominant eye by standing about 3 m in front of a wall, picking a spot on it, and then rapidly pointing to it while keeping both eyes open. Once you have reached your final pointing position, alternately close each eye. You will find that the point on the wall will shift out of alignment with your finger for one eye, and will still be aligned for the other. The eye which is open when the finger and spot are best aligned is your dominant eye. For the purposes of our discussion of the perception of direction, sighting dominance is important because the visual direction associated with straight ahead is more strongly influenced by the dominant eye, and judgments of straight ahead are biased toward the side of the dominant eye.

VI. DEVELOPMENT OF DEPTH PERCEPTION

Various theories of perception tend to diverge on the issue of whether there is a learned component in the perception of depth. In the older literature this has been referred to as the "nativist versus empiricist" question. The nativists argue that these perceptual abilities and our capacity to use them are inborn and automatically invoked by stimulation, whereas the empiricists maintain that interaction with the world, through which we learn about its properties and organization, is crucial to our spatial awareness and abilities.

One of the most common ways to assess whether there is a learned component in depth perception is to observe the behavior of young animals or humans when they are placed in situations that call on their abilities to perceive distance or direction. Since infants and young animals have limited experience with the world, empiricist theories predict poor depth perception relative to adult performance levels.

In certain simpler animals, there is strong evidence that the perception of direction and distance is genetically determined (consistent with a nativist theory). Thus, in salamanders it is possible to invert visual direction by actually rotating the eye 180°. When this is done, animals consistently swim and snap in the opposite direction of the stimulus when presented with a food lure. The same results occur even if these eye rotations are performed during the animals' embryonic stage which suggests that the ability to determine visual direction is "prewired" to the location of retinal stimulation in this species.

In higher animals, investigators frequently use controlled-rearing procedures, such as rearing an animal in total darkness from birth until testing, to determine if there is a learned component to depth perception. Dark-rearing eliminates all externally generated visual experience. If experience with various visual depth cues is necessary for the development of normal depth perception, these dark-reared animals should have noticeable deficits when required to judge depth or distance. If depth perception simply matures as the animal ages, this restriction of the animal's visual experience should not affect its behavior, and the only important variable should be its chronological age.

The *visual cliff* is a simple apparatus used for measuring depth perception in young animals and it is diagrammed in Figure 12. It is made up of two sections, divided by a "start platform." Each section provides a different depth impression. The "shallow" side is a piece of glass that lies directly over a patterned surface. The "deep" side has the same type of patterned surface, but looks like a sharp drop since the surface is placed at some distance below the glass. In a test trial, a young animal is placed on the starting platform that separates the apparently shallow and deep surfaces. It is assumed that from this position the subject can see that the shallow side is near, hence safe, whereas the deep side, with its simulated cliff-like drop-off, would be perceived as being dangerous. Researchers operate under the presumption that if an animal consistently chooses the shallow rather than the deep side, then it can perceive the difference in apparent depth and is attempting to avoid a fall.

The visual cliff apparatus has been used primarily to generate data concerning the development of depth perception. A combination of controlled rearing followed by observations of behavior on the visual cliff has been the experimental technique most commonly used in animal studies. In general, the findings have suggested that experience and innate factors interact to produce an animal's ability to perceive depth. For example, when cats or rats are initially reared in the dark they show little depth discrimination on the visual cliff when first tested. However, as they receive more and more experience in a lighted world their depth discrimination rapidly improves until they are indistinguishable from normally reared animals. When the visual experience

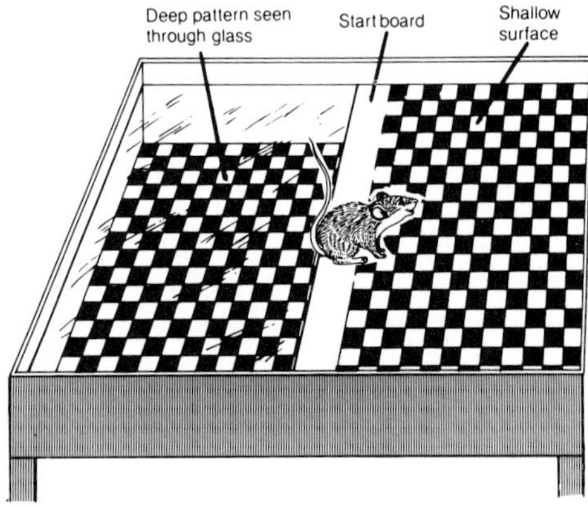

FIGURE 12 A rat crossing to the shallow side of the visual cliff. A piece of glass prevents the animal from falling should he cross to the apparently deep side.

takes place also seems important. There seem to be *sensitive periods* in an animal's development, referring to the fact that there are particular ages and particular durations of time when depriving an animal of a particular type of visual experience may produce the largest perceptual deficits.

An interesting finding is that the developmental time course and the effects of experience (or deprivation of appropriate experience) seem to be different for different classes of depth cues. Binocular depth perception develops quite early, since evidence for the use of binocular disparity for a depth cue may be found in 3- or 4-month-old infants. The use of cues for binocular depth perception differs from the use of monocular, pictorial depth cues in a number of ways. For instance, in rats it has been shown that dark-rearing decreases the accuracy of depth perception when animals are tested monocularly, but has little effect on binocular depth ability.

Sensitivity to other depth cues develops at different rates. Thus, the use of the emergent stereomotion cue seems to develop quite early, and has been measured at ages as young as 2 to 3 weeks. Even at this young age, infants will blink their eyes when presented with an object that seems to be moving closer and seems to be growing close enough to hit them in the head.

The slowest development seems to be for pictorial depth cues, suggesting that experience may play a large role in establishing these cues to distance. Several studies have shown that it takes until 6 or 7 months of age for infants to respond to linear perspective information, familiar size, and texture gradients. Use of more complex cues, such as the perception of relative depth in a picture, based on the direction of shadows cast in the pictorial representation, may not appear until the age of 3 years.

A balanced appraisal of the developmental evidence available indicates that the perception of depth and distance probably is a combination of inborn factors and active experience. These studies suggest that adhering strictly to either a nativist or empiricist viewpoint is too limiting. Innate components of perception must mature and certain types of experience can help or hinder the achievement of a high level of perceptual functioning. In much the same way, some aspects of depth perception are innate and others require memory and experience to properly function. In any event, this cue-driven process, by which the flat image on the retinas is interpreted (usually quite accurately) as a three-dimensional representation of the outside world, remains one of the most valuable and complex aspects of everyday perception. [*See* Perceptual Development.]

Bibliography

Coren, S., Ward, L. M., and Enns, J. T. (1994). "Sensation and Perception," 4th ed. Harcourt Brace, Fort Worth, TX.

Goldstein, E. B. (1989). "Sensation and Perception," 3rd ed. Wadsworth, Belmont, CA.

Hochberg, J. (1988). Visual perception. In "Steven's Handbook of Experimental Psychology" (R. C. Atkinson, R. J. Hernstein, G. Lindzey, and R. D. Luce, Eds.), Vol. 1. Wiley-Interscience, New York.

Matlin, M. W. (1988). "Sensation and Perception," 2nd ed. Allyn and Bacon, Boston.

Schiffman, H. R. (1990). "Sensation and Perception, An Integrated Approach," 3rd ed. Wiley, New York.

DISGUST

Graham C. L. Davey
The City University, London

Glossary

Contamination Contact between a previously acceptable substance and a disgust substance which causes rejection of the previously acceptable substance.

Contempt Expression of scorn or distain accompanied by feelings of superiority.

Disgust A type of rejection response characterized by a specific facial expression, a desire to distance oneself from the object of disgust, a physiological manifestation of mild nausea, a fear of oral incorporation of the object of disgust, and a feeling of "revulsion."

Distaste An oral rejection response triggered primarily by sensory or taste factors.

DISGUST is a basic emotion that appears to develop from the newborn's innate reaction to distasteful substances. When it is fully developed, the disgust reaction comprises a distinctive facial expression and distinctive cognitive, behavioral, and physiological manifestations. Disgust appears to be a universal emotion that possesses both biological and cultural functions. However, under a few extreme circumstances it can be viewed as a contributing factor in a number of psychological disorders.

I. THE EXPRESSION AND FEELING OF DISGUST

Disgust has been recognized as a basic emotion for over a century, and like other emotions it has a distinctive facial expression, distinctive behavioral and physiological manifestations, and a particular subjective experience. The facial reaction specific to disgust in adults is very similar to the facial reactions of newborn infants to bitter or sour tastes, but as we will see later, the adult disgust reaction can be elicited by a much broader range of stimuli than tastes alone.

Figure 1 illustrates the typical facial expression of disgust. The most central features of this response are the wrinkling of the nose and the gaping mouth. The wrinkled nose acts to block olfactory stimulation and to cut off any odor input from the offending stimulus. The gaping mouth is typified by the upper lip being pulled up, the lower lip is pulled down and the tongue is pushed out and up toward the roof of the mouth. This gaping reaction acts to prevent oral incorporation and allows the contents of the mouth to drain out. The typical facial response is often accompanied by a gutteral sound reminiscent of rejection of food from the throat (characterized as the word "yuk" that is often learned at an early stage as a social signal for disgust). These facial expressions appear to develop from innate reactions to unpalatable tastes that are found in newborn children. For example, babies less than 2 hours old and with no previous taste experience react facially to bitter and sour tastes by gaping and nose wrinkling. This suggests that the basic facial expression to distasteful substances may be innate, but may form the basis of the facial disgust reaction to a broader range of stimuli in adulthood. [*See* FACIAL EXPRESSIONS OF EMOTION.]

The subjective experience of disgust can be distinguished by a combination of physiological and behavioral reactions to the eliciting stimulus. The most prominent physiological reaction is a feeling of nausea or sickness. Most often the feelings of nausea are mild, and avoidance of the disgusting object may occur before nausea has become a significant symptom. However, in circumstances where contact with a particularly disgusting object is sustained, this can

Encyclopedia of Human Behavior, Volume 2
Copyright © 1994 by Academic Press, Inc. All rights of reproduction in any form reserved.

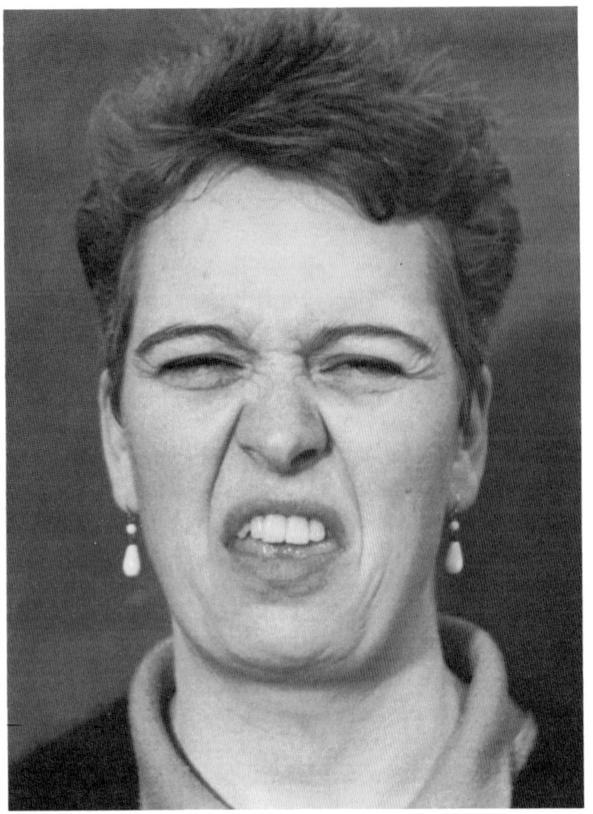

FIGURE 1 The typical facial expression of disgust.

easily lead to physical vomiting. The most prominent behavioral reaction to disgusting stimuli is avoidance (a desire to distance oneself from the offensive object), and it is this avoidance component of the response that can frequently lead to disgust being confused with anxiety or fear. Taken together, the components of nausea and physical avoidance make up the distinctive subjective feeling associated with disgust which is often verbalized as "revulsion."

Some theorists (e.g., Rozin and Fallon) have also argued that as the disgust reaction develops it acquires specifically cognitive components such as a fear of contamination from disgusting stimuli. For example, people come to recognize that many disgusting objects may be physiologically dangerous if orally incorporated (i.e., may cause disease or illness), and this leads to a belief that even nondisgust objects that have come into contact with disgusting objects will then be contaminated with the properties possessed by the disgusting object (e.g., people will often refuse to eat from a bowl that has been in contact with a fly—even if the bowl has been properly washed and sterilized following the contact).

Disgust is known as one of the three emotions in the hostility triad (the others being anger and contempt), and disgust is often closely related to feelings of contempt. However, disgust is usually accompanied by significantly greater physiological arousal than contempt and is seen by some theorists as a reaction that is restricted to the prevention of oral incorporation of disgusting objects. In contrast, contempt is a much more subtle emotion and is most frequently used to demean other human beings. Indeed, the facial expression for contempt is rather different from that of disgust (tilting the head upwards, lifting the brow and corners of the upper lip, and tightening the corners of the mouth), and this suggests that its evolutionary origins and biological function may be quite different to those of the disgust reaction.

II. THE NATURE OF DISGUSTING OBJECTS

In the newborn child, the stimuli that elicit facial expressions similar to disgust are unpalatable tastes such as bitter and sour. However, by the time a child is 2–3 years of age, the range of stimuli that can elicit this facial expression has expanded considerably, and often continues to expand into adulthood.

Rozin and Fallon distinguish between "distaste" (the newborn's reaction to unpalatable tastes) and "disgust." They argue that disgust is a broader-based reaction that develops from neonatal distaste and functions as a global food-rejection response. Hence, disgusting objects are all ones which, for one reason or another, we have good reason for not wanting to orally consume. Most commonly, disgusting objects thus tend to be animals, parts of animals or animal products (such as mucus or feces), stimuli that have been in contact with animals, or stimuli that resemble animals. It is the case that disgust is sometimes used to describe some vegetable items, but most often these are simply bad-tasting rather than items which elicit the full spectrum of the disgust reaction.

The most potent primary disgust substance is arguably feces. This is usually the first disgust item to develop (at around 2–2½ years of age), and is as close as one can get to a universal disgust object. Its potency as a disgust object is reflected in its use in many languages as a debasing and irreverent term.

The fact that animals and their products tend to make up the vast majority of disgusting objects is consistent with the fact that the prohibiting of eating animals tends to be the rule rather than the exception in many cultures, and even in Western cultures the vast majority of animals are disgusting when considered as food (e.g., all insects and most invertebrates, reptiles and amphibians, animals close to humans in appearance, pets, etc.).

So why should animals and their products become the primary focus of the human disgust response? There are a number of possible theories. First, it may be that humans wish to accentuate the human–animal boundary that they see as distinguishing them from the rest of the animal kingdom. In an attempt to maintain this distinction, humans may tend to disguise or reject the internal incorporation of products from the rest of the animal kingdom. That animal meat is frequently presented for consumption in a form which disguises its original form and nature is consistent with this view. Second, the human–animal distinction outlined in the first view suggests that some form of psychological distance from the self may be a critical factor. It is clear that the body products of individuals close to the self, such as sexual partners and offspring, tend to be treated with less disgust than the body products of others (e.g., strangers), and also that there is a tendency to be more disgusted by animals that are disparate from the human form (e.g., creepy-crawly insects, invertebrates) than those that closely resemble the human form (e.g., apes and monkeys). The disgust response may therefore have evolved as a generalized defensive reaction to psychological and physical configurations that are disparate from the self. Third, it may be that animals and animal products are a focus for the disgust response because they represent potent disease vectors. That is, in the course of human history animals have frequently acted as agents for the spread of disease among humans (e.g., the role of the black rat in the spread of the Great Plagues of Europe), or have become associated with the spoiling or putrifaction of human food (e.g., cockroaches, maggots, mice, rats, etc.). It may therefore be quite appropriate that disgust as a food-rejection response should become associated with a wide range of nonhuman animals in this way.

Finally, while disgust can be most frequently characterized as a food-rejection response, there are some objects of disgust which are not so easily interpretable in these terms. For example, psychoanalysts have reported many cases where different forms of sexual activity have become the focus of disgust (e.g., oral–genital and genital–anal intercourse), and some individuals often report that their own self can become a source of disgust (e.g., their body shape or their own eating habits). So, while it is clear that the disgust response develops from the innate reaction to things that simply taste bad, psychologists are still in the process of determining how this primitive response becomes associated with a range of stimuli that cannot obviously be classifed as items that are being "orally rejected."

III. CULTURAL DIFFERENCES IN DISGUST

What is significant about the disgust reaction is its relative universality across a range of very different cultures. For example, experimental studies have shown that subjects from a variety of literate cultures associate the same facial expression of disgust (see Fig. 1) with the equivalent emotion word in their own language. Using experimental techniques that do not require verbal labeling of emotions, similar results have also been obtained with isolated, preliterate subjects (e.g., with the Fore language group from New Guinea). In terms of cultural differences in the understanding of the facial expression of disgust, there is some evidence that Japanese subjects differ from Western subjects in terms of the facial characteristics that they assign to the emotion of disgust. However, this finding is very much the exception rather than the rule, and may result from the Japanese translation of the word disgust conveying a somewhat different meaning in Japanese than in English.

While disgust is a characteristically identifiable emotion across most cultures, there are one or two cultures in which it differs from standard Western connotations. In some cultures disgust is not distinguished from other related emotions. For example, Samoans use only one word for hate and disgust. In other cultures, disgust is more finely differentiated into clear subcategories. For instance, the Ifalukians of Micronesia have words which distinguish between disgust feelings associated with decaying matter and disgust feelings associated with moral indignation. The only known languages which do not have a word that corresponds closely to the English connotation of disgust are Polish and Chewong.

Nevertheless, the fact that most cultures possess a term that translates into the English equivalent of disgust, and that the same facial expressions of disgust are recognized across a wide variety of literate and preliterate societies, suggests that disgust is a universally discriminable emotion.

There is also some evidence that the objects that are the primary focus of disgust tend to be similar across different cultures. Rozin and Fallon have argued that pan-cultural disgusting objects include body waste products, decayed animal matter, carnivorous animals, scavengers, and animals close to humans in appearance (e.g., primates) or social-emotional relations (e.g., pets). Even so there are some cultural variations. For example, Eskimos often happily consume the feces of grazing mammals in the course of consuming their unemptied guts, and many cultures differ in the range of animals that their cultural traditions will allow them to eat—those that are prohibited are then viewed as disgusting (e.g., some Asian cultures permit the eating of dog meat; in Western societies this would be viewed as quite disgusting).

There is also evidence that disgust is a feature of many common animal fears and that these fears may differ across cultures. For example, spiders are a common fear-relevant animal in Western cultures, and fear of spiders is known to be associated with the disgust response. However, in many non-Western societies, spiders do not appear to be the disgust-relevant stimulus they are in the West. In many areas of Africa the spider is revered as a wise creature and its dwelling places are cleaned and protected by the local people; in areas of Indo-China, the Caribbean, Africa, North America, and Australia, spiders are frequently eaten as a delicacy; Indian children in Brazil keep them as pets; and many cultures consider spiders to be symbols of good fortune.

In conclusion, while disgust appears to be a universal emotion with a cross-culturally recognizable facial expression, there appears to be somewhat greater cross-cultural diversity in the nature of disgusting objects. This latter finding is perhaps not so surprising given that disgust can become associated with stimuli as a result of a number of putative developmental and learning processes, and these processes will be discussed in detail in the next section.

IV. DEVELOPMENT OF THE DISGUST RESPONSE

There is no doubt that newborn infants that have never experienced tastes before do exhibit a specific facial expression to unpalatable tastes such as sour and bitter, and this has been taken as evidence for an innate "distaste" reaction. Indeed, the distaste reaction can even be found in newborns whose cerebral hemispheres have been rendered dysfunctional because of disease or congential birth defects. This suggests that the newborn's distaste reaction is one that is fairly old in evolutionary terms, is probably mediated by primitive areas of the brain, and is independent of learning and memory.

However, some theorists (such as Rozin and Fallon) have attempted to distinguish between the neonate's distaste reaction and disgust. While disgust may have developed from the innate distaste reaction (especially since they both share similar facial expressions), the adult disgust reaction is more diverse in terms of its psychological and physiological components (e.g., it is accompanied by mild nausea, physical avoidance, and cognitive features such as fear of contamination), and is elicited by a wide range of objects and situations other than a few basic tastes.

This raises the question of how the full-blown adult disgust reaction develops. It is clear that children under the age of 2 years are quite tolerant of a range of stimuli that adults would call disgusting. They do not appear to reject odors characteristic of decaying materials, and are willing to put a variety of objects that adults would call disgusting into their mouths (e.g., imitation dog feces, slugs, cockroaches, etc.). However, the incidence of rejection of adult disgust substances rises substantially after 2 years of age, and by 7–9 years of age children have acquired the concept of contamination whereby a previously nondisgusting object is rendered disgusting through contact with a primary disgusting object (e.g., a glass of orange juice becomes undesirable because a fly has landed in it).

There are a number of possible processes by which children may develop a schema of disgust. The fact that studies have demonstrated a high correlation between parents and offspring in disgust sensitivity levels (i.e., parents and offspring show disgust responses of similar strength in response to hypothetical contamination scenarios) suggests that parent–offspring transmission processes might be important in this respect. First, it may be that a disgust facial expression in a parent may give rise to an empathic disgust expression in the child, and the child may then come to associate their imitative facial expression with the source of the parent's disgust. Second, it is possible that both verbal and nonverbal expressions may communicate disgust from parents to offspring. Through this kind of social referencing, offspring may become able to identify specific primary disgust objects (e.g., feces, decaying material). Third, from interactional experiences with their parents offspring may learn that certain properties are common to the majority of stimuli to which their parents exhibit disgust (e.g., decayed material, mucosity, feces-like, etc.), so that they evolve a schema of disgust which is transferable to other stimuli that display these properties (e.g., "I'm not touching that snail—it looks slimy").

The disgust schema appears to develop around a small number of primary disgust characteristics such as mucosity, decaying material, bad odors, feces-like features, etc., and these primary disgust characteristics appear to be common to the disgust schemas found in most people from most cultures. However, there are some basic learning processes which can generate secondary disgusts which are specific to individuals. Rozin and Fallon identify Pavlovian conditioning as a possible important process in the development of secondary disgusts. This is where a spatially and/or temporally contingent association occurs between a conditioned stimulus (e.g., a neutral substance or object) and an unconditioned stimulus (a disgust substance or object). For example, when a cockroach falls into a glass of orange juice, there is a simultaneous spatio-temporal pairing of the juice (conditioned stimulus) with cockroach (unconditioned stimulus). Subsequent tests demonstrate that subjects that have undergone this experience show a significant drop in readiness to drink even freshly poured orange juice which is presented in a new, clean glass. The Pavlovian associative process appears to have transferred the affective value of the unconditioned stimulus (cockroach) to the paired conditioned stimulus (orange juice), and this associative process may be one that underlies most, if not all, secondary disgusts. [*See* CLASSICAL CONDITIONING.]

V. THE FUNCTION OF DISGUST

Because disgust is such a universal emotion it is worth discussing its function—both in evolutionary terms ("why did the disgust reaction evolve?") and in terms of its contemporary cultural role ("what is the social significance of the disgust reaction?").

Since the newborn's distaste reaction appears to be unlearned and mediated subcortically, it probably evolved very early on in the evolution of human beings. The distinguishing features of the distaste reaction are ones which block swallowing and allow liquid to drain from the mouth. Furthermore, these features occur most strongly in response to bitter solutions, and bitter substances encountered in nature may be highly poisonous. Hence, the neonate's distaste reaction would appear to be highly adaptive in facilitating the rejection of potentially poisonous substances.

However, the more complex adult disgust reaction may serve a broader range of functions other than simply facilitating the oral rejection of potential poisons.

The fact that disgust is characterized by the rejection of distasteful and potentially dangerous substances has led Carroll Izard to suggest that disgust may have evolved to help animals maintain a nesting environment which was sufficiently sanitary to promote the health of the animal and its offspring. Disgust would also have prevented animals from eating spoiled food and drinking polluted water, and to have helped them to maintain body hygiene. All of these functions would have contributed to the prevention of the ingestion of items responsible for illness, and to have prevented the transmission of disease either intraspecifically or interspecifically.

However, Paul Rozin has argued that the disgust reaction has developed more recently as a powerful way of transmitting cultural values. In effect, the disgust reaction is a way of endowing certain substances with potent negative affect which can be communicated effectively to both offspring and others within the community. This process also functions to ensure that individuals do not consume or come into close contact with substances that might facilitate illness and disease, but the actual disgust reaction serves a communicative rather than a simple oral rejection function.

Nevertheless, all of the putative theories of the distaste and disgust reactions imply that the underlying function of these responses is to prevent the ingestion of substances that may cause illness (e.g., poisons) and to facilitate the avoidance of substances that may transmit disease (e.g., animal feces, body products such as mucus, putrefying foodstuffs, etc.). The contemporary disgust response appears to have developed in such a way as to contribute to this underlying function via a variety of behavioral and cultural processes.

VI. DISGUST AND PSYCHOLOGICAL DISORDERS

Disgust is a particularly powerful emotion, and as a result it can become a factor which underlies a number of psychological disorders.

There are at least two ways in which the disgust reaction may become inappropriate and maladaptive. First, as we have noted in the previous section, secondary disgusts can be generated in circumstances where a stimulus or situation which is normally not a focus of disgust becomes associated with either the disgust reaction or a primary disgust object (perhaps through processes of Pavlovian conditioning). It can frequently be the case, therefore, that disgust will become associated with an inappropriate object or situation, and that this may generate problems in living and seriously affect mental health. For example, for some individuals, disgust may become associated with eating or even with body shape, and as a result it may play a part in eating disorders such as bulimia or anorexia. In such disorders, eating binges—and even just eating—may evoke strong feelings of disgust which lead to subsequent feelings of self-contempt, guilt, and depression.

Second, some individuals may develop a particularly potent disgust reaction which makes them extremely sensitive to potentially disgusting objects. This reaction may become so strong that they have an overwhelming urge to get away from disgusting stimuli, they have a constant fear of contamination, and in many cases they take extreme precautions to ensure that they remain uncontaminated (e.g., by indulging in excessive cleaning or washing rituals). This is known clinically as a form of obsessive–compulsive disorder which is characterized by continual fear of contamination from a wide range of possible sources. For example, an individual with an excessive sensitivity to contamination may show distressingly high levels of anxiety at the possible presence of a single "contaminating" dog hair in the room.

Disgust also appears to play a part in many common animal fears. For instance, there are a number of animals within Western cultures that have acquired a fear-relevant status, yet these animals do not appear to be predatory (in the sense that they may attack and physically harm human beings), nor are they generally venomous. Such fear-relevant animals include spiders, rats, nonvenomous snakes, mice, slugs, snails, lizards, cockroaches, maggots, etc. Matchett and Davey suggested that fear to these fear-relevant animals was in fact mediated by disgust rather than fear of being harmed through physical attack. Consistent with this hypothesis was the finding that self-reported fear of such fear-relevant animals was directly related to individual disgust sensitivity levels—the higher an individual's sensitivity to disgust, the higher their level of fear to fear-relevant animals. In contrast, self-reported fear of predatory animals (such as lions, tigers, snakes, alligators) was entirely unrelated to disgust sensitivity. Graham Davey has hypothesized that fear-relevant animals may have acquired their disgust-evoking status in a number of ways: (i) because they may have acted as agents for the spread of human diseases (e.g., rats), (ii) because they have become spatially or temporally associated with disgusting objects (e.g., the association between maggots and putrefied meat; and between cockroaches, mice, and the spoiling of food stores, etc.), and (iii) because at least some features of the animal may resemble primary disgust stimuli (e.g., some fear-relevant animals are perceived as being mucous or slimy, such as snakes, lizards, worms; or resemble feces, such as slugs). Subsequent studies have indicated that experimentally raising the disgust sensitivity levels of subjects (by showing them a brief video containing revulsive images) also increases their self-rated fear of fear-relevant animals (but this manipulation does not increase fear to predatory animals). This suggests that disgust sensitivity plays a causal role in determining many common animals fears, and, indeed, there is evidence that heightened disgust sensitivity also underlies severe spider fear in clinically referred spider phobics. [*See* PHOBIAS.]

It can be seen from this section that psychologists have only just begun to investigate the way in which the disgust emotion might underlie a variety of psychological disorders. However, as we come to understand the processes that underlie the development of the disgust reaction we may be able to identify its involvement in psychopathology more clearly, and to develop appropriate therapeutic techniques for the relevant disorders.

Bibliography

Angyal, A. (1941). Disgust and related aversions. *J. Abnorm. Soc. Psychol.* **36,** 393–412.

Ekman, P., and Friesen, W. V. (1986). A new pan-cultural facial expression of emotion. *Motiv. Emot.* **10,** 159–168.

Izard, C. E. (1977). "Human Emotion." Plenum, New York.

Matchett, G., and Davey, G. C. L. (1991). A test of a Disease-avoidance model of animal phobias. *Behav. Res. Ther.* **29,** 91–94.

Rosenstein, D., and Oster, H. (1988). Differential facial responses to four basic tastes in newborns. *Child Dev.* **59,** 1555–1568.

Rozin, P., and Fallon, A. E. (1987). A perspective on disgust. *Psychol. Rev.* **94,** 23–41.

Steiner, J. E. (1973). The human gustofacial response. In "Fourth Symposium on Oral Sensation and Perception" (J. F. Bosma, Ed.). U.S. Department of Health, Education, and Welfare, Rockville, MD.

Dissociative Disorders

Etay Shilony
Harvard University

Michael Z. Fleming
Boston University

Glossary

Amnesia Loss of memory or inability to recall either partial or total personal past.

Defense mechanism Any unconscious or subconscious behavior or thinking pattern aimed at reducing anxiety, shame, or guilt.

Dissociation A psychological process in which the psychological parameters that make up experience become fragmented or lack integration.

Personality A combination of traits that can be observed and described as being the unique qualities of a particular individual.

Psychogenic Pertains to behaviors or disorders with no known organic basis (i.e., a functional disorder) and is therefore likely to result from conflict or stress.

Trauma An event that is outside the range of usual human experiences and would be distressing to most people (e.g., war, rape).

DISSOCIATION can be defined as a psychological process in which certain thought processes are split off from conscious awareness or are significantly altered. For over a century, researchers, as well as the popular media, have been fascinated with these processes. Particular interest has been given to the extreme form of dissociation, multiple personality disorder. Lately, research on dissociation has focused on its relationship to trauma, particularly examining dissociation as a defense mechanism activated during and following traumatic experiences.

I. HISTORY OF DISSOCIATIVE DISORDERS

Prior to the 18th century, changes in memory, perception of reality, and personality, the core phenomena associated with dissociative disorders, were seen as resulting from demonic possession. It was only during the middle of the 18th century that the first attempts to differentiate between real and imagined possessions took place. The 18th century marked a shift from religious to secular exorcists, and, by the mid-1800s, hypnotism was established as the method of treatment for patients who were experiencing these phenomena. The clinical literature of the last decades of the 19th century elaborated about patients who presented with disturbances in memory and changes of personality. Almost every significant observer of personality and behavior of that time became interested in such phenomena, which they viewed as being part of the hysterical syndrome. One of the most important of these was Jean Paul Charcot. Charcot, who taught at the elite French Academy Ecole Normale Superieure, was the one who established hypnosis as a legitimate area for scientific investigation. His inquiries involved the use of hypnosis to treat hysteria. He professed that in hysteria, consciousness can be disrupted and shattered into different elements. Pierre Janet, a student of Charcot, is considered to be the first clinician to specifically address the phenomena, which he labeled as dissociation.

Janet's studies with patients suffering from amnesias and fugues led him to believe that, while thoughts and memories are normally coherent, integrated, and available to conscious awareness, they can sometimes be split off or altered. In this abnormal state, the individual can engage in behaviors for which he or she has no explanation or memory. Though outside of conscious awareness, these separated thought processes continue to have power and can affect the actions and emotions of that person. Janet's and Charcot's interest in split-off parts of the self was mirrored in the periods' popular literature,

Copyright © 1994 by Academic Press, Inc. All rights of reproduction in any form reserved.

particularly in John Stevenson's depiction of multiple selves in *Dr. Jekyll and Mr. Hyde*, published in 1886.

It was not only in Europe that there was such a strong fascination with "multiple selves." In the United States as well, clinicians such as Morton Prince, a contemporary of Janet, were writing on the subject. Prince emphasized the simultaneous activity of two or more personalities in one individual as the cornerstone of the dissociative process. Prince is best known for his reports on a multiple personality patient, "Miss Beauchamp," which he published in 1906. William James was another American researcher who was influenced by Janet's work and argued for the existence of a "second self," which he labeled the "subliminal self." While Janet's American contemporaries focused on describing dissociative phenomena, Janet, and later Sigmund Freud, made an effort to explain its etiology. Freud introduced the concept that the psyche actively transfers mental contents from conscious awareness into the unconscious by way of repression. According to Freud, amnesia and other dissociative phenomena were a result of this active process, which protects the individual from emotional pain subsequent to external circumstances, or from internal anxiety-provoking affects and drives. Freud, however, was more interested in the somatic symptoms that followed repression than in amnesia. He focused his interest on the concept of conversion, which he used to explain the occurrence of hysterical symptoms. [*See* AMNESIA.]

During the early decades of the 20th century, dissociation lost its place as a separate area of interest and research, and dissociation was classified under the category of the hysterical syndrome. However, the first edition of the American Psychiatric Association's *Diagnostic and Statistical Manual of Mental Disorders* (DSM-I), published in 1952, created a separate category for memory disturbances (but still under the larger category of hysteria). The second edition of the manual (DSM-II), published in 1968, maintained the distinction between conversion and dissociation and divided the category of hysteria into two types: conversion and dissociative. In the third edition (DSM-III), published in 1980, and later in the 1987 revision (DSM-III-R) dissociative disorders were no longer under the category of hysteria, but appeared as an independent diagnostic category.

Creating a separate diagnostic category for dissociative disorders in the DSM-III marked the renewal of interest in these phenomena. Today, dissociative disorders, particularly multiple personality disorder (MPD), are being increasingly diagnosed. The increased interest in the psychological effects of traumatic experiences, particularly childhood sexual abuse, also contributes to the interest in dissociation. Hypnosis has received renewed attention as a method of investigation and treatment of dissociative pathology. [*See* HYPNOSIS.]

II. TYPES OF DISSOCIATIVE DISORDERS

The DSM-III and later the DSM-III-R established four distinct dissociative disorders: (1) multiple personality disorder; (2) psychogenic fugue; (3) psychogenic amnesia; and (4) depersonalization disorder. A fifth diagnosis covers atypical dissociative reactions under the category of dissociative disorders not otherwise specified. This category includes phenomena such as derealization, trance states, and more.

A. Multiple Personality Disorder

Multiple personality (see Table I) is a dissociative reaction in which an individual manifests two or more distinct personalities or personality states. Each personality has fully developed emotional and thought process patterns that are unique and relatively stable. In some cases, the different personalities have shared memories, common behaviors, and social relationships. Usually, the personalities are dramatically different: One may be sexually overt and seductive, while the other would be restricted and puritan. In adults, the number of personalities reported varies tremendously. Approximately 50% of cases reported have had fewer than 10 personalities, while the other 50% report more than 10, at times up to 100.

TABLE I
Diagnostic Criteria for Multiple Personality Disorder

A. The existence within the person of two or more distinct personalities or personality states (each with its own relatively enduring pattern of perceiving, relating to, and thinking about the environment and self).

B. At least two of these personalities or personality states recurrently take full control of the person's behavior.

Source: "Diagnostic and Statistical Manual of Mental Disorders," third ed., revised. Copyright American Psychiatric Association, Washington, DC, 1987. Used with permission.

The person might change from one personality to another at periods varying from minutes to several years. The transition from one personality to another usually lasts a few seconds or minutes but in rare cases extends to hours or days. The transition is often precipitated by a stressful event or an environmental cue relevant to the individual. At times, the first appearance of an alter personality can be spontaneous, as evidenced in the case of Eve White, who was studied by Thigpen and Cleckley between 1953 and 1957.

Often, personalities are aware of some or all the other personalities to various degrees. One personality might refer to other personalities as friends, companions, or adversaries. Needs, urges, fears, or behaviors can be displayed amongst the different personalities and be expressed to the external environment by one of the personalities with or without the awareness of others.

Most of the personalities are aware of lost or distorted periods of time that cannot be explained. Frequently, one personality will discover activities performed by another personality, such as written notes, purchased clothes, etc. Often, these individuals rationalize stories to cover up for missing periods of time or unexplained activities.

The interest in multiple personality flourished between the end of the 19th century and the beginning of the 20th, particularly in France and in the United States. Eugene Azam studied a patient by the name of Felida X for 35 years. He published the case of this woman, who had a second personality, in 1887 with a preface by Charcot. Janet also reported on several cases, one of which involved an adult women with a child personality. The most famous case of that period, and probably the most detailed in its description, was done by Morton Prince in 1904 on his patient Christine Beauchamp, who had four personalities. This case was the most referenced case in the multiple personality literature until the case of Eve White, which dominated the clinical and popular literature between 1957 and 1973. *The Three Faces of Eve* was replaced by the case of Sybil, who was described as having 15 personalities.

Between the 1930s and the 1970s, the research on multiple personality disorder suffered a major decline. Relatively few articles concerning the subject were published in the psychological literature during these years, with only slightly more than 100 cases being reported. The diagnosis was seen as rare, and many doubted its existence.

Many credit the renewed interest in the disorder, during the 1970s, to the case of Sybil, who was treated by Cornelia Wilbur. While Wilbur's paper, describing the case and the treatment, was rejected by medical journals, the book, written by Schreiber in 1974, gained tremendous attention. The inclusion of MPD as a separate diagnosis in the 1980 publication of the DSM-III served to enhance the legitimacy of the diagnosis and provided a clearer distinction between MPD cases and other disorders, such as schizophrenia, with which it is often confused. Most recently, the research concerning MPD has focused on the relationship between this disorder and child physical and sexual abuse. It has been discovered that up to 80% of MPD cases have experienced early childhood abuse and that dissociating, or creating alter, imaginary personalities, was a defense against the painful aspects of these experiences. It is believed that this mechanism is carried into adulthood as a way of defending against the anxiety and the depression that is associated with memories of the abuse. Hypnosis is quite frequently used in the treatment of these patients to access the different personalities in an effort to integrate them into one. A number of authors have recently challenged the usefulness of hypnosis in the treatment of MPD patients, however. In MPD cases where the client was exposed to severe sexual abuse, supportive psychotherapy is suggested in a context in which the client can recall the abuse in a safe and controlled way, and slowly put in perspective the traumatic experiences and distortions of memory and feeling that were necessary for survival. Hypnosis, however, is also used to draw out painful memories and provide a form of abreaction in the safe context of therapy.

B. Psychogenic Fugue

This disorder involves a sudden, unexpected travel away from home or from the work place with an assumption of a new identity and with an inability to recall one's past (see Table II). The diagnosis of

TABLE II
Diagnostic Criteria for Psychogenic Fugue

A. The predominant disturbance is sudden, unexpected travel away from home or one's customary place of work, with inability to recall one's past.

B. Assumption of a new identity (partial or complete).

C. The disturbance is not due to multiple personality disorder or to an organic mental disorder (e.g., partial complex seizures in temporal lobe epilepsy).

Source: "Diagnostic and Statistical Manual of Mental Disorders," third ed., revised. Copyright American Psychiatric Association, Washington, DC, 1987. Used with permission.

this disorder is made only for individuals who do not suffer from organic mental disorders.

Patients in a fugue state do not appear to have any unusual behaviors. On the contrary, they appear quiet, yet purposeful, and usually do not draw attention or suspicion. In some cases, a completely new identity is assumed; the person may assume a new name, move to a new residence, and engage in complex social and vocational activities without exhibiting symptoms of any mental illness. In most cases, however, the identities that are developed are not as elaborate and complete. Often, the personality features and activities that are developed reflect a rather different lifestyle from the person's previous one. During the period of the fugue state, these patients are completely unaware that they have forgotten their identity and past lives. Often, when the fugue state ends, patients recall the time preceding its onset, but have complete amnesia as to the time they were in the fugue itself.

Since the essential features of psychogenic fugue involve identity disturbances, it can be at times confused with multiple personality disorder. Unlike patients diagnosed with multiple personality disorder, however, the assumption of a new identity in psychogenic fugue is limited to a single episode. Also, in multiple personality disorder, disturbances in identity are often present since childhood, whereas, in psychogenic fugue, there is no history of identity disturbances prior to the onset of the fugue.

C. Psychogenic Amnesia

The essential feature of psychogenic amnesia is a sudden inability to recall important personal information that is too great to be explained by ordinary or normal forgetfulness (see Table III). As is the case with psychogenic fugue, this diagnosis is not made with patients who suffer from organic mental disorders. In most psychogenic amnesia reactions, individuals cannot remember their names, their age, or where they reside. They often do not recognize their relatives, significant others, or friends. In contrast, however, their memory of general knowledge remains intact, and their abilities, such as reading, talking or performing skilled work tasks are unchanged. Psychogenic amnesia patients often present with indifference toward their disorder.

TABLE III
Diagnostic Criteria for Psychogenic Amnesia

A. The predominant disturbance is an episode of sudden inability to recall important personal information that is too extensive to be explained by ordinary forgetfulness.

B. The disturbance is not due to multiple personality disorder or to an organic mental disorder (e.g., blackouts during alcohol intoxication).

Source: "Diagnostic and Statistical Manual of Mental Disorders," third ed., revised. Copyright American Psychiatric Association, Washington, DC, 1987. Used with permission.

Psychogenic amnesia is classified into four types based on disturbances in recall: (1) localized (or circumscribed)—the individual has no memory of the events that took place during a specific period of time, usually the first hours following a traumatic event. (2) Selective—a person forgets some, but not all of the events, during a specific period of time. (3) Generalized—a person fails to remember important personal information from his or her entire life span. (4) Continuous—a person cannot recall events subsequent to a specific time, up to and including the present. Generalized and continuous amnesia are the least common.

The phenomena of psychogenic amnesia, particularly localized or selective, is the most common of the dissociative reactions seen in hospital emergency rooms. Psychogenic amnesia is fairly common as an initial reaction to intolerable, terrifying events, and is often observed in soldiers who experienced combat, or civilians who experienced catastrophic events or disasters. Its onset is sudden and usually occurs immediately following the traumatic events. The course of the disorder is relatively brief, lasting hours or days. The termination of the amnesia is also sudden, and often spontaneous, and the person is usually aware of the fact that disturbance in memory took place.

During the period of the amnesia, the individual might experience unusual somatic sensations, dizziness and headaches for a brief period of time. Also, perplexity, disorientation and purposeless wondering may occur.

D. Depersonalization Disorder

The experience of depersonalization involves an alteration in the person's sense of self (see Table IV). This is manifested by experiencing oneself as being detached from and outside one's body, feeling as if in a dream, or observing oneself from the outside. Some individuals report feeling like a machine, feeling dead, or feeling estranged. These individuals might also suddenly feel that their bodies are chang-

TABLE IV

Diagnostic Criteria for Depersonalization Disorder

A. Persistent or recurrent experiences of depersonalization as indicated by either (1) or (2): (1) An experience of feeling detached from, and as if one is an outside observer of, one's mental processes or body. (2) An experience of feeling like an automaton or as if in a dream.

B. During the depersonalization experience, reality testing remains intact.

C. The depersonalization is sufficiently severe and persistent to cause marked distress.

D. The depersonalization experience is the predominant disturbance and is not a symptom of another disorder, such as schizophrenia, panic disorder, or agoraphobia without history of panic disorder but with limited symptom attacks of depersonalization, or temporal lobe epilepsy.

Source: "Diagnostic and Statistical Manual of Mental Disorders," third ed., revised. Copyright American Psychiatric Association, Washington, DC, 1987. Used with permission.

ing, or that certain body parts are becoming significantly larger. Various forms of numbness to sensory input are reported, as are feelings of not being in control of some of one's actions, such as speech. Although the individual's experience of reality is altered during the experience of depersonalization, one's reality testing remains intact. The person experiencing depersonalization "knows" that the distortions he or she experiences are not "real," but rather that they reflect changes in his or her perception of reality.

Depersonalization can be diagnosed as a disorder in the absence of another psychiatric disorder that includes feelings of depersonalization. The experience of depersonalization is found in a variety (15–30%) of psychiatric patients, and mild symptoms of the experience are quite common in normal adults and particularly adolescents.

The phenomenon of depersonalization was first introduced in 1873 by Maurice Krishaber, a French clinician. Laurent Dugas suggested the name in 1911, but the interest in the disorder was diminished after this period and depersonalization was not studied as a specific syndrome until after World War II. The term "depersonalization neurosis" was first included in DSM-II, and in DSM-III the disorder was included under the category of dissociative disorders.

E. Dissociative Disorders Not Otherwise Specified

This cluster of disorders includes forms of dissociative symptoms, yet without the specific characteristics of the diagnosis described above (see Table V). Included under this category are individuals whose presentation resembles trance states, people who experience derealization (unaccompanied by depersonalization), and victims of prolonged periods of coercive persuasion (e.g., brainwashing) who present with dissociative symptoms. This category also includes Ganser's syndrome. This phenomenon is often associated with amnesia, disorientation, perceptual disturbances, fugue, and conversion symptoms.

The literature on dissociation also refers to other disorders, which are not included in the DSM-III-R as dissociative disorders. Somnabulism (sleep walking) was traditionally included in early investigations as a form of a dissociative disorder. In DSM-III, and later in DSM-III-R, it was listed as a disorder

TABLE V

Diagnostic Criteria for Dissociative Disorders Not Otherwise Specified

Disorders in which the predominant feature is a dissociative symptom (i.e., a disturbance or alteration in the normally integrative functions of identity, memory, or consciousness) that does not meet the criteria for a specific dissociative disorder.

Examples

1. Ganser's syndrome: the giving of "approximate answers" to questions, commonly associated with other symptoms such as amnesia, disorientation, perceptual disturbances, fugue, and conversion symptoms.
2. Cases in which there is more than one personality state capable of assuming executive control of the individual, but not more than one personality state is sufficiently distinct to meet the full criteria for multiple personality disorder, or cases in which a second personality never assumes complete executive control.
3. Trance states (i.e., altered states of consciousness with markedly diminished or selectively focused responsiveness to environmental stimuli). In children, this may occur following physical abuse or trauma.
4. Derealization unaccompanied by depersonalization.
5. Dissociated states that may occur in people who have been subjected to periods of prolonged and intense coercive persuasion (e.g., brainwashing, thought reform, or indoctrination while the captive of terrorists or cultists).
6. Cases in which sudden, unexpected travel and organized, purposeful behavior with inability to recall one's past are not accompanied by the assumption of a new identity, partial or complete.

Source: "Diagnostic and Statistical Manual of Mental Disorders," third ed., revised. Copyright American Psychiatric Association, Washington, DC, 1987. Used with permission.

of sleep and arousal. Some cases of MPD, however, have been reported to present with somnabulism as part of their clinical picture. Possession states can also be classified under the dissociative phenomena since they involve changes in the perception of self, loss of memory, and marked shifts in behavior.

III. DISSOCIATION AS A CONTINUUM

The concept of dissociation as a continuum extends back to the work of its early investigators, Pierre Janet, Morton Prince, and William James. Central to this concept is the notion that dissociation becomes maladaptive only when it becomes frequent and intense, or occurs in inappropriate contexts. Clearly, nonpathological forms of the dissociative phenomena (e.g., day-dreaming) are quite common in everyday life. Furthermore, in some contexts, dissociative phenomena are quite adaptive, as it protects individuals from the full impact of traumatic events (see below).

A review of the dissociative disorders listed above shows that the disorders vary in the magnitude of disruption of memory and identity. For example, psychogenic amnesia involves loss of memory for information relevant to personal identity. Psychogenic fugue involves a loss of memory of the primary identity and an assumption of another identity. In multiple personality, there are multiple assumptions of identity and multiple areas of amnesia with regards to the activities and behaviors of alter personalities, as well as of memory.

In an effort to quantify the concept of the dissociation continuum, Eve Bernstein and Frank Putnam designed the Dissociative Experience Scale (DES) in 1986. The scale is a 28-item self-report questionnaire designed to measure dissociation in normal and clinical populations. It assesses the wide range of the dissociation phenomena by asking respondents to indicate on a 100-mm-line visual analogue scale the frequency with which certain experiences occur. In Bernstein's and Putnam's data the DES scores obtained created a continuum, on which the normals received the lowest DES scores and the MPD patients the highest score.

In discussing people who present with dissociative phenomena, one needs to be aware, therefore, that dissociation can be an adaptive, if not a normal, reaction to stress. It is the level and frequency of the dissociative experience that classifies it as maladaptive and that determines the need for psychiatric treatment.

IV. DISSOCIATION, TRAUMA, AND STRESS

The last two decades have seen an exponential increase in the clinical literature on dissociative disorders. Janet's work is often cited and re-examined in the literature, and dissociative disorders are studied as they are related to different clinical phenomena. A prominent part of this literature deals with the relationship between dissociation and post-traumatic stress disorder (PTSD). [*See* POST-TRAUMATIC STRESS DISORDER.]

Reviewing the literature on the history of PTSD diagnosis reveals that the view that a person who had experienced a traumatic event may develop symptoms not associated with any pre-existing physiological or emotional pathology is an old one. Early accounts of post-traumatic symptomatology can be seen in a diary written by Samuel Pepys, a survivor of the 1666 Great Fire of London, and in Charles Dickens' diary describing his involvement in a railway accident in 1865. Both men described having feelings of terror, nightmares, and different physical symptoms following their dreadful experiences. Their detailed accounts bare striking similarity to the clinical concept of PTSD which was codified over 100 years later in DSM-III.

The psychological damage resulting from uncontrollable terrifying life events became a central focus of psychiatric interest around the turn of the century. The American Civil War and, later, World War I were two major human experiences that created focus on post-traumatic phenomena in soldiers who took part in combat. The psychiatrists who treated soldiers suffering from what would probably be diagnosed today as PTSD first explained the soldiers' symptoms as resulting from shell shock, which produced physical lesions in the brain. It was only in the early 1940s that researchers established the fact that war and combat experiences create syndromes that are caused by psychological stress. [*See* STRESS.]

During the same time period, initial cases of post-accident symptoms with civilians were thought to be caused by lesions in the nervous system that resulted from an injury to the spinal cord or the brain. However, following surgery performed on these patients, with no evidence of physical damage, physicians started to admit that some of these cases may be related to hysteria.

Sigmund Freud's works on hysteria was increasingly of interest as the limitations of brain pathology and lesions as a singular explanation became more apparent. Freud was also interested in the symptoms that followed trauma. Initially, Freud presented his understanding of this matter in a paper he wrote in 1896. Its title, "The Aetiology of Hysteria," referred to Freud's then new theory that the origin of neurosis lay in early sexual traumas which he called "infantile sexual scenes" or "sexual intercourse in childhood." This involved the child witnessing sexual intercourse between parents or being sexually molested. Freud had later retracted his views on this etiology of hysteria and came to believe that the development of neurosis was rooted in childhood Oedipal fantasies and misinterpretations of childhood events—referring to the stories his female patients told him about their seductive fathers. Freud named this neurosis "anxiety neurosis." Freud, however, continued to believe that symptoms can follow a traumatic event and cited accidents, death of a loved one, and combat as examples. These symptoms he defined as "traumatic neurosis."

The shift in Freud's thinking, away from actual traumatic events to instinctual wishes, had a major effect on the research and understanding of trauma. Little attention was paid to the consequences of actual overwhelming events, and the focus of scientific inquiry shifted to internal psychological processes. It was only two decades ago that interest in the research of trauma resulting from external events has re-emerged. This can be explained as related to psychiatry shifting from a dynamic intrapsychic model to a biomedical model. Also, there is little doubt that the Korean and later the Vietnam War, as well as experiences of people working in rape crises centers, focused the attention of the American public and clinicians to the power of trauma. The clinical literature that emerged dealt mostly with the after-effects of combat experience, and different measures were developed to assess these effects. The literature that has emerged from the mid-1970s and on concerning post-traumatic stress led to the inclusion of PTSD as a separate diagnosis in the DSM-III, and later in the revised edition (DSM-III-R). It is noted that even after its inclusion in the DSM-III, PTSD was mainly diagnosed with victims of violence, disasters, and combat. Sexual trauma was still viewed under the category of Freud's anxiety neurosis, i.e., mostly as imagined by children in response to Oedipal wishes. Over the last few years, however, attention has focused on child abuse, its traumatic impact, and its role in creating psychopathology. This interest can be attributed to a number of factors, such as the attention paid by the women's movement to the consequences of rape and incest, and to recent challenges of the traditional viewpoints of the psychoanalytic movement. In any event, a broad literature is surfacing of both research and therapy on children and adults who were victims of sexual abuse, incest, and child physical abuse.

In DSM-III-R, a traumatic event is defined as an event that is outside the range of usual human experience and would be markedly distressful to almost anyone. The DSM-III-R diagnosis of PTSD involves three basic clusters of symptoms: (1) intrusive re-experiencing of the trauma, (2) avoidance and numbing responses, and (3) physiological states of hyperarousal.

Judith Herman has suggested that an expansion of the DSM-III-R diagnosis of PTSD is due in the upcoming fourth edition of the manual (DSM-IV). She believes that the DSM-III-R concept of PTSD is not designed for survivors of prolonged, repeated trauma (e.g., sexual abuse). Currently under consideration for inclusion in DSM-IV is an expansion of the concept of PTSD to include a spectrum of disorders. These will range from the brief, limited reaction to stress to a single, acute trauma, through "simple" PTSD and finally, to what Herman labeled "the complex disorder of extreme stress (DESNOS) that follows upon ongoing and continuous exposure to repeated trauma."

Much of the early thinking about reactions to trauma involved the concept of dissociation. Janet viewed dissociation to be part of the hysterical syndrome, and required the presence of an amnesia as a critical, distinguishing factor. Janet was also the first to point out that dissociated states often followed childhood sexual or physical abuse. Freud, although recognizing the importance of amnesia, as had Janet, was more interested in these phenomena as manifestations of hysteria. Both Janet and, later, Freud considered the appearance of amnesia to result from the removal of a cluster of mental associations from consciousness. Many of the symptoms of hysteria were viewed as the effect of those absent mental contents on certain operations of the patients' conscious mind and physical functions. The dissociation of mental contents that leads to amnesia was perceived as a mechanism for protecting the individual from emotional pain that is caused by either external circumstances or anxiety-provoking drives and affects.

Within this framework, most contemporary writers in the field continue to conceptualize dissociative reactions as an adaptive process, protecting the individual from the intense anxiety experienced during, and often following, terrifying events. It is argued that as a protection from conscious awareness, memories of the dreadful events are split-off from normal consciousness, and are forgotten. Researchers see dissociation as a process by which a person struggles to integrate a traumatic experience into the self-structure, or as a coping mechanism aimed at minimizing emotional pain and preserving the person's functioning. Amnesia is therefore viewed as an essential element of this adaptive process, and much of the symptomatology that follows the traumatic experience is viewed as a form of re-experiencing this forgotten material.

It is noted that the level of amnesia varies with dissociative reactions. For example, depersonalization appears under the category of dissociative disorders in the DSM-III-R, and does not involve amnesia, but rather involves experiences of an altered state of reality, the sense of feeling detached, the feeling of being an observer outside one's body, and feeling as if in a dream. In 1936, Freud introduced depersonalization and derealization as two unconscious defense mechanisms and wrote, "The subject feels that either that a piece of reality or that a piece of his own self is strange to him . . . in the latter case we speak of depersonalization; derealization and depersonalization are intimately connected."

There is evidence that depersonalization is often present in the face of life-threatening danger. It is also often described by survivors that feelings of depersonalization helped them survive a traumatic experience. Its unique quality as a dissociative reaction provides a defense against the impact of terrifying events. Yet, intriguingly, depersonalization does not necessitate forgetting. Research has established that individuals who experience depersonalization during traumatic events experience fewer and less intense subsequent psychiatric symptoms.

V. DISSOCIATION AND THE POPULAR MEDIA

Dissociative disorders, and particularly multiple personality, while reported throughout the history of studies on human behavior, were up until the early 1970s, seen as a rare and questionable condition. While the clinicians showed disinterest or disbelief regarding multiple personality, the disorder continuously fascinated writers, film makers, and the general public. Perhaps it is the common confusion between multiple personality and schizophrenia. Schizophrenia, in its root of schiz, denotes a split, which in turn gets linked to the other classic misunderstanding, "breakdown," all of which condenses into a view of a unified self, breaking into parts. The concept of multiple personality was also fascinating due to the classical assignation of bipolar dichotomies to the different personalities, with one being good and the other evil, or one being male and the other female. Young versus old, hedonistic versus ascetic, artistic versus Philistine, all come to be the polar opposites which comprise the multiples. This archetypal split of existence into a vision of dichotomies was the subject of Stevenson's 1886 *Dr. Jekyll and Mr. Hyde*. The 1931 film version of the book, directed by Reuben Mamoulian, brought to the screen a complex variation on the idea of possession. Where possession emphasizes takeover by a force outside the self, the concept of multiple personality depicted here emphasized the other force as part of oneself. [*See* SCHIZOPHRENIA.]

From its early representation in a film like *Dr. Jekyll and Mr. Hyde*, multiple personality has continued to fascinate the public. Though a small number of cases were reported up until the 1980s, the cases reported found their way into the popular press and into the cinema. The first most important case was Eve, first reported by Thigpen and Cleckely in 1954, and later expanded into a best-selling book, *The Three Faces of Eve*. The movie version of the book, starring Joanne Woodward, was a major success. The introduction to the film *Three Faces of Eve*, by Alistair Cook, was an attempt to make the film a quasi-documentary of a clinical case study. Shortly after the film was produced, the theme of dissociation and multiple personality found a more dramatic representation in Hitchcock's *Psycho*, produced in 1960. Anthony Perkins' transformation from a frightened, meek person into an aggressive murderer depicts a new type of murderer, a person with multiple selves, one of which is purely evil.

Rarely is a popular book credited with having an effect on construction of a psychiatric diagnosis: such is the case, however, with the book *Sybil*, published in 1973, and the subsequent television movie version of 1976. The case of Sybil provided detailed accounts of the symptoms and treatment of amnesias, fugue states, and child abuse, and introduced to the general public, and to clinicians, the complexities of the disorder. Again, as in other reported cases of multiple personality, such as in the 1987 report of the case of Truddi Chase and her 92 personalities, the media's interest not only brought notoriety to the individual who contained the personalities, but endowed their therapists with celebrity status.

The public fascination with multiple personality made the transformation of personality a genre unto itself. Some of the most recent examples of this genre have occurred in a number of feature films such as *The Tenant, The Eyes of Laura Mars, Despair, Dressed to Kill,* and *Magic,* and of course, serves as the basis for the plot line of countless television shows.

Bibliography

American Psychiatric Association (1987). "Diagnostic and Statistical Manual of Mental Disorders," 3rd ed., revised. American Psychiatric Association, Washington DC.

Bernstein, E. M., and Putnam, F. W. (1986). Development, reliability and validity of a dissociation scale. *J. Nerv. Ment. Dis.* **174,** 887–892.

Chase, T. (1987). "When Rabbit Howls/The Troops for Truddi Chase." E. P. Dutton, New York.

Chu, J. A., and Dill, D. L. (1990). Dissociative symptoms in relation to childhood physical and sexual abuse. *Am. J. Psych.* **147,** 887–892.

Fleming, M., and Manvell, R. (1985). "Images of Madness: The Portrayal of Insanity in the Feature Film." Associated University Presses, NJ.

Freud, S. (1896). The etiology of hysteria. In "The Standard Edition" (J. Strachey, Ed.), Vol. 22. Hogarth Press, London, 1964.

Herman, J. L. (1992). Complex PTSD: A syndrome in survivors of prolonged and repeated trauma. *J. Traum. Stress* **5,** 377–391.

Nemiah, J. C. (1989). Dissociative disorders. In "Comprehensive Textbook of Psychiatry" (H. Kaplan and B. Sadock, Eds.), 5th ed., Vol. I, pp. 1028–1044. Williams and Wilkins, Baltimore.

Putnam, F. W. (1989). "Diagnosis and Treatment of Multiple Personality Disorder." Guilford Press, New York.

Putnam, F. W. (1989). Pierre Janet and modern views of dissociation. *J. Traum. Stress* **1,** 49–58.

Ross, C. A. (1989). "Multiple Personality Disorder: Diagnosis, Clinical Features, and Treatment." Wiley, New York.

Rosenzwig, S. (1988). The identity and idiodynamics of the multiple personality "Sally Beauchamp." *Am. Psychol.* **43**(1), 45–48.

Schrieber, F. R. (1973). "Sybil." Regnery, Chicago.

Shilony, E., and Grossman, F. K. (1993). Depersonalization as a defense mechanism in survivors of trauma. *J. Traum. Stress* **6,** 119–128.

Stevenson, R. L. (1886). "Strange Case of Dr. Jekyll and Mr. Hyde." Scribner, New York.

Thigpen, C. H. (1957). "The Three Faces of Eve." Kingsport Press, TN.

Van der Kolk, B. A. (1987). "Psychological Trauma." American Psychiatric Press, Inc., Washington, DC.

DIVORCE

Steven Stack
Wayne State University

Glossary

Alimony An allowance made by one spouse to the other for support pending or after legal separation or divorce.

Child support An allowance made by one spouse to another for the support of dependent children as part of a divorce settlement.

Crude divorce rate The number of divorces per 1000 in the general population.

Divorce A legal dissolution of a marriage.

Joint legal custody An arrangement in a divorce settlement wherein the parents share legal or decision-making power over their children.

Joint physical custody An arrangement in a divorce settlement wherein the parents share physical or residential custody of their children.

Social integration The strength of the bonds between the individual and the social order, including the number and intensity of shared beliefs and practices.

Suicide The act of taking one's own life knowingly and intentionally.

DIVORCE is a significant indicator of the quality of marriages and, more generally, of the quality of life. Divorce often breeds feelings of rejection, loss, and failure. On scales of traumatic life events divorce is second only to death of a spouse. For adults, divorce increases the odds of many social problems including financial strain, depression, a sense of disorientation, and suicide. Divorce is also associated with lower well-being for children both in the short term on such indicators as school performance and psychological distress and in the long term on indicators including social mobility, psychological problems, and divorce as an adult. As divorce becomes more prevalent, it can interfere with the production of the next generation of appropriately socialized and trained persons for society.

While divorce is associated with many stress-producing consequences, more than a million couples seek divorces each year. Recent national survey data indicate that at least half and perhaps as many as two-thirds of the persons currently getting married will ultimately have their marriages end in divorce. That is, divorce is becoming part of the normal "life course" or socialization experience of people. While most people may ultimately seek a divorce at some point in their lives, it is not clear, however, if the benefits of ending an unhappy marriage are, in fact, greater than the costs of a divorce.

I. THE EXTENT OF DIVORCE

A. Descriptive Data and Trends

1. United States

There are currently 15 million divorced adults in the United States and a larger number of remarried, formerly divorced persons (41% of all marriages involve a bride and/or a groom who were previously divorced). The number of children of divorce is approaching the number of children from intact homes.

Divorce rates (divorces per 1000 general population) vary by region and state. The rates of the South (5.4) and West (5.3) are higher than those for the Midwest (4.5) and Northeast (3.5). These differentials have been narrowing over time. States with the highest rates of divorce are Nevada (13.2) and Arizona (7.1). States with the lowest rates are Pennsylvania (3.2) and Massachusetts (3.0).

Divorce rates peak at different ages for men and women. For men, the rate jumps from 38/1000 for

Copyright © 1994 by Academic Press, Inc. All rights of reproduction in any form reserved.

ages 15–19 to a high of 55.9 for men ages 20–24. For women, the rate starts at a peak of 56.3 for those between 15–19 and then falls steadily for the rest of the age spectrum. This difference in peaks by gender is accounted for by the fact that men tend to marry younger women. That divorce peaks at an early age for both genders is associated with the fact that divorces tend to occur in the first 7 years of marriage and that most people are married by their mid 20s. The analysis of age-specific divorce rates indicates that divorce does not peak during midlife crisis or during the empty nest period when the children leave home.

Females, being less likely to remarry than males, are more apt to be divorced than males. In a recent year 6.6% of all males were currently divorced compared to 8.9% of females. Reflecting a higher incidence of marital instability among blacks, both black men and black women (7.4 and 11.6%, respectively) were more apt to be divorced than whites (6.6 and 8.6%, respectively).

In 1988 wives initiated divorce actions in 61% of the cases, down from 67% in 1975. Husbands filed in 32% of the cases, and joint actions constituted the remainder of the filings. When children are present, wives initiate nearly the same percentage of filings (65%), down from 71% in 1975.

Fifty-three percent of divorces in 1988 involved at least one child under the age of 18. The average number of children per divorce has been falling since 1964, a reflection of a decline in overall family size. The median duration of marriages that ended in divorce in 1988 was 7.1 years, up from 6.7 years in 1970.

Prior to the 20th century custody of the children was uniformly given to the father who was legally responsible for providing for the children. Given the spread of Freudian ideas on child development this pattern totally reversed in the 20th century with the courts uniformly awarding custody to the mothers (Phillips 1988). Today, while fathers are increasingly awarded joint (or shared) *legal* (decision making) custody, it is still unusual for fathers to obtain *physical* (residential) custody of their children. However, joint physical custody is becoming more common.

Approximately 15% of divorced women in the 1980s and 1990s were awarded alimony payments. Alimony awards are about equal in size to child support awards, but unlike child support, they can remain in force until death of either party or remarriage of the recipient spouse. Typically property is divided approximately equally and, in almost all states, can include pensions; pensions are often the most sizable form of property in divorce settlements.

Some work explores the relationship between child support and property settlements. It is possible, for example, that a generous child support award might be offset by a less favorable property settlement. However, inequality is inherent in most divorce negotiations. Those who receive favorable support awards also tend to receive favorable property settlements, often through informal agreements. Critics contend that some legal limits should be placed on couples' informal negotiations.

Compliance with child support orders is enhanced by joint custody, an effective coparenting relationship with the ex-spouse, and the frequency of visitation by the noncustodial parent. As a general rule, the greater the involvement of the noncustodial parent in the continued socialization of the child, the greater the compliance with child support. In contrast, noncustodial parents lacking any legal authority over their child, who have hostile relations with their former spouse, and who seldom visit their child, will be likely to default on their child support payments.

Divorce litigation often continues into the decades following the divorce. An increasing amount of divorce court time is spent on divorce modifications. This is, in part, due to new federal guidelines on child support adopted in the states in the late 1980s. Such legislation in many states warrants a periodic change in child support when there has been a "material change in circumstances" of either parent (generally an increase in income of at least 10%).

a. Trends

The incidence of divorce has increased substantially over the last century and a half. The earliest data on the estimated percentage of marriages that ultimately ended in divorce are for 1867. Ultimately 5.3% of the persons who married in 1867 were divorced. This figure doubled to 12.0% for those married in 1900. Currently, most marriages will ultimately end in divorce.

Between 1921 and 1965 divorce had been rising very slowly in the United States. The two noticeable departures from this pattern were a drop in the depths of the Great Depression and a short-term substantial upswing in the aftermath of World War II. As the postwar baby boomers began to wed, the divorce rate nearly doubled between 1965 and 1975.

It reached a record high of 5.3 in 1981. Since that time it has levelled off and stayed at a very high level fluctuating about 5.0.

2. Comparative Perspectives: Other Nations

The United States has the highest divorce rate of any industrialized nation in the world. That the United States has a high rate goes back well into the 19th century. In 1869 the rate was 1.2, a rate higher than some industrialized nations in the 1990s.

Table I presents data on divorces per 1000 population for selected nations of the world. Nations with a high proportion Catholic (e.g., Italy, Spain) tend to have a low divorce rate; one, Ireland, still has no legal provision for divorce. Norms against divorce are especially strong among Catholics. Divorce rates also tend to increase with the level of economic development and urbanization. The Russian federation and the Ukraine have rates above 3.5 and begin to approach that of the United States.

We do not fully understand why the rate of divorce in the United States is so high. One possibility is our high level of individualism, a quest after the maximization of individual goals and pleasures. We are relatively low in "collectivism." For example, the proportion of our labor force that belongs to unions, a collective form of organization, is the lowest in the industrialized world. If the costs of a marriage outweigh its benefits, Americans are apparently more likely than the members of any other nationality to seek a divorce.

TABLE I
Divorces per 1000 Population Circa 1990, Selected Nations

Nation	Divorce rate
Australia	2.5
Austria	2.1
Belgium	1.9
Canada	3.1
Denmark	3.1
Finland	2.9
France	1.9
Greece	0.9
Hungary	2.9
Ireland	0.0
Italy	0.5
Israel	1.3
Japan	1.3
Luxembourg	1.1
Netherlands	1.9
New Zealand	2.7
Norway	2.4
Poland	0.9
Portugal	1.0
Russian Federation	3.9
Spain	0.6
Sweden	2.2
Switzerland	2.0
United Kingdom	2.9
United States	4.7
Yugoslavia	0.9

Source. United Nations (1992). "Demographic Yearbook." United Nations, New York.

II. THE CAUSES OF DIVORCE

A. Macrosociological Explanations

1. Changes in Divorce Legislation

In colonial America there were no divorce courts and divorces were rare events. Divorces were a *legislative* matter, and each was debated in the colonial congress! Further, one alternative to marriage, living alone, was either banned or heavily taxed. With the development of judicial divorce, more lenient divorce legislation, female labor force participation, and other changes, divorce was more common by the late 19th century.

Commonsense might argue that the tightening or loosening up of divorce legislation would affect the incidence of divorce. However, if the reformation of divorce law simply follows normative changes in the culture of a people, there may be no impact. In an analysis of 41 states over a 20-year time frame, the introduction of no fault divorce legislation was found to be related to an overall increase in divorce. In 14 of the states the increase was between 20 and 25%. Laws regarding incompatibility and separate living have the greatest impact. However, sociodemographic variables were found to be more important than shifts in the divorce laws in explaining divorce rates. Similar changes to "no fault" in Australia and Canada witnessed a temporary increase. In Italy, divorce reforms of both 1970 and 1987 had no impact on the incidence of Italian divorce. The low propensity to divorce in Italy has been attributed to the family-centered culture which has strong norms against divorce.

An analysis of 17 industrial nations found that the degree of liberality in the divorce law was the variable most closely associated with the variance in divorce rates, it was more important than economic conditions and female labor force participation. However, the liberality of divorce legislation was largely determined, in turn, by the strength of Catholicism. Divorce law itself may be a reflection of the status of religion in society.

2. Economic Factors

Two conflicting theories link the business cycle to the divorce rate. In the first view, economic prosperity should increase the divorce rate since divorce is less costly in prosperous times. Prosperity provides unhappy couples the financial means for a divorce. Proponents of this first view often note the sizable drop in divorce during the worst years of the Great Depression. According to the second view, economic prosperity should decrease divorce since it reduces stress on families. In this perspective, it is economic depression that increases divorce. Financial strain adds tensions to family life that in turn increases the probability of divorce. While surprisingly little rigorous empirical testing has been done on these opposed perspective, the weight of the evidence, from the post World War II era, suggests that economic prosperity (e.g., low unemployment) has a slight negative effect on divorce. The size of this effect is typically less than that of the age structure and the extent of female labor force participation.

Womens' increased labor force participation is perhaps the most frequently cited factor underlying the increase in divorce since World War II. As economic opportunities for women have increased, more women have obtained an independent financial base. They are less dependent on marriage for monetary support, and more apt to seek a divorce from an unhappy marriage. Increased female labor force participation has often been the leading determinant of shifts in the incidence of divorce. However, other nations have even higher rates of employed women than the United States and these nations, such as Sweden, have substantially lower divorce rates. There is more to the divorce equation, then, than this factor.

The age structure of the population can affect divorce through influencing economic opportunities for different age cohorts. As the proportion of young people in society expands, this sets in motion certain rigidities in the supply of labor. An oversupply of labor results in more competition for employment. An abundance of young workers results in the fall in their incomes, more financial strain on their marriages, and, hence, a higher incidence of divorce.

3. Social Integration

Factors such as religiosity, migration, urbanism, and war can affect the strength of the bond between the individual and society. The extent of shared beliefs and practices and can be affected by these conditions; when bonds to social institutions like religion and neighborhoods are weakened, life can become less meaningful. Urban life can promote a sense of anonymity undermining integration and increasing tolerance for divorce. In such contexts the probability of divorce increases.

In a study of divorce rates in 3000 counties Breault and Kposowa found that indicators of social integration were more important than socio-economic variables in explaining the variation in divorce rates. In particular, the higher the incidence of church membership, the lower the rate of divorce. Also, the higher the rate of population growth the higher the rate of divorce. Finally, the higher the percentage urban, the higher the incidence of divorce.

Wars can reduce divorce through home-front mobilization or greater social cohesion. However, *after* World War II there was a dramatic increase in American divorce. Combat experience and late entry into the war were associated with greater divorce risk. Post-traumatic stress syndrome was a leading contributor to risk of divorce. In contrast to World War II, the Vietnam War (an unpopular war) increased the incidence of divorce independent of other socioeconomic trends of the time. The Korean War had no discernable independent effect on American divorce. Further work on other nations will be needed to resolve these contradictory findings. [*See* POST-TRAUMATIC STRESS DISORDER.]

As divorce becomes more commonplace, the normative climate surrounding divorce is liberalized. The stigma associated with divorce may decline resulting in an increase in divorce; divorced persons can provide role models and encourage others to follow suit. Overtime data for the United States confirm a positive association between divorce and the previous level of divorce. This suggests some support for a cultural perspective.

B. Individual Level Explanations

1. Personality and Dissimilarity in Social Status

Anecdotal accounts sometimes stress personality factors which allegedly contribute to divorce risk.

Persons high in irritability and low in ability to provide social support, for example, may be divorce-prone. Almost no research has been done on these matters. However, clinical work on persons who divorce more than once, repeaters, finds that they tend to be self-involved narcissistic personality types. They have limited capacities for long-term relationships, prefer the emotional highs accompanying new loves, and are attracted to superficial qualities in others. It is not clear, however, if these findings can be generalized beyond repeaters.

Studies tend to find that the greater the differences in status between spouses, the higher the odds of marital disruption. This is especially true for dissimilarities in religious preference, but also extends to differences in age, education, and race. Communication between the spouses is a function, in part, of similarities on these characteristics. The associated value conflicts can increase divorce risk.

2. Social Integration

Social isolation increases risk of divorce. Measured in terms of the number of ties to friends and community organizations, the greater the "integration" the lower the probability of divorce, but only for the first 7 years of marriage. Stronger results are found for "normative integration" or the number of close relatives and friends who have experienced a divorce. In an 8-year panel study of 2000 married couples, the probability of divorce was only 9% among those with no significant others who had divorced, whereas the probability of divorce was 16% among those who had both a friend and relative who had divorced. As normative standards permit or encourage divorce in one's social networks, the likelihood of divorce increases.

One particularly strong predictor of divorce is low religious integration. Catholics have a lower incidence of divorce than Protestants given stronger norms against such in the former.

3. Economic Factors

The occupational status, education level, and income of the husband lower the risk of divorce. Only income tends to remain significant if we hold the other variables constant. Conversely, the lower the socio-economic status, the higher the risk of divorce. Financial strains place the family under stress which, in turn, increases the probability of marital dissolution.

At the individual level, the research on the effect of the labor force participation of wives is mixed. Measured as number of hours worked, wife's employment tends to be associated with a greater incidence of divorce. The physical absence of a wife from the marital home may increase marital stress given a greater chance for conflict over who shall do the unpaid household work. Whether the wife is in the labor force sometimes is associated with greater and sometimes with lesser risk of divorce. Wives' employment may be indicative of greater autonomy in the lives of husbands and wives; personal independence is often thought of as a factor reducing divorce risk.

4. Family Dynamics and Process

While premarital cohabitation might be seen as "preparation" for a successful marriage, persons who cohabit before marriage are at relatively high risk of divorce. Both cohabitation and divorce may be indicators of a predisposition to go against normative behavior regarding marital conventions. For example, a recent decade review of the relevant literature found that in most studies those persons who had cohabited before marriage had a higher probability of divorce than those persons who did not cohabit before marriage.

a. Children

On the one hand, children are often thought to decrease the odds of divorce since they can give an unhappy couple "a reason to stay together"; or perhaps problems concerning the children per se help to prevent a focus on marital problems, thereby lowering risk of divorce. On the other hand children can increase stress; children also represent a source of numerous economic and social demands on parents. The presence of step-children, in particular, substantially increases the odds of divorce even in the short run.

An overtime, 20-year study of 4400 couples found that children can have both destabilizing and stabilizing effects on marriage. Firstborns and younger children decrease the odds of divorce through their preschool years. One study, over a 3-year period, found that childless couples were four times more likely to divorce than couples bearing a child. However, older children and children born before marriage increase the odds of divorce. In the long run, however, couples with children are more likely than childless couples to reach their 20th wedding anniversary. The net effect of children is to only slightly lower the risk of divorce.

b. Esteem for Spouse

Spouses in happy marriages tend to hold each other in a higher regard than divorced persons. The former group is considerably more likely to describe their mate's traits as superior to their own than the latter group.

c. Sexuality

A badly neglected variable, sexual adjustment, distinguishes happily married couples from divorced spouses. The former report significantly more enjoyment and higher actual-preferred sex frequency ratios than the latter. Sexual incompatibility is one of the more frequent explanations that divorced persons, themselves, give for the breakdown in their marriages. Further, adultery is a much cited reason for divorce among divorcees, but there is little research on this issue.

Parental sexual abuse of children is not an automatic antecedent of divorce. The odds of divorce are increased if sexual abuse is combined with three conditions: (1) the victim is relatively young, (2) other types of abuse are present as well, and (3) the child confided in and was believed by the mother. [*See* CHILD ABUSE.]

Alcohol and drug abuse are another two aspects of family dynamics that divorced people frequently cite as a cause of their marital disruptions. The weight of the evidence to date suggests that alcohol abuse, in particular, is more of a consequence than a cause of divorce. [*See* SUBSTANCE ABUSE.]

III. THE CONSEQUENCES OF DIVORCE

Probably the best researched area in divorce studies is that of the consequences of divorce. The effects of divorce include psychological, economic, and social consequences. The literature on the effects of divorce is divided first into that discussing effects on children and that discussing effects on adults. For children, effects are further subdivided into short- and long-term impacts. Finally the sources of variation in the extent to which people are affected by divorce are discussed for both children and adults. Some persons are more negatively affected by divorce than others.

A. Effects on Children

1. Short-Term Consequences

a. Psychological Impacts

A meta-analysis of 92 relevant studies found that parental divorce increases the risk of psychological maladjustment and low self-esteem in the children.

There is some evidence that the children of divorce have lower peer popularity in school than the children of intact families. This may be a social consequence of psychological impairment.

b. School Performance

A meta-analysis of 92 studies found that parental divorce is associated with decreased school performance. However, there is considerable variation in the school performance of children following divorce. Two factors that account for a third of the variance in school performance are the mother's report of conflict between her and her ex-spouse in front of the child, and the child's report of intense arguments between him- or herself and the mother. Other contributing factors to low grade point averages were mothers with high levels of depression and low education levels.

The "task overload" often found in single-parent, divorced families is associated with weaker supervision, increased labor force participation of the custodial parent to offset the loss of the income of their former spouse, and less parental monitoring of school work.

While a divorced noncustodial father might hypothetically still serve as a resource for his child's social mobility through such means as role modeling and frequent visitations, this is unlikely in many cases. Among a National Survey of Children sample, of children who had experienced family disruption, most had not seen their biological father in the past year. Marital disruption effectively destroys the relationship between a child and the noncustodial parent in a majority of cases.

c. Criminal Behavior

Divorce tends to be associated with a higher incidence of criminal behavior. In an analysis of 150 cities, family disruption was the leading predictor of both juvenile robbery and homicide rates, for both blacks and whites. Divorce reduces the amount of supervision and control of children, both within the family and in neighborhoods with high proportions of single-parent families. To the extent that divorce is accompanied by conflict and a disrespect for parental authority, this may be generalized to a disrespect for authority in general, thereby increasing the probability of deviant and criminal behavior. At the individual level, the link between divorce and crime is especially pronounced if there is continued conflict between spouses after the divorce and if there is continued instability and/or divorce in a reconstituted family. [*See* CRIMINAL BEHAVIOR.]

2. Long-Term Consequences

a. Psychological Impacts: Depression

Life course approaches to divorce and depression have established a link between parental divorce and the odds for depression among the children after they become adults. This association is independent of other marital and socio-economic life outcomes of the children. [*See* DEPRESSION.]

b. Divorce

Parental divorce increases the risk of divorce among the children when they reach adulthood. The children of divorced parents tend to have more favorable attitudes toward divorce than the children of intact families. Divorced parents may constitute a role model for their children.

c. Social Mobility

The experience of family disruption during childhood substantially increases men's odds of ending up in the lowest occupational stratum. Family disruption also weakens the association between father's occupational status and the occupational status of the son. These relationships hold for both blacks and whites.

At the macro level of analysis, the increase in divorce rates since the 1960s is tied to the weakening of the association between sons' class of origin and class of destination. As more sons have been coming out of divorced homes, fewer of them are achieving the amount of occupational advancement that you would ordinarily expect on the basis of their father's occupation.

3. Explaining the Variation in Effects among Children

Some children of divorce fair better than others in their level of well-being. Explanations of this variation include those stressing the quality of the custodial parent's mental health and the level of conflict between ex-husband and ex-wife. The empirical findings of over 100 studies on these matters are mixed and a systematic review of them is required in order to present any meaningful generalizations.

Amato's recent review of 180 relevant studies lumps together the following dependent variables as indicators of "well-being": academic achievement, behavior problems, psychological adjustment, self-esteem, and quality of social relations. Five theories were reviewed with respect to the well-being of divorced children: (1) basic parental loss, (2) parental adjustment, (3) interparental conflict, (4) economic hardship, (5) life stress hypothesis.

Loss of a parent through divorce might be compensated for by frequent visitations by the noncustodial parent. However, while 16 studies support this notion, 16 studies reject it. Similarly, one might contend that replacement of a lost parent by a stepparent might improve well-being of children. There is no systematic support for this thesis: 11 studies find that remarriage improves children's well-being while 19 studies reject this notion. In a similar vein, commonsense might tell us that loss of a parent through divorce might have less effect on children's well-being if the divorce occurs at a later age. This notion is, however, supported in only 8 of 26 studies.

Hypotheses derived from the parental adjustment perspective fair better than the parental loss perspective. First, the hypothesis that the well-being of children of divorce is positively linked with the postdivorce psychological adjustment of the custodial parent is supported in 13 of 15 studies. Better adjusted parents are able to foster higher levels of well-being in their children. Further, the higher the quality of the relationship between custodial parent and child, the greater the well-being of the child (19 of 20 studies).

Strong support is found for the interparental conflict perspective. Such conflict generally lowers the well-being of the child. Twenty-five of twenty-eight studies support the notion that children's well-being is inversely correlated with the level of postdivorce conflict between their parents.

From an economic perspective on well-being, one would anticipate that children in postdivorce families marked by financial strain would have lower well-being than children in families lacking in such strain. Six of ten studies support a positive relationship between income and well-being. Only 9 of 29 studies support the associated notion that because remarriage increases income, the well-being of children of custodial parents that remarry is higher than those parents who do not remarry. Because fathers tend to have higher incomes than mothers, we might expect that children of divorce experience higher well-being if fathers are awarded custody rather than mothers. Only 5 and 15 studies support this thesis. In sum, an economic perspective on children's well-being is not generally supported.

The life stress perspective contends that it is not a single stressor that erodes children's well-being, but a series or accumulation of stressors. Changing schools, moving, financial strain, loss of contact with grandparents, and so on, may ultimately wear down the child and threaten his or her basic well-being. Ten of thirteen studies confirm the notion that the greater the number of stressful life events, the lower the well-being of the child. Only 16 studies of 33 which focus on remarriage and repeated remarriage as single stress factors find that these stressors taken by themselves lower well-being of children.

Generally speaking, children of divorce are more apt to have better well-being if their custodial parent is in good mental health, interparental conflict is low or absent, and the number of stressful life events is low.

B. Effects on Adults

1. Psychological and Physical Health

Generally, research has found a strong association between divorce and psychological impairment. For example, national survey data find that the divorced have a level of depression that is 40% higher than the national average. Levels of problems such as loneliness, guilt, anger, and anxiety are higher among divorced persons than married persons. These problems are often attributed to such factors as a deterioration of the standard of living after divorce, a relative lack of confidants, and a deep sense of loss.

Suicide is often used as a barometer of group mental troubles. Divorced persons have a risk of suicide that is two to four times greater than married persons depending on the gender and age group one inspects. For example, divorced males ages 40–44 have a suicide rate of 104.4/100,000, 4.58 times that of married males of the same age (20.3/100,000). At the societal level, the relationship between divorce rates is like a sociological "law." Divorce trends have been linked to suicide trends in Canada, the United States, Norway, Denmark, Sweden, and Finland. Within the United States divorce and suicide are closely linked in the 50 states, the 3000 counties, and for samples of cities. The greater the divorce rate the greater the suicide rate. Divorce is apparently a culturally defined traumatic life event and a good index of the quality of marital life through time and space. [*See* SUICIDE.]

Recent longitudinal research on a national sample of 1300 couples found no evidence that the negative mental health consequences of divorce are permanent. Predivorce stress levels are high among divorcing couples. However, these levels ultimately return to those of married couples.

Turning to physical health, research on both the United States and other nations has tended to find a higher rate of both morbidity and mortality among the divorced than the married. The increased risk of illness among the divorced has been linked to suppressed immunological functioning. Poorer immune functioning is especially pronounced among divorced persons who are still attached to their ex-spouse.

2. Economic Effects

Generally, the standard of living of everyone in a divorce decreases given that two households have to be supported with about the same income. With respect to divorced families, there is approximately a 30% reduction in the income and standard of living of the custodial parent. Remarriage is often cited as the main avenue for restoring the predivorce standard of living. Little research detail is available on the economic state of noncustodial parents. This group is often assumed to have a higher standard of living since their "per capita income" increases upon divorce.

The economic effects of divorce are lessening given new federally mandated guidelines on child support. In some states application of these guidelines indicates that fathers now pay double, on the average, what they typically had to pay before guidelines went into effect. The rate of defaulting on child support payments, approximately 25%, will probably drop in 1994 when child support will be taken directly out of the noncustodial parent's paycheck.

3. Social Effects

Criminal behavior is related to the incidence of divorce. An immediate target for criminal violence is the ex-spouse, a person who is often the perceived source of considerable anger. Crimes of violence occur among one-quarter of all divorcing couples. At the aggregate level, the divorce rate is a fairly reliable predictor of the crime rate in cities.

4. Explaining the Variation in Effects among Adults

Divorce can be conceptualized as a long-term stressor composed of a set of events occurring both before and after the divorce. These social, psychological, and economic events can pile up and have a cumulative impact on people. The impact is in proportion to such conditions as the psychological and material resources of the persons involved.

a. Gender Differences

A key variable explaining differences in psychological reactions to divorce is gender. While males report less stress prior to the decision to divorce than females, the reverse is true for postdivorce adjustment. To the extent that indicators of divorce adjustment are related to self-esteem, predivorce gender differences in self-esteem may account for gendered differences in postdivorce adjustment.

Additional aspects of gender roles serve as moderators of divorce adjustment and differentially benefit women. These include ability to form attachments, social networking, derivation of social support, and the fact that women are more in command of the divorce process; women are more apt to initiate divorce than men. About half of husbands report having had no warning concerning divorce prior to the divorce. Women who initiate divorce are more apt to grieve in the predivorce as opposed to postdivorce process. Finally men tend to be more emotionally dependent or "attached" than women to their spouses, often making men's postdivorce adjustment more difficult.

While both men and women experience an increase in depression following divorce, the causes of the depression tend to be somewhat different. For men loss of emotional support is cited ahead of financial problems. In contrast, for women, financial problems are cited ahead of loss of emotional support.

b. Economic

The economic consequences of divorce are cushioned by the economic resources, such as skills and degree of labor force participation, of the custodial parent. Custodial parents with higher levels of education and training, and who increase the number of hours worked, fare better than their counterparts. Receipt of alimony is, however, associated with lower labor force participation, possibly due to lower skill levels and the advanced age of such recipients.

c. Support Systems/Social Isolation

Persons reporting fewer or no contacts with a social support network experience more difficulty in divorce adjustment. For older divorced persons, relationships with their adult children are often critical to divorce adjustment. Adult children can provide financial, psychological, and service-oriented support.

d. Relations with Ex-spouse

Inter-spousal hostility and bitterness over the divorce impedes divorce adjustment. Positive attachment, such as dependence, to a former spouse may account for long-term psychological distress in some divorces. A relationship with one's ex marked by indifference may be the most healthy mode.

The development of a new intimate relationship with someone of the opposite sex improves divorce adjustment. This may be, in part, a function of the ensuing decrease in any positive attachment to one's ex-spouse.

e. Cultural Beliefs

A belief in the immorality of divorce and few premarital problems are associated with higher levels of psychological stress among divorcing couples. Adherence to liberal gender roles improves divorce adjustment for women.

f. Sexuality

An important aspect of divorce adjustment is reestablishing an intimate sexual relationship. Research by Stack and Gundlach on a national sample of divorces, found that age and gender were the most powerful predictors of the variance in frequency of sex and presence of a sex partner in the past year. The higher the age, the lower the incidence of sex. Males were considerably more sexually involved than females, especially at older ages. Persons low in religiosity, high in education, and high in political liberalism were more sexually active than their counterparts. [*See* SEXUAL BEHAVIOR.]

g. Other

Divorced blacks report less psychological distress, less attachment, and higher self-esteem than divorced whites. This is associated with there being less stigma surrounding divorce among blacks, possibly since divorce is more common among blacks. Being younger, participating in a professionally organized, peer support group, and being geographically mobile (for women) are associated with divorce adjustment.

IV. CONCLUSIONS

A. Social Consequences of Divorce Law Reform

The last quarter century brought an unprecedented degree of change in divorce legislation both in the

United States and in most industrial nations. Changes included the rise of no-fault divorce grounds, the adoption of marital property law, and the introduction of joint custody. The United States was among the leaders of these changes.

It is not clear if this rapid rate of legal change will continue or, given some shortfalls in the marriage and fertility rate, if the legal pendulum will begin to slide in a more conservative direction.

1. Alimony

Recent decisions in such states as Colorado (in re *Dwyer,* 1191 WL 118478) and Oregon (in re *Smith,* 798 P 2d 717) indicate the possible start of a trend wherein alimony will not necessarily cease with cohabitation and/or remarriage of the recipient spouse. In states where remarriage does not automatically cancel alimony, remarriage rates for females may increase. As the costs of remarriage decline, if all else is equal, the remarriage rate should increase. Research is needed to test the impact, if any, of these legal changes on remarriage rates.

Although some legal scholars charge that it is unconstitutional (on the grounds of *equality before the law*), the number of states with judicial authority to order divorced parents (but not married parents) to pay college expenses of nonminor children is increasing. In a review of national appellate cases, the amount awarded for college expenses is generally equal to or exceeds the previous amounts paid for child support. In this sense, support of the children of divorce can, and often does, continue into their mid 20s. Supporters of this new trend contend that divorced parents are sometimes lacking in "generosity" toward their children; the courts need legal muscle to force such parents to pay college expenses that the children probably would have received if their parents had not divorced. In any event, the extension of support beyond the age of majority increases the costs of divorce and, as such, may make marriage less attractive.

Krause links the revolution in divorce law with increased economic risks for those who choose marriage and children over a career. An increasingly proportion of childless couples or "DINKS" (double income no kids) has emerged in middle-class society. For responsible men and women, rigorous child support enforcement may be a deterrent to having children. Further, the absent parent often is required to pay more toward the support of a child than they paid while married. The present system also leaves the noncustodial parent without any power over how the money is spent.

The child-rearing function in society is increasingly delegated to the lower socio-economic strata, often in single-parent families. Twenty-five percent of all children and 50% of black children grow up in poverty. These shifts threaten the social security system to the extent that such is reliant on a healthy, educated population to generate the necessary income for the support of retired persons.

2. New Development in Research

Recent longitudinal research on both the United States and Canada has questioned the notion that divorce per se is the proximate cause of lowered well-being among children of divorce. Cherlin and his colleagues (1991) measured emotional well-being and school achievement of adolescents over time. The children who experienced a parental divorce scored lower on both indicators. However, when controls were introduced for such factors as social class, school achievement, and emotional health before the divorce, the apparent effect of divorce fell by 50% for boys and became insignificant. For girls the effect of divorce fell, but was still significant. The researchers conclude that it is not divorce but the years of growing up in a dysfunctional family that is mainly responsible for lowering the well-being of children. This research is in need of replication. It should also be extended to adult samples. Perhaps divorced adults' well-being is more a product of years of a dysfunctional marriage than a divorce per se. [*See* MARITAL DYSFUNCTION.]

Bibliography

Amato, P. (1993). Children's adjustment to divorce: Theories, hypotheses, and empirical support. *J. Marriage Family* **55,** 23–38.

Becker, G. (1991). "A Treatise on the Family," 2nd ed. Harvard University Press, Cambridge.

Biblartz, T., and Rafferty, A. E. (1993). The effects of family disruption on social mobility. *Am. Sociol. Rev.* **58,** 97–109.

Breault, K. and Kposowa, A. (1987). Explaining divorce in the U.S.: A study of 3,111 counties. *J. Marriage Family* **49,** 549–558.

Cherlin, A., Furstenberg, F. F., Jr., Chase-Lansdale, P. L., Kiernan, K. E., Robins, P. K., Morrison, D. R., and Teitler, J. O. (1991). *Science* **252,** 1386–1389.

Dawson, D. (1991). Family structure and children's health and social well-being. *J. Marriage Family* **53,** 573–584.

Kitson, G., and Morgan, L. (1990). The multiple consequences of divorce. *J. Marriage Family* **52,** 913–924.

Kitson, G. C. (1992). "Portrait of Divorce: Adjustment to Marital Breakdown." Guilford, New York.

Krause, H. D. (1990). Child support reassessed: Limits of private responsibility and the public interest. *Family Law Quart.* **24,** 1–34.

Phillips, R. (1988). "Putting Asunder: A History of Divorce in Western Society." Cambridge University Press, New York.

Seltzer, J. (1990). Inequality in divorce settlements. *Am. J. Sociol.* **19,** 82–111.

Stack, S. (1990). New micro-level data on the impact of divorce on suicide, 1959–1980: A test of two theories. *J. Marriage Family* **52,** 119–127.

Stack, S. and Gundlach, J. (1992). Divorce and Sex. *Arch. Sex. Behav.* **21,** 359–367.

White, L. K. (1990). The determinants of divorce: A review of research in the eighties. *J. Marriage Family* **52,** 904–912.

DREAMING

John S. Antrobus
The City College of the City University of New York

Glossary

Association Learned connection between two or more items or events.

Cataplexy Sleep–waking disorder in which a waking person suddenly moves into a REM sleep-like state.

Cognition Thought.

Dreaming An imagined, visual, hallucinated event that occurs during sleep.

Frontal eye fields A portion of the cortex where the final decision is made about where, when, and how fast to move the eyes.

Hallucination Mental image to which one responds as though it were a perception of a real-world event. A image that is believed to be "real."

Imagery Perception-like event that is not a true perception in that it is not correlated with a corresponding external event or object.

Lateral geniculate nucleus Group of many nuclei that link the cortex with incoming sensory and outgoing motor neurons.

Lucid dream Dream in which the dreamer is aware that he or she is dreaming.

Mentation Thought and/or imagery. Mental events of any kind.

Neurocognition The field of study concerned with the relation of cognition to neurophysiology.

NREM sleep Non-REM sleep: including EEG stages 2, 3, and 4.

Nuclei Clusters of neurons.

Occipital Referring to the visual portion of the cerebral cortex.

Ocular Referring to the eyes.

Parapsychology The study of events, perception, and behavior that cannot be accounted for by psychological relationships. Literally, beyond psychology.

Parietal A portion of the cortex that processes spatial information

PET scan Method of obtaining three-dimensional pictures of the brain and estimates of the distribution of brain metabolism. The metabolic measures estimate neural activity or information processing.

PGO *Pontine* (referring to the pons), *geniculate* (referring to the lateral geniculate), *occipital* (referring to the occipital cortex).

Polygraph A multiple-channel-writing device.

Pons A part of the brain stem, below the thalamus.

Psychophysiology The study of the relation between mind and body, or behavior and physiology.

REM Rapid eye movements.

REM sleep Stage 1 EEG marked by REMs and a waking-like EEG, generally accompanied by more intense dreaming than NREM sleep.

Stressor An event that forces an individual to use his or her resources to adjust, protect, or otherwise respond to that event.

THE DRAMATIC, unpredictable, and often bizarre character of dreaming has fascinated or frightened

Copyright © 1994 by Academic Press, Inc. All rights of reproduction in any form reserved.

men and women since the beginning of written history. Although dreams are produced by the mind/brain of the dreamer, their strangeness has suggest to many people that they are produced by someone else. Until recent times, the someone else was a god or spirit of some kind. Since life is full of uncertainty, and people who have the most power have the most to lose in unpredictable situations, kings and generals routinely consulted dream interpreters prior to going to war to predict their chance of winning. Interpretations were deliberately ambiguous so that, when the war was over, the interpretation could be judged as accurate, regardless of who won. In this fashion, the business of dream interpretation was kept secure, and the faith in the divine source of the dream was unshaken. Of course, some dream interpreters, such as Joseph in the Bible, were more persuasive than others. Eventually, interpretations became codified so that certain objects in a dream were considered symbols of certain events in life, and they were compiled in dream books that are still in use today.

I. FREUD AND HIS INTERPRETATION OF DREAMS

Although we know that dreams are created by the brain of the dreamer, we are a long way from understanding precisely how that process works. Certainly, no one understands it well enough to predict what a person is going to dream about. But that does not seem to dissuade people from interpreting dreams. In his book *The Interpretation of Dreams*, Sigmund Freud, a Viennese doctor, argued that much of our thought and behavior are caused by desires and feelings about which we are completely unconscious. He believed that these unconscious thoughts could produce disorders such as the hysterical fainting spells of Viennese ladies when they were exposed to something shocking, particularly something sexual. In fact, Freud believed that all of these unconscious thoughts were driven by sexual drives forced underground by a society that harshly repressed sexual expression. Since dreams are not under control of the conscious mind, they were, for Freud, an ideal place to observe the working of these unconscious processes. He assumed that all neurotic behavior could be attributed to unconscious processes. Unconscious processes could be understood by interpreting the dreams of the neurotic person, and once the unconscious processes were fully exposed and understood the person would be free of neurosis. Although there is little merit in this argument, it nonetheless remains today as the central strategy of orthodox psychoanalysis.

As the science of psychology began to develop, there were many who were unwilling to accept Freud's dogmatic assertion that his theory was correct and did not need to be subject to scientific test. Freud and his followers could always find an explanation for how *any* dream, indeed, any segment of a dream, was consistent with the theory. Since no one could find a way to test the theory, it became essentially a belief. One either believed or did not.

Meanwhile early cognitive psychologists were trying to find the link between dream images and objects in the everyday world. For example, waving perfume under the nose of sleeper on a hot night resulted in a dream of being on a romantic south sea island. The experimenter deduced that the perfume in the presence of the heat had aroused the sleeper's memory of stories of the south seas, and these memories, in turn, had been played out as a dream. This explanation is based on association theory which describes how objects and events with similar, as well as opposite features tend to activate one another.

Indeed, Freud's theory of dreaming was a special kind of association theory. First, objects and events could be activated because of their previous associations with emotions. Freud believed that dream images were activated by sexual feelings, but sexual images tended to activate fear, and so some form of compromise association took place. For example, sexual feelings might tend to associate to images of sex organs. Since the image of a penis would induce anxiety, the dreamer might dream of a sexual object in a more neutral form, such as a cigarette or a pen. Similarly, any round object might be the compromise association for the unacceptable image of a vagina.

Freud's joining of association and motivational processes created a more sophisticated model of dreaming than that of the early associationists. By restricting the source of motivation to sex, and by discouraging experimental evaluation and revision of his model, however, he established a movement in which his followers were unable to contribute further to our understanding of dreaming. Indeed, nothing of significance to the theory of dreaming occurred in the first half of this century. Constructing theories of what goes on inside the brain when an individual perceives, thinks, learns, and recalls had been of such limited value to early experimental psychologists that they decided to confine the terms of their theories to the publicly observable stimuli, the external stimulus, and the observable behavioral response, the input and the output. This radical behaviorist period of psychology effectively discouraged research on dreaming from 1920 to 1953.

II. THE NEUROCOGNITIVE LINK: ASERINSKY AND KLEITMAN

In 1953, a Ph.D. student in physiology named Aserinsky and his mentor, the father of modern sleep research, Nathaniel Kleitman, stumbled across the Stage 1 sleep electroencephalogram (EEG) rapid eye movement (REM) association with dreaming. That started an explosion of dream research that extended for over 30 years. Multiple pen-writing amplifiers (polygraphs) had just become available for research purposes. Although sleep had been recorded on the polygraph for about 15 minutes, sleep was regarded as a kind of bland monotonous state so there was no incentive to stay up to record an entire night of sleep. But that is what Aserinsky did. To his surprise he found that the brain waves kept changing from one pattern to another through the night in 90-minute cycles. At one phase of these cycles, the brain waves looked remarkably like those of the waking brain, and the *eyes were moving rapidly under the sleepers' lids!*

He could not resist. He did what any of us would have done. He awakened the subject and asked him what was going through his mind. The subject reported a long dream! Aserinsky repeated the awakenings in many other REM periods and nearly always got long dreamlike reports. But in the non-REM (NREM) periods he generally got very brief reports of mental experience, and often nothing at all.

This dramatic discovery indicated that if one wished to study dreams one should get them right at the source, during REM sleep. It also pointed to a particular brain state, Stage 1 REM, as the condition under which dreams were most likely produced. Indeed, the discovery helped to launch the field of cognitive neuropsychology where cognitive processes are understood in terms of their associated neurophysiological processes.

III. DEFINING CHARACTERISTICS OF DREAMING, AND REM VERSUS NREM SLEEP MENTATION

The close association of REM versus NREM sleep with dreaming versus not dreaming has created some confusion about whether we are studying the physiological characteristics of dreaming or the cognitive characteristics of brain states. When reports are matched by subject and time of night, 94% of REM reports are more dreamlike than NREM reports. So, while sleepers are generally dreaming in REM sleep, dreaming and REM are not synonymous.

Nevertheless, research focuses on the neurological, REM–NREM variable because the experimenter cannot see a dream, but she *can* see the polygraph evidence of the sleeper's state. Furthermore, REM and NREM brain states have clear discrete boundaries whereas the definition of dreaming is complex and a little fuzzy. Before the Aserinsky and Kleitman discovery, dreaming was defined as the imagery and thought of a sleeping person. After their discovery, it was clear that the dramatic imagery reported by sleepers as dreaming was produced almost exclusively in REM sleep. Consequently, the definition of dreaming has become indistinguishable from a description of the cognitive characteristics that distinguish REM from NREM sleep.

Dreaming may be defined as hallucinatory imagery and thought that occurs during sleep. By hallucinatory, we mean that the dreamer assumes that the images are occurring in the real or public world, and not until awakening does the individual identify the perception-like objects and events as imaginal. "Lucid" dreams are an apparent exception to this definition. In a lucid dream, the dreamer is aware that he is dreaming, can modify the course of the dream, and can even signal with his eyes or fingers that a lucid dream is in progress. During a lucid dream the brain state is somewhat altered from that of normal REM sleep, so that it may be called an altered, *REM-like,* dream-like state.

Dream images are primarily visual and in color. Their brightness and clarity is approximate 80% that of waking perception. Dreamers sometimes experience a sequence of images as though watching a movie, but they more typically experience participating in the dream. They act and the images respond. Auditory images occur much less commonly. The sense of body movement, pain, and emotions are noticeably reduced or absent during REM dreaming and may appear only as the dreamer makes the transition to waking, or when she sleeps late and the brain moves back and forth between REM and drowsiness.

Dreams are popularly associated with bizarre objects and events. The most common class of bizarreness is sudden or unexpected changes of scene. Much less common are shapes of objects or creatures that are improbable or nonexistent in real life. The least frequent class is persons whose visual identity is different from their known identity. For example, "It was my brother, but he was a girl (in the dream)."

All of these characteristics are expressed in life-like sequences that are longer and more detailed in REM than in NREM sleep. A typical NREM report consists of one or two persons or objects. They are not clear images and they tend not to interact. In one-third of NREM awakenings, subjects cannot remember anything. In summary, the length of the mentation report and the number of reported visual images are the sharpest discriminator of REM versus NREM mental life.

IV. DREAM RECALL

The discovery that an individual spends well over an hour, about 21% of his sleep time, in REM dreaming raised the question of what determines whether the individual remembers a dream in the morning. Over a dozen factors influence dream recall. If you are interested in your dreams, you will pay more attention to them, and you will tend to "notice" them *while* you are sleeping. The same holds for persons in psychoanalytic therapy. Some of this noticing may occur in the brief interval of near wakefulness that prevents one from falling out of bed as one shifts body position at the end on a REM period.

You are more likely to remember an interesting dream than a normal one. If, upon awakening, you lie still and try to remember your dreams you will recall more than if you awaken to a radio or phone call. The lack in the waking state of cues that might help recall events in a dream tends to handicap the recall of dreams that are in memory. Sometimes, chance events of the day will trigger the recall of a dream. Above all, dreams that occur while sleeping late in the morning, a weekend habit for many people, are better recalled than those that occur earlier in the night.

V. THE ACTIVATION PARADOX

The association of the rich mental life of the dreamer in REM sleep with the neurophysiological picture of brain waves that are remarkably similar to those of a waking individual makes a certain amount of sense. The bedroom is quiet, the eyes are closed, and the brain is awake in some way. So the brain makes dreams out of its own memories. But if the brain is awake, why is the individual lying limp on the bed instead of walking around and interacting with the real world?

Several investigators found that the sensory pathways that carry information about the outside world to the brain were functionally turned off during REM sleep. The brain could not, even if the eyelids were taped open, know what was going on. Jouvet found the specific nucleus that during REM sleep inhibits not only sensory input but the output of the neurons of the motor system. By disengaging this nucleus in a cat, he showed that the cat ran about hissing as though it were chasing the image in its dream! Image what night life would be like if all of us ran about for an hour every night acting out our dreams!

In 1949, Moruzzi and Magoun had shown that a small set of nuclei in the brain stem determine whether the brain is awake or asleep. Hobson and McCarley showed that the same nuclei act in REM sleep to awaken the brain. But in REM sleep they are joined by additional nuclei that essentially turned off the sensory input to the brain and turned off the motor neurons that carry out the commands of the motor cortex. Isolated from the outside world, the brain did the same thing as it did when awake, but with nothing coming in from outside, it was no wonder that its mental output was a little odd at times.

Neurologists and cognitive neuropsychologists have clearly established that different parts of the brain are dedicated to different cognitive operations. Although the brain, in REM sleep may be cut off from the outside world, one part of the brain may still send information to another part of the brain. Hobson and McCarley identified a pontine part of the brain stem-lateral geniculate nucleus (in the midbrain)–occipital cortex (PGO) wave in the cat that has a dramatically high electrical potential and is unusually frequent in REM sleep. They suggested that it was the origin of dreaming.

The activity of the pontine nuclei not only reaches the cortex in the form of PGO waves, but through its connections to the ocular motor system it is able to drive the eye movements of REM sleep. Although the eyes are quiescent during most of a REM period, PGO activity within the REM period is always accompanied by bursts of eye movements. Hobson and McCarley reasoned that the high voltage of PGO waves would disrupt any ongoing dream sequence and thereby cause the bizarre or improbable sequences described above. They further proposed that since PGO waves carry eye movement information, the brain must interpret this information as evidence that the eyes are looking at something. For example, if the PGO waves move the eyes in a particular pattern, the brain must invent a story that is consistent with the eye movement pattern. In other words, according to this activation–synthesis model of dreaming, the activated brain produces the images of the dream by "synthesizing" the eye movement information implied by the PGO waves. Finally, they argued, that since the PGO waves originate in the brain stem, well below the cerebral cortex where memories are stored, the pattern of PGO is essentially random. Since it is random, the origin of dream images is random and there can be no basis for interpreting dreams!

Although the suggestion that the brain could somehow create a sequence of dream images to fit a sequence of eye movements may seem preposterous, experimental studies of stimulus "incorporation" in REM sleep show that the activated brain is remarkably adept at interpreting any sensory stimulus in such a way that it is consistent with the context of the preceding dream. For example, if the sleeper is dreaming that he is sitting in a chair on a hot day, a light spray of water on his skin may elicit a dream of spilling a glass of water on his clothes. If she dreams she is in a room, the spray of water may become evidence of that the roof is leaking. If dreaming that he is reading a book, the sound of a bell may be interpreted as a telephone ringing. In the dream context of walking down the street, a loud clap may be interpreted as a gunshot, particularly in times of warfare or violence in the waking world. In short, the brain in REM sleep interprets whatever information it receives in a way that makes the new information as consistent as possible with the context of the preceding dream. The dream reports that are prefaced by phases such as "and all of a sudden. . ." may be instances where the brain fails to find a smooth transition from one image to another.

According to the activation–synthesis model, the brain must know in which direction the eyes move even though no external visual information reaches the eyes during dreaming sleep. Several experiments have obtained detailed reports of the time and direction of looking behavior during REM dreaming and measured the degree of association between eye movement predicted from these imaged events and the actual recorded eye movements. Although the evidence is inconsistent from one experiment to the next, the best studies show that many, but not all, sequences of eye movements are indeed associated with the dreamer's experience of looking. For example, one experimenter noticed that the dreamer's eye movements were moving in a continuous fast right–left pattern. Although the experiment was not concerned with eye movements, the pattern was so unusual that the experimenter felt compelled to find out what the dreamer was imaging. The subject reported that she was riding on a subway car looking out of the window watching the supporting columns flash past. The eye movement pattern matched the sequence of dream images very nicely.

All of this evidence applies to sequences of *individual* eye movements, up, down, left, right, etc. When eye movements occur in rapid bursts of several per second, they are too close together to be correlated with the dreamer's subjective impressions. Since PGO waves are reliably associated with eye movement bursts but not discrete eye movements, the correlation of PGO with the ocular orientation in the dream is unknown.

One aspect of the eye movement–dreaming pattern is clearly incompatible with the activation–synthesis model. Although Stage 1 REM sleep is defined by the occurrence of REMs, and a waking-like EEG within sleep, long stretches of the Stage 1 REM period are without any REMs. But visual imagery as well as all other characteristics of dreaming continue almost undiminished in the absence of PGO waves or eye movements. If these are no PGO waves, what then, is the input to the brain that is interpreted as a dream?

VI. DREAMING AS A SERIAL MODULAR CONSTRAINT SATISFACTION PROCESS

Antrobus has suggested a neural network, serial constraint satisfaction model of dreaming in which the activated brain in REM sleep behaves in much the same way as the activated brain in the waking state would if all of its sensory input was cut off. For example, in waking perception, the lateral geniculate nuclei in the thalamus and the primary occipital cortex carry out the first in a series of interpretations of the visual information that is registered on the retina. Visual perception is a series of neural interpretations that terminates in different brain regions that recognize the shape, color, spatial position, parts, function, and name of an object or person. Although retinal information is inhibited in REM sleep, the lateral geniculate nuclei and primary visual cortex and higher regions of the brain are sufficiently well activated to do exactly what they do in the waking state. Even in the waking state these brain areas do not "see" what the retina sees. They "see," or more correctly interpret, what the information they get from other cortical and subcortical regions.

This interpretation process may be represented by the neural network models of constraint satisfaction described by Rumelhart and his colleagues. Constraint satisfaction is a precise mathematical model for how interpretations may be carried out at levels as small as networks of neurons. Each of these neuronal areas or nuclei essentially interprets the pattern of activation in the neurons to which it is connected. The connections may be positive or negative and are learned during the course of waking perception. For example if neurons in the primary visual cortex interpret some random neural activity as two dark spots, and the spatial regions of the parietal cortex interpret them as approximately horizontal, then the more anterior regions of the brain may interpret them as eyes. Since most of the eyes we see are those of people, the brain may go on to construct the rest of the face, and so on. At the higher levels of constraint satisfaction, the process of dream image construction is precisely like that described above by the incorporation experiments described above. Each segment of the brain makes the best sense it can of what the other segments of the brain tell it. Just as the constraint satisfaction model shows how a fragment of sensory stimuli is sufficient to produce a complete waking perception, so Antrobus shows how nonsensory activity in the visual brain can lead to a complete imagined percept in REM sleep.

How does this model account for the association of dream images with eye movements? Waking eye movements are determined by a large number of neural processes: visual stimuli, auditory stimuli, orientation and motion of the head and body in space, shift in balance, memory, interest, volition, and more. All of these "inputs" are coordinated through the frontal eye fields in a part of the cortex that controls all body movements. In the waking state, a perceptual image would provide one basis for a decision by the frontal eye fields to move the eyes. The execution of the movement would be carried out by a complex subcortical process that ends up in the oculomotor system. The fine tuning of the eye movements is carried out in the cerebellum which is attached to the brain stem by a branch that includes the cells that originate the PGO spikes. [*See* EYE MOVEMENTS.]

Antrobus proposed that the dream image, coupled with the dreamer's interest, sends the decision to the frontal eye fields to move the eyes just as they would in the waking state. Hong and his colleagues, using a PET scan of the brain has recently shown that the frontal eye fields are, indeed, very active during REM sleep, particularly in the right hemisphere. Obviously, the Antrobus model says that the dream determines the eye movements, rather than the dream being an interpretation of eye movements. Although both the Antrobus and the activation–synthesis models start with a random process, the successive interpretations by different brain regions in the Antrobus model make the dream very much the product of the interests and perceptual styles of the dreamer. Since these motivations and perceptual characteristics are learned in the waking state, they do have potential for representing some of the waking characteristics of the dreamer. Whether such interpretations are accurate or valid, however, is another question. The poor agreement by different interpreters of the same dream suggests that the validity of dream interpretations is poor.

The role, if any, of PGO waves in dreaming remains to be determined. Dreaming can clearly proceed in the absence of PGO waves, and PGO waves may be independent of neural decisions made by the frontal eye fields. There is simply not sufficient neurophysiological evidence at this point to determine their role, if any, in dreaming.

The serial modular constraint satisfaction model says that the brain processes in REM sleep and waking are similar, that the output of the brain in the two states differs only because the input during REM sleep and waking is quite different. Compared to REM sleep and waking, the output of the brain in NREM sleep is impoverished because the cortex receives little activation from the pontine brainstem structures that determine the overall activation of the brain.

For many years, experimenters who studied dreaming sleep ignored waking imagery, apparently because they felt it was too familiar to everyone to warrant study. Furthermore, because waking thought and imagery differ so much from one waking situation to another there did not seen to be a single kind of waking thought that could serve as a basis for comparison with mentation produced in the sleep states. Foulkes, and later Antrobus, Wollman, and Reinsel, decided that for the purpose of comparing imagery and thought across the three states, waking mentation should be obtained from individuals in the same quiet, dark bedrooms that are used for the study of sleep mentation.

If the hypothesis that dreaming sleep is simply the output of an active brain that is cut off from external stimuli is correct, it should be possible to observe dreamlike mentation from awake subjects in this environment. The hypothesis was confirmed. Waking visual imagery was just as clear and bright, and the mentation just as storylike and bizarre as in REM sleep. The two differences that did emerge were that the storylike sequences of waking mentation were less continuous and the images were not hallucinatory. Both of these characteristics could be attributed to the lower sensory thresholds (greater sensitivity) of the brain to external stimuli during waking. No matter how dark and quiet the room, the waking subject is intermittently aware of his external environment and therefore knows that the images are *not* real perceptions. In REM sleep, there is no sensory evidence to compare with the dreamer's images, so the dreamer *knows,* wrongly of course, that the images are real perceptions!

Similarly, the intermittent awareness of external stimuli interrupts the imagery from time to time much as Hobson and McCarley assumed that PGO waves interrupt dreaming. But despite the occasional report of "and all of a sudden. . . ," image and thought sequences during REM dreaming exhibited greater continuity than did waking mentation.

Further support for the position that dreaming is the output of an activated brain that is isolated from the outside world by high sensory thresholds comes from a close look at dreams that occur when an individual sleeps late in the morning. Late morning seems to be the ideal time for dream recall, bizarre dreams, and even lucid dreaming. Antrobus, Kondo, Reinsel, and Fein reasoned that by sleeping late into the morning, the brain was activated by both the rising phase of the wake–sleep, 24-hour diurnal rhythm, and the alternating 90-minute REM–NREM cycle. Therefore, both NREM and REM reports should be longer and their images clearer and brighter in the late morning. In the REM phase, dreams should be longer and more vivid that at any other time during sleep. And that is what they found.

In other words, the pattern of activation that is distributed across the brain in REM sleep and waking, and is controlled by nuclei in the pontine portion of the brain stem, is fairly similar in both states. The primary difference in the two patterns of activation is that, as mentioned earlier, the REM activation pattern includes the active suppression of sensory input and inhibition at the spinal level of execution of the motor commands of the cortex. That is, the motor cortex can say "run," but the command to the skeletal muscles is not carried out. Nor is the expected sensation of moving transmitted back to the brain. And so the dreamer is apt to feel paralyzed. The second difference is that waking imagery is predominantly auditory and often verbal, whereas REM imargery is largely visual. The source of this difference is unknown. By way of further comparison, fever and many drug states are accompanied by visual imagery and hallucinations, whereas schizophrenia is associated with auditory hallucinations.

VII. FUNCTION OF DREAMING SLEEP

It is curious that the inhibitory processes of REM sleep are not active in NREM sleep. Clearly they are unnecessary because the brain in not sufficiently active in NREM sleep to either interpret the incoming sensory information or to issue motor commands. For reasons that are buried far back in the history of mammalian evolution, the sleeping brain becomes active in 90-minute REM–NREM cycles, but cuts off its sensory input and motor output during the REM phase so that the individual does not get into trouble by chasing its hallucinated demons in the dark. Although many theories have been proposed to account for this intermittent activation, they are so speculative that they do not warrant extended comment here. The most plausible hypothesis is that neurons require stimulation for their survival and growth. But people and other mammals also require rest in the form of sleep so that certain restorative processes can take place. The period of the wake–sleep cycle is determined by the 24-hour rotation to the earth, however, not by the needs of cortical neurons for stimulation. And so, perhaps, the brain stem developed its own internal form of stimulation which it delivers to the cortex intermittently when the individual is cut off from external stimulation. One strong piece of support for this self-stimulation theory is that REM sleep makes up about 70% of the 24-hour day of the fetus when its nervous system is in the process of rapid development.

The reader may wonder whether the sensory and motor systems are also deprived of this intermittent self-stimulation. The answer is that they are not inhibited during the 79% of the night that makes up NREM sleep. In fact subjects are vaguely aware of their environment during about 30% of NREM sleep. But since the cortex is not sufficiently active to fully perceive this sensory information, much less remember it or issue motor commands, there is no reason for the motor system to be actively inhibited.

Perhaps the most widely known hypothesis of the function of dreaming is Freud's suggestion that it is the guardian of sleep. Freud did not know, of course, that most dreaming occurs within the 21% of the night devoted to REM sleep. There would not be much value to a guardian that guarded only 21% of one's sleep. The notion that dreaming protects sleep comes from the remarkable ability of the brain to "incorporate" into an ongoing dream external stimuli that might otherwise awaken the sleeper. Although this process has not been studied systematically, there is little doubt that a ringing bell that is interpreted as a telephone in one's dream excuses the dreamer from getting out of bed to answer one's real telephone. Freud, however, was more concerned about the sleeper being awakened by the perception of raw sexual energy. He proposed that dreaming protected sleep by transforming this sexual threat to sleep into a more benign form. For example, a penis might be rendered as a cigar.

A recent hypothesis about the purpose of REM sleep deserves some comment because it was proposed by Crick, the Nobel Prize–winning geneticist. In his work with mathematical models of neural networks, he found that networks often become in effect gridlocked. So many neurons may become active that the network cannot process any information. He found that if he stimulated such a network with random information, it became essentially unlocked. Assuming that the origin of PGO waves in dreaming sleep is random, he suggested that they might function to free up cortical networks that might be gridlocked by the cumulative information processing of a days' work. This random, PGO-dreaming process, he suggested, would be a form of cleaning out the trivial memories accumulated during the day.

Of course the function or value of REM sleep is not necessarily the same as the function of dreaming. If the function of REM sleep is to stimulate cortical neurons, then those neurons are bound to produce the images and thought that they do in the waking state. But this does not mean that the particular mentation that is produced during REM sleep has a value for the individual. It may mean that the capability to produce that imagery and thought has value for the individual when in her waking environment, and if that ability is not exercised from time to time, even in sleep, its ability to process information will be weakened where it is most needed, namely in the waking state. [*See* SLEEP: BIOLOGICAL RHYTHMS AND HUMAN PERFORMANCE.]

VIII. REM DEPRIVATION

The discovery that dreaming is closely associated with Stage 1 REM sleep suggested to Bill Dement, another student of Kleitman's, a simple way to determine the function or value of dreaming sleep. He could simply waken the sleeper every time the brain moved into REM sleep. And so he did. And to his surprise, the more often he interrupted an individual's REM sleep the sooner the sleep moved back into REM sleep. That meant that the more often he interrupted the sleeper's dreams, the sooner the brain began to dream again. Moreover, if Dement deprived a sleeper of a hour of REM dreaming, the brain tended to make up the loss, almost minute for minute, during the following nights.

The immediate conclusion was that everyone has a need to dream. One psychiatrist proposed that if one could not get sufficient dream time, one would become psychotic. When subjects were deprived of an equal amount of Stage 4 sleep, a "deep" NREM sleep stage that predominates in the early part of the night, however, sleepers showed the same tendency to make up stage 4 sleep. In fact, if totally sleep deprived, people tend to make up the lost stage 4 sleep first, and the lost REM sleep second. The obvious question about the consequences in the waking state for the individual who is deprived of Stage 1 REM sleep remain unanswered. It has proved too costly to systematically deprive people of REM sleep over a number of days, study their waking thought and behavior all day long, and then compare this behavior with that of individuals deprived of equal amounts of NREM sleep. And so, the deprivation of REM sleep never did tell us about the function of REM sleep. And if it had, it would not necessarily have told us anything about the function of dreaming. Dreaming is one of many characteristics of REM sleep. Any consequence of REM deprivation might well be due to the loss of some characteristic other than dreaming.

IX. PROBLEM SOLVING IN DREAMS

Our tendency to see reflections of our personal concerns and problems in our dreams prompts the notion that dreams are a form of personal problem solving. The suggestion is so general that it is difficult to confirm or disconfirm. Herbert Simon, one of the fathers of artificial intelligence, the science of simulating the mental processes of the brain on computers, maintains that *all* mental processes are forms of problem solving. Even the automatic process of determining if an eye movement should move 10° or 11° to the right is a complicated problem that takes a very large computer to simulate. We are, of course, much more aware of the big problems of life such as whom one should marry, but they are no different in their neuronal representation than are decisions about eye movements. So, yes, dreams are a form of personal problem solving. When the dreamer imagines a strange person in the kitchen, he "solves" the problem by imagining an escape. One might then ask whether a solution imagined in one's dreams will generalize to the waking state. People who "solve" threats in their dreams by running away may well also run away from threats in their waking world. But, like the chicken and the egg, it is difficult to determine which comes first. [*See* PROBLEM SOLVING.]

The strongest support for the notion that large conceptual problems may be solved during dreaming comes from a number of anecdotes by scientists, writers, and creative artists, including Mozart, in which they have imagined substantial scientific solutions or artistic works, while dreaming. Indeed, some poets and surrealistic novelists regularly look to their dreams for images that they could not possibly construe in their waking life. Because sleep removes the individual from the constraints of the waking world, the activated brain of dreamer should be able to produce images and events that are creative in that they are somewhat free of waking constraints. And if there is sufficient motivation and sufficient preliminary knowledge some of these productions may well represent solutions to real world problems.

Nevertheless, the argument should not be overstated. For example, a screen writer might incorporate features of a bizarre dream image in a film. Although the image might well constitute a solution to the writer's problem, the process of generating the dream image would not be a problem solving process unless the original problem had in some way directed the dream process.

There is no way to know whether these anecdotes of creative dreams were produced in REM sleep or in those less well studied dreams that occur late in the morning, where the brain wanders back and forth between and highly activated REM sleep and a drowsy never-never land between sleep and waking. That the most dedicated dream recaller remembers less than 1% of her dreams each night suggests that whatever the solutions that REM dreams provide, they have little chance of being remembered upon awakening.

X. STRESS, GOALS, AND MOTIVATION

In order for a dream to contribute to the solution of a problem, some representation of the problem must be activated within the brain. Because sleep removes the individual from an external problem for 7 to 9 hours, the only cues that might reactivate the waking problem are imaginal ones. Dream images rarely represent objects, persons, or events from the recent past, so current problems are rarely explicitly represented in a dream. The events of the day do make up a large part of the sleeper's images during the interval of falling asleep, but these are not REM sleep dream images. If a waking problem is going to influence the dream, then, the problem must be both significant and long-standing. The horror of some repetitive life stressors such as child abuse, rape, a traumatic divorce, or warfare are so powerful, and they become associated to so many other events in an individual's life, that any of a large number of images are able to reactivate the memories at any time of the night, and may do so for many years after the original stressor. Weaker stressors may also influence a dream to the extent that they share some of the features of these more severe stressors. [*See* STRESS.]

Outside of these traumatic events, there is very little evidence that the stressors of the day influence one's dreams. For example, systematic study of patients before and after surgery show almost no evidence of cutting or threat of any kind. As might be expected, there are individual differences in the response to stress. A very small number of adults who experience persistent night terrors seem to feel vulnerable to many of the minor life stressors to which most people are indifferent.

XI. EMOTIONS IN DREAMS: NIGHTMARES AND NIGHT TERRORS

Stress is normally associated with powerful emotions as an individual strives to escape or cope from a stressor. But these emotions are rarely experienced with the REM dream. On the other hand there are many instances where individuals wake up screaming from a dream. There are several possible explanations for this paradox, none of them well researched. The most dramatic association of dreaming and panic occurs in night terrors, a nonpathological developmental problem experienced by some children during NREM sleep within the first 2 hours of sleep. The child awakens screaming in terror and continues to hallucinate images of being attacked. Occasionally, the child is able to respond to the parents, but may immediately fall back into the hallucinated terror.

The best current explanation for these terrors is that the neural mechanisms that normally inhibit or modulate the experience of emotional arousal are so deeply asleep that the mechanisms that amplify emotions expand without any neural constraints. Anything that lightens the first hour of sleep, such as awakening the child after 30 minutes of sleep, or a small drink of coffee before going to bed, tends to eliminate the terrors. Because most night terrors spontaneously disappear after a year or two it may be assumed that they are not caused by any personal stressor of maladjustment. A serious problem can develop, however, if the parents mishandle the behavior. Some parents are embarrassed because the neighbors hear the screaming. Others are angered because the hallucinating child appears to be completely ignoring their orders to be quiet. If the child is punished or beaten he will become afraid to go to sleep and a serious sleep problem may develop. At that point the family should seek help at a sleep disorders center.

The experience of emotion in nightmares, which occur primarily in REM sleep, seems to begin as the sleeper moves out of sleep. In that brief transition to wakefulness, the psychophysiological indices of emotion, such as elevated and irregular cardiac and respiratory activity, and increased muscle tonus and body movement, move to dramatic levels. Some investigators assume that the cognitive representation of threat is represented in the images of the dream, but the normal connections to the subcortical mechanisms that participate in emotional experience are inhibited during sleep, especially REM sleep, and become active only as the dreamer struggles toward wakefulness.

One reason for our poor understanding of the relation between dreams and emotions is that dreams reported in the laboratory are much less emotional than those reported at home. Although the laboratory setting may put a damper on the expression of emotions, a more likely explanation for the difference is that the home dreams that are emotional are noticed on those mornings when the dreamer sleeps late, where REM dreaming may intermingle with periods of drowsy wakefulness. In other words, the brain is well activated, but the REM sleep processes that normally inhibit the experience of emotion may be weakened by the broad based activation provided by the rising phase of the 24-hour diurnal rhythm.

XII. SLEEP WALKING AND TALKING

Although sleep talking is popularly associated with dreaming, only 20% of sleep talking occurs in REM sleep. Sleep talking and sleep walking both require activated skeletal muscles. Sleep walking requires vision and balance. Because these processes are not inhibited in NREM sleep they predominate in that state. Although most sleep talking is confined to only words, such as, "good," or "okay," some utterances are long enough to establish that they are related to a concurrent dream. Many people have attempted to carry on conversations with sleep talkers. Arkin showed that the brain must move into a NREM–waking transition state in order for the sleep talker to reply to a question from another person.

XIII. MIXED DREAMLIKE STATES

I have already pointed out that while the characteristics of dreaming are strongest in REM sleep, the most dramatic dreams, the most emotional, bizarre, vivid, and lucid, seem to occur in the late morning when the rising phase of the diurnal rhythm overlaps the REM phase of the 90-minute REM–NREM cycle. Sometimes, fortunately rarely, the REM cycle intrudes into the middle of waking experience. In the disordered state of narcolepsy, an emotional incident may trigger a temporary interval of motor weakness, drowsiness, and even a hallucination. Cataplexy, a related, more severe, but rarer disorder, is accompanied by severe loss of motor tonus. Other evidence of REM sleep intruding into the waking state is the occurrence of a drowsy episode accompanied by penile tumescence. Penile erection is common during REM sleep, particularly following a body movement. But only about 10% of these erections in REM sleep are associated with sexual content in the dream.

XIV. PARAPSYCHOLOGY, DREAM INTERPRETATION, AND SPURIOUS ASSOCIATIONS

There is so much information in a dream, that one can find connections or associations between some dream events and some events in real life. Once the associations have been made, it is tempting to assume that a causal relationship holds between the two. For believers of parapsychology, the association of a dream event with a future real life event seems so strong that the dream seems to predict the future. For the dream interpreter, the association between the dream event and some personality characteristic of the individual seems so compelling that the dream seems to be able to reveal some meaning of the person's mental processes. Scientific evidence for both of these positions is close to zero. Yet both practices continue to flourish.

Bibliography

Antrobus, J. (1990). The neurocognition of sleep mentation: Phasic and tonic REM sleep. In "Sleep and Cognition" (R. R. Bootzin, J. F. Kihlstrom, and D. L. Schacter, Eds.), pp. 1–24. American Psychological Association, Washington, DC.

Antrobus, J. (1991). Dreaming: Cognitive processes during cortical activation and high afferent thresholds. Psycholog. Rev. **98,** 96–121.

Aserinsky, E., and Kleitman, N. (1953). Regularly occurring periods of ocular motility and concomitant phenomena during sleep. *Science* **118,** 273–274.

Dement, W. C. (1972). "Some Must Watch While Some Must Sleep." Freeman, San Francisco.

Ellman, S. J., Spielman, A. J., Luck, D., Steiner, S. S., and Halperin, R. (1991). REM deprivation: A review. In "The mind in Sleep: Psychology and Psychophysiology" 2nd Ed. (S. J. Ellman and J. S. Antrobus, Eds.), pp. 329–389. Wiley Interscience, New York.

Ellman, S. J., Spielman, A. J., and Lipschutz-Brach, L. (1991). REM deprivation update. In "The Mind in Sleep: Psychology and Psychophysiology," 2nd Ed. (S. J. Ellman and J. S. Antrobus, Eds.) pp. 369–376. Wiley Interscience, New York.

Foulkes, D. (1966). "The Psychology of Sleep." Scribners, New York.

Hobson, J. A., and McCarley, R. W. (1977). The brain as a dream state generator: An activation-synthesis hypothesis of the dream process. *Am. J. Psychiat.* **134,** 1335–1348.

Moruzzi, G., and Magoun, H. W. (1949). Brain reticular formation and activation of the EEG. *Electroencephalograph and Clin. Neurophysiol.* **1,** 455–473.

Reinsel, R., Antrobus, J., and Wollman, M. (1992). Bizarreness in sleep and waking mentation. In "The Neuropsychology of Sleep and Dreaming" (J. Antrobus, & M. Bertini, Eds.), Erlbaum, Hillsdale, NJ.

Rumelhart, D. E., Smolensky, P., McClelland, J. L., and Hinton, G. E. (1986). Schemata and sequential thought in PDP models. In "Parallel distributed processing: Explorations in the microstructure of cognition," Vol. 2. (J. L. McClelland, D. R. Rumelhart, Eds.) pp. 7–57. MIT Press, Bradford, Cambridge, MA.

Wollman, M. C., and Antrobus, J. S. (1986). Sleeping and waking thought: Effects of external stimulation. *Sleep* **9,** 438–448.

DYSLEXIA

Chris Chase
Hampshire College

Glossary

Aphasia A linguistic disorder caused by brain damage.

Axon Part of a brain cell, called a neuron, which conducts information from one cell to another.

Cortex Part of the brain responsible for higher cognitive functions.

Dyslexia A serious reading impairment caused either by acquired brain damage or by congenital neurological abnormalities.

Irregular word A word with a pronunciation that does not correspond to the phonemic translations of its letters.

Neuron A cell in the nervous sytem which transmits and receives information from other neurons.

Phoneme The smallest unit of sound in speech. In English letters are used to represent phonemes, although there are more phonemes in English than letters so some letters represent more than one phoneme.

Regular word A word with a pronunciation where all the letters have a standard phonemic translation.

Standard deviation A unit of measurement which describes the variability of a group of scores.

Thalamus Part of the brain that receives input from different sensory organs and relays this information to the cortex.

DYSLEXIA is a term used to describe individuals who have serious reading problems. In the case of acquired dyslexia, reading skills already learned have been impaired by brain damage. In the case of developmental dyslexia, children have trouble learning to read despite adequate intelligence and educational and socio-cultural opportunities; the cause is presumed to be the result of congenital neurological abnormalities. Both types of disorders are discussed with a particular emphasis on developmental dyslexia.

I. INTRODUCTION AND HISTORICAL BACKGROUND

Reading is a relatively recent acquisition among the many skills developed by humans. Although difficult to estimate, spoken language is presumed to have developed at least several 100,000 years ago. By comparison written language is probably only several thousand years old. Writing systems probably were invented many times by different cultures, but we only have early historical evidence from five different societies, the oldest of which is the Sumeria cuniform writing made in clay tables that date to 3500 B.C. There certainly could have existed writing systems older than Sumerian; however, there is little doubt that spoken language predates written language by many generations. [*See* READING.]

The fact that reading and writing systems are recent cultural inventions implies that our species did not evolve to read. Spoken language has required many biological adaptations to develop the vocal apparatus and neurological systems necessary for speech production and comprehension, a process that evolved over millions of years. Reading skills have been built upon the linguistic and visual functions provided by evolution. Whereas children learn to speak without formal instruction, reading is learned later in life in school, building upon the vocabulary and grammar already acquired through speech. Stating the obvious, achieving a fifth grade level of reading proficiency (generally considered to be the skill level necessary to read a newspaper)

Copyright © 1994 by Academic Press, Inc. All rights of reproduction in any form reserved.

requires 5 years of instruction and daily practice for most students. Clearly, reading is not a skill that comes "naturally" but in fact requires considerable time and effort to learn. Consequently, there is no reason to think that all children have been biologically endowed with the same capacity for learning to read. As with most skills in life, some individuals are more talented than others.

Developmental dyslexia has social as well as biological origins. The recently discovered neurobiological abnormalities associated with dyslexia have generated considerable interest in the scientific community and will be discussed below. However, the social aspects of this disorder are usually neglected. Developmental dyslexia was only first reported about a hundred years ago in Great Britain at a time when elementary education was made available to all children in an effort to create a literate society. Earlier cases of dyslexia were likely overlooked because reading and writing were not considered essential skills, in fact most children never received any formal education. If a child's family was wealthy enough to provide some written language instruction and he or she failed to progress, the problem probably was attributed to other causes, such as oppositional behavior or poor intelligence, and other career interests which did not require reading and writing were pursued.

Today we have very few jobs which do not require reading skills; consequently, considerable efforts are made to teach all children to read and write, and we are more sensitive to situations in which a child despite opportunity, ability, and effort still fails to learn to read. A comparable situation to the past might occur today for a child who took dance or music lessons, only to discover that he or she had no sense of rhythm or was tone deaf. We do not identify *disrhythmia* and *dismusica* as disorders in need of remediation because these skills, while enhancing the quality of life, are not considered to be necessary to function proficiently in society. It is quite possible that other disorders, such as *computer illiteracy,* could be "discovered" in the future as social demands for skills that require technological proficiency require new ways to use our cognitive abilities.

II. DEVELOPMENTAL DYSLEXIA

A. Diagnostic Considerations

1. Exclusionary Criteria

Recognizing that a child is having trouble learning to read is not too difficult, but understanding why this is so requires considering many factors which could obstruct learning: intelligence, sensory impairments, socio-cultural influences, instructional environment, or emotional or behavioral problems. Dyslexia is the last factor to be considered. Since there are no unique symptoms associated with dyslexia (despite the popular misconception that dyslexics see letters backward), diagnosis is made using exclusionary criteria. In general a dyslexic individual has had serious trouble learning to read and (1) has normal intelligence, (2) has no significant sensory impairments which would affect reading development, (3) comes from a home environment supportive of the learning process and in which English is the primary spoken language (presuming text is being read in English), (4) has had an adequate educational opportunity to learn to read (5 year olds cannot be diagnosed as dyslexic), (5) has no serious emotional or behavioral problems which could be considered to be the primary cause of the reading problem.

2. Degree of Reading Impairment

The severity of the reading problem also must be considered. Half of any group of students who take a reading test will score below the average, since test scores usually are distributed in a normal or "bell-shaped" pattern about the mean score. Identifying a child whose reading score is below average does not mean he or she necessarily has a serious problem learning to read. Some students will score just below the mean, say at the 40th percentile, whereas others may do more poorly and score at the 10th percentile. Where one draws the line and claims that scores below a particular cut-off point represent a serious reading problem is somewhat arbitrary and depends on social, educational, and economic issues. On the one hand, one probably would not set the cut-off point at the 30th percentile or above for many reasons, including the fact that test performance can vary from one day to another and the reliability of the reading test could place the child's "true" value closer to the mean. On the other hand, placing the cut-off at the 2nd percentile would certainly guarantee that all the children scoring below the cut-off have a severe reading problem but omits many children above the cut-off who are quite reading impaired. In practice many schools usually use a cut-off set somewhere between the 10th and 15th percentiles (roughly $1\frac{1}{2}$ standard deviations below the mean).

3. Dyslexic or Poor Reader: The Use of Discrepancy Formula

Not all children whose reading scores are $1\frac{1}{2}$ standard deviations below the mean are considered to be dyslexic. Some children are what you might call "garden-variety" poor readers (sometimes referred to as backward readers); that is, they generally are performing below average in most of their academic subjects including reading. Although they may be intelligent in other ways, such as music or art, they are not very academically talented, as indicated by a low average score on an IQ test. To distinguish poor from dyslexic readers, the discrepancy between an individual's IQ and reading test scores is measured. In practice a discrepancy of $1\frac{1}{2}$ standard deviations between scores is considered sufficient to make the diagnosis of dyslexia, although another more complicated formula also can be used that takes into account the correlation between tests. For example, a child with an IQ of 110 and a reading score of 87 could be considered dyslexic; however, if the child's IQ were 90 then his or her reading score would have to be 67 to make a dyslexic diagnosis. [*See* INTELLIGENCE.]

The use of discrepancy criteria can produce some paradoxical situations. For example, a very bright child with an IQ of 130 could be reading above average with a score of 107 and still be considered dyslexic, whereas a child with an IQ of 90, which is just below average, could be a very poor reader with a reading score of 70 (at the 2nd percentile) and still not be considered dyslexic. This situation has led some researchers to propose abandoning the use of IQ testing and discrepancy formula altogether in making diagnostic decisions and instead only to use reading performance data. However, these situations rarely interfere with educational practice since all children, regardless of whether they meet dyslexic criteria, are referred for remedial help when they are having trouble making adequate progress in their regular classroom. The bright dyslexic student, however, may have to seek private tutoring, since as the result of a Supreme Court decision, public schools are not mandated to develop the full academic potential of each child but only to assure he or she achieves normal academic proficiency. Furthermore, several studies have shown that dyslexic readers have a poorer prognosis than "backward" readers in reading but did better in math, suggesting that the deficits associated with dyslexia are specific and unique.

4. Diagnostic Value of Dyslexia

Given the fact that there are no inclusionary diagnostic criteria, some may argue that dyslexia has little diagnostic value. Since the criteria for measuring reading impairment fluctuate and appear to be somewhat arbitrary, it is difficult to establish a reliable estimate of the prevalence of dyslexia. Some studies have produced estimates as high as 15% of the population, but a more widely accepted figure is around 5%. Although dyslexia is not a diagnostically discrete condition, many other medical conditions also use exclusionary criteria and measure variables on a continuous scale which require cut-off criteria. For example, Alzheimer's disease is now recognized as a unique medical condition with a specific neuropathology. However, a few years ago, only exclusionary criteria were available to make the diagnosis and performance rating scales that measured memory and self-sufficiency functioning were among the best indicators used. There are many other examples of medical conditions which use somewhat arbitrary cut-off criteria, such as obesity, high blood pressure, or high cholesterol levels. In each case the diagnosis is prognostically quite valuable, although the variables being measured are continuous and therefore require the use of cut-off criteria to make proper categorizations. Dyslexia is no different.

B. Neuropathology

1. Introduction

The cortex, a part of the brain which processes higher cognitive functions, is organized into two separate hemispheres. Many functions, such as visual processing, are bilaterally represented: that is, both hemispheres contribute to our view of the world. However, some functions, particularly linguistic ones, are lateralized in one hemisphere for reasons which are not fully understood. Language is processed in the left cortical hemisphere for most people. Should the brain be injured, as the result of a stroke or other head trauma, brain cells, called neurons, die and cannot be repaired or replaced. In many cases the parts of the left hemisphere which are damaged were responsible for language processing and so the damage disrupts linguistic functioning, a condition known as aphasia. Usually people with aphasia also have difficulty reading, but in some cases the damage may predominately affect reading skills and in rare instances be the only linguistic impairment. Such a condition is known as acquired dyslexia. [*See* APHASIA.]

2. Cortical Abnormalities

In modern times, acquired dyslexia was first observed about 100 years ago. The first reports of children with developmental dyslexia, which occurred about the same time, were thought to have similar cortical damage. Recently, Albert Galaburda and his colleagues at Harvard University have published the results of anatomical studies of the brains of six dyslexic individuals. They have shown cortical and subcortical pathology, involving bilateral damage affecting both the auditory and visual systems. At cortical levels these abnormalities appear as localized damage in small areas less than a millimeter in size where neurons are dislocated and the normal layered structure of cortex has been disorganized. Recent animal studies suggest that such cortical abnormalities occur early during fetal development. From an analysis of Galaburda's data, one study reported 23% of the cortical abnormalities occurred in the right hemisphere verses 77% in the left hemisphere.

3. Cortical Symmetries

In addition to these cortical abnormalities, a region of the cortex called the plenum temporale was symmetrically sized in the two hemispheres. Such hemispheric symmetry is not unusual, although 65% of a normal sample showed a left asymmetry, 11% had a right asymmetry, and 24% were symmetric. Since the formation of cortically asymmetrical regions appears to occur early in fetal development, the dyslexic symmetrical plenums also is probably produced early in the first trimester.

4. Subcortical Abnormalities

Abnormalities in subcortical brain structures also have been observed in several dyslexic brains. Cellular disorganization has been found in the auditory and visual areas of the thalamus, a brain structure that serves to relay sensory information from peripheral sensory systems, such as the ears and eyes, to the cortex. A recent study of the visual system of four dyslexic brains by Margaret Livingstone and her colleagues from Harvard was particularly interesting since only one part of the thalamic visual system showed any abnormalities. They were seen in an area called magnocellular region of the lateral geniculate nucleus (LGN). The LGN is the part of the thalamus that processes visual information. Neurons in the magnocellular layer were disorganized and cell bodies were 27% smaller than those measured in a control sample. Other regions of the LGN are made up of layers of neurons called parvo cells, and they looked normal in the dyslexic brains.

Livingstone speculated that smaller magno cells would process information slower than normal. A slower magno system could have interesting effects on how certain aspects of the visual information are processed. For example, the parvo system has been shown to be more selective for processing fine visual details and for encoding color, whereas the magno system handles the processing of global patterns or the "gestalt" of an object but is generally colorblind. Why a slow magno pathway would specifically affect visual processing of text is currently the subject of intense research interest.

C. Cognitive Deficits

1. Phonemic Awareness

Isabelle Liberman and her colleagues were among the first to show that dyslexics are impaired in their awareness of the phonemes in words. A phoneme is the smallest sound unit of speech. Whereas the word *cat* has one syllable, it also has three phonemes which happen to correspond to the three letters in the word. Most phonemes are consonants, and each has distinctive features involved in its vocalization that make it unique. For example, the phoneme/b/ is called a stop consonant because it is produced by cutting off the flow of air from the mouth. Other stop consonants, such as /p/, /d/, /t/, /g/, and /k/, have the same feature. They are distinguished from each other by two additional characteristics: voicing, which describes whether the vocal cord vibrates (found in /b/, /d/, and /g/), and place of articulation, meaning where the sound is formed in the mouth (front for /p/ and /b/; middle for /d/ and /t/; and back for /g/ and /k/). In all the languages of the world there are fewer than 100 phonemes, but most languages only use about 40 of them. Some languages like English use alphabets which are constructed so that each letter represents a phoneme; however, most phonemic alphabets have fewer letters than the phonemes used in the language. In English, for example, we have 26 letters which are used to represent about 40 phonemes. This is one of the reasons why learning to read English can be so difficult; the phonemic pronunciations of some letters or letter combinations change in different contexts and are not always consistent.

Before people learn to read, most are unaware of the phonemes in their language. Illiterate adults and children can count the syllables in words but are very poor at recognizing individual phonemes. When people learn to read, their phonemic awareness improves. For some, this improvement is the direct result of the reading instruction received. Teaching phonics directly trains the reader to pay attention to phonemic sounds in their language and to learn which letters and letter combinations are used in the written language to represent those sounds. There is widespread agreement that teaching phonics is probably the most important technique for reading instruction. Once the beginning reader has learned to "crack" the phonemic code of the language, he or she can rapidly increase their reading vocabulary by sounding out unfamiliar words.

Most dyslexic children have difficulty sounding out words and are less aware of the phonemic structure of language than other children their age; they have difficulty organizing phonemic information in short-term memory and recalling it; and they suffer from auditory perceptual impairments which make it difficult to discriminate between phonemes. Measurements of phonological awareness in prereaders have been shown to be predictive of later reading performance. Early training in phonological awareness also appears to facilitate reading acquisition among poor readers.

2. Temporal Processing Deficits

A new line of research has explored temporal processing deficits found in the sensory systems of dyslexic children. Many studies have shown that dyslexics have impaired temporal resolution in the early stages of processing that can impair the speed of their visual, auditory, and even sensory-motor perception. At present there are no fully developed theories which can explain why and how such deficits specifically affect reading functions, but as described above, this evidence is consistent with known neuropathology and represents an exciting new area for work.

D. Treatment

Two basic treatment strategies have been employed over the years to remediate dyslexia. The first approach attempts to correct the underlying neurological dysfunction through training programs and exercises which are presumed to strengthen and improve cognitive processes necessary for normal reading development. The second approach provides direct reading instruction, usually with a specialized set of curriculum materials or instruction methods.

1. Neurological Training Programs

Many different training programs have been advocated, each with their own particular theory about how dyslexic neurological impairments have affected reading development. Usually each program focuses on a particular behavioral deficit which has been found to occur among dyslexic children and therefore thought to be associated in some causal way with their reading problems. The idea has been to provide exercises that improve functioning in the particular behavior domain of interest with the expectation that if the behavioral problem can be corrected, this will in some way affect the course of reading development as well. One of the most popular programs of this type involves visual–perceptual training. The proponents of this approach argue that dyslexic readers have trouble controlling eye movements while reading and that exercises which strengthen ocular motor control are a necessary part of any remediation program. Another more recent intervention advocates the use of colored lens to correct dyslexic visual perceptual abnormalities. Helen Irlen, who invented this technique, does not have a theoretical justification for why this approach should work, but can offer testimony from many individuals whose reading skills improved. [*See* EYE MOVEMENTS.]

There are many reasons why such training programs should be treated with considerable skepticism and caution. First, most of these programs cannot provide evidence that the behavioral problems they attempt to correct occur more frequently among dyslexics than normal readers. Second, even if the behavioral problem occurs more frequently for dyslexics, it does not mean that this behavior is related to their reading problem. Most proponents for these programs are naive about psychological and neurophysiological aspects of reading and base their theories on antiquated notions about how the brain works. Third, when their treatment programs have been examined under well-controlled experimental conditions, they generally fail to show greater improvement compared to a nonspecific treatment group; that is, people get better because of the "placebo" effect, not because of the particular treatment given.

2. Reading Instruction

In contrast, providing direct reading instruction has, time and again, been shown to be of considerable benefit to dyslexic children. Several different teaching techniques have been popular; most involve the use of novel materials which are interesting and fun for children to use or include practice drills that present the information in many different sensory modalities. Many of these techniques have been incorporated into sets of instructional materials for normal readers, and there is no reason to think that these particular approaches are somehow uniquely important to dyslexic learners; in fact, they appear to be useful for all children learning to read.

Some instructional methods advocate teaching to a child's cognitive strengths and avoiding his or her weaknesses, whereas others stress the importance of remediating weaknesses directly. As described above, teaching phonics is a very important approach for developing good reading skills, and dyslexic children are known to be very poor at learning the phonemic code of the language. So a phonic remedial approach would be valuable, although progress is very likely to be slow. An alternative approach would encourage learning to read by the whole word method. Sight vocabularies are acquired by associating words and their meanings directly without the intervention of phonemic decoding strategies. The whole word method has been around for a very long time, and children can learn to read this way. For many dyslexics, this may be their only recourse. A recent study demonstrated that dyslexic children benefited from both phonemic and whole word methods, although individual progress was quite variable.

III. ACQUIRED DYSLEXIA

A. Methodological Approach

As described above, individuals whose readings skills were disrupted by brain damage suffer from a condition called acquired dyslexia. Neuropsychologists are interested in studying this disorder for several reasons. First, by examining the location of their brain damage they can infer which parts of the cortex are involved in reading functions. Second, acquired dyslexics make interesting types of errors when they read. By studying and classifying these errors, scientists expect to find well-organized patterns that would reveal the structures and processing components involved in reading. They assume that the brain is organized into separate and discrete processing modules, each with a specialized function which is used for reading. Assuming that the brain injury is localized and has only damaged some of the modules, scientists then attempt to reconstruct what the normal system might look like, taking into account how the damaged module(s) would affect normal reading functions to produce the dyslexic error patterns.

There are many reasons to be cautious about this approach. First, the exact location of the brain injury is often unknown, particularly with regard to the site and extent of damage in other, subcortical regions. Second, there is considerable debate about the extent to which mental functions are cortically localized and the degree of individual variability about where such localization occurs. Third, to cope with their disability, acquired dyslexics may adopt unusual strategies when they read which bias their error patterns, making it difficult to generalize from these data to normal reading function. Despite these reservations, this research approach has produced a very influential word reading model (described below) with several features which are widely accepted.

B. Acquired Dyslexic Subtypes

There are at least seven different subtypes or syndromes of acquired dyslexia. Three have been more carefully studied than the others; they are called *deep, surface,* and *phonological* dyslexia. All of the syndromes are based on an analysis of reading error patterns.

1. Phonological Dyslexia

This syndrome is fairly new but has a very straightforward symptom. Phonological dyslexics appear to have trouble reading out loud unfamiliar words or pronounceable nonwords (pseudowords), even very simple ones such as *mab* or *pib*. When the word is familiar, they have no trouble, even when the word may have an irregular pronunciation, such as *island, pint,* or *sword* (irregular because not all of the letters in the word receive the standard phonemic translation—silent /s/ in *island,* long /i/ vowel in *pint,* silent /w/ in *sword*).

2. Surface Dyslexia

Surface dyslexics appear to have the opposite problem of a phonological dyslexic. They read using a phonological strategy by sounding out each letter but are unable to recognize the word directly or on sight. When a word has a regular pronunciation, then sounding it out works well; however, if a word is irregular they usually "regularize" it. For example, silent letters are pronounced (e.g., *island* as *izland*) or vowels, which have a long pronunciation without an "e" at end of the word (e.g., *pint*), are shortened.

3. Deep Dyslexia

Deep dyslexics have a variety of symptoms. Their most characteristic error involves making semantic substitutions when they read out loud, replacing the word they are reading with another that is semantically related. For example, *spirit* is read as *whisky* or *emergency* as *ambulance*. Like phonological dyslexics, deep dyslexics also are very poor at sounding out unfamiliar words or pseudowords. In addition they make a variety of other errors, including derivational (reading *beauty* for *beautiful*), visual (*brush* for *bush*), a combination of visual and semantic (*papers* for *newspaper*), or function word substitutions (*is* for *the*). Furthermore, deep dyslexics are better at reading words which are concrete and easily imaginable than words which are abstract (e.g., *drum* vs *mind*).

4. Attention Dyslexia

Attention dyslexia appears to affect the ability to read letter or word groups. These individuals can read single letters or sometimes individual words without difficulty, but when other letters or words are presented their reading is impaired, even if the target letter or word to be read is highlighted from the others.

5. Visual Dyslexia

Unlike attention dyslexia, visual dyslexics can read all the individual letters in a word without any difficulty. However, when they attempt to pronounce the whole word out loud, they sometimes change part of it, substituting another word which is visually similar (e.g., *incense* is read as *increase*).

6. Word Form Dyslexia

Word form dyslexics appears to read by using a spelling strategy. Words are read only by naming (either out loud or subvocally) each of the letters in the word. As the number of letters in words increases, so does the time it takes for them successfully pronounce the word.

7. Direct Dyslexia

Direct dyslexics can read both familiar and unfamiliar words correctly, but cannot understand what the words mean. They appear to lose access to their semantic memory, although they still retain those cognitive structures responsible for word recognition and phonological decoding. This syndrome usually is found in patients in the early stages of dementia.

8. A Comparison of Acquired and Developmental Dyslexia

Some researchers have been impressed by the similarity of reading error patterns found in developmental and acquired dyslexias, particularly for phonological and surface dyslexia, and have proposed the same models be used for both conditions. There are several reasons why such comparisons are inappropriate. First, the structural damage associated with developmental dyslexia is unlike anything seen in acquired dyslexia—both with regard to the site and particular type of neurological abnormality. In fact, if an individual were to suffer brain damage as extensive as what has been found in developmental dyslexia, such trauma would most likely produce the symptoms of a severe, global aphasia in which all reading skills would be lost. Second, there are just a small number of ways to categorize reading errors. Any similarities between acquired and developmentally dyslexic reading errors may be superficial and do not necessarily provide important clues about the underlying neuropathology.

Third, the neurological abnormalities found in developmental dyslexia have forced these children to take a different path to acquire reading skills. They approach the tasks of learning to read with neurological systems which are different from normal readers, and consequently develop a cognitive architecture for reading which is unique. It is impossible to damage the adult cognitive architecture in a way which will reproduce the mental operations of a developmental dyslexic child. To further illustrate, imagine a young sapling growing into a mature tree. If the sapling was healthy, the adult tree will be large with many branches and a strong trunk. If the sapling started out in poor health, its growth would be stunted. There is no way to damage the healthy adult tree so that it resembles a stunted one. The damage occurred during development and the process cannot be reversed.

IV. MODELS OF READING

A. Symbolic Model

Two performance characteristics stand out when the reading error patterns of acquired dyslexics are reviewed altogether. First, two independent methods for oral word reading are available: either words can be read using a knowledge of phonemes to decode their pronunciation or word recognition can occur directly without phonological mediation. Second, word recognition processing can proceed independently from our comprehension of what we have read. Words can be automatically processed to some degree of recognition without allocating additional resources necessary for attaching meaning to the words. [*See* PHONOLOGICAL PROCESSING AND READING.]

These characteristics have been represented in a model, where boxes have been used to symbolize a particular processing module and arrows between the boxes illustrate the sequence of operations that are performed when reading. Figure 1 shows a simplified example of this type of model. This basic model has been further elaborated over the years by separating each large box or module into many smaller subprocessing components and adding more processing pathways. The phonological route separates each word into individual letters or letter clusters and then assigns a phonemic translation to each part to determine a pronunciation. In the direct route, whole words are processed based on their visual form without phonemic decoding and then memory systems are accessed to recall its pronunciation. Only words which are visually familiar and

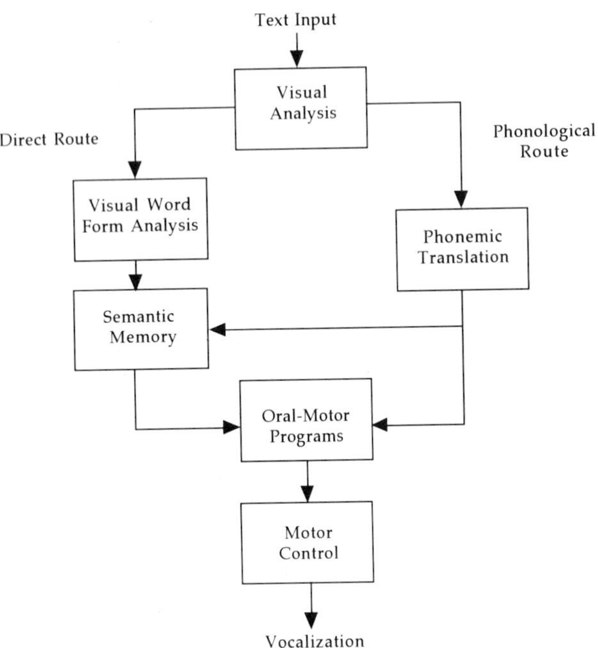

FIGURE 1 A symbolic model of word recognition.

already stored in memory can be read through the direct route. The two pathways operate independently and in parallel. Whichever route's information reaches the oral–motor response system first controls how the word is pronounced. Direct access to memory is presumed to be faster than phonemic translation, so if a person is familiar with a word, his or her memory of its pronunciation controls how it is read out loud.

The reading error patterns of the acquired dyslexics can be understood by assuming that certain processing pathways have been damaged. The intact pathways continue to process information but because systems have specialized functions, the loss of any pathway or processing module will compromise reading performance. In the case of irregular words (see above under phonological dyslexia), the two pathways will produce different pronunciations. The phonological route codes all phonemes in the same way, and so would produce a "regularized" translation of an irregular word with all the phonemes included. The direct route, however, has access to a memory system in which irregular pronunciations can be looked up.

Because of this difference, how irregular words are pronounced can provide important clues about where a dyslexic's damage may be located. For surface dyslexics, who "regularize" the irregular word, researchers believe their direct access to memory for pronunciation has been damaged and they must rely on the phonological route. For phonological dyslexics, their phonological route has been damaged and so they are unable to read unfamiliar or pseudowords but have no difficulty with direct access, even for irregular words. Deep dyslexic damage is more complicated. Since they cannot read pseudowords, their phonological route must be damaged. In addition they make semantic substitutions, suggesting that their memory recall may be impaired. Presuming their verbal memory or recall systems have some sort of semantic organization, in the process of accessing the pronunciation of a word, surface dyslexics may accidentally get the pronunciation of a different word which is semantically related.

B. Neurophysiological Model

The symbolic model described above has been directly mapped to the anatomy of the brain. Figure 2 presents a diagram of the different neurological regions which are located in the left hemisphere of

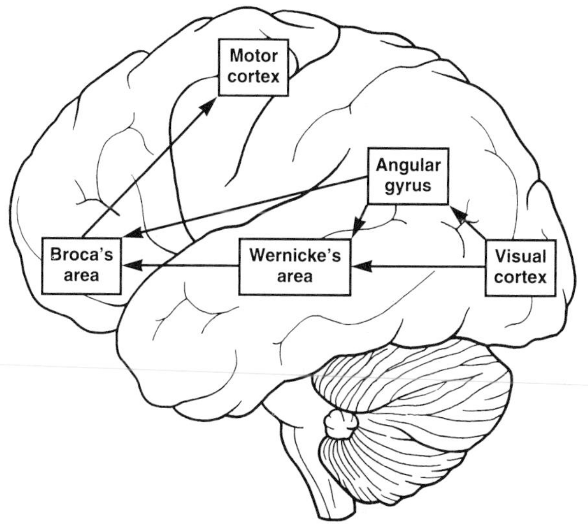

FIGURE 2 A neuroanatomical mapping of the symbol reading model.

the cortex. This map was based upon an analysis of the linguistic and reading impairments found in dyslexic and aphasic patients and the locations of brain damage that affected their verbal functioning. Reading begins in the visual cortex. From there the two parallel pathways diverge. The phonological route proceeds through the angular gyrus where phonemic decoding is processed. The direct route passes information through Wernicke's area where semantic memories can be accessed. Both pathways converge in a region called Broca's area, which stores oral–motor programs for controlling speech production. This information is then relayed to the motor cortex, where signals are sent to the mouth and throat to make vocalizations.

Recently, new neurophysiological evidence has raised questions about this model. A new technology, called positron emission tomography (PET), can measure changes in the blood flow of the cortex during a short period of time. If an individual is reading words while a PET scan is made, the image will indicate which areas of his or her brain were active during reading. Steve Petersen and his colleagues from Washington University have shown that the part of the brain which is most active when recognizing familiar words is located in the left hemisphere in a small region just adjacent to the primary visual cortex. Although activity in this region is consistent with processing in the direct route, the symbolic model predicted more activation should be occurring in Wernicke's area. In fact Wernicke's area is never very active when reading either orally or silently. Furthermore, the same region that was activated by familiar words also was active when reading pseudowords. This result is inconsistent with the symbolic model, which predicted pseudowords should be stimulating different cortical regions along the phonological route, primarily in the angular gyrus.

C. Connectionist Model

The evidence from the PET study along with the results of other psychological experiments have led researchers to construct a different kind of reading model in which phonemic and visual word form processing are handled by one complex system, in which both kinds of information simultaneously interact with each other and with semantic memory. In contrast to symbolic models made up of separate processing modules that function in a sequential and hierarchical fashion, these new systems, called connectionist models, broadly distribute processing across many simple units. Each unit responds to a specific attribute of the word being read. For example, there might be individual phonemic units and phonemic clusters that are activated when those speech sounds are contained in the word being read. Units which represent letters and letter clusters also would be present. Together these units mutually excite and inhibit one another, creating a competitive and dynamic process in which patterns of activation across units change over time. Initially many units may be partially activated, but through competitive interactions, eventually the whole system settles into a stable state in which a group of phonemic and letter units that provide the best representation of the word remain active.

Using computer programs, several different connectionist reading models have been built, and a few have been "damaged" to simulate acquired or developmental dyslexia. Some of the damaged simulations will disrupt functioning altogether, just as many aphasic individuals lose all reading skills. However, with some types of damage, such as reducing the number units available for processing, the reading performance of the network degrades "gracefully"—it continues to recognize words but also make errors. In these simulations the error patterns produced by the connectionist model do a remarkably good job of simulating some aspects of dyslexic performance.

V. CONCLUSIONS

New technologies, like PET, are helping to describe the relationship between brain structures and behavioral functions with a degree of precision which was inconceivable 30 years ago. We now know a good deal more about the neurobiological functions responsible for reading and continue to refine our models in an attempt to make them more biologically plausible. Reading researchers must continue to build conceptual bridges between functions at the behavioral level and neurophysiological processes at the biological level. Until we understand more about the neurobiological processes of reading, we cannot give a full accounting of why some children have trouble learning to read and will be unable to offer remediation strategies that effectively address their problems.

Bibliography

Coltheart, M., Patterson, K. E., and Marshall, J. C. (1987). "Deep Dyslexia." Routledge & Kegan, Inc., New York.

Galaburda, A. M. (1989). "From Reading to Neurons." MIT Press, Cambridge, MA.

Jager-Adams, M. (1990). "Beginning to Read." MIT Press, Cambridge, MA.

Obrzut, J. E., and Hynd, G. W. (1991). "Cognitive Models of Developmental Reading Disorders." Academic Press, San Diego, CA.

Patterson, K. E., Marshall, J. C., and Coltheart, M. (1985). "Surface Dyslexia." Erlbaum, Hillsdale, NJ.

Rayner, K., and Pollatsek, A. (1989). "The Psychology of Reading." Prentice Hall, Englewood Cliffs, NJ.

Seidenberg, M. S., and McClelland, J. L. (1989). A distributed, developmental model of word recognition and naming. *Psychol. Rev.* **96,** 523–568.

Tallal, P., and Galaburda, A. M. (1993). Temporal information processing in the nervous system. *Ann. N. Y. Acad. Sci.* **682.**

Wong, B. Y. L. (1991). "Learning about Learning Disabilities." Academic Press, San Diego, CA.

Ears and Hearing

John R. Pierce
Stanford University

Glossary

Amusia Loss or impairment of musical function.

Aphasia Loss or impairment of language function.

Basilar membrane A very narrow, springy membrane that extends along the cochlea.

Cochlea A part of the inner ear: a narrow, coiled tube about 35 mm long whose function is a rough frequency analysis of sounds.

Decibel (dB) A measure of relative power, 10 times the logarithm to the base 10 of the power ratio.

Frequency Number of times of recurrence per second; called hertz (Hz).

Gain Usually, the ratio of output amplitude to input amplitude. Power gain is the ratio of output power or intensity to input power or intensity. Gains given in decibels represent power ratios.

Impedance The ratio of force to velocity of motion.

Intensity Power density in watts per square meter.

Period The time after which a periodic sound repeats.

Place The position along the basilar membrane at which the oscillation due to a sinusoidal sound is most intense.

Power The rate of transfer or expenditure of energy. It is measured in watts.

IT IS THROUGH our eyes and ears that we perceive the world about us. Except in communication through language, sight ordinarily dominates. In seeking to understand ears and hearing we must have some understanding of the nature and properties of sound waves and some idea of the structure and function of the ear. With this background we can learn something of psychoacoustics, or the measurement and interpretation of the perception of sounds. With such knowledge as a background, we can understand something of kinds of deafness and disfunctions in the interpretation of sounds. Learning to hear and interpret sounds and speech, are both important aspects of ears and hearing. In the absence of sight, the blind use hearing as their chief means of sensing the world about them. But individuals with normal hearing have a remarkable ability to sense the size, direction, and distance of sound sources.

I. SOUND WAVES

Through hearing, we interpret activity in the world about us by means of sound waves that travel from a source of sound to our ears.

The term wave refers to any disturbance that travels from one point to another without carrying along the medium in which it travels. Thus, when a pebble is dropped into a still pool, ripples travel out from the point of impact, as shown in Figure 1, but the water does not move outward as a whole, as it does in a jet from a hose. Unlike waves on the surface of water, which travel out in circles, sound waves travel out in spheres of increasing size as they move away from their source. Whereas ripples on water are transverse waves (meaning that the motion of the water is at right angles to the direction in which

Copyright © 1994 by Academic Press, Inc. All rights of reproduction in any form reserved.

FIGURE 1 As Leonardo da Vinci understood, waves are not a bodily flow, but a traveling disturbance. Here the disturbance is a slight change in the height of the surface of still water. After we drop a small object into still water, ripples move out in concentric circles. [From Pierce, J. R., Null, A. M. (1990). "Signals: The Science of Telecommunications." Scientific American Books, New York.]

waves travel), sound waves are longitudinal waves; there is a very small back-and-forth motion of the air in the direction in which the wave travels, and a consequent variation in density and air pressure. Figure 2 contrasts a longitudinal wave (above) with a transverse wave (below).

The speed at which sound travels depends on both the springiness and the mass of the air. The more a gas resists compression, the faster sound travels through it. The more massive or dense a gas is, the slower sound travels through it. Helium is a very light gas, and sound travels through helium almost three times as fast as it travels through air. Sound waves travel through air at a speed of 344 m/sec or 1128 ft/sec. The speed of sound waves increases slightly with temperature.

FIGURE 2 The lower curve depicts a transverse wave, such as a ripple on the surface of water. The wave travels along the surface of the water; the surface moves up and down, at right angles or transverse to direction of the wave. As sound waves travel through air, there are alternate regions of higher pressure, where the molecules of air are squeezed closer together, and of lower pressure, where the molecules are farther apart. The regions of higher and lower pressure are depicted in the upper part of the figure as changes in spacings between lines.

At ordinary sound levels, the speed of a sound wave does not depend on sound intensity, which is defined as watts per square meter. The sound wave consists of very small fluctuations of air pressure, and of very small back-and-forth motions of the air. The accompanying changes in density are illustrated in the upper part of Figure 2. The intensity I of a sound wave is the difference p in air pressure due to the sound wave, times v, the small local longitudinal velocity caused by the sound wave. The pressure p is a constant K, times the velocity v. Hence, we can write

$$I = pv = Kv^2 = p^2/K.$$

The intensity is proportional to the square of v, or to the square of p.

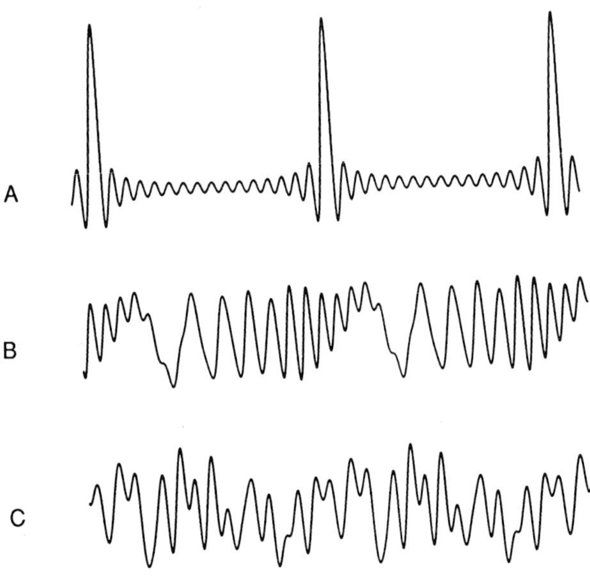

FIGURE 3 Three periodic sound waves, depicted by variations of sound wave pressure as a function of time. All three sound waves consist of 16 harmonic frequency components with the same amplitudes; only the relative phases are different for the three waves. In wave A the component sine waves are so phased that their amplitudes add and cause a peak at the beginning of each period. In wave B the phases are artfuly chosen so as to give the effect of periodic chirps, or rises in frequency. In wave C the phases are random, and the waveform looks like a repeating section of noise. For low fundamental frequencies the ear can respond to changes during a single period of the sound wave, and the waves A, B, and C sound a little different.

In the sound waves which reach our ears, the air pressure varies with time in a complicated manner. Figure 3 shows how pressure varies with time for three different sound waves. Similar curves may be used to represent the way pressure varies with distance along a sound wave at an instant in time.

The ear sorts a sound wave into various ranges of frequency. A sound wave may be thought of as the sum of many frequencies, of many simpler component waves.

Fourier analysis is the representation of a complicated wave as the sum of sine waves of various frequencies. Figure 4 shows a complicated wave (above) and its representation as the sum of three sine waves (below). Each sine wave is completely specified by three quantities: the frequency, the amplitude, and the phase. The frequency f in hertz (Hz) is the number of times the sine repeats in a second (the period T, the time between repeats, is the reciprocal of f, that is, $T = 1/f$). The amplitude is how much the sound pressure increases and decreases. Phase represents the time at which the pressure fluctuation changes from negative to positive. The wavelength of a sound wave, λ, is the distance between crests of the wave, and is the velocity of sound, V, divided by the frequency f

$$\lambda = V/f.$$

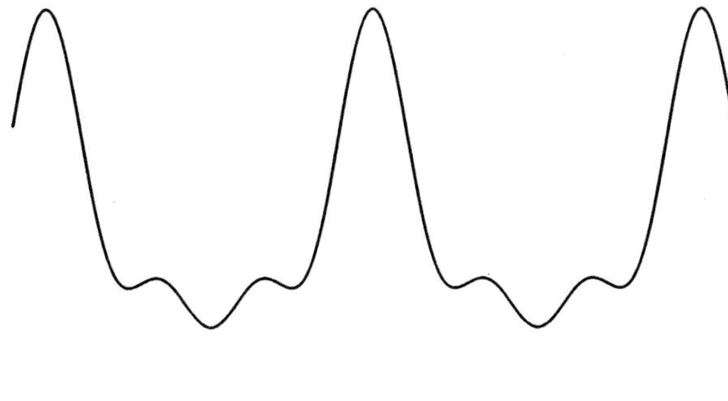

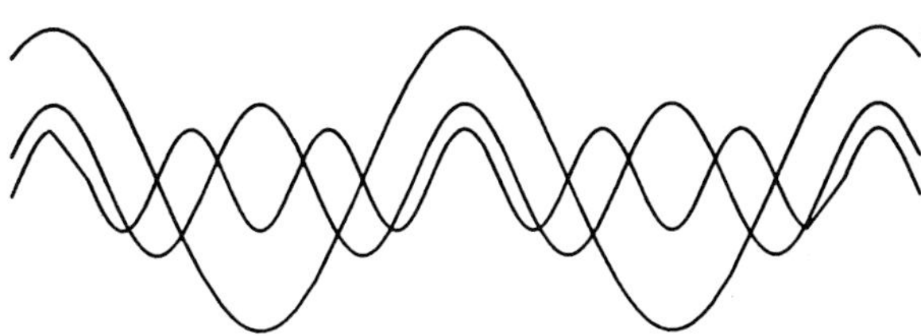

FIGURE 4 The upper curve depicts a "complicated" waveform. This waveform is simply the sum of the three sine waves of different frequencies that are shown in the lower part of the figure.

The shape of a wave depends on the amplitudes and phases of its its sinusoidal components. In the waves of Figure 3, the relative amplitudes of the sinusoidal components are equal for the three waves, but the relative phases are different. Each of the three waves is made up of 16 sinusoidal components of the same 16 frequencies and intensities, but for each of the three different waves, the sinusoidal components reach their peaks at different times.

Sound waves can be of short duration, like a short pulse or click, or of longer duration, such as a broad pulse or a persistent noise. How short a wave *can* be depends on its bandwidth B, the range or band of frequencies present measured in hertz. The bandwidth of the sound waves shown in Figure 3 is about 16 times the lowest frequency in hertz. Waveform *a* consists of a number of short pulses, each about one-sixteenth as long as the time between pulses. The shortest pulse that a wave with a bandwidth of B Hz can have is about $1/B$ seconds. Thus, there is a reciprocal relationship between bandwidth and minimum duration.

Unlike waveform A of Figure 3, waveforms B and C are not sequences of pulses. Waveform B looks like a sine wave whose frequency changes periodically with time. Waveform C looks like a repeated noise, a repeated random up-and-down oscillation of roughly constant amplitude. Waveform depends on the relative phases of the sine waves, which represent a sound, as well as on their amplitudes and frequencies.

As in the case of the waves in Figure 3, many natural sound waves are periodic or nearly periodic; they repeat over and over again. The waves of Figure 3 are all periodic. Examples of other periodic sound waves are the puffs of air going through the holes of a siren, the sound of a circular saw or a gasoline motor, the sound waves of sung vowels, many animal vocalizations, and the sounds of musical instruments such as violins, horns, and pianos.

In the Fourier representation of periodic sounds, all frequency components must go up and down an integer number of times in one period of the overall wave. Thus, the only frequencies that can be present are whole numbers divided by the period T ($T = 1/f$). These frequency components ae called harmonic partials or harmonics. These frequencies consist of the lowest frequency f (the fundamental frequency), a frequency $2f$ (the second harmonic), a frequency $3f$ (the third harmonic), and so on. Thus, a vowel or other musical sound of pitch-freuqency or fundamental frequency 261.6 Hz (middle C) will contain sinusoidal components of frequencies 261.6, 523.2, 784.8 Hz, and so on.

The distribution of power among the harmonics of a periodic wave affects what we hear. When high frequencies are removed, as when the bass control of a radio is turned up, a voice will sound muffled. When low frequencies are removed, removing the fundamental and lower harmonics, the sense of pitch does not change, but the voice sounds tinny.

The frequencies we can hear range from around 30 to around 20,000 Hz for young people, and around 10,000 Hz for old people. The frequencies in musical and voice sounds may or may not include the fundamental or first harmonic, but they do include many higher harmonics. While the lowest note of the piano keyboard has a fundamental frequency of 27.5 Hz, most of the sound power of such a low note is in high harmonics. While the highest note of the piano keyboard has a fundamental frequency of 3729 Hz, it contains harmonics of much higher frequency. If the higher frequencies are removed from a sound, it may be difficult to interpret the sound. Hence, it is difficult to distinguish *f* and *s* over a telephone because telephones transmit no frequencies above 3200 Hz.

The wavelength of sound is important in listening through a horn, or with the outer ears, and also in the reflection of sound by solid objects and the casting of sound shadows. When a sound is directly in front of the head and shoulders, the sound is reflected off the body and increases the sound intensity.

When a sound source is to the right of the body, the left ear is in a sound shadow. The difference between what is heard between the left and right ears is important in sensing the direction of the sound source. A substantial shadow occurs only when the object casting the shadow is a wavelength or more in size. The wavelength of a 112 Hz sound is 10 feet; that of a 1120 Hz sound is 1 foot; that of a 13,440 Hz sound is 1 inch. Sound reflection and shadowing by the head is important only in high frequency sounds.

The wavelength of sound is also important in tubular resonators, such as trombones. Sound waves travel the length of such tubes and are reflected at the ends. Resonance depends on the time it takes the sound to travel repeatedly from end to end. The frequencies of these resonances are such that the wavelength is two times the length (tube open or closed at both ends) or four times the length (tube open at one end and closed at the other). In musical instruments, the tubes determine or influence the pitch of the sound produced. In the human vocal tract, the resonance is determined by the relative amplitudes of the various harmonics generated in speaking.

II. THE EAR

Figure 5 depicts the various parts of the ear in a schematic way. A sound wave travels through the air and reaches the outer ear (the pinna, plural pinnae), modified in intensity and spectrum by the head, body, and head position. High frequency components have shorter wavelengths and are more modified most. When the sound comes from one side, the head shadows and reduces the sound level at the farther ear. This plays a part in sensing the azimuthal left or right) direction from which the sound comes.

The pinna itself modifies the spectrum of the sound that enters the auditory canal. The pinna can substantially modify only high frequency, short wavelength components of the spectrum (roughly, components above 6000 Hz). The modification changes with the angular height or elevation of the sound source, and this change is important in judging the height of a sound source. The reader can verify this by holding the tops of the ears down and noting the difficulty in judging the elevation of clicks or jingling keys.

Various spectral modifications due to the pinnae and to the head and body appear to be important in externalizing the sound source, in hearing the sound as coming from some place distant from the head. Such externalization is generally absent or poor for stereo sound heard with headphones. It is best when the microphones for the two stereo channels are fed from tubes in the auditory canals.

The auditory canal or meatus is a tube about 3 cm long and 6 mm in diameter that leads from the pinna to the ear drum. A tube of this length which is open at one end and closed at the other is resonant at 2900 Hz. Hence, the ear is most sensitive to sound at around 3000 Hz.

The cochlea is a coiled, bony, fluid-filled tube or canal about 35 mm long and 1 mm in diameter. Along its whole length, the tube is divided by the long, narrow, springy basilar membrane which is stretched across a bony gap.

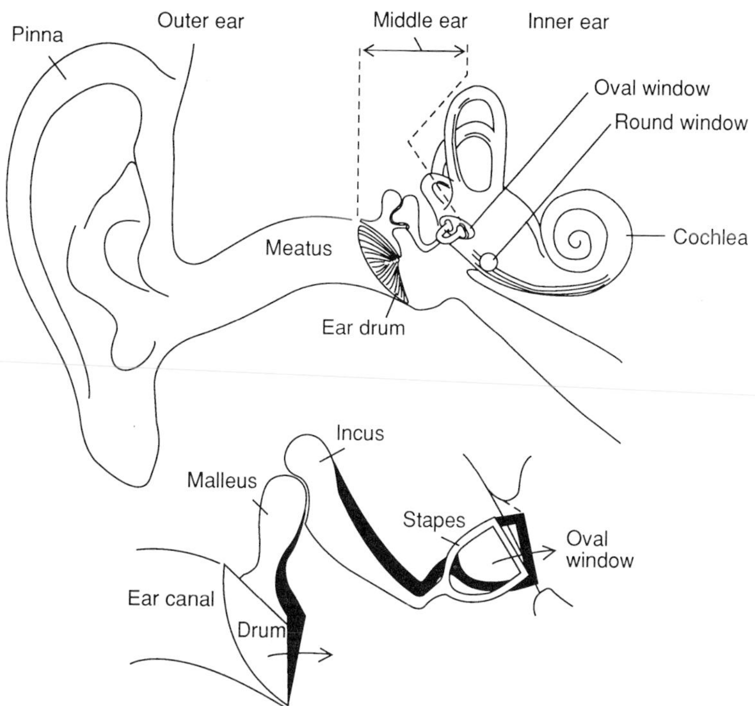

FIGURE 5 A schematic picture showing the outer ear (pinna), the auditory canal or meatus, the middle ear (shown in the lower drawing to a larger scale), the eardrum and 3 bones that transmit vibration from the eardrum to the oval window of the inner ear, and the coiled cochlea that analyzes vibration into various frequency ranges and sends nerve messages brainwards along the auditory nerve. The semicircular canals above the cochlea are not involved in hearing. [From Pierce, J. A. (1992). "The Science of Musical Sound" rev. ed. W. H. Freeman, New York.]

Three interconnected little bones in the middle ear transmit vibrations from the eardrum to the flexible membrane of the oval window. These vibrations cause waves that travel along the basilar membrane of the cochlea, from the basal end (at the oval window) toward the apical end 35 mm away. These bones are the malleus (hammer), the incus (anvil), and the stapes (stirrup).

The chain of these three bones can be stiffened and their transmission of sound decreased by the contraction of the stapedius muscle. Loud sounds cause contraction of the muscle and a reduction of the vibration transmitted to the oval window. This stapedius reflex is one automatic gain control function in the ear.

We have noted that the cochlea is a coiled tube about 35 mm long and 1 mm in diameter. The diameter varies somewhat along the length. The long, narrow, springy basilar membrane varies in width along the cochlea, being narrowest at the basal end and widest at the apical end. At the apical end there is an opening called the helicotrema between fluid-filled channels separated by the basilar membrane.

If the stapes pushes the oval window in slowly, the fluid moves along a channel on one side of the basilar membrane, goes through the passage to the other side of the basilar membrane, moves back along that side, and pushes out the flexible membrane of the round window.

A rapid sinusoidal oscillation of the oval window creates a wave which travels along the basilar membrane and increases in amplitude with distance from the oval window. The amplitude rises to a sharp peak of vibration at a particular place along the basilar membrane. Beyond this place, the vibration falls rapidly to zero. The distance from the oval window of this place of maximum vibration decreases as the frequency of the sinusoidal sound increases.

Figure 6 illustrates the overall amplitude of vibration along the cochlea caused by two simultaneous sine tones with frequencies of 120 and 960 Hz. Each causes a peak of vibration along the cochlea at the "place" of the frequency. Very high frequencies cause peaks of vibration to the left, near the basal end of the cochlea; very low frequencies cause peaks

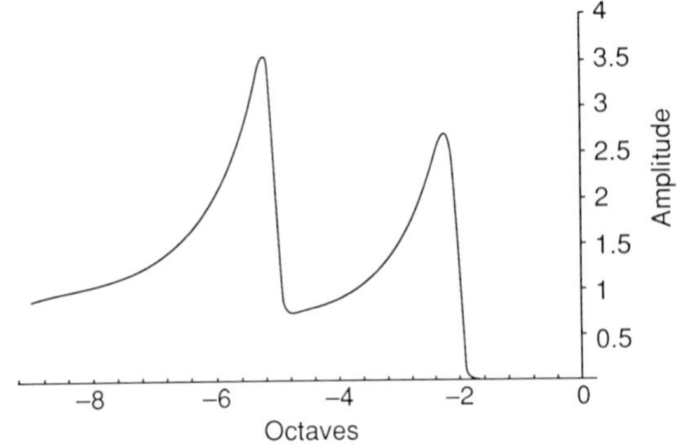

FIGURE 6 The overall amplitude of waves that travel along the cochlea. Two sine waves of frequencies 120 and 960 Hz travel to the right, from the basal end of the cochlea which begins at the oval window, toward the right or apical end which terminates at the helicotrema. The vibration associated with each wave peaks at the "place" of the frequency and then falls rapidly to zero. A sound of higher frequency cannot reach the place of a lower frequency and mask it.

of vibration to the right, near the apical end of the cochlea, at the helicotrema. The frequency scale is in octaves: 0 at the right corresponds to a frequency of around 30 Hz; 9 to the left corresponds to a frequency of around 15,000 Hz. A frequency component causes no vibration to the right of its place, and a higher frequency cannot mask or interfere with hearing a lower frequency. The vibration falls off less rapidly to the left of its place. If the two peaks lay very close together, the two peaks would coalesce, and both frequencies would lie in the same critical bandwidth.

Thus, the cochlea sorts out the frequency components of a sound. The higher frequencies cause strongest vibration near the oval window; the lower frequencies cause strongest vibration farther along toward the helicotrema. The vibrations activate some of the 3500 inner hair cells which lie along and in contact with the basilar membrane. Vibrations of the hair cells result in the generation of electric (strictly, electrochemical) nerve pulses which travel along fibers of the auditory nerve. Several fibers innervate each inner hair cell.

The nerve pulses of the auditory nerve excite nerve pulses in ascending nerve pathways that join a number of complicated way stations between the brainstem and the auditory cortex of the brain. The nerve pulses that finally reach the cortex carry information from all lower parts of the auditory system.

Some fibers of the auditory nerve transmit nerve pulses from the brain to the 12,000 outer hair cells which also lie along the basilar membrane. The outer hair cells are also interconnected along the cochlea. They act as a sort of gain control which makes the level of vibration along the cochlea more nearly uniform than it would otherwise be.

Outer hair cells may be thought of as tiny muscles which increase the relative vibration of the basilar membrane. In one type of tinnitis, or ringing in the ears, the basilar membrane oscillates locally in the absence of sounds, and this vibration can be picked up by a sensitive microphone placed near the ear.

The ear is most sensitive around 3000 Hz; a person with very good hearing can hear a 3000-Hz sine wave with an intensity of about a millionth of a millionth of a watt per square meter. For 50% of people, the intensity of the sound that can just barely be heard is around 15 dB (30 times) as great. The maximum tolerable sound intensity is about one watt per square meter, 120 dB (a million million times) as great as the intensity which can just barely be heard by a person with very good hearing. The automatic gain control features of the little bones and of the outer hair cells makes it possible to hear such a range of intensities.

The greatest tolerable sound intensity does not change much with frequency or with acuteness of hearing, but the just hearable intensity does. Compared with the value for 3000 Hz, the just hearable intensity is about 50 dB greater at 60 Hz and about 16 dB greater at 10,000 Hz.

The way stations between the auditory nerve and the auditory cortex are a sequence of interconnected pairs, one for each ear. At each way station a tonotopic mapping is preserved, whereby the location at which nerves fire changes smoothly with the frequency of the sound causing the firing.

Signals from the two ears first come together at a way station called the superior olive complex. One part of the superior olive compares the relative intensities of sound from the two ears, while another part compares the relative times of the arrival of the sound at the two ears. From these comparisons, the direction of the sound source may be determined.

"Listening in one direction" refers to one's ability to focus on sounds from a specific direction. If one is focused on sounds that occur to the left of the body, equally intense sounds from other directions seem less loud. One example of this is the cocktail party effect: the ability to hear what one nearby speaker says in a room full of chatter.

An individual nerve fiber can fire a few hundred times per second. After a nerve fiber has fired, there is a refractory period during which it can no longer fire despite any ongoing stimuli. Each inner hair cell is innervated by several nerve fibers. In response to the same stimulus, related nerve fibers fire preferentially near the same parts of the sound waveform. Thus, many nerve fibers are available, and the sums of their firings collectively preserve time features of a sound wave.

The period of a 1400 Hz sine wave is about 700 μsec (millionths of a second). But, in detecting what direction such a sound comes from by relative time of arrival of sound waves, the error can correspond to a time difference of a few tens of microseconds. This corresponds to a difference in direction of the sound source of about one degree.

The ear performs many tasks, including recognizing parts of the sound waves that reach the ear as coming from a particular source, and identifiying the nature of that source. The exact function of intermediate way stations is not well understood, but they are thought to be responsible for analyzing aspects of sounds and sending the results of the analyses to the auditory cortex, directly or after further processing.

III. PSYCHOACOUSTICS

It is important to know something about the anatomy and function of the various parts of the ear in order to understand the experience of hearing. But, it is sounds themselves that are primary in our lives. The critical bandwidth is a measure of the range of frequencies that excite a single hair cell. If a single hair cell is substantially excited by two sine waves, their frequencies lie within a critical bandwidth and they cannot be heard as separate and independent sounds. If no or very few hair cells are excited by both sine waves, their frequencies are separated by more than a critical bandwidth, and the two sounds can be heard separately. If there are many harmonics of a low fundamental frequency within a critical bandwidth, what we hear depends on their relative phases. For low fundamental frequencies, the waveforms A, B, and C of Figure 3 will sound a little different.

The critical bandwidth increases with frequency. Above a few hundred hertz the critical bandwidth around a frequency f is about $f/5$.

Critical bandwidths are related to what we hear in a variety of ways. If many hair cells in different critical bandwidths are excited at the same time, we hear this as a "click." Similarly, if a sine wave is turned on or off suddenly, we will hear a "click." If a sound wave that produces a click arrives at the right ear a few tens of microseconds before it reaches the left ear, we hear the sound as coming from a source a little to the right. We are not, however, consciously aware of having heard the clicks at two slightly different times. Any given tone must start 20 msec or more after the other if it is to be heard as a separate, later starting tone.

The amplitudes of most musical tones and speech sounds do not rise or fall abruptly. If one is to hear a tone without a click, a sine wave or other waveform must change slowly. If a sine wave is gradually turned on and gradually turned off during a period of some tens of cycles, a short tone will be heard without an accompanying click.

A musical tone is made up of many harmonics, yet it is heard as a single sound of a definite pitch. Either successive lower harmonics or (in the absence of low harmonics) clusters of high harmonics can give a sense of pitch. A cluster of successive high harmonics is heard as a succession of clicks whose rate is equal to a (missing) fundamental frequency. For low rates corresponding to musical tones of low pitch, such a succession of clicks sounds buzzy, but it gives some sense of pitch, for the rate can be matched to the pitch of a musical tone. At rates above a few hundred per second the click sequence becomes a crude musical tone. Either successive low harmonics or successive high harmonics that are a series of clicks can evoke the sensation of pitch, presumably by different mechanisms.

There are a number of traditional measurements of sound, including jnds (just noticeable differences) of intensity and pitch, and judgments of reported loudness. The sum of jnds was once thought to be a numerical measure of the percept of pitch or of loudness, but this has proved not to be the case.

Timbre is another attribute of sounds. Distinct vowel sounds are an instance of a timbre that depends strongly on spectrum. The addition of vibrato makes synthesized vowel sounds more natural and acceptable. Changes in frequency with time affect timbre. A good instance is that the timbre of the sounds of brass instruments depends on the higher harmonics rising in amplitude later than the lower harmonics. In speech, change of spectrum with time plays a crucial part in distinguishing consonants and dipthongs.

Hearing goes far beyond distinguishing loudness, pitch, and timbre. When there are multiple sources of sound, it is possible to distinguish the parts of sound that belong to different sources. When sounds bounce off walls, reflections delayed by from 1 to around 50 msec are not heard as separate sounds coming from different directions; they are absorbed into the direct sound that arrives first. This is called the precedence effect; the sound wave that arrives first takes precedence in whatever mechanism gives us our sense of direction of arrival of a sound wave. We hear reflections as echoes only when their arrival at the ear is substantially delayed.

Other things help us to sort out sounds from a single source. Continuity (also called common fate) is important. Things that change together are heard together. A common vibrato or tremolo can fuse frequency components into one sound. Proximity in pitch or timbre can also be important. In listening to melodies, tones sounded at long intervals are heard as one sequence, whatever their pitches. But if the notes of two melodies in different ranges of pitch are interleaved and played rapidly, the two melodies are heard as simultaneous. Differences in timbre increase the distinction among melodies.

The quality of the sound plays a crucial part in judging the distance of a sound source. In a shout, or in the striking and clanging of a huge bell, we sense physical effort, partly from experience, but partly from the nature of the sound. When we hear such a sound as having a low intensity, we judge that it comes from far away. A whisper in one ear seems very close partly because we hear it in one ear only; if the source were farther away, more sound would get to the more distant ear.

There are other clues to the loudness and distance of a sound source. Most of the sound we heard from a distant source in a room with the listener may be successive reflections from the walls. Adding reverberation to a sound can thus make it seem farther away. The farther a sound travels from its source, the more likely we are to be shielded from higher frequency components. A familiar sound with reduced high frequencies can seem far away.

IV. DEAFNESS, APHASIAS, AND AMUSIAS

Most people suffer some impairment of hearing with age. Common deficiencies are a loss of the ability to hear high frequencies, some general loss of sensitivity, and tinnitus, or ringing of the ears.

A conductive hearing loss refers to a hearing impairment of the middle ear, usually caused by a stiffening of the connections between the malleus, incus, and stapes, so that vibration is not transmitted efficiently from the eardrum to the cochlea. Treatments for severe conductive hearing loss include the use of a hearing aid, surgical breaking or loosening of the chain of three bones, or replacement of the chain by a prosthesis.

A sensorial hearing loss refers to a hearing loss associated with the cochlea and its hair cells, which transduce vibration into neural firings. Sensorial loss is often more severe for faint sounds, while loud sounds are heard normally. This is called recruitment. Recruitment makes hearing aids less satisfactory than in the case of conductive hearing loss.

When the outer hair cells fail to function, the frequency selectivity of hearing is reduced, and so is a satisfactory response to a wide range of sound levels. If the inner hair cells are severely damaged, they may fail to cause neural firings in response to vibration. This results in total deafness. The insertion of electrodes into the cochlea is the only treatment for this type of deafness. The electrodes are connected to an electronic apparatus that picks up sounds and fires the nerves directly. Results of this treatment are mixed; sometimes a fair degree of intelligibility of speech can result; sometimes there is only an aid to lipreading; sometimes the procedure is almost totally useless in restoring useful hearing.

Hearing may be impaired even when the middle ear and the inner ear function well. Injury to the brain through wounds, operations, or disease can result in aphasia (loss of language function) or amusia (loss of musical function). A Russian composer suffering from severe left hemisphere lesions was unable to distinguish consonants, yet he wrote his best symphonies during his 3-year illness. Injury to the left hemisphere of the brain can result in the loss of ability to sing a tune, yet a patient whose entire left hemisphere had been removed and who had lost the ability to speak could sing familiar songs with few articulatory errors. [*See* APHASIA.]

Language is associated with the left hemisphere of the brain, while tasks involving form, such as putting together a jigsaw puzzle, are associated with the right hemisphere. Music has been associated with the right hemisphere, but it not yet clear what functions occur in the different hemispheres, and to what extent there is flexibility of function between the hemispheres.

V. LEARNING TO HEAR

The sounds of speech form a very special and important part of our environment of sound. For mankind, the capability of speaking and understanding words is inherent. Other mammals, with the possible exception of whales and dolphins, cannot imitate sounds that they hear. Some songbirds (*Passeriformes oscine*) must learn their songs, and the dialects in which they sing, from mature birds. The ability to learn is greatest when the birds are young, indeed, before they can sing. They remember the birdsongs they heard when very young, and through practice, gradually learn to sing them as they become older.

This process resembles human production of speech. Babies must be taught to speak through imitation of their primary care giver. Humans, like the song birds, are best able to distinguish between similar sounds and imitate such sounds while young. An adult may no longer be able to distinguish or imitate sounds of other languages, despite having had this capability as a child. In all cultures and in all languages, babies are spoken to in a slow, simplified way, and with extreme intonations reminiscent of music. From hearing and interacting with such speech, the child learns to form the sounds of the language, and eventually learns to talk.

VI. HEARING AND THE BLIND

Man is primarily a visual animal, but blind people have an amazing ability to perceive the world about them through sound. They learn to identify and sense the location of sound sources, whether these sounds stem from objects, creatures, or actions. They have an ability to sense silent objects, such as walls, and even tables and chairs through reflected sounds. This acute sense of hearing is most evident when the individual has been blind from birth or from an early age. It is an acquired skill, not an analytical process.

Blind people often make use of a cane, which is used not only to explore the surface and coutours of the ground before them, but also as a sounding device. Taps of the cane are reflected by walls and objects, and the reflections give a sense of direction, distance, and size.

Blind people have also used compact ultrasonic sonar devices, similar in function to the bat's squeaks and hearing. These devices produce audible tones whose frequencies are proportional to distance. Because they are binaural, the direction of the reflecting object can be sensed. While these devices have proven to be technically successful, the general experience is that they do not provide enough additional information to make them worth their cost and the inconvenience.

Bibliography

Aslin, R. N. (1987). Visual and auditory development in infancy. In "Handbook of Infant Development" (J. D. Osofsky, Ed.), 2nd ed. Wiley, New York.

Bregman, A. S. (1990). "Auditory Scene Analysis." MIT Press, Cambridge.

Edelman, G. M., Gall, W. E., and Cowan, W. M. (Eds.) (1988). "Auditory Function: Neurological Bases of Hearing." Wiley, New York.

Fernald, A. (1991). "Prosody in Speech to Children." In "Annals of Child Development" (R. Vasta, Ed.), Vol. 8, Jessica Kingsley, London.

Handel, S. (1989). "Listening: An Introduction to the Perception of Auditory Events." The MIT Press, Cambridge.

Moore, B. C. J. (1989). "An Introduction to the Psychology of Hearing," 3rd. ed. Academic Press, San Diego.

Pickles, J. O. (1988). "An Introduction to the Physiology of Hearing," 2nd. ed. Academic Press, San Diego.

Ecological Psychology

Robert Sommer
University of California at Davis

Glossary

Affordances Invariant cues in the environment which have survival value for the organism.

Behavior setting A bounded, self-regulated, and ordered system composed of replaceable human and physical components that interact in a synchronized fashion to carry out the setting program.

Invariants Higher order properties of stimuli which remain constant despite movement of the observer, the environment, or both.

Proprioception The sense of movement and positioning of the body in relation to the environment.

ECOLOGY has traditionally emphasized the study of organism–environment relationships. Ecological psychology focuses specifically on the interdependence of humans and their environments, which is typically studied under real world conditions rather than in the laboratory. This approach has given rise to two separate theories and lines of research: one concerned with perception, and the other with social behavior.

I. ECOLOGY IN THE BIOLOGICAL SCIENCES

Ecology, from a Greek word meaning "household," is the branch of biology that studies relationships between organisms and their surroundings, especially with regard to the adaptations of organisms to environments and the resulting population distributions.

The ecological study of a species requires description of its habitat and its relationship to that habitat, its social organization, and its relationships with other species, emphasizing functional adaptations. Because of its broad scope, the term has been introduced into the social and behavioral sciences, and used in several different ways, often in combination with other terms such as social ecology, psychological ecology, ecological psychiatry, and human ecology. All these fields describe how organisms are influenced by their surroundings and, in turn, contribute to changing those surroundings through their behavior. Studies of human populations from an ecological perspective are less frequent than is the case for other species. Reasons for the lesser importance of an ecological perspective in the human sciences have been the great diversity of human habitats, the ability of humans to adapt to different environments, and the ability of humans to change the environment.

II. EARLY ECOLOGICAL APPROACHES IN PSYCHOLOGY

The specific term "psychological ecology" was probably introduced by K. Lewin in 1943 in an attempt to shift the emphasis in psychology away from individual organisms and their mental processes to organism–environmental relationships. Lewin's usage of the term was primarily psychological, referring to a person's interpretations of the external environment in terms of goals, barriers, and boundaries. Lewin defined psychological ecology as the relationship between psychological and nonpsychological factors. In approaching a problem, the researcher studies nonpsychological data first to find out how they determine the actual conditions of life for an individual or group. Only after the nonpsychological factors are known can research begin to focus on the psychological dimensions of a problem. At the same time, another psychologist from the gestalt tradition, E. Brunswik, was developing an ecologi-

Copyright © 1994 by Academic Press, Inc. All rights of reproduction in any form reserved.

cal model of preception in an attempt to widen the scope of research beyond the narrow range of stimuli used in laboratory experiments. Brunswik maintained that research on perception should employ stimuli typical of real life situations in an approach called "ecological sampling." According to Brunswik, the task of the researcher is to locate within the richness and variety of real world stimuli those invariant patterns capable of representing a stable, external world and relevant to the functional adaptations of species.

The approaches of Brunswik and Lewin gave rise to two separate lines of research and theory in psychology, both calling themselves "ecological," one emphasizing perception and the other behavioral adaptations. Although the two lines of research share the ecological perspective of examining functional adaptations of organisms to their environments, they are concerned with different issues, employ different methods, and publish their studies in different journals intended for different audiences. The perception research has been most closely identified with J. J. Gibson, who was influenced by E. Brunswik. The behavioral studies identified with R. Barker and his associates were influenced by K. Lewin. The former studies are almost entirely experimental and theory-driven, while the latter are largely observational and atheoretical. Because the two approaches to ecological psychology are so different, they will be described separately. At the conclusion, an attempt will be made to examine commonalities and differences between them, and to chart the future of ecological approaches in psychology.

III. GIBSON'S ECOLOGICAL PSYCHOLOGY

During the Second World War, J. J. Gibson was engaged in pilot training for the U.S. Air Force. This convinced him of the importance of studying perception and locomotion in the real world. Flying was movement, but there was little in the research literature dealing with the perception of motion since most laboratory studies employed stationary observers and stationary stimuli. In contrast, practical problems of flying involved take-off and landing, navigation, evasive action, and targeting; all carried while the organism is moving. Gibson argued that the distinction between sensory and motor aspects of behavior, which was virtually inherent in the laboratory approach where a stationary observer viewed stationary stimuli, was highly artificial and misleading. Gibson regarded perception as an activity taking place in constant motion which made it a construction of sequential images and interpretations of stimuli based on the integration of visual information over time, rather than at a single instant. This view linked visual perception to proprioception, or the sense of movement and positioning of the body in relation to its environment. Movement mediated through the human proprioceptive system is central to Gibson's view of how humans perceive the environment. [*See* VISUAL MOTION PERCEPTION; VISUAL PERCEPTION.]

Following classical ecological theory, Gibson regarded organism and environment to be an inseparable pair. Each term implied the other. No organism could exist without an environment surrounding it. Equally true, Gibson maintained, although not as obvious, environment implied an organism to be surrounded. A critical feature of this conception is that environment is not defined independently of organisms, or organisms defined independently of environments. Gibson's views had been influenced by the work of the physiologist, G. P. Walls, who described the functional adaptation of visual organs in relation to particular environment. Walls documented how vision evolved in different species to improve chances for survival.

Gibson considered the first task of ecological psychology to be an adequate description of the environment as what is out there to be perceived. Environment consists of a medium, substances, and surfaces that separate the substance from the medium. The medium for terrestrial animals such as humans is air, which is insubstantial, and thus permits locomotion. Substances are solids and liquids that vary in composition and resistance to change. The surface of a substance has a characteristic texture, reflectance, and layout. In a successful adaptation, organisms need to perceive what aspects of surface, substance, and medium persist and what aspects change in regard to specific environment events. The ecological approach to visual perception starts with the flowing array available to an observer who walks from one vista to another, or moves around any object of interest with the possibility of approaching it for scrutiny, thus extracting the invariants underlying the changing perspective and noticing the connection between hidden and obvious surfaces. For Gibson, the senses represent evolved adaptations to an organism's environment. These adaptations develop in relationship to environmental factors that contribute to an organism's survival. Evolutionary success requires sensory systems that directly and accurately depict the environment, requiring a minimum of interpretation and analysis. The key stimulus features that contribute to an organism's survival which Gibson termed "affordances" are invariant. Gibson interpreted the classical concept of ecological niche as a set of affordances. Affordances differ according to situation and species, as in a tree affording shelter to a small rodent, visibility to a bird, and shade or fuel to humans under different circumstances. Affordances are perceived directly from the pattern of stimulation arising from them, with a minimum of synthesis or interpretation. Unlike values and meanings which are considered to be subjective phenomena, an affordance has both objective and subjective properties, becoming a fact of the environment and a fact of behavior. The affordance of something does not change as the needs of the observer change; it is always there to be perceived. Gibson's approach is sometimes known as the theory of direct perception, which has received support from the research by E. J. Gibson, who studied the development of perceived invariance in infancy, investigating how the human child becomes able to recognize the many permanent properties of objects, even though the stimulus information about these objects is always changing. When a toy falls on its side, providing a different perceptual pattern, it is perceived as the same toy and not a different one. It is the increasing ability to extract information about the permanent properties of objects that characterizes perceptual learning and development. [*See* Perceptual Development.]

IV. BARKER'S ECOLOGICAL PSYCHOLOGY

Roger Barker was strongly influenced by the field theory of K. Lewin with whom he collaborated on several classic studies in child psychology. Barker subsequently became disenchanted with laboratory experimentation which he believed failed to provide information about the frequency, duration, and the complexity of behavior as it occurred in actual life. While admiring the way that Lewin selected problems from real situations, Barker maintained that behavior should be studied without outside manipulation or imposition of structure. Rather than contrive artificial settings, he advocated the study of behavior settings that already existed, using methods that would exert as little influence as possible upon the situation. Barker developed an approach to research that relied almost exclusively upon nonreactive observation of people in their ordinary settings. With his associates H. Wright and P. Gump, Barker initially called this approach psychological ecology, then ecological psychology, and subsequently eco-behavioral science. The approach drew more heavily on natural sciences such as botany and geology, which encouraged documentation of processes as they naturally occurred, than from physical sciences such as physics and chemistry, whose laboratory experiments isolated elements from their natural context.

To collect systematic records of behavior in natural contexts, Barker argued for the establishment of field stations. More than a home base for researchers, a field station is an established organizational unit continuing over time, whose staff includes a cadre of continuing researchers and space for visiting researchers. There would be facilities for collecting, preserving, and retrieving naturalistic data; archives of primary data comparable to those collected in other natural sciences over long periods of time, and accessible to other researchers who can analyze them in their own ways; and methods of statistical analysis appropriate to ecological data, perhaps similar to those used in quantitative botany and geography.

Barker and his associates established the Midwest Psychological Field Station in Oskaloosa, Kansas, where, for a period of 24 years, detailed systematic records were kept of community life. Observers were stationed throughout the town, and recorded everyday activities of children, using various sampling methods. Occasionally, a researcher followed a child for a designated period of time, recording where the child went, who was there, and what the child did. At other times, a researcher remained in a designated location and recorded which children visited, and what they did while they were there. Based on these observations, Barker concluded that the behavior of a child could often be predicted more accurately from knowing the situation that the child was in, than from knowing individual characteristics of the child. Throughout the 24 years of the Midwest Field Station, there were continuous, deliberate attempts to keep the community informed about the goals and methods of the project. Subsequently, Barker and P. Schoggen replicated these methods in Yoredale, UK. Like Oskaloosa, Yoredale was a rural community surrounded by farmland.

Barker maintained that the ecological environment has an objective reality with observable, geographical, physical and temporal attributes. Barker stated the agenda for ecological psychology as a series of questions, such as "What are environments like?" "How do environments select and shape the behavior of their occupants?" And "What are the structural dynamic properties of environments to which people must adapt?" Barker's conception of ecological psychology rested on several assumptions: (1) human behavior must be studied at a level that recognizes the complexity of systems of relationships linking individuals and groups with their social and physical environments; (2) such systems cannot be understood piecemeal; (3) environment–behavioral systems have properties that develop and change over long periods of time; (4) change in one part of the system is likely to affect other parts of the system; and (5) the challenge of ecological psychology is to obtain sufficient understanding about environmental systems to be able to predict and control the effects of planned and unplanned interventions.

The initial practical problem of ecological psychology, as Barker saw it, was to identify the natural units into which environments could be divided. These units, called behavior settings, are in no way imposed or created by the experimenter. To the lay observer, behavior settings such as a gas station or lunch counter are as objective as a building or a river. Units are identified through a behavior setting survey, a comprehensive inventory and description of all the public behavior settings of a community or institution. A behavior setting has replaceable human and physical components that interact in a synchronized fashion to carry out an ordered sequence of events called the setting program. Even though the occupants may change, the behavior setting will persist. Behavior settings are common phenomena in everyday life and lay people have no difficulty recognizing them, thereby linking ecological psychology to concepts readily understood. The same behavior setting might provide different inputs to different persons, and different inputs to the same person as that individual's behavior changed.

Differences between the behavior of inhabitants of underpopulated, adequately populated, and overpopulated settings provide a test of the theory that the ecological environment is an interdependent whole and has predictable effects on its human inhabitants. According to behavior setting theory, when there are too few people to perform the necessary roles, the number and range of pressures on each inhabitant increases because the same pressure to perform the necessary roles will be distributed over fewer inhabitants. From this, it follows that inhabitants of underpopulated settings, in comparison to those in adequately populated settings, are likely to be more active within the setting and engage in a greater variety of actions. Admission standards may be lowered and differences among applicants may be virtually ignored, and occupants must work harder at more difficult tasks to keep the setting going. Each occupant will be more valued and given greater responsibility. Overpopulated settings encourage the creation of mechanisms to control the number of applicants along with attempts to increase the capacity of the setting, through either enlargement or shifts to alternative larger settings. Predictions based on population size have generally been confirmed by studies in schools, churches, and workplaces. [*See* CROWDING: EFFECTS ON HEALTH AND BEHAVIOR.]

Barker's conception of ecology psychology as a naturalistic behavioral science has been extended and refined in recent years. K. Fox has linked it to social accounting theories, showing how data from large-scale inventories of behavior settings can reveal changes in the quality of life in communities, thereby complementing other social and economic indicators. J. Barker has extended the approach to political science, showing how residents can make behavior setting inventories to obtain valid self-knowledge about community activities in order to improve their situation. A. Wicker has attempted to extend both the methods and objectives of ecological psychology. Wicker recommends a combination of quantitative and qualitative approaches with the latter being used to study the purposive goal-directed behavior of individuals in behavior settings. Wicker also suggests that ecological psychology provides a framework for positive interventions in community life, to improve behavior settings or to develop new settings to meet new community needs. To Barker, ecological psychology was almost entirely nonreactive and noninterventionist; Wicker presents a more activist and cross-disciplinary view.

V. FUTURE OF ECOLOGICAL PSYCHOLOGY

Ecological psychology developed from research in gestalt psychology, which itself arose as a reaction against the reductionism of behavioristic psychology. The chain of intellectual development has not stopped, since ecological psychology is a forerunner of environmental psychology, which involves the study of relationships between organisms and the physical environment. Environmental psychology is more eclectic in method, theory, and subject matter. Field and laboratory studies are done on the same issues, and there is no overriding approach or framework as is typically the case in ecology psychology. Environmental psychology is also less holistic than ecological psychology, and typically studies limited classes of phenomena such as the effects of noise upon performance or the influence of crowding upon altruistic behavior. The latter type of research is more manageable, less time-consuming, and easier to summarize and publish than is work in ecological pyschology since it fits the conventional stimulus–response model used in other branches of psychology. Most researchers engaged in the psychological study of person–environment relationships identify themselves as environmental rather than ecological psychologists. However, the latter term remains appropriate for researchers using the approaches developed by either J. J. Gibson or R. Barker. Coincidentally, at the end of their respective careers, both Gibson and Barker rejected "ecological psychology" in favor of more specific terms. Recognizing the dominance of visual perception in his theory, Gibson suggested "ecological optics" to describe the visual information available for perception. Barker, in his last books, desired to move the field away from psychology and called his approach "eco-behavioral science." However, their associates continue to use ecological psychology because of its explicit emphasis on interdependence between organisms and their surroundings. [*See* ENVIRONMENTAL PSYCHOLOGY.]

Related approaches in the social sciences include human ecology, social ecology, and population ecology; all of which take a holistic view of individuals and groups in their surroundings. Presumably, an intellectual niche exits for additional applications of an ecological model on an individual level such as cognitive ecology, dealing with the interdependence of an organism's thought processes and surroundings; and personality ecology, focusing on the mutual dependence of personality style and the organism's milieu; and so on. The defining characteristic of all such attempts to employ an ecological model in psychology is a holistic research strategy which recognizes interdependence between the psychological processes of organisms and their surroundings.

Bibliography

Gordon, I. E. (1989). "Theories of Visual Perception." Wiley, Chichester.

Reed, E., and Jones, R. (Eds.) (1982). "Reasons for Realism." Erlbaum, Hillsdale, NJ.

Schoggen, P. (1989). "Behavior Settings: A Revision and Extension of Roger Barker's 'Ecological Psychology'." Stanford University Press, Stanford.

Wicker, A. (1987). Behavior settings reconsidered. In "Handbook of Environmental Psychology" (D. Stokols and I. Altman, Eds.), Vol. 1. Wiley, New York.

ECONOMIC BEHAVIOR

Harinder Singh
San Diego State University

Glossary

Expectations What individuals think about future values.

Expected utility The anticipated satisfaction from a good/service.

Experimental Controlled or laboratory economics

Neoclassical The traditional or orthodox approach.

Optimal The ability to make fully rational and objective decisions.

Preference Reversal To switch your options for the same choices.

X-inefficiency Unexplained inefficiencies in production.

THE TRADITIONAL economic model of human action assumes optimal behavior. Nontraditional approaches are modifying this model by including psychological, institutional, and sociological considerations. Five research areas are analyzed to demonstrate how the narrow traditional model results in anomalies. Incorporating psychological and institutional considerations results in more realistic economic models. Whether the nontraditional approaches will ultimately replace traditional models depends not only on their descriptive reality but also on their simplicity, predictive power, and universality.

I. INTRODUCTION

Both economists and psychologists analyze human behavior. However, the methodological approaches adopted by the professionals of these disciplines are quite different. As far as economics is concerned, Alfred Marshall, one of the founding fathers of the discipline, put it best when he wrote, more than a century ago, "Economics is a study of men as they live and move and think in the ordinary business of life. But it concerns itself chiefly with those motives which affect, most powerfully and most steadily, man's conduct in the business part of his life." This quote from Marshall provides some clues about the differences of both approaches. Unlike psychology, economics is primarily concerned with the business part of an individual's life; the competitive pressure of market forces nudges individuals to be more motivated and vigilant about decision making. Psychologists are concerned with the *process* of decision making, whereas economists focus on final *outcomes*. This divergence also springs from different goals: the psychologist wants to understand and improve decision-making procedures, whereas the economist is interested in the final results (actions) of the decisions and how this activity affects his economic condition. In terms of empirical analysis, psychologists will typically analyze individual-specific observations involving sequential decision-making, usually generating data by controlled experiments. On the other hand, economists generally study aggregate, discrete data which are generated by the final actions of economic agents, such as buying/selling behavior. [*See* CONSUMER PSYCHOLOGY.]

However, despite these apparent differences between traditional economics and psychology, some economists have consistently and persuasively questioned the methodological foundations of traditional economics. These subdisciplines within economics are adopting a more descriptive, psychological, and institutional approach to economic behavior. These "nontraditionalists" include behavioral economists, socio-economists, and institutional or evolutionary economists. This "internal rebellion" among economists has been going on for a long time, but it has accelerated in the last decade

Copyright © 1994 by Academic Press, Inc. All rights of reproduction in any form reserved.

or so. Traditional ways of analyzing economic behavior are being increasingly challenged; interdisciplinary work with psychology, sociology, and political science is accelerating.

This article proceeds as follows: At the onset, justification is provided for the conventional approach. Subsequently, the objections of the nontraditionalists are presented and the modifications and extensions of the conventional approach suggested by them are discussed. In order to analyze specific cases, a range of economic issues is discussed where methodological battles are being fought, the so called "trenches" or "applications." The article concludes with some thoughts on the future prospects of analyzing economic behavior. This methodological debate is packaged in traditional and nontraditional terms, thereby giving an under-dog status to new ways of approaching old issues. This type of rhetoric is employed because working outside or against the prevailing paradigm is always an uphill battle.

A. Traditional Analysis of Economic Human Behavior

The model most economists work with is termed the "rational choice" model. A individual maximizes his objective function: a consumer maximizers their utility or satisfaction, a producer maximizes his profits or sales. The key word is "maximize" within a constrained, objective, measurable environment. The rational choice paradigm is appealing because of its simplicity and universal applicability. Based on the rational choice model, economists can deduce or make inferences with a relatively limited amount of aggregate data. The external constraints within which economic behavior is analyzed can be extended to improve the sophistication of the model. The behavior of other individuals can be incorporated by adopting a game theoretic approach. The prices of different competing inputs and outputs can be included in the objective function. Organizational and market structure variables can be employed to explain differences in economic behavior. For instance, the implications of economic behavior in a competitive or monopoly environment can be analyzed with respect to buyers or sellers. Despite the increasing complexity of these models, one underlying attribute characterizes these traditional economic models: the individual or organization is assumed to be "optimizing" or "rational." This does not mean that individuals or organizations are not subject to suboptimal behavior. Of course there are periodic lapses from the rational ideal. However, it is generally asserted that these individual errors are not significant enough to override the general implications of the rational model. A widespread evidence of errors or suboptimal behavior would be disturbing to traditional economists. First, because it violates a common assumption. Second, because traditional economists contend they do not have a "theory of errors" which could be reasonably incorporated into the rational decision-making model. I labor this point because, in contrast, a psychologist would "celebrate" the finding of widespread errors because he now has an opportunity to improve decision-making procedures. An economist being concerned with final outcomes based on rational decisions would term such behavior as an "anomaly." In fact, the *Journal of Economic Perspectives,* a major journal of the American Economic Association, has started featuring a periodic "Anomalies" section, which discusses economic behavior which is inconsistent is some way from traditional thinking.

B. Nontraditional Approaches to Economic Behavior

The nontraditional approaches to economic behavior have one common element: they modify the conventional approach by incorporating new psychological, institutional, and sociological considerations. The relevant issues can be formalized by decomposing the rational choice model into different components. When an individual is making a complex decision subject to external constrains, the *degree* of rationality exhibited by him can be evaluated by considering the following stages:

1. Whether the goal of the decision maker coincides with the goal the analyst "thinks" the decision maker is employing.
2. Whether the decision-making process is based on objective and/or subjective considerations.
3. Whether the decisions are influenced by noneconomic considerations such as institutional, sociological, and political factors.
4. Whether the actions of the decision-maker are consistent with his or her final goal, i.e., they are reasoned and deliberate.
5. Whether these actions are fully optimal, i.e., they are the *best* conceivable choices.

Note that the conventional economic model would typically consider rational behavior to be actions guided by objective economic variables assuming fully optimal behavior, i.e., jump to the fifth proposition. Nontraditional economists attempt to consider and incorporate factors related to the initial four propositions.

One way to consider the controversy is the distinction between normative and descriptive analysis. Traditional economics is normative, in the sense that it analyzes individuals as they *should* behave, rather than being descriptive, focusing on how the *actually* do behave. Nonconventional economists contend that the traditional orthodoxy imposes conditions on human behavior which are too stringent, it assumes unfailing, fully optimal behavior.

Extensions based on first proposition can proceed in several ways. First, it may simply be the case that the decision-making unit may have a different goal than the one the economist assumes. For instance, an economist may assume that a firm is maximizing profits, whereas the firm may be maximizing sales, market share, employee satisfaction, etc. If an economist has an open mind, this kind of slip is relatively easy to track down and rectify. Second, traditional economists assume an individual maximizes his own welfare. Generally, inadequate consideration is given to utility which transcend individual considerations. Some economists are now focusing on "group utility" and "social objectives," which may transcend individual concerns. A good example in this regard is the "paradox of rebellion." From an individual maximizing point of view, it is not at all clear why an individual should join a collective rebellious movement, since the gains of the movement are going to accrue to him regardless of whether he joins. So why should he put himself at risk? This paradox is solved by adopting a group utility norm, where the individual is motivated not only by individual considerations but also by general commitment to his group.

Now consider the second proposition, whether the decision is based on subjective or objective factors. It seems obvious that some forms of behavior are predominantly economic, such as buying and selling stocks, maximizing sales, etc. However, economists have began analyzing a wide array of areas which are beyond the narrow confines of economics, such as analysis of crime, divorce/marriage behavior, inefficiencies within organizations, etc. It is to expected that once we analyze noneconomic phenomena, the amount of subjective factors considered in the decision-making process is likely to be higher; consequently, the traditional objective rational model will not be a good approximation of human behavior. However, traditional economists continue to employ the narrow objective model in areas which have a high subjective component.

Another point to keep in mind is whether rational behavior is required by all or some participants for a phenomenon to be suitable for the conventional assumptions. For instance, in the stock market, *everyone* does not have to behave rationally, that is, as long as *some* market participants at the margin are rational, the market price will reflect rational behavior. In this example, rationality is a "marginal" concept. However, in other cases, such as consumer behavior, rationality may be an "average" concept, in the sense that we are interested in how the typical consumer behaves. In the first example, the conventional rational choice model may be a good approximation of economic behavior. However, in the second case, the conventional model may impose unrealistic conditions. Consequently, it is important to analyze what type of rationality requirement is needed for a specific economic phenomenon.

As regards the third proposition, it is important to note that reality is multi-faceted, almost any behavioral phenomenon has economic, sociological, political, and institutional dimensions. However, traditional economics focuses on a narrow range of economic variables. Two groups taking exception to this are institutional or evolutionary economists and socio-economists. American institutionalists such as Thorstein Veblin and Wesley Mitchell have a long tradition of disagreeing with the traditional notions of economic behavior. Institutional economics is often regarded as holistic, systemic and evolutionary. It is holistic because it relates to the whole sequence of human behavior. It is systemic because it asserts that economic behavior can be understood only within the context of the general process. It is evolutionary because human action is evaluated in the context of historical and institutional change. Evolutionary economists actively seek contextual validation when they analyze economic behavior. In other words, their analysis takes into account the specific institutional and social context which influences human behavior. Socio-economists have a similar approach in that they focus on the interaction between the societal environment and economic behavior. Economic man is not a rarified individual who pursues narrow economic goals; he is also influenced by social norms, peer pressure, group interests, and institutional constraints. As Etzioni, one of the founders of socio-economic approach, points out, "The paradigm advanced here seeks to characterize the context within which the forces that the neoclassical approach focuses on are played out, a context that sets limits and provides direction to these forces." The socio-economic approach is also characterized by focusing on less observable behavioral variables such as emotion, commitment, beliefs, and moral values.

The fourth proposition raises some fundamental issues about the cognitive limitations of individual decision-making. Herbert Simon has contended for almost four decades that individuals attempt to simplify their decision-making by adopting minimally acceptable thresholds, i.e., they indulge in "satisficing" rather than "optimizing," behavior. This approach is consistent with the general psychological framework which recognizes the computational limitations of individuals and their desire to reduce cognitive overload. One very important implication of Herbert Simon's approach is that it provides an important guide to how decision-making models should incorporate reality. Some extensions of neoclassical decision-making models attempt to be realistic by including information search costs, pay-off matrices, implicit incentives, and constraints. However, these modifications are included not as psychological characteristics of the decision-maker but as additional details in his computational environment. Consequently, these extensions typically assume "optimal" ability to make decisions in a progressively more complex environment. Herbert Simon's work and the literature in psychology and experimental economics suggests that this approach imposes unrealistic assumptions about human behavior.

These modifications in the technical environment of the decision-maker are generally done as "ex post rationalizations." Consider for example, a worker who is not producing up to full capacity. He is not classified as exhibiting suboptimal behavior, but rather the conventional neo-classical explanation is that he is optimally purchasing leisure on the job. In another situation, an individual who is not transferring his money to a high-yield asset (with comparable risk and liquidity) and prefers to keep his savings in a low yield checking account is still behaving optimally (i.e., maximizing his utility) because the psychological comfort of a "savings" buffer has its own utility. Note that this approach of analyzing human behavior can be tautological and circular in explaining away suboptimal behavior. With ex post rationalizations almost any behavior can be asserted to be "optimal" by including unobservable transaction costs and implicit incentives.

The fourth proposition also highlights another important issue. Obviously a whole spectrum of behavior exists between the two extremes of completely irrational behavior and full optimization. In some cases, decision making could be suboptimal yet reasoned, deliberate, and consistent with the subjective goals of the decision maker. Obviously, the degree of rationality may well have to do with the pressures to be rational. Generally, in a competitive environment, rational behavior is more likely. However, in extremely tense or competitive situations, excessive pressure can generate suboptimal behavior. The Yerkes-Dodson law postulates an upside down U-shaped relationship between the quality of decision making and the pressures on an individual/organization. Initially, the pressure improves the quality of decision making but after a point, additional pressure can lower the quality of decision making. The important implication of this law to economic behavior is that a rigid premise of "optimal behavior" may be too simplistic for a range of performance which exist in a complex world. The neo-classical assumption of "fully optimal behavior" can be regarded as a special case which provides a good approximation in some instances, particularly when market pressures are at appropriate levels. [*See* DECISION MAKING, INDIVIDUALS.]

The foregoing discussion of analyzing various stages of rational behavior should convince us that proposition 5, the traditional neo-classical assumption of fully optimal behavior, is a special case, in a wide range of possible behaviors. The ultimate decision about which propositions apply in a specific case should not be based on rigid a priori assumptions but rather on careful empirical evaluation of a specific situation.

II. CASE STUDIES OF ECONOMIC BEHAVIOR ANALYSIS

So far, we have explained how the nontraditional approaches to economic behavior attempt to adopt a broader and more flexible approach to rational decision-making. This controversy is ongoing not only in general methodological terms, but also in specific research areas. In order to provide a more concrete focus, we sketch out five research issues in which the rational decision-making model has been controversial and subject to modifications. These five case studies are meant to be illustrative; the range of issues is by no means limited to these applications.

A. Subjective Utility Analysis

One feature of expected utility analysis is that losses and gains are evaluated symmetrically. By expected utility, we mean the anticipated satisfaction from alternative choices. For instance, if (a) you win an unexpected lottery of $1000 and (b) an unexpected break down of your car rakes up a $950 bill, simultaneously, then, according to the expected utility model, you are still ahead, by the net gain of $50. However, a large amount of experimental literature reveals that an individual may feel "disadvantaged" after the two events. Daniel Kahneman and Amos Tversky, two psychologists working on economic issues, have found that individuals code gains and losses differently. In this particular case, the loss is given considerably more subjective weight than a corresponding gain. This type of asymmetric coding of losses and gains is contrary to the traditional rational choice model.

In fact, Kahneman and Tversky have modified the conventional utility function to an "asymmetric value function." In the orthodox neo-classical model, any additional gain has positive, but declining marginal utility. Losses and gains are treated symmetrically, because an individual's change in utility is represented by a movement on the same expected utility curve (which is increasing at a decreasing rate from the origin). In the asymmetric value function, gains are still subject to diminishing utility. However, incremental losses are evaluated more negatively than positive utility yielded by gains (i.e., the loss function is relatively steeper than the gain function). They emphasize that this asymmetric S-shaped value function is a purely descriptive device which incorporates the notion that losses are coded more negatively than comparable gains.

Once the traditional model is extended along these lines, a host of economic behavior which might appear irrational within the narrow confines of the orthodox rational choice model actually begins to make sense. For instance, conventional theory asserts that "sunk costs" (costs which cannot be retrieved) should be ignored in decision making. However, in reality, it is found that decision makers find it difficult to ignore sunk costs. This is probably because sunk costs are psychologically coded as large negative losses.

This "value function" representation of economic behavior which is validated in a variety of experimental settings has important implications for successful marketing strategies. Robert Frank points out the following marketing implications: segregate gains into smaller components, combine losses into a larger chunk, offset a small loss with a large gain by lumping the two. These marketing strategies based on the asymmetric value function can reduce the negative psychological impact of higher prices on consumers without actually costing anything.

Kahneman and Tversky have identified other subjective biases that are widespread and prevalent. The "anchoring bias" indicates that most subjective decisions are based on a historical reference point. The "availability bias" implies that individuals evaluate the likelihood of a phenomenon not on the basis of objective probabilities but rather on the ability to recall similar events. Psychologists have identified many other heuristics and biases in subjective decision making. Economists have found these subjective lapses from the conventional model disturbing, but they have clung to the conventional thinking because of the consistency and universality of the traditional model. However, investigators such as Kehneman and Tversky are showing that these biases are widespread, robust, and can be incorporated into traditional decision-making framework to improve the predictive performance of these models. These type of extensions of the conventional model are more useful and persuasive than merely criticizing orthodox thinking.

B. Expectations Formations

The word *"expectations"* relates to what economic agents "expect" the future values of economic variables to be. For example, inflationary expectations and interest rate expectations have to do with subjective impressions about the future course of these variables. In economic relationships, expectations play a crucial role. An acceleration of inflationary expectations can cause current market interest rates to creep upward, and the resultant wage increases (in anticipation of inflation) can further worsen the inflation outlook as costs of production increase. A basic problem arises in the measurement of expectations. Subjective internal decisions are, by definition, unobservable. Generally, economists have relied on two proxies for the underlying process of expectations formation: subjective values gleaned from survey data or econometric forecasts generated by statistical procedures. Given the preference for objective data, it is not surprising that economists have been skeptical about the reliability of survey forecasts, partly because respondents may not have a strong incentive to make correct responses. On the other hand, econometric forecasts are preferred because they utilize all available information objectively. From a psychological point of view, survey values are directly associated with cognitive decision-making and should be closer to the underlying expectations process compared to a normative, statistical model.

Again, one aspect we have to consider is the distinction between normative and descriptive behavior. If for the sake of argument, we agree that statistical forecasts are more rational and reliable, that does not necessarily imply that we should employ this proxy all the time. George Katona was one of the earliest economists to build a systematic rationale for analyzing survey expectations of consumers. He contended that it is important to analyze subjective views of consumers, even if they are somewhat "irrational" because consumers do act on the basis of these subjective impressions and their total expenditure is about two-thirds of our gross national product. Consequently, descriptive analysis is important in order to figure out what is happening to a significant portion of our economy.

Now, let us proceed to a more difficult question: which proxy is more reliable? Reliability is evaluated by how close subjective surveys or statistical forecasts are to the final realizations of the variables, i.e., the extent of forecasting errors. Consider the case of a well-known price survey data set collected by Joseph Livingston, a financial columnist from Philadelphia. Traditional economists have analyzed this data set to ascertain whether the respondents of this survey made rational decisions about future prices. Economists who subscribe to the "rational expectations" methodology argue that an individual is not rational if he makes *systematic* mistakes. In other words, if there is a statistical pattern in the data which is not taken into account by economic agents, than they are not learning from their past mistakes.

Almost all the sophisticated rationality tests performed on the Livingston data indicated that these survey forecasts were not rational. These results reflected the fact that during the 1970s, economic agents consistently underestimated the upward creep in prices. This finding resulted in discrediting survey data in general and further fortified the skepticism about subjective data. In 1985, John Caskey, applied the same information constraints that the Livingston data had (i.e., he looked at the 8-month and 14-month ahead forecasts) and investigated the forecasting errors of reputable forecasting houses such as DRI. His results indicated that these reputable forecasting establishments made errors similar to those of the respondents of Livingston survey data. So what is going on?

Two points need to be made about reconciling these conflicting results. First, it appears that respondents underestimated inflation rates in the 1970s because there was an underlying structural shift in the data. Since this was a new phenomena, some amount of learning had to take place before respondents identified this shift to a different data regime. Typically, rational expectations methodology does not allow adequate time for learning behavior. Second, learning does not always occur at neat quarterly intervals. Statistically, when models employ quarterly data, the correlation of error terms across quarters is regarded as systematic errors. However, as Milton Friedman points out, this methodology confuses the distinction between "chronological" and "psychological" time.

From a psychological point of view, learning periods are related to the availability of new information. For the sake of argument, if there is no new information available for 1 year, there will be no change, although when the model is evaluated on a quarterly basis ex post, there will be correlation in the forecasting errors across four quarters. This fundamental flaw in the statistical methodology shows that it very difficult to operationalize and test the rationality hypothesis with a widely acceptable statistical procedure. Both the subjective survey responses and the forecasts of reputable consulting services appeared "irrational" because an adequate learning time was not incorporated and the periodicity of learning updates was measured wrongly. The premature conclusion about the reliability of survey data shows that economists are generally more skeptical about subjective values, even though objective forecasts may have problems of their own.

C. Preference Reversals

Since economists view decision making as an objective, rational exercise, it is not surprising that adequate attention is not given to different ways by which information (about decisions) is elicited. To put it in a specific context, economists are interested in knowing the "preferences" of consumers or producers; however, little attention is devoted to how the preference is made operational. When a consumer "prefers" a Honda Accord rather than a Toyota Camry, What does this exactly imply? Is the Honda "ranked" higher than a Camry? Is it "demanded at a higher price" or "offered to be sold at a higher price?" Traditional economists would contend that if the Accord is "preferred" to the Camry, it does not matter how the preference is elicited, the results should all be consistent. This traditional notion is under attack because preferences switch around when they are elicited with a different procedure. This kind of switching, known as "preference reversals" goes against the grain of objective rational decision making.

Let us formalize the argument by a simple, traditional example. Let us assume there is one lottery with a high chance of winning a small price (probability of 9/10 of obtaining $10). This high chance gamble is called the "H" bet. An alternative gamble has a low probability of winning a high value (probability of 1/10 of getting $90). This low probability bet is termed the "L" bet. It is important to realize that the expected value of both lotteries is $9.00. Laboratory experiments indicate that most respondents choose the H bet when asked to pick one over the other. However, when they are asked the lowest price they are willing to sell each lottery, they place a relatively higher selling price on the L bet. The stated preference of the H bet when the decision is elicited by one procedure and the subsequent switch to the L bet when the elicitation procedure is altered is a typical preference reversal.

Economists were initially defensive when this phenomenon was reported by two psychologists, Paul Slovic and Sarah Lichtenstein. The initial reaction of traditional economists was that something is inherently wrong in the way these behavioral experiments are set up. For instance, Grether and Plott designed a series of experiments to show that preference reversals either do not exist or were not relevant to economic theory. The possible reasons for the reversals included lack of motivation, income effects, strategic behavior, intransitivity of preferences, and the nature of the auction process. However, most of their results indicated that preference reversals phenomena could not be explained away by traditional economic reasons.

When confronted with this anomaly, there were two reactions. Some traditional economists have reacted to these robust preference reversals results by developing theoretical models which are generalized to incorporate a certain category of reversals. Behavioral economists have reacted by investigating potential psychological explanations. After a large number of controlled experiments, behavioral economists are concluding that the primary reason for preference reversals is "the compatibility hypothesis." That is, when respondents are asked to pick the gamble they prefer, choice is *compatible* with probabilities. Consequently, they focus on the high probability and pick the H bet. On the other hand, when respondents are asked to rank in terms of selling price, they focus on the *comparable* higher dollar value of the L bet and prefer it to the H bet.

In fact, Slovic and Lichtenstein, being psychologists, had recognized preference reversals as a special case of the general notion that decision making is influenced by the context and procedures employed. Knowing that buying and selling behavior is more correlated with payoffs, whereas choices of gambles is more closely associated with winning/losing, they had constructed laboratory choices where the preference switching would occur because of these compatibility considerations. This result has being generalized to postulate that the amount of weight (in decision making) given by a respondent to each stimulus attribute is linked to its compatibility with a response scale. The literature on the preference reversal phenomenon is an important lesson in the different ways in which economists and psychologists view lapses in the traditional decision-making model. Economists view it as an anomaly which can be explained by a better experiment. Psychologists and behavioral economists view it as an example of the fact that preferences are context dependent.

D. Evaluating Nonmarket Behavior

This section relates to another controversy in which laboratory experiments about human behavior are developing important insights. The problem has to do with a basic question: How do you value services which do not have an established market? Traditionally, in economics, services which have a market can be priced in terms of the demand and supply auction process. However, some services such as establishing "clean air" have two problems of evaluation: externalities and the lack of a market price. Externalities arise because the benefit of clean air accrues to the general public at large. The lack of a market which internalizes these externalities implies that it is difficult to put a dollar value on clear air. The Environmental Protection Agency (EPA) is generally confronted with this type of question: How much value do Americans place on reducing air pollutants by a specific amount? To put it in specific terms, we could ask a representative sample of Americans, the following alternative questions:

(a) How many (dollars per year) are you willing to pay to obtain a 10% reduction in air pollutants (termed the WTP estimate)?

(b) How many (dollars per year) are you willing to accept as compensation for *not* having a 10% reduction is air pollutants (termed the WTA estimate)?

Note that the questions are basically asking respondents to value the same gain in clean air by two comparable ways. Traditional economic theory would predict that the WTA estimate will be marginally higher because of an "income effect." The income effect arises because there is a change in endowments when the question is switched from (a) to (b). However, economists have found that in a typical survey the WTA estimates are, in some cases, 10 times higher than WTP values. This kind of discrepancy results in a theoretical and a practical dilemma. Economic theory cannot explain such widespread deviations from rational responses. EPA does not know which estimates (WTP or WTA) to rely on. Policy responses are contingent on how much value Americans place on clean air.

One general finding is that this discrepancy between WTP and WTA estimates is significantly lower in laboratory experiments. More importantly, if learning behavior is allowed to occur, by establishing an auction market, the discrepancy is reduced significantly. The ratio of WTA to WTP can range from 1.3 to 5, depending upon the different experiments and the degree of learning. Richard Thaler has argued that the discrepancy may be due to an "instant endowment effect." This effect is a special case of "loss aversion" in which respondents who receive a gift (WTA) may value it less (so they want more dollars) and persons who are asked to pay an amount have significant loss aversion (i.e., they are only willing to part with a lower dollar value). It has also been suggested that, if the questions are somehow "bounded," perhaps by asking the *percentage* of monthly income respondents are willing to pay or accept, the results are more symmetric than if the respondents are free to indicate *any* dollar value. This literature about the valuation of nonmarket services provides another example of economic behavior which does not appear to conform to the traditional model of rational choice. It also shows that most of the persuasive hypotheses about this discrepancy are psychological in nature.

E. Production X-Inefficiencies

Our last example of deviations from rational choice model is from firm behavior. This example illustrates that the traditional rational choice model may not always be a good approximation of individual behavior in a group environment. Microeconomic theory generally asserts that firms operate as efficiently as possible, i.e., they are constantly minimizing their costs of production. This contention is based on the notion that perfect competition will force firms to be efficient, otherwise the inefficient firm will be driven out of business. In 1966, Harvey Leibenstein challenged this traditional notion by asserting that this concept of optimal efficiency *within* the firm is not always realistic. He attempted to generalize firm behavior by focusing on the behavioral causes of inefficiencies. One reason is that labor contracts are incomplete: we can contract a person's time but it is difficult to directly control a worker's effort level.

The working environment "inside" the firm may also be sheltered by behavioral conventions, habits, strategic behavior, and interpersonal dynamics. Since the causes of internal inefficiencies of the firm were to a large extent unknown, Leibenstein called his concept "X-efficiency." The practical significance of this approach was that it implied that market structure, such as a monopoly (sole producer), not only had pricing consequences but also had potentially significant production inefficiencies. This indicated that there was something close to a "free lunch"; reducing these X-inefficiencies could potentially result in an improvement without additional costs.

The reaction of traditional economists was either to assert that this inefficiency was too small to worry about or to provide ex post deductive arguments about why this "inefficiency" was really something else. It is important to note that the critics did not investigate the existence or the causes of this inefficiency by empirical analysis. In the first instance, I will discuss some of the arguments provided by the critics. Subsequently, I will refer to the widespread validation of the X-inefficiency concept based on empirical analysis.

One major form of rationalization was that employees are not inefficient or suboptimal, rather they consciously decide to obtain more "on-the-job leisure" by forsaking earned income. This spin on inefficiency while ruling out any suboptimal behavior is difficult to test at an empirical level. These critics did not go out and investigate whether workers make ex ante avoidable mistakes, they merely asserted ex post, that since workers are assumed to be rational, they must be making an optimal decision to forsake income for leisure at the work site. Another line of argument contended that the amount of welfare loss attributed to X-inefficiency is actually "rent seeking" activity by the monopolists. Rent seeking is the amount spent by a monopolist to retain market share. By making inefficiency and rent seeking substitutes, the critics asserted that a monopolist is not inefficient because he makes an optimal allocation between traditional production costs and rent seeking costs. Again, the argument was an ex post rationalization with no empirical verification.

However, other economists who concede the possibility of suboptimal behavior inside the firm have validated the existence of X-inefficiency in over 60 empirical studies. Most of these investigations were conducted at the industry level. In order to pin down the magnitude of X-inefficiency and investigate its potential causes, more firm-level studies need to be done. Nevertheless, the empirical evidence generally supports Leibenstein's initial hypothesis that productive activity inside the firm can and often does deviate from its theoretically optimum levels.

III. FUTURE OUTLOOK

In the previous section, I have discussed five cases in which the conventional economic model of human behavior has been modified by the existence of activities which are different from what economists consider "optimal" or the "norm." Nontraditional economists have began to focus on the process and the context in which decisions are made. It should be pointed out that the conventional economic model of human behavior is a very powerful paradigm, in that it explains universally and simply a significant portion of human actions. In situations where the market pressures are significant (such as financial markets and highly competitive firms), the quality of decision-making is generally closer to the traditional norm. However, in other areas (such as production in sheltered firms, consumption and saving behavior, leisure–work decisions) where group interaction is involved and noneconomic factors (psychological biases, social conventions, societal goals, etc.) impinge on human behavior, the traditional normative model may be an inaccurate approximation of reality and consequently may loose it predictive qualities. The neo-classical normative model should be regarded as an initial skeletal approximation of human behavior, which can be modified by contextual validation procedures to approximate reality more closely.

Initially, most nontraditional economists were merely criticizing the orthodox model of economic behavior. It is relatively easy to point out different types of lapses from the optimal norm. At present the focus has shifted to improving the traditional model by augmenting it with other contextual considerations. Both orthodox and unorthodox economists complicate their models by augmenting them. The critical difference is that traditional economists usually include information search costs and other constraints at the theoretical level, still requiring the individual to make optimal decisions. However, nonorthodox economists incorporate additional considerations based on social and psychological constraints as part of the decisions-making process. As the discussion of the five applications has demonstrated, these considerations include incorporating robust subjective biases and heuristics, being cognizant of different elicitation procedures, work conventions, and institutional constraints. These modifications generally result in a more realistic approximation of human behavior and improve the predictive power of these models. However, they do so by adopting an ad hoc approach. The ultimate success of nontraditional approaches to economic behavior will depend upon achieving four goals: developing models which are simple, realistic, predictive, and widely applicable. A tall order, but the battle goes on.

Bibliography[1]

Dugger, W. (1979). Methodological differences between institutional and neoclassical economics. *J. Econom. Issues* **13,** 899–909.

Etzioni, A. (1988). "The Moral Dimension." The Free Press, New York

Frank, R. (1991). "Microeconomics and Behavior." McGraw Hill, New York.

Frantz, R. (1988). "X-Efficiency: Theory, Evidence, and Applications." Kluwer, Boston.

Harless, D. (1989). More laboratory evidence on the disparity between willingness to pay and compensation demanded. *J. Econom. Behav. Organization* **11,** 359–379.

Hogarth, R., and Reder, M. (Eds.) (1987). "Rational Choice: The Contrast between Economics and Psychology." University of Chicago Press, Chicago.

Marshall, A. (1920). "Principles of Economics," 8th ed. Macmillan, London.

Mullen, J., and Roth, B. (1991). "Decision Making: Its Logic and Practice." Rowman and Little Field, Savage, MD.

Roth, A. (Ed.) (1987). "Laboratory Experiments in Economics: Six Points of View." Cambridge University Press, New York.

Singh, H. (1990). Relative evaluation of subjective and objective measures of expectations formation. *Quart. Rev. Econom. Bus.* **30,** 64–74.

Thaler, R. (1992). "The Winner's Curse: Paradoxes and Anomalies of Economic Life." The Free Press, New York.

[1] The best source about differences in the approaches adopted by economists and psychologists is the book by Hogarth and Reder. A good explanation of the traditional model of rational choice is provided in Frank (Chapters 3 and 6) and Mullen and Roth (Chapters 3 and 7). Both authors also discuss well-known subjective biases. The book by Richard Thaler is a good collection of controversial anomalies in economics. Dugger outlines the basic features of institutional economics. Experimental economics and its contribution in different areas is reviewed extensively in the book by Roth. As regards applications, preference reversals are discussed in Thaler's book (Chapter 7). Singh provides a brief discussion about issues related to expectations formation. Harless has a good review of WTP/WTA studies. Frantz provides a comprehensive analysis of X-efficiency issues.

EDUCATIONAL PSYCHOLOGY

Philip H. Winne
Simon Fraser University, Canada

Nancy E. Perry
University of Michigan

Glossary

Attribution Interpretations a learner makes about causes that underlie outcomes of the tasks undertaken in a given learning environment.

Cognitive mediation A learner's perceptions about how to engage with instructional tasks based on interactions between the learner's knowledge and beliefs, and features of tasks posed in a learning environment.

Cognitive strategy Deliberate choices a learner makes among procedures for addressing and completing a task.

Efficacy expectation A learner's judgments about capability to reach a goal.

Goal orientation Beliefs a learner holds about why instructional tasks have utility, distinguished mainly as opportunities to expand one's competence or as jobs to complete that prove one's competence.

Learning environment Factors contributing to a learner's conception of the interactive milieu in which instructional activities are introduced, engaged, and evaluated.

Metacognition Knowledge about and awareness of one's cognitive processing.

Schema A general structure for knowledge of a category or an event structured in terms of slots that are filled by specific values for attributes of the category or event.

Self-regulation A learner's intentional monitoring and managing of cognitive and motivational strategies and the learning environment to advance toward goals of instructional tasks.

EDUCATIONAL PSYCHOLOGY is a specialized area of scholarly and practical inquiry within the broader field of psychology. Like its parent discipline, educational psychology has two main goals: to create theories that offer valid accounts for learners' and teachers' behavior; and to develop principles that, when applied in instructional situations, enhance learners' capabilities to achieve their own goals as well as those set for education by the society in which learners live. What distinguishes educational psychology from psychology in general is a focus on situations in which a teacher or a surrogate for a teacher, such as a text book or a computer program, intentionally seeks to influence a student's knowledge, motivation, and beliefs.

I. THE HERITAGE OF CONTEMPORARY EDUCATIONAL PSYCHOLOGY

The origins of educational psychology reach back at least to the 16th century when the Spanish scholar Juan Vives set forth principles for educating in *De Tradendis Disciplinus*. Further links between views of education, psychology, and teaching were forged in the 1860s in courses taught in America at normal schools for teachers. In this early period, principles were descriptions of very general scope, such as: a student's active involvement is essential to learning, interest underlies all learning, and practice stabilizes newly learned skills. These maxims were not grounded in systematic empirical inquiries, a reflection of the close tie between philosophy and psychology at that time. And, they did not explain phenomena of teaching and learning. Modern research has validated some of these ideas and overturned others.

Copyright © 1994 by Academic Press, Inc. All rights of reproduction in any form reserved.

The quarter century inaugurated in 1899 by William James' *Talks to Teachers on Psychology and to Students on Some of Life's Ideals* and chronicled in experimental work by G. Stanley Hall, James McKeen Cattell, and Edward L. Thorndike saw much growth in the field. This period was marked by a transition to empirical methodologies for grounding proposals concerning processes that constituted learning and how teaching affected those processes. The discipline emerging in this period stressed studies of individual differences in students' mental capacities and sought laws governing simple associations.

Over the next decades, the field continued to evolve and diversify. A signal development was B. F. Skinner's operant model of learning in the 1930s. This model emphasized environmental consequences of an active learner's behavior as factors that shaped how the learner would behave in the future. Later theorizing developed models about processes of memory that operant models ignored, and postulated structures of information that were constructed and manipulated by mental processes. These structures of information were resources upon which the learner drew in transferring knowledge to new situations. Also prominent in this period were studies of motivational drives and incentives as informational structures that acted in concert with a learner's goals to orient and govern learning processes. Earlier notions of mental capacity gave rise to investigations of how learners' aptitudes influenced how they participated in instruction.

In the 1960s, educational psychology was swept up in a wider and forceful cognitive revolution. This movement adopted a metaphor of the computer in its inquiries. Organized structures of information in a student's mind—prior knowledge—and the series of particular cognitive processes that operated on new information in the context of prior knowledge were hypothesized to determine what the student achieved as a result of engaging in instructional experiences. The work in this era shaped the field of educational psychology as it is today.

II. THE COGNITIVE MEDIATIONAL MODEL AND LEARNING

The cognitive mediational model proposes that prior knowledge and the student's cognitive processing while engaging in instructional tasks are primary determiners of the effects of instruction. According to this model, to each instructional event, students bring an array of prior knowledge: about themselves as learners, beliefs about how tasks unfold in this particular instructional environment, expectations about goals that they and that a teacher have for learning, and conceptual knowledge about the subject matter(s) being instructed. This panoply of information, new subject matter presented in an instructional task, and cues the teacher provides about how the student might cognitively process information to learn all are informational resources on which the student draws. The result is an interpretation or mediation of instruction in which the student makes choices, either consciously or tacitly, about how to learn as the instructional engagement unfolds. Thus, students determine which information is important and which cognitive processes will be applied to it. Because different forms of cognitive processing lead to different kinds and different amounts of achievement, the student's cognitive mediations determine what the student learns.

Within the framework of the cognitive mediational model, two formats are theorized to represent knowledge. Declarative knowledge describes a topic. It can be a simple proposition (e.g., water is a compound of hydrogen and oxygen). Or, it can be a schema that characterizes a complex topic (e.g., the scientific method) in terms of values for attributes that typify that topic (e.g., accuracy of measurement, experimental control) and interrelations among the attributes (e.g., how controls affect the validity of an experiment). When learners cognitively process information during instruction, new propositions can be added to their existing network of information in long-term memory through a process called elaboration. Or, when new information is substantially discrepant with prior knowledge, the learner can accommodate a schema to that discrepant information. This may result in tuning the schema to make slight modifications to it, or radically restructuring the schema to reflect fundamental changes in its attributes and their organization.

Procedural knowledge is the second form of knowledge. It can be written as IF–THEN rules that describe how to classify a thing (e.g., distinguishing the main character in a story) or how to transform information by applying a process to it (e.g., creating a summary of a text by deleting details and organizing similar ideas). Organized collections of IF–THEN rules constitute skills. Skills are acquired in three stages. First, each rule that comprises a skill is represented declaratively. At this stage, each rule is independent of others that ultimately will form a complete skill. Second, through practice and feedback, each rule is transformed into a dynamic action and automated so that it does not demand attention to be performed. At this stage, the learner can carry out the skill's components one by one, but the complete skill is performed in staccato fashion as each component is linked to the next. Finally, with further practice, the set of rules becomes an orchestrated whole so that they are preformed as one smooth and automatic act, a skilled act.

Prior knowledge—especially (a) declarative knowledge that reflects motivational views of self, (b) schemata that give structure to the subject matter being studied, and (c) skills for engaging strategically in purposeful learning—is both an outcome of previous instruction and an important aptitude that affects learning from instruction. Three main impediments to instructional effectiveness relate to the student's prior knowledge. First, students may lack essential prior knowledge. Second, students often fail to activate prior knowledge that is useful in learning. If relevant prior knowledge remains inert, the student's progress is impeded and final achievements are incomplete. Third, students can enter instruction with debilitating misconceptions: some concern the subject matter under study and others are misunderstandings about how instructional tasks evolve. In these situations, if students do not restructure schemata or reconfigure skills, such misconceptions seriously interfere with learning. These issues are taken up in later sections.

III. TACTICS AND STRATEGIES FOR LEARNING AND SOLVING PROBLEMS

Strategies are orchestrated sets of procedures (skills) for completing a task. What distinguishes strategies from complex but otherwise straightforward procedures is that strategies require learners to imagine subgoals and deliberate about alternative approaches to achieving a task's goal. Most researchers agree that there are two categories of strategies: domain-specific or cognitive strategies, and general executive or metacognitive strategies. Metacognitive strategies, discussed under Section V, facilitate learning in general and are applicable across a variety of subjects. They include strategies for planning, monitoring, and evaluating learning. [*See* PLANNING.]

Domain-specific strategies are particular tools for working within a subject matter. They manipulate and create information in instructional tasks to advance the learner toward the task's subgoals. When students use strategies, they are actively processing information and this enhances learning. Examples of domain-specific strategies in reading are identifying main ideas, drawing inferences, paraphrasing, and summarizing. In writing, common strategies are outlining and proofreading. A useful problem-solving strategy in mathematics and in science is translating symbolic expressions into figural representations, as in graphing and flowcharting.

Accomplished learners have three kinds of knowledge about strategies. First, they have declarative knowledge about what strategies are, that is, they can describe which procedures constitute a strategy and the products that those procedures create. For example, students usually know that they can evaluate their understanding by asking themselves questions as they study. Second, accomplished learners have proceduralized these rules so that they can carry out strategies. For instance, to identify the main idea in a section of text, these students select what appears to be an important idea and then monitor the extent to which other ideas refer to or elaborate it. Third, expert learners have conditional knowledge that identifies situations in tasks or entire tasks in which a particular strategy is appropriate. For example, when preparing a summary of a reading assignment but not when searching for specific facts, expert learners judge that identifying the main ideas in a text is a useful strategy to use.

Domain-specific strategies are not useful for all students. If learners already have extensive knowledge or competence in the subject, strategies for extending knowledge about that domain are generally unnecessary because the expertise in the domain per se supports further learning. In fact, requiring accomplished learners to use prescribed strategies in place of their prior domain knowledge typically interferes with learning. In sharp contrast, strategies are especially useful for students whose knowledge of a domain is limited or not well organized. Under these conditions, strategies help to clarify information that a task contains and guide the student's processing of that information. A common finding in schools, however, is that students who could profit most from applying domain-specific strategies are unlikely to use them, that is, these strategies remain inert. Research has vigorously investigated why students do not apply strategies when it would be appropriate.

One obvious explanation for students' lack of strategic approach to learning is that they do not know about strategies. Indeed, many students fail to discover effective domain-specific strategies on their own and most school curricula do not explicitly teach such cognitive strategies. Thus, learners commonly have a limited range of cognitive strategies and, among strategies they do possess, many are elementary and relatively weak. Unfortunately, learners generally are reluctant to abandon these weak strategies despite these strategies' obvious low utility. Learners misjudge that the time and energy it would take to learn a new, more potent strategy will not yield sufficient return for their investment.

When students have capabilities to use cognitive strategies, another common reason they do not use them is that monitoring progress toward learning goals is infrequent or incomplete, as discussed later under Section V. This is particularly characteristic of young children and students with learning difficulties. When students fail to recognize difficulties or impasses during instructional tasks, they miss opportunities to hone strategies and observe beneficial effects that result. Consequently, strategies remain unpracticed and are not perceived to be helpful.

As well as weaknesses in the three components of strategy knowledge, young or unskilled learners often have limited domain knowledge. Since cognitive strategies work with domain knowledge, gaps in domain knowledge enforce limits on the utility of strategies students do use. This increases students' difficulties in judging which cognitive strategies might be helpful in addressing tasks. A predictable consequence of this configuration of knowledge is that, when strategies' impact on learning falls well below students' expectations, incentives decrease for using them again.

Fortunately, strategies can be taught and, when this is coupled with effective teaching of domain knowledge, achievement and motivation are both positively influenced. Two approaches to strategy instruction have proven particularly successful: direct strategy instruction and reciprocal teaching. Direct strategy instruction mirrors the principles of effective instruction in any subject matter. First, explanations about the strategy clearly describe elements that comprise the strategy and describe why the strategy is useful. Conditional knowledge about when and where the strategy might be applied and means by which students can evaluate their use of the strategy also are provided. Then, modeling by the teacher or a competent peer of when and how to use the cognitive strategy exposes how the strategy unfolds and how it coordinates with successive stages of task performance. When demonstrations include self-talk through which the model reveals how to cope with challenges and setbacks, learners can observe how motivational dispositions can contribute to productive learning. In the next stage, students practice using the strategy and extending domain knowledge with guidance from the teacher or a more competent peer. Gradually, responsibility for performing tasks is transferred to the student and practice becomes independent. Throughout guided practice, informative feedback is a critical ingredient, both to improve the students' use of the strategy and to model when and how the student can self-evaluate.

Reciprocal teaching supplements features of direct instruction and extends them to a collaborative setting where learners work together on tasks that elaborate both domain knowledge and learning strategies. The teacher begins by describing information to be learned, demonstrating cognitive strategies that support learning of the subject and discussing how strategies articulate with domain knowledge. After this introduction, the reciprocal features of this teaching model emerge. As students continue learning, they and their peers (and, initially, the teacher) alternate in the roles of discussion leader and learner. The discussion leader (a) generates questions about information to be learned to which others in the group respond, (b) summarizes as learning proceeds, (c) notes or solicits points that need clarifying, and (d) makes predictions about what should be learned next and about strategies that will be useful in approaching the next subgoal. Other students (and perhaps the teacher) comment and elaborate on the discussion leader's contributions. As students gain competence, the teacher retreats from these interactions to coach learning by giving feedback and encouragement, inviting students to evaluate their domain knowledge and learning strategies, and re-modeling and re-explaining as needed.

IV. MOTIVATION

Theories of motivation seek to identify factors that explain what people choose to do, qualitative features of their behavior such as its intensity or joyfulness, and their persistence. Before the cognitive revolution, theories of motivation had a functional orientation. Motivation was seen as a relatively simple switch that, in the presence of a particular arrangement of environmental stimuli, activated, altered, or deactivated behavior. As a result of the cognitive revolution, these theories were replaced with ones in which a person's knowledge and perceptions of situations jointly create opportunities for choosing how to behave. Whereas prior behavioral theories of motivation emphasized hedonistic tendencies to seek pleasure and avoid pain, cognitive theories expanded notions of psychophysical pleasure and pain to include thoughts about self and surroundings that were valued. Based on knowledge gained from prior experience, people were hypothesized to predict consequences (using IF–THEN rules) that would follow each of several alternative behaviors, thereby creating outcome expectations. They evaluated the values associated with those different outcome expectations and then decided which alternative would maximize value. In the expectancy-value models of motivation, behavior was thus jointly influenced by (a) people's expectations about the consequences of obtaining a particular outcome if they behaved in a particular way and (b) the relative values they placed on those alternative outcomes. Expectancy-value theories gave rise to several more specific views linking motivation and learning: efficacy theory, goal theory, and attribution theory. [*See* MOTIVATION, EMOTIONAL BASIS.]

In generating an outcome expectation, it is reasonable that students assess beliefs about whether they are capable of carrying out cognitive processing that achieves the goal of a task. The result of this self-assessment is an efficacy expectation, a prediction about ability to learn or one's capability for demonstrating achievement. Efficacy expectations are powerful influences on whether students approach tasks about which they have a choice. Several characteristics of a task's goal influence students' efficacy expectations. The first is the perceived proximity of the goal, that is, how close the goal is perceived to be in time or relative to the student's current state of knowledge. Other things being equal, more proximal goals give rise to stronger or more positive efficacy expectations and, hence, a greater likelihood that the student will choose to engage a task. The student's perception of how difficult the task is also influences the student's motivation. The more steps the student judges it will take to complete a task, the more information to be processed in the task, and the more novel the task, the more difficult a task is judged to be and the lower the efficacy expectation. Finally, provided that the goal is proximal and the task is not deemed too difficult, the more clear and precise the standards for determining whether the task's goal is met, the more positive the efficacy expectation. Instructional tasks that optimize efficacy expectations are ones that students perceive to be challenging but also see as being within reach, and that have clear goals. Tasks with goals that are vague do not motivate students to try them. Similarly, tasks that students see as extremely easy are not motivating because the student perceives little gain to follow. [*See* SELF-EFFICACY.]

At major transition points in a task, and upon completing it, students evaluate the match between their accomplishments and the task's subgoals or goal. At these points, attribution theory proposes that students inherently strive to understand what causes their successes or failures. Four main kinds of attributions are used to account for performance: ability, effort, the difficulty of the task, and luck. These can be classified in terms of how stable the cause is (e.g., task difficulty is stable but effort varies), whether the cause originates internally with the student (ability and effort) or externally (task difficulty and luck), and whether the cause can be controlled by the student (e.g., effort can be but luck cannot). [*See* ATTRIBUTION.]

Achievements attributed to ability lead students to raise their sense of efficacy. Thus, when posed a similar task, they are likely to have a positive efficacy expectation. Students have tendencies to overestimate efficacy, however, probably because memories for past performances selectively highlight successes over failures. Failures attributed to task difficulty or to low effort do not negate efficacy or necessarily lower motivation for similar tasks. If the student believes it is possible to be more effective next time, by calling on external resources (such as teacher help) or by adapting strategies to span gaps in learning, improvement is within the student's zone of proximal development where, with help, the student can succeed. These kinds of failures can be positively motivating. Students with this view believe that ability is incremental rather than a static or stable entity. However, if a student has spent substantial effort on a task and failed, this is often interpreted as a reflection of low ability. If the student does not hold an incremental view of ability, efficacy expectations for similar tasks will be much reduced and the student likely will not be motivated to approach such tasks in the future.

Linked to students' beliefs about the causes of their successes and failures are perceptions of control. When students can have input to selecting the tasks they attempt, goals have intrinsic worth and are valued more. Typically, this translates into more intense cognitive engagement with the task than when goals are set for the student by someone else. Also, when students perceive that performance on a task can be improved by applying effort and cognitive strategies, factors that they control, this tends to enhance efficacy and, in turn, elevates motivation. We describe this as a tendency, however, because along with control comes responsibility. Should the student fail, attributions for poor performance point toward factors under the student's control. Failure in these situations can lead to feelings of guilt if effort was not fully applied, or to low ability, if effort was applied but the task's goal was not attained. Under Section V, we discuss a phenomenon known as the double-edged sword wherein some students maladapt to responsibility by withdrawing from tasks. [*See* CONTROL.]

Evaluations about task performance also are provided by feedback the student receives from peers, the teacher, and the task environment (e.g., a computer program that will not run because it has bugs). Teachers frequently praise or encourage students, but these kinds of feedback are not universally motivating. When students interpret positive feedback as an attempt to control their work rather than being genuinely supportive, motivation declines. Also, when students are praised for succeeding at what they judge to be very easy tasks, they interpret praise as a sign that the person praising them believes they have low ability. In turn, this can lower efficacy expectations and depress motivation. Teachers should realize that feedback they provide is interpreted by students as a reflection of expectations the teacher holds for them. This is subtle instruction for students about how they should think about their ability and motivation.

Incentives are the "payoffs" students seek from the goals they perceive are associated with tasks. Incentives are powerful influences on engagement in learning. Some students have a mastery orientation that governs their view of incentives. They perceive tasks as opportunities to extend competence and explore new ideas. Mastery oriented students prefer moderately challenging tasks because these afford the best chance to learn the most. Mastery oriented students also believe that effort is an inherent part of learning since, if a task entails minimal effort, it is one that cannot teach much that is new. In contrast, other students interpret tasks as occasions to prove to peers and teachers that they have ability or as occasions where they might err in public. These students believe tasks are assignments to perform rather than events from which to learn and, hence, are described as holding a performance goal orientation.

Some general principles for motivating students are implied by these cognitive theories of motivation. When students can set goals that have intrinsic value for them, cognitive engagement is intensified with instructional tasks that lead toward those goals. This does not mean that students should dictate the curriculum but that students' interests should be accommodated in a fair manner. Teachers can increase students' efficacy by guiding them to address goals that are proximal, specific, and challenging but not too far beyond present capabilities. This invites students to assume responsibility for their learning and creates a setting within which to promote an incremental view of ability. Attributing successes to purposeful effort, as when students use appropriate strategies, forges tools for students to succeed and means for them to take credit for their work. This, in turn, bolsters efficacy, further intensifies engagement, and enhances overall motivation. Fostering a mastery orientation recasts errors as occasions for reconsidering how to apply effort in learning. This is a productive first step toward coping with and profiting from mistakes and novice performance.

V. METAKNOWLEDGE, METACOGNITION, AND SELF-REGULATED LEARNING

Over the course of thousands of experiences with tasks in instructional environments, students develop knowledge about how to study and how, by varying their approaches to studying, they affect their achievements. This knowledge about (a) knowledge and (b) about how to regulate one's construction of knowledge is metaknowledge. A belief that pitfalls in problem solving can be avoided by planning as a first step in problem solving is an example of declarative metaknowledge. Engaging a cognitive tactic that assembles new information presented in a text with a personal experience, because the learner believes this enhances the memorability of new information, illustrates procedural metaknowledge. Cognitive events that have metaknowledge as their subject of thought are metacognitions. Three main categories of metaknowledge can be usefully distinguished: self-metaknowledge, task metaknowledge, and self-regulation. [*See* METACOGNITION.]

Self-metaknowledge is knowledge or beliefs students have about themselves as learners. Predominantly, this consists of the student's self-efficacy and attributions, discussed previously under Section IV. These propositions establish a context within which students choose tasks that will be engaged. Self-metaknowledge also affects whether students persist at the task and shapes qualitative features of their engagement with the task, such as the effort they give to it and their openness to exploring alternative avenues toward the task's goals.

Self-metaknowledge develops with experience. Younger students, before approximately the age of 9 or 10 years, typically believe that applying copious effort ensures learning. They do not recognize competence as a separable contributor to achievement. Teachers of this age group may inadvertently perpetuate this belief when their feedback consists of abundant praise for effort and little corrective information. Students usually interpret such feedback as meaning that learning was successful rather than that effort is one critical component in successful learning activities. As they mature, however, students begin to distinguish effort and competence, and come to understand that effort does not guarantee success in learning. Accompanying this developmental change in the higher grades is a greater emphasis on achievement, and this can spawn a condition known as the double-edged sword. Students who view themselves as lacking competence perceive that applying full effort in a task at which they might fail will force them to conclude that competence is truly weak. To avoid this unwanted conclusion, students limit effort or choose tasks far beyond their competence, providing a ready excuse for failure: "I didn't really try my best" or "No one could do that." Either choice practically assures that competence cannot be increased by engaging in tasks, and this affirms the student's initially negative view of self as a learner. The other edge of the sword also cuts self-worth should the learner elect to apply full effort. If the task is simple relative to the learner's competence, achievement evidently must be attributed to that fact rather than the learner's competence. For tasks that are relatively challenging in relation to the learner's competence, failure is probable since prior knowledge needed to achieve the task's goals has become deficient by avoiding tasks through which is might have been increased. That failure also confirms the student's sense of incompetence. The combination of these views of self can lead to a successively downward spiral in which competence grows minimally and self-worth declines. The repair for this syndrome is supportive, well-designed instruction that extends the student's competence per se as well as elaborating self-regulation of learning.

Another major component of a student's self-metaknowledge is the extent to which learning ability is viewed as innate versus the degree to which learning is understood to depend on effort that is expressed as the application of appropriate cognitive strategies. These beliefs reflect the entity-incremental view of ability, discussed under Section IV. A particularly debilitating condition, called learned helplessness, can develop if learners perceive that, no matter how much effort they spend, achievements remain beyond their grasp. Helplessness is inadvertently abetted when a collection of conditions jointly characterize learning tasks: namely, when tasks assigned are substantially beyond the student's subject matter competence; when the student lacks cognitive strategies that might bridge the gap between subject matter competence and the task's requirements; and, if the teacher's or peers' attributions for performance stress stable, internal, and uncontrollable factors. Helpless students completely abandon effort because they misattribute failure to ability rather than to ignorance, a malleable condition that can be overcome with effective instruction and the use of appropriate cognitive strategies. Fortunately, a reversal of this debilitating metaknowledge has been demonstrated in programs that couple effective instruction in cognitive strategies with retraining students to attribute failures to lack of knowledge and inappropriate effort. [*See* LEARNED HELPLESSNESS.]

Tasks through which students develop subject matter competence, cognitive tactics and strategies, and beliefs about themselves and their environment can be characterized in terms of five main features: (a) the conditions under which the task is performed, (b) cognitive and behavioral operations that accomplish the task, (c) products that result from applying operations, (d) the timing and characteristics of evaluative information that the student can access to guide performance, and (e) standards by which intermediate and final products of the task are judged. As a student addresses a task, past experiences with analogous tasks provide a basis for the student to make predictions about these five features of the present task. Task metaknowledge, the knowledge upon which the student bases these predictions, is acquired from the teacher, peers, directions for an assignment, and students' own analyses of experiences with tasks. Task metaknowledge can be both general and specific to a particular task at hand.

One facet of general task metaknowledge is the student's view of whether learning is accomplished quickly and with ease versus a process requiring persistence and considerable effort. When students are set a complex task, one that obliges them to coordinate and integrate information from several sources, students who perceive learning to be a quick and straightforward process typically lapse in integrating information. Hence, they do not construct comprehensive, interconnected responses. Because these same students typically overestimate the level of their understanding at transitions or the end of the task, they also bypass opportunities to sharpen and deepen subject matter knowledge. A belief system that highlights a view of learning as rapid and easy, then, is doubly problematic: it does not invite students to restructure schemata about tasks that properly reflect complexity, and it obstructs their development of full representations of subject matter knowledge.

Students' task metaknowledge may be underdeveloped and even contaminated with misconceptions that impede or seriously interfere with achieving instructional goals. For example, resources that authors add to texts to guide learners in elaborating and monitoring comprehension often are not understood or used. Beginning readers usually do not know that pictures accompanying a text can supply information useful in understanding the text. Across the grades, students often do not know how to take advantage of many of the devices—sidebars, diagrams, adjunct questions, and invitations to investigate elaborations to the text's primary information—that commonly embellish contemporary text books. Misconceptions about the products a task calls for also affect learning. In the middle elementary grades, many students misconceive assignments to write an essay as meaning that one should merely list all that is known about a topic. They are ignorant of more fundamental qualities of essays, such as organizing their points at both local and global levels or considering how well their text helps a reader draw inferences that contribute to the message carried in the essay. Students in early adolescence have a different misconception about the standards for judging essays. They typically regard primary criteria for high-quality essays to be correct spelling, proper punctuation, and other mechanical features. By overstressing these standards when they edit essays, students focus on mechanics and fail to edit essays to be better vehicles for meaning.

Another topic within task metaknowledge fuses two kinds of information: the learner's general beliefs about the instrumental value that accrues when cognitive tactics and strategies, discussed under Section III, are applied; and knowledge the learner has accumulated from past experiences with instructional tasks about the appropriateness of specific cognitive tactics and strategies for accomplishing the particular task at hand. Together, these two elements of task metaknowledge constitute conditional knowledge. Conditional knowledge can be represented as sets of IF–THEN rules. The student uses these rules to determine IF the conditions of a task at hand and one's current state of self are well-matched to a particular cognitive tactic or strategy, THEN adopt that tactic or strategy. Thus, conditional knowledge is how the student recognizes and prepares to use resources that can help in approaching goals. Applying conditional knowledge is a crucial step toward developing a plan about how to accomplish a task.

Whenever the student has choice in instructional tasks or controls the steps taken toward goals, conditional knowledge is the gateway to or the bottleneck for students' use of cognitive tactics and strategies. Students in the earliest grades often lack conditional knowledge. For instance, if young elementary grade students are asked to learn the steps in a sequence, many will merely say each step once aloud, then stop. Their recall is quite poor. If these same students are asked to rehearse the items in order or to apply a simple organizational strategy, such as creating a sentence in which each word starts with the same first letter as does the name of each item in the series, they are able to use this cognitive tactic. This indicates that the THEN segment of conditional knowledge, the tactic or strategy, is available in memory and, when it is applied, a doubling of recall is common. Similar findings are observed in upper elementary students' failures to apply comprehension strategies to reading and high school students' missed opportunities to use organizational and elaborative strategies while studying. This is an example of how knowledge, in this case tactical or strategic knowledge, can be inert. Such knowledge could be put to good use in tasks but, due to deficiencies in conditional knowledge, it remains inert.

Two explanations can be offered for why cognitive tactics and strategies remain inert. The first is that the student lacks conditional knowledge about instrumental value that can be obtained by using a cognitive tactic or strategy to address a task. This deficiency can be corrected by posing tasks where that cognitive tactic or strategy is useful, and then guiding the student to consider inert knowledge. For instance, the student might be provided a reference sheet that prompts to inspect the task for features that indicate a tactic or strategy might be useful, and check boxes where the student verifies which particular elements of the task have been explored. Or, informed feedback can be given during work on a task. Informed feedback guides the student to identify errors in the task, asks the student to identify probable reasons for committing those errors, thus exposing conditional knowledge, and offers clues about tactics and strategies that could avoid those errors in future tasks.

The second explanation for inert knowledge points toward the third main facet of metaknowledge, self-regulation. A student who is well equipped with subject matter knowledge prerequisite to a new learning task, whose self metaknowledge about learning is positive, and whose stock of task metaknowledge is extensive has many resources to support learning. All these cognitive resources, however, need to be orchestrated and applied productively. Self-regulation refers to the cognitions and behaviors that a student engages to (a) select tasks that the student predicts will amplify knowledge, (b) organize the malleable features of assigned tasks (conditions, operations, and evaluations) so that work on them is as productive as possible, and (c) audit their work on tasks to investigate how cognitive tactics and strategies, and how metaknowledge might be extended and adapted, to increase their utility when the learner addresses analogous tasks in the future.

It might seem that students do not have much latitude to select tasks in school, but this is a narrow view of students as enterprising co-creators of instructional settings. Students always have options to set tasks for themselves beyond or within the tasks assigned by a teacher or posed in a text book. Self-regulating students seek out supplemental tasks that they predict will enhance their competence. As discussed under Section VI, the learning environment is an important influence on how easily students can develop and exercise this aspect of self-regulation.

When tasks are assigned, self-regulating learners reconfigure them. For example, they do not immediately start the task itself but first plan how to approach it. Plans often include heuristics, that is, generally useful but not usually sufficient rules for carrying out a task. One such heuristic is to survey a task before starting it to discern qualities of products that will meet the task's goals. This information can provide criteria the student can use in monitoring whether progress is being made during the task. Another pretask heuristic is to scan for subject matter knowledge involved in the task or introduced in it. The student can use this information to probe long-term memory for related knowledge that, in turn, can help to elaborate new information and monitor comprehension of it. Failing to apply this self-regulatory heuristic is the second explanation for inert knowledge that we postponed in an earlier section.

The third principal feature of self-regulation is monitoring. Two domains of knowledge are monitored: subject matter information and metaknowledge. During the task, self-regulating learners compare qualities of their intermediate products or subgoals to their understandings about final products or goals. Based on these checks, they elaborate and tune schemata and domain-specific strategies in the subject matter being studied. If necessary, they also will engage in restructuring those schemata and strategies. As well as monitoring developments to subject matter knowledge, self-regulating students examine the metaknowledge they have used to carry out the task. This is forward-looking thinking because its purpose is to make preparations for having better approaches to similar tasks that the student will address in the future. Learners who evidence all these qualities of self-regulation adopt an active approach toward selecting, shaping, and engaging in learning tasks. They view themselves as accountable for adding to, tuning, and restructuring their subject matter competence, and they strive to evolve metaknowledge so that it becomes more and more useful in future learning.

Predictions from theory and findings from research converge in four main principles for promoting metacognition and self-regulation in classrooms. First, the subject matter that students are presented should be within their conceptual grasp. If tasks are too complex or demanding, students' cognitive resources will be so absorbed that few will be available for metacognitive and self-regulative activities. Second, to have procedures with which to be metacognitive and self-regulating, students should be taught cognitive strategies and task metaknowledge directly and informatively. If this information is left as a secondary target embedded within assignments, it is unlikely that students will acquire cognitive tactics and strategies, and articulate them with the demands of learning tasks. Direct instruction, described under Section III, has proven effective in achieving this instructional objective. Third, the skills that comprise subject matter, on the one hand, and cognitive tactics and strategies, on the other, require extensive and appropriately varied practice before they become automatic effective elements in students' knowledge. This implies that teachers should be patient and design curricula to revisit skills taught earlier to hone and extend them. Finally, in addition to assessing and rewarding students for their achievement of subject matter knowledge, they also should be directly evaluated and praised for growth in metaknowledge.

VI. LEARNING ENVIRONMENTS

Over weeks, months, and years of their schooling, as they cognitively mediate thousands of tasks, students' collate and articulate personal beliefs, observations of social exchanges, and accumulating achievements. These create an overarching framework of metaknowledge for interpreting the activities of instruction and the milieu in which those activities unfold. This metaknowledge of classroom environments shapes students' cognitive mediations of schooling, influencing how they engage in tasks and what they learn.

Students discern that sets of tasks have structures. One major distinction is between ability-focused versus task-focused structures. In contrast to ability-focused structures, task-focused structures offer (a) a measure of choice about goals to pursue and means for pursuing them, (b) opportunity for collaboration, and (c) a view of success that emphasizes effort, progress, and improvement. Task-focused structures invite students to choose tasks matched to their capabilities and, because different students choose different tasks, direct comparisons with peers' achievements are blurred. These factors contribute to developing strategic, motivational, and self-regulatory knowledge. As well, they create an environment that encourages students to adopt a mastery orientation toward learning.

Students are astute observers of qualities of their teacher's interactions with classmates and aspects of feedback the teacher offers about performance. Unknowingly, teachers can convey subtle messages about their beliefs concerning students' ability and whether it is incremental versus static. For instance, in response to pressures to cover curricula, teachers may inadvertently but systematically address more difficult questions to students who have more subject matter knowledge, reserving less difficult questions for the other students. Observing this correlation between the distribution of tasks and peers' competence invites students to make social comparisons. If this pattern persists, it affords an interpretation that the teacher views ability as static rather than incremental. Should the teacher notice this correlation, an attempt to compensate may ensue wherein questions are asked that are beyond less competent students' current grasp which, in turn, typically requires abundant and public help. This can signal to students that the teacher believes the student is unable to address the task solo. The student's attributions to low ability are re-affirmed. A remedy is straightforward: address questions of approximately the same difficulty and complexity to all, reserving differentiation of tasks for other venues, such as cooperative groups in which students themselves negotiate the distribution of assignments.

Another factor shaping students' perceptions of the classroom environment is grouping for instruction. When there is a wide spread of ability in classrooms, or when students are assigned to fixed groups that homogenize ability within groups and differentiate ability across groups, individual differences in ability become salient in students' accounts for performance and in their beliefs about how the teacher adapts tasks to individual differences. The usual result is that students' motivation becomes focused on completing tasks rather than learning for mastery, and levels of achievement become further differentiated.

The content, frequency, and public nature of evaluations also influence students' interpretations about their ability and their views of the teacher's expectations for their academic development. Evaluation that provides means for and encourages improvement (as in reciprocal teaching), rather than emphasizing mistakes, encourages students to view challenge as a means toward progress rather than a test of competence. Private or, at least, individualized evaluations of performance reduce perceptions of tasks as vehicles for demonstrating ability. These views can be undermined, however, if tasks are a steady diet of merely rehearsing facts or producing answers to straightforward problems.

In summary, complex interactions among all the factors of teaching and learning contribute to students' views of the classroom environment. This overarching view establishes meanings about what learning is, how it can be approached, and why it is undertaken. Research in educational psychology is now striving to construct theories capable of coordinating this multiplicity of factors as the next steps in advancing research and improving practices of instruction.

Bibliography

Berliner, D. C., and Calfee, R. C. (Eds.) (1994). "Handbook of Educational Psychology." Macmillan, New York.

Glover, J. A., and Ronning, R. R. (Eds.) (1987). "Historical Foundations of Educational Psychology." Plenum, New York, NY.

Jones, B. F., and Idol, L. (Eds.) (1990). "Dimensions of Thinking and Cognitive Instruction." Erlbaum, Hillsdale, NJ.

Meece, J. L., and Schunk, D. H. (Ed.) (1992). "Students' Perceptions of the Classroom." Erlbaum, Hillsdale, NJ.

Pintrich, P. R. (Ed.) (1991). Current issues and new directions in motivational theory and research [Special issue]. *Educational Psychologist* **26.**

Weinstein, C. E., Goetz, E. T., and Alexander, P. A. (1988). "Learning and Study Strategies: Issues in Assessment, Instruction, and Evaluation." Academic Press, San Diego, CA.

Wittrock, M. C. (1986). Students' thought processes. In "Handbook of Research on Teaching" (M. C. Wittrock, Ed.), 3rd ed., pp. 297–327. Macmillan, New York, NY.

Zimmerman, B. J., and Schunk, D. H. (1989). "Self-Regulated Learning and Academic Achievement: Theory, Research, and Practice." Springer-Verlag, New York, NY.

EEG, Cognition, and Dementia

Duilio Giannitrapani
Veterans Affairs Medical Center, Perry Point, Maryland

Glossary

Alzheimer's disease A progressive brain degeneration of unknown etiology occurring in senescence; particularly affects cognition and is believed to be characterized by neurofibrillary tangles and neural plaques.

Axon potential An electrical charge traveling along the length of the neuron (axon), carrying information from one neuron to another.

Cortex The most recently developed portion of the brain which presides over more complex functions. It is the outermost layer, closest to the scalp. All EEG data being derived from scalp electrodes are therefore a reflection of cortical activity subject to modification due to lower brain structures. Because of folding, not all cortical regions can be effectively recorded from scalp electrodes.

EEG rhythms EEG activity is characterized by its frequency in five major bands: delta, 1–3 Hz; theta, 4–7 Hz; alpha, 8–12 Hz; low beta, 13–21 Hz, and high beta 22–30 Hz.

Electroencephalogram (EEG) Literally, the electric writing of the head. The first use of the technique in its present form is attributed to Berger (1929). While the nature of electrical activity in single neurons is fairly well understood, it is not clear whether the EEG is the resultant of synchronous firing of millions of neurons or of changes in electrical fields only indirectly related to the firings of these neurons.

Factor analysis A multivariate analysis technique developed by Spearman for analyzing the structure of covariance or correlation matrices. The aim of factor analysis is the explanation of relationships among numerous correlated variables in terms of relatively few underlying variables or factors.

Frequency analysis Used here synonymously with spectral analysis: See spectral analysis.

Hz Abbreviation for hertz, representing a unit of measure for the frequency of sinusoidal waveforms. It is synonymous with cycles per second (cps or c/sec).

Neuron The cell which carries information between brain areas and between the brain and body and vice versa.

Neurotransmitter A chemical released by the neuron to facilitate the transport of an axon potential between neurons.

Spearman ρ A measure of correlation which makes no assumption about the distribution of the two variables. It is a rank order correlation because it is computed from each subject's rank on the two variables rather than from computation of actual scores as is the case in the computation of the Pearson r.

$$\rho = 1 - \frac{6 \sum d^2}{N(N^2 - 1)},$$

where $d = R_{x_i} - R_{y_i}$.

Spectral analysis (Used here synonymously with frequency analysis and Fourier analysis.) A mathematical procedure which performs the transformation of data from the time domain into the frequency domain by fitting the time domain points with a sum of harmonically related sine and cosine waves.

Synapse The junction between the end of the axon of one neuron and the dendrites of another neuron.

Thalamus A subcortical brain structure which mediates sensory, regulatory, and affective functions and has strong connections with the cortex.

Copyright © 1994 by Academic Press, Inc. All rights of reproduction in any form reserved.

EEG (electroencephalographic) correlates of cognition, the most complex brain function, have been studied with different methodologies, but major advances have been reached with the advent of computerized EEG spectral analysis. A sampling of current thoughts concerning electrophysiological models is given, followed by a discussion of correlation and factor analysis studies between EEG and cognition. These studies are aimed at demonstrating the presence of EEG parameters and their topography, which might reflect different types of cognitive involvement in normal subjects and in pathological conditions such as dementia.

I. THEORETICAL ISSUES

Among various brain functions (e.g., cognition, perception, affect, preservation of vital functions, homeostasis), cognition is by far the most complex, least understood, and developmentally most recently acquired. Descartes, in his quest for demonstrating his own existence, concluded that he did exist on the basis of *cogito ergo sum* and cognition only was capable of defining his existence. In early times the heart or the diaphram or a large vein was attributed cognitive functions. Later it was recognized that the brain was a necessary component. Since the brain upon inspection was silent, the dilemma consisted in ascribing cognitive functions to a structure that did not exhibit any perceptible cognitive activity. This dilemma has been passed down to us. The best minds have attempted to deal with the problem by developing philosophical schemata, all of which fall short of the mark.

The investigator who, through studying electrophysiological activity, attempts to gain some understanding of how cognition occurs is bound to be inextricably intermeshed *voli noli* with the mind–body problem. No matter how finely the brain tissue is dissected either structurally or functionally, an understanding will probably never be attained as to how the activity of structure (brain tissue) can give rise to an ethereal nonstructural phenomenon (thought). Perhaps a structure more complex than the brain itself will be required to fully comprehend the more complex functions of the human brain. It is possible even though incomprehensible to us that the brain develops cognition when in the execution of a certain process a staggering number of neuronal circuits get recruited and interact with each other. Embedded in the act of raw neuronal functioning somehow a transformation occurs so that consciousness arises.

Except for clinical observations of loss of functions resulting from different types of brain injuries, studies dealing with the brain's role in performing cognitive functions had to await the availability of physiological measures obtainable *in vivo* with noninvasive procedures. Hans Berger introduced the study of electrophysiological activity detectable from the intact scalp with a string galvanometer and a smoked cylinder but was unsuccessful in establishing relationships between EEG alpha activity and cognition. Serious research in this area required the availability of more precise measurements which occurred with the advent of solid-state electronics and ultimately the computer.

Subsequent investigators did not have much success in their attempts to understand the nature of cortical potentials in the study of cortico–mentation relationships. Relatively little systematic work has occurred in determining how cognitive activity is concurrent with physiological activity as measured by the EEG.

An implicit assumption is that the human cortex is organized for performing, among other things, cognitive tasks. The presence in the EEG of repetitive rhythmic activity lends itself to the expectation that the rhythmicity is somehow related to cortical organization. It is particularly difficult to theorize about EEG rhythmicity because how this electrical activity is generated is neither known nor understood. The locus of origin of cortical EEG activity is also a source of conjecture. Some exceptions, e.g., alpha activity (8–12 Hz) or spindle activity (14 Hz), seem to have at least some thalamic components.

Eccles theorized that the EEG is attributable to gross synchronization of synaptic potentials and maintained that frequency of alpha activity at around 10 Hz is readily explained if it is due to circulation of impulses in closed self-reexciting chains. After the discharge of an impulse (axon potential), recovery from depressed excitability is almost complete by 100 msec. When a neural network is stimulated continuously at a low intensity, such as when cortical activity is at a low level, the probability of a subsequent discharge will reach a maximum after 100 msec. In a network of closed self-reexciting chains at a low level of cortical activity, therefore, frequencies in the alpha range (8–12 Hz) would be those most likely generated.

It would also follow that with a higher cortical excitation level, a higher level of stimulation at the synaptic junction would occur with the result that the neuron would be excited earlier than in the above mentioned 100 msec. The earliest would be approximately 15 msec, at the end of the absolute refractory period during which a stimulus of any strength is incapable of developing an axon potential. The theoretical upper limit of the frequency generated by closed self-reexciting chains would be therefore 1000/15 or 66 Hz. This does not preclude the existence in the EEG of frequencies higher than 66 Hz, which could be the resultant of either the interaction of several of these circuits or different methods of generation.

However complicated this rationale may sound, it consists of a gross over-simplification of brain events. First of all is the assumption that the rhythmical activity of the EEG derives from a summation of axon potentials. Other possibilities are changes in ion concentrations in sodium and potassium unrelated to membrane changes occurring during the axon potential. As amply demonstrated, ion exchanges also occur consequent to neurotransmitter activity.

Some of the rhythms can be postulated to perform a scanning function, a rationale which was used primarily to interpret alpha activity. Grey Walter postulated, in addition, the existence of other scanning mechanisms and discussed specifically the appearance of theta activity in conjunction with pleasure withdrawal. He indicated that this slow potential may represent scanning for pleasure. Much work also has been generated relating intrinsic animal rhythms and theta activity.

One of the earliest investigators and one having the longest series of investigations in this area is W. T. Liberson who demonstrated the presence of a relationship between the frequency of dominant activity and "passive" and "active" intelligence. Instead of grouping the intelligence subtests of the Wechsler Intelligence Scale into the traditional performance and verbal subdivisions, he regarded as measuring "active" intelligence those subtests involved in conceptualization (e.g., arithmetic, digit span, picture completion, and picture arrangement) and "passive" intelligence those relying more on old funds of knowledge (e.g., information, vocabulary, comprehension, and similarities). [*See* INTELLIGENCE.]

Liberson demonstrated that EEG power (amplitude^2) in the slower frequencies was found to have greater correlative strength for "passive" than for "active" intelligence subtests. The latter showed greater correlative strength with the higher frequencies, but power alone did not give a clear picture because correlative strength was not the same in different brain areas. The power varied, being higher in those brain areas known to serve a function in the execution of the intellectual task whose scores were being correlated with the EEG activity.

EEG beta activity, because of its small amplitude, was not studied in this context before Mundy-Castle's work. He concluded that a portion of this activity, appearing at the inception of the stimulus and disappearing soon after, could represent scanning of cortical projection and association areas.

The plausibility of scanning hypotheses in EEG is therefore supported by the disappearance of certain EEG rhythms (e.g., alpha) in conjunction with the introduction of a stimulus or with an increase of other rhythms in response to specific stimulation (e.g., low beta). The importance of understanding mechanisms that could subsume the rhythms which present, evaluate, and ultimately select alternatives in rapid succession cannot be overstated.

II. AGE AND MATURATION

The study of mental abilities is limited to our current understanding of mental functions. This understanding governs current theories which in turn determine what is accepted as fact. Relationships between electrocortical brain activity and scores of currently used mental ability measures have been demonstrated and are studied not only for the purpose of furthering the understanding of mental abilities but also to determine the existence of mechanisms governing cognition in the brain. The relationships found to exist between mental abilities and brain activity studied via frequency analysis of the electroencephalogram are presented here.

Measurement of mental abilities has been restricted almost exclusively to behavioral correlates obtained from performance on selected individual tasks. Since intelligence is a process that cannot be measured directly, it is inferred at the present time from scores obtained through performance on verbal/behavioral tests. The major drawback of this method lies in the presence of the inferential step between the mental functions that the individual is capable of performing (process) and the scores (outcome). By removing that inferential step from the measurement of mental abilities, i.e., by testing the validity of a process measure (EEG scores), the intervening behavioral component is eliminated. One can then attempt to understand the electrophysiological variables that may either preside over or constitute the more central or physiologically meaningful elements of cognitive functions.

The search for cognitive correlates of spectral analysis of the EEG is a novel endeavor necessitating the establishment of some baselines. Since the EEG is known to evolve with maturation, it is relevant to separate age-related variables from those related to cognition per se. Figure 1 shows a matrix of correlations (Spearman ρ) obtained in a sample of 56 subjects between age in months (11 through 13 years) and EEG power in 16 frequency bands each 2 Hz wide.

It is quite evident from this figure that all significant correlations are negative. A decrease of delta and theta activity had been observed by previous investigators, while a decrease of high beta had not. The power of alpha activity instead does not show in this study any significant correlations with age. There are some indications that alpha activity reaches a developmentally mature level at about age 10. The absence of positive correlations for the dominant alpha band (11 Hz band for this group) confirms no further increase in the 11 to 13-year-old range, while the absence of negative correlates in this frequency would support the notion that the decline in alpha power which occurs in a portion of adults has not yet begun.

The fact that the bulk of EEG power in the sample is negatively correlated with age acquires special meaning when attempting to separate the role of maturation from that of cognition. These two dimensions in their various manifestations are usually positively related. Finding EEG power negatively related with age and positively related with mental functions, as shown later, presents an unprecedented and welcome possibility to differentiate the role of the two parameters.

The reader should be cautioned that the relationships with EEG power mentioned above refer strictly to studies dealing with power spectral analysis of the EEG and not to studies of EEG evoked potentials. The latter, and in particular the late components of EEG evoked potentials, have their own topographic characteristics which are not being discussed here. The interested reader should refer to the work of Roy John or Alan Gevins.

III. HARMONIC ACTIVITY AND SCHIZOPHRENIA

Harmonics are sinusoidal waveforms at frequencies which are integral multiples of a basic frequency

		Frequency bands															
		1	3	5	7	9	11	13	15	17	19	21	23	25	27	29	31
Prefrontal	left	−•											−•	−•			
	right			−•									−•	−●	−●		
Lat. frontal	left	−•	−•	−●	−•							−•	−●	−●	−•		
	right			−•										−•			
Frontal	left		−•	−●	−•								−●	−●	−•		
	right	−•	−●	−●	−•									−•	−•		
Central	left		−●	−●	−•												
	right	−•	−●	−•	−•												
Temporal	left	−•	−●	−●										−•			
	right		−•	−•	−•					−•			−•	−•	−•		
Post-temporal	left	−⬤	−●	−●						−•			−•	−•	−●		−•
	right	−●	−●	−•									−•	−•	−•		
Parietal	left	−●	−●	−●	−•												
	right	−●	−●	−•													
Occipital	left	−●	−•														
	right	−•															

• Rho with $p < 0.05$ (0.26–0.34); ● rho with $p < 0.01$ (0.35–0.42); ⬤ rho with $p < 0.001$ (0.43–0.48); ■ rho with $p < 0.0001$ (> 0.48).
A minus (–) preceding the dot indicates a negative rho.

FIGURE 1 Age in months (11–0 through 13–11) vs 64 sec of EEG $\log_{10}$ power, $N = 56$ (number). Spearman ρ's were computed for each of the 16 frequency bands and 16 brain areas; only significant ρ's (all negative) are shown as indicated in key. Dot size is proportional to significance of correlation in each cell. [From Giannitrapani, D. (1985) "The Electrophysiology of Intellectual Functions," p. 87. Karger, Basel, Switzerland. Reproduced with permission.]

called the fundamental or first harmonic. It appears that harmonics in the steady-state EEG are found in conjunction with an impairment in cognitive functioning. In mechanics a perfect idealized gear train is one that transmits force from input to output without production of heat, sound, or harmonics. The greater presence of these artifacts indicates a greater loss of force from input to output, with a consequent reduction in the efficiency of the gear train. In the brain, harmonics could be generated by "chatter" or impaired transmission at the synaptic junctions, thereby decreasing the synchronization of neuronal circuits and consequently decreasing the efficient transmission of information.

In a study with schizophrenic patients, a greater presence of harmonic activity was observed (Fig. 2) among the patients when compared to normal controls. In the figure each tracing represents the log of power in 17 frequency bands each 2 Hz wide for each of 10 schizophrenic patients and 10 normal controls, averaged over 8 conditions and 16 brain areas for a total of 64 sec of EEG. It can be seen that even though some of the normals show in the higher frequencies low level peaks that could consist of harmonics of lower frequencies, the schizophrenics show much greater harmonic power. Obvious elevations of peaks in the beta range and more specifically in frequencies which are integral multiples of the dominant activity in the 9-Hz (8–10 Hz) band are demonstrated. [*See* SCHIZOPHRENIA.]

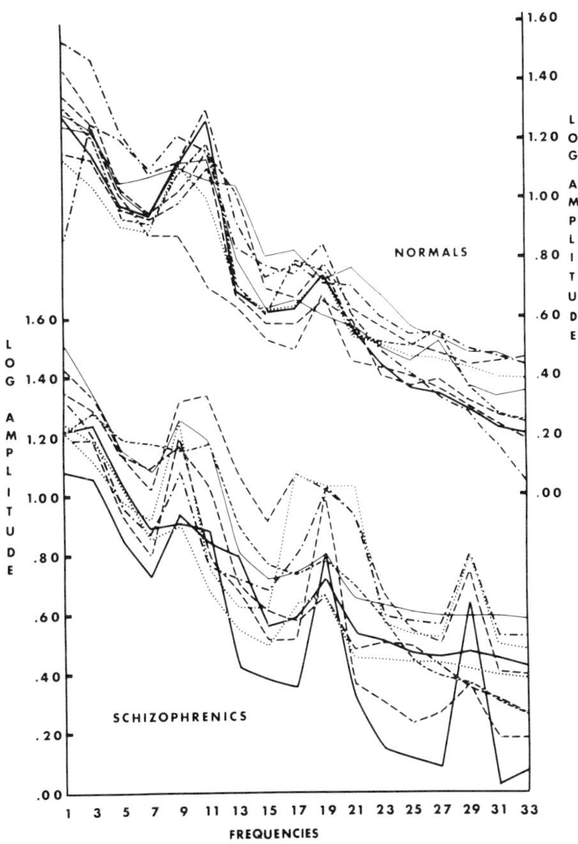

FIGURE 2 EEG $\log_{10}$ power in 17 frequency bands (2 Hz wide) for 10 schizophrenic subjects and 10 normal controls, averaged over 16 brain areas and 8 conditions for a total of 64 sec of EEG. [From Giannitrapani, D., and Kayton, L. (1974) Schizophrenia and EEG spectral analysis. *Electroenceph. Clin. Neurophysiol.* **36,** p. 382. Reproduced with permission.]

Among the schizophrenics a major loss of cognitive functions is characterized by not being able to categorize and evaluate the relevance of a particular response in a given context. Some investigators relate this to a deficit in frontal lobe function. We can theorize that in those patients the search for an appropriate response is impaired by the desynchronization of neuronal circuits necessary for the orderly progression of the search for a contextually appropriate response. This anomaly in the availability of circuits could originate from an impairment of electrochemical regulation at the synaptic junctions which could constitute one of the main factors in the impairment of cognitive functions.

IV. THE TOPOGRAPHY OF COGNITION

In the study of cognitive correlates of EEG activity two methods are contemplated. In the first more obvious one the EEG spectra are obtained while the subject is performing the task under consideration. Any observed change should be due to the task. The problem with this method is that the observed changes may be unrelated to the cognitive components but may be related to some peripheral component of the task under consideration. An alternate method, which at first sight seems more inferential but which yields clearer results, is to obtain the spectra under conditions unrelated to the cognitive variable and to correlate the EEG spectral values with the behavioral scores obtained for the cognitive task. This second method which proved to be fruitful assumes the presence of ubiquitous EEG frequency components which correlate with conceptual capacity.

One must differentiate thus between mentation and the capacity for mentation. The second method favors the notion that the impulses of the resting EEG which correlate with some form of cognitive activity would also continue to be present during the cognitive activity in question. It is conceivable that certain EEG values which may be a correlate of mentation may be orthogonal or inversely related to a measure of the capacity or ability for engaging in mental activity.

Intercorrelation matrices between EEG spectral scores and WISC scores are shown in Figures 3–5. In all of these matrices the EEG spectral scores are identical to those in Figure 1. They consist of 64 sec (8-sec averages of six stimulus and two awake-resting conditions).

Figure 3 shows the matrix of significant correlations between EEG spectral values and Wechsler coding subtest scores. In this particular task the subject is asked to substitute a series of digits with the symbols found in a given key. Coding constitutes a measure of visuo-motor functioning and thus requires a minimum amount of cognition. Figure 3 shows that this relatively unitary function of visually searching for and processing information correlates with the presence of several frequencies of EEG activity only in occipital areas, primarily on the left side. The occipital electrodes are placed on the scalp regions that approximate the visual projection areas. This finding therefore has face validity.

A group of significant negative correlations occurs in the anterior areas in a slow frequency band where the power of eye-movement artifacts clusters. Some subjects' involuntary eye movements are known to increase during mental arithmetic, one of eight conditions comprising the 64 sec of EEG selected for the study. By separating the matrices for each of the eight conditions, it was ascertained that the cluster of significant negative correlations was present only in the arithmetic condition. Since WISC coding requires efficient and speedy eye movements between the code and the target, it can be hypothesized that the subject who generates involuntary eye movements during mental arithmetic also finds it difficult to engage in volitional eye movements with speed and precision and will consequently be penalized in this timed visual task.

To further explore the existence of relationships between EEG and cognition, the same EEG power scores are correlated with scores on the WISC comprehension subtest which requires practical information and an ability to evaluate appropriate responses to situations. Wechsler avoided specifying what functions might be involved in the performance of this task. It seems that among the unique features of comprehension is not only the ability to elicit responses from within but more important the ability to evaluate the appropriateness of each elicited response, i.e., to form a judgment regarding which response is appropriate or relevant within the given context and at what point to terminate the search

		Frequency bands															
		1	3	5	7	9	11	13	15	17	19	21	23	25	27	29	31
Prefrontal	left																
	right																
Lat. frontal	left																
	right																
Frontal	left		–•														
	right		–•														
Central	left													•			
	right																
Temporal	left																
	right																
Post-temporal	left																
	right																
Parietal	left																
	right																
Occipital	left				•					•	•		•				
	right										•						

• Rho with $p < 0.05$ (0.26–0.34); • rho with $p < 0.01$ (0.35–0.42); ● rho with $p < 0.001$ (0.43–0.48); ■ rho with $p < 0.0001$ (> 0.48). A minus (–) preceding the dot indicates a negative rho.

FIGURE 3 WISC coding vs 64 sec of EEG $\log_{10}$ power ($N = 56$). Spearman ρ's were computed for each of the 16 frequency bands and 16 brain areas; only significant ρ's are shown as indicated in key. Dot size is proportional to significance of correlation in each cell. EEG scores used to correlate with coding scores are identical to those in Figures 1, 4, and 5. [From Giannitrapani, D. (1985) "The Electrophysiology of Intellectual Functions," p. 98. Karger, Basel, Switzerland. Reproduced with permission.]

for a response. It could be called a test of contextual appropriateness.

Comprehension (Fig. 4), among all the WISC subtests, shows the highest number of correlations with the EEG scores used. There is a broad band of significant correlations from 1 to 23 Hz with the exclusion of the 19-Hz band. It is as if the reasoning required for efficient performance in the comprehension subtest is utilizing the presence of EEG frequencies in a broad spectrum and in all brain areas with the notable exception of the occipital areas which were significant in the coding subtest.

Current neuropsychological knowledge is mute in regard to the topography of comprehension except for some relatively vague inferences concerning the frontal lobes. The data shown here more specifically suggest a smaller involvement of the prefrontal areas but a greater involvement of the frontal and central brain areas, with some noted emphasis on the left lateral frontal, right frontal, and central areas, in particular.

V. THE TOPOGRAPHY OF ARITHMETIC

Arithmetic functions have eluded strict localization perhaps (1) because great variance occurs between different brains while performing these functions and (2) because they have been attributed lateralization on the left side due to the verbal component and on the right side due to findings from patients with spatial deficits. Clinical findings have never been clear partly because of the many brain areas involved. In the Gerstmann syndrome, for instance, acalculias involve the left angular and supramarginal gyri while performance of simple arithmetic on paper may be compromised by right parietooccipital lesions; also concentration deficits may affect the ability to do numbers "in the head," with right-sided lesions. Therefore, one infers left, right, or bilateral participation in the complex array of doing calculations. [*See* CALCULATION.]

The WISC arithmetic subtest measures the ability to solve arithmetic story problems and requires both reasoning and speed of performance, the latter because it is a timed test. Scores, therefore, may be affected by fluctuations of attention as well as motivation. Figure 5 shows significant correlations obtained between the same EEG power scores used in Figures 1, 3, and 4 and the respective WISC arithmetic scores.

This matrix is unique among those obtained for the verbal subtests in that significant correlations are absent in the lower frequencies, no correlation

		Frequency bands															
		1	3	5	7	9	11	13	15	17	19	21	23	25	27	29	31
Prefrontal	left						•	•					•				
	right																
Lat. frontal	left				•		●	⬤					•				
	right						•	•									
Frontal	left			•	•	●	•	⬤	•			●	●				
	right			●	●	●	•	⬤	•	•		•	●				
Central	left	●	●			●	●	■	•			•					
	right	•				•	●	⬤	•				•				
Temporal	left	•		•	•	•	●	●									
	right	•		•	•	•	•	●									
Post-temporal	left			•		•		•									
	right		•			•											–•
Parietal	left	•	●	•		•	•	•	•								
	right	•	●	•		•	•										
Occipital	left																
	right																–•

• Rho with $p < 0.05$ (0.26–0.34); ● rho with $p < 0.01$ (0.35–0.42); ⬤ rho with $p < 0.001$ (0.43–0.48); ■ rho with $p < 0.0001$ (> 0.48).
A minus (–) preceding the dot indicates a negative rho.

FIGURE 4 WISC comprehension vs 64 sec of EEG $\log_{10}$ power ($N = 56$). Spearman ρ's were computed for each of the 16 frequency bands and 16 brain areas; only significant ρ's are shown as indicated in key. Dot size is proportional to significance of correlations in each cell. EEG scores used to correlate with comprehension scores are identical to those in Figures 1, 3, and 5. [From Giannitrapani, D. (1985) "The Electrophysiology of Intellectual Functions," p. 93. Karger, Basel, Switzerland. Reproduced with permission.]

		Frequency bands															
		1	3	5	7	9	11	13	15	17	19	21	23	25	27	29	31
Prefrontal	left																
	right																
Lat. frontal	left							●									
	right							•									
Frontal	left							●	•			•	•				
	right							●	•	•							
Central	left							●	•	•							
	right							●		•							
Temporal	left							●	•	•							
	right							●	•								
Post-temporal	left							•		●			•				
	right																
Parietal	left							•		•			•				
	right							•		•							
Occipital	left									•			•	•			
	right									•				•			

• Rho with $p < 0.05$ (0.26–0.34); ● rho with $p < 0.01$ (0.35–0.42); ● rho with $p < 0.001$ (0.43–0.48); ■ rho with $p < 0.0001$ (> 0.48).
A minus (–) preceding the dot indicates a negative rho.

FIGURE 5 WISC arithmetic vs 64 sec of EEG $\log_{10}$ power ($N = 56$). Spearman ρ's were computed for each of the 16 frequency bands and 16 brain areas; only significant ρ's are shown as indicated in key. Dot size is proportional to significance of correlation in each cell. EEG scores used to correlate with arithmetic scores are identical to those in Figures 1, 3, and 4. [From Giannitrapani, D. (1985) "The Electrophysiology of Intellectual Functions," p. 94. Karger, Basel, Switzerland. Reproduced with permission.]

being significant below the 13-Hz band. The highest correlations are again away from the anterior and posterior poles of the brain and are stronger in general on the left side. While the 13-Hz band is ubiquitously significant in the verbal subtests, the low beta frequencies and especially the 15- and 17-Hz bands become significant only in correlations with the arithmetic, comprehension, picture arrangement, and block design subtests of the WISC.

The EEG under scrutiny was obtained during several conditions: arithmetic (sequential subtractions), noise (listening to white noise), and voice (listening to a story), all with eyes closed, and two with eyes open—vision (looking at a poster) and diffuse vision (looking through diffusing goggles). Since these conditions were unrelated to arithmetic story problems but one condition was performance of mental arithmetic (sequential subtractions), it was relevant to determine whether EEG activity obtained during these conditions showed specific clustering in certain frequencies and brain areas. It was of interest, for instance, to study EEG activity in the left temporal areas known to be involved in language functions.

A factor analysis of EEG power scores was performed for each condition separately, utilizing the topographic distribution of loadings of a given factor to study the relative dependence of a given EEG frequency in a given frequency band to other frequencies of the same or other brain areas. Figure 6 shows the factors having loadings in the temporal areas for each of the conditions. The similarity between factors of the arithmetic, diffuse vision, and noise conditions can be observed. Loadings are located primarily in the anterior temporal and temporal areas, consist primarily of beta activity, and are lateralized with greater loading on the right side. In contrast, the factor for the voice condition, while still being loaded on the same frequencies, is localized on the left side, confirming the involvement of left-sided linguistic areas. It is simple to interpret the similarity of the loadings on the right side of the diffuse vision and white noise conditions, both being obtained by figureless stimuli, one visual and one auditory, but mental arithmetic shows also a greater amount of loadings on the right side. Consisting of sequential subtractions, it could be argued that the similarity with the two previous conditions is that for both diffuse vision and white noise there is an instinctual search for a figure in stimuli that are intrinsically figureless. In the arithmetic condition the similarity lies in the search for the next appropriate number, a number which acquires figure qual-

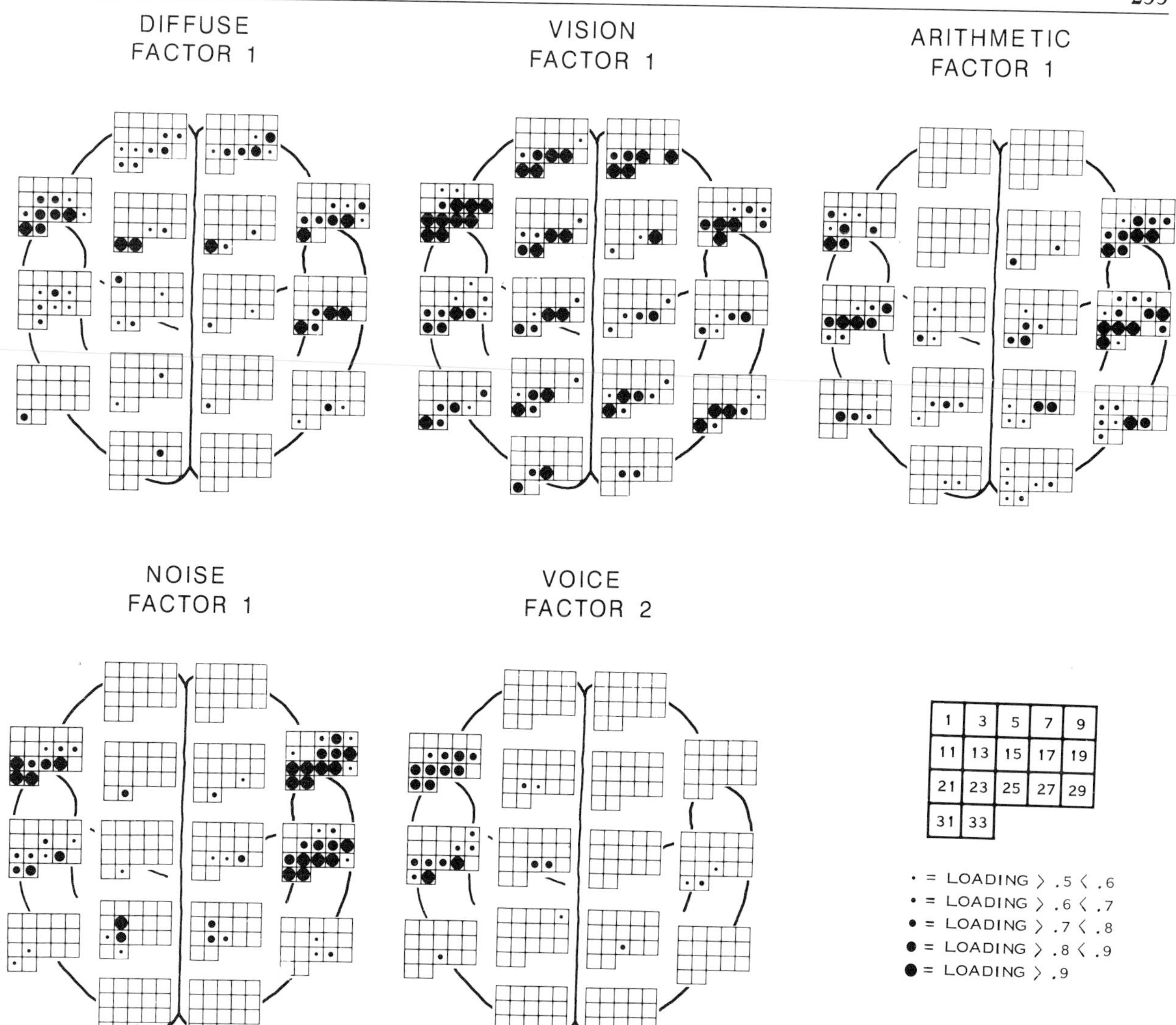

FIGURE 6 Temporal factors. For each of five indicated conditions a factor analysis was performed and factors having loadings primarily in temporal and anterior temporal areas were selected. Dot size indicates magnitude of loading for each EEG frequency as per key. [From Giannitrapani, D. (1985) "The Electrophysiology of Intellectual Functions," p. 206. Karger, Basel, Switzerland. Reproduced with permission.]

ity when the mental check to determine whether the computation is correct is satisfied.

The commonality between the three conditions is a mental search for figure–ground relationships. This hypothesis is reinforced by the distribution of loadings in the patterned vision condition, which has a greater involvement of the left anterior temporal area, reminiscent of the voice condition. This latter observation might suggest the presence of verbal activity during this task. Obviously, verbal activity is not as dominant during the perceptual search which occurs in the noise, diffuse vision, and arithmetic conditions.

VI. EEG AND DEMENTIA

Dementia, which consists of the loss or deterioration of cognitive functions, is a process not well understood primarily because the brain mechanisms governing mental functions are not well understood. It can be subdivided into two organic groups, one which is consequent to any number of irreversible brain damages and the other which is reversible in nature and is consequent to transitory conditions such as vascular insufficiency, uremia, or anoxia. A third group, not a true dementia, is functional or pseudodementia which is consequent to, e.g., depression. The diagnosis of pseudodementia is at times very difficult and is expected to and does have EEG characteristics quite different from those exhibited by true dementia. All of these groups (except pseudodementia) show an increase in delta and theta activity both in traditional and in quantitative analysis of the EEG. Even though this effect seems to be stronger for Alzheimer's dementia patients, the slow wave increase in itself is not pathognomonic of Alzheimer's dementia. [*See* ALZHEIMER'S DISEASE; DEMENTIA.]

Dementia can be further subdivided into its different etiologies, but to date it is not clear whether each of these etiologies produces a dementia with different electrophysiological characteristics reflecting the different types of brain damage. If the EEG is assumed to reflect cognitive functions, it should be expected to have characteristics common to all types of dementia as well as specific characteristics depending on the multifactorial etiology of the disorder.

Traditional EEG has demonstrated that when the dominant frequency becomes slower than alpha activity, the subject is in general either an infant, not alert, asleep, or suffering from brain damage. It seemed reasonable that the degree of slowing could be used as a measure of the level of cognitive functioning. A partial test of this hypothesis was attempted by the author with an analysis of the EEG frequency spectra of three groups of subjects: Group 1, 16 patients with diagnosis of severe Alzheimer's dementia; Group 2, 16 patients with the diagnosis of non-Alzheimer's dementia (including anoxias, multi-infarct or secondary to alcohol abuse) and matched with those of Group 1 for severity of dementia and age; Group 3 consisting of 10 normal control males matched for age with the two other groups. This design permitted determining whether the presence of EEG slow activity correlates with dementia. To test this hypothesis an 11-point ordinal dementia scale was developed. This scale provided a simple instrument able to rank patients on a broad spectrum of developmental deficits which progressively ranked impairments in naming, memory, abstraction, speech, voice, orientation, and perception. Scores from the scale were correlated with the EEG power in 18 frequency bands each 2 Hz wide.

The means of power scores for 16 scores for 16 brain areas are plotted in Figure 7, which shows that the control group retains a previously observed alpha peak at 9 Hz. This represents a slowing from a mean dominant frequency of 11 Hz observed in younger ages. It also shows that for the slow frequency bands (1–5 Hz) the control subjects have significantly lower power scores than those in either the Alzheimer's or non-Alzheimer's group, reemphasizing the role of slow activity in dementia.

Of particular interest in the normal group is the hump in power of the 15- to 21-Hz frequencies. Figure 7 shows that a broad spectrum of low beta activity is significantly decreased in the non-Alzheimer's group and is further decreased in the Alzheimer's patients in comparison with the normal subjects.

Early investigators had observed an increase in fast activity with increase in age. This increase in beta activity was not positively correlated with dementia but rather seemed to relate to intact functions. The problem was in interpreting the role of a frequency whose power increased with age but decreased with dementia. In a young population, the author had observed that an increase in low beta activity occurred in the presence of unstructured stimuli or stimuli that required structuring on the subject's part and thus could represent the presence of a mechanism for scanning for structure.

The author's observations in another set of experiments with a young adolescent group indicated that the power of low beta activity, among other frequencies, correlated positively with the capacity for performance on the WISC comprehension, arithmetic (Fig. 5), picture arrangement, and block design subtests, all of which require a structuring effort on the subject's part.

In senescence, with a generalized decrease in cognitive functions, increase in low beta activity may indicate the presence of a coping mechanism which becomes manifest via the electrophysiologic byproduct of this scanning effort. It is possible that with a further increase in severity of the process responsible for the dementia, this coping mechanism is no longer adequate for the retention of cognitive functions and either is curtailed severely or ceases to operate. As a result, low beta power decreases in the dementia groups as evidenced in Figure 7.

Two hypotheses can be considered suggesting that low beta power is a correlate of (1) a scanning function or (2) a search for structure, both necessary components of cognitive ability. They are not mutually exclusive and are consistent with the Alzheimer's experiment findings which show a significantly higher level of low beta activity in the normal control group and no significant differences in this activity between the two demented groups. The role of age in the presence of this activity needs to be studied further.

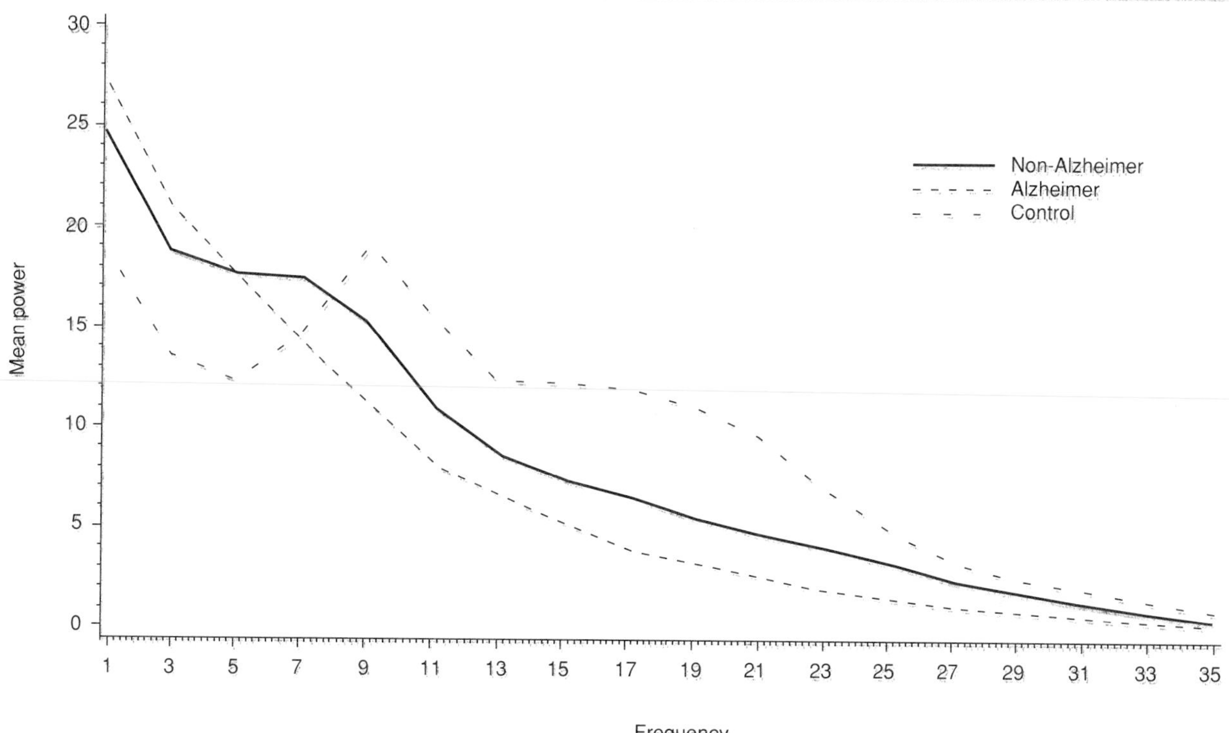

FIGURE 7 Mean $\log_{10}$ power in 18 frequency bands (2 Hz wide, 0–36 Hz) of 12 brain areas for three groups: Alzheimer's dementia patients (N = 16), non-Alzheimer's dementia (N = 16), and normal controls (N = 10). [From Giannitrapani, D., and Murri, L. (eds.) (1988). "The EEG of Mental Activities," p. 33. Karger, Basel, Switzerland. Reproduced with permission.]

The Alzheimer's study findings furnish strong support for the notion that slow wave activity correlates with dementia while low beta activity correlates with some component of cognitive functions. There is less evidence for supporting the notion that different types of dementia are distinguishable in the EEG. The only statistically different power score between the Alzheimer's and non-Alzheimer's dementia groups is significantly higher power in the 9-Hz band for the non-Alzheimer's dementia patients. In addition, the Alzheimer's group is conspicuous for having a spectrum void of features. It consists of an exponential curve decreasing in power with increase in frequencies which was not observed previously perhaps because other studies used broader frequency bands that could have masked the finding.

Utilization of frequency bands 2 Hz wide permitted the observing of a fundamental difference in the shape of the curve of the two groups. This finding can be interpreted as resulting from two different mechanisms generating dementia in the two groups.

The non-Alzheimer's dementia group shows an absence of dominant peaks but a semblance of dominant activity on or at about 7 Hz. This indicates that dominant activity is less prominent and, in general, slower than in the normal control group. The non-Alzheimer's dementia group also shows significantly more slow activity and significantly less fast activity (low beta) than the normal control group.

These findings indicate that in the case of non-Alzheimer's dementia it is meaningful to speak of slowing of dominant activity because the rhythmical organization of dominant activity is retained albeit slower in these patients. In the case of the Alzheimer's patients, however, since there is not even evidence of the vestige of a peak of dominant activity in the slower frequencies, one could speak of a removal of EEG rhythmicity (rather than slowing of dominant activity) which could constitute evidence of a different mode of EEG desynchronization resulting in dementia for the two groups.

The data support the notion that EEG slow activity is not the only correlate of loss of cognition. It seems that for dementia to occur, there needs to be present one of at least two mechanisms, first the slowing of dominant activity with the prima facie implication of slowing of cortical functions and second the absence of rhythmical dominant activity. If this hypothesis is correct, a search must be made for the correlates of these and other factors producing dementia in the hope of gaining a better understanding of the elements necessary for cognition to occur.

VII. CURRENT DEVELOPMENTS AND SUMMARY

The mapping of cortical areas in their role in cognitive functions is expanding rapidly. During the period of writing this article, three new techniques have emerged. The first two are offshoots of MRI (magnetic resonance imaging); the first becomes possible by greatly increasing the power of the magnetic field while the second utilizes the maxo-planar technique developed in Great Britain. Both permit the production of snapshots in less than a second while traditional MRI requires at least 5 to 10 min for each image. Both techniques are sensitive to the oxygen content of venous blood and, given the oxygen decrease during brain tissue activity, can lend themselves to the study of transitory brain activity such as higher cortical functions rather than being relegated only to structural studies as in traditional MRI.

The third technique consists of computer super enhancement of cortical images obtained during brain operations using the open skull technique. Correlations were found between changes that occur in the tissue's color density and the utilization of those brain areas. These changes, invisible to the naked eye, become quite apparent when submitted to computerized super enhancement procedures. These changes may represent the flow of ionic currents, oxygen delivery, changes in blood volumes, potassium accumulation, or glial swelling.

While these developments are very exciting, the MRI examination is expensive, and the open skull technique is restricted because it is available only for brief periods of time in patients undergoing surgery. The EEG retains certain advantages including its low cost and the noninvasiveness of the procedure.

In conclusion, it has been amply demonstrated that EEG components carry information concerning the functional role of brain areas. Some of this information relates to cognitive functions, but the basic mechanisms governing the execution of these functions in the brain are not understood yet. The challenge remains to study and discover these mechanisms.

Bibliography

Basar, E. (Ed.) (1988). "Dynamics of Sensory and Cognitive Processing of the Brain." Springer, Berlin.

Chen, A. C. N., and Buckley, K. C. (1988). Neural perspectives of cerebral correlates of giftedness. *Int. J. Neurosci.* **41**, 115–125.

Edelman, G. M. (1989). "The Remembered Present. A Biological Theory of Consciousness." Basic Books, New York.

Giannitrapani, D. (1985). "The Electrophysiology of Intellectual Functions." Karger, Basel, Switzerland.

Giannitrapani, D., and Murri, L. (Eds.) (1988). "The EEG of Mental Activities." Karger, Basel, Switzerland.

Johnson, R., Jr. (1988). The amplitude of the P300 component of the event-related potential: Review and synthesis. *Adv. Psychophysiol.* **3**, 69–137.

Lopes da Silva, F. (1991). Review article, Neural mechanisms underlying brain waves: From neural membranes to networks. *Electroenceph. Clin. Neurophysiol.* **79**, 81–93.

Steriade, M., Gloor, P., Llinas, R. R., Lopes da Silva, F. H., and Mesulam, M.-M. (1990). Basic mechanisms of cerebral rhythmic activities: Report of IFCN Committee on Basic Mechanisms. *Electroenceph. Clin. Neurophysiol.* **76**, 481–508.

EMBARRASSMENT AND BLUSHING

Robert J. Edelmann
University of Surrey, United Kingdom

Glossary

Blushing Spontaneous reddening or darkening of the face, ears, neck, and/or upper chest caused by blood vessels dilating and increasing blood volume in those areas in response to social evaluation or public scrutiny.

Embarrassment A state of emotional discomfort resulting from the projection of an undesired image to others present.

Face saving All coping actions, both verbal and nonverbal, taken by both the embarrassed person and observers to the event to overcome feelings of embarrassment in an attempt to regain social composure.

Self-consciousness The focusing of attention upon oneself either as a result of the situation (e.g., in the presence of an audience) or as a result of individual differences in the tendency to be self-attentive.

Self-presentation Attempts to control the image of ourselves that we present to others.

EMBARRASSING blunders, faux pas, and improprieties are everyday social occurrences. However, because embarrassment is essentially a state in which a person has failed to maintain social poise or a desired image in the presence of others, it is an uncomfortable state which people seek to avoid. In addition to external cues, which can relate to either the nature of the social accident or the reactions of others to our faux pas, a feeling of embarrassment can also be elicited by internal cues (notably blushing) in the absence of an intrinsically embarrassing situation. Indeed, for some people the fear of blushing can be a socially debilitating experience. Because of the aversive nature of embarrassing situations people try to avoid them when possible or, if embarrassment has occurred, make efforts to restore their identity or self-view as well as attempt to save face or preserve a desired identity in the eyes of others present.

I. THEORETICAL EXPLANATIONS FOR EMBARRASSMENT

Although embarrassment is a common and dramatic experience with which nearly everyone is familiar, there is a lack of agreement about the precise psychological events which give rise to it. Three broad theoretical explanations have been advanced: the first focuses upon self-presentational concerns subsequent to a faux pas or social accident; the second emphasises the individual's flustered uncertainty about how to continue an interaction in the wake of such social accidents; and the third focuses upon anxiety and worry about the need to create a desired impression.

Theories focusing upon self-presentational concerns suggest that embarrassment has to do with a failure to present a desired image to others whom we regard as evaluating our performance. This assumes that the individual concerned is motivated to make a particular impression on others. Falling over in front of friends is likely to cause us less concern about the impression we create than falling over just as we are about to introduce a guest of honor to a large audience at an important function. Factors that increase the negative consequences of failure, such as larger, more competent audiences, novel or ambiguous interaction contexts, or facets of one's own

Copyright © 1994 by Academic Press, Inc. All rights of reproduction in any form reserved.

personality, are likely to increase our desire to protect our image before others.

A further assumption, however, is that the prevailing circumstances during an interaction do not allow us to present a desired image to others present. The latter circumstances involve the violation, witnessed by others, of some taken-for-granted social rule. This, in turn, assumes that the person concerned has violated the rule unintentionally while at the same time being aware that a violation has occurred. Someone unaware of the rules of conduct will remain unembarrassed by their "inappropriate" behavior no matter how concerned they are with the evaluative reactions of others, unless others present make it clear that their behavior is inappropriate. If we are unaware of the rules of etiquette at a social function, transgressing such rules will not cause us concern unless others present draw our failings to our attention. Similarly, someone aware of the rules but unconcerned with evaluative reactions is likely to remain unembarrassed by social mishaps. Conversely, someone acutely concerned with negative audience evaluations is likely to be embarrassed by seemingly trivial events. It is only when our knowledge of, and motivation to concur with, these rules exists that embarrassment is a consequence of social failure.

Others have argued that it is not self-presentational concerns *per se* that cause embarrassment but flustered uncertainty about how to proceed once an unexpected or disruptive social event has occurred. Thus, forgetting someone's name or falling over in public disrupt the working concensus of identities that exists in social interaction, leaving a new concensus to be created. Until such a new concensus exists, awkwardness or flustered uncertainty predominates. Although such a reaction may well be important, flustered uncertainty is itself likely to be directly related to a concern with the evaluation of others. Appearing to be flustered or uncertain is not an image we would wish to present to others and hence may be embarrassing in its own right.

Finally, some have pointed out that anxiety and worry about whether one has actually created, or indeed will create, an undesirable impression is a central feature of self-presentational concerns. Indeed, some people seem to be so concerned about the impression they will create that they suffer extreme embarrassment in the absence of any clearly defined evoking event. Indeed, they may be so concerned that they might behave in a way which is humiliating or embarrassing that they actively seek to avoid social situations.

Clearly, there are common features to the three theories described. Although flustered uncertainty and anxiety about one's social performance do seem to be important aspects of embarrassment, self-presentational concerns are central. Thus, the emphasis in each theory is that embarrassment has to do with the actual, or anticipated, occurrence of an unwanted event that communicates undesired information about oneself to real, or imagined, others, whom we regard as evaluating our performance.

II. CAUSES OF EMBARRASSMENT

There have been a number of attempts to collect descriptions of, and categorize, embarrassing events on the basis of the situations involved. One factor illustrated by such endeavors is the sheer variety of embarrasing circumstances people document. It is perhaps not surprising therefore that the various attempts to systematically categorize embarrassing acts produce a variety of different solutions. Thus, some refer to inappropriate identity (e.g., uncontrollable laughter or tears) and loss of poise. The latter includes loss of physical poise (e.g., tripping over furniture), impropriety (e.g., failure to control bodily behavior, for example, when fainting), forgetting someone's name or introducing them by the wrong name, and awkward interactions (e.g., asking inappropriate or unfortunate questions or simply not knowing how to proceed). Others have referred to false identity (i.e., telling someone untruths about oneself and being found out), breaches of privacy (e.g., unintentional exposure of body parts, touching or coming too close to someone, or revealing feelings that the person wished to hide), and being made to feel conspicuous as when over-praised (e.g., discomfort occasioned by excessive compliments). Still others have included a category of empathic or vicarious embarrassment to describe instances when we feel embarrassed for another person who is in a seemingly embarrassing situation (e.g., when an actor forgets his lines). Although there are clearly a number of ways of classifying embarrassing events, these tend to reflect the methodology used; there do not tend to be radical differences in the general descriptions of embarrassing events obtained. Thus, some categorization schemes refer to specific actions (e.g., tripping and falling) while others pinpoint dimensions (e.g., who is embarrassed, as in empathic embarrassment).

Therefore, rather than considering categories of acts, a more useful strategy for classifying embarrassing episodes is to consider psychologically meaningful underlying dimensions. Two such dimensions appear to be of particular importance: who is embarrassed by the event and who is responsible for causing the embarrassment. The first dimension, who is embarrassed, considers whether it is one individual, both (or all) the interactants, the audience, or the bystander/viewer. The second dimension, who is responsible for causing the embarrassment, considers whether it is the embarrassed person themselves (i.e., the actor) or an observer to the embarrassment. By combining these two dimensions, four broad categories of situation can be recognized: (i) those in which the individual is responsible for their own embarrassment (individual behavior, actor responsible); (ii) those in which the interaction itself is embarrassing (interactive behavior, shared responsibility); (iii) situations in which embarrassment is caused by an observer (audience provocation, observer responsible); and (iv) an empathic reaction of embarrassment to someone else's behavior (bystander behavior, audience responsible).

The actual types of embarrassing episode described by earlier classification schemas can readily be incorporated by the dimensional categorization approach. Examples from the first category (individual behavior, actor responsible) include loss of poise (e.g., forgetting someone's name), impropriety (e.g., wearing the wrong clothing to a social function), and false identity (i.e., telling someone untruths about onself and being found out). Examples from the second category (interactive behavior, shared responsibility) include any awkward interaction when neither person is sure what to say, when there are long mutual silences, unsuccessful attempts by both parties to end the conversation, and so on. Examples from the third category (audience provocation, observer responsible) include conspicuousness (e.g., being the "victim" of people singing "happy birthday to you" or when being complimented or congratulated), being the victim of teasing, or when people make public our past embarrassing predicaments. Examples of the final category (bystander behavior, audience responsible) include any occasion of empathic embarrassment when we feel embarrassed because of someone's or something's behavior (e.g., going to the zoo and seeing animals engage in sexual behavior).

Central to each is a desire to present oneself in a way that meets one's own standard for self-presentation and/or a desire to avoid focusing attention toward the public aspect of oneself. Thus, any event that involves the transgression of an unwritten social rule (e.g., falling over in public, dressing inappropriately for social occassions, awkward interactions) results in both the presentation of an undesired image and self-attention. Being made the center of attention (e.g., through teasing) inevitably draws our attention to the public aspect of ourselves and a concern with the image we are likely to present.

Interestingly, blushing, which is often regarded as the hallmark of embarrassment, may actually make us more self-aware and lead us to assume we are presenting an image (i.e., embarrassment) that is discrepant from the image we wish to present. We tend to assume that people feel embarrassed when they blush, although visible facial reddening also occurs with other emotional states such as anger. Thus, it is possible to make someone embarrassed simply by telling them they are blushing, even in nonembarrassing situations. Blushing may then be sufficient to generate embarrassment in the absence of specific situations that are defined as embarrassing. People who are over-attentive to internal and expressive cues may be particularly prone to generate a feeling of embarrassment from a perception of their own blushing. Because of the negative experience of embarrassment with which blushing is associated, this may, in some cases, lead to a chronic fear of blushing. This issue is developed further in the following section.

III. BLUSHING AND THE EXPRESSION OF EMBARRASSMENT

Embarrassment is marked by a well-defined set of behaviors. Eye contact is reduced, body movements, speech dysfluencies, and smiling all increase, and blushing is likely to occur. This reaction seems nearly universal, although the intensity and relative importance of different components of the reaction seem to differ across cultures. Indeed, the display of embarrassment is readily recognizable by others. But why should an emotion we wish to hide be so evident to others? There are a number of suggestions for the functions of behaviors associated with embarrassment.

The desire to look away or hide behind one's hands when embarrassed has been studied in laboratory experiments as well as being widely referred to in people's self-reports of their embarrassment. A common feeling when embarrassed is a wish to disappear or escape from the situation. Unfortunately, departing the scene of an embarrassing mishap is rarely possible to achieve without attracting even more attention to oneself. Hence, as we are unable to increase our physical distance from others, we may use avoidance of eye contact, turning away, or covering our eyes as a way of increasing our psychological distance from them. A further possible explanation is that people look away when embarrassed to avoid seeing the signs of rejection on the faces of other people. Alternatively, reduced eye contact may be a reflection of the tension or anxiety associated with embarrassment. Such nervous responses may also include manipulative gestures (such as fingering one's clothes, hair, or surrounding objects), turning one's body away, and stammering.

There are a number of ways in which anxiety associated with embarrassment might interfere with speaking. First, a preoccupation with the reason for our embarrassment may make it difficult to pay attention to what we wish to say. Alternatively, anxiety may make us pay too much attention to what we wish to say with the result that we stumble over our words. Finally, anxiety may interfere with normal breathing, with shorter, faster respiration interfering with speech output.

A "silly" self-conscious grin and a "strangled" laugh are also common reactions to embarrassment. The fact that, during embarrassment, smiling usually occurs while the person looks away, distinguishes it from a smile of pleasure. There are four possible explanations for such a reaction. First, people may use smiling in an attempt to hide or conceal their embarrassment; such attempts may occasionally succeed, as embarrassment can be mistaken for amusement. Second, smiling and laughter when embarrassed may serve as an admission of the person's inappropriate behavior, while at the same time attempting to reduce the importance of the event giving rise to the embarrassment. Third, laughter may serve to reduce the tension or anxiety engendered by the embarrassing event. Fourth, it may be a purposeful nonverbal strategy used by the embarrassed person to change the meaning and focus of the situation in an attempt to save face. By diminishing the importance of the event, the identity "victim" can be transformed to "co-actor" and the label "embarrassing" transformed to "humorous." Finally, the "silly" grin of embarrassment may be related to the submissive, appeasement grin which occurs in other primates when threatened. Embarrassment presents a threat to the persons sense of self and, in such circumstances, smiling may serve to conciliate a potential "aggressor."

Although it is possible to feel embarrassed without visibly blushing and to visibly blush without experiencing embarrassment, blushing and embarrassment have been inextricably linked by a number of authors. Although the faces of nonhuman primates redden or "flush" with rage, blushing is a peculiarly human expression that is restricted to certain specific regions of the body. The "blush region" is located in the face, ears, neck, and upper chest. The redness itself is caused by the bed of capillaries close to the skin filling with blood in order to allow the body to lose heat. It seems that the blood vessels in the face and upper body differ structurally from blood vessels in other parts of the body. In addition, people seem to differ in their responsivity, hence, individual differences in actual intensity of blushing. But, how might blushing and embarrassment be interlinked?

One possibility is that people use their own expressive behaviors to interpret their inner feelings. Thus, skin blood-flow changes associated with blushing may play a significant part in influencing the intensity of reported embarrassment. Our attention shifts between ourselves and the environment on a continual but nonrandom basis. If a social accident has occurred, attention may initially be directed toward an evaluation of the event itself. This may be followed quickly by an inward focus of attention directed specifically toward those aspects of the self that are presumed to be associated with embarrassment, most notably blushing. The subsequent environmental focus of attention may be directed toward a search for the evaluative reaction of others, again followed by inward focus toward our blushing. The fact that the process is rapidly repeated serves to explain why blushing and embarrassment escalate. Further, for those who are particularly sensitive to, or predisposed to attend to, their bodily reactions, the sequence of reactions might be initiated internally, perhaps by a mere suspicion that one is blushing, rather than by a specific external event. Reactions to the suspicion that one might be blushing could explain why people can be made to blush by telling them that they appear to be blushing even when they are not. Such information leads them to infer that they are embarrassed, thereby leading them to blush.

Blushing is additionally curious in that it is a clearly visible sign of an emotion that, in most cases, we would prefer to conceal. Its very visibility has led some to argue that blushing is indeed communicative and acts as a "nonverbal apology." It is a visible statement to others that we are aware that our behavior was untoward, inappropriate, or inadequate and, because we care about other people's evaluations, our blushing is a way of seeking forgiveness from other group members. It is also possible that blushing, like the silly grin serves a function similar to nonhuman appeasement gestures. For nonhuman primates, appeasement frequently results in loss of interest in the victim by the threatening animal. One purpose of blushing may, paradoxically, be to reduce attention from observers. Although some people may deliberately embarrass or humiliate others, or deliberately draw attention to another's blushes, in general we tend to avoid focusing on people when they are blushing.

IV. INDIVIDUAL DIFFERENCES IN EMBARRASSMENT

People differ markedly both in their tendency to blush and in their reported frequency of embarrassment experienced. Four factors related to such differences are examined here: age, gender, personality, and culture.

A. Age

Embarrassment is systematically built into our social system. Societies everywhere have unwritten rules which regulate everyday behavior. It seems that the aversive consequences of embarrassment are such that one reason for our tendency to follow the rules, conventions, and behaviors expected by others is our fear of the possibly embarrassing consequences of not so doing. Indeed, laughing at, ridiculing, or, in short, embarrassing another person for rule-breaking is likely to result in attempts to avoid such rule-breaking in the future. Some have argued that, via such mechanisms, embarrassment exerts a powerful influence on the acquisition of social rules in children and adolescents. Thus, children are introduced to modesty, self-control, and manners by means of teasing, laughter, and ridicule for mistakes. During adolescence, there is an increasing desire to manage the impressions we create for others and hence we are increasingly motivated to avoid being singled out for laughter and ridicule. Embarrassment thus becomes a particularly powerful method by which social rules can be acquired.

Although little conclusive evidence exists about developmental aspects of embarrassment, there seem to be discernible age-related changes. Embarrassment does not seem to occur with any great frequency in very young children. The first signs seem to be around the ages of 2 to 3 years. Over the next few years the occurrence of embarrassment increases until, by the ages of 6 or 7 years, embarrassment is experienced as frequently as in adulthood. A peak period of embarrassment seems to be during adolescence. There then seems to be a decline in embarrassment and blushing in later adult life.

The appearance of embarrassment is linked to the emergence of the social self and associated self-consciousness. Some have argued that there is little evidence of self-consciousness in younger children (less than 10 years), a marked increase during early adolescence, with a peak at 13 or 14 years of age, followed by a gradual decline. Thus, while children of 2 years and younger recognize and react to reflected images of themselves in a mirror, this may merely illustrate that they are aware of themselves, but not necessarily indicate that they are self-conscious. It would seem unlikely that very young children would be able to evaluate themselves vis-a-vis some standard behavior in order to create a desired impression in the eyes of others present. Thus, while children as young as 18 months may show embarrassed behaviors in situations that might be anticipated to elicit embarrassment, whether they actually experience the emotion of embarrassment is a different matter.

Even at a relatively young age children play games in which they portray fictional characters. In such enactments the child is concerned to portray the character in a way they consider to be "real." However, their ability to view things from someone else's perspective is limited. The child's behavior is thus more likely to be directed by what appears to be right to him or her, rather than by what appears to be right to others. Although they may be aware that certain behaviors provoke ridicule or laughter they may not be aware of why such reactions occur. At this age they are thus likely to experience a fairly "primitive" form of embarrassment.

By the age of 8 years the child is more aware of how the impression he or she creates is viewed by others. The child is concerned with creating an appearance that fits the occasion and is evaluated positively. Thus, for the older child, a social transgression or social accident is likely to result in "mature" embarrassment, similar to that experienced by adults. [*See* IMPRESSION FORMATION.]

The peak in embarrassment during adolescence parallels the peak in self-presentation concerns and self-consciousness which occurs at this time. Conformity is at its height during adolescence, marked by a need to wear the correct clothes and have the right interests. The desire to win approval from others is an important goal. In addition, adolescence is associated with marked changes in physical and psychological makeup. No longer being a child, but not yet being an adult, the adolescent has yet to acquire the necessary repertoire of behaviors to play out the adult role. Lack of knowledge can lead to indecisiveness and lack of confidence and hence more likelihood that behaviors will be viewed negatively or have embarrassing consequences. [*See* ADOLESCENCE.]

There is then a gradual decline in self-consciousness after adolescence which is paralled by both a decrease in experiences of embarrassment and a decrease in the tendency to blush. With increased age, novel experiences and hence the potential for embarrassment are likely to decline; this is paralled by an apparent decrease with age in the propensity for blood vessels in the face to dilate.

B. Gender

There is a popular view that women are more likely to blush and are more easily embarrassed than men. Certainly, within a historical context, coy, shy reactions, such as exhibited by the "blushing bride," were considered appropriate signs of modesty for women. In general, however, such stereotypical differences are not supported by the limited research findings, although women report experiencing more intense embarrassment than men and men and women may find different circumstances embarrassing. It is possible that women are socialized to be more acutely aware of and sensitized to disapproval from others. Indeed, socialization differences may create pressure for women to be more modest in certain circumstances. Thus, women may be more likely to blush when talking about a personal topic, when they are the center of attention or when receiving a compliment. However, any gender differences that do exist may be due to differences in skin thickness or likely reporting of emotional experiences. It is possible that blushes are more visible for women than for men because of their finer facial skin. Further, given the greater propensity for women to express their feelings, they may more readily report blushing or experiencing embarrassment.

C. Personality

It is frequently noted that some people are more likely to experience embarrassment than others. A central factor here seems to be the degree of concern people have with others' impressions of them. Those concerned with projecting an image which engenders social approval, or at least avoids engendering social disapproval, are likely to be more easily embarrassed. This is true for people who are publicly self-conscious; they feel as if they are being observed, have a high regard for how other people view them, and feel that the reactions and remarks of others are of particular importance. A proneness to embarrassment may be particularly likely if this is allied to an over-attentiveness to inner thoughts and feelings (i.e., an awareness of blushing). The degree to which people fear social situations in general is also related to degree of blushing and embarrassment. At the extreme, people troubled by chronic fear of blushing obtain scores on measures of social anxiety similar to those clinically diagnosed as socially phobic.

D. Cultural Differences

There seems to be clear evidence that blushing is universal and that embarrassment is expressed in a similar way across cultures. Blacks and other dark-skinned people experience vasodilation in the kinds of social situation that provoke blushing in whites. However, blushing in the former appears to be marked by a further darkening of the skin rather than the reddening which occurs in lighter skinned people. Blushing seems to be more likely in certain cultures (e.g., the UK) than others, while averting eye contact or laughter, which is common in some cultures, seems to occur rarely in others (e.g., Italy). These apparent differences tend to be derived from self-reports, rather than from actual observations in the cultures concerned, and hence any variations may simply reflect reporting differences. However, if the differences are real, they may involve variations across cultures in the meaning attributed to embarrassing events. Thus, embarrassment might be a more serious matter in certain cultures and hence laughter or smiling would be less likely to occur. There may also be variations in skin thickness across cultures and hence variability in the visibility of blushing. It is also important to bear in mind that different situations are likely to elicit embarrassment and blushing across cultures.

V. FACE SAVING AND EMBARRASSMENT

Because of its aversive and disruptive nature, people generally attempt to avoid embarrassing situations when possible. However, as complete avoidance is rarely possible, we often make attempts to redress the situation in order to maintain face, regain social approval, and restore the interaction following an embarrassing event. In dealing with embarrassing events four main face-saving strategies are recognized: apologies, accounts, avoidance/escape (evasive facework), and the use of humor. Two additional strategies, remediation and hostility, have also been discussed. Remediation involves offers or requests of help or comfort, expressions of concerns, or offers to correct the problem, for example, cleaning up after an accident. In contrast to situations inviting remediation, there are some circumstances in which anger or hostility is used as a method of coping with embarrassment. In general, however, this latter reaction is restricted to circumstances in which the person has been criticized or teased by others with the deliberate intent of causing embarrassment. In this context the goal of intentional embarrassment is to negatively sanction the other's behavior, to establish power, or simply for self-satisfaction. The embarrassed person may respond with hostility in an effort to keep the same behavior from occurring again.

The simplest way of dealing with embarrassment is to offer an apology, such as "I'm sorry" or "pardon me." This serves to acknowledge blameworthiness for the undesired behavior in the hope that a minor indiscretion can be passed over quickly and forgotten by those concerned. Indeed, the very act of being embarrassed can itself serve as an apology, the visual signs of blushing indicating that the person accepts responsibility for the untoward act. An interpretation of a sign of embarrassment as an apology is most likely in situations in which the person's undesired behavior may have caused discomfort to someone else who was present. Brazening out the situation may serve to increase both parties embarrassment, while a display of embarrassment accompanied by laughter may diffuse the situation.

While an apology offers an admission of responsibility, an account is an attempt to explain the undesired behavior. Accounts can take two forms: excuses and justifications. The former consists of attempts to play down one's own contribution to the event while at the same time admitting that the behavior was wrong. A justification similarly admits some responsibility for the event while at the same time containing an element of denial that there are any negative consequences of the behavior. Categories of accounts involve appeals to environmental circumstances, lack of intent, highlighting personal characteristics, or scapegoating. Thus, if we embarrass ourselves by tripping in front of others, we might comment "that's the trouble with slippery floors" (environmental circumstances), "I didn't mean to do that" (lack of intent) "that's typical, I seem to have two left feet" (personal characteristics), "the cleaners have polished the floor again" (scapegoating). Categories of justification include "self-fulfillment," which justifies the action on the grounds that it leads to some form of enlightenment, and "effect misrepresented," which justifies the action because the consequences were trivial or because no harm was done. Because they add to excuses, and attempt to minimize or deny the undesirability of the event, justifications may be too strong for dealing with minor transgressions associated with embarrassment. An attempt to justify ones actions may serve to prolong, heighten, and add to the implications of the embarrassing event.

Although a verbal apology or account may be used frequently to deal with embarrassing events, there are occasions when they may be inappropriate or may fail to deal adequately with the situation. In addition, the person concerned may feel unable to offer a verbal apology or account for their action. In such circumstances avoidance may be a common reaction. This may take the form of either withdrawal subsequent to the embarrassing event (escape) or attempts to avoid encounters in which embarrassment might occur (avoidance). However, physically retreating from the situation, rather than achieving the goal of averting attention, is likely to draw further undue attention to the embarrassed person. There are occasions, however, when averting an awkward event can be achieved by changing the topic or remaining silent rather than by escape per se. It is also clear that some people will go to extreme lengths to avoid social situations due to a fear that they will behave in a way which is embarrassing. This is particularly true for people with a chronic fear of blushing. Avoidance in this case is more an attempt to avoid losing face through blushing inappropriately than an attempt to save face.

A further general strategy involved in coping with embarrassment involves the use of humor or laughter and smiling. Laughter serves to reduce the tension, while joking can turn a potential loss of social approval into a gain in social approval.

In order for a face-saving strategy to be successful, it must be acceptable, reasonable, and adequate. In the case of minor, nonserious events, humor and laughter may be appropriate. As events become more important, then apologies and excuses are likely to be used with greater frequency. In general, however, apologizing is seen as the most appropriate response regardless of the type of embarrassing situation. Excuses and justifications tend to be used infrequently, except in social situations involving forgetfulness or awkwardness. In addition, the limited research findings seem to indicate that the face-saving strategy used will depend upon not only the type of embarrassing event, but also the gender and status of those involved. In terms of gender differences, women seem more likely than men to offer an apology or excuses outlining mitigating circumstances. In addition, women are more likely to offer help and more likely to act on such offers, if their embarrassing actions have caused potential distress to others. When the embarrassing event is not serious, people of higher status, in comparison to those of lower status, are less likely to acknowledge responsibility or to account for their actions.

Interestingly, there seems to be very little variation across culture in the type of face-saving strategy used. Both avoidance and a simple expression of embarrassment are common reactions to all types of embarrassing events across cultures. The main variation seems to be in the use of humor, which may be almost absent in cultures with stronger sanctions for rule-breaking.

VI. OBSERVER REACTIONS

When someone becomes embarrassed, others present are likely to react to and become involved in that person's embarrassment. Each may effect the other so that embarrassment can either spiral or be mutually controlled. In seeking to offer assistance, observers may excuse or explain the embarrassed person's behavior, "play along" with them, for example, by the use of humor or offer support or empathy. Such reactions may be used alone or in combination, and seem to be relatively constant across cultures.

The most common reactions from observers seem to be support and empathy. Indeed, these may often be used in combination, most usually with a supportive comment followed by a sign of empathy. Support includes any comment or nonverbal expression intended to reassure the person that they are still viewed positively despite the embarrassing event. A typical comment might be "don't worry, it's not important," while typical gestures include a warm smile or friendly touch. Empathic reactions involve comments intended to assure the embarrassed person that the event that occurred could have happened to anyone. A typical comment might be: "I know how you feel, I'm always doing the same thing." Such a reaction can also be a useful way for the observer to show that they accept an apology offered by the embarrassed person. [*See* EMPATHY.]

Humor is also used by observers with moderate frequency. However, humor and laughter will clearly have a different meaning dependent upon whether the observer laughs alone or whether both the observer and the embarrassed person laugh together. There is a fine dividing line between "laughing with" and "laughing at" someone. If the embarrassed person fails to join in with the observer in his or her attempt to help, they may well end up being the butt of the joke rather than making light of the event. In such circumstances embarrassment is likely to be intensified.

A similar intensification of embarrassment is likely to occur if the observer fails to respond or responds in a manner which is interpreted negatively by the embarrassed person. As with humor, a lack of response can be interpreted as either a sign of or a lack of support. The difference between a positive or negative reaction is often signalled by subtle behaviors such as a fleeting smile or facial expression acknowledging the event, or even an appearance of embarrassment from the observer. Assuming that the observer wishes to provide assistance in remedying the situation, their attempts can fail either because they do not know how to respond or because their attempts backfire.

There are also occasions when an observer may seek to intentionally increase another's embarrassment. For example, if they feel that the embarrassed person has not shown sufficient "remorse," if the embarrassing behavior has disturbed others present, or if the embarrassed person was apparently responsible for the event. Such deliberate intensification of another's embarrassment may be achieved either by drawing their attention to the event or by expressing reproach. The latter may involve criticism or correction. Clearly, such reactions may well serve to further disrupt social interaction.

As well as instances when an observer may seek to intensify another's embarrassment, there are occasions when an observer may seek to intentionally initiate embarrassment in others. Intentional embarrassment is frequently used as a sanction to teach children correct or tactful behavior. Men, in comparison to women, are more likely to intentionally embarrass children and subordinates. This may reflect the fact that males are stereotypically more competitive and engage in controlling behaviors. Intentional embarrassment also occurs frequently among same-sex friends, often as part of a "game" to test each other's social poise.

VII. COPING WITH BLUSHING

Although there have been a number of studies investigating face saving in embarrassing situations, until recently, little attempt had been made to examine strategies for coping with the specific reaction of blushing. Indeed, controlling blushes is difficult to achieve. Blushing may to some extent be beyond voluntary control; it is impossible to prevent oneself blushing, and attempting to do so may actually serve to increase blushing intensity. Conversely, when people are asked to deliberately blush they find it difficult to do so.

Blushing seems to cause most distress when it occurs in the absence of a clearly defined embarrassing event, for example, when someone fears that their red face will be taken as a sign of shyness or a lack of social grace or when others present draw attention to a red complexion. Indeed, the fear of blushing can be psychologically debilitating. Many chronic blushers are unable to cope with their difficulty, resorting to medication in the hope of dampening down their reaction or make-up in an effort to conceal their red face.

Chronic blushers are characterized by two facets of self-consciousness, they are over-concerned with both their internal sensations and thoughts, as well as observers' subsequent reactions to their blushing. This is illustrated by comments from sufferers such as "I'm going red, why? I wish I could stop"; and, "when I blush I think what must other people think of me." The latter concern means that chronic blushers are anxious to avoid drawing attention to themselves. The normal face-saving strategies outlined above, even though they serve to present the embarrassed person in a more positive light, achieve their objective by drawing further attention to the embarrassed person. Thus, chronic blushers may find themselves unable to use such strategies. Their major concern is to escape or hide and this may be achieved by avoidance of social situations.

Because the negative pattern of thinking associated with blushing is sufficient to cause embarrassment in the absence of a clearly defined embarrassing event, the most effective strategy for dealing with blushing is for the person to modify their thinking pattern. This can be achieved by re-evaluating and redirecting attention away from oneself and blushing.

While embarrassment is a common but uncomfortable state which can disrupt social interaction, chronic blushing can severely disrupt the lives of those concerned. There is clearly an interrelationship between the event (either external or internal) giving rise to embarrassment and coping strategies used. Less extreme events or feelings are likely to be dealt with by humor or jokes whereas more extreme events or feelings may require a more fundamental approach by the person concerned.

Bibliography

Crozier, W. R. (Ed.) (1990). "Shyness and Embarrassment: Perspectives from Social Psychology." Cambridge University Press, Cambridge.

Cupach, W. R., and Metts, S. (1990). Remedial processes in embarrassing predicaments. In "Communication Yearbook" (J. A. Anderson, Ed.), Vol. 13. Sage, Newbury Park, CA.

Edelmann, R. J. (1987). "The Psychology of Embarrassment." Wiley, Chichester.

Edelmann, R. J. (1990). "Coping with Blushing." Sheldon Press, London.

Edelmann, R. J. (1990). Coping with embarrassment and chronic blushing. In "Communication Yearbook" (J. A. Anderson, Ed.), Vol. 13. Sage, Newbury Park, CA.

Edelmann, R. J. (1990). Chronic blushing, self-consciousness, and social anxiety. *J. Psychopathol. Behav. Assessment,* **12,** 119–127.

Leary, M. R., Britt, T. W., Cutlip, W. D., II, and Templeton, J. L. (1992). Social blushing. *Psychol. Bull.* **112,** 446–460.

Leary, M. R., and Meadows, S. (1991). Predictors, elicitors, and concomitants of social blushing. *J. Pers. Soc. Psychol.* **60,** 254–262.

Miller, R. S. (1992). The nature and severity of self-reported embarrassing circumstances. *Pers. Soc. Psychol. Bull.* **18,** 190–198.

Sharkey, W. F., and Stafford, L. (1990). Responses to embarrassment. *Hum. Commun. Res.* **17,** 315–342.

EMPATHY

Nancy Eisenberg
Arizona State University

Glossary

Empathy An emotional reaction to another's emotional state or condition that is consistent with the other's state or condition.

Personal distress An aversive, vicariously induced emotional reaction such as anxiety, discomfort, or worry which is coupled with self-oriented, egoistic concerns.

Prosocial behavior Voluntary behavior intended to benefit another.

Sympathy A vicarious emotional reaction based on the apprehension of another's emotional state or condition, a reaction that involves feelings of sorrow, compassion, or concern for the other person(s).

EMPATHY over the years, has been defined in diverse ways in the psychological literature. Although there is not agreement on its definition, many social and developmental psychologists currently differentiate between various vicarious emotional responses to others' emotions and taking the cognitive perspective of another. Specifically, many theorists and researchers studying human development define empathy as an emotional reaction to another's emotional state or condition that is consistent with the other's state or condition (e.g., feeling sad when viewing a sad person).

Some psychologists use the term empathy to refer to related other-oriented reactions such as sympathy and compassion. However, we have found it useful to differentiate among empathy, sympathy, and personal distress. *Sympathy,* which frequently may stem from empathy, is defined as a vicarious emotional reaction based on the apprehension of another's emotional state or condition, a reaction that involves feelings of sorrow, compassion, or concern for the other person(s) rather than experiencing the same emotion as the other. Conceptually, sympathy involves an other-orientation and the motivation to assist the needy or distressed other whereas empathy by itself does not.

Another vicariously induced emotional reaction that frequently is confused with empathy and sympathy is *personal distress*. Personal distress is an aversive vicariously induced emotional reaction such as anxiety, discomfort, or worry which is coupled with self-oriented, egoistic concerns. Experiencing personal distress seems to lead to the motive of alleviating one's own distress. Unfortunately, in real life and in much of the existing research, it is difficult to differentiate among empathy, sympathy, and personal distress.

Perspective taking involves the cognitive comprehension of another's internal psychological processes such as their thoughts and feelings. Sympathy and empathy involve taking the perspective of others; however, they are not the same as cognitive perspective taking. Although perspective taking often may result in empathy and related emotional responses, it is a cognitive process rather than an emotional response.

Empathy and related emotional reactions such as sympathy and personal distress have received increasing attention from theorists and researchers in the last two decades. This is probably due in part to an increased focus on the role of emotion in devel-

Encyclopedia of Human Behavior, Volume 2

Copyright © 1994 by Academic Press, Inc. All rights of reproduction in any form reserved.

opment in the last decade and to the strong theoretical link between empathy (and related constructs such as sympathy) and both positive social behavior (e.g., helping, sharing, comforting) and social competence.

Much of the recent theory and research on empathy and sympathy has concerned a few topics: (a) the development of empathy, (b) gender differences in empathy, (c) the relation of empathy and sympathy to prosocial behavior (voluntary behavior intended to benefit another), (d) whether empathy or sympathy is associated with altruistic motives (i.e., is motivated by the desire to benefit another rather than self-interest), (e) the relation of empathy to aggression, and (f) the origins of empathy and related vicarious emotions. Each of these topics is now briefly reviewed after a discussion of theory.

I. THEORIES OF VICARIOUS EMOTIONAL RESPONDING

Theories concerning the development of empathy have varied over the years. In line with a social learning theory, Aronfreed and Hoffman have suggested that empathy is acquired early by conditioning or association, that is, by repeated pairing of the child's feelings of pleasure or pain with someone else's expression of the corresponding feelings. In contrast, some psychoanalytic theorists believe that empathy develops from early infant–caretaker interactions because the caretaker's moods are communicated to the infant by touch, tone of voice, and facial expressions.

By far the most comprehensive and influential theory of the development of empathy is that of Martin Hoffman. Hoffman has emphasized both the cognitive and affective aspects of empathy, and the link of empathic emotion with prosocial action.

According to Hoffman, empathic distress, defined as experiencing another's painful emotional state, develops early in infancy as a consequence of either built-in, biologically determined human tendencies toward empathy or early classical conditioning. For example, cues of pain or displeasure from another or from another's situation may evoke associations with the observer's own past pain, resulting in an empathic affective reaction. Initially a child who cuts herself feels pain and cries. Later, on seeing another child similarly injured, the sight of the blood, the sound of the cry, or other aspects of the situation having elements in common with her own prior experience can elicit the unpleasant affect initially associated with that experience. [*See* CLASSICAL CONDITIONING.]

Hoffman believes that infants are capable of experiencing empathic distress before they can clearly differentiate themselves from others. Consequently, they are often unclear about who is feeling the distress they witness and may, at times, behave as though what happens to others is happening to them.

Once babies cognitively differentiate themselves from others, their empathic distress may be transformed, at least in part, to concern for the victim. That is, they may continue to respond in a purely empathic manner—to feel uncomfortable and highly distressed themselves—but they also experience a feeling of compassion for the victim, along with a conscious desire to help because they feel sorry for the victim, not just to alleviate their own empathic distress.

Nonetheless, although aware of others as separate individuals, for some time toddlers view the world only from their own perspective and do not understand that other people have their own traits, preferences, and feelings. Instead toddlers attribute their own feelings to others, and may therefore use inappropriate means in attempting to relieve another's distress. Examples of this are a 13 month old who brought his own mother to comfort a crying friend, even though the friend's mother was equally available, and another toddler who offered her own favorite doll to cheer up an adult who looked sad.

According to Hoffman, at about the age of 2 or 3, children begin to view others as distinct physical entities with their own emotions and thoughts. They are capable of rudimentary perspective-taking and are motivated to put themselves in the other's place and find the real source of his or her distress. Hence, children of this age can assist in ways tailored to relieve the other person's distress rather than their own.

Until they are between 6 and 9 years of age, children's vicarious emotional responses are restricted to another's immediate, transitory, and situation-specific distress. With greater cognitive maturity and awareness of their own and others' continuing existence, children begin reacting to others' general conditions (including deprivation, oppression, illnesses, and incompetence) as well as to another's immediate distress. Consequently, an adolescent often is able to comprehend the plight not only of an individual but also of an entire group or class of people—such as the economically impoverished, politically oppressed, or developmentally disabled.

Hoffman's theory is appealing because it places empathy in a broad developmental perspective, changing with increasing age and cognitive capacities. Some aspects of the theory are partially supported by anecdotes and research, such as the shift from helping behaviors based on an egocentric view of the world (for example, confusion between helping that would make oneself rather than another feel better) to those based on an understanding of others and their needs. Moreover, the role of advances in perspective-taking skills in empathy has received some support, as has the relation of self-related processes (i.e., the recognition of self) to empathy and prosocial behavior. However, some of the theory is speculative, and some postulates are extremely difficult to test empirically. Nonetheless, the theory has provided a theoretical basis for recent research on empathy.

II. THE DEVELOPMENT OF VICARIOUS EMOTIONAL RESPONDING

As suggested by Hoffman, evidence of precursors of empathy (or primitive empathy) is found early in life. In the first days of life, infants cry in reaction to the cries of other infants, a behavior that some believe is a precursor to empathic responding (although others question whether this is true). Although 6 to 12 month olds show little reaction to the distress of others, between 12 and 18 months of age many children react to others' negative emotion with agitation or sustained attention. By 18 months of age, toddlers sometimes try to comfort others in distress, and it appears that some children's prosocial actions are based on empathic reactions. With increasing age, as children learn to differentiate their own internal states from those of others, children become capable of experiencing sympathy *for* another person rather than merely vicariously sharing another's negative emotion. Thus, by 2 to 3 years of age, it is not uncommon for a child to demonstrate behaviors that seem to reflect genuine sympathy. By age 4 to 5, children sometimes report or exhibit emotions akin to both sympathy and personal distress, and markers of children's empathic sadness or sympathy tend to be associated with prosocial behavior.

It is not clear whether empathy, sympathy, and personal distress increase after the preschool years. Children sometimes report more sympathy or empathic sadness with age during the elementary and junior high school years, but these age-related changes could be due to increases with age in the desire to appear sympathetic to others and to oneself. Facial reactions indicative of empathic sadness, sympathy, or distress sometimes decrease with age (particularly for males), perhaps because of the general tendency to increasingly inhibit facial displays of negative emotion with age. Older children and adults may be better able to regulate their vicariously induced emotion than are younger children, with the consequence that they are more likely to experience sympathy rather than empathic overarousal and personal distress. However, additional research is needed to determine the nature of changes in empathy, sympathy, and personal distress over the lifespan.

III. GENDER DIFFERENCES IN EMPATHY AND RELATED RESPONSES

A common stereotype is that women and girls are more caring and emotionally responsive than are men and boys. Thus, one might expect females to be more empathic and sympathetic than males. However, the degree to which males and females have been found to differ in their vicarious emotional responding varies with the definition of empathy and the methods used to assess empathy.

In an early review of sex differences in empathy, Martin Hoffman concluded that girls are more affectively empathic than are boys. However, much of the data Hoffman reviewed was obtained from studies involving a picture-story measure of empathy. With such measures, children are presented with brief stories and/or pictures about others in emotionally evocative situations and then are asked how they themselves feel. More recent studies have cast doubt on the validity of such measures of empathy. For example, children's scores on picture-story measures of empathy are influenced by sex of the experimenter; gender differences favoring females have occurred primarily when female experimenters were used. Because female experimenters have been used in most research on children's empathy involving picture-story measures, the higher scores of girls may be a function of their responsiveness to a same-sex experimenter.

In relatively recent reviews, Eisenberg and her colleagues have found that gender differences in empathy and related vicarious emotional responses vary as a function of the measure of empathy. There are large differences favoring females for self-report measures of empathy, especially questionnaires. A modest difference favoring females has been found for self-report of emotional reactions in experimental settings in which subjects were exposed to empathy-inducing stimuli. However, modest or no gender differences have been found when the measure of empathy was either physiological or unobtrusive observations of nonverbal behavior. It is likely that this pattern of findings is due to differences among measures in the degree to which the intent of the measure is obvious and respondents can control their responses. Gender differences are greatest when demand characteristics are high (i.e., when it is clear what is being assessed) and respondents have conscious control over their responses (e.g., when subjects respond to self-report measures). In contrast, gender differences in empathy generally are nonexistent when demand characteristics are subtle *and* respondents are unlikely to exercise much conscious control over their responding (e.g., when subjects' physiological responses are the measure of empathy). When gender stereotypes are activated and people can easily control their responses, they may try to project a socially desirable image to others or to themselves. Females, more than males, may want to believe that they are empathic and sympathetic and, consequently, may tend to interpret their emotional reactions in empathy-inducing contexts as sympathy, even when they are not.

In recent work investigators have attempted to differentiate between sympathy and personal distress using physiological and facial reactions, as well as self-reports. Thus, there are some preliminary data on gender differences in sympathy and personal distress. In general, researchers have found fairly consistent gender differences favoring females for questionnaire measures of personal distress and sympathy, modest self-reported gender differences in sympathy and personal distress in reaction to empathy-inducing stimuli (females tend to report more), occasional differences in facial reactions (generally favoring females), and no gender differences in heart rate findings. Findings for skin conductance are mixed. Regardless of type of measure, there are few gender differences in measures of sympathy or personal distress in the preschool years. However, by mid-elementary school age, there is evidence of a weak tendency for girls sometimes to report and/or display more vicarious affect. Overall, then, the pattern of findings suggests that females are slightly more likely than males to evidence empathy, sympathy, and personal distress, but that the differences are quite weak (except for questionnaire measures) and dependent on method of measurement and the context.

IV. THE RELATION OF EMPATHY AND RELATED REACTIONS TO PROSOCIAL BEHAVIOR

As noted previously, psychologists frequently have hypothesized that empathy and sympathy are associated with prosocial behavior or altruism (i.e., nonegoistically motivated prosocial behavior). People who experience another's distress and sadness or feel concern for the distressed or needy person are expected to be motivated to alleviate the other person's sadness or distress. In contrast, people who experience personal distress are expected to focus on alleviating their own distress.

Generally, this hypothesis has been supported by the empirical research, although the results of existing studies vary as a function of the index of empathy and prosocial behavior. Children's self-reports of vicarious emotion in experimental settings or in response to picture-story measures of empathy generally are unrelated to their prosocial behavior. In contrast, nearly all other indexes of empathy have been positively related to prosocial behavior, including facial measures for children, questionnaire measures for adults and children, and experimental measures in studies primarily with adults. In addition, dwelling on the misfortunes of others appears to increase the likelihood of one's attending to others' needs and helping them. Moreover, in recent studies in which sympathy and personal distress have been differentiated, children's sympathy, as assessed with facial and physiological reactions, has been associated with their helping and sharing whereas personal distress reactions to others' need or distress have been uncorrelated with prosocial behavior or correlated with low levels of prosocial behavior (particularly for boys). Thus, the research indicates that empathy and sympathy are positively associated with prosocial behavior, at least in some contexts.

It is not totally clear when the link between sympathy or empathy and prosocial behavior emerges. However, there is evidence that some children who appear to be emotionally aroused by others' distress attempt to assist as early as the second year of life. It is likely that the quality and probability of prosocial action instigated by vicarious emotional responding increases with age in the early years of life. [*See* ALTRUISM AND HELPING BEHAVIOR.]

V. EMPATHY/SYMPATHY AND ALTRUISTIC MOTIVATION

An ongoing debate in social psychological studies with adults is whether empathy (or sympathy) is associated with true altruism or whether all prosocial behavior, even that engendered by sympathy, is egoistically motivated. C. Daniel Batson has argued that empathy/sympathy is associated with the selfless desire to benefit another and that empathically motivated altruistic behavior is not due to the desire for external rewards, the desire to avoid guilt, or the expectation of feeling good due to vicarious sharing of distressed or needy persons' joy when their condition is improved. In contrast, people experiencing personal distress rather than sympathy are expected to assist others only when helping is the easiest way to make themselves feel less distressed. Thus, individuals experiencing personal distress are expected to assist primarily when it is difficult to escape contact with the needy or distressed other who is causing them to feel distressed and when assisting is not costly. In contrast, if it is easy to escape from the distressed person and the aversive cues emitted by that person, those experiencing personal distress are expected to simply leave the situation and avoid further contact with the other person.

Although Batson and other researchers have gathered considerable experimental data consistent with Batson's arguments, there also are data congruent with the view that people experiencing empathy sometimes help to alleviate their own negative mood or to experience empathic joy. Data on the latter issue are scarce and can be interpreted in conflicting ways. Thus, the debate regarding the motivational status of empathy and sympathy is likely to continue into the future.

A related issue is whether there is an altruistic personality based, at least in part, on sustained individual differences in empathy or sympathy. Many theorists and researchers have assumed that this is the case—that individuals differ in their tendency to experience empathy or sympathy and that these differences underlie personality differences in the tendency to be altruistic. Batson, however, has questioned the veracity of such an assumption; he argues that people who appear to be altruistic may be helping as an instrumental means of enhancing their own welfare by receiving self-rewards or avoiding self-punishment. Although this assertion may sometimes be true, it generally is difficult to determine for certain the nature of individuals' motivation for their prosocial tendencies. Moreover, if individuals sometimes assist for altruistic reasons (an issue for which the research is more convincing), it is reasonable to assume that some people do so more than do others. In addition, the association between individual differences in empathy/sympathy and altruistic motivation likely holds more in some situations (e.g., those in which sympathy inducing cues are relevant) than others. Nonetheless, this is an another issue of continuing debate.

VI. EMPATHY AND AGGRESSION

Numerous theorists have considered empathy to be relevant to an understanding of aggression as well as prosocial behavior. For example, they have suggested that people who tend to experience another's pain or distress are likely to refrain from aggression or cease their aggression because of the discomfort created by their empathic response to the victim's emotional reactions (or imagined reactions). [*See* AGGRESSION.]

There is some empirical support for the link between empathy and aggression, although the association appears to be modest in strength. However, as for research concerning empathy/sympathy and prosocial behavior, the association between the two varies as a function of the method of measuring empathy. When empathy is assessed by using picture-story measures with children (in which children are told stories about hypothetical children in emotion-eliciting situations and then are asked how they themselves feel), empathy is negatively related to elementary children's, but not preschoolers', aggression. There also is a negative association between empathy and aggression /acting-out behaviors when empathy is assessed with questionnaire measures. However, the relations of aggression to adolescents' and adults' reports of empathy in experimental settings and to facial reactions indicative of children's empathy are very weak and nonsignificant.

Of particular interest is the association between low levels of maternal empathy and child abuse. However, findings in regard to maternal empathy and abuse must be viewed as tentative due to the small number of relevant studies. [*See* CHILD ABUSE.]

VII. THE ROLE OF BIOLOGY AND SOCIALIZATION IN VICARIOUS EMOTIONAL RESPONDING

There is debate regarding the degree to which biological versus environmental factors are responsible for individual differences in children's and adults' empathy, personal distress, and sympathy. In studies of adult twins' self-reports of empathy, there is some evidence that genetic factors may account for a considerable degree of variance in empathy. In a recent study of young children, Carolyn Zahn-Waxler and her colleagues found evidence of a significant genetic component for empathic concern, prosocial actions, and unresponsive–indifferent reactions to others' distress at both ages 14 and 20 months. The contribution of genetics to self-distress in empathy inducing contexts was not significant. Moreover, the size of the heritability estimates was modest (generally in the .20s), suggesting that environmental factors also play a role in the development of empathy and symapthy.

In fact, research on the socialization of empathy and sympathy clearly suggests that there is an association between children's vicarious responding and both parental empathy-related characteristics and parents' child-rearing practices. Children's empathy has been associated with quality of the mother–child attachment early in life and with supportive (empathic) parenting, although the findings are not always consistent. In addition, parents' reported sympathy and perspective taking have been positively correlated with same-sex elementary school children's sympathy and negatively correlated with their personal distress reactions. Supportive, empathic caretakers are likely to model and encourage the capacity for empathy in children. However, parental warmth by itself may be insufficient to foster empathy in children. Indeed, practices that involve some discipline or restrictiveness may facilitate the development of empathy. For example, both maternal and paternal demandingness (i.e., the parent's tendency to point at responsibility or say which behavior he or she expects in a situation) have been associated with elementary school children's self-reported empathy.

Parents also may subtly model or communicate acceptance of a variety of emotional responses through their own expression of emotion or their acceptance of others' emotional reactions in everyday life. In homes where negative emotions such as sympathy and apologizing are expressed frequently, children would be expected to learn to express empathy and sympathy and to be relatively uninhibited in doing so. Consistent with this argument, women (but not men) who report growing up in homes high in positive emotion and submissive (nonassertive) negative emotions are particularly likely to report responding emotionally to sympathy-inducing and distressing films. In contrast, expression of hostile or aggressive (i.e., dominant negative) emotions (e.g., anger) in the home is unrelated to women's vicarious emotional responding and has been associated with low levels of sympathy in children.

Parental verbalizations regarding the expression of emotion and others' emotions also appear to affect children's vicarious emotional responding. For boys, parental emphasis on controlling emotion seems to be associated with high levels of personal distress and low levels of sympathy whereas discussion of ways to instrumentally deal with situations that cause the child's negative emotion has been associated with sympathy in response to another's distress. Maternal verbalizations linking the child's own experience to that of a needy person in an empthy-inducing context have been correlated with high levels of children's vicarious emotional responding of all types (sadness, sympathy, and distress). Thus, providing a verbal link between the child's own experience and another's distress seems to elicit an emotional response, but it could be empathy, sympathy, or distress. In contrast, mothers' report to her child of feeling sad or sympathetic in empathy-inducing contexts has been associated with boys' self-reported sympathy.

Finally, parental reinforcement of children's sympathetic and prosocial responding has been correlated with children's empathy or sympathy. For example, maternal reinforcement of elementary school children's sympathetic and prosocial reactions to a needy or distress person (as reported in maternal interviews) has been associated with girls' facial concerned attention and sadness in response to a sympathy-inducing film, with girls' attempts to provide instrumental aid, and with the sensitivity of boys' comforting of a crying baby. Thus, consistent with social learning theory, parental reinforcement of sympathetic and prosocial responding seems to be foster relatively high levels of sympathy and prosocial behavior (although cause and effect have not been ascertained).

In summary, a number of parental characteristics and behaviors recently have been linked with the development of empathy, sympathy, or personal distress in children. However, it should be noted that there is, as yet, little research on this topic. Thus, conclusions from the few existing studies must be viewed as tentative until more research is available.

VIII. SUMMARY

Although relatively detailed theories regarding empathy, its development, and its correlates have been proposed, research concerning the development and origins of empathy, sympathy, and personal distress is limited in quantity. Vicarious emotional responding is evident relatively early in life, and the emergence of sympathy appears to be linked to cognitive achievements such as perspective taking. Although there are gender differences in some measures of vicarious emotional responding, it is not clear whether the differences are due to sex differences in actual emotional responding, to sex differences in how people want to appear to others or themselves, or to differences in how males and females interpret and cope with their vicarious emotional responses. The experience of empathy and particularly sympathy appears to enhance the likelihood of prosocial action, although there is debate regarding whether empathically or sympathetically motivated helping behaviors are truly altruistic in motivation. Empathy also appears to have a modest inhibiting effect on aggression. Finally, the origins of vicarious emotional reactions appear to be both biological and environment (i.e., due to socialization).

Bibliography

Batson, C. D. (1991). "The Altruism Question: Toward a Social-Psychological Answer." Erlbaum, Hillsdale, NJ.

Cohen, A. (1990). "The Brighter Side of Human Nature: Altruism & Empathy in Everyday Life." Basic Books, New York.

Eisenberg, N. (1992). "The Caring Child." Harvard University Press, Cambridge.

Eisenberg, N., and Fabes, R. A. (1991). Prosocial behavior and empathy: A multimethod, developmental perspective. In "Review of Personality and Social Psychology" (M. Clark, Ed.), Vol. 12. Sage, Newbury Park.

Eisenberg, N., and Fabes, R. A. (1989). "Empathy and Related Emotional Responses". Jossey-Bass, San Francisco.

Eisenberg, N., and Strayer, J. (1987). "Empathy and Its Development." Cambridge University Press, Cambridge, UK.

Hetherington, E. M. (Ed.). "Handbook of Child Psychology," Vol. 4: "Socialization, Personality, and Social Development." Wiley, New York.

Hunt, M. (1990). "The Compassionate Beast." William Morrow, New York.

Miller, P., and Eisenberg, N. (1988). The relation of empathy to aggression and externalizing/antisocial behavior. *Psychol. Bull.* **103,** 324–344.

Oliner, S. P., and Oliner, P. M. (1988). "The Altruistic Personality: Rescuers of Jews in Nazi Europe." Free Press, New York.

Wispe, L. (1991). "The Psychology of Sympathy." Plenum, New York.

Environmental Cognition

Christopher Spencer
University of Sheffield, United Kingdom

Glossary

Affordance Gibson uses this term to indicate the kinds of opportunities and activities that a place permits or encourages. He considers that we perceive places in terms of these affordances.

Cognitive map The internal representation of spatial information, stored spatially rather propositionally, and allowing the individual to generate novel routes.

Environmental grammar A set of spatial expectancies, whose rules and contents will be largely culturally determined.

Landmarks Distinctive environmental features, important both in structuring the cognitive map and in the map's use during navigation.

Legibility Clarity of layout of city (etc.), predicting not only ease of wayfinding but also aesthetic preference.

Place and placelessness Relph has contrasted those distinctive—and often valued—places with those unstructured—and often disliked—locations which he describes as being placeless.

Spatial reference system A way of encoding the relative spatial positions of objects (etc.): initially egocentric, then via a fixed system of reference, and ultimately on a set of coordinates.

WHY A SEPARATE section for environmental cognition? Its importance is clear at a biological level: consider the survival value to the organism of spatial knowledge about resources and dangers. At a cognitive level, it is concerned with the most complex of stimuli; and at a social level, it is often linked to the individual's sense of identity and well-being. Two main sections of this article consider the ontogeny and microgeny of environmental cognition: the development in the child of skills to gain, reference, and handle environmental information; and, in the adult, the application of these skills to develop knowledge of a new geographical area.

Finally, the article considers the action and aesthetic implications of environmental cognition: spatial decision-making, movement through space, and updating of present position during travel.

Environmental aesthetics research has included the cognitive image of distant places as determinants of travel decisions; the image and "legibility of the city"; and the dimensions of aesthetic judgment of man-made and natural scenes.

I. INTRODUCTION

Cognition as a topic represents one of the best developed areas of modern psychology. Why then should the Encyclopedia have a separate article dealing specifically with cognition of the environment? In answering this question, first at the biological, survival, level, then at the cognitive–perceptual level, and finally at the socio-individual level, an indication of the distinctive scope of environmental cognition will emerge.

A. Biological Level: The Survival Value to the Organism of Environmental Cognition

Knowledge of space—the spatial layout of resources, refuges, kin, dangers, predators—must rank as one of the most basic universal aspects of cognition. The range over which the organism is knowledgeable will reflect the species' activity patterns—from a few centimeters of rockpool for some mollusks to the pole-to-pole migratory journeys of some terns and shearwaters.

Copyright © 1994 by Academic Press, Inc. All rights of reproduction in any form reserved.

Accurate travel from point to point demands a knowledge of orientation—the vector direction—and the distance to travel. Animal behavior studies have identified the range of information sources that are variously in use to plot such routes: these range from the social to the celestial—from, for example, the waggle-dance of bees returning to the hive which communicates the bearing from there back to a food source; to the use of star patterns and the earth's magnetic field by some birds in night migration.

What is especially impressive is that feats of accurate, long distance navigation can be performed by relatively simple species. Waterman, for example, describes the flight in autumn of the monarch butterfly, from central and eastern states of the United States to a few specific groves west of Mexico City: the flight is so precise that it betokens a highly accurate sense of space.

Environmental knowledge of a more immediate locale is characteristic of most species. Many foraging birds and insects use a polar rather than a grid reference system: many vectors fanning out from the central pole of a home base.

The food-gathering behavior of organisms has been studied by biologists seeking to ascertain whether there are optimal foraging strategies. (As we shall see below, this approach has similarities with the mathematical study of shopping-route behaviors in humans.) Germane to our present concern is that such foraging behavior is spatially organized. Part of the "acculturation" process in those species where the young remain dependent upon the adults for some time is, in effect, the transmission of spatial information about the resources to be found within the familiar territory. Infants may start with a polar system, but with experience come to approximate to the grid reference knowledge of the mature animal; and are thereby enabled to perform novel trips across the territory. Species which store food show evidence of a vast spatial memory: hundreds, thousands of cached nuts or seeds may be recovered, indicating that these many temporary locations can be logged within a grid of familiar and persisting landmarks.

Inferences about the nature of animals' environmental awareness can be made from many aspects of their behavior. Neurophysiological evidence can also contribute: maplike projections of various features of the environment have been found in both arthropod and vertebrate species. In vertebrates, there is strong evidence for the hippocampus being involved in the "cognitive map"; and the "mushroom bodies" of the bee brain undergo rapid change after the insect makes its first exploratory flights, again indicating the localization of function. [*See* COGNITIVE MAPS.]

B. Cognitive Perceptual Level

Environmental cognition demands separate treatment in that it differs from object perception in its complexity, its multisensory nature, and its intimate connection with the activities of the individual: whether as learner about or user of the environment, the individual is *within* the observed in a way not paralleled in object perception.

Environmental cognition is, by definition, concerned with real world perception, at molar rather than molecular level. Environments are continuous, hugely complex, and potentially rich with meaning. Characteristic of many individual transactions with them is that of purposiveness: individuals are seeking resources, association, privacy; they are traveling or searching to fulfill some goal or plan. Such purposeful encounters probably characterized the first, leaning-phase, transactions with particular environments; and thereby they serve to organize the complexity of environments into coherent, knowable wholes. Common language and environmental psychology both describe these as "places"; and one of the distinctive enterprises of environmental cognition research has been to describe what distinguishes places from "placelessness" (Relph). In addition to the coherence of the physical elements of place, researchers soon realized that the defining characteristics also included socially acknowledged place rules and expectations (similar to the "scripts" which enable individuals to recognize and react appropriately to social situations). "Places" also have an aesthetic dimension to them, as will be discussed in the concluding section of this article: in other words, they are nonrandom assemblages of socially significant physical elements, which evoke affective responses in the traveler.

Gibson has, in his accounts of the senses as perceptual systems, emphasized the importance of taking an information processing approach to environments. In his account, places are perceived in terms of their affordances: the kinds of activities that a place permits or encourages. Perception of environmental features is thus seen in functional terms; similarly, storage, access, and use are guided by functional properties. Gibson's account has been perhaps better received by environmental psychologists than by mainstream perceptual psychology, and has helped to shape accounts of the child's development of environmental competencies. It also converges with ecological psychology's account of how children come to realize the social potential of places, which are there usefully described as "behavior settings," a concept which integrates the social with the physical.

Environmental cognition research shares with much of contemporary cognitive psychology an increasing concern for the development of knowledge structures; it too has offered computer models of such structures, and their use in navigation through space, as will be discussed below. It is clear that the amount of central processing capacity available at any one moment is limited; that spatial navigation can claim a considerable portion of this, and thus any further complex task imposed upon the traveler is likely to compete for this cognitive resource.

C. Social–Individual Level: The Link between Environmental Cognition and the Individual's Well-Being

The two preceding sections dealt with the role of environmental cognition in promoting the biological survival of the organism, and in aiding its cognitive efficiency in using the environment. Its final, most sophisticated role is in developing and maintaining personal and social well-being through identification with and attachment to places. Here, the empirically minded psychologist may feel ill at ease, dealing with concepts which are altogether less easy to define and to measure.

However, there exists an extensive literature about the "sense of place": the awareness that some locations have a coherence and identity that allows individuals themselves to identify with these places; to gain pleasure, security, self-understanding from them; and to place considerable importance upon such places in their memories, their self-descriptions, and their decisions. The sense of place literature—in geography, and in planning—points up a need for psychology to examine more closely the higher importance of places for people.

Within psychology, there is a well-developed understanding of the nature of attachment—yet in nearly all of it the attachment is to people. There is only a small literature on displacement: on the nature of homesickness (e.g., children sent away to boarding school); on the deleterious effects of separations when a child is hospitalized; and on the psychological functioning of those who are away from familiar places, whether through enforced exile, or traveling as students to a foreign country. (Even the new interest environmental psychology has shown in periods of short voluntary exile, i.e., tourism, has shown the possibility of some negative effects amid all the positive effects such travel is usually assumed to bring.)

Similarly, practically all of psychology's literature on the development and sustenance of self-identity and well-being tends to describe this solely in terms of the individual's social environment, without considering the possibility that identification with places may interact with those processes. Does self-identity shaped by the earliest memories of place, through to an account of those places where one feels "most at home," "most oneself," seem implausible to psychology? Such an account is certainly not far-fetched for the autobiographer, for the historian, or for the political scientist.

Nor is such discourse unfamiliar to those design professions whose very aim and claim is to be able to create places: interior designers, architects, city planners. In such disciplines, there is perhaps a greater belief in an environmental determinism of behavior, and of feelings and well-being, than is common within psychology.

There is, however, some clear empirical evidence within both environmental psychology and planning that the aesthetics of place can be directly linked to personal well-being in studies of satisfaction with housing: the outward image of a housing project ranks high on the list of factors predictive of satisfaction and well-being in many studies. Similarly, the appearance of particular behavioral settings has been shown to affect behavior within them: for example, Sommer's classic experiment in "softening" a university classroom by changing its decor, which led to the least popular and effective room on campus being the best used. There is clearly an important and diverse future research agenda here for environmental psychology. [*See* ENVIRONMENTAL PSYCHOLOGY.]

D. Conclusion

This section has argued for the study of the cognition of the environment above and beyond the main psychology of cognitive processes on the grounds that environmental cognition has an immediate biological survival value; that the properties of the "object" of the cognition are so much more complex than in usual object perception; and that environmental cognition leads one to discussion of the sense of place, of self-identity, and of individual well-being. Hence, any simple definition of environmental cognition which does not admit to all three of these levels will be imcomplete.

II. THE DEVELOPMENT OF ENVIRONMENTAL COGNITION: ONTOGENESIS AND MICROGENESIS

In order to understand a phenomenon, it is often instructive to study its development. Much of environmental psychology's cognition research has been concerned with the two kinds of development: ontogenesis—the development from infancy of cognitive skills for environmental understanding—and microgenesis—the development of knowledge about the novel area, using these skills.

A. The Ontogeny of Environmental Cognition: The Child Develops Skills for Gaining, Referencing, and Using Environmental Information

In this section we will examine Piaget's account of cognitive development as applied to this area; indicate how environmental psychology has extended this account; and show how, with increasing experience, the child can begin to parse the grammar of the environment. Much of the process is visually led; hence, the blind child has to use alternative sources to construct images of the environment. The section ends considering how the process continues through the lifespan, with differentiating environmental cognitions reflecting the individual's activities and interests. [*See* COGNITIVE DEVELOPMENT.]

1. The Piagetian Perspective

The account given by Piaget of the child's developing concepts of space is based closely on his general stage theory of cognitive development. The child moves from a spatial geometry constructed on topological principles, through projective phase, to one derived from Euclidean principles. Piaget is particularly concerned with small scale space.

Proximity, separation, order, openness, and closure are the basic topological principles, which the child by the age of 2 is beginning to apply. Perspectives and, in particular, the realization of how objects interelate in space independent of own position are slowly developed alongside topology: such projective principles may be discerned at the age of 3, but, according to the Piagetian view, it takes another 8 or 9 years for their full development. The ability to apply metrics to space—the basis of Euclidean principles, may emerge at age 4, and continue developing into adolescence. The child will become better able to estimate distances and bearings, and to operate with proportional reductions in scale.

The environmental psychologists Hart and Moore have extended this approach to the child's understanding of large scale places. During the sensorimotor stage, the child is capable only of egocentric orientations: the environment is understood only as it relates to self. During the preoperational stage, the child begins to use a fixed system of reference: known locations—home, friends' houses, shops, school—provide the bases for this system. By the end of Piaget's concrete operations stage, children will begin developing a coordinated reference system, with abstract geometric patterns and, arguably, referenced against the cardinal directions.

Environmental psychology characteristically goes beyond the Piagetian account, and lays more emphasis upon experience, background, values, and interests as differentiating children's learning about the broad environment: the transactional perspective.

2. Expanding Frames of Reference and Individual Differences

As the infant and child grow older, there is an expanding range of geographical experience. Is there a corresponding developmental sequence?

Does the child first achieve an integrated image of body layout (with much effort expended in body-part coordination), then extend this frame of reference outward to the immediate world (with the focus now being on the location of objects), and then outward from this, as the child explores ever more widely, to consider the spatial interrelationships between places?

Pick and Lockman have shown that the individual does not have to achieve complete mastery of the first frame of reference before working on to the next. Nor does the individual necessarily dispense with earlier frames: the individual can call upon a multiplicity of reference systems. Some life tasks call forth an egocentric frame, others an allocentric, still others a geocentric; and many tasks implicate several frames of reference. (Pick's definition for a frame is "a locus or set of loci with respect to which spatial position is defined".)

The case for a relationship between adequacy of body image (the first such frame) and success in other, broader, spatial skills is not supported by empirical evidence. There is, however, evidence for a clear age-related trend from egocentric responding to allocentric responding on a spatial task; although when this shift occurs varies dramatically both with task type and with the availability and salience of environmental cues. And note "egocentricity" is not here being used in the strict Piagetian sense, but simply to indicate the literal self-centeredness of the frame.

At this point, we should also note that there are stable individual differences in performance on tasks which have some spatial component. Similarly, sex differences have been widely reported in measured spatial abilities: a review of nearly 200 studies has concluded that:

1. Sex differences in spatial perception as measured by, for example, the water level test, exist by age 8 and persist across the lifespan. [*See* SPATIAL PERCEPTION.]
2. There is a small effect for mental rotation—as measured by the rotating figure test.
3. Spatial visualization has been found to be equally difficult for most males and females: tasks usually consist of complex, multistep manipulations of spatially presented information.

3. Developing an "Environmental Grammar"

Not only does the child develop their cognitive skills for processing and retrieving spatial information, but they also, as a result of their transactions with a variety of environments, develop a set of expectancies about the layout and components of typical behavior settings. Just as ecological psychology has demonstrated that individuals learn and apply generalizable scripts about the behavioral roles and rules of behavior settings, so too does the individual come to learn an "environmental grammar" of spatial expectancies.

We can usefully illustrate this with relation to the ever-broadening range of settings the child will encounter: rooms are likely to have standard components (e.g., doors, windows); houses are likely to have a specified subset of designated-use rooms; neighborhoods will usually contain a range of domestic, public, and commercial buildings; and cities can usually be expected to have differentiated regions. Learning an environmental grammar, at any of these scales, consists of developing the appropriate expectancies and, hence, the corresponding search strategies. Note how far the actual rules and contents of such grammars will be very largely determined by local cultural patterns (see, for example, Canter on the striking differences between Japanese and European room-behavior designations). The individual's ability to parse the environmental grammar of a place again represents not just their "developmental stage" but, most importantly, their personal range of transactions with similar types of setting.

4. Using Alternative Sources of Input: The Task of the Blind Child

Not until one examines the blind child's ways of coming to know the physical environment does the centrality of vision to the sighted child's understanding become fully apparent. For the latter, the visual overview—whether of room or region—serves to articulate the elements of experience into a spatial whole. For the blind child, nothing is so directly realized, all has to be constructed, either through one's individual, sequential experiences, or through such spatial aids as maps and models. And, as a consequence, the unaided and untutored blind child tends to be less mobile than the sighted, fearing collision with obstacles, and becoming disorientated or lost. Hence, in this area, environmental cognition research has one of its practical applications, in developing and evaluating the mobility education of the blind.

One of the basic (but until recently untested) assumptions of mobility education has been that the body image provides the base-line frame of reference for cognizing space beyond the body; hence, much practical work has tended to be done with young blind children to develop this image. However, as already noted, the recent empirical evidence does not support this assumption. It would seem more profitable to work directly with the blind child's strategies for exploring and knowing about immediate and then more distant space.

Direct experience is important for building up an integrated internal representation of an area: indeed, the single most important predictor of a blind child's spatial ability (holding level of visual handicap constant) is the amount of life-time freedom to explore space the child has been allowed. Overprotective parents, who limit this experience, may inadvertently produce children who arrive at school age with self-protective, nonexploratory styles.

Whereas mobility training used to concentrate upon route and landmark learning, to equip the individual for the most likely routes through their area, modern mobility education attempts to build up exploratory skills and to encourage the child to integrate geographical information into a coordinated spatial whole. The use of tactile maps not only imparts specific knowledge about an area, but also develops this spatial thinking, which frees the blind child from overdependence on taught routes. A range of audio–tactile–graphics processors, that the child can interact with, interrogate, and input own discoveries into, are likely to become more widely available.

5. Later Lifespan Developments

Development continues through the lifespan, even if the most dramatic changes occur during childhood. We should thus conclude this section with a brief review of such lifespan developments in environmental cognition.

During adolescence and early adulthood, the range of an individual's activities increases considerably; and with it increase not only the range of environmental knowledge but also the subtlety of understanding of environmental grammars. Diversity of knowledge between individuals also increases, as a function of activity patterns, salience, and, in some cases, some formal environmental awareness training. Thus, for example, architects, planners, pilots, and orienteers have all been populations whose spatial and environmental awareness have been studied and compared with untrained control groups. Training in many of these cases offers the individual a novel and extended vocabulary for environmental descriptions—e.g., architectural styles and land features useful for navigation.

In general the activity patterns of the individual, as they change through the lifespan, predict the nature of selective inclusion into our environmental images of the city, region, or world. Clearly, not all "environmental facts" are sought or retained in this schema; and the pattern of search and retention serves the individual's salient activities. The same city district, as known to the young adolescent, the lover, the businessman, the retired oldster, will be remembered (and reported back to the experimenter) in importantly different ways.

Particular research attention has been paid to the environmental needs—and hence patterns of cognition—of two of these: the adolescents and the old. Both groups are heavily dependent upon what the neighborhood affords them; both are likely to discover, at least in Western cities, that environments appear to be designed by and for the mobile adult of middle years, and that as a result, their needs are not fully satisfied.

B. The Microgenesis of Environmental Cognitions: The Skilled Adult Develops Knowledge of a New Geographical Area

The previous section described the development from infancy of the basic skills to process environmental information; but so far we have not fully described what it is that develops, or how the information is stored. In this section, we address this issue, while considering how the skills are used to learn about a newly encountered area.

1. The Cognitive Map

During the 1940s, many rats ran many mazes in the interest of science; and occasionally they escaped the confines of the maze and were able to run in a direct line to the end point of the maze. Tolman, noticing this, suggested that, rather than learning a rigid series of left and right turns, the rats were in fact aggregating all of this information about turns, angles, and distances into a "cognitive map," which enabled them to realize the relative positions of places.

This metaphor of a map has become so persuasive that it threatens to convince us that *all* spatial information is stored analogically: an internal spatial representation. Yet there is clear evidence that spatial information can also be stored and retrieved propositionally—in other words, almost as a string of instructions for movement along a route.

After Tolman, the city planner Kevin Lynch was next to shape our thinking on the nature of the cognitive map. In his empirical investigations of the images travelers developed of the city of Boston, he identified the key elements of the image: route, nodes (where routes intersect), and landmarks, with at a larger scale, city regions and phase changes.

Because routes and landmarks are clearly basic elements in both the ontogenic and the microgenic accounts, it has often tacitly been assumed in the literature that microgenesis recapitulates ontogenesis. Perhaps the predominant reason for this has been the influence of Siegal and White's theory.

They have argued that children first learn as landmarks those places which are of particular interest to them. Once these are established, information about local routes can be fitted to them, forming minimaps. These may be locally accurate and useable; yet children will not initially realize how separate minimaps could interelate. Only later in the developmental sequence can children integrate these minimaps into an overall representation of the environment.

Many published studies support the Siegal and White sequence for both ontogeny and microgeny: adults learning new areas do seem to re-enact the child's developing sequence.

A note of caution, however, should be entered here: many of these studies use indirect methods of testing people's knowledge of the environment—e.g., drawing sketch maps or giving distance estimations—and these methods may not fully reflect such knowledge. Studies in which environmental cognition is tested more directly (e.g., by asking a young child or a newcomer to rewalk a complex route) suggest that much more information can be recalled and acted upon than would be represented in a sketch map.

Route learning in other words may not be the later, constructed process of the Siegal and White account: and indeed being able to retrace a once-traveled route may have high survival value!

2. Measurement Techniques: How to Represent the Cognitive Representations of Environment

Any investigation of the cognitive world of an animal or of a very young child necessarily has to rely heavily on behavioral data—either in natural or experimental situations. Do cetaceans use magnetic fields to navigate? Data on whale-strandings and their association with measured geometric anomalies may provide an answer. Does the preverbal child use egocentric or allocentric coding of events? One can devise an experimental setting to pose the question.

When working with older children and with adults, however, most researchers have preferred to work with methods in which the person represents to the researcher their representation of the environment: methods used include sketch-mapping, model building, distance, and bearing estimation. Such productive methods clearly impose demands upon the person's general representational capacities: their level of graphicacy, for example—their general capacity to draw anything. Young children's spatial knowledge so clearly outstrips their graphic skills that the point is obvious; however, it is one which is often forgotten when the investigator asks apparently competent adults to sketch their "knowledge." Second, each method of representation (sketch map, verbal description or whatever) can be shown to elicit from store a subtly different subset of the information the person holds: some elements are clearly to the fore when the demand is for a map, and others when one asks for a route description as a means of elicitation.

Other experimenters have attempted to construct the implicit cognitive map from apparently more objective questions on, for example, distance estimates. These methods have their advantages—but also begin to reveal the nontransivity of such estimates. (One famous, early finding of environmental psychology was that the same route between town center and suburb was estimated differently according to direction of travel.) Multi-dimensional scaling is conventionally used to integrate such estimate data.

Some experimenters have been bold enough to leave the lab, and investigate environmental cognition in action: for example having people navigate through an area, while tape recording as full a verbal protocol as they could. Such methods elicit exciting data, but often involve as much a voyage of discovery for the navigator as for the investigator, bringing to the surface decisions that the individual had not previously been aware of. Measurement, in other words, may alter the process being measured.

3. Techniques to Capture Individual Strategies

Intensive work with individuals in the real world can eventually build into a detailed model of environmental knowledge. Golledge and colleagues, for example, have studied one individual's route learning over a period of a week; and have combined many of the above methods of investigation to produce such a cognitive model, which they have been able to computer-stimulate using artificial intelligence techniques. (Much of the work on human environmental cognition and navigation has strong implications for those in the AI community concerned with, for example, robot guidance systems.)

Other studies have observed individual styles in the application of environmental cognition: Ottosson has, for example, spent much time running behind orienteers, making detailed commentaries about their behavior. Passini has studied shoppers' strategies in planning travel through a shopping precinct; and Gärling has assessed the evidence for their approximating to a "least distance minimizing heuristic."

Most of the naturalistic, long-term studies of people's spatial behavior has been done with children and adolescents: Torrell asked 6- and 10-year-old children to keep detailed diaries of their outdoor activities; Moore had 9–12 year olds take on a lengthy field trip round their neighborhoods, and, from extensive interviews, has elicited the private worlds of these children. Hart lived among the children of a New England town as would an anthropologist, vividly documenting the way the cognized world expands with the roles and freedoms allowed to children as they grow older.

III. ACTION AND AESTHETIC IMPLICATIONS OF ENVIRONMENTAL COGNITION

Throughout the earlier discussions, environmental cognition has been presented as intimately connected with action. In this final section, we now consider its role as the basis of spatial decision making (i.e., overall strategy choices and the level of broad implementation), and also of movement through space and spatial updating (the level of detailed implementation of journey plans).

Contributing to the first of these, the overall spatial choices, are the aesthetic aspects of environmental cognition: preference choices are not solely functional and instrumental. Hence, the second section here considers the role of aesthetic preferences, from the large scale—the cognitive image of places (e.g. holiday destinations, shopping areas) as determinants of travel and relocation decisions— through middle scale—the appearance and layout of towns (their "legibility")—to the small scale—the dimensions of aesthetic judgment of buildings or rooms. At each scale our preferences for the natural environment should not be ignored.

A. Environmental Cognition as the Basis for Spatial Decision Making

Knowledge of the environment influences both our evaluations of and actions within it; such knowledge uptake itself selectively filtered by the individual's goals and personal plan and the extent to which a place satisfies these goals and plans affects the individual's evaluation of places.

Traditionally, cognitive psychology and behavioral/economic geography have concentrated specifically upon the relationship between cognition and action, leaving out any account of aesthetics. Individuals are seen as making decisions about how to choose and act in the world: actions are taken after the individual perceives and forms preferences for different possible action alternatives, following specifiable decision rules, and observing constraining factors. [*See* DECISION MAKING, INDIVIDUALS.]

The kind of cognitive factors involved include previous experience, perceptual abilities, hierarchical goals, and the decision rules mentioned above. As Gärling and Evans have indicated in their review, the formation of plans and their influence on actions in the environment have become a topic of increasing interest within cognitive psychology. A typical research issue is the influence of individual goals upon travel plans and decisions: spatial problem solving in a world constrained by time pressures, geographic layout, available transport, and so on.

Gärling and colleagues, for example, have asked whether a shopper's travel plans through town could be described by a heuristic for achieving the least possible total distance between all the shops to be visited. Their findings are instructive: under a laboratory simulation, where the spatial relationships between targets are clearly visible (e.g., on a town plan), people *do* choose paths and sequences which approximate this most efficient heuristic. However, in the equivalent task traveling in the real world, real shoppers are much more prone to take less efficient routes, partly as a result of distractions and partly, one can hypothesize, because the real world is less easy to conceptualize in plan-relationships between target places.

Hence, a coldly rational decision rule is unlikely to give a full prediction of much human spatial behavior: actions are based on more than just a clear geographical cognitive map, and must include some reference to preferences and motivations.

And even such an analysis may overstate the purposive, rational character of much travel: the environment itself, rather than prior planning, may suggest much travel.

We can analyze even a relatively simple way-finding task to show that it is composed of many sub processes. In an extensive study of way-finding, Passini recorded travelers' descriptions of their routes and actions as they walked through urban shopping malls. Some subjects recorded more than 100 discrete decisions in completing a task taking 20 minutes.

And analysis of such protocols indicates how responsive rather than thought-through and preplanned is such a decision process. Most people have often only global initial plans, with a few general decisions and a number of specifics at the outset. Particular problems are then tackled as they emerge: Passini observes that generally a new detailed plan is formulated only after the previous plan has been executed. The execution of travel plans is controlled by matching and feedback: matching relates the expected place image to the perceived place. Where there is a match, feedback sets the action part of the decision in motion; where there is a mismatch, it leads to further problem solving.

Environmental psychology and artificial intelligence have both a keen interest in the maintenance of orientation during travel: the tasks include place recognition, keeping track of one's location when moving about, and anticipating features of the environment. Successful travel may appear to be an automatic process, but can be shown to involve a continuous and complex updating process.

B. Environmental Cognition and Aesthetics

Cognitive maps as described above were first conceived by Tolman as the internal representation of space and its routes, junctions, distances, and angles. The apparently similar term, "mental maps," was used by the geographers Gould and White to indicate an altogether less factual representation of space: they were concerned to account for the preferences, prejudices, and images of places that lead individuals to make spatial choices. Thus, for example, some places within one's country are widely agreed to be attractive holiday destinations; others are less attractive. Such consensual views can be aggregated and drawn over a cartographic map as contours of preference, as an outward graphic representation of these inward preferences. Similar mental maps were also constructed to demonstrate consensus about willingness to relocate when seeking employment.

These early, relatively crude exercises nonetheless serve to reinforce the point that environmental cognitions and actions are closely linked to preferences. Later work on the images of distance places has shown how initial preferences can act as a selective filter in the seeking of and processing of new information about these places: in this, environmental psychology links up with the psychology of prejudice and stereotyping of peoples (e.g., Weigand). [*See* PREJUDICE AND STEREOTYPES.]

We can move from this broadest geographical scale to research at the middle scale—the preferences people express for aspects of man-made environment and natural landscapes.

Lynch, in discussing the image we develop of the city, introduced the concept of the legibility of places. Interestingly for the present discussion, the concept as he uses it links ease of understanding the physical layout with aesthetic response.

A legible city (or district) would be one which is relatively easy to comprehend and to remember—with implications for distinctiveness and discriminibility. Areas lacking in clear landmarks, nodes, districts, etc., would rate as low in legibility. And, interestingly it is these poorly structured areas which are also rated as less aesthetically appealing, a finding which has lead many researchers after Lynch to examine in more detail the relationship between particular physical features (and their interrelationship) and aesthetic response to them.

Experimental aesthetics has cropped up at several stages in the history of general cognitive psychology. Within the specifically environmental domain, recent work has been particularly promising, and has introduced some romance back into psychology: where else in this Encyclopedia would one find empirical work on what predicts people's feelings of *mystery* (to take a concept researched by Kaplan)?

Nasar, in identifying the evaluative image of the city as a whole, distinguishes between identity, location, and what he calls likability—the qualities accounting for preferences. His empirical work shows that likability has two broad dimensions: affect and imageability.

Peoples' affect for environments (Nasar works principally with American cityscapes, it should be noted) is predicted by the naturalness of the place, its upkeep, openness, order, and historical significance. Imageability relates to distinctiveness of form, visibility, and patterns of use—which in turn relate to a place's symbolic significance.

Coming finally to the scale of an individual building or room, there has again been much recent research linking form to aesthetic response. Despite perhaps the lay presumption that tastes may differ widely, in practice there tends to be a high public agreement on choices between places: i.e., one can indeed see an emergent consensus on aesthetics. (Group differences, cultural differences, and "expert-group" differences, e.g., architecture students, of course can overlay this observation.)

Such emergent consensus has encouraged work on the predictors of preference at this level. Visual arousal and complexity are among the factors implicated (along with Kaplan's mystery!): there being an empirically determinable optimal level of complexity for a particular building type.

Aesthetical responses might perhaps be thought of as a *superficial* by-product of environmental cognition. But Nasar argues that both cognition and aesthetics are both crucial to the public experience of urban areas.

- ◆ Aesthetics is a major dimension of environmental perception
- ◆ Pleasure and beauty rate as the central dimensions of environmental assessments
- ◆ Aesthetic factors have consistently been found to be closely associated with judgements of community satisfaction

Yet, says Nasar, planners and urban decision makers gloss over aesthetics as subjective and unquantifiable: *they are neither*. (And, most troublesome, such design professionals have consistently been found to differ from the general public's consensus in appraisals of the built environment.)

There is, in addition to all of the above research on the man-made environment, an equivalent empirical literature developing on what factors predict the aesthetic response to the natural environment (e.g., Kaplan and Kaplan). In both areas, environmental psychology has contributed to this more from the speculative level of early aesthetics research to the well-supported principles of current research.

Bibliography

Gärling, T., and Evans, G. W. (Eds.) (1992) "Environmental Cognition and Action: An Integrated Approach." Oxford University Press, New York.

Golledge, R.G. (1987). Environmental cognition. In "Handbook of Environmental Psychology" (D. Stokols and I. Altman, Eds.), Vol. 1. Wiley, New York.

Heft, H., and Wohlwill, J.F. (1987). Environmental cognition in children. In "Handbook of Environmental Psychology" (D. Stokols and I. Altman, Eds.) Vol. 1. Wiley, New York.

Matthews, M.H. (1992). "Making Sense of Place." Harvester Wheatsheaf, Hemel Hempstead, and Barnes and Nobel, Savage, MD.

Nasar, J.L. (1988). "Environmental Aesthetics: Theory, Research and Application." Cambridge University Press, Cambridge.

Passini, R. (1984). "Wayfinding in Architecture." Van Nostrand Rheinhold, New York.

Spencer, C.P., Blades, M., and Morsley, K. (1989) "The Child in the Physical Environment: The Development of Spatial Cognition." Wiley, Chichester.

Waterman, T.H. (1989). "Animal Navigation." Scientific American Library, New York.

Environmental Psychology

Robert Gifford
University of Victoria, Canada

Glossary

Behavior setting A location that consistently evokes certain patterns of behavior in those who are present.

Crowding The experience of insufficient space; to be distinguished from density.

Density A physical measure of persons per unit area.

Personal space Or interpersonal distance; the physical distance component of interpersonal relations.

Place attachment A strong person–place bond that develops through long or intense association; the place becomes part of the self.

Postoccupancy evaluation Evaluating buildings to determine whether and how well the architectural program was executed.

Privacy The process of regulating the amount of social interaction in which one is involved; can mean solitude-seeking but can also mean seeking company.

Programming (architectural) Planning buildings to meet the behavioral and psychological needs of those who will use them.

Social design Architectural design that emphasizes inclusive, grass-roots, democratic participation by those who will use the building; interior function and meaning are more important than exterior aesthetics and ornament.

Social dilemma Situation in which group and individual interests are in conflict, often applied to resource management situations; individuals are rewarded more for self-interest behavior than for group-interest behavior, but if most individuals choose self-interest the resource is extinguished.

Territoriality A pattern of attitudes and behaviors related to the perceived or actual control of a physical space, object, or idea; acts as a mechanism for the peaceful regulation of space use much more often than as a source of source of aggression.

ENVIRONMENTAL PSYCHOLOGY is the study of transactions between individuals and their built and natural settings. It assumes that the actions of persons change the environment and that their behavior, experience, and well-being are changed by the environment. Environmental psychology includes basic research aimed at understanding person–environment transactions and practice that applies this knowledge to improve human settings.

I. BACKGROUND, THEORY, AND METHOD

As an organized discipline, environmental psychology is relatively new but some social scientists have studied person–environment transactions for decades. If one considers the enormous investment society makes in the construction and maintenance of the physical environment, including buildings, parks, and public outdoor settings, the long delay before person–environment relations received ade-

Encyclopedia of Human Behavior, Volume 2

Copyright © 1994 by Academic Press, Inc. All rights of reproduction in any form reserved.

quate attention seems odd. However, many studies have dealt with the major topics within environmental psychology since the late 1960s. Much of this work has been stimulated by the recognition of environmental problems such as crowding, pollution, energy shortages, and unsuitable buildings.

Theories in environmental psychology are diverse and still developing. Some emphasize central psychological processes such as stimulation and control. The common occurrence of too much or too little stimulation is the focus of adaptation-level, arousal, overload, underload, and stress theories, which predict that a wide range of behaviors and experiences will be affected by level of stimulation. Other theories emphasize the importance of the individual's real or perceived control over the environment (e.g., personal control, reactance, learned helplessness, and boundary regulation theories). The ecological approach asserts the importance of the behavior setting, a naturally occurring small-scale social–physical unit consisting of regular patterns of person–environment behavior. Integral or holistic approaches (e.g., interactionism, transactionalism, and organismic theory) attempt to describe the complete interrelationship of persons and setting. Finally, the operant approach downplays abstract principles, adopting a direct problem-solving approach that employs behavior modification techniques to deal with environmental issues such as recycling, littering, and energy conservation. [*See* ECOLOGICAL PSYCHOLOGY.]

Environmental psychologists recognize that person–environment transactions are influenced by many different factors, which has led to multiple paradigms for studying them. Many different research methods are employed—some standard in social science and others devised especially for environmental psychology. A strong preference for performing research in the everyday world means that field studies are common. Sometimes laboratories and simulated settings are necessary, but are primarily used when a field study is not possible. True experiments are sometimes possible; they are desirable when a researcher seeks to isolate particular causes and effects, but quasi-experimental research designs are much more common.

Environmental psychology has taken root in many countries as well as above and below the surface of the earth, including the design of space stations and deep-sea research vehicles. To some extent, the field has a unique character in each country because each country has distinct environmental problems and philosophies.

II. ENVIRONMENTAL PERCEPTION

Environmental psychologists usually study the perception of whole, everyday scenes. In doing so, they sometimes must sacrifice a degree of experimental control, but in return they obtain data on the perception of real, complex settings through which the perceiver may move and feel a connection. Perceivers select certain cues from scenes and ignore many others. Unfortunately, some cues they ignore may be important, at least in the long run (e.g., air pollution's effect on health).

Environmental perception has been studied using verbal reports, time-sampling, behavioral inference, phenomenological methods, and combinations of these. The available evidence suggests that perceptions of qualities such as length and distance are largely dependent on the physical elements in the scene and how these elements are arranged. However, personal factors such as perceptual ability, finding a setting pleasing, culture (such as being raised in a "carpentered" world), and training (for example, in architecture) also affect the very way we see the world.

The theories of Egon Brunswik, James Gibson, and Donald Berlyne each have had major impacts on the study of environmental perception. Each began as a traditional (nonenvironmental) theory, but contained the necessary seed to be fruitful for environmental psychology: an emphasis on properties of stimuli. Each has provoked considerable basic research into the nature of environmental perception, but they have also been extended into the practical domains of city planning, park planning, and architecture.

III. ENVIRONMENTAL COGNITION

How do people think about and find their way around in the space around them? They do not acquire, store, and recall information about locations, distances, and arrangements like cameras or copy machines. Yet their ways of doing so are usually effective and rule-governed.

Spatial cognition—the way we acquire, process, store, and recall information about everyday settings—is studied by examining sketch maps, model construction or manipulation, distance estimation, and naturalistic observation. It is affected by one's stage of life, familiarity or experience with the setting, and certain cognitive biases. The study of cognitive maps reveals that legible places are easier to comprehend: they have clear paths and distinct edges, districts, nodes, and landmarks. The spatial cognition of children generally follows a sequence moving from egocentric to projective to abstract. The spatial cognition of older people differs from that of younger adults. Where their experience is limited by lowered mobility or sensory abilities, they may perform less well. Their memories of the environment are more personalized and are, in some respects, better than those of young adults.

Experience in a setting gives one a fuller and better organized cognitive image of it. Both landmarks and paths facilitate the growth of place knowledge. Where one of these elements is more common than the other, examples of it will be learned first. Male–female differences in spatial cognition exist, but may largely reflect the different travel experiences of men and women. Two common cognitive biases are to envision places as more grid-like or Euclidean than they actually are and to wrongly employ larger geographical entities in placing smaller ones (e.g., Reno is thought to be east of Los Angeles because it is in Nevada, which is generally east of California, but Reno is west of Los Angeles). The environmental cognition of urban forms is improved by clear paths and visible landmarks. Some evidence suggests that visibility without organization, however, may detract from effective environmental cognition. At the architectural level, buildings that are tall, free-standing, distinctively shaped, and used often are better recalled than others.

IV. ENVIRONMENTAL APPRAISAL

Environmental appraisals are personal, subjective judgments of places; they may or may not be consistent with most other people's views of the same places.

Environmental appraisals take six forms: description, evaluation, aesthetics, emotion-eliciting qualities, meaning, and concern. First, environments may be verbally described in many ways; a good poet or novelist is probably best able to select and employ the most apt words to describe any particular setting. Researchers, nevertheless, have tried to develop standard sets of descriptors to assist the average person's attempt to describe places. One outcome of these efforts has been to identify certain descriptive dimensions that commonly emerge when persons describe settings.

Second, environmental appraisals take the form of evaluations or preferences. These are influenced by such personal factors as age, sex, and familiarity with the place and by such objective features as room design, congruity, contrast, and complexity. A newer approach developed by Stephen and Rachel Kaplan advocates the use of concepts that integrate person and place: involvement, making-sense, immediate versus future promise, coherence, legibility, mystery, complexity, and familiarity.

Third, the aesthetics of environments may be appraised. Environmental beauty has been the concern of activists, planners, experimentalists, and humanists. Landscape beauty has been shown to be largely a function of the amount of different landscape elements in a scene and the apparent distance to and the placement of these elements in the scene.

Fourth, emotional response to the environment is a form of appraisal. Emotional responses to environments are usually mild, persistent, and cumulative rather than sharp and brief. Nevertheless, they are a complex mix of behavioral, cognitive, and physiological responses. Individuals report that settings evoke combinations of pleasure, arousal, and perhaps other emotions (e.g., dominance) in them. These reports are linked to behavior in James Russell and Albert Mehrabian's pleasure–arousal hypothesis, which asserts that we approach places that are more arousing when they are also pleasant.

A fifth form of appraisal is the meaning we assign to a place. Two kinds of environmental meaning are the setting's communication of some architectural or philosophical concept and the communication of its purpose or function. Communication, in the sense used here, occurs in some buildings but not others. For example, one study showed that Nazi-built architecture communicated general Nazi philosophy; some plain buildings fail to communicate their function to typical passersby. Part of the art of architecture lies in finding a nonverbal, stylistic way to get a message from the designer of a building to its users. Meaning in the sense of a building's perceived working function has strong effects on its appreciation. Many individuals do not like vagueness in function.

Finally, we appraise places in terms of the concern (or lack of it) we have for them. Environmental concern is a form of appraisal for which behavioral consequences are of particular importance. Early research suggested there are weak links between environmental concern and action, but later work shows that when action is more broadly conceived, the links are stronger.

V. ENVIRONMENTAL ASSESSMENT

Environmental assessments are measurements of a place's qualities that aspire to objectivity; that is, they are attempts to measure the way a population experiences a place. Environmental assessments may aim to measure a setting's physical and spatial properties, artifacts and objects, traits, behavioral occurrences, or social climate.

Environmental assessments, in contrast to environmental appraisals, tend to be place-centered (instead of person-centered), aim to measure physical properties (instead of psychological properties), are more often policy-oriented (rather than oriented to the understanding of individuals), and more often employ observers with an expert or frequent-user relationship to the place being assessed. Environmental assessment researchers have so far concentrated on one family of traits (environmental quality) and one kind of setting (wilderness parks). Environmental assessments may use technical or human means of observations. Each has its place; neither is necessarily more reliable or valid; each employs a variety of instruments (machines for technical assessments, questionnaires or rating forms for human observers). Observer-based environmental assessments or OBEAs, as opposed to machine-based or technical environmental assessments (TEAs), have at least five purposes. They allow for comparisons between TEAs and OBEAs, assist in the development of physical measures of environmental quality, provide data on environmental quality trends from the human perspective, provide assessments of quality along dimensions with particular human relevance, and educate the staff of the assessed setting as to its strengths and weaknesses.

Four OBEA paradigms may be identified: expert, psychophysical, cognitive, and humanistic. Each has its own values and purposes, resulting in different kinds of assessments. The generalizability and utility of OBEAs depend on wise matching of observers to the kind of assessments they are to make.

VI. ENVIRONMENTAL PERSONALITY

The study of personality may seem antithetical to environmental psychology if one assumes that environmental psychology emphasizes the effects of settings on persons. However, personality is part of environmental psychology for three reasons. First, it does not merely refer to persons, but includes consideration of how persons interact with their environments. Second, personality dispositions help predict the behavior of individuals in the environment, because dispositions that specifically characterize our environmental tendencies have been described and examined. Third, dispositions form an important part of the person half of the person–environment relation.

Three early personality theorists are important for environmental psychology: Henry Murray, Kurt Lewin, and Andras Angyal. Murray's personology introduced the concepts of alpha and beta press (the actual and perceived power of the environment to affect one's welfare) and internal and external proceedings (subjective and objective accounts of the initiation and completion of a behavior sequence). Lewin's field theory, which conceptualized persons as actively interacting with their environments in their life spaces, produced the famous formula $B = f(P,E)$. One's representation of the physical environment and some elements of the unrepresented physical environment (the foreign hull) affect one's behavior and experience. Lewin's action research concept, in which theory and application are fused, guides many environmental psychologists today. Angyal's holistic, systems-oriented approach has not been widely acknowledged, yet represents an early version of a theoretical position that is widely held today. An illustrative concept from this organismic–contextual theory is autonomy–homonomy, in which individuals are viewed as ranging from those who wish to blend into the environment to those who wish to re-make the environment into their own image.

Numerous modern systems for conceptualizing personality in relation to the environment have been described, but the most developed is the Environmental Response Inventory created by George McKechnie, which assesses eight dispositions: pastoralism, urbanism, environmental adaptation, antiquarianism, stimulus-seeking, environmental trust, need for privacy, and mechanical orientation. Research involving personality dimensions designed for environmental psychology has so far largely examined the validity of the dimensions. The results have been positive: for example, thing-specialists have more constructs for objects and settings, those with high scores on environmental adaptation like large, new buildings, and screeners adapt to the high-density dormitory better than do nonscreeners.

Some traditional personality measures also assist in the understanding of behavior that has environmental significance. For example, extraverts generally prefer smaller interpersonal distances and may experience less stress in higher density situations. They arrange furniture in a more "open" manner, perceive landscapes differently, and have a better sense of direction than introverts. Persons with an internal locus of control also prefer smaller interpersonal distances and tolerate high density better than those with an external locus of control. Internals often engage in more pro-environment activities, such as recycling, although other factors can alter this. They also may prefer more "controlled" architecture. Psychological health and conventionality have also been linked to environmentally relevant behavior; such behaviors have been shown to be influenced by the joint effects of personality and the physical setting. [*See* CONTROL; EXTRAVERSION–INTROVERSION.]

VII. PERSONAL SPACE

Personal space refers to the interpersonal distance chosen during social interaction. It involves elements of territoriality, spacing, and communication. It varies with and reflects the rise, current status, and decline of relationships. Alpha personal space is the objective distance between interacting individuals and beta personal space refers to the experience of that distance.

Personal space has been measured using simulation, stop-distance, and naturalistic observation methods. The simulation techniques may produce the same results as the others, but are better suited to studying beta personal space than alpha personal space. The stop-distance technique, if performed without the subject's awareness, is probably the best method. Naturalistic observation can be technically difficult and often does not allow the investigator to distinguish among different possible reasons for variations in personal space.

Personal space may be predicted in part from knowing an individual's characteristics. Males typically use larger distances than females. Young adults typically use more personal space than children. Interpersonally warm and nonanxious individuals probably have smaller personal spaces than others. Psychological disturbance often leads to more variable or inappropriate personal space. These personal influences on personal space also have interactive effects: to predict a person's personal space choices accurately, one must know the person's age, sex, race, culture, and personality.

Social and physical features of the situation also affect interpersonal distance. Edward Hall described four zones of increasing distance that depend on the closeness of the relation between the two persons. Attraction, cooperation, and equal status are associated with smaller personal space; stigma and unequal status lead to larger personal space. Orientation, as opposed to distance, is less well understood. People seem to prefer more space when the physical environment offers less room. Again, these factors combine to produce interpersonal distances that are different from what would be expected from consideration of each influence by itself; multivariate research is helping to untangle these complex effects.

Culture is a major modifier of interpersonal distance. There is some evidence for a continuum that ranges from the closeness of Arabs and Latin Americans to the distance of English and Germans. But differences within these groups, occasional results that do not fit this neat pattern, and other factors such as the language one speaks during a particular interaction all may affect personal space.

Personal space is intimately intertwined with numerous facets of human behavior. Changing one's interpersonal distance may allow one individual to exert social control over another. Moving close in a positive relationship may lead to greater attraction, but doing so when the other person is a stranger leads to flight. Impressions are often formed on the basis of interpersonal distances we observe in others, but these attributions are not always valid. Help may be forthcoming when individuals approach close to others *and* impress their need on the other. Cooperation occurs more and leads to better performance when individuals are physically "immediate" (closer and facing one another). When they are less immediate, performance is better in competitive conditions.

The individual's acquisition of the rules concerning interpersonal distance are probably well characterized by social learning theory. The functions of personal space are characterized by numerous minimodels based on concepts such as comfort, protection, communication, stress, optimal stimulation, and affiliative equilibrium. More encompassing theoretical integrations have begun to appear. The social penetration model emphasizes the role of personal space in the rise and fall of relationships. The limits-of-compensation model highlights the outer limits of interpersonal distance, showing that as discomfort grows interaction becomes more difficult. The approach–avoidance model hypothesizes differences between the desire to draw close to someone and the desire to keep one's distance. Discomfort is seen as the discrepancy between the two desires.

VIII. HUMAN TERRITORIALITY

Territoriality is a pattern of behavior and attitudes held by an individual or group that is based on perceived, attempted, or actual control of a definable physical space, object, or idea. It may involve habitual occupation, defense, personalization, and marking of that space.

Environmental psychologists recognize seven types of territory: primary, secondary, public, interactional, body, object, and idea. The seven types of territory may be infringed upon in at least three ways: invasion, violation, and contamination. In turn, territory-holders may utilize preventative, reaction, or social boundary defenses.

Territoriality is nearly always investigated in the field. Researchers occasionally perform true experiments, but more often examine correlations between territoriality and other behaviors or attitudes, ask for the participant self-reports of territorial activities, or observe how individuals mark or personalize territories.

Personal factors, physical and social aspects of situations, and culture can lead to territoriality. For example, males generally manifest more territoriality than females. Dominance (as a personality trait) is inconsistently related to territoriality. As for environmental factors, Oscar Newman's defensible space theory argues that physical arrangements increase territoriality feelings and behavior and that this increase leads to a decline in territorial invasions. These physical arrangements may be at the block or neighborhood level (e.g., altering traffic flow) or at the house level (e.g., fences and plantings). Evidence generally favors the theory, but the evidence is not conclusive and defensible space features certainly do not guarantee that intrusions will not occur. Territoriality appears to increase with three social factors: ownership compared to renting, positive social climate, and greater competition for resources. Cultures differ in their expression of territoriality, although the question of whether some cultures are more territorial than others has not been clearly answered.

Territoriality is associated with a variety of behaviors and experiences: personalization, aggression, dominance, control, and attachment. Personalization and marking are very common, may occur with or without awareness, signal ownership but do not always lead to active defense, and seem to offer psychological benefits to the territory-holder beyond merely informing the world of a territorial claim. Popular writers have exaggerated the relation between overt aggression and territoriality in humans. Territoriality does facilitate control of spaces, but this is usually accomplished through passive means that do not involve direct bullying of others. Place attachment is the experience of belonging to a setting. So far studied primarily by humanistically inclined phenomenologists, place attachment an important process involving some of the closest person–environment bonds we ever experience.

Theories of human territoriality remain diverse, speculative, and largely untested. Ethology, organizational behavior, behavior settings, brain structure, and conflict resolution are some of the disparate concepts that underpin theories of human territoriality. A theory that synthesizes them coherently will surely picture human territoriality as an extremely complex process. The main function of human territoriality probably is the maintenance of order and identity in everyday life. Environmental psychologists do know enough about territoriality to use it in their contributions to better environmental design.

IX. CROWDING AND POPULATION DENSITY

Crowding is an unpleasant experience of spatial restriction, whereas density is a physical ratio of persons per unit area. Perceived density is the individual's estimate of this ratio. Crowding, density, and perceived density are not always correlated with one another. The notions of social versus spatial density, indoor versus outdoor density, and proximity have been advanced as ways to refine the density ratio into a variable with more predictive power. [*See* CROWDING: EFFECTS ON HEALTH AND BEHAVIOR.]

Aggregate (archival) studies offer the best avenue for examining the gross effects of density on entire populations, and laboratory experiments offer the greatest opportunity to draw causal conclusions. The field experiment represents a compromise that is capable of investigating effects on individuals (a drawback of aggregate studies) and of claiming some relevance to everyday life (a drawback of the laboratory experiment).

At the personal level, personality, expectations, and preference influence whether an individual experiences a given situation as crowded or not. Internal locus of control, high affiliative tendency, a tendency to screen unwanted stimuli, a preference for high density, and an expectation for low density predispose individuals to experience less crowding when density is high. Personal experience with high density may reduce crowding stress in secondary (e.g., public) but not in primary (e.g., residential) environments. In confined settings, women usually manage high density better, but men seem to cope better when escape is possible.

Social influences can worsen or ease crowding. Sheer numbers of others will sometimes, but not always, produce more crowding. If others are watching or touching an individual (particularly a male), or one is engaged in disliked activities, crowding is worse even when density is equivalent. Being left out produces more crowding stress than sharing space with another person who is compatible.

Objective, accurate information about high-density settings reduces crowding. Crowding is likely to be worse when density is higher, the building is higher, the corridors are longer, the ceiling is lower, and when sunlight rarely finds its way in. High inside density usually leads to physiological and psychological stress, at least for those who prefer larger interpersonal distances or are socially isolated. Performance may be harmed under high density when the task is complex, when others are watching, and when performers must physically interact to accomplish the task. When a person's expectations about density are unfulfilled, performance may suffer: performance may even be worse in *low* density if the performer expected high density. Some aspects of performance may even improve when density or audience size is increased.

High density often has negative effects, but under some conditions—perhaps when we perform activities in which we are already competent—it may improve performance. Inescapable high inside density harms a wide range of social behaviors, particularly for men. Except in prison, those effects take more passive forms (e.g., lack of helpfulness) than active forms (e.g., aggression). High density may enhance humor, but it almost always creates negative emotion. High density reduces one's sense of control; as a result a variety of coping mechanisms are used.

Centuries of experience may be necessary before a culture can live successfully with high density. If newer cultures wished to learn from older cultures, they might consider encouraging more psychological distance between individuals, allowing times and places for escape, developing stricter norms about what may be said to whom, restricting who may go where within the home and how each space within the home is to be used, discouraging social interaction with acquaintances inside the home but encouraging it in public places, and learning to appreciate higher levels of social stimulation.

X. PRIVACY

A major goal of human social behavior is to regulate the amount of contact we have with others. Privacy concerns the regulation of access to self. This access may be interactional, as in control over who is allowed to be with whom, or informational, as in who is allowed access to archival information about whom. Alan Westin reasoned that interactional privacy has four faces: solitude, intimacy, anonymity, and reserve. Research supports Westin's speculations and adds certain minor refinements. Conceptually, privacy may be considered as preference, expectation, value, and behavior. The measurement of privacy through naturalistic observation of behavior is rare, but measurement via self-report is well-developed.

Privacy preferences, expectations, and satisfaction are influenced by personal characteristics. For example, city-raised individuals prefer more anonymity and intimacy. Women seem to manage privacy in close groups by discussing more interpersonal and intimate matters and men often achieve privacy by removing themselves from the setting and talking less about delicate matters. Individuals who have greater-than-average privacy needs are less sure of themselves and more anxious. Members of different cultures are believed to have similar privacy needs but, depending on how the environment supports those needs, may fulfill those needs in different ways.

The physical setting also has important effects on privacy preferences, expectations, and satisfaction. For example, open space at work often breeds dissatisfaction, whereas at home it is usually preferred. Its physical influences are both immediate, such as the doors and partitions surrounding people, and less immediate, such as the distance between houses and the number of neighbors visible from one's house. Privacy attitudes and behaviors vary from setting to setting.

Informational privacy is primarily affected by who wants the information from us, what information they want, and how they attempt to obtain it. Perceived informational privacy sometimes differs from actual informational privacy. Some privacy fears could be reduced if employees gave informed consent to the gathering of information about them.

Those who know how to use the environment to successfully regulate their privacy may be more successful in areas of life beyond the social realm. Some individuals adapt to or accept situations that would seem to offer too much or too little social contact. Others faced with a shortage of traditional mechanisms of regulating social interaction develop creative solutions to the problem. As a key process in our dealings with others, privacy is inextricably linked to communication, autonomy, identity, emotional release, and growing up. Use of many privacy regulation mechanisms may be one hallmark of success; satisfaction with little privacy a sign of growing institutionalization.

Irwin Altman's model of privacy as an optimizing boundary-control process dominates, but other theorists have contributed ideas. John Archea, for example, observes that privacy has a strong environmental component. Maxine Wolfe and her colleagues note that privacy preferences, expectations, and satisfaction vary over the life cycle. Eric Sundstrom observes that privacy needs vary as a function of status.

XI. HOME AND COMMUNITY SETTINGS

"Home" is a rich personal experience that may develop in a residence, which is the physical setting. Residential satisfaction is a function of person and residence characteristics. The more congruent the residence is with one's stage in the life cycle and role in the family, the more satisfied one is likely to be. As for physical form, the single family dwelling is by far the preferred residence form in North America. Single and elderly individuals, however, often prefer apartments. High indoor density is a key dissatisfier. Moving is one outcome of residential dissatisfaction; it is a source of stress in itself. Individuals who have little residential choice or do not enjoy new settings experience even more mobility stress.

Behavior *in* residences, such as space management, the effects of architectural style on behavior, and home-based leisure, is rarely studied except through interviews, primarily because of the difficulties involved in conducting research inside the home. Privacy and crowding are the biggest problems, primarily as they harm child development. High-rises seem inappropriate for children. Resident lifestyle is reflected in the physical organization of the home. Home is an important place to experience the growth and relaxation that leisure can provide.

Neighborhood satisfaction is related to such physical factors as the availability of nearby green space, general upkeep, and noise. Yet these factors interact to some extent with personal characteristics (e.g., screening tendency, perception of control, and one's residence type). Neighborhood social ties may be less important than they used to be, except for a few determined groups such as religious enclaves.

Cities are stimulating, but their impact does not constitute an overload for everyone. Individuals apparently adapt to some stressors (e.g., air pollution) more than others (e.g., noise). Vandalism and street art are different in motive and expression: vandals destroy settings out of a sense of revenge, whereas artists enhance settings while expressing social concerns. Crime and fear of crime are also important urban problems that may be eased in part through the application of defensible space design principles.

Climate is a complex set of variables, but aggression probably increases with air pollution and with temperature. However, sunshine combined with moderate temperatures seems to increase helping. Noise in the community reduces helping unless the victim's need is serious. Interaction among strangers on the street generally follows a mini–max principle: minimize interaction, maximize order. Frequent exposure to the same strangers, however, leads to a kind of distant affection.

Retail settings are an important part of the community. Environmental factors in shopping include store location and layout, the display of goods, ambient music, and noise, lighting, and shopper density. Research in the retail environment has been slow to emerge. This may be because its commercial value means that researchers report their findings to corporate sponsors rather than public-domain journals.

Most homes are threatened by one or more environmental hazards, some natural and others technological. In the precalamity phase, governments attempt to reduce risk through engineering and education, but when neither of these are effective, many lives are lost. Specific warnings and awareness-raising simulations can help, but effective personal action is often blunted by our tendency to bounded (i.e., limited) rationality: under-preparation for impending disasters, hasty, sometimes inappropriate responses to hazard mitigation once the disaster occurs, and misperception of hazard risks. During most disasters, individuals generally interact in relatively rational and cooperative ways; the exception is a disaster that traps people in a confined setting. The outcome of disaster is stress in many forms. Some forms of coping reduce some forms of stress better than others. Community attachment and economic factors often prevent residents from vacating high-risk areas; they would rather see governments engage in massive public works to protect their homes than leave.

XII. WORK AND TRAVEL SETTINGS

Work begins with getting there. Most research on this has been concerned with encouraging commuters to help save energy. Environmental psychologists have created demographic profiles of car and urban transit riders, devised models of commuter preference, provided positive information about urban transit, evaluated existing transit systems, and studied the effect of reducing fares reduced fares. This research has not yet had very large effects on our automobile addiction, but the more promising approaches are being sorted out from the less promising ones. The impact of commuting on the commuter is real, but that we need to learn more about how commuting stress works and who will experience the most stress. [*See* STRESS.]

Once at work, physical influences play many roles. Noise has many effects. In industrial settings, it can cause serious hearing loss. Loud noise is particularly dangerous when employees do not realize that deafness comes slowly and almost imperceptibly. Despite our suspicion that noise affects performance, research in natural settings shows how complex the issue is and that performance decrements depend on the task, the person, and the type of noise. Noise harms performance under certain combinations of these, but not under others. For certain tasks, noise may even arouse a person enough to improve performance. Noise is a serious problem in modern open-plan offices. Employees find sound a problem both coming and going: sound entering their workspace is annoying and when their own words escape over partitions too easily, their privacy is compromised. Office noise may even affect important interpersonal behavior, from mere impressions of others to important judgments regarding them. There is some suggestion that long-term exposure to loud sounds has physiological effects beyond hearing loss. Music may improve performance of well-learned cognitively simple tasks. Employees naturally dislike noise but, for the most part, like music on the job. They generally think noise hinders and music helps their performance.

The effects of temperature on human behavior are best examined by using effective temperature, a measure which includes humidity and air movement as well as temperature. Relatively extreme effective temperatures do not affect many work behaviors unless core body temperature is altered. The effects of temperature are also usually moderated by access to heavier or lighter clothing. The amazing variety of temperature effects reported are due to these measurement and clothing factors, as well as to many others including degree of acclimatization, knowledge of coping strategies, motivation, and type of work. Engineers have described precise "comfort envelopes," but psychologists have discovered that comfort depends on perception as well as actual effective temperature and that optimal performance may be found outside the comfort envelope. Stress occurs when individuals are initially subjected to effective temperatures farther outside the comfort envelope, but many persons can adapt to these more extreme temperatures after longer term exposure to them.

Several components of air, including carbon monoxide, air ions, and odors (both bad and good), may affect performance, but the effects are not striking under normal conditions. Extremely low concentrations of negative ions may affect some basic cognitive processes and extremely high concentrations may slightly facilitate them, but these effects are not strong for the average person. However, long-term exposure, differential physiological sensitivity, and psychological mediators such as perceived control help to explain why the performance of some individuals is affected but that of others is not. When it carries chemical impurities or disease-causing organisms, air can seriously impair health. Air quality is a growing concern of employees. Lack of control over noticeably bad air may affect persistence at work and, in some circumstances, foster negative feelings among employees.

Light affects work behavior primarily when it is insufficient (leading to low productivity, accidents, and eyestrain) or improperly placed (leading to glare and eyestrain). Lighting often is excessive in North American offices and many individuals dislike the newer forms of lighting, some of which distort color. European lighting standards call for lower levels of illumination. Carefully placed local lighting could resolve some of these problems. Access to natural light and views is psychologically important.

Naturally occurring spatial arrangements have few documented effects on performance, but employees are very sensitive to space and unhappy with many existing arrangements. Many open-plan arrangements reduce desirable communication and increase undesirable communication. Office arrangements lead visitors to form impressions of the office-holder's character and status. Yet many organizations restrict the degree to which employees may arrange or personalize their offices and fail to consult with employees when offices are planned.

The environmental psychology of travel is a new but growing area. Travelers affect destinations and are affected by them. Anticipation, travel itself, and the recollection of travel involve environmental perception and cognition. Recreational travel is a trade-off between familiarity and risk and between economic growth and environmental degradation, but as society is able to provide employees with more disposable income and time, it is a trade-off many are pursuing. Destination selection, acquisition of knowledge about destination, and behavior enroute are a few areas of developing research. Some destinations bring relief from anxiety; others throw travelers into "environment shock." Travelers ruin some physical settings and enhance almost none. "Romantic" tourism (i.e., the search for more and more unspoiled destinations) may be an undesirable luxury. More careful planning of destination sites might spread the impact of visitors, offer more authentic experiences, and educate travelers while offering them solace from the working world.

XIII. LEARNING SETTINGS

Both macro (e.g., school and campus design) and micro (e.g., desk and room design) physical features of learning settings affect learning and related activities. Students in large schools have a slight advantage in the variety of topics they can learn about but, partly because time at school is limited, students in large schools do not actually participate in more activities than students in small schools. Students in large schools more often learn and enjoy as spectators; students in small schools more often learn and enjoy as participants. In most areas of learning, students in small schools achieve more as a result of developing competence through direct involvement in activities. However, when activities in large schools are understaffed and activities in small schools are overstaffed, these outcomes may be reversed. Decentralizing school buildings may decrease student–teacher interaction. If satisfied teachers are better teachers, then sensitive construction or renovations of their workplace (the classroom) should be undertaken when necessary. Students often perform better in the place where they learned the material.

Noise interferes with learning both while it occurs and, if the learner is subjected to noise for long periods, even after the noise is gone. Noisy classrooms may impair the performance of girls more than boys, that of autistic children more than hyperactive children, and that of most children when the task is difficult. Noise may hinder performance by interfering with information processing, lowering the student's perception of control, and increasing blood pressure. Noise is more bothersome in nonlaboratory settings, higher density settings, and when it concerns social rather than schoolwork topics. To combat noise, instructors have changed their methods—sometimes sacrificing a good method for a quiet one—and successfully employed behavior modification techniques such as sound-activated electrical relays that control reinforcers such as radio music and extra recess time.

Incandescent lighting is preferred by many, but it is more expensive than fluorescent lighting. Fluorescent lighting has not been shown to have dramatic negative effects on the performance or health of most students, despite some claims to the contrary. As with noise, light's effects may be on specific subgroups of individuals; when studies of whole classes or schools are done, large effects on a few learners may be obscured by an absence of effects on most learners.

There are few simple, direct relations between climate and educational behavior; some combination of person and setting variables may enhance or reduce the influence of climate. Research is difficult because climate is composed of many possible patterns of temperature, humidity, and air movement. Perhaps the best-supported conclusion is that performance is best in slightly cool but not humid classrooms. Preferred environmental conditions may not be the same as conditions that facilitate performance.

The amount and arrangement of space in educational settings are very important for classroom performance and behavior. High density may affect learning when the activity involves physical movement around the classroom, when learning is dependent on some classroom resource that is not increasing as fast as the number of learners, when a particular situation appears crowded to a particular learner, and when the concept to be learned is complex. Among preschoolers, high density alters the child's choice of activities. Educational benefits appear to accrue in classrooms that have the teacher's desk in a corner, carefully arrange and separate different kinds of activities, possess library corners, and are carpeted. Action zone seating benefits some students. Open-plan classrooms have positive outcomes when teachers use techniques suited to open-space classrooms and students have fewer behavioral or other problems. Such classrooms can be noisy but can foster student autonomy. All these findings depend in part on grade level and teaching style.

Space in classrooms affects student and teacher feelings. Most students and teachers prefer lower density classrooms, because lower densities usually feel less crowded. Providing satisfying physical arrangements within schools is best accomplished by furnishing a variety of layouts. Softer, more home-like classrooms will not become common until attitudes change: school authorities must be willing to spend a bit more, janitors must be willing to deal with rooms that are probably harder to clean, and parents must be willing to believe that a "real education" is possible in a nontraditional classroom.

Increased social density leads to increased aggression and withdrawal when other resources, architectural features, and teaching style do not counteract it. Attempts to provide more privacy for students in the classroom have so far not been very successful. Open-plan classrooms increase social interaction. Classroom arrangements should provide optimal stimulation. The proper amount in any given situation cannot yet be specified, but the student's need for stimulation, the type of activity, and the length of time spent in the activity must be considered.

Environmental competence involves learning *about* the environment. Three kinds include (a) one's personal style, attitudes, and awareness of physical settings, (b) knowledge of physical settings, including technical knowledge, how to unearth new information, knowledge about how social systems control space, knowledge of person–environment relations, and (c) practical environmental skills such as scouting, matching, personalization, and creative custodianship. Programs in and out of school teach many different facets of environmental competence, from basic environmental ethics to campfire starting to architectural design.

XIV. ARCHITECTURAL PSYCHOLOGY

One main purpose of environmental psychology is to use knowledge such as that described to this point in order to create more humane buildings. Some buildings are human disasters; others are merely persistent nuisances to those who occupy or use them.

Reform movements include community architecture and social design. The latter, as described by Robert Sommer, is a way of creating buildings that fit occupants and users better by involving them in the planning process. It is needed in societies that have splintered the building creation process into many specialist roles. Social design is a remedy for the malady in which architects see themselves primarily as artists, ignoring the basic needs and activities of occupants. This malady is now widely recognized, yet many buildings are still constructed without significant user involvement.

Social design aims to match settings to their occupants, to satisfy a variety of principal player needs, to promote personal control in the building, and to encourage social support. Under some circumstances, another goal may be to increase productivity or otherwise change behavior. Obstacles to social design include a lack of communication between those who pay for a building and those who use or occupy it, resistance to the "extra effort" of involving users and occupants, unrealistic expectations that socially designed buildings will directly cure various evils, and inevitable conflict among principal players in the design process.

The design process includes programming, design, construction, use and adaptation, and postoccupancy evaluation. Programming consists of three phases: understanding the needs of users, involving them in the possibilities of design, and translating their needs into design guidelines, goals the actual design should achieve. The first phase involves discerning user needs through surveys and interviews, observing their behavior, and studying the traces they leave.

The second phase, direct user participation in the design process, increases steadily from traditional to directed to joint planning. It includes encouraging, activating, and educating users, and involving them directly in the planning process. Social designers often find themselves in a strong advocacy position, arguing for the interests of the average building user against the interests of other principal players.

The third phase, formulating design guidelines, requires that specific goals be set. These vary from building to building but a widely useful group of them includes the provision of shelter and security, appropriate social contact, positive symbolic identification, task instrumentality, pleasure, and the opportunity for growth. Turning these guidelines into plans and reality is the job of architects and construction companies. The environmental psychologist returns later to monitor user behavior and adaptation of the new building. Postoccupancy evaluation examines the effectiveness of the program and design, using a variety of social science tools. Together with programming, postoccupancy evaluation is perhaps the major activity of practicing environmental psychologists.

XV. RESOURCE MANAGEMENT

A second major application of environmental psychology is to improve the management of nature and its many essential but limited resources. Each individual manages a steady supply of natural resources that have been converted into products. Some of these resources come from limited sources called commons. A commons is a pool of desirable materials that may be harvested by a number of individuals or organizations that share access to it. Commons dilemmas occur when harvesting of natural resources proceeds faster than the resource can regenerate; individuals must decide whether to maximize their own gain or the gain of the group, including themselves. Social traps are similar, but emphasize the time dimension; one is "trapped" as the eventual outcome of repeatedly yielding to short-term rewards while ignoring long-term costs. Social dilemma is the general term for these conflicts. The idea may sound abstract, but it applies to so many everyday situations (e.g., recycling, littering, energy conservation, endangered species, lumbering, fishing, pollution, etc.) that it is useful as a powerful general concept.

Field experiments on social dilemmas are nearly impossible and field studies are uncommon. Many simulations of social dilemmas have been investigated in laboratories, but judging from participants' reactions, these may not be as unrepresentative of everyday behavior as one might think.

The quality of resource management depends on the resource itself, characteristics of the managers, and the rules governing the harvest. Cooperation seems to decline as the importance of the resource increases and to improve as the resource is depleted—two ominous signs. As children develop, their ability to manage commons dilemmas increases. The results of many studies suggest that when a commons dilemma exists, part of the resource should be allocated to each participant to manage, friendship and trust should be encouraged among the participants, the number of participants should be kept small, and participants should communicate, make public choices, and be subject to punishment for selfish decisions, although positive incentives for cooperation are even more effective. Further, we should give individuals experience operating the commons, require minimal contributions where they are suitable (in social dilemmas where the participants must donate to keep the resource alive), and point out the benefits of altruism in the commons. Last but certainly not least, we should try to increase the payoff for cooperation if possible.

Several theories of social dilemmas have been described. Tragic choice theory maintains that self-interest cannot be overcome except by the creation of a very strong central authority; this is unpleasant but necessary for the survival of the commons. Without such a central authority, the production and distribution of resources will be organized so as to benefit the wealthy at the expense of both the poor and the commons. Social trap theory applies a reinforcement perspective social dilemmas, suggesting that better management of the commons would follow from a restructuring of reinforcement timing. Like tragic choice theory, a centralized authority appears necessary. Equity theory emphasizes the importance of perceived equality in resource allocation. Cooperation may increase if participants believe others are receiving goods in proportion to the effort invested, no more and no less. But this could still lead to the extinction of a commons: if everyone works hard and harvests just as hard, depletion will occur; if perceived equity is cognitively altered, over-harvesting can be justified to oneself. Limited processing theory postulates that most individuals act selfishly, not because they are evil but because the dangers of defection simply do not occur to them. Its solution is clear: begin by making more individuals aware of the consequences of over-using resources that are in limited supply. [*See* EQUITY.]

Two social dilemmas are pollution and energy use. Pollution is a "give-some" form of social dilemma: individuals or organizations cleanse their own hands but dirty the commons. Air pollution is one example; it is an old problem caused by individuals as well as industry that occurs in both rural and urban areas, occurs indoors and outdoors, and affects our behavior as well as our health. Its behavioral effects are subtle, but probably include constraining the kinds of activities we engage in, mildly impairing cognitive processing, and increasing interpersonal and psychiatric problems. Efforts directed against air pollution have been blunted by our tendency to adapt to it and by the high perceived cost of correcting it. Litter is another form of pollution; it has multiple costs. Educational campaigns have sensitized most individuals to the problem, but too often behavior does not change accordingly. Littering is usually a mindless activity. Attribution strategies appear to reduce littering behavior, but may be difficult ethically. Certain strategies for combatting the problem reliably cut 15–20% of litter, sometimes more. These approaches include prompts, reinforcements for picking up others' litter, reinforcements for properly disposing of one's own litter, modeling, and environmental designs that make it easy to dispose of litter properly.

Energy use is a social dilemma when it is easier to waste energy, particularly from nonrenewable sources, in the service of a short-term goal than to conserve it for the future. Up to 50% savings could be achieved in ideal conditions, which would include an integration of psychological, economic, and engineering contributions. Conservers include those with enough money to purchase energy-saving devices so they can save over the long haul, those who must conserve because they cannot afford much gasoline, air conditioning, or fuel oil, those who have adopted a voluntary simplicity lifestyle and feel a personal responsibility for energy problems, those who are willing to make moderate public commitments toward energy conservation, and those whose energy use is monitored and frequently fed back to them. Conservation may be enhanced by some appeals from authorities. Educational campaigns seem to change attitudes, priming individuals for changing behavior, but do little the change behavior by themselves. Feedback and goal setting have achieved 20% savings. A housing development that integrated several design innovations with a group of ecologically oriented residents will approach the upper limit of 50% energy savings.

Bibliography

Bell, P. A., Fisher, J. D., Baum, A., and Greene, T. C. (1990). "Environmental Psychology," 3rd ed. Holt, Rinehart and Winston, Fort Worth, TX.

Gifford, R. (1987). "Environmental Psychology: Principles and Practice." Allyn and Bacon, Needham Heights, MA.

Sommer, R. (1983). "Social Design." Prentice-Hall, Englewood Cliffs, NJ.

Stokols, D., and Altman, I. (1987). "Handbook of Environmental Psychology." Wiley, New York.

EPILEPSY

Peter J. Snyder and William B. Barr
Long Island Jewish Medical Center

Glossary

Clonic Alternating contraction and relaxation of muscles.

Congenital Present at birth.

Convulsion Paroxysms of involuntary muscular contractions and/or relaxations.

Electroencephalography The amplification and recording of electrical potentials of the brain from electrodes that are usually attached to the scalp.

Epileptogenic focus A discrete area of the brain wherein the electrical discharges that give rise to seizure activity originate.

Etiology Pertaining to the cause or causes of a disease or illness.

Gliosis A proliferation of neuroglial tissue (largely non-nervous, supporting tissue of the brain and spinal cord) in the central nervous system.

Ictus The period of time during which an epileptic seizure occurs.

Paroxysm A sudden, periodic attack or recurrence of symptoms. A sudden spasm or convulsion of any kind.

Seizure A recurrent paroxysmal event that is characteristic of epilepsy; may or may not include impairments of consciousness and/or convulsions.

Tonic Increased muscle tone sustained over a given length of time, such as during a seizure.

Uncus A "hooked" shape anterior portion of the hippocampal gyrus, within the temporal lobe of the brain.

EPILEPSY is a common neurological disorder characterized by sudden, brief attacks that may alter motor activity, consciousness, and sensory experiences. Convulsive seizures are the most common type of paroxysmal event, but any recurrent seizure pattern is considered "epilepsy." Many forms of epilepsy have been linked to viral, fungal, and parasitic infections of the central nervous system, known metabolic disturbances, the ingestion of toxic agents, brain lesions, tumors or congenital defects, or cerebral trauma. Although the direct causes of seizures are not always readily observable, with the advent of sophisticated histological, neuroimaging, and biochemical methods it is becoming increasingly possible to diagnose the causes of seizure disorders that have, in the past, been difficult to identify (e.g., microscopic brain lesions).

Epilepsy is best thought of as a class of symptoms rather than a "disease" per se. As described above, epilepsy can result from a myriad of differing types of insults to the nervous system, ranging from identifiable structural pathology including space-occupying lesions (e.g., brain tumors, vascular malformations) to pathological processes of unknown etiology and indiscernible by current neurodiagnostic techniques.

I. HISTORICAL PERSPECTIVES

Epilepsy has been known to mankind since the dawn of civilization, and it has been described in the literatures of most of the world's major religions. Until fairly recently, it was thought to result from possession by evil spirits or demons, or from punishment by celestial gods. The Greeks first used the word epilepsy to describe the occurrence of someone "seized by forces from without," with the earliest medical text on this disorder, *On the Sacred Disease,* being written in approximately 400 B.C.E. by Hippocrates. In that text, Hippocrates contended that the Olympian gods were not inclined to inflict evil diseases on mortal beings, and that epilepsy

Encyclopedia of Human Behavior, Volume 2
Copyright © 1994 by Academic Press, Inc. All rights of reproduction in any form reserved.

instead is a natural disease with neurologic causes (i.e., an excess of phlegm rushing into the blood vessels of the brain).

Although Hippocrates' biologic theory of epileptogenesis reflected the physiologic theories of his day, he argued that epilepsy was not the product of supernatural influences, and so treatment should not rely on the use of magic. This great advance in understanding of epilepsy, as well as other major strides in neuroanatomical knowledge, was nearly lost in the middle ages. Medieval physicians (with few notable exceptions, such as the Spanish physician Moses Maimonides) believed that epilepsy, or the "falling sickness," was caused by either demonic possession or regular variations in the lunar cycle.

These widely accepted supernatural explanations for epilepsy were again replaced, during the Renaissance period (14th–17th centuries), by naturalistic theories, but clarity regarding the causes and treatment of seizure disorders lagged behind advances in other medical disciplines. It was not until the mid-19th century that the British neurologist John Hughlings Jackson first proposed that epileptic seizures result from discrete areas ("foci") that may be potentially localized within the brains of his patients.

Throughout the 20th century, great strides have been made in the ability to search for and isolate areas of the brain that give rise to paroxysmal epileptiform activity in individual patients. These advances are largely due to the invention of methods for the electrical stimulation of, and recording from, the cerebral cortex. The foundations of this technology lay in the early work by the German physiologists G. Fritsch (1838–1927) and E. Hitzig (1838–1907). The Fritsch and Hitzig studies, using dogs sedated by ether anesthesia, showed that specific behaviors could be elicited by the electrical stimulation of discrete cortical areas. For example, they found that the stimulation of a specific lateral frontal region, with a weak current, led to muscular contraction of the limbs on the opposite side of the body. Conversely, the application of a stronger electrical stimulus caused a convulsive seizure. Finally, the removal of that area of the dog's brain resulted in contralateral motor deficits.

The Fritsch and Hitzig experiments were undeniably influential to the British physician Sir David Ferrier (1843–1928), a pupil of the Scottish logician and psychologist A. Bain (1818–1903). In 1884, Ferrier published his discovery of both the location of the motor cortex in primates, and that stimulation of discrete portions of the motor area led to highly predictable responses (e.g., leg movements). These early studies led to the later development of reliable methods, by O. Foerster (1936) in Germany, and W. Penfield and H. Jasper (1954) at the Montreal Neurological Institute, for the electrical stimulation of the human cerebral cortex. These stimulation studies were specifically designed to determine the sites of epileptogenic involvement, within the cerebral cortex, in cases of incurable epilepsy.

Throughout the 1920s and 1930s, similar advances were being made in methods for the recording (as opposed to stimulation) of electrical activity in the human brain (electroencephalography, or EEG). The invention of EEG largely resulted from the work of the German psychiatrist Hans Berger (1873–1941). Berger first showed that rhythmic ("spike-and-wave") electrical activity, now considered to be the hallmark of an epileptic seizure, can be recorded from the surface of the brain. The advent of EEG has since led to radical improvements in patient care, in that it provides a painless, noninvasive technique for diagnosing seizure disorders. Electroencephalographic techniques will be discussed in greater detail later in this chapter. [*See* BRAIN ELECTRIC ACTIVITY.]

For a comprehensive historical perspective of epilepsy, the reader is referred to *The Falling Sickness* by Oswei Temkin (1971), which is the most scholarly work on this topic to date.

II. PREVALENCE

Approximately 2% of the population will have at least one seizure some time during their lives, and many of these individuals develop chronic seizure disorders. Although 70% of persons with epilepsy are successfully treated with available medications, about 30% develop chronic seizures that do not respond completely or satisfactorily to anticonvulsant medications.

The existence of this smaller, and yet sizeable, group of people with epilepsy supports the hypothesis that early seizures may serve to intensify any latent predisposition of an individual's central nervous system to produce further seizure discharges (an idea first advanced by the British neurologist William Gowers in 1881).

III. MODERN PERSPECTIVES ON DIAGNOSIS AND TREATMENT

A. Etiology and Classification of the Epilepsies

Epilepsy may be classified by either seizure type or causation, and classification systems have been developed with both views in mind. Several types of seizures are associated with specific cerebral locations of discharging epileptogenic foci. The differential diagnoses of various seizure disorders are important areas of ongoing research and debate.

William Gowers published the first classification system for epilepsy in 1885. He was the first clinician to conceive of two groups of epilepsy patients, those with structural brain disease (e.g., brain tumors, vascular disease) and those with an unidentified tendency toward seizures (e.g., secondary to toxic or metabolic disorders). Gowers felt that it is inaccurate to assume categorically that epilepsy is due to observable central nervous system (CNS) lesions. Rather, sometimes the CNS disturbance causing seizure discharges may be due to a biochemical disturbance affecting isolated groups of nerve cells. [*See* CENTRAL NERVOUS SYSTEM.]

There are, of course, other ways to separate seizure disorders into specific subgroups. For example, certain epileptic syndromes are common to specific age-groups, such those that are seen in children (i.e., neonatal seizures, infantile spasms, and febrile convulsions). These age-determined syndromes are characterized by specific seizure types, which can be correlated with particular EEG patterns and likely prognoses. Unfortunately, previous attempts to categorize these syndromes have been unsuccessful, resulting in a large number of subtypes that are each rather infrequently seen in clinical settings.

Given the myriad of different ways of classifying a complex set of phenomena (with a wide range of possible motor, sensory, psychological, and behavioral symptoms), dramatic refinements in seizure classification did not occur until the Commission on Classification and Terminology of the International League Against Epilepsy (ILAE) introduced a formal classification system for seizure types in 1970. A new classification system was needed because many old terms for different types of seizures (e.g., grand mal, petit mal) were seen as confusing and often misleading. Several types of seizures that are listed in the ILAE classification system will be reviewed below.

B. Phenomenology and Classification of Seizures

The ILAE classification system, last revised in 1985, separates seizures that are primarily generalized in their origin from within the brain from those that are localized (partial) in their origin. A further separation may be made on the basis of whether individual types of seizures involve convulsions or not. Seizures that involve convulsions, that is, involuntary muscular contractions and/or relaxation ("spasms"), are considered by the mass media, and by general public knowledge, to be the "prototypic" seizure type. A modified and abbreviated version of the ILAE classification scheme is shown in Table I.

As can be seen in Table I, epileptic seizures are not always convulsive. Seizure types are usually divided into two broad groups according to the manner in which the epileptiform electrical activity spreads throughout the brain: generalized seizures and partial (including complex-partial) seizures.

1. Generalized Seizures

Approximately one-third of all epilepsy patients suffer from generalized seizure disorders, including a variety of generalized motor and "absence" seizure types. In primary generalized seizures, meaning that the seizure does not first begin as a partial seizure

TABLE I
Abbreviated Classification of Epileptic Seizures

I. Convulsive seizures
  A. Generalized seizures
    1. Myoclonic seizures
    2. Clonic seizures
    3. Tonic seizures
    4. Tonic-clonic seizures ("grand mal")
    5. Atonic seizures
  B. Partial seizures evolving to secondarily generalized seizures
    1. Simple partial seizures evolving to generalized seizures
    2. Complex partial seizures evolving to generalized seizures
    3. Simple partial seizures evolving to complex partial seizures and then to generalized seizures
II. Nonconvulsive seizures
  A. Generalized seizures
    1. Absence Seizures ("petit mal")
  B. Simple partial seizures
    1. With motor symptoms
    2. With somatosensory or special sensory symptoms
    3. With autonomic symptoms
    4. With psychic symptoms
  C. Complex partial seizures (CPS)
    1. Beginning as simple partial seizures and progressing to impairment of consciousness
      (a) With no other features
      (b) With features as in II.B.1–4 (see above)
      (c) With automatisms
    2. With impairment of consciousness at onset ("psychomotor")
      (a) With no other features
      (b) With features as in II.B.1–4 (see above)
      (c) With automatisms

(see below), the paroxysmal discharges typically arise from deep structures located in the base and middle of the brain (brainstem or thalamus). Unlike many patients with partial seizures, patients with generalized seizures do not experience any psychic or sensory disturbances at the start of the seizure ("aura"), and there are no focal motor behaviors elicited by the seizure (e.g., automatic motor movement of limbs on only one side of the body).

Generalized motor seizures are divided into subtypes (e.g., tonic, clonic) depending on the motor sequence observed during the seizure event (see Table I), and they are collectively the most common of the primary generalized epilepsies. There is some evidence pointing to a genetic basis for some of the subtypes of this group of seizure disorders.

Typical absence ("petit mal") seizures usually occur in childhood, between the ages of 4 and 12, and only rarely persist into adulthood. These seizures are associated with a brief (5- to 30-second) staring spell and a highly characteristic EEG pattern.

2. Partial and Complex-Partial Seizures

Of the 2% of the population with epilepsy, two-thirds have partial or complex-partial seizure disorders. Most behavioral alterations, that may be attributed to the presence of a seizure disorder, are seen in patients with partial and complex-partial seizures.

Partial seizures are those that begin in one part of the brain and that may or may not spread to other regions. Partial seizures usually consist of specific motor, sensory, and/or psychic alterations. The psychic changes are often accompanied by stereotyped automatic movements (leading to the term "psychomotor") such as lip-smacking, chewing, or eye-blinking. These seizures often originate from one or both of the temporal lobes (usually from the hippocampus or amygdala, structures that are buried within the temporal lobes), and they are often accompanied by emotional changes that are quite variable from one person to another. The most common of these emotional changes is fear, but sadness, pleasure, or "deja vu" feelings are frequently reported as well. Hallucinations or misperceptions are also common ictal phenomena of partial and complex-partial seizures. These sensory experiences can be auditory, tactile, visual, or olfactory.

In "simple-partial" epilepsy, there is no alteration in consciousness as a result of the seizure discharge. In "complex-partial" epilepsy, impaired consciousness results directly from the seizure discharge. Although both simple-partial and complex-partial seizures typically result from a localizeable seizure focus, the electrical discharge may spread to other cortical areas and trigger discharges from other possible epileptogenic foci, resulting in secondarily generalized seizures. Often the specific ictal motor and sensory phenomena exhibited by individual patients correspond to the cerebral localization, or focus, of the epileptic discharge, and the progression of symptoms may indicate the degree of spread of abnormal electrocerebral activity during a seizure. Should this electrocerebral activity spread widely enough, it will be associated with readily apparent alterations in consciousness (complex-partial seizures).

In a large scale study of 6000 epilepsy patients, 39.7% of the patients showed symptoms of complex-partial seizures, and most of these patients suffered from temporal lobe epilepsy. This implies that roughly 40% of all epilepsy patients have either unilateral or bilateral temporal lobe epileptogenic foci. More specifically, temporal lobe epilepsy afflicts approximately 25% of children and 50% of adults with epilepsy. Because temporal lobe epilepsy is the largest single type of seizure disorder, and since it is most frequently associated with cognitive, emotional, personality, and behavioral alterations (both during and between seizures), most of the following sections of this article concentrate primarily on this type of epilepsy.

C. Diagnosis

A seizure is basically a natural response to a physiologically noxious stimulus (e.g., lesions, tumors, and/or scars within the brain). Historically, the problem of locating the discharging lesion in temporal lobe epilepsy developed along two lines of investigation: (1) the repeated finding of a specific type of lesion (gliosis) in one part of the hippocampus (Ammon's horn); and (2) research resulting from the demonstration in 1889 by Hughlings Jackson of a focal lesion in the anterior tip of the temporal lobe, including the amygdala, in patients who were prone to "uncinate fits" (temporal lobe epilepsy). The clinical significance of these medial temporal lobe lesions had become firmly established by the early 1950s.

Many investigators have reported specific cognitive deficits, such as memory disturbances, that differentiate temporal lobe epilepsy patients from patients with other types of epilepsy. Other clinical features are also useful in making this diagnostic distinction. For example, in comparison to other types of epilepsy patients, those with temporal lobe epilepsy often have greater difficulty on standard tests of language and acquired factual knowledge. They also tend to show more impairments in peer relations. Temporal lobe epilepsy patients also are more likely to have a family history of epilepsy, a higher incidence of early anoxic episodes, and a higher incidence of febrile seizures in infancy.

Several different diagnostic techniques are routinely used to infer the location of epileptogenic foci, ranging from *structural* brain imaging techniques (i.e., computed tomographic imaging (CT), magnetic resonance imaging (MRI)) and the imaging of brain *function* or metabolism (e.g., measurements of regional cerebral blood flow (rCBF) with positron emission tomography (PET), single-photon emission tomography (SPECT), EEG, and neuropsychological examination). All of these techniques are highly complex, and no single diagnostic approach, in isolation, provides a definitive set of answers that can be used to guide surgical decisions. The proper diagnostic evaluation of epilepsy patients who are not easily controlled by medications (see below) thus requires the collective efforts of a multi-disciplinary team, all members of which are typically on staff at epilepsy centers. At the very least, these teams consist of a neurologist, neurosurgeon, neuropsychologist, social worker, and neurological nurses. Two broad types of diagnostic methods that are employed at such centers are described below.

1. Electroencephalography (EEG)

In the late 1800s the German physiologist Hermann L. F. von Helmholtz (1821–1894) became the first scientist to accurately measure electrical impulses that travel along the nerve fibers. Helmholtz's initial groundbreaking work, and the subsequent flurry of discoveries proving that the brain both is electrically active and it produces rhythmic waves, led to what is considered to be the single greatest breakthrough in the history of epilepsy research.

Later work in the 1920s by Professor Hans Berger, which was initially regarded with a great deal of skepticism, showed that the currents generated by the brain could be amplified electronically in order to permit recording through the human skull and scalp. The technological underpinnings of EEG are difficult to understand without some rudimentary background in the physics of electricity. Briefly put, each EEG channel has two inputs, and these inputs are typically derived from electrodes placed within an inch or two of each other on the scalp. The EEG recording from each channel is, then, an algebraic sum of the electrical signals that are picked up from each input. These electrical signals, in turn, are generated by large groups of neurons in the area of the brain located directly below each electrode that is placed on the patient's scalp.

As it is used today, EEG studies of epilepsy patients require several separate channels. The standard placement of multiple electrodes over the scalp (a predetermined "montage") is necessary because the brain is quite large, and some electrical waveforms (especially epileptiform activity) may emanate from discrete cortical regions rather than from the entire brain. Hence, without the use of multiple electrode sites, any degree of specificity in identifying the general location of epileptiform activity would be impossible.

As mentioned above, the application of EEG has become the single most important method with which to diagnose seizure disorders and to track progress in treating patients with epilepsy. EEG provides a set of diagnostic procedures that are equally powerful for the evaluation and treatment of both patients who respond well to treatment with anticonvulsant medications and patients who are being considered for epilepsy surgery because treatment with medications have not been successful. Differing types of electrical patterns, observed with EEG, are particularly useful in diagnosing specific types of seizure disorders. For example, absence seizures (see Table I) are characterized by generalized spike-and-wave complexes at a fast rate of 3 to 4 discharges per second. In comparison, the convulsive seizures that are observed in children with Lennox-Gastaut syndrome are characterized by spike-and-wave complexes at a much slower rate of 1 to 2.5 discharges per second.

In the case of patients who are being considered for possible surgical intervention, seizures are recorded from the surface of the skull, or by electrodes that are either placed on the surface of the brain (after the removal of a section of the patient's skull) or inserted into the brain itself. Their actual seizures as well as the EEG data are simultaneously recorded on closed-circuit television (CCTV). These recordings are typically made over the course of several days (24 hours per day), and they enable the neurologist to define the diffuse or focal origin of seizures.

The clinical application of EEG provides a window into the electrophysiological functioning of the human brain. Recent advances in neuroradiology have allowed for other methods, such as SPECT, PET, and fast-MRI images, to directly observe where, in a patient's brain, there might be areas of decreased blood flow or oxygen uptake. Similarly, other types of diagnostic procedures provide detailed analyses of how well different areas of the brain are functioning, for the mediation of higher cognitive and behavioral functions.

2. Other Neurodiagnostic Procedures

In addition to the recording of seizures by CCTV/EEG studies, functional neuroimaging studies and a comprehensive neurophsychological examination all serve to provide corroborating evidence for focal cerebral dysfunction. Hence, these studies further help to identify the specific location of epileptogenic activity in the brain. For example, the neuropsychological examination is useful both for the verification of the site of structural lesions and for the identification of lesions that are not observable with neuroimaging techniques (and for which EEG data are equivocal). Additionally, the neuropsychological examination is useful in the presurgical identification of surgical candidates who are likely to suffer debilitating functional impairments following surgery.

Patients with intractable epilepsy who are being considered for focal resection of a temporal lobe are especially at risk for developing impairments in memory and speech functions postsurgery. To diminish such risks, cortical and subcortical regions that are crucial for cognition, in particular for memory and speech/language functions, must be identified before surgery. Therefore, the choice of which psychological assessment tests to use must be based on two criteria: the first is the isolation of the cognitive functions typically subsumed by the brain region that is presumed to contain the epileptogenic focus; the second is the range of important abilities potentially affected by surgery. The type and extent of behavioral/cognitive impairments that can be predicted to follow surgical intervention will determine whether a patient is an appropriate candidate for surgery, as well as type and extent of surgical resection.

D. Treatment

Patients who experience recurrent seizures are typically given therapeutic dosages of an anticonvulsant medication. Approximately 70% of all epilepsy patients are successfully treated with medications, in that they experience a satisfactory reduction in the frequency of seizures. Although new pharmaceutical agents are continually being developed and tested for the treatment of epilepsy, four compounds are the most commonly prescribed drugs for seizure disorders: carbamazepine (Tegretol), valproic acid (Depakote), phenytoin (Dilantin), and phenobarbital.

All of these drugs, if taken under the supervision of a neurologist who is trained in the treatment of epilepsy, are both safe and usually effective. Patients who are placed on these medications must be monitored on a regular basis because of the risk of potentially harmful side-effects if the required dosage changes, for any of several reasons, and too much of these medications are taken by mistake.

When treatment with medication is unsuccessful in controlling a seizure disorder (for about 30% of persons with epilepsy), surgical intervention is typically considered. Epilepsy patients are suitable candidates for surgical intervention if the seizures are so severe and frequent that they seriously interfere with the patient's quality of life. The type of surgical approach largely depends on the location of the dysfunctional brain tissue that is causing the seizure discharges. For example, if there are multiple epileptogenic foci, located bilaterally (that is, within both left and right hemispheres of the brain), the best approach may be to cut through a large portion of the major bundle of nerve fibers that allow for communication between the hemispheres (corpus callosum), so that a seizure that starts on one side is not able to spread to the other side. This type of treatment does not stop seizures from starting, but it often reduces the severity of the seizures.

For patients with a single, discrete epileptogenic foci, the direct removal of the brain tissue where the seizures originate is typically considered. For these patients, either the entire lobe of the brain (e.g., temporal lobe) that contains the seizure focus is removed ("lobectomy"), or only the specific area of dysfunctional tissue is removed ("lesionectomy").

The anticipated benefits of surgery depend largely on the size and location of the discharging foci. The frequency with which surgery fails to alleviate seizures increases in patients with multiple or bilateral epileptogenic foci (meaning that there are areas of epileptogenic tissue within both sides of the brain), and where only part of the discharging tissue is removed. Nonetheless, the removal of well-defined focal epileptogenic lesions results in a substantial reduction in seizure frequency in 60–80% of patients following surgery. If a comprehensive presurgical diagnostic evaluation leads to the formation of a surgical plan that reduces the risk of postoperative impairments in memory, language, and other higher cognitive functions, the outcome of surgery is generally quite favorable.

IV. BEHAVIORAL CONSEQUENCES

A. Intelligence

The question of whether seizure disorders lead to lowered levels of intellectual functioning has been an important area of study since the early 1940s. This question is actually very complex, and there have been no simple answers as of yet. This issue may be broken down into three parts: whether alterations in intellectual functioning are related to (1) the presence and duration of the seizure disorder; (2) the underlying neurobiological dysfunction that causes (or may be caused by) the seizures; and (3) side-effects of chronic anticonvulsant medication treatment. [*See* INTELLIGENCE.]

Although several investigators have reported a relationship between epilepsy and intellectual deficits in children, studies of children both before and after the onset of seizures found that the occurrence of seizures is not causally related to lower intellectual functioning. Similarly, no significant differences have been found in the performance of children with febrile seizures (between the ages of 1 month and 7 years) who experienced no subsequent afebrile seizures, versus their seizure-free siblings, on standard tests of intellectual functioning. In fact, this finding holds true for those children who experienced febrile seizures lasting 30 minutes or longer.

With regard to adult patients, the relationship between intelligence and the frequency and focal onset of epileptiform activity has been examined. Lower levels of intellectual functioning, as measured by the Wechsler Adult Intelligence Scale—Revised (WAIS-R), are associated with generalized, rather than focal seizures. A strong relationship has also been found between the total amount of epileptiform EEG activity and performance on the WAIS-R.

In studies of temporal lobe epilepsy patients, no significant differences have been found between patients with right- versus left-hemisphere foci on any of the WAIS-R intelligence quotient (IQ) index scores. However, the duration of the disorder has been shown to be positively correlated with the degree of cognitive dysfunction as well as poor surgical outcome after unilateral temporal lobe resection. An early age of onset of the seizure disorder is associated with lower (WAIS-R) IQ index scores.

The frequency of seizure activity appears to exert a strong effect on intellectual functioning. Patients who experience a high seizure frequency (more than one seizure per month) demonstrate greater impairments in overall intellectual functioning than do patients with a low seizure frequency (one seizure every 4–6 months). In addition, an increased frequency of major motor seizures is correlated with increasing levels of neurocognitive impairment. To summarize, there is an increased risk of impairments in intellectual functioning in patients who (1) develop seizure disorders at an early age; (2) experience a high frequency of seizures; and (3) have seizure disorders for a long time. This trend is supported by studies of the hippocampal-dentate complex, using the Golgi staining method to examine the microscopic structure of the neurons (brain cells) in this region (buried within the middle of the temporal lobes). These studies found a wide variation in the degree of cellular changes across patients with varying durations of the disorder, suggesting a continual degenerative process, rather than one due to a single cortical insult prior to the onset of the disorder.

Finally, many studies have been conducted in order to determine the effects of chronic administration of anticonvulsant medications on intellectual functioning. These studies have generally shown that two of the four major medications, carbamezapine and valproic acid, are *not* associated with any undesirable side-effects in cognitive functioning. The chronic administration of the other two medications, phenytoin (at higher dosages) and phenobarbital (a barbiturate), however, has been found to lead to impairments in concentration and motor speed (e.g., how fast an individual is able to pick up and manipulate objects).

B. Cognitive Functioning

Epilepsy is typically a disorder of children and younger age adults, and the etiology of many seizure disorders in this young population can often be attributed to birth or early postnatal trauma. Because epilepsy of childhood origin is common, epilepsy populations are characterized by a greater prevalence of anomalous cortical organization of functions such as speech, language, memory, and handedness. The frequent occurrence of amodal patterns of cortical organization for higher cognitive functions, in this patient population, means that the typical assumptions that are made, based on studies of brain lesions in adults, are only partly applicable or frankly misleading.

A number of variables related to epilepsy (e.g., age of onset of the seizure disorder, frequency of seizure activity) and variables related to the treatment of epilepsy (i.e., side-effects of anticonvulsive medications) exert strong impacts on a diverse range of cognitive functions. This set of reciprocal relationships between the clinical and neural factors that underlie the cognitive deficits, and the potentially affected functions (e.g., attention and concentration, learning and memory, speech and language, perceptual-motor skills, and executive (decision-making) abilities) are too vast to fully explore in this chapter, and so only a few areas of study are discussed below.

One major set neurocognitive functions evaluated by the neuropsychologist relates to language. Speech functions may be assessed by a variety of techniques including controlled word production, confrontation naming, sentence repetition, rapid rote reading with/without distractors. A common finding from this type of evaluation is that patients with left temporal lobe epilepsy, as compared to those with right temporal lobe epilepsy, often show a mild impairment in their ability to name objects ("anomia"). Additionally, in comparison to patients with generalized seizures, patients with psychomotor seizures (most of them presumably being temporal lobe epileptics) had a clear deficit in the fluidity of speech production.

A second major area of neuropsychological investigation that is relevant to the study of epilepsy patients is memory functioning. The identification of the cortical and subcortical areas crucial for memory in presurgical patients has been stimulated by research on both animals and humans that has shown the possibility that the integrity of memory functioning might be at risk for some patients following neurosurgery. In 1957, Scoville and Milner published evidence that damage to the medial temporal region of the human brain causes a profound memory impairment (amnestic syndrome). They found that if bilateral resections of the medial temporal lobe included only the uncus and amygdala, no amnestic symptomatology resulted postsurgery. If, on the other hand, the lesion extended far enough posteriorly to include the hippocampus, a memory deficit developed, the severity of which depended on how large and how far back (posteriorly) the resection is made. [*See* AMNESIA; MEMORY.]

Recent studies have succeeded in establishing a model of medial temporal amnesia in the monkey, and it is clear that bilateral damage to the hippocampus and surrounding temporal lobe cortex produces a global anterograde amnesia in humans. This memory impairment has been found to be selective, in that the ability to acquire new perceptual-motor skills is spared. The neural networks underlying memory encoding, storage, and retrieval are complex and well-integrated, branching to many areas of the brain that are only recently being recognized as important in memory function. However, a common theme running throughout the research in this area is the paramount importance of the hippocampus (in humans) for the encoding and retrieval of new learning. [*See* HIPPOCAMPAL FORMATION.]

This finding is crucial in the diagnostic work-up of epilepsy surgery patients because in many instances, both (left and right) hippocampi do not contribute equally to the overall integrity of the complex neural network for memory. Rather, many patients have a more unilateral distribution of memory patency, favoring one hippocampus over the other, due to an early brain injury. Thus, if the only remaining functional hippocampus happens to also be epileptogenic, the removal of this structure may eliminate the seizure activity but it would also be akin to the removal of both hippocampi—with the associated disastrous results for memory functioning being a likely postoperative result.

There are several ways to examine memory functioning in epilepsy patients. For example, impairment in the encoding, storage, and recall of verbal information may be measured via story narratives or with serial list learning procedures. In the former task, the patient is afforded the benefit of processing information that is embedded in a salient social context, while in the latter task the patient must remember a list of words that may not share any contextual relationship. Patients with temporal lobe epilepsy tend to show a greater short-term verbal/semantic memory deficit (i.e., recall of narrative texts) than do patients with extratemporal epileptogenic lesions. This finding seems to be independent of group differences in overall intellectual functioning, age, education, age of onset of the seizure disorder, and medication.

Some investigators have found significant differences in verbal memory functions between left- and right-temporal lobe epilepsy patients. Specifically, left-temporal lesioned patients are often more impaired, relative to the right-foci group, on verbal learning tasks. An opposite pattern of results is often found on two tasks that measure memory for visual-spatial information, with the right temporal group being significantly more impaired on these tasks than the left temporal group.

C. Personality and Psychopathology

Galen, a Roman physician and student of Hippocratic writings, was the first to observe, in about 200 A.D. that people who suffer from repeated seizures often show alterations in personality. This ancient observation has been corroborated by modern investigators. Specifically, it is generally felt that patients with temporal lobe epilepsy (TLE) show a higher incidence of psychiatric difficulties than do patients with other types of epilepsy. Some authors have suggested that the prevalence of psychotic disorders in TLE patients might be as high as 10–15%.

Early controlled studies of the prevalence of psychotic disorders in epilepsy patients showed that in TLE, psychotic disturbances were significantly associated with epileptogenic foci lateralized to the speech dominant (usually left) hemisphere. Significant correlations have also been reported between left-temporal lobe seizure foci and schizophrenia-like symptoms, and to a lesser degree, between right-sided foci and affective disorders (e.g., depression, obsessive–compulsive disorder). It should be noted, however, that although a number of studies have supported the position that psychoses, not attributable to solely peri-ictal behavioral and sensory disturbances, are prevalent among TLE patients, others have not been able to confirm this relationship. There have been many attempts to determine the effect of unilateral TLE on specific aspects of psychosocial behavior. One example of early work on this topic was the finding that, in interpreting cartoons, TLE patients tended to focus on irrelevant detail, were concrete, egocentric, and had a paranoid style. While these traits are not necessarily indicative of psychopathology, it has been suggested that the frequent occurrence of these behaviors in TLE patients might provide insight into the effect of localized temporal lobe neuropathology on the expression of one's personality.

This type of study led, in the late 1970s, to the development of personality questionnaires for use with TLE patients, to study the impact of specific types of epilepsy on human personality. A major result of this effort was the finding that patients with right temporal lobe pathology reported more elation, while patients with left temporal lobe pathology reported more anger, paranoia, and dependence. Additionally, right-sided TLE patients were significantly differentiated by items stressing externally demonstrated affect (e.g., unusual sexual attractions, helplessness, sadness, emotional arousability, moralistic fervor) and also by an overconcern with details and orderliness. Left-sided TLE patients were attributed with a sense of personal destiny, paranoia, humorlessness, conscientiousness.

Other research has shown that left-sided TLE patients may make more atypical assignments of affect labels to emotionally toned stimuli, while the right-sided TLE patients tend to assign emotional labels to the same stimuli in a fashion similar to that observed in healthy, neurologically normal control subjects. Although these general trends in research on the relationship between (temporal lobe) epilepsy and personality disturbances have been corroborated by numerous investigators, an equal number of scientists have been unable to replicate many of these findings. Thus, the precise relationship between various types of seizure disorders and personality and psychopathology remains very controversial.

Although many comparative studies with structured personality tests [e.g., the Minnesota Multiphasic Personality Inventory (MMPI)] have been conducted, many of them have failed to differentiate between groups of patients with various seizure types and epileptogenic foci. This implies that even if epileptic patients suffer from an increased prevalence of psychopathology, this may be attributable to other factors (e.g., anoxic events, head injury) that are only indirectly associated with the seizure disorder.

In 1984, the neuropsychologist Bruce P. Hermann and his colleague Steven Whitman completed a review of 64 studies published between 1962 and 1984, on the relationships between temporal lobe epilepsy and psychosis, aggression, sexual dysfunction, personality changes, affective disorders, and other types of psychopathology. They found that the results of all 64 studies may be separated into three main categories: (1) brain-related factors (e.g., neurologic, EEG, and neuropsychological variables); (2) non-brain-related factors (e.g., chronic illness, socioeconomic variables); and (3) treatment-related factors (e.g., medication side-effects). These authors argue that the study of the relationship between epilepsy and personality and psychopathology is highly complex. Furthermore, any putative relationship will be impacted on, to differing degrees, by a multitude of variables that form the three general factors that are listed above.

V. SOCIOLOGICAL PERSPECTIVES

A. Social Stigma

Most people with epilepsy are able to enjoy interesting and happy lives, as active members of the societies in which they live. As we have seen, however, some people with epilepsy can show a broad range of alterations in personality, emotional, cognitive, intellectual, sensory, and motor functioning as a result of their seizure disorders. In addition, some of them often face further problems in coping with epilepsy in their homes and communities. All epilepsy patients are at risk of suffering from social stigma, prejudice, or even hostility, which typically results from a lack of information and understanding.

This lack of understanding varies across racial and cultural groups, with some cultures persisting to this day in viewing epilepsy as infectious, "dirty," or due to pernicious supernatural influences. Although Western cultures no longer subscribe to this particular belief system, persons with epilepsy continue to encounter negative attitudes in many areas, ranging from immediate family and school environments to the job market. In fact, in some states in the United States, old laws remain in effect that prohibit persons with epilepsy from marrying and raising families.

B. Epilepsy and the Law

The law in most Western societies serves to both discriminate against and to protect people with epilepsy. For example, people with uncontrolled epilepsy are prohibited from operating motor vehicles. While this regulation is reasonable from a safety perspective, it is hard to accept for someone whose social life and employment opportunities are disrupted by this restriction.

There are considerable differences between states as far as legal restrictions are concerned. As mentioned above, there are marriage prohibition and sterilization laws still in effect in a few states, although they are not currently enforced. Epilepsy patients have also been discriminated against in their attempts to procure health and life insurance policies, although there has been moderate improvement in this legal arena over the past two decades.

Special services for epilepsy patients, including financial assistance, housing, education for handicapped children, and legal assistance services, have recently become more widely available. In the United States, the single most active resource center and organization for people with epilepsy and their families is the Epilepsy Foundation of America, Inc. (4351 Garden City Drive, Landover, MD 20785). This organization maintains a library that is open to any interested person (persons with epilepsy and their families, students, and health care providers) as well as a toll-free information telephone number: 1-800-EFA-4050.

Bibliography

Bennett, T. L. (Ed.) (1992). "The Neuropsychology of Epilepsy." Plenum, New York.

Delgado-Escueta, A. V., and Walsh, G. O. (1983). The selection process for surgery of intractable complex partial seizures: Surface EEG and depth electrography. In "Epilepsy" (A. A. Ward, Jr., J. K. Penry, and D. Purpura, eds.), pp. 295–326. Raven Press, New York.

Hermann, B. P., and Whitman, S. (1984). Behavioral and personality correlates of epilepsy: A review, methodological critique, and conceptual model. *Psychol. Bull.*, **95**, 451–497.

Rodin, E. (1987). An assessment of current views of epilepsy. *Epilepsia*, **28**, 267–271.

Temkin, O. (1971). "The Falling Sickness." Johns Hopkins University Press, Baltimore.

Trimble, M. R., and Bolwig, T. G. (Eds.) (1986). "Aspects of Epilepsy and Psychiatry." Wiley, New York.

Collections of Recent Articles

Issues in epilepsy—An agenda for the 21st century. *Epilepsia* (Suppl. 1) **33**, (1992).

Neuropsychology of partial epilepsy. *Epilepsia* (Suppl. 6) **33**, (1992).

Episodic Memory

Gary Gillund
College of Wooster

Glossary

Autobiographical memory Memory for personally experienced events or the context in which they were presented. Usually considered a component of episodic memory.

Context The spatial and temporal information that is present when material is learned or remembered. This may include environmental and internal context.

Dissociation A result in which an independent variable has one effect on one task and a different effect on another task. A dissociation is often taken as evidence that different memory systems exist.

Episodic memory Memory for information presented in a particular spatio-temporal context or memory for the context itself.

Procedural memory Memory for information that is prescriptive. This form of memory allows us to perform many behaviors.

Recall A memory task that simply requires a participant to report as much as she or he can remember about an event. Familiar examples include most essay exams and open-ended questions on questionnaires.

Recognition A memory task that requires a participant to distinguish previously studied material from new material. A familiar example is the multiple-choice test.

Semantic memory Memory for abstract facts and for information associated with language.

Source amnesia An inability to remember where or when some event was encountered although the fact that it was encountered is remembered.

Stochastic independence Statistical independence. The absence of a correlation between two variables. An inability to predict performance on one task given the score on another task.

EPISODIC MEMORY has been used in a heuristic sense to refer to memory for information that is dependent on the spatio-temporal context in which it was presented and tested. Episodic memory refers both to the memory for the material that depends on the context for efficient retrieval and to memory for the context itself. Episodic memory has also been used in a theoretical sense to refer to a specific memory system, distinct from other memory systems. The theoretical position is outlined in this article and, in the process, the heuristic use of the term also is made clear.

I. CONCEPTIONS OF EPISODIC MEMORY

A. Episodic Memory as a Heuristic

Endel Tulving first used the term episodic memory to label a type of experiment that asked questions about context-dependent and personally experienced events. A typical experiment might include a study phase in which a set of words would be presented to people and a test phase in which their memory for the words would be examined by some procedure, typically recall or recognition. The task is called an episodic memory task because the participants personally experienced the events and, in order for test performance to be successful, the participants must refer to events that occurred in a specific place and at a particular time. That is, they cannot recall just any words, only the words that occurred during the study phase, if they are to be accurate.

Episodic memory tasks were initially contrasted to semantic memory tasks. Semantic memory deals with factual information that appears independent

Copyright © 1994 by Academic Press, Inc. All rights of reproduction in any form reserved.

of context. A typical semantic memory study might be one in which participants are asked the definitions of several words. Successful performance on this task does not require personal experience with the words or definitions and it does not require access to the particular place and time in which the definition was experienced. Such information is typically not available. [*See* SEMANTIC MEMORY.]

Tulving's first use of the term episodic memory was therefore taxonomic. He wanted to distinguish between two types of tasks that appeared fundamentally different. Tulving argued that a categorization of memory experiments along an episodic/semantic dimension would lead to better insight into the nature of memory.

Almost all researchers in memory have acknowledged the usefulness of the heuristic sense of the term episodic memory. However, since Tulving first introduced the term, he has expanded the definition. Tulving, and others, have argued that episodic memory is a memory system. This theoretical position argues that there are several distinct but interdependent memory systems. Each system has its own operations, processes, and functions that distinguish it from other systems. This theoretical account of episodic memory has generated much research and a great deal of controversy. [*See* MEMORY.]

B. Episodic Memory as a Memory System

One goal of memory researchers is to find general principles or fundamental laws that govern memory performance. The search for these fundamental principles has been largely unsuccessful. As a result, many psychologists have sought to divide memory into different parts. The idea is that one reason the search for general principles has failed is that different memory systems use different processes, operate on different kinds of information, and serve different functions. Therefore, we are unlikely to find principles that hold across all systems.

Tulving has been one of the strongest proponents of the memory systems approach. Originally, he argued for just two systems—the episodic and semantic. Later the procedural system was added, and recently he has proposed five distinct systems. These systems differ along several dimensions and a few of the most important distinctions are described below.

Perhaps the most important distinction among memory systems is that they are all designed to deal with different kinds of information. The episodic system deals with information in context. Personally experienced information that depends on context for efficient retrieval defines episodic information. In contrast, for example, the semantic memory system is designed to deal with facts and language. The semantic memory system does not require access to contextual information to work efficiently. Semantic memory contains information not usually associated with any particular spatio-temporal context. As another example, the procedural memory system contains information that allows us to do things like play tennis, ride a bike, or read. This information is also context independent.

Fundamentally different operations are thought to be used by the different memory systems. Each system has a unique set of processes to store, organize, and retrieve information. For example, episodic memory is thought to be temporally organized. In some ways it can be thought of as a movie of a person's life. Portions of a person's past are organized and accessed along some temporal dimension when stored and recalled. In contrast, semantic memory is thought to be organized more like an encyclopedia in which related topics are stored together. Procedural memory is analogous to a set of prescriptions for how to perform certain tasks.

The differences that exist among the memory systems in the kinds of information with which they deal, their organization, and operations result in other differences. For example, the subjective experience of recalling information from each system differs across memory systems. When people recall information from the episodic system they often report an "I remember" sort of experience. That is, they often say things like "*I remember* eating pizza at the party." When recalling information from semantic memory, people often say or report a feeling of "I know." For example, people *know* that Lincoln was the 16th president of the United States or they *know* that the letters "d-o-g" mean dog. The procedural memory system is unique in that most people are not aware that they are using it. For example, most people have a very difficult time describing what they do to maintain their balance while riding a bicycle or even how they hold a pen while they write (without looking). Though these skills are well learned and people exhibit a memory for the skills by performing them, they probably cannot describe them without difficulty unless they have recently tried to teach someone else how to use those skills.

There are many other ways in which memory systems differ. Space limits the coverage of them in this article. Instead, I now turn to a brief evaluation of the kinds of experiments designed to test the idea of distinct memory systems.

II. EVIDENCE REGARDING AN EPISODIC MEMORY SYSTEM

A. Empirical Dissociations

The basic assumptions of the memory systems approach are that episodic memory differs from other memory systems in the type of information it uses, the operations performed on that information, and the functions it performs. However, episodic memory must interact with other memory systems and there is no reason some similarities cannot be found across memory systems. Therefore, the experimental work that is most important for confirming the existence of a distinct episodic memory system is research that shows a different pattern of performance for episodic and one or more of the other proposed memory systems. Much of this research has been devoted to testing for a difference between episodic and semantic memory systems or between episodic and procedural memory systems.

One important piece of evidence for the proposition that there exists a separate episodic memory system comes from studies that show that factors that have one effect on the episodic memory system have either no effect or a different effect on other proposed systems. The differential effects of one independent variable manipulation on the proposed memory systems are called dissociations. Many empirical dissociations take the form suggested in Figure 1. In this case, moving from treatment X to treatment Y has the effect of decreasing performance on a task thought to involve the episodic memory system while the same manipulation has no effect on a task thought to involve the semantic (or procedural) memory system. Again, the logic of this kind of dissociation is that if two different memory systems have different operations and use different processes, then they should be sensitive to, at least some, different variables. Therefore, it should be possible to show that some variable has differential effects on two memory systems.

Several dissociations between episodic and semantic memory have been reported. Most these studies have shown that some variable (including such factors as the tasks performed while learning the words, the relationship between studied words,

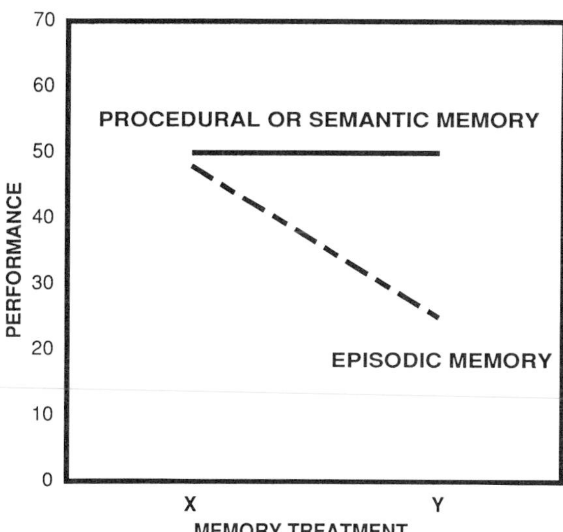

FIGURE 1 Hypothetical data showing a dissociation between an episodic memory task and either a semantic or procedural memory task.

and the hypnotizability of subjects) has a large effect on episodic memory performance but effectively no impact on semantic memory performance. Other studies have shown a similar pattern of results for episodic and procedural memory. Some variables that have resulted in a dissociation between these two tasks include test delay, processing instructions, and the physical appearance of the stimuli.

Of course other patterns of dissociations are possible. More compelling evidence for a separate episodic memory system comes from experiments showing a double dissociation. A double dissociation exists when one variable influences an episodic memory task but leaves another memory task unaffected or changes performance in the opposite direction. A second variable influences the other memory task but leaves performance on the episodic task unaffected (or changes performance in the opposite direction).

These dissociations support the idea that there is a distinct episodic memory system by showing that certain variables differentially influence episodic tasks and tasks thought to tap other memory systems. However, there are certain cautions that must be taken before accepting the results as unconditional support for the memory systems approach. First, there is a growing literature showing dissociations within a single proposed memory system. That is, it is possible to show that one manipulation has one effect on one kind of episodic memory task (say, recall) and either no effect or a different effect on another episodic memory task (say, recognition). Similar sorts of findings can be found for tasks thought to tap the procedural or semantic memory systems. In fact, all that is needed to explain a dissociation is that at least one process differs for any two tasks and that the independent variable that results in a dissociation affects that process. Because each memory system has several processes, the finding of dissociations does not require the postulation of distinct memory systems.

A related issue follows from the one above. Namely, if it is not necessary to postulate separate systems to explain dissociations, why do so. Unitary memory theorists argue for a certain parsimony in proposing just one memory system. Although a presentation of a unitary memory position is beyond the scope of this paper, many theorists have presented and supported such a position.

A third criticism of dissociation experiments is that they often suffer from confounds that make unambiguous interpretations of the results impossible. For example, if the episodic memory task differs from the semantic task, for example, in the level of difficulty, the instructions given, or in the prior exposure to the to-be-remembered material, then any dissociation may be the result of the confounded variable and not because of the existence of two different memory systems. Such precautions are not often heeded in the research that has been conducted. Experiments that have tried to control for these extraneous factors have often given mixed results.

In sum, the evidence from experimental dissociations presents a necessary but not sufficient line of evidence for the memory systems approach. The evidence to date is largely consistent with the memory systems approach but the evidence does not require the postulation of distinct memory systems to be explained.

B. Neuropsychological Evidence

Perhaps the most compelling evidence for a distinct episodic memory system approach comes from a variety of neuropsychological data. These data take the form of a dissociation as well. The evidence is of the form that one region of the brain is important for episodic memory but another region of the brain is important for a different memory system. The clearest evidence of a dissociation in this literature is between episodic memory and procedural memory although other evidence suggests a distinction between episodic and semantic memory.

An important piece of evidence comes from brain-damaged individuals. There have been several individuals studied who, because of some brain trauma, have showed impaired episodic memory but relatively intact procedural memory. Other individuals have shown impaired episodic memory but relatively spared semantic memory. These individuals usually show amnesia for some type of information (often episodic) but spared memory when tested on semantic or procedural tasks.

A second line of evidence comes from the study of the brains of healthy individuals. Event-related potentials (a measure of the brain's electrical activity) have revealed different functions for episodic and semantic memory tasks. Pictures of cerebral blood flow (a measure of brain activity) have implicated different brain region involvement for semantic and episodic tasks.

Additional evidence comes from the study of brain lesions in animals. Although researchers argue over the presence of episodic memory in animals other than humans, much of the evidence does appear consistent with the idea of multiple memory systems.

New techniques in brain research that allow for the study of intact brain performance are expanding our knowledge of memory and other cognitive processes. So far, they have provided support for the multiple memory systems approach and the concept of episodic memory. However, as with the other types of evidence discussed, the evidence is not conclusive. Some researchers have argued that the neurological evidence can and should be interpreted within a single memory system.

C. Developmental Research

Older adults (aged 65 years or older) typically perform much more poorly on episodic memory tasks than younger adults (ages 18–30) when tested with recall or recognition for recently encountered material. These same older adults often perform as well as, or better than, younger adults on tests of general knowledge or vocabulary which are considered to be semantic memory tasks. This pattern of results is, of course, another example of a dissociation that supports the idea of a distinct episodic memory system. Similar patterns of results have been found with episodic and procedural memory tasks. That is, older adults perform comparably to younger adults when tested on a procedural memory task while showing large declines relative to young adults on episodic memory tasks. Many of these conclusions are drawn across, rather than within studies, and thus more research is needed. This sort of research also suffers from the same problems discussed in the empirical dissociations section.

Similar sorts of studies with young children are difficult to find or evaluate. It is very difficult to assess the episodic memory of a young child because young children find it difficult, because of their language skills, to talk about or report their recollective experiences.

D. Stochastic Independence

If there existed just one memory system, then an individual would perform somewhat similarly across various memory tasks. That is, levels of performance across tasks should be correlated. A person with a good memory on one kind of task should be pretty good on another memory task because the same system would underlie performance in both conditions. A perfect relationship would not be expected because different processes might be used on different tasks, there might be differences in experience with the different tasks, etc. On the other hand, if there are different memory systems, no such correlations need be expected. That is, a person with a good semantic memory may have a very poor episodic memory. Here, one might expect performance on tasks thought to tap different memory systems to be independent of each other. In fact, if performances on tasks thought to tap two memory systems were independent of each other, then such a result would suggest two different systems (or at least different processes) were involved in the two tasks. Such independence is statistical in nature in that knowing someone's score on a semantic memory task would not allow accurate prediction of that person's performance on an episodic memory task. This sort of independence is known as statistical independence or stochasitic independence.

Several studies have revealed stochastic independence between episodic and semantic memory performance. On the other hand, some studies have shown some correlation between the two tasks. In addition, stochastic independence does not require the assumption of independent memory systems. In general, the results (as with empirical dissociations) appear not to be sufficient to rule out a unitary memory system approach. The results are generally supportive of the multiple memory systems approach, but problems in interpretation of the data do not allow absolute conclusions.

E. Evidence against Episodic Memory as a System

So far, the evidence reviewed is largely consistent with the idea of a distinct episodic memory system. The bigger problem is that it is not inconsistent with a unitary memory system approach. That is, neither approach is ruled out. There do exist several experiments that have attempted to challenge the multiple memory system account. Examples of this type of research have demonstrated that episodic and semantic memory tasks show similar patterns of results and so need not make reference to different systems, that inferences are possible in the episodic memory system (an operation thought to be available only in semantic memory) and that episodic information influences performance on a semantic memory task, or vice versa.

Proponents of the multiple memory systems approach typically respond to these data in one of the following ways: (1) There are flaws either in the design of the experiment or in the interpretation of the data. (2) Episodic memory and other memory systems are unique, but they certainly interact. Therefore, one would expect that there should be similarities in performance on tasks that involve more than one system. (3) Although the systems have unique operations, it is really a matter of degree. For example, although inferences are natural in the semantic memory system and rare in the episodic memory system, it is surely possible, albeit difficult, to draw inferences from within the episodic memory system.

These sorts of arguments are reasonable, but they make it difficult to provide convincing evidence either for or against episodic memory as a system. What is needed is a detailed theory of episodic memory that specifies the conditions under which dissociations should be found, when different memory systems interact, and how variables influence the system. A detailed theory would allow more definitive tests to be conducted and further progress to be made in this area.

III. EXTENSIONS OF EPISODIC MEMORY

The idea of episodic memory as a distinct system is extremely controversial. However, the debate over how many memory systems there are has generated a great deal of research. The answer to the basic question has not been answered but we know a good deal about basic memory processes and the variables that influence these processes. In addition, the heuristic use of the term and its emphasis on context and personally experienced events has generated much research that at its core is not theoretical. Instead it has demonstrated the importance of personal and spatio-temporal information for much of our everyday memory functions. Two of these areas of research stemming from episodic memory are described below.

A. Context Effects

Context is a vague term that has been used in the literature to refer to such factors as the words that surround a to be remembered word, the physical surroundings in which a set of material is studied and tested, internal moods, and drug states. A classic design for these sorts of experiments is depicted in Table I. In this experiment, a set of material is presented in one of two contexts (with word A or word B, in room A or room B, on land (A) or in water (B), while intoxicated (A) or while sober (B), while happy (A) or sad (B), etc.). Half the participants in each study condition are tested in the same context and the other half of the participants change contexts. The general finding of studies with free recall procedures is that maintaining the same context during study and test leads to better performance than changing context between study and test. Although there are exceptions to this finding, it has been replicated enough times under enough conditions that it is clear that context is associated with new material when it is learned and context plays an important role as a cue when memory is probed.

TABLE I
Typical Design for a Study That Examines the Effect of Context on Episodic Memory

	Study context	
Test context	Context A	Context B
Context A	(a) Context match	(b) Context mismatch
Context B	(c) Context mismatch	(d) Context match

It is interesting that the context effects are much less robust when recognition is used as a test than when recall is used as a test. This presumably results because recognition tests involve other good cues (the to-be-remembered item itself is presented and the participants are typically asked simply whether it was one of the items studied) that are not available for free recall (where subjects are simply asked to recall as much as they can). Presumably, context plays a bigger role when other cues are not available.

Context effects in free recall are less consistent when internal mood states are used as the context or when drugs are used to induce a context. These results can be at least partially explained by the difficulties in inducing moods and by the additional effects of the drugs and moods on cognitive functioning. For example, both depression and alcohol slow down performance on a variety of cognitive tasks.

An issue related to context effects is source amnesia. Source amnesia is indicated when a person can recognize having seen some material before, for example, but not where or when it was originally presented. That is, memory for the source of the information is lost. If the source of the information is considered a kind of context, then this is an example of a loss of memory for context information. It is interesting that individuals who have poor memory for the source of information, such as old adults, typically also show poor episodic memory performance. [*See* AMNESIA.]

B. Autobiographical Memory

Recent years have witnessed a great increase in research activity in the area of autobiographical memory. Autobiographical memory refers to the (usually important) personal memories that make up one's life history. In some ways this can be considered a subset or subsystem of episodic memory. Episodic memory is more general in that any event that was experienced is potentially part of episodic memory. However, the event is unlikely to become part of autobiographical memory unless it is important in defining oneself. In addition, a typical episodic memory task in the lab requires the recall of events that occurred in a specific spatio-temporal context, but not usually the recall of the spatio-temporal context itself. Autobiographical memory is often composed of that very specific spatio-temporal context. [*See* AUTOBIOGRAPHICAL REMEMBERING AND SELF-KNOWLEDGE.]

Some researchers prefer to treat autobiographical information as distinct from episodic memory to differentiate more naturalistic and real world tasks used in autobiographical research from the somewhat artificial tasks used in most traditional episodic memory research. In addition, a different term frees researchers in the area of autobiographical memory from the theoretical baggage associated with the term episodic memory. However, even given these differences and preferences, clearly autobiographical memory has much in common with episodic memory and much of the work can be traced back to lab work in episodic memory.

Much of the work on autobiographical memory stems from an increased interest in taking memory research out of the (artificial) laboratory and into more real world settings. It is expected that an increased ecological validity will improve our knowledge about how memory works. Autobiographical memory is also of interest because of its ties to social psychology and personality. Much of how we define ourselves in relation to others can be attributed to our personal memories or studied through them. Thus, autobiographical memory, which shares much with episodic memory, is proving to be a fruitful area of research.

Bibliography

Davies, G. M., and Thomson, D. M. (eds.) (1988). "Memory in Context: Context in Memory." Wiley, Chichester.

Gillund, G., and Perimutter, M. (1988). Episodic memory and knowledge interactions across adulthood. In "Language, Memory, and Aging" (L. L. Light and D. M. Burke, eds.), pp. 191–208. Cambridge University Press, New York.

Matlin, M. W. (1989). "Cognition," 2nd ed., pp. 84–90. Holt, Rinehart, and Winston, Orlando, FL.

Medin, D. L., and Ross, B. H. (1990). "Cognitive Psychology," pp. 217–264. Harcourt, Brace, Jovanovich, Orlando, FL.

Nelson, K. (1993). The psychological and social origins of autobiographical memory. *Psychol. Sci.* **4,** 7–14.

Precis of Elements of Episodic Memory (with Commentaries) (1984). *Behav. Brain Sci.* **7,** 223–268.

Roediger, H. L., III, and Craik, F. I. M. (Eds.) (1989). "Varieties of Memory and Consciousness: Essays in Honour of Endel Tulving." Erlbaum, New York.

Rubin, D. C. (Ed.) (1986). "Autobiographical Memory." Cambridge University Press, New York.

Tulving, E. (1993). What is episodic memory? *Curr. Direc. Psychol. Sci.* **2,** 67–70.

EQUITY

Charles G. McClintock
University of California at Santa Barbara

Terry L. Boles
University of Iowa

Glossary

Equality An equity rule prescribing allocating outcomes equally.

Equity A set of rules or standards that define fair procedures or outcomes.

Distributive equity Concerning the etiology, nature, function, and fairness of decisions regarding the allocation of resources.

Fairness Here, a synonym for equity; the perceived "rightness" or "wrongness" of a procedure in an outcome.

Justice Here, a synonym for equity; standards of fair political and legal procedures and outcomes.

Need An equity rule prescribing allocating outcomes on the basis of need.

Proactive equity Where fairness judgments and behaviors are treated as dependent variables and are subject to the influence of personality and situational variables.

Procedural equity Concerning the etiology, nature, function, and fairness of the processes leading to decisions on how to distribute resources.

Proportional equity An equity rule prescribing allocating outcomes proportional to inputs.

Reactive equity Where perceived judgments of fairness or unfairness are treated as independent variables and their effects upon subsequent judgments and behaviors are observed.

EQUITY in its most general sense, refers to a set of norms or rules that help to ensure allocations of valued resources between individuals and/or groups are perceived to be fair. Such rules either (1) prescribe what the final distribution or allocation of resources between individuals or groups should be (distributive equity) or (2) prescribe what procedures should be followed to ensure that such distributional or allocative decisions are reached and then implemented in equitable and just ways (procedural equity).

In its most narrow sense, the term equity is used to specify a particular rule of distributive justice which asserts that the resources received by individuals or groups should be proportional to their relative contribution or input. Within some theoretical systems, the term proportional equality is employed to describe this narrower definition of equity.

In this article we will focus upon the more inclusive of the two definitions of equity. In doing so, we will use the terms *fairness* and *justice* interchangeably with the term equity, even though these alternative terms sometimes carry somewhat different nuances of meaning. Fairness, for example, has a stronger motivational connotation than equity. Justice often refers to equity within a legal context. We will use the term *proportional equity* when referring to the more specific definition of equity, namely, the allocation of outcomes proportional to inputs.

I. THE ORIGINS AND FUNCTIONS OF EQUITY

A fundamental assumption in most, if not all, theories of equity is that achieving equitable resource allocations and following fair procedures are essential to maintaining relationships of exchange. Resources exchanged within relationships include, among other things, effort, talent, money, commodities, status, kindness, love, anger, and laughter. It follows from this assumption that perceived inequity, unfairness, or injustice in procedure or outcome will increase the likelihood of social conflict and produce instability within social relationships,

Copyright © 1994 by Academic Press, Inc. All rights of reproduction in any form reserved.

whether these relationships involve dyads, fraternal organizations, commodity markets, or nation-states.

Various approaches to understanding the etiology, the nature, and the functioning of the rules of equity within human relationships have been taken by economists, philosophers, evolutionists, political scientists, anthropologists, sociologists, and social psychologists. We next briefly review some of these approaches.

A. Social Philosophy

Social philosophers have for centuries attempted to develop a prescriptive theory of fairness which would define what is equitable, and permit one to assess the relative applicability and/or merits of various rules of distributive and procedural fairness. Aristotle, for example, distinguished *rectificatory justice,* the restoration to a party of something unjustly lost to another party, from *distributive justice,* the allocation of goods employing the principle of equity, from *justice in exchange,* the perception of what is a fair and appropriate amount of one commodity to trade for another. He assumed these various forms of justice were more or less applicable in particular contexts and that they played an important role in facilitating interaction and in regulating conflict between members in a society.

Later, the philosophers T. Hobbes and J. Locke argued for a strongly utilitarian definition of equity, namely, fairness in outcomes was defined by the relative utility of contributions made to the common good. For Hobbes, distributive justice or equity first implied keeping one's word, one's covenant. And, for both Hobbes and Locke, equity or fairness in resource allocation implied that individuals who contributed more to the common good should be afforded more rewards than those who contributed less.

More recently, the contemporary philosopher J. Rawls has set forth a very much qualified view of Hobbes' and Locke's utilitarian ethic. Rawls describes two fundamental principles of fair allocation: *political equity,* which affords everyone equal political rights; and *economic equity* which affords everyone economic opportunity. Rawls recognizes, consistent with utilitarianism, that inequality in economic outcomes will occur as a function of differences in members' contributions to society. He argues that in choosing between alternative ways to allocate rewards as a function of individuals relative contribution to the common good, the principle of *need* should also be taken into consideration. He suggests the specific relative contribution rule selected should be the one that provides the greatest benefit to the least advantaged members of society.

In effect, Rawls acknowledges the long recognized difference between political and economic fairness. In doing so, he establishes two fairness principles that allow for a discontinuity between political equality on the one hand, and a need-qualified utilitarian model of economic and social equity on the other. As is true for all philosophical models of fairness, the appropriateness of Rawls' modified utilitarian model of justice has been challenged on a variety of formal, ethical, and pragmatic grounds.

B. Economics

Economists also view utilitarian models of fair allocation as providing the more rational and effective strategies for maximizing economic efficiency, and for assuring the success of economic systems. Utilitarian models make two strong assumptions: (1) that of substitution, where one individual's pleasure (utility) is considered to be as important as that of any other; and (2) that of joint maximization, where an appropriate distribution procedure should maximize the sum of the utilities of the members in a given economic system.

Based on the above assumptions, economists recognize two resource distribution processes that promote efficient and fair outcomes but which operate in different ways. The first assumes that the accumulation of individual wealth within a laissez-faire economy encourages efficient work and investment which in turn contributes to overall economic growth. The second, which follows from the concept of marginal utility, assumes that as wealth accumulates its per unit value decreases at the margin. Therefore, redistributing wealth to those with fewer resources through the imposition of some form of graduated taxation is assumed fair because it increases the overall sum of society's utilities, and thereby contributes to the common good. [*See* ECONOMIC BEHAVIOR.]

C. Sociology and Social Evolution

Sociologists traditionally define fairness as a standard for evaluating allocation behavior which is embodied in the norms or rules of societies. Their work has been primarily descriptive in nature, and relatively little effort has been expended in assessing the etiology of those norms, rules, or practices that facilitate fair or constrain unfair organizational practices and outcomes.

Sociologists identified with the subdisciplines of ethnomethodology and symbolic interactionism have described the role that various norms, including fairness, play in the functioning of organizations. Norms are assumed to function as referential standards. That is, they are employed by members of organizations to comparatively evaluate the resource allocations made to self across time, to members of one's own groups, and to members of other groups. Fairness is judged by comparing actual allocations with normatively defined expectations of appropriate allocations. Discrepancies between expected and obtained allocations of resources, including that of social status, lead to perceptions of injustice.

The actual form of injustice perceived and its organizational consequences depend upon the direction of the disparity in outcomes from a standard, as well as by the nature of the reference groups involved in the comparison. Reference groups are defined demographically in terms of characteristics such as race, gender, education, occupation, and social class, and comparatively in terms of such associated states as power and social status.

Although traditional sociology has not expended much effort exploring the etiology of fairness norms and behavior, the neighboring field of evolutionary anthropology has recently begun to explain the emergence and the current status of fairness norms as the result of an evolutionary process. One central role that fairness rules or norms are assumed to play within society from the standpoint of evolutionary theory is that of reducing the likelihood of cheating behaviors when valued resources are exchanged between members of societies.

Social evolutionists argue and cite behavioral evidence that suggests that the detection of cheating is so important that humans have evolved ways to process information which facilitates determining whether others have behaved unfairly. The detection of cheating, of course, is assumed to increase the likelihood that resource allocations are made justly, and that certain individuals do not obtain a disproportionate share of those resources which have been mutually created.

Behaviors that result in an organism obtaining more of a commonly valued resource than they deserve are likely to become dominant because they increase the likelihood of the genetic survivability of those who display them. Such behvaiors, if widespread and unchecked over the long term, can become a threat to the successful continuance of a society.

Recent studies suggest that humans process information "illogically" in certain contexts to increase the likelihood of detecting whether a norm of fairness has been violated. Such processing is seen by evolutionists to be consistent with the assumption that the human brain has evolved to evaluate information in ways that decrease the likelihood of social cheating and increase the probability of fairness in exchange.

II. THE DEVELOPMENT OF FAIRNESS JUDGMENTS AND BEHAVIORS

In recent years, the more significant theoretical and empirical attempts to define and understand equity have occurred within the fields of developmental and social psychology. The remainder of this article first evaluates work on the development of equity judgments and behaviors, and then examines the social psychology of fairness.

The field of developmental psychology has been concerned primarily with two aspects of fairness: (1) describing the progressive, inevitable, step-wise development of children's cognitive and social abilities and evaluating the effects of this process upon their judgments of what is fair and moral; and (2) describing how children acquire fairness rules as a function of age, and understanding how individual differences and environmental factors interact to influence their judgments of others' allocations or their own allocation behavior.

A. Structural Models of the Development of Fairness Judgments

A structural approach to the development of fairness judgments assumes that children's conceptions of what are equitable procedures and outcomes follow a series of developmental stages. These stages are assumed to be necessary, irreversible, universal, and goal-directed. Three major theories, namely, those of J. Piaget, L. Kohlberg, and W. Damon, dominate the structural approach to development. [*See* MORAL DEVELOPMENT.]

1. Piaget's Theory of Moral Development

Piaget, within his general theory of moral development, described the etiology of equity or fairness judgments. Piaget assumed that children inevitably go through three fixed stages. In the first, children's judgments of appropriateness of an allocation are dominated by self-concern. In the second, equalitarianism clearly dominates other rules. And, in the third, equity, in which fairness is defined by the relationship between own and other's inputs and outcomes, dominates. In describing the development of these judgmental processes, Piaget did not specify the ages at which children reach each, but did insist that they represent a sequence that is necessary, inevitable, and universal in its progression.

2. Kohlberg's Theory of Moral Development

Kohlberg sets forth a more elaborate structural theory of moral development. Like Piaget, Kohlberg uses children's responses to a series of moral dilemma vignettes to define the various stages of development. Kohlberg sees the rules of equity or justice emerging as a series of compromises between the conflicting demands of interdependent persons. At the youngest ages behavior is judged as appropriate if it is hedonistic and aimed at maximizing the child's own resources independent of others. Next, children's moral judgments become conventional showing conformity with important significant others. And finally, judgments of moral behavior, including equity, either become autonomous or assume the form of social contracts that are negotiated with others.

These three general developmental states are further subdivided by Kohlberg into a more differentiated set stages. Kohlberg has sought to demonstrate the validity of his stage model of development by conducting a series of descriptive studies of scenario based moral reasoning in various social and cultural environments. His findings show some step-wise consistency in development of moral reasoning, but not to the extent assumed by the theory.

3. Damon's Model of Distributive Justice

The most elaborate strutural model of distributive justice has been set forth by Damon. Like Piaget and Kohlberg, Damon observed the reactions of children to stories or scenarios that contained moral dilemmas. He found, in terms of fairness, young children initially believe resources should be shared equally and at later ages become concerned with the norms of reciprocity and the principle of proportional equity. Only at later ages do they take need into consideration as a criterion for resource allocation.

Damon also carefully examined both the manner in which children reason about justice and their actual behavior. The correlations observed between the two were not sufficiently strong to provide major support for his expectation that moral judgment and moral behavior are both sequential and strongly linked. In this regard, Damon has observed, "predicting a child's social conduct from his or her reasoning remains a complex and risky task. . . . [Such] predictions must also consider the different ways in which self-interest may influence different modes of reasoning in different contexts."

In evaluating the existing evidence in support of structural models of the step-wise development of equity, one is forced to several conclusions. First, relatively minor variations in the moral stories or scenarios employed to estimate children's developmental stages have been found to produce significant and unexpected differences in children's judgments, and their subsequent assignment to particular developmental stages. Second, numerous exceptions have been observed for individual children in the fixed order of stages through which all children are assumed to progress. Finally, Damon has stressed, to account for the variability in moral judgment, both within and between children, self-interest and environmental factors must be taken into account by structural models of development.

B. Empirical Studies of the Acquisition and Expression of Fairness Rules

The acquisition and expression of fairness rules implies the mastery of what I. Kant described as a set of regulative rules. Such rules take the form "If *X*, then *Y*," and represent culturally shared beliefs about how a set of prior conditions (*X*) influences a set of outcomes (*Y*). Throughout history, societies have set various allocation rules or norms for its members to learn; for example, "if one is king, then one has divine rights," and "if one is a winner, then one can take all," and "if a resource is scarce, then one should take turns using it."

The three "if. . .then" fairness rules that have been empirically observed to dominate children's behavior in contemporary Western societies are those described earlier: (1) *equality*, e.g., if one is a member of a group, then one should share outcomes equally; (2) *proportional equity*, e.g., if one contributes more to a classroom project, then one should be afforded a higher grade and more praise; and (3) *need*, if one is a member of a group and in need, then other members with more resources should share some of their resources with you.

Very young children do not follow any of the above rules. Rather, they allocate resources in such a manner as to maximize their own personal utilities independent of what happens to others. Because such allocations often occur in interpersonal situations where resources are limited, children's egocentric choices negatively impact others and lead to conflict. Early socialization efforts by parents and teachers are frequently directed toward encouraging children to begin to use fairness rules to reduce the likelihood of social competition and conflict.

As a result of these efforts, children's behaviors begin increasingly to conform to one or more of the rules of fairness. The dominance of particular rules varies not only as a function of the development of numerical skills and age, but also as a result of environmental contingencies such as task structure, self-presentation needs, and expectations of reciprocity. For example, if adult observers are present, children, because of an increased concern with self-presentation, are more likely to choose fairness rules that are less favorable to self and more favorable to another than they do when adult observers are absent.

As regards children's capabilities to use various fairness rules, empirical evidence suggests that equality is recognized as a rule of fairness by as early as 5 years of age. By 6 to 7 years, children understand an ordinal representation of proportional equity, namely, they recognize that someone who has contributed more to a task should receive greater outcomes than someone who has contributed less. By the age of 8, most children have an appreciation of the concept of proportionality at the concrete level which allows for a one to one matching of inputs to outcomes, e.g., "If I correctly spell six of eight words, then I should receive six of eight points." Because of the nature of the development of children's numerical abilities, a more abstract understanding of proportional equity does not occur until about age 12.

As regards children's actual allocation behavior across settings, research indicates that most of those under 6 years of age are strongly self-interested and uninfluenced by consideration of fairness. When a fairness rule is used, which is relatively infrequently, it is most likely to be the most simple rule computationally, equality. As children develop, they begin to mask or modify their strictly self-interested allocations by selecting from the fairness rules that they have mastered the one which most benefits themselves. By middle childhood, about age 10, equalitarian choice rules tend to dominate the self-interested use of fairness.

Strict proportional equity does not appear to serve as a general allocation rule for children. Even those in early adolescence make allocations that are consistent with "niceness" to others. Early adolescents have been observed to afford more to another when the other contributes more, and to distribute outcomes equally when they themselves contribute more.

The rule of proportional equity, however, does dominate the allocations of college-age students except in situations where they believe their choices are strictly anonymous and self-presentation is not a concern. In these situations, college students have been observed systematically to select a fairness rule in their own self-interest. Specifically, an equality rule is selected when they find themselves disadvantaged in inputs relative to another, and an equity rule is chosen when they are advantaged in inputs. Such behavior cannot be considered totally self-interested insofar as students under conditions of "anonymity" could have kept all the resources for themselves without others' knowledge, but did not.

In summary, theory and research suggest children's acquisition of fairness rules are a combined function of socialization and the development of relevant cognitive–numerical skills. With socialization and with cognitive development, children acquire and use differing fairness rules in a progressive, though not invariant, order.

III. THE SOCIAL PSYCHOLOGY OF EQUITY

Over the past 50 years, the field of social psychology has expended considerable energy attempting to understand the role which equity plays in human relationships. These efforts have focused on two primary forms of equity or fairness: fairness in allocation (distributive justice), and fairness in procedure (procedural justice). These two forms of fairness have been treated, both theoretically and empirically, sometimes as independent variables (reactive studies of the effects of perceived fairness and unfairness), and sometimes as dependent variables (proactive studies of the causes or correlates of fairness judgments and behaviors).

The major approaches to the social psychology of equity are summarized in Table I. In the remainder of this article, we consider theoretical and empirical work that falls within the cells of this 3 × 2 matrix. First, we describe the major models that dominate work on distributive justice (Cell 1), then, we consider several more recently formulated models of procedural fairness (Cell 2).

Subsequently, we examine empirical work which treats equitable and inequitable allocations as independent variables and assesses their effects upon judgments and behaviors (Cell 3). Next, we evaluate studies which employ procedural justice as an independent variable, and assess its effects upon judgments and behaviors (Cell 4). Then, we look at distributive justice as a dependent variable, and examine its causes and correlates (Cell 5). Finally, we examine empirical work that treats procedural fairness as a dependent variable, and describe its causes and correlates (Cell 6).

A. Distributive and Procedural Justice: An Overview

Before undertaking the detailed description of social psychology theory and research outlined above, we will make a few general observations about the ways in which distributive and procedural justice are viewed in the field. As described previously, three allocation rules have been of central theoretical and empirical concern: (1) equality, (2) proportional equity, and (3) need. Some social psychologists regard these rules to be but three forms of the same general equity principle but as having different inputs. Thus, for proportional equity, the input is the contribution an individual or group makes to the goals of a relationship; for equality, the input is equal membership in a group; and for need, the input is the level of deprivation experienced by a group or a member of a group.

Other social psychologists view these three allocation rules as distinct and operating in competition with one another. They assume that equality and need, unlike proportional equity, cannot be adequately conceptualized in terms of a mathematical relationship between inputs and outcomes. Despite these theoretical arguments, the manner in which the rule or rules are measured and the role they are assumed and observed to play in human behavior are similar, if not identical.

Social psychologists studying procedural fairness assume that in judging the equitableness of a particular outcome, people consider not only the allocation rule employed, but also the circumstances or procedures followed in reaching the allocation decision. Work in the area of procedural justice has focused primarily upon the fairness of the procedures followed by third parties in legal, plea bargaining, mediation, and arbitration settings.

TABLE I
The Social Psychology of Equity

	Distributive fairness	Procedural fairness
Major models of equity	Cell 1	Cell 2
Equity as an independent variable: reactive fairness or justice	Cell 3	Cell 4
Equity as a dependent variable: proactive fairness or justice	Cell 5	Cell 6

B. Models of Distributive Equity (Cell 1)

The major models of distributive fairness in social psychology are reactive in the sense they attempt to describe and understand the effects of perceived distributive equity and inequity upon individuals' subsequent judgments, attitudes, and behaviors. One of the first reactive theories emphasizing the effects of perceived unfairness in allocation was formulated by the sociologist G. Homans as part of a more general theory of social behavior.

1. Homans Theory of Equity

Homans assumed that judgments of equity are based on the learned expectation that outcomes to self and others will conform to the rules of distributive justice. When these rules are violated, perceptions of unfairness result. The reactions to these perceptions include anger, when one perceives oneself as underrewarded, and guilt, when one perceives oneself as overrewarded. Of the two, anger is assumed to be more likely to occur and to influence subsequent behavior more than guilt because individuals are likely to be more versatile in finding rationalizations for their being overrewarded than underrewarded. Homans examined and found confirmation for the above expectations in the work place.

It is a short conceptual step from Homans' assumptions concerning the occurrence and effects of the violation of expectations to Festinger's theory of dissonance and dissonance reduction. And it is the marriage of the motivational principles of dissonance theory with the normative theory of distributive justice that provides the conceptual foundation for contemporary social psychological theories of equity and fairness, including those of J. Adams and of E. Walster, E. Berscheid, and W. Walster.

2. Adams' Equity Theory

Adams' equity model stresses the effects which perceived injustice has upon subsequent behavior. He assumes that perceptions of inequity give rise to motivational states that are resolved when equity is restored. That is, perceived inequity is assumed to produce a condition of dissonance accompanied by tensions and stresses which individuals are motivated to reduce cognitively or behaviorally. The theory specifies the antecedents to and the responses that follow from the aversive motivational state that is associated with perceived inequity. [*See* MOTIVATION.]

More specifically, Adams assumed that equity is realized when outcomes to person *P*, and to another person, *O*, are strictly proportional to their relative inputs. For *P*, *O* is any person with whom they share an exchange relationship, or with whom they compare themselves when they are both in an exchange relationship with a third party, such as an employer. In Adams' model, the stress of inequity occurs when *P* perceives that the norm of distributive justice has been violated. Namely, it occurs whenever the ratio of *P*'s inputs to outcomes differs from that of *O*'s.

Given this formalization of the principle of equity and equity violation, Adams examined various alternative reactions made by individuals to perceived inequity. Following earlier theoretical and empirical work on the effects of cognitive dissonance upon judgments and behaviors, he proposed five specific ways in which perceptions of inequity could be reduced: (1) by actually altering inputs or outcomes; (2) by cognitively distorting own inputs or outcomes; (3) by cognitively distorting the inputs or the outcomes of the other; (4) by changing the object of comparison, that is, finding others with whom to exchange resources; and (5) by leaving the situation, that is, the exchange relationship.

According to Adams' theory, actors choose from among the above five alternatives the one which is most consistent with their own self-interest, and which is least costly for maintaining their self-esteem. The theory does not provide a basis for explaining why inequity is aversive. Parts of the theory have been tested including the frequently, but not always, observed effect that perceptions of being under- or overpaid produce the expected decrease in effort with underpayment and increase in effort with overpayment.

3. The Equity Model of Walster, Berscheid, and Walster

Walster, Berscheid, and Walster extend Adams' model to include an explanation of the etiology of perceived inequity. The first assumption of their model is that without normative controls, humans are predisposed to maximize their own outcomes and to follow predominantly self-interested forms of behavior.

Consistent with the earlier reported findings in developmental psychology, Walster *et al.* assume that before being socialized, children are unconcerned with others' outcomes. In an effort to reduce the various interpersonal and intergroup conflicts that follow from strictly self-interested behavior, Walster *et al.* assume that societies develop and administer rules of fair procedure and allocation to reduce conflict and to achieve equitable distributions of valued resources among their members.

Early in childhood, these procedural and allocation rules of fairness are enforced through the administration of rewards and punishments. Over time, they become internalized. The socialization of fairness rules is not, however, assumed to cause children to proactively pursue equitable strategies or goals. Rather, in Walster *et al.*'s model of fairness, as in those of Homans and Adams, the motivations underlying equity are reactive. Fairness follows either from the guilt associated with violating internalized norms of fairness or from the objective fear that one will be punished by other group members for norm violation.

In a second assumption, Walster *et al.* assert that inequity produces a level of psychological distress proportionate to its perceived magnitude. The level of stress affects the degree to which individual's perceptions, attitudes, and behaviors are mobilized to restore both "actual" and "psychological" equity.

Thus, like other reactive or need reduction theories of behavior, Walster *et al.* focus principally upon the ways in which actors attempt to restore balance, both materially and cognitively, once it is disrupted by perceptions of unfairness. Compared to prior theories, the model greatly extends the range of social relationships that are assumed to be influenced by the stress of perceived inequity including: (1) production relationships in industrial settings; (2) trials and other legal settings; (3) recipient–donor exchanges; (4) victim's interactions with harm-doers; (5) communal and intimate forms of interaction; and (6) economic, political, and social exchanges between nation-states.

4. Berger, Zelditch, Anderson, and Cohen's Model of Distributive Justice

A more sociologically oriented status-value theory of reactive fairness has been formulated by J. Berger, M. Zelditch, B. Anderson, and B. Cohen. The theory assumes that evaluations of fairness or justice are based upon whether the outcomes obtained under a particular set of conditions correspond with an observer's or actor's normative expectations concerning fairness. These expectations are assumed to be based upon a referential structure that specifies how particular states of social characteristics should be related to the allocation of rewards.

More specifically, a referential structure serves as a frame of reference for evaluating fairness. It is composed of a set of generalized others who possess given states or levels of one or more social characteristic such as age, education, gender, and occupation. Differing states or levels are associated with varying amounts of status-value goal objects or rewards. Unfairness is assumed to occur and will be recognized when the reward expectations associated with a given referential structure are violated. Considerable theoretical and empirical effort has been expended to determine what are the relevant social characteristics (status, education, race) or inputs (effort, ability, need) that define a referential structure, as well as how they are measured and combined to provide a single standard for evaluating the fairness of an outcome.

C. Models of Procedural Equity or Fairness (Cell 2)

The development of models of fair procedure is a relatively recent area of intellectual effort within social psychology. Work in this area assumes that people's judgments and behaviors not only relate to the perceived fairness of outcomes, but are also influenced by perceptions of the manner in which allocation decisions are reached, that is, the procedures followed. Perceived variations in procedure or process are frequently reported to influence judgments of fairness in formal legal trials, in plea bargaining, in mediation and arbitration, in police–civilian interactions, in labor–management relationships, and in supervisor–worker interactions.

Three theories of procedural justice or equity will be briefly described here: (1) J. Thibaut and L. Walker's control-based model, (2) G. Leventhal's description of rules of procedural fairness, and (3) A. Lind and T. Tyler's group-value model.

1. Thibaut and Walker's Control-Based Model

Thibaut and Walker provided the initial theoretical statement of procedural equity within social psychology. They observed that process is important because if procedures are judged to be unfair, the viability of relationships at all levels, international, societal, intergroup, and interpersonal, can be seriously jeopardized. They further observed that many social decisions involve outcomes which are inherently difficult to judge in terms of their "correctness" or "fairness," and hence procedures are often evaluated instead.

For example, it is often difficult on an a priori basis to determine whether one social policy will lead to better outcomes than another. For this reason, given such indeterminacy, perceptions of the appropriateness or fairness of one policy over another are strongly influenced by perceptions of the appropriateness of the selection process.

Having rationalized the importance of process, Thibaut and Walker go on to set forth a control-based model of procedural fairness. In doing so, they argue that the fundamental process that influences judgments of fairness is that of control, namely, the power that participants have to affect those processes that determine the allocation of outcomes they will eventually receive.

Thibaut and Walker distinguish two primary forms of control, process and decision. *Process control* refers primarily to the disputants' power to express their opinions, to have voice, and thereby to influence the manner in which information is evaluated before a decision is made. *Decision control* refers to the power to influence the actual allocation decisions made by another. Access to these two forms of control is assumed to affect observers' and disputants' judgments of the fairness of both procedures and outcomes.

2. Leventhal's Normative Rules

In a second conceptualization of procedural equity, Leventhal sets forth a number of normative rules of equitable process that are seen to influence judgments of the fairness of procedure and ultimately of allocation. These process rules include the requirement for: (1) a consistent use of procedure across persons and time; (2) the suppression of self-interested biases; (3) the employment of accurate information; (4) the noncorruptible processing of information and decision making; (5) the availability to decision makers of the relevant parties' positions; and (6) the ethical processing of information and decision making. Behaving consistently with these normative rules is assumed to increase the likelihood that both process and outcomes will be perceived as fair.

3. Lind and Tyler's Group-Value Model

Lind and Tyler have recently proposed an alternative model, namely, a group-value model of procedural equity. The fundamental assumption underlying this model is that evaluations of procedures are most strongly influenced by peoples' perceptions of how such procedures influence their long-term relationship with legitimate authorities and institutional decision-makers. Procedures provide information in three highly important areas relevant to a person/third party authority relationship, namely, information about standing, about neutrality, and about trust.

People are assumed to evaluate as fair those procedures that maintain and improve their standing in groups thereby validating their self-identity and their self-worth. People also consider as fair, procedures that are unbiased, honest, and treat people with respect. Finally, procedures are considered equitable if individuals trust that decisions-makers will behave fairly both now and in the future.

D. Distribution as an Independent Variable: Reactive Fairness I (Cell 3)

Reactive theories of fairness have generated a significant body of empirical research. Representative findings will be briefly described in each of the following areas: (1) individual differences in reactions to injustice; (2) attitudinal effects of perceived unfairness; (3) performance effects of perceived unfairness; and (4) coping strategies used by victims to reduce or to avoid the stress of perceived unfairness.

1. Individual Differences

One individual difference variable that has been extensively evaluated in both proactive and reactive models of fairness is gender. One might expect, given acutely different experiences in terms of job level, prestige of job, and payment for identical work, that women would characterize the work place as being less fair than men. However, empirical results are inconsistent with this expectation, as well as with one another. In part, the observed inconsistencies may occur because most studies have failed to control for a number of job characteristics that covary with gender.

In one sophisticated study that controlled on a number of the relevant covariates, male and female governmental employees' satisfaction was assessed as a function of a series of demographic characteristics including age, education, tenure in the organization, and gender. Satisfaction was broken down and assessed for five job characteristics: pay, promotion policies, co-worker characteristics, nature of one's immediate supervision, and characteristics of the work itself.

An overall analysis found, as a main effect, that males were more satisfied with promotions and work than were females. However, the effect was strongly qualified by an analysis of covariance that controlled for pay, age, and job tenure in the organization and in the present position. Following this analysis, only one significant sex difference was observed. "Everything else being equal," women were more satisfied with their pay than were men.

2. Attitudinal Effects

One might also expect that perceived inequity should have strong effects upon a variety of attitudes. However, the research findings to date in this area have not been consistent. Results of studies on the attitudinal effects of overreward or overpayment, for example, have been mixed. Some studies have found a decline in satisfaction given overreward. Others have found no reduction, and in some instances increases in satisfaction were observed.

As regards being underrewarded, which theoretically should motivate more attitude change than being overrewarded, the findings again are mixed. Although satisfaction is not observed to increase with the perception of being underrewarded, the expected decrease in satisfaction is not always found. Some studies report that some underrewarded individuals are not distressed by the unfairness of outcomes, but are concerned that they in some way may not have made an adequate input or contribution to the task.

Research on changes in attitudes toward allocators who afford one rewards or punishments also is characterized by somewhat mixed findings. In general, allocators who follow the rules of equity are liked more than those who underreward. On the other hand, those who overreward have been observed sometimes to be liked more, sometimes less, and sometimes the same as those who reward equitable.

Finally, the observed difference in attitudes between tasks performed under conditions of fairness versus unfairness tend to be inconsistent with the expectations that would follow from equity theory. The latter would predict, consistent with dissonance theory, that if there are no alternative means to reduce perceived inequity, individuals should enhance the value of the task following overreward and depreciate it following underreward. In studies to date, the observed effect is either in the opposite direction or not significantly different. [*See* ATTITUDE CHANGE; COGNITIVE DISSONANCE.]

3. Performance Effects

The behavioral or performance effects of perceived equity and inequity are less mixed and more consistent with equity theory. Equity theory predicts that underpaid hourly workers will be less productive or produce a greater amount of low-quality output than equitably paid ones. Research tends to confirm these two predictions.

Equity theory also predicts that overpaid hourly workers will raise their performance level, and will be more productive or produce higher quality output than equitably paid ones. Although the findings are not as strong as those for underpaid workers, the outcomes of the majority of studies performed on the influence of overpayment are consistent with the expectation that overpaid workers produce improvements in either the quality or quantity of performance, or both.

4. Victim's Coping Responses

Recently there has been a concern with how perceptions of inequity or unfairness may influence the attitudes and behaviors of those who have experienced some form of life changing unfairness, namely, victims. Theories of fairness, like social comparison theory, assume that one is most likely to experience feelings of fairness or unfairness when one compares one's own inputs and outcomes with those of similar others. If one is a victim of a natural catastrophe, crime, illness, job loss, etc., there is often cause to feel that one has been treated unfairly relative to others.

If one assumes that victims perceive their outcomes as unfair, and that such perceptions are stressful, then one can ask whether there are characteristic ways in which victims reduce stress. S. Taylor, in setting forth a program of research to account for changes in the attitudes and behavior of victims, assumes being victimized, like experiencing inequity, is aversive. Not only is the primary victimization event stressful, but so are the implied secondary effects of loss of control and of self-esteem.

Victims have been observed to employ various strategies to reduce both perceptions of unfairness and the associated stress. One strategy victims use is to change their reference group and to compare downward with a different population of individuals or groups who are worse off then they. A second strategy they follow is to imagine an even worse scenario than the victimizing one, e.g., "I could have been killed." A third strategy that victims have been observed to employ to reduce the stress of perceived unfairness is to find benefits in their present state that help justify it, e.g., seeking and finding more meaning in one's life after being victimized than before. A fourth strategy is to pat oneself on the back for successfully coping with the cause of one's stress, and/or for helping others.

The preceding four strategies employ a number of perceptual and cognitive processes for reducing the stress of being a victim. When unfair outcomes are produced by the actions of another, there are other more direct behavioral methods that can be pursued to reduce the resulting perceptions of unfairness. One can seek economic restitution from the other; one can pursue legal means to blame and to punish the harmdoer; one can demand apologies; and if a relationship exists between oneself and a harm doer, one can threaten to or actually leave the relationship. [*See* COPING.]

E. Procedure as an Independent Variable: Reactive Fairness II (Cell 4)

Only a limited amount of research has evaluated individual's reactions to their perceiving that given allocation procedures are fair or unfair. In organizational settings, it has been observed that perceptions of procedural fairness increase employee satisfaction and their commitment to an organization. Such perceptions are also associated with an increased trust of supervisory personnel, and with greater wage satisfaction.

Within the legal system, it has been found that perceived fairness of process leads to higher general levels of satisfaction, as well as more positive evaluations of the system's outcomes. Within the political system, it has been observed that perceptions of procedural fairness are related to stronger endorsements of political leaders, and to increased compliance with their requests, even when the leaders' actions may not produce favorable outcomes for the observer. Perceptions of fairness in political process by observers may also reduce the amount of attention they pay to outcomes and to the evaluation of whether they are beneficial to oneself.

Finally, research based upon Thibaut and Walker's control model of procedural equity has reported several basic relationships between perceived procedure and fairness judgments. The most strongly documented of these is between voice or control over process and outcome. Studies in legal and organizational settings indicate that giving voice, that is allowing participants to express opinions, in third-party decision settings, significantly increases judgments of procedural fairness.

Recent research indicates that the effects of having voice may not be, as initially assumed, due to participants beliefs that opinion expression plays an instrumental role in influencing outcomes. Rather, research suggests that perceiving one has voice may influence fairness judgments simply because one has the opportunity to express one's view even when one recognizes that one's opinions will not influence the final outcomes received.

The latter finding is more consistent with the central assumptions of the group-value model of procedural fairness than those of the control model. The group-value model assumes that perceptions of fairness of process and outcome are enhanced when the procedures followed by authorities afford people status under conditions of perceived neutrality and trust. [*See* CONTROL.]

F. Distribution as a Dependent Variable: Proactive Fairness I (Cell 5)

Considerable theoretical and empirical effort has been devoted to describing and understanding the causes and correlates of fairness judgments and behaviors. In addition to age and developmental stage, described earlier, a variety of other specific proactive factors have been studied. These include: (1) the characteristics of the allocator, (2) the characteristics of the task, (3) the nature of the resources being distributed, and (4) the nature of the relationship which exists between individuals in an allocation task, and (5) the nature of group membership.

1. Characteristics of the Allocator

Two of the characteristics of the allocator that have received considerable attention are gender and interaction orientation. Gender, of course, refers to the sex of the allocator. Interaction orientation (IO) refers to fundamental differences in goals recognizing that some persons are more strongly oriented toward the interpersonal side of relationships, trying to develop and sustain cordial relationships with others, while other people are more task oriented, focusing upon individualistic forms of problem solving and being either relatively indifferent toward others or concerned with outdoing them.

In terms of gender, women have been found more likely to be equalitarian in their allocations than men who tend to make choices that afford themselves higher outcomes than others. It has also been found that women in their interaction orientations tend to be more relationally oriented whereas men are more task oriented. It has been assumed this latter difference mediates the observed gender differences in fairness behaviors. There is, however, a difficulty with this explanation. Gender and interaction orientation are not found to be highly correlated. Rather, both act independently as factors in determining fairness rule preference.

A third variable, the nature of the task, has been found to interact with gender to produce results that are sometimes consistent, sometimes inconsistent, with the assumption that the gender differences in fairness are mediated by interaction orientation. In work related settings, gender differences in allocations are found to occur in a direction consistent with the IO hypothesis, namely, women are more relational and equalitarian in their allocations, whereas men are more task oriented, allocating equitably. In relational or affective tasks, however, differences in allocation rule use as function of gender are not observed.

A number of other personality variables have been hypothesized to be related to differences in fairness behavior. Frequently these variables are observed to interact with situational factors to influence choice behavior. For example, individuals high in affiliative needs are found to be more likely to mimic the fairness choices of others than individuals high in achievement needs. The latter are more likely to follow an equity rule independent of others' rule use.

The effects of one person's allocation rule use upon another's have been examined when the latter differ on the personality variable of self-esteem. Persons low in self-esteem are more likely to imitate an interdependent other's fairness rule use. Those high in self-esteem are more likely to make allocations based on differences in performance independent of other's allocation strategy. It can be argued that those low in esteem are more susceptible to influence because they are more concerned about self-presentation. But, it is also possible that they are less confident about which rule is appropriate to use, and hence are more likely to mimic others. [*See* SELF-ESTEEM.]

Research has also assessed whether individuals who are cooperative or competitive in orientation vary systematically in their use of fairness rules. Using a minimal group paradigm, where subjects are assigned to groups randomly or on the basis on some trivial difference in preference for an object or behavior, it has been observed that cooperative individuals are more likely to assign outcomes equally between an ingroup and an outgroup member whereas competitive individuals are likely to select an allocation rule that favors the ingroup member. [*See* SOCIAL VALUES.]

The relationship between self-consciousness, self-awareness, self-presentation, and equity rule use has also been evaluated. In this analysis, public (attuned to other's impressions) versus private (attuned to own feelings) self-consciousness is measured and treated as an individual difference variable. Being self-aware versus non-self-aware is introduced as a manipulated situational variable. The interaction of the two is assumed to affect an allocator's concern with managing others' impressions, and this concern is further assumed to affect the selection of equity rules.

Research indicates that a concern with others' impressions is highest for those high in public self-consciousness who are not made self-aware, and lowest for those high in private self-consciousness who have been made self-aware. Further, those highest in concern with other's impressions were observed to be most likely to use an equality rule in self/other allocations; those lowest in concern were most likely to select an equity rule.

In summary, the characteristics of allocators have been found to influence the choice of fairness rules. In most instances, the explanatory power of individual difference variables is increased substantially by understanding how they interact with conceptually relevant situational variables. This is hardly surprising since most forms of social behavior are influenced by an interaction between the dispositions of individuals and the situational forces operating upon them.

2. Characteristics of the Task

Research has also examined how specific characteristics of a task can influence the selection of allocation rules. Here, we will briefly review research in which two factors were manipulated: (1) task instructions, and (2) information about own and other's task inputs.

One instructional variable manipulated is whether a task is perceived to be one of production or one of maintaining an interpersonal relationship. As hypothesized, allocations have been found to be more consistent with proportional equity when work and productivity are stressed, and more equalitarian when interpersonal harmony and friendship are emphasized. The complexity of input information also can influence rule choice. It has been observed with both children and adults that when input information is complex, there exists a tendency to fall back on an equality rule of allocation. There are several possible reasons why equality serves as the default rule given informational complexity.

First, equality tends to be the easier fairness rule to compute. Second, given informational complexity, it may have primacy in recall since as noted earlier, developmental studies indicate that equality is the first fairness rule to be acquired by children. Third, equality may be the normatively dominant fairness rule, and given informational complexity, it may be more difficult to find reasons to deviate from using it.

3. The Nature of the Resources

The nature of the resources being distributed may also affect allocation judgments and behavior. In one study, fairness rule use as a function of resource type was examined using Foa and Foa's classification of resources into six types: money, goods, services, status, information, and love. In three countries, Germany, Sweden, and the United States, the following was observed: (1) equality is the preferred distribution rule when the commodities to be allocated are love, goods and services; (2) equity is preferred when the allocated commodity is status; (3) equity and equality are equally preferred when allocating money; and (4) equality and need are equally preferred when allocating information.

A second resource characteristic found to influence fairness rule use is the valence of the outcomes. Resources can be positive or negative in sign, and thereby valued as gains or losses, rewards or punishments. In the legal system, outcomes are often punishments which are judged as more or less fair on the basis of their severity. In third-party allocation studies, it has been observed that judgments of the appropriateness of allocations vary as a function of nature of the inputs, the sign of the outcomes distributed, and the nature of the relationship existing between individuals.

For example, when outcomes are negative and no information is available as to why one person has a higher input than another, equitable allocations are judged fairer in competitive than in cooperative relationships. Given positive outcomes, proportional equity is judged as a fairer distribution rule when performance is attributed to diligence than when it is attributed to ability.

Few studies have evaluated how negative outcomes are allocated. One might expect, however, that in integrative relationships, negative outcomes would be more likely to be shared equally, whereas in nonintegrative relationships equity would dominate, particularly if one's input implied one should receive less of a negative resource.

4. The Nature of the Relationship

The nature of the relationship that exists between individuals or groups undoubtedly influences their choice of fairness rules. One might expect, regardless of whether the outcome is positive or negative, that strangers would be more likely to employ the rule of equity; friends more likely to employ the equality rule; and intimates, including family members, more likely to invoke the rule of need.

Results from empirical studies on the effects of the form of relationship upon rule use are, however, somewhat ambiguous. Inconsistent with the above expectations, friends are found in a number of studies to be no more likely to allocate resources equally between themselves than are nonfriends. However, there are also findings consistent with the above expectations. Individuals in cohesive relationships have been observed to be more likely to make equal distributions of outcomes between self and others. And, individuals are judged by observers as more likely to be in a friendship relationship if they split meal checks equally rather than by the rule of proportional equity.

A significant body of research has contrasted the allocations of individuals within one-to-one exchange relationships versus those within more altruistic and intimate forms of communal or identity relationships. Although the empirical findings are again mixed, some of the evidence is consistent with the theoretical assumption made by M. Clark and J. Mills that need is more likely to be used as an allocation rule within communal or intimate relationships whereas equity is more likely to be used within relationships based upon the exchange of resources.

Clark and Mills argue that persons in communal relationships are strongly concerned about other's welfare and do not keep track of the relative contributions made to a relationship. On the other hand, individuals in exchange relationships are assumed to engage in careful bookkeeping and to expect to receive returns consistent with the quantity and quality of their inputs to the relationship.

Although it seems likely that bookkeeping is not as important within communal as exchange relationships, there would seem little doubt that within communal relationships, such as marriage, bookkeeping goes on over time. And, the perceived balance of own and spouse's input influences perceptions of the fairness of the outcomes each has received within the relationship.

5. Group Membership

Finally, fairness judgments or behaviors are likely to be influenced by whether those who allocate and receive allocations are individuals, members of groups, or groups themselves. Most of the research findings described thus far relate to the allocations of resources between two individuals. Research employing the minimal group paradigm, as described earlier, provides evidence that at a group level, there often exists a general attitudinal or distributional bias or unfairness, namely, own group members are favored over outgroup members.

The above finding of a general ingroup bias, however, must be qualified in several ways, First, the bias on group members may vary as a function of their interpersonal orientations. For example, as noted earlier, cooperative individuals, who are concerned with both own and other's welfare, have been observed to prefer equal ingroup–outgroup allocations to ingroup biased allocations. Individualistic and competitively oriented individuals, on the other hand, who are concerned with being outcome advantaged in either relative or absolute terms, strongly prefer allocations that favor their own group members. Second, communication can influence group bias. When communication occurs between ingroup and outgroup members before an allocation, the level of ingroup bias decreases and ingroup and outgroup members tend to be treated more equally and fairly.

Third, the relative input of ingroup and outgroup members can influence group bias. When ingroup members outperform outgroup members, group members afford more resources to their own group members than to outgroup members. However, when outgroup members outperform ingroup members, individuals tend to allocate resources consistently with the rule of equality affording the same outcome to an ingroup and an outgroup member. This, of course, reflects another form of ingroup favoritism.

G. Procedure as a Dependent Variable: Proactive Fairness II (Cell 6)

Relatively little theoretical work has been undertaken to develop a conceptual framework for evaluating factors that increase or decrease the likelihood that specific fairness procedures will be followed, or that once manifested, the procedures will be perceived as fair. M. Lerner does, however, describe how perceptions of fairness of procedure are influenced by three fundamental forms of personal relationship: nonunit, unit, and identity.

Lerner defines nonunit relationships as having the properties of zero-sum games where participants strive to demonstrate their dominance and superiority over others. In such relationships, certain procedural rules are assumed to exist to protect societal members from excessive competition by legitimizing, neutralizing, and depersonalizing the conflict. In some instances, the court system performs this function although, as Lerner points out, court battles at times further personalize the conflict. Arbitration, mediation, and other dispute resolution procedures also provide ways to reduce the types of conflict that may occur in nonunit relationships. [*See* ARBITRATION.]

Persons within unit relationships perceive themselves as sharing a similar fate with one another. They expect those within the relationship to hold common values, and therefore engage in cooperative and helpful behavior. There are times, however, when resources cannot be equally divided within this form of relationship, and hence conflict may arise.

To manage such conflict in a manner congruent with the cooperative orientations of unit members, certain fairness procedures are followed. First, process is emphasized rather than outcome. Thus, the way a game is played is viewed as more important than its outcome. Second, the stability of the unit relationship across time is stressed providing another way to ensure that short-term inequities will not produce conflict but will eventually balance out thereby maintaining overall fairness.

Finally, it is assumed in identity relationships that others are often to be psychologically indistinguishable from self. Thus, the rewards and punishments, happiness and sadness of another become one's own as well. Being fair in procedures within identity relationships is comparable to being fair in procedure with oneself.

Society may also intercede at times to define what are appropriate procedures for dealing fairly with others with whom one "should" share a close relationship. In the case of dependent children, for example, laws specify procedures that are fair in regards to the nature and length of parental care. Or, a society may set forth fair procedures to be followed in allocating resources for educating its less fortunate, more needy members.

In terms of the existing empirical work on procedural equity, correlational studies have identified processes that when followed enhance judgments of fairness. These include: suppressing bias, giving consideration to other's views, following procedures consistently, providing timely feedback to participants, maintaining ethical standards, trying to be fair, producing good decisions, and providing opportunities to present and correct information, as well as to voice one's concern.

In addition, experimental research, mostly involving individuals who do not share close unit relationships, indicates that variations in the structure of the decision-making process can influence judgments of procedural fairness. Thus, arbitration, a procedure where the parties to a dispute have some control over the process whereas a third party controls the outcome, is judged to be fairer than autocratic decision-making, a procedure where a third party controls both process and outcomes.

In general, the greater the perceived opportunity for those involved in a conflict to provide information and to express their values during the decision-making process, the greater the perceived fairness of both procedures and outcomes. Further, the effects of an increased opportunity to express one's beliefs and to provide information tend to increase the likelihood of judgments of both procedural and distributive fairness, even when the outcomes distributed to oneself are unfavorable.

Other research, concerned with the nature of outcomes and the perception of procedural fairness, reports that when the outcomes received are moderately or highly rewarding, procedures tend to be viewed as fair regardless of the process. When, on the other hand, rewards are low or are negative, processes perceived to be fair were rated as fair, and those perceived as unfair were rated as unfair.

Other findings relating to the perception of procedural fairness include: (1) given apparent improprieties in judicial process, procedures are rated as less fair given unfavorable outcomes, and more fair given favorable outcomes than when there are no perceived improprieties; (2) the degree of rated unfairness of an apparent procedural impropriety is related to the level of acceptability of the justification provided for its occurrence; and (3) individuals who experience outcomes resulting in a loss accompanied by unexplained changes in procedure perceive the procedure as more unfair than those who experience such unexpected changes without a loss. When such changes are strongly justified, however, there is no difference in perceived fairness regardless of whether individuals experience a loss.

IV. SUMMARY

One of the principal reasons that humans interact is to exchange resources, an activity which is requisite to their survival. The rules of equity provide an important set of prescriptions that help effectively to govern both the processes and the outcomes of these interactions. For purposes of scientific inquiry, equity in procedure and allocation equity can be treated as independent variables. Variations in perceived fairness of procedure or resource allocation are assumed to produce more or less stress which in turn importantly impacts subsequent social judgments and behaviors, as well as the nature of interpersonal and intergroup relationships. The procedures and rules that define equity can also be treated as dependent variables, and one can assess how various maturational, personality, and situational factors interact to influence the manner in which they are acquired and expressed.

In this article the nature and functions of equity, as viewed by the major disciplines in the behavioral sciences, are reviewed. Then, the development of fairness judgments and behavior is described. First, three models are set forth. Each model assumes that the processes underlying the development of fairness judgments and behaviors are cognitively built in, strictly ordered, and universal in expression. Second, empirical work on the development of fairness is described in terms of children's variations in rule use. Variations are examined as a function of age, experience, and various environmental contingencies.

The largest body of scientific knowledge concerning equity falls within the domain of social psychology. To facilitate our description of the previous theoretical and empirical efforts of social psychologist, we ordered work in the fairness area on two dimensions. The first contrasts fairness as procedure (procedural equity) with fairness as allocation rule use (distributive equity). The second dimension has three levels.

The first level, includes historical and existing theoretical models of distributive and procedural equity. This level can be contrasted to the other two which both focus more upon the empirical analysis of fairness judgments and behaviors. At level two, equity is treated as an independent variable and its effect upon perceptions of fairness and unfairness in procedure and distribution are empirically evaluated. At level three, distributive and procedural equity are treated as dependent variables, and various factors that influence the expression of fair evaluations and behaviors are empirically evaluated.

As depicted earlier in Table I, the content of the six cells created by crossing the two dimensions described above provides one with a meaningful way to summarize social psychological theory and research on equity and fairness. In reviewing the content of cells in Table I that consider procedural equity (Cells 2, 4, and 6), one finds that both theory and research in this area are relatively recent and not extensive. In particular, there have been few attempts to understand the environmental and individual difference variables that may underlie the etiology and selection of fair procedures and allocations. In contrast, there have been major and sustained theoretical and empirical efforts over the past 50 years to understand distributive fairness (as described in Cells 1, 3, and 5 of Table I).

Future theoretical and empirical work on equity and fairness undoubtedly will be directed not only toward further evaluating procedural and distributive fairness, both as independent and dependent variables, but also toward exploring the relationship between the two. Defining and understanding equity, in all its various forms, are essential to formulating and testing comprehensive and valid theories of social development as well as to achieving an understanding of many of the more important aspects of individual, interpersonal, and intergroup behavior.

Acknowledgment

The authors acknowledge their indebtedness to Dr. Holly A. Schroth for her unpublished paper entitled "Fairness and Justice: A Review of Recent Social Psychological Research," which describes recent empirical efforts in the domains of distributive and procedural fairness.

Bibliography

Cohen, R. L. (Ed.) (1986). "Justice-Views from the Social Sciences." Plenum, New York.

Greenberg, J., and Cohen, R. L. (1982). "Equity and Justice in Social Behavior." Academic Press, New York.

Deutsch, M. (1985). "Distributive Justice." Yale University Press, New Haven, CT.

Lerner, M. J. (1987). Social science perspectives on justice. *Soc. Justice Res.* **1,** 1–125.

Lind, E. A., and Tyler, T. R. (1988). "The Social Psychology of Procedural Justice." Plenum, New York.

Steensma, H., and Vermunt, R. (1991). "Social Justice in Human Relations," Vols. 1 and 2. Plenum, New York.

EXPECTATION

Warren W. Tryon
Fordham University

Glossary

Cognition Thought processes mediating behavior.

Conditioning When responding is conditional upon a stimulus or stimuli. In operant conditioning, the discriminative stimulus sets the occasion for the emission of a response which is contingently followed by reinforcement. In respondent (classical) conditioning, the conditioned stimulus comes to elicit the conditional response after being paired with the unconditional stimulus.

Expectation Conscious anticipation of future events on the basis of prior experience.

Information That which reduces uncertainty.

Self-efficacy An expectation about one's ability to perform specific tasks.

EXPECTATION can be defined as the anticipation of future consequences based on prior experience, current circumstances, or other sources of information. Expectation is a quintessential psychological term. All psychologists have had to address it in one manner or another. This article provides a cognitive, behavioral and psychoanalytic perspective on expectation. The behavioral perspective contains the greatest number of subheadings to emphasize that behaviorists have long been concerned with this issue despite criticism to the contrary. Moreover, the most controversial issues associated with expectation stem from the behavioral perspective. The final section presents a novel fourth perspective based on connectionism, also known as neural networks or parallel distributed processing. It is presented because neural networks provide a synthetic perspective from which to integrate the seemingly irreconcilable differences presented in the previous perspectives.

I. COGNITIVE PSYCHOLOGY

Cognitive psychology emphasizes information processing. Expectation is taken as the final common pathway of cognition leading to behavior. Expectation is therefore integral to all psychological explanation. People are said to behave in accordance with their expectations. They usually approach what they expect will be pleasurable and/or beneficial and avoid what they expect will be painful and/or problematic.

One must be careful to avoid circular reasoning when explaining behavior in terms of expectation. Arguments are circular when expectation is inferred from behavior and then used to explain the behavior from which they were inferred. For example, it is circular to first conclude that a person carrying an umbrella expects rain and second to explain that the reason they are carrying the umbrella is because they expect it will rain. An independent confirmation of expectation is needed before it can be used as an explanatory variable despite the fact that an independent assessment of expectation would often confirm the suspected expectation of rain. This point emphasizes an important difference between scientific and lay explanations.

Placebo effects, by definition, are mediated by expectation. Inert substances by definition, placebos can reduce pain (produce analgesia) or function as tranquilizers or stimulants (alter mood) if one strongly expects such effects. Placebo alcohol can increase sexual arousal, decrease sex-related guilt, and increase or decrease aggression and social anxiety depending upon context. Placebos can also induce nausea and vomiting, produce or inhibit con-

Copyright © 1994 by Academic Press, Inc. All rights of reproduction in any form reserved.

tact dermatitis, and cure warts. Strong expectation is the common element in all of these phenomena.

The following four factors have been identified to account for psychotherapeutic placebo effects: (1) A therapeutic relationship with a professionally trained care giver. (2) Conducting therapy in a setting that suggests therapeutic responsiveness such as a hospital, clinic, university, or professional office. (3) Therapy based on a clear rational. (4) A specific therapeutic procedure or ritual. All four factors exert their effect by inducing a positive outcome expectation. Positive expectation is an important component of the working alliance between therapist and client in all forms of psychotherapy regardless of therapeutic rationale.

II. BEHAVIORAL PERSPECTIVE

Behaviorism is often criticized as though it were a single unified position having no interest in psychological events; the "black box" approach. The following sections reflect a broad range of behavioral and cognitive–behavioral approaches to expectation.

Whereas cognitive psychologists accept explanations based on expectations as complete once they connect observable behavior with an associated psychological state, behavioral psychologists regard explanations based on expectations as necessarily incomplete until the source of the expectation is identified. Prior experience is where behaviorists look for the basis of expectation. When an experiential basis is found to account for the expectation, behaviorists explain both the expectation and the consequent behavior in terms of this prior experience. This fundamental theory construction difference accounts for most differences in how cognitive and behavioral psychologists use terms like expectation.

A. Pavlov's Conditional Response

Pavlov spoke and wrote of condition*al,* not condition*ed,* responses. We read of conditioned responses today due to a mistranslation of his work from Russian into English. A conditional response is one that is predicted on previous experience. Though born in 1849 and trained as a physiologist, it was not until 1902, when Pavlov was 53 years old, that he noticed that the dogs who served as his subjects anticipated (expected) the arrival of food upon hearing their keeper's footsteps. Pavlov subsequently renovated his laboratory and embarked on a second career in what today would be called neuropsychology. His research focused on the ability of the cerebral hemisphere to form associations between stimuli and responses. Though the term "expectation" does not appear in the index of his 1928 magnum opus *Conditioned Reflexes: An Investigation of the Physiological Activity of the Cerebral Cortex,* this is clearly what his work was about. [*See* CLASSICAL CONDITIONING.]

In addition to the famous bell–meat powder–saliva paradigm so widely discussed in introductory psychology texts, Pavlov also studied temporal conditioning where a time interval serves as the conditional stimulus. Food is presented at regular intervals resulting in increased salivation at those times. If, after acquisition of this conditional response, food is omitted at one of the regularly spaced feeding intervals, increased salivation occurs at that time. Pavlov succeeded in creating food expectancies in dogs with temporal intervals as long as 30 minutes!

As a physiologist, Pavlov explained the increased salivation at a regular feeding time as a response mediated by the cerebral cortex rather than as the product of a psychological expectation. The cerebral cortex was hypothesized to play an important mediating, but not initiating, role. The "cause" of salivation at times when food is routinely presented but occasionally omitted was attributed to the equal temporal spacing of food presentation scheduled by the experimenter rather than to the presence of a psychological state called expectation. It can be argued that the regular presentation of food gave rise both to the expectation and to anticipatory salivation.

B. Tolman's Expectation

In 1932 Tolman wrote *Purposive Behavior in Animals and Men* where he argued, and presented data, supporting his thesis that animals, as well as people, learn to expect, anticipate, the consequences of their actions and behave accordingly. Clearly, these expectations are driven by the subject's experience. Enough trials where lever pressing was followed by shock necessarily generated the expectation that shock would occur if the lever was pressed again. Only during acquisition would there be any variability in expectation. This conception pertains equally well to obtaining food for a lever press or any other consequence which regularly follows a behavior. In sum, expectation is hypothesized to mediate behavior but both behavior and expectation are determined by prior experience.

C. Rotter's Social Learning Theory

Rotter applied Tolman's expectation theory to social and clinically relevant behaviors. The two key concepts of social learning theory are expectancy and reinforcement value. The generalized expectancy of "locus of control" concerns the extent to which one expects that events are controlled by one's own behavior rather than by external forces like luck or the behavior of other people. Internal locus of control is the expectation of control whereas external locus of control is the expectation of helplessness. A huge literature developed in which persons with internal and external locus of control are compared. [*See* CONTROL.]

D. Rescorla's Relational Learning

Rescorla demonstrated that a conditioned (conditional) stimulus (CS) and an unconditioned (unconditional) stimulus (US) become associated because the CS provides *information* about the US. The proof of this assertion is that one can transform an effective learning schedule into an ineffective one through extra presentations of the US that are temporally uncorrelated with (do not predict) the CS.

Information is technically defined as a reduction of uncertainty. Pavlovian conditioning works because the CS reduces uncertainty about the onset of the US. Classical conditioning is an explicit recipe for producing expectations. Adding extra CS presentations reduces the amount of information communicated by the CS onset resulting in decreased learning about the CS–US relationship.

E. Bandura's Self-Efficacy

Bandura presented self-efficacy as a unifying theory of behavioral change. All psychological procedures were hypothesized to influence behavior through expectations of personal efficacy. The fact that personal estimates of performance are highly correlated with actual behavior is not disputed. Controversy emerges over why this correlation should exist. It has been argued that the correlation between performance estimates and actual behavior exists because self-concept governs (causes) both events. Alternately, it has been argued that people have long histories of being rewarded for doing what they say they will do; especially in situations where exceptions to this rule are easily noticed and likely to be punished. [*See* SELF-EFFICACY.]

F. Seligman's Learned Helplessness

Normal dogs, and other animals, quickly learn to jump over a low barrier to escape shock. Dogs who have previously received uncontrollable shock do not learn to escape shock under these same conditions. These results have been interpreted to mean that prior experience with inescapable shock led to the expectation of uncontrollability resulting in decreased motivation, impaired learning, and other signs of depression. Analogous results have been found with humans on a variety of tasks. These results clearly show that the expectation of helplessness and the consequent behavioral deficits both derive from prior experience with uncontrollable aversive experience.

A subsequent theoretical revision holds that expectation of uncontrollability is a necessary but not sufficient condition for the induction of depression in humans. Attribution of uncontrollability to internal (personal), stable, and global factors is hypothesized to be required before depression results. Attribution of uncontrollability to external, temporary, and circumscribed factors is predicted not to result in depression. This revision combines expectancy theory with attribution theory. [*See* ATTRIBUTION; LEARNED HELPLESSNESS.]

G. Skinner's Selectionism

Skinner was most definitiely *not* a stimulus–response (S-R) psychologist. He was a R-S psychologist. New behavior is shaped from old behavior. Complex behavior is refined from simple behavior. Skinner explicitly applied Darwin's evolutionary logic of variation and natural selection to behavior. Phylogenetic evolution entails selective death prior to reproduction. The surviving animals are better adapted to their environment because the less well-suited ones are no longer present. This is like raising the average IQ of a group of subjects by removing those with the lowest IQ from the group. Said otherwise, if one is allowed to choose a subset of subjects from a larger group according to some characterisitc or quality, then the average of the select sample regarding the quality will be greater than the initial group. Hence, average characteristics of populations change over time given consistent selection.

Skinner applied Darwin's reasoning by variation and natural selection to behavior; a process he termed ontogenetic evolution. He reasoned that variation is an unavoidable characteristic of all behavior. For example, it is virtually impossible to perform exactly the same behavior twice in succession. Even a simple lever press cannot be duplicated exactly. The force and therefore speed with which the lever is pressed will not be exactly the same from trial to trial. The number of microseconds that the lever remains fully depressed will differ from trial to trial. Hence, every behavior consists of a population or class of related behaviors called an operant; they are similar operations on the environment.

A response–reinforcement contingency specifies an if–then relationship which constitutes a selection criteria. It requires that only those particular behavioral variations meeting the selection criteria will be followed by the reinforcing stimulus. For example, one might present food only for lever presses exceeding a specified force. In this case, the distribution of lever press forces will increase above baseline levels. Gradually increasing the force criteria, changing the selection contingency, produces predictable behavioral changes; ontogenetic behavioral evolution results.

Discriminative stimuli are events which predict when the selection process is in effect. Through repeated experience, the subject behaves differently when the discriminative stimulus is present compared to when it is absent. For example, if the above mentioned lever press contingency results in food only when a green light is on, then lever pressing will eventually be restricted to times when the green light is on regardless of how hungry the subject is. The act of discriminating when the contingencies are in effect is functionally equivalent to expecting that the if–then contingent relationship will hold. Consistent environmental experience is therefore an important cause of one's expectations; experience drives expectation. Because Skinner maintained that both expectation and behavior derived from prior experience, he attributed the cause of behavior to prior experience rather than to expectation despite the fact that expectations are highly correlated with contemporaneous behaviors. The human perception that expectations exist concurrently with behavior did not change Skinner's causal attributions.

While it is easy to appreciate the origin of expectation and behavior in experimental settings where the observer is aware of the selection criteria used to grant access to the reinforcing stimulus, a naive observer would probably not suspect the presence of a selection scheme but would return to the everyday practice of explaining the subject's behavior entirely on the basis of expectation. If the naive observer could interview the subject, he or she would almost certainly inquire about the subject's expectations rather than their experiential basis. Consequently, an expectation-based explanation would be even more likely. While the expectancy explanation would be correct, as far as it goes, it would also be incomplete since it would not account for the origin of the expectation. Because lay people, and many psychologists, do not agree that expectation-based explanations are incomplete, a search for the origin of these expectations is typically not undertaken. The view that explanations based on expectations, and other psychological states, are incomplete and stand in the way of identifying the source of both the psychological states and the associated behavior are the two primary reasons why Skinner consistently resisted cognitive explanations of behavior. Cognitive psychology could bridge the theoretical gap with operant conditioning by examining the experiential basis of expectations and other psychological states. The few attempts to do so are evidence that the proponents of expectation explanation do not find such accounts incomplete.

H. Staats's Psychological Behaviorism

Staats has written about the corrosive crisis of disunity within psychology and has sought to construct a framework theory to promote unification. Behavior and its supportive, underlying, psychological processes are divided into three major categories called basic behavioral repertoires (BBRs).

The sensorimotor (S-M) repertoire consists of coordinated skills including visual tracking, grasping, manipulating, throwing, catching, standing, walking, self-care skills, and imitation.

The emotional–motivational (E-M) repertoire distinguishes among stimuli on the basis of their personal value; what one is willing to work for. This repertoire consists of all learned and unlearned associations which elicit emotional responses and therefore serve as incentives. It defines whether one will respond positively or negatively to an event; whether one will approach or avoid an object.

The language–cognitive (L-C) repertoire entails expectation, language, and all other higher mental functions. The intimate connection between language and cognition is explicitly recognized.

Development is understood as the process by which more complex BBR's are formed through cumulative–hierarchical combinations of simpler ones. Personality consists of all individual BBR differences. Explaining why one child benefits from a specific educational opportunity while another does not entails examining a broad range of BBR's pertinent to both the instructional topic and mode of presentation. For example, students who are expected to discuss a story must first be able to read and comprehend what they read. Dyslexic students may need to listen to taped versions of the story rather than read it.

BBR's are the product of prior learning and interact with present circumstances to produce contemporary behavior. Expectations develop as part of the L-C repertoire and are important behavioral causes. The primary advantage of the BBR approach for the psychology of expectation is that it explicitly specifies prior experience as the origin of expectation. Expectation functions as the proximal cause whereas prior experience functions as the distal cause of present behavior.

III. PSYCHOANALYTIC PERSPECTIVE

Psychoanalysis, like behaviorism, is not a single entity but represents a broad evolving spectrum of opinion. However, the following points are generally characteristic of this position.

A. Ego Psychology

Extraordinary parallels exist between contemporary cognitive behaviorism and ego psychology. In the late 1930s, Heinz Hartmann identified the problem of adaptation to reality as the central psychological question. While psychoanalysis concerned itself with id–ego conflicts and ego defense mechanisms, ego psychologists emphasized development depending upon preception, intention, thinking, language, memory and other rational processes including expectation. The term "conflict-free ego sphere" was used to accentuate this distinction.

Modern cognitive psychologists distinguish themselves from psychoanalysis in the same important ways that ego psychologists do. Anticipating future events, expectation, is accorded the same important role in explaining human behavior by ego psychologists as by cognitive psychologists. A list of ego functions and a list of cognitive processes are essentially the same list. Expectation is discussed in the same causative fashion by ego psychologists as by cognitive psychologists making all of the aforementioned comments regarding the cognitive perspective pertinent here.

B. Unconscious Ego Defenses Distort Expectation

Psychoanalytic theory posits unconscious motives in addition to conscious ones. The ego not only defends consciousness against unconscious impulses but, through defense mechanisms, is hypothesized to distort consciousness including expectation. Unconscious processes are typically described as primitive and highly emotional. Hence, a neurotic person might marry an undesirable partner *expecting* a bright future. This positive expectation could be viewed as a secondary cause of deciding to get married. Primary causation is usually attributed to unconscious motives. Unconscious motivations to leave home could produce unrealistically positive expectations of future happiness through marriage. The same processes can work toward underestimating negative consequences. Unconscious motives to engage in particular behaviors may be manifested in a diminished expectation of loss. [*See* DEFENSE MECHANISMS.]

IV. NEURAL NETWORK PERSPECTIVE

Recent developments outside of psychology have provided psychologists with an extraordinary opportunity to develop a unified theory of behavior and associated psychological states including expectation. I refer to connectionism and the parallel distributed processing models also known as neural networks.

A. Architecture

Neural networks consist of interconnected elemental processing nodes, described below. The architecture of a neural network refers to the specific way in which the artificial "neurons" are interconnected. One of the simplest architectures is to fully interconnect a set of input neurons with a set of output neurons such that each input neuron is connected to every output neuron. Much greater capability is achieved through the insertion of a "hidden" middle layer where input neurons are connected to mediating neurons which, in turn, are connected to output neurons. No direct input–output connections are allowed. The strength of each connection is designated by a number called a connection weight. This weight is intended to represent a functional property of the synapse which connects real neurons.

B. Neural Principles

Each of the middle and output nodes functions, to a first approximation, like real neurons in the following ways. First, all inputs are summed and if the result exceeds a threshold, then the neuron fires. Summation is implemented by multiplying the status of the neuron from which the connection originates ($1 = \text{on}$, $0 = \text{off}$) by the connection weight. These products are added across all inputs. Second, a nonlinear sigmoidal threshold function connects the summed inputs (X axis) with a probability of firing (Y axis). It is critical to the effective functioning of the neural network that this transfer function be nonlinear. It is noteworthy that the transfer functions of real neurons are also nonlinear.

C. Learning Function

Connection weights are initialized to random values within a specified range. Neural networks are then trained to either a supervised or unsupervised mode rather than programmed. The response of a neural network to experience is to increase the values of some connection weights and decrease the value of others according to a learning function expressed as a mathematical equation. It is noteworthy that learning in simple neural systems entails changes in synaptic strength modeled here as altered connection weights.

Back-propagation is a common method of systematically altering connection weights as a function of experience. The network's first response is on the basis of the initial random connection weights. The discrepancy between the current and desired response is evaluated and propagated backward by first changing the weights connecting all of the middle to output nodes and then changing all of the weights connecting the input to middle nodes. This gradient decent algorithm gradually optimizes the weights for performing the specified task. Other methods for altering connection weights exist.

D. Emergent Properties

Neural networks can learn anything they can represent. Learning reduces to coding appropriate responses to different stimuli. The final pattern of weighted interconnections among neurons constitutes a complex code which enables the network to behave intelligently in response to training situations and to novel situations, within limits.

A broad spectrum of rule-based-like learning has been demonstrated without rules of any kind or any type of central processing unit. Parallel distributed processing (PDP) networks of homogeneous units are capable of many psychological functions including: operant and respondent conditioning, human categorical learning, memory, facial perception, letter perception, word recognition, and learning to pronounce English.

E. Unified Perspective

Neural architecture is an important aspect of a functional neural network. Genetic and maturational factors determine the necessary physical substrate for the learning, including expectations. When neural networks are excessively pruned, loose associations result which can result in psychotic expectations. A neural network capable of normal Wisconsin Card sorting can be altered so that it shows symptoms of frontal lobe damage; it perseverates and is unusually attracted by novelty. Said otherwise, this altered network mistakenly expects the correct response to be the previous response or a novel opportunity. These finidngs explicitly recognize that expectation has a biological basis.

Neural networks are consistent with both behavioral and cognitive values. The following two sentences illustrate one pair of supporting points. The learning/representation duality (that neural networks can learn anything that they can represent) emphasizes that expectations are cognitive representations which mediate behavior; they function as proximate causes of behavior. The fact that connection weights, which encode every representation, change over time in a manner that is highly consistent with Skinner's principles of variation and selection (evolution through reinforcement) emphasizes that expectations are systematically derived from experience.

F. Proximal Causal Mechanism

Neural networks provide a biologically inspired proximal causal mechanism capable of simulating many psychological processes and behaviors. That functional networks are trained rather than programmed emphasizes learning from prior experience as fundamental to all psychological and behavioral development. That neural networks are implemented within a digital computer means that all of their parameters are under complete experimental control. The complex developmental processes by which present expectations develop from prior experience and interact with current context to yield contemporary behavior and altered expectations (cf. Staats BBR's) can be studied one cycle at a time if desired.

V. CONCLUSION

Expectation has been addressed by cognitive, behavioral, and psychoanalytic psychologists. Neural networks provide a unified perspective from which these investigators plus neuroscientists, mathematicians, physicists, and computer scientists can all discuss expectation using the same vocabulary. Each discipline can articulate important principles within a common context. Having a explicit proximal causal mechanism for generating expectations from prior experience that is under complete experimental control greatly facilitates conducting rigorous scientific research on this topic. A new and productive era of high-quality theoretically unified research on expectation is therefore anticipated.

Bibliography

Frank, J. D., and Frank, J. B. (1991). "Persuasion and Healing: A Comparative Study of Psychotherapy," 3rd ed. Johns Hopkins University Press, Baltimore, MD.

Kirsch, I. (1990). "Changing Expectations: A Key to Effective Psychotherapy." Brooks/Cole, Pacific Grove, CA.

Rumelhart, D. E., and McClelland, J. M. (1986). "Parallel Distributed Processing," Vols. 1 and 2. MIT Press, Cambridge, MA.

Wasserman, P. D. (1989). "Neural Computing: Theory and Practice. Van Nostrand Reinhold, New York.

EXTRAVERSION–INTROVERSION

D. H. Saklofske
University of Saskatchewan, Canada

H. J. Eysenck
Institute of Psychiatry, London

Glossary

Correlation A statistical method for determining the degree and direction of relationship between psychological variables.

Extraversion A major personality dimension that includes measureable traits such as sociability, activity, and dominance.

Factor analysis A statistical technique that combines clusters of correlated variables into broader categories.

Personality A field of study that focuses on describing individual differences in human behavior and identifying the causes that characterize our unique ways of thinking, feeling, and acting across situations.

Traits Relatively consistent and enduring ways of thinking, feeling, and behaving.

EXTRAVERSION has been recognized as a major personality variable in contemporary psychological writings. It may be thought of as a personality dimension that describes a number of more specific personality traits ranging from sociability and liveliness to dominance and adventure-seeking. Extraversion is thought to have a biological basis associated with cortical arousal. The lower level of cortical arousal found in extraverts is used to explain their greater need for activity, excitement, and general stimulation. Extraversion has, in turn, been linked with various human behaviors such as occupational performance and antisocial behaviors.

I. EXTRAVERSION: AN OVERVIEW

Mary and Deborah are a study in contrasts. Both young women have entered their first year of university and have been assigned to share a room in the university residence. Mary is described as a "bubbly" person, full of charm and wit, a real go-getter. She is active in many campus clubs and can always be found with a group of friends. She enjoys dancing and lively music, plays various sports with other friends, loves to travel, and seems willing to try most things at least once. She is well-liked and popular and often at the center of events. She has indicated that she would enjoy work that has lots of action and change to it rather than an office job.

In contrast, Deborah is a somewhat shy and retiring person who is much more content to work on her studies in the library or at her desk in the residence. She prefers quiet meals and going to movies or reading a book to the more outgoing activities of her roommate. She is not especially well known by fellow students as she tends to move rather quietly from class to class. She has several close friends that she knew from her public school days. Her expectation is to major in history and English and hopefully author books or work as an archivist.

What ever commonalities and differences exist between these two people, one particular personality dimension comes to the fore. The various behaviors, actions, and preferences would suggest that Mary and Deborah vary along the personality continuum defined as extraversion–introversion. Extraverts, like Mary, manifest a relatively consistent and stable profile characterized by such descriptors as

Encyclopedia of Human Behavior, Volume 2
Copyright © 1994 by Academic Press, Inc. All rights of reproduction in any form reserved.

sociable, lively, active, carefree, and sensation-seeking. Deborah more clearly falls toward the other end of the continuum which defines introverts, people who are quiet, reserved, passive, controlled, and less sociable and outgoing.

Extraversion is seen by many psychologists as a major personality dimension that is very important in formulating a description of human behavior and particularly of individual differences. Psychologists have created numerous concepts in an effort to explain, understand, predict, and even change or modify human behavior. Thus, variables such as intelligence, anxiety, achievement motivation, sensation-seeking, self-concept, and extraversion have been suggested as important ones in describing behavior. Some of these variables have been cast within very elaborate theoretical frameworks that have both a formal and empirical basis. As well, they may vary in importance from serving as very minor to major descriptors of human functioning.

In order to understand the nature and relevance of extraversion (E), consideration must be given to a number of basic questions that are of critical importance when examining any personality description. To follow is a discussion of E that focuses on the following themes: historical perspectives, current views of personality, personality measurement, the biological basis of E, cross-cultural studies, and relationships with other human characteristics.

II. HISTORY

Efforts to understand ourselves, to show how we differ from other animals, to discover what makes us alike and yet different from each other, certainly predate the creation of psychology as both a scientific discipline and a profession. In fact, personality is derived from "persona," the Latin wording meaning mask. The earliest descriptions of human personality originated from the observations of such important Greek philosophers as Theophrastus and Hippocrates, and the Roman physician Galen. It is at this earliest time that the underpinnings of what is now termed extraversion were first witnessed. Arising from these observations of some 2000 years ago was the doctrine of the four humors, which classified individuals into four types; i.e., phlegmatic (controlled, calm), sanguine (carefree, sociable), choleric (egocentric, hot-headed), and melancholic (worried, serious). It is the sanguine temperament that most closely corresponds to our current picture of the stable extravert. This representation of human personality was further elaborated upon by Immanuel Kant in the late 1700s. Of interest is that these four temperaments were seen as quite discrete and unrelated suggesting that only four categories or types of human personality were possible. [*See* INDIVIDUAL DIFFERENCES IN TEMPERAMENT.]

It was not until Wilhelm Wundt, frequently referred to as the founder of the first psychological laboratory in Leipzig, Germany, in 1879, challenged the notion of a categorical system and instead proposed a dimensional view of human behavior. A view of personality began to emerge that may be represented in Figure 1. This representation of human personality shows that individuals may fall at any position or even combination of positions along the emotional–nonemotional and changeable–unchangeable dimensions. This two-dimensional system further shows the more dynamic nature of the four basic temperaments and a much clearer description of extraversion–introversion (i.e., changeability).

During the early years of this century, the Austrian psychiatrist Otto Gross and the Swiss psychiatrist Carl Jung formulated causal theories to account for the behaviors suggested by the typology. Jung has been credited as one of the first to elaborate on the pair of what he considered as opposite personality traits labeled extraversion–introversion.

As psychology continued to flourish and grow in the 20th century, the efforts to describe personality

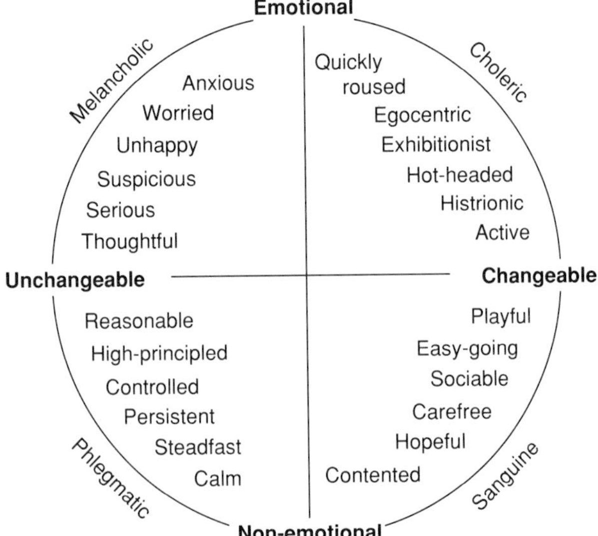

FIGURE 1 Diagrammatic representation of the classical theory of the four temperaments as described by I. Kant and W. Wundt.

within a scientific framework also increased. What psychologists have attempted to do is to employ scientific methods in the study of human behavior. Psychologists are very rigorous in the research methods used to gather and analyze information, use carefully controlled investigative procedures to acquire new information, and insist on replication of results. Thus, the discipline and practice of psychology are grounded in the scientific study of behavior rather than subjective and personal views and nonscientific pseudopsychologies such as astrology. Earlier speculations about human personality began to give way to more rigorously controlled research investigations cast within the framework of carefully constructed theoretical models. The I-E dimension continues to receive considerable attention from personality theorists and researchers. [*See* PSYCHOLOGY AND PSEUDOSCIENCE.]

III. CONTEMPORARY VIEWS OF EXTRAVERSION

Personality psychologists have been and are still actively engaged in the debate as to whether human beings can be best and most meaningfully described with the aid of only a few or many "words." One can very quickly create an exhaustive list of personality descriptors: e.g., happy, bright, friendly, kind, assertive, honest, sullen, patient, etc. The static four temperament approach is obviously too limited but the open-ended idiographic approach, that taken to extremes, which suggests that each individual is absolutely unique, is similarly not useful. We can accurately describe individuals along such major dimensions as extraversion–introversion when we recognize that some human characteristics or behaviors share much in common with others (e.g., shy, withdrawn, nonassertive, untalkative, quiet, loner, etc.). Psychologists' attempts to reduce human behavior to a finite set of descriptions are not an attempt to impose an artificial and nonworkable solution onto a truly complex personality description. Rather, psychologists attempt to find the most meaningful and parsimonious means of representing human personality.

Extraversion has its roots in the early Galen-Wundt theory of the four temperaments but has been more recently elaborated by such notable contemporary psychologists as R. B. Cattell, H. J. Eysenck, J. P. Guilford, J. Wiggins, and P. Costa and R. McCrae. Extraversion is also included in other personality models but under different names. Further, E scales appear on a number of personality questionnaires ranging from the Eysenck Personality Questionnaire where it comprises one of the three major personality variables to the well-known Minnesota Multiphasic Personality Inventory.

The description of individuals according to a small number of personality dimensions is frequently referred to as the trait approach. Essentially, through the use of sophisticated statistical techniques, such as correlational and factor analysis, psychologists have reduced the large number of behavioral descriptions to a much smaller number of stable and generalizable characteristics that make possible the explanation and prediction of individual differences and similarities. This view rests on the assumption that a meaningful model of personality can be based on a smaller but more powerful set of traits that are remarkably stable across time and differing situations. [*See* TRAITS.]

Very briefly, E appears as a major personality variable in almost all of the current trait descriptions, whether by name or as a result of further research investigations stimulated by these theories. An ongoing debate is whether personality is best described by the 16 primary traits suggested by Cattell (various other numbers are suggested by other psychologists such as the 8 domains of interpersonal behavior reported by Jerry Wiggins), or the "big 5" trait dimensions emphasized by Costa and McCrae, or by the "3 super factors" described by Eysenck. A consistent finding from the research studies is the emergence of a robust factor that may be called extraversion. Analysis of large numbers of responses to the various personality questionnaires seems to invariably produce an E factor. The two most influential trait theories today both agree that E is one of the major dimensions. Eysenck adds two other major personality dimensions labeled neuroticism (N) and psychoticism (P). Costa and McCrae add neuroticism, openness to experience, agreeableness, and conscientiousness to their extraversion factor to produce the "big 5" trait dimensions.

Some of this confusion may be clarified by examining how Eysenck has developed his personality model with particular reference to E. His system is a hierarchical one and begins with single acts or thoughts. The second level focuses on more consistently occurring acts and cognitions. Next comes the level of traits and finally types which reflect a composite of various correlated traits. Thus, each level is more encompassing and inclusive than the

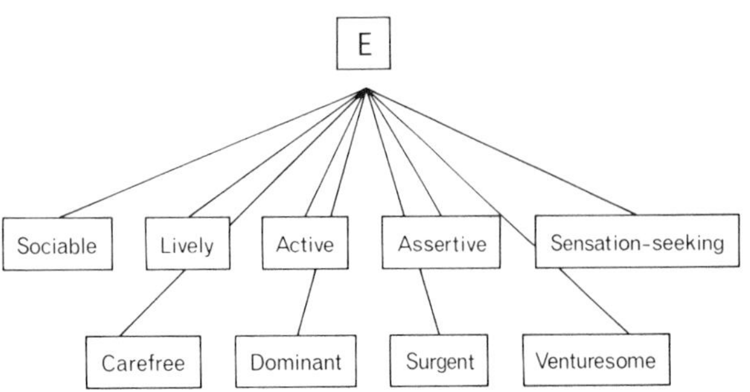

FIGURE 2 Some traits defining extraversion.

previous level. With respect to E, it is a dimension that encompasses a number of trait descriptors such as sociable, lively, active, assertive, and carefree. It is the observed intercorrelations between these traits that justify us in postulating the existence of extraversion. This structure is shown in Figure 2. Similarly, for the other major higher-order concept, neuroticism, the traits that intercorrelate and thus define it are shown in Figure 3.

How can we justify such a typology? Table I shows six questions supposed to measure E, and six questions supposed to measure N. We can collect large numbers of answers from random samples of the population, intercorrelate the answers, and check whether the patterns of intercorrelations give us two independent factors corresponding to E and N. When the necessary calculations are done via sophisticated statistical techniques, called factor analysis, we obtain the results shown in Figure 4; it will be obvious that the results support the theory.

We do not have to rely on self-ratings to obtain such evidence. Figure 5 shows the results of such a factor analytic investigation of the relation between ratings made of thousands of children in a child guidance clinic, using items of behavior. It will be seen that extraverted children demonstrate conduct problems, and introverted children personality problems.

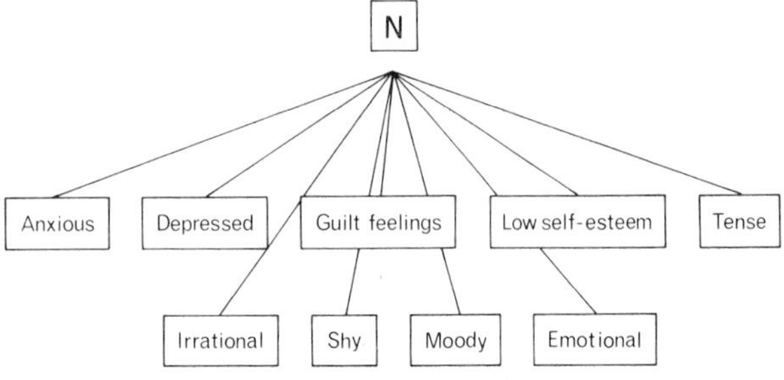

FIGURE 3 Some traits defining neuroticism.

TABLE I
Questionnaire Items Measuring Extraversion–Introversion

Questions	Key
1. Do you sometimes feel happy, sometimes depressed, without any apparent reason?	N
2. Do you have frequent ups and downs in mood, either with or without apparent cause?	N
3. Are you inclined to be moody?	N
4. Does your mind often wander while you are trying to concentrate?	N
5. Are you frequently "lost in thought" even when supposed to be taking part in a conversation?	N
6. Are you sometimes bubbling over with energy and sometimes very sluggish?	N
7. Do you prefer action to planning for action?	E
8. Are you happiest when you get involved in some project that calls for rapid action?	E
9. Do you usually take the initiative in making new friends?	E
10. Are you inclined to be quick and sure in your actions?	E
11. Would you rate yourself as a lively individual?	E
12. Would you be very unhappy if you were prevented from making numerous social contacts?	E

Of course all of these children are essentially high N scorers; children with low N scores would simply be more outgoing behaviorally when extraverted, and unsociable when introverted.

Jung had earlier put forward the hypothesis that introverted neurotics would show psychasthenic or dysthymic symptoms (anxiety, depression, apathy), while extraverted neurotics would show hysterical symptoms (hysterical attitude, conversion symptoms). A study of the behaviors and attitudes of

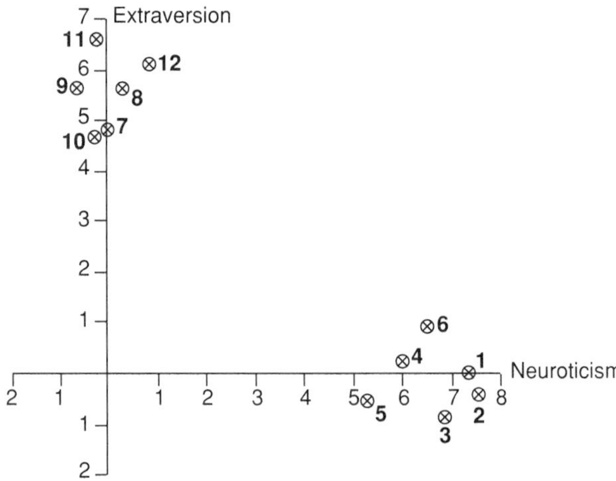

FIGURE 4 Relative position in two-dimensional space of six neuroticism and six extraversion questionnaire items.

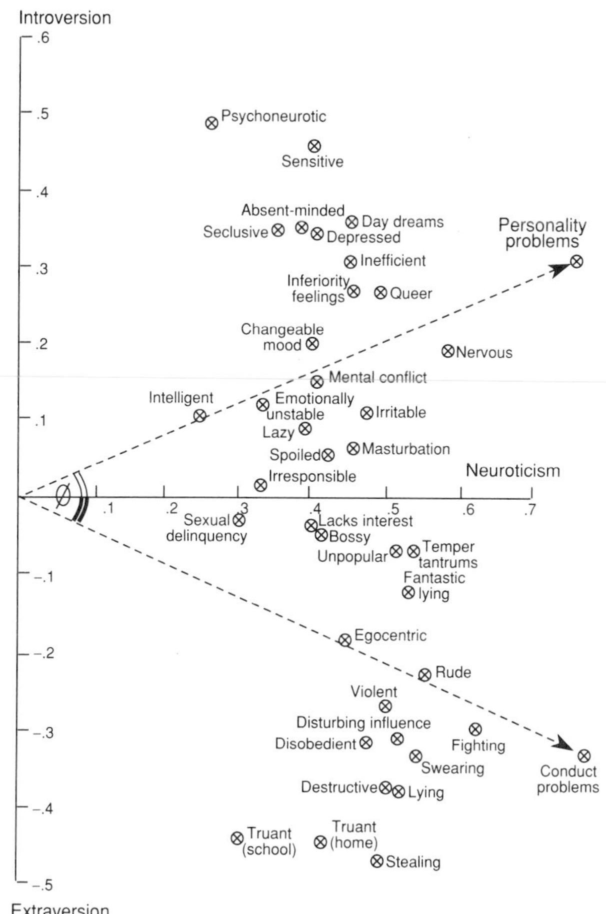

FIGURE 5 Two-factor representation of conduct and personality problems in children, showing breakdown into extraverted and introverted groups.

hundreds of neurotics bore out this theory as shown in Figure 6. These empirical studies will give a idea of the structure of personality.

To follow is a discussion of various studies and findings that help us to better understand extraversion. It is important to know about the theories and models that psychologists have created to account for and explain extraversion. The most thorough and widely accepted is the theory put forward by Hans Eysenck of the Institute of Psychiatry, University of London. Much of the ensuing discussion will draw from the theoretical and research contributions of Professor Eysenck. A question that is frequently asked is how psychologists measure variables such as extraversion. A number of questionnaires have been developed and will be mentioned below. While a description of the structure of personality is important, it is equally important to examine its causes. Extraversion would not be a very useful personality description if it only served as a summary label for a collection of human behaviors. Of considerable importance are questions related to whether extraversion is learned or whether genetic factors determine a persons position on the extraversion dimension? What are the biological underpinnings of extraversion and are there certain brain structures or functions that underlie an individual's behavior along the introversion–extraversion dimension? Further points that must be addressed relate to the robustness of extraversion such that we may question if it can be identified cross-culturally. Of relevance is what extraversion, or any other personality factor, tells us about other aspects of human functioning. For example, are extraverts more or less prone to certain psychiatric illness, are there differences in various performance indicators between extraverts and introverts?

IV. THE MEASUREMENT OF EXTRAVERSION

Psychologists may employ various procedures for gathering information about human behavior. We may observe a person in a structured situation or in more natural settings. The person may be interviewed or we can ask others to tell us about the person. Various tests can be conducted to determine, for example, how an individual reacts to stressful situations or responds to tasks that require the learning of new behaviors. In some instances, we gather information that tells about the person's internal condition such as the level of cortical arousal (EEG or electroencephalography). Various biochemical influences on personality can be examined by extracting samples of hormones such as testosterone or neurotransmitters including monamine oxidase or serotonin. We may also assess personality with self-report questionnaires. It is this personality test, inventory, or questionnaire method that is most commonly used to assess variables such as extraversion.

Hans and Sybil Eysenck have developed the most well-known and frequently used personality measures of extraversion. The recent versions include the Eysenck Personality Questionnaire (EPQ) for which there are both adult and child forms. This questionnaire contains items that are answered "yes" or "no" and measure the three superfactors of extraversion, neuroticism, and psychoticism. It also includes another scale that measures untruthful-

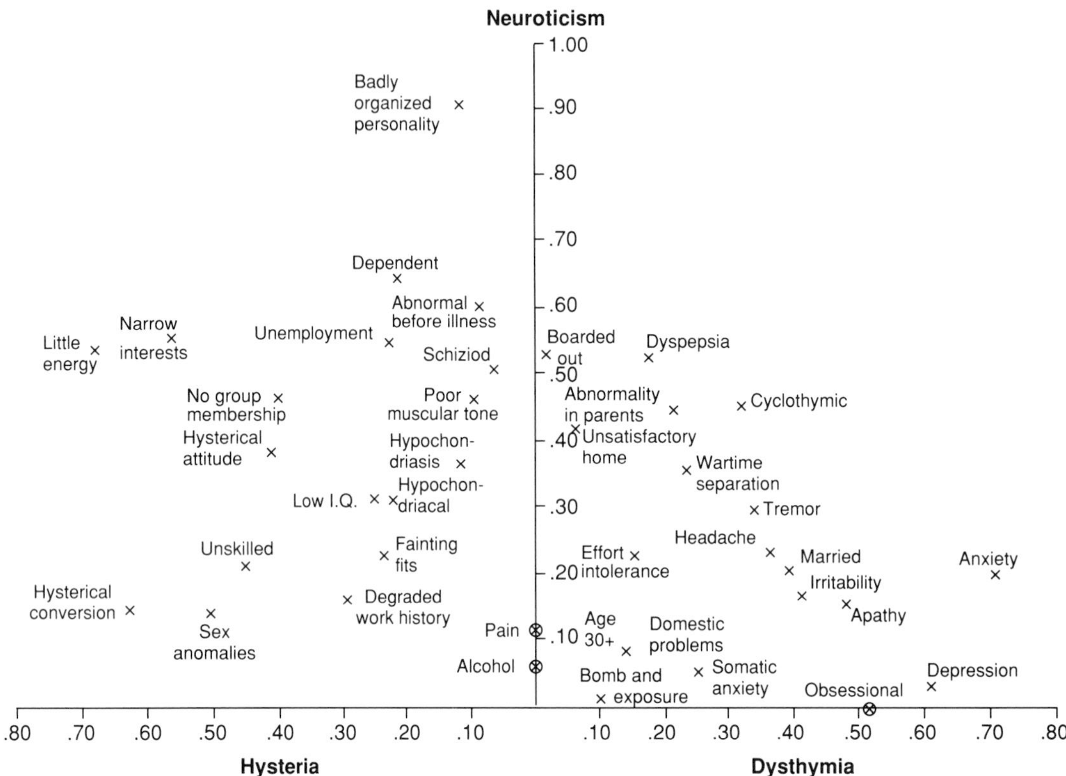

FIGURE 6 Behaviors and characteristics of introverted and extraverted neurotics.

ness, faking, or social desirability (e.g., answering questions in a way that presents a supposedly more "desirable" profile of the person).

Since extraversion, in the main, taps such traits and behaviors as shown in Figure 2, the kinds of items that might be found on such inventories may look like the example questionnaire to follow:

Please respond to the following statements with "yes" if you agree that they more or less describe you. Answer "no" if the statement is not a reasonably accurate description of you. There are no right or wrong answers.

---

1. I like loud music.
2. I would much prefer a quiet evening at home to going to a party.
3. Driving fast cars would appeal to me.
4. I am easily bored.
5. I enjoy meeting new people and having lots of friends.
6. I make decisions in a very methodical and deliberate way.
7. I would not enjoy traveling to new and different places.
8. Others see me as an easy-going and carefree person.

While these are not actual items from the EPQ, they do reflect the kind of content and appearance found in measures of extraversion. If you answered yes to questions 1,3,4,5,8, and no to questions 2,6,7, then you would likely be more of an extravert than introvert.

Many hundreds of studies have been conducted that focus on how useful and "good" these questionnaires are for assessing introversion–extraversion. Interested readers may wish to examine the journal *Personality and Individual Differences,* for research papers reporting results of studies with the EPQ and related measures. Both the children and adult versions show consistently high reliability (an indication of the test's precision, consistency, and stability) and validity (an indication of whether the test measures what it was intended to measure). Researchers and practicing psychologists can rely on the EPQ to provide reliable and accurate measures of E, as well as N and P.

V. THE BASIS OF EXTRAVERSION

Trait models of personality are sometimes criticized for apparently pretending to explain differences in behavior by simply postulating the existence of traits based on that behavior. How do we describe social shyness? We correlate a number of questions related to that trait, extract the factor of social shyness, and then describe the observed behaviors by the very trait label based on the analysis of these behaviors! But this criticism is incorrect. In the first place we carry out the statistical analyses in order to discover whether our original notion was correct; i.e., that there was in fact only one factor of social shyness. At first sight it may seem obvious that this is so, but it many not be. When we take a large sample of items relating to sociability, social shyness, and similar notions, calculate the correlations, and factor analyze the resulting table of correlations, we find, not one factor, but two. There is an introverted social shyness, defined by items which tell us that introverts do not like particularly being with other people, and prefer being by themselves most of the time. However, they are not worried about being with other people and can perfectly sustain social interactions. There is also a quite independent type of neurotic social shyness, where people are actually afraid of others, and avoid them for that very reason. They would like to socialize with others, but are prevented from doing so by their worries and anxieties about social relations. Thus, a statistical analysis of this kind is carried out in the main to see whether our commonsense beliefs are justified or not, and in many cases what is found is that they are not. In other words, we have to solve the problem of personality description before we can go on to attack the problem of causality. Factor analysis and other correlational methods are not meant to tell us anything about causality, but to act as tools for the discovery of a proper personality taxonomy. Having solved the problem we may then go on to carry out the more difficult task of finding out why some people are sociable, others shy, why some people are extraverted, others introverted.

VI. HEREDITARY INFLUENCES

The first step in such a causal analysis must be to discover to what extent differences in behavior are determined by heredity, and to what extent they are determined by environmental factors. For many years personality theorists took it for granted that environmental factors, and particularly the influence of the family, were the major, if not sole, determinants of individual differences in human behavior. Early studies of identical and fraternal twins seemed to support such a view, but the studies used unreliable and invalid tests, and failed to attack the problem properly.

There are several ways of assessing the relative importance of nature and nurture. The first, and probably the most important, is to study identical twins (monozygotic twins, MZ) who were brought up from birth in different environments, i.e., were adopted. Identical twins share 100% heredity, being the product of a single ovum, fertilized by a single sperm, and then separating into two separate entities. MZ twins separated at birth share identical heredity, but have completely different environmental influences determining their behavior. We get an accurate estimate of the importance of heredity by looking at the intercorrelations between such MZ twins; if environment were all important, there should be no correlation at all. In fact several studies have shown quite high correlations, suggesting that heredity accounted for at least 50% of the total difference observed.

Similarly, we can compare MZ twins and dizygotic twins (DZ); i.e., fraternal twins who share on the average only 50% heredity, and are no more alike than ordinary siblings. If heredity was important, we could expect MZ twins to be much more alike than DZ twins, and this is precisely what is usually found. So here again, we have evidence for the importance of heredity. These and other studies, such as whether adopted children are more alike in personality with their biological or their adoptive parents, leave us in no doubt that heredity is extremely important. They also show that the theory implicating only the family is quite wrong. We can divide the environmental factors determining differences in personality into those between family, emphasizing the importance of family upbringing, and those within family, emphasizing the environmental differences between different children coming from the same family, such as one having a good teacher, the other a poor one, or one marrying a good person, the other an abusive, unsupportive one. Several very large-scale studies have now shown that it is the within-family environmental factors that affect individual differences in personality between children, not those between family, a finding that demonstrates that practically all the usual theories of personality are in fact inadequate, and have to be replaced. [*See* BEHAVIORAL GENETICS.]

VII. THE LINK BETWEEN BIOLOGY AND EXTRAVERSION

Let us consider the consequences of these findings. The major finding is that causal factors involve DNA, and inevitably also physiological, neurological, or hormonal intermediaries; DNA cannot directly affect behavior, but can only affect biological structures which mediate behavior. Hence, our task becomes one of finding these intermediaries, and a beginning has been made in that direction with respect to E. Figure 7 illustrates the major theory that links biology and personality.

When nervous impulses originating in the outer world go to the brain via the ascending afferent pathways, they send collaterals into the ascending reticular activating system (ARAS). This area, in turn, sends "arousal" messages to the cortex to keep it in a state of functional readiness. Without this signal to maintain arousal, the cortex would effectually go to sleep, and fail to transmit the incoming messages to other neurons and finally to the motor neurons which cause activity in the muscles and produce the active response to the incoming stimulation.

Cortical arousal is known to vary from high to low in any given individual. Cortical arousal is high when you are taking an important examination, watching or playing an important game of baseball or tennis, or preparing to propose marriage to your beloved. Cortical arousal is low when you sit at home in the evening, tired from the day's work, and watch an incredibly boring television program. The actual degree of arousal can be measured by the electroencephalogram (EEG); high arousal is characterized by fast, low-amplitude alpha waves, and low arousal by slow, high-amplitude alpha waves. [*See* BRAIN ELECTRIC ACTIVITY.]

Current theory suggests that extraverts are characterized by a habitual low level of arousal in the resting state, while introverts are characterized by a high level. Such a theory is of course relatively easy to test; we would only have to measure the EEG of samples of resting introverts and extraverts, and see whether introverts have an EEG characterized by a fast, low-amplitude alpha, while extraverts would be characterized by a slow, high-amplitude type of alpha. Or we might look at the electrodermal level (i.e., skin conductance) of extraverts and introverts. The greater the arousal, the greater the level of skin conductance. These and many other measures of arousal have been used to test the theory, and in general the results have been positive.

Consider Figure 8 which shows the skin conductance of groups of extraverts and introverts taken once per hour from 7:00 AM till midnight. The values are determined by the subjects themselves, on a portable device, and they also wrote down what they were doing at the time. Compare the age-corrected figures for the introverts and extraverts (the number of sweat glands decline with age, so a correction has to be made). It will be seen that throughout the day, until about 9:00 or 10:00 PM, introverts are definitely characterized by higher degrees of arousal. The figures for the two groups come together for the rest of the evening. Why is this so?

It has generally been found that most people prefer intermediate degrees of arousal to extremes. Very high arousal is produced by stimuli that are painful—very bright lights, very loud noise, etc. Simi-

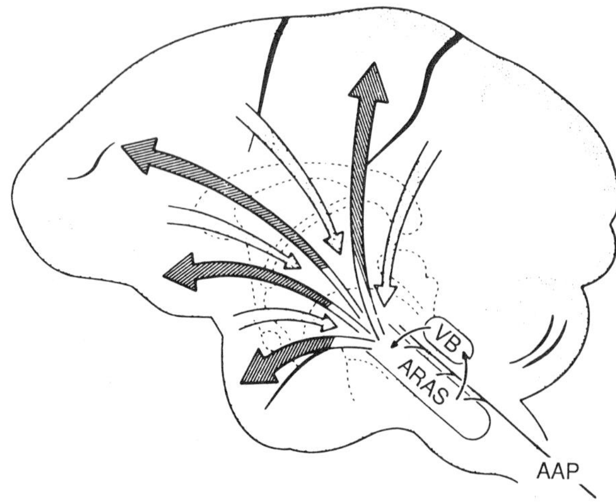

FIGURE 7 Diagrammatic representation of the interaction between the limbic system (visceral brain) and the reticular-cortical arousal system. [Copyright © 1967 H. J. Eysenck.]

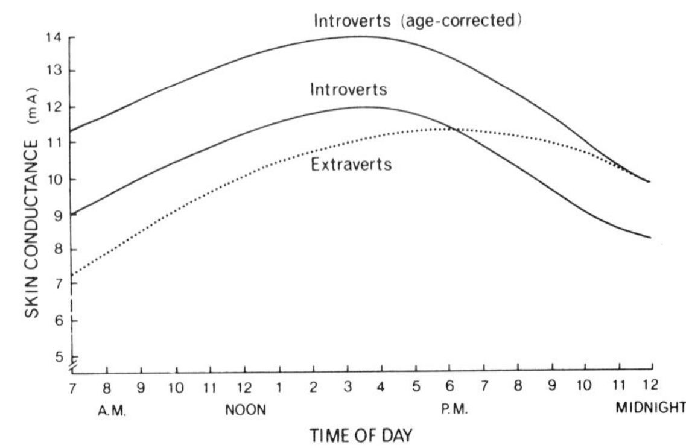

FIGURE 8 Skin conductance of extraverts and introverts from morning to night.

larly, very low degrees of arousal, such as are produced by sensory deprivation experiments, are felt to be boring and for any length of time insupportable. This means that extraverts, having too low levels of arousal, would seek arousing stimuli, such as the presence of other people, loud music, etc. Introverts, already having too high levels of arousal, would seek to avoid such arousing stimuli, and prefer withdrawal. Thus, each person can regulate his own level of arousal, but for most people this is only possible in the evening; during the day they are constrained to do whatever their job demands. What was found in the experiment diagrammed in Figure 8 was that extraverts raise their arousal level by going out, visiting clubs, having a lot of fun, while introverts lowered their level of arousal by going home, reading a book, and generally avoiding arousing stimuli.

The general theory is shown in Figure 9. The solid line in the middle shows the preference of the average person for intermediate levels of arousal, and their dislike (negative hedonic tone) for high or low levels. The same is true of introverts and extraverts, but the optimum level is shifted to the right for extraverts, to the left for introverts. It is obvious that extraverts should be more tolerant of high degrees of arousal, such as pain, while introverts should be more tolerant of low levels of arousal, such as sensory deprivation. Many experiments have shown that this is true, adding further support for the general theory.

We can see why this is a causal theory. Extraverts are sociable because their heredity has given them an ARAS which is functioning in a way that generates a general low level of arousal. To achieve a satisfactory equilibrium they have to raise their level of arousal by behaving in certain ways, such as socializing with other people and engaging in risky activities such as mountaineering or ski-jumping, while introverts avoid these activities in order to lower the high arousal level, which they were given by nature, through an overfunctioning ARAS.

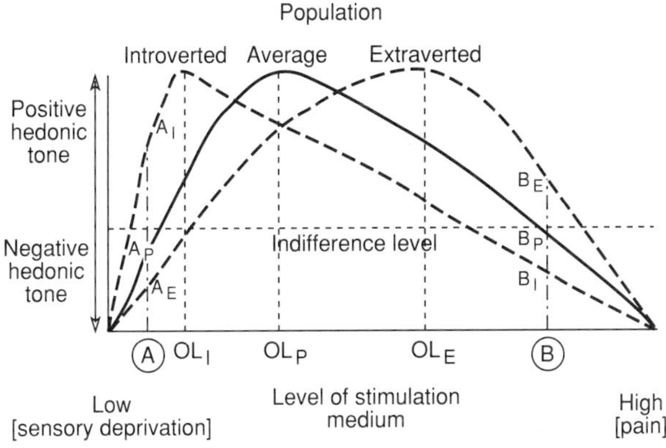

FIGURE 9 Personality and tolerance for arousal.

Referring back to Figure 7, we can see in diagrammatic form the limbic system, which mediates the expression of the emotions, and fulfills a similar role as far as differences in neuroticism are concerned. A limbic system which is working overtime would make a person behave in highly emotional and ultimately neurotic ways while a limbic system underfunctioning would have the opposite effect, making the person very stable and unemotional. [*See* LIMBIC SYSTEM.]

These physiological and neurological structures and functions may determine not only personality factors like E and N, but also mood changes. Extraversion generally is related to postive feelings and moods, while neuroticism is generally related to negative, unpleasant feelings and moods. Now consider the choleric person, i.e., one high on both N and E. This person would likely show marked mood swings from high-negative to high-positive. The melancholic would vary between indifference and negative moods, while the sanguine person would vary between very positive moods and indifference. The least variable would be the phlegmatic, showing neither highly positive nor highly negative moods at any time. These differences are shown in Figure 10.

We can now see why Wundt called the extravert "changeable." One way of raising the level of arousal is by changing features of the environment, and this suggests experimental ways of testing the theory. In one experiment, extraverted and introverted subjects were given a large number of pictures, with instructions to pick out the two they liked best. They were then shown one of these pictures in an apparatus, with instructions to push a button when they wanted to let that picture disappear and the other one to come up. It was predicted and found that extraverts would change from one to the other more rapidly than would introverts. Predictions have also been made for much more important variables, such as individual sexual behavior. It was predicted that extraverts would have sex earlier, more frequently, with more partners, in more positions, etc.; it was also predicted that they would divorce more readily. In other words, to accommodate their low arousal level they would need more and stronger stimulation, and would need more changes in respect to their sex partners, the actual

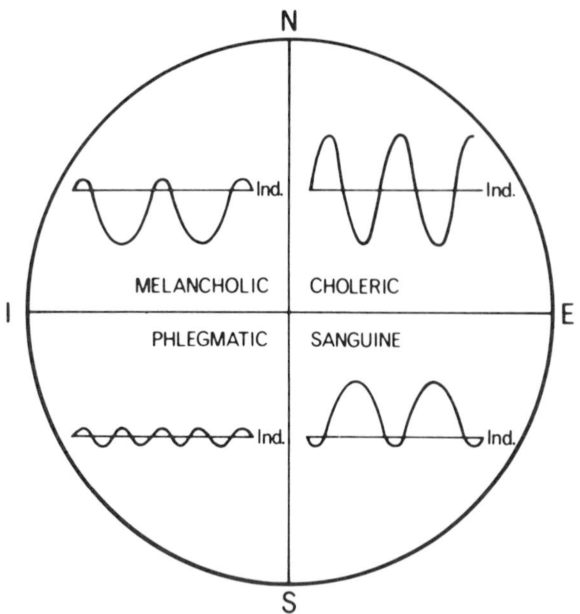

FIGURE 10 Mood variations and introversion–extraversion.

practices they indulged in, etc. Such a causal mechanism postulated by the theory explains a great deal of human conduct.

VIII. CROSS-CULTURAL RESEARCH INTO EXTRAVERSION

There are other consequences of the general theory that E and N are determined very largely by heredity, and that their behavior is mediated by biological structures in the central nervous system and the autonomic nervous system. One of these is that E and N not only should appear in those cultures where the original studies were made (essentially the European–North American culture) but should be equally characteristic of all other countries. What is asserted is not that all these cultures would be equally extraverted, or equally neurotic, but rather that the same factors would emerge in these countries as were found in North America, Australia, etc. The experiments were done in over 35 different countries, including a large number of European countries, Scandinavian countries, Slavic countries (e.g., Russia, Hungary), Mongoloid countries (e.g., Japan, China), South American countries, and African countries (e.g., Uganda, Nigeria). In all of these countries, over 500 males and 500 females were administered the EPQ, and the items were then intercorrelated and factor analyzed to see whether the resulting factors would be the same as we found in England and the United States.

It was found that in all these countries there were practically identical structures of items, verifying the existence of N and E. Of course not all countries had identical levels of E and N; Japan was very high on N but lower on E. The United States was very extraverted. Thus, the prediction is verified. Identical factors emerged in many different countries and cultures. Of interest is that similar findings have been obtained across large samples of children from different countries such as Denmark, Greece, Spain, and Singapore.

IX. DRUG STUDIES AND EXTRAVERSION

There is another way of testing the hypothesis that personality is mediated by biological mechanisms in the central and autonomic nervous systems. If true, then it should be possible to shift the person on the various dimensions involved by means of drugs known to be relevant to the hypothetical underlying structures. Thus, stimulant drugs should make people more introverted because they are known to raise the cortical arousal level, while depressant drugs should have the opposite effect, making people more extraverted. It is well known that alcohol, which is a depressant drug, does make people more extraverted (except in excessive doses, of course), while stimulant drugs have the opposite effect. Similarly, andronergic drugs lead to greater neuroticism, anxiolytic drugs to greater stability. Figure 11 illustrates these effects. Also shown is the third major personality dimension, psychoticism, which is increased by

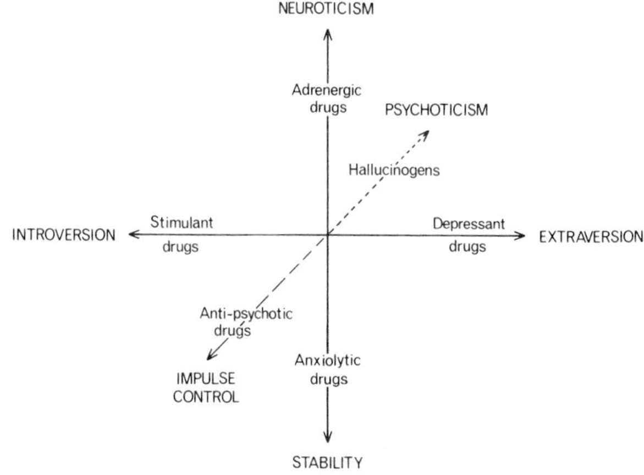

FIGURE 11 Psychotropic drugs and personality.

hallucinogens, and diminished by antipsychotic drugs. A great deal of work done along these lines has given positive results.

X. EXTRAVERSION AND OTHER PERSONALITY FACTORS

In looking at E as a dimension of personality, one must always remember that it is never found in isolation, but always interacting with other dimensions of personality and with intelligence. Thus, an intelligent extravert behaves very differently from a less intelligent one, and a neurotic extravert very differently from a stable one. Furthermore, of course extraverts may have the same score on E scales of the EPQ but nevertheless differ to some extent from each other because they may be characterized in the main by different traits. The sociable extravert is not necessarily assertive, the carefree one not necessarily dominant. These traits are all intercorrelated, but the correlations are far from perfect. Different extraverts may sometimes show different facets, and therefore subtle differences. It should never be assumed that knowing the main dimensions of personality of a given person tells us all there is to know. The hierarchical system outlined earlier in this article simply tells us that knowing the position of a person on the major dimensions will tell us more about that person than any other similarly restricted data set. If we know a person's IQ score as well as degree of E and N, we will know more about him or her than any other three figures could tell us. This does not mean that there is not a great deal more to be known; if we characterize the person in terms of 40 or 50 traits, we would certainly have a much more detailed picture. But much of this information would be redundant and we would have great difficulty in absorbing it all. Having a hierarchical theory means that for different purposes we may choose different levels of analysis. We may be particularly interested in one aspect of E, say sociability, or dominance, and under these conditions we would obviously prefer to make use of a questionnaire measuring sociability or dominance. Thus, a hierarchical system is very flexible for it is not committed to working only at the highest level. R. B. Cattell, for instance, prefers to focus on his 16 personality factors, although these are intercorrelated and give rise to higher-order factors very similar to E (which he calls "envia") and N (which he calls "anxiety"). There is no essential contradiction between the Cattell and Eysenck systems. For all practical purposes they simply lay emphasis on different levels of analysis.

Essentially what a proper theory of personality must do is to look at all the steps from distal causal factors, like heredity, to proximal causal factors, like differences in the functioning of the limbic system or the ARAS, to the major dimensions of personality like E and N. The theory must then proceed to the study of proximal consequences, such as the study of changeability already mentioned, which is best done in the laboratory. And finally it must proceed to distal consequences, mainly in the social field, such as sociability or the differences in sexual behavior discussed above. In the case of E, we have a complete chain from DNA, through ARAS, to E, to laboratory behaviors, and then on to social behavior. It is not suggested that each element in the chain has been finally located and that no further progress is either required or possible. The concept of cortical arousal presents many difficulties and there are many anomalies in the experimental analysis of extraverted behavior in those terms. These will be analyzed and solved in future research; at the moment all we can say is that the theory has much going for it.

XI. EXTRAVERSION AND SOCIAL BEHAVIOR

In a complete chain of events, our main interest of course is in the final link, i.e., social behavior. We have mentioned sexual behavior as one example but there are many others. For example, it has been shown that traffic accidents are much more frequent in people who are high N and high E. It has also been shown that by using this knowledge in the selection procedure for drivers, the accident rate can be halved.

A rather different field is education. There has been a great deal of interest in the last 20 years in the so-called "discovery learning" methods, i.e., students are encouraged to discover basic principles and rules. It has been found comparing classes taught by either discovery or reception learning methods that there is little difference in achievement. This may be due to the fact that both methods are equally good but it may also be that extraverts learn better by means of discovery methods, and introverts by means of reception methods, as predicted on theoretical grounds. Figure 12 shows the results of one such study, where pupils were taught

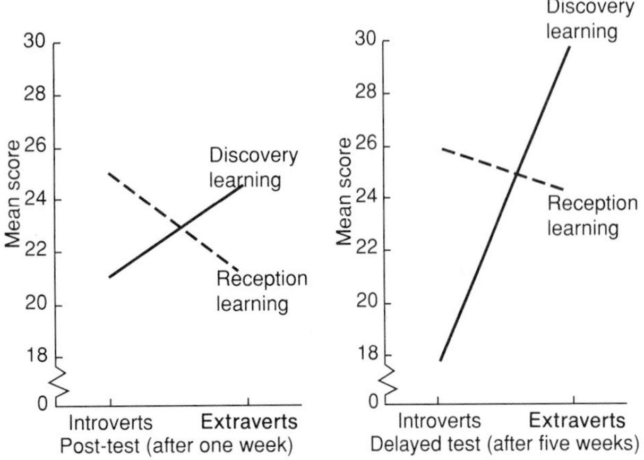

FIGURE 12 The performance of introverts and extraverts using different learning methods.

by one method or the other and then were separated into introverts and extraverts. The post-test was done after 1 week, and again after 5 weeks. It is obvious that extraverts do indeed benefit much more by discovery learning, and introverts by reception learning.

An examination of the current research literature implicates E in a wide variety of real-life behaviors including social interactions, sexual activity, work performance, school achievement, psychiatric disturbance, and antisocial and criminal behavior.

XII. CONCLUSION

Most people underestimate the very large individual differences in personality which heredity has created. We tend to think that most people are like us, just slightly different because of environmental events, particularly events characteristic of a given family. Such a view grossly underestimates the very real differences, which are largely genetic, or, if environmental, have little to do with the way children are brought up in a given family. Theories of personality characteristic of the last 50 years have now been shown to be essentially contradicted by the facts of behavior genetic research. We will have to develop new theories in order to do justice to the facts as described. The above descriptions of extraversion are contemporary. While there is every good reason to suggest that E will continue to be recognized as a major personality dimension, the specific findings reported here ranging from its biological basis to behavioral manifestations are currently being examined and reexamined.

Bibliography

Eysenck, H. J., and Eysenck, M. W. (1985). "Personality and Individual Differences." Plenum, New York.

Eysenck, H. J. (1990). Biological dimensions of personality. In "Handbook of Personality: Theory and Research" (L. Pervin, Ed.), Guilford, New York.

Monte, C. (Ed.) (1991). "Beneath the Mask: An Introduction to Theories of personality," 3rd ed. Holt, Rinehart, Winston, Chicago.

Strelau, J., and Eysenck, H. J. (Eds.) (1987). "Personality Dimensions and Arousal." Academic Press, New York.

Zuckerman, M., Kuhlman, D. M., and Camac, C. (1988). What lies beyond E and N? Factor analyses of scales believed to measure basic dimensions of personality. *J. Pers. Soc. Psychol.* **54,** 96–107.

EYE MOVEMENTS

Bruce Bridgeman
University of California at Santa Cruz

Glossary

Accommodation Change in focus of the lenses, normally accompanied by a vergence eye movement.

Conjugate Both eyes moving with the same speed and direction at the same time.

Fixation Steady gaze at an object or texture of the visual world, maintained by compensatory eye movements.

Fovea The area of best detail vision, at the fixation point of the retina.

Oculomotor Referring to the six muscles that move each eye, and the neurological system that controls them.

Pursuit Smooth, conjugate eye movements that track moving objects.

Saccade A rapid change of visual fixation from one point to another, accompanied by a suppression of vision.

Vergence A horizontal rotation of the two eyes toward or away from one another.

EYE MOVEMENTS change the orientations of the eyes relative to the head. Vision is concentrated on a line of sight from each eye: the point where the lines of sight from the two eyes meet is the point of sight, where both eyes have the best vision. Eye movements act to stabilize the eyes relative to the visual world, and also to move the point of sight around in three-dimensional space, allowing clear binocular vision at any location. Three types of eye movements—saccadic or jumping movements, slow pursuit movements, and the convergences and divergences that move the point of sight in the third dimension—perform these functions.

I. FUNCTIONS OF EYE MOVEMENTS

In the course of evolution the earliest vertebrate animals, fish and sharks, became highly mobile. But their eyes were poor at picking up information from objects and textures that were sweeping quickly across their retinas. The solution was compensatory eye movements. As the fish turned, for instance clockwise, the eyes would track the background, moving counterclockwise in their orbits. When the eyes had moved as far as they could go, they jumped rapidly in the opposite direction to begin another cycle. In this way, the image remained nearly stationary on the retinas, and vision remained clear (except during the return jumps). This pattern of alternating slow and fast movements remains in humans and all other vertebrates as well. It can be observed when someone looks out the side window of a car or a train. It happens involuntarily, and is difficult or impossible to suppress. The pattern defines the oldest function of eye movements, to maintain a clear image on the retinas despite the retinal motion caused by one's own locomotion.

Simple vertebrates such as sharks have panoramic vision and see about as well in one direction as in any other. Humans, however, have a different strategy of seeing. Our sharpest vision and best color perception are in a small region of the retina called the fovea, which views an area of the visual world about the size of the moon. When we fixate an object, we place the fovea on the image of the object. It is here that vision for such tasks as reading and recognizing faces takes place. Nature has invested a disproportionate share of the visual apparatus in this small region; about one quarter of the visual area of the brain is devoted to processing informa-

Encyclopedia of Human Behavior, Volume 2
Copyright © 1994 by Academic Press, Inc. All rights of reproduction in any form reserved.

tion from the fovea. Since the region of sharpest vision is so small, eye movements are essential to examine objects in detail. So in addition to compensatory eye movements, humans have added exploratory eye movements. The exploratory eye movements are jumps of the eye called saccades. They have the same characteristics as the return jumps that occur during compensatory tracking, and they evolved from those return movements. Their function is to move the point of fixation from one place in the visual world to another as rapidly as possible.

There is another function of eye movements as well. If the eyes remain absolutely immobile with respect to the world, the visual image fades out and does not return. This is because the visual receptor cells in the retina cannot signal steady states. They respond only to changes in illumination. To guarantee that there is always a little movement of the retinal image on the retina, the eyes are always jittering with very small amplitude oscillations. There are slow drifts of the eye interrupted with tiny saccades. The drifts are adequate to prevent fading on the fovea; the small saccades prevent fading in the retinal periphery, which has less precise focus and requires the quicker movements to prevent its blurry image from fading. So eye movements function to prevent the image from moving either too quickly or too slowly across the retinal receptors.

In summary, then, eye movements have three functions: first, to compensate for motions of the images on the retinas due to locomotion or to movement of objects in the world; second, to move the point of sight to a new location in the world; and third, to prevent fading of the visual image from immobility of the retinas.

II. TYPES OF EYE MOVEMENTS

Eye movements are controlled by parts of the brain that, together with the eye muscles themselves, are called the oculomotor system. There are three basic types of movements: pursuits, vergences, and saccades.

A. Pursuit Movements

1. Tracking the Visual Array

The slow eye movements that track the visual array are called pursuit movements. There are two types. The first type, the compensatory movements already discussed, cancel motions of the entire visual world relative to the eye. They occur in all vertebrates, even those without a fovea, and are guided by an inborn feedback system that tracks the visual world in much the same way that a guided missile tracks its target. If the image of the world begins to drift across the eyes, the motion is processed in the visual system and fed back to the muscles that move the eyes. The processing takes about 0.1 sec, so for this amount of time the drift is not compensated. Then the eyes begin to move. Initially the movement is in the correct direction, but its speed is uncontrolled. Then the eye begins to match the velocity of the drift of the image, continually adjusting its speed and direction as the drift changes. The process is never perfect, and usually there is some remaining drift that is not compensated.

The job of preventing the image from moving on the retina is shared by several mechanisms using different inputs. In addition to visual feedback control, there are other sources for the information that drives compensatory eye movements. Whenever the head begins to turn, the vestibular sense picks up the acceleration in the semicircular canals of the inner ear. These organs feed a signal forward to the eye muscles to compensate for the predicted slip of the image against the retinas. This occurs even in darkness, when vision cannot generate corrective movements. In the vertical direction the compensation is called the "doll reflex" because the eyes, like those of a doll, roll downward when the head tilts back. The reflex compensation works in all directions, though, including tortional eye movements (the eye rotating about the line of sight as an axis) to compensate for tilts of the upright head toward one shoulder.

The system even predicts image motions, by monitoring motor commands sent to the neck muscles. There is another compensation for active movements of the head. Commands sent to the neck muscles to move the head also have accompanying discharges to the eye muscles. These signals are feedforwards, compensating a predicted motion of the retinal image rather than an actual motion. Because they are copies of the efferent signals sent from the brain to the neck muscles, they are called efference copies. The corrective eye movements can begin at the same time as the head movement that will create the disturbance. The anticipated drift of images on the retina is compensated before it begins.

2. Tracking Moving Objects

In animals with foveas, such as humans, a problem arises when an object that is being fixated begins to move relative to the background. To maintain fixation on the object, the eyes should begin to track it. But the stabilizing system just discussed will lock onto the visual background as a whole, preventing the eyes from tracking the object. To solve this problem there is a second system that drives pursuit movements. This more recently evolved system tracks anything that happens to be on the fovea, regardless of the motion of the background. When the two tracking systems come into conflict, the newer foveal pursuit system wins out, and the eye tracks the object on the fovea. Like the stabilization system, though, this system is reflexive and cannot be turned off. Whenever the image on the fovea begins to drift, the pursuit system acts to cancel the drift. This means that the image on the fovea has some peculiar properties: it never moves very much, and changes only when the eye jumps to a new fixation point.

Pursuit movements have a rather slow top speed. They track moving targets well if the velocity of the image on the retina is less than about 30°/sec. Above this speed they begin to fall behind. The eyes can move faster than 30°/sec, but above this speed they do not track as fast as the target motion. Pursuit can range as fast as 80°/sec for brief periods, but only for a target that is moving substantially faster than this. To keep up, the eye movement system introduces quick saccadic eye movements that are interspersed with pursuit.

B. Convergence and Divergence

Another aspect of compensating for movements of objects in the world is in the third dimension. While pursuit movements track objects moving horizontally, vertically, or obliquely, convergence and divergence movements track objects moving toward or away from the observer. Together these are called vergence movements. Again they are involuntary; they occur whenever the object that is imaged on the foveas of the two eyes moves in depth. Movements of targets that are not imaged on the foveas have little effect on vergence movements. [*See* DEPTH PERCEPTION.]

When an object moves closer to the eyes, the image in the right eye shifts to the left while the image in the left eye shifts to the right. The two eyes track this motion with equal and opposite movements. The two eyes move in opposite directions, either toward one another (convergence) when an object approaches or away from one another (divergence) when it recedes. Vergence movements are linked to movements of the lens and the pupil that also help to focus images as their distances change. When an object moves both toward the eyes and across the field of view, vergence and pursuit movements work simultaneously to track accurately. Each kind of movement is distinct, though, and they are controlled by nerve cells in different locations in the brain. For both kinds of slow eye movements these controller cells are located in the brainstem, the oldest part of the brain in evolution.

Vergence movements too are relatively slow; the fastest vergences are driven by abrupt movements of a target in depth. These result in an abrupt change in innervation to the eye muscles, but because of the resistance of the eyes to quick movement, the eyes drift slowly into place. There is no point in driving the eyes faster, because the change in accommodation in the lenses of the eyes could not keep up in any case. Figure 1 illustrates the response of the eyes to an abrupt shift of a target in depth. The bottom of the figure represents positions distant from the observer's eyes, and the top represents closer positions. Time runs from left to right. When the target (T) jumps closer to the observer at time A, there is a brief delay; then the eyes converge. Trace E represents the difference in the gaze positions of the two eyes. Both at the original vergence position and at the new position, there is some oscillation of the two eyes relative to one another, represented by the oscillations in the trace. The motor system is always "hunting" for the best vergence position. Five seconds later, at time B, one of the eyes is occluded. There is now no error signal to hold the eyes in a converged position, and they gradually relax back to the original vergence angle.

C. Exploratory Movements

In humans, periods of compensatory tracking are punctuated by rapid jumps of the eye called saccades. These are brief sprints to a new location in the visual field. Both eyes move simultaneously,

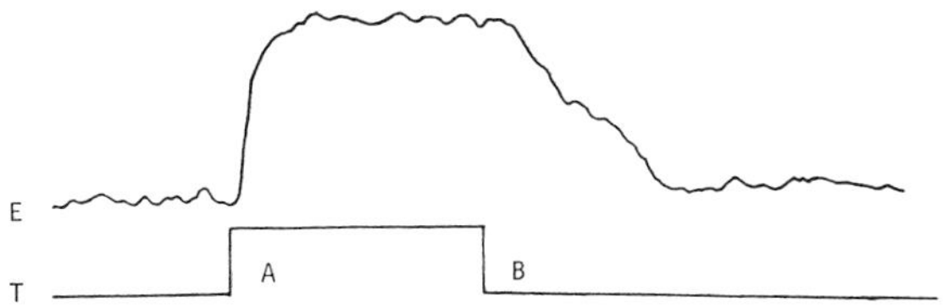

FIGURE 1 Vergence eye movements (E) in response to a target (T) step. The target remains on for 5 seconds (A to B).

in the same direction. During these jumps, the eye moves so quickly that no useful visual information can be picked up. In addition, the visual system actively suppresses vision during saccades. During these movements, the pursuit tracking system is also suppressed, to allow the eye to move away from the target that is being tracked by the retinas. Pursuit locks onto the image again as the saccade ends.

A saccadic eye movement is ballistic in the sense that once started, it cannot be stopped. Starting a saccade is like throwing a ball—once the ball leaves your hand, its path cannot be altered. If you begin a saccade, then change your mind, the movement must be completed anyway, and corrected later by another saccade.

The ballistic property of saccades is illustrated in Figure 2. The left side of a screen is represented at the bottom of the diagram and the right side at the top. Time goes from left to right. The figure begins with the observer fixating on the target at the left side of the screen. The target jumps to the right by an amount a_1, remains steady for about one-fifth of a second, and then jumps back slightly to the left by the amount a_2. Since the eye has just begun to move when the target jumps back to its final position, it would seem that the eye should saccade directly to that position. But it does not. The first saccade has already been programmed in the brain, and the control mechanism is committed to the large saccade r. This saccade will be completed even though the target has already jumped away from the saccade's goal point. To get to the displaced target, the observer must program a new saccade, with a new delay, and finally gets to the final position after this second saccade. The delay is the time that the motor system needs to set up the new saccade.

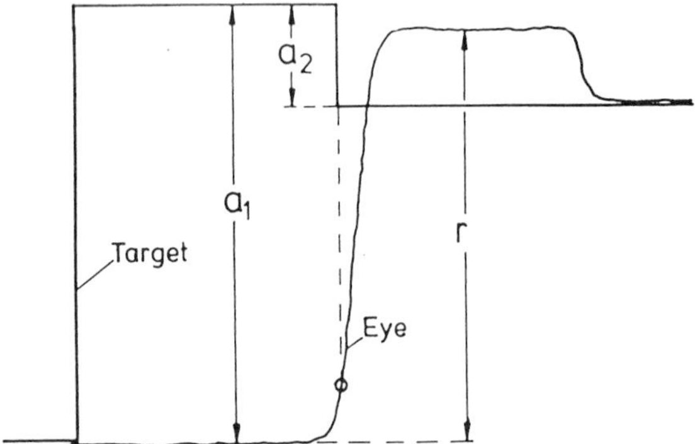

FIGURE 2 The ballistic nature of saccadic eye movements. The eye must go to its originally targeted position, even though the target jumps away from the goal point just as the eye begins to move. The target remains at position a_1 for one-fifth of a second.

Figure 3a shows some other properties of saccadic eye movements. In this example, the eye begins 15° left of the center, and moves abruptly to 15° right. The eye does not quite reach the target. There is a little undershoot, that is corrected about 170 msec after the completion of the primary saccade. This is the situation when the head is prevented from moving. When the head is free, however, most large saccades are accompanied by head movements in the same direction (Fig. 3b). Since the head rotates at a much smaller rate than the eye, there is a quick saccade that brings the eye to the target just as the head movement is getting under way. Then, to keep the eye fixating on the target, a compensatory eye movement begins in the direction opposite the head movement. As a result the gaze position relative to the target remains stable while the eye and head rotate in opposite directions at equal speeds. Again there is a small corrective saccade to correct a saccadic undershoot. At the end of the process the eye is again centered near its original position in the orbit, but the head is deviated to the right.

1. Neural Control of Saccades

At the start of a saccade, the agonist eye muscles (the ones pulling in the direction of the movement) receive a pulse of innervation that activates them to their maximum extent. The size of the pulse is always maximal, even for small saccades; the size of the intended movement affects only the pulse's duration. About halfway through the movement, the innervation drops back to the level required to hold the eye in the new position. This is the pulse–step pattern of innervation. It allows saccades to be accomplished much faster than vergence movements or pursuit. For large saccades, there is a braking pulse in the antagonist muscles near the end of the movement. This helps to keep the rapidly rotating eye from overshooting its target.

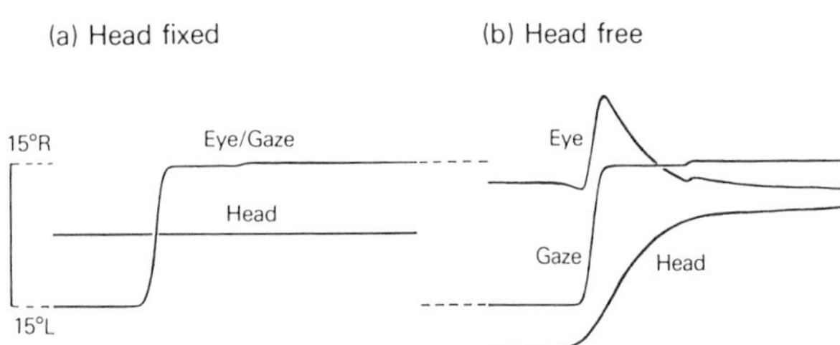

FIGURE 3 Saccadic eye movements (a) with the head fixed and (b) with the head free to rotate. Gaze is the sum of eye motion and head motion. The small corrective saccade occurs one-sixth of a second after the end of the main saccade.

The strategy of the oculomotor system in driving a saccade is like an automobile driver's strategy in entering a crowded freeway. To reach cruising speed as quickly as possible, the driver presses the gas pedal to the floor. The faster he wants to go, the longer the pedal stays on the floor. This is the pulse of the pulse–step strategy. When cruising speed is reached, the driver lets back on the pedal to maintain a steady speed. This corresponds to the step of innervation.

2. Initiation of Eye Movements

Normally, the only conscious decision involved in oculomotor behavior is the initiation of saccades. Even this is often automatic, without the owner of the saccadic system thinking about its behavior. Accordingly, two separate systems can initiate saccades. One resides in an ancient part of the brain in evolutionary terms, the superior colliculus of the midbrain. Another is located in the newest part of the brain, in the lateral part of the frontal lobe of the cortex. The midbrain branch of the saccade control system initiates automatic actions such as the return jumps during locomotion, while the frontal cortex system is responsible for jumping to a new target that is determined by the observer's motivations for visual exploration. We know that these are the only two saccade control areas, because removing both of them causes permanent loss of all saccades.

The functioning of these systems can be observed by recording from tiny electrodes that pick up signals from single nerve cells. For a long time it was thought that the nerve cells in the frontal cortex played little role in initiating saccades, for most of them fired only after the beginning of a saccade. These recordings were made when the animal was only casually looking about a laboratory. But when a monkey makes a deliberate saccade, to obtain a reward, many cells in a part of the lateral frontal cortex called the "frontal eye field" become active just after the change in the visual stimulus but before the eye begins to move.

III. EYE MOVEMENTS AND ATTENTION

A. Scanpaths

When a human observer encounters a new visual scene, the eyes jump first to the area of greatest interest, where the density of information is greatest. They then jump to another spot determined by information content, distance, and one's own interests. A series of saccadic jumps generates a *scanpath*, a pattern of fixational eye movements.

The scanpath is the meeting point of oculomotor physiology and cognitive psychology. Decisions about where to move the eye next are made with great rapidity (up to five per second) and usually without awareness of the decision process, yet they involve some sophisticated use of information. Separation of figure and background is important in guiding the scanpath. In ambiguous figures that can be interpreted in several ways, the scanpath depends on the interpretation of the moment.

After the identity of the scene is established, higher-level questions govern visual scanning patterns. A Russian researcher, A. L. Yarbus, showed subjects a painting while asking them questions about the people in the painting; the scanpaths depended on the nature of the question being asked. When asked to estimate the material circumstances of the people, for example, observers fixated largely on the clothing and furniture in the painting. When asked about the ages of the people, though, they fixated mostly on the faces. Observers still scan the most information-rich regions of the painting, but the definition of what provides the most information changes with the question that is being asked.

B. Shifts of Attention

Normally, when a person shifts attention from one part of the visual world to another, the first thing that happens is that a saccadic eye movement is generated to shift the eyes to the new location. These shifts are very frequent—normally, the eye makes a saccade about three to four times each second. Even when the eyes are not actively exploring, the tiny saccades that punctuate fixational drifts continue at about the same rate. This makes saccades, unaccompanied by any other behaviors, by far the most frequent of all human behaviors. As such, they are of central interest to psychologists who are interested in studying behavior.

There are three parts to shifting attention: attention must be disengaged, shifted to the new location, and reengaged. The process is analogous to shifting gears in an automobile with a manual transmission. Stepping on the clutch corresponds to disengaging attention, moving the shift knob is the transfer to the new location, and releasing the clutch pedal is the reengaging. Each of these steps has a corresponding feature in oculomotor control. The disengagement is the active inhibition of the tracking systems that automatically lock the fixation point to a particular feature of the visual world. If tracking were not disengaged, the start of the saccade would conflict with the fixation function and the two systems, tracking and saccadic, would fight against one another. The saccade itself corresponds to the shift of attention, and the reestablishment of fixation occurs at the end of the saccade. Though vision is inhibited during and just before the saccade, it is more sensitive immediately after the eye comes to rest.

Each of these steps takes time. The whole process requires at least 0.2 sec, limiting saccades to about five per second. If attention is disengaged before the eye retargeting process starts, though, the shift can take place more quickly. Attention can be disengaged by turning off a fixation target, leaving an observer staring into empty space. Then when a new target appears, the saccade to it can begin after only 0.1 sec instead of the usual 0.2 sec. These short-latency saccades are called express saccades. Attention can also be shifted without an eye movement, but this is an unnatural act and takes some concentration.

1. Reading

a. Normal Reading

One of our most skilled and highly practiced oculomotor skills is reading. Reading can be considered as a specialized and stereotyped scanpath made on a particular kind of visual pattern (printed text). An experienced reader normally fixates a new word on each fixation, with a normal saccade between fixations. Small words such as "of" or "but" are frequently skipped. Occasionally a reader will look back to a previously fixated word, especially if the text is difficult (a "reverse saccade"). At the end of each line, a single large saccade returns the eyes to the beginning of the next line. This pattern is called a staircase, since it looks like a staircase in an eye movement record when position of the eye is plotted against time. [*See* READING.]

Since they are exploratory saccades, the eye movements of reading are limited to about five per second, with a fixation period of about 0.2 sec between them. Normally, reading generates about four saccades per second. Under these circumstances, how can one read faster? The only way is to make larger saccades, skipping more words. Especially if the text is easy or redundant, the reader can often fill in the context even if some words are not picked up by the visual system. This requires extra effort, though. The technique of tracking a finger, advocated by some speed-reading techniques, results in pursuit eye movements that make it difficult to see the text.

Dyslexia, a severe reading deficit in a person who is otherwise normal intellectually, is often accompanied by abnormal saccadic patterns during reading. One symptom is a "reverse staircase," repeated eye movements in the wrong direction. The input to the brain from such a sequence must be difficult to interpret. [*See* DYSLEXIA.]

b. Reading on Computer Screens

Though computer screens look a lot like paper, people read more slowly from computer screens than from paper. There are several reasons for this; glare, sharpness, and resolution on the screens are problems. Another, less obvious problem is the flicker of the screens. Most computer screens flicker between 60 and 72 times per second, as a spot of light flies across each line of the display in succession. Any given point on the screen is illuminated for only an instant during each scan; the rest of the time it is dark. As a result, there is usually nothing on the screen when the fixation point lands at a new location following a saccade. The visual system must wait for up to a 60th of a second before the reading process can resume. These tiny delays, repeated several times per second, add up to a small decrease in reading speed. Skilled readers can overcome this deficit with practice, but they must make larger saccades, and fewer reverse saccades, to do it. This is more work for the information-processing centers, and may lead to fatigue.

IV. EVOLUTION AND ANATOMY OF THE EYE MOVEMENT SYSTEM

A. The Shark

The eye movement (oculomotor) system evolved along with the earliest vertebrates. To look at the structure of the eye muscles and the orbits, we can return to the shark, the basic vertebrate pattern. In the shark each extraocular muscle has a simple job. The six muscles are arranged in three opposing pairs: one member of each pair pulls in one direction, while the other pulls in the opposite direction. Two muscles pull the eye up and down, two turn it right and left, and two rotate it like a wheel with the line of sight as the axle. The eyes point in opposite directions from each side of the head. The muscles serve to compensate for the shark's locomotion.

B. The Human

Humans have the same six muscles as the shark, but their arrangement and functions are more subtle and flexible. During evolution the orbits have moved to the front of the head, so that we can have binocular vision. The muscles that move the eye are always activated to some extent. A lateral set pulls the eye to the left and right; a superior–inferior set pulls up and down, and a little inward at the same time; and an oblique set twists the eye in a complex motion. All eye movements can be resolved into actions of these three pairs of muscles in each eye.

The three dimensions of space are built into our eye movement control system. Consider the double-eye as a single organ, handled by a single neurological control system. The double-eye controls the point of sight, where the lines of sight from the two eyes intersect. Thus, each direction of visual space is represented by a pair of eye muscles, operating in various combinations. Rectangular coordinates were not invented by mathematicians; they were there all along in the oculomotor control system. [*See* MOTOR CONTROL.]

V. EYE MOVEMENTS IN SLEEP

A. Slow-Wave Sleep

The eye movements of slow-wave sleep, the sleep that occurs just after going to sleep, are simply slow drifts of the eye and a general upward trend. It is in another phase of sleep, named rapid eye movement (REM) sleep, that spectacular eye movement activity occurs. This phase begins abruptly about 1½ hours after falling asleep, and has several signs; the body muscles become paralyzed, the brain shows signs of intense activity, and the eyes begin to move vigorously. [*See* SLEEP: BIOLOGICAL RHYTHMS AND HUMAN PERFORMANCE.]

B. Paradoxical Sleep

REM sleep is also dream sleep; sleepers awakened during REM usually report vivid dreams, while those awakened during slow-wave sleep seldom do. This does not mean that all dreaming occurs during REM sleep, and it is now almost certain that some dreams occur in other sleep stages. Toward the end of a night of sleep the distinction between dream reports from REM and from slow-wave sleep begins to break down, but for most of the night REM dreams are the most common and the most vivid. [*See* DREAMING.]

Dreams are maddeningly subjective as subjects of experimental inquiry. Some techniques have been successful in revealing characteristics of these mysterious experiences, however. For instance, we can ask whether the subjective impression of time in dreams matches the actual duration of the dream. Because dreaming often starts along with a REM episode, subjects can be awakened after varying durations of REM sleep and asked to relate their dreams. Later awakenings result in longer dream reports, but the effect peaks after about 15 min of REM. Awakenings after longer intervals than this lead to about the same length of dream report. The dreams seem to occupy about as much time as it would have taken to act out the action in real life, as far as we can tell, but apparently memory for the dreams stretched back only about 15 min. Sometimes an external sound is incorporated into a dream; the ringing of an alarm clock might become a telephone ringing in a dream palace. Experiments show that these sounds, too, become inserted into dreams at about the intervals one would expect from the duration of corresponding events during waking.

A further step toward relating the content of dreams to the physiology of sleep would be to relate the scanpaths of eye movements to the contents of the dreams. Early studies reported such a relationship, but later results have been mixed. Some groups find a relationship between eye movement patterns and reported dream experiences, while others find no correspondence. Interpreting such studies is difficult: how strong must a relationship between dream reports and eye movements be to have significance?

Another way to examine the relationship between dreams and scanpaths is to look not at the scanpaths but at the movements themselves. If the eye movements of REM sleep are exploratory movements driven by visual imagery, they should have the characteristics of normal waking eye movements: saccades, pursuit tracking, or vergence movements. These movements are driven by specialized control systems, permitting only a few kinds of movements. Saccades have a fixed peak velocity for each amplitude of movement. But pursuit movements cannot exceed a velocity of about 80°/sec. Convergence and divergence are even slower. These restrictions create a "forbidden zone" for eye movements, consisting of movements that are faster than 80°/sec but slower than saccades for the corresponding amplitude of movement. Such movements can be neither saccades nor pursuits.

To learn whether REMs of sleep are exploratory, one need only look in the forbidden zone of large eye movements too fast to be pursuits but too slow to be saccades. Unfortunately, this is not as easy as it sounds. The electrical method usually used in sleep studies cannot measure the dynamics of movements with the necessary precision, and most other methods require the eyes to be open. One technique, however, fulfills all the requirements. The procedure is to sew a small coil of fine wire into the sclera surrounding the cornea of a monkey's eye, leading the two ends of the wire out to a recording apparatus. Using the same principle as a conventional transformer, alternating currents are induced in this coil with three huge induction coils surrounding the monkey. Eye movements can be recorded quite accurately, either with the eyes closed or with the eyes open.

Sleep studies with implanted search coils show that the fastest REMs of sleep match the dynamics of waking saccades, while other movements are slow enough to be pursuits. Many so-called REMs, though, fell into the forbidden zone; the movements were not related to visual exploration. The cat also has REMs inconsistent with visual exploration, for all of the movements are in the same plane.

The eye movements of REM sleep are not continuous, but occur in bursts of a few minutes' duration. A typical burst in humans begins with slow movements, continues with more rapid movements up to saccadic velocity, and concludes with slow movements. All of these observations contradict the idea that REMs are the same as exploratory saccades.

Do dreams help to review the experiences of the day? If this were their main function, we should expect to see less REM in organisms with fewer experiences. REM sleep is seen even in unborn fetuses, however. Shortly before birth infants spend most of their time in this state. If they are dreaming, it is difficult to imagine what they dream about. If dreams review or consolidate the day's experiences, we should be able to manipulate the amount of eye movement allowed during the day and find a corresponding change in sleep REMs that night. In fact, the opposite change occurs; people induced to make smaller eye movements during the day make larger ones at night. So the evidence does not support a role of eye movements in dream experiences.

VI. CONCLUSION

Eye movements perform many functions. They stabilize the images on the retinas of the eyes, allowing clear vision despite movements of the self and of objects in the world. They also allow rapid shifts of visual attention and processing from one object to another. In addition, they communicate the direction of a person's attention to others, and even help to express emotional states. In sleep, their role seems to be limited to physiological responses to sleep-related brain processes.

Bibliography

Carpenter, R. H. S. (1988). "Movements of the Eyes," 2nd ed. Pion, London.

Chekaluk, E. Llewellyn, K. (Eds). (1992). The role of eye movements in perceptual processes. *Adv. Psychol.* **88.**

Guitton, D. (1992). Control of eye-head coordination during orienting gaze shifts. *Trends in Neurosci.* **15**(5), 174–179.

Kowler, E. (Ed.) (1990). "Eye Movements and Their Role in Visual and Cognitive Processes." Elsevier, Amsterdam.

Luer, G., Lass, U., and Shallo-Hoffman, J. (Eds). (1988). "Eye Movement Research: Physiological and Psychological Aspects." Hogrefe, Toronto.

Pola, J., and Wyatt, H. J. (1993). The role of attention and cognitive processes. *Rev. Oculomotor Res.* **5,** 371–392.

Rayner, K. (Ed). (1992). "Eye Movements and Visual Cognition: Scene Perception and Reading. Springer-Verlag, New York.

Rayner, K., and Pollatsek, A. (1992). Eye movements and scene perception. *Can. J. Psychol.* **46,** 342–376.

EYEWITNESS TESTIMONY

Kipling D. Williams
University of Toledo

Elizabeth F. Loftus
University of Washington

Glossary

Acquisition The first stage of memory in which the details of the event are initially interpreted by the witness and subject to influence by expectations, stress, and opportunity to observe.

Confirmation bias The process of selecting from one's memory or attention the information that tends to confirm one's beliefs or expectations, while ignoring information that tends to disconfirm one's beliefs or expectations.

Memory The flow and interpretation of information into the human mind, the storage of information there, and the retrieval of that information for the higher mental processes or remembering, thinking, judgment, and decision making.

Retrieval The third stage of memory in which the process of extracting the memory (line-ups, photo arrays, questioning procedures) may influence the stored memory.

Storage The second stage of memory in which the information is potentially influenced by information received between the time of initial exposure and subsequent tests of recall or recognition.

EYEWITNESS TESTIMONY is one of the most pervasive and powerful types of evidence routinely introduced in courts of law. "That's the man that attacked me. I will never forget his face." Who among us is not moved by this statement and compelled to believe it without question? Psychological research in memory, perception, and social psychology, however, informs us that jurors' assign too much credibility to eyewitness memory. Memory is not like a videotape. The original perception of an event is affected by the perceiver's level of stress, and is biased according to what the perceiver knows and expects. Once acquired, the memory is continually constructed and reconstructed to make sense, and changed so that it will fit incoming information from others. Studies indicate that there are numerous factors that routinely impair eyewitness accuracy, yet jurors tend to ignore many of these. They rely heavily on the confidence of the witness which can be unrelated to accuracy. Expert testimony on eyewitness memory is one way to inform jurors and improve their analysis of the eyewitness aspects of the case.

I. JURORS' BELIEFS ABOUT EYEWITNESS TESTIMONY

There are several ways to assess the extent to which jurors believe in eyewitness testimony. Questionnaire studies reveal that the public ranks eyewitness testimony as high or higher than any other single piece of evidence. Mock trial experiments, in which people are asked to play the roles of jurors, listen to testimony that either does or does not include eyewitness testimony, and reach a verdict, establishes that eyewitness testimony strongly increases the likelihood of a guilty verdict. In one study, mock jurors were given a description of a grocery store robbery in which the owner and his granddaughter were killed. The jurors also received a summary of the evidence and arguments presented at the defendant's trial, after which each juror was asked to arrive at a verdict of guilty or not guilty. Some of the jurors were told that there had been no eyewitnesses to the crime. Others were told that a store clerk had testified that he had seen the defendant shoot the two victims, although the defense attorney claimed he was mistaken. In the first instance, where there was no eyewitness but only circumstantial evi-

Copyright © 1994 by Academic Press, Inc. All rights of reproduction in any form reserved.

dence, 18% of the jurors felt that the defendant was guilty. This rose to 72% when a single eyewitness account was added to the circumstantial evidence. Interestingly, a third group of jurors had heard that the eyewitness had been substantially impeached because he had not been wearing his glasses and his vision was very poor. This information was largely ignored: 68% of the jurors still voted to convict.

Another way to assess jury belief in eyewitness testimony is to have mock jurors indicate their impressions of an eyewitness who testified during the mock trial. For instance, one study was conducted in two phases, the crime phase and the trial phase. In the crime phase, three people sat in an experimental room thinking they were going to participate in an experiment. At one point a "thief" entered the room, pretending to be part of the group. She soon "discovered" a calculator that had apparently been accidently left in the room. She picked it up and put it in her purse, mumbling something about wanting it and then left. The entire incident lasted just a few minutes. A little while later the remaining people, the witnesses, were asked to describe the thief and to try to identify her from a set of six photographs. In the second phase of the study, a new group of people, the jurors, were told about the theft and the witness identifications. The jurors watched as each witness was cross-examined. The jurors' job was to decide whether a particular witness was or was not mistaken. The results indicated that the jurors tended to believe the eyewitness testimony about 80% of the time. What is striking, however, is that these jurors were just as likely to believe a witness who had made an incorrect identification as one who had made a correct identification. The confidence of the eyewitness was a crucial determinant of believability. The jurors tended to believe those witnesses who were highly confident more than they believed those who were not.

In a recent study, mock jurors observed one of several versions of a re-enactment of a real trial, in which real lawyers played the roles of the trial attorneys. The authors varied 10 factors that might seem to be related to the accuracy of the eyewitness. These included whether the perpetrator wore a disguise, whether a weapon was visible, the level of violence in the incident, the retention interval between the time the eyewitness saw the event and the time he made his identification, whether the eyewitness was exposed to mugshots before viewing the lineup, the suggestive nature of lineup instructions, the number of people in the lineup, the similarity between the "suspects" in the lineup, whether the lineup members spoke, and the degree of confidence expressed by the eyewitness. Although the mock jurors recalled testimony relevant to each of these factors indicating that they had attended carefully to the trial information, the information presented on nine of these factors had no reliable effect on the jurors verdicts. Only one factor swayed the jurors, eyewitness confidence. Like the student jurors, jurors relied heavily on the confidence with which eyewitness testimony was given in making judgments as to witness accuracy. As we will see, the jurors ignored the factors that would have better predicted the accuracy of that testimony. We shall also see that the only variable that the jurors were sensitive to, the level of the eyewitness confidence, is not a particularly reliable predictor of accuracy.

A. Summary

Clearly, eyewitness testimony is powerful, and jurors appear to be readily convinced by it when it is presented confidently, even when there are present factors that would better predict its level of accuracy. These factors affect accuracy at all stages of memory, from the moment the event is first perceived, through the period of time memory is in "storage," to the suggestive and biased procedures authorities use to retrieve the memory. We will review these factors with respect to this sequence of memory stages. [*See* MEMORY.]

II. FACTORS AFFECTING ACCURACY OF EYEWITNESS MEMORY

A. Acquisition

At the acquisition stage, information about an event is perceived by the witness and is processed for memory storage. Many factors influence the pieces of information selected for encoding and how much and how well it gets encoded into storage. Several of the more salient variables affecting the acquisition of eyewitness memories include the witness' opportunity to observe various details, witness expectations, the capacity of the situation to elicit heightened arousal in the witness, the witness's age and race compared to the race of the perpetrator, and the extent to which they might have had prior eyewitness training.

1. Opportunity to Observe

Intuition has it that the opportunity for the witness to observe and his or her memory accuracy should be strongly and positively related. In fact, the U.S. Supreme Court has accepted this notion as a criterion for judging eyewitness reliability. Certainly the opportunity to observe any particular portion of the scene, such as the perpetrator's face, depends on the length of the witness' exposure to it. One study showed that for briefly displayed unfamiliar faces, increases in exposure duration up to 4 sec improved recognition accuracy. As a matter of fact, the results of several studies indicate that increases of a few seconds of exposure time for unfamiliar faces result in moderate-size increases in face recognition accuracy. Longer exposure durations result in a higher correct identification rate and a lower false identification rate.

Time to observe a critical item such as the perpetrator's face would clearly be reduced by increased complexity of the scene being viewed and by the presence of a focus of attention away from the critical item, a weapon focus, for instance. Defining complexity in terms of the number of perpetrators present, recall and recognition of the principal perpetrator are adversely affected when five perpetrators are present as opposed to one or three. The effects of event complexity are greater also at higher levels of event violence.

When a weapon is wielded by a perpetrator of a crime, it seems likely that its life-threatening potential would capture a considerable amount of eyewitness attention, attention not available for concentrating on the suspect's face. In one study, subjects in two experiments viewed a slide sequence scenario in which the target person held either a weapon or a control object, a check. Subjects made more frequent and longer eye fixations on the weapon than on the check, and recognition memory for the person holding the gun on the cashier was poorer than that for the same target person handing the cashier a check.

2. Expectations and Stereotypes

Past research has shown that our expectations, beliefs, and stereotypes can affect the way we categorize, organize, delete, and modify information during acquisition. Research and theory on confirmation bias suggest that individuals perceive an event in ways that confirm their expectations. [*See* CATEGORIZATION; PREJUDICE AND STEREOTYPES.]

Suppose, for instance, that a gang of four young males are often seen together by members of a small community. They are easy to spot because of their distinctive clothing. One night, four young males dressed in this distinctive clothing are seen robbing a liquor store. An eyewitness clearly sees three of the four boys, and recognize them as the gang members. The fourth boy is not seen well, but the eyewitness *assumes* it is the same boy that has been seen before with that gang, and modifies her memory in such a way to recall seeing that boy. In fact, the fourth boy did not participate in the robbery, and another had taken his place. But, because of prior expectations of the eyewitness, she recalls seeing the boy she had seen in the past. This is an example of confirmation bias due to prior expectations.

Jurors may also be affected by such confirmation biases. Much like we selectively search for similar features between an infant and its parents, jurors may do the same when comparing a defendant to a poor quality bank videotape of the perpetrator in a robbery. Juror's confirmation biases may direct them to see one similar feature between the defendant and the videotaped image, and to ignore five dissimilar features.

3. Elicitation of Heightened Arousal

Many jurists appear to hold to the view that heightened arousal increases accuracy of memory. The notion that an attacker's face is "carved in the brain" of the victim is a compelling notion. What does the laboratory evidence show? Generally speaking, accuracy of acquisition is related to levels of stress and arousal, but differently than that assumed. Instead of increasing accuracy with increasing arousal, the pattern of data more closely fits an inverted-U function (called the Yerkes–Dodson law), such that poorer accuracy occurs under very low and very high levels of stress, whereas greater accuracy occurs under moderate levels of stress. This relationship between arousal and performance holds true across many organisms and many types of performance. It has been found not only when rats try to find their way through a maze, but also when law students take their bar exams. Similarly, the ability to comprehend and remember aspects of an unexpected and traumatic event is impaired by the accompanying levels of fear and stress. Indeed, in many studies where the violence level or intensity of personal threat has been successfully manipulated, higher arousal levels have resulted in reduced eyewitness accuracy.

In one study, a male perpetrator appeared before a large class of college students briefly during which time he either exited (low arousal) or snatched a female student's purse before exiting (high arousal). Two days later 42 witnesses who said they had gotten a look at the perpetrator were shown either a target-present or target-absent lineup by the same policeman. Pilot data had indicated that physiological arousal as indexed by changes in skin impedance was four times as great for bystander witnesses in the high arousal as compared to the low arousal condition. Overall identification accuracy taken across both lineup conditions was 49% for those viewing the suspect in the low arousal setting and only 24% for those having viewed him in the high arousal setting.

In another recent field study, witnesses provided physical descriptions and identifications from photo lineups of a nurse who had recently inoculated them at an immunization clinic and of a second person who had taken their pulse 2 min later. Physiological arousal as indexed by heart rate was significantly higher at inoculation as compared with when their pulse was taken. Physical descriptions of the inoculating nurse were less accurate as compared to those of the pulse-taking nurse.

As mentioned earlier with respect to the presence of a weapon, however, such fear can channel or focus attention on a single stimulus (i.e., the weapon), thus improving memory for that particular stimulus.

4. Age of Eyewitness

Intuitions regarding the age of the eyewitness are mixed. People believe either that the word of a child is more susceptible to imagination and suggestion and, therefore, should not be trusted or that children have no reason to lie and are more likely to be truthful. Furthermore, stereotypes abound regarding the accuracy of elderly eyewitnesses. Nearer the beginning of the lifespan, it would appear that memory for unfamiliar faces is developmentally sensitive across the years of childhood and early adolescence. In fact, adult-like levels of face recognition performance may not be achieved until well into adolescence. There seems to be general agreement, as well, that children provide less complete reports of event details in free verbal recall than do adults. Though the result is not universally obtained, children younger than about 9 years of age also typically show greater susceptibility to suggestive or leading questions. Nevertheless, children as young as 6 years of age *may* show adult-like accuracy in answering objective questions, particularly when details are salient, when the event can be assimilated to his/her level of social and cognitive competence, and when the event context can be appropriately reinstated.

In one study comparing young adults to the elderly, young adults were equally as adept as elderly adults at recognizing elderly faces and yet were superior to the elderly at recognizing faces of young adults, those more likely to be perpetrators of a crime. There is evidence for certain kinds of recognition deficit in the elderly. Several studies have shown that the elderly experience a decline in the ability to recognize photographs of faces seen only once before. That is, older persons show a reduced ability to recognize faces seen in only one view relative to the ability of young adults. On the other hand, if a face has been seen from multiple viewpoints, there appears to be no age-related deficit. Older adults seem to suffer a deficit, as well, in verbal recall of details of witnessed episodes. [*See* FACE RECOGNITION.]

5. Other-Race Phenomenon

When faced with trying to recognize or describe a member of a racial group different from one's own, there is the folk expression, "They all look alike." Although many regard such a statement as evidence of prejudice or narrow-mindedness, there is a substantial core of truth to the statement and it applies to whites, blacks, Hispanics, and Asians.

In laboratory and field research, witnesses do better at identifying suspects of their own race than they do at identifying suspects of another race. For instance, in studies of staged thefts in convenience stores, there was an other-race impairment for white store clerks such that 33 to 55% accurately identified blacks, whereas from 53 to 68% accurately identified whites. The impairment also occurs for blacks and Hispanics trying to identify whites. Even whites who attend predominantly all-black colleges suffer from such inaccuracies.

6. Training or Experience

Even though a substantial majority of laypersons believe that police should be uniformly better at eyewitness memory tasks by virtue of their training, the evidence thus far accumulated is that it is impossible to train adults to become better at face recognition, at least for faces of the same race. It is true that as many as 30 studies have been done in an effort to show that more thoroughly (deeply) processed faces should be better recognized later. Indeed any encoding strategy that forces a person to scan an entire face is more effective than one that limits the scan. Intensive short-term training in any of the deep encoding strategies discovered thus far does not seem to improve one's same-race face recognition capabilities. It does appear possible, however, that training can yield permanent gains in the capacity to recognize other-race faces. One training procedure found that in as few as six 45-min training sessions distributed over a 2- to 3-week period, there were large gains by Caucasian trainees in the ability to recognize Japanese faces which persisted even after 5 months.

7. Summary

Many factors present the situation and in the specific characteristics of the eyewitness can adversely affect the accuracy of interpretation and memories of these eyewitnesses. In whatever imperfect form the memory is acquired, it then becomes susceptible to a variety of outside influences and internal reconstructions. This first occurs in the storage stage of memory.

B. Storage

Storage of a memory trace occupies the interval between the end of its acquisition and its subsequent access at retrieval, and of course intervals between subsequent retrievals, if any.

1. Retention Interval

In recent years, a primary concern of researchers studying memory for faces and/or eyewitness testimony has been to determine whether there are predictable negative effects of increases in the length of this interval during which stored traces must be retained, the retention interval. Sometimes there is a gradual decay over time, but this is not always the case. A common pattern of forgetting is to see a large amount of forgetting at the very early stages of retention, and then there is a gradual decline. One study that reveals this pattern showed that in the first 5 min after encoding, 13.5% of initial trace strength was lost, while it took the remainder of the 2 days to lose another 13.5%. Five more days resulted in the loss of 4% more. Clearly it would be ideal if police were able to test eyewitness memories for unfamiliar faces within 48 hr, an ideal that obviously cannot always be achieved.

2. Postevent Information

A variety of events occurring during the retention interval have been shown to interfere retroactively with initially encoded information so as to lower subsequent memory performance. Among the phenomena that have been shown to interfere with accurate memory is misleading verbal information.

The common finding is that misleading postevent information reduces the accuracy of subsequent recollection, a phenomenon referred to as the "misinformation effect." In these studies subjects who have previously encountered misleading information have misrecalled the color of a car that was green as being blue, a yield sign as a stop sign, broken glass or tape recorders that never existed, and even something as large and conspicuous as a barn when no barn was ever seen.

Postevent information can also occur when the witness hears others provide their rendition of the event or what the perpetrator looked like. Research on group discussions often finds that group members' memories for an event converge, forming a consistent, yet not necessarily correct, memory. Additionally, seeing or hearing descriptions provided by the police in the newspaper or on television, as well as viewing artist's compositions of the perpetrator, can alter the stored memory.

3. Unconscious Transference

Another type of information, which may have been acquired before the witnessing of the event, could also intrude upon memory resulting in another modification. We often can remember a face, but not the context in which we originally saw it. Sometimes, witnesses get a "feeling of familiarity" when examining a particular individual in a mug shot or lineup, a feeling they misattribute to one of a positive identification of the perpetrator. In many instances, witnesses have relied upon this feeling of familiarity to an identification, unconsciously transferring the face of a person they have seen at a bus stop, the grocery store, on television, or from another mugshot, to that of the face of the perpetrator.

4. Summary

Significant decay occurs with increasing intervals of time between viewing the event and retrieving the information. Much of this decay occurs soon after the exposure, resulting in impaired memory. In addition, various forms of postevent information can affect the memory once it has been acquired. During the storage stage, the memory is subjected to constant revisions and reconstructions to conform to this incoming information, so that it makes sense and is consistent with current versions of the event. We will now examine various forms of retrieving the memory that may also serve to modify it.

C. Retrieval

In the previous section, we discussed how various types of postevent information could intrude upon the memory to alter it. Indeed, some of this post-event information occurs during the retrieval stage of memory, the point or points at which the witness is ask to recall the description of the perpetrator or to recognize the perpetrator in a mug shot, photo array, or line-up. When authorities have a specific suspect in mind, various forms of interrogation and identification techniques can subtlely "suggest" the desired description of a suspect or the selection of a such suspect from a photographic array or live line-up. The witness then integrates the suggestions and assertions made during the retrieval stage with the stored memory resulting in a newly constructed memory that is consistent with these suggestions.

1. Leading Questions

Suggestive questions imply a correct fact or answer within the context of the question. The form of these implied facts can often be quite subtle. Asking how fast an automobile was going when it smashed into another car compared to when it hit another can can dramatically increase the reported speed. Additionally, those who are asked the "smashed into" question later report having seen broken glass in the accident when there was none, whereas those asked the question with the word "hit" in it do not report seeing broken glass. In another study, subjects were presented with a film of an automobile accident and immediately afterward were asked a series of questions about the accident. Some of the questions suggested the existence of an object that did not exist. Half the subjects were asked "How fast was the sports car going when it passed the barn while traveling along the country road?" In fact, no barn existed. The remaining subjects were asked "How fast was the sports car going while traveling along the country road?" Later all subjects were asked if they had seen a barn. When questioned again about the accident a week later, more than 17% of those exposed to the false information about a barn said they had seen one. Apparently, the "assumption of a barn" during the initial questioning caused many subjects to incorporate the nonexistent barn into their recollections of the event.

In other studies, new information does more than simply supplement a memory: it apparently alters or transforms the memory. In one study, the subjects saw a simulated accident involving an auto and pedestrian. A red Datsun was seen traveling along a side street toward an intersection at which there was a stop sign for half the subjects and a yield sign for the others. After stopping at the intersection, the Datsun turned right and knocked down a pedestrian who was trying to cross the street. Immediately after the accident the subjects answered questions. Some subjects then received a question containing a piece of misinformation: for example, the question "Did another car pass the red Datsun while it was stopped at the stop sign?" contains a piece of misinformation when asked of subjects who actually saw the yield sign. Finally, subjects were given one last test. They were instructed to report whether they had actually seen the stop sign or yield sign. Depending upon the time intervals that occurred between the slides, the intervening questions, and the final recollection, as many as 80% of subjects indicated that their recollections were consistent with the misinformation. This experiment suggests that erroneous presuppositions are capable of transforming a person's recollection as well as merely adding to it.

2. Line-Up Fairness

One particular occasion in which the retrieval process can substantially interfere with memory is when an eyewitness is attempting to recognize the perpetrator from an array of photographs or from alternatives in a live line-up. Considerable research has been conducted on what constitutes a fair versus biased procedure for such identifications. A number of post hoc measures of line-up fairness have been developed by psychologists in recent years. Probably the least fair recognition and most coercive procedure is the "show up" technique, in which the witness is asked to look at one individual to determine if "this is the perpetrator." The problem with this is that there is substantial pressure upon the witness to affirm the authority's suspicion that they have apprehended the suspect. Confirmation biases also play a role, such that witnesses selectively look for similarities between the suspect and their memory for the perpetrator, but may disregard dissimilarities. The in-court identification is similarly flawed in that only one reasonable suspect is present, the one sitting next to the defense attorney.

Line-ups of at least five alternatives is most desirable. Furthermore, research has been done showing that sequential line-ups are more fair vis-a-vis the diagnosticity ratio than are simultaneously presented ones. That is, the correct identification rate is about the same with each type of line-up, but the false identification rate is lower with sequential line-ups. When sequential line-ups are combined with neutral instructions allowing explicit rejection of the line-up by the witness, an even greater increase in diagnosticity occurs. The selection by the police of nonsuspects (or foils) is also quite important. Fewer false identifications are made when the nonsuspects match the physical description provided by the eyewitness. Witnesses tend to use a "resemblance" strategy and select the person who most closely resembles the perpetrator in their memory. To the extent that only the suspect matches this description, the functional size of the line-up is one. A fair line-up is one in which nonwitnesses, given only the original physical description, are equally likely to select all alternatives. Still another booster of diagnosticity is the reinstatement of strong physical context cues associated with the suspect, posture, gait, voice, and three-quarter profile. Hence, police can increase the power, sensitivity, and fairness of identification procedures by using sequential line-ups and photospreads composed of persons who match the suspect on all characteristics mentioned in the initial verbal description. These displays should be accompanied by unbiased instructions allowing rejection of the entire set of individuals, and, where possible, additional physical cues characteristic of each line-up member should be presented.

3. Retrieval Enhancement Techniques

There have been some new developments that permit less biased, more complete, more accurate assessments of the relevant contents of memory at the end of the retention interval. These retrieval procedures cannot, however, compensate for difficulties of acquisition and storage. They can only increase the likelihood of accurate retrieval of what has survived the retention interval. For instance, error rates in recall can be reduced if leading questions are avoided and if all specific questions employ the indefinite article rather than the definite article. Two other procedures have been proposed to improve both eyewitness recall and recognition, the hypnotic interview and various forms of the guided memory interview. The hypnotic interview, however, does not appear to facilitate recognition performance on line-ups and photospreads. Evidence is mixed regarding its ability to promote eyewitness recall. Hypnosis, however, does increase susceptibility to leading questions and enhance witness confidence, two factors that should deter its employment. Research testing the guided memory interviews is more favorable. This procedure involves getting the witness to reinstate mentally the environmental and personal context prevailing at the time of the incident and to recall the event, as completely as possible, from various perceptual perspectives and in a variety of orders. Versions of this interview process have been shown to be more effective than the traditional police interview in terms of correct items recalled, while eliciting a similar rate of incorrect items recalled, although face recognition fairs less well.

4. Summary

Substantial modifications to stored memory can occur in the retrieval stage, when eyewitnesses attempt to extract their memories from storage. Leading questions and biased line-ups impose suggested correct answers that may contaminate memory. New procedures have been attracting attention that can reduce these forms of bias.

III. ASPECTS OF TESTIMONY INFLUENCING JUROR BELIEF

Triers of fact are faced with the unenviable position of trying to determine the accuracy of an eyewitness' memory. This section reviews the social psychological research that shows that often jurors discount the factors discussed above that may contribute significantly to eyewitness accuracy, and instead place more weight on factors that are not predictive of eyewitness accuracy. Several studies have been conducted recently regarding characteristics of the testimony or the witness that may affect the believability of eyewitness testimony for jurors. These include witness confidence, amount of detail provided, age of witness, whether the witness has been discredited, and whether the witness makes a nonidentification statement ("That isn't the person who robbed the store").

A. Witness Confidence

People believe others who appear credible. One aspect of credibility is the speaker's confidence, the strong and assured belief in what he or she is saying. If people did not already use confidence as a clue to credibility, the court system itself encourages them to do so. Instructions to the jury often direct jurors to reconcile inconsistent testimonies by giving more weight and substance to the confident witness.

The conclusions of several experiments suggest that confidence is extremely influential, even more than the accuracy of the testimony. The relation between confidence and accuracy, however, is much weaker than we might imagine. It is concluded that confidence is not a useful predictor of either the accuracy of particular witnesses or the accuracy of particular statements made by the same witness.

The reason for this low correlation is that confidence of one's memory is a social phenomenon, as well as a memory issue, and as such, is subject to social influence. After repeating the same story several times, one's confidence about the accuracy of the story amplifies. This is partly due to wanting to maintain consistency after publicly committing oneself to a specific rendition of what one witnessed. Social psychological research informs us that asserting something publicly increases our belief in what we say, and that the more important the consequences of such an assertion, the stronger our confidence will be.

The external pressures on a person to maintain one's story are also strong. It would be very difficult to change one's mind on the 10th retelling of the event, after so much time and work have been put into the trial process, based upon the first 9 tellings. In fact, eyewitness confidence increases as one simply prepares mentally to be cross-examined.

Eyewitnesses may use other cues than the "feeling of knowing" to assess their own confidence. People tend to use their own response latencies (how long it takes to make the identification) as indicators of their confidence levels. However, response latencies are not related strongly to either confidence or accuracy. Furthermore, there may be relatively stable individual differences regarding how confident one is, regardless of one's accuracy. People who are confident of correct memories are also confident of incorrect memories. So, although the accuracy level of an eyewitness at best remains stable or, more typically, declines over time, confidence in the accuracy of such a memory may increase substantially over time and may be related to factors unrelated to accuracy.

B. Amount of Detail

People are more convinced by eyewitness testimony that contains specific details, even if these details are unrelated to the description of the suspect. People assume that those who remember trivial details possess better memories in general, and hence are more credible. Actual eyewitnesses who were cross-examined about errors they made for trivial details were found to be less reliable overall by mock jurors. Interestingly, in another study, eyewitnesses who paid attention to trivial details were *less* likely to have paid attention to the culprit's face. So, as with confidence, it may be that jurors give weight to factors that are unrelated or inversely related to accuracy.

C. Witness Age

As mentioned before, the age of the witness sometimes affects the degree of accuracy of the memory. How do people regard the testimony of children? Do we possess stereotypes about the quality of children's memories, how well they resist manipulation under questioning, and whether they are credible (i.e., honest and/or expert)? In two experiments, mock jurors produced a consistent yet unexpected pattern of results: The child witness was believed more than the elderly witness, and the elderly witness was believed more than the young adult. Yet, a third study indicated that people *said* they would typically believe the child the least, followed by the elderly witness, and that they would believe the young adult the most. At this point, we can conclude little about how credible people view the eyewitness testimony of children. It is possible that child witnesses (or elderly witnesses) who competently and articulately express themselves during examination may violate our stereotypes and, as a consequence, increase their credibility. Further research will be needed to determine if the inconsistent results of past studies have been due to the fact that some of the child witnesses have been portrayed as "adult-like children."

D. Discredited Eyewitnesses

If the eyewitness is discredited during testimony, will jurors persist in believing the eyewitness? In a study mentioned earlier, even when it was pointed out that a witness who required glasses was not wearing glasses at the time of the event, mock jurors continued to be heavily influenced by the witness. On the other hand, if an eyewitness admits poor eyesight and apologizes for her testimony and asks for the court to ignore her testimony, then the testimony is largely ignored. Of course, the likelihood of such a scenario is probably very low, as any defense attorney would attest.

E. Nonidentifications

How do people react to an eyewitness who asserts that the defendant is *not* the person they saw commit the crime compared to one who says it is? Research suggests that a nonidentification is less informative and influential. Apparently, people are more likely to assume memory failure as a reason for a nonidentification than as reason for a false identification. The results of another study, however, indicate that the nonidentifier's effectiveness is greater if the nonidentifier chose to testify rather than when the attorney simply relayed the nonidentification to the mock jurors.

F. Summary

The persuasiveness of the eyewitness can be more important than the accuracy of the eyewitness in terms of the jury's decision. There are a number of factors people use to determine credibility of witnesses, and these factors can be misleading. People rely on witnesses' apparent confidence and their use of detail and on those who identify the suspect rather than those who were at the incident who do not identify the suspect. Furthermore, age is an important, albeit inconsistent, factor and the effects of discrediting the eyewitnesses yield inconsistent findings.

IV. COMMUNICATING EYEWITNESS RESEARCH TO TRIERS OF FACT

The question persists as to whether it is desirable to transmit to triers of fact relevant portions of the body of research on eyewitness memory, and if so, which means of communicating research results would be more effective, expert testimony or judicial instructions. Some research psychologists believe that jurors should not be exposed to research evidence on eyewitness memory. They argue that there are inconsistencies in the results of studies, that knowledge of the exact nature of memory reconstruction is not adequately grounded, or that the jury already has a basic understanding of the important issues. Those in favor of allowing information to be disseminated to the jury argue that no science is without controversy, that consistent findings that link certain factors to faulty memory reports are sufficiently important and should not be withheld from the jurors, and that jurors' intuitions are not consistent with the actual research findings. At this point, some courts, but not all, have opined that there is considerable agreement within the field of psychology regarding eyewitness research, that the results are not typically within the common knowledge of the jury, and that jurors are assisted by such knowledge.

Regarding agreement within the field, a recent survey of experts on eyewitness testimony determined that more than 80% of them felt that nine different phenomena associated with eyewitness behavior were sufficiently reliable for psychologists to present in court: wording of questions, line-up instructions, postevent information, accuracy/confidence, attitudes and expectations, exposure time, unconscious transference, show-ups, and the nature of the forgetting curve. Over 70% of the experts also believed as sufficiently reliable the phenomena of cross-racial difficulties experienced by white witnesses, line-up fairness, time overestimation, and stress effects.

There are three different lines of research whose results all converge on the conclusion that laypersons do not have well-informed intuitions regarding the effects of a number of variables on eyewitness behavior. Questionnaire studies have yielded evidence of considerable ignorance of the actual implications of many factors that bear on the reliability of eyewitness testimony. Studies that ask laypersons to read the methods of eyewitness research and to predict the results indicate that their predictions have little or no relationship to the results. Finally, perceived confidence of witnesses, rather than accuracy, has correlated relatively strongly with verdicts in most studies in which mock jurors view cross-examinations of both accurate and inaccurate witnesses to a staged crime.

Research on the effects of exposure to eyewitness research results suggest that expert testimony increases juror sensitivity to witnessing and identification conditions, conditions whose effects are not generally part of jurors' common-sense knowledge. Expert testimony accomplishes this, while not increasing skepticism or introducing confusion, provided testimony is clear and concise. In addition, expert testimony appears to increase jurors' ability to integrate evidence and may well improve the criminal justice process in the long run.

An alternative way to expose jurors to research evidence on eyewitness memory is through judicial instructions. Expert testimony costs more and takes more time than judicial instructions, and there is the possibility that in some cases both the prosecution and the defense would hire experts, leading to a potential "battle of the experts."

There are three important disadvantages to judicial instructions. For one thing, results of two studies have shown the ineffectiveness of the most commonly used pattern instructions. These instructions did not increase juror knowledge of eyewitness testimony research and either did not increase juror sensitivity to witnessing and identification conditions or actually decreased juror sensitivity. Second, judges do not have a lot of latitude in commenting on the evidence and therefore can only call the jury's attention to eyewitness memory problems without being able to explain all the cautions. Third, even if judges could comment on the evidence in greater detail, they could not provide the necessary information because of their lack of expertise. Presumably a court-appointed expert would be needed to supply the expertise.

Until further development and testing produce judicial instructions that are demonstrably effective, it appears that expert testimony will be necessary. It is even possible that judicial instructions can never be developed that will be as effective as expert testimony because judges are not free to comment in detail concerning eyewitness evidence and do not have the expertise to do so in any event. Allowing expert testimony will provide jurors who are exposed to eyewitness testimony a scientific basis from which they can determine for themselves the proper weight to give it.

Bibliography

Buckhout, R. (1974). Eyewitness testimony. *Sci. Am.* **231,** 23–31.

Ceci, S. J., Toglia, M. P., and Ross, D. F. (Eds.). (1987). "Children's Eyewitness Memory." Springer-Verlag, New York.

Cutler, B. L., Penrod, S. D., and Dexter, H. R. (1989). The eyewitness, the expert psychologist, and the jury. *Law Hum. Behav.* **13,** 311–332.

Cutler, B. L., Penrod, S. D., and Stuve, T. E. (1988). Juror decision making in eyewitness identification cases. *Law Hum. Behav.* **12,** 41–55.

Deffenbacher, K. A. (1984). Experimental psychology actually can assist triers of fact. *Am. Psychol.* **39,** 1066–1068.

Loftus, E. F. (1979). "Eyewitness Testimony." Harvard University Press, Cambridge.

Loftus, E. F., and Doyle, J. M. (1992). "Eyewitness Testimony: Civil and Criminal." Michie, Charlottesville, VA.

Loftus, E. F., and Ketcham, K. (1991). "Witness for the Defense." St. Martin's Press, New York.

Wagenaar, W. (1988). "Identifying Ivan: A Case Study in Legal Psychology." Harvard University Press, Cambridge.

Wells, G. L., Ferguson, T. J., and Lindsay, R. C. L. (1981). The tractability of eyewitness confidence and its implications for triers of fact. *J. Appl. Psychol.* **66,** 688–696.

Wells, G. L., and Lindsay, R. C. L. (1980). On estimating the diagnosticity of eyewitness identifications. *Psychol. Bull.* **88,** 776–784.

Wells, G. L., and Loftus, E. F. (1984). "Eyewitness Testimony: Psychological Perspectives." Cambridge University Press, New York.

Williams, K. D., Loftus, E. F., and Deffenbacher, K. A. (1992). Eyewitness evidence and testimony. In "Handbook of Psychology and Law." (D. K. Kagehiro and W. S. Laufer, Eds.), Springer-Verlag, New York.

Face Recognition

Raymond Bruyer
Louvain University, Belgium

Glossary

Cognitive neuropsychology A method of cognitive psychology by which dissociations between representations and the subcomponents of a given normal cognitive architecture are sought by studying the defective effects of natural variables such as aging or brain damage.

Cognitive psychology Experimental study of the mental (i.e., not directly observable) representations and operations involved in the complex process by which a given event (stimulus, mental image, etc.) triggers a given behavior (response), and analysis of the relationships and interaction between these representations (i.e., a cognitive architecture).

Covert recognition Recognition without awareness (as opposed to overt recognition), perhaps a form of implicit memory.

Prosopagnosia A rare but spectacular neurological symptom, resulting from certain brain lesions, and characterized by a specific inability to visually recognize faces that were well-known before the cerebral damage as well as faces which were frequently encountered after the brain injury, while the recognition of persons by other cues (like the voice, the silhouette, etc.) is spared; the trouble cannot be explained by severe perceptual, intellectual, and memory deficits.

FACE RECOGNITION is fast and automatic but is certainly not a single operation. Rather, it is the end-product of a lot of underlying subprocesses operating on many different representations. Both subprocesses and representations can be selectively disturbed by pathology (brain injury), natural factors (aging), and experimental manipulations. Moreover, overt responses of the subjects are not the sole source of information for researchers, since physiological and behavioral signs of covert face recognition have been reported. First of all, the domain under investigation and the methods used are introduced. Then, the main cognitive operations and representations underlying the recognition of persons from the sight of their face (visual analyses, recognition of the face, recognition of the person, access to semantic pieces of information and to the name of the person seen) are described. Finally, a broad outline of a hypothetical cognitive architecture is suggested, which summarizes what is currently known about this complex process.

I. DOMAIN AND METHODS

Face recognition is an impressive human faculty which probably results from the great importance of this behavior in daily life. So, numerous experimental studies and detailed observations of failures of this process due to brain damage, aging, and experimental manipulations have been reported over the past three decades.

Copyright © 1994 by Academic Press, Inc. All rights of reproduction in any form reserved.

During the 1980s, a unified conceptual framework progressively emerged within the general "information processing approach," which is the major feature of cognitive psychology (that is to say, the overt behavior triggered by a stimulus is assumed to be the result of a series of operations made on representations and conceived as computations on the available information). The purpose of such an approach is to use methods of experimental psychology and of neuropsychology in order to, first, dissociate the numerous subprocesses involved in face recognition and, then, describe and understand the cognitive architecture of this complex behavior. The dissociation between two kinds of representation (say A and B) can be established by observing a factor (e.g., an experimental manipulation, a particular brain injury, aging) which impairs A but not B and another factor which impairs B but not A (the so called "principle of double dissociation"). These general methodological rules apply because the studied variables (mental or cognitive representations) are not directly observable. Additionally, data concerning face recognition in infants, connexionnist simulations, and cellular recordings in animals contribute to our knowledge in this matter.

Albeit fast and automatic (i.e., unavoidable), face recognition is not a single operation but rather the end-product of many underlying subprocesses operating on a lot of different representations as will be seen below. Both subprocesses and representations can be selectively disturbed by pathology (brain injury), natural factors (aging, daily-life incidents), and experimental manipulations. In addition, recognition of a specific, individual face (identification) is not the sole process that can be triggered by the vision of a face. First, the face must first be categorized as "a human face," probably by mechanisms similar to those ensuring the recognition of objects. Second, face recognition results from visual analyses that can be performed on known as well as unknown (new) faces. Third, some visual operations can be performed on faces which are not mandatory for face recognition (for instance lipreading, detection of the direction of the gaze of the face seen, recognition of facial expressions, detection of the apparent age or the gender of the person seen, etc.). Fourth and finally, face recognition is only an intermediate step toward a deeper operation thanks to which pieces of semantic information as well as the name of the person met can be retrieved from memory. More generally, the broad cognitive architecture underlying the identification of a particular face

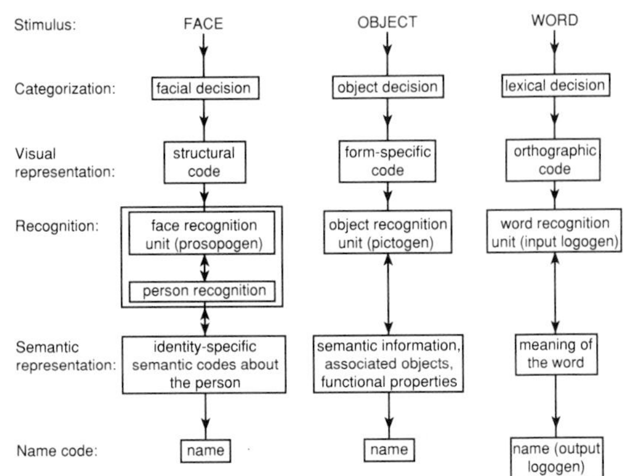

FIGURE 1 The general cognitive architecture of the face identification process (left), and its similarities with the recognition of other kinds of visual stimuli (objects, words).

seems to be similar to that involved in the visual recognition of other kinds of stimuli (see Fig. 1).

It is also worth noting that face recognition is not the only way for recognizing people. So, this operation has to be situated in a more general process ensuring person recognition, including in parallel the recognition of the voice, gait, silhouette, handwriting, name, etc., of the person seen (see Fig. 2).

II. VISUAL ANALYSES

When a face appears in the visual field of a viewer, a series of visual or perceptual operations are made. Some of them are not specific to faces, since their output is a representation of "the human face" as different from any other visual object. The other

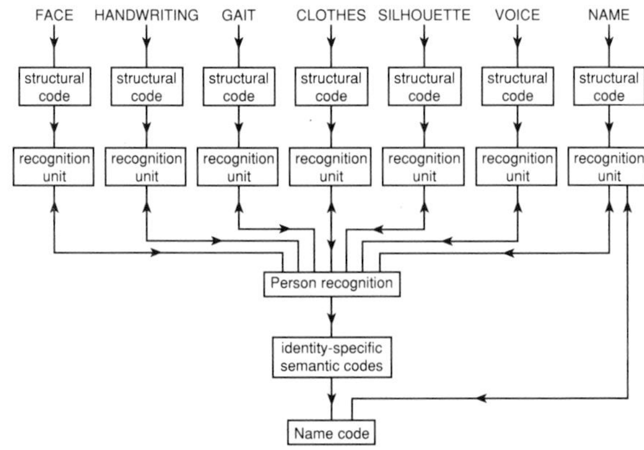

FIGURE 2 Face recognition is not the sole way of ensuring a person's recognition, since people can also be recognized by their voice, silhouette, handwriting, clothes, gait, name, etc.

visual operations are probably specific to faces. Some of them are not mandatory for the identification of the particular face seen, and the others can be made no matter whether the face is already known by the viewer.

A. Facial Decision

When something "falls" in the focus of visual attention, it is first "recognized" at a broad categorical level. That is to say, it is recognized as a fork, a sofa, a car, a bird, or a human face. Obviously, this perceptual stage of the processing cannot be specific to faces, but rather, it underlies the recognition of any category of objects. [*See* CATEGORIZATION.]

Object recognition has been dissociated into four main steps. First, a primal sketch is computed on the retinal image generated by the input. The retinal image (one for each eye) is a curved bidimensional matrix of points of luminous intensities. The primal sketch is a representation of the loci of changes in the luminous intensity at several levels of precision, and of the spatial organization of these changes. Second, a 2.5-dimensional (D) sketch is derived from the primal sketch, which explicits the surfaces and their orientations in the perceived object. This computation is made by taking into account and in parallel several kinds of information such as colors, textures, movements, shadows, differences between the two primal sketches (one from each eye), etc. However, this three-dimensional representation is still dependent on the actual viewpoint, i.e., the distance and orientation of the object (which explains the expression "2.5 D"): the frame of reference is that of the viewer. Therefore, a third representation is computed which is independent of the actual viewpoint and based on the structural organization of the object: this 3-D model is organized around the proper structure of the object, its internal axes, and the spatial organization of these axes. In other words, an invariant structural description is derived. Fourth and finally, this structural invariant description is compared to descriptions already stored in long-term memory and, if a match emerges, the object is "recognized" at a categorical level (a fork, a car, and so on). It should be noted here that an alternative, but not incompatible, theory suggests that object recognition results from the recognition of parts of objects and the spatial organization of their assembly. The underlying assumption is that objects, like words, are specific sets of elements or parts issuing from a limited set of about 30 different volumetric elements.

The result of this first series of perceptual operations is that a given object is categorized as human face, because the structural invariant description of a human face has been reached (the "syntactic properties" of the object met: an oval form, with two symmetrically located blobs, a central vertical nose, and so on = a human face). For many kinds of objects, this output authorizes usual daily-life behaviors. Indeed, it is generally sufficient to recognize a car, a fork, or a chair to manage daily-life activities. Some objects require a true individual identification, but at a broad level: I have to recognize my own car, my house, or my tea cup among several cars, houses, or cups, but all other cars, houses, or cups can be confused. However, where faces are concerned, a real individual identification is at work: for social purposes, one has very often to individualize faces in daily-life activities. Thus, the following operations are devoted to this individual identification of exemplars within the category of human faces.

Before proceeding, however, let us note here that this individual identification of exemplars is probably not an indication of specific, neurally encapsulated mechanisms of face recognition in humans. Indeed, properties of face recognition (for instance, the inversion effect, that is to say, the dramatic effect of vertical inversion upon face recognition) have been replicated with other kinds of mono-oriented stimuli with subjects specifically trained to individualize these types of materials (e.g., dogs in dog breeders and handwriting in graphologists). Moreover, neural cells selectively sensitive to faces are not affected by inversion in monkeys (which are "arboreal" animals) but are in sheep. Thus, it seems that face recognition is a particular perceptual skill but that this expertise, unlike other forms of expertise, is largely shared by human beings.

B. Structural Analyses

Once a visual object has been classified as "a face," the processor generally performs computations to recognize it at an individual level. Since this series of operations precedes the individual recognition, it can be computed on both known and unknown faces. In addition, some operations can be made which are not necessary to recognize the encountered face.

1. Toward Individual Face Recognition

The currently seen face is perceived at a particular distance, with a momentary facial expression and in a specific pose. Therefore, an early description is derived which is dependent on the distance, expression, and pose (a 2.5-D representation). It could be that, for faces, this derivation is particularely sensitive to properties like shadows and textures. In addition, while the object categorization stage ("a human face") is probably governed by the derivation of categorical spatial relationships (two symmetrically placed eyes, a centrally located vertical nose, etc.), the specific exemplar recognition results more probably from the computation of precise coordinate or metric or distance relationships (two faces differ by the distance between the eyes, the length of the nose, etc.). At this stage of the process, individual features (mouth, eyes, nose, etc.) are recognized. It is worth noting that this recognition of individual features is strongly dependent on contextual effects, the so-called "face superiority effect": just like the processing of individual letters is influenced by the string of letters displayed (a word, a pronounceable nonword, an unpronounceable series, etc: the "word superiority effect"), the processing of isolated facial features is more difficult than the processing of features shown in a "facial context."

However, a face is always changing and the purpose of perceptual analyses is to derive a face representation which is invariant from the actual viewpoint. Thus, a 3-D model is built, and which explicits the invariant properties of the face seen. This would explain why one is able to recognize a particular face which has never been seen in this particular pose or expression (actually, this explicit computation of a 3-D model for face recognition is disputed; for instance, it could be that 3-D structure is coded implicitly via the analysis of image intensities). This representation would be compared to representations already stored in long-term memory, and if a match appears, recognition takes place.

These kinds of computations can be made on known as well as unknown faces, but it is worth noting that face familiarity can influence visual analysis. For instance, visual analysis is generally limited to inner features (eyes, nose, mouth) when a familiar face is encountered, but extends to inner and outer features (chin, hair, etc.) when an unfamiliar face is met. Another illustration is that the detection of local alterations of features is virtually impossible when a known face is shown.

2. Optional Visual Operations

View-specific (2.5-D) and invariant (3-D) representations of faces can also be used to compute representations which are not mandatory for face identification. For example, from a single, particular view of a face, one is able to recognize its expression (a categorical process of noncategorical stimuli, like color and speech recognition), the specific mouth movements linked with speech production, or the direction of its gaze. Similarly, from both the particular view and the invariant description of a face, one is able to derive some representations linked with the apparent age, gender, "race," and attractiveness of the person seen (the so-called "semantic visually derived codes").

III. FACE RECOGNITION

If the encountered face is already known by the viewer or resembles a known face, then face recognition takes place because the structural invariant description of the input matches a previously stored representation. It is hypothesized that the processor includes a register of face-recognition units, that is to say, a store of visual descriptions of faces already met in the past.

A. Familiarity Decision and Face-Recognition Units

Technically speaking, face recognition occurs when, and only when, a correct decision of "already seen" is taken. That is to say, a previously met face (old) gives rise to a hit, and a never seen face (new) triggers a correct rejection. Methodologically, this stage is generally assessed by means of familiarity decision tasks. Several faces are shown one by one, and the subject has to decide whether the current face is known or not.

Face recognition is assumed to be the result of a match between the structural invariant representation derived from the face seen and a recognition unit stored in long-term memory (the register of face-recognition units) and built up from the previous encounters with that face. There would be just one or a few recognition units for each already known face, and the nature of these units is more probably a structural visual representation (a form of "mental image," probably caricature-like) than a propositional verbal-like representation. Also, it is assumed that the firing of a face-recognition unit is not the result of a threshold, all-or-none mechanism but, more likely, of a gradual response depending on the degree of similarity between the recognition unit and the invariant representation actually derived. This accounts for the "repetition (or identity) priming," that is to say, the recognition of a face is facilitated if the same face (not necessarily under the same pose or expression) has been seen recently by the subject during the current experiment. Finally, the activation of face-recognition units is conceived as resulting from the number of individual facial features recognized, as well as the number of recognized spatial configurations between these features.

B. Prosopagnosia

Even if humans are expert in face recognition, this ability is not uniform (age and sex differences have been reported). A well-known phenomenon is the "race effect," which can be understood by considering the store of face-recognition units as a multidimensional space of which the zero point would be a prototypical face (the "mean" of all faces already met). However, the major sign of defect is prosopagnosia.

Prosopagnosia, i.e., "agnosia for faces" (from the greek word "prosopon," which means "face"), is a rare but spectacular neurological symptom characterized by an inability to visually recognize faces that were well-known before the cerebral damage (including sometimes the face of the patient himself). Generally, the subject is also unable to recognize faces that are frequently encountered after the brain injury (members of the nursing staff, neuropsychologists, physicians, etc.). According to autopsy examinations, prosopagnosia often results from a damage in the occipito-temporal regions of both cerebral hemispheres, but the right hemisphere could be more involved than the left in face processing.

Strictly speaking, prosopagnosia is a defect specific to faces. That is to say, other objects should be well recognized visually. However, other defects are often associated with—but cannot be considered as responsible for—prosopagnosia, such as some kinds of visual agnosia for objects and/or for verbal symbols (letters, words, etc.). In addition, even when prosopagnosia seems to be pure, it could be the manifestation of a subtle deficit of the recognition of specific exemplars within a given category (a car among cars, a house among houses, a coin among coins, etc.). Given these considerations, it could be that several types of prosopagnosia should be distinguished.

Many, but not all, prosopagnosic subjects are able to perform the various visual operations described above. Thus, the patient recognizes human faces among other complex and mono-oriented visual pictures and he is able to recognize facial expressions, to evaluate the apparent age of the face seen, to categorize faces by gender or race, and to recognize isolated facial features. The prosopagnosic subject is even capable of discovering the copy of a target face among distractors of the same age and gender, even when the target and its copy are two different photographs of the same face (i.e., two different poses or expressions). Thus, in many cases, the cognitive locus of the trouble cannot be found in operations or representations which precede the register of face-recognition units. However, there are some exceptions with deficits in these stages, another argument inviting us to distinguish several forms of prosopagnosia.

On the other end of the processing (see below), the recognition of persons is spared in prosopagnosia. That is to say, familiar and/or famous persons are well recognized, provided the stimulus is not their face alone. Thus, prosopagnosic subjects correctly identify the persons from their voice, silhouette, gait, kind of clothes, handwriting, car, house, name, etc. In addition, known persons can be named from semantic pieces of information. Thus, the cognitive locus of the trouble cannot be found in operations or representations which follow the register of face-recognition units (note, however, as will be seen below, that the defect can be found in the output of this register).

Obviously, the store of face-recognition units is the best candidate for the cognitive locus of the defect of which prosopagnosia is the clinical manifestation. However, two interpretations are still possible. According to one interpretation, prosopagnosia points to the destruction or loss of face-recognition units and the impossibility to generate new recognition units from recently met faces. Therefore, albeit adequately derived, the structural invariant representation of the currently seen face cannot be matched to a structural representation stored in long-term memory. According to the other interpretation, prosopagnosia indicates a defective access to the register of face-recognition units. In other words, a structural representation of the face seen is correctly derived and there is a corresponding representation in long-term memory, but the link between them is broken.

In fact, it is perhaps unnecessary to make a choice between these two interpretations. Indeed, once again, there are probably several kinds of prosopagnosia, as testified by the discovery of signs of covert face recognition in some, but not all, reported cases of face agnosia.

C. Covert Recognition

Usually, the cognitive operations performed or not performed by a subject are assessed by considering his performance in a series of precisely defined tasks. In other words, overt or manifest responses are analyzed (verbal productions, speed of verbal or manual responses, etc.). A given response results from a decision made by the subject, and the subject is aware of the decision. However, awareness is not the entire story, and the overt response is often the result of a lot of processes not reaching the level of "consciousness." For instance, in normal subjects the recognition of a face is speeded up if the same face has been seen shortly before (repetition or identity priming: see above), even when the subject is not aware of having seen the same face twice (other examples will be given below).

Signs of covert recognition of faces not recognized overtly have been observed in some, but not all, prosopagnosic subjects. This phenomenon reveals that these patients are still able to covertly use representations that they cannot use overtly. This covert knowledge has been revealed by means of two main procedures. There are, first of all, physiological indexes, either peripheral (variations of skin conductance, pupil dilation) or central (event-related visual brain potentials). Both peripheral and central physiological measurements revealed dissociations in the recognition signs between overt, explicit, or behavioral responses on the one hand, and covert, implicit, or physiological responses on the other. For example, a patient did not "recognize" the face of a famous person but when the name of this person was shown together with the face, a specific variation of the subject's skin conductance was recorded, a variation not observed when other names were shown. Also, electrical brain potentials of another patient were sensitive to the proportions of known vs unknown faces in a particular display, while all faces were overtly judged as unknown.

Thus, some prosopagnosics did not overtly recognize faces covertly recognized by their "processing system." However, one could argue that the argumentation is a bit weak and that we are perhaps comparing uncomparable events, i.e., controlled behavioral responses could be expressing processes other than those revealed by automatic physiological responses. Fortunately, there also exist overt, behavioral indexes of covert recognition of overtly unrecognized faces in some prosopagnosic subjects. These indexes can be classified into three main categories: semantic priming effects, interference effects, and the learning of face–name associations. Priming and interference effects are described below but let us note here that the effects observed in normal subjects have been observed too in some prosopagnosic patients who did not recognize overtly the faces shown. Concerning face–name associations, prosopagnosic subjects, who had difficulties in learning the wrong name of unrecognized famous faces but no or less difficulties in learning the true name of unrecognized famous faces, have been reported.

Some other behavioral measures were also taken, such as forced-choice procedures (when obliged to decide which member of a pair of faces—one unknown and one famous—was famous, a prosopagnosic subject produced nonrandom decisions; however, another prosopagnosic patient with signs of covert face recognition performed at random when forced to guess), the episodic recognition of familiar and unfamiliar faces (in a prosopagnosic subject, familiarity increased the episodic recognition of famous-but-not-identified faces), the mere-exposure paradigm (the normal subject tends to prefer stimuli to which he has been exposed to previously, which was observed in a brain-injured patient who was not aware of having seen the face previously), and the recording of eye movements during the inspection of the to-be-recognized faces (like normal subjects, prosopagnosic subjects inspected more inner than outer features when a famous face was shown—and equally inner and outer features of unfamiliar faces—while all faces were overtly judged as unknown).

Three lessons can be derived from these studies. First of all, despite their overtly ascertained prosopagnosia, some prosopagnosic subjects produce signs of a covert access to the face-recognition units (including for those precise faces that were not overtly recognized). This suggests that the face-recognition units are not destroyed, but that the access to them is defective. Note here that these signs of covert recognition can be found even for faces met after the onset of the brain damage, i.e., that new recognition units can still be formed. However, in some other subjects, the "locus" of the defect was found to be the link from face-recognition units to identity-specific semantic codes (see below). Second, in some subjects, it was even possible to show a covert access to the identity-specific semantic codes, and even more to the name codes, concerning the "unrecognized" faces (for these codes, see below). This suggests that, in these subjects, the face-recognition units, the semantic codes, and the name codes are not cancelled but that the deficiency should be interpreted in terms of (overt) access to these representations. Third, these signs of covert access are not universal in the small world of prosopagnosics. Indeed, on the one hand, even those prosopagnosics with covert signs did not necessarily display them in every task. On the other hand, since the "discovery" of these indexes, covert signs have been sought, without success, in some patients. Therefore, this suggests that prosopagnosia with covert recognition is the clinical manifestation of a defective access to spared face-recognition units, while prosopagnosia without covert recognition is the clinical manifestation of a loss of recognition units.

IV. PERSON RECOGNITION

As already mentioned, face recognition is not the sole way toward the recognition of persons. People can be recognized from other inputs, like their voice, handwriting, or name and prosopagnosics, albeit unable to recognize faces, remain able to recognize persons. Therefore, a specific stage of "person recognition" has been provided that can be activated by several kinds of recognition units (face-recognition units, voice-recognition units, etc.). It thus follows that all components that remain to be described are no longer specific to the processing of faces. Two features of this stage deserve mention.

First, relationships between the face-recognition units and the person-recognition stage are bidirectional. That is to say, the firing of this operator can activate face-recognition units. In this way, it is understandable that the recognition of a face can be facilitated by the previous hearing of the voice of that person or that the reading of a famous name can induce the generation of a mental image of the corresponding face, which facilitates the visual recognition of this face.

Second, the person-recognition stage is not a register of representations per se, but just a multimodal (i.e., it can be activated by several types of input—sounds, pictures, written words, etc.) gateway toward the semantic representations.

V. SEMANTIC CODES

Identity-specific semantic codes constitute the "concept" of the person met. These codes are formed with several abstract pieces of information not visually derivable from the current face (unlike gender, race, age, etc., mentioned above) but, instead, arbitrarily linked to the person and associated to it by means of a learning process which took place during each encounter of that person (this link is "arbitrary" in the sense that there is no a priori reason to observe a relationship between a given face and the semantic pieces of information: the link must be learned, it cannot be inferred from observation). These codes represent information like the occupation of the person, her hobbies, other persons frequently met together with that person, etc. As will be explained below, the name of the person must be kept separate from these codes. [*See* SEMANTIC MEMORY.]

Several empirical data invite us to consider this register as separate from and later than the register of face-recognition units. First, semantic decisions (i.e., to decide whether a famous face is that of a politician or of an actor, for example) are made less quickly than familiarity decision (i.e., to decide whether a face is known). Second, many prosopagnosic subjects are unable to make familiarity decisions but carry out correctly semantic decisions about people (provided the input is not the face). Third, analysis of everyday natural and normal failures reveals that a given face can be recognized while no semantic information about the person seen can be retrieved, but that the correct access to semantic information from the face without recognition of that face never occurs.

In addition, this register is useful in explaining some classical experimental data. For instance, the recognition of a person whose face is shown is speeded up by the previous exposure to a closely related face or to the name of a closely related person (example: the familiarity decision on the face of Oliver Hardy is facilitated by the previous reading of "Stan Laurel"). This "semantic priming" is of shorter duration than the repetition (or identity) priming mentioned above, but is cross-modal (while the repetition priming is face specific). Similarly, "interference effects" have been shown where semantic decisions about a famous face are lengthened by the previous exposure to the face or the name of another famous face concerning a person whose semantic category is not shared by that of the target.

VI. NAME CODES

In a cognitive architecture, the names of the persons must be kept separate from the identity-specific semantic codes for several empirical reasons. First, chronometric studies have shown that the retrieval of a person's name occurs later than the retrieval of specific semantic pieces of information about that person. Second, enquiries about natural daily-life errors have demonstrated that one sometimes retrieves semantic properties about a recognized person while the name cannot be retrieved, while the inverse pattern of errors never occurs. Third, normal aging perturbs more the retrieval of names than face recognition and the access to semantic information.

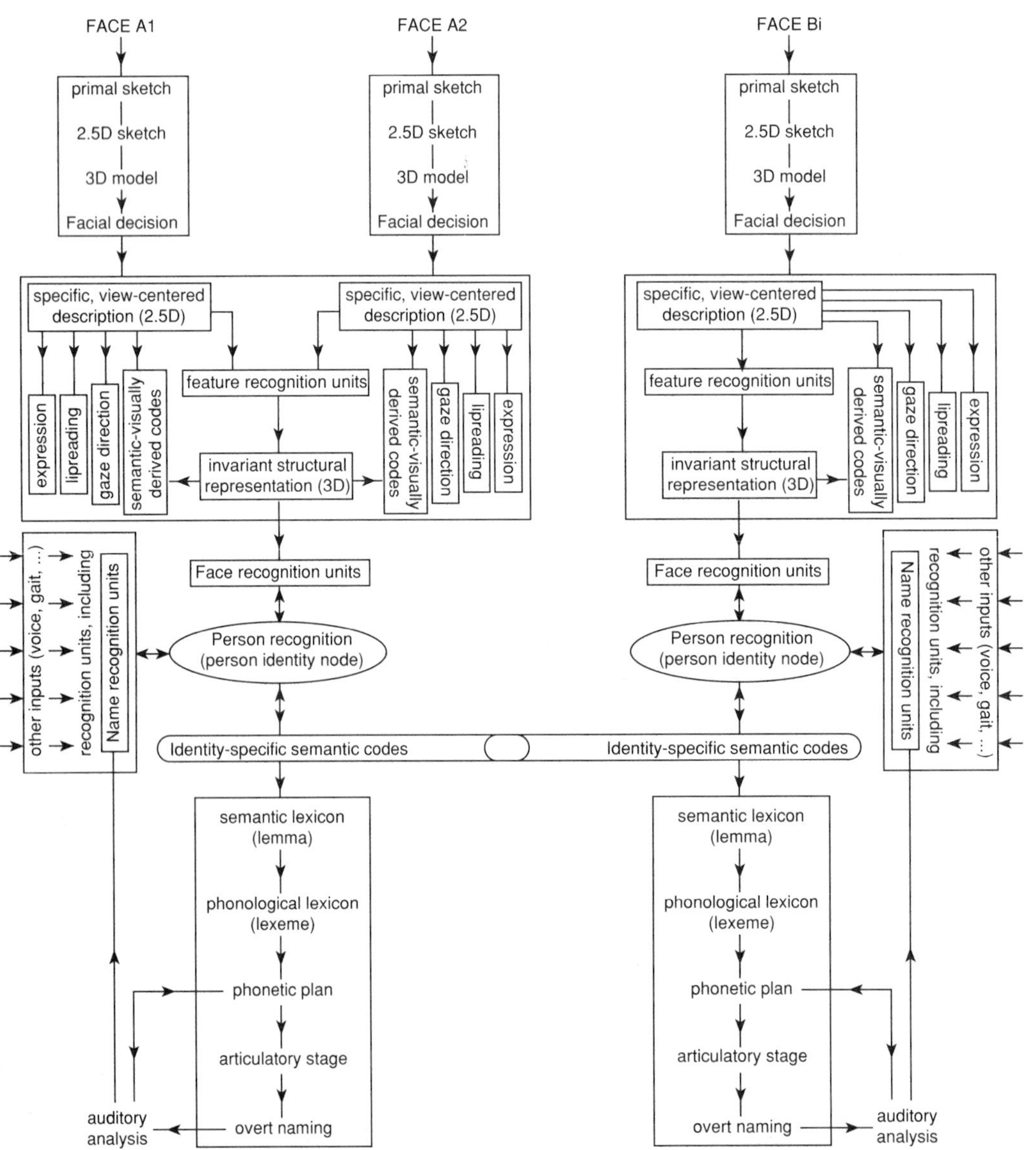

FIGURE 3 A general and hypothetical cognitive architecture of the operations underlying the identification of a person from his face, which summarizes both the available empirical data and the various architectures published over the past years. The tentative model concerns the recognition of two different views (1 & 2) of a given person (A) and the recognition of another person (B) from a given view (i).

Fourth, cases of brain-damaged patients have been reported where the deficit concerns specifically the retrieval of persons' names. In addition, this dissociation cannot be accounted for by formal differences between semantic properties and names, since it is less easy to retain that a given person "is Mr. Baker" than that person "is a baker."

However, the access to, and the production of, a name is, in turn, a complex process which is abundantly debated in psychology of language. Thus, the semantic information about the person encountered activates an element of the semantic lexicon, which is the store of the semantic and syntactic representations specific to a given, to-be-pronounced, name (the lemma). Then, this semantic lexicon gives access to the corresponding components, or lexemes, of the phonological lexicon (a store of phonemes or linguistic sounds). In the next step, the phonetic plan is at work, and it assembles the several to-be-pronounced sounds in a correct sequence in order to "say" the name of the person. This is followed by the articulatory stage which plans the adequate motor sequence of laryngeal movements and, as a result, the overt naming of the person.

It must be noted here that an "auditory analysis" device is provided, in order to account for the (voluntary) control of the to-be-pronounced name. Thus, this analyzer is able to compare the output of the phonetic plan to the overt naming to verify whether they match; it is able to compare the output of the phonetic plan to that of the name-recognition units to verify whether the to-be-named (or subvocally named) person corresponds to the perceived person; and it is able to check the overt naming with respect to the activated name-recognition unit for the same purposes. This device allows to take into account the empirical observations according to which naming errors (in particular tip-of-the-tongue phenomenon) are rarely random: often, the erroneous planned or overtly produced name shares some semantic or phonological relationships with the correct name.

VII. SUMMARY: OUTLINE OF A COGNITIVE ARCHITECTURE

To recap the various processing stages mentioned in this article, Figure 3 is a tentative proposal summarizing the main empirical findings about face recognition. The figure is structured to simulate—or to model—the various cognitive steps involved in the recognition of a given person (A) from two different views (A1 and A2) of its face, and the recognition of another person (B) from one view (Bi) of its face. This was essentially made to illustrate, first, that the processes of the two views of a given person should converge toward the recognition of a single person and the production of a single proper name whatever the facial appearance (A1 vs A2) and, second, that two different persons (A and B) can share some semantic properties (the partial overlap of the two sets of semantic codes), which could explain the semantic priming, that is to say, the faster recognition of a given person when a related person has been shown before.

Bibliography

Bruce, V. (1988). "Recognising Faces." Erlbaum, London.

Bruce, V. (1990). Face recognition. In "Cognitive Psychology: An International Review" (M. W. Eysenck, Ed.). Wiley, Chichester.

Bruce, V., Cowey, A., Ellis, A. W., and Perrett, D. I. (Eds.) (1992). "Processing the Facial Image." Clarendon Press, Oxford.

Bruyer, R. (1991). Covert face recognition in prosopagnosia: A review. *Brain Cognition* **15,** 223–235.

Bruyer, R. (1993). Failures of face processing in normal and brain-damaged subjects. In "Handbook of Neuropsychology" (F. Boller and J. Grafman, Eds.), Vol. 8. Elsevier, Amsterdam.

Milders, M. W., and Perrett, D. I. (1993). Recent developments in the neuropsychology and physiology of face processing. In "Baillière's Clinical Neurology: Visual Perceptual Defects" (C. Kennard, Ed.). Baillière Tindall, London.

Schweich, M., and Bruyer, R. (1993). Heterogeneity in the cognitive manifestations of prosopagnosia: The study of a group of isolated cases. *Cog. Neuropsychol.* in press.

Young, A. W., and Ellis, H. D. (Eds.). (1989). "Handbook of Research on Face Processing." North Holland, Amsterdam.

Facial Expressions of Emotion

Dacher Keltner
University of Wisconsin at Madison

Paul Ekman
University of California at San Francisco

Glossary

Autonomic specificity The thesis that different emotional states are marked by specific autonomic nervous system activity, including changes in heart rate, respiratory activity, and glandular response.

Display rules The set of norms that a culture or subculture teaches its people regarding the appropriate display of emotion.

Duchenne smile The smile associated with actual enjoyment that involves the activity of the orbicularis oculi, which raises the cheeks.

Nonverbal leakage Nonverbal signs of inhibited emotion observed in facial behavior, posture, and vocal activity.

Universality The finding that distinct cultures agree upon the meaning of facial expressions of anger, disgust, fear, happiness, sadness, and surprise.

FACIAL EXPRESSIONS OF EMOTION are composed of the contractions of facial muscles that accompany the experience of emotion. There is solid evidence showing that distinct cultures agree upon the meaning of facial expressions for anger, disgust, fear, happiness, sadness, and surprise, suggesting that these are universal expressions of emotion. Social interaction often requires that people inhibit their emotion (for example when lying) or simulate emotion when it is not felt. The signs of inhibited emotion and differences between simulated and spontaneous facial expressions are discussed. In the final section evidence is presented that shows that voluntary facial expressions of emotion generate emotion-specific changes in autonomic nervous system activity, which is consistent with the view that at least certain emotions have distinct autonomic nervous system responses.

I. UNIVERSAL FACIAL EXPRESSIONS OF EMOTION

More than a century ago in *The Expression of the Emotions in Man and Animals,* Charles Darwin claimed that we cannot understand human emotional expression without understanding the expressions of animals. He proposed that our emotional expressions are in large part determined by our evolution, that the facial actions seen in emotional expressions originally served purely biological or instrumental functions in our progenitors, but were maintained in our repertoire because of their communicative value. For example, the brow lowering of anger, it could be argued, protects the eyeballs from blows that are likely in antagonistic contexts. This facial action, and those of other emotions, also conveyed information to others about an individual's possible future behavior, or what might have happened to elicit the action. Because this communicative value was also adaptive, the facial actions were maintained even if the original function was lost, or the actions were modified as a result of natural selection to enhance their efficacy as signals. Ethologists use the term ritualization to describe the process by which a behavior is modified through genetic evolution to enhance its efficacy as a signal.

Darwins's analysis suggested that there are facial expressions of emotion that should be observed across human cultures. Despite the importance of this view, only relatively recently has relevant evidence been gathered. To understand the findings on cross-cultural facial expressions of emotion, it is helpful to first examine the culture-specific view of facial expressions, which dominated the field until recently.

Copyright © 1994 by Academic Press, Inc. All rights of reproduction in any form reserved.

A. The Culture-Specific Viewpoint

The culture-specific view proposes that the information signaled by facial expressions of emotion is specific to each culture. One compelling observation made by those who espouse this view is that some cultures do not show facial expressions of certain emotions despite there being events that should elicit those emotions: for example, it has been claimed that Eskimos show no anger. Even more central to the culture-specific view was the observation that people of different cultures smile in diverse circumstances. For example, Klineberg said

> Not only may joy be expressed without a smile, but in addition the smile may be used in a variety of situations . . . a smile may mean contempt, incredulity, affection . . . [quoting from Lafacadio Hearn's observation of the Japanese] Samurai women were required, like the women of Sparta, to show signs of joy on hearing that their husbands or sons had fallen in battle.

The observation that smiles occur in diverse settings, both pleasurable and unpleasurable, highlights methodological and conceptual problems that have been clarified by subsequent theory and research. The first problem is due to the use of imprecise behavioral description. The term "smile" unfortunately refers to too many different facial expressions. Dozens of different smiling expressions have been distinguished, which involve the deployment of different sets of muscle actions. Each of these smiles differs in appearance, although in each the lip corners are drawn upward. It is therefore confusing to call these all smiling, implying that they are a singular, unified category of behavior. When these different lip-corner-up appearances are treated by the observer as one entity, it will appear that the smile has no common meaning. Evidence to be described later shows that smiles that occur in unpleasant circumstances and those that occur in pleasant circumstances when enjoyment is felt differ in their muscle actions. Imprecise terms such as frown, grimace, and scowl, like smile, encourage observers to miss what may be important distinctions.

A second problem raised by the example of smiles is the failure to consider that differences in observed facial expressions may be due to culturally imposed attempts to manage universal expressions. Facial expression was often viewed as a totally involuntary system, not capable of being voluntarily controlled. This approach fails to consider the set of norms developed in each culture that dictate who can show which emotion to whom, and when—norms that have been called "display rules" and will be discussed later. The smiling appearance of the grieving Samurai women could be the behavior required by a display rule to cover their sadness or grief with the appearance of polite smiling.

It would be quite damaging to the conclusion that there are universal expressions of emotion if there was clear evidence that when people are in a negative affect situation, experiencing pain, sadness, disgust, fear, or anger, they show an expression in which the lip corners go up, only if the following explanations can be ruled out: (1) The subject who shows this smiling countenance does not believe that negative feelings must be masked with a simulated, deliberate smile. (2) The smile is not a comment added by the subject to signal that the negative experience can be endured (a grin-and-bear-it smile, or what Ekman and Friesen called a "miserable smile"). (3) The smile incorporates the features which Ekman and Friesen have found to occur when enjoyment is experienced (see description below), as distinct from polite or masking smiles. There is no such evidence.

A third problem raised by the culture-specific view of smiles is the failure to distinguish facial expressions of emotion from other facial expressions that do not correspond to the experience of emotion. These expressions or gestures include illustrators, which are movements that punctuate and illustrate simultaneous speech (e.g., an emphatic raising of the eyebrows), emblems, which refer to movements that have a direct verbal translation known to all members of a culture or subculture (e.g., the flirtatious tongue protrusion in the United States), and referential expressions, which refer to emotions but are performed in a way that signals that the emotion is not felt when the expression is made (e.g., feigned surprise when being told something already known). The message conveyed by an emotional expression is, by definition, a feeling of the moment, providing information about likely antecedent and consequent events. Every facial movement is not an emotional expression, however, and evidence will be discussed that bears upon the distinctions between facial expressions that attend the experience of emotion and those that do not.

B. Evidence for Universal Facial Expressions of Emotion

In the early 1970s there were two challenges to the culture-specific view of facial expressions of emotion. The first was a critical reevaluation of the experiments that had supported that position, and a more precise theoretical characterization of facial expressions that attend the experience of emotion and those that do not. The more significant challenge to the culture-specific view was cross-cultural data that addressed the question of whether people in diverse cultures are able to recognize the same facial expressions of emotion.

In this research, in each culture subjects chose the emotion term that fit photographs of posed Caucasian facial expressions. Different photographs were shown, subjects were given somewhat different lists of emotion terms, and people in different cultures were examined. This research, however, obtained consistent evidence of agreement across more than a dozen Western and non-Western literate cultures in the labeling of enjoyment, anger, fear, sadness, disgust, and surprise facial expressions.

To rule out the possibility that such agreement could be due to members of every culture having learned expressions from a shared mass media input, visually isolated preliterate cultures in New Guinea and what is now West Irian were also studied. Agreement in labeling the facial expressions of emotion was replicated, although surprise expressions were not distinguished from fear expressions in one of the preliterate, visually isolated cultures. The research design was also reversed and led to the finding that when New Guineans posed facial expressions of emotion they were understandable to Western observers.

These studies show that there is a set of facial expressions of emotion that are understandable across cultures. To reconcile these findings of universality with the many reports of cultural differences in facial expressions, another line of research examined the effects of display rules on facial expressions of emotion. Display rules are defined as norms that govern the individual's expression of emotion, and are presumed to be taught to individuals during the process of socialization. Cultural variations in display rules—for example, one culture might emphasize the intense expression of an emotion and another the nonexpression of that emotion—could explain how universal expressions might be modified to create the impression of culture-specific facial expressions of emotion. This research compared the spontaneous expressions of negative emotion (primarily disgust) of Japanese and Americans while watching a videotape of a graphic circumcision ritual. In each country subjects were videotaped when they were alone, and presumably no display rules should operate, and when they were with another person. As predicted, there was no difference between cultures in the expressions shown when subjects thought they were alone. However, when an authority figure was present the Japanese more than the Americans masked negative expressions with the semblance of smile.

A new line of studies has identified one way in which cultures do differ in regard to facial expression. Recent evidence suggests that there are cultural differences in the perception of the strength of an emotion rather than which emotion is shown in a facial expression. Japanese made less intense attributions than did Americans regardless of the emotion shown or whether the person showing the emotion is Japanese or American, male or female. This difference appears to be specific to the interpretation of facial expressions of emotions, since it was not found in the judgment of either nonfacial emotional stimuli or facial nonemotional stimuli.

A number of empirical questions remain about universals in facial expression of emotion. We do not know how many expressions for each emotion are universal, for no one has systematically explored a variety of expressions for each emotion in multiple cultures. For example, based on the different muscle movements involved, it has been proposed that there are over 60 variants of the expression of anger. How many of these are observed across cultures, and with what frequency? Nor is there certain knowledge about whether there are other emotions with universal expressions. There is some evidence, but it is contradictory, for universal facial expressions for contempt, interest, shame, and guilt. Nor is much known about cross-cultural differences in display rules, as a function of sex, role, age, and social context.

Virtually all of these questions concerning the universal facial expressions of emotion are relevant to the developmental appearance of the facial expressions of emotion. For example, research generally suggests that the same facial expressions that appear to be universal in adults appear quite early in the development of the infant, although less is known about the variants of the facial expressions shown. Research in developmental psychology is beginning to address whether some facial expressions of emotion (for example anger) are elaborations upon simpler expressions (distress) or distinct in their initial appearance, and also the role of facial expression in regulating parent–child interactions.

II. INHIBITING AND SIMULATING FACIAL EXPRESSIONS OF EMOTION

Anyone who has felt like laughing when it is inappropriate, or been disappointed and not wanted others to know, has encountered the task of inhibiting facial expressions of emotion. The inhibition of emotion is complex, because emotion is expressed not only in the face, but also in posture, hand gestures, the voice, and gaze activity. People inhibiting emotion would ideally prevent others from perceiving their emotion across all channels. This, however, is quite difficult. Research has shown that when people inhibit their emotion, for example when attempting to hide feelings of disgust with smiles, they tend to inhibit their facial expressions of emotion rather than other nonverbal signs of emotion. They may do this because many of the facial muscle actions of emotion are under voluntary control, the face is more scrutinized than the other nonverbal channels, and people may not be aware of the influences of their emotional state on their voice, gaze, or posture to the extent that they are aware of it in their face.

Given that the inhibition of emotion is likely to occur in the face, how will it be evident? Research and theory suggest four ways. First, people may intensify or de-intensify the facial expression: smiles may be intensified, frowns restrained, and the tightened brown of anxiety relaxed. Second, the timing of the inhibited facial expression may change, either in the onset of the expression (when the expression is first evident) to the offset of the expression (when it is last evident on the face). Third, the location of the expression in the stream of behavior may also be altered, for example, being most visible after it would be appropriate to see facial expressions of emotion (e.g., delayed laughter at someone's pratfall). And finally, people may show other micro-expressions of emotion when inhibiting facial expressions of emotion. For example, in holding back laughter, micro-expressions of fear may be evident as part of the anticipation of the disapproval that will ensue.

People are also more likely to inhibit certain facial actions than others. Namely, people are more likely to inhibit lower facial behavior than upper facial behavior. Thus, people inhibiting fear are likely to show less of the lip stretch characteristic of fear but continue to show the raised and pulled in eyebrows; people inhibiting sadness are likely to show less of the downward pull of their lip corners but continue to show the pulled in and raised inner corners of their eyebrows. The tendency to inhibit lower facial actions rather than upper facial actions may occur for different reasons. Many of the upper facial actions of emotion are more difficult to control voluntarily than the lower facial actions. Additionally, the most distinct signs of emotion may be emitted vocally (e.g., a shriek of fear, a wail of sadness), which would prompt people to concentrate on that area to hide their emotion.

A recent line of research has documented individual differences in how people inhibit facial expressions of emotion. In the study, subjects were instructed to convey positive emotion with verbal descriptions and smiles while they watched a film that elicited strong disgust. Some subjects revealed their negative emotion in elevated voice pitch but successfully inhibited their facial expressions of emotion. Other subjects were able to inhibit vocal cues of their negative emotion, but showed facial signs of negative emotion. And some subjects' negative emotion was evident in both facial expressions of emotion and their vocal pitch. Because individual differences are likely to be pronounced in how people reveal their inhibited emotion, observers are likely to be more accurate in identifying inhibited emotion in people they know. Observers may also be especially prone to fail in detecting whether others are inhibiting emotion when they apply general strategies (e.g., "inhibited people always have higher pitched voices").

B. Simulated Facial Expressions of Emotion: Distinctions between Smiles of Enjoyment and Nonenjoyment

Social interaction often requires that people simulate facial expressions of emotion. Upon receiving a Christmas present of little appeal, people politely smile to the giver. The smile, in fact, is perhaps the most commonly simulated facial expression of emotion and, as discussed, was at the heart of a conceptual confusion that led anthropologists to proclaim that facial expressions of emotion are culture specific. As an illustration of how people are able to simulate facial expressions of emotion, this section will examine the differences between smiles that simulate enjoyment or have other meanings and those that are part of the experience of enjoyment.

Recent research has found that there is an anatomical difference between smiles that accompany the experience of enjoyment and those that occur in circumstances in which the individual is being polite or hiding negative feelings. This anatomical difference was first described by the French neuroanatomist Duchenne de Boulogne, who, writing in 1862, said that the smile of enjoyment could be distinguished from deliberately produced smiles by considering two facial muscles: zygomatic major, which pulls the lip corners up obliquely; and, orbicularis oculi, which orbits the eye pulling the skin from the cheeks and forehead toward the eyeball.

> The first [zygomatic major] obeys the will but the second [orbicularis oculi] is only put in play by the sweet emotions of the soul; the . . . fake joy, the deceitful laugh, cannot provoke the contraction of this latter muscle (page 126). [This muscle] . . . does not obey the will; it is only brought into play by a true feeling. . . . Its inertia in smiling unmasks a false friend.

Duchenne's observation is consistent with the finding that most people cannot voluntarily contract the outer portion of the muscle that orbits the eye, and would therefore not be able to include this action when they deliberately smile. Duchenne had not distinguished between the inner and outer part of the orbicularis oculi muscle, and it has been found that most people can voluntarily contract the inner portion of the orbicularis oculi muscle. Duchenne's formulation was modified based on this finding, and it is just the actions of the outer part of this muscle that is now considered crucial for distinguishing the smile of enjoyment from other smiles.

Enjoyment smiles have also been proposed to be distinguished from other forms of smiling by the presence of certain other muscles, and by the symmetry and the timing of the smile. Based on these variations that can occur during smiling, 18 different forms of smiling have been described. Enjoyment smiles are those smiles associated with pleasure, relief, amusement, etc. Nonenjoyment smiles include masking smiles (in which the smile at least partially covers muscular movements associated with another emotion), false smiles (smiles intended to mislead another into believing enjoyment is felt when it is not), miserable smiles (grin-and-bear-it smiles), etc. And recent evidence has identified the facial actions that are part of the embarrassed smile, which include gaze aversions down, head turns to the side, face touches, and attempts to reduce the intensity of the smile with such actions as lip presses and puckers.

Although there has been some empirical support for each of the proposed markers that distinguish enjoyment smiles from other smiling, the largest number of studies have examined Duchenne's observation. In all of these studies the smile with the contraction of the outer portion of the orbicularis oculi muscle was compared with other kinds of smiling that do not include that muscular action. Three types of evidence provide remarkable convergence supporting Duchenne's distinction.

1. Social Context

More Duchenne smiles were observed when subjects truthfully described pleasant feelings than when they followed instructions to claim to be feeling pleasant while watching gruesome surgical films. In another study in which subjects simply watched emotion-inducing films while alone, more Duchenne smiles were observed when the films were pleasant as compared to unpleasant, and there were no differences in how often other kinds of smiling occurred. Ten-month-old infants showed more Duchenne smiles when approached by their mother, more of other kinds of smiling when approached by a stranger. Five- to seven-year-old children showed more Duchenne smiles when they succeeded, and more other kinds of smiling when they failed in a game. Psychiatrically depressed patients showed more Duchenne smiles at time of discharge from a hospital as compared to time of admission, with no difference in other kinds of smiling. Similarly, there was more Duchenne smiling in late as compared to early psychotherapy sessions, but only among patients who had improved.

2. Persons

Schizophrenic patients showed fewer Duchenne smiles than normal individuals but there was no difference between the groups in other kinds of smiling. Mothers who were referred to a clinic by the courts because of they had abused their child showed less Duchenne smiles when interacting with a child than a control group of mothers who had evidenced no child abuse. Happily married couples showed more

Duchenne smiles than unhappily married couples, but there was no difference in other kinds of smiling.

3. Other Emotional Responses

Only the Duchenne smile correlated with self-reports of positive emotions after subjects had seen two films intended to induce positive affect, and only the Duchenne, not other kinds of smiling, predicted which of the positive films each subject reported liking best. In that same study different patterns of regional brain activity were found when the subjects showed the Duchenne as compared to other smiles, a finding replicated in the study of 10-month-old infants. And, recently different patterns of regional brain activity were observed when subjects deliberately performed a Duchenne smile as compared to a non-Duchenne smile.

Recent work has also shown that the Duchenne smile is recognizable to observers, who were able to distinguish enjoyment from nonenjoyment smiles when they viewed a series of smiles. One of the questions remaining about smiles is whether the different positive emotions (e.g., amusement, contentment, relief, etc.) have distinctive forms of smiling, or if they share one signal and can be inferred only from other behavioral or contextual cues. Similar questions can be raised about whether various forms of nonenjoyment smiles (compliance, grin-and-bear-it, etc.) are marked in the smile itself. It should also be possible to use the same emphasis on dynamic and morphological markers to distinguish actual instances of each of the negative emotions from deliberate performances of those emotions. The actual negative emotional expression will include muscular elements that are difficult for most people to perform voluntarily and that will not be seen in deliberate performances of the expression (e.g., in anger, the contraction of the portion of the muscle in the lips which narrows the lip margin; in sadness, the pulling of the eyebrows together and raising them).

C. The Detection of Failures in the Inhibition of Emotion

A basic issue in social relations is how well people can detect other's attempt to hide their emotions in the context of detecting deceit. The telling of lies may require several kinds of inhibited facial behavior. Liars may show facial expressions of emotion, such as guilt and fear, because of the tension and anticipation of punishment. People often lie by masking one emotion (e.g., disgust or contempt at seeing a disliked individual) with smiles, which, as has been discussed, may reveal the masked emotion underneath or seem unauthentic. Liars may betray themselves with the words they use, including convoluted answers, slips of the tongue, unusual tirades, higher pitched voice, and more frequent pauses, which tend to occur during lying. And during lies people's behavior in different channels is more frequently inconsistent (for example, someone will show calmness in the face and arousal in the voice) than when people are telling the truth.

The problems in detecting deceit based upon nonverbal behavior are twofold. First, many of the signs of lying are subtle and difficult to detect in the stream of behavior. And second, many of the signs of lying are the consequence of the emotion aroused by the prospects of being caught lying, and these emotions are likely to occur in truthful people as well. In basing judgments of truthfulness on demeanor, people run the risk of committing a false negative, in which a liar is incorrectly judged to be truthful, or a false positive, in which a truthful person is incorrectly judged to be lying. Either type of mistake, whether it occurs in the courtroom, marriage, therapy, or international negotiations, can have serious consequences. Consequently, it behooves people to know how much confidence should be placed in judgments based on demeanor about whether someone is lying or telling the truth.

Given the subtlety of the nonverbal signs that reveal lying, it is of interest to know who is good at catching liars, and what sort of people are better able to deceive without being caught. In the usual study on how good people are at detecting deception, observers are given video- or audiotapes and are asked to judge whether each of a number of people is lying or telling the truth. Average accuracy in detecting deceit has rarely been above 60% (with chance being 50%), and some groups have done worse than chance. Most of these studies have examined college students, who may not have had any special reason to learn how to tell when someone is lying. This raises the question of whether people who have good reason to detect lying, for example when it is integral to their profession, are better able to detect lying.

In recent research, videotapes of people lying and honestly expressing pleasure were shown to a variety of professional groups to whom detecting lying is important. These groups included members of the secret service, federal polygraphers, robbery investigators, judges, psychiatrists, special interest individuals, and college students. The accuracy rates of all of the groups except one were comparable to typical accuracy rates of around 55%. The one group whose accuracy rate was better than this rate was that of the U.S. Secret Service, whose rate was 64%. Interestingly, many of these Secret Service members had done protection work, guarding important government officials from potential attack. Such work may force reliance on nonverbal cues, and that experience may have helped their performance. [*See* NONVERBAL BEHAVIOR.]

Are some people better able at getting away with deception than others? Research indicates that, indeed, certain people, because of their facial appearance or style of emotional expression, are more frequently judged as telling the truth when lying than other people. It has been shown that some people simply look more honest than others, although this effect is stronger when observers' base their judgments solely on people's voices than their faces. Other research, in which people are asked to make counterattitudinal statements, has shown that people who are emotionally expressive tend to be more frequently judged as telling the truth when lying, whereas socially anxious and shy people tend to be more erroneously judged as lying when in fact they are telling the truth. Emotionally expressive people may show the fluency and intensity of expression that people intuitively associate with the truth, whereas shy people show many of the behaviors (pauses in speech, expressions of fear or anxiety) people associate with lying. The danger, and compelling message of this research, is how difficult it is to know, simply based on behavioral observation, whether someone is lying or telling the truth.

III. FACIAL ACTION GENERATES EMOTION PHYSIOLOGY

Most emotion theorists emphasize the involuntary nature of emotional experience, ignoring those instances in which people choose to generate an emotion through reminiscence or by adopting the physical actions associated with a particular emotion, (e.g., speaking more softly to de-intensify anger or smiling to generate enjoyment). Facial expression from this vantage point is seen as one of a number of emotional responses, which is generated centrally when an emotion is called forth by an event, memory, image, etc.

A new role for facial expression has recently been examined, in which voluntarily performing certain facial muscular actions generated involuntary changes in autonomic nervous system activity (ANS). Subjects were not asked to pose emotions, but instead to follow muscle-by-muscle instructions to create on their face one of the expressions which had been found to be universal. For example, rather than ask a subject to pose anger, instructions stated: "pull your eyebrows down and together, raise your upper eyelid and tighten your lower eyelid, narrow your lips and press them together." There was greater heart rate acceleration and increased skin conductance when subjects made the expressions for negative emotions (anger, disgust, and fear) as compared to the positive emotion of happiness. There was greater heart rate acceleration when subjects made the expression for anger, fear, and sadness as compared to disgust, and increased finger temperature in anger as compared to fear. [*See* ANGER; ANXIETY AND FEAR; DISGUST.]

These differences in the autonomic physiology generated by different facial configurations have since been replicated in three more experiments and a number of a possible artifacts that could have been responsible for this phenomenon have been ruled out: it occurs when subjects cannot see their own faces or the face of the person giving the instructions; it is not an artifact of somatic muscle activity; and, it is not due to differences in the difficulty of making the different facial configurations. The finding that voluntary facial action generates different patterns of ANS activity was also replicated in an older population. And recently an experiment was conducted in another culture to determine whether these findings are specific to Americans or are more general. A cultural group was selected—the Minangkabau of Sumatra—who differ from Western societies in language, religion (fundamentalist Moslem), and social organization (they are matrilineal, with inheritance through the mother's side of the family). The autonomic differences replicated and additionally showed that the facial configuration of sadness elicited a physiological response distinct from the other emotions. Most generally, these findings suggest that emotion-specific ANS response may be pan-cultural.

The function of these physiological differences is illuminated when one adopts the perspective that the physiological response of emotion should serve the organism's adaptive needs. For example, the two negative emotions of fear and anger are usually associated with the behavioral responses of fleeing and fighting, both of which involve high degrees of somatic activity. Thus, it is reasonable to expect that these two emotions would be associated with greater heart rate acceleration than would the negative emotion of disgust, the positive emotion of happiness, or the emotion of surprise, none of which is associated with increased levels of somatic activity and thus makes no increased metabolic demands on the heart. Further, if fear is primarily associated with fleeing, it would be functional for blood flow to be diverted away from the periphery and redirected toward the large skeletal muscles. This would be consistent with the decrease in peripheral finger temperature that was found for fear. Similarly, anger, with its close association with fighting, might recruit increased blood flow to the muscles of the hand to support grasping weapons and opponents. This would be consistent with the increase in peripheral finger temperature that was found for anger. Disgust, with its association with ridding the body of noxious materials, could be accompanied by increased vagal outflow resulting in greater salivary and gastrointestinal activity. One side-effect of such vagal outflow could be a restraining of the heart rate increase associated with other negative emotions, which would be consistent with the finding of unchanged or small decelerations in heart rate during disgust.

The finding that voluntarily performing certain facial muscular actions generates involuntary changes in autonomic nervous system activity raises important conceptual and theoretical issues. The most pronounced is whether these voluntary facial muscular performances generate emotion or only the physiology of emotion. The problem in answering that question is what to use as the criterion for emotion. The research described could not use either the face, which generated the response, or the physiological changes that occurred when the facial actions were made, since the researchers wanted to know whether an emotion is experienced when these physiological changes are generated. Instead it had to rely upon self-report. When subjects reported actually feeling the emotion associated with the expression they made, the ANS distinctions among the negative emotions were more pronounced.

There is also the matter of whether the changes in ANS activity generated when subjects make the different facial expressions are unique to this specific task or would occur when emotion is brought about by more usual means. This raises the general question about whether ANS patterning is emotion specific or context specific. It has been proposed that the changes in both physiology and expression are emotion specific. Consistent with this view, a recent study found similarities in the specific ANS patterns generated by the voluntary facial action task and by a task in which subjects were instructed to relive past emotional experience.

Before turning to broader theoretical implications, it is useful to examine three alternative accounts for these findings. The first explanation posits a central, hard-wired, connection between the motor cortex and other areas of the brain involved in directing the physiological changes that occur during emotion. Usually when emotions are aroused by perception of a social event a set of central commands produce patterned emotion-specific changes in multiple systems, including (but not limited to) such peripheral systems as facial expressions, vocalizations, skeletal muscular actions, and autonomic nervous system activity. When there is no emotion operative, as in the described experiments, but one set of those commands is generated deliberately, the established emotion networks transmit the same patterned information thereby generating the other emotion-specific response changes. The initiating actions need not be a facial expression; emotion-specific vocalizations, or respiratory patterns, for example, should do just as well.

A second group of alternative explanations could propose that any connection between expression and physiological change is learned and not hard-wired. The extreme version of this viewpoint sees emotions as totally socially constructed, and has no reason to expect that there always will be both an expression and a unique pattern of physiology in every emotion, let alone any connection between the two. Emotion-specific ANS activity might only be learned in those cultures that teach its members specific adaptive behaviors for an emotion, and there would be no reason for every culture to do so, or if they did, to teach the same adaptive pattern. If anger exists in two cultures, and it certainly need not in every culture, there would be no necessary reason why anger would be associated with fighting and the physiology that subserves such actions in any two cultures. Nor would there be any reason for expressions to be learned and associated with any physiology. The findings of the same emotion-specific ANS physiology and the capability for voluntary facial action to generate that activity, in a Moslem, matrilineal Indonesian culture, challenge such a radical social constructivist view. A more moderate social learning position, which allowed for universals both in expression and in physiology, might still claim that the link between the two is learned not hard-wired, established through repeated co-occurrence.

A third set of alternative explanations emphasizes peripheral feedback from the facial actions themselves, rather than a central connection between the brain areas which direct those facial movements and other brain areas. This view includes variations in terms of whether it is feedback from the muscles, skin, or temperature changes and whether it is hard-wired or requires learning.

For now, there is no clear empirical basis for a definitive choice among these explanations. Studies of people with facial paralysis who have no possibility of peripheral facial action or feedback it is hoped will challenge that explanation. If there is a direct central connection, and if these people know how to deliberately contract their facial muscles, then we should observe patterned changes in their physiology, even though no facial action occurs. That study is not yet complete, and the results may not be unambiguous. The findings may be negative not because the mechanism is not a central one, but because these patients may not be able to follow the instructions to attempt to contract specific facial muscles. There is no way to verify with these subjects, as can be done with normal subjects, that they actually produced the required facial muscle configuration.

The implications of these findings for theories of emotion are significant. One of the oldest issue in the field of emotion, and psychology for that matter, is whether emotions have distinct autonomic responses or whether all the emotions are characterized by a similar pattern of general arousal. The specific differences found between the negative and positive emotions and within the negative emotions argue against a general arousal view. It will remain for future research to determine how many of the negative emotions and positive emotions possess distinct autonomic responses, and what the nature of those differences is.

The same issue of emotion-specific physiology has captivated researchers in their search for specific central nervous system activity associated with the different emotions. Most strikingly, it appears that the different hemispheres of the brain are involved in the production and perception of different emotions. Research suggests that the right hemisphere is associated with negative emotion and the left hemisphere with positive emotion, although this view is being challenged. It also appears that voluntary and involuntary facial expressions have different hemispheric localizations. This research, like that on the autonomic specificity of emotion, offers long awaited answers to questions regarding the structure and function of emotion.

Bibliography

Campos, J. J., and Barrett, K. C. (1984). Toward a new understanding of emotions and their development. In "Emotions, Cognition, and Behavior" (C. E. Izard, J. Kagan, and R. B. Zajonc, Eds.), pp. 229–263. Cambridge University Press, New York.

Camras, L. A., Malatesta, C., and Izard, C. E. (1991). The development of facial expressions in infancy. In "Fundamentals of Nonverbal Behavior" (R. Feldman and B. Rime, Eds.), pp. 73–105. Cambridge University Press, New York.

Darwin, C. (1872). "The Expression of the Emotions in Man and Animals." Philosophical Library, New York.

Davidson, R. J. (1992). Anterior cerebral asymmetry and the nature of emotion. Brain and Cognition **20,** 125–151.

Davidson, R. J. (1984) Hemispheric asymmetry and emotion. In "Approaches to Emotion" (K. Scherer and P. Ekman, Eds.), pp. 319–344. Lawrence Erlbaum, Hillsdale, NJ.

Ekman, P. (1984). Expression and the nature of emotion. In "Approaches to Emotion" (K. Scherer and P. Ekman, Eds.), pp. 319–344. Lawrence Erlbaum, Hillsdale, NJ.

Ekman, P. (1992). "Telling Lies: Clues to Deceit in the Marketplace, Marriage, and Politics, 2nd ed. Norton, New York.

Ekman, P. (1992). Facial expressions of emotion: New findings, new question. *Psychol. Sci.* **3,** 34–38.

Ekman, P. (1992). An argument for basic emotions. *Cognition and Emotion* **6,** 169–200.

Ekman, P., Friesen, W. V., and O'Sullivan, M. (1988). Smiles when lying. *J. Pers. Soc. Psychol.* **54,** 414–420.

Levenson, R. W., Ekman, P., and Friesen, W. V. (1990). Voluntary facial expression generates emotion-specific nervous system activity. *Psychophysiology* **27,** 363–384.

Lutz, C., and White, G. M. (1986). The anthropology of emotions. *Ann. Rev. Anthropol.* **15,** 405–436.

Rinn, W. E. (1984). The neuropsychology of facial expression: A review of the neurological and psychological mechanisms for producing facial expressions. *Psychol. Bull.* **95,** 52–77.

Family Systems

David J. Miklowitz
University of Colorado at Boulder

Glossary

Alliances The joining together of two or more members of a family in such a way that the needs of one or more of these members are met. Alliances exist on a continuum from healthy (e.g., a stable, interconnected, intimate marital relationship) to unhealthy. When an alliance is cross-generational and takes the form of a coalition against a third party (e.g., a father and daughter ally against a mother), a dysfunctional "triangle" has developed that may lead to psychopathology in one or more members of the family.

Boundaries The degree to which persons or relations between persons are amenable to outside influence or engagement. Boundaries exist around any given family member, around dyadic or triadic relations between this member and other members of the family, and between the family and the outside world. Individual or family boundaries can be conceived as impermeable (inaccessible), semipermeable (partially accessible), or overly permeable (too easily influenced or accessible). Boundaries in dyadic relations (e.g., mother-son) have often been viewed as existing on a continuum from enmeshed (overly close or involved) to disengaged (disaffected, distanced, underinvolved).

Cybernetics The study of self-corrective and self-regulatory phenomena, in which a family uses information from its past to direct its functioning in the future. Cybernetics focuses on a family's attempts to use new information to grow and change in the face of an external challenge or, alternatively, to "right itself" and bring back a state of stable regulation (see "homeostasis").

Differentiation The defining of the self as unique and distinct from that of others. Often, differentiation is discussed in terms of the degree to which a person has separated or become autonomous from his or her family of origin.

Hierarchies The order of dominance or power in a family. In a healthily organized family, the parents have more "say-so" than the children, whereas certain children may be more or less privileged relative to their siblings as a function of their age and abilities.

Homeostasis The self-regulatory processes of a family, which are driven toward maintaining an internal sense of stability and predictability. Families often attempt to return to this steady state when threatened by an external event (e.g., financial problems) that pose the necessity of change.

Identified patient The person in the family who, because of dysfunction in the family as a whole, develops psychopathology. This person is also referred to as the family "scapegoat" or "crucible."

Life cycle A series of stages most families pass through in their development, from an initial courting phase through marriage and childbearing, raising of children, and eventually, old age. Each stage of this cycle presents new challenges. Healthy families are able to adapt and change in accordance with these challenges, whereas dysfunctional families will attempt to regain their steady state (homeostasis).

Paradoxical intervention A therapist may choose to support the homeostatic balances of the family by "prescribing the symptom," or by encouraging the continuation of the family's existing problems and their transactions around these problems. Often, these interventions have the reverse effect of enabling the family to modify itself and grow, and lead at least temporarily to an improvement in a key family member's illness.

Reframing The stating of a family problem in a way that it is more amenable to solution, and that encourages the family to view the problem in a new way.

Copyright © 1994 by Academic Press, Inc. All rights of reproduction in any form reserved.

System An interlocking set of elements (persons, behaviors) that are interdependent on and mutually influenced by each other. In a family system, one can only understand the behavior of one family member by considering the behavior of other members of the family, as well as the matrix of family relationships in which these behaviors occur.

FAMILY SYSTEMS THEORY is a relatively new way of thinking about families, although the concept of a system in science is quite old. A "system" is a collection of organisms that are interconnected in mutually influential, interdependent relationships with each other. If one thinks about organisms as people, and the interdependent relationships as emotional attachments, then it is easy to view a family as a system. What systems theory states is that the family, being a system, is superordinate to the behavior, wishes, needs, or attributes of any individual within this system: The whole (the family) is different from and greater than the sum of its parts (its members or their individual behaviors, thoughts, or feelings). The behavior of any one person in the family can only be understood in the context of the behavior of the entire family unit. This way of thinking about families has a number of implications for the study of psychopathology. Psychopathology in a key family member is viewed as reflecting dysfunctional patterns of interaction or structure within a family system. In parallel, the successful treatment of a disordered person is viewed as coming about through changing the organization and transactional processes that characterize the family, via the techniques of family therapy.

I. KEY ASSUMPTIONS

A. Interdependence

In family systems theory, one cannot understand the behavior of one member of the family without understanding the behavior of other members of the family, as well as the matrix of family relationships in which this behavior occurs. In parallel, the behavior of these others is a function of the behavior of the first party. Thus, if one person within the family begins to show more independence (e.g., a mother who was previously a homemaker enrolls in a college program), others may also change (e.g., the children may become more self-sufficient, but the father may become more emotionally demanding and expressive). A person's ability to change, grow, or improve is likewise seen as limited by the ability or willingness of others in the family to allow this change or growth to occur.

B. Reciprocal Causality

We are used to thinking about behaviors as linearly, causally related to subsequent behaviors in a chain of events. Family systems theory argues that causality goes in multiple directions. To use a simple example, person A criticizes person B, who then responds by criticizing A back. Person A then withdraws, which causes B to feel guilty. In this example, persons A and B are involved in a mutually determined, bidirectional transactional process that cannot be attributed to either party alone. Although person A may have begun this chain of events, his or her actions are dictated in part by other events that have occurred within the system, some of which have involved B and some of which have not. Thus, family systems thinkers are not interested in assigning blame or credit for the outcome of family transactions, viewing these as chains of events that have multiple determined origins.

Reciprocally caused, mutually determined patterns of interaction can have healthy or unhealthy consequences for a given individual. For example, a marital couple that solves problems via exchanges that indicate openness, acceptance, and mutual positive regard will be less likely to engender depression in one member than a couple that attempts to solve problems through coercion or arguments that escalate into personal affronts and accusations.

C. Boundaries

Some family systems thinkers, particularly those from the structural school (discussed below), focus less on sequences of behavior and instead think about the family as organized in terms of interpersonal boundaries. A boundary defines the interpersonal distance between persons or sets of persons. There is a boundary that distinguishes each person from every other person in the family, as well as a separate boundary that defines, for example, how close the parents are to the children, or how much access each child will have to each parent. Another boundary defines the degree of interconnection between the family unit and the outside world.

Family structures have been described as existing on a continuum from "enmeshed" to "disengaged." An enmeshed family is one in which boundaries between persons within the family are fluid, too easily penetrated, or even nonexistent. A family is enmeshed when each member in the family talks for every other, or in which persons are not allowed to keep in confidence their feelings, thoughts, or wishes. A family is disengaged when members do not interact with each other or do not know or care about each others' "comings and goings." Of course, one dyadic pair within the family (e.g., a mother and son) may have a very enmeshed relationship whereas this same mother may have a very disengaged relationship with her husband.

The boundaries between a family system and the outside world have been described on a continuum between "fluid" or excessively permeable to "rigid" or impenetrable. A family with fluid external boundaries might be one in which there is no distinction between persons who are inside versus outside the family: The family as a unit has no clear identity separate from its environment. With no forewarning, friends and neighbors may come over to the house, eat dinner, and spend the night; one or both parents may disappear from the household for unpredictable periods of time; the children may live in the households of various relatives or friends with no apparent agreements as to when they will return to the home. In contrast, rigid families are closed to the outside world and relationships within the family are overly close or confining. In these families, friends of the children are not allowed to come to the house, doors are always locked, and the parents have few or no social contacts outside of the home. In rigid families, members may be bound together by secrets or unusual, shared beliefs (e.g., "We must stick together to protect ourselves from outside evils").

Ideally, a family should have "semipermeable" boundaries, both for the relations inside the family and for those between the family and the outside world. Thus, children should be allowed to visit friends but should still be expected to come home after playing; every child should have access to each parent, but the parents should have a marital life separate from their children; parents should be dedicated to family life but also have interests, hobbies, and friendships separate from it.

D. Hierarchies

A healthy family is one in which certain members or combinations of members have more power or "say-so" within the family than do others. This assignment of power or decision-making capacity should roughly follow the age and generational standing of the member. That is, parents should have more power to make decisions than their children, whereas extended relatives (i.e., aunts, grandparents) who live in the household may have less power than the parents but more than the children. Children should be assigned privileges and input into family decisions in proportion to their age and degree of development. For example, a 16 year old should not be expected to keep the same hours as a 9 year old. Children who have been given an excessive and inappropriate role in family decision making (e.g., an 8 year old who is frequently consulted by her father as to what house the family should buy) have been described as "parentified."

The hierarchical structure of the family will vary to some degree as a function of ethnicity or culture. For example, research by McGoldrick, Pearce, and Giordano suggests that mothers are greater authority figures than fathers in Irish families, whereas fathers have more authority in Puerto Rican families. Thus, the well-trained family therapist keeps in mind cultural norms when comparing the hierarchical structure of a family to a predetermined normative template.

E. Psychopathology as a Symptom of Systemic Dysfunction

As indicated above, there are many ways in which family interaction patterns or structures can be deviant or unhealthy. Family systems theory views different forms of mental illness, whether these be schizophrenia, depression, anorexia nervosa, or childhood conduct disorder, as symptomatic of dysfunction in the family as a whole. Psychopathology occurs when the family is destabilized by some event in the family's "life cycle" (e.g., a death in the family, a marriage of one of the offspring, divorce, loss of employment) such that the family's regulatory (homeostatic) mechanisms, or its habitual ways of interacting, are disrupted. One member (the "identified patient," "scapegoat," or "crucible") then develops psychopathology as a way of rebalancing the system (regaining homeostasis). This member is often already genetically predisposed to develop psychopathology, and tensions within the family system serve to elicit this vulnerability to dysfunction.

For example, a child may develop a school phobia shortly after his father has admitted to having an extramarital affair. The child's disorder serves to focus the parents' attention away from their troubled marriage and onto a mutual concern, the child's health. Thus, the parents begin to work together again, and the system has been temporarily restabilized, albeit at the expense of the child's welfare.

F. Family Therapy

Because disorder in an individual is viewed as directly stemming from dysfunction in the family as a whole, most family systems therapists involve the entire family in therapy. The core belief is that changing the family from the "top down" will alter the behavior of the symptomatic family member(s). Altering dysfunctional patterns of communication, pathological alliances or coalitions, unstable boundaries, and ineffective hierarchical power structures will help the family and individuals within the family to more closely approximate a state of health. Many schools of family systems theory and therapy exist, as will be discussed later.

II. HOW DO FAMILY SYSTEMS CHANGE?

There are three forms of systemic change that have been described in the family systems literature. These are *first-order* change, *second-order* change, and *growth*. First-order change refers to temporary changes that can be accomplished by directly manipulating in family therapy the preexisting patterns of intrafamilial alliance. For example, in a family containing an aggressive boy with whom the mother engages in frequent battles, a first-order change might be accomplished by assigning the father the role of disciplinarian and asking the mother to act as his adviser. Although these sorts of structural changes can be rather short-lived, the ease with which they can be accomplished may suggest the degree to which more permanent changes can be effected in treatment.

Second-order change refers to more permanent changes in the patterns of alliance, boundaries, or interactional sequences within the family. In the example above, second-order change might be accomplished by (a) helping the parents to understand that their child becomes aggressive as a way of diverting the parents' attention from the distress within their marriage, and (b) working with the parents to reduce this level of marital distress so that the child's misbehavior is no longer functional.

Growth refers to a pattern of change that follows a predictable sequence of stages. Duvall and Miller have articulated the notion of a "family life cycle" for describing and explaining the developmental stages through which most families advance. In this model, families must master certain conflicts and tasks that accompany natural advances in the life of the family (i.e., from courting to marriage, from childbearing to raising children, from middle age to old age and retirement). For example, the family must be able to allow a 10-year-old child to go away to summer camp or a teenager to begin to develop romantic relationships without introducing transactions that undermine these developmental advances.

If the tasks relevant to each stage are not mastered, the family may become "stuck" at certain stages and be unable to emotionally advance to later stages. Thus, the teenage boy who was earlier denied romantic attachments may become depressed during his first semester at college and be unable to recover without returning home to the family.

As Steinglass has suggested, an even flow of information exchange within the family (i.e., good communication skills), flexible, adaptable patterns of interaction (i.e., transactions that do not always have the same outcome), and a structure that is responsive to new environmental input (i.e., semipermeable interpersonal boundaries) enable the family to adapt to new circumstances and change in growth-promoting ways. A family with poor communication skills, inflexible patterns of interactions, or overly rigid or very fluid boundaries will have trouble adapting to the demands of a new situation, and will attempt to preserve sameness (homeostasis) in the face of unexpected challenges.

III. WHAT KEEPS A FAMILY SYSTEM FROM CHANGING?

Opposed to any changes in the system are the family's *homeostatic* mechanisms. Homeostasis refers to a family's steady-state, regulatory functions and internal stability. It is the property of the system that keeps the family from growing before it is ready, even if this growth would potentially benefit the family. Homeostatic mechanisms exist in all families, and are not in themselves pathological. A family without stabilizing, regulatory forces would "change with the wind" in a manner that would not enhance the emotional health of any of its members. [*See* HOMEOSTASIS.]

A family's homeostatic mechanisms are best described as certain preexisting, identifiable, and predictable patterns of interaction or alliance. These are most obvious when an external stressor is introduced (i.e., a pending life cycle stage advance, such as the youngest child getting married). The stressor leads to a struggle within the family between the need to change and the desire to preserve the family's internal sense of stability. It is often during these life cycle transitions that psychopathology develops, and this pathology may reinstate the family's homeostatic patterns of interaction and free the family from the threatening tasks that accompany the stage transition it is facing. Thus, as Steinglass has suggested, psychopathology often reflects a conflict between the growth-promoting drives of the family and the desire to preserve homeostasis.

For example, consider a family in which the father has so much power that most of the activities of the family are oriented around satisfying his needs (the family's homeostatic state). The father decides to retire from his job (a life cycle transition), and the mother, uncomfortable with the husband's now continual presence, begins to spend more and more time away from the home. Shortly therafter, the youngest son becomes truant from school and the oldest daughter threatens to move out. The father, in response to these events, develops symptoms of a severe depression, forcing the rest of the family to take care of him. The family's original homeostatic pattern (transactions that support the father's dominance) has been restored in the face of an external threat (his retirement).

IV. MODELS OF FAMILY SYSTEMS THEORY AND FAMILY THERAPY

Many schools of family therapy have arisen since the inception of this movement in the 1950s. Each of the primary schools will be described and distinguished from each other. Other schools of thought exist as well, and the reader is referred to Gurman and Kniskern (1991) for additional information.

A. The Bowen Model

Murray Bowen is often considered one of the founders of family therapy. Much of his work focused on the notion of a person's *differentiation* from his or her family of origin as a necessary condition for emotional and physical health. Differentiation is the process of being able to define one's own boundaries, to integrate conflicting sides of the self, and to tolerate and empathize with the emotional conflicts and reactions of others. A person in a family or in any other system is constantly battling between his or her discomfort with autonomy or independence and the desire to differentiate or self-regulate. The primary goal of therapy is to encourage the differentiation of all members of a family, including but not limited to any symptomatic members.

Differentiation must also occur multigenerationally, such that the parents in the family are differentiated from their own parents. Thus, members of a family are often encouraged to go back to their families of origin and attempt to resolve conflicts that have inhibited their degrees of differentiation. None of these therapeutic processes can successfully occur, however, unless the therapist has achieved an adequate degree of differentiation him or herself.

Bowen viewed schizophrenia as the end-point result of a lack of interpersonal differentiation that is transmitted from generation to generation. He noted a pattern in which mothers of schizophrenics and their (typically male) offspring were connected in an overinvolved relationship, in which the offspring was treated as a child and not encouraged to perform age-appropriate behaviors. Fathers in these families were often seen as weak, ineffectual, and underinvolved with their children. Parents in these families were viewed as undifferentiated from their own families of origin (e.g., mothers were still largely dependent on their own mothers for emotional nurturance). Bowen created inpatient facilities in which whole families were hospitalized for treatment that centered on these concepts. [*See* SCHIZOPHRENIA.]

B. The Palo Alto Communication Model

This group, headed by Gregory Bateson, was interested primarily in the role of communication in family systems. They were the first to describe the family as a "cybernetic system" that either modifies itself to become more adaptive through incorporating new information (self-corrective feedback or growth) or returns to a state of homeostasis when new, disruptive information is introduced (error-activated feedback). The Palo Alto group was interested in the ways families transact: Who speaks to whom and how often? To what degree is information shared in a way that is understood by others? Are messages validated or invalidated? Do statements lead to intrafamilial growth or do they serve to maintain homeostasis?

The Palo Alto group is perhaps best known for its work on the "double-bind" hypothesis of schizophrenia. A double-bind experience is one in which the recipient (usually the schizophrenic or preschizophrenic person) receives a message (usually from a parent) in which there are two conflicting, inconsistent meanings communicated on the verbal and/or nonverbal level. Furthermore, the patient is unable to comment on this inconsistency or escape the situation. For example, a schizophrenic patient was told by his mother, "You should do more things on your own, away from the house." He responded that he wanted to spend some time with his friends, and she countered, "I don't think you're ready for that kind of independence." Repeated experiences of this form of parent-to-offspring communication were viewed as having a strong causal role in the development of thought disorder and delusional thinking in schizophrenia.

Although the Palo Alto group contributed a great deal to our understanding of family systems and spawned many of the later family models, the double-bind theory of schizogenesis has not received support in experimental studies.

C. The Strategic Model

This model, pioneered by Jay Haley and his associates, grew directly out of the Palo Alto model but introduced certain new family intervention strategies and modes of conceptualizing family dysfunction. The focus of the strategic model is on the family's dynamic patterns of interaction, particularly as these surround a specific problem.

Strategic family therapists believe that it is not usually a specific problem that causes a family distress, but rather, their attempts to solve it. Families, they believe, often attempt to solve problems through first-order changes that really do not alter the family's homeostatic steady state. Strategists are particularly interested in the problem of "triangulation," in which two members of a family form a coalition that excludes a third party. For example, if a mother with marital problems develops an overly close relationship with her daughter that excludes the father, a triangle has developed. The daughter becomes caught between the two parents, and may develop psychiatric symptoms as a means of returning the family to homeostasis. Thus, the original problem may have been marital tension, but the "solution" is for the mother and daughter to develop an alliance and for the daughter to develop symptoms as a way of joining her parents together. The original problem, and the family's attempts to solve it, are the foci of strategic therapy.

Strategic therapists use rather dramatic techniques to restructure the transactional patterns of families. These include *reframing* (redefining a problem so that it is more workable and modifiable) and *paradoxical intervention* (prescribing or encouraging the continuation of the symptom and the family dynamics surrounding the symptom). An example of reframing in the above example might be the statement, "Your daughter has done the family a great favor by developing symptoms. She has brought her parents back together." A paradoxical intervention might take the form, "Mother and daughter should spend all of their time together, because daughter is ill and needs the constant care that only a mother can give. Dad should not interrupt this relationship if he wants his daughter to get well." Interventions of this sort, which on the surface appear to support the homeostatic mechanisms of the family, often have the paradoxical effect of promoting growth.

D. The Structural Model

Salvador Minuchin developed structural therapy for the treatment of delinquent boys from lower socioeconomic backgrounds, believing its tenets could be applied to families from all social and ethnic groups. Structural theraptists believe that pathology in a key family member occurs as a direct result of abnormal and dysfunctional hierarchical family structures. That is, the parents do not have appropriate power in relation to their children, a pathological alliance has developed between one parent and a child, or certain children have too much "say" over the lives of other family members. Much emphasis is placed on boundaries between subsystems of the family (e.g., the emotional distance between the parental subsystem and the child subsystem) as well as the boundary separating the family from the outside world.

The structural therapist keeps in his or her mind a "map" of how a normal family should look in terms of boundaries and hierarchies, and encourages via systemic interventions the restructuring of the family to approximate this template. He or she often directly manipulates the hierarchy of the family by restructuring pathological alliances (e.g., by moving members of an enmeshed dyad away from each other during a session; by assigning a parent the role of confidant for a child from whom this parent has become estranged; by "empowering" members of the family who are in positions of weakness). Unlike the strategic therapist, structuralists will not generally focus on the presenting problem but will try to modify symptoms by focusing immediately on pathological family structures, thereby working "from the top down."

E. The Milan School

Based on the work of Mara Selvini Palazzoli, Luigi Boscolo, and Gianfranco Cecchin in Italy, the Milan school grew out of the strategic model but was influenced by the structural approach as well. Therapists from this school proceed by the information-gathering technique of "circular questioning," in which the therapist forms hypotheses about the family's dynamics on the basis of asking each member of the family to comment on the relation of two other members of the family, or perhaps by asking one member to clarify another's views, behavior, or conflicts. The therapist's hypotheses about the family are constantly revised on the basis of the information gathered from these questions.

The hypothesis formed by the therapist is often that the family has developed a "game" in which various members of the family are trying to gain control over the rest of the family. For example, in a very enmeshed family containing a schizophrenic patient, the "game" might consist of the patient becoming delusional or hearing voices when the topic of the father's relationship with the patient's sister is broached. The "signature" technique of this group is the "counterparadoxical" intervention, in which the game is identified and the family is encouraged to continue this game or even exaggerate it (i.e., the schizophrenic patient is encouraged to remain ill in order to protect the rest of his family, and the family is encouraged to become more protective of the patient). These counterparadoxical maneuvers underline the homeostatic mechanisms of the family while covertly challenging the family to modify itself and grow.

F. The Symbolic–Experiential School

Carl Whitaker developed a school of family systems therapy that takes into account the role of unconscious factors and motivations in systems. Like other psychoanalytic thinkers, Whitaker believes that families communicate through symbols rather than words. Unlike the strategic school, which focuses on the interactions surrounding the family's presenting problem, Whitaker chooses to define and manipulate the symbols expressed by the family, whether or not these directly pertain to the identified problem. For example, he views suicide in one family member as a symbol of the family's conflict over whether it, as a unit, should continue to survive. Likewise, he views marital distress as symbolizing a conflict between husband and wife over whose family of origin ought to be imitated.

Whitaker uses a very idiosyncratic treatment style that focuses heavily on bringing to light unconscious motivations. He tends to regularly share his own inner feelings about or reactions to the family. He also employs the technique of "seeding the unconscious," in which conflicts that are being expressed by the family symbolically are verbalized by the therapist before the family is able to verbalize these feelings themselves (e.g., to a father who is highly dependent on his wife, he might say, "I miss my mommy too"). His style is a rather flamboyant one, and often communicates to the family that he is comfortable with his own vulnerabilities in a way that makes them more comfortable with their own.

G. The Psychoanalytic Family Model

Influenced by the work of Bowen, Whitaker, and the Freudian individual psychoanalytic and object relations movements, the psychoanalytic–family school believes that one can only understand the matrix of transactions, dynamics, and structures presented by a family if one also understands the configuration of unconscious conflicts, drives, and wishes of each family member and of the family as a whole. Like the Bowenians, proponents of this school believe that symptoms in one key family member to some degree symbolize that person's lack of differentiation from his or her parents. Thus, this school differs from the strategic or structural schools in its focus on unobservable factors that may motivate the development of pathological alliances, boundary difficulties, and other growth-inhibiting phenomena.

Conflict within the family is often viewed by this group as due to "projective identification," in which one family member experiences aspects of the self that are intolerable. These aspects of the self are then "projected" onto another member, who then "identifies" with these attributes and starts to experience them. For example, a wife working at a high-level job who herself feels incompetent—perhaps due to the repeated experience of receiving devaluing and disconfirming messages from her mother—may rail against her husband in a way that makes him feel inadequate. If this husband in turn fears that expressing his own competencies will lead to competitions with his father, the stage is set for him to accept these accusations of incompetence by identifying with them and "acting the part."

Much like individual psychoanalytic therapy, family therapists of this school will interpret to the family certain dynamics like projective identification (e.g., to the wife in the couple described above, the therapist might say, "I think you are expressing your own feelings of discomfort with yourself by encouraging your husband to feel those same feelings"). The psychoanalytic therapist will also help the family to work through its "transference" reactions to the therapist and to each other (the process by which unconscious feelings about a significant person from the past are experienced in a new, close relationship). However, the matrix of transferences and countertransferences (the emotional reactions of the therapist to the family and each of its members) is far more complex in family work than in individual treatment. In the latter, transferential phenomena are mainly analyzed as these occur between client and therapist.

H. The Behavioral Family Model

Behavioral approaches, based in learning theories, view family interactions in terms of reward/punishment ratios. According to this view, how we behave in a family setting depends in part on which aspects of our behavior are selectively reinforced and which are punished or negatively reinforced. Furthermore, our behavior is in part a function of what we have learned through modeling of others in our past, including our parents. Our prior learning history may have resulted in certain skill assets or deficits (e.g., the inability to solve problems), the latter of which are viewed a remediable through family therapy.

The satisfaction level experienced by a couple or family is viewed as a function of the ratio of rewarding to punishing interchanges: Families, and couples in particular, often come to therapy when they have sacrificed pleasing, reinforcing transactions for coercion, mutual invalidation, aversive control tactics, or negatively escalating arguments. Whereas the psychoanalytic school might view these negative exchanges as a product of projective identification, behaviorists believe that families maintain these exchanges because to discontinue them is more costly to the family than their retention.

Behaviorists often use a predetermined series of assessments and interventions with couples or families. Often, a behavioral assessment will first be conducted, in which each family member's skill assets or deficits (and those of the family as a whole) are evaluated, the degree to which interactions rely on mutual reward versus aversive control or punishment is clarified, and each member's cognitions or attributions about family relationships are elucidated. Based on the conclusions drawn from these assessments, the therapist may work with the family in any one or combination of ways: (1) Through skill building, such as training the family in communication or problem-solving skills. This training often involves encouraging the family to role-play and rehearse new ways of speaking to and resolving conflicts with other family members; (2) through challenging and restructuring the beliefs, attributions, or "dysfunctional cognitions" of each member of the family; (3) through suggesting concrete ways of increasing the benefit : cost ratio of family interactions, such as encouraging the couple or parents to plan time alone together. Therapists of a strategic or structural orientation might also suggest the latter intervention, but the purpose would be to strengthen the boundary around the marital subsystem and differentiate it from the child subsystem. In comparison, the behavioral school would view this intervention, when combined with skills training, as a means of increasing positive reinforcement and decreasing aversive interchanges within the marital couple.

To illustrate the technique of behavioral family therapy, consider again a family containing an aggressive boy. A behaviorist might first ask the parents and child to discuss among themselves a specific family problem so that the therapist can assess the degree to which interchanges achieve their stated goals (e.g., are the parents' statements effective in controlling the child's behavior?). Interventions might then consist of encouraging one or both parents to verbally praise the child's positive behaviors and ignore his negative, aversive behaviors; challenging the mother's stated belief that she is not a good parent; and teaching the child to verbalize to the parents his needs and frustrations instead of expressing these in his behavior. Later, the efficacy of communication within the couple might be examined and new modes of interaction modeled and rehearsed.

The behaviorists have been most conscientious in providing empirical evidence for their approaches. For example, research has shown that among couples with distressed marriages, aversive or punishing styles of communication and conflict resolution are predictive of later divorce. Behavioral marital therapy, in turn, has been found in controlled clinical trials to be efficacious in preventing divorce and increasing marital satisfaction among such couples. There is also increasing evidence that behavioral family therapy approaches are useful in the treatment of severe psychopathology: Schizophrenic outpatients who receive regular medication and whose families undergo behavioral family treatments are at lower risk for psychotic relapses over time than are those who only receive medication or medication with individual therapy.

V. CONCLUSION

Many schools of family systems theory and therapy exist. Each school places its emphases on different family processes: Some focus on verbal or nonverbal transactions within sessions, others on the family's structures or power hierarchies, others on underlying or unconscious conflicts, and others on skill assets and deficits, individual cognitions, and family-wide reward : punishment ratios. What these schools have in common is the notion that the family is an interlocking, interdependent set of elements, that one person's behavior is directed, shaped, influenced, or reinforced by that of others, and that psychopathology in one member reflects dysfunctional interactions in the family as a whole. They also share the belief that the best way to treat psychopathology in a family member is to modify or restructure the transactions of the entire family. Family systems therapy can be very powerful in the treatment of individual or relational dysfunctions.

Acknowledgment

Preparation of this article was supported in part by grants MH43931 and MH42556 from the National Institute of Mental Health.

Bibliography

Anderson, C. M., and Stewart, S. (1983). "Mastering Resistance: A Practical Guide to Family Therapy." Guilford Press, New York.

Duvall, E. M., and Miller, B. C. (1985). "Marriage and Family Development," 6th ed. Harper & Row, New York.

Gurman, A. S. (1978). Contemporary marital therapies: A critique and comparative analysis of psychoanalytic, behavioral and systems theory approaches. In "Marriage and Marital Therapy" (T. Paolino and B. S. McCrady, Eds.), Brunner/Mazel, New York.

Gurman, A. S., and Kniskern, D. P. (Eds.) (1991). "Handbook of Family Therapy," Vol. II. Brunner/Mazel, New York.

Guttman, H. A. (1991). Systems theory, cybernetics, and epistemology. In "Handbook of Family Therapy" (A. S. Gurman and D. P. Kniskern, Eds.), Vol. II. Brunner /Mazel, New York.

Hahlweg, K., and Goldstein, M. J. (Eds.) (1987). "Understanding Major Mental Disorder: The Contribution of Family Interaction Research." Family Process Press, New York.

Hoffman, L. (1981). "Foundations of Family Therapy: A Conceptual Framework for Systems Change." Basic Books, New York.

Jacobson, N. S., and Margolin, G. (1979). "Marital Therapy: Strategies Based on Social Learning and Behavior Exchange Principles." Brunner/Mazel, New York.

McGoldrick, M., Pearce, J. K., and Giordano, J. (1982). "Ethnicity and Family Therapy." Guilford Press, New York.

Minuchin, S. (1974). "Families and Family Therapy." Harvard University Press, Cambridge, MA.

Steinglass, P. (1987). A systems view of family interaction and psychopathology. In "Family Interaction and Psychopathology" (T. Jacob, Ed.). Plenum, New York.

FORENSIC PSYCHOLOGY

Tony D. Crespi
Meriden, Connecticut

Glossary

Civil (involuntary) commitments The process whereby the state commits an individual to a psychiatric facility.

Forensic psychology The interface of psychology and law.

Police psychology A specialty of forensic psychology in which psychologists work with police departments.

Psychological evaluations A process whereby psychologists administer special tests to clients (i.e., intelligence tests, personality tests, etc.).

Voluntary commitments The process whereby a person voluntarily requests admission to a psychiatric facility.

FORENSIC PSYCHOLOGY is the interface between psychology and the law. Since 1962 when the United States Court of Appeals for the District of Columbia first stated that appropriately qualified psychologists could testify in court on matters pertaining to emotional disorders (*Jenkins v. United States*), the involvement of psychologists in court-related issues has grown. Their work has encompassed corrections, civil commitment, police psychology, child custody, and competency, as well as diverse legal areas where expertise is requested on questions surrounding psychological dynamics.

I. BACKGROUND AND CONTRIBUTIONS

Forensic psychologists are uniquely qualified to contribute psychological expertise to the legal process. With the legal system confronted by a potpourri of complex issues, the forensic psychologist's specialized training provides the legal system with psychological insights on matters ranging from the prediction of dangerousness to situations involving involuntary hospitalization.

In an ideal situation, the collective expertise of the forensic psychologist's specialized knowledge enhances the wisdom of the legal community and provides judges, attorneys, and juries with information to make better informed decisions. Certainly the courts are faced by a challenging array of cases where psychological participation can be useful. At present, for example, more than 1.5 million juveniles are arrested annually and more than 600,000 adults are reported as incarcerated in correctional programs. Equally distressing, there has been an increase in psychiatric admissions for adolescents. Particularly noteworthy about these groups, it has been estimated that approximately 80 to 90% of psychiatric and correctional populations have a history of physical, sexual, or psychological abuse.

Selecting from a growing roster of problems facing children, approximately 270,000 children are reported in foster care in the United States. Removed from homes for such problems as abuse and neglect, the court system plays a critical role in the placement of such children, but court personnel are not typically trained in the mental health issues facing children or families. The forensic psychologist brings this expertise.

These data, then, buttressed by information on such matters as violence in the home (reported to occur in 1 in 14 marriages) or sexual abuse (by the age of 18, 1 in 3 women have been reported to be a victim of sexual abuse), lead to the conclusion that for the legal system, the forensic psychologist can

Copyright © 1994 by Academic Press, Inc. All rights of reproduction in any form reserved.

be a useful resource. That is, the forensic psychologist can answer questions and provide information helpful to judges, attorneys, juries, parole officers, and juvenile justice personnel. For example, a person who hears voices and who cannot tell what is real from what is not would not be expected to generally understand their rights if arrested. In such a case, a forensic psychologist can provide clarifying testimony about the client's reasoning and understanding. In another example, a forensic psychologist can provide testimony on the background of a defendant who was sexually abused and violently sodomized by a parent prior to murdering that parent.

Given the importance of the issues faced by the legal system, the forensic psychologist can serve an educative role in clarifying psychological dynamics and providing rich details and information through the use of psychological assessment instruments. The courts face difficult cases in which psychological factors influence behavior. The forensic psychologist helps serve as a bridge in the interaction between psychology and the law.

II. PROFESSIONAL TRAINING

The clinician asked to provide the court with psychological expertise must be appropriately trained and credentialed. In view of the importance of psychological testimony in the judicial system, it is important to understand the depth and extent of training required of psychologists for licensure/certification: psychologists providing services to the public are required to hold licensure/certification by their respective states.

To be eligible for licensure or certification (a designation which varies by individual state statutes), psychologists classically complete undergraduate baccalaureate degrees of approximately 4 years duration followed by graduate training leading to a doctoral degree including practicum and internship training. Appropriately, forensic psychologists must earn their doctoral degrees in a designated area of professional psychology (e.g., clinical psychology, school psychology, or counseling psychology) and may hold the Ph.D. (Doctor of Philosophy), Ed.D. (Doctor of Education), or Psy.D. (Doctor of Psychology). Doctoral training must involve a balanced program of training as outlined by the licensing boards for psychologists of each state.

Following receipt of the doctorate, candidates for licensure complete 1 to 2 years of postdoctoral experience under the supervision of a licensed psychologist. Prior to independent practice, they subsequently complete state and national examinations for practice.

Forensic psychology, as a unique area of practice of psychology, involves specific areas of expertise separate from that typically learned during graduate school. Therefore, just as physicians complete specialty training following medical school, so too, the forensic psychologist typically (with the exception of those who complete programs offering integrated training with a law school) acquires specialty training following receipt of their doctorate.

Through postdoctoral specialty training, often augmented by participation in workshops and symposia involving specific areas of forensic practice, psychologists acquire the necessary training for forensic work. For clients, attorneys, and the public, as in selecting a physician, it is worthwhile to make specific inquiry about each psychologist's background, training, and professional credentials. Ultimately, the best fit between client's needs and psychologist's background requires careful attention.

III. THE ROLE OF THE FORENSIC PSYCHOLOGIST

Forensic psychologists must use their knowledge of human behavior and various psychological assessment instruments to provide the legal system with an assessment, diagnosis, and recommendations for a range of clients. As examples, forensic psychologists may be asked to provide a psychological assessment to aid in the disposition of a case for a convicted child molester, rapist, or murderer, or they may be asked to conduct a comprehensive psychological evaluation to aid in the determination of placement for a child in a custody hearing.

A forensic psychologist may also be involved in a subsection of forensic psychology called police psychology which can involve such areas as police selection, hostage negotiation, or stress reduction. The demands of involvement in screening police candidates versus intervention as a psychotherapist for a police officer who shot a criminal in the line of duty can represent two extremes for the forensic psychologist.

Forensic psychologists, then, are asked to offer testimony, expertise, and guidance in a wide array of cases. Today, a sampling of cases that the forensic psychologist might be involved with might include arson, murder, rape, foster care, drug addiction, sexual abuse, child welfare, or psychiatric commitment. Indeed, the legal system presents a wide array of cases to the forensic psychologist. Still, while the actual cases vary, in a general way the role of forensic psychologists can be construed to involve the general areas of practice which characterize professional psychology: assessment, intervention, consultation, and research. Each shall be discussed briefly.

A. Assessment

The unique role of psychological testing (i.e., psychological assessment) has remained an important area of practice for forensic psychologists. Psychological testing provides the court with both quantitative and qualitative data which can encompass intellectual abilities, cognitive reasoning, personality strengths and weaknesses, competency, mental status, and neuropsychological functioning. Although specific tests chosen for forensic practice vary, selected psychological tests often used include the Minnesota Multiphasic Personality Inventory, Wechsler Intelligence Scales, California Psychological Inventory, 16 Personality Factor Questionnaire, Myers-Brigg Type Indicator, Rorschach, Thematic Apperception Test, Bender-Gestalt, and House–Tree–Person. [*See* CLINICAL ASSESSMENT; PERSONALITY ASSESSMENT.]

For many professionals in the court system, psychological testing is an integral aspect of the testimony of the forensic psychologist. The expectation, generally, is that psychological test results provide objective, impartial, psychological information. However, psychological tests provide data only about current functioning and do not accurately predict future behavior. Nonetheless, psychological testing can provide comparisons with the normative sample on which the test was developed, and provide indications of psychological and psychiatric disorders.

The questions asked of the forensic psychologist often fall directly to the results of the psychological evaluation. What is the intellectual level of the defendent? Is the client suicidal? The data from the psychological testing must be integrated into a comprehensive picture which can be presented to the court. In presenting testimony, the forensic psychologist may be presented with additional questions, and must present findings which can help the court system render a decision.

B. Intervention

Forensic psychologists are confronted by a wide range of challenges since the services to be provided can vary widely from one client to the next. A police officer referred for counseling because of depression will require different treatment than a psychiatric patient committed to a hospital to restore competency for trial. As such, forensic psychologists must be knowledgeable about the advantages and disadvantages of different interventions and treatments and may utilize individual, group, or family treatment as deemed appropriate.

Obviously, not all clients seen by the forensic psychologist are willing participants in the treatment process. The court may require treatment for clients for different reasons. One client may be ordered to receive treatment to restore competency while another may be ordered to receive treatment as a condition of parole. Thus, the contours of psychological treatment are often governed by the court rather than by the psychologist or the defendent, and the treatment atmosphere for a client who may or may not believe they need intervention, but must participate because of a court mandate, can dramatically effect the process of treatment.

The inherent problems of designing an effective treatment program for a client mandated by the court for treatment or committed to a forensic psychiatric hospital for treatment can vary from the treatment plan designed for a police officer or parollee, for instance, who voluntarily requests psychotherapy services. In short, one especially challenging aspect to forensic psychology is the fact that while there *are* clients who will voluntarily desire psychological services, the forensic psychologist will also encounter many clients who participate in treatment only because of the court: their denial or avoidance of treatment will necessitate the need for a persuasive treatment plan.

C. Consultation

Consultation is the area of practice for forensic psychology in which psychologists provide information to many different agencies. Consultation with courts, police departments, judges, attorneys, court personnel, and staff in correctional and forensic psychiatric settings illustrates agencies and individuals with whom forensic psychologists work.

The forensic psychologist must possess strong communication skills, both written and oral, and be able to explain psychological terminology to many individuals not familiar with the language of psychological practice. The forensic psychologist who is asked to provide an evaluation of a client as to whether they are competent to stand trial must be able to explain relevant findings to the judge, trial attorneys, and the jury. Because of the need to effectively communicate psychological data to so many different individuals, consultation skills are critical for the forensic psychologist.

Obviously, the forensic psychologist working with a police department to construct a psychological battery of tests to aid in police selection procedures will present different information and utilize different consultation strategies than the forensic psychologist asked to provide a psychological consultation in a child custody case. As consultants, the forensic psychologist must effectively choose the techniques most germane to each case and strive to present psychological expertise in a fashion which can most effectively meet the needs of each client.

D. Research

Psychological research may ultimately provide the courts with definitive answers for questions which cannot at present be fully understood. What intervention is most effective with sexual offenders? What are the implications of long-standing sexual and/or physical abuse? What are the effects of witnessing repeated acts of violence in the home versus living in a neighborhood characterized by street violence? What differences exist between individuals who commit different crimes, including arson, rape, or murder? What factors affect juries? What behavioral characteristics affect court deliberations?

Clearly, there is a large area of research where the forensic psychologist may ultimately help the court. Research involving eyewitness testimony is one area which has already begun to yield important information. Other areas include advances in the understanding of neuropsychological deficits of adolescents on death row. [*See* EYEWITNESS TESTIMONY.]

The utility of psychological research is undeniable. Even so, there remains a great dearth of knowledge. In general, greater research attention is needed on the predictors of dangerousness, on the developmental characteristics of different types of offenders, and on the effectiveness of different treatment interventions with children, adolescents, and adults. In short, psychological research conducted by forensic psychologists can be of tremendous value to the courts and society by offering greater scientific precision and understanding about the most effective ways the courts can intervene in cases involving psychological dynamics. Of course, the full range of knowledge and information which can potentially be learned through psychological research endeavors involving forensic psychology has yet to be fully ascertained.

IV. PREDICTION OF DANGEROUSNESS

Testimony surrounding the prediction of dangerousness remains one of the more frequently asked questions for the forensic psychologist. Whether involved in the civil (involuntary) commitment of the mentally ill to psychiatric hospitals or providing a psychological evaluation involving the possible confinement of a defendant to a correctional facility, the concern for potential for dangerous behavior endures as one of the more problematic issues for the forensic psychologist.

You might ask, then, *can* forensic psychologists predict dangerousness?

Regardless of theoretical position or quality of training, from a psychometric standpoint, any psychological prediction involves a degree of error. In psychological terms, the forensic psychologist can err in two ways. The first way is to suggest that a person will be dangerous when they will not (false positive). Basically, this involves overpredictions of dangerousness. The second way is to suggest that the person is not likely to be dangerous when they will (false negative). This involves underpredictions of dangerousness.

More false positive errors are made than false negative errors. This means that forensic psychologists overpredict dangerous behavior and suggest imprisonment or involuntary psychiatric hospitalization when it is not necessary. However, even with the fact that psychologists predict dangerous behavior more times than is actual, this does not reduce the fact that there still exists a group whom are seen as not dangerous and who are. That means that while the error is reduced, it is not eliminated.

Over the past 25 years, research involving predictions of dangerousness leads to the unavoidable conclusion that there exists a high incidence of error involving the prediction of dangerousness. Some studies report that greater than 80% of individuals were *inaccurately* predicted to be violent! In other words, these individuals did not display the violent behavior which was predicted.

Empirically, it is important to remember that the science of human behavior is not sufficiently well-developed to allow reliable predictions to be made about future behavior. Thus, while courts are pressing for determinations and predictions surrounding the possibility of future violence, forensic psychologists know that such predictions cannot be made without error. At the present time, this means that psychological determinations risk either the release of clients who may act violently or confining clients who will not be violent.

Over the long run, we have yet to know whether forensic psychologists will someday be able to make such predictions with ideal accuracy. This may indeed, come to pass. It is not, however, a reality at this point in time. Mostly, we can expect that the forensic psychologist can provide considerable psychological information about how a client is functioning during the examination itself. And a psychological evaluation can be helpful in clarifying whether the client understands their behavior. This type of information can be quite helpful, and can help the judge, attorneys, and jury in rendering a decision.

In short, while the prediction of dangerousness remains a commonly asked question for the forensic psychologist, the ability to predict future behavior remains a murky issue at best. Still, the forensic psychologist can be helpful in clarifying and explaining dynamics which may have contributed to past behavior, and in clarifying present behavior. However, the available research indicates that the prediction of future dangerousness, while potentially invaluable to the court system, cannot be reliably predicted.

V. COMMITMENT

Commitment to psychiatric hospitals can be either voluntary or involuntary. In the United States, civil (involuntary) psychiatric hospitalization—civil commitment—has loomed as one of the critical areas where forensic psychologists must effectively interface with the courts. The ability to hospitalize a patient, whether the patient wishes this or not, is the basis for involuntary commitments. Historically, the basis of civil commitment has rested in the concept of the "parens patriae" power of the state to act as guardian on behalf of those in need. Thus, commitment was not viewed as punishment. Rather, it was viewed as a way to protect the welfare of the individual.

Unquestionably, our history is filled with instances where commitment has been inappropriate, including instances where a parent sought hospitalization for children and husbands sought psychiatric commitments for wives because of disagreements far removed from the need for psychiatric care. Fortunately, civil commitment laws have been altered and rewritten in order to more effectively protect patient rights. However, for forensic psychologists, involuntary commitment remains a critical area of practice. In fact, most psychologists employed in psychiatric hospitals today routinely complete psychological evaluations used, at least partially, to determine whether certain patients require commitment.

As previously stated, psychiatric commitments are of two types: (1) voluntary commitments, and (2) involuntary commitments. Each shall be described in brief.

A. Voluntary Commitments

Voluntary commitments involve the willing, "voluntary" agreement by a patient to undergo psychiatric treatment. The fact that an individual voluntarily is admitted for psychiatric treatment, though, does not necessarily indicate the patient will necessarily be released on request. Voluntarily commited patients must request their release in writing. When this discharge request is received, the hospital is obligated to subsequently either release the patient or file for involuntary commitment.

Generally, then, even if a patient voluntarily requests psychiatric treatment initially, there is no guarantee that the patient will subsequently be released on their request. When appropriate—when the treatment team believes that a patient is in need of further treatment—the hospital may petition the court for a civil commitment. If the court agrees with the hospital that the patient meets the statutory requirements for a civil (involuntary) commitment, the patient may subsequently be ordered to remain hospitalized. On the other hand, if the court rules that the patient does not meet the criteria for an involuntary period of hospitalization, the hospital will be ordered to release the patient. What is striking about this, then, is the fact that not all "voluntary" patients remain voluntary, and not all patients voluntarily admitted for psychiatric treatment will necessarily be discharged simply by virtue of their requesting such a release.

B. Involuntary Commitments

Involuntary commitments are characterized by the ability to hospitalize a patient, whether the patient wishes this or not. Involuntary commitments have their roots in the concept of the "parens patriae" power of the state, which is to act as guardian of those in need.

From a historical standpoint, the Supreme Court addressed the status of civil commitment in the 1975 case of *O'Connor v. Donaldson*. This case involved a patient, Donaldson, who spent approximately 14 years hospitalized. The Supreme Court ruled that civil commitment was unconstitutional based solely on mental illness and that the patient must be dangerous to either self or others: Donaldson was not dangerous and was ordered released.

Addressing standards and guidelines for commitment, it is noteworthy that the commitment guidelines which follow are general in as much as civil commitment laws vary from state to state. As a result, the interested reader will want to refer to individual state laws for specific details. Generally, the criteria which follow are provided to serve as introduction to the area of civil commitment. Those confined for forensic evaluation or for reasons involving criminal justice may be confined under different standards.

Patients who meet the commitment criteria generally: (a) demonstrate a mental disorder, and (b) are considered dangerous to either self or others, and (c) are committed consonant with the principle of the least restrictive placement, and (d) lack the ability to make an informed decision involving treatment.

Procedurally, an individual can be committed for up to 6 months duration, with renewals. State statutes vary from state to state, with varying lengths of time allowed relative to placement and the lapses of time after which hearings must be held. The latter is noteworthy as admissions can come from a variety of referral sources. For instance, if a patient is admitted from an emergency room, hearings must be scheduled within certain time parameters—generally 48 hours. On the other hand, court ordered commitments may possess a longer time parameter.

It is during the initial examination and admission period that the patient undergoes an assortment of examinations, one of which is often a psychological evaluation (i.e., psychological testing) completed by the forensic psychologist. The forensic psychologist is not the sole person completing examinations, but lawyers and judges often place great weight on the opinion of the forensic psychologist and on the results of the psychological examination.

Today, the psychiatric commitment of individuals to psychiatric facilities remains an area of considerable discussion, despite changes and refinements in the various laws governing the process of commitment. For forensic psychologists, the ability to make contributions involving civil commitment is of considerable importance as psychological evaluations offer an important vehicle for interviewing and examining patients. Indeed, although exact predictions about the need for psychiatric commitments can appear as much art as science, the use of a psychological evaluation serves as a useful adjunct to the clinical interviewing typically completed by the psychiatrist (M.D.) and psychiatric social worker (M.S.W.).

VI. CONCLUSIONS

How many clients interacting with the legal system display psychological issues of sufficient magnitude to warrant the involvement and expertise of a psychologist? How many court decisions are made without the necessary input of experts in mental health? Because of the divergent number of cases confronting the judicial system, it is unknown how many individual cases are adjudicated without the expertise of the forensic psychologist.

As a general rule, the courts are faced with difficult if not seemingly impossible questions. Because many cases involve psychological dynamics—cases ranging from child custody disputes to cases involving the necessity for psychiatric hospitalization—forensic psychologists who blend specialized knowledge of psychology and the law provide valuable input for attorneys, judges, juries, and families. In addition, forensic psychologists are actively working with staff, administrators, and families in the correctional system, in psychiatric settings, in police departments, and are providing valuable input in legal matters involving many differing cases involving the interaction of psychology and the law.

Unfortunately, the compendium of questions facing both psychologists and the courts remains too voluminous and complex to yet be completely unravelled. Should an adolescent murderer with severe neuropsychological disorders be put to death? What are the best predictors of dangerousness? What differences exist between someone who murders a stranger versus a family member? Clearly, the questions are many. Fortunately, forensic psychologists are working to provide society with responsible information in which to better understand these and related issues. For although the judicial decisions are rendered by the court, the psychological input of the forensic psychologist can be an invaluable aid to the court system. As has been noted in this chapter, the forensic psychologist brings to the court specialized knowledge about psychology and the law. And it is this expertise which can help the court face a wide array of challenging cases.

In general, forensic psychology is still a young science, which has yet to completely unravel many of the questions posed by the courts and society. At the same time, forensic psychologists are active contributors to the court system and are providing expertise in highly specialized matters. It is safe to say that some day we may yet unravel mental illness and criminal behavior. In the meantime, the challenge for the forensic psychologist, the courts, and society, is tremendous.

Bibliography

Appelbaum, P. S., and Gutheil, T. G. (1991). "Clinical Handbook of Psychiatry and the Law, 2nd ed. Williams & Wilkins, Baltimore, MD.

Campbell, T. W. (1992). The "highest level of psychological certainty": Betraying standards of practice in forensic psychology. *Am. J. Forensic Psychol.* **10**(2), 35–48.

Crespi, T. D. (1989). "Child and Adolescent Psychopathology and Involuntary Hospitalization: A Handbook for Mental Health Professionals." Charles C. Thomas, Springfield, IL.

Heilbrun, K. S. (1992). The role of psychological testing in forensic assessment. *Law Hum. Behav.* **16**(3), 257–272.

Heilbrun, K. S., and Annis, L. V. (1988). Research and training in forensic psychology: National survey of forensic facilities. *Prof. Psychol. Res. Practice* **19,** 211–215.

Lockwood, J. L. (1992). Juvenile criminal responsibility and the courts. *Am. J. Forensic Psychol.* **10**(2), 5–15.

Melton, G. B., Petrila, J., Poythress, N. G., and Slobogin, C. (1987). "Psychological Evaluations for the Courts: A Handbook for Mental Health Professionals and Lawyers. Guilford, New York.

Monahan, J. (Ed.) (1980). "Who Is the Client? The Ethics of Psychological Intervention in the Criminal Justice System." American Psychological Association, Washington, DC.

Roesch, R., Grisso, T., and Poythress, N. (1986). Training programs courses, and workshops in psychology and the law. "The Impact of Social Psychology on Procedural Justice" (M. F. Kaplan, Ed.), pp. 83–108. Charles C. Thomas, Springfield, IL.

FREE WILL

Howard Rachlin
State University of New York at Stony Brook

Glossary

Compatibilism The view that even though all behavior of organisms originates in principle outside of their bodies, the concept of free will (the distinction between voluntary and involuntary behavior) is nevertheless meaningful.

Determinism The view that because all behavior of organisms is in principle predictable as the outcome of prior causes originating outside of their bodies, there is no room in psychology for the concept of free will.

Libertarianism The view that at least some important actions by some organisms are not predictable on the basis of external causes. These actions are held to be due to free will, an autonomous internal cause.

PHILOSOPHERS have bequeathed to psychologists three fundamental positions on the question of free will: *determinism, libertarianism,* and *compatibilism.* Determinism says that all interesting or important behavior—of humans, of organisms in general, as well as of inorganic objects—is in principle predictable on the basis of prior events. Therefore, say the determinists, there is no such thing as free will. Determinism implies that the concept of free will is useless in psychology or, worse than useless, a cloak for ignorance of the true causes of behavior. Libertarianism (not necessarily the same as political libertarianism) says that at least some interesting or important actions of people and maybe even some actions of nonhuman animals are truly free. These actions are vitally important for the organisms in which they originate but they are unpredictable on the basis of either past behavior or anything else. Such actions, libertarianism implies, are outside the realm of scientific study. According to libertarians, psychology can at best vaguely predict free behavior perhaps through empathy or some other undefined process. But a psychology of purely voluntary behavior can never be "scientific." Libertarians and determinists agree that if one is right, the other must be wrong. Compatibilism on the other hand says that some acts may be both determined and free at the same time—depending on how you look at those acts. Compatibilism implies that the distinction between voluntary and involuntary behavior is a useful and meaningful distinction even while a scientific psychology is possible.

I. LIBERTARIANISM

An explicitly nonscientific psychology is nevertheless possible within a libertarian framework. Humanistic, phenomenological, existential, and hermeneutical branches of psychology take this tack. Existential psychology, for instance, holds that the fundamental psychological reality ("being") consists of immediate phenomenal appearances. Our perception of objects in the world, as well as our mental representations of those objects, contains more or less "nothingness" (like jigsaw puzzles with more or fewer pieces missing). The essential function of our wills is to construct our physical and mental worlds ("essence") from appearances ("existence"). Thus, the concept of free will plays a very important part in existential psychology. It is the basic mechanism by which an abstraction (a chair, for instance) arises from particulars (appearances of chairs). This primary function of the will determines in turn the distinctly secondary function of controlling overt behavior. Behavior is uncontrollable and unpredictable according to existential psychology because individuals might always have behaved otherwise than they did. Two individuals with identical

Encyclopedia of Human Behavior, Volume 2
Copyright © 1994 by Academic Press, Inc. All rights of reproduction in any form reserved.

histories may see the world differently, see themselves differently, and behave differently, not because of different genetic composition but because of different innate, and free, wills. Psychologists today are mostly determinists or compatibilists because to be a libertarian is to confess that much of what is usually considered the domain of psychology (the areas of motivation, choice, rational thought, and so forth) is at once important and beyond systematic understanding.

II. DETERMINISM

Those modern psychologists who are determinists are usually reductionists of one sort or another. They say that while the mind (and the will) is crucially important it is nothing but . . . (and here they specify some deterministic system). The most common sort of reductionism is physiological reductionism. In modern philosophical psychology, physiological reductionists are also called "materialists." Modern materialists hold that the mind is nothing but the workings of the brain (or the wider central and peripheral nervous systems combined). The creed of modern physiological reductionists was perhaps nowhere better argued than by the Russian reflexologist Ivan Michailovich Sechenov in 1863. Sechenov said

> All the endless diversity of the external manifestations of the activity of the brain can be finally regarded as one phenomenon—that of muscular movement. Be it a child laughing at the sight of toys, or Garibaldi smiling when he is persecuted for his excessive love for his fatherland; a girl trembling at the first thought of love, or Newton enunciating universal laws and writing them on paper—everywhere the final manifestation is muscular movement. In order to help the reader to reconcile himself with this thought more readily, I will remind him of the frame-work created by the mind of humanity to include all manifestations of brain activity; this frame-work is "*word and deed*." Under *deed*, the popular mind conceives, without question, every external mechanical activity of man based exclusively on the use of muscles. And under *word*, as the educated reader will realise, is understood a certain combination of sounds produced in the larynx and the cavity of the mouth, again by means of muscular movements.

From the strict materialistic point of view, animals including humans are machines explicable by physical and chemical principles; it is the job of the psychological determinist to uncover the workings of these machines. What seems like voluntary behavior is just involuntary behavior of a more complex kind. For Sechenov, Newton enunciating universal laws is just a more complex version of Newton kicking his leg when his knee is struck by a hammer. From this viewpoint physiological psychology is the only truly scientific psychology. Other forms of psychology would be mere holding actions, rough classifications with which we make do until our knowledge of the physiological basis of behavior catches up.

But not all modern determinists are materialists of this physiological sort. The deterministic system inserted in the blank space of: "The mind is nothing but . . ." need not be a strictly physiological system. B. F. Skinner, a modern radical behaviorist, believed that an animal's apparently voluntary actions are caused by what Skinner called its "history of reinforcement," the pattern of prior rewards and punishments for classes of acts (called *operants*) defined by common consequences. For Skinner, an operant's consequences determine its subsequent occurrences. It is this characteristic of operants that, according to Skinner, makes them seem (but not really be) voluntary. For example, a rat may press a lever with its left paw, its right paw, its nose, etc. All constitute the same operant, the rate of which is predicted by the theory. Since operants are what Skinner's theory predicts, the rat is within the theory "free" to press the bar as it may—with any particular movement. But according to Skinner this sort of freedom is unimportant. Therefore, Skinner was right to declare himself a determinist. In *Beyond Freedom and Dignity* Skinner claimed that free will is a myth and that people's "desire" for freedom is *nothing but* a behavioral tendency to replace control of operants by aversive consequences with, equally deterministic and ultimately more precise, control by reward. [*See* OPERANT LEARNING.]

A similar kind of determinism is claimed by modern cognitive scientists. The sort of behavior these scientists are interested in predicting is largely verbal or informational—the sort that could go into or come out of a computer. A successful theory, according to cognitive science, is one that can be translated into a program that passes the "Turing test." A computer program held to embody a theory of the mind may be tested by human observers who feed questions into the computer and receive answers from it. To the extent that the machine's answers are indistinguishable from those given by a real human being, the computer's program is an adequate model of the mind. Any program that passes this test will necessarily be highly complex, perhaps involving probabilistic neural networks, perhaps not. It is that complexity of our actual minds, a complexity not generally available to our conscious introspection, which according to the cognitivist creates in us the illusion that our behavior is free. When the true program by which our minds are governed is uncovered we will see, says the cognitivist, that our behavior was never really free.

The cognitive scientist's theory of the mind is *nothing but* the program itself. But a given program may be instantiated in many ways—by transistors, vacuum tubes, relays, analog circuits, a number of connected abacuses, and so forth. For the cognitive scientist, however, the particular mechanism by which the program is instantiated, while "free" to vary within the system, is held to be unimportant, not the aspect of behavior that makes it seem voluntary. Thus, modern cognitive science is generally deterministic.

III. COMPATIBILISM

If there are several conceivable kinds of determinism there is an even greater conceivable multiplicity of kinds of compatibilism. Compatibilism implies a dualistic approach to scientific activity (if not to existence in general). To understand the compatibilist point of view it might be easiest to go all the way back to the founder of philosophical dualism, the ancient Greek philosopher Plato. In the famous Allegory of the Cave in his dialogue *The Republic,* Plato asked us to conceive a group of prisoners in a cave chained so that they can see only shadows on the wall. The shadows are two-dimensional projections of a three-dimensional world consisting of objects, other people, and even *themselves;* the prisoners cannot even perceive themselves in three dimensions. Then one prisoner is freed and exposed to the three-dimensional world, first the world in the cave behind the prisoners (where a fire projects the shadows), then the real world outside the cave in the sunlight. The main difference between the free man and the prisoners is that the free man has gained knowledge of the three-dimensional world while the prisoners remain ignorant. When in the allegory the free man is returned to the cave the prisoners do not believe his stories of the three-dimensional world and either laugh at him or, worse still, persecute him (a reference to the behavior of the Athenians to Plato's teacher Socrates). In the allegory the prisoners' chains correspond to our own ignorance of reality. Plato sees us as being bound by our own ignorance. The prisoners' two-dimensional world is analogous to *our* three-dimensional world, the world of our perceptions, our pleasures, and our pains. This world, a world of *illusions,* is contrasted with a multidimensional *real world* of what Plato called "Forms." The sun, in the allegory, is compared to The Good; what is seen in the full light of the sun is the real world of Forms. The benefit of behaving in accordance with our pleasures and pains (seeking pleasure) is illusory and *temporary* as contrasted with the benefit of behaving in accordance with the Forms (seeking goodness) which is true and *permanent.* A person whose behavior is guided by mere pleasure and pain is supposed by Plato to be like the prisoners in the cave while a person whose behavior is guided by the Forms is said to be free. According to Plato, everyone *wants* to behave in accordance with the Forms; none of us would willingly trade a worse for a better alternative given that we could accurately weigh worse and better alternatives. The problem is that we are blinded by our pleasures; only the most intelligent of us are capable of accurately weighing all of our alternatives; therefore, only the most intelligent of us are capable of true freedom of behavior. Thus, Plato tied freedom, knowledge, and goodness into one package. We would necessarily have all three of these virtues if our behavior were determined by the Forms. What are the Forms? Where are they located relative to us? How can we bring our behavior into line with them? How can we know if we are succeeding or not? All of these questions were discussed at length in Plato's philosophy and taken up in interpretations and extensions of Plato from Aristotle to present-day philosophers and psychologists. Let us consider three interpretations: *strict dualism, internal/external dualism,* and *molar/molecular dualism.*

A. Strict Dualism

The Forms are to be found not in this world but in another world located somewhere else, perhaps in heaven. We have access to this other world only by revelation from God. This sort of mystical dualism has had little effect on modern psychology. We will therefore not discuss it further.

B. Internal/External Dualism

The Forms are to be found not in the outer world but inside of us. We have access to the inner world of Forms only through deliberate insight exercised by our free wills. This view was formalized in the neoplatonic philosophy of St. Augustine (fourth century A.D.). It separates an illusory *external* freedom of the sort Skinner referred to as freedom from aversive contingencies from true *internal* freedom (freedom of the will). According to Augustine our souls are naturally directed outward to the chaotic world with its random pleasures and pains; our behavior naturally follows this chaotic pattern; when our souls face outward we are like leaves in the wind. However, by an effort of the will (aided by the Christian religion), we can turn from the outer world to an inner world where we can find direction of another kind—from God (equivalent to the world of the Forms). Obeyng God is thus a consequence of turning inward, away from the world, an action we do of our own free will. Even if every move we make is strictly determined by God, our wills are said to be free because by an internal effort of will we freely chose *this* form of control rather than control by essentially random pleasures and pains.

Leaving aside the question of God's foreknowledge of our behavior, Augustine's distinction between behavior controlled by rewards and punishments in the external world (living in "The City of Man") and behavior controlled from the internal world (living in "The City of God") is a kind of compatibilism: looked at one way, behavior is *controlled*—either by rewards and punishments or by God. Looked at another way, we are *free* to determine the *source* of control—from without or within. For Augustine this internal freedom is God's greatest gift to human beings and is also the reason why evil exists in the world. If there were no evil, we could only do what was good; we would never have to choose. God, not us, would be responsible for our good behavior. But, because we *may* do evil, we are responsible for our own good behavior (at the cost of also being responsible for our own evil behavior).

The difference between Augustine and Plato is that for Plato the effort a person has to make to be guided by the Forms is (in modern terms) a *cognitive* effort. For the Forms to guide our behavior, we have to *calculate,* said Plato. Plato's true Forms are thus accessible only to an intelligent elite. For Augustine, the City of God is available not to a cognitive elite but to a *motivational* elite—those who have the spiritual strength (foreknown by God) to turn inward for direction. Once we do turn inward we will automatically do the right thing (our soul will be at peace).

Ironically, while Augustine's conception of an inner world has had a very strong influence on modern psychology, his compatibilism has not. Augustine viewed everyone's inner world as one world; for Augustine, when two individuals both turn inward for direction they both turn to a common God, common principles, common social rules such as the Ten Commandments. Their behavior in such a case would be in synchrony *due* to this common control. For Augustine, we all *inwardly* see the same thing although if we turn outward we see different things—our individual versions of a chaotic world.

More than a thousand years later, during the Renaissance, the French philosopher and mathematician René Descartes was to turn Augustine's conception inside out. For Descartes, the outer world was the source of *common* control; Renaissance physics had just begun to find remarkable regularity in that world. The human commonality of Augustine's inner world, on the other hand, was replaced by the concept of an isolated (and "Free") individual inner soul, identical with the individual mind, with which we are familiar today. Descartes believed that the individual human soul is absolutely free. Although he conceived of people's bodies as just machines and all nonhuman behavior and some human behavior (like the knee jerk and pupillary dilation) as controlled by machinelike reflexes hence strictly determined, Descartes claimed that the most important human actions are controlled by the free, individual mind working through the body (the "ghost in the machine"). Descartes thus abandoned Augustine's compatibilism for libertarianism.

As indicated previously, libertarianism denies the validity of scientific psychology because it exempts the most important human actions from scientific understanding. Descartes' philosophy has therefore been modified by modern psychologists via two routes, both of them deterministic. One route, that of Sechenov and his modern followers in neuropsychology, expands the territory of the bodily machine from simple reflexes to more and more complex ones—from Newton's knee jerk to "Newton enunciating universal laws.'' This form of determinism simply banishes the ghost from the machine—or threatens to do so once physiology has developed to the point where it can explain complex human behavior.

The other route to a scientific psychology, *psychic* determinism, retains the ghost alongside the machine but claims that the ghost itself is not free; the ghost's operations, like the machine's, are said to be lawful. This second route led from Descartes to the beginnings of experimental psychology. The initial impetus of experimental psychology was to discover the ''laws of the mind'' and to give them causal status equivalent to that of physical laws. Once the ''laws of the mind'' were discovered it would be seen that all behavior of all organisms is as involuntary as the behavior of a leaf in the wind. The German philosopher Gottfried Wilhelm Leibnitz (late 17th century) compared the individual mind and the physical world to two clocks (originally set by God) running in parallel, both reading the same time. The workings of the mind were no less clocklike (no less lawful) than the workings of the body—different but corresponding in form.

A common characteristic of this branch of determinism from Gustave Fechner, the founder of psychophysics, to Wilhelm Wundt, the founder of the first psychology laboratory (at Liepzig, Germany, mid 19th century), through Wundt's student, Edward Bradford Titchener, the founder of the first American psychology laboratory (at Cornell University, at the turn of the 20th century), to modern-day cognitive psychology, is the desire to get past *mere* overt behavior to understand the inner laws of the mind. For Wundt and Titchener these laws were structural and associationistic: elementary sensations combined in more complex perceptions combined in turn in still more complex cognitions—all strictly determined, none free in any way—no matter how you look at them.

The anti-structuralists of the early 20th century, the gestalt psychologists, differed from the structuralists on the nature of the mental laws. The gestalt psychologists believed that the laws of the mind worked more like electrical fields than like discrete circuits. But for them the laws of the mind were just as deterministic as the laws of those electrical fields. The deterministic computer model of modern cognitive psychology discussed previously is a continuation of early experimental psychology's search for the laws of the mind.

All psychologies of internal/external dualism have in common the hope of eventually coordinating the laws of the mind with the laws of the body (coordinating one of Leibnitz's clocks with the other). The 18th century British associationist philosopher and physician David Hartley divided his book *Observations on Man, His Frame, His Duty, and His Expectations* into alternate chapters on physical and mental explanation of all human behavior, including moral behavior. Modern cognitive neurophysiology is a much more sophisticated, more rigorous, and more experimentally based endeavor than was Hartley's but it rests upon a corresponding parallelistic determinism—a functional organization of the nervous system running parallel to a functional organization of the mind.

A common feature of parallelistic determinism from Wundt to the present day is its focus on internal causal systems—interactions between one part of the body and another or one part of the mind and another. If the body and the mind are each machines then psychology must be fundamentally directed at discovering the workings of these machines. What are the units of the mind? How are they connected? How do they operate? These are the questions that parallelistic determinism substitutes for Plato's questions about the Forms. The cognitive mechanism is seen as a mechanism for transforming the particulars of everyday experience into abstract conceptions. Trying to understand human behavior (the sort of understanding sought by Plato's wise man who journeyed out of the cave) is for cognitive determinists like trying to understand the program of a computer from analysis of its inputs and outputs. According to some modern cognitivists, understanding of the human mind will be obtained when we can build a computer that successfully simulates it.

Thus, while *strict dualism* leads to libertarianism, *internal/external dualism* has led to the sort of determinism characterized by modern cognitive psychology. We now turn to a third interpretation of Plato's distinction between particulars and abstract Forms—*molar dualism*. This form of dualism leads, as we will see, to modern compatibilism.

C. Molar/Molecular Dualism

The interpretation of Plato's Forms that has led to modern compatibilism is that of his immediate follower and the other great ancient Greek philosopher, Aristotle. For Aristotle (and perhaps for Plato himself), the Forms, as abstract conceptions of objects in the world (objects including other people and ourselves), exist not in another world (as strict dualism says) and not inside us (as internal/external dualism says) but in the world itself. Aristotle saw the dimension of particular-versus-abstract as a dimension of *functional* interaction with one natural world. Thus, although Aristotle was a monist in the sense that he believed in the existence of a single world, he was a pluralist as regards our understanding of the world. Consider a modern example. When we watch a movie we see only one thing—the movie. Our understanding of the movie is usually at the level of character and plot. But in some sense the movie is nothing but colored shadows on a screen. In the usual case, we see *through* the many particular shadows, the many particular "projections" that represent a character in the movie so that we recognize the character immediately each time he or she appears on the screen. In that sense the lights and shadows on the screen may be said to be "perceptually transparent." But we understand this phrasing as a metaphor. The characters do not exist in the room behind the screen—they exist on the screen. Similarly it would be wrong (Aristotle would have said) to think that the particular shadows exist on the screen but the characters exist in our heads. Shadows and characters are just two ways of looking at the screen. (And of course both exist in our eyes and brains as well as on the screen but, as Aristotle insisted, we see the world, we do not see our eyes. Nor do we see our brains).

With some effort we can look at a movie as pure shadow and light—i.e., we can see the movie in terms of particulars and with some effort (plus some considerable experience) we can see the movie at a still more abstract level than characters and plot; a critic for instance might see the movie in terms of the director's style or might even be able to discern the school where the director was trained.

Understanding the Forms, Aristotle said, is just an abstract way of perceiving the world. Aristotle agreed with Plato that the more abstract our vision of the world is, the better we will be able to deal with it. Why? For the same reason Plato gave—because abstract conceptions of the world are relatively *permanent* while particular conceptions are relatively *temporary*.

Since Aristotle lived and died 300 years prior to the birth of Christianity and more than 600 years prior to St. Augustine, he did not conceive freedom as an *internal* attempt to turn away from the particulars in the world but rather as an external and successful attempt to see *through* them and to conceive the world abstractly.

A person who does this is, according to Aristotle, free from particular influences in the same sense that an ocean liner is free from the influence of small waves. A modern concept of *self-control* (inherited from St. Augustine) would view a person on a diet who eats an extra hot dog as *externally controlled* by the smell and taste of the hot dog; the same person refusing the hot dog would be viewed as *internally controlled,* as self-controlled (hence as free). Aristotle, on the other hand, would have seen the eating of the hot dog as caused by the particular qualities of the hot dog, its *particular* taste, its *particular* smell, while the refusal of the hot dog is caused by its abstract qualities: the hot dog as part of an unhealthy diet. Both goals (good taste, good health) are what Aristotle called *final* causes, rather than efficient causes in the sense that they are consequences rather than antecedents of acts. But the good taste is a final cause of the *particular* act of eating the hot dog while the good health comes from no particular act but rather an extended pattern of acts over time. Looked at one way, viewers who respond to the most abstract features of a movie, like eaters who respond to the most abstract features of their diets, are free: free from (in some sense normal or typical) influence by particulars, by immediate forces, by temporary pleasures and pains. Looked at another way their behavior is controlled—controlled by abstractions.

The more complex an organism's behavior is, the more abstract are the principles that explain it. The life of the philosopher, Aristotle said, is the most abstract, and therefore the best and freest life. For Aristotle, even though all of a person's actions are caused (by both efficient and final causes) it is still meaningful to talk of better and worse acts; it is still meaningful to talk of free acts and unfree acts: final causes of free acts are consequences that are beneficial in the long run (to society as well as the individual) while final causes of unfree acts are consequences that may be beneficial only in the short run and possibly harmful in the long run. Thus, Aristotle was a compatibilist.

The influence of this point of view on modern psychology has come through studies of *self-control* or *delay of gratification* discussed elsewhere in this volume [*see* CONTROL]. Nevertheless it will be instructive to briefly summarize one procedure that epitomizes the conflict between particular and abstract. The procedure is a game originally designed for a single player but extended also to groups. In its group form, it is a version of the famous prisoners' dilemma of game theory and is easiest to understand in that form.

The instructions to a group (of 10 members, for example) are as follows:

> Each of you is asked to choose alternative A or alternative B. If you choose alternative A you will get \$$N$. If you choose alternative B you will get \$$(N + 4)$. N will equal the number of members of the group who choose A. (No other member of the group will know what you chose.)

In this game, if all 10 members choose A, each gets \$10. If all 10 members choose B, each gets \$4 ($N = 0$). However, any individual will get almost \$4 more (actually \$3.90 more in a group of 10 members) by choosing B than by choosing A, *regardless* of what the rest choose.

With this game some people choose A and some choose B depending on a host of factors. But the central question the game asks is how do people perceive themselves in relation to the group? Choice of A benefits the group as a whole but hurts the particular individual (relative to choice of B) while choice of B does the reverse.

In its original, within individual, form the game treats the individual from time to time (or trial to trial) as analogous to a group of individuals. Thus, an individual chooses repeatedly between A and B, and is rewarded with N points for choosing A and $N + 4$ points for choosing B. But N is equal to the number of A choices made by the individual over the past 10 trials. As trials go on, N for the present trial is determined by the subject's choice on the previous 10 trials while the 11th-trial-ago is dropped out. Clearly it is better for the individual over time to always choose A, since the person will then average 10 points per trial, than to always choose B (averaging 4 points). Even a single choice of B will lose points on the average.

Again, the degree to which people choose A or B is a measure of the degree to which they see their choices as particular events or as abstract patterns over time because in this game those two perceptions are made to conflict with each other (much like the figure–ground conflicts constructed by the gestalt psychologists).

The only conception of free will that remains meaningful in modern scientific psychology is this originally Platonic conception: when people act for the long-term good of themselves and their society in cases where such acts conflict with their immediate and individual pleasures they may meaningfully be said to be acting freely; they are not constrained by pleasures and pains. This freedom is compatible with a determinism that sees even their choice of abstract good over particular pleasure as in principle predictable.

Bibliography

Ainslie, G. (1992). "Picoeconomics. The Strategic Interaction of Successive Motivational States within the Person." Cambridge University Press, New York.

Beakley, B., and Ludlow, P. (Eds.) (1992). "The Philosophy of Mind" MIT Press, Cambridge, MA.

Dennett, D. C. (1984). "Elbow Room. The Varieties of Free Will Worth Wanting." MIT Press, Cambridge, MA.

Loewenstein, G. F., and Elster, J. (Eds.) (1992). "Choice Over Time." Sage, New York.

Rachlin, H. (1994). "Behavior and Mind." Oxford University Press, New York.

Skinner, B. F. (1971). "Beyond Freedom and Dignity." Random House, New York.

Friendship

Timothy S. Hartshorne
Central Michigan University

Glossary

Intimacy A process involving feelings of being understood, respected, and cared for.

Life task By virtue of being born into society, each individual is confronted with certain conditions or tasks which must be addressed.

Loneliness The affective experience of a discrepancy between desired and achieved levels of social contact.

Social relationship An interpersonal bond in which both individuals recognize and acknowledge the connection; includes friends, family, neighbors, significant others.

Social support The various kinds of aid, emotional, instrumental, informational, individuals receive from their network of social relationships.

FRIENDSHIP is most basically a particular type of social relationship. It can be defined by distinguishing it from other kinds of social relationships such as family and kin, neighbor, and collegial or strict work relationships. These latter relationships, among others, have socially prescribed role characteristics, and occupants can be objectively identified. Friendship, on the other hand, is a voluntary and informal relationship, focused on a particular person, rather than a role occupant. Friends cannot be objectively identified; they must be claimed by an individual as friends.

I. CHARACTERISTICS OF FRIENDSHIP

Friendship can be an ambiguous construct. Just as soon as a defining characteristic is identified, exceptions can be found. For example, the above definition suggests friendship is voluntary, informal, and personal. However, the extent to which it is voluntary is limited by opportunities and prior notions of eligibility. Informality may be compromised when friends come from organizational membership. Also, friendships may be less personal when they are based on group membership.

The ambiguity of this construct is also illustrated by the problem of degrees of friendship. Studies where participants were asked to list their friends, and where those nominated were subsequently contacted and asked to list their friends, have found that mutual choice does not always exist, even when one is nominated as a close friend. This suggests that either some individuals are poor judges of the quality of their friendships, or that different definitions are operating. There is a person I see on a weekly basis at a meeting we both attend. At the end of each meeting we frequently chat, and find we have a lot in common. I look forward to these conversations, and I list this person as a friend. He does not list me. Is this because I am exaggerating the meaning of our relationship, or because I have a broader definition of friend?

In this section we will review how friendship is coming to be understood by social scientists. We will begin by considering the place of friendship in the social setting. We will then examine the dynamic components of friendship (what takes place between friends), the provisions of friendship (what people get out of friendship), and contextual factors (factors that impact on the friendship). Finally, we will look at theories of friendship formation. Why do friendships happen?

A. Friendship as Life Task

People typically consider friendship a voluntary, or freely chosen relationship. This is in contrast to family, who are not freely chosen, or interactions with people at work which are not voluntary. However, a number of social scientists have noted that social

Encyclopedia of Human Behavior, Volume 2
Copyright © 1994 by Academic Press, Inc. All rights of reproduction in any form reserved.

factors which lie outside the immediate control of the individual impact on the patterns and structure friendship takes.

Humans are by nature social beings. But this is not by choice; it is a matter of survival. The strength of humans as a species is certainly in their intelligence, but they use this intelligence to form social groups, or societies. This allows for specialization in roles, and such specialization means no one person must be an expert in everything, and the pooling of individual expertise facilitates the development of the society. To be cut off from the group, or from society, would limit a person's ability to develop, or even to survive. If many individuals chose to cut themselves off from the group, the development or even survival of the society would be threatened. It is therefore imperative, from society's viewpoint, that individuals remain in the group.

Group maintenance requires that people feel that they are an important part of the group, and that they belong with the group. This may be accomplished by society in three ways. First, individuals are expected to find someone to live and bond with, forming thereby and thereafter a family. Belonging should be basic to families. Second, individuals are given functional roles to play that contribute to the well-being of society. If the group needs a teacher, someone is encouraged to take that role, and then they belong by virtue of their contribution. Third, and most important for our purposes, society expects people to get along with each other; in other words, to be friendly. These friendly interactions make people feel that their presence is valued. Note that being friendly is therefore something that society requires of its members, along with love and occupation, for their mutual survival.

Alfred Adler identified these three (love, occupation, and friendship) as life tasks, because they are expectations placed on each individual by life, or by society. Thus, in choosing a friend, an individual is both doing something which is voluntary and free, and meeting a major societal expectation.

The implication of this analysis is that friendship is a relationship with both personal and societal dimensions. It meets both personal and societal needs, its formation is influenced by both personal and societal factors, and the kind of relationship that is formed is an outgrowth of personal and societal dynamics.

B. The Dynamic Components of Friendship

Friendship should be conceptualized as a process rather than as a state. In this manner, every interaction between friends serves to express the relationship as well as to impact upon it. Three processes seem particularly significant to friendship: reciprocity, spending time, and shared connections.

Reciprocity suggests that both members of the friendship dyad get something from the relationship. Friendship is seen as an equity relationship, where the norm is that what a friend does for you needs to be reciprocated in some form. In some friendships this is done on an equal basis, so that if one friend invites the second to dinner, there is an expectation that this second friend will in turn invite the first to dinner. In other friendships this reciprocity is not so much equal as equivalent. One friend may invite the second to dinner, but the second will reciprocate by spending time listening to the first friend's problems. A difficulty is to set an appropriate rate of exchange. Research has found that friends who feel their actions have not been reciprocated may withdraw from the friendship. Also, friends who feel unable to reciprocate may withdraw themselves.

The nature of this reciprocity is sometimes described as either communal or exchange. The norm in communal relationships is to provide services out of concern for the needs of the other person, while the norm in exchange relationships is to expect appropriate returns. This distinction is believed to differentiate between close and casual relationships, with closer friendships following a communal norm. However, in both cases, friendship is supported when something is received in return.

Reciprocity helps to distinguish between friendship and other social relationships. Family members, neighbors, and co-workers may or may not reciprocate services, but they will remain family members, neighbors, and co-workers anyway. Friends who give nothing back stop being considered friends.

Spending time means that friends seek out each other's company. While it is true that people can remain friends for a lifetime with very little contact due to long distance or other excusable reasons, this lack of contact is experienced as negative, and these friends repeatedly express a wish to be reunited.

The experience of separation is one that differentiates between friends and non-friends. We are typically saddened to be separated from a friend. While this may also be true of separation from family, neighbors, or co-workers, their status does not change if we do not experience such emotions. However, it is unlikely that a friendship will continue if we have little interest in spending time together, and experience little sense of loss when separated.

Nevertheless, while friends wish to spend time together, friendship is typically not experienced as exclusive, such as a romantic relationship. There is an expectation and acceptance that friends will have other friends with whom they also wish to spend time.

Shared connections implies that over time friends come to develop a history of shared experiences which is expressed through their friendship. This can sometimes be detected in their language, which comes to express their connection. Some researchers have used the game "Password" as a measure of friendship closeness. This game involves giving verbal clues to a partner about a hidden word. Close friends can often use words based on a shared experience that would have meaning only to them, and could not be used as a clue with any other partner.

Community psychologists have identified a shared emotional connection as being a significant component of a sense of community. This means having a shared history, a common place and time together, and similar experiences, and leads to a sense of belonging. It is this sense of belonging together that serves to maintain a friendship. Shared connections are quite common among family members, and may exist among neighbors and co-workers. However, once again, they appear to be essential dynamics of friendship.

C. What Friendship Provides

Many lists of the benefits of friendship have been proposed by different social scientists. Some of these are thought to vary with the developmental stage of the individual, with gender, or with type of friend. These variations will be considered later. In this section we have selected the three most commonly noted benefits: intimacy, companionship, and social support.

Intimacy has been variously operationally defined, most commonly by measures of self-disclosure, but also by measures of trust, or closeness. It is typically considered a process involving feelings of being understood, respected, and cared for. In this way, it seems very similar to the qualities expected to be demonstrated by a psychotherapist. In fact, intimacy in relationships has been found to be associated with positive mental health.

As will be discussed below, males and females usually differ in degree of intimacy in friendship. However, this may be due to different gender based definitions or understanding of what this term means. In a study of self-disclosure of particular topics, females rated sexual activity as higher on intimacy than males, while males rated family history, personal habits, opinions, feelings, and tastes are more intimate. It is also possible that males and females express intimacy differently. [*See* LOVE AND INTIMACY.]

Companionship means having someone to do and share things with. This is an obvious benefit of friendship. If a person wants company, they can call on a friend. However, socializing can be done to be friendly, and does not necessarily imply friendship. A study of college students found companionship to be listed as a benefit of both close and casual friendships. In fact, having fun together is strongly associated with feeling positive about the relationship.

Social support refers to the various kinds of aid individuals receive from their network of social relationships. Such aid may be in the form of emotional support (reassurance and comfort, being valued and cared for), instrumental support (material or physical assistance, problem solving), or informational support (ideas, suggestions, facts, advice). [*See* SOCIAL SUPPORT.]

Social support has been found to have both direct and indirect benefits. People with good social support seem to experience less stress in their lives (direct effect). In addition, people with good social support seem to cope with stress better than those with limited support (indirect). Social support seems to operate in some cases by directly removing the source of stress, changing perceptions about the threat, or increasing one's personal sense of control.

Social support from family differs from that given by friends due to the problem of reciprocity, which operates in the latter relationship. For that reason friends tend to provide more emotional and informational support than instrumental.

Emotional support from friends often takes the form of moral support, and may occur in both mundane and crisis situations. Acceptance has been found to be the most desired form, and most related to positive outcomes. Reassurance has not been found to be helpful.

Informational help is usually in the form of advice, and is usually appreciated more for problem solving than coping with personal distress. Passing on information about jobs, services, and how-to's is typical.

Instrumental help from friends typically takes the form of practical support such as rides, pick ups, shopping, brief child care, care of house or pets when out of town, etc. Financial assistance is rare between friends, except for a quick loan such as for dinner or a movie. Major instrumental help is usually sought from family and kin.

D. Contextual Factors in Friendship

Friendship takes place in a context. In this section we very briefly review factors that have been found to impact on friendship.

Some friendships are of long duration, while others are relatively brief. Research has found that two-thirds of older persons have had friendships that lasted throughout their life. Little is known about how friendship differs in the context of length. The most obvious difference might be with the shared connections dynamic. People who have been friends a long time have shared a lot of history, and may have a strong sense of "we-ness."

Another context would be depth, or the extent to which people know each other. Some people have a lot of contact, and become very familiar and comfortable with each other. So much contact is not necessarily related to liking, however, but rather propinquity, or the state of being near each other. Propinquity does often lead to friendship formation.

Geographical distance, time, and costs are obstacles that can limit the accessibility of friends to each other. Such distance will limit intimacy, companionship, and social support, thus reducing the benefits of the relationship. However, it is clear that these friendships may in certain circumstances last for many years. Such circumstances still need to be discovered, but may be related to shared connection, based on past benefits.

People enter relationships with different expectations for intimacy, companionship, and/or social support. Such expectations may be related to gender, age, or personality. For example, individuals who are high on self-monitoring (strive to be what is called for by situations) differ from those who are low (behave based on their own dispositions and attitudes) in the way they choose and interact with friends. [*See* EXPECTATION.]

Finally, friendships will differ based on whether the current situation is one of crisis or routine for one or both of the individuals. Clearly the need for certain types of social support will vary, creating issues of reciprocity.

While these kinds of contextual factors would seem to be important, they have tended to be ignored by researchers, who have generally lumped friends and situations together in one group. One exception to this has been the distinction between close and casual friendships. For example, close as opposed to casual college friends have been found to interact more often, for a longer period of time, across a wider range of days and locations, more often in their homes, more often excluding other parties, more often deliberately initiating the interaction, and to gain a greater number of benefits from the interactions. Other research has tried to predict whether a friendship will become close. Variables found to be predictive for males included status similarity, proficiency at "Password," having been roommates, less tendency to avoid certain conversational topics, and less present time geographical distance.

E. Theories of Friendship Formation

Given the number of social encounters each person experiences during the course of a lifetime, it is reasonable to speculate why certain of these encounters turn into friendships, while others do not. We will briefly review four theoretical viewpoints on this question, and then report some of the more frequently identified factors.

Reinforcement theory postulates that when we receive reinforcement from, or in the presence of, another individual, that person will take on a positive value for us, and we are more likely to seek out that person's company. An extension of this position would be that we choose friends from among those individuals with whom we have the best time, or other positive experiences. It has been found that children who receive rewards as part of a group, are more likely to choose group members for further interaction.

Exchange theory postulates that rewards or benefits of a relationship need to outweigh the costs, at least in terms of other alternative relationships, in order for a friendship to develop and maintain. Costs may be such things as wasted time, irritation, or boredom. It has been found that profit value (benefits minus costs) is correlated with the perception of how interaction affects a friendship. However, benefits were more strongly related to close friendships, while costs were significant for casual friendships.

Cognitive consistency theories postulate that friendships are formed in part to maintain a balance in relationships, so that if A is friends with B and C, then B and C are likely to form a friendship. B and C are also likely to become friends if A dislikes both of them. This position is supported by research findings that people are attracted to those who share similar values and beliefs and who like the same people they do.

Development theory postulates that the attraction in a relationship is based on different factors as the friendship develops. For example, external attributes such as physical attractiveness may influence the early stage of a relationship, followed by perceived similarity in values and beliefs. Next, increases in intimacy, companionship, and social support become significant. Finally, friends experience dyadic crystallization, or commitment to a long-term relationship. Of course, a negative appraisal at any stage may lead to deterioration or ending of the friendship. This theory tends to be supported by retrospective accounts, where people recall how their friendship developed. However, this theory is contradicted by research showing that people can predict rather quickly whether a friendship will develop, and that they immediately behave differently with these people. Unfortunately, the research on both sides of the issue has tended to lump together different kinds of social relationships.

A number of factors have been listed by researchers as important in friendship formation. These include propinquity (we become friends with people we are near to), familiarity (we come to like people we spend time with), similarity (we are attracted to people who seem to be like us in social status, career, education, values, attitudes, etc.), complementarity (we like to be with people who are our complement in various ways), and rewardingness (we like those who reward us).

F. Summary

Friendship is a task, or problem, significant to society, and so cannot be ignored. Friends reciprocate with each other, spend time together, and construct a shared history. As a benefit they experience intimacy, companionship, and social support. Friendship is experienced in different contexts such as duration, depth, accessibility, expectations, crisis, and closeness. Finally, friendship develops from propinquity, familiarity, similarity, complementarity, and rewardingness.

II. GENDER AND ETHNIC DIFFERENCES IN FRIENDSHIP

In reviewing above the characteristics of friendship, group differences in how these characteristics might be experienced were not discussed. This section considers gender and ethnic differences in friendship. Then the following section considers age differences.

A. Gender Differences in Friendship

Males and females have same-sex friends, and they also have cross-sex friends. Research suggests that males and females experience friendships differently, and that same-sex and cross-sex friendships also differ.

The primary gender differences identified are that females have a slightly smaller network of friends, spend more time with friends conversing and sharing, and experience more intimacy. Males, on the other hand, have a somewhat larger friendship network, spend more time engaged in specific activities with their friends, and experience more companionship.

Social scientists at one time saw significance in the social network size differences between males and females, claiming that females either had inferior skills at forming friendships, or that their role as housewives limited out of the home contact. Today it is recognized that while men maintain larger networks, they tend to have weaker ties, while women's networks, regardless of size, are more intimate and expressive.

Female relationships have been described as more "face to face," while male friendships are more "side by side." Women spend time talking with their friends, and see this as central to their relationship. Men like to engage in activities such as sports, where they are focused on some external goal. This may be one reason why similarity as a variable in friendship formation differs by gender, with females oriented toward shared values, and males toward shared interests.

It has also been noted by a number of researchers, as mentioned above, that males and females may have different definitions of intimacy. Nevertheless, on most measures of intimacy (such as self-disclosure), females do experience more with their friends than do males. However, these are mean differences, and the total range is generally the same for both genders; that is, some males experience as much self-disclosure as the most self-disclosing females. Men also tend to be more self-disclosing to their female friends than to their male friends, while females are less self-disclosing to their male friends than to their female friends.

Recognizing the dangers in overinterpreting mean differences, some researchers have looked at how sex-role orientation influences these gender differences. The results tend to be mixed, and difficult to interpret, but in general gender differences in friendship become less significant when measures of masculinity–feminity and androgyny are taken into account. Most researchers therefore point to socialization into sex roles as the primary source of gender differences in friendship. [*See* SEX ROLES.]

Cross-sex friendships, other than romantic ones, have received less attention. This may be because nonromantic, nonfamilial, personal relationships between men and women are viewed as rather ambiguous and even deviant, in that the norms are unclear, role models are lacking, and such friendships tend to be viewed with suspicion. However, today, more than ever, professional men and women interact together in many ways and contexts. Friendship would seem a logical outgrowth, as well as an appropriate context within which men and women can come to better understand, respect, and appreciate each other; providing an "insider's perspective" to the opposite gender.

Cross-sex friendships do present some challenges: determining the type of emotional bond the relationship represents, dealing with the issue of sexuality, coping with the barrier of inequality, and learning how to present the relationship as authentic to relevant audiences.

B. Ethnic Differences in Friendship

It seems reasonable, since friendship exists in a cultural milieu, that ethnic and racial differences would exist in how it is experienced. Very little research has addressed this question. One study found that taboo topics for self-disclosure to friends differed for British and Chinese students. Another study found British students to value sensitivity and humor in friendships, while Chinese students stressed money-mindedness and creativity. In addition, a study found middle-school black children to have larger neighborhood friendship networks than white children. Clearly, this is an area in need of more investigation.

Slightly more research has looked at cross-ethnic friendships. With similarity, familiarity, and propinquity as major variables in friendship formation, it is not surprising that cross-ethnic friendships are less common, and not well researched. Children in the early grades are more likely than later to have friends from other ethnic and racial groups. Cross-racial friendships have been found to be less stable for children in grades 4 to 6. While most students from an integrated school said they had cross-racial friends, only about a quarter reported seeing these friends outside of school. Blacks, and children from integrated neighborhoods, reported more friendships in nonschool settings. Three school organization factors have been found to be related to interracial friendships in school: classroom racial composition (affecting opportunities), instructional practices (especially those like grouping that intensify status differences), and reward structure (cooperative being more facilitative than competitive).

III. FRIENDSHIP THROUGH THE LIFESPAN

Simple observation suggests that the nature of friendship changes through the lifespan. While friendship as a life task remains constant, the focus of friendship undoubtedly varies. Stage theory has been a popular way to examine human development, and stages of friendship development have been proposed. We will review friendship within major developmental periods. It is important here to make a distinction between friendship and peer relations. The latter are more general group interactions, involving such issues as conformity, popularity, and reference group.

A. Infancy

Can infants under the age of 18 months form friendships? Freudian and Piagetian influences have led to a focus on the mother–infant bond for personality and cognitive development. However, infants as young as 12 months do interact with peers, and show preferences for some over others, although the source of such preference seems restricted to familiarity.

In a laboratory setting, including mother, stranger adult, and stranger peers, the infant seeks to maintain physical contact with the mother, but does make more distal contact with peers, while mostly avoiding the stranger adult. When a familiar peer is included, the infant is more likely to engage in positive proximal activities with that peer. When given a chance to play with a stranger peer outside the laboratory for several weeks prior to coming to the lab, the infant shows a preference for interaction with the now familiar versus a new stranger peer, including more positive affect, and more willingness to share a toy.

Propinquity and familiarity appear to be the keys to infant friendship, along with the ability to use a parent as a secure base for social exploration.

B. Childhood

Preschool friends might better be described as "playmates." While they can now name particular children as their friends, and they spend more time interacting with those they so identify, activities are largely games, object sharing, and pretending.

However, by kindergarten and first grade, precursors to social support can be noted. Friends may be conceptualized as helpers; for example, the child who helps to pick up something spilled. Reciprocity is also noted, although self-interest predominates. Friends can be more clearly differentiated from acquaintances, being observed as more involved with their partners, more emotionally expressive, and more competitive.

Middle childhood friendships may be longer lasting than infant and preschool, possibly because they are increasingly based on similarity. Most friends are of the same age and sex, and increasingly the same race or ethnicity. These friendships also involve more self-disclosure, especially for girls, and thus more intimacy. Gender differences are emerging, as boys tend to have more friends, and spend more time with friends in active play. [*See* PEER RELATIONSHIPS AND INFLUENCES IN CHILDHOOD.]

C. Adolescence

It is during adolescence that intimate and mutually shared relationships with friends fully develop. A key factor in judging close versus casual friendships is trust. Key concerns with friends are revealing a secret and backstabbing. This is due to the identity concerns of the adolescent, as they are defined by various audiences (family and peers) and as they are coming to know themselves. This can produce a tension between public comportment (the basis of popularity) and private communication (the basis of intimacy). By their public comportment, adolescents test their ability to fit in, and be accepted by society. By their private communication, adolescents test the acceptability of their more private selves through their intimate self-disclosure. Should a friend violate the confidence, peer acceptance is threatened, and the risks of intimacy are heightened. [*See* ADOLESCENCE.]

Friendship during adolescence changes from a more superficial relationship in early adolescence, to a more intimate sharing in middle adolescence, and then to a more realistic relationship, which is more autonomous and interdependent, in later adolescence. The early adolescent is still largely concrete in thinking, and this is reflected in the sharing of things, time, and favors, as opposed to ideas and possibilities which characterize formal operational thinking. The middle adolescent is excited by the hypothetical, and enjoys testing the limits of the possible, and their sharing with friends may take a bizarre turn from time to time, as they self-disclose outlandish possibilities for themselves, trusting in the friendship to keep them from going too far into extremes. By late adolescence, individuals have a better sense of who they are, and no longer need friends to be a continuous sounding board. Friendships can now be based more on who the other person is, and what they bring to the relationship. Friendship is now less possessive, and based less on superficial characteristics such as physical attractiveness and popularity.

D. Adulthood

Because most research is conducted on the American college student, less is known about postcollege adults, and this is certainly true in the area of friendship. The friendship as life task orientation would suggest that in adulthood there is a greater orientation toward the community as a whole, and on being friendly and socially responsible. Most surveys find the average adult lists 5 or 6 friends, although the range extends from no friends to as many as 25 or more.

The basis of friendship changes. Middle aged persons typically list good judgment, family commitment, and viewing others as valued individuals as the basis of friendship. Being perceived as polite, friendly, having similar values, interests, and background are important now. Living near each other and working together are a factor in friendship choice. Physical appearance, however, has disappeared as a variable.

Both middle aged men and women report spending less time with their friends than they once did; however, the strength of the relationship and amount of self-disclosure have increased over time. Women report their friendships to be more important and intimate than do men. However, men's friendships seem to have lasted longer.

Marriage has an influence on friendship patterns, particularly for men. Many men identify their wife as their best friend. While unmarried men self-disclose to friends about as much as do married and unmarried women, after marriage they report less self-disclosure. However, while marriage affects men's self-disclosure to friends, they report high self-disclosure to their spouse. Married women also report a high degree of self-disclosure to their spouse, but they maintain their high levels of intimate self-disclosure to friends, although their nonintimate self-disclosure is lower than for unmarried women. [*See* MARRIAGE.]

E. Old Age

As the population ages, researchers have directed more attention to the elderly, and friendship in old age has been a topic of concern. As people age their needs for social support may increase as they are confronted with mobility, health, and stamina difficulties. At the same time, the death and retirement moves of friends may reduce the size of their social network.

The stereotype of old person as nursing home resident clearly distorts the life experience of the majority of older persons who are living independently and enjoying themselves. Friendships in old age have the same characteristics as before, providing intimacy, social support, and companionship. Best friends are associated with a communal as opposed to an exchange orientation. Women have fewer, but more intimate friendships. Older women are also more likely than men to still have a close friend from the past.

Friendship may be defined in terms of particular individuals who are viewed as irreplacable, or friendship may be defined as a kind of relationship which is more important than the individuals involved. Older persons holding the first definition are viewed as more vulnerable to the loss of friendship in old age, while those holding the latter are more open to acquiring new friends. One study found that about one-third of the elderly in their sample had made a new friend in the past year.

Some elderly are placed in nursing homes. Friendships there have been found to be less intimate, but to still provide pleasant interaction, companionship, and social support. While these elderly may not discuss personal matters with friends, feelings about life in the home are frequent topics of conversation, with the focus on happy or angry feelings, and less so on sad feelings.

Family continues to play a significant role in the life of the older person; however, these relationships may involve problematic obligations and conflicts from the past. Friendships provide an alternative set of relationships that are more flexible and less encumbered.

IV. THE CONSEQUENCES OF HAVING OR NOT HAVING FRIENDS

A recent study presented 45 adult women with a stressful task to perform at home, in the presence of a female friend, a pet dog, or neither. Participants in the friend condition demonstrated higher physiological reactivity and poorer performance, than those in the other conditions.

Does this study mean that friends are a bad thing, leading to poorer life performance? Certainly there are times when we may experience friends as looking over our shoulder and evaluating our actions. Researchers have found that negative interactions with friends are associated with less satisfaction with the relationship. However, friends may also, as we have seen, be an important source of support for us as we go through life. In this section we will briefly review some of the areas where friends have been found to have a positive impact, or the lack of friends a negative one.

A. Self-Concept

It is said that you are judged by the company you keep. The fact that a person makes a particular friendship choice says something about the kind of person he or she is. Some social scientists suggest that we form friendships because they support, reward, or reaffirm our sense of who we are. Friends may help us to express or recognize important attributes of ourselves. They may encourage our positive self-evaluation. They may facilitate our personal growth. We may feel safe to risk self-disclosure of our authentic selves with friends.

Studies have found a relationship between the extent to which friends are seen as displaying empathy, congruence, and unconditional positive regard, and measures of self-esteem. While all three were significant for females, only the first two proved significant for males.

B. Mental Health and Adjustment

The direct and indirect effects of social support on stress were noted above. Here some recent research regarding the elderly and adolescents will be briefly summarized.

Depression in the elderly has been of concern. Research has found a correlation between friendship activity and depression. For example, frequency of contact with friends is related to a less depressed mood. Due to its correlational nature, it may be that friends help reduce depression, or that people who are less depressed engage in more activity with friends, or some other variable may account for the association. [*See* DEPRESSION.]

The healthy adjustment of adolescents has also been of concern. Research has found intimacy more closely associated with psychological adjustment than popularity. Other studies have examined the influence of friends on such behaviors as delinquent acts and substance abuse. Friends' use of drugs, engagement in delinquent acts, lack of achievement, and religious orientations have been found to be correlated with adolescent substance abuse. Interestingly, what adolescents believe their friends do is more highly related to their own choices, than what friends actually do. [*See* SUBSTANCE ABUSE.]

C. Interpersonal Competence and Social Skills

The ability to form friendships may involve some skill. In broad terms, one needs to recognize, select, and make the most of opportunities for friendship. One needs strategies and techniques for enticing likable persons into a friendship. One needs to know ways to help relationships develop and grow. It is also useful to have skills for maintaining and repairing relationships. It has been suggested that people actually engage in strategic planning to create perceived desirable friendships.

Programs and interventions to develop social skills have recently been developed, and are used in the schools with positive outcomes. However, it is clear that not all children or adults need social skills training. They seem to be able to form friendships without formal training. Little is known about how such skills develop, although the literature on friendship development suggests that these skills are learned through the experience of friendships while growing up. Friendships perform an educative function. Children experiment with tactics for including and excluding, and thereby learn friendship skills. Friendship can thereby be viewed as contributing to an individual's interpersonal competence.

D. Loneliness

Is loneliness the absence of friends? In an absolute sense, this is clearly not the case. There are people who have no friends, but do not experience loneliness, and there are others who have many friends, but who still describe themselves as lonely. Thus, loneliness is most often defined as a discrepancy between desired and achieved levels of social contact. While not all social contact consists of friends, it is reasonable to assume that friendships have an impact on the experience of loneliness.

Studies of lonely college students find that they spend more time alone, have fewer close friends, and date less frequently. In addition, they tend to be more anxious, depressed, neurotic, and shy, and report lower self-esteem and a more negative outlook on life. Major predictors of loneliness in college males include social competence and sex-role orientation, while for college females they include friendship satisfaction and perceived social support.

A relationship between friends and loneliness is not only found with college students. A study of working adults found loneliness correlated with the degree to which a person's friends are friends with each other. Studies of the elderly have found that contact with friends reduces the experience of loneliness. Interestingly, contact with family members produces no such effect.

E. Summary

Having friends seems to make a difference in people's lives. It may foster self-esteem, mental health, social competence, and inhibit loneliness. Such a relationship is predicted from the idea of friendship as a life task, expected by society of each individual. Perhaps the most basic contribution of friendship, and one which is made reference to by a number of writers, is a sense of belonging. Through the experience of intimacy, companionship, and social support, people come to feel that they are valued as human beings, that their presence in these relationships has meaning both to themselves and to their friends, and that they are indeed a part of a community: in other words, they belong.

Bibliography

Allan, G. (1989). "Friendship: Developing a Sociological Perspective." Westview Press, Boulder.

Derlega, V. J., and Winstead, B. A. (Eds.) (1986). "Friendship and Social Interaction." Springer-Verlag, New York.

Duck, S. (Ed.) (1988). "Handbook of Personal Relationships: Theory, Research, and Interventions." Wiley, New York.

Hartshorne, T. S. (1991). The friendship life task and family life satisfaction. *Individual Psychol. J. Adlerian Theory, Res. Practice* **47,** 477–481.

Ladd, G. W. (1988). Friendship patterns and peer status during early and middle childhood. *Dev. Behav. Pediatr.* **9,** 229–238.

Rizzo, T. A. (1989). "Friendship Development among Children in School." Ablex, Norwood, NJ.

Youniss, J., and Haynie, D. L. (1992). Friendship in adolescence. *Dev. Behav. Pediatr.* **13,** 59–66.

Genius, Eminence, and Giftedness

Nancy Ewald Jackson
University of Iowa

Glossary

Creativity The production of problem solutions, ideas, or products that are novel, unusual, and valued by a society.

Eminence Prominence within a field of expertise valued by a society, as indicated by expert colleagues' judgments or by the frequency with which an individual's work is used by others in the field or mentioned in history.

Genius Sustained production of problem solutions, ideas, or products that are extraordinarily unusual and valued extremely highly by a society; an individual whose creative acts or products have changed the nature of a discipline or the lives of others in important ways.

Giftedness Although the term sometimes is used as a synonym for creativity or superior intelligence, in this article it is used more broadly to include these two phenomena; a demonstration of excellent performance on any task that has practical value or theoretical interest. This use includes excellent performance on tests of intelligence and exceptionally rapid learning of new knowledge or skills. Because it does not focus on the social value of products, giftedness as defined here is of interest primarily in the study of children.

Intelligence An individual trait that is somewhat stable across the lifespan and is expressed in superior performance on standard tests of knowledge and reasoning as well as in adaptive functioning in everyday life. Intelligence has diverse aspects.

GENIUS, EMINENCE, GIFTEDNESS, and the other terms that are listed above are all used in multiple ways by behavioral scientists, and what one researcher calls genius might be described as eminence, creativity, or giftedness by another. These are fuzzy, overlapping concepts, but they are distinguishable. Different individuals would be cited as prototypes of each concept. For example, most of us would choose different labels from the set above as the best descriptors for Albert Einstein, Georgia O'Keefe, Martin Luther King, Ronald Reagan, and Elvis Presley. Furthermore, many people who would be identified as highly intelligent by both behavioral scientists and their own friends and associates never achieve eminence or demonstrate any remarkable degree of creativity, much less genius. The purpose of this article is to describe and attempt to explain these various forms of exceptional superiority, emphasizing how giftedness, genius, and eminence develop across the lifespan.

I. INTRODUCTION

A. Brief History of the Field

Common usage of the term *genius* traditionally has emphasized the idea that such extraordinary ability must reflect some extraordinary process, such as the giving of a gift by the gods. Throughout the history of Western civilization, genius has been linked with

Encyclopedia of Human Behavior, Volume 2
Copyright © 1994 by Academic Press, Inc. All rights of reproduction in any form reserved.

other extraordinary, equally inexplicable, phenomena such as madness and physical illness.

The scientific study of genius can be traced back to the mid-19th century and the work of the English aristocrat-scientist Sir Francis Galton. Galton observed that eminence tended to run in families and assumed that eminence reflected genius. Like his contemporaries, Galton also assumed that genius was the result of an inborn ability, transmitted genetically.

Galton proposed that genius could be measured and quantified much as physical traits such as height and weight can be. However, systematic measurement of what was then called genius and would now be called superior intellectual performance was not possible until the early 20th century, when the first practical intelligence test was developed by Alfred Binet and Lewis Terman. Like Galton, Terman initially believed that genius was an inborn trait that should be readily detectable in childhood. He used the Stanford-Binet Intelligence Scale to identify 1500 California schoolchildren whom he described as geniuses by virtue of their superior performance on the test. Most of the children in Terman's sample earned IQs of 140 or more, far above the average score of 100. [*See* INTELLIGENCE.]

Partly as a result of Terman's longitudinal research, which has continued throughout the lives of the original sample of children, psychologists gradually began to realize that superior performance on a test of intelligence administered in childhood was no guarantee of genius as defined in this article. The contributions of individual experience and cultural context to the development of both intelligence and genius began to be recognized. For example, Terman and his colleagues found that those highly intelligent boys in his sample who had successful professional careers were more likely than equally intelligent, but less successful, boys to have had well-educated, relatively affluent parents. Factors other than degree of superiority in childhood intelligence seemed to determine which of the gifted group were most successful professionally.

Terman and his colleagues also demonstrated that high intelligence was not generally associated with poor mental or physical health. This conclusion was consistent with Sigmund Freud's theory of creativity as a healthy channeling of instinctual energy into productive work. However, the idea that there is a link between mental superiority and mental illness did not disappear from the scientific literature when Terman's findings appeared. Freud also suggested that creativity might be related to neurosis, and researchers such as Leta Hollingworth pointed out the socioemotional challenges faced by individuals whose development was so exceptional that they did not fit easily into their social worlds. [*See* CREATIVE AND IMAGINATIVE THINKING.]

Research on the intellectual and personality characteristics of creative individuals began to flourish in the 1950s, and tests were developed to measure individual differences in the fluency and originality of people's responses to open-ended questions. Some progress was made in identifying the characteristics of highly creative individuals in various professions, but the new tests of creative thinking processes were not strong or unique predictors of meaningful creative productivity. These tests do tap abilities distinct from those displayed on tests of intelligence, but the problems they pose are necessarily trivial. Research in the past 20 years has demonstrated that creative achievement within a professional domain depends in large part on having access to a mental store of richly interconnected knowledge about the domain.

B. Current Issues, Perspectives, and Methods of Study

Current approaches to the study of genius, eminence, and giftedness include retrospective biographical studies of eminent individuals, prospective longitudinal studies of the intellectual, professional, and socioemotional development of children or young adults identified as gifted, and cognitive psychological studies of the mental processes involved in producing creative products or problem solutions. The study of exceptionally superior individuals and exceptionally superior performance is becoming more and more closely tied to basic research and theory on the nature of individual differences in cognition, motivation, and personality. For example, one important approach to studying basic questions about human problem solving is to analyze the performance of experts in domains such as chess or physics. In a related line of research, computer programs have been written to mimic aspects of human creative problem solving and problem finding. These programs have been used to test theories about the nature of creative-thinking processes. [*See* PROBLEM SOLVING.]

Longstanding questions continue to guide studies of genius, eminence, and giftedness. Can we identify children who have especially high potential for becoming creatively productive adults? What kinds of families and schools nurture the development of genius and creativity? How and why does creative productivity wax and wane across the lifespan? What is the link between genius and madness?

II. GENIUS AND GIFTEDNESS IN CHILDHOOD

A. Childhood Genius and Giftedness: Domains of Superiority

One confusing legacy of Terman's research is that children who have earned extremely high scores on intelligence tests are sometimes described as geniuses or as having "genius-level IQs," even though they have not accomplished anything that would justify calling them geniuses by adult standards. Contemporary researchers prefer to describe superior intellectual or creative performance in childhood as an instance of giftedness. Expressions of giftedness change with age.

Researchers have not yet identified any pattern of infant behavior that strongly predicts gifted performance in later years. However, there is some suggestion in the literature that highly intelligent infants are efficient information processors who quickly become bored with familiar sights and sounds and turn their attention to novel events from which they can continue to learn something new. In children of preschool age, giftedness often is manifest in a remarkable memory for information encountered in everyday life, in the ability to learn new things very quickly, in sophisticated use of language, in early mastery of complex concepts, and in precocious reading. However, giftedness in early childhood can develop and be expressed in diverse ways. For example, Einstein is reported to have begun talking unusually late, but to have spoken in complex sentences as soon as he began to converse.

Some theorists have suggested that intellectual giftedness in children is a general phenomenon that becomes more specialized with age. According to this theory, one of two children who appeared equally gifted at the age of 6 years might develop special strength in the use of language and verbal reasoning and become a historian or lawyer, while the other might develop special strength in manipulation of visual–spatial patterns and become a physicist or architect. This theory is plausible because the development of a high level of talent in any domain requires the investment of a great deal of time and energy, and individual children's opportunities and choices might focus their talents in one area or another. However, we do not yet know enough to exclude the possibility that specialized aptitudes are present and potentially detectable in very young children.

Children display specialized gifts earlier in some domains than in others. A child is more likely to produce work good enough to attract widespread professional attention in domains such as musical performance, chess, computer science, or mathematics than in creative writing or the social sciences. Those domains most conducive to the production of child prodigies tend to be those in which a limited and clearly structured body of information can be mastered rapidly by systematic study.

The most extreme kind of specialized giftedness is the savant syndrome, from the French term *idiot savant,* or wise fool. Children and adults who have been diagnosed as mentally retarded or autistic sometimes show remarkable islands of talent for doing mental arithmetic, using systematic information from calendars, maps, or timetables, performing complex piano music after a single hearing, or creating sophisticated drawings from memory. Savants intrigue many researchers interested in genius because they display some aspects of genius-like intellectual power without showing even average intelligence in other aspects of their lives [*See* AUTISM; MENTAL RETARDATION.]

B. Cognitive and Socioemotional Characteristics of Highly Intelligent or Gifted Children

Most studies of gifted children actually have been studies of children who, like those in Terman's sample, earned high scores on intelligence tests. One simple and at least partly adequate way of describing the thought processes of very intelligent children is that their thinking is precocious, that is, similar in form to that of older children of average intellectual ability. However, this description is not perfect. It works only as a description of preadolescent children. By the time they have reached the age of about 12 years, intellectually superior children are beginning to show a degree of efficiency and power in their thinking that less able individuals never will attain.

The description of high intelligence or giftedness as precocity also fails to allow for the unevenness of gifted children's development. Intellectually superior children are likely to be less advanced than older children of average ability in performing tasks that depend heavily on physical (possibly neurological) maturation or the acquisition of world knowledge and strategies that are likely to be accumulated only with life experience. On the other hand, recent evidence suggests that intellectually superior children are especially well able to understand the requirements of new tasks and figure out effective ways of doing them.

Children who have developed remarkably mature knowledge and ability to solve problems in one specialized domain, such as chess or music, often do not show comparably advanced performance on other intellectual problems. For example, a 10-year-old chess whiz would be likely to be better than most adults at remembering positions of chess pieces on the game board but inferior to adults and comparable to her age-mates at remembering other kinds of information.

Children identified as gifted according to a criterion such as high performance on a test of general intelligence are diverse in their socioemotional characteristics. In general, high intelligence gives a child some advantage in identifying, analyzing, and solving social or emotional problems. Highly intelligent children tend to be popular with their peers and generally well adjusted. Nonetheless, aspects of gifted children's socioemotional development may lag behind their intellectual development. Even the brightest 3 year old may sometimes have the temper tantrums common at that age, and a gifted 12 year old may giggle and gossip with her friends in typically preadolescent ways. [*See* SOCIOEMOTIONAL DEVELOPMENT.]

Children whose intellectual gifts make them extremely different from their peers also face special challenges. The 13-year-old boy who is capable of doing college-level academic work needs to struggle to create a life in which he can find intellectual challenge and rewarding work, friends who share both his intellectual and his recreational interests, and acceptance of his age-dependent physical and social limits. Children who have been identified as gifted also face the burden of living up to their own and others' high expectations, possible guilt about access to special privileges or attention, and, sometimes, hostility from others.

C. Origins of High Intelligence and Giftedness in Childhood: Genetic, Family, and Sociocultural Factors

Superior intellectual performance, as manifest in high scores on standard intelligence tests, seems to be influenced by both genetic and environmental factors. The extent to which one or the other influence is a more important source of individual differences depends on the particular group of children being studied and the circumstances in which they are growing up. In the United States today, the circumstances in which children grow up are so variable, and so often suboptimal, that many children do not have the opportunity to develop their full genetic potential.

On the average, families whose children develop superior intellectual ability, creativity, and giftedness in various forms are characterized by at least moderate socioeconomic status, by involvement in childrearing, and by parenting behaviors that show warmth and nurturance combined with firm but reasonable discipline. Among children who all have high potential for superior intellectual performance, differences in achievement that are related to family characteristics often become evident during the high school years. Mihaly Csikszentmihalyi and Kevin Rathunde have suggested that adolescents who translate their intellectual ability into high achievement come from homes in which their parents have set high standards and provided enough structure to foster a sense of security, while also allowing opportunity and support for creative expression and encouraging independence.

Eminent individuals often have had abundant opportunities during their childhoods to become seriously engaged in study related to their ultimate area of achievement. They also are likely to have been omnivorous readers with numerous hobbies and interests.

The achievement of eminence is more likely among only or oldest children or those who hold a family position that marks them for special parental attention in some other way. Robert Albert has concluded that highly creative, as opposed to merely effective, individuals are likely to have lost a parent in childhood through death or divorce or to have experienced other sorts of family tension or turmoil. However, Csikszentmihalyi has argued that the careers of eminent individuals who came from harmonious, supportive homes are less troubled and in some ways more productive than those of individuals whose creativity grew out of an unhappy childhood.

The best way to get a sense of the kinds of families that cradle genius is to read biographies and autobiographies of great artists and scientists. For example, the kind of structured encouragement common in the backgrounds of many eminent scientists is evident in the way Nobel laureate physicist Richard Feynman describes his father's behaviors:

> Before I was born, my father told my mother, "If it's a boy, he's going to be a scientist." When I was just a little kid, very small in a highchair, my father brought home a lot of little bathroom tiles—seconds—of different colors. We played with them, my father setting them up vertically on my highchair like dominoes, and I would push one end so they would all go down.
>
> Then after a while, I'd help set them up. Pretty soon, we're setting them up in a more complicated way; two white tiles and a blue tile, two white tiles and a blue tile, and so on. When my mother saw that she said, "Leave the poor child alone. If he wants to put a blue tile, let him put a blue tile."
>
> But my father said, "No, I want to show him what patterns are like and how interesting they are. It's a kind of elementary mathematics." So he started very early to tell me about the world and how interesting it is. [R. P. Feynman, as told to R. Leighton (1988). "What Do You Care What Other People Think? Further Adventures of a Curious Character," p. 12, Norton, New York]

Feynman's younger sister also earned a Ph.D. in physics, although she did not achieve the same degree of eminence as her brother.

Circumstances beyond the family influence the development of giftedness and genius. A child's potential is most likely to develop if there is a good match between his or her aptitudes and cultural values. Potential chess prodigies, musical virtuosos, or extraordinary computer programmers are more likely to develop in a society in which children are exposed routinely to chess games, musical instruments, or personal computers and encouraged to become engaged with them. These circumstances tend to be unevenly distributed, and different social groups are likely to be under- or overrepresented among the eminent in various disciplines. For example, in the United States today, women and members of several ethnic minority groups are much less likely than white males to pursue high levels of study in mathematics or to achieve eminence in the mathematically oriented sciences. Some theorists have attempted to attribute these group differences in achievement to differences in innate ability, but biological explanations have not convinced most behavioral scientists who study genius and giftedness. Nonbiological explanations include gender and ethnic stereotypes such as those that influenced parental attitudes in the Feynman family, differences in propensity for risk-taking and tolerance for confusion, and differences in values that influence career choices.

III. GENIUS, EMINENCE, AND SUPERIOR ACHIEVEMENT IN ADULTHOOD

A. Predicting Genius and Eminence in Adulthood from Performance in Childhood

When Terman identified 1500 California schoolchildren as, he thought, potential geniuses, he succeeded in selecting a number of men who would be highly successful in their professions, including the eminent behavioral scientists Lee J. Cronbach and Robert Sears. However, he failed to pick a single child who would become a Nobel laureate or achieve comparable prominence in the arts, politics, or industry. Two future Nobel laureates were reportedly among the children his screening system could have picked up, but rejected. The most promising children do not always become the most eminent adults, and genius cannot be predicted from any simple combination of child and environmental characteristics. Theorists have proposed several hypotheses about why the emergence of creativity, genius, or eminence is hard to predict, even though tested intelligence has moderate stability from childhood to adulthood. One hypothesis is that requirements and opportunities for success in a discipline change as an individual matures cognitively and socially, moves to more sophisticated levels of achievement, and interacts with a discipline in different contexts. For example, as a developing artist matures from a young child scribbling at the kitchen table to work as a mature professional, he or she must deal with a succession of personal and professional challenges. Time to complete artistic projects may compete with other interests or responsibilities, more sophisticated instruction and more expensive materials may be needed, and the standards by which the artist's work is judged will change.

Many excellent students never are able to go beyond efficient solution of problems that are set for them to the identification and solution of important novel problems. Some individuals may lack the risk-taking propensity or sustained commitment and self-discipline needed to do creative work at a professional level. In general, a child is likely to reach a high level of creative productivity and eminence only with the most fortunate convergence of individual aptitude, opportunity, support, and societal circumstances.

Biographies of Nobel laureates and other eminent scientists reveal the importance of factors other than sheer intellectual power in the development of genius and creativity. As students, future Nobel laureates are likely already to be aware of the importance of working with the right mentors and identifying the right problems to study. Becoming a successful scientist involves making and using the social connections that will permit access to important new ideas and research tools and developing a sense of how the field is moving. A few scientists have achieved eminence despite spending their early careers pursuing an independent path outside the mainstream of work in their field, but they are the exceptions.

B. Age-Related and Domain-Related Patterns in Achievement

Becoming a genius takes time and study. Although we may delight in the spontaneous creativity of young children, the ability to generate important new ideas seems to rest heavily in thorough knowledge of the discipline in which one is working. Artists, scientists, and public leaders all need time to develop their own unique voice or creative perspective.

Across a number of different fields, it seems to take about 10 years of study in a discipline to become an expert capable of doing creative original work. However, the age at which individuals begin doing important creative work varies across disciplines. For example, poets and mathematicians tend to do their best work at an early age, often while still in their 20s. In contrast, novelists, historians, geologists, and behavioral scientists peak later.

Dean Keith Simonton has proposed a mathematical information-processing model in which creative productivity is related to two characteristics of a discipline, *ideation rate* and *elaboration rate,* and two characteristics that can vary across individuals, *age at career onset* and *creative potential.* The rate at which new ideas are produced (ideation rate) and the rate at which these ideas can then be transformed into completed projects (elaboration rate) are set at different levels for each discipline because the time course of the creative process differs across fields. It takes longer both to get a good idea for a novel and to write and publish the novel than it does to conceive, complete, and publish a poem.

The chronological age at which one can begin producing important work within a discipline varies depending on the amount of formal education required. Therefore, on the average, poets and musicians are likely to achieve eminence at earlier ages than scientists. However, a poet who begins late in life should, according to Simonton, suffer no disadvantage other than a time-based restriction in total productivity.

Within a given field, a few eminent individuals contribute most of the important creative work. Those individuals who have the most creative potential produce the most work, both good and bad, throughout a lifetime, but their careers will wax and wane much as the careers of their less able colleagues do. Figure 1 depicts the life course of productivity for four hypothetical individuals working within the same discipline but varying in their initial creative potential and chronological age at career onset. The two top curves represent early-starting individuals with low or high creative potential and the two bottom curves represent later-starting individuals with low or high potential. An individual with a high level of creative potential who enters this field at age 20 is likely to make his or her best contribution at about age 40, but a late starter with identical potential who begins working at 30 will peak at age 50. The total productivity (area under the curve) for both of these individuals will exceed that of an individual with less potential. Also note that both the high-potential and the low-potential individuals take about 20 years to reach their most productive year; this span is determined by the constant ideation and elaboration rates for their common discipline.

Simonton's model has been developed and tested by examining the productivity of eminent historical figures in various fields. For example, the life course of a musician's first, last, and most important creative contributions could be estimated by looking at the frequency with which works composed in different years have been recorded and performed.

C. Creativity, Personality, and Mental Health

The link between genius and madness assumed by the ancients has not disappeared with systematic scrutiny, but the boundaries of the association have become clearer. Eminence in the sciences does not seem to be associated with high risk for mental illness of any sort. However, some groups of creative artists,

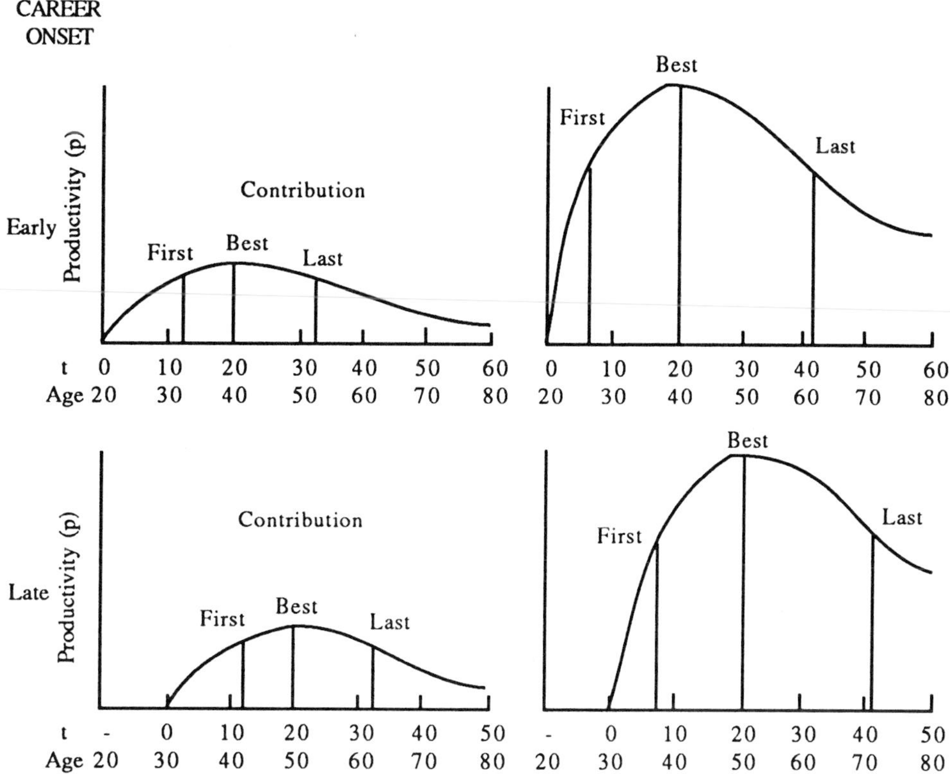

FIGURE 1 Four hypothetical curves expressing annual productivity as a function of career age, with ideation and elaboration rates held constant, but with individual variation in initial creative potential (high or low) and in career onset (early or late). [Reproduced with permission from D. K. Simonton (1992). The child parents the adult: Getting genius from giftedness. In "Talent Development: Proceedings from the 1991 Henry B. & Jocelyn Wallace National Research Symposium on Talent Development" (N. Colangelo, S. G. Assouline, and D. L. Ambroson, Eds.), pp. 278–297. Trillium, Unionville, NY.]

especially writers, seem to be likely to come from families with high rates of mental illness and to be unusually at risk for developing illness themselves.

Some of the most systematic research into links between creativity and mental illness has been done by Nancy Andreasen, who has studied creative writers and their families. Andreasen hypothesized that the fluid, unconventional thought processes characteristic of schizophrenics might make this illness especially common among creative writers. However, the eminent writers she studied were not especially prone to schizophrenia. The kind of mental illness most common in writers, relative to other professionals, is affective illness, especially disorders that involve drastic mood swings from elation (mania) to depression. Writers also seem to be especially prone to alcoholism, which can be both a cause and consequence of depression. Perhaps a high rate of productivity is facilitated by manic energy. Also, people who suffer from some degree of affective mental illness may tend to choose the independent life of a creative artist, free to reject social norms and to set their own standards and schedule. Yet another possibility is that there is some genetic linkage between a potential for verbal creativity and potential for affective illness, even though there is no direct behavioral link between the two phenomena. [*See* DEPRESSION; SCHIZOPHRENIA.]

More and less creative individuals also have been found to differ within the realm of normal variation in personality. For example, Donald MacKinnon and his colleagues found that, relative to their less successful colleagues, architects who were especially creative and successful were more open to new experience, self-assertive, impulsive, competitive, and domineering, but less likely to be sociable, accommodating, and appreciative of others. Personality differences between the more and less successful architects remained stable and increased across their later careers. This is one of several studies in which creative people have shown characteristics that might make them difficult to get along with in everyday life. Robert Albert has suggested that confidence in and commitment to one's own critical perspective, a tendency to see what is wrong with the current state of affairs, contributes to creative productivity.

IV. CURRENT ISSUES AND DIRECTIONS FOR FUTURE RESEARCH

Research currently is moving toward greater attention to the diverse realms in which people can be intelligent or creative and to the potentially different thought processes involved in, for example, verbal, social, or visual–spatial problem solving. The search for simple links between childhood giftedness and adult eminence is being replaced by preliminary models designed to capture the complexity of development. Behavioral scientists are becoming more comfortable thinking about individual accomplishment as something that must be understood in a sociocultural context. Finally, studies of giftedness, creativity, and genius are becoming more theoretically and methodologically sophisticated and attracting the attention of a wider group of behavioral scientists.

Bibliography

Albert, R. S. (1992). "Genius and Eminence," 2nd ed. Pergamon, New York.

Horowitz, F. H. & Friedman, R. C. (Eds.) (in press). "The Gifted and Talented: Theories and Reviews." American Psychological Association, Washington, DC.

Klein, P. S., and Tannenbaum, A. J. (Eds.) (1992). "To Be Young and Gifted." Ablex, Norwood, NJ.

Ochse, R. (1990). "Beyond the Gates of Excellence: The Determinants of Creative Genius." Cambridge University Press, Cambridge, UK.

Rothenberg, A. L. (1990). "Creativity and Madness: New Findings and Old Stereotypes." Johns Hopkins University Press, Baltimore.

Shurkin, J. N. (1992). "Terman's Kids: The Groundbreaking Study of How the Gifted Grow Up." Little, Brown & Co., Boston.

Sternberg, R. J. (Ed.) (1988). "The Nature of Creativity: Contemporary Psychological Perspectives." Cambridge University Press, New York.

Treffert, D. A. (1989). "Extraordinary People: Redefining the 'Idiot Savant.'" Harper & Row, New York.

Gestures

Peter Bull
University of York, United Kingdom

Glossary

Aphasia Any disorder of speech resulting from brain damage.

Emblems Refers to those nonverbal acts which have a direct verbal translation such as nodding the head when meaning "yes" or shaking the head when meaning "no."

Illustrators Movements directly tied to speech which amplify and elaborate the verbal content of the message.

Phonemic clause Consists of a group of words, averaging five in length, in which there is only one primary (or tonic) stress indicated by changes in pitch, rhythm, or loudness. It is terminated by a juncture, where these changes in pitch, rhythm, and loudness level off before the beginning of the next phonemic clause.

Regulators Movements which guide and control the flow of conversation, influencing both who is to speak and how much is said.

THE TERM GESTURE may be used to refer to communication through the hands and arms (manual gesture), but is also used in a wider sense to refer to communication through other parts of the body (the head, trunk, legs, and feet). As a form of movement, gesture is conventionally distinguished from posture, which refers to static positions. Gestures typically occur in conjunction with speech, but not always: they may occur as a substitute for speech, when talking is difficult or impossible.

I. INTRODUCTION

The study of manual gesture can be traced back to Cicero and Quintilian, who both wrote treatises on rhetoric, which included a number of observations on the use of the hands in oratory. However, it was only during the 17th century, with the publication of works such as Bonifacio's *L'Arte dei Cenni* (1616) and Bulwer's *Chirologia . . . Chironomia* (1644) that gesture acquired the status of a subject in its own right. Bulwer's work was exclusively concerned with gesture, with what he called "the naturell language of the Hand, as it had the happiness to escape the curse at the Confusion of Babel." As the title indicates, there are two sections in the book: Chirologia and Chironomia. Chirologia comprises a descriptive glossary of 64 gestures of the hand and 25 gestures of the fingers. Chironomia is a prescriptive guide to the proper usage of an additional 81 gestures during well-delivered discourse, as well as cautions against the improper use of "manual rhetoricke."

The scientific study of gesture has only become possible with the development of sophisticated recording apparatus; most contemporary studies of gesture have used either film or videotape as the main technique of observation. The great advantage of working with recorded material as compared with "live" observation is that it allows for repeated viewing; this is particularly important for complex sequences of movement, which can be replayed time and again, if necessary, in slow motion. The great disadvantage of using videotape or film is that it is dependent on a human observer to transcribe and, if necessary, to code the behavior into appropriate categories. It is customary to check an observer's scoring by carrying out a reliability study in which his coding of behavior is correlated with that of an independent observer. Nevertheless, manual methods of transcription are still extremely time consuming and fatiguing, and limited in their accuracy.

As an alternative, people have more recently started to work with fully automated systems of mea-

Copyright © 1994 by Academic Press, Inc. All rights of reproduction in any form reserved.

surement. One such system is known as polarized-light goniometry. This operates by projecting strong light from a single source through a plane polarizer material and a rapidly rotating disk onto a photosensor (or photosensors) attached to the subject. The reflected light is automatically processed by the goniometer to provide immediate information on properties of movement such as its rate, duration, range, and speed. One particular advantage of this apparatus is its sensitivity to small movements, which a human observer working from videotape might miss or find very difficult to classify. Another advantage is its precision—by taking direct readings of speech amplitude, it is possible to make fine measurements of the relationship between head movements and speech. A disadvantage of the system is that it does not allow a detailed description to be given of the visual appearance of particular movements.

An automated system which does give a visual representation of movement involves attaching a data glove to the subject. The glove is linked to a computer which can generate a detailed graphic representation of hand movement, which may then be subjected to further analysis. However, both these automated systems suffer from the necessity of attaching recording apparatus to the body; this has the disadvantage of making the subjects aware of the focus of the investigation, which may make them self-conscious. Furthermore, there are many situations in which the use of such devices would not be practical. For these kinds of reasons, videotape analysis will undoubtedly continue to play a significant role in research on gesture for the foreseeable future, and most of the studies described below are based on this technique.

II. EMOTIONS AND INTERPERSONAL ATTITUDES

A. Cultural Universals in the Facial Expression of Emotion

Particular importance is commonly ascribed to nonverbal cues in the communication of emotion. However, in this respect gesture appears to play an essentially subordinate role to the face. Charles Darwin proposed that if the emotions are expressed in the same way in different cultures, then these expressions are probably inherited, whereas if they differ between cultures, then they are probably learned. Modern research has shown that the facial expressions associated with seven emotions (anger, fear, happiness, sadness, surprise, disgust, and contempt) are decoded in the same way by members of both literate and preliterate cultures. However, even if one accepts the existence of universals in decoding, it is only necessary to hypothesize that whatever is responsible for common facial expressions is constant for all mankind: inheritance is one such factor, but learning experiences common to all mankind could equally well be another. Nevertheless, children born both deaf and blind show the basic repertoire of facial expressions of emotion, and all but one of the discrete muscle actions visible in adults can be identified in neonates born without any such handicaps. It is also the case, however, that we can learn to control our facial expressions through the learning of what are called display rules—norms governing the expression of emotion in different contexts. Display rules may take the form of attenuation, amplification, substitution, or concealment of particular expressions. It is now generally accepted that there are at least seven fundamental emotions with innate facial expressions, but that these can also be modified through the display rules described above. [*See* FACIAL EXPRESSIONS OF EMOTION.]

B. Gesture and Facial Expression

There is no such evidence for cultural universals in gestural expression. However, a number of studies have been carried out in which people were asked to make judgments of emotion from the face alone, the body alone, and the whole person. If body movement is important in the judgment of emotion, then the accuracy of judgments from the whole person should be superior to that from the face alone. But in practice this seems not to be the case. Decoders appear to base their judgments on the face more than on the body, they found it easier to agree on the face and their judgments from the face were more accurate. Nevertheless, one potential problem with these studies is that the facial expressions and body movements may have differed in their degree of informativeness; the decoders may simply have paid more attention to whichever feature was carrying the most information. Moreover, there seems to be no reason in principle why gesture should not convey information about particular emotions, since we speak of people jumping for joy, or clenching their fists in anger, or cowering in fear. However, it is possible these gestures only occur under conditions of intense emotion, and were not reflected in the studies described above. In fact, in certain situations gesture does convey significant information about emotions and interpersonal attitudes. One such situation is deceptive communication. Because the face is so visible and has the capacity to send many different sorts of messages quickly, it is important to control facial expression when engaged in deception. In one study, students of nursing were asked to watch two films, one intended to be pleasant, the other intended to be stressful (showing amputations and the treatment of severe burns). The nurses were interviewed after seeing the films, and were asked to describe their reactions to the pleasant film honestly, but to conceal any negative reaction they might have had to the stressful film. Videotapes of the interviews were shown to observers, who were asked to guess which film the nurses had just seen; they were significantly more accurate when making these judgments from the body than from the face. When the nurses were asked what expressions they should control or what they should do in order to avoid detection, significantly more of them mentioned the face than the body.

Embarrassment is another emotion which people often try to conceal. One ingenious experimenter contrived to study embarrassment in the laboratory by arranging a structured interview: the subject was asked to select from a collection of pictures the one which he or she most disliked and was then asked a series of 15 questions concerning the reasons for that choice. In the eighth question, the interviewer revealed that he himself had painted the picture (he had in fact painted all the pictures in the original collection). After the interview was over, each subject was shown a videotape of the interview and asked to rate their response to the eighth question on a list of 19 emotion categories which included embarrassment, to check that the experimental manipulation had been successful. Subsequently, the videotapes were shown to another group of observers, who were asked to identify embarrassment or amusement from the face, the body, or the face and the body together. Accurate recognition of embarrassment required both facial and body cues, while amusement required only facial cues; in fact, embarrassment was incorrectly identified as amusement by those observers who saw the face alone. The decoders who saw both the face and the body were also asked which cues they had used to identify embarrassment; those which were significantly associated with accurate recognition were the eyes, the hands, the mouth, and the lower legs. [*See* EMBARRASSMENT AND BLUSHING.]

C. Gender Identification Signals

Gestures are also important in conveying information about sexual attitudes, through what are sometimes called "gender identification signals." In one study, on the basis of a questionnaire intended to measure sex-role attitudes, three groups of men and women were selected: one with strongly masculine characteristics, another with strongly feminine characteristics, and a third described as "androgynous" (with characteristics of both sexes). Each subject was then asked to role play being a junior high school math teacher, and each performance was videorecorded. The videotapes were then shown to observers, who were asked to rate the encoders in terms of masculinity/feminity under five different conditions: from the vision alone (head and body), the head only, the body only, the voice, and a still photograph. The observers were only able to accurately guess the sex-role attitudes of the encoders in the vision alone and the body alone conditions. Physical appearance or clothing seemed to be unimportant, since the observers could not make accurate guesses when they saw only the still photographs. Thus, movements of the body seem to be important in conveying information about sex-role identification. [*See* SEX ROLES.]

In fact, sex differences in the use of gesture seem to occur as young as 4 or 5 years old. This has been highlighted by studies of children with sexual identity problems, who appear to make exaggerated use of gestures which are associated with the opposite gender. In two studies of normal children, researchers found that girls made significantly greater use of five of the "effeminate" movements used by gender-disturbed boys. These were referred to as the limp wrist, flutters (rapidly moving the arms up and down), walking with a flexed elbow (where the angle between the upper arm and forearm is between 0 and 135°), the hand clasp (touching the hands together in front of the body), and palming (a grooming movement which involves touching the palm to the back, front or sides of the head above the level of the ears). Thus, it appears that there are significant differences between the sexes in the use of gesture, and furthermore, that gesture is of considerable importance in conveying information about sex-role attitudes and sex-role identification.

D. Dominance and Submission

Gesture also conveys information about other interpersonal attitudes, such as dominance and submission. It was Charles Darwin who proposed that "making oneself smaller" appeases and inhibits human aggression. This suggestion has been taken up by modern researchers studying how fights between boys are resolved. They found that just before the fighting stopped, the boy under attack would often reduce his body stature in some way, for example, by bowing his head, slumping his shoulders, lying motionless on the ground, kneeling, or through what was called "waxy flexibility" (the child allows the aggressor to manipulate his body without offering muscular resistance). An interesting alternative which achieved the aim of reducing body stature indirectly was the use of shoe tying.

In another study, the researchers observed fights which were terminated by the intervention of a third person. In a significant number of cases, the third person intervened against an antagonist who continued to attack a child exhibiting some kind of appeasement display, which involved a diminution of body stature. Thus, both these studies suggest that making oneself smaller does function as an appeasement gesture in human conflicts, which is also likely to provoke intervention by other people if the signals are ignored by the aggressor. In fact, the way in which these boys inhibit aggression through making themselves smaller finds obvious parallels in formal status systems where an inferior greets a superior by bowing, kneeling, or even by kowtowing, a custom in Imperial China whereby the inferior touched the ground with his forehead in absolute submission. [*See* AGGRESSION.]

III. THE SYNCHRONIZATION OF BODY MOVEMENT

The central importance of nonverbal cues in the communication of emotion has led some writers to regard body movement as an alternative system to speech, offering a more reliable indicator of people's true feelings. This has been especially true of the popular literature on "body language," in which it seems to be represented as a kind of "royal road to the unconscious," providing a vital source of information about people's "real" feelings and attitudes. One particular danger of this viewpoint is that it neglects the extent to which speech and body movement complement one another in communication; indeed, it may be the case that incidences in which nonverbal communication conflicts with speech are the exception rather than the rule. In fact, frame-by-frame analysis of film has shown how the body of the speaker moves closely in time with his speech, a phenomenon which is referred to as self-synchrony. These observations have not been confined simply to hand gestures; it is movements of all parts of the body which are believed to be closely synchronized with speech. [*See* NONVERBAL BEHAVIOR.]

It has also been claimed that body movement is closely synchronized between conversationalists, sometimes referred to as interactional synchrony. It has been said not only that "the body of the speaker dances in time with his speech," but also that "the body of the listener dances in rhythm with that of the speaker." It has been claimed that interactional synchrony is a fundamental, universal characteristic of human communication, which provides constant feedback from the listener to the speaker concerning the listener's level of attention and interest. These claims for interactional synchrony were based on detailed frame-by-frame analysis of filmed conversations. They were subsequently criticized by other researchers, who found that body movement coordination between the participants in a group conversation did not significantly exceed that which might have been expected by chance alone. Thus, the concept of interactional synchrony is very much open to dispute. [*See* INTERPERSONAL COMMUNICATION.]

There is much more evidence for self-synchrony, although it is not the case that every bodily movement is related to discourse. In a study of psychotherapy sessions, it was only noncontact hand movements (movements which do not involve touching the body) which were judged as related to speech; contact hand movements were considered for the most part to be unrelated to speech. In political speeches, it has also been found that it is principally noncontact rather than contact hand movements which are related to vocal stress. Thus, for the most part it seems that contact movements serve different functions from noncontact gestures. This is further supported by a study which found that nonsignalling movements (e.g., stroking oneself) were used significantly more by high anxious patients, while low anxious patients made significantly greater use of signalling movements (e.g., pointing). Self-touching movements are often used not for communication but as a grooming activity, so that under conditions of high anxiety they may be used as a means of reassurance.

There are several ways in which nonverbal behavior has been shown to be related to speech, and these are discussed below.

A. Syntax

The relationship between syntax and body movement was studied by analyzing the speech of a patient in a psychotherapy session. Observations were made of the number of postural shifts, leg movements, and foot movements and it was noted whether they coincided with syntactic boundaries. A movement was scored as coinciding with syntax if it took place within but not across the duration of a clause. It was found that most of the observed body movements fell within syntactic boundaries, and hence it was concluded that body movement is closely related to syntax. [*See* Syntax.]

B. Vocal Stress

Discourse has a discernible structure based on strings of words which seem to be spoken as a unit, known as the phonemic clause or tone group. A phonemic clause consists of a group of words, averaging five in length, in which there is only one primary (or tonic) stress indicated by changes in pitch, rhythm, or loudness, and which is terminated by a juncture, where these changes in pitch, rhythm, and loudness level off before the beginning of the next phonemic clause. It has been observed that most speakers of American English accompany their primary stresses with slight jerks of the head or hand, while junctures are accompanied by a movement of the head, eyes, or hands. In a study of informal conversation, it was found that over 90% of tonic stresses were accompanied by body movement; these were movements not only of the head or hands, but also trunk movements and movements of the legs and feet. In a study of political speeches, it was found that a large proportion of the speaker's hand movements were related to vocal stress. Repeated movements, where, for example, the speaker extends and flexes his forearm continuously for two or more occasions, always occurred within the duration of a tone group and never violated tone group boundaries. These repeated movements seem to serve a dual function: they both pick out stressed words and demarcate the extent of the tone group. [*See* Phonological Processing and Reading.]

C. Meaning

Body movement is also closely related to the meaning of speech, and a number of different semantic units have been identified which are articulated by posture. So, for example, it has been observed that an American speaker may hold the position of his head and eyes for a few sentences before shifting the attitude to another position. Each of these shifts has been regarded as marking the end of a structural unit at the next level higher than the syntactic sentence. It has been called "a point," because it corresponds roughly to making a point in a discussion. A sequence of several points go to make up a "position," which corresponds roughly to a point of view that a person may take in conversation; the position is marked by a gross postural shift involving at least half the body. The totality of one person's positions go to make up the "presentation," which may last from several minutes to several hours; it is terminated by a complete change in location.

These observations have been confirmed in studies carried out in a number of different social settings. In a detailed analysis of a conversation filmed in a London pub, it was found that the trunk and leg movements of one speaker occurred only with changes of what was called a "locution cluster"; this refers to a change in what the speaker is talking about, and appears to be very similar to the concept of the position. Similarly, in a study of television news, two BBC newsbroadcasters were found to use distinctive hand movements when introducing the next item, clearly marking out topic changes through specific changes in posture. Again, in a study of informal conversation, it was found that speech which introduced new information was significantly more likely to be accompanied by distinctive changes in posture. Thus, body movement appears to be clearly related to the meaning of speech, as well as to syntax and vocal stress.

IV. THE FUNCTIONS OF GESTURE IN CONVERSATION

It has also been argued that nonverbal behavior serves a variety of functions in relation to speech, which can be divided into emblems, illustrators, and regulators. The term "emblem" refers to those nonverbal acts which have a direct verbal translation, such as nodding the head when meaning "yes," or shaking the head when meaning "no"; their function is communicative and explicitly recognized as such. Illustrators are movements directly tied to speech, which amplify and elaborate the verbal content of the message. Regulators are movements which guide and control the flow of conversation, influencing both who is to speak and how much is said.

A. Emblems

Emblems are generally assumed to be specific to particular cultures or occupations, but there do appear to be pan-cultural emblems such as the "eyebrow flash," where a person raises his eyebrows for about a sixth of a second as a greeting; this has been observed in a wide number of differing cultures. In one study, the geographical distribution of 20 emblems was mapped across western and southern Europe and the Mediterranean. The findings showed that whereas some emblems were specific to one particular culture, others were much more widespread. In Italy, for example, pressing and rotating a straightened forefinger against the cheek (sometimes referred to as the cheek-screw) is a gesture of praise; it is, however, little known elsewhere in Europe (see Fig. 1). Another gesture referred to as the nose-thumb, in which the thumb touches the tip of the nose with the fingers pointing upward spread out in a fan, is widely known throughout Europe as a form of mockery (see Fig. 2). The meanings of other emblems vary between cultures. For example, a gesture sometimes called the ring, where the thumb and forefinger touch to form a circle, in Britain means something is good, in parts of France means something is worthless, while in Sardinia it is an obscene sexual insult (see Fig. 3)!

Some emblems have a long history. The Roman author Quintilian, writing in the first century A.D., describes a hand gesture which is formed by the first finger touching the middle of the right-hand edge of the thumb nail; this graceful gesture he says was well suited to express approval. It seems to correspond almost exactly to the ring emblem described above,

FIGURE 1 The cheek-screw. [Based on a photograph in D. Morris *et al.*, 1979, "Gestures: Their Origins and Distribution," Jonathan Cape Ltd., London. Reproduced by permission.]

FIGURE 2 The nose-thumb. [Based on a photograph in D. Morris *et al.*, 1979, "Gestures: Their Origins and Distribution," Jonathan Cape Ltd., London. Reproduced by permission.]

FIGURE 3 The ring. [Based on a photograph in D. Morris *et al.*, 1979, "Gestures: Their Origins and Distribution," Jonathan Cape Ltd., London. Reproduced by permission.]

since Quintilian's precise description of the relationship between the thumb and the first finger almost necessitates the adoption of a circular ring-like position. Again, the emblem known as the nose-thumb is referred to as early as 1532 in the writings of the celebrated French author Francois Rabelais, who devotes a whole chapter to a duel of gestures between two of his characters. The nose-thumb is also depicted in a 1560 print entitled "La Fete des fous" by Pieter Brueghel. In fact, in the 17th century, John Bulwer in his *Chirologia . . . Chironomia* gave a detailed description of a whole number of emblems; this represents the first such book of its kind in the English language.

Clearly the function of emblems is communicative, and they constitute a form of nonverbal communication of which people have explicit awareness. The question arises, however, why emblems should have emerged as an alternative form of communication to speech. It has been argued that they are often used when speech is difficult or impossible, and hence function as an alternative system to speech. For example, the policeman directing traffic on points duty and the deaf-and-dumb person using sign language can both be said to be using emblems in situations where speech is not possible. Emblems are also useful for communicating at a distance; many familiar signing systems are used in a variety of sports by officials communicating at a distance with other officials, players, and spectators. Some of the most notorious emblems are, of course, insults; it may be advisable to use emblematic insults at a distance, since it makes it more difficult for the insulted person to retaliate!

B. Regulators

Regulators are movements which are assumed to guide and control the flow of conversation, for example, in the way in which people exchange speaking turns. In an intensive set of studies of turn-taking it was found that attempts by the listener to take over the turn could be essentially eliminated by the speaker continuing to gesture; this was called the attempt-suppressing signal. Observations also showed that ceasing to gesture was one of five turn-yielding cues, signals that offer a speaking turn to the other person. It was proposed that the effect of these five cues is additive: a linear relationship was found between the number of turn-yielding cues displayed and a smooth switch between speakers. The other cues were the completion of a grammatical clause, a rise or fall in pitch at the end of a clause, a drawl on the final syllable, and stereotyped expressions such as "but er" and "you know."

C. Illustrators

Illustrators are movements which are directly tied to speech, and it is maintained that they facilitate communication by amplifying and elaborating the verbal content of the message. Whether illustrators do in fact facilitate communication was tested in one study in which a silent film was made of various events, such as a car making a series of turns, or a tennis ball bouncing into a corner. Observers were asked to view these events and to describe them to another person who was unable to see the film. These descriptions were videotaped and shown to a second group of observers with sound and vision, with sound only, or in a modified audio-visual condition where the contrast was reduced to obliterate facial information and hence prevent lip-reading. Comprehension was found to be significantly better in the modified audio-visual condition than in the audio only condition, thus suggesting that illustrators do facilitate speech comprehension independently of the information obtained from lip-reading.

V. THE DISTINCTIVE PROPERTIES OF GESTURE

Gesture clearly has a variety of functions in interpersonal communication, but the question naturally arises as to why gesture is used in addition to speech. The concepts of "illustrators" and "regulators" imply that gesture is essentially subordinate to speech, amplifying and elaborating the spoken word. However, gesture and speech have very different characteristics as media of communication. First, since gesture requires sight for its transmission whereas speech requires hearing, the conditions that are suitable for the reception of the two do not necessarily coincide. Second, whereas in speech it is the sequential and syntactic structure which is important, this is not the case with gesture; but it can be used to directly represent action sequences. Despite these radical differences, it is important to note that these two modes of expression are employed together in a highly integrated fashion, participants often freely choosing between them to meet the requirements of the communication task at hand. The distinctive features of gesture are discussed below and their implications for interaction considered.

A. Gesture as a Visual Means of Communication

The most obvious feature of gesture is that it is a visual means of communication. It is often easier or quicker, for example, to point to an object than to describe it verbally. Similarly, some gestures are like representative pictures in that they attempt to represent the visual appearance of an object, spatial relationship, or bodily action, sometimes referred to as "physiographic." This hypothesis was tested in an experiment in which English and Italian students were asked to communicate information about two-dimensional shapes to other students from their own culture, both with and without the use of hand gestures. The decoders drew what they thought the shapes were, and these were rated by English and

Italian judges for their similarity to the originals. The results showed than when gesture was permitted, the drawings were judged as significantly more accurate; furthermore, this effect was significantly more pronounced for the Italians, thus providing some evidence in support of the popular view that gesture is of particular importance in Italian culture.

B. Gesture as a Silent Means of Communication

Because gesture is visual, it is also of course a silent means of communication. So, for example, gesture is often employed when it is difficult or impossible to use speech because of distance or noise. The speech channel may be momentarily blocked by noise, but it may also be blocked because it is already occupied. In multiparty conversations, the use of gesture may occasionally be observed by people who are not participating in the conversation. In this context, gesture may be used to comment on an interaction, without interrupting the flow of speech. This may be done cooperatively or critically, so that the commentator does not have to take a speaking turn.

An additional feature of gesture is that for its use people do not seem to have to enter into the same kind of mutual obligation as they do in conversation. As a consequence, in certain circumstances gesture may be a quicker means of communication, because gestural exchanges do not require the ritual conduct associated with conversation. A comparable feature of gesture is that it may often be used in situations where the speaker seeks to be less fully bound or committed to what he or she has to say. So gesture is sometimes adopted as a substitute for speech, where speech might be regarded as too explicit or indelicate.

C. Gesture as a Form of Bodily Action

Gesture by its very nature is a form of bodily action and this also gives it certain advantages in communication. The appearance of an action can never be as adequately described in words as it can be represented through gesture. So, for example, gesture may be of particular importance in mimicry or in demonstrating how particular skills should be performed. Because gestures can be reminiscent of physical actions, they may acquire additional forcefulness as a consequence: a clenched fist may convey anger more effectively than a torrent of words. This may give gesture especial importance in the communication of emotions and interpersonal attitudes.

D. Gesture as a Visible Means of Communication

Another important feature of gesture is that it is not only visual but also a highly visible means of communication. So, for example, one study of a birthday party showed how people used gesture as an initial salutation to capture one another's attention before entering further into conversation. In a study of medical consultations, it was found that when the doctor's attention was focused on his notes, patients would use more flamboyant gestures as a means of attracting his attention. In this context, gesture has the additional advantage of indirectness as well as visibility, since a direct request to a higher status figure like a doctor might well prove unacceptable.

A situation characteristically associated with the flamboyant use of gesture is that of public speaking. In this context, gesture has distinct advantages over other forms of nonverbal communication such as facial expression or gaze which may be less discernible to a distant audience. This can be illustrated through the detailed analysis of a political speech delivered in the 1983 British General Election campaign by the leader of the National Union of Mineworkers, Arthur Scargill. Scargill made extensive use of a number of rhetorical devices which have been identified as being effective in evoking applause, in particular, contrasts (e.g., "there's something criminally insane about a government which puts war before peace") and three-part lists (e.g., "Soviet Marxism is ideologically, politically, and morally bankrupt"). Analysis showed that Scargill used gesture to illustrate both these devices. In the case of contrasts, he employed ambidextrous gesturing, switching from one hand to the other as he moved on to the second part of the contrast: through his gesture he is literally saying "one the one hand" and "on the other hand" (see Figs. 4 and 5). With regard to three-part lists, the three items in each list were invariably marked out by carefully synchronized gestures. Where the list comprised three words, each word was stressed vocally and accompanied with a single hand gesture: where the list included a phrase or clause with more than one vocal stress, then a repeated movement was usually employed picking out two or more vocal stresses and terminating at the end of the list item, then a new gesture started on the next item (see Figs. 6 and 7).

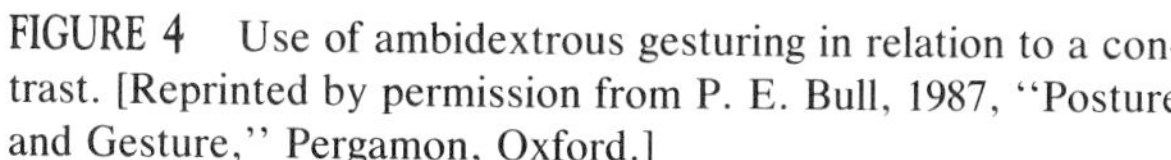

FIGURE 4 Use of ambidextrous gesturing in relation to a contrast. [Reprinted by permission from P. E. Bull, 1987, "Posture and Gesture," Pergamon, Oxford.]

FIGURE 5 Another example of ambidextrous gesturing in relation to a contrast. [Reprinted by permission from P. E. Bull, 1987, "Posture and Gesture," Pergamon, Oxford.]

Another common rhetorical device which Scargill used to evoke applause was what has been called the "headline–punchline" device, in which the speaker states that he is going to make a declaration, pledge, or announcement, and then proceeds to make it (e.g., "I'll tell you the most important task [headline]: it's to say to the Lord Matthews, it's to say to the Lord Rothermeres, it's to say to the Rupert Murdochs that the first obligation of a new Labour government will be to take into common ownership the press" [punchline]). On three occasions, Scargill progresses from unilateral to bilateral gestures for the final part of the punchline (see Figs. 8 and 9). This seems to have the effect of bringing the rhetorical device to a climax, highlighting the fact that here was an appropriate point in the speech for the audience to applaud.

If Scargill's hand gestures are closely intertwined with rhetorical devices which have the effect of arousing applause, they also constitute a significant part of the way in which he attempts to control applause. On 12 occasions he uses gesture to control applause either by holding his hand or index finger outstretched; on two-thirds of these occasions he uses such a gesture just before a point in the speech where applause might have been considered appropriate, in that he was about to present a statement in one of the rhetorical devices discussed above (see Fig. 10). This is a noteworthy example of the use of gesture as a regulator, since the speech channel is, so to speak, "jammed" by the applause; in effect, he cannot make himself heard, so he uses gesture instead as a means of controlling the applause. In

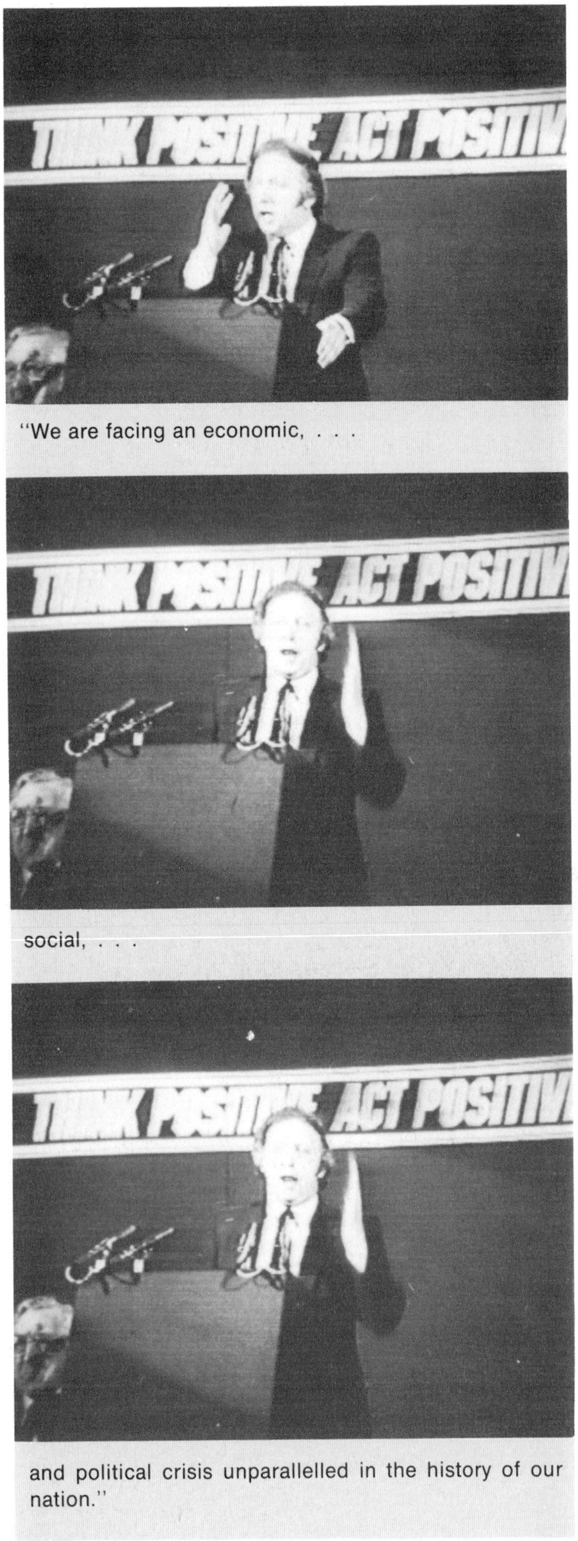
"We are facing an economic, . . .
social, . . .
and political crisis unparallelled in the history of our nation."

FIGURE 6 Gesture in relation to a three-part list. [Reprinted by permission from P. E. Bull, 1987, "Posture and Gesture," Pergamon, Oxford.]

"We want an end to cruise, . . .
an end to trident, . . .
an end to polaris."

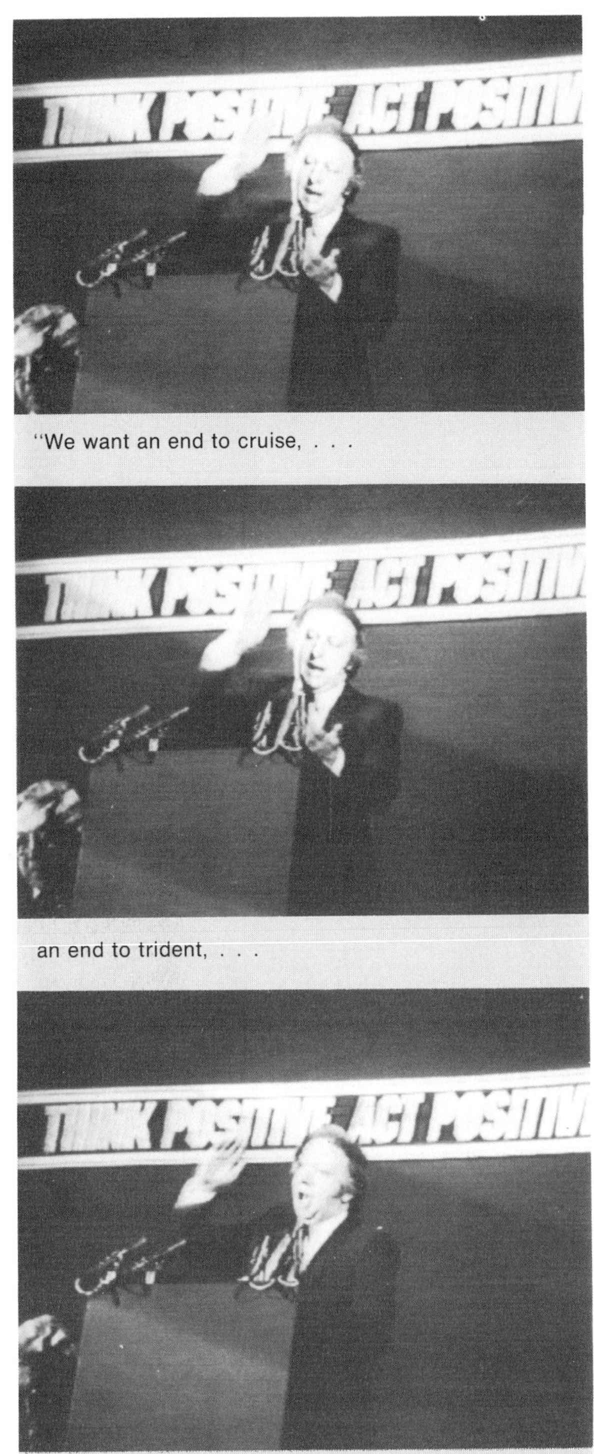

FIGURE 7 Another example of gesture in relation to a three-part list. [Reprinted by permission from P. E. Bull, 1987, "Posture and Gesture," Pergamon, Oxford.]

"All I want to say to those lads and lasses who say that they're members of the NUJ is that those people who were guarding the concentration camps also pleaded that they had no alternative [gesture occurs on 'no alternative']."

FIGURE 8 Bilateral gesture in relation to a headline–punchline device. [Reprinted by permission from P. E. Bull, 1987, "Posture and Gesture," Pergamon, Oxford.]

"I'll tell you the most important task: it's to say to the Lord Matthews, it's to say to the Lord Rothermeres, it's to say to the Rupert Murdochs that the first obligation of a new Labour government will be to take into common ownership [bilateral gesture begins on 'will be to take into common ownership'] . . .

the press."

FIGURE 9 Another example of bilateral gesture in relation to a headline–punchline device. [Reprinted by permission from P. E. Bull, 1987, "Posture and Gesture," Pergamon, Oxford.]

fact, Arthur Scargill actually seems to conduct his audience: his gestures not only accompany rhetorical devices which evoke applause but also curtail the applause once it has been aroused—even to the extent of indicating to the audience the points at which they should, or should not, applaud.

E. Differences in Visibility between Different Gestures

Arthur Scargill's use of two-handed movements in relation to the climax of the headline–punchline device can be used to illustrate another of the distinctive properties of gesture. Not only is gesture a highly visible form of communication, but there are also differences in visibility between different forms of gesture, so that more important aspects of speech can be indicated by larger movements and/or movements involving more than one part of the body. This can be further illustrated from studies of conversation, where it has been shown that making a point may be indicated by a movement of the head or eyes, whereas the more important semantic unit of changing the point of view that a person takes may be indicated by a much larger postural shift involving at least half the body.

F. Gesture as an Optional Means of Communication

A further feature of gesture is that it is to some extent optional. Whereas features like vocalization, speech rate and amplitude are intrinsic to speech, that is, it is impossible to converse without them, it is perfectly possible to converse without the use of gesture. Thus, the presence or absence of gesture may in itself be seen as a form of communication. Certainly, gestures related to speech are clearly intended to be communicative. For example, gesture is used more frequently face to face than when talking over an intercom. Gesture is also part of the turn-taking system in conversation; it may be used as an attempt suppressing signal to prevent someone else taking a turn, while ceasing to gesture acts as a turn-yielding cue.

"We've had a number of speeches here tonight, including one from the leader of our party and the next prime minister, about the important tasks [applause-suppressing gesture occurs after 'important tasks']. . . ."

FIGURE 10 Use of gesture as an applause suppressor. This applause-suppressing gesture is followed by the rhetorical device illustrated in Figure 6. [Reprinted by permission from P. E. Bull, 1987, "Posture and Gesture," Pergamon, Oxford.]

These findings can all be taken as supporting the view that gesture is intended to be communicative; but the use of gesture in conversational turn-taking also suggests a further proposition: that gesture may be taken as indicating a wish to communicate. This proposition has a number of intriguing implications. Gesture may be used when a person is interested in the topic he is talking about, or to accompany certain parts of speech which the person regards as more important. Gesture may also be used when a person is interested in communicating to another person or group of people: for example, it has been found that people attempting to be persuasive used significantly more gesture than when asked to present a message in a neutral fashion. Conversely, an absence of gesture may indicate a lack of desire to communicate; for example, people suffering from depression used significantly fewer illustrators on admission to hospital than on discharge.

G. Gesture as Part of a Multichannel System of Communication

Finally, it needs to be stressed that gesture forms part of a multichannel system of communication, operating principally not as an alternative to speech, but essentially in conjunction with it. This view is supported by recent cognitive research on gesture: it has been argued that gesture and speech are part of the same psychological structure and share a common computational stage. This is because not only do gestures occur primarily during speech, they are also synchronized with linguistic units; indeed, they have semantic and pragmatic functions that parallel those of speech. In addition, gesture develops simultaneously with speech in children, and dissolves together with speech in aphasia. [*See* APHASIA.]

That gesture is part of a multichannel system has important implication for its role in communication. In fact, four main functions of nonverbal signs in conversation have been distinguished: semantic, syntactic, pragmatic, and dialogic. Thus, nonverbal signs may either affect the meaning of speech or signify meaning in themselves (semantic function); they may regulate the simultaneous and sequential occurrence and organization of verbal signs and other nonverbal signs (syntactic function); they may indicate characteristics of the message sender and receiver (pragmatic function); finally, they may indicate the nature of the relationship between the conversationalists (dialogic function). Gesture can convey any or all of these functions; hence, through using gesture in conjunction with speech it is possible to communicate simultaneously on a number of different levels.

VI. CONCLUSIONS

Interest in gesture has a long history, but it is only in recent years that it has become the focus of systematic scientific investigation. Research has shown that gesture is important in communicating emotions and interpersonal attitudes; it is also closely synchronized with speech in terms of syntax, meaning, and vocal stress. Three main types of gesture have been identified, referred to as emblems, illustrators, and regulators. The concepts of illustrators and regulators, however, seem to imply that gesture is essentially secondary to speech, amplifying and elaborating the spoken word. But gesture and speech, considered as media of communication, have very different properties. Gesture can be shown, through a consideration of its distinctive features, to be not so much subordinate to speech, as different. The key elements are that gesture is visual, that it is silent, and that it constitutes a series of bodily actions. In addition, it is highly visible, there are differences in visibility between different types of gesture, it is to some extent optional, and it constitutes part of a multichannel system of communication. As a consequence, it is particularly useful for communicating certain kinds of information and this has significant consequences for the way in which it is used in social interaction.

Acknowledgment

The author thanks Matthew Thomas for typing the manuscript, and for his useful comments on earlier versions of this article.

Bibliography

Argyle, M. (1988). "Bodily Communication," 2nd ed. Methuen & Co., New York.

Bull, P. E. (1987). "Posture and Gesture." Pergamon, Oxford.

Heath, C. (1986). "Body Movement and Speech in Medical Interaction." Cambridge University Press, Cambridge.

Kendon, A. (1985). Some uses of gesture. In "Perspectives on Silence" (M. Saville-Troike, Ed.) Ablex, Norwood, NJ.

McNeill, D. (1985). So you think gestures are nonverbal? *Psych. Rev.* **92**(3), 350–371.

Glial Cells

Leif Hertz
University of Saskatchewan, Canada

Elijah Ocherashvili
The Beritashvili Institute, Tbilisi, Republic of Georgia

Brona O'Dowd
La Trobe University, Australia

Glossary

Energy metabolism Metabolism of glucose (and in astrocytes also of glutamate) in order to maintain energy-requiring processes (e.g., active ion uptake). Metabolism of both glucose and glutamate is illustrated in Figure 1; note that glucose metabolism occurs in two stages: glycolysis (glucose to pyruvate or lactate) and oxidative metabolism (of pyruvate or glutamate) in the citric acid cycle.

Glial cells (astrocytes, oligodendrocytes, and microglia) Nonneuronal cells co-existing with neurons in the central nervous system.

GLIA and neurons are the two primary cell types in the central nervous system. Glia can be further subdivided into the myelinforming oligodendrocytes; microglia, primarily performing phagocytic and immunological roles; and astrocytes. Astrocytes are crucial in regulation of transmitter, ion, and metabolic substrate concentrations in the neuronal microenvironment.

I. INTRODUCTION: RELEVANCE OF GLIAL CELLS FOR HUMAN BEHAVIOR

Behavior may be regarded as all observable actions resulting from outgoing nervous instructions composed by the brain in response to internal bodily needs/desires or external stimuli in the individual's immediate environment. It is generally assumed that the brain processes associated with behavior occur exclusively in nerve cells, and there is no a priori reason to believe that this might not be the case. Evidence will, nevertheless, be provided that this may represent an immense oversimplification. A crucial involvement of glial cells has been suggested based on two different memory models. The first is the proposal by Alexander I. Roitbak that oligodendroglial cells enhance synaptic efficiency by myelinating presynaptic previously naked nerve fibers during the development of classical Pavlovian conditioning. The second is the recent supposition that astroglial cells play an essential role during a pivotal stage of memory formation. The evidence for this second proposal comes from one-trial passive avoidance learning in newborn chicks—a task originally introduced by Cherkin in the late 1960s and further developed over the years by Marie Gibbs and Kim Ng. In this contribution we will first briefly describe the complexity of the central nervous system with emphasis on a neuronal–glial interaction occurring around an interstitial space. Subsequently, different types of glial cells are described, and it is discussed in what manner cellular phenomena taking place in glial cells may contribute to the establishment of memory. In the final part, we identify specific events in the two behavioral paradigms and in some abnormal conditions that produce behavioral dysfunction, which appear to provide compelling evidence that

Copyright © 1994 by Academic Press, Inc. All rights of reproduction in any form reserved.

glial cells are essential for at least certain aspects of memory formation and behavior.

II. BRAIN CELLS AND EXTRACELLULAR SPACE

A. Cell Types

The brain is the most complex of body organs. Although brain tissue is made up by two main cell types (i.e., nerve cells and glial cells) each of these may be divided further into several subgroups. Nerve cells were originally characterized morphologically but are now increasingly being classified according to the transmitter they utilize for synaptic transmission (e.g., glutamatergic neurons, noradrenergic neurons, peptidergic neurons, etc.). Nerve cell bodies account for at most 5–10% of the volume in gray matter of the mammalian central nervous system (CNS). [*See* SYNAPTIC TRANSMITTERS AND NEUROMODULATORS.]

Glial cells are traditionally divided into protoplasmic and fibrous astrocytes, oligodendrocytes, and microglia. In gray matter, the most abundant glial cell is the protoplasmic astrocyte, whereas the fibrous astrocyte is found mainly in white matter. Oligodendrocytes produce myelin in white matter but are also found close to some neurons in gray matter. Again, the volume occupied by easily recognizable cell bodies is relatively small, although glial cells in large vertebrates outnumber nerve cells by a factor of 5–10.

After the volumes occupied by nerve cell and glial cell bodies have been added up, a considerable fraction of the tissue volume remains to be accounted for. In gray matter the main part of this fraction is made up by the so-called neuropil. The neuropil is the part of the tissue where interactions occur between neurons and glial cells. It is composed of an intricately interwoven network of minute neuronal and glial processes, which often taper into thin lamellar sheets. Although the input-receiving dendrites on neurons may generally constitute the largest fraction of the neuropil, both nerve endings and glial cell processes also account for a large part of the volume.

Excitation of nerve cell processes in the neuropil leads to an entry of sodium ions and an exit of potassium ions from the cells to the extracellular space, and it is the subsequent restoration of normal balance between intracellular and extracellular ions by the aid of active, energy-dependent transport mechanisms which accounts for most of the energy requirement associated with function in the CNS. It is a reflection of the immense surface area and the intensity of the active ion movements, that it is the energy metabolism in the neuropil, not in the nerve cell bodies, which is increased during functional activity.

B. Interstitial Space

The interstitial or extracellular space shared by neurons and glial cells is of critical importance during functional activity in the brain. This space is isolated from the rest of the body by the blood–brain barrier and is mainly localized in the narrow extracellular clefts penetrating the neuropil. The importance of alterations in the composition of the neuronal–glial microenvironment has only been realized during the last 20 years. Aided by newly developed microelectrodes that can be inserted into the extracellular space, it was shown that the extracellular potassium concentration rises dramatically during functional activity or pathological conditions: a few millimolar during normal nerve cell activity (e.g., from 3 to 4 m*M*), to a ceiling level of 10–12 m*M* during seizures, and to exceedingly high levels (more than 50 m*M*) during energy failure. In many other tissues such alterations in extracellular ion concentrations would be greatly reduced and eventually abolished by diffusion into the vascular system. This does not occur in the CNS on account of the blood–brain barrier, which only allows a very selective transport, primarily of glucose, oxygen, and carbon dioxide, between brain tissue and circulating blood. Therefore, the extracellular concentrations of potassium ions and other neuroactive compounds are regulated by (1) release and (2) subsequent uptake into adjacent cells. There is now overwhelming evidence that a large part of the uptake of excess extracellular potassium occurs into glial cells.

Another important methodological advance made it possible to estimate extracellular glutamate concentrations by the aid of microdialysis. Extracellular glutamate content increases during stimulation of glutamatergic neurons; again, a large part of the reuptake occurs into astrocytes, depleting neurons of a neurotransmitter. Therefore, glial cells must also be involved in replenishing neurons with precursors for transmitter glutamate. This transmitter is probably important for the establishment of long-term memory. As will be discussed later, the return of glutamate precursors to neurons is remarkably complex.

III. WHAT ARE GLIAL CELLS?

A. Astrocytes

Astrocytes are the most abundant glial cells in gray matter of the mammalian brain and are located at strategic positions, e.g., around synapses and abutting microvessels as capillary endfeet. They also form a multilayered structure (glia limitans) covering the surface of the brain. Astrocytes extend a large number of finely branched processes and extremely thin veils and may constitute the cell in the vertebrate organism which has the largest surface to volume ratio. These cells originally received the name "astrocytes" on account of their sometimes stellate appearance. The presence of a specific protein, glial fibrillary acidic protein (GFAP), is conventionally used as an indication of the astrocytic character of a glial cell. This protein is found in both protoplasmic and fibrous astrocytes. In cultured cells it is expressed not only in the so-called type 1 astrocyte which is the tissue culture equivalent of "normal" astrocytes in gray matter of the central nervous system, but also in the so-called type 2 astrocyte. The latter cell is quite often studied in tissue culture and is for this reason also mentioned here. However, the importance of the type 2 astrocyte *in vivo* has not been established. It may not correspond to any astrocyte of relevance for events occurring in gray matter and will not be discussed further.

B. Oligodendrocytes

The oligodendrocyte is the central nervous tissue equivalent of the Schwann cell in the peripheral nervous system. As indicated by their name, oligodendrocytes have relatively few processes. The establishment of the role of Schwann cells in the myelination of axons by Geren in 1954 was the first solid information about the role of any glial cell. Each oligodendrocyte in the mammalian central nervous system myelinates more than one axon and during the peak of myelination it produces several times its own weight of myelin per day. The functional importance of myelination is that the rate of impulse propagation in axons increases substantially after the establishment of an insulating myelin sheath at all points except at the nodes of Ranvier, and that the nerve fiber becomes capable of carrying impulses at much higher frequency. This is important because the intensity of stimulus is coded in the CNS in terms of frequency and because increased stimulus intensity helps to consolidate neuronal pathways.

The number of oligodendrocytes in brain cortex continues to increase during adulthood, and the total amount of myelin in the rat brain rises rectilinearly throughout life as a function of the logarithm of the age of the animals. This suggests a continuous myelination of fibers which were previously nonmyelinated, and even in the normal adult brain cortex there is a substantial amount of nonmyelinated presynaptic fibers. A moderate elevation of the extracellular potassium concentration, as occurs following neuronal excitation, not only causes a proliferation and differentiation of oligodendrocytes, but also leads to an actual increase in myelination. This response is a central feature of the first memory model to be discussed later in this paper.

In older literature it is stated that oligodendrocytes surround many nerve cell bodies as satellite cells. Although some perineuronal oligodendrocytes do exist, it has often not been possible to verify the oligodendrocytic character of perineuronal cells histochemically, and at least some of these cells appear to be microglia. Also, in cases where oligodendrocytes do border upon neurons, thin astrocytic membranes have been observed to be interposed between the two other cells.

C. Microglia

Microglia play a role in the CNS similar to that of macrophages outside the CNS. Like other cells within the immune system they both secrete cytokines and respond to cytokines. Cytokines (e.g., interleukins, interferons) are relatively high molecular weight polypeptides which are produced during the effector phase of immunity and mediate immune and inflammatory responses. An increasing amount of evidence suggests a bidirectional communication between the immune system and the CNS. Cytokines act on the same second messenger systems (the adenylate cyclase system and the phosphoinositol system) as neurotransmitters. Thus, both can be characterized as signaling agents.

IV. GLIAL FUNCTIONS

A. Metabolism

In the following we elaborate on characteristics of glial cells that may make them suitable for playing a role both in the determination of normal behavior and in abnormalities connected with behavioral dysfunction. Since behavior is intricately associated with a neuronally mediated response, these glial actions must eventually modify neuronal function. In this section we describe what ultimately amounts to neuronal–glial interactions in metabolism.

Metabolically, astrocytes behave like most ordinary cells in the body, e.g., liver cells or muscle cells. For example, the high molecular weight carbohydrate energy-store glycogen is found in liver, muscle, and brain (see Fig. 1). Under normal conditions brain glycogen is present in astrocytes, but not in neurons, as is its degrading enzyme, phosphorylase. In liver, glycogen can be released as glucose after degradation (a means of increasing the blood concentration of glucose), whereas muscle glycogen cannot be released as glucose, but only as the glucose metabolite pyruvate. This applies also to brain, indicating that the energy obtained during conversion of glycogen to pyruvate can only be utilized by the astrocytes themselves, not by neurons. In contrast, the energy generated during subsequent oxidative degradation of pyruvate might be available for both astrocytes and neurons.

Remarkably, astrocytes appear to utilize energy obtained by breakdown of glucose or glycogen to pyruvate (Fig. 1) rather than the larger amount of energy generated by further oxidative degradation of pyruvate (to carbon dioxide and water) for several energy requiring processes, possibly including active ion uptake. In this context it should be noted that glycogen granules, but not mitochondria (the organelles carrying out oxidative metabolism), can be observed in even the thinnest processes. Active uptake processes, especially of potassium ions and of glutamate, are in general much faster into astrocytes than into neurons. This is of importance in regard to behavior because the rapid uptake of excess extracellular potassium into astrocytes after neuronal activity may be essential for the establishment of the long-lasting "undershoot" of the extracellular potassium concentration which appears to play a major role in memory formation.

The rapid uptake of glutamate into astrocytes means that glutamate, after its release from neu-

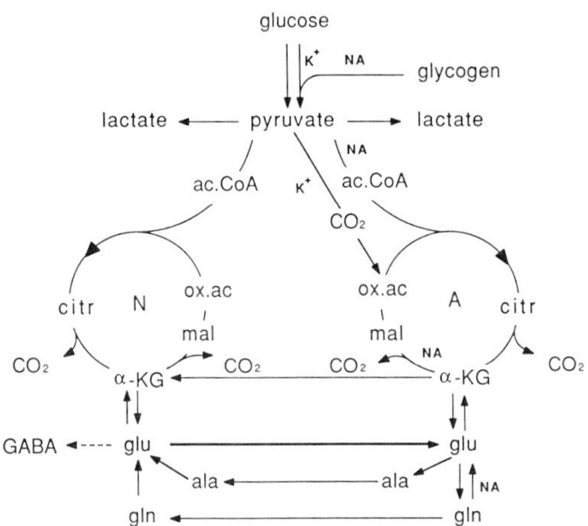

FIGURE 1 Glucose and glycogen are metabolized to pyruvate–lactate (during glycolysis) and via acetyl co-enzyme A (ac.CoA) to carbon dioxide (CO_2) and water in the citric acid cycle in both neurons (N) and astrocytes (A). Only astrocytes have pyruvate carboxylase activity allowing a net synthesis of oxaloacetate (ox.ac.) and other citric acid cycle constituents, e.g., α-ketoglutarate (α-KG) from glucose. Glutamate (glu) is released from glutamatergic neurons and partly accumulated into astrocytes (heavy line). Synthesis of glutamine (gln), an astrocyte-specific process, release of gln from astrocytes, its reaccumulation into neurons, and hydrolysis to form glu and GABA contribute to replenish neuronal transmitters. However, astrocytic glu is also metabolized to CO_2, and its amino group is partly transaminated into other amino acids, e.g., alanine (ala), which is formed by transamination with pyruvate. Additional glu precursors must, therefore, exist in glutamatergic neurons. α-KG and gln are synthesized in astrocytes, released, accumulated into neurons, and used to form the carbon skeleton of glu and GABA. Incorporation of amino nitrogen from ala (and/or other amino acids) supplies the amino group. Stimulation by noradrenaline or elevated potassium concentrations is indicated by NA and K^+, respectively. As indicated in text, the energy-yielding processes stimulated by NA may be of special importance during certain learning tasks. [From Hertz and Peng in Yu *et al.*, 1992.]

rons as a transmitter, is mainly accumulated into astrocytes, where it is partly converted to glutamine (Fig. 1). This, together with the demonstration that glutamine synthetase activity is present only in glial cells (astrocytes and to a lesser extent oligodendrocytes) led to the concept of a "glutamate–glutamine cycle," in which astrocytic glutamine (which has no transmitter properties) after its synthesis from glutamate is released to the extracellular space and re-accumulated into glutamatergic neurons, where it is used as a glutamate precursor, and into GABAergic neurons which produce γ-aminobutyric acid (GABA) from glutamate. However, a substantial fraction of the glutamate which has been taken up into astrocytes is not converted to glutamine but used as a metabolic fuel, i.e., oxidized to carbon dioxide and water. This obviously means that there is a net loss of glutamate from the cycle. Moreover, extracellular glutamine is not preferentially accumulated into neurons, and glutamine can be metabolized to glutamate (and thereafter used as a metabolic substrate) in astrocytes. Therefore, besides glutamine, also other glutamate precursor molecules must be supplied to the neurons.

Glutamate does not readily cross the blood–brain barrier, whereas glucose does. Net synthesis of glutamate within the CNS occurs from glucose. In order to accomplish such a synthesis of glutamate, the glucose metabolite pyruvate must be carboxylated to a citric acid metabolic cycle constituent, e.g., oxaloacetate or malate, which in turn can be further converted in the citric acid cycle to α-ketoglutarate, a direct precursor for glutamate (see Fig. 1). The quantitatively dominating, and perhaps only, pyruvate carboxylation process in brain is formation of oxaloacetate, catalyzed by the pyruvate carboxylase. Like glutamine synthetase, this enzyme is present in astrocytes but absent in neurons, so that neurons on their own are not able to produce glutamate from glucose. In contrast, astrocytes readily synthesize α-ketoglutarate from glucose, and glutamatergic neurons can utilize extracellular α-ketoglutarate for *net* synthesis of transmitter glutamate. Astrocytes also synthesize the amino acid alanine in large amounts from pyruvate, and alanine is reconverted in neurons to pyruvate during the formation of glutamate from α-ketoglutarate (see Fig. 1). The pyruvate thus formed can be used by the neurons as a metabolic substrate. Because alanine originates from astrocytes, this constitutes a transfer of a metabolic substrate from astrocytes to neurons. Since an elevated potassium concentration causes release of transmitter glutamate from neurons it is noteworthy that the production of a glutamate precursor by pyruvate carboxylation in astrocytes also is enhanced in the presence of an elevated extracellular potassium concentration.

In sum, an astrocytic–neuronal interaction must occur in order for normal glutamatergic transmission to take place, and *de novo* synthesis of glutamate from glucose leads at the same time to the transfer of a glucose metabolite from astrocytes to neurons where it can be used as an energy substrate. Since glutamate is the most important excitatory transmitter in the CNS (and probably is implicated in long-term memory formation) the functioning of such a neuronal–astrocytic glutamatergic unit constitutes an important link between energy metabolism and neuronal activity.

B. Ion Homeostasis

1. Potassium

In most cells, the membrane permeability for potassium ions is higher than that for other ions, for which reason the membrane potential is relatively close to a potassium equilibrium potential. This is especially the case in glial cells where the potassium conductance is so high that the cells behave as virtually perfect potassium electrodes. Therefore, the resting membane potential in glial cells is generally higher than in neurons, and a small alteration in extracellular potassium concentration will cause a more pronounced change in membrane potential than it would in neurons. However, regardless of the extent of the depolarization, it does not lead to any depolarization-induced influx of sodium ions into glial cells because glial cells, in contrast to nerve cells, are not excitable and show no action potentials. Thus, the continuing demonstration that astrocytes display characteristics which were previously presumed to be exclusively neuronal (e.g., receptor expression, calcium channels) does not mean that astrocytes behave like neurons, but that the two cell types complement each other with their separate but unique characteristics and functions.

Astrocytes constitute an electrically coupled syncytium, through which potassium ions can move extremely rapidly by a passive, current-carried transport mechanism (the "spatial buffer") from a region with a local elevation of the extracellular potassium concentration to different extracellular locations. The electrical circuit is initiated by the local depolarization and it is closed by extracellular flow of sodium ions back to the origin, or of chloride ions in the opposite direction. This redistribution of potassium ions from a local increase is not directly dependent upon energy metabolism, although it does depend on membrane polarization which, in turn, is a result of energy metabolism. This process does not transfer potassium ions from the extracellular space into glial cells, but it does remove potassium ions from the outside of the neuron(s) from which a potassium ion release has occurred during excitation, to other locations. In this way it can dissipate a local increase in extracellular potassium ions, and it has been suggested by Peter Laming that it may also be able to reach an initially not excited area more rapidly than impulses following conventional synaptically regulated neuronal pathways and in this way prime the neuronal microenvironment for subsequent activity.

The "spatial buffer" mechanism was originally described on the basis of experiments in the invertebrate brain. For some time it was thought by many investigators that this was the only mechanism involved in potassium ion homeostasis at the cellular level of the mammalian CNS. This concept has now been shown to be incorrect. Two mechansims for active, energy-requiring uptake of potassium ions into astrocytes in the mammalian brain have been firmly established: (1) the conventional active uptake of potassium in exchange with sodium, which is catalyzed by the Na^+, K^+-ATPase and found in most cell types, including both neurons and glial cells, and (2) an electroneutral co-transport of K^+, Na^+ and Cl^- (chloride), which is present in, e.g., astrocytes and certain renal epithelial cells, but not in neurons.

An increase of the extracellular potassium concentration above its normal, resting level stimulates potassium ion uptake into astrocytes by both mechanisms. In contrast to astrocytic Na^+, K^+-ATPase, the neuronal type of Na^+, K^+-ATPase reaches its maximum activity at normal resting extracellular potassium concentrations, and can be further activated by only the increase in intracellular sodium concentration, which occurs during neuronal excitation. The driving force for the co-transport system for K^+, Na^+, and Cl^- ions in astrocytes is the sodium ion gradient across the cell membrane; this gradient can be maintained despite a continuous coupled uptake of K^+, Na^+, and Cl^-, because the increase in intracellular sodium ion concentration brought about by the co-uptake will stimulate sodium efflux by activation of the intracellular sodium sensitive site of the Na^+, K^+-ATPase in astrocytes. Thus, simultaneous activation of both mechanisms for active uptake of potassium into astrocytes leads to an accumulation of potassium ions without any corresponding extrusion of sodium ions.

The extremely rapid active uptake of potassium into astrocytes after neuronal excitation is likely to normalize the extracellular potassium concentration before completion of the active extrusion of excess intraneuronal sodium ion concentration resulting from the excitation. Operation of the "spatial buffer" mechanism can achieve a similar result locally. A remaining activation of the intracellular sodium sensitive site of the neuronal Na^+, K^+-ATPase will therefore bring about a lowering of the local extracellular potassium concentration below its resting level because of the obligatory sodium/potassium exchange during enzyme activity. This "undershoot" of the extracellular potassium concentration, in turn, leads to neuronal (and glial) hyperpolarization. Because the undershoot is long-lasting, it may mark or isolate the recently activated neuronal assemblies for more permanent structural/functional changes.

2. Calcium

The concentration of free intracellular calcium has repeatedly been shown to serve as an essential intracellular messenger in virtually all cell types and in mammalian cells amounts to about 1×10^{-7} *M* (100 n*M*). This value is much lower than the extracellular calcium concentration (approximately 1×10^{-3} *M*). The steep calcium gradient across the cell membrane is maintained by control of channel-mediated calcium entry into the cell, active carrier-mediated transport of calcium out of the cell, and controlled sequestration of calcium in the cell interior by binding to or release from intracellular organelles (mainly the endoplasmic reticulum). It was previously believed that mitochondria also served as storage sites for cytosolic calcium, but it is now becoming recognized that the level of intramitochondrial free calcium responds to certain alterations in free cytosolic calcium concentration and serves as an important regulator of energy metabolism in at least some cell types, including astrocytes. This phenomenon is important for transmitter action on energy metabolism.

Channel-mediated calcium entry into the cell may occur either by transmitter activation of receptor operated channels, or through one of at least three different voltage-sensitive calcium channels, physiologically described as L, N, and T channels. Calcium is displaced from its intracellular binding sites by stimulation with the second messenger inositol-triphosphate (IP_3), which is formed by receptor stimulation with, e.g., α-adrenergic, some serotonergic, and some peptidergic agonists. In addition to the formation of IP_3, another messenger, diacylglycerol (DG), is also produced by activation of these receptors. In the presence of free calcium ions, DG evokes a translocation of cytosolic protein kinase C (PKC) to the membrane and a PKC activation. The activated and membrane-bound PKC is calcium-sensitive, and its activity can be further increased by calcium ions entering the cell via calcium channels. In turn, PKC activity regulates a multitude of events within the cell or on the plasma membrane.

An extremely interesting phenomenon is the oscillatory increase in free cytosolic calcium concentration in cultured hippocampal astrocytes in response to glutamate, which has recently been described by the Cornell-Bell/Smith group. This glutamate-induced increase in free cytosolic calcium concentration may be propagated as waves between contiguous astrocytes. Neuronal signaling must be able to elicit such calcium waves in adjacent astrocytes, since astrocytic calcium waves can be elicited in an organotypic hippocampal slice preparation either by the application of NMDA, which has no direct effect on the astrocytes, but causes the neurons to release glutamate, or by stimulation of the afferent mossy fiber pathway. Three important questions which remain to be answered are: (1) whether the pathways for the waves through the astrocytes can be regulated; (2) what effect the calcium wave has on the astrocytes through which it passes; and (3) whether the wave has any effects on the neurons it encounters.

V. ASTROCYTES AS TARGETS FOR AN AUTONOMIC NERVOUS SYSTEM

The primary function of the autonomic nervous system in the periphery (the sympathetic and parasympathetic nervous system) is to regulate bodily functions like muscle contraction and glandular secretion (e.g., in the gastrointestinal system), as well as metabolism and vascular perfusion according to functional demands. It has, for many years, been a dogma that the CNS, in contrast to all other organ systems, does not possess an autonomic nervous system. The main reason for this belief is probably the presence of the blood–brain barrier, which anatomically is based on tight junctions between endothelial cells, and makes receptors located on the abluminal side of the endothelial cells as well on other target cells within the CNS inaccessible for most systemically administered receptor agonists. Moreover, specific nuclei of origin for noradrenergic, serotonergic, and cholinergic fibers to the CNS have only been discovered relatively recently, and even less information is available about intracerebral peptidergic pathways. Noradrenergic and serotonergic fibers ascend from, respectively, locus coeruleus and the raphe nuclei in the brain stem and supply cells all over the cerebral and cerebellar cortex as well as in the hippocampus with their entire afferent adrenergic and serotonergic input. Both these nuclei are part of a supraspinal system which also controls autonomic output in the peripheral nervous system, and they receive afferent fibers from the hypothalamus (which synthesizes the pituitary hormones), allowing coordination of hormonal and neuronal activities. The cholinergic nucleus basalis magnocellularis of Meynert, which is located in the forebrain, receives an important direct input from both locus coeruleus and the raphe nuclei. The best known dopaminergic pathway is the nigrostriatal tract, extending from the substantia nigra in the brain stem to the corpus striatum. This pathway is mainly involved in control of movement, but there are also dopaminergic pathways reaching the cerebral cortex.

Many of the ascending monoaminergic fibers (e.g., serotonergic, dopaminergic, and noradrenergic) in the brain cortex show a structural anomaly from other nerve fibers in the brain, i.e., they do not terminate in true synapses but in varicosities, from which transmitters reach their target cells (neurons, glial cells, microvessels) by diffusion. This is an arrangement similar to that in the peripheral part of the autonomic nervous system. Peptidergic transmitters to a large extent function in a similar manner and also reach different kinds of cells.

Neurons, astrocytes, and microvessels all express noradrenergic receptors. In the rodent brain most β-adrenergic receptors appear to be located on astrocytes and microvessels with only a sparse neuronal innervation. α-Adrenergic receptors are more evenly distributed between neurons and astrocytes, although there is a distinct postsynaptic expression of α_2-adrenergic receptors especially on astrocytes. Serotonergic (5-HT) receptors are also found on both cell types. The 5-HT_{1C} receptor, which mainly has been demonstrated in choroid plexus cells, appears to be important in astrocytes. Dopaminergic receptors have been observed on striatal astrocytes.

Both noradrenaline and serotonin stimulate glycogenolysis as well as Na^+, K^+-ATPase activity in astrocytes. Noradrenaline also stimulates different aspects of oxidative metabolism, probably secondary to an increase in free cytosolic calcium concentration which, in turn, increases free intramitochondrial calcium concentration and thereby exerts a direct stimulation of different dehydrogenases (see Fig. 1). Noradrenaline also stimulates glycolysis as well as glutamate uptake into astrocytes. In addition, activation of PKC, probably by a receptor agonist, appears to be capable of reducing the ionic coupling for potassium in the astrocytic syncytium. This may mean that transmitter activity enhances active ion transport and may reduce passive ion distribution.

Astrocytes also express receptors for many peptide transmitters. At least some of these act by stimulation of the phosphoinositol second messenger system and an increase in free cytosolic calcium concentration. Thus, exposure to the peptide transmitter vasopressin, which is of behavioral importance because of its involvement in certain aspects of memory, leads to an increase in free cytosolic calcium concentration in some, but not all, astrocytes.

VI. GLIAL CELLS AND LEARNING

A. Pavlovian Conditioning

In classical Pavlovian conditioning, two factors, usually a biologically meaningless factor (the conditioning stimulus) and a biologically significant factor (the unconditioned stimulus), eventually become coupled or associated if they are presented in close temporal contiguity a number of times. As a result of this pairing, the organism will emit the usual biological response when confronted with the conditioned stimulus alone. This procedure has often been viewed as the essence of simplicity, but research during the last decades has suggested that conditioning even in relatively simple systems may be much more complex than previously suspected and involve cognitive events. [*See* CLASSICAL CONDITIONING.]

A potential role of myelination of previously nonmyelinated presynaptic nerve endings during the establishment of a conditioned reflex has been pointed out by Roitbak. During the initial conditioning period, the hypothesis proposes that an oligodendrocytic process under the influence of the unconditioned stimulus approaches its target, a nonmyelinated axon which shortly before had been excited by the conditioning stimulus, and begins to envelop it. Thus, there is no formation of new synapses, but an existing synapse is consolidated by myelination. Since myelination dramatically increases the capacity of an axon to follow a high rhythm of stimulation, coating of the axon with myelin enhances the effectiveness of synaptic action and the amount of released transmitter becomes increased in the synaptic cleft of the myelinated circuit. Once synaptic effectiveness has been consolidated by myelination, increased synaptic activity will lead to other morphological and functional changes, including an increased width of postsynaptic densities and an increased size of dendritic spines.

The Roitbak hypothesis requires that the conditioning stimulus leaves a trace that is still recognizable during the presentation of the unconditioned stimulus. It is well established that neuronal excitation evokes an initial increase in extracellular potassium concentration. This is generally followed by a long-lasting "undershoot" in the extracellular potassium concentration which may owe its existence to the glial mechanisms for active uptake of potassium as was discussed above. In turn, the "undershoot" results in a prolonged hyperpolarization of adjacent cells. Experiments in which post-tetanic potentiation was evoked showed that the hyperpolarization was abolished by administration of ouabain or hypothermia, and therefore appears to depend upon the lowering of the extracellular potassium concentration below its resting level by active, energy-requiring transport.

The unconditioned stimulus which follows slightly later, will generally be of sufficient biological relevance to stimulate the nonspecific activation system of the brain stem, which we now know includes the noradrenergic pathways ascending from the locus coeruleus. The second phase of neuronal potassium release, which results from this neurohormonal activation, will lead to an increase in oligodendrocytic proliferation and differentiation and an enhancement of myelination of previously naked neuronal processes, all of which can be mimicked experimentally by moderately increasing the extracellular potassium concentration. Although the activation system of the brain stem will be stimulated globally, it is only "at the locations where the nerve fibers had already been excited (by the combination of the conditioned and the unconditioned stimulus) that the conditions will be right for myelination." These conditions probably include the oligodendrocytic hyperpolarization resulting from the "undershoot" of the extracellular potassium concentration. Modifications of the axonal membrane, especially with respect to neuronal–glial adhesion molecules, may also play a role for the recognition.

The proposed mechanism for the development of the conditioned reflex displays clear analogies with elements of developmental biology of the CNS. For example, the suggested differentiating role of an elevated extracellular potassium concentration is identical to the role of a depolarizing potassium concentration during neuronal development. Cell culture experiments have clearly established that a signal like a partly depolarizing potassium concentration (or another modification simulating afferent neuronal activity) is essential for normal development of certain neurons, e.g., glutamatergic cerebellar granule cells. Also, the extracellular potassium concentration is known to regulate the development of Muller cells (a glial cell) in the retina.

The mechanism proposed by Roitbak might physiologically be of special importance for the establishment of use-dependent connections in the CNS during an early postnatal period, when myelination occurs at extremely high rates. This hypothesis is also consistent with a phylogenetic correlation between myelin content and activity of myelinating enzymes in the brain of vertebrates and their ability to develop conditioned reflexes. Finally, several conditions leading to deficiencies in myelination (X-ray irradiation, hypothyroidism, vitamin deficiencies) also impair the ability of the animal to develop conditioned reflexes, although no direct causal correlation has been established.

B. One-Trial Passive Avoidance Learning

Memory refers to the cognitive ability to recall a past experience and, if the experience is associated with learning, memory commonly results in a change in behavior. The passive avoidance learning task (PAT) capitalizes on the fact that the day-old chick at birth is equipped with a well-developed CNS which enables the newly hatched bird to quickly learn about critical aspects in its environment (e.g., the chick needs to peck while exploring the environment for edible food). The PAT entails pretraining chicks to peck at water-coated red and blue beads. If one of these beads (typically the red) is then coated with the chemical adversant methyl-anthranilate and presented to the chicks for pecking, the chicks peck once and display a strong disgust reaction; about 75% of the chicks avoid the red bead thereafter. [*See* MEMORY.]

Pharmaco-behavioral experiments have shown that discrimination memory for the single-trial passive avoidance experience in neonate chicks is formed in three sequential stages: a short-term (STM) stage, available for 15 min following learning; an intermediate (ITM) stage, operating between 15 and 55 min postlearning; and a long-term (LTM) stage formed by 60 min after learning (Fig. 2). The ITM stage appears to consist of two phases: a first phase (ITMA) which is susceptible to inhibition by the uncoupler of oxidative phosphorylation 2,4-dinitrophenol (DNP), and a second DNP-insensitive phase (ITMB), during which glucose utilization is increased in the neostriatal/hyperstriatal complex of the forebrain, a region which is intimately associated with memory processing in the chick. Given that this phase is not inhibited by DNP (which inhibits oxidative metabolism in the citric acid cycle), the increase in glucose utilization must indicate an enhancement of exclusively glycolysis, i.e., formation of pyruvate/lactate from glucose (see Fig. 1). Since the 2-deoxyglucose used for determination of glucose metabolism is partly incorporated into glycogen, part of the increase might represent an increased glycogenolysis.

Each of the memory stages is dependent upon the establishment of the previous stage. Long-term memory requires protein synthesis and can be inhibited by protein synthesis inhibitors; short-term memory appears to be correlated with the increase in extracellular potassium evoked by the sensory event (aversive taste), and it is abolished if a more widespread depolarization is evoked by artificially increasing the extracellular potassium concentration or administering glutamate intracranially (Fig. 2). Active uptake of potassium ions must be involved during the induction of ITMA since administration of ouabain, an inhibitor of the Na^+,K^+-ATPase, abolishes memory at the beginning of ITMA, but has no effect during short-term memory. Ethacrynic acid, an astrocyte-specific inhibitor of the Na^+, K^+,

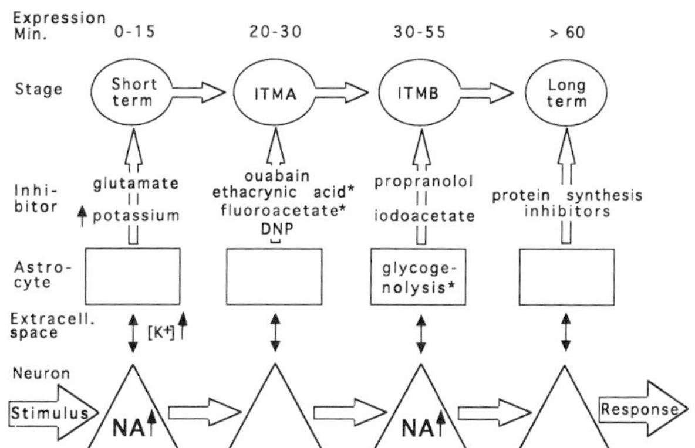

FIGURE 2 Schematic representation of the Gibbs-Ng model for one-trial passive avoidance learning in the neonate chick. The different stages are indicated together with the time after learning at which each stage is expressed, selected inhibitors of each stage, the stage at which glycogen (an astrocyte-specific carbohydrate energy store) is decreased, the stage at which the extracellular potassium concentration ($[K^+]$) is elevated by sensory stimulation, and the stages at which noradrenaline (NA) is increased. Events marked with an asterisk are astrocyte specific.

Cl^- co-transport, has a similar effect. The extinction of memory by either of these two inhibitors of active potassium ion transport is consistent with the concept that cellular hyperpolarization due to lowering of the initially increased extracellular potassium concentration below its resting level is essential.

The learning task itself is associated with an initial, probably arousal-induced increase in the noradrenaline level of the tissue which subsequently rapidly returns to normal values. If the task has caused sufficient arousal, there is a second, equally large increase in noradrenaline, beginning abruptly at the start of ITMB (Fig. 2). If a weaker reinforcing stimulus is used (e.g., a diluted concentration of the chemical adversant), the second increase in noradrenaline is reduced, and neither ITMB nor the long-term memory stage develops. In this situation a lasting memory of the experience can only be formed if the noradrenaline signal during ITMB is artificially increased, e.g., by intracerebral injections (immediately after learning) of vasopressin, noradrenaline, or adrenocorticotropic hormone (ACTH), all of which cause an elevation of noradrenaline levels during ITMB. Consistent with this, birds trained with a stimulus of normal strength and treated with propranolol, a blocker of β-adrenergic agonists, show no evidence of ITMB and, in turn, fail to consolidate the adversive experience.

Iodoacetate, a specific inhibitor of glycolysis, also blocks ITMB (Fig. 2) verifying the dependence of this ITM phase on glycolysis, possibly including glycogenolysis. An inhibition by iodoacetate does not distinguish between neuronal and astrocytic glycolysis (Fig. 1). However, glycogen, a carbohydrate energy store with an exclusively astrocytic localization, was specifically depleted during ITMB, yielding unequivocal information that astrocytic energy metabolism is mobilized during ITMB. This does not necessarily indicate that neuronal glycolysis is not also important at this stage. Nor does it mean that astrocytic energy metabolism is unimportant during other memory stages. On the contrary, ITMA can be inhibited by fluoroacetate, a specific inhibitor of oxidative metabolism in glial cells (Fig. 2).

In sum, there appears to be a threshold level in the memory-related rise in forebrain noradrenaline at the end of ITMA, which must be reached if the adversive experience is to be consolidated. Glycolysis and astrocyte-specific glycogenolysis are essential during ITMB and both glycogenolysis and astrocytic glycolysis can be stimulated by noradrenaline acting at β-adrenergic receptors. It may be speculated that this enhancement of glycolytic metabolism in astrocytes and the resulting energizing of energy-requiring processes, perhaps first and foremost active uptake processes, are indispensable for further memory processing. Since the strength of the learning stimulus is directly related to the level of noradrenaline at the ITMA–ITMB transition, this scenario may be the biological equivalent of the psychological concept of "reinforcement."

VII. GLIAL CELL INVOLVEMENT IN BEHAVIORAL DYSFUNCTION

Glial cells have often been implicated in organic diseases of the brain, e.g., in epilepsy. Verification of a possible correlation between behavioral dysfunction and glial cells is often difficult because neuronal degeneration generally is accompanied by proliferation and hypertrophy of astrocytic cells, differentiating into the so-called reactive astrocytes. It has, however, repeatedly been suggested that astrocytic mechanisms for maintenance of potassium homeostasis are altered in glial cells located in epileptic brain foci. More recently, effects of several commonly used antiepileptic drugs have been found on cultured astrocytes, but not on cultured neurons, with a rank order comparable to their *in vivo* efficacy. At least some of these drugs may affect astrocytic calcium channels, and Ann Cornell-Bell and her co-workers have directly demonstrated profound modifications in the waves of free cytosolic calcium concentrations through astrocytes obtained from the vicinity of surgically removed epileptic foci. [*See* EPILEPSY.]

Alzheimer's disease is a degenerative neurological disease with progressive and severe cognitive disability developing in parallel with a reduction of energy metabolism in the brain. During the last couple of years the possibility has been suggested that Alzheimer's disease may represent an interruption of normal astrocytic–neuronal interactions. It is an indication in this direction that glutamate and potassium homeostasis appears to be impaired. Perhaps these abnormalities might be secondary to a well-established cell loss in locus coeruleus and the raphe nuclei, since adrenergic and serotonergic fibers from these nuclei regulate both energy metabolism and transport of potassium and glutamate in astrocytes. There is also evidence that glial cells (astrocytes and/or microglia) are instrumental in the formation of Alzheimer amyloid from the amyloid precursor protein. An unequivocal abnormality in brains from patients with Down's syndrome or Alzheimer's disease is an increase in the glial S-100 protein. In this context, it should be kept in mind that patients suffering from Down's syndrome invariably develop Alzheimer's disease if they live through middle age, that the increase in S-100 in these patients is present already at birth, and that S-100 appears to be an astrocytic component of a serotonergic–astrocytic–serotonergic developmental interaction. Microglial cells appear also to be involved in these conditions since the cytokine, interleukin I, is present in brains from patients with Down's syndrome and Alzheimer's disease and is localized to microglia. [*See* Alzheimer's Disease.]

Depression is a major psychiatric disease disabilitating numerous people from all walks of life. Symptoms include a dampened mood, inability to perform daily activities, and quite often various somatic complaints. This disease is often very successfully treated with antidepressant drugs. Long-term treatment (2–3 weeks) with classical antidepressant drugs causes a down-regulation of β-adrenergic receptors in the brains of experimental animals, which timewise correlates with the required treatment period before clinical improvement is seen in patients. This receptor is exclusively or preferentially localized on astrocytes, suggesting an astrocytic involvement in depression, a concept that is reinforced by the finding that a similar down-regulation of β-adrenergic receptors has been demonstrated in primary cultures of astrocytes. Also, the recently introduced antidepressant drug, fluoxetine, has a stimulatory affect on serotonergic 5-HT_{1C} receptors in these cultures and causes an increase in glycogenolysis. This finding indicates that fluoxetine, in addition to its well-known inhibition of serotonin uptake into neurons (which is generally assumed to be the mechanism of its antidepressant action), causes a direct receptor stimulation in astrocytes. [*See* Depression.]

Astrocytes may also be involved in addiction to certain drugs, e.g., cocaine. Continuous exposure of developing astrocytes in primary cultures to a toxicologically relevant concentration of cocaine leads to an abolishment of the metabolic stimulation of oxidative metabolism normally observed during exposure to noradrenaline. This impairment appears to be chronic even after cessation of the drug exposure. This finding may be of special relevance since behavioral studies have suggested abnormalities specifically of responses presumed to involve noradrenergic mechanisms in the offspring of rats treated with cocaine during a comparable period. Other authors have found an abnormal volume response to elevated potassium concentrations in astrocytes cultured from rat puppies born to dams who had been treated with cocaine during the pregnancy.

VIII. CONCLUDING REMARKS

In this presentation we have tried to provide compelling evidence that glial cells are, indeed, of importance in relation to behavior. No attempt has been made to review the topic comprehensively, and it seems likely that additional glial cell functions in the future will be found equally relevant for behavioral responses.

Bibliography

Benveniste, E. N. (1992). Inflammatory cytokines within the central nervous system: Sources, function, and mechanisms of action. *Am. J. Physiol.* **263,** C1–C16.

Hertz, L. (1989). Is Alzheimer's disease an anterograde degeneration, originating in the brainstem, and disrupting metabolic interactions between neurons and glial cells? *Brain Res. Bull.* **14,** 335–353.

Hertz, L. (1992). Autonomic control of neuronal–astrocytic interactions, regulating metabolic activites and ion fluxes in the CNS. *Brain Res. Bull.* **29,** 303–313.

Laming, P. R. (1989). Central Representation of Arousal. In "Visiomotor Coordination: Amphibians, Comparisons, Models and Robots" (J. P. Ewert and M. A. Arbib, Eds.), pp. 693–727. Plenum, New York.

MacDonald, J. F., Schlichter, L., and Ransom, B. R. (1991). Ions water, and energy in brain cells. *Can. J. Physiol. Pharmacol.* **70,** (Suppl.), S100–S373.

Ng, K. T., Gibbs, M. E., Crowe, S. F., Sedman, G. L., Hua, F., Zhao, W., O'Dowd, B., Rickard, N., Gibbs, C. L., Sykova, E., Svoboda, J., and Jendelova, P. (1991). Molecular mechanisms of memory formation *Mol. Neurobiol.* **5,** 333–350.

Peters, A., Palay, S. L., and Webster, H. deF. (1991). "The Fine Structure of the Nervous System. Neurons and their Supporting Cells" 3rd ed., pp. 1–494. Oxford University Press, New York.

Roitbak, A. I. (1993). "Glia and Its Role in Nervous Activity" pp. 1–392. Nauka, Saint Petersburg (in Russian).

Stone, E. A., and Ariano, M. A. (1989). Are glial cells targets of the central noradrenergic system? A review of the evidence. *Brain Res. Bull.* **14,** 297–309.

Yu, A. C. H., Hertz, L., Norenberg, M. D., Sykova, E., and Waxman, S. G. (1992). Neuronal–astrocytic interactions: Implications for normal and pathological CNS function. In "Progress in Brain Research," Vol. 94, pp. 1–409. Elsevier, Amsterdam.

GRIEF AND BEREAVEMENT

Vicki Gluhoski, Julie Leader, and Camille B. Wortman
State University of New York, Stony Brook

Glossary

Bereavement Objective situation of an individual who has recently experienced the death of someone significant.

Grief Emotional response to one's loss which includes a number of psychological and somatic reactions.

Mourning Actions and manner of expressing grief which are shaped by social and cultural forces.

THE LOSS OF A LOVED ONE is a challenge most people encounter during the course of their lives. Each year 8 million Americans must cope with the death of a close family member. Eight hundred thousand lose a spouse and 400,000 experience the death of a child under the age of 25. In addition, over 50% of all women 65 and older are widows, and the vast majority stay widowed for the rest of their lives. For each of these deaths, bereaved persons are left behind to deal with the loss. Available evidence suggests that exposure to the loss of a loved one increases one's risk of subsequent mental and physical health problems.

This article reviews and discusses several areas which are relevant for a comprehensive understanding of bereavement. These domains include the socio-cultural context of grief, symptomatology, theoretical perspectives, normal and pathological grief, consequences of bereavement, bereavement and well-being, risk and contextual factors, intervention, dealing with the social environment, and future research directions. In each domain, an attempt is made to integrate the classic studies in this field with more recent and methodologically rigorous research. In so doing, we hope to dispell many of the misconceptions people may hold about the grief process. Although some of the original findings have continued to be supported, others have not. We report on these discrepancies and discuss new and provocative results. Since the majority of methodologically rigorous studies have examined how people cope with the loss of a spouse, we will focus on that particular loss in this review. However, we will include some information about how individuals cope with other losses, including the loss of a child, parent, or sibling. Several researchers considered the leaders in the field are referred to throughout the chapter. These include Clayton, Osterweis, Parkes, Rando, Raphael, Stroebe and Stroebe, and Weiss.

I. SOCIO-CULTURAL DETERMINANTS OF GRIEF

In any attempt to understand the impact of bereavement, the social and historical context of death must be considered. The way death is viewed in contemporary Western society may be a historical anomaly. Never before in history have mortality rates been so low, and life expectancy rates so high. Consequently, death is a relatively rare occurrence, and is often viewed as a tragic loss rather than a normal, expected life event. In fact, living conditions and medical technology have advanced to such a degree that as a culture we hold the illusion of immortality and are thus shocked and distressed when someone close to us dies. In contrast, at other points in history disease, famine, and wars were rampant and mortal-

Copyright © 1994 by Academic Press, Inc. All rights of reproduction in any form reserved.

ity rates were tremendously high. Because death occurred so frequently, and was therefore defined as routine, there is evidence that people experienced the death of another with less suffering than is typical today.

While some argue that grief is experienced universally, that it is biologically driven, and that it is triggered when attachment figures are lost, sociologists and anthropologists see grief and mourning as shaped by social and economic, as well as historical, circumstances. Cross-cultural differences attest to this, for much variability exists in such factors as (1) the openness, intensity, and control over the expression of grief and anger; (2) the proscribed length of mourning; (3) the amount of emotional and financial support given to the bereaved; (4) the opportunities or prohibitions in forming new intimate relationships; and (5) the conceptualization of the bereaved person's future in the face of the loss.

Of particular interest is the way in which cultures differ in the extent to which the emotional expression of grief is tolerated. Paul Rosenblatt, a leader in the field of cross-cultural bereavement, found that the bereaved typically cry in 72 of the 73 cultures he studied. Other researchers have noted that the Balinese do not show their sorrow with tears but still report experiencing sadness. However, Tahitians view the emotions of bereavement as symptoms of illness and thus are less likely to admit having these feelings. There are also cultural variations in the time course allotted for the grief process. In the United States it has been widely accepted that the individual will complete grieving within the first year after the loss. More recent research, however, has indicated that this assumption is erroneous, and that it usually takes much longer for the bereaved to recover from their loss. Navajo Indians are expected to grieve only during the first 4 days immediately following the death. Conversely, Orthodox Jews have an initial intense 7 days of mourning called *shiva,* and limit the mourning period in total to 30 days for all losses except that of a parent. In those instances, the individual is expected to grieve the loss for 1 year.

Nancy Scheper-Hughes, an anthropologist who has studied infant mortality and mother–infant attachment in the shantytowns of Northeast Brazil, elucidates how culture, as well as economic and emotional scarcity have shaped the way mothers view, care for, and eventually grieve or fail to grieve for their infants when they die. In this environment of poverty, scarcity, deprivation, and loss, women must often compete with their own offspring for survival. Because the living conditions are so poor, and infant mortality rates so high, mothers often do not emotionally bond with their infants until after their first year of life when their chances of survival are better. Thus, when infants die, mothers often express little or no grief.

These cross-cultural differences are intriguing because they demonstrate that there is no single correct way to mourn another's death. Within each society, however, there are proscribed norms and individuals who do not fulfill these expectations may be ostracized or labeled as deviant. These cultural norms are relevant for our subsequent discussion of grief symptoms and when mourning is viewed as abnormal.

II. SYMPTOMATOLOGY

Lindemann (1944) and Eliot (1930) were two of the early researchers to document common reactions to the death of a significant other. Eliot viewed grief as a process and believed it included stages of shock, denial, yearning, guilt and anger, and recovery. Lindemann described the typical response as including somatic distress, a preoccupation with the image of the deceased, guilt, hostility, and a loss of activity. The classification of grief reactions has been refined and elaborated since this early work. Currently, grief is regarded as a set of responses that may be experienced in four different ways: psychologically, behaviorally, socially, or physically. Psychological responses fall into three different categories: emotions (principally depression, anxiety, yearning, anger, guilt, and sometimes relief), cognitions (such as disbelief, inability to concentrate, and preoccupation with the deceased), and perceptions (including visual and auditory hallucinations, or a sense of the deceased person's presence). Behavioral responses include searching behavior (i.e., scanning the environment for the deceased), crying, restless hyperactivity, sleep disturbance, a tendency to sigh, and either avoiding or seeking out people, situations, or objects that are reminiscent of the deceased. Social responses include social withdrawal, decreased interest in initiating or maintaining relationships, feelings of alienation or detachment, and heightened dependence on others. Physical responses include appetite disturbances, decreased sexual interest, sleep disturbance, and fatigue. Other symptoms, such as trembling, heart palpitations, hypervigilance, or headaches, may also be involved. For a more complete discussion of the symptoms of grief, the reader is referred to Rando (1993).

III. THEORETICAL PERSPECTIVES

Several different theoretical formulations have influenced current conceptions of the grief process. One of the most important approaches to loss has been the classic psychoanalytic model of bereavement, which is based on Freud's important paper "Mourning and Melancholia." According to Freud, the major task of mourning is the gradual surrender of psychological attachment to the deceased. Freud viewed the process as an internal struggle, since the person experiences intense yearning for the lost loved one, but yet is faced with the reality of the loved one's absence. Freud saw this struggle as inherently painful and involving turbulent emotions. As thoughts and memories are reviewed, Freud maintained that ties to the deceased person are gradually withdrawn. At the conclusion of the mourning period, the bereaved person is said to have "worked through" the loss and to have freed himself or herself from an intense attachment to an unavailable person. Freud maintained that once the process is completed, the bereaved person is able to invest emotional energy in new relationships.

Another theoretical model that has been extremely influential is the attachment model of grief developed by John Bowlby. In this formulation, Bowlby drew heavily from psychodynamic thought, from the developmental literature on young children's reactions to separation, and from work on the mourning behavior of animals. Bowlby maintained that during the course of normal development, individuals form instinctive affectional bonds or attachments, initially between child and parent and later between adults. Bowlby maintained that when such bonds are threatened, powerful attachment behaviors are activated, such as clinging, crying, and angry protest. Unlike Freud, Bowlby suggested that the function of this behavior is not withdrawal from the loved one but rather reunion. He was the first to recognize that behaviors arising from separation anxiety, such as pining and restlessness, are critically important features of grief.

Drawing in part from these theoretical notions and in part from available research, Bowlby maintained that successful resolution of grief involved passing through four stages of mourning. The first stage is characterized by numbness, disbelief, and shock. As the individual processes the loss, he or she will experience a stage of yearning and protest in which searching and pining are prominent. The third stage, despair, occurs when the individual gives up the search and recognizes the loss is permanent; this is accompanied by feelings of depression and lethargy. The final stage, called recovery or resolution, is experienced when the person accepts the death, detaches from the lost object, and resumes an active life. The individual returns to prior levels of functioning, adapts to his or her new role and status, and begins to form new relationships.

In the bereavement literature, a number of different theorists have proposed models which, like Bowlby's, involve stages or phases of reaction to loss. An influential stage model has been advanced by Horowitz and his associates (see, e.g., Horowitz, 1985). Horowitz maintained that initially following a loss, a person will appear stunned and unable to process what has happened, responding with what is termed outcry. Outcry is a sense or feeling "Oh no, it can't be true." However, Horowitz believed there was a tension between denial and intrusion of painful thoughts regarding the loss. Denial is characterized by numbness, and intrusion is characterized by working through the painful reality of what has happened. Over time, an individual is expected to experience oscillating periods of denial and intrusion. The loss is denied until reality begins to break through, and then the person experiences a period of intrusion. When that becomes too painful, the person will shift to denial again. Over time, these cycles are assumed to become less and less intense as the person successfully copes with the loss.

These models are important because they specify the processes people go through in attempting to come to terms with the loss of a loved one. One stage model, recently advanced by Rando, provides a particularly thorough account of the grief process. Her model, like Horowitz's, begins with an avoidance phase. She maintains that during this phase, the mourner must acknowledge the reality of the death and come to some sort of understanding as to why the death occurred. Next comes the confrontation phase, where the mourner must react to the separation by feeling and expressing his or her psychological reactions to the loss. The mourner must also recollect and reexperience the deceased and the relationship realistically, and relinquish attachments to the deceased. Finally, the bereaved person reaches the accomodation phase, where he or she must readjust and move adaptively into the new world, forming a new identity while not forgetting the old. The mourner must also reinvest in ways that the investment can be returned to the mourner.

Stage or phase models have received a great deal of attention not only from those interested in bereavement, but from those studying other life events, including miscarriage, rape, and life-threatening illness. One stage model that has received a great deal of publicity over the past two decades is Kubler-Ross's model on how people react to their own impending death. Kubler-Ross identified five stages of emotional response to such a loss, including denial, anger, bargaining, depression, and, ultimately, acceptance. Kubler-Ross has estimated that each year, her stage model has been taught in 125,000 courses in colleges, seminaries, medical schools, hospitals, and schools of social work.

Over the past several years, descriptions of stage models like Kubler-Ross's have also appeared in numerous textbooks and articles written for and by physicians, nurses, therapists, social workers, members of the clergy, and patients and their families. As a result, these models have become firmly entrenched among health-care professionals. In fact, there is evidence to suggest that professionals sometimes use the stages as a kind of yardstick to assess a person's progress. People who do not follow the stages are likely to be labeled as deviant, neurotic, or pathological diers, and clinical personnel may become angry at people who do not move from one stage to the next. They may also dismiss a person's legitimate emotional reaction (e.g., becoming angry after being kept waiting two hours) as merely indicative of a stage ("He's just going through the anger stage"). A lot of pressure may be put on individuals to grieve as the stage models would indicate that they should.

As research has begun to accumulate, it has become clear that although stage models of response to loss are widely believed among health care professionals, there is little empirical evidence that supports them. We undertook a careful review of dozens of studies purporting to focus on stages of reaction to loss. Surprisingly, only a few studies had assessed feelings of shock, denial, anxiety, anger, and depression longitudinally following the death of a loved one. In contrast to the stage approach, research evidence suggests that there is considerable variability in the intensity of the emotional response, in the kinds of specific emotions that are experienced, and in their sequence. In fact, the Institute of Medicine has issued an authoritative review of bereavement research in which they cautioned against the use of the word stages, noting that this might lead people to expect the bereaved to proceed from one specific reaction to another in a more orderly fashion than usually occurs.

In recent years, there has been considerable interest in applying a new theoretical model, generally referred to as the stress and coping approach, to the problem of bereavement. According to stress and coping theorists, life change creates a disequilibrium which imposes a period of readjustment. Supposedly, this readjustment period can leave a person more vulnerable to stress and its consequences. The available research evidence suggests that mere exposure to stress, such as the loss of a loved one, accounts for little of the variance in the development of mental or physical disorder. For this reason, a major thrust of work within this theoretical framework has focused on the identification of variables—so-called vulnerability or resistance factors—that can account for the variability that exists in response to stress. Several different types of factors have been examined in the literature, including various personality predispositions, resources such as financial assets, and social support. Investigators have projected that the speed and completeness of recovery from bereavement would depend on the coping resources available to the individual. A major advantage of this stress and coping approach to bereavement is that, unlike the stage models, it can account for variability in response to such a loss.

IV. NORMAL AND PATHOLOGICAL GRIEF

In this section, we summarize what we believe to be the current understanding of the normal grieving process. We also describe various types of grief that are not considered to be normal. We then ask whether available evidence substantiates current, widely shared views of the grieving process. Our judgment, after a thorough review of the literature, is that it does not. There are many studies which suggest that we need to reevaluate our current understanding of normal grief.

As noted above, most researchers no longer see grief as a series of specific stages that always unfold in the same way. However, they do see grief as a process, and there are a number of widely held assumptions about how this process operates. First, when people experience a major loss, they are expected to go through a period of intense distress, which lessens over time. Second, failure to experience intense distress is regarded as indicative of pathology. A number of investigators, including Bowlby, have identified the absense of distress as one of the two types of pathological grief. Third, it is believed that if individuals fail to experience distress shortly after the loss, problems or symptoms of distress will emerge at a later time, either in the form of a delayed grief reaction or subsequent health difficulties. It is also widely believed that if a person does not manifest intense distress following a major loss, then he or she was not really attached to the person who died, or that he or she is continuing to deny the implications of the loss.

Once a person has become depressed or distressed as a result of the loss, it is expected that he or she will "work through" or process what has happened. Implicit in this assumption is the notion that individuals need to focus on what has happened, and that attempts to deny or block feelings about the loss will ultimately be unproductive. Also implicit is the belief that this process will break down the feelings of the attachment toward the loved one so that energy can be directed toward new activities and relationships.

Finally, after a relatively brief period of time—a calendar year in the case of losing a spouse, and 1–2 years after losing a child—the person is expected to achieve a state of recovery and return to normal role functioning. Those who do not recover according to the expected timetable are regarded as experiencing a type of pathological grief called chronic mourning. Individuals are also expected to achieve a state of resolution following the loss. This means that the person must be able to understand cognitively what has happened. The person must also be able to come to terms with the loss emotionally. This means that the lost person can be recalled, and reminders can be encountered, without intense emotional pain.

Available evidence fails to provide support for any of these assumptions, although they are widely accepted by clinicians and lay persons alike. Wortman and Silver undertook a systematic evaluation of those bereavement studies that have used standardized outcome measures and structured interviews of relatively large, unbiased samples. First, most studies assessing depression find that between 15 and 30% of respondents are depressed in the first few months following the loss. However, a depressed reaction is certainly not universal. In some individual studies, such as those by Lund and his associates which focus on the elderly bereaved, only a small percentage of bereaved individuals (14.6% of the men and 19.2% of the women evidenced "at least mild" depression on the Zung Depression Inventory at three weeks postloss). Many other studies have shown similar results, suggesting that the initial response to conjugal loss is actually quite variable. [*See* DEPRESSION.]

In longitudinal studies in which bereaved persons are followed over time (see Wortman and Silver, 1989, for a review), there is little evidence to suggest that those who do not show initial distress will develop subsequent problems. In fact, delayed grief seems to be a very unusual and uncommon response. There is also no empirical evidence to support the claim that failure to exhibit distress is associated with subsequent health problems. In fact, numerous studies show that people who show relatively little distress after the loss, and who rate themselves as strong and capable of handling what has happened, are those who cope best with the loss in the longer run. Consequently, those who show intense distress shortly after the loss are those who are most likely to experience subsequent difficulties.

To date, relatively few studies have focused on the impact of "working through" the loss. Parkes and Weiss's work shows that those respondents who initially show the greatest evidence of yearning or pining for their loved one—possible indicators of "working through"—were most likely to evidence poor mental and physical health at 13 months postloss. As Parkes and Weiss expressed it, "We might suppose that people who avoid or repress grief are the most likely to become disturbed a year later, yet this is not the case." Like early signs of intense distress, early signs of intense efforts to "work through" the loss may portend subsequent difficulties. Other investigators have obtained similar findings.

Regarding the expectation of recovery, there is considerable evidence that the timetables previously believed to be accurate are in fact incorrect. In a nationally representative prospective study conducted by our research team, we found that following the loss of a spouse, there were large differences between bereaved and control respondents in depressed mood and in major depression. These differences persisted for two full years after the loss. Studies focusing on loss of a child have also shown that parents typically experience intense distress for several years. There is growing consensus that in many cases, it may take longer for individuals to recover from a major loss than was previously believed.

There is also evidence to suggest that the bereaved person may remain attached to the loved one for much longer than was formerly believed, and that such attachments may not be maladaptive. This was the case, for example, for studies recently conducted by Silverman and Worden on children's reaction to the loss of a parent. They found that the majority of children devoted considerable energy to connect with their deceased parent. Many talked with the deceased, had dreams about him or her, or frequently thought about him or her. Studies with adults have similarly shown that people often sense the presence of their dead spouse and that they find this comforting rather than disturbing. Clearly, more research is needed to determine the consequences of such continuing attachment, but we should not implicitly assume it is maladaptive.

Finally, available evidence suggests that people are not always able to resolve what has happened to their loved one. In the study by Parkes and Weiss, 61% of those respondents who had suddenly lost their spouse, and 29% of those who had forewarning, were still asking why the event had happened 2–4 years later. In a study from our research program of the long-term impact of losing a spouse or child in a motor vehicle accident, we found that even after 4–7 years, most respondents were unable to find any meaning in the loss, had thoughts that the death was unfair, and had painful memories of their spouse or child during the past month. In a second study from our research program, we focused on a nationally representative sample of nearly 800 widows and widowers who had lost a spouse from 1 month to 60 years previously. Even after decades had passed, the majority of respondents continued to have memories and conversations about their spouse that made them feel sad or upset.

V. CONSEQUENCES OF BEREAVEMENT

The models discussed above have led to a vast body of literature examining the sequelae of the death of a loved one. Below, we review the impact of bereavement on a number of different indicators of well-being, including health, mortality, mental health and personal growth. Each of these areas is discussed in turn.

A. Physical Health

At the forefront of this research are the studies examining the impact of bereavement on physical health and mortality. Widowhood is linked to increases in illness, as well as higher mortality. The bereaved report more somatic distress including headaches, dizziness, fainting, and chest pains than controls and also make more doctor visits and consume more medication. Widowers are at greater risk to develop cardiovascular and infectious diseases, with fatal consequences. Widows are particularly at risk for developing cirrhosis. These findings have been supported in epidemiological, clinical, and questionnaire studies. Although the literature is not entirely consistent, most studies support the idea that bereavement has a negative effect on health.

B. Mortality

The impact of bereavement on mortality has generated even more interest and debate than the effects of bereavement on subsequent illness. There is widespread agreement that the death of a spouse has a very significant impact on mortality. There is also evidence to suggest that an increase in mortality is associated with the death of a child. Widowers and the younger widowed have a particularly elevated risk of death. In a sample of over 9000 subjects whose progress was followed for 4 years, it was discovered that the first 6 months presented the greatest risk for widowers under the age of 60. For women under 60, the second year after the loss was associated with the highest mortality rates. Others have found a sevenfold risk of mortality in the first year after the loss; with the greatest risk being for widowers during the first 6 months. In another landmark study in this area researchers retrospectively calculated death rates for widowed and married subjects. Consistent with previous results, they found that widowed subjects, under the age of 45, had a risk of death that was seven times greater than that for controls. Men were at greater risk than women. In a more recent report, these findings were again confirmed. In a random sample of 500 widowed subjects, significant rates of mortality were evident in widowers up to 6 years after the loss. Those who had low self-reported happiness levels, little social support, but higher socio-economic status had an enhanced risk. Based on this most recent work, it appears that the mortality rates for widows in every age group are significantly higher than for married individuals, especially in the first 6 months. Men who remarry are at less risk, although the mechanisms responsible for this remain unclear. For women, the risk period is extended, but not as elevated. Causes of death differ for widows and widowers. Men are most likely to die from tuberculosis, influenza and pneumonia, cirrhosis and alcoholism, suicide and accidents, and heart disease. Widows are more likely to die from cirrhosis and alcoholism, heart disease, and cancer. In addition, the elevated risk of suicide among the widowed must be highlighted and may last for several years. Deaths in the first year are usually due to heart disease.

Despite so many studies which have found an association between bereavement and mortality, a few studies have not found this relationship. In one study, comparisons were made between three groups: parents of the 2518 Jewish Israeli soldiers killed in the Yom Kippur War of 1973, parents of 1128 men between the ages of 18 and 30 who died between 1971 and 1975, and a matched control group. These groups were followed for 10 years; there was no evidence of elevated mortality rates in the bereaved samples as compared to the control population, throughout the timespan covered.

One shortcoming of past research linking bereavement with mortality and morbidity is the lack of attention to mediating mechanisms. Virtually all studies conducted to date have been designed to determine *if* bereavement affects health, rather than *how* health changes come about.

A number of possible processes have been discussed in the literature. There is some evidence that bereavement, through its influence on depression, may cause immune system changes, although there has not yet been research linking immune changes to health outcomes. Investigators have also maintained that bereavement may be linked to changes in sleep, nutrition, or diet, ultimately affecting health, although research demonstrating such links has yet to be conducted. Bereavement may also cause negative health outcomes by causing people to be less attentive to, and less likely to seek treatment for, symptoms. Bereavement may also impair health by increasing the bereaved person's level of chronic strain (e.g., financial strain, lack of assistance with household tasks) and resulting in what some investigators have called "bereavement overload." As will be discussed, there is some evidence that such strains are important. The absence of one's spouse may also reduce the likelihood that a person takes his or her medicine or makes regular visits to the doctor. It may even cause health problems by increasing behaviors known to be injurious to one's health, such as smoking and drinking. Such substance-use problems are discussed in more detail below.

Focus on such mechanisms is a high priority for future research. Only if we clarify the process through which bereavement influences health can we design effective interventions to ameliorate these effects.

VI. BEREAVEMENT AND WELL-BEING

In addition to its impact on health, bereavement has an impact on many different indicators of well-being, including depression, anxiety, substance abuse, daily stress, and social and financial strain. We will consider each of these matters in turn.

Much attention has focused specifically on the relationship between bereavement and depression. Most investigations have concluded that conjugal loss leads to an increase in depression in the weeks and months following the loss. However, there have been inconsistencies from study to study concerning the size of the effect. Several studies have found that between one-third and one-half of widowed respondents experience clinically significant depression during the first year after the death. In contrast, a few investigators have found minimal effects of widowhood during the first year of the loss. In most cases, these latter studies focused on elderly widowed respondents. Such respondents may be more psychologically prepared for widowhood than their younger counterparts and therefore fail to show such an intense reaction.

Depression is not the only psychological consequence of loss. In one study 44% of widowed subjects reported having at least one type of anxiety disorder during the first year after the loss. Some subjects were interviewed 6 months after the loss and other subjects 12 months after their loss. Both groups had rates of panic disorder and generalized anxiety disorder that were substantially higher than community rates. Studies also suggest that rates of other anxiety disorders, including obsessive–compulsive disorder and post-traumatic stress disorder, are also elevated among the bereaved. [*See* ANXIETY DISORDERS; PANIC DISORDER.]

Despite their prevalence, anxiety disorders have received relatively little attention from past theorists or from practicing clinicians. One exception is John Bowlby, who maintained that the primary response to loss of a loved one is separation anxiety. According to Bowlby, this type of anxiety is associated with restlessness and continual scanning of the environment in hopes that the loved one will return.

Only when the reality of the loss is acknowledged and internalized does the anxiety dissipate, at which point the depression and despair of mourning ensues. Parkes maintained that intense separation anxiety usually portends subsequent difficulties with the mourning process. Unfortunately, few investigators have assessed feelings of anxiety among the bereaved. In one study that did provide an assessment of both anxiety and depression, anxiety was found to be more prevalent than depression among individuals who lost their spouse during the past year. Research suggests that an anxiety reaction is especially likely to occur when the loss is sudden and unexpected, particularly if the death was traumatic or violent.

A question that has generated some controversy over the years concerns the prescription of psychotropic drugs for the bereaved. Some therapists believe that it is a mistake to medicate the bereaved, because medications like antidepressants hinder their ability to get in touch with their painful feelings and work through the loss. For similar reasons, lay groups often maintain that their members should avoid medication at all costs. One of us (CBW) was seeing a woman who lost her only child and had been prescribed antidepressants. She subsequently went to a Compassionate Friends support group for bereaved parents, where she was admonished to throw away her medication. Within two days, her symptoms had become so serious that she had to be hospitalized. Despite the strong feelings of some groups and individual therapists, however, the weight of the evidence suggests that antidepressants should indeed be prescribed for bereaved individuals who are clinically depressed, especially if the depression has endogenous symptoms or where the symptoms are unremitting.

As the prevalence of intense and disabling anxiety among the bereaved has been recognized, a number of investigators have maintained that there are advantages to initiating treatment with an anti-anxiety drug, which may work more quickly than an antidepressant. If the anxiety is relieved and the bereaved person is still depressed, most clinicians would advise using an antidepressant drug at that point. Although the use of anti-anxiety drugs is becoming increasingly accepted among clinicians who treat the bereaved, there is little empirical research on the matter at this point in time.

There are also several studies which suggest that bereavement places people at risk for substance abuse. Because of the intense emotional pain associated with a major loss, it is not surprising that people attempt to dull their feelings with alcohol. Tranquilizer use has also been found to increase, as has the use of tobacco. Some investigators have argued that if the mourner continues to use substances to avoid the pain associated with the loss, he or she will become chemically addicted. Unfortunately, the conditions of bereavement make it difficult for caregivers or friends to take the necessary "hard line" with bereaved persons who become substance abusers. Most available research suggests that the use of these substances is a risk factor for poor psychological outcome. Of course, most of these substances are known to have a deleterious effect on health; their use may thus influence mortality and morbidity as well.

In addition to influencing physical and mental health, bereavement has social implications as well. The survivor has lost a sexual partner, protector, source of reassurance of worthiness and social support, companion, financial and status provider, recreation partner, and helper for child rearing. The survivor is faced with daunting new challenges: he or she has sole responsibility now for all decisions, may be challenged by unfamiliar tasks such as household chores, employment, or the development of social relationships. The loneliness the widowed experience may seem unbearable; not only have they lost their closest companion, but their other relationships may have changed as well. They may become distant from in-laws, and may not be included in activities with couples. They must conform to social expectations of recovery and may be ostracized if they do not fulfill these assumptions.

Another important consequence of bereavement is financial strain. In a study which followed widowed subjects for 10 years researchers found diminished income for both men and women. This may be a particular problem for women because they are less likely to remarry and thus may never regain their prior financial status. Approximately 25% of widowers remarry within 5 years after the loss, but the typical widow never remarries and outlives her husband by about 15 years. Those who have few economic resources may have less opportunity to choose the living arrangements they would prefer after their spouse's death, and may be unable to purchase some of the services the spouse performed, such as household maintenance.

There also is evidence to suggest that bereavement affects well-being and life satisfaction. In one recent study, respondents' reactions to subsequent negative and positive events were examined in three samples: people who lost a spouse, people who recently became physically disabled, and matched controls. Not surprisingly, undesirable events had a negative effect on the psychological health of all groups. Although the disabled group was helped by desirable events such as celebrating special occasions, such events had no impact at all on the well-being of the bereaved. Similar findings were obtained in our own research. We found that it took our bereaved sample almost 10 years after the loss of a spouse until their life satisfaction scores were comparable to control subjects' scores.

An interesting question that might be raised is whether an experience like losing a loved one can ever have positive consequences for well-being. Helen Lopata has maintained that as a result of having to manage on their own, the women she studied developed an enhanced sense of independence and personal competence. Other investigators have suggested that one positive consequence that often accompanies loss is that it leads to a change in personal priorities. After the loss of a child, for example, greater emphasis may be placed on family activities and on friendships, and relatively less emphasis may be placed on work and on the accumulation of possessions. However, this shift in values is often accompanied by an underlying state of anxiety triggered by the death. Hence, people's ongoing feelings seem to include both positive and negative components, as the remark of one of our respondents illustrates: "We should enjoy our loved ones while we can because we never know when we might lose them."

A completely separate line of research initiated by Blair Wheaton has suggested that the consequences of a life event like widowhood may not be negative if the event represents the end of a chronic stress (e.g., the burden of caring for an ill spouse or being involved in a bad marriage). There is some evidence to suggest that the widowed become less depressed under these conditions than when the spouse was previously well and when the marriage was good.

VII. MEDIATING FACTORS IN THE GRIEF RESPONSE

Now that it is becoming clear that there is considerable variability in response to bereavement, there is increasing interest in identifying those mediating factors that may enhance or ameliorate the impact of the loss. Without such mediators, general theoretical models of the grieving process have limited utility in predicting reactions to loss. Several different types of mediating variables have been studied, including type or mode of death, circumstances surrounding the death, demographic factors, individual differences, and relationship factors. Each of these is discussed in turn.

A. Type or Mode of Death

There is considerable evidence that sudden and unexpected deaths result in more subsequent mental and physical health problems than deaths that are not. This is particularly the case for deaths that are untimely, caused by the maliciousness or negligence of another, or associated with violent circumstances. Rando has maintained that in today's culture, violent deaths are becoming increasingly common.

The death of a child, which is typically sudden and often the result of a traumatic incident, is recognized as enhancing a parent's risk for a variety of health problems. In one study, respondents who lost a child in a motor vehicle crash 4–6 years earlier showed significantly higher mortality and were significantly more likely to obtain a divorce than control respondents who did not suffer such a loss.

There are also studies suggesting that the loss of a spouse poses enormous difficulties. Mental and physical health problems are typically exacerbated if the loss is sudden, untimely, preventable (caused by another's negligence or maliciousness), or violent. As Parkes and Weiss have written, such losses may have their impact through their "transformation of the world into a frightening place, a place in which disaster cannot be predicted and accustomed ways of thinking and behaving have proven unreliable . . . ."

Sudden losses are not the only type of loss that place the surviving spouse at risk for mental and physical health problems. There is some research which suggests that death caused by a lengthy illness can also pose difficulties, particularly for elderly spouses. Such illnesses can exhaust coping resources and lead caregivers to ignore their own health problems.

Deaths that are associated with stigma are also more likely to cause difficulties for survivors. The guilt, anger, and confusion felt by survivors of suicide may complicate the mourning process and exacerbate symptoms. Similar processes may operate for those whose loved one died of acquired immunodeficiency syndrome (AIDS). Such individuals commonly have difficulties obtaining adequate medical care during their illness. They may be excluded from intensive care units, for example, and their loved ones may be frustrated by their inability to ensure adequate care. Research suggests that dissatisfaction with the medical care received by the loved one is an important predictor of depression following the loss.

At present, the vast majority of bereavement studies have focused on loss of a spouse. Some investigators have studied the impact of loss of a child. Only a handful of studies have investigated other kinds of losses, including loss of a parent, sibling, or grandchild. Also, very little is known about the issues faced by those whose loved ones have died of AIDS. Gaining a fuller picture of the psychological and health consequences of these other losses, which affect hundreds of thousands of people annually, is an important research priority.

B. Circumstances Surrounding the Death

It is well-established that perceptions of social support availability are associated with adjustment to life stress. Social support is one of the most commonly studied risk factors in the bereavement literature. Although the literature is not entirely consistent, several studies have shown that those who express feelings of lack of support, such as "nobody understands or cares" or the feeling that there is no one available to talk with following their spouse's death, are more likely to report subsequent difficulties. However, some well-designed studies have failed to find a relationship between support and subsequent mental or physical health. Moreover, little progress has been made in identifying the components of support that are most important in protecting people from the stress of losing a loved one.

In addition to the loss, the surviving spouse or loved one may be dealing with other chronic difficulties, which may increase vulnerability to subsequent mental and physical health problems. In some cases, these difficulties may have existed prior to the loss, as when the surviving spouse has a longstanding chronic health problem. In other cases, such problems may stem directly from the loss itself, as when a widow must move out of her home as a result of financial problems brought on by her husband's death. There is reasonably consistent evidence that the presence of such chronic strains can exacerbate the impact of the death. Financial strain appears to be particularly important in this regard, perhaps because those with few economic resources have less freedom of choice concerning such issues as their living arrangements and lifestyle.

C. Demographic Factors

1. Age

Some researchers have suggested that the older bereaved will be less depressed by the loss of a spouse because older people are more likely to expect the death and to be psychologically prepared for it. Consistent with this reasoning, several studies have indicated that the young are hit harder by the loss of a spouse than are the elderly. This seems to be the case for mental and physical health consequences. Interestingly, however, two studies have found that while the younger bereaved show greater initial distress following the loss, the death of a spouse has a more enduring effect on the older bereaved.

2. Gender

Although the research evidence is not entirely consistent, most studies suggest that men suffer more as a result of losing a spouse than do women. In one study, it was suggested that the strains following widowhood were actually quite different for men and women. For women, the major source of vulnerability was an increase in financial strain. In contrast, men's greater vulnerability appeared to stem from their more limited social relationships and from the difficulties they had in assuming household tasks previously handled by their wives. Interestingly, the results show that widowhood is associated with significantly more strained relationships with children for men, but not for women. Many men may have relied on their spouses to maintain relationships with children and may find it difficult to assume that role in widowhood. Previous lack of closeness between fathers and children, combined with male difficulty in expressing the need for support, may underlie the strained relationships that were found.

D. Individual Differences

1. Personality

It has frequently been argued that premorbid personality variables play an important role in adjustment to the loss of a spouse. However, only a small number of empirical studies have investigated this possibility. In one study, women who were assessed six months after the loss of their spouse and found to be more conscientious, conservative, emotionally mature, controlled, and socially precise were less likely than other widows to experience distress two years after the loss. In another study, the investigators measured self-esteem among recent widows and found that those who felt competent 3–4 weeks after the loss were least likely to show enduring depression or distress at an interview two years later. Finally, it has been shown that personality variables sometimes interact powerfully with the mode of death to influence outcome. One set of investigators assessed bereaved individuals and classified them as high or low in internal locus of control. Those individuals who had a low internal locus of control, and who suffered the unexpected loss of a spouse, were the most likely to experience intense and prolonged grief reactions.

E. Past History of Major Depressive Disorder

Are those who have a past history of major depressive disorder more vulnerable to the loss of a loved one than those who do not? A relatively small number of studies have addressed this problem, and the results have been inconsistent. About two-thirds of the studies suggest that a prior history of depression places individuals at risk, while one-third find no effects for this factor.

1. Major Depression following the Loss

There are a number of studies which have demonstrated that those individuals who respond to bereavement with a clinically significant depression in the first few months following the loss are most likely to have enduring difficulties with depression. In several studies, early diagnosis of depression was the single most important variable in predicting long-term mental health outcome following the loss of a spouse.

F. Relationship Factors

The two relationship qualities that have been most frequently discussed in the literature on bereavement are ambivalence and dependence. Psychologists have generally assumed that relationships characterized by ambivalence or dependence have their roots in the early experiences of childhood. Individuals who are predisposed to ambivalent relationships are primed to feel disappointments, betrayal, or abandonment by their loved ones and typically react to such feelings with intense hostility. For this reason, marriages in which one partner is ambivalent are generally characterized by considerable marital conflict. In Parkes and Weiss's important study, those who were involved in conflictual relationships were found to experience more long-term difficulties with bereavement than those who were not. In the few other studies that have examined this matter empirically, some have found no relationship between marital conflict or marital problems and subsequent difficulties, and some have found that those who have a good marriage experience the most severe grief. In one recent study, the impact of the marriage interacted with whether the spouse was ill prior to his death. Among women with an ill spouse, those with a bad marriage became less depressed when their spouse died, whereas those with a good marriage became more depressed.

Dependence also has been discussed as a vulnerability factor for chronic grief reactions, with most investigators viewing emotional dependence as a form of insecure attachment. Such individuals supposedly have a tendency to form clinging relationships and react to real or threatened separation with intense fear or distress. Dependence has been examined only in a handful of studies, but most of these have found it to predict a poor outcome. This was the case for the study by Parkes and Weiss in 1983, which found that those involved in highly dependent relationships were more likely to experience intense yearning for the person who had died, as well as feelings of helplessness and indecisiveness shortly after the death.

VIII. THE ROLE OF CONTEXTUAL FACTORS

In predicting reactions to loss, there has been a growing recognition that it is important to have information about the context in which the loss occurred. As many investigators have pointed out, the loss of a loved one means different things to different people. When they lose their spouse, for example, some people lose their best friend, some lose their only source of financial support, some lose their business associate, some lose a coparent, and some suffer all of these losses. By "unpacking" the life event to determine exactly what was lost, it is possible to gain a more precise understanding of the relationship between exposure to bereavement and subsequent health problems.

One recent study suggested that it is important to take both moderating and contextual factors into account. Eight classes of risk factors were examined separately for women who lost their spouse in two different contexts: those who lost an ill husband and those who lost a husband who was well. Interestingly, there was virtually no overlap between those variables which predicted depression for women who lost a husband who was ill and those which predicted depression for those whose husband had been well. Modifiers of the impact of loss of an ill spouse included high involvement in productive activities, good mental health, and a good marriage prior to the loss. Factors enhancing the impact of losing a well spouse included low involvement in productive activities, a belief in a just world, and high dependency on the spouse prior to his death.

IX. INTERVENTION

The evidence reviewed above leaves no doubt that for a significant percentage of bereaved individuals, loss of a loved one causes considerable pain and distress. In many cases, especially when the loss involved is a spouse or child, or the incident was sudden, unexpected, or violent, this distress may last much longer than was previously believed. Nonetheless, studies have suggested that the bereaved rarely seek out professional help. A small percentage (5–10%) turn to their clergy or to their physician for assistance; an even smaller percentage attend support groups, and fewer still undergo psychotherapy. Freud once described bereavement as a malady that runs its course, and he maintained that treatment is unnecessary and perhaps even counterproductive. It would be desirable to know more about how the typical layperson views bereavement and why he or she does not usually seek professional help.

There is some controversy about whether more effort should be made to encourage the bereaved to seek treatment. Some practitioners maintain that as long as the grief is normal, it can be handled with the assistance of family, friends, and community supports (e.g., the church), and that professional intervention is not necessary. However, others maintain that given the intense pain usually associated with even normal bereavement, virtually all bereaved could benefit from some form of intervention. Of course, many treatment options are available for the bereaved; the options include individual psychotherapy, group or family therapy, peer support groups, and widow-to-widow programs.

A number of practitioners have discussed specific goals concerning treatment for the bereaved. It has been argued that interventions should facilitate the expression of grief, provide reassurance that feelings and responses are normal, ensure time for grieving, monitor risk of suicide and coping failure, and ensure that the mourner has appropriate medical attention and medication when symptoms warrant. Other major goals of treatment involve encouraging the expression of distressing emotions and developing the capacity to tolerate and modulate the painful feelings associated with grief. The bereaved should also be assisted in reviewing the lost relationship so that they can gain perspective on the relationship and move on to develop new relationships, in enhancing social support, and in developing strategies for dealing with specific problems brought on by the loss. Certain of these goals are facilitated by particular types of treatment; hence, individual psychotherapy would be the best treatment to provide monitoring of the necessity for medication and a referral if it is needed. A peer-support or widow-to-widow program may be most effective at providing reassurance that particular emotions are normal.

Most practitioners agree that a given strategy may be more appropriate under some circumstances than others. For example, support groups may be indicated for those with lower levels of distress while psychotherapy may be appropriate if the individual is greatly distressed or if he or she has a number of risk factors known to exacerbate the pain of the loss (e.g., concomitant stressors, sudden and unexpected loss, child loss). Below, we summarize available evidence for each of the major treatment strategies.

There is clear evidence in the literature that individual psychotherapy is generally helpful, particularly among those who are at high risk and/or who have inadequate social support networks. Although the literature is not entirely consistent, a number of controlled studies have suggested that those who undergo psychotherapy show benefits in comparison to those who do not. For example, cognitive–behavioral interventions have been shown to be successful in reducing the bereaved's tendency to avoid reminders of the loss and the distress that typically occurs when such cues are encountered. Over time, these cues stop evoking strong painful responses.

Treatment studies of this sort have produced significant differences between treatment and control groups. While initial studies focused primarily on exposure to cues, more recent cognitive behavior therapists have added additional components, including graded involvement in roles and activities, and exercises designed to focus on cognitions of hopelessness and negative self-esteem. It remains to be seen whether these latter techniques will prove to be successful. There is also evidence from controlled studies to suggest that brief, focused psychodynamic therapy can be very effective in helping the bereaved. Other therapeutic techniques, such as the gestalt empty chair technique, where the bereaved person converses with the lost loved one, have generated considerable enthusiasm in case reports but have not yet been subjected to careful empirical study.

A long-standing and widely used treatment option is the community-based widow-to-widow program developed by Phyllis Silverman in the late 1960s. Recently widowed women receive a telephone call from a widow contact, called an aide, who has undergone training on bereavement, supportive counseling, and community resources. These aides offer emotional and practical support for as long as the mourner requires in the form of telephone calls, home visits, and group meetings with other recently widowed women. Silverman developed the program based on her view of grief as a normal reaction to loss that requires support from the community, rather than as a psychiatric illness that needs to be treated by a professional.

Controlled intervention studies testing the outcome of this type of mutual-help intervention have had mixed results. Some studies find no differences in adjustment between those who participate and those who do not, while other studies indicate that participants do, in fact, benefit from the programs. In the most widely cited controlled study of a widow-to-widow intervention, Mary Vachon and her colleagues found that this type of intervention was beneficial, especially to those widows at high risk. Vachon followed 162 widows for 2 years, 68 of whom were paired with a widow contact. She found that those widows receiving the intervention who were initially assessed as being in "high distress" were more likely to move to low-risk status than were similar members of the control group. In general, widows who received this support recovered faster than those who did not. Those who had low levels of social support particularly benefitted from the program. Differences between the treatment and control group were especially apparent in interpersonal adaptation. The treatment group had made new friends, were involved in new activities, and felt less anxious and depressed.

The treatment literature provides encouragement for the wider application of treatments for the bereaved, but leaves us with a number of unanswered questions. First, while there is considerable evidence that treatments are effective, virtually nothing is known about why they are effective, or how they influence the grief process. Hopefully, future studies will include more dependent variables so that we can learn more about which outcomes are impacted by which therapeutic processes. Second, there is an enormous need for the development of new treatments for special populations at risk. This is particularly the case for those who experience the sudden, unexpected, traumatic loss of a spouse or child. Because such individuals are motivated to avoid cues associated with the loss, they may be particularly unlikely to seek psychotherapy or to remain in treatment. Third, we need more information about the optimal timing of therapeutic treatment. Most professionals have suggested that the period between about 1 and 3 months is the best time to start therapy, but no research has focused on the subject. Finally, it has been suggested that different treatments might be appropriate for those with different symptoms of grief. For example, those who are in a state of delayed or inhibited grief might benefit from emotional expression of their distress, while those who are in a state of chronic grief may not be helped by this strategy. An interesting finding to emerge from the treatment literature is that in many studies, a minority of individuals have become worse as a result of intervention. We must enhance our understanding of the specific conditions under which a certain therapeutic technique, such as exposure or encouragement of expression, has negative consequences.

X. COPING WITH THE SOCIAL ENVIRONMENT

As noted above, there are strong cultural norms for how long it should take to recover from a major loss. Individuals are typically expected to be "back to normal" within 6 months or a year after losing a spouse, and within 1 or 2 years after losing a child. The available research provides clear evidence that, particularly when the loss is sudden and unexpected, the recovery period may last much longer. One study found that, even among older women who lost their husbands, a large percentage of women experienced clinical depression lasting for a two-year period.

As a result of a pervasive belief that people should recover relatively quickly from a major loss, those in the bereaved person's social network are often uncomfortable with displays of grief that fall outside the proscribed timetable. Moreover, they communicate this to the bereaved. Widows frequently report that even intimates do not support the need to mourn their loss beyond the first few days after the death.

Research has demonstrated that those in the bereaved person's social network use a variety of specific strategies to get them to inhibit displays of grief. These strategies include discouraging the grieving person from expressing feelings (e.g., "tears won't bring him back"), minimizing the loss (e.g., "you had many good years together"), and encouraging the grieving person to recover more quickly (e.g., "you should think about dating," "you should get married again"). There is clear evidence to suggest, however, that the bereaved do not find such comments helpful. In fact, such reactions may place a burden of guilt on the bereaved that adds to their distress from the loss. There is consensus that what they do find most helpful is an opportunity to express their feelings if they want to, an opportunity to interact with others who are bereaved, and a sense that family members and friends are there for them—that is, available to meet their needs.

Clinicians frequently admonish the bereaved to express their feelings rather than hold them inside. Yet there is evidence to suggest that those who express their distress and elicit negative reactions from others may fare less well than those who do not reveal their distress at all. It is hoped that future research will help to clarify the interpersonal dynamics of coping with loss and provide answers to questions such as: Does social suppression of one's distress lead to increased ruminations about the loss, and does this contribute to subsequent health problems or inability to concentrate and function? Are there alternative ways of expressing one's distress that are more beneficial than talking, such as artistic expression (poetry, painting, writing, or keeping a diary)? Are there ways that the bereaved can express their distress that are less likely to evoke negative emotions in others (e.g., bereaved persons may elicit less rejection if they convey anxiety or depression than if they convey bitterness or rage)?

XI. FUTURE DIRECTIONS

In this article, we have attempted to make two major points. First, the grief process is extremely variable. Some people are devastated by a major loss, while others seem to emerge relatively unscathed or may be even strengthened by the grieving process. Second, many ideas about grief from popular culture—for example, that people must experience distress following a loss, and that failure to do so is indicative of pathology; and that people "work through" their feelings and return to normal functioning within a proscribed timetable—have not been substantiated by empirical research. While researchers have identified several factors that influence how people react to a major loss, much remains to be learned. In this section, we spell out the implications of the current state of knowledge and suggest some areas for subsequent research.

Considering what we know at present, what can any of us do to ease the pain of a grieving person? The evidence suggests that the most important thing we can do is remain nonjudgmental about how the bereaved person is grieving. Some people will return to work quickly and may even become involved in another relationship within a few months. Others may show intense depression for well over a year and may cry when reminders of the loved one are encountered. Conveying that the person's coping reaction is inadequate or inappropriate will only intensify his or her distress. On the other hand, a nonjudgmental attitude is much more likely to be perceived as supportive and healing.

One potentially important area of research highlighted by this review concerns subjects who fail to show intense distress following a major loss. This review suggests that such a reaction is not at all uncommon. Moreover, there is little evidence from these studies to suggest that these respondents develop subsequent problems. Hence, there are a number of questions that it would be useful to address. Do these individuals exhibit classic signs of grief and mourning despite their lack of intense distress? Do they show fewer ruminations about the loss than individuals who are more distressed? Do they devote a lot of energy to avoiding reminders of the loss, and are they able to encounter reminders with equanimity? Is such a lack of distress best understood as occurring because the relationship was not a close one, because the person is in a phase of denial, or because he or she is demonstrating resilience or coping strength?

There is also evidence to suggest that respondents who are most distressed shortly after the loss are likely to be highly distressed one or two years later. The question is, what predicts initial high distress? Unfortunately, this question can only be answered through research designs that are prospective (i.e., in which individuals are asked questions about variables such as their health, marriage, and social support network prior to the loss as well as following the loss). Since many of these variables are likely to be affected by the loss, it is highly desirable to assess them before the loss. At present, there are a number of prospective studies in progress.

In addressing the question of why some individuals show little distress following a major loss, it will be important to move beyond self-report methodology and use measures that are indicative of real physiological change. Such a study would help us to determine whether those who do not show intense distress develop subsequent physical health problems.

In addition to using measures of actual physiological status and health change, it will be important to supplement typical measures of grief and distress with measures of personal growth. Many individuals have suggested that people may undergo positive changes as a result of a major loss, but this has rarely been shown empirically. It would also be interesting to determine whether people must go through a period of intense distress in order to achieve personal growth, or whether those who do not become as distressed are just as likely to exhibit personal growth.

This review has revealed that there are a number of areas that, despite their importance, have received relatively little research attention. First, only a few studies have focused on the long-term effects of a major loss. It is especially important to enhance our knowledge of the long-term effects of losses that are sudden, traumatic, or violent, since there is clear evidence in the literature that such losses are very damaging. Moreover, in addition to understanding the long-term mental and physical health consequences of a major loss, it is important to augment our current knowledge about thoughts, memories, dreams, nightmares, and anniversary reactions. Many bereaved persons find that they react with intense distress to cues associated with their loved one for many years. A difficult aspect of this process is that it is impossible to predict when one will encounter such a cue, and hence, lose one's equilibrium. One man who was working with one of us (CBW) had dinner with his boss several years after the loss of his daughter. He dissolved into tears at the restaurant when they encountered the hostess, who looked exactly like his daughter. We believe that reactions of this sort are far more important than was previously suspected. For example, they may account for the social withdrawal so often witnessed among the bereaved.

Much more needs to be known about the processes that inhibit healing and promote a continuing high level of distress. One possibility is that people who have suffered a loss, especially if it was sudden and traumatic, may come to process information about the world differently from those who do not experience such a loss. For example, people who lost a child in a drunk-driving incident may be more sensitized to, and more disturbed by, advertisements for liquor, news stories about drunk-driving crashes, etc.

To date, there has been little diversity in the subject populations studied in bereavement research. Most studies have focused exclusively on Caucasian women. Relatively little is known about men, and there is virtually no information about how African Americans or Latinos react to a major loss. Moreover, as noted earlier, most studies have focused on loss of a spouse or young child. Much less is known about how people react to the death of a sibling, a parent, or an adult child.

In this article we have reviewed evidence regarding the importance of risk factors like social support and concomitant stressors. Two risk factors that have received relatively little attention, but that we feel are important, are views of the world and prior stressors. In working clinically with the bereaved, it has been our observation that if a person's view of the world is shattered by a given loss, intense and prolonged stress is likely. In contrast, if a person's philosophical perspective or view of the world can be incorporated into what has happened, we believe that intense distress is far less likely. The reason why we feel prior stressors may be important is that they can influence a person's current view of the world. Moreover, a loss might cause intense distress by evoking or stirring up memories of a prior loss.

Finally, much more needs to be known about the medical establishment's beliefs about the bereaved and what constitutes appropriate treatment. Evidence reviewed in this article suggests that because the bereaved are expected to suffer, those in the medical establishment practice a kind of pharmacological Calvinism in treating the bereaved. Tranquilizers and antidepressants that have been shown to benefit the bereaved are often not prescribed because it is commonly believed that the person needs to experience pain associated with the loss in order to recover.

In summary, we have attempted to provide an overview of what is currently known about bereavement, what so-called "truths" believed about the grieving process have not been supported by available research, and what research directions might be fruitful to pursue. It is hoped that awareness of the state of current bereavement research will lead to greater appreciation of the variability in response to loss and of the importance of remaining nonjudgmental about bereaved persons' responses to their loss. Ideally, this will enhance the likelihood that the bereaved are treated with the compassion and respect they deserve.

Bibliography

Raphael, B. (1984). "The Anatomy of Bereavement: A Handbook for the Caring Professions." Hutchinson, London.

Osterweiss, M., Solomon, F., and Green, (1984). "Bereavement: Reactions, Consequences, and Care." National Academy Press, Washington, DC.

Parkes, C. M., and Weiss, R. S. (1983). "Recovery from Bereavement." Basic Books, New York.

Rando, T. A. (1993). "Treatment of Complicated Mourning." Research Press, Champaign, IL.

Stroebe, W., and Stroebe, M. S. (1987). "Bereavement and Health: The Psychological and Physical Consequences of Partner Loss." Cambridge University Press, Cambridge.

Stroebe, M. S., Stroebe, W., and Hansson, R. O. (1993) "Handbook of Bereavement: Theory, Research, and Intervention." Cambridge University Press, Cambridge.

Wortman, C., and Silver, R. C. (1989). The myths of coping with loss. *J. Consult. Clin. Psychol.* **57,** 349–357.

Group Dynamics

Paul B. Paulus
University of Texas at Arlington

Glossary

Additive task Group tasks in which the contributions of individual members are added together to form a group product.

Compensatory task A group task in which the contributions of individuals are averaged to form a group product.

Competition A relationship among individuals in a group in which the success of one member is associated with lack of success for other group members.

Conjunctive task A group task in which all of the group members must complete a specific action before it is finished.

Cooperation A relationship among individuals in a group in which the success of one member increases the chances of success of the others.

Deindividuation A state of decreased self-awareness and a lowering of self-control that can occur when individuals are actively involved in groups.

Disjunctive task A group task in which there is one correct solution. As soon as it is discovered by one member and accepted by the group, the task is solved.

Group Two or more individuals having some common bond, goal, or task.

Group brainstorming Generating as many ideas in groups as possible without concern for quality and evaluation.

Group development The stages through which groups go during their existence.

Group norms Strong expectations for behavior that develop and exist in groups.

Group polarization The tendency of group members to become more extreme in their attitudes or opinions after discussions with individuals who have similar attitudes or opinions.

Group socialization The process by which individuals become full-fledged members of groups.

Groupthink Defective decision making in groups that results from in-group pressure to reach consensus.

Intellective task Verbal or mathematical tasks on which there is a demonstrably correct solution.

Judgmental task Tasks that involve evaluations for which there do not exist demonstrably correct answers.

Leader The person who has the responsibility or capability of directing group activities.

Mixed motive Situations in which group members are confronted with the choice of whether to cooperate or compete with other group members.

Social comparison The tendency to compare our opinions and abilities with others when we are uncertain about them.

Social facilitation A term used for the study of the effects of the mere presence of co-workers or observers on task performance.

Social loafing Reduction in effort by individuals in groups when their individual performances are not easily identified or evaluated.

Work teams Groups of workers that are provided some autonomy in carrying out their assigned tasks as an organized unit.

GROUP DYNAMICS is the study of the forces or processes that are responsible for various group phenomena. Groups influence individual behavior in many ways, but individuals can also have an impact on these groups. Groups appear to satisfy many needs, but they often lead to performance or decision making that is less than optimal. Several of the

Encyclopedia of Human Behavior, Volume 2
Copyright © 1994 by Academic Press, Inc. All rights of reproduction in any form reserved.

processes that underly group behavior and ways of improving group functioning are discussed.

I. MAJOR CHARACTERISTICS OF GROUPS

Group dynamics is the study of group behavior. Groups come in many forms and have many different reasons for their existence. Some groups are merely short-term aggregations of people with no strong interrelationship, such as groups at spectator events. Other groups such as clubs, churches, and families have strong bonds and maintain long-term relationships. Some groups develop simply to have a good time while others are concerned with accomplishing specific tasks. It is difficult to use a single description for all types of groups, but most would agree that groups consist of two or more individuals who have some common bond, goal, or task. Many groups are part of an organization or large social system such as a corporation or college.

A. Reasons for Joining Groups

There are many different reasons why people join groups. They may choose a group because they share with other members a desire to reach a certain goal (e.g., a political party), to perform a particular task (e.g., play basketball), or to have social connections. The decision to join a particular group may also be motivated by a variety of personal needs. Groups may fullfill needs for belonging, attention, affection, approval, and support. Individuals who are motivated by such needs are likely to seek groups that consist of individuals that have similar values and beliefs. By involvement in groups, individuals can also establish an identity as in the case of joining a fraternity, sorority, or a political activist group. In addition to personal needs, individuals may join groups for other needs such as achievement and influence, to make money, to obtain information, or to learn a skill.

B. Group Socialization

Groups differ greatly in the process by which individuals join and become full-fledged members of the group. Some groups have stringent entrance requirements while others have few if any (e.g., political parties). Most individuals who join groups appear to go through some sort of socialization process. At first the prospective member and the group will investigate each other to determine whether group membership should be considered. Once someone joins a group, groups typically have various procedures and programs to help the newcomer become a full-fledged group member. Once this socialization process is complete, full acceptance as a member of the group occurs. At this point, the new member presumably feels a strong commitment to the group. This commitment may wane over time due to conflicts, boredom, or competing interests. The group may attempt to resocialize the individual, but if these efforts are not successful, the individual may exit the group.

C. Group Development

Groups go through various stages during their existence. In the forming stage individuals get to know each other and the various group rules. This is often followed by a storming stage in which members compete for positions, roles, and leadership. If the conflicts associated with this stage are resolved effectively, the group enters the norming stage in which there is the development of a deeper emotional bond and common perspective about how the group should function. At this point the group can focus on the achievement of its goals and tasks in the performing stage. As long as groups function satisfactorily in pursuit of various goals or tasks, they should be able maintain their existence rather easily. However, if the major goals for tasks are achieved or if the group is having difficulties in achieving its goals, the group may disband or adjourn.

D. Group Structure

Groups typically have a structure that defines how work is to be accomplished and who is responsible for various tasks. There are a number of different dimensions of group structure. In decentralized groups, decisions are shared by most or all members of the group, whereas centralized structures place the responsibility for decision making in the hands of leaders. Decentralized groups tend to have higher degrees of satisfaction but are not necessarily more effective than centralized groups. *Vertical specialization* is the degree to which there exist levels from the top to the bottom of the organization. Groups with much vertical specialization require effective communication up and down the hierarchy. In some groups there is much division of labor with group members doing highly specialized activities. In other cases group members work on broader tasks that require a range of activities and skills. *Horizontal specialization* is the degree to which the group is divided into subgroups for various tasks. There appear to be trends in organizations to increase decentralization, reduce vertical specialization, and to have less division of labor. While these changes may lead to greater worker satisfaction, their impact on improved productivity depends on many factors such as the type of work, phase of the group, type of leadership style, and the culture.

II. INFLUENCE PROCESSES IN GROUPS

A. Arousal

Although groups differ along many dimensions, there are certain forces that play an important role in most groups. One of the most basic impacts is that of degree of arousal. When others are observing us or working with us, we seem to be in a state of heightened arousal or emotionality. This may be in part due to a concern about what others are thinking about us or how they are going to react to our behavior. This enhanced stimulation or arousal may increase our ability to do simple tasks or behaviors but it may hinder the performance of relatively difficult tasks or behaviors. This is often seen in the performance of athletes in front of spectators. The general study of effects of the presence of audiences or coworkers on performance is termed *social facilitation*.

B. Diffusion of Responsibility

When one becomes immersed in group activities in which one's individual actions or unique contributions are difficult to separate from those of the other group members, group members may experience a diffusion of responsibility. That is individuals may not feel personably accountable for their actions. In extreme cases this may take the form of *deindividuation* in which the person loses a sense of self-awareness or experiences a lowering of self-control. In this state the individual may be very susceptible to the influence of others in the group. Therefore, if others are exhibiting antisocial behaviors, the individual may be prone to act in similar ways. Diffusion of responsibility can also take its toll on group task performance. When individuals work on a task as a group, they may not feel individually accountable for their performance. The larger the group, the less the accountability and the more likely that individuals will demonstrate social loafing or reduced efforts. [*See* SOCIAL LOAFING.]

Diffusion of responsibility in groups is not inevitable. It is most likely to occur when it is difficult to identify the individual group members, there is no individual evaluation of performance, the task being performed is easy or boring, and members of the group are all doing the same task. Alternatively, it can be reduced or eliminated by increasing individual evaluation or identifiability, by using tasks that are difficult or interesting, and by having individuals in the group doing different tasks.

C. Social Comparison

1. Comparison of Opinions

Groups of course perform a variety of activities. They make decisions, solve problems, perform tasks, set goals, make plans, or engage in a social activities. Each of these activities provide opportunities for individuals in groups to compare themselves with others. This tendency or drive toward social comparison is seen as one of the basic social influence processes in group situations. It is motivated by one's uncertainty about the accuracy of one's beliefs or opinions and a desire to evaluate one's adequacy or ability along a variety of dimensions. Individuals can use this social comparison process to evaluate their opinions, attitudes, personal characteristics, and abilities. For opinions and attitudes, the tendency is to compare oneself with individuals who are generally similar to oneself in a variety of characteristics that are salient to the group members such as age, gender, religion, values, and other opinions or attitudes. This implies that individuals will seek out groups consisting of individuals who already appear to be similar to them on a number of dimensions. As a result, many groups form on the basis of similarity of interests, attitudes, and characteristics. Moreover, interaction among such group members should increase the extent to which the members receive support for their existing opinions or ideas. Thus, groups should increase the confidence of individual group members in their collectively shared ideas, opinions, and values. [*See* SOCIAL COMPARISON.]

2. Comparison of Abilities

Comparison of abilities among group members involves a slightly different type of process. Comparing one's ability or characteristics with those of others has potential implications for one's self-esteem. If one compares favorably, one's self-esteem is likely to be enhanced. If one compares unfavorably, one's self-esteem may be reduced. One way to increase the probability of a favorable outcome is to use someone who is slightly superior to oneself as a basis of comparison. If as a result of this *upward comparison* process (e.g., a game of tennis, a sales contest) this other person is indeed superior to oneself, the negative impact on one's self-esteem should be minimal. That outcome should have been expected. Yet if one actually performs in a way superior to that of the comparison person, one's self-esteem should receive a strong boost.

Sometimes individuals appear to engage in *downward comparison*. This involves comparing with someone of less ability, or lower status, or who is less fortunate than oneself. This is most likely among people of low self-esteem or have low expectations or self-confidence. Because these people do not expect to compare favorably with others of superior ability or status, this can be seen as a way in which they can ensure maintenance of their self-esteem or positive perceptions of their performance or situation. This type of comparison is often observed when people have had some serious disease or illness. They may compare their situation favorably with those who have had even worse health problems.

D. Conformity and Independence

Individuals in groups have a variety of social needs. Most have a need to be accepted by others and to be seen in a favorable light. People also have a strong desire to have certainty about different aspects of their social world. Although certain physical features of our world are subject to little disagreement (e.g., color, shape, and size of objects), there is potential for significant disagreement about issues for which there are no objective or commonly accepted answers (e.g., religion, values, and politics).

Our social needs are often met in groups. Other group members can provide acceptance and approval or help increase one's certainty about subjective issues. This fact is the basis for power of group members over the behavior of other members. This power may be exerted to make group members adhere to social norms of the group. *Norms* are strong expectations for behavior that develop and exist in groups. Groups may expect certain types of dress, manners, and beliefs. Individuals who do not adhere to the group norms may face disapproval or possible rejection. To the extent that individuals are concerned with maintaining positive acceptance by other group members, the group has *normative influence* over the individual. The degree to which the individual depends on the group as a basis for deciding subjective or social issues (e.g., how to vote) is the extent to which the group has *informational influence*. As a result of the social and informational influence processes, group members often adhere closely to arbitrary social norms and share a high degree of similarity in opinions and attitudes. When individuals deviate from the group norms, other group members may exert pressure to have the individual change their behavior or opinions to match those of the group more closely. The degree to which individuals match the standards of the group as a result of such pressure is known as *conformity*. If they do not change their behavior, they may be rejected or ignored by the group. [*See* OBEDIENCE AND CONFORMITY.]

E. Leadership

Although group members are often a source of directive pressure within groups, certain group members have special positions of power that enable them to exert greater influence than other group members. Individuals who have the capability of, or responsibility for, directing group activities are called *leaders*. These leaders may be appointed as in business enterprises, may be elected as in political groups or organizations, or may achieve their positions because of their status in the group (e.g., age, wealth). The capability of a leader to influence groups derives from various bases of power. *Reward power* is the ability of the leader to provide desired rewards such as money, promotions, and approval. *Coercive power* is the ability to punish group members for failure to comply with requests. This type of power is often the basis for the control exercised by dictators over their populations. Leaders have *expert power* if they are seen as being very knowledgeable and able to provide correct solutions to problems. If group members desire to emulate characteristics of the leader, the leader has *referent power*. Followers may strongly identify with leaders who have physical or socially attractive features. When someone has been elected or appointed to an office on the basis of appropriate procedures, this person has *legitimate power*. Individuals may obey their requests or commands because social norms suggest that this is appropriate.

F. Communication in Groups

Communication involves the exchange of information in groups. Most groups or organization have both formal and informal means of communication. Formal communication networks can vary in degree of centralization. In centralized networks information from all group members goes through one individual. This is an effective structure when transmission of information is the primary group task. In decentralized networks group members freely communicate with one another. Centralized networks may lead to overloading of the central communicator and are associated with less satisfaction for peripheral members but may be very efficient for relatively simple tasks. Decentralized networks are best when the group is confronted with complex problems that require full exchange of information. *Downward communication* in an organization or group goes from the top to the bottom of the organizational hierarchy. This typically involves directives and information related to performance of tasks. *Upward communication* goes from the lower levels of the hierarchy to higher ones and often is used to provide feedback about performance and effectiveness of procedures or policies. Lateral communication is the exchange of information among members or subgroups at a similar level of the hierarchy. Effective functioning of groups requires accurate and efficient communication throughout the organization using all available channels.

Groups also have various informal means of communication. For example, *grapevines* are informal communication networks based on interpersonal relationships. They are often involved in the transmission of rumors. Informal communication can take various forms such as verbal, nonverbal, written, or electronic. Communication appears to be most effective if multiple channels are employed. Verbal messages followed up by written ones may optimize both impact and clarity. When messages are delivered in person, the receivers have access to nonverbal cues such as facial expressions, eye contact, and bodily movements. These may allow individuals to look for hidden meanings in the verbal message. For example, bodily cues may be helpful in assessing whether someone's verbal message reflects this person's true feelings. Electronic communication is becoming increasingly important in many organizations. It can be very efficient and may facilitate high levels of communication across different levels of the group hierarchy. However, important messages may have greater impact if they are delivered verbally or in person.

G. Environmental Influences

Group activities take place in a variety of physical environments. Sometimes people work or play in very crowded situations. At other times groups may be isolated in quiet rooms. These environmental conditions may influence the quality and nature of the interactions. Workers in crowded or noisy office environments may be less productive and less sociable than those in less crowded ones. Noisy conditions can also increase the chances of aggressive incidents. Even the arrangements of the furniture in a room can affect the interaction among group members. Furniture that is arranged to encourage interaction may lead to more communication and positive group feelings. Size of the group is also important. In meetings or classrooms, large group sizes may inhibit individuals from participating in the group process. [*See* ENVIRONMENTAL PSYCHOLOGY.]

III. WORKING IN GROUPS

A. Types of Group Tasks

Many of our daily tasks are done in group situations. We may prepare meals at home with family members, fix a car with a friend, play basketball with our neighbors, and work in an office with our coworkers. While some tasks can be done only with groups, in other cases individuals could do them in isolation. One interest has been to determine to what extent groups are a help or hindrance to the solution of problems or performance of various tasks. This of course depends on the type of task or activity. Much research has investigated tasks that simply involve the addition of individual products such as counting money or generating ideas. These are *additive tasks*. While groups obviously will produce more than any single individual, they may not outproduce a similar number of individuals performing alone. On the other hand, if the group members are in competition with one another or there is evaluation of individual performance, individuals in groups may outperform solitary individuals. These patterns of results hold only for relatively simple tasks in which motivation is closely related to performance level. On relatively complex or learning tasks, the individuals in groups may perform more poorly than solitary individuals because of increased anxiety associated with accountability or evaluation in groups.

Some tasks involve averaging the contributions of group members such as estimating the number of beans in a jar. This is called a *compensatory task* because the biases in judgment of specific member can compensate for the biases of the other members. *Disjunctive tasks* require members of a group to discover a correct solution to a problem. As soon as one member comes up with a correct solution that is accepted by the group, the task is complete. However, unless the solution is fairly obvious, groups may sometimes not accept correct solutions and therefore function more poorly than comparable groups of individuals working alone. On *conjunctive tasks,* all of the members must complete a certain action before that task is completed. This is exemplified by a mountain-climbing team. Here the performance of the group is determined by its least able member.

Group tasks can also vary in the extent to which it is possible to demonstrate that there is a correct answer. There are no demonstrably correct answers for *judgmental tasks* that involve evaluations such as the attractiveness of art or the appropriateness of social positions. *Intellective tasks* involve verbal or mathematical problems for which demonstrably correct solutions do exist. On judgmental tasks group consensus is the main determinant of the group judgment. For intellective tasks, the correct answer will be chosen if it is recognized by one or more of the group members. In fact, groups appear to be quite good at detecting errors or wrong solutions in the process of determining the correct answers on such problems.

Another important dimension of group tasks is whether group members are in a competitive or cooperative relationship with one another. *Cooperation* exists when the task success of one member enhances the probability of success of other members of the group. Sports teams are typical of such groups. Cooperative relationships minimize conflict, lead to positive interpersonal feelings, and may enhance performance on complex or learning tasks or on tasks requiring a wide range of skills. *Competition* exists when the success of one group member comes at the expense of failure by other group members, as in classes where teachers limit the number of high grades. Not surprisingly, this relationship is often associated with negative interpersonal feelings and conflict. However, competition may enhance performance by increasing motivation, especially on well-learned or simple tasks. Most situations involve both cooperative and competitive elements and are referred to as *mixed motive*. When individuals are confronted with these types of situations, they are often tempted to compete even though cooperation would be the best strategy for the group in the long term. This dilemma may be reflected in the difficulties societies face in getting individuals to sacrifice personal gain for the common good. [*See* SOCIAL VALUES.]

B. Group Brainstorming

1. Perception of Group Performance

It is obvious from our discussion that the effectiveness of groups depends on the task, group members, and the context of the group. Although groups may excell in some situations, they often perform below expectations. Individuals seem to believe that groups will be quite productive, as in the case of group brainstorming. This involves the generation of ideas in groups under a set of rules designed to encourage free exchange of novel ideas. Group members are encouraged to generate as many ideas as possible and instructed not to criticize or evaluate the ideas of others in the group. While most individuals expect this to be an effective procedure, brainstorming groups actually generate fewer ideas than do a comparable group of solitary individuals (nominal groups).

2. Processes in Group Brainstorming

The relatively poor performance of brainstorming groups appears to be caused in part by the blocking or interfering effects of the activity of other group members that occurs when one is trying to generate ideas in a group. In addition, group members may be concerned about others' reactions and inhibit the number of ideas they contribute. Group members may also reduce their efforts or loaf in the group because they typically are not held accountable for individual ideas. All of these factors tend to inhibit performance of individuals in groups. Furthermore, group members may be inclined to match their level of performance to that of the less productive members.

3. Procedures for Effective Brainstorming

Various techniques may help counteract and overcome some of the problems of brainstorming groups.

Group brainstorming should be used only with individuals who are comfortable working in groups. Group members should generate ideas alone first until they cannot generate additional ideas. At that point they may find the group useful in stimulating additional ideas.The group should be given a challenging goal and held accountable for it.

C. Teamwork

It has been popular in recent years to organize workers into teams to accomplish their assigned tasks. For example, the quality control circles that have been promoted in the automotive industry involve having a small team of workers meet periodically to identify and solve work-related problems. Other work teams may consist of small groups that are given a high degree of autonomy in setting goals and work procedures. Having group members work cooperatively in this manner should be beneficial for morale and motivation, but it does not guarantee success. Work teams should be used only if cooperative interaction is likely to facilitate productivity. Once they are formed, they should be provided with the necessary resources and develop clearly defined tasks and role differentiations. As with most groups, the monitoring and assistance of a skilled outside supervisor is required to help the group overcome the problems inherent in group interaction such as conflict and social loafing.

IV. GROUP DECISION MAKING

A. The Nature of the Process

Much decision making occurs in groups. Committees, task forces, legislatures, and social organizations are just a few examples of groups that often have to make group decisions. The advantage of group decisions is the opportunity for input from a wide variety of members. This also helps distribute responsibility for the decision among the group members. As with group brainstorming, the effectiveness of group decision making appears to be in doubt. Unless formal procedures are in place, groups often do not effectively organize their decision-making process. One major problem is that groups tend to go along with the first plausible idea. When the majority of the group has accepted a particular idea or solution, the group consensus rarely changes. The direction of the group decision in juries and other similar groups can be predicted quite well from a knowledge of the prior support for a position among group members. It appears that the direction of influence typically goes in the direction of the largest faction. So if a plurality of a group initially favors a particular position, the final group decision is likely to be consistent with that position. This strength-in-numbers effect may reflect a domination of the information exchange process by the larger faction as well as pressures to conform to the dominant group position. Of course, this effect is most likely to occur on judgmental tasks where there is no objective right or wrong decision.

B. Decision Rules

When groups make decisions they can employ various decision rules to govern their decision such as plurality, majority, or unanimity. The more agreement that is required of the group, the more difficult will be the process of coming to a group decision. However, demanding decision rules, such as unanimity, may get all of the members involved in the decision and discussion process. As a result, the discussion of the issues may be more thorough and group members may be more satisfied with the decision.

C. Group Polarization

Groups often come together to discuss issues or opinions. Although there is typically a wide range of opinions among individuals, sometimes group members have similar attitudes or opinions about a topic. This is particularly true in the case of groups that form on the basis of agreement on important issues (special interest groups, political groups). When groups of individuals who are biased to a particular side of an issue discuss this issue as a group, they tend to move their opinions further in the already favored direction after the group discussion. This shift toward more extreme opinions in groups is termed *group polarization*. It appears to be caused by two different processes—social comparison and information exchange. Individuals in a group who perceive themselves as favoring a particular side of an issue may discover during the group discussion that others more strongly endorse that position than they do. As a result, they may feel some pressure to change their opinions to more strongly reflect the valued direction. In addition, most of the ideas exchanged in such a group would tend to support the favored direction. These then provide additional support for the individual taking a more extreme position. [*See* ATTITUDE CHANGE.]

The group polarization phenomenon applies to groups that have a fair degree of homogeneity of opinions, attitudes, or values. Because people tend to select groups on the basis of similarity of interests and beliefs, many groups are fairly homogeneous. The social comparison and information exchange processes in such groups should tend to move the group's attitudes in more extreme directions. It is therefore not surprising that there is so much conflict among groups who are divided along political, religious, and ethnic lines or any other dimension that is related to strong differences in values (e.g., management versus labor, environmentalist versus developer). To minimize such polarization tendencies, it may be useful to increase interaction in cooperative ventures among members of the different groups.

D. Groupthink

1. The Nature of Groupthink

Even if members in a group have a broad range of opinions, this does not guarantee that these will be carefully examined in a group discussion. Sometimes decision-making groups have strong pressures to come to agreement. They may be under time pressure to make a decision. This pressure may come from competitors, from crises that demand quick solutions, or from arbitrary deadlines. Groups that are under such pressures may come to decisions without carefully evaluating alternative courses of actions. The processes related to such defective decision making are known as groupthink.

2. Characteristics of Groupthink

There are a number of features that appear to facilitate the occurrence of groupthink. Consistent with the polarization effect, groupthink is most likely to occur if the group is fairly homogeneous in member characteristics and is insulated from other groups. In addition, a directive leader who champions a particular point of view and exerts pressures for consensus is likely to lead to groupthink.

In groups that are prone to groupthink there is pressure toward uniformity of opinion, with direct pressure being applied to dissenters. Group members may also rationalize away information inconsistent with their decision. Obviously groups in which pressure to uniformity and cognitive distortions predominate are unlikely to make well-informed decisions. They are not going to carefully examine a broad range of alternatives or information. They will tend to overlook the risks of the favored alternative or fail to develop contingency plans. Information in support of the impending decision will be given more weight than information inconsistent with it. Decisions approached in this fashion may be disastrous for businesses and governments. The Bay of Pigs invasion under the direction of President Kennedy, the decision to escalate the war in Vietnam, and the Challenger disaster are among some of the highly publicized instances of groupthink. Detailed analyses of the decision making involved in these events has revealed much evidence for symptoms of groupthink and the related defective decision-making process.

3. Preventing Groupthink

A number of procedures may minimize or eliminate the occurrence of groupthink. The group should set a goal of making the best possible decision rather than simply developing consensus quickly with a minimum of conflict. Group leaders can play an important role by promoting this goal and not pressuring the group in a particular direction. Procedures should be developed to assure a wide-ranging and full discussion of the alternatives. Breaking the group into small subgroups at various points in the decision-making process may increase the chances of diverse perspectives being carefully considered. If these groups come to similar decisions, confidence in the correctness of the decision is increased. Input from knowledgeable outsiders who are not subject to the pressures of the groups may also be helpful in providing some assessment of the reasonableness of the decision.

V. INFLUENCE OF INDIVIDUALS ON GROUPS

A. Minority Influence

There are many forces within the group that constrain or limit the behavior of its group members. Groups generally do not respond favorably to those who disagree with the majority consensus or position. This fact often inhibits individuals from expressing deviant opinions. When they have the courage to deviate, group members typically attempt to persuade them they are wrong and move them in the direction of the group. If these attempts are unsuccessful, opinion deviants are often rejected or ignored.

While opinion deviants are not liked, they do have some potential positive impact on groups. Because of their distinctive position, they gain the attention of group members and may stimulate them to rethink the issue. The fact that someone is willing to go against the grain of the group may give them some additional credibility and influence. This is particularly true if they persist forcefully in the face of attempts by the majority faction to produce compliance with their position. As a result, the members of the majority may actually change their opinion in the direction of the majority position. This change tends to be a "true one" in the sense that it is an actual change in their personal opinions that may not be expressed during group interaction but is evident in anonymous measures of beliefs taken after exposure to minority influence. In contrast, individuals who change their position in response to majority influence typically are only complying publicly with the group norm. Assessments of private beliefs often indicate little personal change. The ability of minority factions to stimulate cognitive reevaluation on the part of members of the majority may be one reason that exposure to minority positions in groups can produce subsequent increased creativity in individual problem solving.

B. Leadership in Groups

1. Characteristics of Leaders

Most groups have leaders. As discussed earlier, these are individuals who have the capability or responsibility of directing the group's activities. They may be informal or temporary leaders who derive their status from actively contributing to the welfare of the group. Those who dominate the discussion in a group are often seen as leaders. Leaders may also attain more formal positions of leadership by means of election or appointment.

The types of skills, traits, and interpersonal styles required of leaders will depend greatly on the type of group. Certainly, military units and research teams require different types of leaders. However, there are some characteristics that appear to be generally important for successful leadership. Leaders must desire to have influence over others, need to be motivated to achieve goals, and should have the determination to persist in this process. Successful leaders tend to be self-confident, honest, and flexible. Intelligence, creativity, and relevant knowledge are also important. Although it makes a great deal of sense that leaders should be motivated and capable, these characteristics do not ensure attainment of positions of leadership or leadership effectiveness. The behavioral style of leaders and situational factors often appear to be more influential than personal characteristics.

2. Leader Behavior

Analyses of leadership behavior have revealed the existence of two distinct styles. Some leaders are consideration or person oriented. They are concerned primarily with maintaining good relationships among group members. Their approach to group members is one of interpersonal warmth and trust and involves open communication between leader and followers. A second style is known as production or structure oriented. The main concern is structuring the situation so that the task is done well and efficiently. This involves developing ways for the group members to function more effectively without concern for developing positive interpersonal relationships. Actually, it is possible for leaders to exhibit a wide variety of combinations of degree of concern for people and concern for productivity. A *hybrid leader* or team manager who is able to exhibit both a concern for people and who has the ability to structure the work environment for productivity may be ideal. [*See* LEADERSHIP.]

3. Situational Factors

The effectiveness of a particular style of leadership appears to depend on characteristics of the situation such as follower support of the leader, degree of task structure or clarity, and leader power over followers. These features influence the degree of control the leader has over the situation. With low degrees of situational control, production-oriented leadership may be required for effective group performance. Under these conditions group members need direction and structure, and attempts at improving interpersonal relations may have little impact. With moderate degrees of situational control, a person-oriented style may yield more positive group relations and motivation to perform. A task-oriented leader may alienate group members by using a directive or autocratic approach and as a result further weaken the situational control. With high degrees of interpersonal control, a person-oriented style is not necessary and the group may respond positively to the task- or production-oriented behaviors of the leader. Group member satisfaction as well as performance tends to be highest in groups with the appropriate match of situation with leadership style.

4. Transformational Leaders

Sometimes leaders excite the imaginations of their followers and are able to motivate them to perform at high levels or make extreme sacrifices. Franklin Roosevelt, Winston Churchill, Martin Luther King, and Ross Perot are just a few examples of leaders who fall into this category. These types of leaders have a vision, act in a confident manner, and are good communicators who have a dynamic personal style. They are also skilled in judging others and manipulating their own attractiveness and appeal to their followers. Transformational leaders tend to emerge when groups face crisis situations and need both a strong and visionary leadership and an emotional commitment to a cause by the followers. These types of leaders are not necessary and probably not useful when groups are focused primarily on routine activities.

VI. SUMMARY

We have learned much about group dynamics. Groups are subject to a wide range of processes as they go about their various tasks. Our present state of knowledge can aid us in getting the most out of these groups. However, there is still much to learn and there are many interesting new issues on the horizons. Electronic technology allows for new ways of organizing group interaction and structuring group tasks. These interactions and tasks will be mostly cognitive or informational in nature. New developments in cognitive psychology may allow for the development of more sophisticated understanding of such cognitive interactions among group members. However, it seems likely that many of the principles of group dynamics uncovered with face to face interacting groups will be applicable to understanding the interactions of electronic groups.

Bibliography

Forsyth, D. R. (1990). "Group Dynamics." Brooks/Cole, Pacific Grove, CA.

Hackman, J. R. (1987). The design of work teams. In "Handbook of Organizational Psychology" (J. W. Lorsch, Ed.), pp. 315–342. Prentice–Hall, Englewood Cliffs, NJ.

Hendrick, C. (Ed.) (1987). "Group Processes: Review of Personality and Social Psychology," Vols. 8 and 9. Sage, Beverly Hills, CA.

Janis, I. L. (1982). "Groupthink," 2nd. ed. Houghton-Mifflin, Boston.

McGrath, J. E. (1984). "Groups, Interaction and Performance." Prentice–Hall, Englewood Cliffs, NJ.

Moreland, R. L., and Levine, J. M. (1989). Newcomers and oldtimers in small groups. In "Psychology of Group Influence" (P. B. Paulus, Ed.), pp. 143–186. Erlbaum, Hillsdale, NJ.

Paulus, P. B. (Ed.) (1989). "Psychology of Group Influence." Erlbaum, Hillsdale, NJ.

Paulus, P. B., and Garcia, J. E. (1991). The dynamics of groups and organizations. In "Social Psychology" (R. M. Baron and W. G. Graziano, Eds.). Holt, Rinehart and Winston, Fort Worth, TX.

GUILT

Donald L. Mosher
University of Connecticut

Glossary

Affect Primary innate biological motivating system, consisting of nine primary affects, each defined by a discrete pattern of facial, vocal, breathing, neural, and endocrine responses to innate or learned activators.

Central assembly All functionally joined units of the minding system during a quantum of time, including the transmuting mechanism which renders conscious a report selected from the larger set of messages.

Moral ideology Module of moral rules, within a world view, that define which aspects of human conduct are to be celebrated as virtues or sanctioned as vices.

Scene Unit of analysis of the stream of life, defined as a happening with a beginning and an end, forming an organized pattern that includes affects, objects, times, places, events, actions, psychological functions, props, and outcomes.

Script Unit of analysis of personality, defined as a psychologically magnified set of rules for ordering information in a family of connected scenes to predict, control, defend, and evaluate variants and analogs of the family of scenes. *Sex* is to scene as *sexuality* is to script.

GUILT can be defined as the feeling of remorse for violating a moral rule. Within the script theory of Silvan Tomkins, guilt is the affect of shame when centrally assembled with a moral judgment that the self is blameworthy. Such moral barriers interrupt ongoing excitement and enjoyment to trigger guilt. Shyness, shame, and guilt are identical as an innate affect, but as moral shame, guilt amplifies an evaluation that the self is responsible for violating a moral rule. Although free-floating guilt may not be assembled with perceptions of specific causes and consequences in consciousness, whenever moral self-blame is so assembled, a specific moral urgency is manifested. Guilt is the primary human motivator that prevents, inhibits, avoids, escapes, modifies, amends, or defends against possible or actual immoral fantasies or conduct. "Guilt" refers primarily to the affective–cognitive report of anticipatory, coincident, or consequent moral remorse and secondarily to the motivational disposition to minimize guilt.

I. A SCRIPT THEORY OF SEXUAL GUILT

The human infant is born into a world in which she quickly learns to continue or repeat good scenes and to escape or avoid bad scenes. Inevitably, the human being comes to want to maximize the discrete positive affects of interest–excitement and enjoyment–joy and to minimize the discrete negative affects of fear–terror, distress–anguish, anger–rage, shame, disgust, and dissmell (an auxiliary to olfaction, like disgust is to gustation). Disgust and dissmell are innate defensive responses that are auxiliary to the hunger, thirst, and oxygen drives and which generalize to learned sources. Shame is an affect auxiliary response that specifically inhibits interest and enjoyment whenever a temporary barrier interrupts those activated positive affects. Examples of temporary barriers include all sources of shyness, discouragement, exposure, and guilt. Surprise–startle resets the central assembly, commanding an immediate response to its activator regardless of the nature of the ongoing scene. [*See* ANGER; ANXIETY AND FEAR; DISGUST.]

Positive affects are experienced as rewarding and inherently acceptable from birth; just as the negative

Encyclopedia of Human Behavior, Volume 2
Copyright © 1994 by Academic Press, Inc. All rights of reproduction in any form reserved.

affects, in addition to their distinct qualia, are invariably experienced as punishing and inherently unacceptable. Just as pleasure and pain require no learning and are distinctive in their qualia, so too are innate affects unlearned and distinct in experience. Affects are innate biological entities, encoded in subcortical centers and activated by gradients of neural stimulation that match distinct innate programs. Learned activators of affect must match or mimic these gradients. Whether activated by innate or learned sources, each discrete affect conforms to its innate profile of activation. Tomkins's theory and empirical research on affect stimulated Paul Ekman's and Carrol Izard's independent demonstrations of the universal recognition of facial affect. Ekman's research continued to identify neural and physiological correlates of discrete affects; Izard's research demonstrated the unlearned appearance of affect in children. [*See* FACIAL EXPRESSIONS OF EMOTION; MOTIVATION, EMOTIONAL BASIS.]

The experience of affect is primarily the experience of patterned changes in the facial skin and secondarily in breathing and vocalization which may or may not be associated with perception, analysis, or memory in the central assembly. When in consciousness, however, the nine discrete affects acquire their nuance and meaning from the information that is centrally assembled and transmuted into a report. Affect is activated by only three classes—nonoptimally intense, accelerating, or decelerating gradients—of neural firing. Consciousness is biased toward the inclusion of affect because the governing principle for filling the limited channel of consciousness selects messages to report with the most dense neural firing from the larger set of messages until the limited channel is filled.

The human infant quickly learns to repeat, create, and evaluate whatever scene is the source or target of excitement and joy; just as she learns to predict, defend against, and evaluate whatever object poses a barrier to such excitement and joy (thereby, activating shame or guilt) or whatever activates fear, distress, anger, disgust, or dissmell.

Discrete affects motivate through their capacity to amplify by analogy any ongoing or recruited responses; such responses are correlated with their sources, both sharing a distinct affective qualia and a similarity to the innate profile of activation of the discrete affect. So, the activation of excitement from a sexual partner touching the sexual skin amplifies both the source (being touched) and target (the sexual partner) of that affect, giving both an excited qualia with a moderately accelerating profile as the specific gradient that triggers interest–excitement.

Any temporary barrier or interruption of ongoing sexual excitement or sexual enjoyment innately activates shame. Guilt is the variant of shame in which moral cognitions regard the source, the target, or sexual affect itself as violating a moral rule within an ideology of what sexuality means and how it is to be celebrated or sanctioned. The moral ideology of parents and other significant socializers affects their style of socialization of guilt, including their tolerance of sexual affect and how they link moral cognitions to sexual scenes.

Experience in sexual scenes or in vicarious sexual scenes that involve moral rules can be connected as sharing a family resemblance, including the interruption by guilt of sensory pleasure, excitement, and enjoyment. Whenever a good scene turns bad, it becomes a candidate for psychological magnification. Psychological magnification increases the urgency of rules concerned with interpreting and understanding, with predicting and managing, with creating and defending, and with evaluating and justifying a connected set of scenes that have been so amplified by affect that they have become urgent to understand and manage. The individual attempts to order the information from the family of scenes by sets of rules: psychological principles that govern psychological functions.

Like their rules, scripts are selective in the scenes they govern; incomplete, requiring auxiliary information as the scenes unfold; often conditional upon variables as alternatively specifying response, tactic, or strategy; variously accurate and inaccurate in their interpretation and management of the scene; and continually changing with disconfirmation or as new scenes are added to the family.

Fresh affect is activated during the process of ordering information in the family of scenes, thereby re-amplifying the already once amplified scenes *and* their rules. The principal script factor is repeated dense change in the polarity of affect within the set of scenes. Thus, the good sexual scene turned bad—sexual guilt interrupting sexual excitement and enjoyment—becomes the primary source of the sex-guilt script.

Scripts are modular, capable of combination, recombination, and partitioning. Sexual scripts are composed of modules of rules ordering information from several families of scenes, including affect socialization scenes, moral scenes, interpersonal scenes, sexual scenes, and gender scenes. For example, gender, interpersonal, and moral rules are learned respectively in scenes concerned with the socialization of gender, of interpersonal relations, or of morality. Later, these modules become connected with developing sexual scripts within the encompassing family of scenes relevant to sexuality.

The broadest classification of sexual scripts would order them based upon the overall ratio of positive to negative affect within the plot of a life, including sexual scenes: (a) affluent, (b) damage–reparative, (c) limitation–remediation, (d) contamination–decontamination, and (e) toxic–detoxification. Given its stable equilibrium of positive over negative affect, an affluent sexual script provides flexible and alternative paths to deepening sexual involvement. In damage–reparative sexual scripts, perceived damage activates shame–guilt that may be temporary when it is repaired by seeking forgiveness, avoiding specific sexual objects or sexual linkages, or by making amends for harming the partner. In limitation–remediation sexual scripts, some life-long limit in the nature of the self (e.g., gender dysphoria) or sexuality (e.g., sin) or world (e.g., homophobia) requires remediation by continuing effort to remedy it (e.g., by a sex-change, or chastity, or coming-out). In contamination–decontamination sexual scripts, sexuality is replete with plurivalent conflict, impurity, and ambiguity—often creating nuclear scripts that constellate more and more scenes to the family—that require continual but failing efforts to decontaminate the multiple deep disgusts that a sexual scene activates. In the toxic–detoxification sexual script, which has a stable equilibrium of negative affects over positive, a lust-murderer, for example, must recast the scene in which he trembled in terror by venting his rage against a dissmelling oppressor (mother) or her analog (prostitute).

The sexual guilt script is a modular component of sexual scripts. It functions as an affect control script, in which guilt (in contrast to distress, fear, disgust, anger, or dissmell) controls sexual excitement and enjoyment. An affect control script regulates the density, display, vocalization, consciousness, communication, conditionality, and consequences of affect.

Sexual scenes and sexual guilt can be either rewardingly or punitively socialized. Ideology includes a world view about the nature of sexuality and affect that varies from left-winged humanist ideology, identifying with the oppressed and social change, to right-winged normative ideology, identifying with the dominant authority and the status quo. For the humanist, children and their playful affects, like human nature, are to be celebrated as exciting sources of enjoyment. For the normative, children must be taught to adhere to the norms, and, thus, positive affect should only occur when a norm is met. So, for the normative, the only good sex should be marital, monogamous, passionless sex in the missionary position to procreate. A rewarding socialization of sexuality contrasts with a punitive socialization in which sexual excitement and enjoyment must be interrupted or further controlled (as contaminating or toxic) by socializers who activate negative affect in an attempt to offset sexual affects. Thus, the punitive versus rewarding socialization of sexual affects, often joined with specifically stated moral rules that are either normatively inviolate or humanistically contextual, respectively, create either intolerance or tolerance of the density, display, vocalization, consciousness, communication, conditionality, and consequences of sexual excitement and enjoyment. Thus, a psychologically magnified sexual guilt script often produces a damage–reparative sexual script in which the conditionality of sex is inhibited and limited by invariant moral rules, the density of sexual affect is interrupted or diminished by guilt, the display and vocalization of sexual interest–excitement and enjoyment–joy are attenuated or suppressed, the consciousness of sex as perception and fantasy is selective and reduced, the communication of sexual interest and information is decreased or stopped, and the consequences of sexuality are often feared as sexual and moral failure or, still worse, as disgusting and dangerous. Shame–guilt is not a highly toxic affect; in contrast, the more strongly that sexuality is psychological magnified by more toxic disgust or still more toxic terror, rage, and dissmell, the more problematic the sexual script becomes. In the punitive socialization of sexual affects, these affects are both suppressed and conceptually linked to sexual sin (guilt) and dirt (disgust) and danger (fear) by the Normative socializer. The sexual sinner is perceived either as contaminated (disgusting) and as requiring decontamination or as so evil and perverse (dissmelling) as to be toxic and beyond redemption, activating righteous rage.

Whenever the punitive socialization of sexual affects has been predominantly associated with the use of disgust to minimize sexual affects, then a contamination–decontamination script becomes likely as the major sexual affect control script. Whenever the punitively socialization of sexual affects produces an affect control script based upon the socializer's rage and dissmell to sanction sexual affects, producing terror and dissmell and hidden rage in the child, then a toxic–antitoxic sexual script may be the outcome. Although such anti-sexual ideological scripts are intolerant of communicating about sex, the same inflexible, anti-sexual, moral rules may have been offered by the parent or inferred by the child as a rationale for their cruel behavior; the less toxic but still moderately punitive parent may use this same anti-sexual ideology when inducing shame–guilt. The rewarding socializers of sexual affect communicate conditional rules for sexual guilt that are flexibly tied to issues of caring and responsibility in interpersonal relations rather than to fixed and exceptionless rules (e.g., no masturbation or premarital sex or oral–genital sex *ever*.). A rewarding socialization of sexuality celebrates sexual interest–excitement and enjoyment–joy as rewarding affects to be maximized in life; sexual scenes are good scenes, rewarding and valued.

II. THE MEASUREMENT OF GUILT

By the mid-1960s, Donald Mosher had developed sentence completion, true–false, and forced-choice inventories to measure the personality disposition of guilt. The items included: (a) admissions of feeling guilty, sinful, ashamed, disgusted, or revolted by sexual, aggressive, or other immoral acts, intentions, or fantasies; (b) moralizing attitudes that characterized sexuality or aggression as abnormal, self-destructive, or detrimental to society; and (c) self-reports that judged the self to be blameworthy, even as evil and unworthy of forgiveness, as desiring punishment, as practicing ascetic denial, or as engaging in acts of confession, contrition, and restitution. Nonguilty items included: (a) denials of shame or guilty feelings over immoral acts, intentions, or fantasies; (b) nonmoralizing attitudes toward sexuality and aggression as normal, expected, or pleasurable; and (c) self-reports of self-acceptance following sexual or aggressive behavior, plans to avoid detection, or to enjoy transgressions brazenly.

The construct of guilt is given meaning by a script theory that specifies the processes by which it effects scenes and scripts; *guilt* is given meaning by the rules for its use in the scientific context. As a script (or personality variable), guilt is a disposition to activate the affect of guilt and guilty responses that minimize guilt in a moral-conflict scene. An inventory of guilt should include psychometric referents faithful to the theory that reliably orders individuals' dispositions to guilty affect and responses. Construct validation requires using the measure of guilt to test theoretically generated hypotheses. Favorable empirical outcomes both corroborate the theoretical hypotheses and provide evidence of the construct validity of the inventory.

Influenced by the classic papers of Cronbach and Meehl on construct validity and Fiske and Campbell on the multitrait–multimethod matrix, Mosher, in a classic paper, demonstrated that his three measure of three aspects of guilt (sex guilt, hostility guilt, and morality conscience) converged appropriately within subscales and discriminated guilt from social desirability and anxiety. However, these promising multimethod matrices used multiple psychometric measures of the same trait—guilt, not maximally dissimilar measures. Thus, they demonstrated the reliability more than the validity of the three aspects of guilt. These measures of guilt represented the state of the art in personality scale development in the mid-1960s, leading to 300 empirical studies.

Later, a factor analysis of the Forced-Choice Guilt Inventory demonstrated that the internal structure of each subscale was similar for males and females and that the factor structure was complex within each subscale. The four-factor structure for sex guilt was: (a) *childhood sexual experiences,* (b) *sexual relations before marriage,* (3) *feelings about adultery,* and (4) *sociosexual guilt*. Another study of the concept of item bias in item-response theory used a pool of 72 sex-guilt items; the authors concluded that, within items, the relationships of items to guilt were the same for men and women, but, across items, the relationships of items to guilt were different for men and women. Men had higher thresholds than women for feeling guilty over prostitution, adultery, childhood sexual play, sexual desires, and petting; men and women had about equal thresholds for guilt over obscene literature, unusual sex practices, sex relations, before marriage, masturbation, and dirty jokes; and men had lower thresholds than women for guilt over homosexuality. Only 2 of the 72 items yielded poor item responses. Several studies had demonstrated that women usually scored lower on sexual guilt than men. These item-response results indicated that this is a function of differences to particular stems which appear to reflect differences in socialization and, consequently, in the gender and sexual scripts of men and women; the pattern of the data generated no real surprises, since men were known to be more homophobic than women and more accepting of heterosexual contacts outside of courtship or marriage.

To measure the affect of guilt, six adjective prompts (guilty, remorseful, repentant, sinful, blameworthy, and conscience stricken), usually embedded within Izard's Differential Emotions Scale, provided reliable and useful in many studies.

In 1975, Paul Abramson and Mosher developed an Inventory of Negative Attitudes toward Masturbation as a measure of masturbation guilt. Three factors were (a) *positive attitudes toward masturbation* ("Masturbation can provide harmless relief from sexual tensions"), (b) *false beliefs about harm* ("Masturbation can lead to homosexuality"), and (c) *negative affect over masturbation* ("When I masturbate, I am disgusted with myself.").

After 20 years, the means of sex guilt had fallen, the Revised Mosher Guilt Inventory (Mosher, 1988) was developed by using the old items with contemporary samples. The response format was altered to a limited-comparison format, which is like a forced-choice format in pairing stems, but uses a Likert rating scale on each item. This strategy of renewing the item pool, using contemporary internal consistency analyses from both sexes, permitted the retention of past evidence of construct validity while improving the predictive power of the inventory.

In 1988, Mosher and James Sullivan developed the Sexual Polarity Scale to measure sexual ideology (also included were items from Tomkins's Polarity Scale of Normatives and Humanists). *Sexual ideology:* (a) consists of a more or less organized set of ideas about sexuality that orders information about norms and vices within a sexual world view; (b) polarizes individuals into communities that believe and share either a left-winged naturalist or a right-winged Jehovanist view of the sexual world; and (c) serves as an ideological script that interprets, manages, defends, evaluates, and criticizes ongoing, remembered, and imagined sexual scenes.

III. A SUMMARY OF RESEARCH ON SEX GUILT

A. Double-Entendre Words

The earliest research on sexual guilt examined reports of recognition and word association in a double-entendre (e.g., screw, rubber, prick, balls, snatch) paradigm. Across several studies, high-sex-guilt men and women delayed recognition of sexual words and gave fewer sexual associates, although sexual associations were elicited from them by repetition of the list or by instruction. Frequency of sexual associations also were influenced by sexual arousal or priming by pin-ups, expectations of the experimenter's response, and the "approachability" and sex of the experimenter.

In a series of studies, Gary Galbraith succeeded in reconciling the initial failures to find the expected, delayed reaction times to double-entendre words by high-sex-guilt participants. By an instruction requiring either a sexual or a nonsexual association to a color-coded stimulus word, sexual responses produced longer latencies than nonsexual associations and high-sex-guilt men and women had longer response latencies to sexual responses but not to asexual responses.

B. Premarital Sexual Behavior and Moral Decisions

Several studies demonstrated that the personality disposition of guilt is negatively correlated with delinquent and criminal status and behavior. Among felons, their undetected and unreported totals of crimes were correlated in the .60s with sex guilt for sex crimes; hostility guilt for violent crimes, and total crimes with both hostility guilt and morality conscience. Among college students, similar negative correlations were reported with self-reported drug-use and delinquencies. Not only did high-guilt men and women use marijuana, depressants, stimulants, and hallucinogens less, but when they did use these drugs they found the drug experience less pleasant and reported more "bad trips."

A frequently replicated result found sex guilt to be inversely related to the cumulative level of premarital sexual experience. Also, sex guilt was inversely related to sexual standards, virginity, age of first coitus, lifetime and last-year frequencies of coitus, number of coital partners, and orgasmic frequency across several samples of men and women. As predicted, high-sex-guilt men and women expected to feel guilty, giving moral reasons for not participating in premarital sex. High-sex-guilt men, who have affiliative needs, attempted fewer passes and used less exploitative tactics when dating; just as, high-sex-guilt women reported experiencing less aggressive sexual behavior.

Decision making about beginning premarital coitus was studied by combining an interest in sex guilt with Lawrence Kohlberg's approach to moral judgment. Delinquents scored low on guilt and moral judgment, yielding a positive correlation in a truncated range without any postconventional scores. Within samples of college women or of men and women, high-sex-guilt subjects scored highest on the law-and-order stage of morality. Whether a couple decided to have coitus was predicted best by male sex guilt, then by male moral judgment, and then by female sex guilt. Males, but not females, with a law-and-order orientation reported more standing decisions not to begin coitus; the lesser power of women and the traditional norm that women should accept male dominance may overcome high-sex-guilt women's sexual restraint. Although uncorrelated with sex guilt in men, the need for autonomy was inversely correlated with sex guilt in women.

Among noncollege women, low-sex-guilt women were more sexually aroused or orgasmic: to fantasy and erotica, sex-play, masturbation, and coitus. Anorgasmic women reported greater discomfort communicating about the need for clitoral stimulation, more masturbatory guilt, more belief in sex myths, and more sexual guilt.

Using an interpersonal pleasuring paradigm, modeled after the aggression machine, high-sex-guilt males administered less pleasure to women. When they anticipated meeting the woman, they gave still lower levels of pleasure to her. All of the men increased their level of interpersonal pleasuring across trials, suggesting that giving pleasure is a rewarding response, but a less acceptable one for high-guilt men.

C. Contraception, Abortion, and STDs

Several studies reported an inverse correlation between sex guilt and attitudes toward and the use of effective premarital contraception. Masturbation guilt appeared specifically to inhibit women's use of the diaphragm that requires, for them, a disgusting (when imagined or when inspecting) manipulation of the vulva for vaginal insertion. Also, high-masturbation-guilt women reported more distress from genital herpes, less sexual interest, and less willingness to tell partners; Abramson also found that high fear combined with high masturbation guilt led to more frequent outbreaks of genital herpes among infected women.

High-sex-guilt men and women not only disapproved of abortions but were reluctant to grant them, particularly when pregnancies resulted from casual sex. Yet, an abortion clinic reported their clients were higher on sex guilt than nonpregnant, sexually active women; high-sex-guilt women cannot plan to sin by seeking oral contraceptives. High-sex-guilt men know less about condoms and are reluctant to use them, even when they have a sexually transmitted disease.

Having found that high-sex-guilt women had coitus despite their reservations, failed to contracept or delayed the onset of contracepting, and had unwanted abortions, Meg Gerrard's research program sought answers. Noting that it was easier to prefer and recognize high levels of moral reasoning than to produce and articulate high levels of moral reasoning, Gerrard demonstrated that college women's level of endorsed moral reasons from a prepared list was higher than their ability to verbally articulate their own moral reasoning. The less sexually experienced, high-sex-guilt women had the largest gap between their preferences and their articulated moral reasoning. Gerrard concluded that the relationship between sex guilt and specifically sexual moral reasoning was strongly negative and was mediated by sexual experience. She argued that these women's maladaptive sexual behavior (coitus without contraception) resulted indirectly from their lack of sexual experience and, thus, their relative inexperience in coping with moral dilemmas. Pursuing this hypothesis, Gerrard and her associates studied the effects of sexual experience and sex guilt on the recall of sexual and nonsexual moral dilemmas. In particular, high-sex-guilt, sexually active women were compared to low-sex-guilt, sexually active women. Women whose sexual behavior violated their sexual norms had difficulty remembering sexual vignettes. What they did remember were the reasons *in favor of*, rather than against, participating in sexual activities, which the authors' interpreted as an avoidant and repressive defense against guilt.

D. Sexual Fantasy and Pornography

High-sex-guilt women who read erotica were sexualy aroused but felt guilty. While viewing sexually explicit films, high-sex-guilt men and women not only felt guilty but also rated the films as more pornographic, disgusting, and offensive; they considered oral–genital sex to be abnormal.

In general, men reported sexual arousal and positive affect to pornographic stimuli, whereas women reported a mix of sexual arousal and disgust. This reflects the bias in commercial pornography toward a male audience who reports more exposure to pornography. Nonetheless, high-sex-guilt men had less exposure to pornography in the past and looked less at *Playboy* while waiting for an experiment to begin. Viewing time of pornographic slides generally increased as a positive linear function of ratings as pornographic—highly arousing but disgusting images. But, unobtrusive timing during the viewing of sexually explicit slides revealed that high-sex-guilt men did not increase their exposure to more explicit slides, thereby minimizing their exposure to "forbidden" porn.

In a study of sex guilt and gender, "correct" choices in a discrimination task were followed by erotic slides, "incorrect" choices by nonerotic slides. Both females and high-sex-guilt subjects made fewer erotica-producing choices and also were less positive in their affective responses to the erotica. For individuals who experienced positive affect to the slides, they were experienced as rewarding; whereas for others, they were punishing.

When men and women viewed experimental films of a male or a female masturbating, the men were turned on by the female and turned off by the male masturbating; women were about equally responsive to both. Men and women high on either sex guilt or masturbation guilt reported more disgust, guilt, shame, and anger; men high on masturbation guilt reported the most disgust to the film of the male masturbating. Women, but not men, wrote a more elaborate sexual fantasy to the same-sex film of masturbation. For both sexes, high masturbation guilt was associated with less positive affect about the fantasy or about orgasm.

Given this difference in the ability of women relative to men to identify positively with same-sex masturbation, another study tested two plausible hypotheses that such negative responses were due either to guilt over masturbation or to homosexual threat in men. Results indicated that men's adverse reactions to a film of a male masturbating were consistent with both masturbation guilt *and* homosexual threat.

Recent research demonstrated that women responded more positively to X-rated videos designed for and by women than to X-rated videos intended for a male audience; men were responsive to both. Ideological beliefs about the harms of pornography—moral corruption and incitement to violence—influenced subject's rating of harmful effect on others.

Like the studies of pornography, studies of guided imagery of sexual encounters continued to find that high sex guilt was associated with less sexual arousal and more negative affect during imagined sexual scenes across a variety of experimental conditons. A causal model was posited and supported across free fantasy, remembered interpersonal sex and masturbation, and guided imagery of a sexual scene. Derived from script theory, the model specified: (a) sex guilt and masturbation guilt have both direct and indirect effects on subjective sexual arousal, (b) positive affects amplify, whereas negative affects attenuate, sexual arousal, and (c) affects mediate the indirect effects of sex guilt and masturbation guilt.

Sexual guilt was associated with: fewer sexual fantasies during intercourse, more guilt over such "abnormal" and "immoral" fantasies, and more sexual dissatisfaction and dysfunction. Studies of sexual fantasy production found that high-sex-guilt men and women produced more restricted content and shorter fantasies and reported more embarrassment and less sexual arousal while writing them.

E. Guilt and Defensive Processes

Defensive processes are inferred from correlates rather than directly observed in action. Still, a number of studies have documented the potential role of the modulation of various responses from guilty motives. When watching erotic videotapes, high-sex-guilt women reported less subjective sexual arousal but had more vaginal engorgement according to vaginal photoplethysmyography. Because women low in sexual arousability and sexual experience showed a similar pattern, Patricia Morokoff concluded that a history of inhibited sexual behavior facilitated increased responsiveness to "forbidden" stimuli. Although difficult to untangle, it appeared that sexual guilt mediated differential past exposure to sexual stimuli (a known outcome) or inhibited awareness of subjective sexual arousal despite physiological signs of arousal.

In a balanced placebo design (alcohol dosage crossed with expectancy), alcohol expectancy, but not alcohol itself, yielded greater penile tumescence and subjective sexual arousal to audiotapes of consenting intercourse, rape, and sadistic sexual aggression. High sex guilt (and hostility guilt) was inversely correlated with subjective sexual arousal for the consenting and rape tapes. Another investigation using a balanced placebo design had individual's watch sexual slides that were unobtrusively timed. The high-sex-guilt men reported less sexual and masturbatory experience and fewer orgasms; they rated the slides as more pornographic, had less experience with porn, and more negative attitudes toward it. Nonetheless, believing that they had imbibed alcohol permitted them to view the more pornographic material longer; thus, they now showed the same positive linear function of time with ratings of pornographic explicitness as the low-sex-guilt men.

A similar study with women had a less clear-cut outcome. More inhibited or less interested, women did not show a linear increase of viewing time with pornography ratings. It was only the low-sex-guilt women in both the placebo (expect alcohol/receive tonic) and antiplacebo (expect tonic/receive alcohol) who viewed the slides significantly longer than the control women (expect tonic/receive tonic). Thus, only the least inhibited women were responsive to either alcohol expectancy or alcohol dose. Although, the high-sex-guilt women did not change their viewing behavior, they reported the highest level of subjective sexual arousal.

Using a balanced placebo design in an information processing context, high-sex-guilt men increased penile tumescence to both heterosexual and homosexual videos only in the placebo condition of falsely expecting to receive alcohol. From these studies, it appears that, although many men may use alcohol to minimize the affective inhibition of sexual affects, high-sex-guilt men need only to expect alcohol/receive placebo to reduce their personal responsibility and to permit them to respond sexually to "forbidden" sources.

In 1974, false heart rate feedback was shown to influence high-sex-guilt men's ratings of attractiveness of sexual slides. In 1978, Frederick Gibbons demonstrated increased consistency between preexperimental attitudes toward erotica and laboratory response to erotica when men were self-focused, using a mirror to create self-focus. Women were more consistent in their rating as a function of self-focus, but high-sex-guilt women were less capable of enjoying erotica when self-focused.

Other investigators pointed out that less subjective sexual arousal in high-sex-guilt subjects might represent either suppression or denial of arousal in self-focused conditions. Supplying high-sex-guilt men with alternative attributions (either sexual arousal or undifferentiated arousal) produced denial, reports of decreased sexual arousal, and somewhat more undifferentiated arousal when viewing slides of nude women. Gibbons continued by examining motivational biases in causal attribution of arousal by introducing a placebo pill, asserted to create arousal. High-sex-guilt men and women who viewed an erotic video attributed their arousal to the drug rather than to the erotica. Attributing their arousal to a nonthreatening source reduced their guilt over transgressing a sexual standard that prohibits sexual arousal to erotica.

In self-awareness theory, self-focused attention increases consistency with standards of "correctness," whether such standards are internal or external. Gibbons asked what happens when a personal standard conflicts with external standards? Self-focused, high-sex-guilt women conformed more than others, supporting the *social* standards hypothesis. But, postexperimentally, they also had maintained their own personal standards. After modifying their responses in the liberal direction in response to conformity pressure, they reasserted their personal standards.

IV. IMPLICATIONS FOR THE SOCIALIZATION OF GUILT

The critical question in the socialization of sexual affect is whether the parent regards the sexuality of the child as positive or as an alien entity to be shaped to fit antisexual norms. If the parent can empathize with the child's sexual excitement and with the complexities of an emerging gender and sexual identity, then sexuality is neither an affront to the authority of the parent and society nor sinful, dirty, and dangerous. Instead, it is another aspect of interpersonal relationships. A humanist morality requires a rewarding socialization of sexual affect while helping the child tolerate the negative affect triggered by the inevitable shameful and guilty failures and distressing limitations that must be faced and tolerated before the young adult can be said have mastered a moral sexuality. The parent will attempt to minimize shame and guilt and to remedy limitations, but will neither contaminate sexuality with disgust nor make it toxic by fear, rage, or dissmell. Sexual morality will be justified by reasoned argument from moral principles, rather than consisting of draconian threats of punishment for engaging in sexual scenes defined as either conditionally or forever taboo.

Sex guilt is associated with religiosity, generational differences, and a normative and Jehovanist ideology, creating a continual tension between the sexuality of youth and the "morality" of conservative adults. Yet, a moral view of sexuality requires the same moral rules that govern all human relationships; it does not require an ideology that sex equals dirt and danger nor an affect socialization that instills sexual disgust, fear, and dissmell. Sexual dissmell motivates hatreds that cannot be morally justified. Social acceptance of sexual diversity requires tolerance of sexual affect in children and adults. At its best, sexual guilt is only a temporary barrier, not a permanent wall forbidding sexuality. At its best, a critical morality fosters nonmalevolence and benevolence in sexual relationships, not a moralistic intolerance of sex and sexuality.

Bibliography

Creighton, M. R. (1990). Revisiting shame and guilt cultures: A forty-year pilgrimage. *Ethos* **18,** 279–307.

Kelly, M. P., Strassberg, D. S., and Kircher, J. R. (1990). Attitudinal and experiential correlates of anorgasmia. *Arch. Sex. Behav.* **19,** 165–177.

Kugler, K., and Jones, W. H. (1992). On conceptualizing and assessing guilt. *J. Pers. Soc. Psychol.* **62,** 318–327.

Mosher, D. L. (1988). Revised Mosher Guilt Inventory. In "Sexuality-Related Measures: A Compendium" (C. M. Davis, W. L. Yarber, and S. L. Davis, Eds.). Graphic Press, Lake Mills, IA.

Mosher, D. L., and Sullivan, J. P. (1988). Sexual Polarity Scale. In "Sexuality-Related Measures: A Compendium" (C. M. Davis, W. L. Yarber, and S. L. Davis, Eds.), Graphic Press, Lake Mills, IA.

Mosher, D. L. (in press). Sexual guilt. In "Encyclopedia of Human Sexuality" (V. L. Bullough and B. Bullough, Eds.). Garland Press, New York.

Scheff, T. J. (1988). Shame and conformity: The deference emotion system. *Am. Soc. Rev.* **53,** 395–406.

Tomkins, S. S. (1991). "Affect Imagery Consciousness: Anger and Fear," Vol. III. Springer, New York.

HABIT

Paul Reading
Cambridge University, United Kingdom

Glossary

Dopamine Neurotransmitter primarily associated with behavioral activation. It is released mostly from neurons originating in midbrain nuclei, including the substantia nigra, and terminating in the striatum. Its release is enhanced by psychomotor stimulant drugs such as amphetamine.

Obsessive–compulsive disorder Disabling chronic psychiatric disorder which interferes with a patient's normal life and is manifested through obsessions or compulsions. The former refer to recurrent or persistent ideas, thoughts, or impulses that are perceived, at least initially, as intrusive and irrational. The latter represent repetitive, seemingly purposeful behavioral routines performed in response either to an obsession or according to certain rules that are often perceived as unnecessary or bizarre.

Procedural memory A form of long-term learning that refers to the acquisition of motor skills and habits in both humans and animals. It is separable from the capacity to learn and remember incidents and events and is often spared in subjects rendered amnesic by brain damage.

Reinforcement The tendency of stimulus–response associations to be strengthened by certain stimuli usually of an arousing nature. It is related to but distinguishable from reward processes in which certain stimuli elicit approach behavior.

Striatum An area of basal forebrain that can be divided into dorsal and ventral subregions, corresponding loosely to "motor" and "limbic" areas and largely comprising caudate nucleus and nucleus accumbens, respectively. The striatum receives inputs from the majority of cortical areas and sends outputs to thalamic and midbrain nuclei.

HABIT can be defined as behavior that has become automatic and removed from conscious awareness through a process of learning. The concept of habit has a rich history in early philosophies of human behavior and more recent formulations of animal learning theory. Humans and animals have at least two forms of long-term learning, one of which, termed procedural memory, can be considered as more primitive, based on stimulus–response memories or habits. Modern neurobiological evidence points to the striatum as a critical brain structure involved in the formation and expression of habits. When the striatum is dysfunctional, disorders of habit may occur, including obsessive–compulsive syndromes.

I. INTRODUCTION

The word "habit" has numerous connotations whether used in the field of psychology or in modern parlance. It derives from the Latin verb "habere" ("to have") and originally referred to the characteristic external appearance, manner, or bearing by which one would recognize an individual or class of individuals. The attire worn by some religious orders represents one specialized example of this. More

Copyright © 1994 by Academic Press, Inc. All rights of reproduction in any form reserved.

relevant to the ensuing discussion, however, is the more contemporary meaning that relates to the customs or practices characteristic of a social group or individual. In particular, the tendency for an animal or human to respond in a predictable and apparently automatic fashion to a stimulus, external or internalized, will serve as a working usage here. Even in this sense, however, the term covers many aspects of behavior when used in popular language or by psychologists. For example, a lay person may identify habits variously as mechanical movements or routine actions that might include dressing or washing; actions such as smoking related to acquired cravings; mannerisms or tics; characteristic modes of thinking leading to immutable attitudes about issues and events; or as actions evaluated on ethical grounds as being "good" or "bad." Even within the arena of psychology, the term may be applied to a spectrum of behavioral acts ranging from molecular aspects of behavior such as specific measurable components of a simple conditioned reflex to broader patterns of behavior extended over periods of time. In either connotation, however, there are two key underlying elements. First, the behavior being considered is evoked by a configuration of conditions, in turn dependent on an intrinsic "set," disposition, or readiness to respond to them. Second, a habit is invariably acquired, representing the end-product of a process of learning.

The concept of habit has a rich and influential history. Starting in the early 17th century, Descartes' dualist view of body and mind led to a conception of habit as the gradual easing with practice of "animal spirits" through the pores of a hydraulic system proposed as a model of physiological functioning. Following on, the concept of habit formed the bedrock of early English empirical philosophy. By placing emphasis on sensory processes, Hobbes used the concept of habit to provide a psychology of learning, proposing that all ideas stemmed from stimulation of the sensorium. The notion was taken further by Locke at the end of the 17th century who conceptualized the mind at birth as a "tabula rosa," an empty slate potentially influenced by early teaching and the installation of habits. Finally, habit formed the universal law of mind for Hume in the mid-18th century. His doctrine proposed that all perceptions and experiences, including beliefs of causation, were explained by habits, themselves established by consistencies between experiences.

It is toward the end of the 19th century, however, when the notion of habit was refined and integrated into a theory of behavior that was to have persisting implications for modern constructs. At that time, primarily as a result of Darwin's influences, the ancient dichotomy between animal and human mind was beginning to evaporate. William James' inspirational exposition *The Principles of Psychology* provided the foundation for an overdue conceptual reorganization. As one of the last proponents of a traditional mentalistic approach to behavior, James provided a prescient and eclectic model, comprising three distinct devices to explain behavior: (1) the ideomotor theory of voluntary action in which the idea of an occurrence of a voluntary act was sufficient to make the act occur; (2) habit, conceived as a short-circuiting of consciousness which occurred with repetition of a voluntary act; and (3) instinct. This last aspect was defined as "the faculty of acting in such a way as to produce certain ends, without foresight of the ends, and without previous education in the performance." It defied the popular view that since man possessed a superior intellect, he expressed few, if any instincts. Rather, James argued that man had many more varied instincts than animals but that they were more apt to be obscured by man's advanced mental apparatus. Habits were also deemed to be commoner in man as a result of increased neural plasticity, thereby allowing the performance of routine tasks and freeing the higher mental processes for more important and challenging tasks. Habit, according to James, was "the enormous fly-wheel of society, its most precious conservative agent." James even speculated on the existence of connections or fixed neural pathways, established after repetition, in order to explain the neural basis of habit formation. By conceptualizing instinct as a short-circuiting of habit that occurred over evolutionary time, a position subscribed by the majority of commentators including, perhaps surprisingly, both Lamarck and Darwin, a hierarchical scheme for the explanation of behavior became apparent: all behavior is originally voluntary, but after sufficient practice it becomes habitual, and after sufficient exercise of the habit it becomes, in turn, instinctive or hereditary.

Aspects of this simplistic view of habitual behavior, however, were challenged by the pioneering experimental results of a contemporary of James. Just before the turn of the 20th century, Thorndike was performing his classic studies on "animal intelligence" in which cats gradually became proficient at escaping from "puzzle boxes." He observed that after much varied, apparently random, responding, the cats would, by trial and error, strike a lever that led to their release and food reward. Over subsequent trials, the animals took less and less time to "solve" the task. In contradistinction to the relatively new and revolutionary view that animals' actions were governed by intelligence or by the memory of elicited pleasure, Thorndike contended that what was learned in the puzzle box was a direct association between sense impression and impulse to action, namely, a habit. Further, he argued that an idea per se had no power to initiate action. Rather, pleasure or the alleviation of pain was hypothesized to produce an automatic strengthening of a stimulus–response association, a contention that marked the birth of connectionism. His experimental findings, he argued, implied a process of selection and were not explainable in terms of mere repetition alone. The so-called *Law of Effect* was invoked, stating that, of several responses made to the same situation, those accompanied or closely followed by satisfaction would be more likely to recur when the situation recurred. Responses that led to dissatisfaction would have their connections with the situation weakened. Rewards and punishments in this context were termed reinforcements in later formulations. Although Thorndike's ideas have been exposed to fierce criticism in the intervening years, the clear fact that behavior is modifiable by its consequences and that appropriate reinforcement is an integral part of habit formation continues to influence modern theories of the neurobiology of motor learning as will be seen later.

While Thorndike was formulating the Law of Effect, the groundwork for a behavioristic revolution was being laid. Watson devised an entire system of psychology based on the formation of habits, forcefully abandoning concepts of hedonism and subjectivity. For him, habits were integrated systems of conditioned reflexes built around available innate patterns of movement. Language habits were special cases since they could become "implicit," representing the behaviorist equivalent of thought. Even personality was deemed as reflecting the end-product of hierarchical habit systems. In his scheme, man differed from animals only in his increased capacity for developing verbal, manual, and emotional habits. This extreme standpoint attracted an almost cult-like following and in a diluted form has been strikingly influential in subsequent theories of animal and human learning theory.

Of the neo-behaviorists concerned with "habit," Hull is particularly remembered as developing a quasi-mathematical theory concerned with explaining motivated behavior and establishing the fundamental behavioral phenomena underlying motivation. One of the main thrusts of his argument was to highlight the distinction between the actual performance of a learned act and the internalized tendency to perform the act when appropriately stimulated. This latter hypothetical construct corresponded to "habit strength," designated $_{S}H_{R}$, and it reflected a more or less permanent but latent change in the animal's nervous system. Its value was dependent on antecedent variables such as the number of reinforced trials. $_{S}H_{R}$ was strictly an intervening variable and not manifest in behavior directly. Rather, observable behavior was dependent on a reaction potential (SER), itself the product of $_{S}H_{R}$ and drive (D). The incorporation of drive in the equation SER $= f(_{S}H_{R} \times D)$ is, perhaps, the most perspicacious aspect of Hull's theory. Although it had been generally presumed that the strength of a learned response increased with practice and motivation, Hull's theory implying a multiplicative relationship was the first to address the interaction. It was based on data from two similar experiments conducted between 1938 and 1940 which provided virtually the whole of the empirical basis for his drive theory of motivation and, arguably, were the most important studies ever performed on rats. Briefly, in 1942 Perin trained four groups of rats to press a bar for food. All animals were deprived of food for 23 hours but were exposed to differing numbers of reinforced training trials (5, 8, 30, or 70). Tested in extinction (i.e., with no food available) and only under 3 hours of deprivation, the relationship between the number of previous trials and the resistance to extinction was examined, the latter defined as the mean time taken for the animals to exhibit a response-free period of 5 minutes. A negatively exponential curve was obtained. The results were compared to Williams' study from 1938, which used a higher level of deprivation (22 hours) when testing in extinction. The form of the two curves was mathematically similar providing the basis for Hull's famous equation. Hull later added further intervening variables representing inhibitory and other factors but the essence of his treatise was simple: habit must be energized by a drive state in the presence of appropriate stimulation if an actual response is to occur.

On this background, the role of habit in modern theories of animal and human learning theory can now be addressed.

II. CONTEMPORARY LEARNING THEORY AND THE FORMATION OF HABITS

A. Animals

Modern theories of animal learning have attempted to incorporate mechanistic models of behavior into more teleological accounts. Traditionally, it has been assumed that at some level of causal analysis the occurrence of a particular activity can be explained simply by the presence of an eliciting, releasing, or triggering stimulus. This concurs with the physiologist's notion of a reflex, the ethologist's concept of fixed action pattern, and the psychologist's conditional and unconditional responses. Indeed, it has been customary to refer to any behavior as a "response," implying the presence of an eliciting stimulus whether or not there is evidence for one. In contrast to such a stimulus–response model, an alternative account emphasizes that a particular behavior is controlled at the time of performance by an animal's knowledge about the consequences of this activity. In other words, an animal's behavior can be truly purposeful and goal-directed, referrable as an "action" to distinguish it from a response. There is little doubt that such a teleological system exists in humans but proving whether animals are capable of displaying true purposive actions has been far from an easy matter. Traditional S-R theorists such as Guthrie went as far to ridicule the concept with the famous quip that "the animal is left buried in thought." However, it is clear that such an ability would have considerable implications for behavioral flexibility and adaptability. This is especially apparent if the value of a goal object is changed either by an alteration in motivational state or by the acquisition of new knowledge about the goal. For example, if an animal has learned two separate routes to two sources of water when thirsty, one of which has a much higher saline content than the other, could it immediately select the route to the saline goal when subsequently salt-deficient? It is clear that a stimulus–response or "habit" account would not predict appropriate selection since the training received while thirsty should have simply strengthened the capacity of various stimuli to elicit approach without providing precise knowledge of the goals. The evidence for the existence of "actions" will not be addressed further here since we are concerned with the role of habit. Suffice it to say that there are considerable data supporting the propositional model of animal behavior which has given rise to "expectancy theory."

However, if the capability of animals to exhibit true goal-directed behavior is accepted, the question of whether a particular behavior is an action or a response arises. Clearly, during habit formation the same activity can be both an action and a response at different times. The popular contemporary account implies that an instrumental behavior starts as an action controlled by knowledge about its relation to the goal but becomes autonomous of its current value, simply triggered by the stimuli in whose presence it has been repeatedly formed. Contemporary theories have tended to neglect the study of habits, concentrating on more "intelligent" forms of behavior. However, there is no doubt that even complex human chains of behavior can become automatic as a result of life's goal devaluation. These have recently been called "slips of action" but were well characterized by James' who claimed: "very absent-minded persons in going to their bedroom to dress for dinner have been known to take off one garment after another and finally get to bed, merely because that was the habitual issue of the first few movements when performed at a late hour." In other words, for the middle-class of the last century, the stimuli associated with the bedroom at night could trigger the response of going to bed, even though this was inappropriate or "devalued."

However, from a modern perspective, surprisingly few studies have examined the anecdotal surmise, alluded to previously, that habit formation results from repeated practice and that extended training renders behavioral control autonomous of the current value of the goal. A simple experiment by Adams has recently helped to redress this imbalance. He trained two groups of food-deprived rats to lever-press for sucrose pellets on a so-called random ratio schedule where there is a fixed probability that each press will be rewarded. Each group received a total of 50 rewards per session. One group was allowed to perform a total of 100 rewarded trials whereas the other group was "over-trained" and received 500 rewarded trials. The sucrose reward was then "devalued" for half the animals in each group by pairing the consumption of the sucrose with "illness-inducing" lithium chloride injections. The remaining half of each group received the same injections but given noncontingently with the sucrose consumption. All rats were then tested for their rate of lever-pressing under conditions of nonreward, i.e., extinction. As might be expected, the rats with experience of 100 rewards and subsequent devaluation performed at significantly slower rates than those animals who had not been exposed to contingent lithium injections. However, this differential effect was not apparent in the two subgroups of rats having received 500 training trials. The 500-press group could, therefore, be interpreted as having performed in a habitual fashion, relatively unaffected by goal devaluation. Importantly, a subsequent reacquisition test implied that the difference in sensitivity in the overtrained animals to goal devaluation was not due to the ineffectiveness of the aversion procedure per se.

Although the above findings lend support to the notion that habits evolve from repetition, another more subtle explanation has been expounded by Dickinson with some supporting experimental evidence. He considered the changing experiences of animals as training is extended. Taking the above study as an example, in which there was a fixed probability that each lever press would produce a reward, the rats that were trained for 500 sessions would be expected to show a negatively accelerated acquisition function. In other words, early in training there would be a relatively large increasing change in the rate of performance between the early sessions as the animals learned the contingency between lever-pressing and sucrose delivery. Later, the increases in rate of performance from day to day would be considerably less. In turn, the relation between rate of pressing and reward rate would be experienced over a large range of values during the first few sessions, but, if the animals training were to continue, only over a restricted range later. In fact, during the later stages of extended training, the variation in the animals' performance is so limited that little contact is made with the instrumental contingency which, of course, is defined by the way in which the occurrence of the reward varies with behavior.

From this, the development of behavioral autonomy can be deduced. When an animal's performance is varying during early training, it experiences and consequently stores knowledge about the strong relation between behavior and reward rates. If the reward is devalued at this stage, performance rate is depressed via this knowledge, as in the group of rats with limited training (100 trials) and goal devaluation in the example above. However, overtraining means that the behavior–reward correlation is no longer experienced and that performance is no longer controlled by knowledge about this relation. Reward devaluation has little effect in the absence of such knowledge and a habit has been established.

This hypothesis predicts that if an animal's experience of a strong behavior–reward correlation is minimilized in some other way while maintaining performance, then habit formation should develop even with limited training. Dickinson, therefore, compared the effects of goal devaluation on two groups of rats that had received comparable training periods and total quantity of rewards but had been exposed to different schedules of reinforcement. Briefly, one group was trained on a random ratio schedule as in the Adams' study and the other on a random interval schedule in which reward became available with a constant probability in each unit of time. The subsequent lever press then delivered the reward. The linear behavior–reward rate function seen in a ratio schedule is not seen when random intervals separate the availability of reward. Instead, at low levels of performance, there is a strong positive relation between behavior and reward rate which rapidly weakens as the response rate rises. At modest levels of performance, the reward rate is relatively immune to variations in the behavior rate. By corollary, a habit should be acquired much more rapidly on this random interval schedule by virtue of the weak behavior–reward relation seen after minimal training. The results of the experiment confirmed this. Without detailing the procedure to match the random ratio and interval groups, it was found that the performance of the latter was impervious to reward devaluation. There was no difference in the rates of lever-pressing of animals trained on the random interval schedule for whom the reward had and had not been devalued, in contrast to the random ratio group.

In summary, the results suggest that, contrary to popular belief, habits do not result merely as a consequence of overtraining. Instead, they appear to arise because overtraining usually tends to reduce the variation in behavior and thus the animal's experience of the behavior–goal correlation which initially controls actions. A similar state of affairs occurs with limited training on a random interval schedule. In both situations, performance is no longer controlled by knowledge about behavior–goal correlations in the absence of the relevant experience.

B. Humans

The dichotomous nature behind the mechanisms of instrumental control of animal behavior alluded to above can equally be applied to human long-term learning. It seems likely that there is one form of learning that is influenced by the capacity to verbalize a strategy, open to conscious reflection and perhaps based on instrumental conditioning. The other is implicit and independent of verbalization, perhaps based on Pavlovian conditioning. This fractionation of human long-term memory has been widely hypothesized from a variety of perspectives over recent years and a plethora of labels has resulted. The distinction most relevant to this discussion is that which divides memory into procedural and declarative types. [*See* CLASSICAL CONDITIONING; OPERANT LEARNING.]

The origins of this particular distinction have come from studies of brain-damaged subjects. As early as 1911, the Swiss neuropsychiatrist Claparade noted that severely amnesic patients were nevertheless capable of learning certain things. A memorable if eccentric example of this is his observation of a woman with Korsakoff's syndrome who refused to shake hands with him after he had hidden a pin in his palm on the previous morning's ward round. In keeping with her profound amnesia, she had no accessible knowledge or recollection of the reasons for her refusal but clearly had learned *how* to avoid pain. Since then, numerous studies on patients rendered amnesic for a variety of reasons have revealed the existence of preserved learning skills. Examples include the remembering of pictures or words when cued by their fragments and the learning of simple motor skills such as keeping a stylus in contact with a moving target or the use of novel tools. It has been also observed that these subjects solve jigsaw puzzles and visual mazes with increasing efficiency over subsequent "training" sessions. The striking unifying feature about these tasks is the frequent denial by the subject of having encountered them before while showing clear and, on occasion, totally unimpaired learning. Clearly, learning has been determined by performance rather than any conscious awareness of previously encountering the task.

It is natural to wonder whether such dichotomous learning effects also exist in intact individuals. A wide range of equivalent studies has investigated this. For example, Jacoby and Dallas allowed subjects to process words at differing levels, involving either superficial judgments about their appearance or sound when spoken or more deep judgments about their semantic meaning. Learning was then tested in two ways: either directly by recognition or indirectly by the speed by which the word was identified when presented tachistoscopically. The deeper the processing of the word, the more consistent its recognition, as might have been expected. However, the perceptual identification of the word was totally uninfluenced by the level at it had been previously processed. This effect has been repeated in several other paradigms and has led to the general surmise that those measures of learning that are relatively intact in amnesic patients are also insensitive to the level of processing in normal subjects.

It is, therefore, widely accepted that there exists more than one kind of long-term learning. However, the theoretical understanding of the underlying processes is far from complete. Although the term "procedural learning" captures the fact that skills, habits, or "motor learning" is preserved in amnesics incapable of knowledge acquisition, it is almost certainly a concept of excessive generality. For example, some skills or habits are learned very slowly by amnesics. Further, it is difficult to justify the grouping together of tasks as varied as conditioning and the solving of complex puzzles. Rather, it would seem parsimonious to suggest that the acquisition of new information about ourselves and the environment could be termed episodic, whereas memory processes not requiring this autobiographical component, such as skill learning, require further taxonomy. In other words, broader explanations than those based on an assumed dichotomy are needed.

III. THE NEUROBIOLOGY OF HABITS

Having examined the nature and psychology of habits, the neurobiology of their formation and expression will be addressed. The classical approach of physiological psychology is to damage part of an animal's brain and deduce its function by subsequent analysis of the resulting behavioral deficit. This is fraught with problems in the context of automatic stimulus–response behavior. Clearly, from a superficial perspective, if such a system is disrupted and the animal fails to respond to some eliciting stimulus, there could be many reasons for the deficit, ranging from a problem of stimulus detection to one of muscle activation. Nevertheless, a variety of studies of brain-damaged experimental subjects, both animal and human, has provided substantial evidence that the part of the brain primarily concerned with the automatic expression of learned motor acts is the area of basal forebrain termed the basal ganglia, in particular its major component, the striatum.

A suitable starting point concerns a series of studies that has examined the localization of an archetypal form of automatic stimulus–response learning, namely, filial imprinting in the domestic chick. Chicks develop an attachment toward any visually conspicuous object soon after hatching and, later, approach such objects automatically in preference to other novel objects. This phenomenon has been studied quantitatively by placing newly born chicks in a running wheel and exposing them to distinctive objects, including rotating boxes or stuffed birds. The intensity of approach activity can be measured by the number and rate of revolutions of the running wheel. Several days following the initial stimulus exposure, the running response of the chicks may be recorded for a variety of stimuli. Normal chicks are seen to exhibit more than three times the approach activity to the imprinted stimulus as compared to the unfamiliar one.

Initial biochemical studies on the chicks' brains during imprinting have highlighted increased metabolic activity in a small area of anterior forebrain, termed the intermediate zone of the medial hyperstriatum ventrali (IMHV). Metabolic activity was assayed by measuring the incorporation of uracil into macromolecules. A number of control experiments ruled out the influence of certain nonspecific factors such as locomotor activity per se to explain the increased activity. Further, split-brain chicks were prepared with division of their optic pathways such that each eye was connected to one-half of the brain only. After training with one eye open, there was no transfer of learning to the previously closed eye on subsequent testing. Of note, increased uracil incorporation was observed only in that hemisphere receiving input from the eye open during training, emphasizing the role of this area of brain in the expression of imprinting. Additional studies used chicks with bilateral lesions in the region of the IMHV, performed either before or within 3 hours of training, and demonstrated permanent obliteration of any imprinting response. Importantly, other forms of associative learning and performance were left intact. These included the speed and accuracy of pecking responses to moving beads and the ability to learn a visual pattern discrimination to obtain heat reinforcement, even using the discriminanda of the imprinting study.

Clearly, analogies of imprinting to habit formation in higher species and the nature of brain areas homologous to the IMHV in mammals remain subjects of some speculation. Nevertheless, in the rat, a creature apparently well adapted to the formation of motor habits, lesion studies have implicated the striatum in the performance of automatic stimulus–response behavior. Traditionally, however, animal experiments concerned with the study of learning and memory have concentrated on the hippocampal formation in attempts to model brain-damaged human amnesics with corresponding limbic lesions. Although the acquisition of various learning tasks can be severely compromised by damage to the rat hippocampus, types of learning that involve the consistent performance of a single response in the presence of a specific sensory cue are generally spared. Such tasks include simultaneous brightness discriminations in which the lesioned rat consistently approaches a positive discriminative cue. In addition, the learning of successive "go/no-go" olfactory discriminations is unimpaired in which the animal is presented with successive individual odor stimuli either paired with reward or nonreward. By contrast, there is evidence that damage to the caudate nucleus, the major component of the striatum, is sufficient to disrupt the learning of all these types of tasks by affecting a system concerned with habit formation. [*See* HIPPOCAMPAL FORMATION.]

For well over a hundred years, the caudate nucleus has been asssociated with motor function. In order to demonstrate its specific role in habit formation, therefore, it is important to demonstrate preserved indices of general motor performance following its destruction. One such study by Packard and White has used a radial arm maze with eight arms projecting from a central "hub." On each training trial, four of the eight arms were consistently baited with food reward. Normal hungry rats are particularly adept at "solving" such tasks by using spatial cues associated with the maze and, over a series of daily trials, learn to visit the baited arms while eventually ignoring the unbaited ones. Importantly, during each trial, intact rats learn to avoid those baited arms already visited on that trial, efficiently exhibiting a so-called "win-shift" strategy. When bilateral electrical lesions were made to the caudate nucleus, a pattern of deficit emerged consistent with the disruption of a reference memory system concerned with the performance of motor habits that were stable from trial to trial. The lesioned rats failed to avoid the consistently unbaited arms over a series of trials, in contrast to control rats. Importantly, however, on each individual trial, having successfully visited a baited arm, the experimental rats were equally efficient as controls at remembering and subsequently avoiding these arms. The preservation of intra-trial "working memory" argues strongly against lesion-induced deficits of motivation, motor performance, disinhibition, sensitivity to nonreward, or general learning impairments. Rather, the animals with caudate damage were interpreted as having deficits of stimulus–response long-term memory with preservation of learning dependent on the short-term "working" memory of relationships between stimuli in each trial. Of interest is the observation that rats with hippocampal damage exhibited an opposite constellation of deficits, namely, impairment of working memory with preservation of reference memory. Other studies that have analyzed the behavior of rats with striatal damage have obtained results comparable to the one above. These have demonstrated impaired learning of avoidance behaviors, cued water maze performance, and left/right maze discrimination, all of which involve stimulus–response learning. [*See* MEMORY.]

A study by the author and colleagues investigated the acquisition of a learned motor habit after discrete lesions to separable areas of the rat striatal complex. The task was a paradigmatic example of a conditional visual discrimination in which an arbitrary stimulus, either a slow or fast flashing light, was associated with an arbitrary response, the pressing of a left or a right lever in a standard operant chamber. In order to obtain food reward, the rats were trained to apply a procedural rule, such as "push the right lever when exposed to a fast light and the left when it is slow." Normal rats have been found to learn this particular task slowly and, once performance is at asymptotic levels, accuracy is remarkably stable from trial to trial and few omissions are made. Since accuracy is preserved whether or not the rats are food-deprived, performance becomes relatively divorced from primary motivational states, further emphasizing the habit-like qualities of the task once acquired. The arbitrary stimulus–response association means that efficient responding cannot result from simple Pavlovian associations whereby the animal merely approaches a reward-related conditioned stimulus. Using a neurotoxin that specifically destroyed intrinsic neural circuitry, it was found that ventro-lateral striatal lesions severely impaired the acquisition of the task. Since other indices of learning were unaffected, the deficit was interpreted as a failure to acquire and use a conditional response rule. Manipulating task parameters, making it "easier," failed to improve performance significantly. The inability of the rats with the ventro-lateral striatal lesions to acquire the habit contrasted with the relatively normal performance of rats with neighboring lesions in the medial striatum.

A large body of data has accrued over the last two decades concerning the behavior of rats with unilateral striatal lesions. The theoretical advantage with this approach is that behavior controlled by the intact striatum can be compared to that elicited from the lesioned side, the animal acting as its own internal control. Here, too, the results can often be interpreted within a stimulus–response framework. Early studies that unilaterally depleted the striatum of its predominant neurochemical, dopamine, revealed an animal severely deficient in attending to space contralateral to the damaged side, producing so-called "striatal neglect." Later experiments that examined skilled paw-reaching led to an interpretation based on the role of the striatum in a rather general concept of "sensorimotor integration." Further investigation, however, has implied that the unilateral deficit is best described as reflecting an inability to initiate a learned prepotent response into contralateral space. Once the lateralized behavior has started, it is performed with virtually normal speed and topography. The type of study that has exemplified this approach and best examined the precise behavior of animals performing with unilateral striatal lesions has used lateralized reaction time tasks.

The details of the reaction time paradigm and the theoretical implications of data from a series of experiments have been described by Robbins and Brown. Briefly, rats were highly trained to hold their heads in a central location monitored by a photocell beam until a brief visual stimulus (200 msec) was presented unpredictably to either side of the head. They were then required to withdraw their heads from the central location and report the occurrence and location of the stimulus by nose-poking in a side hole. Two groups of rats with profound unilateral striatal dopamine depletions were trained, one to respond to the side where the light had been presented, the other to the side opposite. Accurate monitoring of a number of behavioral parameters using computerized technology allowed detailed comparison to be made between the two groups. In essence, both groups had retained abilities to detect and locate events in space contralateral to the lesioned striatum but had a strong spatial bias to respond to the side ipsilateral to the lesion. However, whenever a contralateral response was made, although its initiation was slowed, as measured by the time to withdraw the head from the central location, its performance was normal in terms of speed. Detailed analysis of further studies led to the conclusion that the striatum functions at an early stage of response selection to constrain, or weight, potential response tendencies. This process was referred to as "response set," defined as the prior assignment of probability of selection from a repertoire of available responses. In this context, the striatum has no role in motor programming per se, more likely a function of cortical structures, but acts to affect responses crudely by affecting bias in terms of spatial vectors and temporal aspects. The theory, detailed elsewhere, emphasizes that the functions of the striatum in "response set" are not just to affect the activation of prepotent responses ("attention to action") but also the efferent control over the stimuli eliciting those responses. During training, the establishment of "set" is seen as facilitating stimulus–response links, enabling the response to become habitual or automatic. This aspect of the striatum's role in habit formation arose from molecular considerations of the dynamic performance of visual-reaction time tasks yet has clear parallels with its role in habit consolidation and the learning of arbitrary response rules alluded to above.

The neurochemical basis of simple stimulus–response learning has received a considerable amount of attention in recent years. To put some of this work in context, Thorndike's original Law of Effect is of relevance, stating that the general activation of a (reward) process unrelated to the stimulus or the response is able to improve memory by strengthening the connection between them. This was given original empirical support by demonstrations of a phenomenon known as the Spread of Effect. Here, the experimenter cited a list of words to subjects and required them to respond with whatever word came into their minds. Some of the responses were randomly "rewarded" by the experimenter saying "good" following them. On rereading the original list back to the subjects, the "rewarded" words were remembered most frequently, in accordance with the Law of Effect. However, of note, words either side of the "rewarded" ones were also remembered significantly more frequently than other words, even though they had not been "rewarded." This demonstration implied that rewarding events can improve memory even when they are not contingently related to the behaviors they affect, the mere temporal contiguity is sufficient. It is now clear that many types of arousal can affect learning in positive or negative ways if present in the immediate post-training period. For example, electroconvulsive shocks have been found to disrupt the retention of an avoidance response in rats when applied in the immediate post-training period, but not when applied at a later time. This finding concurred with original ideas of memory as a labile trace, temporarily susceptible to external influences before a process of "consolidation."

More recently, marshalling evidence from a variety of experimental paradigms, White has developed these ideas to suggest that neurochemical changes in the striatum are responsible for certain types of stimulus–response memory, habit consolidation or reinforcement. First, it was found that rats could improve their memory if they were allowed to self-stimulate their brains electrically, immediately following the training period. Of note, it was only those groups of rats that had self-stimulating electrodes in some part of the dopaminergic pathway from midbrain to striatum, the nigrostriatal tract, that showed this effect. Additionally, blocking dopamine receptors with systemic drug administration eliminated the beneficial effects of post-training self-stimulation. It was suggested that dopamine release in the striatum lay behind the improved memory consolidation.

Further experiments using microinjections of the drug amphetamine into the brains of rats added fuel to this notion. It is established that the mechanism of pharmacological arousal or activation following the administration of amphetamine is via increased subcortical dopamine release. Experiments in the early 1960s had already implied that amphetamine given in the early post-training period could improve memory in a variety of situations. White extended this observation by microinjecting the drug into discrete parts of the rat brain and investigating stimulus–response learning in a task requiring the animal to associate a stimulus with a mild footshock. Improved learning, as measured by foot withdrawal on presentation of the stimulus, was seen after injections of the dopamine-releasing drug only when into specific areas of the striatum. Of special interest was that the precise location of the injections within the striatum improved memory depending on the modality of the training stimulus. More specifically, if an auditory stimulus such as a tone was used, that part of the striatum receiving topographical input from auditory cortex was the only area where injections of amphetamine were effective. Similarly, when visual or olfactory stimuli were used, the only effective injection sites were areas of striatum associated with visual or olfactory cortical input, respectively. In summary, it was proposed that the effect of reinforcement on stimulus–response memory, a process distinguished from reward and associated hedonia, was localized in the striatum, particularly dorsolateral areas. In particular, consolidation of the memory was enhanced by dopamine release in a site-specific way within subareas of the striatum. Since dopamine release occurs naturally under certain conditions of arousal, the experimental findings of White have provided a neurobiological basis for Thorndike's Spread of Effect.

Since the neurobiological theories adumbrated above have centered on studies using rats, it is now appropriate to consider if data collected from humans and primates are consistent with the general notion of striatal involvement in habit formation. As far as primates are concerned, Mishkin has been influential in proposing a habit system dependent on corticostriatal pathways. This arose from consideration of monkeys with limbic lesions that were severely impaired at memory tasks involving object recognition among distractor items in unique-trial tests, a type of task performed particularly adeptly by intact animals. These same lesioned animals, however, were perfectly able to learn at virtually normal rates a difficult visual pattern discrimination if presented repeatedly. This finding in apparently amnesic monkeys presented the same paradox of normal learning in the context of rapid forgetting exhibited by amnesic patients. In the case of the monkeys, in fact, the paradox was particularly pertinent since the rules and format of training, such as inter-trial interval, were essentially the same in the tasks not acquired as in those mastered. Moreover, subsequent studies using large inter-trial intervals of 24 hours showed that the preserved learning was not due to the original 2-minute interval being simply too short a separation to prevent the steady accumulation of information over trial repetitions. It appeared, then, that if a recognition task was based on a single acquisition trial, even though this was presented just a few seconds earlier, animals with limbic lesions failed to learn, yet if the choice was made on the basis of several acquisition trials, even though separated by 24 hours, the operated animal was just as successful as controls. Initially, this led to the proposal of a rapid-learning system, dependent on the limbic system, and a slow-learning system, requiring repetition, independent of it. However, this concept failed to square with the human experience that profound amnesics do not benefit from numerous repetitions of an experience. Rather, as previously alluded to, the spared learning ability spared in human amnesics appears qualitatively different to that which has been lost. In the context of preserved monkey learning, Mishkin was, therefore, led to propose a learning process completely independent of both the limbic system and associative memory. It represented a noncognitive stimulus–response bond, that is, not a memory but a habit. By corollary, the neural information stored in the habit formation system was not related to "representations of . . . objects, places, acts, emotions and the learned connections between them but simply the changing probability that a given stimulus will evoke a specific response due to the reinforcement contingencies operating at that time." [*See* LIMBIC SYSTEM.]

Mishkin hypothesized that there existed a trade-off between the long-term reliability afforded by a cortico-striatal habit system and the short-term flexibility of an associative limbic memory system. Additionally, since present in animals even with the simplest nervous systems, it was argued that a habit system based on cortico-striatal interactions was phylogenetically older than a contrasting limbic memory system. On the basis of this assumption an experiment was conducted to investigate the ontogenetic development of memory. Briefly, it was found that immature monkeys aged 3 months could not acquire a simple memory task using trial-unique objects in contrast to animals aged 12 months. However, the young monkeys were as proficient as adults at learning long lists of discrimination problems if they were presented concurrently at 24-hour intervals. The similarity in performance of the infant monkeys to adults with limbic lesions led to the proposal that, compared to habits, memories presumed to be dependent on a cortico-limbic system underwent a relatively slow ontogenetic development.

Despite an abundance of empirical evidence implicating the striatum in habit formation in primates, the direct experimental evidence has been relatively sparse. This situation has arisen largely due to a lack of relevant data. Certainly, visual pattern discrimination habits are markedly affected by damage along the cortico-striatal pathway. However, since the sensory input to the striatum may be interrupted by such lesions, it is not clear what element in the formation of the stimulus–response bond is disrupted.

In the human arena, studies of neurologically impaired subjects have lent some support to the striatal theory of habit formation. In particular, data from patients with Huntington's disease have been illuminating. In this distressing disease, early pathology is characterized by relatively selective degeneration of the intrinsic neural ciruitry within the striatum. At this stage, before more widespread cortical involvement becomes apparent, patients may appear relatively intact, perhaps presenting only with a mild movement disorder. However, although conscious or "explicit" memory is grossly spared at this stage, the learning of certain tasks that necessitate the learning of a "subconscious" motor skill is significantly impaired. One example is a pursuit-rotor motor learning task in which the subject has to maintain contact between a stylus held in their preferred hand and a small metallic disk on a rotating turntable. In contrast to Huntington's disease sufferers, normal subjects and, notably, those with moderate dementia of the Alzheimer type learn the task well and perform with improving efficiency from trial to trial as the turntable speed is increased. This implies that one of the earliest deficits to appear after damage to the human striatum is the inability to acquire a motor skill or habit. [*See* ALZHEIMER'S DISEASE.]

IV. ABNORMAL HABITS

Now that the nature, psychology, and neurobiology of habit formation have been considered, the consequences and theoretical implications of abnormal or excessive habit formation and expression will be addressed. Paradoxically, during the last 25 years, while the theoretical impact of the animal-based associationist theories has been waning, their applied importance in the human context of abnormal habits has increased enormously. The technology associated with modifying habits tends to go under the general rubric of "behavior modification" and is now part of accepted practice in a wide spectrum of areas ranging from marital therapy to the treatment of brain-damaged subjects with "behavioral problems." Drawing particularly on Skinner's work demonstrating how complex chains of behavior could be entrained in subhuman species, behavioral programs have developed based on the simple underlying approach of strengthening and weakening responses by reward and punishment, respectively. One area in which this approach has been especially successful is in the education and treatment of children with severe mental handicap. For example, in the rare condition Lesch-Nyhan syndrome, an inborn error of purine metabolism, a behavioral syndrome of psychomotor retardation and self-mutilation usually develops. The latter aspect can be particularly recalcitrant to symptomatic management, requiring the use of complex behavioral modification techniques.

A spectrum of human mental disorder can also be understood in terms of the abnormal release of habits, perhaps from a malfunctioning striatum. More specifically, obsessive–compulsive syndromes characterized by the intrusion of recurrent thoughts, impulses, or purposeful behavioral stereotypies have been hypothesized to result from the automatic triggering of prepotent responses from the striatum. This approach implicitly treats mental thoughts as actions not connected to motor neurons, a position increasingly held by cognitive psychologists and behavioral neurologists alike. For the purpose of analysis, this allows abnormal acts such as compulsive or ritual hand-washing to be grouped together with intrusive or impulsive ruminatory thoughts. From this, fixed behavioral routines, perhaps with an innate component, and prepotent thoughts can be conceived as representing uncontrolled automatic output via dysfunctional striatal mechanisms. In other words, responses, including obsessional thoughts, are "released" by internal stimuli as a result of a lowered threshold for their expression. The evidence that the striatum is involved in the pathogenesis of obsessive–compulsive disorders comes from several sources. [*See* OBSESSIVE–COMPULSIVE BEHAVIOR.]

First, original descriptions of Tourette's syndrome invoked basal ganglia or striatal damage as representing pathognomonic pathology. Recently, many commentators have included Tourette's syndrome, a disorder of motor tics and uncontrolled obscene utterances, as part of the obsessive–compulsive disorder spectrum. Second, the entity of postencephalitic parkinsonism, described by von Economo in 1917 and known to arise from neurotoxic damage to the striatum, had features of "motor disturbances . . . reminiscent of compulsive movements and compulsive actions, with frequently ensuing utterances of speech and trends of thought of a compulsive character." In addition, brain-damaged subjects with resulting compulsive syndromes have often been found to have bilateral striatal involvement at postmortem examination. Third, radiographic evidence has implicated the striatum in sufferers of obsessive–compulsive disorder. This has come from structural and functional brain imaging using CT and PET scans, respectively. The former method has demonstrated that patients have relatively shrunken caudate nuclei. The latter has revealed increased metabolism in circuits connecting cortex, striatum, and thalamus, particularly involving anterior cingulate cortical areas. Finally, the neuropharmacology of the drugs successfully used to treat obsessive–compulsive disorders implicates the striatum. More specifically, drugs that either inhibit the uptake of the neurotransmitter serotonin, such as clomipramine, or block dopamine receptor blockers, such as haloperidol, have been used to treat compulsive syndromes and Tourette's syndrome, respectively. Both neurotransmitters have particularly high concentrations in subregions of the striatum. In summary, in accordance with the idea that the striatum normally serves to facilitate the expression of stimulus–response habits, excessive release of prepotent response tendencies, including thoughts, may result in obsessive–compulsive syndromes. It should be emphasized that this phenomenon may result from damage to brain areas that normally keep the striatum "in check," such as limbic cortical areas, and not necessarily from direct damage to the striatum itself.

Although obsessive–compulsive syndromes are usually classed as anxiety disorders, some commentators have suggested that they may be categorically more closely alligned to the schizophrenic constellation of disorders. Indeed, stereotypies of behavior and thought are core problems in acute and chronic types of schizophrenia. Additionally, low-dose psychomotor stimulants such as amphetamine have been seen to "release" quite complex behavioral stereotypies in animals and humans and have been used to produce influential and credible animal models of psychosis. Modern theory suggests such drugs act by releasing dopamine from the ventral striatum or nucleus accumbens which, in turn, may disinhibit the expression of prepotent motor tendencies, habits, or even thoughts via the dorsal striatum. [*See* ANXIETY DISORDERS; SCHIZOPHRENIA.]

V. CONCLUSIONS

In summary, the influential notion of habit has been instrumental in the formation of the earliest theories of human psychology and animal learning. In recent decades, it may be argued that behavioral research has concentrated more on "intelligent" or purposeful forms of behavior. However, with the realization that a significant proportion of human actions are subconscious or automatic, there has been something of a renaissance of interest in the study of habits. In addition, the dichotomous nature of long-term memory, demonstrated initially by observations of brain-damaged amnesic subjects, has implied that learning as well as performance can be divided into "conscious" and "automatic" forms. Since the habit system is phylogenetically ancient, it is claimed that extrapolations from animal studies to elucidate its nature in human behavior is wholely justified.

The evidence, largely from animal experiments, points to the striatum as playing a central part in both the acquisition of habits and their subsequent expression. In particular, the neurotransmitter, dopamine, when released onto striatal circuitry from midbrain afferent neurons under conditions of arousal or activation, is important for the consolidation of stimulus–response memories. Subsequent release of dopamine, not necessarily in the same striatal subregion, may act to trigger the now prepotent responses. It is not proposed that the striatum forms a simple repository for stimulus–response links. Rather, activity within the striatum can act to run a motor program smoothly once subconsciously selected, perhaps preserving cortical neural "resources" for more challenging tasks. This idea adds neurobiological flesh to James' early surmises concerning habit.

In the realm of abnormal habits, it is maintained that neurobiological and pharmacological studies of the striatum will provide useful information for the understanding and treatment of a variety of human disorders. These range from behavioral problems in brain-damaged subjects to obsessive–compulsive syndromes and may include phenomena such as addictive behavior and pyschoses. The addage that the art of psychology is "pulling habits out of rats," as one pithy commentator once observed, would appear to be as relevant now as ever.

Bibliography

Dickinson, A., Nicholas, D. J., and Adams, C. D. (1983). The effect of the instrumental contingency on susceptibility to reinforcer devaluation. *Q. J. Exp. Psychol.* **35B,** 35–51.

Mishkin, M., Malamut, B., and Bachevalier, J. (1984). Memories and habits: Two neural systems. In "Neurobiology of Human

Memory and Learning" (G. Lynch, J. L. McGaugh, and N. M. Weinberger Eds.), Guilford, New York.

Packard, M. G., and White, N. M. (1990). Lesions of the caudate nucleus selectively impair "reference memory" acquisition in the rat. *Behav. Neurol. Biol.* **53,** 39–50.

Rapoport, J. L. (1990). Obsessive compulsive disorder and basal ganglia dysfunction. *Psychol. Med.* **20,** 465–470.

Reading, P. J., Dunnett, S. B., and Robbins, T. W. (1992). Dissociable roles of the ventral, medial and dorsal striatum in the acquisition and performance of a complex visual stimulus-response habit. *Behav. Brain Res.* **45,** 147–161.

Robbins, T. W., and Brown, V. J. (1990). The role of the striatum in the mental chronometry of action: A theoretical review. *Rev. Neurosci.* **2,** 181–213.

Squire, L. R. (1987). "Memory and Brain." Oxford University Press, New York.

White, N. M. (1989). Reward or reinforcement: What's the difference? *Neurosci. Biobehav. Rev.* **13,** 181–186.

Handedness

Joseph B. Hellige
University of Southern California

Glossary

Analogous systems Biological systems that are similar in function but not in origin or structure (e.g., the wing of a bird and the wing of a bat).

Corpus callosum Major fiber tract that connects the left and right cerebral hemispheres in humans and is important for transmitting information from one hemisphere to the other.

Dizygotic twins Twins that occur when each of two egg cells are fertilized by two different sperm cells and have, on the average, 50% of their genes in common.

Handedness The tendency for humans to prefer the use of one hand over the other and for motor performance to be better with the preferred hand.

Hemispheric asymmetry Biological and functional differences between the left and right sides of the cerebral cortex.

Homologous systems Biological systems that share a common structure and origin (e.g., the foreleg of a mouse and the wing of a bat).

Laterality Hemispheric asymmetry or any one of a number of behavioral manifestations of hemispheric asymmetry.

Monozygotic twins Twins that begin life as a single egg cell and single sperm and are genetically identical.

Sylvian fissure Deep groove on the lateral surfaces of the cerebral hemispheres which marks the boundary between the frontal and parietal lobes above and the temporal lobe below.

Thymus gland Gland located in the lower neck region and known to be important for normal function of the immune system.

HANDEDNESS is the most obvious behavioral asymmetry in humans, with most of us having a strong preference to use one hand more than the other for a wide variety of activities. Furthermore, performance of many tasks is considerably better with the preferred hand than with the nonpreferred hand. Strong hand preferences exist despite the fact that the two hands are very similar in appearance, size, and structure, so that the factors that underlie handedness must involve such things as asymmetry in the neural control of the hands. Consequently, understanding the mechanisms that underlie human handedness will provide important clues about motor control and neural asymmetries in general. In addition, handedness can be used as a marker for other biological and behavioral factors, including such varied things as cerebral hemisphere asymmetry, susceptibility to certain diseases, and longevity. With these things in mind, the present article reviews what is known about human handedness, its development over the lifespan of an individual, its emergence over evolutionary time, and its relationship to other behavioral factors and asymmetries.

I. CHARACTERISTICS OF HUMAN HANDEDNESS

One characteristic of human handedness is consistency across tasks. That is, a typical individual prefers to use the same hand for a wide variety of tasks, with this being especially true of right-handed people. The extent of hand preference and ability differences between the hands is stronger, however, for skilled activities (such as writing, drawing, using a

Copyright © 1994 by Academic Press, Inc. All rights of reproduction in any form reserved.

toothbrush, holding a needle to sew) than for unskilled activities (such as picking up a small object).

A second characteristic of human handedness is a very strong population-level bias toward right-handedness. Approximately 90% of humans are right-handed, with the proportion of right-handedness being somewhat lower for males (approximately 88%) than for females (approximately 92%). Most of the remaining 10% of humans are typically referred to as left-handed, often because they prefer to use the left hand for writing and drawing. In general, the direction and strength of hand preference across tasks is more variable for so-called left-handed people than for right-handed people (although there is a small percentage of people with a strong and consistent left-hand preference). There is also a very small percentage of truly ambidextrous people, who have virtually no hand preference or ability difference between the hands.

As suggested by the foregoing discussion, there is an important distinction to be made between the direction and magnitude (or degree) of human handedness. Direction generally refers to whether it is the right or left hand that an individual prefers to use and magnitude refers to such things as the consistency of hand preference across tasks, the strength of the stated preference for the dominant hand, and the magnitude of the ability differences between the hands. Among other things,there is evidence that the magnitude or degree of handedness is more heritable in both humans and animals than is the direction of handedness. In fact, some have suggested that what is inherited is a predisposition to be either more rigid or more plastic in handedness, with individuals who are more plastic being more likely to alter their hand preference in response to environmental stimulation. Possible genetic determinants of the direction of handedness are discussed later in the present article.

II. IS HANDEDNESS UNIQUE TO HUMANS?

There are many examples of motor asymmetry in nonhuman species, with some of these asymmetries being very striking at the level of an individual organism. None of these asymmetries show both of the characteristics of human handedness noted above, however. Despite this, some of the motor asymmetries in other species may be related to human handedness in interesting ways.

In considering the extent to which handedness is unique to humans, it is instructive to consider a distinction made in biology between analogous and homologous systems. *Analogous systems* are similar to each other in function but not in origin or structure. For example, the wing of a bird and the wing of a bat are analogous because of their similar functions but they have distinct structures and distinct evolutionary and developmental origins (e.g., a bat is a mammal, more closely related to a mouse than to a bird). By way of contrast, *homologous systems* share a common structure and origin. Homologous systems often have similar functions, but the functions may not be identical. For example, the wing of a bat and the foreleg of a mouse are homologous because they share a common structure and origin—even though their functions are not identical. The distinction between analogous and homologous systems is important because a behavioral asymmetry found in one species (e.g., paw preference in rats) is likely to be a better model system for an asymmetry found in another species (e.g., hand preference in humans) to the extent that the two are homologous. Certain asymmetries in nonhumans seem to be at least analogous to handedness in humans, but there is considerable disagreement about whether they are also homologous.

The conventional point of view has been that other primates do not show population-level asymmetries of hand preference. More recently, however, it has been argued that there are, in fact, several population-level asymmetries, but the direction of those asymmetries is not consistent across tasks. Thus, the population-level asymmetries are obscured if a single global measure of handedness is derived by collapsing across a variety of tasks. One generalization that has received some support is that there is a left-hand preference for reaching in several species of nonhuman primates accompanied by right-hand preference for manipulation, with these effects interacting with age and sex. It has also been suggested that manual asymmetry in these primates tends to be found for high-level tasks such as making a discrimination on the basis of touch but not for low-level tasks such as reaching for a piece of food. Note that this is similar to the fact that hand preference in humans tends to be greater for skilled than for unskilled activities.

Interesting motor asymmetries are also found in rats and mice, with the two most-studied asymmetries involving paw preferences and circling biases. For both of these behaviors, individual animals often show a strong preference for one side or the other, with the direction and magnitude of the preference varying widely from animal to animal. For example, a given animal may prefer to use the same paw across a variety of tasks, but there is little evidence for any dramatic population-level asymmetry such as that found in humans. That is, there are approximately equal numbers of left- and right-pawed individuals. It is interesting that it has not been possible to breed selectively for the direction of paw preference in rats and mice. That is, two "right-pawed" mice are no more likely to produce "right-pawed" offspring than are two "left-pawed" mice. However, it has been possible to breed selectively for the magnitude or degree of asymmetry. That is, the offspring of two strongly asymmetric mice are more likely to be strongly asymmetric than are the offspring of two weakly asymmetric mice. Note that this suggests that the direction and magnitude of paw preference are, to some extent, independent of each other. Furthermore, the fact that *magnitude* or degree of preference is more heritable than *direction* of preference is consistent with similar claims that have been made for human handedness. In both cases, this may come about because the direction of preference is influenced by a variety of early, even prenatal, environmental factors—some of which are discussed in the next section.

While the ubiquity of motor asymmetries in other species suggests that, in some sense, handedness is not unique to humans, more work is clearly needed to determine which (if any) of these motor asymmetries in other species are truly homologous to human handedness. At the very least, the emergence of so many animal models opens the door to a variety of techniques to study the genetic and environmental mechanisms that may contribute to motor asymmetry in humans.

III. HANDEDNESS FROM WOMB TO TOMB

An individual's handedness is determined in complex ways by both genetic and environmental factors. There is a clear genetic contribution to handedness, but the nature of that contribution is not yet understood. For example, I. C. McManus of University College in London in the United Kingdom and M. P. Bryden of the University of Waterloo in Canada review evidence indicating that handedness runs in families. Furthermore, they show that concordance for handedness does not differ from binomial (chance) expectations for dizygotic twins (who, on the average, have 50% of their genes in common) whereas concordance for handedness is slightly higher than would be expected on the basis of chance for monozygotic twins (who are genetically identical). These facts suggest a genetic contribution to handedness. However, it is equally clear that the direction of hand preference is not determined in any straightforward way by a single gene with a dominant allele for right-handedness and a recessive allele for left-handedness. Among other things, the concordance for handedness among monozygotic twins (approximately 88%) is far less than the 100% predicted by such a simple genetic model. Consequently, several more elaborate genetic models have been proposed.

One of the more promising genetic models is the right-shift model proposed by Marian Annett of the University of Leicester in the United Kingdom and another is the genetic model of handedness proposed by McManus. Although these models differ in detail, they both contain the idea that biological asymmetries are, to some extent, influenced by random processes. For example, according to the right-shift model, handedness is determined by a single gene whose dominant allele produces a bias toward right-handedness (and toward dominance of the left cerebral hemisphere for language) and a recessive allele that leads to the absence of this "right-shift bias." In the absence of the right-shift bias, the direction of asymmetry is determined randomly. The right-shift model does a reasonably good job of predicting such things as the proportion of left-handers in the population. However, some predictions do not fare as well. For example, this model predicts that a larger number of left-handers will be right-hemisphere dominant for language than is actually the case.

There appear to be a host of additional factors that interact with any genetic predisposition to produce the phenotypic expression of handedness in a particular individual. One such factor is likely to be pre- or postnatal trauma. For example, the incidence of left-handedness is positively correlated with such things as birth stress and low birth weight. In fact, some have argued that all left-handedness is the result of such trauma. A more likely possibility is that only some left-handedness comes about for these reasons, with the majority of left-handedness occurring for genetic and other environmental reasons, such as the nature of the intrauterine environment during certain critical phases of fetal development.

One of the most interesting theories about the importance of the intrauterine environment was first proposed by the late neurologist Norman Geschwind and his colleagues, most notably Albert Galaburda of Harvard Medical School. This theory concerns likely effects of the levels of certain hormones, especially testosterone, during certain phases of fetal development. According to this theory, higher levels of fetal testosterone promote the intrauterine development of the right cerebral hemisphere relative to the left cerebral hemisphere, by either slowing the development of the left hemisphere or speeding up development of the right hemisphere. The movements of each hand are controlled primarily by the motor cortex of the contralateral cerebral hemisphere. Consequently, this theory argues that higher levels of fetal testosterone produce a bias away from strong right-handedness and toward left-handedness.

Although considerably more testing is needed, there is at least some circumstantial evidence for the fetal testosterone theory. For example, studies of other species indicate that fetal levels of testosterone and other hormones can influence brain development in many ways, including the development of anatomical asymmetry. Males tend to be exposed to higher levels of fetal testosterone than females. Thus, the fact that the incidence of left-handedness is higher in males than in females is consistent with this theory. Furthermore, recent research on the developing fetal brain indicates that fetal males are more likely than fetal females to have a size difference between the developing hemispheres, with the developing right hemisphere being slightly larger than the developing left hemisphere in males. There is also evidence that higher levels of fetal testosterone predispose an individual toward diseases of the immune system, probably by influencing development of the thymus gland. This leads to the interesting prediction that the incidence of such diseases should be higher among left-handers than among right-handers. Some studies have, in fact, reported that the incidence of certain autoimmune diseases and allergies is twice as great in left-handers as in right-handers. However, this relationship to handedness does not hold for all diseases of the immune system and the results across studies are not completely consistent.

There are also indications that handedness is related to the asymmetric positioning of the fetus *in utero* during the final trimester of pregnancy. During the final trimester of approximately two-thirds of human pregnancies, the fetus is positioned with its head down and its back toward the mother's left side. As a result of this position, the left arm is pressed against the mother's pelvis and backbone and the right arm is positioned against the front of the uterus. This position of the fetus may contribute to the predominance of right-handedness in the human population. At the very least, there seems to be a moderately strong relationship between this particular fetal asymmetry and later handedness. One hypothesis advanced to explain this relationship argues that a critical factor is which arm and hand are freer to move late in pregnancy. Note that, for the fetal position described earlier, the right hand and arm are freer to move than the left because the left tends to be pinned against the rigid barrier provided by the mother's pelvis and backbone. Fred Previc of the Armstrong Laboratory at Brooks Air Force Base in Texas has proposed a second hypothesis, arguing that, when the fetus is positioned in the manner described earlier, the forward and backward acceleration forces caused by the mother as she walks create asymmetric shearing forces on the head of the fetus that favor development of the left otolith (the organ of the inner ear responsible for balance) and its neural pathways. On this view, there is a left-otolith advantage in most humans (a claim for which there is, in fact, reasonable evidence) and this otolith asymmetry creates a tendency to rely on the left side of the body for postural control. This reliance on the left side for postural control frees the right side to become dominant for skilled motor behavior.

Despite evidence for the possible effects of fetal position, there is also evidence of handedness in the human fetus well before the last trimester of pregnancy. For example, ultrasound observations of fetuses indicate a strong bias toward thumb sucking of the right hand (approximately 90% of the observations), with the proportion of right-hand thumb sucking being constant from 15 weeks of gestational age onward. Thus, asymmetries of fetal position are unlikely to be the sole determinants of later handedness. Instead, at least some of the seeds of later handedness are sown even earlier.

Various motor asymmetries are present from the time of birth, with some of the asymmetries being correlated at least moderately with later handedness. For example, when newborn infants are placed on their stomachs, approximately 70% show a bias to turn their heads toward the right side and those infants who show a rightward head-turning bias are somewhat more likely than others to show right-hand biases later. Of course, it is very difficult to assess handedness in very young children and there tends to be a great deal of inconsistency until approximately 3 years of age. From that age on, however, the direction and, to some extent, the magnitude of hand preference for certain tasks remains constant into middle age and beyond. That is, once an individual's hand preference has been established for a particular task, its direction and magnitude tend to remain constant throughout the lifespan.

In view of the foregoing, it is interesting to consider the success of attempts to change an individual's handedness, usually attempts to force a naturally left-handed child to use the right hand. In the United States, such attempts were commonplace a generation or more ago but are now much less frequent. From all indications, the attempts meet with only limited success. Consider the case of a naturally left-handed child who is forced to write with her right hand. Such a child may well become "right-handed" for writing, but this kind of training has proven to be very task-specific. That is, the newly acquired right-handedness does not tend to generalize spontaneously to other activities such as using a fork or striking a match. Thus, although there may be many cultural pressures to become right-handed, it is generally the case that only those tasks that are specifically singled out for training become more right-sided. Furthermore, in order for this specific training to succeed, it must take place at an early age.

Although an individual's handedness typically remains constant from childhood through old age, at the present time the proportion of left-handers in the population is not constant across age. At least in the United States and other Western cultures, the percentage of left-handers decreases with increasing age. For example, in one large-scale study Stanley Coren of the University of British Columbia and his colleagues found that approximately 15% of 10 year olds were left-handed, approximately 5% of 50 year olds were left-handed, and fewer than 1% of 80 year olds were left-handed. Some of this decrease in the percentage of left-handedness can be attributed to the fact that today's 80 year olds were children at a time when naturally left-handed individuals were forced to perform many tasks in a right-handed way. Perhaps some of the decrease can also be attributed to the fact that, over the lifespan, left-handers learn to adapt to a world set up for the convenience of right-handers. However, when Coren and his colleagues estimated the likely size of these environmental effects by studying such things as the percentage of left-handers reported in studies published at various times during the 20th century, they concluded that only part of the age-related change can be explained in this manner. This raises the possibility that the percentage of left-handers decreases with increasing age because left-handers do not, on the average, live as long as right-handers—a possibility considered in more detail later in the present article.

IV. EVOLUTION OF HANDEDNESS

Although there is still considerable uncertainty about the evolution of handedness, the existence of analogous asymmetries in other species suggests that at least some asymmetry existed before the emergence of our species, *Homo sapiens,* and even before other species of primates branched off from the ancestral line that led eventually to humans. Once some amount of asymmetry had been established, further evolutionary changes might well have acted to enhance that asymmetry in a variety of ways.

It is important to note at the outset that symmetry and asymmetry are equally the result of evolutionary adaptation. Examples of both symmetry and asymmetry can even be found in the molecules and physical particles of which living organisms are composed as well as in primitive single-celled organisms. This being the case, it is useful to consider the environmental pressures that are likely to have favored symmetry versus asymmetry.

Michael Corballis of the University of Auckland in New Zealand has observed that there is considerable pressure favoring bilateral symmetry for sensory and motor processes. As he notes, freely moving organisms must be equally responsive to stimuli on the left and right sides, favoring sense organs that are placed symmetrically. In addition, limbs must be placed symmetrically so that locomotion can proceed in a straight line. However, even in sensory and motor systems, asymmetry has been favored over symmetry when it happens to be more adaptive. For example, in the flounder, which swims on one side along the ocean bottom, both eyes are on the side of the head facing upward. Evolution may have favored this particular asymmetry because the sensory capacities of an eye facing downward would be wasted. With respect to handedness and its precursors in our primate ancestors, the pressure for symmetry may have depended on the extent to which the hands were used in locomotion and in making direct responses to environmental stimulation as opposed to engaging in other activities.

In organisms that are already functionally asymmetric to at least some extent, further evolutionary adaptations favored by the environment may be implemented more efficiently on one side than on the other. Such adaptations are also likely to be asymmetric when they emerge and set the stage for even more dramatic asymmetries in the future. Given that a certain amount of asymmetry probably characterized living organisms from their first moments on Earth, these types of snowball effects could have led gradually to various forms of motor asymmetry in other species and from there to human handedness. Although there is still much to learn about our evolutionary history, the following scenario seems plausible on the basis of existing evidence.

The existence of motor asymmetries in present-day animals provides clues about when certain precursors of human handedness may have been present in our ancestral chain. For example, there are indications of left-hand preference for reaching and right-hand preference for manipulation in several species of primates. This includes some species of prosimians, which branched off more than 50 million years ago from the ancestral line that led eventually to humans. Prosimians are thought to have changed very little since this branching and, to the extent that this is the case, it suggests that some amount of motor asymmetry was present well before the emergence of hominids. In fact, similar asymmetries are found in New World and Old World monkeys, which branched off from our ancestral line approximately 50 and 40 million years ago, respectively. Recent studies with chimpanzees, our closest present-day primate relatives which branched off from our ancestral line 5–10 million years ago, indicate a moderate amount of right-handed dominance for skilled manipulation. What this suggests is that some amount of manual asymmetry was present before the emergence of the first hominids and that a variety of evolutionary pressures acted on these already asymmetric ancestors to create even more asymmetry. In fact, several evolutionary milestones may have been particularly important for shaping human handedness.

One important milestone was the emergence of an upright posture and bipedal locomotion (i.e., walking on two legs). In contrast to the apes, early hominid species of *Australopithecus* (which emerged approximately 4 million years ago) walked upright much of the time. The transition to an upright posture and bipedal locomotion seems to have been complete by the time the first species of *Homo* emerged, approximately 2 million years ago. For several reasons, walking upright is an important milestone in human evolution and may have played a role in the evolution of handedness. Among other things, standing and walking upright free the hands from the need to provide postural support and from use in locmotion, thereby removing important environmental pressures for functional symmetry. At the same time, the hands could become adapted for a variety of activities that represent manipulations of rather than reactions to the environment. Such activities include carrying food and infants and manufacturing and using tools. Many of these new activities require the hands to engage in complementary activities (e.g., one hand steadies a stone while the other strikes it with a second stone to fashion a primitive tool). This need for complementary functions likely added to the pressure for asymmetry. A somewhat different way in which the emergence of an upright posture might have influenced handedness is related to a hypothesis discussed earlier about asymmetric shearing forces during the last trimester of pregnancy favoring development of the left otolith. Such shearing forces are present when the mother walks upright but would be much smaller or nonexistent if the mother were to walk on all fours.

It is interesting that a strong population-level bias toward right-handedness seems to have been present in various species of *Homo* for at least 1.5–2 million years. For example, an analysis of the flaking patterns on primitive stone tools suggests that right-handers outnumbered left-handers by a ratio of approximately two to one. This strong population bias toward right-handedness (rather than left-handedness) may have been a by-product of the smaller directional asymmetries that existed in primates. Further pressures in this direction may have been related to the emergence of language and to increasing dominance of the left cerebral hemisphere for certain aspects of language (e.g., speech production). Next to handedness, the most obvious functional asymmetry in present-day humans is dominance of the left cerebral hemisphere for producing speech. Both skilled use of the human hand and human speech require sequential, precisely timed movements. It is possible that there were evolutionary pressures for the same cerebral hemisphere to become specialized in some sense for programming such movements, regardless of whether the movements are made manually or orally. Thus, environmental pressures that favored the emergence of such diverse things as upright posture, tool manufacturing and use, speech, and language may have interacted synergistically over the last million years or so to create a variety of hemispheric specializations. In many cases, the direction of those specializations may have depended, like the direction of handedness, on smaller asymmetries in our primate ancestors.

V. HANDEDNESS RELATED TO OTHER BEHAVIORAL FACTORS

Among the reasons for continuing interest in handedness are claims that handedness is related to a variety of other behavioral and biological factors. There is a long history of the view that left-handedness in particular is associated with a host of negative characteristics. This view can even be seen in the very language used to refer to the two sides of the body. For example, in many languages the word for the right side [e.g., "right" (English) "droit" (French), "rechts" (German), "dexter" (Latin)] is also associated with positive characteristics such as correctness, goodness, skill, and dexterity. By way of contrast, the word for the left side [e.g., "left" (English), "gauche" (French), "links" (German), "sinister" (Latin)] is also associated with negative characteristics such as evil, weakness, ugliness, and clumsiness. In view of these historical views that left-handedness is a sign that something is not "right," it is important to consider what is shown by contemporary research.

There are, in fact, contemporary studies showing that the incidence of left-handedness is greater in groups of people with certain negative characteristics than it is in the population at large. Among the characteristics are such varied things as alcoholism, allergies, bed-wetting, criminality, drug abuse, epilepsy, immune disorders, learning disability, mental retardation, schizophrenia, and sleep disorders. To be sure, the elevated incidence of left-handedness associated with these characteristics is often small and there are some equivocal findings. In addition, relationships between handedness and such things as intellectual ability may interact in complex ways with other variables such as sex and overall intellectual ability. For example, several studies indicate that, among males with high reasoning ability, left-handers score lower than right-handers on tests of spatial ability. This relationship between handedness and spatial ability is reversed, however, for females with high reasoning ability. To make matters even more complex, for both males and females the relationship between handedness and spatial ability is reversed for individuals who have low reasoning ability. Nevertheless, for the specific characteristics listed above, evidence of at least a slight increase in the incidence of left-handedness seems too consistent to ignore.

There are also indications that the incidence of left-handedness is greater in certain groups of people with special talents and abilities. For example, the incidence of left-handedness is elevated among architects, artists, chess masters, championship players of the game "Go," those with increasing amounts of higher education, mathematically precocious children, and adults who study mathematics. A particularly interesting example comes from studies conducted by Camilla Benbow of Iowa State University and her colleagues comparing mathematically precocious boys and girls to boys and girls of more typical ability. Among other things, the incidence of left-handedness is elevated among boys and girls who score at least 700 on the math portion of the Scholastic Aptitude Test before the age of 13 years. Only 1 in 10,000 children score in this range, so that such a group is extremely precocious. It has been suggested that the increased incidence of left-handedness in these precocious children is related to enhanced functioning of the right cerebral hemisphere, possibly as the result of early exposure to testosterone during fetal development. The notion is that the sort of mathematical reasoning that is necessary to score so well depends on superior spatial abilities of the sort for which the right cerebral hemisphere is dominant and, as discussed earlier, left-handedness suggests right-hemisphere dominance for motor control. This fetal-testosterone hypothesis receives some support from the fact that, among these mathematically precocious children, the ratio of boys to girls is very high—perhaps as much as 13 : 1. Recall from earlier portions of the present article that elevated levels of fetal testosterone are more likely for males than for females. In addition, the rate of allergies and immune disorders is also elevated in the precocious children, which is at least consistent with the fetal-testosterone hypothesis.

The fact that left-handers tend to be overrepresented at both ends of some dimensions (e.g., intellectual ability) has led to the suggestion that left-handers as a group are more variable than right-handers. To the extent that this increased variability is a reality, it is consistent with the possibility that left-handedness occurs for somewhat different reasons in different people. That is, a bias toward left-handedness may result from a variety of different factors that, in addition to influencing handedness, have diverse effects on other aspects of biology and behavior.

Among the more interesting and controversial claims made in recent years is the claim that handedness is related to such health-related variables as accident rate, the incidence of certain diseases of the immune system, and, perhaps as a result of these things, to longevity. The fact that diseases of the immune system are more likely among left-handers than among right-handers has already been discussed and related to possible effects of elevated levels of fetal testosterone. Studies also indicate a higher rate of various types of accidents among left-handers than among right-handers. For example, in one recent study, left-handers were nearly 90% more likely than right-handers to have an accident-caused injury requiring medical attention during the 2-year period preceding questioning. Much of this increased accident rate may be attributable the fact that left-handers have a difficult time using utensils, appliances, tools, and machinery that have been designed for efficient use by right-handers. To illustrate this possibility, you need only watch a left-hander attempt to cut neatly along a curved line while using right-handed scissors held in the left hand.

Earlier in the present article, it was noted that at the present time the proportion of left-handers in the United States decreases with increasing age, so that fewer than 1% of living 80 year olds are left-handed. After concluding that various artifacts and switches of handedness during adulthood could not account for all of this decrease, Stanley Coren and his colleagues have suggested that the percentage of left-handedness decreases with age because left-handers, on the average, die at a younger age than right-handers. In one investigation of this possibility, Coren and his colleague Diane Halpern obtained information about handedness for a sample of individuals who had recently died. When they examined the mean age of death for men and women who were left- versus right-handed, they found some striking differences. On the average, the age of death was 75 years for right-handers and 66 years for left-handers, with the difference between handedness groups being larger for men than for women. In addition, the rate of death from accidents was higher for left-compared to right-handers—although not all of the handedness difference could be attributed to death by accident. As might be expected, these findings and their interpretation have proven to be controversial. Among other things, differences in the average age of death are likely to be related to the fact that the average age of living left-handers is lower than the average age of living right-handers. Furthermore, at least one longitudinal study indicates that once an individual has lived to age 65, the mortality rate over at least a 6-year period is identical for left- and right-handers. Given the potential practical as well as theoretical importance of resolving this controversy, there is great need for additional longitudinal and epidemiological investigation of possible relationships between handedness and longevity.

VI. HANDEDNESS AND HEMISPHERIC ASYMMETRY

Despite a good deal of similarity, the left and right cerebral hemispheres of humans have somewhat different information processing biases and propensities. Among the most well-established functional hemispheric asymmetries is left-hemispheric dominance for several aspects of language, including speech production and recognition, reading, and the use of syntax. By way of contrast, the right hemisphere is typically dominant for processing spatial relationships and is thought to play a more important role than the left in producing and recognizing emotion. There is a popular belief that the direction of these hemispheric asymmetries is reversed for left-handers compared to right-handers. Thus, we see slogans on T-shirts and bumper stickers proclaiming such things as "Left-handers are the only ones in their right mind." To be sure, there is a relationship between handedness and these types of functional hemispheric asymmetry, but the relationship is far from perfect. In fact, the general finding is that, on the average, hemispheric asymmetry for a typical group of left-handers is in the same direction as for a typical group of right-handers, but the magnitude of the difference is smaller. This difference in magnitude is often attributable to the fact that a greater proportion of left-handers than right-handers show an asymmetry opposite the direction that is considered prototypical.

The foregoing conclusions are illustrated nicely by considering what studies of patients with injury to one hemisphere or the other have revealed about hemispheric asymmetry for speech production. Such studies have led to estimates that approximately 95% of right-handers are left-hemisphere dominant for speech, approximately 5% are right-hemisphere dominant for speech, and very few if any have speech represented equally in both hemispheres. Similar studies of left-handers have led to estimates that approximately 60% are left-hemisphere dominant for speech, 20% are right-hemisphere dominant for speech, and 20% have speech represented equally in both hemispheres. Studies of brain-injured patients have also been used to estimate the proportion of right- and left-handers who show hemispheric asymmetry for certain spatial processing tasks. For right-handers, it is estimated that 32% are left-hemisphere dominant for certain types of spatial processing, 68% are right-hemisphere dominant, and virtually none have equal ability in both hemispheres. The corresponding values estimated for left-handers are 30% with left-hemisphere dominance, 38% with right-hemisphere dominance, and 32% with equal representation in both hemispheres. For both speech and spatial processing, a smaller proportion of left-handers (relative to right-handers) is estimated to have the prototypical direction of asymmetry and more left-handers (compared to right-handers) are estimated to have no asymmetry. The same general pattern of handedness differences is obtained in studies using other techniques to determine functional hemispheric asymmetry.

Certain biological asymmetries of the human cerebral cortex are also related to handedness. One example concerns asymmetry of the sylvian fissure, which is a deep groove on the lateral surfaces of the cerebral hemispheres and marks the boundary between the frontal and parietal lobes (above the fissure) and the temporal lobe (below the fissure). In right-handers, the sylvian fissure is longer and straighter in the left hemisphere than in the right hemisphere in approximately 67% of the cases studied, equal in the two hemispheres in approximately 26% of the cases studied, and longer and straighter in the right hemisphere in approximately 7% of the cases studied. The corresponding percentages estimated for left-handers are 22, 71, and 7%, respectively. The relationship between this type of biological asymmetry and functional hemispheric asymmetry is unknown. Nevertheless, it is interesting that, once again, the pattern for left-handers (relative to right handers) contains a smaller proportion with the typical direction of asymetry and a larger proportion with no asymmetry. Still, for both biological and functional asymmetry, when an asymmetry is present for left-handers, it is more often in the same direction as that seen for right-handers than in the opposite direction.

Although not related directly to hemispheric asymmetry, there are also indications that the size of certain regions of the corpus callosum is related to handedness. The corpus callosum is the major fiber tract that connects the left and right cerebral hemispheres and is known to be important for transmitting information from one hemisphere to the other. Certain regions of the corpus callosum tend to be smaller in the brains of individuals who are consistently right-handed than in the brains of individuals who are inconsistent in their hand preference (there have been very few consistent left-handers in these studies) and this pattern of handedness differences has been larger in the brains of males than in the brains of females. Unfortunately, it is not known what effect, if any, the size of the corpus callosum has on functional hemispheric asymmetry and there is no unequivocal behavioral evidence that handedness is related to the ability to transfer information efficiently from one hemisphere to the other.

VII. SUMMARY AND CONCLUSIONS

Handedness is the most obvious behavioral asymmetry in humans, with approximately 90% of the population having a strong preference to use the right hand for a wide variety of activities. In both humans and other species, there is a clear genetic contribution to the magnitude of hand preference. However, the direction of hand preference is clearly not determined in any straightforward way by a single gene with a dominant allele for right-handedness and a recessive allele for left-handedness. Instead, the direction of handedness seems to be influenced by a number of additional factors that interact with any genetic predisposition to produce the phenotypic expression of handedness in a particular individual. Among the potentially relevant factors are pre- and postnatal trauma, effects of testosterone during fetal development, and asymmetric positioning of the fetus *in utero*. Once handedness is established for a particular task, it generally remains constant from childhood into middle age and beyond.

Even concerted attempts to change handedness meet with only limited success and do not generalize beyond the specific tasks used in the attempt to change handedness.

The ubiquity of motor asymmetries in other species suggests that, in some sense, handedness is not unique to humans and that some form of manual asymmetry was present in our primate ancestors. It is likely that a variety of evolutionary pressures acted on these somewhat asymmetric ancestors to create even more asymmetry. In particular, such diverse things as upright posture, bipedal locomotion, tool manufacturing and use, speech, and language seem to have interacted synergistically to create a variety of hemispheric asymmetries. Perhaps for these reasons, there is at least some relationship between handedness and other types of functional hemispheric asymmetry.

Handedness continues to be studied, in part, because of its relationship to a variety of other behavioral and biological factors. One of the most controversial claims is that left-handers tend to die at a younger age than right-handers, perhaps because left-handers are more likely to be involved in accidents and because left-handers are more susceptible to certain diseases of the immune system. More research is needed to determine the validity of these claims. Regardless of outcome, such research will shed considerable light on both the theoretical mechanisms that produce handedness and the practical consequences of being right- or left-handed.

Bibliography

Annett, M. (1985). "Left, Right, Hand and Brain: The Right Shift Theory." Erlbaum, Hillsdale, NJ.

Bradshaw, J. L. (1989). "Hemispheric Specialization and Psychological Function." Wiley, Chichester, England.

Corballis, M. C. (1991). "The Lopsided Ape: Evolution of the Generative Mind." Oxford University Press, Oxford.

Coren, S. (Ed.). (1990). "Left-Handedness: Behavioral Implications and Anomalies." Elsevier, Amsterdam.

Coren, S. (1992). "The Left-Hander Syndrome: The Causes and Consequences of Left-Handedness." Free Press, New York.

Geschwind, N., and Galaburda, A. M. (1987). "Cerebral Lateralization: Biological Mechanisms, Associations, and Pathology." MIT Press, Cambridge, MA.

Hellige, J. B. (1993). "Hemispheric Asymmetry: What's Right and What's Left." Harvard University Press, Cambridge, MA.

McManus, I. C., and Bryden, M. P. (1993). The neurobiology of handedness, language, and cerebral dominance: A model for the molecular genetics of behavior. In "Brain Development and Cognition: A Reader" (M. H. Johnson, Ed.), pp. 679–702. Blackwell, Cambridge, UK.

Hate

Gerald Schoenewolf
The Living Center

Glossary

Anaclitic depression A psychoanalytic term denoting depression caused by an infant's relationship—usually with the mother or mother-surrogate.

Castration complex A psychoanalytic term describing a fixation during the early stages of sexual development that results in fears of castration in men and penis envy in women.

Ideal self In psychoanalysis, the grandiose self-image towards which one aspires—the saint, the hero, the genius.

Somatize To express emotional stress through a bodily symptom.

HATE can be defined as a state of arousal or excitation in humans in which anger, negative judgments, and impulses of destruction predominate. This state is produced by a combination of biological and environmental factors. Manifestations of hate are numerous, ranging from subtle indirect expressions to outright violence and war. However, not all hate is bad; some hate is destructive, while other hate can be constructive and beneficial.

I. THE BIOLOGICAL ROOTS OF HATE

Hate itself is not innate; however, the emotion of anger and the impulse toward aggression are part of the human constitution. And since hate is generally associated with anger and aggression, we can therefore say that it is indirectly innate. [*See* ANGER.]

An innate aggressive drive has been observed throughout the animal kingdom. Countless investigations have proven that fighting behavior in animals is genetically preprogrammed, and they have uncovered innate, species-specific patterns of fighting. For example, cichlids (a species of fish), even when they have been isolated from parents at birth, begin to fight with rivals by beating them with their tails and pushing or pulling them with their mouths; marine iguanas reared in isolation fight by butting their heads together; lava lizards lash one another with their tails; fighting cocks kick at one another with their claws; and roe buck attack with their antlers. All of this fighting happens spontaneously at a certain point in development.

An innate aggressive drive has also been observed in human beings and has primarily been linked to the "struggle for survival" (Charles Darwin's term) or to a territorial instinct. Aggression in human history is associated with the hunting and gathering of primitive men, with the territorial separation of—and strife between—individuals, groups, and nations, and to the formation of social hierarchies, or ranking orders. One can also see manifestations of this drive in the rough play of young boys and in athletic competition of adults. Indeed, all humans show the unmistakable tendency to keep their distance from strangers due to a fear of their aggression. [*See* AGGRESSION.]

Ethologists have noted that the disposition for aggression can be found in all human societies throughout the world. Threat displays by means of ornament, weaponry, feathers, masks, skins, boots, and phallic exposure as well as facial expressions of threat and rage are universal. People from around the world stomp their feet and clench their fists when they are angry. Also widespread throughout the world is the glorification of aggression through heroic sagas, coats of arms, and medals. Indeed, the history of humankind is a history of conflict and war. [*See* WAR.]

Biologically, aggression is associated with a "fight or flight" response that arouses the sympathetic ner-

Copyright © 1994 by Academic Press, Inc. All rights of reproduction in any form reserved.

vous system and the endocrine system (see Fig. 1). This is a coordinated operaton that goes into effect when an individual feels stress. The stressor excites the hypothalamus (firing brain cells) to produce a substance that stimulates the pituitary and adrenal glands to discharge corticoids (such as adrenalin) into the blood. This in turn elicits thymus shrinkage and releases sugar; and at the same time it also arouses the sympathetic nervous system, which contracts muscles and blood vessels. If an individual is in a state of arousal over a period of time, that can further affect the body's operation and chemistry. In addition, sudden increases of sexual hormones such as testosterone and estrogen can also arouse aggression. [*See* HORMONES AND BEHAVIOR; HYPOTHALAMUS.]

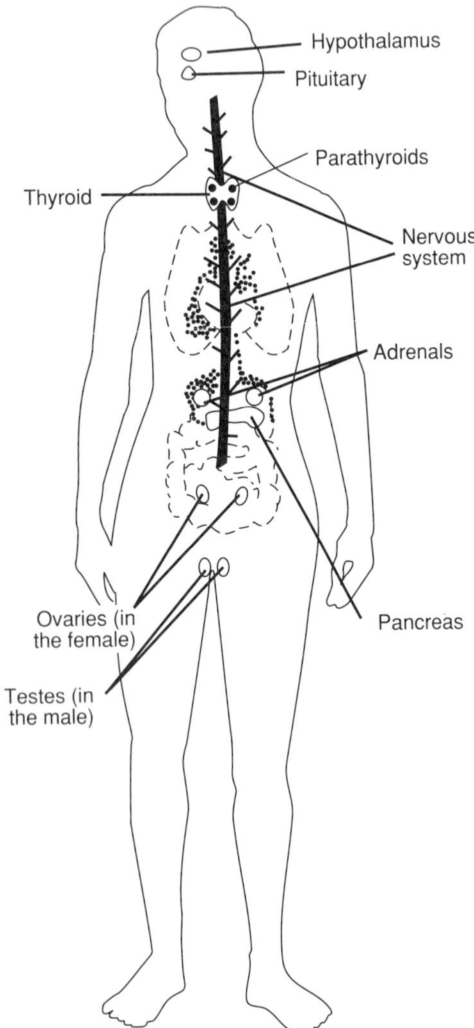

FIGURE 1 The physiology of hate.

Experimental psychologists have demonstrated a rage reaction by attaching electrodes to the hypothalamus. Subjects have been induced to states of extreme anger and have been impelled to perform acts of violence. Such experiments have also shown that while subjects are in such a state of induced rage, their cognitive abilities change; anger leads to negative judgments (hate) and the desire to eliminate the source of the anger (the stressor) by destroying it.

There is some variation in the amount of innate aggression in each individual at birth. Some infants are "cranky babies" while others eat and sleep without much trouble. It is not clear, however, whether this variation in infant aggressiveness is due to genetics or to environmental conditions during pregnancy. Research has shown, for example, that mothers who are depressed (a state of anger and hate turned inward) during pregnancy give birth to hyperactive infants. On the other hand, not all cranky babies have depressed mothers. [*See* INDIVIDUAL DIFFERENCES IN TEMPERAMENT.]

Hate, then, is the cognitive component of the "fight or flight" arousal state. This state of aggressive arousal differs from other states of excitement such as anxiety or nervous anticipation, although these too involve the sympathetic nervous system; the environmental factors are different in these various states of excitement. We hate that which frightens, frustrates, or unsettles us. This hate (and the state of arousal that underlies it) can be temporary or long term, and it can be conscious or unconscious. In some cases people can be in a state of chronic tension and not know it, and they can feel hate and not be aware of it. [*See* ANXIETY AND FEAR.]

II. THE ENVIRONMENTAL ROOTS OF HATE

While there is undoubtedly an innate aggressive drive in humans, that drive cannot become aroused in and of itself. Aggression and hate depend on an interplay of innate and environmental factors. The extent of latent (biological) and environmental factors may differ from individual to individual.

There are numerous theories about what kinds of environmental factors lead to aggression and hate. One theory focuses on the changes in the environment that disrupt homeostasis; getting a divorce, getting fired, getting married, having a child, losing a loved one—these are all changes that cause stress, produce irritability, and arouse hate. Another theory centers on frustration, holding that aggression and hate are linked to frustration of some kind (unrequieted love, envy, unfulfilled ambitions, etc.). Another posits that aggression and hate are connected with threats to survival, as when a rival threatens to take one's job, or the government takes away one's food stamps. Another theory holds that hate may be transmitted through various psychological means such as identification (as when a child identifies with a parent) or indoctrination (as when an individual or group is "brain-washed" into adapting a negative attitude toward another individual or group).

Studies of infants shows a relationship between bonding and aggression. There is a period of life in which bonding with a loving caretaker is essential for survival. In one study, 91 infants in a foundling home during a war were separated from their mothers after the age of 3 months and fed by a succession of nurses. Thirty-four of the infants died by the second year, and a pattern was observed. Upon first being separated from their mothers, infants would typically cry and cling angrily to whatever nurse was feeding them (aggression turned outward); then they would go through a phase of anaclitic depression, lying sullenly in their cribs (aggression turned inward); then motor retardation would set in; and finally they would develop marasmus and die. These studies show that bonding is critical during this early phase of development, and that aggression and destruction erupt as a defense against the loss of this bonding.

Hence, the seeds of the environmental contribution to the formation of aggression and hate are laid in earliest childhood and are transmitted in the milieu of the family. Our first experience of love stems from this earliest bonding with our maternal caretaker, a bonding that evokes feelings of gratitude, security, fulfillment, and contentment. Our first experience of hate also stems from this period. If this first relationship is deficient, we feel cut off, frustrated, threatened, and enraged. We want to destroy this deficient caretaker (bite the breast that feeds us) or, if that is not possible, to destroy ourselves. In other words, when our survival is threatened, the biological "fight or flight" response kicks in, our system is aroused, and we become enraged and hateful. This first relationship is not only the prototype and precursor of what is to come, it may also create fixations or "faults" that establish a tendency toward hating. Like underground faults that lead to future earthquakes, human development fixations may lead to to future emotional disturbances, aggression, and hate.

As we develop, other environmental factors also help to shape our capacities for loving and hating. Other figures—the father, siblings, grandparents, aunts, and uncles—begin to exert an influence in how we love or hate. We form identificational bonds with those we admire and those we fear and tend to incorporate their way of loving and hating. If the parenting is punitive or abusive (and thereby hateful), we may grow up to be punitive and abusive to others (or to submit to abuse and abuse ourselves). If the parenting is permissive (a disguised form of hate), we may grow up to be self-indulgent and bratty (hatefully inconsiderate and demanding), but permissive to our own children and those who ally with us. If our family values are religious and distrustful of those who are not, we may grow up to adopt this religion. We may feel that anybody who is not of our faith represents a threat to our security and hence is to be hated (i.e., pitied and saved). If our family values are ideological and distrustful of anybody who does not share our ideology, we may grow up to adopt this ideology. We may feel that anybody who is not of our ideological or political persuasion represents a threat to our security and hence is to be hated (i.e., ridiculed and dismissed).

Envy and jealousy are often closely related to hate. When we feel envious or jealous, our "fight or flight" response is also aroused and we feel resentment (a form of hate) toward those we envy and experience their existence as an insult and threat to or own. However, the extent to which envy and jealousy prevail in each individual's psychodynamics depends upon upbringing. A tendency toward feeling envy or jealousy may result from childhood spoiling and pampering, from an identification with a parent who has this tendency, or from early childhood fixations that result in inferiority or castration complexes, which cause individuals to feel that they, their bodies, their sexual organs, and their lots in life, are inferior, disadvantaged, or threatened. [*See* JEALOUSY.]

Later, in adulthood, both personal and larger social and cultural factors can influence our hatred. If we already have fixations from early childhood, any situations in our adult lives that repeat the events of those fixations will upset us, arouse us, and induce a hate reaction. If we have lost our mother at 2 years old, any loss later on may bring about a breakdown into depression (self-hate). If we have felt severely deprived, any deprivation will be severely upsetting; if we have felt extremely indulged and pampered, any failure of our later environment to duplicate this indulgence and pampering will arouse rage, etc.

In addition, those who have had deficient bonding (or socialization) in early childhood and who have developed fixations or tendencies toward negative thinking and hating will be most influenced by adversive social or cultural factors. They will be the first to join movements that give them a justification for hating some designated enemy. They will be the first to rail against another nation that has temporarily been designated as our country's enemy. They will be the first to discriminate against others or other groups (while accusing the other group of discriminating against them). They will be the first to join any angry mob.

Psychological tests show that how we perceive things is greatly influenced by our personality. For example the Rorschach Inblot Test may be shown to several individuals and each will see different things in the ink blots. In a section from one of these blots some individuals may see two angels with wings, while othes may see two boys urinating, and still others may see two scuba divers roasting fish over a fire. What we see in these blots depends on our personality make-up (i.e., whether we are obsessive–compulsive, hysterical, paranoid, psychotic, or the like). In other words, our early childhood conditioning influences how we perceive the world; we may perceive some event as being threatening (and respond with anger and hatred), while another person may perceive the same event differently. Threats and hate are often in the eye of the beholder.

Numerous social and cultural factors may arouse aggression and hate. Times of war and economic depression are two of the most dramatic examples of this. During such times, social hysteria runs high, and each individual in a society feels threatened and insecure and becomes aroused and hateful of that which is designated as to blame for this misfortune (the enemy country, the government, Republicans, Democrats, etc.) Social or cultural changes may also arouse aggression and hated. For example, an anthropologist studied how an abrupt change in the system and values of a primitive village resulted in an increase in community stress and aggression. Before the change, the community as a whole cultivated and distributed food more or less in a communistic fashion. When it was decreed that all individuals would henceforth be responsible for their own subsistence, there was an aggressive scramble to acquire the uncultivated wet valleys and a subsequent increase in animosity and criminality. People became hostile to one another, feared one another, envied one another, and became ruthless in dealing with one another. Something like this occurred in Russia when the Communist government toppled in 1991. Poverty and overcrowding can also arouse aggression and hate, as can a lack of meaningful job opportunities. The range of social factors is myriad.

Authority figures can arouse and shape hatred. Stanley Milgram's famous experiment at Yale in the 1970s provided a scientific basis for this phenomenon. He told his subjects—men and women from all walks of life—that they were participating in an experiment to test the effects of punishment on learning. Each subject was asked to take the role of teacher and to deliver electric shocks to a "learner" who was actually a paid actor. The "learner" was strapped into a chair in a separate room and was apparently hooked up to electrodes. The teacher was instructed to ask the "learner" questions, and if the "learner" gave the wrong answers, the teacher was to give him various doses of electric shock by pressing buttons on an electric generator. The shocks ranged from 15 to 450 V. The teachers were instructed to give increasingly stronger shocks, and the "learners" (actors) would cry out and moan in agony and beg the teachers to stop. If a teacher seemed doubtful about going on, the leader, standing behind them, would say in a firm, authoritarian voice, "You must go on." Although some subjects showed signs of great conflict, 65% of them continued to deliver what they thought were shocks to a screaming human being with a weak heart right up to the highest possible voltage, which was labeled "Danger: Severe shock" (see Fig. 2).

This experiment showed that to some degree or another people are willing to administer electric shocks (act out hate) if an authority figure gives permission to do so. There are several explanations for this. Throughout the history of humankind we have shown a need to believe in something greater than ourselves and to obey it—whether it is a king or a president or a Pope or wizard, whether it is one God or many gods or an entire mythology or advanced creatures from another planet, whether it is an idea or philosophy or political movement. This higher authority absolves us of responsibility. We particularly look for ways in which we can act out hate without feeling responsible or guilty about it. Hence, to the degree that we have not fully separated

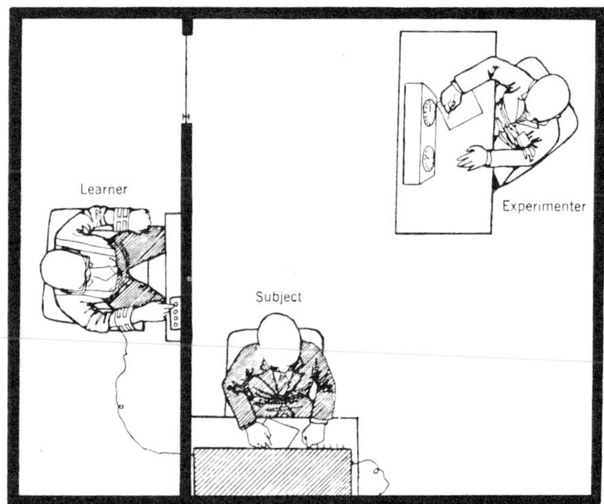

FIGURE 2 Milgram's experiment: 65% (26 out of 40) went to maximum 450 V; 22.5% (9 out of 40) quit between 300–450 V; 12.5% (5 out of 40) quit at 300 V; none quit before 300 V.

from our parents and fully matured, we will need such surrogate authorities to believe in and take responsibility for our decisions. In addition, to the extent we have developed fixations and faults, we will have pent-up rage and potential hatred, and we will look for an excuse (an authority figure's permission) to vent it.

The state of hating, then, is the culmination of a complex process involving the interplay of the innate human aggressive drive, early childhood conditioning, and later personal and societal environmental forces. Sometimes hatred erupts for a short time and is a temporary response to a specific event; while in other cases hatred is chronic and becomes an ingrained trait resulting from deeply traumatic or ongoing adversive events.

III. MANIFESTATIONS OF HATE

Manifestations of hate range from the obvious and simple to the subtle and complex. Obvious and simple forms include direct verbal expressions such as, "I hate you!" or "You stupid idiot!" as well as acts of violence such as murder, rape, or war. More subtle and complex manifestations comprise a multitude of manipulations, ploys, stings, attitudes, and acts through which hate is indirectly expressed. These include, to name just a few examples, forgetting an appointment, pretending to like people whom one hates and thereby "killing them with kindness," having an affair with a married man or woman, stealing memo pads or paperclips from the company for which one works, or telling a child to "stop crying or I'll give you something to really cry about."

Looking at manifestations of hate from an overall perspective, those people who have attained emotional health, established genuine bonds with others, and feel connected to their vocation will manifest the least hate. Those who have not matured emotionally, who have not established genuine bonds with others, and who do not feel connected to a vocation will manifest the most hate. Such people will feel less secure and hence their aggressive response and hatred will be more easily aroused. They will act out in various ways in order to try to compensate for their feelings of insecurity, alienation, and rage—such acting out being the manifestation of their hate. The more innate aggression they bring into the world and the more deficient their upbringing has been, the more disturbed will be their relation to the world. Hence, the worlds of severely sociopathic, paranoid, or schizophrenic individuals are full of agression and hate.

Hate can be expressed in three basic ways: it can be expressed in a direct, verbal way, it can be acted out, and it can be somatized. Direct verbal expressions of hate include any verbal statement of hate, curses, insults, threats, death wishes, and the like. The acting out of hate includes any action that is rude, hostile, rejecting, excluding, manipulative, deceitful, defiant, shaming, ridiculing, contemptuous, threatening, violent, and the like. Somatizing hate has to do with the "bottling up" of aggression so that it takes a toll on our own bodies, as when one develops an ulcer due to a stressful, hate-inducing relationship. Somatizing also includes using illness to manipulate others, as when a individual develops a hysterical paralysis out of resentment at not being cared for, such paralysis forcing a family to care for this individual.

Some manifestations are active and conscious, while others are passive and unconscious. We may actively express hate to a rival in business or love, a mother-in-law, a boss, a neighbor, or a drunk driver who almost runs into us. In such instances we are also quite aware of our aggression and hatred. In other instances, we may not wish to be aware of our aggression so it is expressed passively and we remain unconscious of it. We may not wish to acknowledge that we hate our brother, for there is a strong social taboo against such hatred; so instead we may show great kindness to this brother and even convince ourselves that we love him, but at the same time we may constantly forget his birthday, neglect to write to him, flirt with his wife, and in other ways act out unconscious hate. We chop down tropical forests and drive gasoline-fueled automobiles to advance our immediate goals while at the same time passively killing our planet and remaining, collectively, unconscious of our own mass death wish (mass self-hatred).

The most destructive manifestations of hate occur in families. "Power does not corrupt men," Bernard Shaw said, "fools, however, if they get into a position of power, corrupt power." He was on the right track. To be a parent is to be in a position of absolute power over another human being. Nowhere in any occupation is there as much power as there is in being a parent, and that power is held paractically sacred and shielded from the public eye. Parents who were abused, neglected, pampered, exploited, or impeded as children will grow up to do likewise to their children. As children, each of us are slaves to our parents; thus, we have all experienced slavery. Some slave owners are loving, most are not.

Parental expressions of hate can begin even before birth. Mothers can express passive hate during pregnancy if they take drugs that they know will harm the fetus, if they are careless about their diet, or if they are overactive. Fathers can express hate by mistreating the mother during pregnancy. Once the child is born parents can express hate in numerous ways, including obvious ones such as beatings, sexual molestation, scapegoating, degradation, or neglect, and more subtle and indirect ones. Rene Spitz, observing 203 mother and infant dyads in an institution, wrote of the indirect and unconscious ways mothers express hate during the first year of life. For example, he described mothers who related to their infants with "primary anxious overpermissiveness" and others who acted out "hostility in the guise of anxiety." In each of these cases, the mothers were compensating for unconscious feelings of hate toward the child (usually an unwanted child) through an exaggerated anxiety and overconcern with the child's welfare. He noted a high degree of eczema in the infants of such mothers. It is a general principle in psychoanalysis that an obsessive overconcern with somebody's welfare masks an unconscious wish for their harm.

Another common manifestation of hateful mothering is postpartum depression, which results in a mother's completely rejecting her infant during the weeks right after birth. Research has shown that maternal deprivation during the earliest stage of infancy can lead to severe disturbances, creating fixations that program an individual with a tendency to withdraw from contact with others. This tendency underpins maladies such as nonorganic autism, schizophrenia, and depression.

Parents also act out hate to their children through their personality rituals. For example, an obsessive–compulsive parent may be obsessed with neatness and order to an extent that he or she will not allow any of the children to ever enjoy their existence. Or a parent may be a masochistic martyr type, continually bemoaning his or her life, so that the children can get no real love or attention but must cater to and sympathize with this "victimized" parent. Or a parent may be a passive type, married to an abusive spouse, who sits by and allows the abusive parent to have his or her way with the children. If the children complain to the passive parent about the abuse, the passive parent may promise to put a stop to it, but when the abuse happens again, the passive parent will again remain passive and the child will feel betrayed. Passive hate may be even more devastating than active abuse.

Another common manifestation of parental hate occurs when children become the pawns in a custody battle. Here the hate between the divorcing parents gets displaced onto the children, who are bribed, threatened, and pulled apart by both parents, who are little concerned with the child's welfare but only with their own desire to "win." This desire to win stems from the arousal of their aggressive drive by the threat of divorce, which at the same time rekindles long repressed feelings from childhood connected to similar events.

On a broader spectrum, cultural forms of hate, such as racism and sexism, have become a cause for much concern today, and history is replete with instances of mass discrimination, crusades, and exterminations aimed at one group or another. For example, in Nazi Germany 6 million Jews were rounded up and exterminated in death camps. The Nazis decided that the Jews were evil exploiters of Germany, poisoning the purity of the German people, and therefore had to be eradicated. To understand this gross expression of prejudice and cruelty by one people against another, we must understand the environmental conditions that led to it. After Germany lost World War I, it became the scapegoat and laughing-stock of Europe. It was left thoroughly demoralized and sank into a psychological and economic depression. In the midst of this depression, when the mass aggressive drive of Germany was aroused and people were looking for somebody (or some group) on whom to blame their misfortune, along came Hitler. Here was an authority figure who gave them permission to blame it on the Jews.

During the course of history, certain prejudices are sanctified while others are condemned. Hence, the early Catholic Church condemned as heresy any other religious groups, while sanctifying its own bigotry and prejudice in the form of inquisitions and witch hunts against "heathens" and "wild women." In China during the 1970s the notorious "Gang of Four" formed the Red Guards and sent them out to rid the country of people who were politically incorrect; they roamed the countryside imprisoning and killing innocent people, burning houses, destroying monuments, and generally terrorizing China. Later those who had been Red Guards were condemned. In America, during the McCarthy hearings of the late 1940s, there was a mass persecution of communists (or anybody who looked as if he or she might have communist leanings). Later, McCarthy and his followers were condemned. Social movements often start out with idealistic goals of reforming some social problem, and they just as often end up as hotbeds of hatred that lead to mass hysteria. [*See* PREJUDICE AND STEREOTYPES.]

Mass hysteria represents a gradual or sudden eruption of collective pent-up aggression and hate. If, say, many individuals have had abusive childhoods, and have had to "swallow" their resentment during those childhoods because their parents told them, "Stop crying or I'll give you something to really cry about," that resentment lies dormant until they are adults and there is an opportunity to vent it. When a movement comes along that provides them with that opportunity, they are quick to join it, and their collective pent-up rage may eventually get out of hand until another group (playing the role of the punitive father of childhood) checks it.

Prejudice is a knife that cuts both ways. There are instances of real prejudice (unfounded hatred of an individual or group) and there are other instances in which charges of prejudice are a manipulation the aim of which is to discredit an opponent, to avoid taking responsibility for one's own hate, and to gain special privilege (for being a victim of prejudice). A cause, religion, or movement becomes an extension of one's identity, mirroring one's ideal self, while that part of the self one wishes to disown—that is, aggression and hatred—is projected onto the "out" group. We and our group are "in," good, righteous, and without ulterior motives, while the "out" group is bad, morally repugnant, and imbued with bad motives. The more disturbed individuals are, the more they are prone to splitting others into stereotypes of good and bad, rather than seeing people as complex human beings. In our time, many liberals view conservatives this way, and many conservatives view liberals this way.

Acts of interpersonal violence as well as wars are the most extreme manifestations of hate. When people are aroused to an extent that they kill each other, it is always due fears that their own lives are in jeopardy. Jealous lovers kill because they feel that they themselves have been psychologically murdered by their lover's infidelity. But not every jealous lover kills—only those with fixations in childhood that make them susceptible to this way of expressing hate. Wars are in part innate battles over territoriality (preprogrammed by human genetic endowment) and in part due to adversive environmental conditions. Narcissism (in the form of patriotism) often plays a part. German pride was hurt by the loss of World War I and by their economic depression. To "save face" they started World War II. Japan, wishing to expand its territory (and hence its feeling of power and security), joined in. Other nations felt threatened by them and like dominoes, one by one, were drawn into the war as each of their aggressive drives were aroused.

IV. CONSTRUCTIVE AND DESTRUCTIVE HATE

Not all hate is destructive. In general, the more mature an individual or country is, the more it can be aware of its hateful feelings and verbalize them in a constructive way—that is, in a way that resolves conflict rather than feeding it. Hence, most direct verbal expressions of hate are constructive, while most acting out or somatizing of hate is destructive. There is a popular misconception that "love cures all." If by love one means, "Let's all be nice to each other and suppress our aggression and hate," then such sentiments, no matter how lofty, are misleading. They fail to appreciate fully the nature of aggression and hate; it cannot be willed away through calls for unity. The antidote to destructive hate is constructive hate, not guilty pseudolove.

Donald Winnicott, a British psychoanalyst, tells a story that illustrates this point. He once had an orphan boy live with him and his wife. This boy, who was about 9, was quite unsocialized and would go on binges in which he manaced Winnicott and his wife and destroyed their furniture. Winnicott noted that each of these incidents would arouse intense feelings of hate in him. The boy, he interpreted, had a need to induce others into hating him in order to feel worthwhile. To help the boy develop, Winnicott believed he had to let him know that he hated him. "If the patient seeks objective or justified hate, he must be able to reach it, else he cannot feel he can reach objective love," he writes. Therefore, each time the boy went on a binge, Winnicott would pick him up and take him outside and set him down on the front porch, rain or sleet or snow. There was a special bell the boy could ring, and he knew that if he rang it he would be readmitted into the house and nothing would be said about his fit. Each time Winnicott put him outside, he told the boy, "I hate you for what you just did." It was easy for Winnicott to say that, because it was true. Moreover, he believed it was not only necessary for the boy's development, but also necessary for himself, for had he not expressed his hate in this constructive way he could not have continued to live with the boy "without losing my temper and without every now and again murdering him."

In other words, constructive expressions of hate involve mature ego control of the aggressive drive and hate; they consist of expressing it in such a way as to counter destructive expressions of hate without overdoing it—i.e., without hostile aims of revenge. Constructive hate is generally conscious hate, while destructive hate is often acted out unconsciously. If we act out hate in an unconscious way, there is little chance of a resolution. If we say, "I'm not doing anything, he's the one who did it," or "He started it," we are denying our own aggression, hence preventing resolution. Likewise, we cannot resolve a conflict if when somebody expresses extreme rage at us we look at them in askance and laugh at them. This is simply "throwing salt on their wounds"—an expression of destructive hate which makes them even madder.

Sigmund Freud thought that civilization itself was a cause of discontent and therefore a breeding ground of aggression and hate. Manifestations of destructive hate do seem to be spiraling as civilization becomes more crowded and technological (and thereby alienating). We now have the power to push buttons and kill millions without actually experiencing what we are doing (an expansion of Milgram's experiments). Technology has made our lives easier and spoiled us to a point where we have become addicted to ease and cannot do without it, even though it is destroying our planet and ourselves. Like caged animals, we have become imprisoned by our own civilizations, and have developed a variety of new illnesses, such as AIDS.

The solution to interpersonal as well as world problems lies in a deeper understanding of hate, and in particular, in a deeper understanding of the differences between constructive and destructive hate. At the deepest level, every expression of hate is a defense against a real or imagined threat, a compensation for feelings of inferiority or powerlessness, and a plea for attention. To understand this is to react appropriately, not with a guilt-ladden sentimental cry for unity, nor with a punitive cry for revenge, but with a firm expression of constructive hate. Love is relating genuinely to another human and to the world. Constructive hate is a form of love.

Bibliography

Eibl-Eibesfeldt, I. (1974). "Love and Hate: The Natural History of Behavior Patterns." Shocken, New York.

Freud, S. (1930). "Civilization and Its Discontent." Hogarth, London.

Milgram, S. (1974). "Obedience to Authority." Harper & Row, New York.

Schoenewolf, G. (1989). "Sexual Animosity between Men and Women." Jason Aronson, Northvale, NJ.

Schoenewolf, G. (1991). "The Art of Hating." Jason Aronson, Northvale, NJ.

Spitz, R. (1965). "The First Year of Life." International Universities Press, New York.

Winnicott, D. W. (1949). Hate in the countertransference. In "Through Paediatrics to Psycho-Analysis," pp. 194–203. Basic Books, New York.

Hippocampal Formation

David G. Amaral
State University of New York at Stony Brook

Glossary

Anterior Toward the front of the brain.

Anterograde amnesia Loss of the ability to acquire and/or recall new information.

Axon Output process of neurons which forms connections between brain regions.

Cytoarchitectonics Characteristic organization and packing density of neurons. A major criterion used in defining boundaries of brain regions.

Dendrites Treelike processes of neurons which form their receptive surface.

Lateral Toward the side of the brain.

Medial Toward the middle of the brain.

Posterior Toward the back of the brain.

Temporal lobe One of the four lobes of the human brain, the others being the frontal, parietal, and occipital. The temporal lobe is located on the side of the brain in the region below and behind the temple.

Ventricles System of cavities in the brain that are filled with cerebrospinal fluid.

THE HIPPOCAMPAL FORMATION is a brain region located in the inner, or medial, portion of the temporal lobe. It comprises four subregions: the dentate gyrus, the hippocampus, the subicular complex, and the entorhinal cortex. These four subregions are linked by prominent connections which tend to unite them as a functional entity. The major behavioral function associated with the hippocampal formation is memory. Damage to the human hippocampal formation results in anterograde amnesia. The hippocampal formation is particularly sensitive to a variety of traumas and disease states and is often damaged in anoxia/ischemia, epilepsy, and Alzheimer's disease.

I. LOCATION AND STRUCTURE OF THE HIPPOCAMPAL FORMATION

The most distinctive subregion of the hippocampal formation, and the one from which it takes its name, is the hippocampus. The term *hippocampus* (or sea horse) was first applied in the 16th century by the anatomist Arantius, who considered the three-dimensional form of the grossly dissected human hippocampus to be reminiscent of this sea creature (Fig. 1). Others likened the hippocampus to a ram's horn, and De Garengeot named the hippocampus "Ammon's horn" after the mythological Egyptian god. The terms *hippocampus* and *Ammon's horn* (or Cornu Ammonis) are now used synonymously.

The hippocampal formation is located in the medial portion of the temporal lobe, and the hippocampus and dentate gyrus form a prominent bulge in the floor of the lateral ventricle (Fig. 1). The hippocampal formation is widest at its anterior extent, where it bends toward the medial surface of the brain. The subtle bumps (or gyri) formed in this region give it a footlike appearance, and the name *pes* (foot) *hippocampi* has classically been applied to this area. The main portion, or "body," of the hippocampus becomes progressively thinner as it bends posteriorly and upward toward the corpus callosum (Fig. 1).

The medial surface of the hippocampus contains a flattened bundle of axons called the fimbria (Figs. 1 and 2). Axons originating from neurons in the hippocampus and subicular complex travel in a thin layer called the *alveus* that sheaths the hippocampus and coalesce in the medially situated fimbria. At

Copyright © 1994 by Academic Press, Inc. All rights of reproduction in any form reserved.

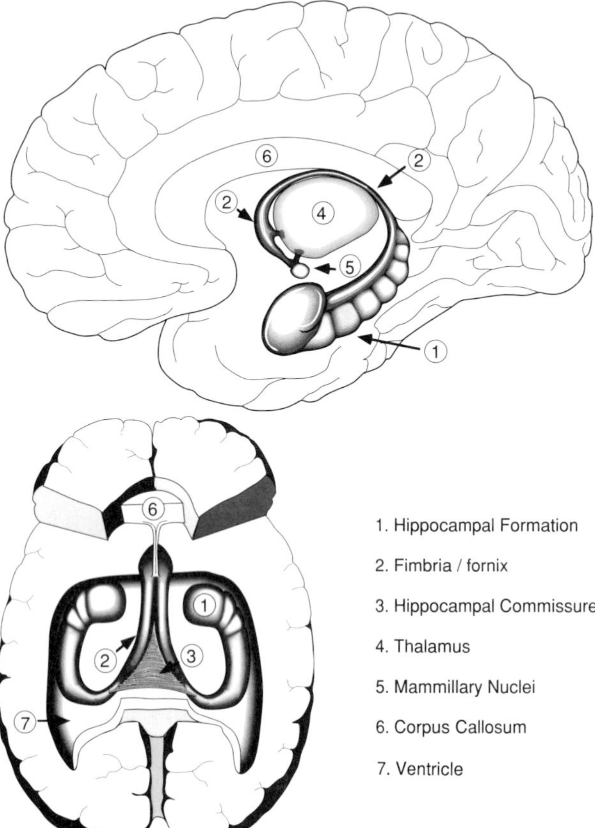

FIGURE 1 The position of the hippocampal formation and related structures in the human brain. The top image represents the medial surface of the human brain. The front of the brain is to the left. The position of the hippocampal formation in the medial portion of the temporal lobe is illustrated. The subcortically directed output bundle of axons, here labeled the fimbria/fornix, can be seen to arc over the thalamus and to ultimately descend into the diencephalon. Connections are made both with the mamillary nuclei and with the thalamus. The drawing in the lower left of the illustration is a cutaway of the brain as viewed from above and behind. The front of the brain is at the top of the image. The C-shaped structure of the hippocampal formation can be seen to occupy the floor of the lateral ventricles.

rostral levels, the fimbria is thin and flat but it becomes progressively thicker caudally as fibers are continually added to it. As the fimbria leaves the posterior extent of the hippocampus, it fuses with the ventral surface of the corpus callosum and travels anteriorly in the lateral ventricle. The major portion of the rostrally directed fiber bundle is called the body of the fornix. At the ends of its anterior trajectory, the body of the fornix descends and is called the column of the fornix. The fornix then divides around the anterior commissure to form the precommissural fornix, which enters the basal forebrain and the postcommissural fornix, which terminates in the diencephalon. Near the point where the fimbria fuses with the posterior portion of the corpus callosum, some of its fibers extend across the midline of the brain to form the hippocampal commissure. A variety of gross anatomical terms have been applied to the commissural fibers but the term *psalterium* (alluding to a harplike stringed instrument) is most common.

The four subregions of the human hippocampal formation can be differentiated cytoarchitectonically in neuroanatomical preparations in which thin sections of the brain have been stained to show the distribution of neuronal cell bodies (Fig. 2). The dentate gyrus is the simplest of the subregions and has a trilaminate appearance. The principal cell layer of the dentate gyrus (the granule cell layer) is populated primarily by one class of neuron, the granule cell. The human dentate gyrus contains approximately 9 million granule cells on each side of the brain. The dendrites of the granule cells extend into the overlying molecular layer, where they receive their main input from the entorhinal cortex.

The human hippocampus can be divided into three distinct fields labeled CA3, CA2, and CA1 (Fig. 2). The distinction of the three fields relates primarily to differences in their connections and more subtle differences in neuronal size and shape. All of the hippocampus has essentially one cellular layer, the pyramidal cell layer, which is populated by neurons with triangularly shaped cell bodies (the pyramidal cells). Pyramidal cells have dendrites emanating from their top (or apical) and bottom (or basal) surfaces. On each side of the brain, there are about 2 million neurons in the CA3 region, 220,000 in CA2, and almost 5 million neurons in field CA1. The relatively acellular layers above and below the pyramidal cell layer all have distinctive names. The outside limiting surface of the hippocampus located deep to the pyramidal cell layer is formed by axons of the pyramidal cells and is called the alveus (Fig. 2). Between it and the pyramidal cell layer is stratum oriens, which contains the basal dendrites of the pyramidal cells. The region above the pyramidal cell layer contains the apical dendrites of the pyramidal cells and is divided into several strata (stratum lucidum, stratum radiatum, stratum lacunosum-moleculare). Different connections are formed in each of these strata.

The subicular complex can be subdivided into three distinct fields, the subiculum proper, the presubiculum, and the parasubiculum (Fig. 2). As in the

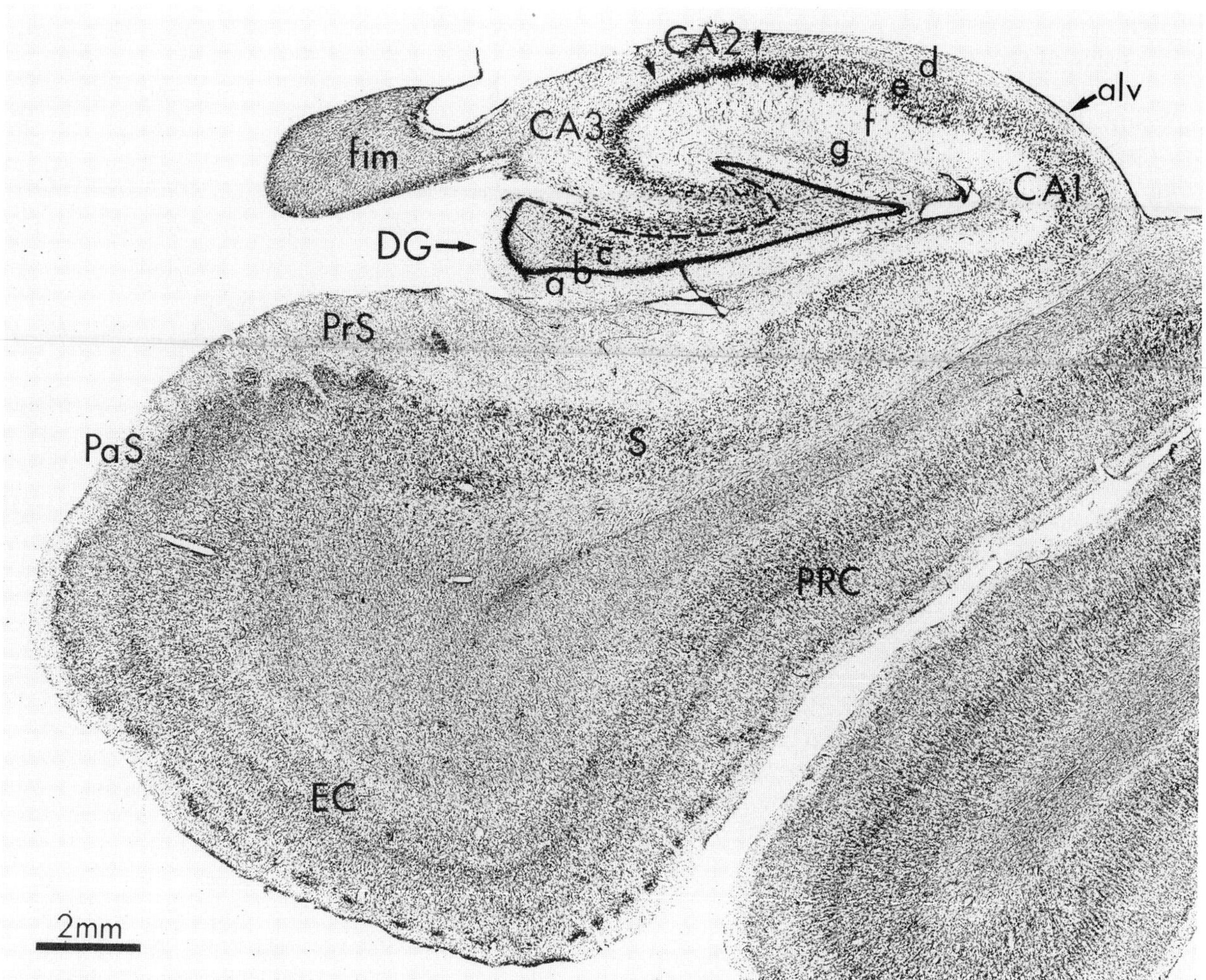

FIGURE 2 A thin section cut through the hippocampal formation of the human brain that is stained for the visualization of neurons. Each dark spot indicates the location of one neuronal cell body. The four major fields of the hippocampal formation can be differentiated in this type of preparation. The dentate gyrus (DG) has three layers: the molecular layer (a), granule cell layer (b), and polymorphic cell layer (c). The hippocampus can be divided into three fields, CA3, CA2, and CA1. The covering of the hippocampus is composed of axons originating from the pyramidal cells and is called the alveus (alv). The next layer, stratum oriens (d), contains the basal dendrites of the pyramidal cells. The cell bodies of the pyramidal neurons are contained in the pyramidal cell layer (e). The apical dendrites of the pyramidal cells extend into the overlying stratum radiatum (f) and stratum lacunosum-moleculare (g). The subicular complex comprises three distinct regions: the subiculum (S), the presubiculum (PrS), and the parasubiculum (PaS). The last subregion of the hippocampal formation is the entorhinal cortex, which is a multilaminate cortical area that resembles the neocortex. The adjacent perirhinal cortex (PRC) is one source of sensory information to the hippocampal formation.

hippocampus, one principal cell layer in the subiculum is populated by about 2.5 million neurons on each side. Details concerning the laminar organization of the other components of the subicular complex, the presubiculum and parasubiculum, are complex and not yet well understood. The subicular complex is an important region of the hippocampal formation, however, because it originates the major connection with subcortical regions such as the thalamus and hypothalamus. [*See* HYPOTHALAMUS.]

The term *entorhinal cortex* was coined by the early neuroanatomist Korbinian Brodmann to name the region that lies adjacent to the shallow rhinal sulcus in nonhuman brains. More than any other subregion of the hippocampal formation, the entorhinal cortex has undergone substantial regional and laminar differentiation in the human brain. Unlike the other hippocampal subregions, the entorhinal cortex is a multilaminate cortical region that resembles the cytoarchitectonic appearance found in the neocortex. It is distinguished from the neocortex by the presence of clusters of darkly stained neurons that constitute the first cell layer (layer II) located just below the surface of the brain. It is also distinct in lacking a layer of small granular cells that typically forms the fourth layer in neocortex.

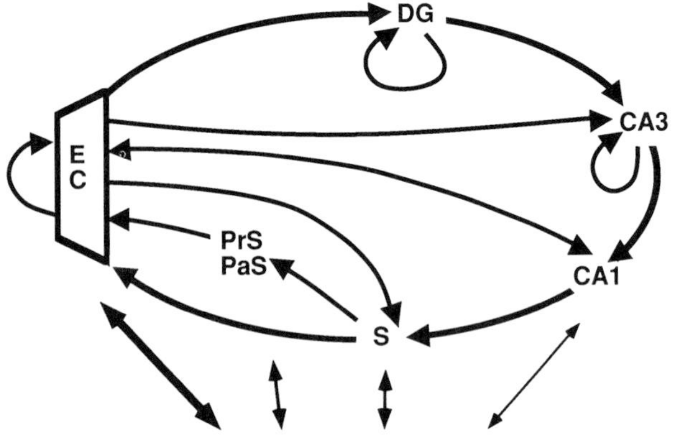

FIGURE 3 Summary of the major intrinsic and extrinsic neural connections of the hippocampal formation. The oval in the center of the illustration represents the hippocampal formation. Arrows indicate the direction of the major intrinsic hippocampal connections. The major subcortical inputs and outputs of the hippocampal formation are listed at the top of the illustration. Several cortical areas that are interconnected with the hippocampal formation are listed on the bottom of the illustration. The cortical interconnections with the hippocampal formation are primarily made with the entorhinal cortex.

II. CONNECTIONS OF THE HIPPOCAMPAL FORMATION

The connections between the four subregions of the hippocampal formation, i.e., the intrinsic connections, and between the hippocampal formation and other portions of the brain, i.e., the extrinsic connections, have been the topic of extensive neuroanatomical study for more than a century. The fundamental intrinsic circuitry of the hippocampal formation and its major inputs and outputs are illustrated in Figure 3.

The four subregions of the hippocampal formation are connected by unique and largely unidirectional connections (Fig. 3). The entorhinal cortex can, for convenience, be considered the first step in the intrinsic hippocampal circuit. Cells located primarily in layers II and III of the entorhinal cortex project to the molecular layer of the dentate gyrus. The connection between the entorhinal cortex and the dentate gyrus is called the *perforant pathway*. Some of the entorhinal projections also terminate in the subiculum and in the CA1 and CA3 fields of the hippocampus.

The dentate granule cells give rise to axons, the mossy fibers, that form connections with pyramidal cells of the CA3 region of the hippocampus. The other main constituent of the granule cell layer is the dentate basket pyramidal cell that gives rise to a dense plexus of fibers and terminals that surround the granule cell bodies. These basket cells are known to use the inhibitory neurotransmitter, γ-aminobutyric acid (GABA). Other classes of neurons in the dentate gyrus form a variety of feedback and feedforward circuits within the dentate gyrus.

The pyramidal cells of CA3 give rise to axons that project to other levels of CA3 (associational connections) and to subcortical regions, especially the septal nuclei. CA3 cells also contribute the major input system to hippocampal field CA1 (the Schaffer collaterals). The CA3 field of the hippocampus also contains a number of nonpyramidal cells, many of which form local circuits within CA3. The pyramidal cells in the CA1 field have a pattern of connections that is quite distinct from the one in CA3. What is perhaps most striking is that CA1 pyramidal cells do not project significantly to other levels of CA1, i.e., there are virtually no associational connections within CA1. Rather, CA1 pyramidal cells project predominantly to the subiculum. The subiculum, in turn, projects to the presubiculum and parasubiculum, and all three components of the subicular complex project to the entorhinal cortex.

One of the more striking features of the intrinsic circuitry of the hippocampal formation is that it is largely unidirectional. The CA3 field does not project back to the granule cells of the dentate gyrus, for example. Nor do CA1 pyramidal cells project back to CA3. Thus, aside from the initial entorhinal input that reaches all of the hippocampal fields in parallel, information flow from the dentate gyrus through the other fields follows an obligatory serial and largely unidirectional pathway. This is in marked distinction to the situation in most other cortical regions, where connections are usually reciprocated.

A variety of chemical substances (neurotransmitters) mediate the transfer of information within the hippocampal circuitry. As in all other cortical regions, some of these substances excite the neurons onto which they are released and some are inhibitory. The hippocampal formation is particularly rich in the glutamate family of transmitters and receptors. One class of receptor, the *N*-methyl D-aspartate (NMDA) receptor, has been implicated both in the modulation of neural activity that accompanies learning and memory and with the pathological activation of neurons that accompanies ischemia-induced neuronal cell death. [*See* SYNAPTIC TRANSMITTERS AND NEUROMODULATORS.]

The fimbria and fornix form the classical efferent, or output, system of the hippocampal formation, and the human fornix is said to contain about 1.2 million axons. The precommissural fornix, which primarily innervates the septal nucleus and other basal forebrain structures, arises mainly from neurons of the hippocampus and, to a lesser extent, from the subiculum and entorhinal cortex. Axons originating in the subicular complex are mainly connected to the diencephalon, i.e., the thalamus and hypothalamus, particularly the mammillary nuclei (Fig. 1).

Connections from one brain region to the same region on the other side of the brain are called *commissural connections*. In nonprimate brains, the hippocampal formations of both sides are heavily interconnected. However, in the primate brain, including humans, the side-to-side interconnections of the hippocampal formation appear to be rather meager. This anatomical observation is consistent with the behavioral finding that damage to the hippocampal formation on one side of the human brain preferentially impairs memory for either verbal (on the left) or spatial (on the right) types of information. This indicates that memory function may be lateralized in the human hippocampal formation.

One fact that has been uncovered about the human hippocampal formation comes from the analysis of patients who have had bilateral damage to the hippocampal formation. These people are unable to learn or retrieve new information about their day-to-day existence. Their ability to recall old memories, however, remains largely preserved. This implies that memory is not stored in the hippocampal formation but perhaps in one of the brain areas that the hippocampal formation communicates with. Thus, it is important to know from what brain regions the hippocampal formation receives its information about ongoing events (sensory information) and to what brain regions the hippocampal formation delivers its processed information. These latter regions would be strong candidates for memory storage sites. [*See* MEMORY.]

For many years it was thought that the hippocampal formation received little input from the higher processing centers of the neocortex. This view was based largely on neuroanatomical studies conducted in rodents. However, with neuroanatomical studies of the organization of the nonhuman primate hippocampal formation, it has become clear that this area is in receipt of substantial sensory information from the highest levels of the neocortex. Several cortical regions, located mainly in the frontal and temporal lobes, are connected to the entorhinal cortex. Information is then relayed to the other hippocampal fields via the intrinsic connections. It is also quite clear that the entorhinal cortex sends return projections back to the neocortex. Thus, the hippocampal formation is privy to high-level sensory information processing that takes place in the cortex and has the connections necessary to send its own processed information back to potential storage sites in the neocortex. [*See* NEOCORTEX.]

III. BEHAVIORAL FUNCTIONS OF THE HIPPOCAMPAL FORMATION

The hippocampal formation has historically been implicated in a variety of functions. In the latter part of the 19th century, for example, the neurologist Wilhelm Sommer considered the hippocampal formation to be a component of the motor system because he found that damage to the hippocampal formation correlated with the seizure disorder associated with temporal lobe epilepsy. For much of the first half of this century, the hippocampal formation was thought to be primarily related to olfactory function and was consider to be a prominent component of what was called the rhinencephalon, or olfactory brain. But evidence that indicated that the hippocampal formation was as prominent in anosmic species as in species which rely heavily on the sense of smell put this notion to rest. In the 1930s the neurologist James Papez considered the hippocampal formation to be a central component in a system for emotional expression. In his view, the hippocampus was something of a conduit by which perceptions could be collected and channeled to the hypothalamus to recruit appropriate emotions. Unfortunately, there has been little substantiation of Papez's theory, and the role of modulator of emotional expression is now more closely linked with another prominent medial temporal lobe structure, the amygdaloid complex.

Perhaps the most widely accepted and long-lived proposal of hippocampal function relates to its role in memory. It has been known for nearly a century that damage to certain brain regions can result in an enduring amnesic syndrome that is characterized by a complete, or near complete, anterograde amnesia. Affected patients are incapable of recreating a record of day-to-day events although most past memories remain largely intact. It is now clear that damage isolated to the human hippocampal formation is sufficient to produce this form of memory impairment. [*See* AMNESIA.]

While fairly convincing evidence now exists that the hippocampal formation plays a prominent role in the formation of enduring memories, the mechanism by which it exerts its influence is far from clear. Since damage to the hippocampal formation does not cause a loss of distant or well-established memories, it appears that the hippocampal formation cannot be the final repository for stored information. Rather, it appears that the hippocampal formation must interact with storage sites in other, presumably cortical, regions to consolidate ephemeral sensory experiences into long-term memory.

Electrophysiological studies conducted primarily in rodents have demonstrated that neurons in the hippocampus are preferentially activated by certain aspects of the environment. If one records the neural activity of a single hippocampal cell while a rat is running around in a maze, for example, the cell might be activated only when the rat travels through a certain location of the maze. Data of this type have prompted the suggestion that the hippocampus can form a "cognitive map" of the outside world. In a more general sense, it might be thought that the neurons of the hippocampal formation, acting as an assembly of differentially activated units, can form a representation of ongoing experience. Perhaps the interaction of this hippocampal representation of experience with the more detailed information of the experience located in the neocortex is the route through which long-term memories are formed. One implication of the electrophysiological data is that neurons in the hippocampal formation are not uniquely sensitive to certain types of information. Rather, neurons in the hippocampal formation may act more like random-access memory (RAM) in a computer and are therefore potentially activated by all types of information. Since it would be difficult for evolution to anticipate all the various forms of information that might need to be stored as memory, a generalized memory buffer system would be highly adaptive. [*See* COGNITIVE MAPS.]

IV. SENSITIVITY OF THE HIPPOCAMPAL FORMATION TO ILLNESS

Various clinical conditions result in morphological alterations of the human hippocampal formation. While the causative factors are not yet known for most of these disease states, it is clear that each of the different hippocampal cytoarchitectonic fields are more or less vulnerable to damage. In ischemia and temporal lobe epilepsy, for example, the field CA1 of the hippocampus (the so-called Sommer's sector) suffers the greatest neuronal cell loss. In other neuropathological conditions, such as Alzheimer's disease, the entorhinal cortex may suffer greater pathology. Several neuroscientists have suggested that the physiological "plasticity" inherent in the hippocampal formation as a biological memory device may predispose it to selective vulnerability to a variety of environmental and biological stressors.

Among the many conditions that produce pathological changes in the hippocampal formation, Alzheimer's disease is probably the most devastating. Alzheimer's disease is an age-related neurodegenerative illness that results in profound memory impairment and dementia. A number of pathological profiles, including senile (or neuritic) plaques and neurofibrillary tangles are consistently seen in some of the hippocampal fields, especially the entorhinal cortex. Ultimately, Alzheimer's disease leads to a massive death of neurons in the hippocampal formation and other brain regions. There is good reason to suspect that the memory impairment associated with Alzheimer's disease is due, in large part, to the devastation of the hippocampal formation by the disease. [*See* ALZHEIMER'S DISEASE.]

Temporal lobe or complex partial epilepsy is another neurological disorder in which the hippocampal formation is severely affected. This most common form of epilepsy was first associated with damage to the hippocampal formation in the late 1800s by Sommer who conducted the first postmortem microscopic examination of a brain from a long-term epileptic patient. Sommer noted a dramatic loss of neurons in the hippocampal formation that was relatively selective and involved a region that in modern terminology would encompass CA1 and part of the subiculum. In approximately two-thirds of the cases of temporal lobe epilepsy, the hippocampal formation is the only structure that shows pathological modifications. During the first part of this century, it was generally believed that hippocampal pathology was a consequence of the epileptic seizures rather than their cause. Currently, however, increasing emphasis is being placed on the idea that disruption of normal hippocampal function may be an iniating factor in temporal lobe seizures. [*See* EPILEPSY.]

In a number of other pathological conditions the hippocampal formation is preferentially damaged. Among these is the loss of neurons, primarily in CA1, consequent to the ischemia associated with cardiorespiratory arrest. As noted above, these patients often demonstrate an anterograde memory impairment apparently resulting from the hippocampal damage.

Bibliography

Amaral, D. G., and Insausti, R. (1990). The hippocampal formation. In "The Human Nervous System." (G. Paxinos, Ed.). Academic Press, San Diego.

Chan-Palay, V., and Kohler, C. (Eds.) (1989). "Hippocampus New Vistas." A. R. Liss, New York.

Squire, L. R., Shimamura, A. P., and Amaral, D. G. (1989). Memory and the hippocampus. In "Neural Models of Plasticity" (J. Byrne and W. Berry, Eds.), pp. 208–239. Academic Press, San Diego.

HOMEOSTASIS

Pascale Lapeyre
College de France, CNRS UPR2, France

Pierre-Marie Lledo
Institut Alfred Fessard, France

Glossary

Cybernetics A word introduced by the mathematician N. Wiener (1894–1964) from the Greek *kubernetes,* "steersman." This word, which defines a theory of feedback systems, namely self-regulating systems, could be applicable not only to living systems but also to machines.

Emotion From the earliest philosophical speculations outward, emotion has often been seen as interfering with rationality, as a remainder of our pre-sapiens inheritance: emotions seem to represent unbridled human nature "in the raw." The current flux of speculations about emotions started with a very specific event, the publication in 1884 of an article by W. James (1842–1910) in *Mind* entitled "What Is an Emotion." He turned conventional wisdom completely around. Instead of the outward signs of emotions (first stated in 1872 by C. Darwin in *The Expression of the Emotions in Man and Animals*), such as facial expressions and visceral reactions, being the result of some prior emotional, neural signal, he insisted that "our feeling of the [bodily] changes as they occur is the emotion."

Homeostasis It was the physiologist C. Bernard (1813–78) who introduced the concept of the constancy of the *milieu intérieur*. This internal milieu ensures the biological unity of the organism and confers a certain autonomy relative to the external milieu. The term "homeostasis" was coined some years later by W. B. Cannon (1871–1945) in his germinal book, *Wisdom of the Body* (1932). He developed the concept of homeostasis, which in modern terminology is the feedback control of servo-systems. This concept was not mathematically expressed until the 1940s, when it became the basis of cybernetics.

Hypothalamus A brain area which encompasses the most ventral part of the diencephalon, where it forms the floor and, in part, the walls of the third ventricle. The hypothalamus consists of several nuclei which form a neuronal continuum. It plays a central role in homeostasis by controlling: (i) the autonomic nervous system; (ii) the neuroendocrine system through its control of both the anterior and posterior parts of the pituitary gland; (iii) the motivational states.

Limbic system P. Broca in 1878 was the first to describe an annular ring of tissue on the medial face of the cerebral hemisphere which represents the free edge of the cerebral cortex. He named this part of the brain *le grand lobe limbique,* "the great limbic lobe," which led to the concept of the limbic system. This system includes the hippocampal formation, entorhinal area, olfactory regions, hypothalamus, and amygdala. Functionally, the limbic system is generally thought to be concerned with visceral processes, particularly those associated with the emotional status of the organism. In fact, the interaction of all the structures in the complex, from the entorhinal area to the hypothalamus, plays a major role in the elaboration of the final actions of an organism in a particular environment, and in the formation of adaptive behavior patterns.

HOMEOSTASIS is a widely and somewhat loosely used term for describing all kinds of responses following the principle of negative feedback control. The main concept of homeostasis is founded in the production of stability in dynamic systems by negative feedback. This concept is now the basis of cy-

Encyclopedia of Human Behavior, Volume 2
Copyright © 1994 by Academic Press, Inc. All rights of reproduction in any form reserved.

bernetics, whose founding fathers were N. R. Ashby and G. Walter in the 1950s. However, the term *homeostasis* was coined some years before cybernetics by the founders of modern physiology, C. Bernard, W. B. Cannon, and W. R. Hess. In Cannon's germinal book, *Wisdom of the Body,* the basic idea of feedback as a fundamental physiological principle is stated. In this context, constancy in the internal environment of the body is the result of a system of control mechanisms that limit the variability of body states. It is now clear that this is an extremely important principle for almost all physiological processes as well as for the guiding of skilled behavior. Such a concept serves, indeed, as a theoretical basis for the physiology of regulation.

I. INTRODUCTION

Cell theory is inseparable from the concept of the internal milieu. Each organism is composed of cells grouped in tissues. These cells are bathed with water-like fluid which forms the extracellular space, providing a medium for diffusion and homogenization around the cells. This space including the blood and lymph is indeed a unifier of the organism. Unlike the external environment which is subjected to uncontrollable change, the internal milieu oscillates slightly around normal values. Thus, the autonomy acquired by the organism relative to its external environment gives it an independent and free life since the constancy of the internal milieu does not mean fixity but rather a possibility to evolve.

Although virtually all of the brain is involved in homeostasis, neurons controlling the internal environment are mainly concentrated in the hypothalamus, a neuronal structure located at the interface of the brain and a range of critical regulatory peripheral functions. In this review, we shall first focus on the anatomy of the limbic system and then on the anatomy of the hypothalamus, a small area which belongs to the diencephalon and which comprises less than 1% of the total brain volume. We shall then consider how the hypothalamus and other closely linked structures in the limbic system receive information from the internal environment and how they act directly upon it to keep it constant by regulating endocrine secretion and the autonomic nervous system. Finally, other parts of the brain which may indirectly affect the internal environment by acting on the external environment through emotions and drives will be described.

II. ANATOMY OF THE LIMBIC SYSTEM AND OF THE HYPOTHALAMUS

In 1953, J. Olds and P. Milner reported that the weak electrical stimulation of specific sites, most of them located in the hypothalamus or in its rostral continuation, the septum, could elicit in experimental animals an internal state of pleasure, or in any case what psychologists describe as a state of *reward.* This work gave, for the first time, a basis to the claim that the hypothalamus, and more generally a *continuum* of brain tissue in which the hypothalamus is central, is implicated not only in endocrine and visceral functions, but also in affect and motivation. We will first consider the structures and connections of the brain tissue related to the hypothalamus which belong to this neuronal continuum before examining the anatomy and numerous functions of the hypothalamus. [*See* HYPOTHALAMUS; LIMBIC SYSTEM.]

A. The Limbic System and Its Connections with the Hypothalamus

The neural continuum in which the hypothalamus is central is composed of a part of the brainstem and of the limbic system.

A part of the brainstem, the mesencephalic reticular formation, which receives inputs from spinoreticular fibers, possesses axons that ascend to the hypothalamus. There are also connections formed by axons directed upward to the hypothalamus from the nucleus of the solitary tract, a cell group in the medulla oblongata. These connections are quite revealing. Hence, the nucleus of the solitary tract is the only known instance of a circumscribed secondary sensory cell group whose primary sensory input is from the visceral domain.

A second part of the continuum in which the hypothalamus is central lies rostral to it. It is largely interconnected with the phylogenetically primitive cortical tissue that surrounds the upper brain stem. A little more than a century ago, P. Broca observed an almost annular ring of tissue on the medial face of the cerebral hemisphere which represents the free edge of the cerebral cortex. This part of the brain called *le grand lobe limbique:* the great limbic lobe by P. Broca has led to the concept of the limbic system. This "lobe" surrounds the diencephalon and the cerebral peduncles. He called it *limbique* from the Latin *limbus* because he conceived it as a threshold to the newer pallium. It is sometimes also called the rhinencephalon to show that these regions of the brain derived in the course of evolution from structures previously associated with the sense of smell. The limbic lobe includes the parahippocampal, the cingulate, and the subcallosal gyri. It also includes the underlying cortex of the hippocampal formation, which is composed of the hippocampus, the dentate gyrus, and the subiculum.

In the 1930s, it became evident to J. W. Papez that the limbic lobe formed a neural circuit that provides the anatomical substratum for emotions. He proposed that the hypothalamus is connected with higher cortical centers since it plays a crucial role in the expression of emotion. According to this idea, the neuronal circuit originally proposed by Papez consists of the cortex which influences the hypothalamus through connections of the cingulate gyrus to the hippocampal formation. Informations are then processed by the hippocampal formation and projected to the mammillary bodies of the hypothalamus by way of the fornix. The hypothalamus in turn provides information to the cingulate gyrus through a pathway from the mammillary bodies to the anterior thalamic nuclei and from the anterior thalamic nuclei to the cingulate gyrus (Fig. 1). P. MacLean's resynthesis of Papez's "theory of emotions" resurrected Broca's concepts and breathed new life into the concept of the all-pervasive limbic system. He included in the limbic system other structures anatomically and functionally related to those described by Papez. These included parts of the hypothalamus, the septal area, the nucleus accumbens, neocortical areas such as the orbitofrontal cortex, and the amygdala (see Fig. 1). [*See* HIPPOCAMPAL FORMATION.]

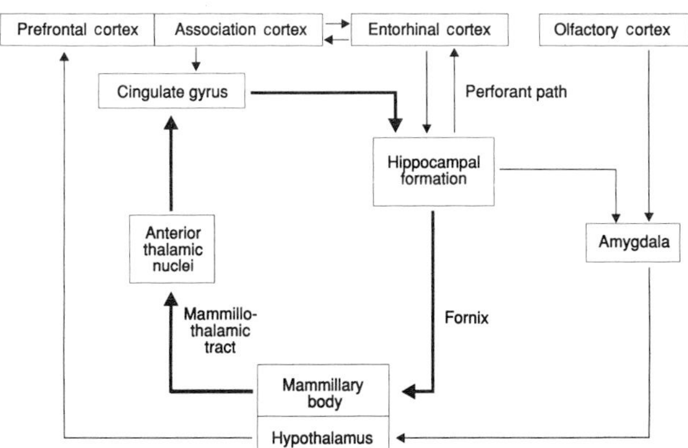

FIGURE 1 The neural pathways for emotion. The first circuit proposed by Papez is indicated by thick lines, while fine lines illustrate recently described connections.

It is also noteworthy that all of the senses represented in the neocortex—vision, hearing, and the somatic sense—direct part of their information toward either one or both of two cortical districts: the frontal association cortex and the inferior temporal association cortex. The two are interconnected by a massive fiber bundle called the *uncinate fasciculus*. In turn, the inferior temporal cortex projects to the entorhinal area. The entorhinal area could be considered as a cortical gateway for projections to the amygdala. In fact, in primates it gives the amygdala its single most important input. The projection is reciprocated; indeed, the amygdala directs its cortical projections to the inferior temporal cortex and to the frontal cortex (specifically the orbital surface of the frontal cortex). Therefore, the amygdala projects to the parts of the neocortex in which are embodied the final stages of the cascade of sensory informations. Evidently, the amygdala also screens its neocortical input. Therefore, it has been tempting for many scientists to speculate that such a brain region could intervene in ideation and cognition. Ordinarily, one thinks of brain function as working inward, i.e., sensory informations being directed from sensory receptor organs over a sequence of synapses to the sensory cortex, and from there (in what Papez called "the stream of thought") toward the limbic system. Here we encounter the opposite: a set of connections directed outward. It is indeed as if the amygdala were participating in the brain's appreciation of the world. [*See* NEOCORTEX.]

The interoceptive and exteroceptive data reaching the neural continuum in which the hypothalamus is central are clearly distinguishable. The former consist of visceral sensory signals from the spinal cord and the brainstem. These data are unconditional stimuli pertinent to the maintenance of life itself. On the other hand, what enters the limbic system from the neocortex is fundamentally different. One might call it a repeatedly preprocessed, multisensory representation of the organism's environment. In this situation, the perception of the world is only biased by physiological needs.

It is also remarkable that among all the senses, olfaction possesses a particular link with the limbic system which was taken to be the "nose–brain." Today, it is clear that the primary olfactory cortex projects to the entorhinal area, which in turn projects to the hippocampus. Thus, we see reintroduced, after years of fervent affirmation followed by years of fervent denial, the idea that the hippocampus receives olfactory signals. Indeed, the pathway which links olfaction with the limbic system is privileged. Hence, the path from the olfactory epithelium is more direct than the path from sensory surfaces such as the skin. Moreover, the primary olfactory cortex projects to the amygdala, in large part onto a particular cell group, the lateral nucleus of the amygdala, by bypassing the neocortex (see Fig. 1). However, while it is clear that the olfactory bulb projects to the amygdala in rodents, one wonders whether this connection is still present in man. Indeed, the existence of a specialized area of the nasal mucosa called the vomeronasal organ, which sends informations to a compartment of the the accessory olfactory bulb, has been demonstrated in animals such as rats. The vomeronasal organ and the corresponding region of the accessory olfactory bulb are thought to form an apparatus dedicated to the processing of sexually significant odors, but in the fully formed human body none of these structures has been identified. Finally, to emphasize the privileged link between olfaction and the limbic system, it can be noted that the primary olfactory cortex projects also to the hypothalamus. [*See* SENSE OF SMELL.]

B. Structure of the Hypothalamus

The hypothalamus in the mammalian brain encompasses the most ventral part of the diencephalon where it forms the floor and, in parts, the walls of the third ventricle. Its upper boundary is marked by a sulcus in the ventricular wall, the ventral diencephalic or hypothalamic sulcus, which separates the hypothalamus from the dorsally located thalamus (Fig. 2).

Caudally, the hypothalamus merges without any clear limits with the periventricular gray and the tegmentum of the mesencephalon. However, it is customary to define the caudal boundary of the hypothalamus as represented by a plane extending from the caudal limit of the mammilary nuclei ventrally and from the posterior commissure dorsally. Rostrally, the hypothalamus is continuous with the preoptic area, which lies partly forward to and above the optic chiasm.

By means of the above-mentioned external landmarks at the ventral surface of the brain, the hypothalamus can be subdivided in the anterior–posterior direction into an anterior part which includes the preoptic area, a middle part and a posterior part. Another subdivision in the lateral–medial direction consists of three longitudinal zones recognized as the periventricular, the medial, and the lateral zones. The periventricular zone consists mostly of small cells which, in general, are oriented along fibers parallel with the wall of the third ventricle. The medial zone is cell-rich, containing most of the well-delineated nuclei of the hypothalamus which include: (i) the preoptic and suprachiasmatic nuclei in

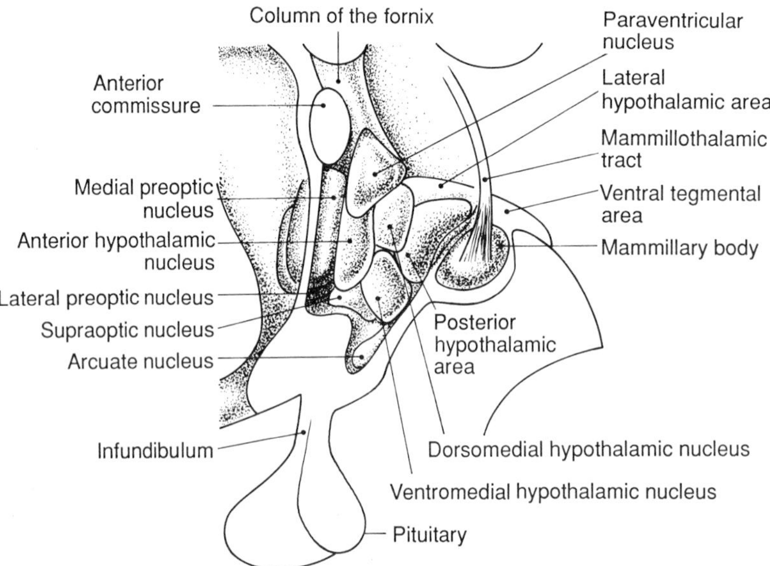

FIGURE 2 The location of the main hypothalamic nuclei shown in a medial view. The hypothalamus contains a large number of neuronal circuits that regulate vital functions such as body temperature, heart rate, blood pressure, blood osmolarity, water and food intake, emotional behavior, and reproduction.

the anterior region; (ii) the dorsomedial, ventromedial, and paraventricular nuclei in the middle region; (iii) the posterior nucleus and mammillary bodies in the posterior region (see Fig. 2). The lateral zone contains only a small number of cells interposed between the longitudinal fiber system of the medial forebrain bundle. This region possesses long fibers that project to the spinal cord and cortex, as well as extensive short-fiber, multisynaptic ascending and descending pathways. The basal portion of the medial region and the periventricular region contains many of the small hypothalamic neurons which secrete the substances that control the release of anterior pituitary hormones (see below). Most fiber systems of the hypothalamus are bidirectional. Projections to and from areas caudal to the hypothalamus are carried in the medial forebrain bundle, the mammillo-tegmental tract, and the dorsal longitudinal fasciculus. Rostral structures are interconnected with the hypothalamus by means of the mammillothalamic tracts, fornix and stria terminalis. However, there are two important exceptions to the rule that fibers are bidirectional in the hypothalamus. First, the hypothalamo-hypophyseal tract contains only descending axons of paraventricular and supraoptic neurons, which terminate primarily in the posterior pituitary. Second, the hypothalamus receives one-way afferent connections directly from the retina. These fibers terminate in the suprachiasmatic nucleus which is involved in generating light–dark cycles. We shall see later, the role of these rhythms in the control of motivated behaviors.

The following section will describe the interrelated functions of the hypothalamus and the pituitary gland as well as some of the major functions of the limbic system.

III. PARTICIPATION OF THE HYPOTHALAMUS AND THE LIMBIC SYSTEM IN HOMEOSTASIS

The internal environment of the body, a term embracing tissue fluids and organ functions, such as blood pressure, heart rate, respiration rate, and so on, is under the control of three independent processes. The autonomic nervous system plays an important role in homeostasis. Hence, in the brain, neurons that affect the activity of the preganglionic motor neurons of the sympathetic and of the parasympathetic nervous system as concentrated in the hypothalamus. The evidence is clear: when the hypothalamus of almost any animal, emphatically including man, is suddenly destroyed, the animal dies, as a consequence of severe disruption of what Bernard called the internal milieu of the body. However, controlling the autonomic nervous system is not the only means by which the hypothalamus maintains homeostasis. In addition, the hypothalamus governs the neuroendocrine system through its control of both the anterior and posterior parts of the pituitary gland, which in turn, play a major role in the constancy of the *milieu interieur*. Finally, the internal environment of the body is also regulated by motivational states and, therefore, we shall also consider some of the hypothalamic functions involved in a repertoire of voluntary behavioral responses.

A. The Autonomic Nervous System

The autonomic nervous system is primarily an effector system which innervates smooth musculature, heart muscle, and exocrine glands. It is a visceral and largely involuntary motor system. It can be noted that anatomical principles underlying the organization of both somatic motor and autonomic nervous systems are similar (Fig. 3) and that the two systems function in parallel to adjust the body to environmental changes. Nevertheless, the two systems greatly differ in several ways. Within the autonomic nervous system, two subsystems, the sympathetic and the parasympathetic, have long been distinguished by means of anatomical, chemical, and functional criteria. The sympathetic is the most extensive of the two systems. Its preganglionic motor neurons are located in the spinal cord, where they occupy a region called the latteral horn of the spinal gray matter. The preganglionic fibers employ the neurotransmitter acetylcholine while the postganglionic fibers often have a substantial distance to travel and employ the neurotransmitter norepinephrine. The sympathetic divison of the autonomic nervous system promotes the organism's ability to expend energy (Hess called it *ergotropic*) and governs an endocrine gland, the adrenal medulla, considered as a modified autonomic ganglion. It is indeed a universal mobilizing mechanism, valuable in emergencies, with postganglionic ramifications throughout the visceral realm. [*See* ADRENAL GLANDS.]

In contrast, Hess described the parasympathetic nervous system as *trophotropic,* to signify that it promotes the restitution of the organism. The parasympathetic nervous system in fact antagonizes the

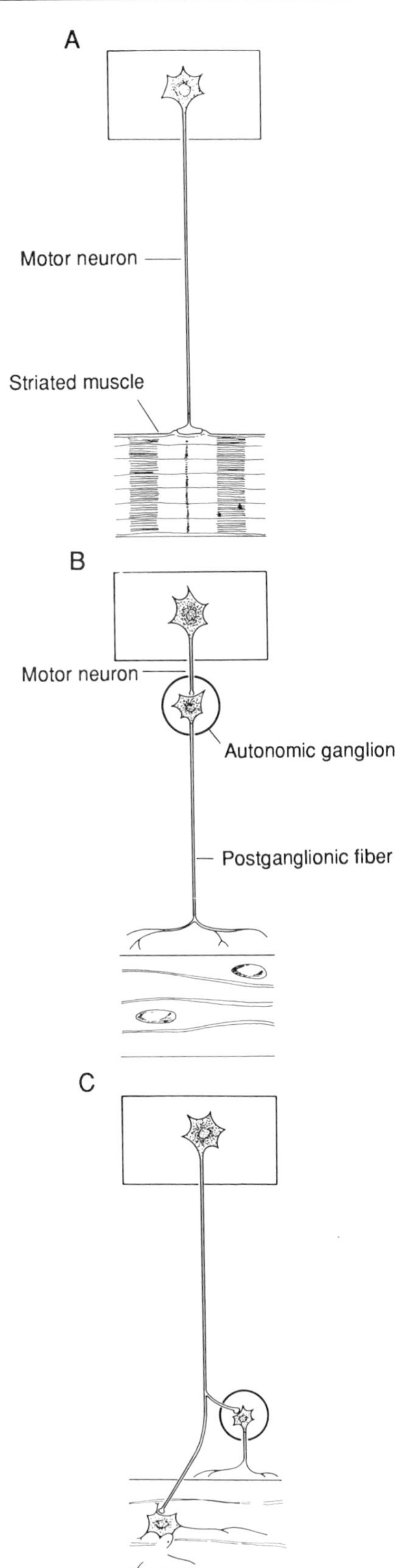

sympathetic's effects. The preganglionic motor neurons of the parasympathetic nervous system are in the brainstem and in a short stretch of the spinal cord near its caudal tip. Like the preganglionic motor neurons of the sympathetic nervous system, they employ acetylcholine as their transmitter but the postganglionic transmitter of the parasympathetic is also acetylcholine. Their axons are long because the ganglia to which they project lie near the tissues of the viscera, and sometimes even inside them (see Fig. 3). The resilence of autonomic control is in good accordance with what is known about the conduction lines descending from the hypothalamus. Indeed, the hypothalamus emits axons that descend toward both sympathetic and parasympathetic preganglionic visceral motor neurons, thus regulating the viscera. Hence, the hypothalamus may function as the so-called head ganglion of the autonomic nervous system which mediates conventional reflexes involving neural inputs and outputs. Fibers passing directly from the hypothalamus to the lateral horn of the spinal cord's gray matter, where the preganglionic motor neurons of the sympathetic nervous system are situated, have recently been found. These fibers seem, however, to constitute a small minority of hypothalamic efferents; the hypothalamus has nothing similar to a pyramidal tract to carry its descending outputs. Instead it appears in large measure to project no further than the midbrain, where neurons of the reticular formation take over. It is noteworthy that pathways descending to autonomic motor neurons are interrupted at numerous levels in which further instructions can enter the descending lines.

Most of the regions of the brain which influence the autonomic nervous system's output (e.g., the cerebral cortex, the hippocampus, the entorhinal cortex, parts of the thalamus, basal ganglia, cerebellum, and the reticular formation) produce their actions by way of the hypothalamus which integrates the information it receives from these structures into a coherent pattern of autonomic response. The hypothalamus controls the output of the autonomic

FIGURE 3 Three different motor innervations. (A) In the somatic motor pattern, a motor neuron from the spinal cord or in the brainstem animates striated muscles directly. In the visceral motor pattern, a two-neuron chain is required. (B) The sympathetic nervous system stations a "preganglionic" visceral motor neuron in the spinal cord. (C) The parasympathetic nervous system employs a two-neuron pathway. The first neuron is situated in the brainstem or toward the bottom of the spinal cord, and the ganglion is close, or even inside, the viscera.

nervous system in two different ways. The first one is direct and consists of projections to nuclei in the brain stem and the spinal cord that act on preganglionic autonomic neurons to control respiration, heart rate, temperature, and blood pressure. Thus, stimulation of the lateral hypothalamus leads to general sympathetic activation (increase in blood presure, piloerection, etc.). The hypothalamus governs the autonomic nervous sytem in a second way, by controlling the endocrine system which releases hormones that influence autonomic functions. This indirect modulation is depicted in the following section.

B. The Neuroendocrine System

The Scharrers first (1940) hypothesized that the peptides of the neurohypophysis were in fact synthetized by specialized hypothalamic neurons and transported within their axons to the neural lobe to be released into peripheral blood. In the late 1940s, Harris and collaborators proposed the hypophysial portal chemotransmitter hypothesis of anterior pituitary control, which stated that the factors regulating the anterior lobe are formed by hypothalamic neurons (later termed hypophysiotropic neurons) and transported to be released into the hypophysial portal circulation and carried to the anterior pituitary, where they control the synthesis and release of anterior pituitary hormones into the general circulation. Both of these hypotheses have been confirmed and rationalized into a unified theory of neurosecretion in which the nervous system controls endocrine function. Neurosecretion is the phenomenon of synthesis and release of specific substances by neurons. Some neurosecretions are exported into the peripheral or hypophysial blood and act as true hormones; others, released in close apposition to other neurons, act as neurotransmitters or neuromodulators. Translation of neuronal signals into chemical ones has been termed "neuroendocrine transduction," and the cells themselves "neuroendocrine transductors," by R. J. Wurtman and F. Anton-Tay. Two types of neurotransducer cells regulate visceral function: (i) neurosecretomotor, in which the neurosecretion acts directly through synapses on gland cells; (ii) neuroendocrine, in which the neurosecretion passes into the blood and acts on distant targets. [*See* HORMONES AND BEHAVIOR; SYNAPTIC TRANSMITTERS AND NEUROMODULATORS.]

Neurosecretory cells possess in common with other neurons the usual aspects of neuron functions. Most of the insight into the physiology of neurosecretory systems has been gained from studies of the hypothalamo-hypophyseal system. This system brings nervous and endocrine cells together in one anatomical entity in which that the nervous system and the glandular cells of the anterior hypophysis communicate. These two structures share common properties. They both secrete peptidergic hormones (releasing and inhibiting hypothalamic factors and the hypophyseal stimulins), and both exhibit electrical properties such as excitability, with production of action potentials. Thus, electrophysiological techniques, which were previously reserved for studies of nerve and muscle cells, can be applied to the hypothalamo-hypophyseal system, in both its nervous and endocrine structures. The electrophysiological properties of these cells reveal the existence of: (i) stimulus-secretion coupling, in particular at the level of neurosecretory terminals in the posterior hypophysis, the median eminance, and the endocrine cells of the anterior hypophysis; (ii) modifications in membrane electrical properties exerted by the binding of different regulatory factors to their receptors. These observations are used to explain the modulatory mechanism of membrane properties brought into play by each factor in order to enhance or inhibit hormonal release. Thus, the electrical properties play a central role in the regulation of endocrine secretion in the anterior hypophysis. These electrical properties, common to nervous and endocrine cells, are linked to changes in membrane permeability to different ions, i.e., Ca^{2+}, Na^+, K^+, and Cl^-.

The pituitary gland is divided into two main functional units, the neural lobe (posterior lobe) and the adenohypophysis (anterior lobe or pars distalis). In many mammalian species, such as the rat, an intermediate lobe (derived embryologically from the same tissue as the anterior lobe) is also present. However, in humans the intermediate lobe cells are dispersed throughout the pituitary gland.

In the neurohypophyseal system, hypothalamic neurons transmit action potentials along their axons in a manner similar to that used by unmyelinated neurons, and each action potential triggers the release of secretory granules from nerve endings by calcium-dependent exocytosis into the general circulation. The neural lobe is an anatomical part of the neurohypophysis which is commonly viewed as consisting of three portions, the neural lobe itself (infundibular process or posterior pituitary), the stalk, and the infundibulum. This latter portion forms the base of the third ventricle (Figs. 4 and 5). In fact, there is a fourth intra-hypothalamic component of the neurohypophysial system that consists

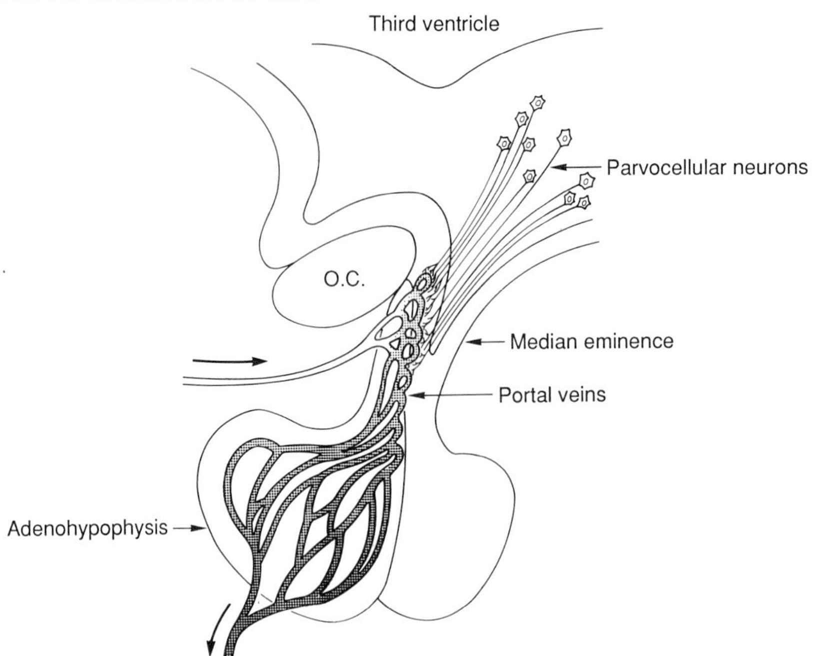

FIGURE 4 The anterior lobe of the pituitary gland. The anterior lobe synthetizes several hormones. Their release is induced by chemical signals, called releasing factors, which are secreted by hypothalamic neurons. These factors enter the hypothalamo-pituitary portal system, comprising first a capillary bed in the hypothalamus, then a venous drainage channel, and in the anterior lobe, a second capillary bed.

of the cells of origin of the two principal nerve tracts that terminate in the neural lobe, supraoptico-hypophysial and paraventriculo-hypophysial.

The neurohypophysial hormones secreted by the magnocellular neurons are vasopressin (antidiuretic hormone, ADH) and oxytocin, which are synthesized within the cell bodies in association with specific proteins, the neurophysins. Like most peptidergic hormones, vasopressin and oxytocin are cleaved from a larger prohormone. These prohormones are synthesized in the cell bodies of the magnocellular neurons, and are cleaved within vesicles during their transport down the axons. Vasopressin, oxytocin, and at least two forms of neurophysins are secreted into the blood circulation and are known to be under the control of the nervous sytems, to be responsive to appropriate physiological stimuli, and to be altered by certain stressful conditions.

While the anterior lobe does not receive any direct nerve supply, its secretions are however under control exerted by the hypothalamus. This control is mediated by chemical factors (hypophysiotropic hormones or releasing factors) secreted by the parvocellular neuroendocrine neurons located in several hypothalamic regions: the medial basal and periventricular regions and the arcuate, tuberal, preoptic, and paraventricular nuclei. Parvocellular neurons secrete peptides in the interstitial space of the base of the third ventricle and then diffuse into the capillary plexus of the median eminence that is interposed between the peripheral arterial system and the pituitary sinusoidal circulation (Fig. 4). By this anatomical arrangement, neurohormonal mediators synthesized and released by hypothalamic neurons are brought into direct contact with the cells of the adenohypophysis.[1]

A different functional link leads from the neurons of the hypothalamus to the posterior lobe of the pituitary complex. This link is more direct since it does not include a part of the circulatory system (Fig. 5). It begins in two circumscribed magnocellular nucleus. They are the first hypothalamic nuclei whose function has been identified with some precision. All, or nearly all, of the axons originating in

[1] The hormones released by the anterior lobe of the pituitary gland are called tropic (literally "switch-on") hormones. Each is the second and final messenger in a sequence of chemical signals leading from the brain to a particular endocrine gland. All the tropic hormones of the anterior lobe are at the same time trophic hormones, in whose absence their target glands atrophy.

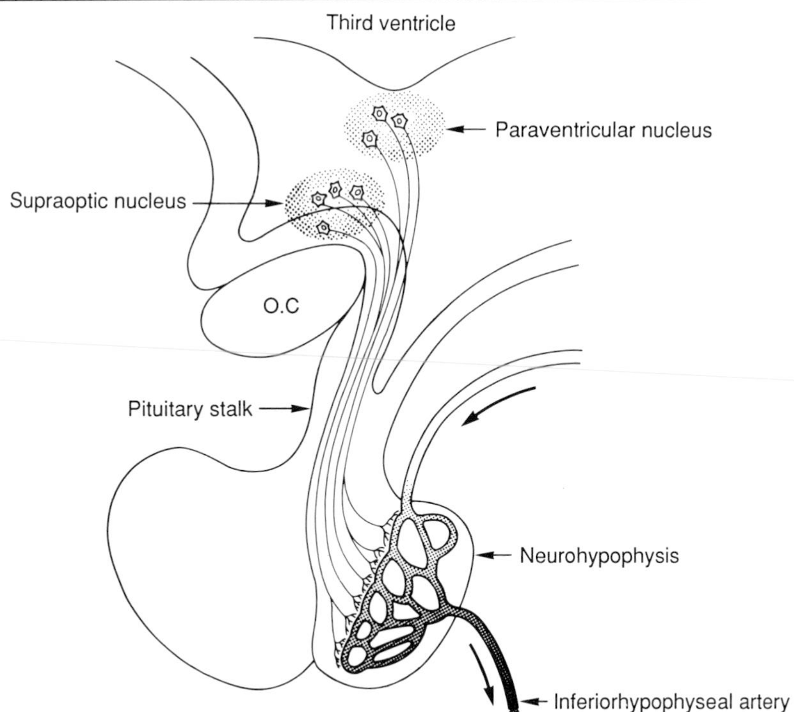

FIGURE 5 The posterior lobe of the pituitary gland. In the posterior lobe, axons from hypothalamic cell groups called supraoptic and paraventricular nucleus release vasopressin and oxytocin into the systemic circulation (inferior hypophyseal artery). O.C., optic chiasm.

the supraoptic nucleus, along with some 30% of the axons originating in the paraventricular nucleus, pass through the pituitary stalk and reach the posterior lobe of the pituitary.[2] Unlike the anterior one, the posterior lobe is a part of the brain. Nevertheless, it contains no neurons; the terminations of the supraoptic and paraventricular axons make no synaptic contacts. Instead, they lie embedded in a tissue composed of modified glial cells called the pituicytes and a dense plexus of capillaries. The glandular products of the supraoptic and paraventricular nuclei are synthesized in the cell body and packaged in neurosecretory vesicles in which some hormonal maturation may occur. These neurosecretory vesicles are transported down the axon to the neural terminal, where hormones are stored and released by secretion when the neuron is stimulated.

Recently, it has been demonstrated that a type of ependymal glial cell called tanycyte, which ensheaths the terminals of hypothalamic neurons, regulates the release of luteinizing-hormone releasing factor (LHRH) from the hypothalamus and may therefore play a key role in the onset of puberty. LHRH axons which travel with the processes of tanycytes can be covered by slips of glioplasm. At the perivascular space level, the nerve terminals may be partially covered or exposed, potentially impeding or enhancing the secretion of LHRH into capillaries. Such observation, realized at a cellular level, illustrates the tremendous plasticity of the hypothalamus. Interestingly, it was found that these glial cells in the median eminance possess estrogen and epidermal growth factor (EGF) receptors, whereas LHRH neurons apparently do not. Taken together, these observations provide strong evidence that, at puberty, glia is a crucial target for estrogenic action which may induce morphological changes accompanied by release of chemical signals which modulate hypothalamic neurons.

[2] The remaining 70% have several destinations, of which one is especially notable: the paraventricular nucleus is a substantial contributor to the pathway descending from the hypothalamus direct to the lateral horn of the spinal cord, which contains the spinal cord's preganglionic sympathetic motor neurons.

C. Behavioral Responses

When Hess succeeded in implanting electrodes in the brain and permanently fixing them to the skull of animals, he found that stimulation of different parts of the hypothalamus produced a array of behavioral responses. For example, electrical stimulation of the lateral hypothalamus in cats elicited autonomic and somatic responses characteristic of anger: increased blood pressure, raising of body hair, pupillary constriction, raising of the tail and other characteristic emotional behaviors. Thus, the hypothalamus is not only a motor nucleus for the autonomic nervous system, as well as a neural part controlling the neuroendocrine system, but rather is a coordinating center that integrates various inputs to ensure a well-organized, coherent, and appropriate set of autonomic and somatic responses. In line with this view, vasopressin, oxytocin, and other regulating hormones are not the only peptides of neurobiological interest which can be found in the hypothalamus. Indeed, the opioid peptides, β-endorphin, and the enkephalins can also be detected in this structure, as are angiotensin II, substance P, neurotensin, cholecystokinin, and a host of other peptides known to be involved in multiple of behavioral responses. Interestingly, almost every type of peptidergic neurons previously studied, including both parvocellular and magnocellular hypothalamic neurons, has been found to contain more than one type of peptide which could act synergistically. Furthermore, peptides released by the hypothalamic magnocellular and parvocellular neurons are not unique to these cells and have also been found in other regions of the nervous system. Such peptidergic projections are well suited for coordinating neuroendocrine and autonomic responses. For example, regulatory peptides released at brain sites other than the median eminence may modulate behavior by actions independent of the release of pituitary hormones. The behavioral effects of regulatory peptides are thematically related to the type of endocrine effects produced by the same peptide acting on the pituitary. Corticotropin-releasing hormone (CRH) is an example of such a regulatory peptide. On one hand, it acts on the pituitary to stimulate the release of adrenocorticotropic hormone (ACTH) in response to stress. On the other hand, when injected intracerebroventricularly, CRH evokes many of the behavioral and autonomic reactions normally seen in response to stress.

D. Limbic Functions

In 1937, Papez suggested that the limbic lobe formed a neuronal circuit that provided the anatomical substratum for emotions. Based on experimental results suggesting that the hypothalamus plays a critical role in the expression of emotions, Papez argued that, since emotions reach consciousness and thought, and conversely, higher cognitive functions affect emotions, the hypothalamus must communicate reciprocally with higher cortical centers.

The representation of the outside world and the internal milieu are superimposed in the limbic system. All the sensory information about the perceiver's environment is inscribed in the neuronal network of the limbic cortex, the hippocampus and the amygdala. The vegetative, nervous, and humoral functions which contribute to homeostasis are represented simultaneously in the limbic system. Moreover, the hippocampus has been described as a gatekeeper embodying the brain's ability to commit things to lasting memory. Evidences for such a role of the hippocampus are clear. For instance, the neurosurgical removal of the hippocampus on both sides of the human brain, as a treatment of otherwise intractable forms of epilepsy, leads to a central disorder called hippocampal amnesia. The patient retains the memories he collected well before the surgery but can not collect new ones. [*See* AMNESIA.]

Other evidences suggest that the amygdala, despite its extensive olfactory input, is not essential for olfactory discrimination but rather commands a number of adaptative responses. Lesions and electrical stimulations of the amygdala produce a variety of effects on autonomic responses, emotional behavior, and feeding. Consequently, the amygdala has been implicated in the process of learning, particularly those tasks that require coordination of information from different sensory modalities, or the association of a stimulus and of an affective response.

Finally, it has been extensively described that the interplay between the neural activity of the hypothalamus and the neural activity of higher centers results in emotional experiences that we describe as fear, anger, pleasure, or satisfaction. For example, the behavior of patients from which a part of the limbic system (frequently the prefrontal cortex) has been removed supports this idea. Indeed, these patients are no longer bothered by chronic pain or, alternatively, when they do perceive pain and exhibit appropriate autonomic reactions, the perception is no longer associated with a powerful emotional experience. [*See* PAIN.]

In summary, neurons from the limbic system form complex circuits that collectively play an important role in numerous behavioral responses such as learning, memory, and emotions. Such a role played by motivational states in homeostasis is discussed in the next section.

IV. ROLE OF MOTIVATIONAL STATES IN HOMEOSTASIS

We have described above the role of the hypothalamus and the limbic system in the neuroendocrine and autonomic regulation of homeostasis. We shall consider now the control of homeostasis by motivational states, the internal conditions that arouse and direct elementary behavior. Motivational states (also called drives) are inferred mechanisms to explain the intensity and direction of a variety of voluntary behaviors, such as temperature regulation, feeding, consuption of water, and sexual behaviors. It is the internal state which creates drives by deviations from the norm which defines the conditions of equilibrum for the milieu. A drive is not the stimulus which triggers the behavioral response but rather the internal force that underlies it. However, a stimulus may cause a drive when it has been associated in the past with a particular internal state. Because of the flexibility of internal parameter which defines a pseudo-equilibrium for the internal milieu of a living organism, it would be more appropriate to refer to the internal state as a "fluctuating central state."

Specific motivational states possess two components: needs and rewards participating in homeostatic drives. Drives represent urges or impulses based upon bodily needs that lead animals into action. This concept is central to Freudian psychology which is related to needs and experiences of satisfaction. Needs are experienced as an intolerable internal situation which must be stopped. This internal state, called motivation by psychologists, induces a drive to accomplish the act that will relieve it. For example, a temperature-regulating drive is said to control behaviors that directly affect body temperature such as rubbing one's hands together. Therefore, physiological deprivation may lead to the satisfaction of a need and this, in turn, will lead to response reinforcement. This means that this action will become more likely in similar future situations. Such a psychological process is considered by some behaviorists to be the basis of learning.

We have so far dealt with the role of tissue needs in generating appropriate behaviors and physiological responses to fight against a bodily deficit. However, another component linked with motivated behaviors is reward, which may lead to a profit. For example, sexual responses do not appear to be controlled by the lack of specific substances in the body, but are rather oriented toward hedonic factors. In this case, drives, by producing goal-oriented behaviors, are defined by the goal to be reached and justified by the reward obtained. One form of reward is pleasure and, therefore, the duality of profit and pleasure is the major component of drive. On the other hand, the couple drive–reward constitutes one of the rules of learning.

Finally, in describing the factors which regulate motivated behaviors, we should also point out the role of ecological constraints and anticipatory mechanisms. The characteristics of most behavioral responses are determined by evolutionary selection which retains only appropriate responses in a defined ecological surrounding. In this context, one of the most determinant parameters which participates in keeping a specific behavioral response is the cost:benefit ratio. The other component which also controls motivated behaviors, namely anticipator mechanisms, gives to the homeostasis concept its temporal dimension. Sometimes, lack rather than need is able to activate drives. In the case of sexual arousal for example, a feeling of lack becomes a simulation of need. Accordingly homeostatic regulation is often anticipatory and can be initiated before any physiological deficit occurs. Such a role is played by clock-like mechanisms which turn physiological behavioral responses on and off before the occurrence of any tissue deficits. The master clock mechanism that drives and coordinates many rhythms is located in the suprachiasmatic nucleus of the hypothalamus. One such common cycle is a daily rhythm called the circadian rhythm, which controls feeding, drinking, locomotor activity, and several other responses. After jet lag due to long distances, travelers can always confirm the important role played by circadian rhythms.

V. OVERALL VIEW

Homeostatic processes can be analyzed in terms of control systems or servomechanisms, comprising a set point, an error signal, controlling elements, a controlled system, and, finally, feedback detectors. This approach has provided a convenient and precise language to describe both concepts and experimental results. Moreover, it has been successfully applied to temperature regulation, feeding, and drinking. For example, in the temperature regulation system, the integrator and many controlling elements appear to be located in the hypothalamus. The normal body temperature is the set point and the feedback detector collects information about body temperature from two main sources: peripheral and central temperatures. The analysis of feeding and thirst behaviors can also be approached in terms of a control system as for temperature regulation, although at every level of analysis, the understanding is less complete than for the control of temperature.

We have seen that the hypothalamus is concerned with the regulation of various behaviors directed toward homeostatic goals such as consumption of food and of water or sexual gratifications. Through its control of emotions and motivated behavior, the hypothalamus acts indirectly in maintaining homeostasis by motivating animals and human beings to act on their environment.

In regulating emotional expression, the hypothalamus functions in conjunction with higher control systems in the limbic system and neocortex. In addition to regulating specific motivated behaviors, the hypothalamus and the cerebral cortex are involved in arousal, namely the maintenance of a general state of awareness (the level of arousal varies from different degrees of excitement to coma, sleep, and drowsiness). However, because of its intimate relationship with both the autonomic and the endocrine systems, the hypothalamus appears to play a central role in regulating homeostatic behaviors. The hypothalamus contributes to these adaptative behaviors by integrating information from both external and internal stimuli that report on the homeostatic state of the animal.

Acknowledgments

The authors thank Drs. Catalina Betancur and Jean-Didier Vincent for their comments on earlier drafts of the manuscript.

Bibliography

Cannon, W. B. (1929). "Bodily Changes in Pain, Hunger, Fear, and Rage." D. Appleton & Co.

Papez, J. W. (1937). A proposed mechanism of emotion. *Am. Med. Assoc. Arch. Neurol. Psychiat.* **38,** 725–743.

Sacks, O. (1987). "The Man Who Mistook His Wife for a Hat and Other Clinical Tales." Harper Collins, New York.

Scharrer, E., and Scharrer B. (1940). Secretory cells within the hypothalamus. In "The Hypothalamus." Res. Publ. Ass. Nerv. Ment. Dis., Hafner, New York.

Vincent, J.-D. (1990). "The Biology of Emotions." Basil Blackwell, Oxford.

Wurtman, R. J., and Anton-Tay, F. (1969). The mammalian pineal as a neuroendocrine transducer. *Rec. Prog. Horm. Res.* **25,** 493–513.

HOMICIDE

David Lester
Center for the Study of Suicide

Glossary

Involuntary manslaughter Death that results from negligence on the part of the killer.

Justifiable homicide Killings which are sanctioned by law, as when a police officer kills a felon within the rules established by the police department for such actions.

Second-degree murder Killing that is malicious (that is, it has elements of cruelty, recklessness, etc.) but not necessarily intentional.

Voluntary manslaughter Killing that takes place in the sudden heat of anger without premeditation or malice.

HOMICIDE is the killing of one person by another. There are several types of homicide, ranging from excusable homicide—killing that is unintentional and in which no blame attaches to the killer—to first-degree murder—unlawful killing that is willful, deliberate, and premeditated. The term *homicide* typically is used by government agencies dealing with causes of mortality, while *murder* and *manslaughter* are used by criminal justice agencies.

I. THE EPIDEMIOLOGY OF HOMICIDE

The homicide rate in the United States in 1989 was 8.9 per 100,000 per year, and the rate has remained quite steady during the 1980s, decreasing a little. Homicide rates are higher in the Southern states than elsewhere, and the majority of murders in the United States are committed with firearms (61% in 1987).

Homicide rates do not vary much with the season, but the rates are higher on weekends and on major national holidays which suggests that leisure (perhaps combined with increased alcohol consumption) increases the risk of homicide. In a study of murder in Memphis, Tennessee, 75% of victims and 86% of murderers were intoxicated at the time of the murder. There is no evidence for a lunar variation in the risk of homicide.

The age at which people in the United States are at greatest risk for being killed is 20–24. The risk is higher for men than for women, and higher for African Americans than for whites. In 1985, the race of the killer and the killed was the same for 88% of the murders. Murder by an acquaintance, friend, or relative (primary murder) is more common in the United States than murder by a stranger (secondary murder)—the ratio in the 1970s was about 2 : 1. However, Martin Daly and Margo Wilson have noted that murder between members of the same nuclear family is relatively uncommon and that the phenomena of murder are consistent with the theory of evolutionary psychology, which argues that human behavior typically operates so as to promote genetic posterity (the survival of one's genes).

The most common method for homicide in the United States in 1987 was firearms (61%), followed by cutting/piercing instruments (20%), and hanging/strangulation (4%).

In 1980, Guatemala had the highest homicide rate (64 per 100,000 per year), followed by Columbia and El Salvador, all nations with internal unrest. The United States had a homicide rate of 10, higher than all other industrialized nations. For example, the English homicide rate was 0.8, the French rate 1.0, and the Finnish rate 2.9.

The rate with which babies are killed (in the first year of life) is low in nonindustrialized nations (where the overall homicide rate is relatively high)

Copyright © 1994 by Academic Press, Inc. All rights of reproduction in any form reserved.

and high in industrialized nations (where the overall homicide rate is relatively low). For example, in Austria in 1970, the overall homicide rate was 1.5 while that for babies was 10.7, while the corresponding rates in Venezuela were 7.9 and 2.0, respectively.

II. INFANTICIDE

Infanticide has been common in many societies in the past. Defective children, twins, first-born sons, daughters, or those coming too soon after the birth of an earlier child were often killed. Sometimes the motive was connected with religious and cultural customs (as in the killing of first-born sons in ancient Carthage); sometimes the motive was simply economic (daughters were seen as less valuable than sons) or a matter of survival (parents who tried to raise twins in primitive conditions might lose both to starvation).

Infanticide refers to the killing of any child. If a parent murders his or her own child, the technical term is *filicide*. Since parents who murder newborns differ considerably from parents murdering older children, the term *neonaticide* has been proposed for the murder of newborns.

In one study, 78% of children murdered by parents were more than 1 day old. About a third of the filicides were in the first 6 months of life, a high percentage which probably results from postpartum depression and psychosis, particularly in the mother.

Twice as many mothers murdered their children as fathers, but the children murdered were equally likely to be boys as girls. About 60% of the parents were judged to be psychotic.

The motives for filicide are varied. In *altruistic filicide,* the aim is to prevent the child from suffering pain. However, the pain experienced by the child may not always be real. For example, parents intending to commit suicide may also murder their children in order to spare the children suffering after the parent dies. In *unwanted child filicide,* the child is unwanted, perhaps because it is illegitimate or the offspring of an extramarital affair, or perhaps the child interferes with the parents' desires and aspirations.

In *spouse revenge filicide,* the child is murdered as a way of hurting the parent. *Accidental filicide* occurs when a child abuser carries the abuse too far and kills the child. Finally *psychotic filicide* is murder committed by a psychotic parent, and the psychiatric disturbance makes it difficult to identify motives for the murder.

Neonaticide was almost always committed by the mother, and these mothers were usually younger than mothers murdering older children, typically under the age of 25. Depression and psychosis were less common in parents murdering newborns and, whereas about a third of filicidal mothers committed suicide, almost none of the neonaticidal mothers did so.

The most common reason for neonaticide is that the child is unwanted, whereas the most common motive for filicide is altruistic. In rare cases, the neonaticidal mother is callous and strong-willed, but the majority are immature women who kill the newborn as a desperate way to deal with a situation with which they had no plans to cope.

III. HOMICIDE AND THE POLICE

Over one hundred police officers are killed on the job each year. In the 1970s as a whole, the rate with which police officers were killed ranged from 105 per 100,000 officers per year in Atlanta, Georgia, to zero in El Paso, Texas. Ninety-nine percent of officers were killed with guns, 14% with their own guns. Internationally, the rate with which police officers were murdered in the 1970s ranged from 198 per 100,000 per year in Northern Ireland (the scene of civil unrest) to 1 in England. The number in the United States was 22 per 100,000 per year.

Police officers also kill civilians. These killings are supposed to be justifiable homicides, but occasionally officers are found to have used their firearms inappropriately. In the 1960s, the rate of justifiable homicide ranged from 0.71 per 100,000 civilians per year in Miami to 0.04 in Boston. In a study in Chicago, the police department found only 1% of the killings to be unjustifiable, but an academic researcher reckoned that 15% were unjustifiable.

A study of American cities found that cities with the highest rates with which police officers were killed by civilians tended to be those in which civilians were killed by police officers at a high rate and in which civilians killed one another at a high rate. These appeared, therefore, to be generally "violent" cities.

IV. THEORIES OF MURDER

A. Subcultural Theory

Marvin Wolfgang and Franco Ferracuti proposed that subcultures exist within some cultures that have values and norms which predispose them to violence, and perhaps murder. Some groups of young males, for example, seem to have attitudes about murder that are deviant from the major culture in America, and they accept murder as an everyday occurrence and everyday risk. After murders occur, they do not feel particularly distressed or guilty.

A study of the town of Acan in the Tarascan region of Mexico found a murder rate of 200 per 100,000 per year. There were two rival political parties in the region, and almost all of the murders were politically motivated. There were rules governing killing. Women were not killed, nor people working in their fields or coming from and going to work. This appears, therefore, to have been a "subculture of violence" as Wolfgang and Ferracuti defined the concept.

B. Frustration and Aggression

In the 1930s, a group of social scientists at Yale University proposed the frustration–aggression hypothesis. They argued that aggression is usually a result of frustration, though they were aware that frustration could result in a variety of responses of which aggression was only one. [*See* AGGRESSION.]

Applied to murder, then, researchers have explored the history of frustration in the backgrounds of murderers. Stuart Palmer compared murderers with their nonmurdering brothers and found a much higher incidence of childhood frustrations in the backgrounds of the murderers. The murderers had more often experienced such events as a difficult birth, forceps injuries, serious operations, serious illnesses, serious accidents, beatings by people other than parents, congenital deformities, postnatally acquired deformities, negative maternal attitudes, more rigid mothers, more severe toilet training, repressive sexual education, slower intellectual development, negative school experiences, symptoms of disturbance such as phobias, compulsions, stuttering, and bedwetting, and temper tantrums. Palmer noted that some of these experiences were signs of frustration already experienced while others were sources of later frustration. For example, physical deformities will lead to the child being insulted and ridiculed at school by his peers.

Palmer found that the murderers had experienced an average of 9.2 of these events whereas their brothers had experienced an average of only 4.2 events. Palmer also found that the murderers had developed less effective and less socially acceptable ways of releasing their frustration than had their brothers.

C. The Role of Control

Edwin Megargee suggested that murderers differed in their control over their aggressive impulses. *Overcontrolled* murderers do not permit themselves to express their anger to any frustration, and so the unreleased anger builds up and up, until one day a new frustration creates enough new anger to overcome the controls. All of the pentup anger is now released, resulting in a brutal murder, after which the person may remain unaggressive for many years.

In contrast, *undercontrolled* murderers release their anger at the each frustration, so that they are continually aggressing against those whom they think have insulted them. As a result, the likelihood that they will kill someone eventually is quite high.

D. Are Murderers Psychiatrically Disturbed?

The answer to this question depends on the nation. A study of Iceland, for example, found only 30% of a sample of murderers to be psychiatrically normal, whereas a study of Scottish murderers found 82% to be normal. However, evidence from studies of psychiatrically disturbed people in general does not indicate that they commit violent crimes at a higher rate than normal people.

The percentage of murderers with brain damage (detected from electroencephalograms) ranges from about 25 to 50%. In the only study to include comparison groups, 24% of murderers had abnormal encephalograms as compared to 12% of normal people and 65% of habitually aggressive offenders. Thus, there is no good evidence to suggest that brain damage is especially relevant to murder in general.

V. THE DIRECTION OF AGGRESSION

Some investigators see suicide and homicide as alternative reactions to frustrating situations. Andrew Henry and James Short suggested that the degree to which people's behaviors were constrained by external factors would determine the choice. If people have clear external factors to blame for their misery or frustration, then they will become angry and, in the extreme, assaultive and murderous. If there are no clear external causes for their misery or frustration, then outward-directed anger is not legitimized and the anger is turned inward onto the self as depression and self-destructive behavior and, in the extreme, suicidal behavior. For example, in many societies, including the United States, oppressed groups (such as African Americans) have higher rates of murder while the oppressors (European Americans) have higher rates of suicide. [*See* SUICIDE.]

At the psychological level, Henry and Short suggested that love-oriented punishment and punishment and nurturance by the same parent would increase the chance of suicide (since children raised in these ways would learn to inhibit the expression of anger and aggression after frustration by the parent), whereas physical punishment and punishment by a parent other than the nurturer would increase the chance of murder. However, some phenomena show that suicide and murder may be more complexly related.

A. Psychic Murder

Joost Meerloo described cases of where people committed suicide in response to the conscious and unconscious hostile wishes of significant others. Joseph Richman has documented this hostility toward the potential suicide clearly in his studies of the families of suicidal people. Meerloo called this phenomenon *psychic homicide*.

B. Victim-Precipitated Homicide

Marvin Wolfgang studied all the murders in Philadelphia in 1 year and found that about a quarter of the victims had played a role in precipitating their own murder. They may have started the fight, for example, which led to their murder. This was especially common in husbands who were murdered by their wives and rare in wives who were murdered by their husbands. Wolfgang called this behavior *victim-precipitated homicide*.

C. Murder followed by Suicide

Many murderers commit suicide after their murder. This is relatively common in mothers who murder children and criminals who kill police officers. More husbands commit suicide after killing wives than do wives after killing husbands, perhaps because wives are less likely to precipitate their own murder than are husbands and so the husbands feel greater guilt. Today, it is not uncommon for couples to commit suicide together, and often one spouse kills the partner and then commits suicide.

Interestingly, studies of suicidal psychiatric patients find them to be quite angry and violent, suggesting that self-destructive and assaultive tendencies can occur in the same individual.

VI. DETERRING MURDER

The two major debates in the problem of deterring murder today concern the effectiveness of capital punishment and gun control.

A. The Role of the Death Penalty

Much of the research on the effectiveness of the death penalty at the societal (aggregate) level has been conducted by economists who have applied their sophisticated statistical techniques to the problem, both over time (from year to year) and over regions (from state to state). However, the results of the research are in conflict, and any conclusion by a reviewer of the research may be colored by the reviewer's own opinion. A cautious conclusion must be that the deterrent effect has not yet been proven.

An alternative methodology has been to explore the number of murders committed in the days following an execution. Steven Stack has shown that, in general, the murder rate drops a little after the majority of executions. However, much more research needs to be done on this topic before reliable conclusions can be drawn.

B. The Role of Guns

Advocates of gun control often argue that gun control would prevent violent crime and, in particular, murder. The problem in testing this assumption is that strict gun control in the United States is quite weak by the standards of other nations where guns are rarely owned by private citizens.

David Lester has found only a very weak effect from strict gun control laws on homicide, much weaker than the effect of strict gun control on suicide. Again, much more research is needed on this important topic.

VII. HELPING THE VICTIMS

For each murder, there is one obvious victim, the person murdered. But friends and relatives, particularly those who witnessed the person killed, also suffer. Increasingly, mental health professionals are working with "survivors" to help them cope with the trauma and adjust to life without their loved one.

Bibliography

Danto, B. L., Bruhns, J., and Kutscher, A. H. (Eds.) (1982). "The Human Side of Homicide." Columbia University Press, New York.

Henry, A. F., and Short, J. F. (1954). "Suicide and Homicide." New Free Press, New York.

Lester, D. (1986). "The Murderer and His Murder." AMS, New York.

Lester, D. (1991). "Questions and Answers about Murder." Charles Press, Philadelphia.

Hope and Optimism

C. R. Snyder
University of Kansas

Glossary

Agency A cognitive sense of energy for the goal or goals that a person envisions.

Appraisal A cognitive analysis of an imagined or real event.

Attribution The cognitive process of determining the underlying cause of an event or events.

Cognitive Any mental process pertaining to the awareness of a given object or event.

Coping Interactive attempts aimed at lessening the physical or psychological pain that is associated with stressors.

Dispositional Pertaining to enduring characteristics that individuals display across time and in differing situations.

Expectancy A cognitive evaluation of the probability of attaining a goal.

Goal Any object, event, or outcome that is cognitively represented and desired by an individual.

Pathways A cognitive sense of being able to generate routes to an envisioned goal or goals.

Placebo The change potential that is inherent in the cognitive belief that change is going to happen.

Psychometric Statistical procedures related to measurements of people.

Situational Pertaining to the influence that a given environment has on the individual.

Stressor An event that is perceived as being the cause of physical or psychological pain.

Validity The extent to which a scale measure what it purports to measure.

HOPE AND OPTIMISM share a definitional core reflecting a positive cognitive set that people have about their outcomes in life. Hope and optimism may be influenced by particular situational factors (e.g., "Today I am especially hopeful because I just found out my promotion went through"), or they may tap underlying dispositions that the person exhibits across different situations and time periods (e.g., "I'm the sort of person who looks on the bright side of things. Just call me an optimist").

I. HISTORICAL SKEPTICISM OF HOPE AND OPTIMISM

Although hope and optimism appear to be positive assets, the historical picture is lacking in praise for these concepts. In the myth of Pandora, for example, hope is the only creature that remained in the box after such negative forces as envy, spite, and revenge had escaped. It is not clear from this story, however, whether hope was to be the antidote for the other evils, or it was just an illusion that would prolong the suffering of humankind. Sophocles and Nietzche echoes these latter concerns, suggesting that hope only increases our pain in the long run. Similarly, Francis Bacon lamented the fact that "Hope is a good breakfast, but a bad supper." Optimism has not fared much better in the eyes of critics. In *Candide,* Voltaire asserted that "Optimism is a mania for maintaining that all is well when things are going badly." James Cabell, in the *Silver Stallion,* offered the observation that "The optimist proclaims that we live in the best of all possible worlds; and the pessimist fears that this is true." Or, consider the words of Donald Marquis, "an optimist is a guy that never had much experience."

Common threads in the historical biases are that hope and optimism are whimsical emotions, that they are difficult to measure, and that they are potentially harmful. Against this backdrop of mistrust, however, psychologists in the last several years have begun to develop cognitive-based models and valid

Encyclopedia of Human Behavior, Volume 2
Copyright © 1994 by Academic Press, Inc. All rights of reproduction in any form reserved.

measures of hope and optimism; moreover, emerging evidence builds a positive case for these concepts. The subsequent paragraphs give the reader an overview of how hope and optimism are being defined and measured, as well as the adaptive role that they play in our daily functioning.

II. DEFINITIONS AND MEASUREMENT OF HOPE

Psychologists and psychiatrists over the last several decades have built models that are related to the common dictionary definition of hope as a "perception that something desired may happen." Interestingly, the various versions of hope all involve an overall perception that goals can be met. Three theories of hope are described next, along with the corresponding ways in which it is measured.

A. Averill and Colleagues

Using a questionnaire approach in order to ascertain the circumstances in which hope is deemed to be appropriate, Averill and his colleagues conclude that hope is a "relatively short-term response tendency, usually initiated and terminated by specific environmental conditions." According to respondents, hope is most appropriate when a person's goal is perceived as being (1) under some degree of control; (2) intermediate in terms of probability of attainment; (3) important; and (4) morally and socially acceptable. To experience hope, therefore, means that an important goal is involved, and the individual has moved into the intermediate range in terms of perceptions about attaining the goal. One implication of this definition is that very low or high perceived probabilities of obtaining a goal are not evocative of hope.

This approach is explicitly tied to an understanding of the rules that people espouse for the appropriate use of hope. This is a social–constructionist perspective in which it is assumed that hope, or any other construct for that matter, is best understood when it is tied to the rules and norms that individuals learn for particular social contexts. The way of measuring hope, therefore, is to use a questionnaire format in which the parameters of hope are charted according to the responses given by people.

B. Stotland

Grounded in the common dictionary meaning of hope, as well as the literatures involving goal-related behaviors, the effects of success and failure on performance, the factors influencing persistence in human behavior, and previous social psychological theory on cognitive schemas, Stotland posited that the essence of hope was ". . . an expectation greater than zero of achieving a goal." As such, the individual's level of hope reflected the expectation or perceived probability of achieving a goal. Furthermore, Stotland assumed that some level of perceived importance needs to be attached to a goal in order for hope to be operative. Given that the threshold of perceived goal importance has been met, hopefulness is a necessary cognition for action to occur.

Hopefulness, in this context, is a mediating construct that enables us to better understand how a given antecedent event resulted in a subsequent behavioral outcome. Although asking the person his or her level of expectation in terms of goal achievement is one means of measuring hope, Stotland reasons that this technique is rarely employed, and that it is not always feasible. As such, hope often rests upon an inference that we make about another person's phenomenological state in a given set of circumstances. That is, as the person reacts to one set of antecedent events with a subsequent behavioral outcome, we infer that a higher level of hope is operative in the degree to which the outcome is obtained. Although hope is inferred to occur in particular situational contexts, Stotland allows for the possibility that some people may have higher levels of hope across situations. Thus, dispositional hope is a possibility in this framework.

C. Snyder and Colleagues

Based upon the previous notion that hope reflects an expectation of goal attainment, Snyder and colleagues posit that goal-directed expectations comprise two separable, additive cognitive components. A first component, which is called agency, taps the person's sense of successful determination in meeting goals in the past, present, and future. The second component, which is called pathways, taps the person's perceived capability to generate successful plans to reach goals. In terms of a common saying, therefore, hope represents the cognitive "will and ways" to achieve goals. More specifically, Snyder *et al.* define hope as "a cognitive set that is based on a reciprocally derived sense of successful (a) agency (goal-directed determination) and (b) pathways (planning of ways to meet goals)." In order for goal-directed movement to occur, within this model of hope it is reasoned that both the sense of agency and the sense of pathways must become operative. Relative to the previous definitions of hope, this latter one adds a new cognitive component—pathways—to the equation.

Using the aforementioned two-component model of hope, Snyder and his colleagues have developed a brief self-report scale that measures a person's dispositional hope. This scale, known as the Hope Scale, comprises four items that tap the agency component and four items that tap the pathways components, as well as four distracter items. Persons respond on a 4-point continuum in regard to the extent to which each item is applicable, and the total Hope Scale score is the sum of the four agency and four pathways items. The Hope Scale is shown in Table I. Results on the psychometric properties of the Hope Scale show that is it surpasses the requisite standards for self-report scales. The agency items intercorrelate positively with each other, as do the pathways items; moreover, factor analyses reveal that the agency and pathways subcomponents are identifiable. Furthermore, all eight items of the Hope Scale intercorrelate positively with each other, and as such the overall hope score is appropriately derived by summing the eight items. Additionally, how persons score on the Hope Scale at a given point in time is consistent with how they score several weeks later on the same scale.

TABLE I
The Future Scale (the Hope Scale)

Directions: Read each item carefully. Using the scale shown below, please select the number that best describes YOU and put that number in the blank provided.

1 = Definitely false 2 = Mostly false
3 = Mostly true 4 = Definitely true

___ 1. I can think of many ways to get out of a jam. (Pathways)
___ 2. I energetically pursue my goals. (Agency)
___ 3. I feel tired most of the time. (Distracter)
___ 4. There are lots of ways around any problem. (Pathways)
___ 5. I am easily downed in an argument. (Distracter)
___ 6. I can think of many ways to get the things in life that are most important to me. (Pathways)
___ 7. I worry about my health. (Distracter)
___ 8. Even when others get discouraged, I know I can find a way to solve the problem. (Pathways)
___ 9. My past experiences have prepared me well for my future. (Agency)
___ 10. I've been pretty successful in life. (Agency)
___ 11. I usually find myself worrying about something. (Distracter)
___ 12. I meet the goals that I set for myself. (Agency)

Note: The total Hope Scale score is derived by summing the four Agency and the four Pathways items. When administering the scale, the information in parenthesis following each item is deleted, and the scale is labeled The Future Scale. [From C. R. Snyder, Harris, et al., *The Journal of Personality and Social Psychology*, ©1991, Vol. 60, p. 585. Reprinted with permission of the American Psychological Association and the author.]

The concurrent validity of the Hope Scale is shown in several studies where it has correlated positively or negatively with other self-report scales in predicted directions. For example, persons scoring higher on the Hope Scale have *elevated* (1) generalized positive goal expectancies; (2) optimism; (3) perceptions of control in their lives; (4) perceived problem-solving capabilities; (5) self-esteem; and (6) positive affectivity. Conversely, persons scoring higher on the Hope Scale have *diminished* (1) anxiety; (2) negative affectivity; (3) depression; and (4) social introversion.

III. IMPLICATIONS OF HOPE

Researchers have explored the role that hope plays in several different life arenas. In this section, hope will be discussed in relationship to perceptions about one's life, coping, and performances.

A. Perceptions of Self and Life Experiences

Generally, one assumption of the various models of hope is that the phenomenology of goal-directed activity should influence the emotions. Thus, a person who is experiencing positive movement toward a goal also should experience positive emotions. Conversely, the individual who is having difficulty attaining a goal should experience negative emotions, especially anxiety. These predictions, which are supported by research examining the emotional states of people under varying degrees of success in their goal-directed activities, highlight the importance of the ongoing cognitive appraisal process. Emotions are not necessarily irrelevant to hope, but they are tied to the goal appraisal process. Further, research shows that it makes a difference whether the probability of goal attainment is decreasing or increasing. For example, the person with a 50% probability who sees the chances of goal attainment *decreasing* should experience anxiety and apprehension due to a sense of loss; on the other hand, the person with a 50% probability who perceives that the chances of goal attainment are *increasing* should experience happiness and other positive emotions due to a sense of gain.

In the previous paragraph, the results of situationally induced changes in hope are discussed irrespective of the individual's dispositional level of hope. In this latter regard, dispositional studies with the Hope Scale suggest that high versus low hope persons approach their life goals differently. High hope people, armed with their cognitive sense of sufficient agency and pathways for goals, appear to approach their particular goals with a (1) sense of challenge; (2) focus upon succeeding rather than failing; (3) perception of a high probability of goal attainment; and (4) positive emotional state. Conversely, the low hope person's sense of insufficient agency and pathways is related to approaching particular goals with a (1) sense of ambivalence at best, and doubt at worst; (2) focus upon failing rather than succeeding; (3) perception of a low probability of goal attainment; and (4) negative emotional state. In other words, life and its accompanying goals are experienced in a qualitatively more positive manner by persons who are dispositionally high as compared to low in hope.

B. Coping

In terms of coping with stressors, persons who are higher as compared to lower in dispositional hope appear to appraise their goals more positively (as discussed above). When blockages occur to these goals, higher hope persons perceive these as being a normal inevitability of life, and they are not unduly disturbed by such situational stressors. Higher hope persons report that they can generate alternative pathways to their goals, and that they use a sense of humor when things look particularly bleak. Furthermore, high hope people report that they have helpful social support networks to be called upon during times of stress, and that they have coping skills to sustain their well-being. Other research has shown that higher as compared to lower hope persons engage in more behaviors aimed at reducing the risk of cancer, that they are less likely to experience burnout in a high stress job, and that they recover better from a physical injury. [*See* COPING.]

C. Performances

Both situational and dispositional research suggest that the cognitive set of hope accompanies successful performances in varying arenas. Manipulations that enhance goal-directed expectancies result in behaviors aimed at goal attainment. In surveys conducted on the concomitants of hope, people in American culture (as well as Korean culture) report that hope is linked to action toward goals through hard work and organization. It should come as no surprise, therefore, that changes toward elevated hope appear to result in enhanced performances. Both laboratory and applied research support this contention. In fact, it has been argued that the positive effects of psychotherapy are basically mediated by increases in hope. For example, persons who are judged to have improved as compared to those who have not improved in psychotherapy have increased their sense of positive goal-related expectancies in their lives. Additionally, the two ingredients of successful psychotherapy outcome, the placebo effect of being in treatment and the specific effects related to particular intervention techniques, have been equated with the agency and pathways components of one hope model.

Just as situational performance gains appear to result because of increases in hope, results also show that persons who are higher as compared to lower in dispositional hope have performance advantages. For example, based on scores on the Hope Scale, college students who score higher in hope garner better grades. These effects have been replicated in several studies, and they occur even when the potentially confounding influences of previous school achievement are removed statistically. Furthermore, Hope Scale scores evidence only a small positive correlations with measures of intelligence. Together, these latter two sets of findings suggest that dispositional hope is more than just one's intellectual capability or previous history of academic achievement.

IV. DEFINITIONS AND MEASUREMENT OF OPTIMISM

The two most recent theories pertaining to optimism are built upon somewhat different conceptual bases, and they are reviewed in the next section. Additionally, the corresponding measurement approaches are described.

A. The Seligman/Peterson and Colleagues Approach

The concept of learned optimism is an outgrowth of an earlier theory known as learned helplessness, in which it was assumed that prolonged exposure to uncontrollable events leads to motivational, cognitive, and emotional problems. In order to make the theory more applicable to humans, the reformulated learned helplessness theory emphasized the importance of the attributional explanations that people make for the bad events that happen to them. In this regard, people are postulated to use three dimensions in appraising the causes of events in their lives: (1) locus (internal to external foci); (2) stability (stable to variable in terms of consistency over time); and (3) globality (global to specific in terms of the number of applicable situations). Originally, the thrust of this theoretical approach was upon the person with the learned helplessness attributional style of making internal, stable, and global attributions for negative outcomes. Over time, however, this set of attributions came to be known as a pessimistic attributional style, with the opposite end of the dimensions (i.e., external, variable, and specific attributions for negative events) being called optimism. In other words, the essence of the evolved theory was that an optimist has a way of thinking about bad events in his or her life such that these events are externalized (locus) and circumscribed (stability and globality). The pessimist, on the other hand, has a way of thinking about bad events such that these events typically are internalized and generalized. These attributional cognitive styles are assumed to be precursors to expectancies that people form about the future. This notion of explanatory style, with the pessimistic to optimistic continuum, represents a dispositional conceptualization. [*See* ATTRIBUTION; LEARNED HELPLESSNESS.]

The attributional style questionnaire (ASQ) is a self-report questionnaire that was developed in order to have a reliable measure of pessimism–optimism. Respondents imagine themselves in six negative situations (e.g., "You give an important talk in front of a group and the audience reacts negatively"), and for each event the person is asked to imagine what the major cause would be. Thereafter, the person rates each cause on a 7-point scale in terms of internal/external locus, stable/variable consistency over time, and global/specific in regard to number of situations to which it would apply. The optimist scores toward the external, variable, and specific end of the continua for the six negative outcomes. The psychometric analyses of the ASQ suggest that the items do not intercorrelate very highly, although the test–retest over several weeks is relatively high. In order to increase the internal consistency of the ASQ, an expanded attributional style questionnaire was developed by increasing the original pool of negative events from 6 to 24. This resulted in higher intercorrelations for the items, and this latter scale is preferable because of its internal consistency.

In order to derive a score for explanatory style based on naturally occurring statements made by people, the authors also have developed the content analysis of verbatim explanations (CAVE). In this regard, a written document (e.g., a letter or diary) of a target person is scanned for events in terms of how these events are explained. Thereafter, the attributions for these events are rated by judges on the internal/external, stable/variable, and global/specific dimensions, and an overall pessimism/optimism score is derived.

B. The Scheier and Carver Approach

Scheier and Carver note that previous expectancy-based theorists have often assumed that the best way of predicting human behaviors is to measure expectancies in a particular response domain (e.g., to predict academic outcomes in school, one would ask about academic-related outcomes). They reason, however, that broad-ranging outcomes (such as successful adaptation to the various difficulties that one encounters over time) should be influenced by expectancies related to more than just one given arena. Therefore, their approach is to tap a dispositional sense of optimism, which is based on a people's generalized outcome expectancies. The authors reason that optimists approach their goals with the assumption that good things will happen. (The reader will note that this latter definition of optimism is very similar to the previously described definitions of hope as an overall perception that goals can be met.) The Life Orientation Test (LOT) represents their efforts to measure dispositional optimism. The LOT comprises eight items reflecting generalized outcome expectancies, and four filler (or distracter) items. People respond on a 5-point continuum in regard to how much they agree with the content of each item, and the total optimism score is the sum of responses to the eight items (four are reverse keyed). The LOT is shown in Table II.

Subsequent statistical analyses have shown that the LOT has acceptable internal consistency in that factor analytic procedures yield one factor, and the items intercorrelate highly with each other. Additionally, people's scores on the LOT taken several

TABLE II
Life Orientation Test (Optimism Scale)

Directions: There are no correct or incorrect answers to these questions. Please be as accurate and honest as you can throughout, and try not to let answers to one question influence your answers to other questions. Indicate the extent to which you agree with each of the following items using the following response format:

0 = Strongly disagree 1 = Disagree 2 = Neutral
3 = Agree 4 = Strongly agree

___ 1. In uncertain times, I usually expect the best.
___ 2. It's easy for me to relax. (Filler item)
___ 3. If something can go wrong for me it will.*
___ 4. I always look on the bright side of things.
___ 5. I'm always optimistic about my future.
___ 6. I enjoy my friends a lot. (Filler item)
___ 7. It's important for me to keep busy. (Filler item)
___ 8. I hardly ever expect things to go my way.*
___ 9. Things never work out the way I want them to.*
___ 10. I don't get upset too easily. (Filler item)
___ 11. I'm a believer in the idea that "every cloud has a silver lining."
___ 12. I rarely count on good things happening to me.*

Note: The total LOT score is derived by summing the eight nonfiller items (after the scores for the items followed by an asterisk are reversed). When administering the scale, the information in parenthesis following each item is deleted, and the scale is labeled The Life Orientation Test. [From Michael F. Scheier and Charles S. Carver, *Health Psychology*, 1985, **4**, 225. Reprinted with permission of Lawrence Erlbaum Associates, Inc., and the authors.]

weeks apart correlate highly, lending support to the contention that the generalized outcome expectancies are dispositional in nature. In terms of concurrent validity, the LOT evidences relationships that would be predicted theoretically. That is, the LOT correlates positively with internal loss of control, expectancy for success, and self-esteem; furthermore, it correlates negatively with negative affectivity, depression, hopelessness, social anxiety, and alienation.

V. IMPLICATIONS OF OPTIMISM

In this section, the role of optimism will be explored in terms of perceptions about one's life, coping, and performances. In each section, the situational and dispositional explanatory style results (i.e., the Seligman/Peterson paradigm) will be reviewed first, followed by the situational and dispositional generalized outcome expectancy results (i.e., the Scheier/Carver paradigm).

A. Perceptions of Self and Life Experiences

In the extent to which one can make externalizing and circumscribing attributions about past or upcoming difficult life experiences, this situationally derived optimism should result in more positive emotion-related responses. Laboratory studies support the inference that manipulated optimistic as compared to pessimistic attributions after failure-like experiences result in higher self-esteem, as well as lower negative affect and anxiety. Turning to the dispositionally measured optimism as derived by instruments tapping explanatory style (e.g., the ASQ, the expanded ASQ, and the CAVE), research consistently suggests that optimism is not characteristic of depressed populations. Likewise, there is support for the inference that an optimistic attributional style precedes decreases in depression.

By increasing the outcome expectancies that a person has in a particular situation context, research routinely reveals that persons increasingly display positive emotions about themselves and the environment. Positive feedback and the associated rise in outcome expectancy associated with the anticipated attainment of a desired goal, which is the essence of situationally derived optimism, apparently lead to a temporary inflation of self- and environment-directed perceptions. Although the aforementioned conclusion is one of the most consistent findings in the social sciences, it is also important to address the repercussions of the more enduring, dispositional type of generalized positive outcome expectancies posited by Scheier and Carver. In this regard, higher as compared to lower optimism persons (as measures by the LOT) report that they are (1) more in control of the contingencies leading to goal attainment; (2) less alienated in relationship to other people; (3) less socially anxious; (4) higher in self-esteem; and (5) more optimistic in terms of their attributional style (as measured by the ASQ).

B. Coping

Several studies in the attributional explanatory style paradigm have suggested that the optimist has coping advantages relative to the pessimist. For example, a situational manipulation to externalize the cause of an impending poor performance has resulted in lowering of pulse rates. Elderly people with an optimistic as compared to pessimistic attributional style have displayed better immune system functioning. Optimists have been shown to make half the number of doctor visits, even when controlling statistically for the health conditions. Using the CAVE methodology, optimists tended to be in better health after a 24-year period than were pessimists. When they become ill, optimists relative to pessimists report that they engage in a variety of activities in order to take care of themselves (e.g., "I increase my rest and sleep," "I decrease my work load," "I eat more nutritious food than usual," "I increase my fluids [juice, soup, and so on]," "I put aside any worries I might have"). In a study of homosexual and bisexual men, although there were no differences in knowledge about AIDS, the optimists reported that they engaged in "safer sex" practices (e.g., using condoms, reducing the number of partners, etc.) to a greater degree than did the pessimists. Lastly, when stressors necessitate that people persevere in the pursuit of their goals, studies reveal that optimists are more likely to do this than are pessimists.

Using the LOT as an optimism index of generalized outcome expectancies, several studies suggest advantages for optimists as compared to pessimists. In particular, optimists appear to utilize problem-focused coping, they seek social support, and they accentuate the positive rather than the negative characteristics of stressors; furthermore, if the stressing event is truly uncontrollable, the optimist accepts the situation. Optimists are less likely to report that they are bothered by physical symptoms than is the case for pessimists, and this holds even when level of physical symptoms is statistically controlled. In another study, dispositional optimism was significantly related to faster recovery from coronary bypass surgery, faster return to normal life activities after discharge, and enhanced perceptions of quality of life 6 months after surgery. Optimists report that they have an average of 6 less days with the flu than pessimists, and optimists appear to have fewer symptoms related to the flu; moreover, the optimists employ specific strategies in order to reduce their probability of getting the flu (e.g., eating well, sleeping, reducing stress, staying away from sick person, exercising, etc.).

C. Performances

To date, the research bearing directly on the topic of performance outcomes has been conducted with the attributional model rather than the generalized outcome expectancy model. In this regard, situational manipulations of attributional style toward the optimist perspective (i.e., external, variable, and specific attributions for potentially negative outcomes) usually result in gains in performance. Two particularly effective approaches are to train people in the optimism-related attributions that their failures are due to lack of effort, or due to the fact that they have used the wrong strategy. These latter attributions evidently free the person from being stuck in their failures; moreover, they enable the person to become energized for the next performance arena, such that they actually performed better. Relatedly, tasks that are described as having performance impediments appear to elicit a seemingly paradoxical situational optimism; that is to say, people approach such activities with their anticipatory externalizing attributions in mind should they do poorly, and because of this they actually perform quite well. Research also suggests that the successful changes obtained by psychotherapy clients reflect, in part, their change from a pessimistic to an optimistic attributional style over the course of treatment.

Beyond the situational evidence for the beneficial effects of an acquired optimistic attributional style, the evidence on dispositional optimism also is suggestive of adaptive sequelae. For example, students with an optimistic as compared to pessimistic attributional style perform better in college, and this positive correlation is significant even when the influence of high school grades is removed statistically. Additionally, other data suggest that optimists are less likely to drop out of school than pessimists. Moving to another performance arena, that of sales, optimists are more successful in terms of products sold than are pessimists; furthermore, optimists last longer in their sales positions than do pessimists. Athletic outcomes tell a similar story in that dispositional optimists as compared to pessimists appear to be more successful at their particular sports.

VI. HOPE AND OPTIMISM IN PERSPECTIVE

Contrary to the skepticism that has been displayed toward hope and optimism throughout previous centuries, an emerging viewpoint among psychologists is that these concepts are not loose, philosophical notions that preclude measurement. In fact, several self-report measures of hope and optimism are available, and they provide theory-driven, psychometrically sound, and valid measurement indices. Additionally, in contrast to the historical prejudice about the counterproductiveness of these concepts, research on coping and performance reveals that elevated levels of hope and optimism are quite adaptive. Furthermore, the principles of hope and optimism can be readily translated to educational and therapeutic approaches that enhance the goal-directed cognitions of people. Indeed, hope and optimism provide useful ways of understanding how people engage in positive change and growth in their lives.

Bibliography

Abramson, L. Y., Seligman, M. E. P., and Teasdale, J. D. (1978). Learned helplessness in humans: Critique and reformulation. *J. Abnormal Psychology* **87,** 49–74.

Averill, J. R., Catlin, G., and Chon, K. K. (1990). "Rules of Hope." Springer-Verlag, New York.

Kirsch, I. (1990). "Changing Expectations: A Key to Effective Psychotherapy." Brooks/Cole, Pacific Grove, CA.

Peterson, C. (1991). The meaning and measurement of explanatory style. *Psychol. Inquiry* **2,** 1–10.

Peterson, C., and Bossio, L. M. (1991). "Health and Optimism." Free Press, New York.

Peterson, C., Schulman, P., Castellon, C., and Seligman, M. E. P. (1992). CAVE: Content analysis of verbatim explanations. In "Motivation and Personality: Handbook of Thematic Content Analysis" (C. P. Smith, ed.), Cambridge University Press, New York.

Peterson, C., Semmel, A., vonBaeyer, C., Abramson, L. Y., Metalsky, G. I., and Seligman, M. E. P. (1982). The attributional style questionnaire. *Cog. Ther. Res.* **6,** 287–300.

Peterson, C., and Villanova, P. (1988). An expanded attributional style questionnaire. *J. Abnormal Psychol.* **97,** 87–89.

Scheier, M. F., and Carver, C. S. (1985). Optimism, coping, and health: Assessment and implications of generalized outcome expectancies. *Health Psychol.* **4,** 219–247.

Scheier, M. F., and Carver, C. S. (1987). Dispositional optimism and physical well-being: The influence of generalized outcome expectancies on health. *J. Pers.* **55,** 169–210.

Seligman, M. E. P. (1991). "Learned Optimism." Knopf, New York.

Snyder, C. R., Harris, C., Anderson, J. R., Holleran, S. A., Irving, L. M., Sigmon, S., Yoshinobu, L., Gibb, J., Langelle, C., and Harney, P. (1991). The will and the ways: Development and validation of an individual-differences measure of hope. *J. Pers. Soc. Psychol.* **60,** 570–585.

Snyder, C. R., Irving, L. M., and Anderson, J. R. (1991). Hope and health. In "Handbook of Social and Clinical Psychology: The Health Perspective" (C. R. Snyder and D. R. Forsyth, Eds.), pp. 285–305. Pergamon, Elmsford, NY.

Stotland, E. (1969). "The Psychology of Hope." Jossey-Bass, San Francisco.

Hormones and Behavior

Christy M. Buchanan and Deborah L. FormyDuval
Wake Forest University

Glossary

Androgens A class of steroid hormones that includes testosterone, and that occurs in higher quantities in males than in females.

Estrogens Often called the "female sex hormones." Refers to a class of steroid hormones secreted by the female gonads (ovaries). Also present in males as a result of testosterone conversion.

Hormone A chemical carried by the circulatory or lymph system from one bodily organ to another, where it is engaged by specific receptors and subsequently influences the action of cells at the remote site.

Hypothalamus Portion of the brain involved with motivated and emotional behaviors; regulates hormone release from the pituitary gland.

Luteinizing hormone A hormone released by the anterior pituitary gland under the influence of the hypothalamus and circulating estrogen; stimulates ovulation and secretion of estrogen in females.

Peptide hormone A hormone derived from amino acids (protein).

Steroid hormone A hormone derived from cholesterol (lipid).

Testosterone Often called the "male sex hormone." A steroid hormone secreted in large quantities from the male gonads (testes), but also in lesser quantities from the female gonads (ovaries).

HORMONES instigate physiological changes in the body and brain and these changes have the potential to influence emotions and behavior. Among humans, emotions and behavior are powerfully influenced by psychological, social, and cultural factors. Yet, humans are clearly still biological animals. To what extent, then, do hormones exert observable or important influences on our behavior? Evidence for hormonal influences on a wide array of human behaviors is discussed.

I. MECHANISMS OF HORMONAL EFFECTS ON BEHAVIOR

Much of this review will be concerned with *steroid* hormones, the hormones that have most commonly been studied in connection with human behavior—especially psychological and emotional aspects of behavior. Other types of hormones (e.g., peptide hormones) act primarily at the cell membrane, where they stimulate a secondary chemical messenger that enters the cell and alters cell processes (e.g., permeability to particular ions). Steroid hormones may act at the cell membrane, but, in addition, act by entering cells and binding to the cell nucleus, influencing the production of RNA (ribonucleic acid), which subsequently directs other cell processes. Steroid hormones thus have the ability to influence gene expression in a way that nonsteroid hormones do not. Ultimately, hormones have the capacity to influence a wide variety of neural structures and processes, from the number and differentiation of cells present in a certain location to a cell's sensitivity or receptivity to particular neurotransmitters.

Hormonal effects on behavior have long been seen as either organizational or activational in nature. Organizational effects refer to the influence of early (i.e., prenatal or neonatal) hormones on the development of the brain and on behavior via those effects on structural brain development. Activational effects on behavior refer to contemporaneous hormonal influences, or influences that typically occur through a change in the state or functioning of structures already present. The great majority of research

Copyright © 1994 by Academic Press, Inc. All rights of reproduction in any form reserved.

on hormones and behavior has been performed against the backdrop of this dichotomy, which, although helpful in understanding some very different types of hormonal action, has been criticized as a simplification of the entire range of hormone action in the body. We begin by summarizing what have traditionally been seen as the critical distinctions between organizational and activational effects, and conclude with specific comments about how these distinctions might be oversimplifying actual mechanisms of hormone action.

A. Organizational Effects

As stated above, organizational effects refer to hormonal influences on organization of the nervous system, including the brain. Organizational effects occur early in development, during the prenatal and neonatal periods, and are, to a large extent, the result of the presence or absence of one particular hormone: testosterone. An obvious effect of differential exposure to testosterone in fetal life is the sex-differentiated pattern of genital development. If a fetus is not exposed to testosterone, the female genital structure results (i.e., labia and vagina). With androgen exposure, male genitalia form (i.e., scrotal sacs and a penis).

In a similar manner, it has been documented that, in rats, the presence of testosterone during early periods of development (i.e., both before and immediately after birth) results in a different pattern of structural development in the hypothalamus than occurs in the absence of testosterone. If testosterone is present, characteristics of the male hypothalamus develop; if testosterone is absent, characteristics of the female hypothalamus develop. In addition, early exposure to testosterone influences how receptive cells in the hypothalamus will be to particular sex steroids later in life. Early testosterone leads to greater binding capacity for testosterone while a lack of such exposure leads to a greater cellular affinity for estrogen. Thus, early hormonal effects on brain organization affect future sensitivity of the organism to circulating concentrations of specific steroids.

Interestingly, although testosterone is the determining hormone in these organizational effects in the rodent brain, it has its effects via conversion, or aromatization, to estrogen. Why then does estrogen itself not have direct effects on early brain formation? Early in fetal development, a chemical present in the blood (α-fetoprotein) binds estrogen unless estrogen is present in abnormally high amounts. Thus, estrogen typically is inactivated in the fetal circulatory system, and is unavailable for use at the cell level. On the other hand, testosterone is not bound, and is free to enter cells. It is only once the testosterone has entered the cell that it is converted into estrogen, which subsequently can influence structural development.

The differences in brain organization provoked by testosterone underlie further physical differences between male and female rat. The area of the hypothalamus that differs between the sexes controls ovulatory cycling of hormones at puberty, so that with the female pattern of hypothalamic development, cyclic patterns ensue, and with the male pattern of hypothalamic organization there is no cyclic pattern. We know that the same part of the hypothalamus controls cyclic hormone activity in humans. Although they are more difficult to demonstrate, differences in behaviors between the sexes in nonhuman animals may also be related to the differential brain development. For example, experimental manipulations of hormones in studies with a variety of animals (rats, monkeys, dogs) have demonstrated that early exposure to testosterone can influence a variety of behaviors, including rough and tumble play, aggressive behavior, and type of sexual activity. Among humans, "experiments of nature" suggest that early hormones may have similar organizational influences. Evidence for influences on specific behaviors will be discussed further at a later point in this review.

Hormones other than the sex steroids can modify brain growth if present in deficient or excessive quantities prenatally, but these are less commonly considered in the context of hormonal influences on development of normal brain and human behavior. We will not cover these hormonal influences in detail, but simply note that organizational influences of other hormones (i.e., thyroid hormones, adrenal glucocorticoids) on behavior may occur.

In sum, organizational effects of hormones imply structural changes that are relatively permanent, that happen early in development, and that have an impact on behavior. As originally conceptualized, there was also believed to be a critical period involved for organizational effects: the presence or absence of testosterone during a certain (early) period of development influences structural changes that are in large part irreversible once established.

B. Activational Effects

Hormones are released in varying quantities and patterns throughout an individual's lifetime. Activational effects of hormones are those that result from alterations in contemporaneous peripheral or central processes, and that are either immediate or slightly delayed in time following hormone release or change. As mentioned earlier, organizational effects (e.g., hormonal effects on neural receptivity to testosterone or estrogen) can influence the later activational impact of specific steroids. Activational effects may occur through (a) contemporaneous alterations of discrete bodily structures, which subsequently influence the ability to act or behave in certain ways; (b) alteration of activity to peripheral sensory systems (e.g., taste, touch, vision); (c) changes in autonomic systems controlling bodily metabolism and excitability; and (d) action on the central nervous system, which has receptors for the various steroid hormones throughout. In contrast to organizational effects, activational effects are characterized as occurring throughout life in a periodic and temporary manner. In general, they refer to hormonal activation of already-existing neural structures, rather than the creation of long-term or permanent structural changes.

C. A Critique of the Dichotomy

This relatively clean dichotomy between organizational and activational effects of hormones has been called into question. Arthur Arnold and Marc Breedlove reviewed evidence inconsistent with several of the assumptions concerning the different kinds of effects. For example, there appear to be some hormonal effects on bodily structures that are relatively long-term, but that have no critical period for their occurrence (e.g., seasonal fluctuations in the size of the brain in birds). In addition, it appears possible for hormones to cause permanent changes in the adult brain. These authors also point out that the major modes of action of steroid hormones on neural structure (e.g., influencing number of neurons in particular brain regions, dendritic growth, size and form of neurons, biochemical processes, and steroid binding and accumulation) all appear to occur both perinatally and at later points in life. Given the lack of clear qualitative differences in mechanisms and types of effect, these experts suggest that it would be more productive to move away from a categorical conceptualization of hormone activity to a conceptualization based on a continuum of hormone-effect duration. In other words, there may be many varying types of hormone effects—ranging from short term to long term—that involve a variety of potential mechanisms—ranging from temporary activation (or inhibition) of existing neural structures to permanent neuronal change. A shift in thinking of this type would open up the study of hormone–behavior relations to consideration of a broader range of ways in which hormones may influence behavior.

II. CONCEPTUALIZATIONS OF CONCURRENT HORMONE–BEHAVIOR RELATIONS

Often when we think of hormonal effects on emotions and behavior, we think in linear terms: we expect certain levels of hormones to be linked rather directly with certain levels of an emotion or behavior. Certainly much of the empirical work has been driven by such a linear model (e.g., are higher levels of testosterone linked with higher levels of aggression? are lower levels of estrogen linked with higher levels of depression?). The research on hormonal influences on behavior, however, has revealed several possible alternative conceptualizations of hormone activity. The revelations have in many cases been "accidental" in that investigators, in the process of searching for linear relations, found that any linear relations were modified by other factors. Other evidence for nonlinear relations has been discovered by specific plan and intent.

What are some of the factors that need to be accounted for in a consideration of hormones and behavior? First, it is quite possible that there are individual differences in sensitivity to hormones at the cell level. Sensitivity to hormones may depend, for instance, on previous hormone exposure, both perinatally and at later periods of development; on age or developmental stage; or perhaps on environmental variables that can influence neuronal receptivity (e.g., nutritional state, arousal). Second, personality or contextual variables may influence how the hormonal effect at the cell level will be translated into behavior. Two individuals who are equally sensitive to, and aroused by, testosterone, may differ in their response to that arousal depending on personality predispositions to, say, aggressive behavior, or depending on environmental restraints on such behavior. Third, the *regularity* of hormonal action may be important with regard to behavior. If hormones are in a state of fluctuation, especially if those fluctuations are irregular, irregular nervous functioning may result and have implications for moods and behavior. Finally, it is clear that environmental circumstances (e.g., aggressive provocation, light or dark) and individual states (e.g., nutrition, sleep) can influence hormonal activity. Sometimes contextual variables influence hormones in a way that stimulates behavior adaptive for that particular situation. In this way, context and physiology work together in an adaptive and integrative manner. In any case, there are reciprocal relations between hormones and emotions/behavior that must be taken into account. In the discussions of hormonal influences on specific behaviors that follow, we consider evidence for such alternative conceptualizations of hormone activity.

III. HORMONAL ASSOCIATIONS WITH SPECIFIC BEHAVIORS

As much as possible, evidence for hormonal effects on specific behaviors will be drawn from the study of humans. However, we draw upon animal research when necessary to provide a framework for theories and evidence regarding humans. Obviously, the fewer data available for humans, the more we emphasize animal data. In addition, because hormones can never be controlled and manipulated in humans in the way they can be with nonhuman animals, there are important insights that can be gained from work with animals. We assume throughout, however, that hormone–behavior relations in human beings are much more complicated phenomena than are hormonal–behavior relations in nonhuman animals. Psychological, social, and cultural factors impinging on any of these behaviors, interacting with and modifying influences, cannot be ignored.

A. Gender Identity

Gender identity refers to the sex with which one identifies. Unfortunately, we know very little about the extent to which gender identity is linked to hormonal versus social experiences. After all, the concept of "gender identity" is not relevant to nonhuman animals, and the kind of research needed to distinguish between possible influences is unethical among humans. Some data relevant to biological and social influences on gender identity have been garnered from individuals who experience prenatal hormone environments that are atypical for their genetic sex, either because of abnormal levels of androgen exposure or because of individual insensitivity to androgens that might be present. Sometimes the prenatal hormonal environment is so atypical that a person develops genitalia for the opposite sex, or genitalia intermediate between male and female. Such individuals are called pseudohermaphrodites, and usually are reared as whatever sex their genitals most closely resemble. Thus, genetic males may be reared as females, and vice versa. In general, data collected on such individuals suggest that pseudohermaphrodites typically are satisfied with the gender they have been assigned, although their behavior may be more likely to deviate from traditional sex roles (e.g., females are more likely to be "tomboyish" and to hope for a career rather than motherhood) than the behavior of same-sex individuals whose assigned gender matches their chromosomal sex. Unfortunately, it is unclear whether the satisfaction with gender identity indicates the importance of socialization or of early differences in brain organization (which are likely to be consistent with the gender label assigned). In addition, the more frequent "nontraditional" behaviors might result directly from brain functioning, indirectly from effects of the prenatal hormones on other characteristics (e.g., physical build; energetic or aggressive play), or from differential socialization based on people's conscious or unconscious knowledge that the individual may in fact be a member of the opposite sex. [*See* SEX ROLES.]

Evidence from an unusual group of men living in the Dominican Republic has been cited as supporting the importance of testosterone in determining gender identity. These men experienced normal levels of testosterone at birth and throughout their lives, but had a genetic abnormality that prevented development of the penis. Thus, these men were reared as females. At puberty, elevated testosterone provoked penile growth, and the individuals were then considered male. Most of these men switched their gender identity without problem. This may indicate that testosterone is more important than early rearing in the eventual development of gender identity; it may, however, indicate that socialization during puberty is as or more important than early socialization. Obviously, our knowledge of hormonal versus social contributors to gender identity is quite limited.

B. Sexual Orientation

Whereas gender identity refers to the sex with which one identifies, sexual orientation has to do with the sex to which one is sexually attracted. Is sexual orientation dependent on hormone activity, either in an organizational or activational sense? We know that the normal hormonal events of fetal development lead to sex-differentiated genital structure, and potentially to differences in areas of the brain that are linked with sexual activity. Theoretically, alternative sexual orientations could result from different hormonal influences on the developing brain. What do we know about the importance of the prenatal hormone environment, the concurrent hormone environment, and social factors in development of sexual orientation? [*See* SEXUAL ORIENTATION.]

Evidence from animal studies has often been garnered as support for a biological model of sexuality. For example, female rats and monkeys treated with testosterone early in development are more likely, as adults, to attempt to copulate with other females than are females without early testosterone exposure. Male rats not exposed to testosterone after birth are more likely to copulate with other males as adults.

In another important set of animal experiments, male rats whose mothers were subjected to stressful conditions during late pregnancy did not demonstrate typical sexual behavior with females, and assumed the female sexual position (lordosis) when approached by other males. Stress-induced alterations in the hormonal environment in the final trimester of pregnancy—that interfered with normal testosterone production—are hypothesized to account for these atypical sexual behaviors, via changes in neural structures. Interestingly, however, the male rats' sexual tendencies were also influenced by the environment in which they were reared: if they were reared in isolation, the female-like sexual tendencies were much more pronounced than if they were reared together with other heterosexual male rats and female rats.

Studies linking prenatal hormone exposure to sexual orientation in humans are, of course, more difficult to come by, and the studies that do exist have strong methodological limitations. Studies of pseudohermaphrodites described earlier are inconsistent in their conclusions about sexual orientation (i.e., some studies suggest higher rates of homosexuality among females exposed to high levels of prenatal androgens while some do not), and are limited by the fact that differences in sexual orientation may have resulted from differences in physical build or socialization of girls born with partially masculinized genitalia rather than from different brain structures. A study of women whose mothers took a synthetic estrogen (diethylstilbestrol, or DES) to prevent miscarriage found a slightly higher rate of homosexual or bisexual orientation among the women exposed to the estrogen (which mimics the effects of androgens in the womb) when compared to unexposed women. Of course, this represents only one study, with a relatively small sample size, but it has a strength in that the women exposed to DES, unlike the pseudohermaphrodites, were not born with masculinized genitalia. Thus, it is less likely that these women were subtly treated like males, or that they somehow perceived themselves as more like males anatomically.

With regard to possible organizational effects on sexual orientation, a recent study based on human autopsies found that one portion of the hypothalamus was half as large in homosexual men as it was in heterosexual men; in fact, the size of the brain area of interest was about the same in homosexual men as it was in heterosexual women. This research is certainly provocative, because it may reflect different organization of the hypothalamus in response to different prenatal hormonal environments. This inference, of course, is speculative—simply demonstrating that the size difference exists does not tell us what caused the difference. In fact, it is possible that differences in sexual orientations or sexual experiences led to differences in brain structure, rather than vice versa.

Studies linking concurrent levels of hormones to sexual orientation have been even less successful in demonstrating a link between the two. For example, testosterone levels do not appear to differ between homosexual and heterosexual men or women. One study suggested that homosexual and heterosexual men differ in their hypothalamic response to estrogen. In this study, the release of luteinizing hormone in response to circulating estrogen in homosexual men was intermediate between that of heterosexual men and that of women. The findings of this study were unclear in several respects, however, including whether the hormonal differences resulted from homosexuality or contributed to it. More importantly, attempts to replicate the results have not succeeded. Currently, then, there is no solid evidence that concurrent circulating levels of hormones are related to sexual orientation.

In sum, animal studies suggest that early hormonal influences on brain organization may be linked to later sexual orientation. The mechanism for prenatal hormones to influence later orientation is theoretically plausible for humans as well, although we do not know how influential such hormonal events are in relation to environmental conditions. Certainly, if rearing conditions of *rats* can alter the effect that hormonal conditions will have on sexual orientation, the rearing conditions of humans—together with humans' capacity to interpret and reflect on their own experiences—has the potential to even more powerfully modify the influence of hormones.

C. Sexual Behavior

In rats, sexual behavior is completely hormone-dependent. Without proper levels of estrogen (for females) or testosterone (for males) sexual behavior does not occur. In fact, the female rodent is not *able* to engage in coitus without estrogenic stimulation. It is anatomically impossible for the male rodent to display intromission unless the female exhibits the sexual posture, and this occurs only at the height of the estrous cycle, when estrogens are at their highest level. The link between hormones and sexual behavior is present but less powerful among nonhuman primates; sexual behavior is facilitated by hormones, but can occur in their absence. Among humans, the link between hormones and sexual behavior is even weaker and more complex.

It is necessary to distinguish sexual ability and sexual desire from the outset. The two are not the same, and it is becoming clear that hormone activity affects these two aspects of sexuality differently. Sexual ability refers to the capacity to engage in sexual activity, particularly coitus, while sexual desire refers to the motivational component of sexual activity. Among lower animals, different mechanisms of action for the two types of effects have been delineated. Sexual motivation stems from central effects of testosterone on the brain, via aromatization to estradiol. Sexual performance is linked to peripheral effects of testosterone on the genitals, via transformation to dihydrotestosterone.

Present research indicates that androgens, especially testosterone, play a significant role in human sexual motivation. In part, this evidence comes from studies of aging men who report a decrease in sexual interest, accompanied by a decline in testosterone activity. In addition, young and middle-aged men with abnormally low sexual desire have been found to have significantly lower testosterone levels than men with normal sexual interest. However, low-sexual-desire men display normal penile erections throughout the night, suggesting that low testosterone levels do not necessarily affect sexual ability.

Unlike female rats, human females have the anatomical capability to engage in intercourse at any given time. Thus, the human female's sexual ability is not hormonally controlled. What about her sexual desire? Studies of the menstrual cycle have not documented consistent phase differences in sexual activity. There are indications, however, that birth control pill users have fewer cyclical fluctuations in sexual activity than do non-pill users. Hormone activity might, thus, have a small role in sexual interest.

Which of the cycling hormones might be important in sexual motivation of women? Evidence concerning estrogen and sexual behavior indicates that, while estrogens may not influence sexual motivation directly, they do have an indirect role by providing vaginal lubrication, which serves to make intercourse less painful. Other studies suggest that testosterone serves to enhance sexual motivation in women as well as men, and that the enhancing effects in women occur at levels of testosterone that would impair the sexual motivation of men. This evidence suggests that women are sensitive to much lower levels of testosterone than are men, a paradoxical finding given the fact that lack of perinatal testosterone exposure is linked to *decreased* neuronal sensitivity to testosterone in rodents. The explanation for the paradox may center around the fact that adult females are accustomed to much lower levels of testosterone than are men, and that relative increases may be more important than absolute levels of hormones in influencing behavior. We will return to the potential importance of an individual's typical levels of hormones again when we discuss the role of estrogens in depression.

Does demonstration of a relation between hormones and sexual motivation necessarily indicate that hormones *cause* sexual interest? The answer to this question is still controversial. Most researchers assume that hormone levels influence behavior, but it is possible that behavior also influences hormone levels. At least one study examined changes in hormone–sexual behavior relations and the results strongly suggest that testosterone levels increase *as a result of* sexual stimulation. In fact, the influence of behavior on hormones presents another possible explanation for the finding that sexual behavior and testosterone are linked at such low levels (in absolute terms) of testosterone among women. Perhaps sexual activity in these women leads to high levels of testosterone compared to other women, levels that are still low compared to those in men. Given the present state of our knowledge, it is necessary to be cautious in drawing inferences about direction of influence.

Behavioral and environmental factors, in addition to influencing hormone activity in and of itself, may modulate the influence of hormones on sexual behavior. For instance, when rhesus monkeys are housed in male–female dyads, sexual activity occurs throughout the female's cycle with no evidence of a peak at any point. However, when housed in larger groups with at least one male present, sexual activity for females is strongly predicted by estradiol–progesterone cycles. Studies of adolescent humans suggest that social control (as measured by parental attitudes, church attendance, and family structure) plays a significant role in the link between hormones and behavior. For example, in one study, testosterone was more strongly related to sexual activity among girls who did not have a father living in the home than among girls whose father did live in the home. For boys, the relation between testosterone and sexual activity was more strongly influenced by degree of parental permissiveness, such that the more permissive the parents, the stronger the relation between testosterone and sexuality.

In sum, human sexual behavior appears to be linked to hormone levels, especially testosterone, although there are many factors that affect the relation. Evidence that females may be more sensitive than males to androgenic effects—perhaps because females are more accustomed to lower levels of testosterone—implies that there are individual differences in sensitivity to hormones that moderate behavioral effects. The effects of experience or context on both hormone activity and sexual behavior, and the link between the two, also cannot be discounted.

D. Aggression

Many lines of evidence point to a role for hormones in aggressive behavior, specifically, a link between higher concentrations of testosterone and a greater likelihood of aggressive behavior. First, in humans and nonhuman primates, males typically demonstrate more aggressive behavior than do females. Among humans, of course, it would be virtually impossible to rule out the important role of socialization in creating this sex difference. Even though the differences in aggressive behavior occur early in development, so do sex-differentiated expectations for behavior and other patterns of socialization. There is evidence, however, from those individuals who have experienced unusual hormonal environments perinatally that testosterone may influence the sex difference in aggression. Genetic females who are exposed to androgens prenatally show more physically active and aggressive play than do other females. Although less well studied, it also appears that genetic males who are not exposed to typical concentrations of androgens perinatally are less active and aggressive in their play than are other males. The limitations of these data have been noted previously, and apply here as well. For example, the "hormonal effects" may be mediated by different body types or different socialization experiences between the androgenized and nonandrogenized groups. [*See* AGGRESSION.]

In another line of work, Lee Ellis has detailed specific sex differences in brain organization and functioning that appear to be related both to early hormone exposure and to criminally aggressive behavior. These are: (1) Different levels of arousal of the reticular activating system. Low levels of arousal are related to lowered sensitivity to pain and lowered responsiveness to ordinary events and conditions, thereby raising the likelihood that an individual will seek out higher than usual levels of sensory input. (2) Different seizure thresholds in the limbic system. Lower thresholds mean more acute responses to stressful events in the environment. (3) Different centers of cortical functioning. When the center for logical thought processes is shifted toward the right hemisphere, which is more closely associated with the limbic system functions responsible for negative emotions (e.g., anger, distrust) than is the left hemisphere, logical thought may be more likely to become entangled with aggressive emotions. Thus, there are a variety of ways in which early hormones might influence later aggressive behavior; the actual importance of these mechanisms in explaining aggressive criminal behavior is not clear.

With a few exceptions, studies of nonhuman animals and humans also show concurrent relations between aggression and circulating androgens, especially testosterone. The relation appears stronger and more consistent among males than females, perhaps indicating a dependence of activational effects on prior organization of the brain, or the effects of differential socialization on hormone–behavior relations. Associations between testosterone and aggression or violence are also more consistent among criminal populations, and this has been documented in both adolescent and adult populations. If an individual is predisposed toward aggressive or antisocial behavior (e.g., temperamentally or due to a provoking environment), levels of testosterone may play a role in determining the degree of that aggression, whereas any influence of testosterone on aggressive behavior within a normal range may be overriden by more powerful personality or social influences. Further support for such an interactional model comes from studies that demonstrate a link between testosterone and moods or behaviors that might, in turn, be linked to aggression: energy level, irritability, tolerance for frustration, sensation-seeking behavior. Depending on how such personality characteristics or emotions are channeled, testosterone may or may not also lead to aggressive behavior. The relation between testosterone and aggressive behavior in humans also appears to be stronger when behavioral or observational measures are used to measure aggression, rather than pencil-and-paper tests, especially among females.

Even among animals, the environment or context moderates testosterone–aggression links. For example, among monkeys, dominant males have higher levels of testosterone than subordinates, and also display more aggressive behavior. However, aggression will not be displayed against prepubertal monkeys, and often only against postpubertal subordinate males if those males attempt to mate. Increasing testosterone in subordinate males does not increase their aggression. It should not be surprising, then, that contextual influences operate to influence hormone–aggression links in humans. Typically, testosterone explains a very small amount of the variance in aggressive behavior, another indication of the importance of additional independent or moderating influences on such behavior.

The context of an individual's own aggressive behavior can also influence levels of testosterone, as shown in nonhuman animals whose testosterone concentrations fall following defeat in an aggressive encounter. This appears to be adaptive in that the probability of further aggressive behavior is lowered in those situations where past aggressive behavior has not met with "success." Men who have been exposed to severe aggression (e.g., war) have lower testosterone levels than do men not exposed, indicating that a similar mechanism may operate in humans. Further data suggest that the mechanism may apply even to less overtly aggressive encounters—encounters that are simply competitive in nature. For example, testosterone concentrations in men are lower among losers than among winners after both physically and mentally taxing competitive situations (e.g., tennis matches, chess games).

We pointed out that testosterone was a less potent motivator of aggression in females than in males. There are a variety of possible explanations for the sex difference, including greater social prohibitions for aggression, less willingness to report aggression, or lower sensitivity to testosterone among women. Is it possible that a different hormone—estrogen—is related to aggressive behavior in women? In studies of the menstrual cycle, the low concentrations of estrogen and progesterone that occur premenstrually have been linked with emotional states (e.g., irritability, instability of mood) that could be related to aggression under certain circumstances. Some studies have purportedly shown an increased frequency of criminal behavior by women during the premenstrual phase; such studies, however, are generally unsound methodologically. In general, research on the menstrual cycle suffers from several problems, among them the fact that studies rarely collect direct measures of hormones, there is inconsistency in definition of cycle phases, and control groups are often not used. Thus, we really know very little about the contribution of estrogen and/or progesterone to aggressive behavior; in fact there are some studies indicating a link between aggression and high, rather than low, levels of estrogen. [*See* PREMENSTRUAL SYNDROME.]

E. Depression and Mood

Research has demonstrated that estrogen and progesterone are associated with thresholds of brain excitation and levels of physical activity among nonhuman animals. In general, estrogen is linked to lower thresholds of excitation and higher levels of activity, and progesterone to higher thresholds and lower activity. It is possible, then, that estrogen and progesterone influence affective experience through their effects on both central and autonomic nervous system responsiveness. Much of the evidence for the role of hormones (particularly estrogen and progesterone) in mood states and disorders (within a normal range) among humans has been gleaned from studies of the menstrual cycle, pregnancy and childbirth, or menopause. These events are difficult to study, especially given the obvious and powerful social expectations and implications associated with each. Nonetheless, there is a fair amount of consistency in the literature linking hormones and mood, including studies that are more methodologically sound, and studies that examine the role of hormones outside of the context of these highly socially defined events or transitions.

The evidence suggests that moderate concentrations of estrogen may be associated with positive moods, and lack of estrogen with negative mood or depression. Progesterone, not surprisingly given its antagonistic influence on brain excitation, may modify these estrogenic effects. For example, a study of postmenopausal women with low estrogen who were suffering from depression and/or anxiety, and who received treatments of estrogen and progesterone, demonstrated associations between different combinations of estrogen and progesterone and specific mood states. After treatment, moderate concentrations of estradiol were linked to positive mood with no unpleasant symptoms. Low concentrations of estradiol were linked to high depression and anxiety, but low aggression; progesterone administered to women with low estradiol resulted in lowered anxiety but not lowered depression. Excessively high post-treatment estradiol was linked to high aggression and anxiety, although progesterone had the effect of decreasing both aggression and anxiety among these particular women. This particular study had some methodological weaknesses, but many strengths, and indicates that estrogen and progesterone work together to influence mood. [*See* Depression.]

Other research with nondepressed, psychiatrically and physically healthy postmenopausal women confirms findings that estrogen within a normal physiological range can enhance mood, and suggests that testosterone may do the same. In addition, some studies have linked higher testosterone to better mood among males. The mechanisms by which testosterone enhances mood are not clear, however, and may include aromatization to estrogen.

Effects of estrogen on moods may vary depending on age or developmental stage. In line with findings that moderate concentrations of estrogen have positive effects on mood but that excesses of the hormone can have negative influences, there is evidence that when estrogen begins to rise among adolescent girls, its effects are negative. Because early-adolescent girls are accustomed to low levels of estrogen, initial estrogen increases, even if low in absolute terms, may be experienced in the body as relatively high. The studies suggest that during the phases of most rapid estrogen rise, estrogen is linked to more depressive affect. These findings, along with those concerning testosterone and female sexual behavior, indicate that emotional and behavioral effects of hormones may depend in part on relative, rather than absolute, concentrations of the hormone.

Some studies of the menstrual cycle have linked cyclicity, or irregularities in cyclicity, of hormone activity to negative mood and behavioral symptoms. Factors such as unusual timing of hormonal peaks and declines, unusually high or low concentrations of estrogen or progesterone at particular points in the cycle, or difficulty predicting when different phases of the menstrual cycle would occur have been linked, for instance, to symptoms of negative mood. In other studies, treatment to reduce or stop cyclic hormone activity while maintaining steroid concentrations within a normal range eliminated negative mood symptoms associated with premenstrual symptoms. The implication of such findings is that cycling and/or irregularity of hormone activity may lead to instability of nervous functioning, which has negative implications for mood. There findings are intriguing, but need more theoretical development (i.e., to explain the mechanism of effect) and empirical replication. The fact that some women with apparently normal hormone cycles experience no negative mood and behavioral symptoms while others with equally "normal" cycles can experience extreme problems and fluctuations in mood suggests that the regularity of cycling is not the whole story. Differences in physiological sensitivity to hormones, as well as personality and environmental factors, are undoubtedly important in explaining the hormone–mood associations.

As with sexual behavior and aggression, environmental, social, and cultural factors certainly represent powerful influences on moods, and events that provoke negative moods have the capacity to influence hormonal states as well. Once again, hormones (in this case, estrogen and progesterone) probably play a small but sometimes significant role in moods and affect, a role that should not be seen as linear or unmodifiable, but that is most likely limited and directed by a host of nonhormonal variables.

F. Maternal Behavior (Nurturance)

The fact that there are huge hormonal changes that accompany pregnancy and childbirth raises questions about the role of hormones in the creation and establishing of maternal behavior, or nurturance and caring of the young. A great deal of research exists concerning hormones and the maternal behavior of rats. This research indicates that hormones of pregnancy (estrogen in particular) facilitate the establishment of care-taking behavior, but that they are not *necessary* for such behavior to be established, and they are not related to the maintenance of such behavior once established. It appears that hormones facilitate maternal behavior immediately after birth, perhaps in part by changing olfactory thresholds in a way that makes rats less timid about approaching infants. Willingness to approach infants obviously increases the probability of nurturant behavior toward those infants. As we have seen with other behaviors, experience can interact with hormones in affecting care-taking behavior. For example, the highest levels of care-taking behavior are found among rats who are both experienced (they have cared for infant rats in the past) and hormonally primed.

There is also evidence that the nurturant behavior of other nonhuman animals, including some primates, is influenced by hormones. If the data from animals have any relevance to humans, it is possible that the hormonal events of late pregnancy and early childbirth serve to heighten maternal receptiveness to the infant, perhaps through changes in sensation, but perhaps through changes in affective states as well. Unfortunately, with humans it is virtually impossible to separate the tremendous social and psychological influences on moods and behavior from their potential biological roots. What, then, are the data that provide evidence of hormonal influence on human maternal behavior?

The observation that parent's responses to infants immediately following childbirth are remarkably similar across the world suggests potential biological roots for that behavior. Other data come from studies that have compared physiological reactions to infants between nonpregnant women, pregnant women, and new mothers. These data suggest that during pregnancy there is an increased likelihood of anxious (heart acceleration) versus attentive (heart deceleration) responses to infant cries. Because hormones were not measured, however, it is also possible that psychological factors affecting the salience of infants are at the root of the differential experience.

Further evidence from humans concerns the role of cortisol in maternal behavior. Higher concentrations of cortisol, a hormone of the adrenal system, heighten general arousal, which, given certain environmental conditions (e.g., a positive attitude toward parenting on the part of the mother; a vocal infant) increases maternal approaches toward the infant. In general, however, evidence for direct hormonal influence on maternal moods and behavior is weak. Studies of hormones and postpartum moods have failed to reveal any strong or consistent differences between the hormonal states of individuals who, for instance, experience postpartum depression and those who do not. In all likelihood, concurrent biological influences on nurturant behavior in humans are small and much less important than one's prior experience with parenting and expectations for parenting.

Is there any evidence for organizational hormone influences on maternal behavior? Might differential brain organization that results from early hormone exposure account for sex differences in nurturant behavior? Studies indicate that doll-play during childhood and interest in infants during adulthood is lower among females who were exposed to androgens prenatally than among females who were not exposed to androgens. It is difficult to know whether such differences should be attributed to differences in brain organization, differences in treatment by others (girls exposed to androgens may look more masculine, or parents may detect even subtle differences in genitalia that influence their parenting), different expectations about the likelihood that one will become a mother (girls exposed to androgens are often sterile), or differences in other dispositional attributes linked to nurturance (these girls may have higher energy levels that predispose them to outdoor, active, play rather than indoor, quiet, doll-play). In sum, maternal behavior is a complex phenomenon determined by a multitude of factors, one of which may be hormonal experiences that increase one's predilection toward infants. The current research, however, indicates that hormonal influences are probably not large, and that they are likely limited in time (i.e., strongest immediately following birth).

G. Stress and Coping

The term "stress" implies some generally unwelcome (e.g., uncertain, unpleasant) physical or emotional event or set of circumstances that, in turn, is associated with increased physiological arousal. In fact, the experience of stress has sometimes been *equated* with activation of the adrenal system, including release of adrenaline, noradrenaline, and cortisol. "Coping," on the other hand, implies attempts to adapt to the stressful situation, with successful coping reflected in a reduction of the physiologically excited state. [*See* COPING; STRESS.]

Cortisol, in particular, appears to play a central role in adaptive responses to stressful situations. Megan Gunnar identifies the central functions of cortisol in response to stress as follows: stimulation of glucose metabolism, increasing energy available to the body; alterations of brain processes that are involved with learning, memory, and emotion; and suppression of other bodily immune systems so that they do not "overreact" as a result of the stimulation. The importance of cortisol in successful coping is illustrated by the observation that animals who have impaired pituitary–adrenal functioning will not survive outside of a highly protected environment. Given these physiological effects, it also becomes evident why chronically high stress is often associated with physical illness. In a well-functioning adrenal system, not only is cortisol elevated in response to stress, but it quickly drops off after the initial stressful incident, except, perhaps, when the stress is extremely traumatic. [*See* STRESS AND ILLNESS.]

The question of specific behavioral responses linked with cortisol elevation is complex and not fully understood. Individual differences in hormonal responses to stress have been documented in nonhuman primates, as well as in humans. In addition, it appears as though individuals show behavioral adaptation in different ways (e.g., withdrawal, quietness, active display of distress, active problem-solving) depending on the type of stressor experienced (e.g., novel, painful, involving loss of control) and individual temperament. Different behavioral responses may result in part from different hormonal responses, but there is also evidence for individual differences in behavioral response to similar hormonal activation. Further, there is evidence that genetic factors (e.g., temperament) and early social experiences *lead to* different adrenal responses in situations of stress. For example, cortisol elevations in response to the stress of an impending exam differ for males and females (with females typically having a weaker cortisol response) and depending on an individual's self-reported method of coping (with rumination associated with a more extreme cortisol response than active coping). Among nonhuman primates, physiological and behavioral responses to stress vary depending on whether the primates were raised with their mothers or with peers (and not mother), with more acute stress responses among the peer-reared monkeys. Even when average group differences are documented, however, large individual differences have been found within groups.

Thus, although the link between cortisol or other stress hormones and specific behaviors is not completely clear, it *is* clear that these hormones play an important role in helping the body to marshal both physical and mental resources to react quickly and intelligently to difficult situations. Individual differences in successful coping may be linked to individual differences in physiological activation, as well as to differences in behavioral responses to similar physiological activation.

IV. SUMMARY

This review provides evidence for hormonal influences on a wide variety of human behaviors. Without question, the physiological mechanisms are in place for such influence to occur. The human brain develops in response to a particular hormonal environment, and differences in brain development certainly have the potential to influence later behavior. In addition, hormones affect many bodily processes (e.g., arousal, metabolism) that may, in turn, have behavioral implications. Human beings are, undoubtedly, biological creatures.

The fact that we are biological creatures does not, however, negate the fact that we are also social creatures. For each of the behaviors reviewed, we have pointed to evidence that any effects of hormones on that behavior are influenced by aspects of the context and of the individual. In addition, it is possible for a person's behavior, or the environmental context, to influence hormonal activity itself. The historical emphasis on searching for hormonal effects on behavior has most likely limited the discovery of instances where behavior influences hormones, yet recent evidence strongly supports the latter causal direction. And as we have noted, a typical weakness of studies currently available has to do with the inability to infer a causal direction.

It is of note that this evidence for contextual influences, and effects of behavior on hormones, is not limited to humans. Even in nonhuman animals, hormonal influences on behavior are modulated by circumstances (e.g., living conditions) and individual characteristics (e.g., status). Even in nonhuman animals, behavior (e.g., aggression followed by defeat) can influence hormones. Certainly, if hormone levels, and the effects of hormones on the behavior of nonhuman animals, can be altered by such factors, the role of hormones in human behavior is even more complex. We have pointed to intriguing research documenting some of these complexities.

Although we have not explicitly discussed the difficulties in carrying out research on hormones and behavior, some of these difficulties should be obvious from the discussion of the research available. The reality that hormones can influence behavior, that behavior can influence hormones, and that both kinds of influences can depend on a myriad of other factors make it extremely difficult to pin down just what cause-and-effect relations exist and are important in explaining human behavior. Of course, this complexity exists in its most extreme form among humans, where we cannot ethically manipulate hormones, and where the number of influences on behavior is great.

In addition to the methodological challenges posed by these conceptual possibilities, there are many additional challenges to measuring both hormones and behavior accurately and meaningfully. For example, as we have noted, hormonal effects may depend on combinations of hormones, and not just on single hormones in isolation. In addition, there are many characteristics of hormone activity that have been explored very little, including frequency and amplitude of hormone release, rates of increase and decrease, and the regularity of hormone release. Measures of these characteristics are particularly difficult to obtain because they necessitate multiple measures over time, but they may be critical to an accurate understanding of hormone activity. Multiple and repeated measures of behavior may also be necessary to adequately characterize a person's behavior with regard to hormonal activity; once again, however, such a strategy requires extensive time, effort, and resources, and has not often been done, at least with humans.

Given the many conceptual and methodological complexities, it is somewhat amazing that there is as much consistency as there is in the findings we have reported. The field of hormone–behavior relations in humans is at an exciting but difficult place. Mechanisms to account for relations are known, and models of potential relations are available; the challenge lies in overcoming some of the daunting methodological difficulties in distinguishing among the potential models.

Bibliography

Arnold, A. P., and Breedlove, S. M. (1985). Organizational and activational effects of sex steroids on brain and behavior: A reanalysis. *Horm. Beh.* **19,** 469–498.

Beach, F. A. (1975). Behavioral endocrinology: An emerging discipline. *Am. Sci.* **63,** 178–187.

Buchanan, C. M., Eccles, J. S., and Becker, J. B. (1992). Are adolescents the victims of raging hormones: Evidence for activational effects of hormones on moods and behavior at adolescence. *Psychol. Bull.* **111,** 62–107.

Ellis, L. (1989). Evolutionary and neurochemical causes of sex differences in victimizing behavior: Toward a unified theory of criminal behavior and social stratification. *Soc. Sci. Information* **28,** 605–636.

Erhardt, A. A. (1984). Gender differences: A biosocial perspective. *Nebraska Symp. Motivation* **32,** 37–57.

Fleming, A. S., and Corter, C. (1988). Factors influencing maternal responsiveness in humans: Usefulness of an animal model. *Psychoneuroendocrinology* **13,** 189–212.

Gunnar, M. R. (1989). Studies of the human infant's adrenocortical response to potentially stressful events. *New Directions Child Dev.* **45,** 3–18.

Hofer, M. A. (1981). "The Roots of Human Behavior: An Introduction to the Psychobiology of Early Development." Freeman, San Francisco.

Kalat, J. W. (1992). "Biological Psychology," 4th ed. Wadsworth, Belmont, CA.

Sherwin, B. B. (1988). A comparative analysis of the role of androgen in human male and female sexual behavior: Behavioral specificity, critical thresholds, and sensitivity. *Psychobiology* **16,** 416–425.

HYPNOSIS

Steven Jay Lynn
Ohio University

Judith W. Rhue
Ohio University College of Osteopathic Medicine

Nicholas P. Spanos
Carleton University, Canada

Glossary

Hypnotherapy Addition of hypnotic procedures to accepted psychological or medical treatment.

Hypnotizability or hypnotic susceptibility Observed or reported responsivity to suggestions following a hypnotic induction, as indexed by behavioral and subjective measures.

Indirect suggestion Compared to traditional authoritative suggestions, they generally contain more subtle, indirect, or implicit cues, are more permissive, ambiguous, and less obviously related to the response sought by the hypnotist.

Induction Verbal or nonverbal communications or procedures intended to induce a "hypnotic state" or increase subsequent responsivity to hypnotic suggestions.

Simulator Low hypnotizable subject instructed to fake the behavior and/or subjective reports of an excellent hypnotic subject. This is typically done in accordance with Orne's simulation paradigm in which the simulator is informed that the experiment will stop if the hypnotist sees through the deception.

THE TERM HYPNOSIS refers to a social influence situation in which a person designated as a hypnotist attempts to influence the experiences and behaviors of a subject or patient. The suggestions administered in the hypnotic situation typically call for changes in sensation, perception, affect, cognition, and control over behavior or psychophysiological processes. It is useful to think of these suggestions as divided into two phases, induction and application, although in practice these may not be entirely distinct.

I. INTRODUCTION

Historically, a wide variety of induction procedures have been used. These include waving hands over patients and having them ingest substances. Many of these methods are rarely if ever used now. Procedures that are currently in vogue involve asking subjects to close their eyes and telling them to sleep, instructing them to relax, having them fix their gaze on an object or their attention on an idea, suggesting various images or automatic movements, confusing them with indecipherable verbal communications, telling them stories, and so on.

Most inductions include suggestions for deep relaxation. However, inductions stressing physical tension and alertness are as effective as relaxation inductions in enhancing suggestibility. Many people are more responsive to direct and indirect suggestion after an induction than they were before; the nature of the induction appears to have little bearing on hypnotizability.

A hypnotic induction is not, in itself, a treatment for psychological disorders. After the induction, a wide variety of applications have been used in hypnotherapy, which often involves a blending of ideas and techniques from different theoretical perspectives. Although one can speak of psychodynamic hypnotherapy, cognitive–behavioral hypnotherapy, and so forth, most clinical applications can be referred to as "eclectic hypnotherapy." Often, per-

Encyclopedia of Human Behavior, Volume 2
Copyright © 1994 by Academic Press, Inc. All rights of reproduction in any form reserved.

haps in the majority of the cases in which hypnosis is used clinically, hypnotic procedures are framed in terms of self-hypnosis. Many clinicians inform clients that all hypnosis (even hetero-hypnosis) can be thought of in these terms insofar as clients are ultimately responsible for generating suggestion-relevant imagery, experiences, and behaviors. Self-hypnosis is most frequently taught by first introducing the client to hetero-hypnotic techniques and related experiences and then encouraging the client to assume increasingly greater responsibility for devising suggestions appropriate to achieving treatment goals. In self-administering therapeutic suggestions, the client replaces the therapist as the active agent in the therapeutic proceedings. Therapists often make customized tapes for clients to listen to at home or at work. This is done in order to minimize dependency on the therapist, generalize treatment gains, and encourage mastery of self-suggestions that can be implemented, in the absence of the tape and the hypnotist, in a variety of situations.

II. HISTORY OF HYPNOSIS

Since the beginning of recorded history procedures that today are labeled "suggestive" have been used to treat a wide range of physical disorders and psychological disturbances. For example, religious healing rituals such as "dream healing" in Ancient Greece and exorcism in Medieval Europe attest to the importance of psychological factors in easing discomfort and, at times, producing beneficial physiological changes.

In 17th and 18th centuries Western Europe religious explanations and treatments for physical and psychological disturbance were gradually replaced by naturalistic explanations and treatments. One of the best known 18th century naturalistic explanations was developed by a Viennese physician named Franz Anton Mesmer. Mesmer believed that the universe, including all living organisms, was permeated by an invisible fluid that he labeled animal magnetism. Supposedly sickness resulted from a disruption in the harmonious flow of this fluid through the body, and a cure was produced by transmitting magnetic fluid from the body of the healer to that of the patient.

The healer (i.e., magnetizer) transmitted his fluid to the patient by passing his hands close to the patient's body. During this process patients frequently experienced a range of unusual sensations and behavioral changes that ended in convulsions and in a diminution of symptoms. Mesmer moved his practice to Paris where he quickly became a sensation among the cultural elite, and where he developed ardent supporters as well as powerful enemies among the medical establishment.

Eventually, two Royal commissions investigated Mesmer's claims. With a series of clever experiments the commissioners demonstrated that the behavioral changes seen in magnetized patients did not result from the flow of an invisible fluid, but instead reflected the patients' expectations, beliefs, and imaginings. On the basis of the negative reports by the commissions, French physicians were banned from practicing magnetism. Despite the ban, magnetism flourished. It soon became associated with the occult as well as with healing and, in various forms, it was transported to countries throughout Europe and also to America.

In England, as in France, magnetism underwent oscillating periods of acceptance and rejection by the medical establishment. In the middle of the 19th century, a Scottish physician named James Braid witnessed a stage demonstration in which a subject was magnetized by staring at a shiny object. Braid rejected the fluid theory of magnetism and hypothesized instead that the behaviors of magnetized subjects resulted from neural inhibition that flowed backward from the eyes (strained by staring) to the brain and produced a condition akin to sleep. Braid labeled this phenomenon as neurohypnosis, and the shortened name "hypnosis" came gradually to replace the name magnetism.

As Braid gained more experience, he realized that the behavior of hypnotic subjects was greatly influenced by ideas and expectations transmitted to them by the hypnotist. He modified his earlier theory of neural inhibition and developed the notion of monoideism. Monoideism was based on the notion of ideo-motor action. According to this notion, vivid ideas or images that remain uncontradicted in the mind of a subject lead automatically to the corresponding action. Thus, if a person vividly imagines that her arm is light and rising in the air, and if this vivid imagining is not contradicted by other thoughts, then the vivid imagery will lead the arm to rise automatically.

Braid's early ideas about neurohypnosis strongly influenced the famous French neurologist Jean Martin Charcot. Unfortunately, Charcot was not influenced by Braid's later notion of monoideism or by his emphasis on how the hypnotist's expectations influence the subject's responses. Charcot studied patients who were diagnosed as hysterics, and came to believe that hypnosis, like hysteria, reflected a neurological weakness and that only hysterics could be hypnotized. According to Charcot there were three stages to hypnosis, and each stage was associated with invariable behavioral symptoms. Charcot's notion of an association between hypnosis and hysteria influenced his colleague Pierre Janet, who came to believe that both hysteria and hypnosis involved dissociations between sets or subsystems of ideas.

Braid's work also influenced Hippolyte Bernheim, a well-known French physician from Nancy. Bernheim's theory of hypnosis was also based on the notion of ideo-motor action. According to Bernheim hypnotic behavior resulted from suggestion. People differed in terms of suggestibility, and suggestions produced their effects by leading subjects to develop corresponding ideas that led via ideo-motor action to hypnotic behavior. Bernheim rejected Charcot's notions that hypnosis was related to hysteria, and that degrees of hypnosis were associated with invariant behavioral symptoms. Instead, Bernheim argued that Charcot inadvertently suggested to his hysterical patients those very behaviors that he came to erroneously believe resulted automatically from hypnosis.

Freud studied briefly with both Charcot and Bernheim. Nevertheless, he rejected the therapeutic use of hypnotic procedures. Freud's psychoanalysis became highly influential in both Europe and America and his rejection of hypnosis served to relegate it to the fringes of medicine and psychology for much of the first half of the 20th century, with notable exceptions including the work of Clark Hull and P. C. Young, whose systematic experimental studies constituted important contributions. Toward the beginning of World War II, R. White reviewed the available data concerning hypnosis and concluded that, because of their overly mechanistic nature, neither the theory of dissociation nor the theory of ideo-motor action could adequately explain hypnotic responding. White argued that hypnotic behavior was goal-directed social action, and that hypnotic subjects responded in terms of their ideas about what the hypnotist wished them to do. At the same time, however, White continued to believe that hypnotic behavior occurred during an altered state of consciousness that was characterized by subtle cognitive changes.

White's work ushered in the modern period of research on hypnosis. His ideas greatly influenced the work of T. R. Sarbin and T. X. Barber who, in the 1950s and 1960s, expanded on the notion of hypnosis as goal-directed social behavior and developed social psychological theories of hypnosis. White also influenced the work of M. T. Orne who, along with emphasizing the role of social factors in hypnosis, has attempted to delineate subtle cognitive changes unique to hypnotic responding. E. R. Hilgard questioned White's dismissal of dissociation as an account of hypnosis and has attempted to reformulate an acceptable dissociation theory of hypnotic responding. M. H. Erickson's writings and his creative use of indirect hypnotic suggestions generated a great deal of interest in a wide range of clinical applications of hypnosis.

The development of well-constructed, reliable standardized hypnotizability scales has done much to advance the scientific study of hypnosis. Early scales developed by Davis and Husband and by Sarbin and Friedlander in the 1930s were important precursors to the more psychometrically sophisticated tests devised by Ernest Hilgard and Andre Weitzenhoffer at Stanford University in the 1960s.

Since these pioneering efforts, many hypnotizability scales have been developed for different purposes and populations. These include brief tests for hypnotizability, and tests for assessing waking suggestibility, hypnotizability in a group context, and hypnotizability with child populations. Scales of hypnotic "depth" have also been developed, along with scales that tap the subjective aspect of hypnotic responsiveness. In general, hypnotizability tests are highly and positively correlated with one another.

As Hilgard has noted, a domain of hypnosis can be identified. The suggestions included in many hypnotizability scales are related to diverse phenomena within this domain. These suggestions involve motor behaviors (e.g., hand levitation), challenges to the subject (e.g., "try to lift that heavy hand, just try"), positive and negative hallucinations, dreams within hypnosis, and posthypnotic amnesia.

Subjects range on a continuum of hypnotizability according to how many suggestions they pass. For example, subjects who pass 3 or fewer suggestions on a 12-point scale are, conventionally, regarded as low hypnotizable (about 15–20% of the population), subjects who pass 4 to 8 suggestions are regarded as medium hypnotizable (about 60–70% of the population), and subjects who pass 9 to 12 suggestions (about 15–20% of the population) are regarded as high hypnotizable.

Hypnotizability is relatively stable. A study by Piccione, Hilgard, and Zimbardo using a 25-year follow-up of subjects first tested in college reported a .71 test–retest correlation. This stability has been variously described as a reflection of the trait-like aspects of hypnotizability versus a reflection of subjects' attitudes and beliefs about hypnosis, and interpretations of hypnotic suggestions that remain stable over time.

III. MISCONCEPTIONS AND HYPNOTIC "FEATS"

A. Misconceptions

The study of hypnosis has done a great deal to eradicate many misconceptions about hypnosis. These include the belief that hypnosis produces a sleep-like state; that hypnotized people lose control of themselves and that their willpower is compromised; that hypnosis involves a radically altered state of mind, and that one cannot "come out" of this state; that hypnotized people are unable to remember what occurred during hypnosis; and that only weak-willed people are able to be hypnotized.

We now know that hypnosis is not related to sleep, that it is something done by the subject rather than by the hypnotist, that subjects control their behavior and do not lose touch with their surroundings, that many people do not experience hypnosis as much different from waking consciousness, that spontaneous amnesia is very rare, and that responsive subjects are no more weak-willed than nonresponsive subjects.

B. Hypnotic "Feats"

Public education about hypnosis is important insofar as misconceptions (e.g., the Svengali-like power of the hypnotist) persist in the general population, partly as a result of the media's sensationalized depiction of hypnosis. Yet many of these misconceptions were promulgated by mesmerists and early hypnotists. Indeed, since the 19th century, mesmerism and later hypnosis have been associated with the idea of unusual and even supernatural capabilities. For instance, some 19th century investigators argued that magnetized (and later hypnotized) subjects could see without the use of their eyes, travel mentally to distant planets and report back accurately about the inhabitants, spot disease by seeing through the skin to the internal organs of sick individuals, and communicate with the dead.

Although most of these outlandish ideas are no longer taken seriously by scientific investigators, unusual claims for hypnosis continue to be made. For example, some investigators argue that the use of hypnotic procedures enables people to recall their earlier abduction by space aliens, and others argue that hypnotic regression to past lives supports the theory of reincarnation. There is no more scientific evidence to support notions like space alien abduction and reincarnated past lives than there was to support 19th century notions of mental space travel or seeing without the use of the eyes by magnetized somnambulists.

Many of the "feats" attributed to hypnotic subjects involved supposed changes in sensory functions. Supposedly, these subjects could be made much more sensitive or much less sensitive (i.e., hypnotic deafness and pain reduction) to sensory stimulation. Modern laboratory studies have found little support for the notion that hypnotic procedures can enhance sensory function. When testing procedures are used that enable actual enhancements in sensitivity to be distinguished from expectation-induced response biases dramatic increments in sensitivity are not found in hypnotic subjects. Some studies do indicate that small increases in perceptual sensitivity may occur following hypnotic induction. However, increments in sensitivity of equivalent magnitudes can also be obtained in motivated nonhypnotic subjects.

The role of hypnotic and nonhypnotic suggestion in reducing perceptual sensitivity remains controversial. Hypnotic and nonhypnotic subjects given suggestions for blindness, deafness, pain reduction, etc., sometimes report dramatic reductions in sensory activity. Typically, the magnitude of these reductions correlates with subjects' pretested levels of hypnotizability. Although some investigators interpret such findings to mean that hypnotic suggestions produce actual reductions in sensory and perceptual activity, there is little evidence to support this view. For instance, Sutcliffe and other investigators have shown that objective measures of perceptual functioning typically remain unchanged despite subjects' reports that they are unable to hear, see, or feel pain. In addition, recent studies indicate that subjects given hypnotic suggestions often bias their perceptual reports independently of any actual change in perceptual experience. Moreover, such reporting biases correlate with pretested hypnotizability. Although these findings do not necessarily mean that subjects are simply lying when they report perceptual changes, they do indicate that subjects' verbal reports should be treated cautiously, and that inferences about changes in perception should not be made on the basis of such reports alone.

Most of the experimental work on hypnotically induced sensory reductions has focused on suggested reductions in pain. In these experiments subjects are administered painful stimulation (e.g., limb immersion in ice water for 60 sec) before and again after some treatment (e.g., hypnotic suggestion, placebo). This work indicates that (a) suggestions for pain reduction given without a prior hypnotic induction procedure are as effective as the same suggestions preceded by an hypnotic induction at producing reports of decreased pain, (b) subjects' expectations concerning the extent to which they will reduce pain strongly influences the degree to which they report pain reductions, and (c) the relationship between hypnotizability and suggestion-induced reductions in reported pain is context dependent.

Context dependency has been demonstrated by showing that high hypnotizables reported greater reductions in reported pain than low hypnotizables only when subjects connected their prior hypnotizability testing with the situation in which pain reduction was tested. Low and high hypnotizables reported equivalent reductions in reported pain when the suggestions for pain reduction were given in a nonhypnotic context that did not create expectations of greater pain reduction for highs than for lows.

These findings are generally consistent with theories of hypnosis that emphasize social psychological and cognitive determinants of hypnotizability. Bowers and his colleagues (Davidson and Woody), however, contend that hypnotic analgesia may be quite unlike cognitive–behavioral pain control insofar as certain subjects do not report spontaneously using any deliberate cognitive strategies (e.g., engaging in counter-pain imagery) and that a number of studies indicate that highly hypnotizable subjects tend to show greater benefit from hypnotic analgesia than from a nonhypnotic cognitive–behavioral procedure. They maintain that these and other findings are consistent with the position that social psychological and cognitive determinants may be less influential than dissociative processes that involve the direct activation of an analgesic response by way of hypnotic suggestions.

Questions about the mechanisms of hypnotic pain control are important and are as yet not completely resolved. However, the available evidence (see Spanos, Liddy, and Ellis) fails to support the idea that hypnotic procedures enable people to surpass their nonhypnotic capacities or that hypnotic procedures provide an avenue for obtaining transcendent knowledge.

IV. HYPNOSIS AND ANTISOCIAL BEHAVIOR

Along with its public report the Royal Commission that investigated magnetism in 18th century Paris also sent a secret report to the King of France. The secret report warned that magnetism was potentially dangerous to the morals of the young women who frequently became the patients of the magnetizers. The commissioners noted how such women often seemed to be sexually attracted to their magnetizer and how an unscrupulous magnetizer could easily take advantage of them in their magnetized condition. The view that magnetized subjects somehow surrendered their will and became automata controlled by the magnetizer has persisted down to the present day, and has been a staple of fiction writing since the 19th century.

In the later 19th and early 20th century, numerous attempts were made to test the coercive power of hypnosis in the laboratory. In these experiments hypnotic subjects were given suggestions to carry out such mock crimes as stabbing the experimenter with a paper knife. Although the subjects frequently carried out the suggested "crimes," the ecological validity of these findings was suspect.

As pointed out by Orne and others, hypnotic subjects who are given the suggestion to carry out some anti-social or self-destructive action are well aware that they are participating in an experiment, and well aware that the norms of scientific experimentation in North American universities and hospitals preclude allowing subjects to hurt themselves or others. In other words, hypnotic subjects who commit criminal or anti-social acts in response to experimentally administered suggestions may do so only because they are implicitly or explicitly aware that they will not be allowed to really hurt themselves or anyone else.

Evans and Orne examined these ideas by comparing the responses of highly hypnotizable hypnotic subjects to low hypnotizable simulators. Subjects in both groups were given suggestions to carry out self-destructive behaviors such as reaching into a beaker of bubbling liquid that they were told was acid. Although a few of the hypnotic subjects carried out the suggestions, an equal number of the simulators did the same. The fact that simulators responded to these suggestions indicated that they had not been fooled into believing that the experiment was really dangerous. Evans and Orne concluded that the subjects in both groups who carried out the self-destructive behavior probably did so because they assumed (quite correctly) that the experimenter would not really allow them to hurt themselves.

Coe attempted to circumvent the fact that subjects feel protected in experiments by giving suggestions for anti-social behavior outside of an experimental context. Subjects who had been previously tested in Coe's hypnosis laboratory were approached outside of the laboratory by a confederate who asked them to sell what they were told was a packet of heroin. For half of the subjects the confederate first administered an hypnotic induction procedure, and for the remainder the request was made without an hypnotic induction. An equivalent number of hypnotic and nonhypnotic subjects sold the "heroin" as requested. Interestingly, whether or not subjects sold the "heroin" was predicted by their attitudes toward drugs. Those with strong anti-drug attitudes were less frequently induced to sell the drug than those without negative attitudes toward heroin.

The experiments by Coe and his associates, like the famous experiments by Milgram, are important in indicating that normal subjects, to a greater extent than assumed, often comply with even the difficult and unpleasant requests of authority figures. Another important implication of Coe's findings is that people differ dramatically in what they consider to be anti-social: Not all of Coe's subjects felt that selling heroin was wrong. The work in this area fails to support the view that hypnotic subjects lose control over their responding or that they are transformed into automata who respond mechanically to signals from the hypnotist.

V. CONTEMPORARY THEORIES AND RESEARCH

A. Psychoanalytic Theory

Freud was so impressed by the apparent submissiveness of certain hypnotized subjects that he likened hypnosis to being in love. There is no evidence to support the idea that hypnosis fosters an erotic or sexual relationship between the therapist and patient. More contemporary psychoanalytic theorists, including Baker, Gill and Brenman, Fromm, and Nash, have instead relied more on concepts allied to ego psychology such as "regression in the service of the ego," and "ego receptivity" (Fromm) to account for subjects' reports of primary process thinking (e.g., fantasy, imaginative activity) and subjects' ability to temporarily relinquish critical judgment, strict reality orientation, and deliberate control of behavior.

Based on a review of more than 100 studies, Nash concluded that hypnosis does not permit subjects to literally reexperience the events of childhood or function in a truly child-like fashion. Instead, Nash maintains that hypnosis engenders a topographic regression with specific properties. These include an increase in primary process material, more spontaneous and intense emotion, unusual body sensations, the experience of nonvolition, and the tendency to displace core attributes of important others onto the hypnotist.

Support for psychoanalytic concepts have come from a number of quarters. Several studies are consistent with the proposition that hypnosis increases primary process thinking that cannot be accounted for in terms of compliance with role demands. Nevertheless, it is unclear whether increased primary process during hypnosis is attributable to suggestions for eye closure, relaxation, and attention to imagery, rather than to unique characteristics of hypnosis.

Many subjects report unusual perceptual and bodily experiences during and after hypnosis. However, studies by Coe and Ryken, Lynn and his colleagues, and Kirsch and his associates indicate that hypnotized subjects' reports are indistinguishable from nonhypnotized subjects reports in a variety of test conditions that involve eye closure, relaxation, imagining suggested events, and focusing on body parts that parallel body parts that are the target of hypnotic suggestions. Thus, altered bodily experiences are by no means unique or specific to hypnotic conditions.

Studies from Nash's, Sheehan's and Lynn's laboratories support the hypothesis that certain hypnotic subjects evidence an especially motivated involvement with the hypnotist or cognitive commitment to respond to hypnotic tasks. However, research has shown that improving hypnotic rapport may increase the responsivity of low hypnotizable subjects, while degrading hypnotic rapport has no appreciable effect on the responding of high hypnotizable subjects, who seem prepared to respond to the hypnotist regardless of the nature of the hypnotic relationship.

The evidence for shifts in affect is mixed. Whereas some studies indicate that hypnotized subjects experience affective shifts that cannot be duplicated by simulating subjects, other studies have shown that simulators can mimic hypnotized subjects' emotions. Finally, although psychoanalytic constructs have been used to account for reports of suggestion-related involuntariness, a variety of theories we review provide equally plausible accounts of hypnotic nonvolition.

B. Neodissociation Theory

After a long hiatus of interest in dissociation, in 1977, Hilgard published an influential book that revitalized the concept by proposing a neodissociation theory based on a contemporary cognitive model of divisions of consciousness. Hilgard's neodissociation theory is based on the idea that there exist multiple cognitive systems or cognitive structures in hierarchical arrangement under some measure of control by an "executive ego." The executive ego or "central control" structure is responsible for planning and monitoring functions of the personality. During hypnosis, relevant subsystems of control are temporarily dissociated from conscious executive control and are instead directly activated by the hypnotist's suggestions. This lack of conscious control is largely dependent on an amnesic barrier or process that relegates ideas, imaginings, and fantasies to unconsciousness. This diminished executive control is responsible for the subjective impression of nonvolition that typically accompanies hypnotic responses. [*See* ID, EGO, AND SUPEREGO.]

Bowers has recently presented a modified version of E. R. Hilgard's neodissociation model of hypnosis that rejects amnesia as fundamental to dissociation. Instead, Bowers proposes that dissociation is largely a function of the direct and automatic activation of subsystems of control by the hypnotist's suggestions. Kihlstrom has also extended neodissociation theory in interesting directions that incorporate concepts of modern cognitive psychology, including memory models and the distinctions between procedural and declarative knowledge.

The empirical roots of neodissociation theory can be traced to Hilgard's introduction of the metaphor of the "hidden observer" to describe the phenomenon by which a person registers and stores information in memory, without being aware that the information had been processed. Hilgard and his associates' initial research on the hidden observer phenomenon involved experimental studies of pain and hearing. In a typical pain study, high hypnotizable subjects are able to recover concealed experiences or memories of pain during hypnotic suggestions for analgesia when they are informed that they possess a hidden part that can experience high levels of pain during analgesia and that this part can be contacted by the hypnotist with a prearranged cue. Research in Hilgard's laboratory has demonstrated that hidden observer reports can penetrate hypnotic blindness, hypnotic deafness, and positive hallucinations.

Hidden observer studies and their interpretation have been controversial. For instance, Spanos and his associates have shown that hidden observer reports vary as a function of the nature and explicitness of the instructions that subjects receive about the nature of the hidden observer. According to this perspective, the hidden observer is implicitly or explicitly suggested by the hypnotist. It therefore can be thought of as no different from any other suggested hypnotic phenomenon that is guided by the subjects' expectancies and situational demand characteristics. Whether the hidden observer reflects a true or pre-existing division of consciousness that is directly accessed by hypnotic suggestions or whether it is a product of suggestion continues to stimulate research and theoretical controversy.

The neodissociation perspective is one of the dominant contemporary hypnosis perspectives. Many researchers and clinicians accept its tenets, and it has inspired a great deal of contemporary hypnosis research.

C. Socio-Cognitive Perspective

Despite its popularity, neodissociation theory is by no means universally accepted. In fact, another influential view of hypnosis—the socio-cognitive perspective—rejects dissociation as an explanatory mechanism and challenges many widely held beliefs about hypnosis. The term *socio-cognitive* captures this perspective's dual emphasis on the social and cognitive dimensions of hypnosis. Socio-cognitive hypnosis theorists contend that hypnotic behavior is fundamentally mundane role- or expectancy-governed social behavior.

The socio-cognitive perspective can be traced to attacks on the concept of hypnosis as an altered state of consciousness. In 1950, Theodore Sarbin challenged the traditional concept of hypnosis as a state (e.g., hypnotic trance, hypnotic state). Sarbin contended that hypnosis could be conceptualized as "believed in imaginings" and developed a theory that relied heavily on the metaphor of role to capture parallels between the hypnotic interaction and a theatrical performance in which both the hypnotist and the subject enact reciprocal roles. Sarbin and his colleague, W. C. Coe, elaborated the theory and conducted research that highlighted the contribution of the following variables to subjects' hypnotic responsiveness: knowledge of what is required in the hypnotic situation, self- and role-related perceptions, expectations, imaginative skills, and situational demand characteristics.

T. X. Barber was influenced by Sarbin's theorizing and criticized the state concept because of its logical circularity (i.e., hypnotic responsiveness can both indicate the existence of a hypnotic state and be explained by it). In an extensive series of studies in the 1960s and early 1970s, Barber and associates N. P. Spanos, J. Chaves, and D. Calverley demonstrated the important roles played by subjects' attitudes, expectations, and motivations in hypnotic responding, and that nonhypnotized subjects showed increments in responsiveness to suggestions that were as large as the increments produced by hypnotic procedures. This research supported the idea that despite external appearances, hypnotic responses were not particularly unusual and therefore did not require the positing of unusual states of consciousness.

Spanos has conducted an extensive research program that has drawn particular attention to the importance of social psychological processes (e.g., subjects' attributions and interpretations of their own behaviors and hypnotic communications, response biases) and the importance of subjects' goal-directed activities and strategic responding (e.g., imagery, fantasy, allocation of attention) in the hypnotic context. This emphasis can also be seen in the writings of Lynn and his colleagues' (Rhue, Weekes, and Sivec), who view hypnotizable subjects as creative problem-solving agents who seek and integrate information from an array of situation, personal, and interpersonal sources to respond to hypnotic suggestions. These investigators place less emphasis on compliance than Spanos and Wagstaff, a British theoretician.

Spanos and his colleagues have developed a social-learning, cognitive-skills-based hypnotizability modification program that provides low hypnotizable subjects with information designed to modify their attitudes about hypnosis, increase their involvement in suggestion-related imaginings, and interpret hypnotic communications in a manner consistent with passing hypnotic suggestions. This program has successfully modified the hypnotizability of about half of the low hypnotizable subjects tested so that after training they test as high hypnotizable subjects. This research has thus challenged the idea that hypnotic responsiveness is trait-like and cannot be substantially modified.

Kirsch's response expectancy theory, which is an extension of Rotter's social learning theory, is based on the idea that expectancies can generate nonvolitional responses. Kirsch's research has shown that a wide variety of hypnotic responses (e.g., amnesia, experienced nonvolition, response to motoric suggestions) covary with people's beliefs and expectancies about their occurrence. Council and Kirsch have argued that the modest relation between hypnotizability and personality traits such as imaginative involvement and absorption may be an artifact of the fact that these trait measures have routinely been administered in a hypnosis test context. When Council and Kirsch measured hypnotizability and absorption in separate contexts so that subjects could not connect the two measuring instruments, no correlation between the measures was evident. The reliability and meaning of these findings have been questioned by researchers, including Bowers, Kihlstrom, and Nadon, who have challenged some of the tenets of socio-cognitive theories.

Indeed, socio-cognitive theories have drawn critical fire from proponents of competing hypnosis paradigms. Bates, Hilgard, Bowers, and Banyai have all, for example, questioned whether treatment gains that eventuate from hypnotizability training represent genuine changes in hypnotic ability or whether they can be accounted for in terms of compliance and conformity with demands for improved performance that are inherent in the training program.

Spanos has addressed this critique by showing that treatment gains generalize to a variety of novel items and subjective measures; that trained subjects respond comparably to nontrained "natural" high hypnotizable subjects; and that skill trained subjects continue to respond to hypnotic suggestions while they are surreptitiously observed, while untrained simulating subjects cease responding when they believe they are not being observed. In the long run, hypnotizability modification research promises to shed light on what aspects of hypnotic responsiveness are amenable to change versus what aspects are recalcitrant to modification and are, consequently, more "trait-like" in nature.

Bowers and Perry each maintain that socio-cognitive models exaggerate the extent to which hypnotic behaviors are strategic and goal-directed. Perry, for instance, argues that purposefulness and nonvolition may coexist in hypnosis. Bowers, in turn, asserts that hypnotically suggested behavior is purposeful in the sense that it is goal-directed—that is, achieves the suggested state of affairs. However, hypnotic behavior is nonvolitional in the sense that it is not performed on purpose—that is, does not flow from executive initiative and effort.

Bowers's more general critique of socio-cognitive theories is based on three points of contention: (1) research by Woody, Bowers, and Oakman suggests that compliance and social influence may account for the behavior of low hypnotizable subjects, but that different (dissociative) mechanisms apply to high hypnotizable subjects; (2) research indicates that response to hypnotic analgesia suggestions can occur in the absence of goal-directed fantasies (e.g., suggestion-related fantasy activity such as imagining that a hand and arm are made of rubber following an analgesia suggestion), indicating that such patterns of imaginative activity are more limited in their ability to account for the experience of nonvolition and response to suggestion than socio-cognitive theorists acknowledge; (3) when goal-directed fantasies accompany suggested responses, they are in many cases indicative of dissociated control rather than direct mediators of hypnotic action. Socio-cognitive theorists (Lynn, Spanos, Wagstaff) have responded to these or related criticisms in a number of publications. These issues will undoubtedly elicit continued debate and dialog between adherents of the two competing hypnosis perspectives.

D. Phenomenological/Interactive Models

Theories that place particular emphasis on understanding the subjects' experience, and the interaction of multiple variables during hypnosis, have been termed "phenomenological/interactive" theories. Whereas parallels can be drawn between phenomenological/interactive theorists and the socio-cognitive theorists, phenomenological/interactive theorists focus more on the differences between hypnotic and waking behavior and cognitive activity than do socio-cognitive theorists.

In the late 1950s, Orne underscored the importance of understanding the subjective experiences and subtle cognitive changes of hypnotized subjects. While never rejecting the concept of a hypnotic state, Orne has argued that subjects are actively involved in interpreting and responding to the social demands of the hypnotic situation.

Orne devised a simulator control methodology that he initially believed would enable the separation of those subtle cognitive characteristics that constituted the "essence" of hypnosis from what he considered to be behavioral artifacts produced in response to social demands. Research using Orne's simulation design was important in demonstrating that a wide range of hypnotic responding that had been assumed to reflect a hypnotic state could instead be explained more parsimoniously in terms of the expectations transmitted to subjects by the social demands of the experimental situation.

Orne's simulation paradigm has been criticized on the grounds that it confounds hypnotizability levels across hypnotized-simulator conditions (simulators are selected from low hypnotizable subject populations) and that the simulation instructions differ in significant ways from standard inductions and may account for hypnotized-simulating differences obtained. These criticisms notwithstanding, research using this design has drawn attention to the pervasive influence of demand characteristics and their potential role in accounting for a wide range of hypnotic phenomena.

Sheehan's contextual model highlights the interactive reciprocal relations between an active organism and an active context, the "fine-grained variation" in responsiveness to suggestion that exists among very hypnotizable subjects. Sheehan's research has also established the relevance of hypnotic rapport to a range of hypnotic phenomena (e.g., hypnotic dreams, hypnotically created memories). Sheehan contends that hypnosis can be distinguished from waking behavior by hypnotized subjects' "motivated cognitive commitment" or problem-solving attempts to respond appropriately to suggestions.

According to McConkey, in order to understand the essential variability that characterizes subjects' hypnotic responses, it is necessary to examine the meaning that subjects place on the hypnotist's communications, the idiosyncratic ways in which they cognitively process suggestions, and intra-individual differences that can occur in responding across suggestions. McConkey's research has supported the hypothesis that high hypnotizability reflects the ability to process information that is both consistent and inconsistent with a suggested event in such a way that facilitates the belief in the reality of the event.

Sheehan and McConkey's models are related to other interactional models (e.g., Nadon, Laurence, and Perry; Banyai) of hypnosis insofar as they call attention to the need to examine multiple, potentially interactive determinants of hypnotic responding.

VI. CLINICAL HYPNOSIS

Magnetic and later hypnotic procedures were initially developed as clinical procedures and, since the 18th century, have been employed to treat a very wide range of physical disorders and psychological disturbances. For instance hypnotic procedures are used routinely to help people stop smoking, lose weight, overcome phobias, and control pain and distress in a variety of dental and medical situations. In addition, hypnotic procedures are also sometimes employed to treat physiological disorders such as warts and asthma.

There are empirical grounds to be optimistic about the therapeutic potential of hypnotherapy. Smith, Glass, and Miller conducted a meta-analysis of psychotherapy outcome studies and found that psychodynamic hypnotherapy produced substantially greater effects than all nonhypnotic therapies. Kirsch conducted a meta-analysis that suggested that hypnosis can substantially enhance the effects of cognitive–behavioral therapies.

Unfortunately, evaluating the clinical efficacy of hypnotic procedures is difficult because most studies in this area contain serious methodological limitations. Most clinical studies consist of one or a series of anecdotal case reports. In these reports the actual treatment procedures employed are often not specified, the procedures for indexing improvement may not be clear or may simply consist of the clinician's statement the improvement occurred, and control or comparison groups are not employed. Under these circumstances no conclusions are possible concerning treatment efficacy.

In the last decade the situation has improved somewhat with the publication of an increasing number of controlled studies. Nevertheless, interpretation of many controlled studies remains problematic because these studies often confound antecedent variables. For instance several studies on clinical pain have compared hypnotic induction procedures coupled with suggestions for comfort, relaxation, and pain reduction against nonhypnotic procedures that involved relaxation and/or distraction, but no suggestion for pain reduction. Although most of these studies found no differences on indexes of pain reduction for hypnotic and nonhypnotic treatments, a few reported more pain relief in the hypnotic than in the nonhypnotic treatments. However, because these studies confounded hypnotic induction procedures with suggestions for pain reduction, it is impossible to conclude that the hypnotic component of the procedures contributed to the success of the treatments.

A number of relatively recent clinical studies have controlled for confounding of this type by comparing hypnotic induction procedures plus suggestions to suggestions alone. These studies have examined such diverse clinical problems as smoking reduction, dental distress, headache pain, chronic pain of various types, and wart reduction. The results of these studies have consistently indicated that suggestions without prior hypnotic induction are as effective as hypnotic induction plus suggestions at producing improvement across a wide range of clinical problems. In summary, the available clinical evidence suggests that hypnotic treatments are often times effective in helping to treat a wide variety of clinical problems. However, it has not been conclusively demonstrated that hypnotic treatments are more effective than nonhypnotic treatments for a variety of problems.

Some investigators have hypothesized that, in clinical settings, hypnotic and other suggestive treatments are only likely to be effective with highly hypnotizable subjects. Interestingly, however, hypnotizability correlates with the outcome of hypnotic treatments much less consistently than it correlates with responsiveness to suggestions for perceptual and cognitive alterations in laboratory experiments. For instance, one recent review of hypnotic treatments (see Spanos *et al.*, in press) for clinical pain found that hypnotizability failed to correlate significantly with indexes of pain reduction in the majority of studies that assessed this relationship. Hypnotizability has also frequently failed to correlate with outcome in studies that assessed the effects of hypnotic treatments for smoking reduction, wart reduction, phobias and weight reduction.

The reasons that hypnotizability correlates significantly with treatment outcome in some studies but not in others remain unclear. The nature of the problem treated does not appear to be important in this regard. According to one hypothesis the relation between hypnotizability and clinical outcome is moderated by the extent to which the hypnotizability test situation and the hypnotic treatment situation call up similar expectations and motivations. Subjects who do not see their hypnotizability test performance as related to or important for how well their hypnotic treatment works may bring very different motivations and expectations to the two situations and, consequently, may respond differently to the two situations.

VII. FORENSIC ASPECTS OF HYPNOSIS

One common misconception holds that hypnotic procedures can greatly enhance the ability of people to accurately recall forgotten events. On the basis of this misconception police departments in a number of countries have often arranged to have eyewitness to crimes hypnotized in the hope that the recall of the witnesses would thereby be enhanced.

Most of the available laboratory evidence now indicates that hypnotic procedures do not dramatically enhance accurate recall and do not enhance the accuracy with which witnesses identify perpetrators whom they have observed commit mock crimes. Although subjects sometimes do recall new information following an hypnotic interview, they may also recall as much new information when motivated by nonhypnotic instructions. When hypnotic (and sometimes nonhypnotic) procedures are used in order to obtain new information from witnesses, the new information obtained is often inaccurate. Moreover, in most real life situations there is nothing that enables either the witnesses or the interviewer to discriminate between the accurate and inaccurate aspects of the recall. [*See* EYEWITNESS TESTIMONY.]

Some investigators have argued that hypnotic subjects are particularly likely to be influenced by leading questions. According to this idea hypnotic witnesses asked a leading question such as, "What color was the suspect's moustache?" are likely to respond to this question by creating an image of the suspect they saw and supplying the suspect with a moustache, even though the actual suspect did not have a moustache. If these witnesses later see a lineup that contains a suspect with a moustache, they are likely to misidentify that suspect as the perpetrator.

The proposition that misleading questions influence and degrade the accuracy of recall is not in dispute. This effect of leading questions has long been known and has been elegantly demonstrated in the laboratory in a large number of studies conducted by Elizabeth Loftus as well as others. However, whether or not hypnotic procedures augment the detrimental effects of leading questions remains a controversial issue. Several recent studies conducted by McConkey and his associates and by Spanos and his associates indicate that misleading questions interfere with accurate recall to the same degree in hypnotic and nonhypnotic subjects.

In a number of studies, witnesses who received hypnotic interviews were more confident about the inaccurate aspects or their recall or about their misidentifications than were nonhypnotic witnesses. On the basis of these findings, and the findings purporting to show that hypnotic subjects are particularly susceptible to the influence of leading questions, Martin Orne proposed that the recall of hypnotic witnesses often reflects pseudomemories—false memories that are confidently believed in as real memories. Orne further argued that because hypnotic witnesses believe so confidently in their pseudomemories they are effectively immunized against cross-examination.

Contrary to these assertions, recent studies from the laboratories of McConkey, Lynn, and Spanos have found that pseudomemory reports occur as frequently in nonhypnotic as in hypnotic subjects. In addition several recent studies also indicated consistently that hypnotic testimony was no more resistant to cross-examination than nonhypnotic testimony.

A ban on hypnotic testimony in the courtroom, as legislation has established in several states, cannot be fully justified by the available evidence. In the future, closer cooperation between psychologists and the legal community might allow issues such as these to be examined empirically before, rather than after, the passing of laws that bear on psychological questions. Less controversial than the issue of admitting hypnotic testimony in the courtroom is the fact that extreme caution needs to be exercised in administering hypnotic procedures to victims and witnesses.

Many theoretical and empirical issues pertinent to hypnosis are unresolved, and the clinical utility and role of hypnosis in the treatment of various psychological and medical conditions remains to be established. The field of hypnosis will advance apace with careful experimental and clinical research, and by way of theoretical tensions and rapprochements between competing paradigms. In this process, the study of hypnosis will continue to enrich the broader field of psychology by contributing insights into the affective, cognitive, behavioral, and relational dimensions of human experience.

Bibliography

Brown, D. P., and Fromm, E. (1987). "Hypnosis and Behavioral Medicine." Erlbaum, Hillsdale, NJ.

Brown, P. (1991). "The Hypnotic Brain." Yale University Press, Westhaven, CT.

Fromm, E., and Nash, M. R. (Eds.) (1992). "Contemporary Hypnosis Research." Guilford, New York.

Hilgard, E. R. (1986). "Divided Consciousness," 2nd ed. Wiley, New York.

Lynn, S. J., and Rhue, J. W. (Eds.) (1991). "Theories of Hypnosis: Current Models and Perspectives." Guilford, New York.

Rhue, J. W., Lynn, S. J., and Kirsch, I. (Eds.) (1993). "Handbook of Clinical Hypnosis." American Psychological Association, Washington, DC.

Spanos, N. P., and Chaves, J. (Eds.) (1989) "Hypnosis: A Cognitive–Behavioral Perspective." Prometheus Books, Buffalo, NY.

Spanos, N. P., Liddy, S., and Ellis, J. A. (in press). In "Textbook of Pain" (3rd Ed.) (P. Wall and R. Melzak, Eds.). Churchill-Livingston, New York.

HYPOTHALAMUS

Quentin J. Pittman
University of Calgary, Canada

Glyn Goodall
Institut National de la Santé et de la Recherche Medicale, France

Glossary

Autonomic nervous system A part of the nervous system which is concerned with involuntary body functions through an action on glands, smooth muscle, and cardiac tissue.

Baroreceptor Receptors located on arteries that signal changes in blood pressure.

Blood–brain barrier An anatomical and functional feature of brain capillaries that restricts passage of many circulating substances into the brain.

Hedonism The doctrine that one will behave so as to achieve pleasure and avoid pain.

Homeostasis A relatively stable state of equilibrium (of the internal body environment).

Neurohypophysial neuron A neuron with a cell body in the hypothalamus and an axon which extends into the posterior pituitary.

Nucleus An aggregation of neuronal cell bodies.

Set point The level about which a controlled system is regulated.

Synapse The junction between a neuron and another neuron or effector.

Tuberoinfundibular neuron A neuron in the medial basal hypothalamus which projects to the median eminence where it secretes either (i) hypothalamic releasing or (ii) hypothalamic release-inhibiting hormones which are transported by the blood through capillaries to the anterior pituitary.

THE HYPOTHALAMUS is composed of a number of groups of cells lying close to the base of the brain and bordering on the third ventricle. As an important area of the brain involved in the control of homeostatic functions as diverse as eating, drinking, sleep, thermoregulation, cardiovascular regulation, and hormone secretion, the hypothalamus receives a variety of inputs, both of a neural and of a humoral (blood-borne) nature. Outputs from the hypothalamus result in hormonal, behavioral, and autonomic responses designed to maintain homeostasis. A wide variety of neurotransmitters is utilized within hypothalamic neural networks to accomplish these integrative and control functions.

I. BACKGROUND

Despite its small size (less than 4 g), the hypothalamus exerts enormous control over the body. An appreciation of this influence developed over the first few decades of this century as descriptions emerged of syndromes associated with hypothalamic lesions and dysfunction in humans. However, much of our information about the hypothalamus comes from animal experiments. It is such studies that have brought the hypothalamus out of the shadow of the overlying cortical areas to establish its important role in the control of homeostasis. As a result of these studies, the discipline of neuroendocrinology is virtually synonymous with that of the study of the hypothalamus. The identification and structural characterization of many of the chemicals important in brain function have arisen from analyses of extracts of hypothalami, where they are synthesized and stored in great abundance. Finally, the concept of neurosecretion, i.e., that a neuron could synthesize and release a hormone (peptide), which is now a commonly accepted fact in the neuropharmacological literature, had its infancy in studies of hypothalamic–pituitary relationships in lower vertebrates.

In order to understand hypothalamic function, it is necessary to have an appreciation of its anatomy.

Copyright © 1994 by Academic Press, Inc. All rights of reproduction in any form reserved.

II. ANATOMY

A. Intrinsic

The hypothalamus is an ill-defined area of neural tissue lying on each side of the midline and bordering on the walls of the third ventricle. As its name would indicate (hypothalamus), it is situated ventral to the thalamus at the base of the diencephalon. The pituitary stalk which joins the hypothalamus to the pituitary exits from the ventral surface. Its anterior border is considered the plane of the anterior commissure and its posterior border the mammallary bodies which lie at the junction between the diencephalon and the mid-brain. This small area of tissue, which in coronal section is barely the size of an adult's thumbnail, comprises a number of nuclei. These are packed tightly together and have been named, as indicated in Figure 1, on the basis of their location within the hypothalamus, their relationship to neighboring structures and the organization of their afferent and efferent connections. In many, (but not all) cases a particular nucleus is associated with specific functions.

Anterior to the hypothalamus proper is the preoptic area. This loosely packed group of neurons is often considered to be anatomically distinct from the hypothalamus, but is so closely related functionally to the hypothalamus, that it is generallly included in any description of hypothalamic anatomy and physiology. The preoptic area gives way another ill-defined group of cells, the anterior hypothalamic area, which is functionally very closely related to the preoptic area. Near the walls of the third ventricle, we can identify a broad sheet of cells known as the periventricular nucleus. Just above the optic chiasm, we find small, well-defined groups of cells (nuclei) including the suprachiasmatic nucleus and the supraoptic nucleus, which is especially characterized by its large magno-cellular cell bodies. The latter nucleus and the more dorso-medial paraventricular nucleus are important in the control of posterior pituitary function. An important nucleus for endocrine control, the arcuate nucleus, logically sits above the exit of the pituitary stalk. The larger, ventromedial nucleus, which lies dorsal and slightly lateral to the arcuate nucleus is also involved in endocrine control, but also has important behavioral outputs. As can be seen in Figure 1, the dorsal and posterior portions of the hypothalamus are occupied by the dorsal medial nucleus and posterior hypothalamus, respectively. A prominent, midline landmark is provided by the ventral projection of the mammillary nuclei; this protuberance, or mamillary body, marks the posterior border of the hypothalamus and provides an important output to the cortex and limbic system via the mammillo-thalamic tract. Running throughout the length of the hypothalamus and abutting laterally upon the subthalamic region and internal capsule is an anatomically indistinct area of tissue called the lateral hypothalamus.

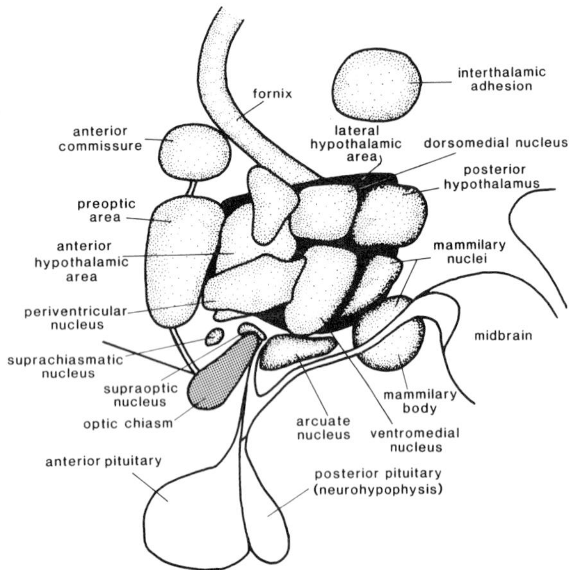

FIGURE 1 Diagram of intrinsic hypothalamic nuclei and surrounding structures. This is a sagittal view from the medial aspect of the hypothalamus with anterior on the left. [Reprinted with permission from Pittman, Q. J. (1991). The hypothalamus. In "The Encyclopedia of Human Biology" (R. Dulbecco, Ed.). Academic Press.]

B. Inputs to the Hypothalamus

In light of the predominant role played by the hypothalamus in a wide variety of internal body functions, it is hardly surprising to learn that the hypothalamus is extensively connected to numerous other parts of the nervous system. These pathways range from large bundles of nerve fibers easily observed upon gross dissection to more diffuse groups of small nerve fibers which eluded anatomical description until the advent of more sensitive anatomical techniques. The hypothalamus is particularly well supplied with information related to the conditions prevailing in the internal body environment. In addition to that provided by the neural inputs, this information comes from a set of intrinsic sensory neurons which monitor local conditions in the extracellular fluid and more distant conditions as revealed by blood content. Thus, through its afferent and intrinsic pathways, the hypothalamus receives a wide variety of information important to its control of the internal body environment (Fig. 2).

1. Neural Inputs

The hypothalamus receives extensive information concerning the internal state of the body via a series of ascending fiber tracts which arise in lower brain stem areas. For example, the nucleus tractus solitarius, a brain stem nucleus which receives vagal inputs from the viscera, has a direct projection to various hypothalamic nuclei. Many of the fibers which originate in other brainstem nuclei pass through the lateral hypothalamus and are especially important in reward mechanisms (see below).

Sensory information from the skin is relayed to the hypothalamus through ascending, polysynaptic pathways which probably reach hypothalamic nuclei either from collaterals of ascending fibers or directly from the thalamus. Receptors in the skin transduce a wide variety of sensory signals; of particular importance to the hypothalamus are sensory fibers whose electrical activities change in response to temperature. Other sensory inputs from the skin carry somatic-sensory information (i.e., touch, pain, etc.).

Although olfactory input is probably of relatively less importance in humans than it is in lower mammals, many of the connections of olfactory areas to hypothalamic nuclei have been retained in the human. Of particular importance is the input from

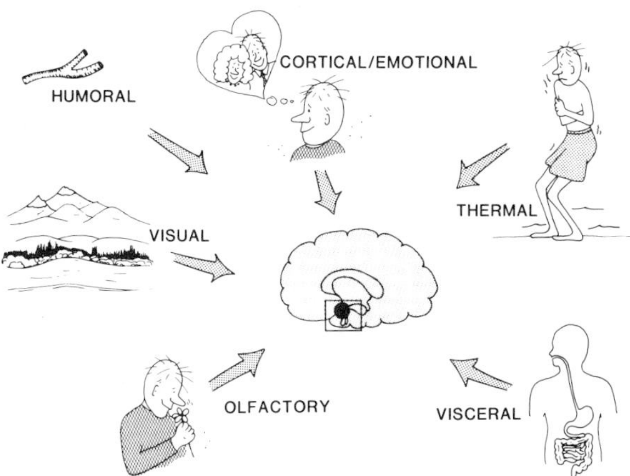

FIGURE 2 Inputs to the hypothalamus [Reprinted with permission from Pittman, Q. J. (1991). The hypothalamus. In "The Encyclopedia of Human Biology" (R. Dulbecco, Ed.) Academic Press.]

olfactory areas of cortex to the amygdala, a nucleus lying in the temporal lobe and which is especially important in motivational function. The amygdala extensively innervates a number of hypothalamic nuclei through two fiber pathways—the stria terminalis and the ventral amygdalo-fugal pathway. Visual sensory information, which is of particular importance in humans for emotional and reproductive behaviors, reaches the hypothalamus directly through the retino-hypothalamic tract or via projections from second order nuclei in visual pathways. [*See* SENSE OF SMELL; VISUAL PERCEPTION.]

The limbic system consists of a number of structures which border on the ventricular system of the brain and are thought to be important in processing emotional behavior. The hypothalamus is one of the major destinations of limbic system information. Much of this information is relayed to the hypothalamus from a temporal lobe structure known as the hippocampus. The hippocampus gives rise to a large bundle of fibers called the fornix, which sweeps into the hypothalamus from its anterior dorsal aspect to innervate the posterior hypothalamic nuclei, in particular the mammillary complex. The septal nuclei are also considered part of the limbic system, and they give rise to descending projections, which run through the medial forebrain bundle to innervate the lateral aspects of the hypothalamus and other descending structures. Cortical input to the hypothalamus arises from prefrontal, infralimbic, and entorhinal cortex. [*See* HIPPOCAMPAL FORMATION; LIMBIC SYSTEM.]

2. Humoral (Blood-Borne) Inputs

In its position at the base of the brain, the hypothalamus is among the first of neural structures to be perfused by blood ascending in the carotid arteries. The hypothalamus contains sensory neurons of a variety of types which respond to local blood-borne elements. Because the blood–brain barrier is somewhat "leaky" in the hypothalamus, many substances which circulate (e.g., hormones, nutrients, etc.) diffuse freely into the hypothalamus where specialized neurons can transduce substance levels into electrical activity. The existence of a short, circulatory feedback loop from the pituitary to the brain provides a means by which pituitary secretions can quickly reach the hypothalamus, where their levels can be monitored.

Other information of importance to the pituitary appears to be that of the metabolic state of the body; in addition to having neurons specialized for monitoring metabolically important substances (e.g., glucose), neurons also are present throughout the hypothalamus which respond to local temperature. As this temperature is largely a function of the blood perfusing this structure, these neurons are uniquely positioned to monitor core temperature as reflected by the temperature of blood arising from the thorax.

Because of its location bordering the walls of the third ventricle, the neurons of the hypothalamus are also in contact with the cerebrospinal fluid which fills the ventricular system and which can diffuse freely into hypothalamic tissue. Although evidence is still fragmentary, it is thought that specialized neurons may exist near the ventricular space which can respond to fluctuations in levels of neurotransmitters and ions which occur in the cerebrospinal fluid.

C. Outputs of Hypothalamus

The anatomical and humoral outputs of the hypothalamus provide this structure with the means to affect many behavioral and physiological functions. An overview of these various controls is described in the following section.

1. Endocrine

The identification and description of the control of pituitary function have provided one of the more fascinating stories of anatomical and physiological investigations of the past 60 years and has given rise to the entire discipline of neuroendocrinology. The intimate anatomical relationship between the hypothalamus and the pituitary is probably best appreciated when one realizes that the posterior pituitary (neurohypophysis) is actually a ventral growth of the hypothalamus. Magnocellular neurons of the paraventricular and supraoptic nuclei project to the neurohypophysis. The peptides arginine vasopressin and oxytocin (as well as a number of other peptides) are synthesized in these nuclei, transported down the axons to the neurohypophysis, and released into the extracellular space from where they enter the bloodstream.

In contrast to the organization of the posterior pituitary, the glandular cells of the anterior pituitary receive no direct neural projections. Rather, a series of neurosecretory neurons (tuberoinfundibular neurons) scattered throughout the various hypothalamic nuclei (but concentrated in the arcuate and ventromedial nuclei) send their axons to the base of the brain (median eminence) and release their contents (releasing or release-inhibiting hormones) into a specialized vascular bed. These portal plexus capillaries transport the hypothalamic releasing or inhibiting hormones from the hypothalamus to the anterior pituitary where they diffuse into this tissue to affect the release of the various anterior pituitary hormones.

2. Cortical/Behavioral

The hypothalamus exerts its control over behavioral functions through mono- and polysynaptic pathways to limbic system structures. Among such projections are those to the septal nuclei, the amygdala, habenula, and medial dorsal nucleus of the thalamus. A particularly important tract providing a relay for hypothalamic information to the limbic system is the mammillo-thalamic tract, which, as its name suggests, arises in the mammillary body and projects to the anterior nucleus of the thalamus. The thalamus, in turn, relays this information to specific limbic structures, in particular, the cingulate gyrus.

3. Autonomic

Because of limitations in anatomical techniques, descending connections from the hypothalamus were originally thought to be few in nature. However, with the advent of more sophisticated anatomical tracing methodology, studies in lower mammals have brought to light the fact that the hypothalamus possesses an extensive system of descending fiber tracts which innervate virtually all of the autonomic nuclei of the brain stem and even descend as uninterrupted axons to the most caudal aspects of the spinal cord where they innervate the sympathetic and parasympathetic preganglionic neurons. A similar system of fibers is found in the human.

4. Intrinsic Connections

In addition to widespread connections to and from the hypothalamus and other parts of the nervous system, the intrinsic hypothalamic nuclei are also extensively interconnected. Throughout the hypothalamus are many short axon interneurons, which receive information from adjacent nuclei either directly or from collaterals of descending or ascending fibers.

D. Neurotransmitters

In the mammalian nervous system, neurons communicate with each other largely through the secretion of low-molecular-weight chemicals called neurotransmitters; these can either diffuse across specialized junctions between neurons (synapses) to affect the electrical activity of neighboring cells or be secreted into the extracellular fluid to influence many neurons at once. The latter form of transmission could be particularly important for changes in "behavioral state." Virtually all of the "classical" neurotransmitters (including acetylcholine, noradrenaline, serotonin, dopamine, adrenaline, γ-aminobutyric acid, and glutamate) are well-represented in the nerve fibers innervating hypothalamic nuclei. As a number of drugs of abuse and medications are known to act through their interference with such classical neurotransmitter systems, it is apparent that hypothalamic function can be altered by exposure to such agents. Of particular interest over recent years has been the realization that the hypothalamus is virtually a cornucopia of peptide hormones which act as neurotransmitters. Experiments describing the neurosecretory nature of hypothalamic neurons and subsequent electrophysiological studies of hypothalamic "neuroendocrine" neurons provided some of the first evidence that peptides could function as neurotransmitters. There have now been well in excess of 50 different peptides described as having putative neurotransmitter functions within the brain and virtually all of these are represented within the hypothalamus. However, the task of identifying the roles of these peptides in specific aspects of hypothalamic anatomy and physiology has barely begun. [*See* SYNAPTIC TRANSMITTERS AND NEUROMODULATORS.]

III. FUNCTIONS OF THE HYPOTHALAMUS

A. Homeostasis and Control Theory

The great French physician and scientist, Claude Bernard, first recognized the fact that the internal environment of the body or "milieu interieur" is maintained constant. Walter Cannon subsequently coined the term "homeostasis" to describe the mechanism by which animals maintain this relatively constant internal environment. The remarkable fact that the internal body environment can be regulated at a constant level in the face of widely varying external conditions of temperature, food availability, metabolic demands, etc., is due, in part, to the hypothalamus. In order to achieve such regulation, the hypothalamus must be able to sense the various internal environments of the body, integrate this information, and compare it to a theoretical "set-point" and then respond to any perturbations with an appropriate effector signal. The means by which the hypothalamus obtains its afferent information and the pathways by which its output is directed to appropriate destinations have been outlined in the preceding sections. The following discussion examines the various functions controlled by the hypothalamus. [*See* HOMEOSTASIS.]

B. Specific Activities

The location of the hypothalamus deep within the brain has not facilitated investigation into the functions of this structure. From the dorsal aspect, one must pass through the entire cerebrum to reach the hypothalamus; from the ventral aspect, the base of the skull limits accessibility. In humans, tumors and cardiovascular accidents have provided the bulk of the experimental material revealing functional correlates to damage or stimulation of particular areas. Even under such circumstances, it has often been difficult to differentiate between a syndrome caused by *damage* to a specific area and that resulting from irritation or stimulation of an area adjacent to, for example, a small hemorrhage. Particularly with respect to the endocrine system, however, a number of diseases which exhibit classical sequelae can now be associated with specific hypothalamic deficits. The information which has been obtained about the human hypothalamus, however, is strongly based upon experimental studies in lower mammals. Fortunately, there appears to be remarkable preservation of form and function throughout the various mammalian genera and experiments in mammals as diverse as the rat and a subhuman primate often give surprisingly congruent results. In these animals, it has been possible to carry out lesion, stimulation, and recording experiments which have revealed important aspects of hypothalamic function. However, even under controlled laboratory conditions, it has still been difficult to achieve clear and easily interpretable results; the various hypothalamic nuclei are closely situated and it has been difficult to affect one area of the hypothalamus discretely without impinging upon adjacent areas. Nonetheless, with these caveats in mind, a description of hypothalamic functions emerges as outlined in Figure 3.

1. Autonomic Control

The pivotal role of the hypothalamus in the control of the autonomic nervous system has long been rec-

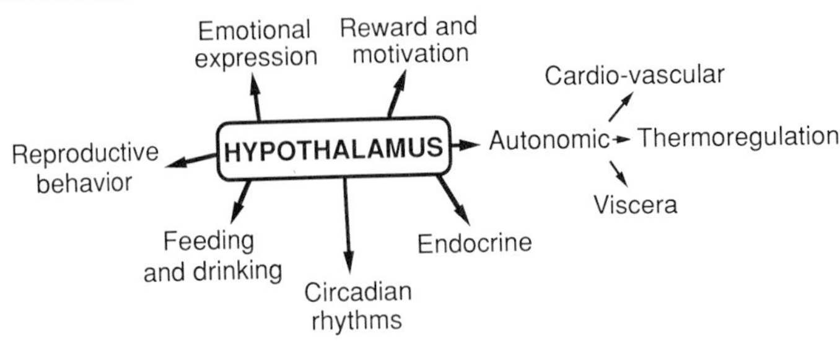

FIGURE 3 Activities under hypothalamic control.

ognized and it is often described as the "head ganglion" of the autonomic nervous system. The autonomic nervous system is divided on the basis of its anatomy, pharmacology, and to a certain extent its function into two components: the sympathetic (involved in arousal of "fight or flight" behavior) and parasympathetic (involved in vegetative function) systems. At one time, it was thought that there was a topographical relationship within the hypothalamus to these two systems with the anterior hypothalamus considered the parasympathetic center and the posterior hypothalamus the sympathetic center. While it is true that in animals "sympathetic" effects can be activated by electrical stimulation of the posterior hypothalamic areas, and "parasympathetic" responses by stimulation of anterior hypothalamic areas, it is equally true that more discrete stimuli throughout a variety of areas of the hypothalamus can cause generalized autonomic effects. The strong interconnections between various hypothalamic nuclei and brainstem and spinal cord autonomic nuclei provide an anatomical basis for the hypothalamus to exert control of cardiovascular function, thermoregulation, and visceral function.

a. Cardiovascular System

With respect to the cardiovascular system, it is known that information is relayed from baroreceptors synapsing in the medulla within nuclei which project directly or via polysynaptic pathways to the hypothalamus. Electrical or chemical stimulation of neurons in hypothalamic areas that receive baroreceptor information causes changes both in arterial pressure and in heart rate; such effects are most likely mediated through descending projections to areas of the ventral lateral medulla and to the spinal cord which control peripheral arterial muscles and cardiac muscle. In addition, a number of circulating hormones influence blood pressure and their release can be influenced by such descending pathways or via hypothalamic connections to the pituitary (described below). Emotional responses to external stimuli can also influence blood pressure via corticolimbic projections to hypothalamic and other nuclei; indeed, stressful conditions may lead to increased blood pressure, causing the well-known (but still poorly understood) problems of hypertension associated with highly stressful lifestyles.

b. Thermoregulation

Classical experiments carried out in the 1930s established that animals with hypothalamic lesions were incapable of normal thermoregulation and gave rise to extensive studies that have unequivocally placed the hypothalamus as a pivotal structure involved in the neural control of body temperature. Thermal sensory information from the skin and other parts of the body is relayed via multi-synaptic pathways to the hypothalamus where it is integrated with information obtained from intrinsic receptors. Through mechanisms not yet well understood, this information is compared to a hypothetical "setpoint" and, where deviations from this temperature take place, appropriate effector mechanisms are brought into play to return temperature to normal. These effector mechanisms include the regulation of peripheral vasomotor tone, alterations in sweat secretion, changes in respiratory rate, changes in metabolism, and alterations of behavior and posture appropriate for changes in heat loss or heat gain. The behavioral mechanisms for regulating body temperature seem to be at least as important as the physiological mechanisms. For example an animal is prepared to work to increase environmental temperature, and general activity levels can be adjusted either to reduce heat loss or to increase heat production. Neonates also can display appropriate mechanisms of behavioral thermoregulation even when the physiological mechanisms are insufficiently developed.

In addition to its control over normal thermoregulation, the hypothalamus, and particularly the preoptic/anterior hypothalamic areas, appears to be important in the development of fever. In lower mammals, application of minute quantities of pyrogens (agents that cause fever) directly to these areas causes prompt, experimental fevers; destruction of neurons in these same areas inhibits fever development in these animals. It has been proposed that fever is in fact not simply a failure of homeostasis, but indeed an adaptative change of the hypothalamic setpoint. A febrile animal will change its behavior in a number of ways, many of which correspond to mechanisms for elevating or maintaining a higher body temperature. Included in the range of behaviors displayed by a febrile animal are behaviors which limit social interactions, reduce food intake, and generally reorientate priorities. Anyone who has been ill will surely recognize that such behaviors apply equally well to humans.

c. Visceral Function

In accord with the hypothalamic control of appetitive behaviors described earlier, the hyothalamus also directly influences gut function to provide complimentary autonomic effects. For example, it has been shown in rats that electrical or chemical stimulation of a number of hypothalamic areas (e.g., paraventricular nucleus, ventromedial hypothalamus, dorsal hypothalamus) can influence gut muscle function, as well as acid secretion from the stomach. It is thought that the pathways from the hypothalamus to brainstem autonomic areas which control acid secretion may be of particular importance in the development of ulcers in response to stress, with the hypothalamus providing the intermediary role in relaying cortical and limbic information to the autonomic nervous system.

2. Endocrine Control

Through its anatomical connections to the posterior pituitary and to the median eminence, the hypothalamus represents the final common pathway for brain control of pituitary secretion. The major hormones released from the posterior pituitary are the peptides arginine vasopressin and oxytocin. Arginine vasopressin is also known as anti-diuretic hormone because of its action within the kidney to enhance water reuptake and concentrate the urine. In addition, this hormone also has other actions within the body to regulate blood pressure through its action on arterial smooth muscle and an action on metabolism through its enhancement of glycogen conversion to glucose in the liver. Oxytocin receptors are also found on smooth muscle, in this case on uterine smooth muscle and on mammary smooth muscle. Thus, its peripheral action is to cause milk letdown via contraction of the mammary smooth muscle and to cause uterine contractions (during the birth of a baby). Oxytocin receptors are also found on fat cells and on selected other peripheral tissues; oxytocin actions on these structures may explain its presence in men.

More direct influences of these two peptides on behavior, even after peripheral administration, have become very apparent in recent years, especially relevant to various social situations. For example, arginine vasopressin has been shown to play a major role in social recognition memory and both it and oxytocin have been implicated in certain features of tolerance and addictive behaviors. [*See* HORMONES AND BEHAVIOR.]

Regulation of the secretion of these hormones is brought about through specialized receptors in the hypothalamus and afferent stimuli arising from peripheral receptors. Neurons in the anterior hypothalamus, and possibly the vasopressin neurons themselves, are capable of sensing the osmolality of the blood and, in response to increases in osmolality cause increased synthesis and release of vasopressin. Reductions in blood pressure and blood volume, signaled via specialized cardiovascular receptors in the periphery, are also potent stumuli for vasopressin release, as are some types of stressful stimuli (e.g., pain and nausea).

Oxytocin is released in response to tactile stimulation of the nipples (i.e., when a baby suckles) and following distention of the birth canal during delivery. Cortical inputs are thought to provide a behavioral influence on oxytocin release; this is sometimes manifested by the spontaneous milk letdown experienced by a mother in response to the cries of her baby. Emotional stress, on the other hand, appears to inhibit oxytocin secretion, thereby making breastfeeding difficult for such a mother.

Hormones responsible for the release or inhibition of release of anterior pituitary hormones are synthesized in tuberoinfundibular neurons scattered throughout the hypothalamus and terminating on the median eminence. The secretory products of these neurons control glandular cells of the anterior pituitary which synthesize and release many hormones. The control of the tuberoinfundibular neurons is beyond the scope of this article. Nonetheless, in terms of general principles, there appear to be negative or positive feedback mechanisms which affect the release of their products. Thus, there are receptors in the hypothalamus which respond to circulating hormones produced both in distant parts of the body (i.e., steroids, such as estrogen produced in the ovary) and from the anterior pituitary. In addition, afferent stimuli from both viscera, as well as cortex and limbic system, can affect release. Secretion of the anterior pituitary hormones is often synchronized to the light–dark cycle and this circadian control is thought to be exerted via retinal signals entering the suprachiasmatic nucleus.

3. Circadian Rhythms

Many animals exhibit behaviors which show a remarkable periodicity which approximates a 24-hr day. These circadian rhythms are thought to be generated by an oscillatory mechanism in the suprachiasmatic nucleus and entrain to the light–dark cycle via impulses arriving from retinal–hypothalamic tracts. In fact, destruction of the suprachiasmatic nucleus in such animals will cause these rhythms to become totally disrupted. Human beings also have a suprachiasmatic nucleus and have also been shown to display circadian rhythms in such functions as body temperature, endocrine functions, etc. Of particular interest, is the hypothalamic control of rhythms of sleep and wakefulness, which appear to be mediated by hypothalamic connections to the reticular activating system of the midbrain. Stimulation of the posterior hypothalamus leads to behavioral and physiological signs of activation or arousal. Inversely, sleepiness and a slowing of behavioral responses follow stimulation of the anterior region of the hypothalamus. This ties with findings that destruction of this region causes insomnia in experimental animals, and continuous sleep follows destruction of the posterior hypothalamus.

Certain psychiatric disturbances have been linked to disrupted circadian rythms, including depression. Specifically, it is suggested that a desynchronization of the various body rhythms is one factor in depression (which is frequently associated with severe insomnia). Partial remission of depressive symptoms can indeed be obtained by resetting the circadian clocks centered in the suprachiasmatic nucleus. [*See* DEPRESSION.]

4. Feeding and Drinking

By the early 1950s it was widely known that the ventromedial nucleus and the lateral hypothalamus play opposing roles in the regulation of feeding behavior. Specifically, it was shown that lesions of the former induce uninterrupted eating, resulting in extremely obese animals, whereas bilateral lesions of the latter result in aphagia, to the extent that animals refuse even to eat food placed directly in their mouths. Electrical stimulation of these hypothalamic regions results in stimulation or inhibition of eating, in ways corresponding to lesions of the opposing structure. While we now know that there are a number of other hypothalamic nuclei (in particular the paraventricular nucleus) which also participate in the control of food intake, the lesioned animals described have been most intensively investigated and are particularly illustrative of possible control mechanisms. Rather than a direct effect on the appropriate behavior (eating, chewing, food seeking, etc.), the lesioned animals display alterations in affective components of eating (choice of diet, etc.). Furthermore, lesioning appears to cause an actual change in the setpoint of body weight regulation. These changes in food intake are associated with corresponding changes in metabolism, which suggest that they are part of an integrated response to the regulation of caloric balance. The findings concerning hypothalamic control of eating behaviors may very well be applicable to humans. For example, many of the behavioral aspects of lateral hypothalamus lesioned rats are similar to those observed in humans suffering from Froelich's syndrome, which results in severe loss of appetite and emaciation, and is linked to hypothalamic lesions. [*See* APPETITE.]

While the actual mechanisms responsible for the regulation of food intake are numerous, such findings indicate that the hypothalamus plays an important role. Among other regulatory events is one in which neurons in the hypothalamus respond to changes in blood glucose level with changes in electrical activity. For example, cells in the ventromedial hypothalamus respond with increased activity to high blood glucose levels, whereas neurons throughout the lateral hypothalamus more often decrease their activity in response to elevations in glucose. These changes seem to be appropriate in terms of our understanding of the relative roles (discussed above) of medial and lateral hypothalamus in regulating food intake. Thus, as is expected for a controlled system, both the sensory mechanisms are present and the necessary connections exist from the hypothalamus to the limbic system to elicit the appropriate behaviors.

The debate as to the exact cue for signaling thirst as well as the location of cells responsible remains vigorous to this day. It would appear that changes in blood osmolality and possibly sodium content activate neurons in areas near the hypothalamus (organum vasculosum of the lamina terminalis and subfornical organ) which in turn send strong projections to the hypothalamus. In addition, osmoreceptors are located in the anterior hypothalamus and preoptic area, which directly respond to changes in plasma osmotic pressure (concentration of solutes in the blood). The hypothalamus appears to integrate signals from the various brain structures and activate drinking behavior via pathways to the limbic system in a manner similar to that described above for eating behavior. It is of interest that the two behaviors appear to be closely related, not only from a hedonic point of view, but possibly also from a motivational one. For example, animals on food restricted paradigms can be induced to drink to excess in the intervals between the appearance of the food pellets. Could this be related to the well-known pairing of food and drink in humans celebrating festive occasions?

5. Reproductive Behavior

Hypothalamic nuclei play major roles in all aspects of reproductive behavior, from courtship, through copulation, to parental investment. Certain differences appear between males and females both in terms of anatomy and in terms of the specific roles played by various hypothalamic structures. One striking difference is found in one nucleus of the preoptic area which is termed the sexually dimorphic nucleus of the preoptic area, which is larger, with more neurons in male rats than in female rats. This morphological difference is observed in many other mammals, including humans, although its functional significance has not yet been elucidated. [*See* SEXUAL BEHAVIOR.]

Lesions of the preoptic area abolish sexual behavior of male rats, but increase it in females, suggesting that the control system is not organized in the same way for the two sexes. Stimulation of the posterior hypothalamus or anteromedial region can elicit sexual responses by males, provided an appropriate stimulus is present, and activity can be measured in lateral hypothalamus neurons during sexual behavior. It is pertinent that administration of hormones such as testosterone or progesterone does not elicit sexual responses in these lesioned animals, suggesting that the hypothalamic centers are involved in the neural control of the behaviors, and not just in the release of hormones.

In male doves, different hormones perfused directly into the anterior hypothalamus induce different components of reproductive behaviors. A mixture of testosterone and estrogen evokes courtship behaviors, whereas testosterone alone yields a behavior that is somewhat later in the logical sequence: the collection of nesting materials. A perfusion of progesterone into the same area results in incubation behavior in male doves. This suggests that the same small region of the hypothalamus can coordinate the appropriate behavioral responses to the varied chemical environment within the body.

In mammals, the sex hormones also influence neural function by binding to receptors throughout the hypothalamus and other brain areas. One of the consequences of this interaction is to modify the expression of certain neurotransmitters and their receptors. One of the most important neurotransmitter systems involved in reproductive behavior is that using oxytocin. Throughout the estrous cycle, pregnancy, and postpartum periods there are significant variations in the concentration and distribution of oxytocin and ocytocin receptors. Application of oxytocin to the hypothalamus initiates maternal behavior in female rats and the antagonist to the peptide interferes with these behaviors. High levels of oxytocin have been suggested to be necessary for the formation of mother–infant bonds. There are also indications that certain aspects of male sexual behavior are under the control of hypothalamic oxytocinergic systems.

6. Emotional Expression

In lower mammals, electrical stimulation of several areas in the medial and posterior hypothalamic nuclei cause impressive displays of aggressive and vicious behavior; because it is thought that such behaviors are merely a behavioral output rather than the "thought" associated with anger, this phenomenon is known as sham rage. Destruction of other areas of the hypothalamus (for example, the ventromedial nucleus) will also lead to such behavioral alterations. [*See* AGGRESSION.]

Two distinct types of aggressive behavior have been postulated to involve distinct neural systems involving the hypothalamus. The first, known as affective (or irritable) aggression, involves a circuit linking the amygdala to the brain stem, through the medial areas of the hypothalamus. Stimulation of this system seems to have a negative hedonic value, since animals will learn a task that causes stimulation of the medial hypothalamus to be stopped. The second form of aggression is of a predatory nature, and involves the lateral hypothalamus. In this case, the fact that animals will learn a task that produces stimulation (that triggers such aggression) of this region suggests that this stimulation involves positive affect. Pharmacological studies also confirm the distinction of these two forms of aggression on neurochemical grounds.

7. Reward and Motivation

The idea is now widely accepted that the hypothalamus is involved more generally in the coordination of the motor and endocrine responses underlying emotional behaivor. Strong support for this arises from the original demonstration of self-stimulation by Olds and Milner and the many subsequent investigations into this phenomenon. If an animal is given the possibility of controlling the delivery of electrical stimulation to electrodes placed in the hypothalamus or many associated structures, it will perform the required response at a very high rate. The rewarding characteristics of such self-stimulation are sometimes so high that animals will totally neglect essential activities, such as feeding and drinking, or cross highly charged grids to reach a place where the self-stimulation could be produced.

This phenomenon has been interpreted either as being based on the brain's "reward system" or as involving its "motivational system." Although self-stimulation can be obtained without any specific drive-state being present, it has often been found that electrodes placed in the lateral hypothalamus generate higher self-stimulation rates as food deprivation is accentuated. The link with motivation is also suggested by the fact that the hypothalamic sites where stimulation of electrodes will cause eating will also support self-stimulation. On the other hand, the idea that self-stimulation taps the reward mechanisms is supported by an elegant study which showed that rats with two implanted electrodes would stimulate one when hungry and the other when thirsty. The fact that self-stimulation rates for electrodes in extra-hypothalamic sites are not influenced by deprivation conditions strengthens the interpretation that the hypothalamus is indeed involved with linking the motivation to the rewarding consequences of the animal's behavior.

Subjective aspects of fear, rage, pleasure, etc., are also associated with hypothalamic damage or irritation in humans; in contrast, pleasurable, euphoric feelings are reported by patients undergoing surgical investigation when forebrain regions are electrically stimulated. This evidence is consistent with the idea that the hypothalamus is one relay in the pathway involving limbic and cortical areas that are associated with emotional behavior. [*See* MOTIVATION, EMOTIONAL BASIS.]

C. Integrative Aspects

While the control of hypothalamic function has been discussed for each regulated function, it must be emphasized that response to perturbations in our internal body environment is accomplished through recruitment of many of the functions of the hypothalamus. For example, the response to a severe hemorrhage will include both autonomic responses designed to elevate blood pressure (e.g., vasoconstriction of peripheral arteries and increased heart rate), hormonal responses mediated via descending autonomic fibers (e.g., adrenal secretion from the adrenal gland), and pituitary secretion of vasoactive hormones and behavioral responses designed to minimize the impact of the reduced blood volume on neural function (assuming a prone position). Similarly, the response to cold will include behavioral (warmth-seeking behavior, putting on warmer clothes, etc.), autonomic (vasoconstriction and shivering), and endocrine (increased secretion of thyrotropin releasing hormone) responses.

The importance of these regulatory functions controlled by the hypothalamus cannot be understated. A lesion or deficit in the afferent circuitry, the central organization or the output of the hypothalamus for the control of these homeostatic and behavioral functions, has serious consequences for the individual. As an "ancient" part of the brain present even in the lowest vertebrates, the hypothalamus has maintained its essential role in supporting bodily functions and survival behaviors.

Acknowledgement

Parts of this article are reproduced here with permission from Pittman, Q. J. (1991). The hypothalamus. In "The Encyclopedia of Human Biology" (R. Dulbecco, Ed.), Academic Press.

Bibliography

Ganten, D., and Pfaff, D., (Eds.) (1986). "Morphology of the Hypothalamus and Its Connections." Springer-Verlag, New York.

Ganten, D., and Pfaff, D. (Eds.) (1990). "Current Topics in Neuroendocrinology," Vol. 10. Springer-Verlag, New York.

Gordon, C. J., and Heath, J. E. (1986). Integration and central processing in temperature regulation. *Annu. Rev. Physiol.* **48**, 595–612.

Kent, S., Bluthé, R. M., Kelley, K., and Dantzer, R. (1992). Sickness behavior as a new target for drug development. *Trends Pharmacol. Sci.* **13,** 24–28.

Kupfermann, I. (1991). Hypothalamus and limbic system:motivation. In "Principles of Neural Science," (E. R. Kandel, J. H. Schwartz, and T. M. Jessell, Eds.), 3rd ed., pp. 750–760. Elsevier, New York.

Nerozzi, D., Goodwin, F. K., and Costa, E. (Eds.) (1987). Hypothalamic dysfunction in neuropsychiatric disorders. *Adv. Biochem. Psychopharmacol.* **43.**

Pedersen, C. A., Caldwell, J. D., Jirikowski, G. F., and Insel, T. R. (Eds.) (1992). Oxytocin in maternal, sexual and social behaviors. *Ann. N.Y. Acad. Sci.* **652.**

Smith, O. A., and DeVito, J. L. (1984). Central neural integration for the control of autonomic responses associated with emotion. *Annu. Rev. Neurosci.* **7,** 43–65.

Swanson, L. W., and Sawchenko, P. E. (1983). Hypothalamic integration: Organization of the paraventricular and supraoptic nuclei. *Annu. Rev. Neurosci.* **6,** 269–324.

Id, Ego, and Superego

Daniel K. Lapsley
Brandon University, Canada

Glossary

Eros One of the two classes of instincts that motivate behavior. It is described as a "life" instinct, the "preserver of all things," incorporating the elements of sexuality and self-preservation. This is in contrast to the opposing tendency to reduce life to an inanimate state, or the "death instinct," which is revealed by aggression and sadism.

Erotogenic zones The zones of the body (oral, anal, phallic) that are sequentially invested with sexualized energy (libido), and are hence the source of autoerotic pleasure. The sexual instinct is thus a composite instinct, only to become organized in the service of reproductive, genital sexuality upon maturity.

Libido The name reserved for the sexual instincts.

Oedipus complex The libidinal cathexis of the phallic erotogenic zone leads to a desire for union and contact with the opposite-sex parent, and a concomitant desire to displace the same-sex rival parent. The competition for the opposite-sex parent engenders anxiety, insofar as the retaliation of the rival is feared ("castration complex"). This is resolved by repressing incestuous desires, and identifying with the same-sex parent, which is the foundation of superego formation. Freud once suggested that the course of Oedipal development between boys and girls was exactly analogous, but later formulations postponed the resolution of the Oedipal conflict for girls until marriage and childbirth.

Pleasure principle The motivating principle of behavior is the pursuit of tension reduction, which is experienced as pleasure.

Primary process The workings of unconscious (id) processes. Instinctual energy is freely mobile, and capable of displacement and condensation. In contrast, secondary process, attributed to ego functioning, attempts to postpone, revise, or otherwise deflect instinctual motivations.

Transference In the therapeutic situation, the (unconscious) incorporation of the analyst in the internal conflicts of the patient.

THE TRIPARTITE PERSONALITY refers to the division of mental life into three agencies or "provinces," id, ego, superego. The id is the oldest and most primitive psychic agency, representing the biological foundations of personality. It is the reservoir of basic instinctual drives, particularly sexual (libidinal) drives, which motivate the organism to seek pleasure (tension reduction). The ego is a modification of the id that emerges as a result of the direct influence of the external world. It is the "executive" of the personality in the sense that it regulates libidinal drive energies so that satisfaction accords with the demands of reality. It is the center of reason, reality-testing, and commonsense, and it has at its command a range of defensive stratagems that can deflect, repress, or transform the expression of unrealistic or forbidden drive energies. The superego is a further differentiation within the ego which represents its "ideal." The superego

Encyclopedia of Human Behavior, Volume 2
Copyright © 1994 by Academic Press, Inc. All rights of reproduction in any form reserved.

emerges as a consequence of the Oedipal drama, whereby the child takes on the authority and magnificence of parental figures through introjection or identification. Whereas the id operates in pursuit of pleasure, and whereas the ego is governed by the reality principle, the superego bids the psychic apparatus to pursue idealistic goals and perfection. It is the source of moral censorship and of conscience.

I. FREUD IN CONTEXT

Psychoanalysis is one of those rare intellectual achievements that has had the effect of radically transforming human self-understanding. Indeed, Freudian notions have so thoroughly permeated human culture that the jargon (if not the substance) of psychoanalysis is accessible to even the most untutored observers of human behavior, so much so that the poet W. H. Auden could write, with ample justification, that to us Freud is not so much a person but rather "a whole climate of opinion under whom we conduct our differing lives." By Freud's own estimation psychoanalysis effectively completed the intellectual revolution begun by Copernicus, and advanced by Darwin, a revolution that undermined human conceit regarding its putatively special and privileged position in the cosmos and in nature. Whereas Copernicus displaced mankind's planet from the center of the heavens, and whereas Darwin showed that no comfort can be taken in the conceit that we are nonetheless above the forces of nature, Freud completed the assault on human pretence by showing that even human reason is not what it has been supposed, that human psychology is, in fact, besieged and driven by irrational, unconscious motivations. Indeed, Freud's discovery of a hidden psychic reality that has beyond the pale of sensible consciousness was thought (by Freud) to be an application of the same Newtonian dualism that accepted the distinction between human sensory abilities (percepts) and a hidden physical reality that could only be apprehended by mathematics and the armamentum of physical science. The Newtonian scheme, which revolutionized our understanding of the physical universe, was invoked by psychoanalysis to advance an understanding of psychic life, an application that hinges on the distinction between conscious and unconscious mental life. And just as physical science develops the techniques to apprehend a physical universe that is beyond immediate human sensibility, so too does psychoanalysis attempt to pierce hidden unconscious realities with its special clinical techniques. Psychoanalysis, then, according to Freud, is to be counted among the natural sciences; it is a specialized branch of medicine (with the caveat that medical training gives no necessary expertise in psychical affairs), with mental life the object of inquiry.

Although psychoanalysis appeared to shock Victorian sensibilities, particularly with its claims regarding unconscious mental dynamics and infantile sexuality, it was nonetheless grounded in themes common to 19th century science. The Freudian theory of instincts seemed at home in a culture that was getting used to the ideas of Darwinian biology. Freud's use of spatial models to locate psychic structures was in keeping with efforts in neurology to localize brain functions. And the mechanistic Freudian image of the psychological architecture as an apparatus for channeling instinctual drive energies was not out of step with the energy mechanics of 19th century physics. Yet, for all the trappings of scientific positivism that Freud was wont to claim for psychoanalysis, the Freudian project was met with considerable resistance, and the history of the psychoanalytic movement is a history of a struggle for academic, clinical, and popular respectability, a respectability that is still not completely won. Freud himself was at pains to recount this struggle in a number of histories, outlines, and encyclopedia articles. Although one aim was certainly to popularize the new science of mental life, Freud was also keen to demarcate psychoanalysis from rival depth psychologies (e.g., Jung, Adler), and to show that controversial psychoanalytic claims were the result of careful scientific investigation of the positivist, natural science kind. He would claim, for example, that the hypothetical entities and forces of psychoanalysis were not different in kind from the hypothetical entities and forces claimed in the ostensibly harder, more respectable sciences. It will be of interest for our purposes to recount the early development of psychoanalysis in order to set the proper context for considering Freud's account of the tripartite personality. The structural notions of id, ego, and superego were rather late theoretical developments that can only be properly understood in light of the prior history of theoretical revisions—revisions that Freud would claim, forced upon psychoanalysis by the evidential warrant.

II. THE CORNERSTONES OF PSYCHOANALYSIS

Freud was initially drawn to the dynamics of depth psychology by the inability of the neurological community to come to grips with the problem of hysteria. Hysterics appeared to suffer a host of somatic and physical maladies (e.g., motor paralysis, glove anesthesia) that had no apparent neurological basis. One promising treatment approach was the use of hypnosis. Josef Breuer, a medical colleague of Freud, claimed to have relieved the hysterical symptoms of a female patient ("Anna O.") by such means. In *Studies on Hysteria* (1895) Breuer and Freud presented a series of case studies and theoretical articles on the etiology of hysteria and the role of hypnosis in treating it. The authors claimed that hysterical symptoms have a symbolic meaning of which the patient had no conscious knowledge. Symptoms are substitutes for mental acts that are diverted from normal discharge because the charge of affect associated with the mental processes becomes "strangulated" (as a result of trauma) and channeled into somatic innervation ("conversion"). That is, a strong affect is prevented from being consciously worked out, and is instead diverted from consciousness into "the wrong path," taking the form of somatic symptoms. Under hypnosis this strangulated affect can be set free or purged ("abreacted"), allowed normal discharge into consciousness, thereby leading to a removal of symptoms. This treatment modality was called *the cathartic method*. Patients, under hypnosis, tended to recall "psychic traumas" from a remote past, extending to early childhood, so that Breuer and Freud could claim that hysterics "suffer from reminiscences." When these traumas are allowed expression in the hypnotic state, strangulated affect is abreacted and redirected away from somatic innervation into normal conscious discharge. One sees in these studies, and in the papers that followed, the preliminary delineation of some of the foundational notions of psychoanalysis. To observe that traumatic "reminiscences" could be recalled only under hypnosis suggests that their conscious expression is met with certain resistances (defensive repression). And, though resisted, these reminiscences continue to exert pathogenic effects (as symptoms), which are suggestive of unconscious mental processes. [*See* Hypnosis.]

Freud was soon to abandon the hypnotic technique for the good reason that not all of his patients were amenable to hypnotic induction. In addition, Freud observed that the amelioration of symptoms seemed to depend more on the nature of the patient–analyst relationship. If this relationship was disturbed, symptoms reappeared. This clinical insight was to later become reformalized as *transference love*. Transference describes a phenomenon that emerges during the course of psychoanalytic treatment whereby the patient comes to involve the analyst as a substitute for past object relations, a finding that some consider to be one of Freud's great discoveries. The hypnotic technique was replaced by the method of free association, a method that requires the patient to honestly read off the content of conscious experiences and memories without judgment or embarrassment. The choice of this technique hinges on the assumption of strict determinism, that is, that associated ideas and memories are not randomly yoked but are instead determined by a dominant (and often pathogenically repressed) trend of thought which is unconscious (but is causally active nonetheless). Given the assumption that symptoms have sense and meaning, and are substitutes for actions that are omitted or repressed, the task of the analyst was to interpret the free associations in a way that successfully deciphered their meaning, a meaning that was otherwise obscured by censorship. To distinguish this technique from the cathartic method, Freud called this method of treatment "psychoanalysis." Freud claimed that this transition from catharsis to psychoanalysis yielded two important novelties: the extension of psychoanalytic insights to phenomena associated with normality, and the discovery of the significance of infantile sexuality for understanding the etiology of neuroses.

In *The Interpretation of Dreams* (1900) and in *The Psychopathology of Everyday Life* (1901) Freud extended this notion of mental determinism to include not just the symbolic character of neurotic free associations which of necessity require analytic interpretation, but also the various parapraxes of normal life ("Freudian slips," accidental self-injury, and other putatively "haphazard" acts) and dreams. These too are like neurotic symptoms in that they express a meaning that can be deciphered by analytic interpretation. The difference between normality and neurosis was not so great as had been supposed. Indeed, the interpretation of dreams was to provide important clues to the nature of the unconscious and the process of symptom formation.

Freud distinguished between the manifest and latent content of dreams. The manifest content was simply the recollected dream, often bizarre and strange. The latent content is provided by analytic interpretation. Latent dream thoughts are distorted and condensed "residues" of the previous day. They are arranged so as to allow pictorial representation and, through "secondary revision," are given a sense of coherence. The motivation for dream formation is a repressed unconscious impulse that seeks satisfaction ("wish fulfilment") through the material of latent dream thoughts. Dreams, then, represent a disguised attempt at a fulfillment of an unconscious wish that was denied satisfaction. The attempt is disguised, that is, the manifest content is strange and bizarre, because of the efforts of a restrictive, disapproving agency in the mind (e.g., the ego). Dream censorship, according to Freud, points to the same mental process that kept the wish repressed during the day. So, on the one hand, there is an unfulfilled, repressed wish that is striving for expression. On the other, there is a disapproving, censoring ego that is striving to repress it. The result is a compromise formation that takes the form of dreams, in normality, and of symptoms, in the case of neurosis. Dream formation and symptom formation, then, are expressions of identical mental dynamics. Both are compromise formations that reflect the conflict between unconscious impulses (wishes) and the censoring ego. [*See* DREAMING.]

The second novelty revealed by the psychoanalytic method was that the search for pathogenically significant traumatic experiences typically took one back to early childhood. And these experiences were invariably a reflection of a disturbance of infantile sexual life. This remains one of the most controversial aspects of Freud's theory, although it is often misunderstood. Infantile sexuality refers to the sensations of pleasure that accompany holding, maternal caressing, and oral and anal satisfactions. What counts as "sexual," in Freud's theory, is thus much broader and more general than what the layperson normally has cause to assume. What Freud claimed was that the development of human sexuality was diphasic, interrupted by a latency period where the sexual motivations are diverted to other purposes. There is, first of all, an infantile period where the sexual instincts are sequentially invested in different zones of the body ("erotogenic zones"), and then a more adult form when the component sexual instincts (oral, anal, phallic) are organized in the service of genital, reproductive sexuality. The sexual instinct is thus an organization of component instincts that takes the adult form only at puberty.

Yet the organization of the infantile expressions of sexuality (sensations of pleasure associated with oral, anal, and phallic zones of the body) is of decisive significance for understanding the etiology of the (transference) neuroses. This is particularly true with respect to the libidinal investment of the phallic region, which encourages the emergence of the Oedipus complex in young children (ages 2–5). More will be said about the Oedipus complex below, insofar as its resolution is foundational for the emergence of the superego. Suffice it to say here that this emotionally charged triangular complex of family relationships is the etiological source of the neuroses. As Freud noted, normal individuals survive and master their Oedipal feelings; neurotics continue to be mastered by them.

At this point we have reviewed what Freud has called the "cornerstones" of psychoanalytic theory: the discovery of unconscious mental processes, the theory of repression and of transference, and the importance of infantile sexuality and the Oedipus complex for understanding neuroses. No one could be called a psychoanalyst unless one accepted these foundational tenets. Yet we are still far from articulating the tripartite structural features of the personality (id, ego, superego). This must await a fuller account of some important theoretical amplifications that anticipate Freud's mature description of id, ego, and superego.

III. THEORETICAL REVISIONS AND THE EMERGENCE OF THE TRIPARTITE PERSONALITY

The division of mental life into that which is conscious and unconscious suggests a topographical hypothesis, viz., that mental life can be demarcated into psychic portions or regions. Unconsciousness is at once a quality that can be attributed to a repressed idea or impulse, and also a region or "province" (the "system *Ucs*") to where the idea is banished. Consciousness, and its precursor ("preconsciousness") too, was formulated as a psychic province ("system *Cs, Pcs*"), and attributed to the workings of the ego. Psychic conflict, then, was a matter of unconscious ideas, emanating from the system *Ucs*, struggling against the repressive forces of the conscious ego. Furthermore, unconscious and conscious processes are seen to follow different laws. The *Ucs* consists of "instinctual representatives" which seek discharge, that is, are wishful impulses. They are exempt from mutual contradiction, are timeless (are not ordered temporarily), are not oriented to reality, and follow the pleasure principle. They are also characterized by *primary process,* which means that the cathectic intensities of wishful, instinctual impulses are freely mobile (amenable to *displacement* and *condensation*). This is in contrast to *Cs* (*Pcs*), where *secondary process* is dominant. Secondary process is a later developmental achievement associated with ego functioning. As a reality oriented process it revises, censors, or *binds* the discharge of instinctual impulses.

Although Freud never abandoned the notion of primary and secondary process, he did come to revise the provisional topographical model of the psychic architecture as one involving "systems," and also the dynamic hypothesis that the unconscious was in conflict with the conscious ego. These notions were revised in light of Freud's clinical observation that his patients were often unaware of the fact that they were employing certain resistances. If the ego is responsible for repression but is also the seat of consciousness, then it was inexplicable how one could not be conscious of one's own resistances and one's own act of repression. Freud concluded that much of the ego, too, must be unconscious. In other words, the unconscious does not consist entirely of that which is repressed (although all that is repressed is unconscious), a fact that makes the division of the psychic architecture into systems *Ucs* and *Cs* (*Pcs*) less compelling.

The ego concept was further clarified as a result of revisions to the instinct theory. According to Freud instincts arise from internal sources, exerting a constant force or pressure demanding satisfaction. The relentless pressure of instinctual drive energies makes it impossible for the nervous system to remain in an unstimulated condition ("principle of constancy"), and hence motivates psychic adaptations so as to effect the satisfaction of internal needs. The *pressure* of an instinct, then, is a "motor" factor, that is, a demand for psychic work. The *aim* of an instinct is gratification through tension reduction. The *object* of an instinct is anything through which satisfaction can be achieved. The *source* of an instinct is a somatic process, experienced as a kind of "hunger" or "need." Indeed, Freud often described instincts as the "psychic representatives" of somatic processes.

In *The Three Essays on Sexuality* (1905) Freud identified the sexual instincts as "libido." Libido is both a quantitative and a qualitative variable—quantitative in the sense that it serves as a measure of the forces of sexual excitation, qualitative in the sense that it can be distinguished from other kinds of psychic energy (contra Jung). Psychoneurotic conflict could then be described as a clash between sexuality and the various functions of the ego (e.g., reality-testing, resistance, repression). However, in addition to libidinal (sexual) instincts, Freud later identified a second group of primal instincts, called *ego instincts*. Ego instincts subsumed the functions of self-preservation, repression, and all other impulses that could be distinguished from sexual (libidinal) instincts, and these instincts are attributed to the ego. By identifying a second group of primal instincts Freud could now characterize psychoneurotic conflict as a clash between libidinal (sexual) and the self-preservative (ego) instincts.

Matters are further complicated, however, by the pivotal paper *On Narcissism* (1914). Here Freud argues that the sexual instincts are originally attached to the satisfaction of ego instincts (self-preservation). That is, autoerotic satisfactions (e.g., orality) are initially experienced in connection with those functions (e.g., sucking) that serve the purpose of self-preservation. Only later do the sexual instincts detach in search of external objects (e.g., mother). Libido that cathects external objects was called "object libido." Yet Freud observed that libidinal development of the anaclitic–attachment type could be derailed. Instead of seeking an external object it was also possible to libidinally cathect oneself. That is, rather than choose mother as a love object, one chooses oneself. Libido, then, could be apportioned depending on the kind of object choice one made. Libido apportioned to oneself was called "narcissistic" (or ego) libido, to distinguish it from the libidinal cathexis of external objects (object libido). In Freud's view the narcissistic libidinal cathexis of the ego is the original state of things, and that consequently the initial phase of libidinal development was one of *primary narcissism*. It is from the reservoir of narcissistic libido that object cathexes are sent out to engage objects.

In *Beyond the Pleasure Principle* (1920) Freud could state explicitly that the dualism between libidinal instincts and ego instincts was no longer tenable, since the narcissistic self-preservative instincts were also libidinal. Insofar as libido is oriented toward sexual objects, and given the fact that the self, too, could be a (narcissistic) object choice, it readily follows that self-preservative (ego) instincts are also libidinal in nature. It would thus seem that all of instinctual mental life could be reduced to the sexual instincts after all, a conclusion that would either justify Jung's monistic use of "libido" as a term denoting a generalized psychic drive or vindicate those critics who accused Freud of pan-sexualism. One solution to this theoretical problem was to group the libidinal instincts as *Eros,* or the life instincts, the "preserver of all things," and to contrapose the life instincts (Eros) to a contrary instinctual impulse that seeks to restore organic life to an inanimate state, which Freud called the *death instincts*. Freud was led to postulate the existence of death instincts by his reflection on the compulsion of those who suffer from traumatic neuroses to repeat traumatic dreams. The dreams of war neurotics, for example, seemed contrary to the general case that dreams represent symbolic wish fulfillment. The compulsion to repeat traumatic experiences, then, appeared to operate "beyond the pleasure principle," and to point toward an instinctual tendency at odds with libidinal self-preservation.

The struggle of Eros and the death instincts can be observed at every level of biology, in every particle of substance, even in molecular organisms. Eros attempts to preserve life through combinations, and this to neutralize the instinctual striving toward death. The two instincts can also fuse resulting, at the psychic level, in sexual sadism. De-fusion can result in the discharge of death instincts toward objects, which then takes the form of aggression, destructiveness, or sadism *simpliciter*. If the ego is the object of discharge, then masochistic tendencies result. Indeed, if it is possible for erotic libido to cathect the ego and to result in a phase of primary narcissism, it must correspondingly be possible for the death instinct to turn up (cathect) the ego, and result in a phase of *primary masochism,* a possibility that Freud did not reject outright.

Freud's account of the two classes of instincts, Eros (sexuality and self-preservation) and death (aggression), allowed him to preserve a dualistic classification of the instincts. The question now loomed as to how these twin instincts interacted with topographical features of the mind, now that the notions of "consciousness" and "unconsciousness" no longer had any straightforward implications for a structural depiction of mental life. This issue would be taken up in Freud's seminal work, *The Ego and the Id* (1923). In this work Freud reworks the structural theory to include three psychic provinces, id, ego, and superego. He also describes how instinctual drive energies can be economically transmuted among these structures, and how certain neurotic conditions can be explained as a result of this hydraulic model of the mind.

IV. ID, EGO, SUPEREGO

The mature structural theory largely replaces the ill-defined notions of unconsciousness and the system *Ucs* with the "id." The id becomes a psychical province that incorporates instinctual drive energies, and everything else that is part of our phylogenetic inheritance. The id operates unconsciously, accords with primary process, and impels the organism to engage in need-satisfying, tension-reducing activities, which are experienced as "pleasure."

Within the id are undifferentiated elements that would later emerge as the "ego." Freud's conceptualization of the ego and its functions has shown clear lines of theoretical development. In early formulations it was identified with the system *Cs (Pcs),* and known largely in terms of its repressive and self-preservative functions, and for its putative opposition to things unconscious. As noted above a clear change became evident in the paper *On Narcissim,* where Freud argued not only that ego instincts were themselves libidinal, but also that ego functions were largely unconscious. One also sees in this paper two further developments. One is that the ego begins to be described not only as an impersonal "apparatus" whose function is to de-tension the biological strivings of the organism, or as a "device" for mastering excitations, but rather as a personal self. Another development is Freud's tentative hypothesis that ego development entails the renunciation of narcissistic self-love in favour of the idealization or aggrandizement of cultural and ethical ideals, which is represented to the child by the influence of parents. This "ego ideal" becomes a substitute for lost infantile narcissim at which time the child was his or her own ideal. Freud goes on to suggest that perhaps a special psychical agency emerges to observe the ego and to measure it by its ideal. This self-observing agency, and the ego ideal, will later take the form of a third psychical province, the superego.

What is the nature, then, of ego and superego formation, as outlined in *The Ego and the Id?* At the outset the psychic system is described as an undifferentiated id–ego matrix. Topographically, a portion of the id lies in proximity to the boundaries of preconsciousness and external perceptual systems (system *Pcpt*), which brings the influence of the external world upon it. The resulting modification results in the formation of the ego. Hence, the ego is that part of the id that is modified as result of the perceptual system, and by its proximity and access to consciousness, although the ego itself, like the id, is unconscious. The ego takes on a number of functions. It commands voluntary movement. It has the task of self-preservation, and must therefore master both internal (id) and external stimuli. The ego masters external stimuli by becoming "aware," by storing up memories, by avoidance through flight, and by active adaptation. Regarding internal drive stimuli, it attempts to control the demands of the instincts by judiciously deciding the mode of satisfaction, or if satisfaction is to be had at all. Indeed, the ego attempts to harness instinctual libidinal drives so that they submit to the reality principle. If the id is a cauldron of passions, the ego is the agent of reason, commonsense, and defense. Yet the ego is never sharply differentiated from the id. Freud argues that the "lower portion" of the ego extends throughout the id, and it is by means of the id that repressed material communicates with (presses "up" against the resistances of) the ego.

The nature of ego functioning is further clarified, and complicated, by superego formation. One clue to understanding superego formation was provided by Freud's reflection on the problem of pathological melancholia. He suggested that when an object relationship is "lost," the lost object can nonetheless by regained by "identification," that is, the lost object is "set up again inside the ego." Say that the libidinal (erotic) needs of the id are such that an attempt is made to cathect an object. When the sexual object is subsequently given up, the ego is altered, insofar as the abandoned libidinal object is now set up inside the ego. That is, the ego incorporates the object within itself (as an introjection), "identifies" with it, and thereby builds up it structure or "character." In this way an object cathexis is substituted by an introjection. Freud suggests that perhaps the id can give up its objects only by identifications of this sort, and that the ego can consequently be considered a precipitate of abandoned object cathexes. Yet another possibility is that the ego can also deflect the object cathexis of the id by forcing itself upon the id as a love object, and thereby transforming object libido into narcissistic libido.

It was from this sort of reflection on how the ego can be built up and altered by identification that Freud found the theoretical foundation of superego formation. For he argued that the first identifications in early childhood would be those that would have lasting and momentous significance, in the sense that here would be found the origins of the "ego ideal." And the necessity for making these identifications would be found in the triangular character of the Oedipus complex.

For illustrative purposes consider the simple Oedipal situation for boys. The boy develops a libidinal attachment to mother, while identifying with father. Eventually, the erotic investment in mother intensifies, and father now comes to be seen as an obstacle, or as a jealous rival. The boy desires to possess mother and also to displace his rival, who is now viewed with some ambivalence. Yet this engenders considerable anxiety, insofar as the powerful rival is capable of significant retaliation through the threat of castration. Hence, the Oedipal situation is untenable for the boy, given the surge of castration anxiety. The maternal object cathexis must be given up. Although many complications are possible, some with pathological consequences, the standard maneuver is for the boy to repress his Oedipal desires for mother. Yet the infantile ego is still too feeble to carry this out effectively. Since the expression of Oedipal desires was met with an obstacle in the person of the boy's father, one way of repressing these desires suggests itself: set up the obstacle within oneself by intensifying one's identification with father. In this way the boy musters the wherewithal to carry out the required act of repression, insofar as this identification is a way of borrowing the strength of the powerful father. But, as we have seen, identification typically results in an alteration of the ego. Indeed, the incorporation of father (perhaps by means of a regression to oral incorporative mechanisms) as a solution to the Oedipal complex is so momentous that a new psychical agency emerges from within the ego, the superego, which will thereafter retain the character of the father. Furthermore, every act of identification results in a sublimation of libido. Libido is "desexualized." But this sublimation also means that the aggressive (death) instincts are no longer bound to erotic libido—it is now "defused," set free, and no longer neutralized. Freud suggested that herein lies the source of the cruel harshness of the dictatorial injunctions ("Thou shalt") of the superego—it lies in the pool of aggressive energies set free by the act of identification and libidinal diffusion.

The superego is thus a precipitate of family life. It is an agency that seeks to enforce the striving for perfection, as it holds out to the ego ideal standards and moralistic goals. As a consequence the superego is the "conscience" of the personality, and it can retaliate against the imperfections of the ego by inducing guilt. Insofar as the superego is derived from the id's first object cathexis (in the Oedipal situation), the superego remains close to the id "and can act as its representative" (in contrast to the ego, which represents reality). And because the origin of conscience is tied to the Oedipus complex, which is unconscious, the corresponding sense of guilt, too, must be unconscious. Indeed, Freud asserts that the superego reaches down into the id, and is consequently "farther from consciousness than the ego is." This leads to an interesting paradox that was noted by Freud. Because one is unconscious of having irrational libidinal and aggressive desires, one is far more "immoral" than one believes. But because the superego (and the guilt that it imposes as punishment) is also unconscious, one is also more moral than one knows.

Superego formation, then, and the ideals that it represents, allows one to master the Oedipal complex. And because it emerged at a time when the ego was still vulnerable, it retains a dominant position with respect to the ego. Freud was keen to point out that the superego is that part of his theory that expresses the "higher nature" of man. He argued that as children we knew these "higher natures" in the person of our parents, "we admired and feared them; and later we took them into ourselves" as introjections. And if religion, morality, and sociality are held to be what is "higher" in mankind, these too find their psychological origin in the workings of the superego. The "religious" longing for a protective and nurturing God finds its origin in the fact that the superego is a precipitate of our infantile longing for father. Our religious humility in the face of a judgmental God is a projection of the self-criticism of an ego who has fallen short of the ideals held out by the superego. With development the injunctions of the father (which are introjected as the superego) are supplemented by other moral authorities, which then fortifies the workings of conscience and thereby intensifies the feelings of moral guilt. And social feelings of all kinds are rooted in the kind of object identification of which superego formation is the model.

In addition to representing that which is "higher" in human nature, the superego is also implicated in a variety of pathological conditions. It is implicated, for example, in a "resistance to therapeutic recovery," since the prolongation of neurotic suffering is a kind of punishment for failing to meet the exacting demands of the superego. Melancholia results when the superego appropriates the violence of aggressive instincts and directs them against the ego. Certain kinds of obsessional neuroses ("tormenting" the object, as opposed to the self), too, can be linked to the harsh reproaches of the superego.

It should be clear that the ego is besieged from two directions. It must cope with the libidinal and aggressive drives of the id, from "below," and also the harsh moralistic and perfectionistic demands of the superego, from "above." The ego must further reconcile these contrary tendencies with the demands of external reality. "Whenever possible," Freud writes, "it [the ego] clothes the id's *Ucs.* commands with its *Pcs.* rationalizations; it pretends that the id is showing obedience to the admonitions of reality, even when in fact it is remaining obstinate and unyielding; it disguises the id's conflicts with reality and, if possible, its conflicts with the superego, too." Freud also likened the ego to a man who struggles to check the superior power of a horse, to a constitutional monarch who is ultimately powerless to frustrate the will of parliament, and to a politician who too often "yields to the temptation to become sycophantic, opportunist and lying." One has recourse to psychoanalysis when such a struggle batters the personality into neurosis.

A. Summary

One way to summarize Freud's account of the tripartite personality is to make explicit the metapsychological assumptions that have to now remained only implicit. Freud's *topographical* perspective is that the critical determinants of human behavior are unconscious, emanating from a biological province which he calls the "id." The *dynamic* point of view is that these critical determinants are instinctual drives, of which two classes can be identified: Eros (sex, self-preservation) and the death instinct (aggression, sadism). The *economic* point of view is that the "hydraulic" disposition of these drive energies among the psychic regions is a regulator of behavior.

V. SELECTED POST-FREUDIAN DEVELOPMENTS

Although there are still many adherents of Freud's classical theory, a palpable development since Freud has been the proliferation of competing psychoanalytic theories, all of which claim some support or other from the many searching insights to be found in the vast Freudian corpus. The most important post-Freudian development is a collection of related theories that is denoted as the "object relational" school. Although these theories can be cleanly distinguished on both obvious and subtle theoretical points, it is fair to say that they share in common a distaste for Freud's emphasis on energy dynamics as the foundation of human personality, and for his division of personality into tripartite, evolutionary layers. They deny, for example, that the human organism is at first asocial, convulsed by bestial instinctual passions, embedded in primary narcissism, and only later to become social and socialized. To picture the human person as one driven by libidinal and aggressive energies is to liken it to a "centaur"—the mythological creature with a human head affixed to the body of a beast.

One objection to the "Centaur model" is that it is yoked to an implausible notion of "instincts." Freud suggested that human motivation can be explained with reference to two instincts, sex and aggression. But sex is not an instinctual impulse that exerts constant pressure but is rather like an "appetite" that shows a measure of periodicity. Aggression is not even an appetite, but is rather an ego reaction to a threat to the personality. And both sex and aggression are aspects of personhood that are ineradicable from interpersonal relationships. Furthermore, Freud's notion that human psychology is driven by the energies afforded by the struggle between life and death instincts has been dismissed by some critics as mere "biological mysticism." [*See* AGGRESSION.]

A related criticism concerns Freud's account of the ego. In Freud's theory the rational ego emerges from a portion of the irrational id, but only as an impersonal apparatus or device for channelling drive energies and for securing the de-tensioning of the organism. What Freud described is a control system and not a personal self who is involved in motivated relationships from the very beginning. When Freud describes the tripartite personality as consisting of "provinces" that are "extended in space" he is describing a material reality that is based on a biological model of localization, and not the psychodynamic reality that whole human selves are formed in meaningful relationships that begin at birth. Hence, object relations theory rejects the Centaur model, rejects the instinct theory, rejects primary narcissism (and masochism), and rejects the impersonal ego.

Yet the object relations approach is often thought of as a movement that develops Freud's own best object relational insights. The notion of transference, for example, and the Oedipus complex of family relations, and the account of the ego as an "agency" (as opposed to a "province") would be ready examples of object relational insights that counter Freud's own preoccupation with impersonal, biological energy mechanics. It is ironic that the Oedipal theory, which is generally considered to be that which is most unpalatable about Freud's theory, is actually the foundation of the keen object relational insight—that personality is grounded in the nexus of family relationships. Of all the psychic structures the superego is the only one to emerge as consequence of interpersonal relationships. It comes to represent the influence of family and societal institutions on the formation of personality. Transference, whereby the patient involves the analyst in his or her inner conflicts, enshrines the view that the history of our experience of interpersonal relationships provides us with a template by which we attempt to manage our current relationships.

In sum, the object relations approach tends to focus on the agentic whole self (the "person ego") whose personality develops within the dynamics of complicated, meaningful relationships—and the warrant for this conceptualization, too, is often to be found in Freud's own writings.

I noted at the outset that psychoanalysis has revolutionized human self-understanding in this century. Yet, for all that, the theory is still very much a product of 19th century conceptions of science. While one has cause to question Freud's reliance on outdated biological and physical science metaphors, his mechanistic conception of energy dynamics and his preoccupation with brain physiology and with localization, what will survive are the psychodynamic features of his theory, and the clinical insights about human personality that have given everyone a new vocabulary. Defense mechanisms, ego, insight therapy, unconscious processes, the symbolic nature of symptoms, dreams, and parapraxes, and transference—these are notions that are not far from even lay discourse. Although it is not easy to divorce the clinical facts attributed to Freud from the theories developed to explain them, especially when the probative and epistemic status of the theory is at stake, it is fair to say that the contemporary study of psychopathology and personality, the conduct of clinical practice, and the way ordinary people confront themselves and others would be very different were it not for Freud's monumental, pioneering work. When one adds to this the whole domain of "applied psychoanalysis"—the extension of psychoanalytic insights for understanding the artistic process, group psychology, esthetics, religious experience, and other cultural products, then the justice of W. H. Auden's elegy becomes apparent. Freud lurks wherever one considers the human condition: a "whole climate of opinion under whom we conduct our differing lives."

Bibliography

Edelson, M. (1988). "Psychoanalysis: A Theory in Crisis. University of Chicago Press, Chicago.

Gay, P. (1989). "Freud: A Life for Our Times." Anchor/Doubleday, New York.

Greenberg, J. R., and Mitchell, S. A. (Eds.) (1983). "Object Relations in Psychoanalytic Theory." Harvard University Press, Cambridge, MA.

Grunbaum, A. (1984). "The Foundations of Psychoanalysis: A Philosophical Critique." University of California Press, Berkely, CA.

Kurzweil, E., and Phillips, W. (Eds.) (1983). "Literature and Psychoanalysis." Columbia University Press, New York.

Reppen, J. (Ed.) (1985). "Beyond Freud: A Study of Modern Psychoanalytic Theorists." Erlbaum, Hillsdale, NJ.

IMPLICIT MEMORY

Stephan Lewandowsky and J. Vivien Bainbridge
University of Oklahoma

Glossary

Amnesia Loss of memory, usually long-term, as a consequence of some kind of trauma. Amnesia may result from a cerebral insult, psychological trauma, or psychiatric illness. Patients with *anterograde amnesia,* the inability to acquire new memories, form the primary population of interest to those studying implicit memory.

Awareness Term used synonymously with conscious recollection of an event.

Cognitive neuroscience Interdisciplinary approach to understanding mental functions, which attempts to integrate findings from experimental psychology, neuropsychology, and neurology. A promising recent development involves computational modeling, in which theoretical explanations are implemented in neurologically plausible computer-based models.

Data-driven vs conceptually driven tasks *Data-driven* tasks require an analysis of the physical, or surface, characteristics of the stimulus (also called a bottom-up analysis). The stimulus is typically provided, in full, by the experimenter (e.g., word naming). *Conceptually driven* tasks involve a semantic or top-down analysis, often in the absence of full information about the stimulus (e.g., free recall).

Declarative vs procedural Describes qualitatively different types of memories, and perhaps different systems of memory. *Procedural* memory involves skills (in particular motor skills), often without allowing verbal recollection, whereas *declarative* memory supports conscious recollection of facts, often in the form of verbal information.

Direct vs indirect tests Tests used to assess people's memory by interrogating memory either *directly* (also known as explicit tests) or *indirectly* (implicit). Direct tests involve conscious attempts to recollect information about specific episodes. Indirect tests do not require recollective activities, relying instead on performance measures on repeated items as an indication that memories exist (see *priming*). Performance measures include such things as response times for the identification of items and probability of completing a word stem or fragment.

Functional dissociation Variables which are found to influence performance on one test of memory, but do not show the same influence on another test are said to produce a *functional dissociation.* For example, a change in modality across presentations will affect indirect (implicit) measures of memory, but will not affect direct (explicit) measures of memory. Conversely, the nature of encoding operations at study will affect direct but not indirect tests.

Priming Change in performance as a consequence of prior experience. Most commonly, priming is a facilitation of, or improvement in, performance on indirect tests of memory.

IMPLICIT MEMORY refers to an unintentional and often unaware manifestation of retention of previous information. This form of memory stands in contrast to the intentional and conscious form of recollection known as explicit memory. Operationally, the two manifestations of memory fall into the domain of different experimental tasks. Tasks that require reference to a specific prior episode—such as recall or recognition of words from a study list—are said to test explicit memory, whereas tasks that can be completed without reference to prior study—such as deciding whether a letter string is a word or completing a word fragment—tap into implicit memory

Copyright © 1994 by Academic Press, Inc. All rights of reproduction in any form reserved.

processes. It is the fact that implicit memory has appeared preserved in amnesics who exhibited an otherwise complete loss of recollective ability that has provided the initial theoretical relevance and much of the impetus for the early research. More recently, the evolutionary significance of implicit memory has been recognized, and it has been argued that the observed differences between implicit and explicit task performance speak to some of the more fundamental properties of human memory. [*See* MEMORY.]

I. EARLY EVIDENCE FOR IMPLICIT MEMORY

The earliest examples of implicit memory involved amnesic patients. A patient would fail to show any explicit memory for people or for a recently completed task, but would nevertheless show enhanced performance when required to repeat that very same task: for example, a reduction in the time and the number of trials required to solve the Tower of Hanoi problem. Early evidence for implicit memory in subjects with intact memory comes from Ebbinghaus' savings paradigm in which the ease of relearning previously learned material served as an index for memory without any concomitant need for explicit recollection. Subsequent investigations of normal subjects have revealed dissociations between tasks paralleling those obtained with amnesics. This article focuses primarily on the distinction between implicit and explicit memory as it was developed using normal subjects. [*See* AMNESIA.]

II. DISSOCIATIONS BETWEEN IMPLICIT AND EXPLICIT TASKS

Conceptual differentiation between different types of memories or different kinds of memory processes is supported by two principal classes of experimental outcomes. First, experimental variables must be shown to have different, preferably opposing, effects on two tasks that are thought to tap selectively into the two memories or processes under consideration. Second, differentiation is supported even more strongly if performance on the two tasks is also found to be statistically independent. An extensive literature has been built around these two types of outcomes and used to differentiate between implicit and explicit forms of remembering. The reasons for the fascination with and enthusiasm for implicit phenomena are conveyed most readily by presenting an early experiment in some detail.

A. An Early Prototypical Experiment

Suppose one is given a long list of words to study without specific instructions about the form of the impending memory test. Again, suppose that study is followed by two different tasks, a recognition test and a fragment completion test, that are presented together on two occasions, once right after study and again a week later. For the recognition test, several of the study items are shown together with an equal number of new items, and the task is to identify the study items from among the set of distractors. For the fragment completion test, meaningful completions must be provided for word fragments such as A____T_IR, Z____E_IN or _E_D_TT_ without necessarily involving any recollective activity.

Two aspects of the results from this prototypical study come as no surprise: Even in the absence of instructions linking the word fragments to the previously studied list, it appears reasonable that prior study of ABATTOIR, ZEPPELIN, and VENDETTA would facilitate completion performance, compared to other fragments whose completions were not studied. This study advantage for tasks that do not logically require reference to a prior memorial episode is known as *priming* and is typically seen to reflect contributions from implicit memory. In the case of the recognition test, some forgetting appears between the immediate and the delayed tests, which is again unremarkable.

However, other aspects of the relationship between those two tasks do not conform to what intuition might expect. First, in contrast to recognition, very little forgetting is observed for fragment completion; that is, the extent of priming remains virtually the same across the 1-week retention interval. Although subsequent research has placed limits on the generality of this finding, the pattern fulfills the criterion for a *functional dissociation* because performance on the two experimental tasks (recognition and fragment completion) is affected differently by a common experimental variable (the time delay).

A second, perhaps more striking, outcome from this early study is the observed *statistical independence* between the two tasks; for a given item or a given subject, there is no discernible relation between the probabilities of recognition and fragment completion. Suppose the study item ZEPPELIN is presented for recognition and the fragment Z____E_IN for completion a short time later. Statistical independence implies that the probability with which a subject completes the fragment is unrelated to his or her ability to correctly recognize the word on the immediately preceding test. Compare this to the likely relation between two consecutive recognition tests involving the same item: if one recognizes ZEPPELIN a first time, surely one would expect this to be related to the probability of recognizing ZEPPELIN a short while later.

This early study by Endel Tulving and his colleagues opened the search for further pairs of tasks that would be subject to functional dissociation by experimental variables or that would show statistical independence. In all cases, one of the tasks would involve explicit remembering (also known as a direct memory test) whereas the other task would not require reference to a prior study episode and would be thought to tap implicit memory (indirect test). Particularly favored among the latter are lexical decision tasks (where subjects decide whether or not a letter string is a word), word identification tasks (reading aloud a word presented very briefly), completion tasks of various kinds, anagram tasks, spelling of homophones (e.g., "piece" vs "peace") which may be biased by prior presentation of related items, and the like. The next two sections present some of the more important experimental outcomes, thus defining the database to which theories must relate.

B. Statistical Independence

Endel Tulving suggested that statistical independence between measures of memory places tight constraints on theory: If there were any overlap between the processes engaged by two different memory measures, some degree of positive dependence would be observed; the absence of that dependence, therefore, implies complete absence of overlap.

Statistical independence between implicit and explicit tests of memory has been found on a number of occasions. Similar to the experiment outlined in the previous section, most of these studies employed item recognition as the explicit memory test. In a comprehensive early investigation by Carla Chandler, recognition was independent of fragment completion under 32 different conditions, including some in which subjects were informed of the relation between the study list and the test fragments. Recognition memory performance has also been found to be independent of primed anagram solutions (where subjects need to construct a word from a stimulus such as "tinekt," after prior presentation of "kitten") and independent of primed perception of shadow faces (subjects indicate whether they can perceive a face in a contour drawing).

In several other studies, recognition performance has been found to be independent of perceptual identification or naming of primed words, and independent of priming of homophones. In the latter task, subjects must spell auditorily presented homophones ("fair/fare"), and the measure of interest is the extent to which the probability of giving the subordinate spelling ("fare") is raised after prior processing of the item in the context of, say, "taxi." Strong priming is shown in this task, and recognition probabilities are independent of the extent of priming. In another setting, recognition of previously presented pictures has been shown to be independent of facilitation of naming latencies for those same pictures, even at retention intervals of up to 6 weeks.

Recently, in response to several concerns that statistical independence merely reflects some procedural artifact, empirical focus has shifted from simple pairwise independence between tasks to comparisons of the extent of dependence between multiple pairs of tasks. For example, whereas word fragment completion is statistically independent of performance on a preceding recognition task (i.e., the probability of completing Z____E_IN does not relate to the probability of having recognized ZEPPELIN), *dependence* with recognition is observed when the same fragments (e.g., Z____E_IN) are also used to cue explicit recall. The fact that both dependence and independence can occur under similar conditions, differing from each other only in the nature of instructions relevant to the second task, is thought to allay fears that independence is an artifact of the first test affecting the second one.

C. Functional Dissociations

At the most general level, a *functional dissociation* involves a statistical interaction between an experimental variable representing different memory tasks (i.e., explicit vs implicit tests) and some other independent variable. Typically, in early experiments on implicit memory, that other variable would be one whose effects most psychologists thought were well understood. For example, it seemed a general property of memory that material is remembered better after a semantic encoding task (''is this object animate or inanimate?'') than after a phonemic study task (''does this word rhyme with fish?''). However, this ''depth-of-processing'' manipulation has repeatedly been found to have very little effect on implicit tests: The extent to which prior presentation of a word primes its subsequent identification under brief exposure conditions is typically *unaffected* by depth of processing at study.

The occurrence of a large number of these functional dissociations has supported the distinction between implicit and explicit memory. The experimental variables and tasks involved in some of the most prominent dissociations are summarized in Table I. To illustrate, consider the first row in the table, involving a change in physical form or modality. Experiments belonging to this paradigm would first present, say, the spoken word ''aardvark'' followed by a lexical decision on the printed form ''aardvark.'' Although that lexical decision would still be primed relative to a condition in which ''aardvark'' is presented for the first time at test, the benefit is reduced compared to repeating the printed form ''aardvark'' at both study and test. As indicated by the last column in the table, a corresponding change in modality has little effect on explicit measures of retention. Similarly, Table I indicates that the many tasks used to manipulate levels of processing usually

TABLE I
Variables That Produce a Dissociation between Implicit and Explicit Forms of Remembering

Experimental variable	Effect of variable on: Implicit memory task	Explicit memory task
Change in physical form (e.g., language, typeface, modality etc.) between study and test	Reduces performance	No effect except in short-term memory situations or for most recent list items
Memory for material from the more recent of two sets	More auditory than semantic interference, or no effect	Strong reduction in performance, primarily semantic
Levels of processing: elaborative rehearsal, generation of study word, free-association to common idioms	Very little effect on single-item priming or object drawings	Large effect on performance regardless of task (including explicit fragment completion)
Amnesia, age, reading impairment	No effect in general. Exception: certain amnesics have been found to be unable to establish implicit associations	Reduces explicit memory performance, although less so for recognition tasks than for recall tasks
Context	If meaning selected at test differs from encoded meaning, priming is eliminated. If context does not affect meaning, priming is unaffected	Encoding specificity principle holds that only cues encoded at study can be effective at test. Change in context reduces performance even when meaning is held constant
Generation of study item in response to cue	Reduces or eliminates repetition priming	Enhances recognition
Study items presented as pictures	Leads to minimal priming of verbal test but greater priming of picture recognition test	Enhances free recall (well-known picture-superiority effect)
Alcoholic intoxication	No effect on fragment completion	Impairs explicit recognition
Word frequency	High-frequency words lead to less priming than low-frequency words across most tasks	Recall unaffected by frequency or better for high-frequency words, the reverse is true for recognition
Increased study time/rehearsal duration	Does not affect the magnitude of priming	Enhances recognition and cued recall
Maturation in infants	No developmental trends shown from 8 to 12 months on indirect tasks (e.g., habituation, etc.)	Developmental trends shown from 8 to 12 months on direct tasks (e.g., object search, etc.)
Instructions to form mental pictures at study	No effect on primed fragment completion	Large positive effect on free recall

fail to affect performance in implicit tasks despite having significant effects on explicit memory performance.

Functional dissociations can occur in a variety of qualitatively different forms, some of which are summarized in the panels of Figure 1. Memory performance is represented on the ordinate, with the bars on the left representing an implicit test and the bars on the right an explicit test, and with the levels of the other experimental variable shown in the legend. The top-left panel represents an idealized version of the dissociation discussed in the preceding paragraph, involving a strong effect of depth of encoding on performance using a task which requires explicit memory but a null effect for a task used to assess implicit retention. The top right panel shows what is known as a double dissociation, in which a variable affects both types of test, but in opposing ways. These particular data are taken from an experiment in which subjects either read a stimulus ("cold") or generated it in response to an antonym cue ("hot–c______?"). The double dissociation occurs because generation improved explicit memory but *reduced* priming (this in contrast to the null effect of encoding manipulation in the left panel). Finally, the bottom panel shows a *crossed* double dissociation, in which the ordering of absolute performance between explicit and implicit test *reverses* as a function of the other experimental variable. These data are taken from an experiment contrasting free recall and fragment completion after reading or generating the items at study.

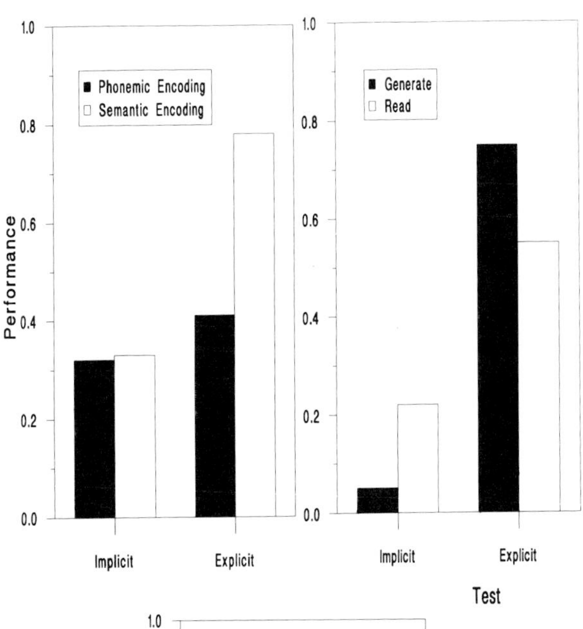

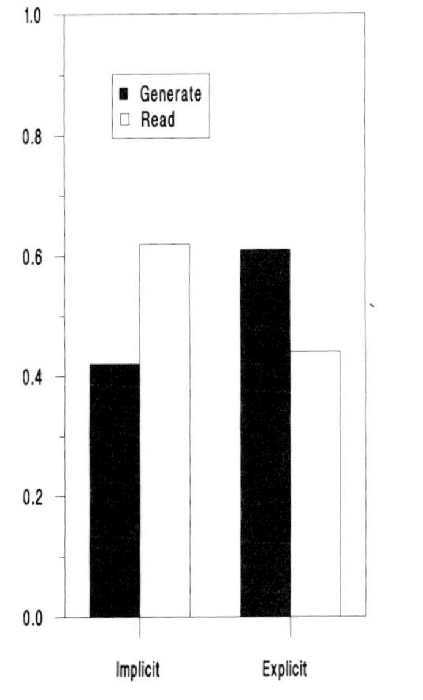

FIGURE 1 Various forms of dissociations between implicit and explicit memory performance.

Lest one think that implicit and explicit tests are always dissociable, the entries in Table I must be compared to those in Table II, which represents variables that have a *common* effect on implicit and explicit tests. For example, repetition priming is eliminated (in bilingual subjects) when language is switched between study and test, and the same is true for data-driven explicit tasks. Likewise, tasks tapping both implicit and explicit memory are sensi-

TABLE II
Variables That Show Parallel Effects on Implicit and Explicit Forms of Remembering

Experimental variable	Comment
Switch in language (e.g., Spanish–French)	Priming is attenuated unless cognates are used. Data-driven explicit tasks are affected in the same way
Repetition of items at study	Repetition of items at study improves naming (a data-driven task) provided repetition is spaced
Level of attention at encoding	Manipulations of attention at study may produce parallel effects in indirect and direct tasks
Directed forgetting	Instructions to either remember or forget items produce parallel effects in both direct and indirect tasks

tive to manipulations of the level of attention at encoding. Typically, neither type of test will reveal much retention if subjects do not attend to the material at input.

The challenge to theory, then, is to explain the numerous dissociations found between implicit and explicit tests, and also to specify why the two are sometimes found to act in concert.

III. THEORETICAL EXPLANATIONS

A. Multiple Memory Systems

One of the earliest theoretical frameworks, tied to the puzzling statistical independence between direct and indirect tests of memory, invoked two structurally and functionally separate memory systems, one devoted to explicit memory and the other one to implicit memory. The former was seen to support intentional and conscious recollection of episodic information whereas the latter was conceived as a largely context-free representation system. Over time, the nature of that implicit memory system has been variously described as "semantic" (meaning-based), "procedural" (skill-based), "perceptual" (presemantic), or "traceless" (not requiring access to a specific episode), which suggests that little is really known about its operation. [*See* SEMANTIC MEMORY.]

The idea that components of mental processing might be handled by structurally or functionally distinct entities has a long history in philosophy (arguably dating back to antiquity when the ancient Greeks formulated a fourfold classification of mental faculties), and also conforms to the long-standing goal of the neurosciences to identify anatomical substrates of specific mental processes. Hence, memory systems theorists often come from—and appeal particularly to—the neuropsychological community, and much relevant evidence consists of the finding that some memorial ability, ascribed to the implicit memory system, is preserved in otherwise dense amnesics.

In conceptual support of the systems argument, reasons are often cited why separate memory systems might have evolved over time. Specifically, multiple memory systems may be the result of evolutionary pressures to deal with *functional incompatibility,* which arises when a given adaptation serving one memorial function cannot, because of its specialized nature, address another memorial demand. It can be argued that humans may have evolved one memory system specifically aimed at building on *invariances* across time (thus allowing habit formation or skill learning and, in this instance, subserving the implicit use of information) and another specifically designed to address *variance* across time (thus allowing explicit recall of specific episodes). Indeed, this argument is supported by evidence relating to how people learn concepts and the most appropriate ways to train people on applied engineering problems. Data from both areas suggest the presence of unanalyzed instance-based recollection as well as more abstract representation of an underlying rule base.

Notwithstanding the apparent success of the systems view, critics have bemoaned the inherent circularity of the multiple memory systems approach and its failure to specify, in advance, exactly which findings would be supportive of different memory systems and which ones would not. For example, why would implicit and explicit tests sometimes act in concert (see Table II), even though they are dissociated frequently enough (see Table I) to warrant the postulation of two separate memory systems? Similarly, the use of statistical independence as a diagnostic for separate systems is problematic because sometimes two apparently *implicit* tests of memory have also been shown to be statistically independent. In consequence, further subdivisions of existing memory systems continue to be proposed: A recent enumeration conducted by Henry Roediger has included as many as 25 different memory systems (5 major ones plus 20 subsystems) that appear needed to account for the existing data within a multiple systems framework. One recent approach embodies additional constraints designed to address the criticisms of circularity (see Section V.A).

B. Transfer-Appropriate Processing

The idea that memory benefits from reinstatement at test of the same cognitive processes that were engaged at study has a long history in cognitive pyschology. Accordingly, the proponents of the transfer-appropriate processing view—primarily Henry Roediger and colleagues—have approached implicit memory from the background of traditional cognitive psychology.

The transfer-appropriate processing view postulates that both implicit and explicit remembering are mediated by a single memory system. One fundamental property of this all-encompassing system is that retrieval—be it implicit or explicit—benefits when the cognitive processes used during test reinstate those engaged at study. With the further assumption that implicit tests are primarily data-driven whereas explicit tests are primarily conceptually driven, the view can explain numerous classic dissociations: Manipulations of the surface structure of stimuli tend to selectively affect (data-driven) implicit memory, whereas other variables that affect top-down processing tend to selectively influence (conceptually driven) explicit memory. Thus, priming of word fragment completion or word identification is reduced or eliminated if modality is changed between study and test. On the other hand, recall or recognition benefit from the presentation of pictures at study.

The transfer view can be differentiated from the multiple systems view if the extent of data- vs conceptually driven processing is manipulated orthogonally to the implicit vs explicit dimension. Consider the classification of tasks shown in the top panel of Figure 2. According to proponents of the transfer view, some of the early experiments showing dissociations between implicit and explicit tasks confounded data-driven and conceptually driven processing, thus artifactually lending support to the multiple memory systems idea. Indeed, when an experiment compares *two* implicit tasks differing in the extent to which they require conceptual processing against several explicit tasks that differ in the same way, then the data-driven vs conceptually driven dimension dissociates performance, *not* the implicit vs explicit distinction. Specifically, suppose items are either read or generated at study, and retention is then tested in one of the four ways shown in the bottom panel of Figure 2: Subjects recall the items either in the absence of cues (conceptually driven explicit task) or in response to graphemic cues, for example the cue "treasure" for the target "treason" (data-driven and explicit). Alternatively, subjects complete the usual fragments (data-driven and implicit) or respond to general knowledge question whose correct responses were the study items, for example "what type of crime is espionage?" (conceptually driven and implicit). The results of this experiment, conducted by Teresa Blaxton, show an advantage of generating over reading on the conceptually driven tests regardless of whether the test is implicit or explicit. Conversely, reading was superior to generating for the data-driven tests of retention, again regardless of whether they were explicit or implicit.

By the time of this writing, most experiments conducted within the transfer appropriate processing framework have shown the data-driven vs conceptually driven dimension to be of critical importance. Several demonstrations exist that underscore how specific the benefits are of reinstatement of processes at test: It has been shown that generation of the target in response to a fragment cue at study—not unexpectedly—leads to high levels of priming on a subsequent fragment completion test. However, if only one letter is changed between the fragment used at study and the one used at test, priming is reduced to the same level that is obtained after simple reading of the study item.

The transfer view has more difficulty acounting for data gathered from amnesics. For example, amnesics typically show intact priming on most implicit memory tasks, including some that are commonly considered to be conceptually driven. Why, then, can data-driven and conceptually driven tasks be dissociated in normal subjects? One possible solution would involve the invocation of separate perceptual subsystems (e.g., a word form system vs a structural description system) that are both preserved in amnesics but can be dissociated in normals. Indeed, recent evidence supports the existence of two systems of this type.

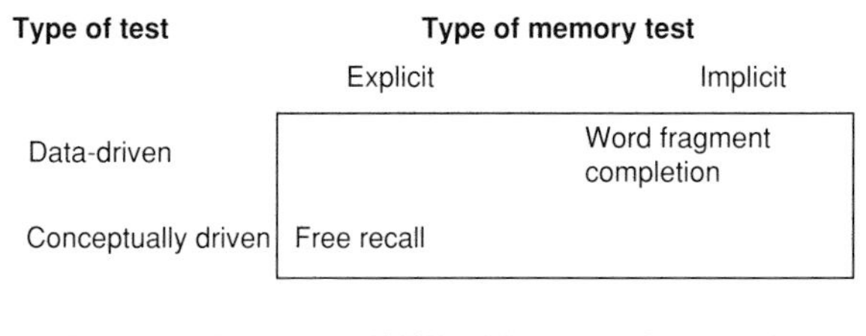

Type of test	Type of memory test: Explicit	Implicit
Data-driven	Graphemic-cued recall	Word fragment completion
Conceptually driven	Free recall	General knowledge questions

FIGURE 2 Classification of memory tests by type of processing required (data-driven vs conceptually driven) and type of memory tapped (implicit vs explicit).

IV. PROBLEMS AND DISTINCTIONS

A. Implicit Memory vs Unconscious Cognition

Implicit memory is only one of several active research areas broadly characterized by an interest in the "cognitive unconscious." One defining feature of most implicit memory experiments is that subjects fully process the information presented for study, although instructions need not emphasize the need for memorization. This is in contrast to work on *unconscious cognitive activation*, or *subliminal activation*, where stimuli are presented too briefly to be fully processed, are made harder to perceive by a poststimulus "mask" of noise, or are otherwise degraded to inhibit conscious perception. Hence, the "implicit" in implicit memory concerns memorial awareness at retrieval, not study, and the discussion so far has rested on the fact that implicit memory tests do not *require* memorial awareness. However, this does not preclude the *presence* of memorial awareness in normal subjects, even on implicit tasks.

B. Control over Conscious Contributions

To what extent, then, do implicit memory tests reflect "contaminations" from explicit recollection? If subjects respond to implicit tests by explicitly remembering the study episode, how can the results speak to the nature of implicit memory at all?

In an early discussion of this problem, Daniel Schacter proposed an empirical *retrieval intentionality criterion*, which can be applied whenever the retrieval cues of a memory task are identical for both explicit and implicit retrieval, with instructions being the only difference. If an experimental manipulation can be found that selectively affects one but not the other retrieval mode, then, by Schacter's criterion, it can be taken for granted that subjects do not use explicit retrieval strategies on the implicit task—otherwise, why would there be a dissociation between the two tasks? While this criterion may serve to rule out that subjects use the *same* explicit retrieval strategies in both retrieval modes, it cannot deal with the somewhat more subtle problem of subjects becoming aware of the memorial quality of their responses while faithfully following implicit test instructions. According to Schacter, these instances of *involuntary explicit memory* can be identified through test-awareness questionnaires. Test-aware subjects have been found to differ significantly from test-unaware subjects; for example, only the former show implicit memory for new associations, defined as the additional priming that is observed in the presence of a previously encoded associative cue. Similarly, it has been suggested that the presence of levels of processing effects in implicit tasks is diagnostic of an intrusion from explicit memory, since they tend to occur only in test-aware subjects.

Larry Jacoby has developed an alternative technique to deal with intrusions from explicit memory that relies on placing implicit and explicit components of recollection in opposition. For example, it has been shown that implicit memory increases the tendency to mistakenly declare a name to be famous after prior exposure to that name. Suppose that one is told, in this situation, that the previously presented names were all nonfamous. Explicit memory for that same stimulus would then support a *non*famous judgment; hence, explicit memory would be in opposition to implicit memory, and any remaining tendency to mistakenly declare a familiar name famous cannot be attributed to explicit memory.

V. RECENT TRENDS

A. Cognitive Neuroscience

In recognition of the limitations associated with searching for additional functional dissociations or manifestations of statistical independence between tasks, Daniel Schacter recently proposed a cognitive neuroscience approach to implicit memory research. The approach seeks to combine cognitive techniques with data from brain-damaged patients and other neurobiological observations. Schacter argues that this approach may help resolve the debate between adherents of the two major theoretical views—multiple memory systems vs transfer-appropriate processing—presented earlier. Specifically, the cognitive neuroscience approach can provide an independent basis for the postulation of different memory systems and can also constrain the transfer-appropriate processing view.

Without independent criteria to confirm the existence of separate memory systems, the multiple systems view can engender a proliferation of memory systems in response to each new experimental dissociation or demonstration of statistical independence. Schacter suggests that although dissociations are a necessary condition for distinguishing between different memory systems, evidence outside the context of those dissociations must be sought before a distinction can be accepted. For example, the fact that certain patients can show intact *perceptual* knowledge of words while suffering severe impairment of *semantic* knowledge of those same words serves to confirm that different memory systems might underlie the dissociations that Roediger and colleagues have observed between data-driven and conceptually driven implicit tasks.

The transfer-appropriate processing view, too, can benefit from constraints provided by a cognitive neuroscience approach, for reasons similar to those just cited. Consider a hypothetical experiment in which a change in typeface between study and test reduces perceptual priming in comparison to repetition of the same typeface. This outcome could be taken to support the transfer view because different typefaces might engage different encoding processes. However, the transfer view could also accommodate the opposite outcome (no effect of changing typefaces) by concluding that typeface is of no relevance to processing. According to Schacter, the danger of circularity can be avoided by importing constraints from neuroscience, in this case the finding that right-hemispheric processing of words leads to perceptually specific representations (which would conceivably be affected by changes in typeface) whereas left-hemisphere representations are more abstract (and thus might not be affected by changes in typeface).

B. Role of Language and Meaning

A remarkable aspect of the evolution of views on implicit memory concerns the extent to which language and meaning are seen to play a role. Whereas implicit memory was initially seen as a low-level perceptual phenomenon reflecting the increased perceptual "fluency" with which stimuli are processed, later experiments necessitated a reshaping of this view to include higher-level processes such as sensitivity to linguistic context or shifts in perceived meaning. It is now known that the presence or absence of priming is a function of whether contextual cues maintain or change a word's meaning between study and test: If meaning is maintained between study and test, then a change of context (e.g., embedding the test item in a different sentence) appears to be of minimal importance. On the other hand, a context-directed change in meaning between study and test reduces or eliminates priming. For example, changing perceived meaning of BANK from its "money" sense to its "river" sense eliminates priming. Results of this kind have forced a reconsideration of the early interpretation that priming necessarily represents a low-level perceptual phenomenon. The distinction between purely perceptual forms of priming and meaning-related priming has recently been clarified and extended by Michael Masson and Colin MacLeod.

Although it has become clear that perceived meaning plays an important role in implicit memory, that role is largely limited to manipulations of context. The repetition of meaning alone, without repetition of the stimulus item, is insufficient to lead to any implicit manifestations of memory. This appears to be true even when context is identical across presentations. For example repetition of the context sentence "He gave five dollars to the old . . . " fails to prime a lexical decision about TRAMP when HOBO provided completion of the sentence during study. Likewise, synonyms fail to prime fragment completion, unless they are presented simultaneously with the fragment. For example, presentation of HEARTH at study does not prime completion of _IRE___AC_ (fireplace) at test: coordinate ("furnace") and associates ("logs") also fail to prime work fragment completion. These results may be contrasted with the benefits of synonym repetition on an explicit free recall task.

Overall, it can be stated that reinstatement of perceived meaning is a necessary but not a sufficient component for implicit memory to be observed. Other more subtle changes in linguistic context are inconsequential.

C. More Formal Models

Most theorizing in implicit memory has involved global "frameworks," such as transfer-appropriate processing or multiple memory systems, that have successfully allowed classification and explanation of numerous results, but that have limited precision and that can be subject to circularity. As distinct from such frameworks, formal models specify in greater detail the underlying encoding and retrieval processes. As of this writing, two models have been formulated that address implicit memory phenomena.

Douglas Nelson and colleagues have extensively investigated the memorial role played by preexisting associations between a study item and related words, and their efforts have recently culminated in a model describing the Processing of Implicit and Explicit Representations (PIER). At the heart of the model is the concept of *set size,* which refers to the number of preexperimental links between a stimulus and other items related by either phonology or meaning. For example, the meaning-related set of "dime" would include "penny" and "nickel," whereas the rhyme-related set would include "lime" and "time." These sets contribute to implicit processing components presumed to occur at study and retrieval: At study, as determined by context, items in the sets attached to a stimulus are activated with the stimulus and thus contribute to the resulting memory trace. At retrieval, these related representations are searched in parallel with conventional explicit associations, and their reinstatement contributes to successful recall.

The PIER model can accommodate the major findings associated with manipulation of the set sizes of targets or cues, for example that a recall cue which is not part of the originally learned list of words is most effective if its set size is small (because fewer implicitly activated items compete for output) and that in most cases targets are also retrieved more easily if their sets are small. Unlike the transfer-appropriate processing and the multiple systems views, PIER not only differentiates between implicit and explicit modes of memory, but also describes precisely how implicit characteristics of memory representations (e.g., set size) can contribute to explicit retrieval. On the other hand, the model's application has been largely limited to studies involving manipulations of set size, and it remains to be seen whether it can accommodate some of the other principal findings in implicit memory.

In contrast to PIER, the other major model in the area, put forward by Michael Humphreys and colleagues, not only describes the contribution of implicit memories to explicit retrieval, but also explains several of the dissociations observed between the two modes of retrieval. At the heart of Humphrey's Matrix model is a neural network consisting of a single layer of connections between input and output units. Like other neural networks, the Matrix model assumes that the weighted connections between input and output "neurons" are adjusted during learning, and are then used to retrieve information when a cue is presented. In contrast to the multiple memory systems view, the Matrix model holds that different forms of memory correspond to different retrieval cues and retrieval processes applied to the common matrix of connections.

There are two major retrieval processes in the Matrix model. A *matching* process involves comparison of a cue (of varying degrees of complexity) to memory and yields a unitary index of matching strength. A *retrieval* process involves recovery of an associate of the cue (which may again differ in complexity) in the form of a complete image. The former process maps into tasks such as recognition or lexical decision whereas the latter corresponds to recall or fragment completion tasks. A further crucial property of the model, orthogonal to the type of process, is the complexity or composition of the cue. Humphreys argues that the implicit vs explicit distinction corresponds to the use of different retrieval cues, as determined by the experimental task demands. Explicit memory tasks, in reflection of the instructions given to subjects, typically require the conjunction of context and item cues: Recognition of "apple" is driven by the conjunction of the item's familiarity and the general contextual cues for, say, "Last list." Implicit memory tasks, on the other hand, typically do not require context cues: Lexical decision performance for the letter string "apple" is primarily driven by its global familiarity match. Because that match includes the most recent presentation of the item on a study list, seemingly implicit repetition priming effects are often observed in lexical decision.

Although quantitative applications have yet to be presented, the Matrix model has been shown to be in qualitative accord with several major dissociations between explicit and implicit memory. Specifically, the model accommodates the fact that implicit memory is largely intact in amnesics by stating that these patients are unable to use specific episodic context cues, although amnesics can cue memory with non-context-specific global familiarity cues.

Notwithstanding the initial successes of PIER and the Matrix model, neither one of them can be considered fully developed. This scarcity of models of implicit memory stands in contrast to other areas, for example recognition memory or categorization, in which computer models play a pivotal role. To a large extent this theoretical deficit may reflect the emphasis that is necessarily given to empirical matters in any new area of inquiry, and it thus stands to reason that more concerted modeling efforts will arise in the near future.

D. Applications to Engineering and Training

Although current research on implicit memory has remained largely unconnected to applied areas of inquiry, a direct link can be constructed between implicit memory and numerous human factors problems. A prevalent issue in engineering psychology concerns the proper form of training for operators of complex plants and assemblies (e.g., nuclear power plants). Should the operator be trained to acquire an explicit mental model of the plant, or should training emphasize crucial IF–THEN action pairs? Is knowledge of the entire set of interrelations between the cooling systems required, or can a meltdown also be averted by memorization of a number of actions that are to be taken in response to some critical event? Experiments involving the training of operators of simulated industrial plants have repeatedly shown that performance is *not* improved by providing subjects with full explicit knowledge of the system, and that training of condition–action pairs often leads to optimal performance. Moreover, satisfactory performance has been observed even in the absence of *any* explicit instructions, when subjects had to learn the behavior of the plant by simply observing the consequences of their actions. (Indeed, in some instances performance has been shown to suffer when subjects are instructed explicitly to discover the rules active in that situation.) Finally, in conformance to more traditional lines of implicit memory research, dissociations between performance and explicit knowledge are typically observed, such that the various different forms of operator training lead to very different abilities to verbally describe the system, without, however, affecting operator performance.

In addition to these empirical parallels, one can also draw a close *theoretical* connection between industrial psychology and implicit memory. Kim Kirsner has recently suggested that the "power law of practice," which describes many aspects of skill acquisition in industrial settings, is also relevant to implicit memory phenomena. The power law holds that it takes an increasingly large number of practice trials to achieve a constant further improvement in performance. In consequence, repetition of high-frequency words leads to less priming than repetition of low-frequency words (see Table I) because the former—having received more "practice" prior to the experiment—benefit less from an additional repetition. It remains to be seen whether Kirsner's application of the power law might provide an alternative single-process account for some of the other prominent dissociations. (John Dunn and Kim Kirsner have shown that a single process, provided it produces a negative correlation between explicit and implicit task performance, can produce dissociations commonly interpreted as reflecting the operation of two processes. It is therefore a priori possible that a single-process account might suffice.)

E. Associated Areas of Inquiry

In addition to the parallels observed in industrial psychology, clear connections exist between implicit memory research on the one hand, and concept formation, social cognition, and perception on the other. Several concept formation experiments report that subjects can learn to identify grammatically correct strings of letters without being explicitly aware of the rules used to generate those strings. Indeed, there is considerable evidence to suggest that when subjects are explicitly instructed to look for structure, their subsequent understanding is less complete and less accurate than that of subjects who received neutral instructions.

Turning to social cognition, it has been observed that reading or generating of trait adjectives (e.g., "industrious") can have a lasting influence on subsequent interpretation of ambiguous descriptions of a person's behavior. That is, subjects are more likely to label that person as "industrious" if they previously studied the trait adjective than if they did not. It is often assumed that this effect of prior exposure is implicit, in the sense that subjects are unaware of the reasons leading to their interpretation of an ambiguously described person. [*See* Social Cognition.]

Finally, Daniel Schacter and his colleagues have recently begun a detailed exploration of implicit memory for nonverbal perceptual objects. Subjects study line drawings of fictitious three-dimensional objects and their memory is later assessed either through an explicit recognition task or through an implicit "object-verification" test, in which subjects must decide whether a briefly presented drawing is structurally possible (i.e., whether it could exist in three-dimensional space). Previously presented items are primed on this implicit test only if the stimulus is structurally possible—no priming is observed for structurally impossible objects, even when explicit memory performance is very high. In addition to requiring structural integrity, the occurrence of priming is tied to subjects making judgments about the stimuli's global 3-D structure at study (e.g., judging which way an object faces). No priming is observed when subjects attend to isolated aspects of the stimulus at encoding (e.g., counting the number of vertical lines). On the other hand, semantic orienting tasks do not improve implicit memory, leading Schacter to suggest that a separate perceptual subsystem—unable to encode structurally impossible objects and insulated from semantic processing—underlies the observed object priming. Parallel evidence for an auditory, presemantic representation system is currently beginning to emerge.

VI. SUMMARY

The evidence is overwhelming that people's memory for attended events is incompletely retrieved by subsequent verbal report. The additional unreportable implicit memories manifest themselves as priming benefits on a variety of experimental tasks. Numerous experimental variables have no effect on these implicit tasks despite having strong effects on explicit tests or the effects are opposite to those found with explicit memory measures. Two theoretical views—multiple memory systems and transfer-appropriate processing—have been offered to explain implicit memory phenomena and their dissociation from explicit memory. A recently proposed cognitive neuroscience approach can be used to reconcile the two major theoretical views. A final goal should be the development of more formal models that can describe and explain the intricacies of the relationship between implicit and explicit modes of remembering.

Acknowledgments

To ensure a balanced list of secondary sources, we asked several leading researchers in the field to suggest what they considered to be key articles. Their efforts are reflected in the list below. We are grateful to Professors Fergus I. M. Craik, Colin M. MacLeod, Michael E. J. Masson, Henry L. Roediger, and Daniel L. Schacter for responding to our request.

Bibliography

Blaxton, T. A. (1989). Investigating dissociations among memory measures: Support for a transfer-appropriate processing framework. *J. Exper. Psychol.: Learning, Memory, and Cognition* **15,** 657–668.

Jacoby, L. L. (1991). A process dissociation framework: Separating automatic from intentional uses of memory. *J. Memory and Language* **30,** 513–541.

Jacoby, L. L., and Dallas, M. (1981). On the relationship between autobiographical memory and perceptual learning. *J. Exper. Psychol.: General* **110,** 306–340.

Lewandowsky, S., Dunn, J. C., and Kirsner, K. (Eds.), (1989). "Implicit Memory: Theoretical Issues." Hillsdale, NJ: Erlbaum.

Masson, M. E. J., and MacLeod, C. M. (1992). Re-enacting the route to interpretation: Context dependency in encoding and retrieval. *J. Exper. Psychol.: General* **121,** 145–176.

Richardson-Klavehn, A., and Bjork, R. A. (1988). Measures of memory. *Ann. Rev. Psychol.* **39,** 475–543.

Roediger, H. L. (1990). Implicit memory: Retention without remembering. *Amer. Psychol.* **45,** 1043–1056.

Roediger, H. L., and Challis, B. H. (1992). Effects of exact repetition and conceptual repetition on free recall and primed word-fragment completion. *J. Exper. Psychol.: Learning, Memory, and Cognition* **18,** 3–14.

Schacter, D. L. (1987). Implicit memory: History and current status. *J. Exper. Psychol.: Learning, Memory, and Cognition* **13,** 501–518.

Schacter, D. L. (1992). Understanding implicit memory. *Amer. Psychol.* **47,** 559–569.

Tulving, E., and Schacter, D. L. (1990). Priming and human memory systems. *Science* **247,** 301–305.

Tulving, E., Schacter, D. L., and Stark, H. A. (1982). Priming effects in work fragment completion are independent of recognition memory. *J. Exper. Psychol.: Learning, Memory, and Cognition* **8,** 336–342.

Warrington, E. K., and Weiskrantz, L. (1968). New method of testing long term retention with special reference to amnesic patients. *Nature* **217,** 972–974.

IMPRESSION FORMATION

Stephanie A. Goodwin and Susan T. Fiske
University of Massachusetts at Amherst

Glossary

Impression formation Process of perceiving, interpreting, and synthesizing information into a coherent understanding of an individual.

Person perception Process of encoding and interpreting perceptual information about another person.

IMPRESSION FORMATION involves the perception, interpretation, and synthesis of information by one person, the *perceiver*, about another person, the *target*. The outcome of the process is a coherent understanding (i.e., impression) of the target. Impressions may be more or less accurate, complex, evaluative, and ambiguous. Ultimately, the resulting impression depends on several factors including the information-processing strategy employed by the perceiver, which is determined jointly by characteristics of the situation, the target (e.g., physical characteristics), and the perceiver (e.g., cognitive-processing strategies, motives, and goals).

As a component of impression formation research, person perception research focuses more specifically on the initial perceptual processes and the interpretation of stimulus information about other people (e.g., how does the perceiver encode information about specific facial features and what does this information mean?). Impression formation research focuses more on how the perceived information is incorporated into a meaningful coherent pattern (impression) of the target. Thus, person perception research typically addresses the first two steps of the impression formation process, but does not address the final step during which target information is unified into a meaningful whole.

Whereas person perception is a component of impression formation, contemporary impression formation research is itself a component of a broader scientific perspective referred to as the study of social cognition. The social cognition paradigms attempt to blend the methods and constructs of cognitive psychology (emphasizing the mechanics of an individual's thought and memory processes) with social psychological concerns emphasizing the interpersonal dynamics of human existence. Social cognition perspectives can be viewed then as a theoretical framework for studying all of the various issues related to human social interaction, including the issue of impression formation. [*See* SOCIAL COGNITION.]

The following sections review several facets of impression formation research, beginning with a brief history of the field and moving into contemporary social-cognitive views. Next, we address several factors related to qualities of the target and perceiver that influence the process, followed by a discussion of the outcomes of the process, including recent perspectives on impression accuracy.

I. HISTORY

Contemporary views of impression formation can be traced to four areas of research earlier this century, mainly in the 1940s and 1950s. Initially, theorists were interested in understanding how accurate perceivers were at forming impressions, the primary objective being to identify those types of individuals who are better than others at forming impressions. This work coincided with, and was later replaced by, a gestalt-inspired interest in how people synthesize pieces of information into unified impressions. During this time theorists also made important distinctions between object perception and person percep-

Copyright © 1994 by Academic Press, Inc. All rights of reproduction in any form reserved.

tion. Perhaps the most important distinction was that perceivers are more likely to ascribe intent or causality to the behaviors of target persons, but not as much to inanimate target objects. This led researchers to ask how perceivers attribute intent to a target's behavior. Finally, researchers began to address how perceivers go beyond available target information to develop theories about personality, an approach that represents a significant transition to current cognitive theories.

A. Accuracy: What Kinds of People Make Good Judges?

Accuracy research was primarily geared toward application, identifying those individuals who are good or bad judges of personality. Following a World War II psychometric emphasis in psychology, the rationale was to select perceivers who might be better suited for particular roles in society requiring especially good interpersonal accuracy. Although the methodology of these studies varied somewhat, the basic steps involved asking subjects and their peers to rate themselves and each other on a number of personality dimensions. This allowed the researcher not only to assess who was accurate (e.g., which participants were superior predictors of their peers' self-ratings), but also to determine the characteristics of a "good" judge (e.g., how did good judges describe themselves). Unfortunately, these studies found little empirical evidence of a general ability to judge personality accurately, a problem that challenged the basic theory behind the research.

In the 1950s, methodological critiques of the accuracy literature brought research in this area to a halt for three decades. Perhaps the most troublesome criticism was Cronbach's objection to accuracy measurement techniques that compared perceivers' ratings with the target's own rating as an index of accuracy. He asserted that these accuracy scores were not pure reflections of accuracy, but instead reflected various kinds of biases and abilities which he termed elevation, differential elevation, stereotype accuracy, and differential accuracy. The elevation component of an accuracy score reflects subjects' tendencies to use the same end of the rating scales as their peers. Perceivers' abilities to rank order the average self-ratings of a group of targets is indicated by differential elevation. In a similar way, stereotype accuracy reflects a perceiver's ability to rank traits across targets. Finally, differential accuracy reflects a perceiver's ability to recognize differences among targets for each trait. It is this last component which represents the perceiver's "true" accuracy score. While Cronbach's intent was to encourage researchers to measure accuracy more carefully, the initial impact of his review was to inhibit research. Only recently have researchers returned to the issue of accuracy, with greater sophistication, as will be discussed later. [*See* TRAITS.]

B. Unified Impressions

As researchers shied away from accuracy research, they shifted their attention to understanding the processes involved in impression formation, allowing them to be agnostic with regard to accuracy. Solomon Asch first addressed the process issue when he noted that people seem to develop consistent overall impressions of other people even when they have limited information. He proposed two competing theories to describe how people form impressions: an additive model and a configural model. According to the additive model, overall impressions are based on the sum of separate evaluative impressions of individual traits. In contrast, the configural model, which Asch himself supported, states that perceivers immediately organize the traits to form a unified meaningful whole or gestalt. In this model, each trait affects the meaning of the others and, following the gestalt perspective, the whole (the impression) differs from the sum of its parts (the traits); the meanings of the traits interact as a function of context.

Asch's research, which set the paradigm for much subsequent work, involved eliciting subjects' open-ended descriptions of a hypothetical target's personality based on lists of the targets' personality traits (e.g., intelligent, skillful, industrious, warm, determined, practical, cautious). Asch found that changing certain central traits in the lists (e.g., *warm* to *cold*) drastically changed subjects' overall impressions. Not all traits had this effect. For example, changing *polite* to *blunt* did not influence the overall impression nearly as much as changing *warm* to *cold*. He concluded that central traits, such as warm or cold, organized the interpretation of the other traits (e.g., warm and intelligent means wise, but cold and intelligent means calculating), whereas peripheral traits (e.g., polite or blunt) did not have this influence on organization. The interaction of traits, as demonstrated by this research, is predicted by the configural theory, but not the algebraic (additive) theory. Thus, Asch concluded that people do not simply sum up their evaluative impressions of traits, but instead, organize their trait impressions into a coherent picture of the person. Other types of mathematical models have taken up the additive model's assertions, in opposition to configural models, all of which will return under contemporary models.

C. Perceived Consistency and Causality

Heider's "naive psychologist" approach to impression formation drew similarly from the gestalt tradition. His analysis focused on consistency and causality as characteristics of a good (i.e., coherent) gestalt. In this, he emphasized the role of the perceiver actively engaged in constructing a meaningful understanding of other people. Heider believed that science could best learn about interpersonal relationships by recognizing how perceivers themselves describe their interactions. In his analysis of naive psychology, cognitive consistency was addressed by Heider's own balance theory, based on the gestalt premise that people prefer consistent cognitions that form a coherent whole. Inconsistent cognitions (e.g., Sheila likes James and she dislikes smoking, but James smokes incessantly) create a tension either to change a sentiment (liking) relationship (e.g., maybe Sheila doesn't like James as much as she thought) or to change a unit (belonging) relationship among the beliefs (e.g., persuade James not to smoke, at least around her). Changing unit or sentiment relationships leads to balance among the beliefs. Balance theory fell victim to its own limitations in application, but the importance of cognitive consistency remains prominent in contemporary impression formation models.

Heider's second major contribution to impression formation theories was recognizing the significance of perceivers' attributions of causality about target behaviors (e.g., explaining *why* James smokes incessantly). This concept has significantly affected the field and has evolved into a strong line of contemporary research. Heider proposed that one way to form a coherent gestalt was to link targets' behaviors to their dispositions. To do this, perceivers must make decisions about targets' intentions and the causes for their behavior. Attributing behaviors to stable internal personality characteristics (dispositional attributions) allows the perceiver better to predict and control future interactions with the target. In contrast, attributing behaviors to external factors (situational attributions) does not improve the perceiver's ability to predict the outcomes of future interactions across different contexts. Unlike enduring dispositions, situations change over time. For example, if a perceiver notes that a target avoids social interaction and attributes this behavior to "shyness," a dispositional attribution, the perceiver can expect the target to behave in a consistently shy manner across situations. However, if the perceiver attributes the same behavior to the target's arrival in a new culture, the perceiver cannot expect the same behavior across situations. [*See* ATTRIBUTION.]

D. Lay Theories of Personality

Concurrent with Heider's development of the naive psychologist approach, Bruner and Taguiri first identified the possibility that people "go beyond the [trait] information [they are] given" when forming an impression. They proposed that people perceive certain traits as related (e.g., someone who is intelligent is also expected to be neat) and others to be unrelated (e.g., someone who is intelligent is just as likely to be generous as greedy). These expectations that certain traits go together constitute the lay perceiver's implicit personality theory (IPT). An IPT can be considered a mental template for generating inferences about personality, which perceivers then use to form an overall impression of a target. For example, if a perceiver learns that a target is inconsiderate, associated traits are likely to come to mind. Based on these relationships, the perceiver may infer that the target is also aggressive, unreliable, and dishonest. The IPT concept had an important influence on research, directing theorists to consider not only the information available to the perceiver, but also what the perceiver may be adding to that information.

E. Conclusion

These four areas of research constitute the roots of contemporary theories of impression formation. Asch's configural and additive models have evolved into theories about, respectively, theory-driven and data-driven cognitive processing. Heider's concerns over cognitive consistency and causal attribution continue to influence theories of how people form particular impressions. Implicit personality theory also endures in modified form, echoed in cognitive views. Even the abandoned work on accuracy has found new life in the contemporary approaches.

II. CONTEMPORARY APPROACHES

The early concerns of understanding the process of forming impressions continue in current theories.

What distinguishes most between past and present perspectives are the tools that current researchers employ to explore these concerns. Heavily influenced by cognitive psychology, and armed with cognitive constructs and techniques, contemporary theorists have focused their attention on the specific cognitive structures, mental representations, and mechanisms involved in forming an impression. Like Bruner and Taguiri, these researchers assume that perceivers have theories about people that can influence impression formation. And, like others before them, many of the most contemporary models address the importance of motivation in the impression formation process.

A. Some Important Cognitive Concepts

Researchers have borrowed and modified several important concepts from cognitive psychology in their endeavor to explain impression formation. Two important concepts that require explanation are categories and schemas.

1. Categorization

Theories of categorization, initially advanced to understand object perception, lent themselves easily to understanding person perception. Categorization theories particularly matter because many current impression formation theories assume that perceivers mentally represent groups of people, with consequences for impression formation. Categorization involves recognition and classification of people, things, or situations. It requires identification and differentiation among instances. A category is a type of cognitive structure that contains classification information about category members. Although classical views of categorization sought to define the necessary and sufficient conditions of membership in various categories, researchers soon realized that there were no hard-and-fast boundaries for natural categories. For example, a Halloween costume could be frightening or not, a fantasy or not, colorful or not. Just about anything *could* be a Halloween costume, and it would be difficult to set down specific rules for saying what is and is not a member of this category. Yet, people still have beliefs that some things are and are not Halloween costumes. In a more social domain, similar definitional issues might arise with regard to defining the necessary and sufficient conditions for being a "teacher."

As an alternative to the classical view of categories, the prototype view proposes categories with fuzzy boundaries and instances that range in typicality from very typical to very atypical. The most typical instance or the average instance, the prototype, best represents the category. For example, many different Halloween costumes may be instances of the category (e.g., monster, super-hero, ancient ruler) but a likely prototype for the category might be "ghost." From the prototype perspective, perceivers classify a new stimulus based on its similarity to the prototype. Things that are more similar will be classified more quickly, consistently, and consensually. With regard to social stimuli, perceivers often categorize different kinds of people according to their personalities. Exposure to prototypical personality information can influence the perceivers' certainty when they later recall information about the target. For example, once perceivers are exposed to a target person who has prototypically extroverted attributes (e.g., friendly, energetic), they are later unsure that they did *not* see other prototypical attributes (e.g., outgoing, lively).

In reaction to the prototype approach, some have argued that perceivers do not always make comparisons to an average category member, but instead recall exemplars, separate specific instances of a category. The fact that people can retrieve concrete counterexamples of category members (e.g., a specific make and model of car that does *not* have power steering) suggests that specific instances may be stored in memory, in addition to or as opposed to abstract averages of the prototype characteristics. According to this approach, perceivers have multiple exemplars available for each category; categorization requires determining how much an instance resembles significant numbers of exemplars from one particular category. Where social stimuli are concerned, evidence for the exemplar model includes research on the perceived variability of social categories. For example, when perceivers' impressions of group members become more differentiated, as when they learn more information about a particular group through increased contact, they also perceive more variability in groups.

Social psychologists soon applied these ideas to the categorization of people. With regard to social categories, research suggests three core categories: gender, age, and race or ethnicity. Categories may be arranged hierarchically, with core categories (e.g., Hispanics) at higher levels than subtypes (e.g., young Hispanic males). Research indicates that perceivers usually operate at the middle of the hierarchy, most often using subtypes. Categories provide meaning by differentiating among people, interpreting information, and evaluating it. [*See* Categorization.]

2. Schemas

Like categories, schemas are cognitive structures for organizing, simplifying, and making sense out of the world. Schemas have been compared to prototypes in that both contain information about stimuli and information relevant to categorization. In most views, schemas are unique in that they also contain information that is *ir*relevant to classification. For example, under the category "computers," there may be a prototype "personal computer" that contains classification information, e.g., "base fits on a desk with monitor and keyboard attached." An associated schema for "computers" may contain not only the descriptive information that facilitates categorization but also information that is associated with the stimulus but irrelevant for classification, e.g., "386SX processors are slower than 486SX; faster processors are expensive." Categories provide mental representation of the labels for different stimuli; schemas contain all the information the perceiver has acquired, directly or indirectly, about the stimulus.

Schemas often are assumed to be hierarchical structures with global and specific layers of information. The contents of schemas are often highly interconnected, or associated, allowing access at various levels within a particular schema and between different schemas. The conditions of schema use resemble those of categorization. Perceivers usually operate at the level of subtypes (e.g., female physicians) rather than more global levels (e.g., female). Person perceivers tend to rely on role schemas first (e.g., teacher, student, politician) and then trait schemas (e.g., friendly, relaxed). Finally, perceivers rely heavily on visual and physical cues when applying schemas. Unique physical characteristics (e.g., being the only redhead in a group, having a physical deformity) are likely to activate particular schemas.

According to Taylor and Crocker, social schemas are "constructions of how the social world works." Of the various types of social schemas, the two most relevant to our discussion are self-schemas and person schemas. Self-schemas, as the name implies, organize information about the self (e.g., self-concept information, self in relationships, etc.). Person schemas organize information about people other than the self. Stereotypes, an important type of person schema, contain generalized information about members of specific socially defined groups of people (e.g., ethnic, gender, and age groups). Information in stereotypes may be *over*generalized, culturally determined, and not especially accurate. [*See* Prejudice and Stereotypes.]

B. Schema-Driven Theories of Impression Formation

One cognitive approach to impression formation posits theory-driven processing of target information. According to this approach, impression formation involves categorization of the target followed by application of associated schemas. Impressions therefore reflect the perceiver's prior expectations. For example, if one's schema for prison inmate includes "dishonest," then one is likely to apply this information to any person who fits the category, whether or not there is evidence that the person is dishonest. The mechanism that is assumed to mediate this process is attention. Schemas guide perceivers' attention to relevant information. Perceivers' schemas can lead them to notice information and behaviors that fit what they expect (e.g., "this inmate's behavior is suspicious") which in turn confirms their initial expectations. The overuse of stereotypes suggests this type of schema-based processing.

However, perceivers can also attend to information that is inconsistent with their prior expectations (e.g., "this inmate refused to collaborate on a scheme to smuggle contraband"). In fact, perceivers give preferential attention to inconsistent information over consistent information in laboratory research. This occurs presumably because inconsistent information, being less redundant, is more informative to the perceiver. In apparent contradiction to the findings of schema-driven research, these findings imply that perceivers should not be apt to apply their stereotypes because they especially attend to counter-stereotypic information. Theorists who promote the schema-driven approaches resolve this contradiction in two ways. First, people do not always have the mental capacity to attend to inconsistencies. When cognitive or motivational capacity is limited (see subsequent sections), as is often true in life outside the laboratory, people may focus on consistencies. Second, theorists suggest that when perceivers do attend to inconsistent information, their schemas can guide them either to reinterpret the information to make it fit their expectations (e.g., "maybe the inmate simply did not get caught participating in the scheme'') or to attribute the information to situational factors (e.g., ''the inmate is just trying to get the guards to trust him''). The schema-driven approach to impression formation explains how stereotypes can lead to inaccurate impressions of individual group members, but does not explain how people can override their schemas to form unique impressions of individuals.

C. Data-Driven Approaches to Impression Formation

In contrast to the theory-driven models, some argue for a piecemeal approach to impression formation, maintaining that people use individual pieces of information to create unique, individuated impressions of targets. Anderson's algebraic model is one such model that has generated empirical support. Much like Asch's linear combination model, this model posits that perceivers evaluate individual pieces of information in isolation before combining them into an algebraic combination that represents the final impression. Anderson's model posits a weighted averaging process, with fixed (context-free) evaluative scale values and weights relative to the context provided by all the information present. Similar models have been proposed in the domains of attitude formation and decision-making. Applied to impression formation, these models account well for the variability in target impressions across perceivers, and for the perceiver's ability to generate impressions that are based on that person's unique attributes (and perhaps not consistent with prior expectations about group members).

D. Integration of the Data- and Theory-Driven Approaches

Recently theorists have tried to resolve the division between data- and theory-driven approaches by integrating them into single models. These models share the assumptions that perceivers use categorization as a default process, but are able to use other strategies, given certain conditions. Brewer's Dual-Process model distinguishes four different levels of processing strategies, the use of which is determined by stimulus characteristics, needs and goals, and similarity between perceiver and target. In contrast, Fiske's Continuum model posits a range of processing from more category-based to more individuating strategies. Goals and stimulus configuration predict the strategy that will be employed, with attention to information allowing the perceiver either to confirm initial expectations or to move beyond those expectations to form idiosyncratic impressions. Individuation is assumed to be more effortful, requiring the perceiver to attend to and make sense of expectation-inconsistent information. Whether the perceiver will engage in this effortful processing depends in part on how motivated the perceiver is to form an accurate impression of the target. Both the Dual-Process and the Continuum models have the advantage of explaining how perceivers form impressions that are consistent *or* inconsistent with their prior expectations. Thus, they can account for stereotyping as well as unique impressions.

E. The Ecological Approach

The ecological approach, emphasizing the interaction between perceiver and target, deserves attention because it provides an alternative to the cognitive approaches. In concert with the Gibsonian approach to object perception, this perspective maintains that targets have certain social affordances (i.e., offer certain opportunities for action). For example, just as a shoe affords covering the foot, certain social targets may afford certain interactions and impressions (e.g., a smiling person affords talking). Because members of a particular group may share characteristics that elicit the same affordances for different perceivers, impressions may be stereotypical. To the extent, however, that perceivers differ in their attunement to particular affordances, impressions can vary across perceivers for the same target. This explains how different perceivers may have unique impressions of the same target, despite prior expectations about group membership. Research on this model is still in its infancy, compared to research on the social cognitive models, so substantial empirical support is still forthcoming. Whatever the future of this model, however, it points out that cognitive models emphasize the internal dynamics of impression formation and de-emphasize the external dynamics of social interaction between target and perceiver. Such alternative approaches serve to remind one that there is more to the impression formation process than the cognitive processing inside the perceiver's mind.

F. Conscious versus Unconscious Processing

The ecological approach argues for a noncognitive process, thereby implying little or no conscious awareness for perceivers regarding how stimulus characteristics influence their impressions. To account for such nonconscious influences, the cognitive approaches argue instead for a number of unconscious cognitive processes, for example, categorization and confirmation. Whether social perceivers have conscious control over their impression formation processes is not a trivial concern. For example, if perceivers are unaware and unable to control these processes, then society can hardly hold them accountable for stereotypic impression formation, nor can society expect conscious efforts to change significantly the content of stereotypes. To clarify this possibility, several theorists have attempted to uncover how much people are aware of and control impression formation processes. [*See* Control.]

Several concepts require discussion before proceeding to the empirical evidence. *Consciousness* implies awareness, either of the mechanisms themselves or of influences on the mechanisms involved in a given process. *Automaticity* refers to situations in which often-used social processes or constructs become less effortful, less conscious, and less controllable. *Control* refers to a perceiver's ability to override automatic mechanisms in favor of more effortful processing. [*See* Consciousness.]

Empirical evidence for automatic processes in impression formation includes Gilbert's exploration of attribution under cognitive load. According to correspondent inference theory, perceivers attribute behavior to corresponding dispositions whenever the situation does not unduly constrain a target's behavior. In these studies, perceivers who are asked to form impressions while simultaneously engaged in another cognitive task are more likely to make dispositional attributions and ignore situational constraints on target behaviors. However, when busy perceivers are immediately given an opportunity to reconsider their judgments, and when they focus attention specifically on the target, they are able to take situational information into account and correct their judgments. These findings imply a default process whereby perceivers attribute behavior to the target's disposition first and consider the situation last. These findings also allude to the possibility that perceivers can control their processing strategies when they are motivated to attend to the target.

Related evidence for controlling the processes comes from research on the Continuum model. This research indicates that when perceivers are motivated to form accurate impressions, as when their own outcomes depend on the target's behavior, they can override their initial schema-based impressions in favor of more effortful individuating strategies.

In sum, evidence indicates that much of the process of impression formation is unconscious and automatic. However, perceivers can control some processes and overcome some automatic strategies when they are motivated to attend to the target and form accurate impressions. Attention is the key; perceivers must first attend to both consistent and inconsistent information in order to later use that information to form accurate impressions.

III. INFLUENCES ON THE PROCESS

In the course of developing theories about how people form impressions, researchers have discovered various factors that can influence the process. We can distinguish among those factors that are roughly attributable to the target, to the perceiver, and to the interaction between the perceiver and the situation.

A. Target Effects

Target effects can be further classified into three groups: target-in-context, target information configuration, and target characteristics. The following summary of these effects is not exhaustive, but is instead intended to illustrate several key effects.

Target-in-context effects refer to how the person information is presented relative to the background of the situation. One interesting context effect, often termed the mere exposure effect, leads perceivers to be attracted to things with which they are familiar. Simply being exposed to a target, thus increasing familiarity, can lead to increased attraction to the target.

Salience is another factor that produces context effects. Physical characteristics or behaviors that are salient stand out relative to their context (e.g., a person wearing a brightly patterned shirt in room full of people in business suits). Salience can influence impression formation in many ways. For example, salient targets are more likely to be perceived as having impact or influence in a situation (e.g., guiding conversation, making contributions to discussion), and are likely to be rated as more extremely positive or negative. People who have solo status (e.g., the only female in a group) are likely to be salient, drawing attention to their behavior, and leading perceivers to make extreme judgments, to view them as disproportionately impactful, but also to see them in stereotypic terms.

Priming effects occur when specific schemas are activated, usually by something in the situation, and consequently influence impression formation. For example, if perceivers are in an informal work setting where sexual jokes are permitted, gender-role schemas are likely to be activated, increasing the likelihood that perceivers will form impressions in those terms. These cognitive effects of the target in the situation occur unconsciously, with perceivers unaware of the influence these factors have on their impressions.

Information configuration effects result from how target information is presented to perceivers. Primacy and recency effects refer to the order in which information is given and how that information will later influence the impression. For example, primacy occurs when information presented first has a greater impact on final impressions than information presented later. Primacy effects have been well substantiated, beginning with Asch's pioneering work in the field. In contrast, there is less evidence for recency effects, later information outweighing early information. Recency effects seem to occur only when an attribute is unstable over time or when attention is specifically focused on later information (e.g., when researchers request several intermediate judgments, indicating to subjects that they should pay specific attention to all the information). Most often, first impressions matter more.

A second configuration effect involves the dilution of the impact of relevant information by the presence of irrelevant information. In this research, perceivers are asked to make a judgment (e.g., how likely is it that this person is conservative?) based on diagnostic category information (e.g., voting behavior) and irrelevant information (e.g., the number of house plants a target owns). Results indicate that the presence of the irrelevant information dilutes the impact of the diagnostic information, leading perceivers to form moderated impressions.

A third configuration effect is illusory correlation, the perceiver's tendency to see a relationship between salient people and salient behaviors. For example, perceivers are likely to assume that minorities (salient people) are more likely to be engaged in violent crime (salient behaviors), when in fact socioeconomic status is a better predictor of such criminal behavior than is race.

Finally, halo effects occur when key traits influence the overall impression, leading perceivers to infer trait information beyond what is actually given. For example, as Asch's initial research indicated, perceivers are likely to infer additional positive traits when one positive central trait is given.

Physical characteristic effects are a direct function of the target's appearance. For example, attractive targets are usually seen as more socially competent, and somewhat more powerful, adjusted, and intelligent. The effect of attractiveness, "what is beautiful is good," and vice versa, may be attributed to a halo effect. Another interesting effect is the "babyface" effect. People with childlike features (e.g., big eyes, small noses, broad foreheads) are likely to be perceived as weaker, more naive, and more honest than mature-looking people. This effect influences impressions of attractiveness and credibility, as well as hiring decisions and parental discipline.

B. Perceiver Effects

Perceiver effects can be broadly classified as relating to cognitive factors and motivational factors.

Cognitive factors influencing impression formation have been well researched, as one would expect given the cognitive tone of current theories. The following is by no means an exhaustive review, but is again intended to illustrate some of the more important effects.

One type of cognitive influence is perceivers' use of heuristics or mental short cuts. These short cuts for processing social information can be efficient strategies for dealing with complex situations, but they can also lead to biases and errors. For example, Tversky and Kahneman's availability heuristic describes the tendency for perceivers to believe that what is easy to recall is also highly probable. This can be an effective strategy because probable, frequent events are likely to be more accessible in memory (e.g., many mid-size cars are sold). However, when memories become accessible because of recency (e.g., having just seen several sports cars) perceivers may come to erroneous conclusions (e.g., sales of sports cars are increasing). Similarly the representativeness heuristic leads perceivers to judge the probability of category membership based on the target's perceived similarity to the average member of the category. This rule is quite logical because one would expect a relationship between similarity (e.g., being extroverted) and membership in a particular category (e.g., stand-up comics). However, this rule also leads perceivers to ignore base-rate information. For example, knowing that a target is extroverted may lead a perceiver to ignore the fact that there are more teachers in the general population than stand-up comics. Thus, one might wrongly assume the extroverted target is a comic because the trait extroverted is more representative of the category comic than the category teacher.

Expectancy effects occur when perceivers' initial expectations influence how discrepant information affects the direction of their impressions. For example, an assimilation effect occurs when information that is mildly inconsistent with prior expectations is assimilated into existing expectations. When new information is too discrepant, however, a contrast effect is likely, moving impressions in the opposite direction of initial expectations.

Finally, perceivers' *goals and motives* can alter impressions via their attention to information. Theorists have proposed several different kinds of motives including accuracy, closure, speed, control, and consistency. The various classifications of motives boil down to a basic distinction between motives to be accurate, versus motives to make decisions quickly.

Motives to be accurate can lead perceivers to disconfirm their expectations. For example, when perceivers are instructed to be accurate, they gather more information about targets and form data-driven impressions. Perceivers also form very different impressions when they are instructed to categorize versus when they are told to be accurate.

In the absence of specific directions to follow accuracy goals, the social structure of the situation can lead perceivers to have accuracy motives. For example, outcome dependency increases accuracy motives, presumably to increase the perceivers' sense of prediction and control. When perceivers' rewards are contingent on targets' performance, perceivers attend to expectancy-inconsistent information, make more dispositional inferences, and form more idiosyncratic impressions. Similar effects occur when perceivers are accountable to third parties, or when personal motives, such as an ideal to be unprejudiced, are activated.

Certain factors increase the costs of being indecisive and lead perceivers to confirm their expectations. When perceivers are at the lowest point in their circadian cycles (i.e., the daily low point in their physical and mental processing capabilities), they gather less information and stereotype more. Similar effects occur under time pressure, and when perceivers are distracted or cognitively busy with other tasks. For example, when perceivers make attributions about targets while simultaneously rehearsing a long digit sequence (i.e., they are cognitively busy), they are unable to take situational constraints into consideration. Compared to non-busy perceivers, busy perceivers are more likely to make dispositional attributions for target behavior. Other factors that reduce cognitive resources have similar effects (e.g., distraction, anxiety, insecurity).

C. Effects of the Perceiver in the Situation

Certain factors unique to the interaction between the perceiver and the situation can influence impression formation, including the perceiver's mood and self-representations. For example, perceivers are more likely to be attracted to targets when they themselves are in a positive mood. Mood effects presumably result from selective attention to mood congruent target information, conditioning of positive or negative affect with the target, and priming. For example, when perceivers are in a negative mood, they attend more to negative information about a target. From a learning theory perspective, perceivers may begin to associate their negative moods with the target or attribute their mood to the target's behavior. As a result, perceivers may become conditioned to respond negatively to the target.

Perceivers' self-schemas and personal stereotypes can influence impression formation by directing attention to consistent or relevant information. These mental representations of self and others can have a great deal of influence by priming the perceiver to attend to particular information. Following Bruner, Higgins has proposed that certain constructs can become chronically accessible and influence impressions across many situations. Markus has proposed a related idea of self-schemas. For example, someone who is dieting may become chronic for body fat and pay particular attention to weight-related information when forming impressions. Similarly, easily accessible personal constructs can direct perceivers to attend to relevant information.

IV. OUTCOMES OF THE PROCESS

Our discussion of impression formation began with the early research on impression accuracy. As mentioned, research in this area came to a definitive halt following Cronbach's measurement critiques.

Recently, however, theorists have returned to the accuracy issue, this time asking when perceptions and memory are accurate. Some current accuracy theories take a pragmatic perspective, asserting that people are "good-enough" perceivers. According to this view, people are as accurate as the situation and their goals demand.

Kenny and Albright's Social Relations model builds on Cronbach's componential approach to accuracy for single traits across judges. According to their model, accuracy is a function of four components akin to an analysis of variance model: elevation accuracy (constant), response-set accuracy (judge), individual accuracy (target), and dyadic accuracy (relationship). Elevation accuracy reflects overall accuracy across judges and targets as a function of general perceptions of a trait. So for example, overall accuracy ratings may be elevated simply because the judges all tend to perceive others as having a particular trait, e.g., aggressive. Response-set accuracy refers to the tendency for individual judges to rate targets using a particular part of the scale; thus, it represents their expectations about trait behavior. Individual accuracy reflects the correspondence between several judges' ratings of one target. Dyadic accuracy is specific to an individual judge and target, and it reflects the unique ability of a judge to rate accurately an individual target. Application of the Social Relations model in laboratory research indicates that when people are already well acquainted with one another, perceptions are determined by the target, and individual accuracy is high. When people are not well acquainted, however, accuracy is predicted by the unique dyadic interaction.

Accuracy is not invariably preferable to bias. Recent theorists have questioned the notion that being accurate is necessarily the most functional goal for perceivers. Stereotypes may sometimes facilitate social interaction because they can implicitly contain information about how to interact with members of a certain group. Thus, consensual stereotypes may serve to smooth interaction, allowing perceivers to predict and control the course of interaction with a particular group member. Still others argue that group categorization can have positive implications for self-esteem. These theorists argue that individuals seek positive self-identification via identification with a valued ingroup. To the extent that categorization and ingroup identification lead individuals to devalue outgroup members, any such identification may incease an individual's self-esteem. This approach to social categorization and bias is changing the way researchers think about the underlying motives and goals that play in the impression formation process. [*See* SELF-ESTEEM.]

V. SUMMARY

This review of the impression formation literature began with a general definition and continued with the history and evolution of current theories. It highlighted several of the more influential perspectives and their findings. However, space limitations preclude an exhaustive review of this vast body of research. We encourage the reader to consider turning to the more comprehensive reviews of the literature that can be found in several of the titles listed in the bibliography.

Bibliography

Fiske, S. T. (1993). Social cognition and social perception. In "Annual Review of Psychology" (M. R. Rosenzweig and L. W. Porter, Eds.), Vol. 44. Annual Reviews, Inc., CA.

Fiske, S. T., and Taylor, S. E. (1991). "Social Cognition." McGraw Hill, New York.

Heider, F. (1958). "The Psychology of Interpersonal Relations." Wiley, New York.

Jones, E. E. (1990). "Interpersonal Perception." Freeman, New York.

Schneider, D. J., Hastorf, A. H., and Ellsworth, P. C. (1979). "Person Perception." Addison-Wesley, Reading, MA.

Zebrowitz, L. A. (1990). "Social Perception." Brooks-Cole, Pacific Grove, CA.

Inbreeding

L. B. Jorde
University of Utah School of Medicine

Glossary

Consanguinity The mating of two individuals who are related to one another.

Inbreeding coefficient The probability that two genes at a locus are identical due to descent from an ancestor common to both parents.

Incest Sibling or parent–offspring mating.

Natural selection An evolutionary process in which an individual's relative success in producing surviving offspring depends at least partly on his or her genetic constitution.

Random inbreeding The amount of inbreeding that would occur in a strictly random-mating population of finite size.

INBREEDING refers to the mating of two individuals who are related to one another. The mating of a man and woman who share a recent common ancestor is said to be "consanguineous" (from the Latin *consanguinitas*, "with blood"). The offspring of consanguineous unions are inbred. Because consanguineous couples share one or more common ancestors, their offspring are more likely to carry identical copies of the same gene at a locus. The probability of this identity is measured numerically by the inbreeding coefficient. A number of cultural and behavioral factors, including socioeconomic status, education, religion, and cultural or geographic isolation, are correlated with rates of consanguineous marriage. Each human is thought to carry several recessive disease genes. By bringing identical genes together in individuals, inbreeding increases the frequency of recessive genetic diseases in populations.

I. HISTORICAL BACKGROUND

For millennia, humans have given special recognition to marriage between relatives. The ancient Hebrews banned several types of consanguineous marriage (*Leviticus* 18:6–18). Meanwhile, the ancient Egyptians, perhaps in observance of the sibling marriage of the deities Isis and Osiris, appear to have encouraged brother–sister mating among the royalty. Cleopatra VII was the product of a brother–sister mating, and she in turn married her two younger brothers but produced no children by these marriages (her relations with Mark Antony and Julius Caesar were both fertile, however). Under Theodosius the Great (A.D. 346–395), a Roman could be put to death for marrying a first cousin. The Catholic Church forbade first-, second-, and third-cousin marriages for centuries, and most Western societies have traditionally had rather low rates of consanguineous marriage. Nevertheless, cousin marriages are seen in the pedigrees of a number of prominent Europeans. Charles Darwin, for example, married his first cousin and produced 10 children (of whom four became scientists of note). Henri de Toulouse-Lautrec was the product of a first-cousin marriage; his short stature is thought to be due to pyknodysostosis, a rare recessive disorder. Queen Elizabeth II of England and her husband, Prince Philip Mountbatten, are related approximately as third cousins. While consanguineous marriage is now relatively uncommon in most Western populations, it remains common, and is in fact preferred, in many of the world's populations. [*See* MARRIAGE.]

Encyclopedia of Human Behavior, Volume 2
Copyright © 1994 by Academic Press, Inc. All rights of reproduction in any form reserved.

II. BASIC CONCEPTS OF INBREEDING

A. Definitions

1. Calculation of the Inbreeding Coefficient

Although the inbreeding coefficient was originally defined by Sewall Wright as the correlation between gametes uniting at fertilization, it is perhaps more convenient to think of inbreeding in terms of probabilities. This approach, developed by J. B. S. Haldane, Charles Cotterman, and Gustave Malécot, defines the inbreeding coefficient as the probability that two genes drawn from a locus in an individual are identical because both have originated from a single ancestor. An individual who carries two identical copies of a gene (or allele) at a locus is said to be a homozygote. One who carries two different alleles at a locus is a heterozygote.

Figure 1 is a schematic illustration of a consanguineous mating between two individuals, labeled A and E, who share one grandparent (they would be termed "half first cousins"). Individuals who are not related to both A and E are omitted from the diagram for simplicity. To calculate the inbreeding coefficient for the offspring (O) of this mating, we need to consider the "path" in this diagram that connects A and E. The path goes from A to B to C (the common ancestor) and then back down to D and finally to E (ABCDE). Our objective is to determine the probability that O has received the same gene from both A and E. The first event to consider is whether the gene that passed from A to the offspring, O, is identical to the gene transmitted from B to A. According to the rules of Mendelian genetics, an individual will transmit to his offspring either the gene derived from his mother or the one derived from his father, each with a probability of one-half. Thus, the chance that A transmitted the gene derived from B to his offspring is one-half. There is also a probability of one-half that the gene transmitted by A is derived from his other parent, who is not related to E and is therefore not part of the path. Next, we want to consider the probability that the gene transmitted from B to A is identical to the one transmitted from C to B. Using the same reasoning as before, this probability must also be one-half. Next, consider the probability that the gene transmitted from C to B is the same as the one transmitted from C to D. Suppose that C's two alleles at a locus are labeled X and Y. There are four possible combinations of alleles that could be transmitted to the two offspring: B and D could each receive Y, B and D could each receive X, B could receive X while D received Y, or B could receive Y while D received X. Since each of these combinations occurs with an equal probability, the overall probability that B and D receive the same allele is one-half. There are two final events to consider, the probability that the gene transmitted from C to D is identical to that transmitted from D to E, and the probability that the gene transmitted from E to O is the one derived from D. Again using the principles outlined above, each of these probabilities equals one-half.

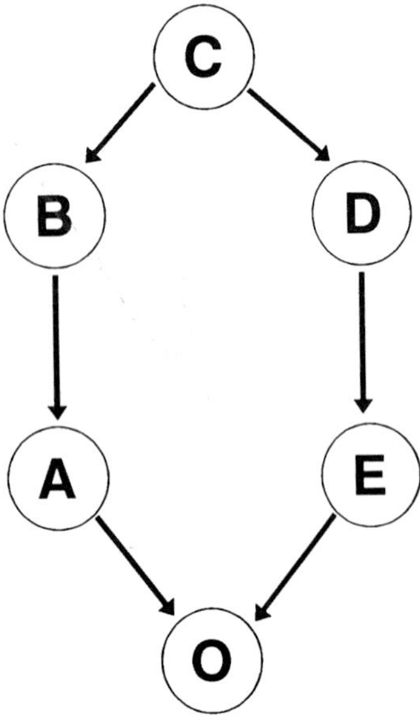

FIGURE 1 An abbreviated diagram of a first-cousin marriage. Only one grandparent is shown.

We have evaluated five independent events, each of which occurs with a probability of one-half. The probability of all five of these events occurring together is obtained simply by multiplying the individual probabilities together: $1/2 \times 1/2 \times 1/2 \times 1/2 \times 1/2$, or $(1/2)^5$. This is the probability that the offspring, O, received genes from each parent that are identical to one another because they both derived from the common ancestor, C. This defines the inbreeding coefficient, usually denoted as f. In this example, f is equal to $1/32$.

Full first cousins share two grandparents instead of one. Then there would be two paths to consider, one going through one grandparent and one going through the other grandparent. Because the transmission of genes through each of these paths would be independent events, one can add the probabilities resulting from each path together in order to obtain the inbreeding coefficient for full first cousins: $1/32 + 1/32 = 1/16$.

Sometimes the common ancestor is himself the product of a consanguineous mating. This increases the probability that he would transmit the same gene to each of his offspring. The degree to which this probability is increased is measured by the ancestor's own inbreeding coefficient, denoted f_A (i.e., the probability that the ancestor carries two genes at a locus that are identical). To incorporate this effect, we multiply the inbreeding coefficient for O by the term $(1 + f_A)$.

In general, then, the inbreeding coefficient for an individual is given by

$$f = \sum (1/2)^n (1 + f_A), \qquad (1)$$

where n is the number of individuals in the path connecting the parents of the individual (including the parents themselves) and the summation is taken over each path that goes through a common ancestor.

The inbreeding level of a population is commonly assessed by averaging the inbreeding coefficients of all members of the population. The average inbreeding coefficient is denoted here as F (in other literature, it is sometimes denoted as α).

Since all humans are probably related to one another to some extent, one might conclude that all matings would be somewhat consanguineous. This would clearly create confusion. In fact, consanguinity is defined relative to a reference population, often the ancestral founders of the current population. Thus, the inbreeding coefficient defined in Eq. (1) actually measures the extent to which the individual's inbreeding level exceeds the average inbreeding coefficient of the reference population.

2. Random and Nonrandom Inbreeding

Many models of population genetics assume that members of a population mate randomly. Given that human populations are necessarily finite in size, random mating implies that relatives would occasionally mate. This component of inbreeding in populations is referred to as random inbreeding. It is typically measured by computing the inbreeding coefficient for each individual assuming random mating in the parental generation: inbreeding coefficients are estimated for all possible pairs of individuals in the parental generation. These coefficients are then averaged. This coefficient can then be compared with the total average inbreeding coefficient for the population (F). A standardized measure of the difference between total and random inbreeding, termed nonrandom inbreeding, is given by

$$F_n = (F - F_r)/(1 - F_r), \qquad (2)$$

where F is the average inbreeding coefficient and F_r is the average random inbreeding coefficient. When $F_r = 0$, nonrandom inbreeding is equal to total inbreeding, F. When random inbreeding exceeds F, F_n is negative, reflecting avoidance of consanguineous matings. This pattern is frequently observed in human populations.

3. Close vs Remote Inbreeding

Population geneticists usually use an arbitrary rule to denote consanguinity. Matings between individuals more distantly related than third cousins (i.e., sharing a set of great-great-grandparents) are not commonly considered to be consanguineous. Matings between distant relatives are however sometimes said to reflect "remote consanguinity" or "remote inbreeding." In a small, closed population, mating couples are often related through a large number of distant common ancestors. The amount of inbreeding due to remote consanguinity can often exceed the amount due to close consanguinity in these populations. It should be apparent that a significant amount of remote consanguinity will be observed in any finite population in which it is possible to trace ancestors back many generations.

B. Measurement of Inbreeding

The method for estimating inbreeding given in Eq. (1) is intended for use with pedigree or genealogical data (the terms pedigree and genealogy tend to be used interchangeably). Genealogical data provide a direct description of the transmission of genes between individuals and potentially yield a highly accurate description of inbreeding in populations. However, there are a number of problems associated with estimating inbreeding from genealogical data. First, the approach is very sensitive to data errors, such as "nonpaternity" (the reported father is not the actual father) and inaccuracies in archival sources. Since the estimation of inbreeding is a multiplicative process (Eq. 1), a single error in a pedigree path will usually render the inbreeding coefficient grossly inaccurate. A second problem is that all pedigree information is truncated: very few genealogies extend more than seven or eight generations into the past. Thus, inbreeding measured in this way is likely to be somewhat underestimated. However, it must be kept in mind that inbreeding coefficients are estimated relative to a founding population. If the genealogical data extend uniformly to a reasonably defined set of founders, then this problem may not be serious. Finally, genealogical data are often difficult and expensive to obtain and manage.

During the past decade or so, several computerized genealogical databases have been developed in order to increase the accuracy and ease of manipulating genealogical data. Computers have made possible calculations of a magnitude that would have been impossible a generation ago. It is now feasible to estimate inbreeding coefficients for hundreds of thousands of individuals in a computerized database (and for millions of pairs of individuals when doing random inbreeding calculations). Some notable examples of large computerized genealogical databases include those of the Laredo, Texas, population, the Saguenay population of Quebec, and the Utah Mormon population.

III. INBREEDING VARIATION IN HUMAN POPULATIONS

A. Interpopulation Variation

Table I summarizes average inbreeding coefficients for a number of human populations, and Figure 2 provides a graphical depiction of worldwide variation in inbreeding levels. The data were gathered from three principal sources: (1) Dispensation records kept by the Roman Catholic Church are commonly available for central and southern European and many American populations. Following the Council of Trent (1542–1563), parishioners were required to obtain dispensations for marriages between individuals related at any degree up to and including third cousins. In Sweden and Finland, dispensations for first-cousin marriages were required by the Crown until the mid-19th century. (2) Many other populations have extensive church or civil registers. It is often possible to reconstruct families and pedigrees from these registers. Computers are now commonly used to perform the arduous task of record linking. (3) A number of studies have employed the direct survey method: married couples are simply asked about their degree of relationship. This method is useful for ascertaining consanguinity at the second-cousin level or closer, but is likely to miss more remote consanguinity.

The data in Table I show that large continental populations tend to have much lower inbreeding coefficients than do isolates (the latter are defined as populations that are nearly closed to immigration). In fact, most of the continental populations have average inbreeding coefficients less than 0.001, while all of the isolates exceed this value. The exceptions to this pattern among the continental populations are Japan, India, and several populations with large proportions of Muslims. Among the Muslim populations in particular, there has been a traditional preference for marriage between first cousins. Consanguineous unions, the great majority of which are first-cousin marriages, account for 54% of marriages in Kuwait, 41% in Jordan, 33% in Syria, 25% in Lebanon, 23% in Algeria, and 22% in Egypt. First-cousin marriage is also common in much of India, and uncle–niece marriage is preferred in regions of South India. Members of these populations often continue to prefer consanguineous marriage even after migrating to other countries in which consanguinity rates are relatively low. High rates of consanguinity are being maintained, for example, among the British Pakistani population.

The highest inbreeding coefficients seen in this table, 0.02 to 0.04, are equivalent to an inbreeding coefficient less than that of first cousins but greater than that of second cousins. The lowest coefficient, 0.0001, is seen in two U.S. populations. This is consistent with the recent origins and high mobility rates of most populations in that country.

B. Temporal Trends in Inbreeding

Some of the most consistent temporal trends in inbreeding values have been observed in western European populations. First, a substantial increase in consanguineous marriage has been observed in many of these populations during the 19th century. This is commonly attributed to the combined effects of population pressure and the loss of primogeniture rights under the Napoleonic code. As population density increased and families were required to divide land among their sons, first cousins often married in order to maintain ever-diminishing land holdings in the same family. The other major trend that can be observed in most of these populations (as well as some others) is a decrease in inbreeding rates during the 20th century (Fig. 3). This trend appears to be due to the breakdown of genetic isolation as population mobility increased.

TABLE I
Average Inbreeding Coefficients in Selected Human Populations[a]

Population	Time period	Sample size	Data source	F
Large continental populations				
Argentina	1980–1981	213,320	Civil records	0.0003
Belgium	1918–1959	2,040,027	Catholic dispensation	0.0005
Brazil	1956–1957	212,090	Catholic dispensation	0.0023
Canada	1959	51,729	Catholic dispensation	0.0005
Egypt	~1960–1980	26,574	Survey	0.0101
England and Wales	1940	49,315	Survey	0.0004
Finland	1810–1920	1,484,126	Royal dispensation[b]	0.0002
France (Loir-et-Cher)	1812–1954	212,837	Catholic dispensation	0.0011
Germany	1898–1953	1,002,175	Catholic dispensation	0.0004
India (Andrha Pradesh)	1957–1958	6,945	Survey	0.0324
India (Karnataka)	1980–1989	107,518	Survey	0.0299
Italy	1956–1960	1,646,612	Catholic dispensation	0.0007
Japan	1900–1960	10,048	Survey	0.0049
Kuwait	1983	5,007	Survey	0.0219
Lebanon (Beirut Christian)	~1950–1980	1,001	Survey	0.0049
(Beirut Muslim)	~1950–1980	1,853	Survey	0.0109
Mexico	1956–1957	28,292	Catholic dispensation	0.0003
Netherlands	1906–1948	1,415,987	National archives	0.0002
Norway	1967–1972	336,818	Medical registration	0.0002
Pakistan (Punjab)	1979–1985	9,520	Survey	0.0280
Spain (Toledo)	1900–1979	25,061	Catholic dispensation	0.0018
Sweden	1750–1844	329,852	Royal dispensation[b]	0.0009
Sudan	~1985	4,833	Survey	0.0317
Turkey	1970–1987	55,175	Survey	0.0065
United States (Wisconsin Catholics)	1853–1981	920,461	Catholic dispensation	0.0001
(Utah Mormons)	1846–1945	435,777[b]	Genealogical database	0.0001
Isolates				
Amish (Old Order)	1800–1960s	3,107	Genealogies	0.0108
(other)	1800–1960s	5,056	Genealogies	0.0032
Arthez-d' Asson, France	1744–1975	5,196	Parish and civil records	0.005
British Pakistanis	~1960–1985	100	Survey	0.0375
Gypsies (Boston area)	—	21	Survey	0.017
Hutterites (S-leut)	1874–1960	667	Genealogies	0.0216
Madison County, Virginia	1850–1939	472	Genealogies	0.0120
Mennonites	1800	640	Genealogies	0.006
Mennonites	1980	570	Genealogies	0.003
Outport Newfoundland	1960–1979	1,534[b]	Parish records	0.0081
Ramah Navajo	1820–1948	1,118[b]	Survey	0.0066
Saguenay, Quebec	1852–1911	7,607	Catholic dispensation	0.0017
Samaritans	1964	381[c]	Genealogies	0.046
Sottunga, Finland	1725–1975	3,030[c]	Parish and civil records	0.0031
Tristan da Cunha	1830–1959	456[c]	Survey	0.0289
Upper Bologna Appennine (Italy)	1565–1980	43,252	Catholic dispensation	0.0013

[a] Sample sizes are number of marriages unless specified otherwise.
[b] First cousins only
[c] Individuals rather than marriages

Another trend, the gradual buildup of remote consanguinity, is usually observed in the small isolated populations for which many generations of genealogical data have been collected. Even though the members of these populations may avoid close consanguineous marriages, they often marry somebody who is related through many distant common ancestors. Thus, their kinship coefficient can still be quite

FIGURE 2 Worldwide variation in the prevalence of consanguineous marriage.

high. In small populations such as Tristan da Cunha and the Ramah Navajo, remote consanguinity accounts for most of the populations' high inbreeding levels.

IV. DETERMINANTS OF INBREEDING

A. Finite Population Size

As has already been discussed, a certain amount of random inbreeding will occur in any finite population. This effect becomes more pronounced as populations become smaller. Most of the isolates listed in Table I are quite small in size, often consisting of only a few hundred individuals. In such populations, it may be impossible to avoid consanguineous mating. An example is the highly isolated Old Order Amish population, in which most individuals are related to one another through multiple common ancestors. Thus, depsite a prohibition against close consanguinity, 98% of marriages taking place since 1960 have been consanguineous, and 25% have taken place between couples related at the equivalent of the second-cousin level or closer.

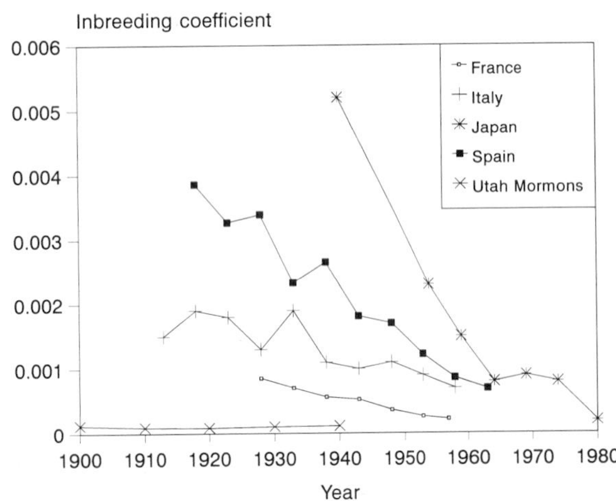

FIGURE 3 The decline of inbreeding during the 20th century in five selected populations.

B. Geographic Isolation

When a population is geographically removed from its neighbors, gene flow (and the availability of unrelated potential mates) will usually be reduced. A number of studies have demonstrated a positive correlation between geographic isolation, usually measured in terms of geographic distances, and inbreeding levels. The combined effect of migration rates and population size on the inbreeding coefficient can be summarized by a simple model, developed by Sewall Wright:

$$F = \frac{1}{4N_eM + 1},$$

where N_e is the "effective population size" (i.e., the population size that would obtain under ideal conditions, including random mating, equal numbers of males and females, and equal numbers of progeny per couple) and M is the migration rate. This equation shows that, as population sizes and migration rates get smaller, inbreeding increases.

C. Cultural and Behavioral Factors

A variety of cultural and behavioral factors influence human population dynamics and mating patterns. Preferential consanguineous marriage systems, such as those mentioned above, can raise inbreeding levels substantially beyond predictions based simply on population sizes and migration rates. The origins of such mating preferences are often obscure, but they can sometimes be related to economic factors, cultural tradition, or religious mandates.

Inbreeding often varies by social class or educational level. Usually, consanguineous marriage is more common among the poorer and less educated segments of society. There are, however, some interesting exceptions. Members of the European nobility usually preferred (or were compelled) to marry within their own relatively small social class, sometimes leading to elevated inbreeding in this stratum of society. Among the first-cousin dispensations issued in 19th century Finland, for instance, 17% were issued to members of the nobility, even though the nobility accounted for only 2% of all marriages. Wealthy landowning families in many parts of the world have practiced cousin marriage in order to maintain holdings within the family.

Another often-studied factor that leads to differences in inbreeding levels is urban versus rural residence. Most studies have found that rural populations experience substantially higher inbreeding than urban populations. This is explained partly by greater geographic isolation and lower population density in the rural setting. Rural residents, being "tied to the land," are also less likely to migrate than are city dwellers. As mentioned above, a need to maintain land holdings within families may further contribute to inbreeding in rural populations.

Inbreeding rates also sometimes vary among different religious groups. A recent study in South India revealed interesting differences in marriage patterns among the three major religious groups, Hindus, Muslims, and Christians. Among Hindus, 21% of marriages took place between uncles and nieces, and 10.8% occurred between first cousins. Uncle–niece marriage is prohibited by the Koran, so only 3.7% of marriages among Muslims were of this type. Marriage between first cousins, which is preferred, accounted for 17.5% of marriages among this group. Christianity discourages both of these types of marriages, so they were somewhat lower among the Christian population (10.2% uncle–niece, 6.8% first cousin). Yet both of these types of consanguineous marriage are relatively high in comparison to European Christians, indicating some acceptance by these Christians of the traditional practices of their Islamic and Hindu neighbors.

Why is consanguineous marriage preferred among a large portion of the world's population? The maintenance of property within families has already been mentioned in other contexts and is doubtless a factor. In addition, consanguineous marriage reduces the financial burden of dowries and bride prices, which are common in many societies. There is often a perception that conflicts are less likely to arise when both marriage partners are members of the same family. In addition, a close family member, such as a first cousin, is usually well enough known to the family so that any financial or health problems are likely to be detected prior to marriage.

V. CONSEQUENCES OF INBREEDING

A. Inbreeding and Genetic Load

Since inbreeding increases homozygosity, it should increase the frequency of recessive diseases among the offspring of consanguineous couples. Such offspring are more likely to die before reaching maturity ("prereproductive" mortality). This results in a reduction of genetic fitness, where fitness is defined in terms of the proportion of offspring who survive to reproductive age. The genetic load in a population is the relative amount of fitness that is lost because all members do not have the optimal genetic constitution. It is defined formally as $(w_{max} - w)/w_{max}$, where w_{max} is the fitness of the optimal genotype and w is the average fitness of the population.

By comparing mortality rates at different levels of inbreeding (including $F = 0$), it is possible to estimate the average number of lethal recessive genes carried by each individual in a population. This statistical regression approach, which was developed by Newton Morton, James Crow, and Herman Muller, has been applied to a large number of human populations. In general, these studies have shown that each human carries the equivalent of approximately one to five genes that would be lethal in the homozygous state (these are termed lethal equivalents). This conclusion must be regarded with some caution, however. It is often very difficult to be certain that the environments of inbred and noninbred individuals are truly equivalent (or adequately controlled statistically). Also, this approach assumes that lethal genes act independently. There are a number of situations in which complex interactions may occur among genes, violating this assumption. While this method of estimating lethal equivalents has its drawbacks, it serves a very instructive purpose in showing that all humans are likely to carry one or more harmful recessive genes.

B. Inbreeding and Mortality: Empiric Data

Table II summarizes the results of several studies in which mortality was measured in several categories of inbred subjects. These studies show that mortality rates among the offspring of first-cousin marriages are elevated substantially above those of the offspring of unrelated couples. There is generally a decline in mortality rates with decreasing levels of consanguinity, as predicted by theory. It is usually impossible to detect a statistically significant increase in mortality beyond the second-cousin level of consanguinity. In the largest comparative analysis of inbreeding and mortality published to date, Muin Khoury compiled data from 31 studies of inbreeding and mortality. Khoury's analysis showed that the median relative risk for mortality among the offspring of first-cousin marriages was 1.4 (i.e., the offspring of these unions would be 1.4 times more likely to die before reaching maturity than would the offspring of unrelated parents). The median relative risks for first cousins once removed[1] and second cousins were 1.21 and 1.28, respectively. While most of the individual population comparisons involving first-cousin marriages yielded statistically significant results, most of the comparisons involving less closely related couples did not. Khoury's study also showed that, even in societies with relatively high rates of inbreeding (up to 15% consanguineous marriages), the proportion of total mortality due to inbreeding is quite small (generally less than 5%).

The studies summarized in Table II deal with postnatal mortality. A number of studies have compared the incidence of stillbirths among inbred and noninbred subjects. In general, these results have not been conclusive. This may be due partly to a lack of ability to detect early fetal and embryonic deaths. It has also been suggested that an advantage may be incurred by inbred fetuses: because they are genetically more similar to their mothers than noninbred fetuses would be, they may be less likely to be attacked by the mother's immune system. This hypothesis is still under investigation.

As mentioned above, inbreeding is usually associated with lower socioeconomic status. Mortality is also elevated in this portion of a population because of factors such as poor nutrition, unsanitary conditions, and inadequate health care. Clearly, these mutual associations could create a spurious association

[1] First cousins once removed are the offspring of one's own first cousins.

TABLE II
Mortality Levels among Cousin and Unrelated Control Marriages in Selected Human Populations

		1.0 cousin		1.5 cousin[a]		2.0 cousin		Unrelated	
Population	Mortality type	%	*N*	%	*N*	%	*N*	%	*N*
Amish (Old Order)	Prereproductive	14.4	1218[b]	—	—	13.3	6064	8.2	17,200
Bombay, India	Perinatal	4.8	3309	2.8	176	0	30	2.8	35,620
France (Loir-et-Cher)	Prereproductive	17.7	282	6.7	105	11.7	240	8.6	1,117
Fukuoka, Japan	0–6 years	10.0	3442	8.3	1048	9.2	1066	6.4	5,224
Hirado, Japan	Prereproductive	18.9	2301	15.3	764	14.7	1209	14.3	28,569
Kerala, India	Prereproductive	18.6	391	—	—	11.8	34	8.7	770
Punjab, Pakistan	Prereproductive	22.1	3532	22.9	1114	20.1	57	16.4	4,731
Sweden	Prereproductive	14.1	185	13.7	227	11.4	79	8.6	625
Utah Mormons	Prereproductive	22.4	1048	15.3	517	12.2	1129	13.2	302,454

[a] First cousins once removed.
[b] Includes 1.5 cousins.

between inbreeding and mortality. Thus, it is preferable to control for the effects of socioeconomic variation when evaluating the relationship between inbreeding and mortality (as well as morbidity, discussed below). Most studies that have controlled for the effects of socioeconomic status find that the association between inbreeding and mortality is somewhat diminished, albeit still detectable. This argues that inbreeding exerts a significant biological effect upon mortality and is not simply the result of socioeconomic differences.

C. Inbreeding and Morbidity

Not all deleterious recessive genes are lethal. Therefore, it is also useful to examine the extent to which inbreeding contributes to morbidity (i.e., the disease rate in a population). Again, a large number of published studies have examined morbidity rates in relation to inbreeding. Compared to mortality results, it is more difficult to compare these studies. While mortality has a fairly exact definition, morbidity does not. When reporting morbidity rates among newborns, different investigators have included diseases of varying levels of severity in their tabulations. Also, the degree of diagnostic accuracy varies considerably among studies, particularly in populations where medical care is not optimal. Keeping these difficulties in mind, it has often been stated that the rate of recognizable disorders among the newborn offspring of first-cousin marriages is approximately double that of the newborn offspring of unrelated couples (in North America, this corresponds to 6–8% versus 3–4%, respectively).

For relatively common recessive diseases like cystic fibrosis and phenylketonuria, it is routine for unrelated heterozygous carriers to mate and produce affected children (the carrier frequencies for cystic fibrosis and phenylketonuria in North America are about 1/23 and 1/50, respectively). Among rare recessive diseases, inbreeding is more frequently the cause of homozygous affected offspring. In one published tabulation, only 5% of phenylketonuria cases were due to consanguineous marriage. In contrast, 50% of childern born with Wilson's disease, a rare recessive disorder of copper metabolism, were the products of consanguineous marriage.

In addition to affecting disease rates, inbreeding has also been shown to have a negative effect on various measures of performance (this phenomenon is often referred to as inbreeding depression). One of the best-studied examples is the intelligence quotient (IQ). At least a dozen studies of inbreeding and IQ have been published, and all of them indicate that the average IQs of the offspring of first-cousin matings are several points lower than those of matched controls. Most of these studies matched the comparison groups for socioeconomic status.

D. Consequences of Incest

Incest, the mating of siblings or parents and offspring, is universally prohibited in human societies. Recent studies indicate that it is even quite rare among other animals, with most bird and mammal species having fewer than 2% incestuous matings. Given the commonness of deleterious recessive genes, it is expected that incest would have serious consequences. This is indeed the case. While data on the outcomes of incestuous human matings are understandably difficult to procure, several small studies have been published. In these studies, between one-fourth and one-half of the offspring of incestuous unions were born with diagnosable anomalies, many of which were severe. Mental retardation is especially common among these children. In part because of small sample sizes (on the order of one or two dozen per study), environmental factors were not controlled in these reports. Since many of the incestuous unions occurred in substandard home environments, nongenetic factors are doubtless partly responsible for the high morbidity rates. [*See* Mental Retardation.]

E. Inbreeding and Fertility

While the effects of inbreeding upon mortality and morbidity have received considerable attention, the relationship between inbreeding and fertility is somewhat less appreciated. A recent survey demonstrated a significant positive correlation between inbreeding and total fertility in 19 of 22 populations. In part, this reflects the influence of socioeconomic factors: higher inbreeding rates and higher fertility are both usually seen among the poorer classes. Another, and somewhat more subtle, factor operates in societies in which consanguineous marriage is preferred. In these populations, the birth of one's cousin often guarantees a marriage partner. Thus, the time and effort devoted to finding a suitable mate can be considerably decreased. As expected, the age of marriage is significantly lower among consanguineous couples in these populations. Consequently, consanguineous couples begin producing children earlier, resulting in higher completed family sizes. The effect is counterbalanced to some degree by the increased mortality of the offspring of consanguineous unions. It has also been suggested that increased fertility among consanguineous couples may reflect the phenomenon of reproductive compensation: couples consciously produce additional children in order to compensate for losses due to increased mortality.

F. Inbreeding and Natural Selection

Natural selection acting against a harmful recessive gene can only affect individuals with the homozygous genotype, *aa*. Since the great majority of recessive genes are "hidden" in the heterozygous state, selection against recessive genes is quite slow. Inbreeding increases the proportion of homozygotes in a population, enabling natural selection to work more quickly.

In a population in which inbreeding has been occurring for a long period of time, one might expect that natural selection would have eliminated a substantial proportion of deleterious recessive genes. It has been argued that this has taken place in South India, where close consanguinity has been common for centuries (possibly for as long as 2000 years). One survey indicated that congenital malformation rates among inbred and noninbred newborns were not significantly different in this population, supporting the idea that a large share of deleterious recessive genes have been eliminated. However, most subsequent studies of the same population did show significant differences. These differences were comparable to those seen in populations such as that of Brazil, where inbreeding has not persisted for a long period of time. Thus, it is debatable whether this phenomenon has occurred in a human population.

VI. SUMMARY

While comparatively rare in Western populations, consanguinity is quite common in many other populations throughout the world. Variation in consanguineous marriage rates reflects a variety of cultural, economic, and religious influences. Numerous studies have shown that consanguinity causes increased mortality, morbidity, and fertility. Consequently, it has significant implications for demographic projections and public health practice, and it is a topic of relevance for anthropologists, psychologists, biologists, medical practitioners, and others.

Acknowledgments

This work was supported by NIH Grant HG-00347 and NSF Grants BNS-8703841 and DBS-9209262.

Bibliography

Bittles, A. H., Mason, W. M., Greene, J., and Rao, N. A. (1991). Reproductive behavior and health in consanguineous marriages. *Science* **252,** 789–794.

Freire-Maia, N., and Elisbao, T. (1984). Inbreeding effect on morbidity. III. A review of the world literature. *Am. J. Med. Genet.* **18,** 391–400.

Hartl, D. L., and Clark, A. G. (1989). "Principles of Population Genetics," 2nd ed. Sinauer, Sunderland, MA.

Jorde, L. B. (1989). Inbreeding in the Utah Mormons: an evaluation of estimates based on pedigrees, isonymy, and migration matrices. *Ann. Hum. Genet.* **53,** 339–355.

Khlat, M., and Khoury, M. (1991). Inbreeding and diseases: Demographic, genetic, and epidemiologic perspectives. *Epidemiol. Rev.* **13,** 28–41.

Khoury, M. J., Cohen, B. H., Chase, G. A., and Diamond, E. L. (1987). An epidemiologic approach to the evaluation of the effect of inbreeding on prereproductive mortality. *Am. J. Epidemiol.* **125,** 251–262.

McCullough, J. M., and O'Rourke, D. H. (1986). Geographic distribution of consanguinity in Europe. *Ann. Hum. Biol.* **13,** 359–367.

Schull, W. J., and Neel, J. V. (1965). "The Effects of Inbreeding on Japanese Children." Harper and Row, New York.

Schull, W. J., and Neel, J. V. (1972). The effects of parental consanguinity and inbreeding in Hirado, Japan. V. Summary and interpretation. *Am. J. Hum. Genet.* **24,** 425–453.

Individual Differences in Temperament

Louis A. Schmidt, Ariana Shahinfar, and Nathan A. Fox
University of Maryland

Glossary

Difficult temperament Temperaments comprising irritability, fussiness, and negative emotionality, which may place a child at risk for subsequent behavioral and emotional disorders.

Easy temperament Temperaments comprising easy soothability and positive emotionality, which may be predictive of a positive developmental outcome.

Electroencephalogram (EEG) A measure of brain electrical activity used by researchers to index central nervous system correlates of behavior.

Heredity The genetic basis of temperament.

Resiliency The ability of particular temperaments to withstand environmental stress.

Temperament A manner of reacting, feeling, and thinking which is innate and specific to an individual.

Temperament structure Dimensions that comprise temperament (e.g., activity level, emotionality, heritability, stability).

Trait An innate characteristic that remains enduring and stable over time.

Vagal tone A measure of heart-rate variability during respiration which is used to index peripheral nervous system correlates of temperamental differences.

Vulnerability The susceptibility of particular temperaments to negative outcome when exposed to environmental stress.

THE CONCEPT of individual differences is germane to all branches of science that study living organisms. For researchers interested in the biological antecedents of personality and emotional development, the study of individual differences in temperament is of particular interest. In general, temperament can be defined as innate traits which characterize the manner in which one expresses emotions. Recent temperament research has focused on conceptualization and structure, biological antecedents and correlates, measurement issues, and predictive outcomes. These topics are discussed in this article.

I. THEORETICAL NOTIONS AND STRUCTURE OF TEMPERAMENT

The study of individual differences in temperament has a long history. In 2 A.D., the Greek physicians Hippocrates and Galen categorized four temperamental subtypes: choleric, melancholic, phlegmatic, and sanguine. These four subtypes were thought to have emerged from differences in bodily "humors." It was not until the first half of this century, however, particularly in Eastern Europe, that the scientific study of temperament emerged. In fact, many of today's notions of temperament can be traced to the work of Pavlov and his followers such as Teplov, Nebylitsyn, Strelau, Eysenck, and Gray.

This section will trace and critique the development of temperament theory in Europe. In addition, recent notions of temperament according to U.S. researchers will be described, with a particular emphasis on the structure of temperament.

A. European Perspectives

One of the earliest accounts of the scientific study of temperament can be linked to Pavlov and his work

Encyclopedia of Human Behavior, Volume 2

Copyright © 1994 by Academic Press, Inc. All rights of reproduction in any form reserved.

on conditioned reflexes in dogs. Pavlov theorized that individual variation in the innate organization of the nervous system was related to the speed and strength with which an organism conditioned. He observed individual differences in the speed of conditioning and the strength of associations that were formed. Pavlov argued that these differences had a physiological basis in the nervous system. [*See* CLASSICAL CONDITIONING.]

Pavlov's neurophysiological approach to the study of temperament motivated research among Soviet and Eastern European psychologists. The work of Russian scientists Teplov, Nebylitsyn, and Rozhdestvenskaya, in the 1950s and 1960s, on central nervous system arousal and cellular excitation in relation to individual differences in temperament and personality are good examples, as is the recent work of Jan Strelau.

Strelau argued that a balance between excitation and inhibition in the autonomic nervous system as well as neuroendocrine individuality, was related to individual differences in temperament. He constructed a questionnaire (the Strelau Temperament Inventory, STI) which incorporates Pavlovian concepts such as strength of excitation, strength of inhibition, and mobility. The STI has recently been used cross-culturally and has been found to be a reliable and valid measure of biologically based temperamental dispositions.

Two other important personality psychologists whose work influences research on temperament are Hans Eysenck and Jeffrey Gray. In defining the structure of personality, Eysenck wrote that temperament could be defined as a person's "more or less stable and enduring system of affective behaviour." Moreover, Eysenck argued that individual differences in temperament arose from a balance between excitation and inhibition in the reticulocortical arousal loop.

The neurophysiological explanation into the causation of individual differences in temperament was soon expanded by Gray. Gray argued that temperamental differences in anxiety and impulsivity were related to a balance between a behavioral activation system (BAS) and a behavioral inhibition system (BIS). These systems were purported to be subsumed under distinct neuroanatomo-physiological systems. As with Strelau's theory, attempts have recently been made to index the psychometric properties of Gray's theory.

Although rich in theory, European temperament research, however, has been confronted by a number of shortcomings. First, despite a large corpus of data on adults, relatively little research has been conducted with infants and/or children. Recent reviews of this literature revealed a disproportionate number of adult to child studies of temperament, and few reports of longitudinal investigations of temperament. In addition, there is little information on the stability or heritability of temperament as defined by these theorists.

B. U.S. Perspectives

Unlike the long tradition of temperament research in Europe, the study of temperament in the United States has a relatively short history and much of it has been done with children. One of the earliest discussions of temperament in the United States was by Gordon Allport in 1937, who defined temperament as the "characteristic phenomena of an individual's emotional nature, . . . susceptibility to emotional stimulation, . . . strength and speed of response, the quality of his prevailing mood, and . . . fluctuation and intensity in mood."

After Allport, the study of temperament in the United States then laid relatively dormant for approximately the next three decades, until Thomas and Chess, in the latter 1960s, undertook a major longitudinal study examining temperamental differences in newborn infants. This study, the New York Longitudinal Study (NYLS), provided a description of infant behavior patterns and categorized these patterns along nine dimensions of temperament (activity level, rhythmicity, approach/withdrawal, adaptability, intensity, sensory threshold, mood, distractibility, attention span/persistence). Subsequent analyses revealed that these nine dimensions clustered around three types of children: (1) "easy children," (2) "difficult children," and (3) "slow to warm up children." Their findings suggested that each of these groups remained somewhat stable over time and each was at differential risk for subsequent behavioral outcomes. Both Thomas and Chess argued that temperamental differences interacted with environmental influences in the formation of personality early in life. They discussed the notion of "goodness-of-fit." Thomas and Chess proposed that when infants of a certain temperamental type were raised by parents who somehow matched this type, there would be a positive outcome in child rearing. Research in the tradition of Thomas and Chess has relied on questionnaires which parents fill out about their child's behavior. Their child's score on each

TABLE I
Summary of Recent Models of Infant and Child Temperament

Investigator	Dimensions
Thomas and Chess (1963)	Activity level, rhythmicity, approach/withdrawal, adaptability, intensity, sensory threshold, mood, distractibility, attention span/persistence
Bates *et al.* (1979)	NYLS dimensions plus fussiness, sociability, changeability, and soothability
Rothbart (1981)	Activity level, smiling and laughter, distress to limitations, fear, soothability, duration of orienting
Buss and Plomin (1984)	Emotionality, activity, sociability, impulsivity
Kagan *et al.* (1991)	Motor arousal, emotionality

of the nine dimensions is computed from the individual item responses.

Much of the current work in temperament now supplements questionnaire assessment with behavioral observation and psychophysiological methods to examine infant and child temperament.

Current models of infant and child temperament in the United States have been proposed by researchers such as Bates, Buss, Kagan, Plomin, and Rothbart. A summary of the major dimensions surrounding each model is presented in Table I. While each of these scientists may differ on the importance of any one defining dimension of temperament, their definitions do converge to some degree. All researchers appear to agree on the notion that temperament has biological, genetic, and emotional components. Moreover, these researchers have suggested multi-dimensional models of temperament which incorporate dimensions such as activity level, smiling and laughter, fear, reaction to frustration, soothability, attention span, sociability, emotionality, attention, and self-regulation. And they have also argued that stability, predictive outcomes, and particular patterns of central and peripheral nervous reactivity are important dimensions affecting the structure of temperament.

II. THE MEASUREMENT OF TEMPERAMENT

The number of instruments used to measure individual differences in infant and child temperament is as large as the number of theoretical positions proposed to understand behavioral variation. Among the approaches most often used are maternal questionnaire, laboratory observation, and physiological assessment.

A. Questionnaire Approach

Of the three temperament assessment approaches, the parent-report questionnaire is the most widely used. The prevalence of this technique is due, in part, to practical reasons such as the low cost of implementing the measure and its ease of administration. Perhaps more importantly, however, parents serve as a broad information base in that they are able to report on how their child usually behaves under normal circumstances and in various situations. In addition, validational studies between parent reports and home observations have found substantial enough agreement to assure correspondence between the questionnaire and objective measures of the child's behaviors.

In general, temperament questionnaires require the parent to report the frequency or quality of their child's behavior in response to particular situations during a recent, specified period of time. The situations presented are common and vary according to the target age of the child being assessed. For example, the Infant Behavior Questionnaire (IBQ) asks a parent to rate how often in the last week their 3–12 month old tossed about in the crib during sleep. The Toddler Behavior Assessment Questionnaire (TBAQ), on the other hand, asks how often their 18–24 month old ran through the house or climbed over furniture during the last month.

Many of the temperament questionnaires share a common theoretical basis in the nine dimensions originally proposed by the NYLS group (e.g., the Infant Temperament Questionnaire, the Toddler Temperament Scale, and the Behavioral Style Questionnaire). Others derive dimensions representing those of a particular theorist (e.g., the Infant Behavior Questionnaire, the Toddler Behavior Questionnaire, and Colorado Child Temperament Inventory). A selection from among the most widely used questionnaire assessments, including response format and targeted age range, is presented in Table II.

Despite a demonstrated high inter-judge reliability, moderate internal consistency, and moderate levels of test–retest reliability, there are several methodological concerns associated with the questionnaire method that must be addressed. One of

TABLE II
Selected Index of Questionnaires Used to Measure Infant and Child Temperament

Instrument	Targeted age	Response format
Infant Characteristic Questionnaire (ICQ) (Bates *et al.*, 1979)	4–6 months	7-point rating scale describing behavior
Revised Infant Temperament Questionnaire (RITQ) (Carey and McDevitt, 1978)	4–8 months	6-point rating scale based on frequency of behavior
Infant Behavior Questionnaire (IBQ) (Rothbart, 1978)	3–12 months	7-point rating scale based on frequency of behavior
Toddler Behavior Assessment Questionnaire (TBAQ) (Goldsmith, 1987)	18–24 months	7-point rating scale based on frequency of behavior
Colorado Child Temperament Inventory (CCTI) (Rowe and Plomin, 1977)	5 months–9 years	5-point rating scale indicating likeness to child
EASI-I Temperament Survey (EASI-I) (Buss *et al.*, 1973)	1–9 years	5-point rating scale indicating likeness to child

Source: Adapted from Hubert, Wachs, Peters-Martin, and Gandour (1982).

these potential sources of concern lies in the possibility that the characteristics of the informant interfere with the report. For example, the caregiver's degree of comprehension of instructions, items and response options, inaccurate memory, biased recall, and concern with social desirability may affect accuracy. In addition, characteristics of the rater–child relationship, such as behaviors which occur in response to caregiver behaviors and biases in parental interpretation of behaviors, may also interfere with objective response to the questionnaire items.

Other criticisms that have been leveled against the questionnaire approach to measuring temperament include the fact that this technique measures behavior along a continuum rather than according to qualitative differences. In addition, for those questionnaires based upon the NYLS dimensions of temperament, there is the added problem that the nine dimensions do not maintain conceptual independence. That is, the NYLS definition of distractibility (the items used to compute the dimension) overlaps with persistence and attention span. This suggests that questionnaire items designed to elicit any of these characteristics will inevitably be confounded.

A third and final concern involved in the questionnaire approach to measurement is that the samples upon which the techniques are standardized do not necessarily represent all children. Therefore, it is necessary to norm these questionnaires on different ethnic and cultural groups.

Taken together, the evidence for and against the questionnaire approach to measuring temperament suggests that it may be a useful tool, provided that issues such as conceptual interdependence and the possibility of caregiver interference or bias in reporting are taken into consideration. Although the issue of conceptual interdependence is one which can only be addressed by a trend toward research into more specific dimensions of temperament, the potential sources of problems associated with the characteristics of the reporter may be reduced by utilizing observational measures of temperament in addition to the questionnaire approach.

B. Observational Approach

Laboratory observation of a child's behavior is an important assessment tool in the study of individual differences in temperament. Not only does observation provide a source of objective validation of caregiver report on the questionnaire, but the recording of a child's actions in a particular novel situation provides a source of information that cannot be obtained through the standardized questionnaire approach. Although methods of observation are sometimes subject to distortion because of a limited period of observation which, in turn, constricts the range of behaviors observed, research has shown that observation over the course of several visits allows for expression of many of the behaviors tapped by questionnaires.

The development of systematic procedures for observing temperament has primarily derived from home observation. The main advantage of this method is that it allows for the study of temperament in a naturalistic setting. While researcher observations in the home have shown concordance with parental report over the course of several sessions, there remain possible sources of error and bias in that setting may vary widely, there is no way to standardize the content or sequence of events, and the observed features of temperament may be confounded with features of the home.

In order to address these methodological concerns, several theorists have developed specific formats of laboratory observation in which the child is assessed in terms of the same dimensions tapped in the questionnaires during various planned situational activities that may involve interaction with the experimenter, the mother, or another child. Observation may be quantified according to *frequency* (or *rate* of response), *duration* of response, and *amplitude* of response. Laboratory assessment validates different temperament constructs and allows researchers to identify characteristics of clinical importance.

While the observational and questionnaire approaches assess the overt behavioral components of temperament, psychophysiological assessment adds the dimension of information on the underlying biological mechanisms of temperament. Just as the observational approach is intended to supplement the questionnaire technique, so the physiological measurement of the processes involved in temperament is meant to work in conjunction with behavioral assessment. The result is a multi-method assessment which addresses both the manifestations of temperament described above by the dimensions of emotionality, activity, and attention, and their biological underpinnings.

C. Physiological Approach

The search for central and peripheral nervous system correlates of infant and child temperament has received much attention over the last decade. Investigators interested in this area of temperament research have primarily used three measures to examine the relation between physiology and temperamental differences: measures of electrocortical (EEG) activity, heart rate, and adrenocortical activity. A discussion of these different approaches is presented in this section.

1. EEG

Although routinely used over the years in clinical environments to diagnosis neuropathology, EEG is currently being used in basic research settings to explore questions related to cognitive and personality development. EEG is a measure of voltage generated within the central nervous system and it is measured off the scalp. With the development of powerful and fast computers, EEG data can now be sampled in large amounts and at faster rates, and frequency analyses can be readily performed. The frequency analysis allows the researcher to derive an estimate of spectral power (energy) within a particular frequency. There is a large corpus of literature suggesting that spectral power is inversely related to activation in that a decrease in power reflects increased cortical activation. From this notion, developmental psychophysiologists have examined the relation between brain activity in particular frequencies and behavioral differences in infants and children. [*See* BRAIN ELECTRIC ACTIVITY.]

Researchers interested in the dynamics in cortical activation between hemispheres have calculated a laterality ratio which reflects the amount of activity in one hemisphere relative to the other. This ratio provides an estimate of power and the degree to which one hemisphere exhibits greater activation than the other.

The pattern of frontal asymmetry has been of particular interest to investigators studying the relation between EEG and temperamental differences early in life. Fox *et al.* for example, suggested that a stable pattern of right frontal asymmetry measured early in life reflects a temperamental vulnerability to negative affect and may predict subsequent inhibited behavior. Recent data from his laboratory appear to support this contention. Results from the Maryland Infant Study have suggested that infants selected for temperamental differences predictive of subsequent inhibition displayed greater relative right frontal activation.

While EEG is a noninvasive measure which provides a window into brain activity, it is faced with several methodological problems. Some of these problems are related to the origin or source of the electrical activity which EEG is purported to measure. Other methodological concerns have been raised about the many variables that can potentially affect electrical signaling, such as individual variation in skull thickness and underlying anatomical structure (e.g., cell density), developmental and metabolic changes, and electrode placement. And several studies have questioned the choice (determination) of frequency bands used and the amount of EEG data required to reach reliable and valid conclusions about brain–behavior relations.

2. Heart Rate

The measurement of autonomic patterning has also been used recently in the study of infant and child temperament. The recording of heart rate activity is a relatively noninvasive procedure; assessment of heart rate is usually conducted while the child is relaxed or attending to a stimulus. Researchers are typically interested in measures of mean heart rate and heart rate variability.

Recent studies have shown that the pattern of heart rate variability may be related to temperamental differences in young children. Kagan and colleagues, for example, found that behaviorally inhibited children displayed faster and less variable heart rates as compared to uninhibited children.

Vagal tone is an additional measure derived from heart rate activity which has recently been used by developmental psychophysiologists. Vagal tone reflects the patterns of heart rate which occur during changes associated with respiration (respiratory sinus arrhythmia). In a series of studies with infants and young children, Porges and colleagues have found that vagal tone is related to emotional reactivity and regulation. Porges argues that vagal tone may reflect emotional health in that infants with high vagal tone tend to display better regulatory skills as compared to infants with low vagal tone.

3. Adrenocortical Activity

A third approach to indexing the physiological correlates of temperamental differences has been that of adrenocortical activity. This approach usually involves the collection of saliva or plasma specimens which are subsequently assayed for levels of cortisol and other immune responses. The measurement of cortisol is usually indexed in terms of changes from some basal level to stressor conditions. Cortisol is a primary hormone of the adrenocortical system whose production varies as a function of time of day and other physiological and psychological stressors. Developmental psychophysiologists are typically interested in the relation between cortisol production and emotional and temperamental differences.

Although recent evidence suggests that differences in infant emotional reactivity may be related to differences in cortisol production (Gunnar, 1991), these findings should be accepted with caution due to the numerous variables affecting cortisol production. For example, cortisol levels are known to vary rhythmically with the diurnal cycle. And there are developmental changes occurring during the first year of life which affect the daily cycle of cortisol production. [*See* HORMONES AND BEHAVIOR.]

III. PREDICTION AND OUTCOMES

The study of temperament provides a framework for research on those behavior patterns of an individual which remain stable and may predict future personality. This section of the article is devoted to describing those elements of temperament which have proven fruitful in terms of understanding subsequent adjustment. While there are certainly many theories of outcome to accompany each temperament style, the two with the most scientific basis and acceptance are those related to the child's level of difficulty and level of inhibition. One reason why the "difficult" and "inhibited" constructs have lent themselves so well to prediction is that they are composed of temperament clusters which have demonstrated stability across ages.

A. Stability vs Continuity

Stability and continuity are terms important to the study of temperament. Stability refers to the extent to which the underlying mechanisms of a certain behavior remain the same over time. While the behavioral expression may change according to an age-appropriate reference, if the basic motivation behind the behavior is the same, then the temperamental construct is said to maintain stability.

Continuity, on the other hand, refers to consistency in a specified behavioral expression over time. For example, continuity is demonstrated when a person responds with fear to a frightening situation each time that situation is presented. Particularly during the transition from infancy to childhood, however, one would not expect to find such continuity of behavior. Rather, researchers have found a connection between a 9 month old who displays fear of novelty and later demonstrates shy behavior when tested at 4 years of age. The proposed mechanism underlying the behavior remains the same while the outward expression follows along with the child's developmental repertoire.

When considering the literature on the use of temperament toward predicting behavioral outcome, one is referring to measurement of stability of behavior rather than continuity.

B. The Difficult Child

The term "difficult temperament" is one which originated with the New York Longitudinal Study and was reserved for children who display irritability, fussiness, and negative emotionality. Although there is some controversy over the use of the label "difficult" because of its negative connotation, the recognition of this unique constellation of behaviors is generally accepted in most of the current literature on temperament. It is also important to note here that the concept of difficult temperament is one which is specifically related to behavioral characteristics displayed by infants and young children.

One reason for the general acceptance of the concept of the difficult infant or young child lies in its clinical usefulness for predicting future behaviors (and behavior problems). A number of studies show a clear and long-lasting correlation between difficult temperament in early childhood and clinical diagnosis of psychiatric disorder in early adulthood. Other studies relate the particular temperament construct to less salient and more immediate outcomes such as infant proneness to colic and excessive crying. Still other studies propose a relationship between difficult temperament and the problems of attention deficit, hyperactivity, hostile/aggressive behavior, and problems with externalizing and internalizing.

It is important to remember that difficult temperament itself is not a risk factor for maladjustment. Rather, Prior states "it is in combination with other significant biological, relationship and environmental variables that it may have significant impact." The need to consider environmental factors in determining the outcome of infants with difficult temperament speaks to the manner in which we view the concept of difficultness. A difficult child is defined in terms of the social relationship that he or she develops with caregivers. While difficulty is a within-child construct, it is an aspect of personality which is measured within the social interaction. What for one set of parents is difficulty may be to another set an endearing or manageable characteristic. In this sense it is useful to remember that caregivers have the ability to reinforce or modify temperamentally based reactions. Maternal personality and her interaction with a difficult child may have a great impact on both the labeling and outcome of this temperamental style. For example, a study conducted by Bates *et al.* found that "multiparous extraverted mothers" tended to rate their infants as easy. While there was a consensus among the mothers that the fussy, hard-to-soothe, labile infant accurately defined the difficult temperament, mothers who displayed these characteristics themselves were more accepting of mild forms of this behavior and thus less likely to label their child as difficult.

There is also evidence to suggest that mothers of "mildly difficult" children were more likely to use intrusive control tactics in dealing with their toddlers than mothers of easy or average children. This is an important element to consider because the same study also found that difficult children were more likely to resist their mothers' control attempts and, thus, experienced more mother–child conflict—a situation which has been shown to produce a pathological outcome in the child.

In addition to lending validity to the predictive value of the concept of difficult temperament, these examples highlight the merit of studying difficult temperament for the purpose of clinical intervention. An example of research in this area is found in the work of Maziade and his colleagues. They found that adolescents assessed as difficult children during infancy, 4 years, 7 years, and/or 12 years were more likely to display clinical disorders at 16 years if they also were living within a family with average or dysfunctional behavior control. While the tendency toward psychopathology was invariably greater for difficult children, those who lived within families described as "superior" in behavioral structure were more likely to have positive clinical outcomes. In this paradigm, the key to managing the difficult temperament lay in adapting those within the child's environment to identify possible problems and to use foresight as a tool in dealing with them.

C. The Inhibited Child

A variety of data from a number of sources indicate that there is a certain constellation of behaviors which can be identified in infancy that predict behavioral inhibition and shyness in young children. The term inhibition refers to a child's reactions when confronted with novel social and nonsocial environmental stimuli.

Early infant predictors of subsequent inhibition include high motor activity and negative emotionality. For example, Kagan and colleagues found that infants classified as high motor/high negative emotionality were more likely to be behaviorally inhibited children as compared to infants classified as high motor/high positive emotionality. And these children also displayed a distinct pattern of central and peripheral nervous system activity.

While inhibited behavior does not necessarily imply a negative outcome, it is an individual difference variable which may serve as a precursor to psychopathology. Data suggest that behavioral inhibition is related to the development of dysfunctional styles of peer relations and social competence. Accordingly, inhibition may be predictive of social withdrawal.

D. Vulnerability and Resiliency

As can be seen from the examples of inhibition and difficult temperament, there are certain mechanisms by which temperament serves not only to predict behavior, but also to put a child at risk for certain pathologies. Just as difficult temperament may produce a vulnerability toward behavior disorders and other psychopathological outcomes, findings on inhibition suggest that a child who exhibits this particular constellation of behaviors is at risk for experiencing social isolation.

There is another side to temperament, however, in which certain behaviors may serve as protective factors that encourage resilience in children exposed to stressors. For example, a child of easy temperament, who displays emotional flexibility, positive emotionality, and persistence in problem solving, has more of the affective resources to express and deal with his or her experience when exposed to stressful situations.

Temperament is not only a factor in protecting children under stress, but also plays a role in adjustment in the general population. During play assessment of a normal sample, those children with high play initiative, good peer relations and involvement who were also rated by their parents as having an easy temperament were found to have positive psychosocial outcomes. In general, not only does easy temperament protect children from stress, but it also promotes positive experience.

There are certain situations, however, in which the tables are reversed for temperament and its utility in resilience. The most notable of these can be illustrated by the findings from a study conducted in East Africa during a drought in which infants with difficult temperaments were found to survive when those with easy temperaments did not. The hypothesis is that the difficult infants' irritable behaviors received more attention and food from the mothers and, thus, ensured the child's survival under high stress.

An interesting parallel to temperament resiliency can be drawn to the concept of "hardiness" in the adult personality literature. In the early 1980s, a large corpus of research was directed toward this concept. Hardiness refers to one's ability to withstand environmental stressors. Apparently, there are certain constitutional dispositions within the individual which serve to buffer or mitigate the effects of stress. Indeed, research has demonstrated that individuals with this particular personality disposition, which encompasses commitment, control, and challenge, were more likely to recover from traumatic events such as cancer. Although the stability of temperament resiliency has not been studied, these data suggest that yesterday's resilient child may be tomorrow's hardy adult.

Bibliography

Allport, G. W. (1937). "Personality: A psychological Interpretation." Holt, New York.

Bates, J. E., and Bayles, K. (1984). Objective and subjective components in mothers' perceptions of their children from age 6 months to 3 years. *Merrill-Palmer Quart.* **30,** 111–130.

Bates, J., Freeland, C., and Lounsbury, M. (1979). Measurement of infant difficultness. *Child Dev.* **50,** 794–803.

Buss, A. H., and Plomin, R. (1984). "Temperament: Early Developing Personality Traits." Erlbaum, Hillsdale, NJ.

deVries, M. W., and Sameroff, A. J. (1984). Culture and temperament: Influences on infant temperament in three East African societies. *Am. J. Orthopsych.* **54,** 83–96.

Eysenck, H. J. (1953). "The Structure of Human Personality." Methuen & Co., London.

Fox, N. A., Calkins, S. D., and Marshall, T. R. (1992). Behavioral and physiological antecedents of inhibition in infancy. Manuscript submitted for publication.

Gunnar, M. R. (1991). The psychobiology of infant temperament. In "Individual Differences in Infancy" (J. Columbo and J. Fagan, Eds.). Erlbaum, Hillsdale, NJ.

Hubert, N. C., Wachs, D. T., Peters-Martin, P., and Gandour, M. J. (1982). The study of early temperament: Measurement and conceptual issues. *Child Dev.,* **53,** 571–600.

Kagan, J., Reznick, J. S., and Snidman, N. (1987). Physiology and psychology of behavioral inhibition. *Child Dev.* **58,** 1459–1473.

Kagan, J., and Snidman, N. (1991). Infant predictors of inhibited and uninhibited profiles. *Psychol. Sci.* **2,** 40–44.

Kobasa, S. C., Maddi, S. R., and Kahn S. (1982). Hardiness and health: A prospective study. *J. Pers. Soc. Psychol.* **42,** 168–177.

Lee, C. L., and Bates, J. E. (1985). Mother–child interaction at age two years and perceived difficult temperament. *Child Dev.* **56,** 1314–1325.

Maziade, M., Cote, R., Bernier, H., Boutin, P., and Thivierge, J. (1989). Significance of extreme temperament in infancy for clinical status in pre-school years. I. Value of extreme temperament at 4–8 months for predicting diagnosis at 4.7 years. *Br. J. Psych.* **154,** 535–543.

Maziade, M., Caron, C., Cote, R., Merette, C., Bernier, H., Laplante, B., Boutin, P., and Thivierge, J. (1990). Psychiatric status of adolescents who had extreme temperaments at age 7. *Am. J. Psych.* **147,** 1531–1536.

McCall, R. B. (1986). Issues of stability and continuity in temperament research. In "The Study of Temperament: Changes, Continuities and Challenges" (R. Plomin and J. Dunn, Eds.). Erlbaum, Hillsdale, NJ.

Porges, S. W. (1991). Vagal tone: An autonomic mediator of affect. In "The Development of Emotion Regulation and Dysregulation" (J. Garber and K. A. Dodge, Eds.). Cambridge University Press, Cambridge.

Prior, M. (1992). Childhood temperament. *J. Child Psychol. Psych.* **33,** 249–279.

Prior, M., Sanson, A., Carroll, R., and Oberklaid, F. (1989). The Australian temperament project. In "Temperament in Childhood" (G. A. Kohnstamm, J. E. Bates, and M. K. Rothbart, Eds.). Wiley, New York.

Rothbart, M. K., and Mauro, J. A. (1990). Questionnaire approaches to the study of infant temperament. In "Individual Differences in Infancy" (J. Colombo and J. Fagen, Eds.). Erlbaum, Hillsdale, NJ.

Thomas, A., and Chess, S. (1981). The reality of difficult temperament. *Merrill-Palmer Quart.* **28,** 1–19.

Trad, P. V., and Greenblatt, E. (1990). Psychological aspects of child stress: Development and the spectrum of coping responses. In "Childhood Stress" (L. E. Arnold, Ed.). Wiley, New York.

Individualism

Thomas J. Schoeneman
Lewis and Clark College

Glossary

Ensembled individualism An individualism that emphasizes an interdependent conception of self that has fluid boundaries, overlaps significant other people and groups, and is part of a larger field or system of controlling forces.

Indigenous psychology Synonym for "individualism"; culturally defined, everyday conceptions of the nature of the person and his or her relations with the world; a layperson's psychology, contrasted to "specialist psychologies" of social science, philosophy, and religion.

Individualism A culture's description of the ideal relationship of the individual person and others.

Primary control The enhancement of reward and avoidance of punishment by attempting to influence or change existing realities.

Secondary control The enhancement of reward and avoidance of punishment by attempting to accommodate to existing realities and by maximizing satisfaction with things as they are.

Self-contained individualism An individualism that emphasizes an independent conception of self that has firm boundaries, excludes other people, and exercises personal control

INDIVIDUALISM, as it is usually defined, is a point of view that puts the interests of the individual before those of the group. Individualism in this narrow sense sees society as a collection of separate individuals who pursue their goals based on a principle of enlightened self-interest; the doctrine also characterizes social institutions as exercising social control that is basically opposed to the freedom and initiative of its individual members. Edward Sampson, Clifford Geertz, and others point out that this view of the relations between individuals and social groups is characteristic of modern Western ideologies; earlier in Western history and currently in the majority of the world's cultures, however, a different individualism was and is operative, an individualism that casts individuals and groups in a more harmonious relationship. Following the lead of Sampson, this article will adopt a broader definition: *Individualism is a culture's description of the ideal relationship of the individual person and others* (where "others" refers to other persons, important social groups such as the family and the work organization, and the state or society as a whole). The article focuses on two contrasting ideologies of person–other relationships: self-contained individualism versus ensembled individualism.

I. OVERVIEW: INDIGENOUS PSYCHOLOGIES

Many social scientists believe that awareness of self is a human universal. This does not imply, however, that all people have similar conceptions of the self and its relation to social groups. Self-awareness may be a universal phenomenon, but the kind of individual that a person believes him- or herself to be is determined by the culture's indigenous psychology.

Indigenous psychology is defined as a culture's everyday beliefs about the nature of the person and his or her relations with the world. An indigenous psychology or individualism, then, is a layperson's social psychology; it is not necessarily the same thing as the "specialist psychologies" of social sci-

Copyright © 1994 by Academic Press, Inc. All rights of reproduction in any form reserved.

TABLE I
Defining Features of Self-Contained and Ensembled Individualism

	Type of individualism	
	Self-contained	Ensembled
Conception of self	Independent (excluding others)	Interdependent (inclusive of others)
Self–other boundary	Firm: sharp, invariant boundary between self and others	Fluid: changeable, less distinct (overlapping) boundary between self and others
Major life tasks	Attain independence from others; discover and express one's unique attributes; stand out from the crowd and speak one's mind; agency	Maintain interdependence and connectedness among individuals and within groups; fit in with and belong to important social groups and read others' mind; communion
Important attributes	Internal/private: abilities, thoughts, feelings, etc.	External/public: roles, statuses, relationships, etc.
Location of agency or control	In the person: within each individual	In the field: the system of forces of which the person is a part
Preferred control method	Primary control: attempts to influence and change existing realities	Secondary control: attempts to accommodate to existing realities
Conception of morality	Asocial: moral principles independent of social networks, reside in individuals, deity or nature	Socially contingent: moral principles embedded in social networks; morality of actions judged based on social effects

entists, philosophers, and theologians, although there is probably a lot of overlap and mutuality between everyday and specialist views of the individual.

While there are many ways of construing the self–other relationship, two kinds of individualism seem to be prominent among human cultures: the self-contained or independent individualism that is familiar to members of Western cultures and the ensembled or interdependent individualism that characterizes non-Western cultures and earlier periods of Western history. The next two sections of the article describe these individualisms more fully, and Table I gives an overview of the two ways of construing the individual.

II. SELF-CONTAINED INDIVIDUALISM: THE INDEPENDENT SELF

Most people in Western nations, and Americans in particular, take it for granted that every person is a unique individual, separated from other unique individuals by a skin that contains an entity known as the self. The defining features of self-contained individualism are given in the middle column of Table I.

The self-contained individual is separate from the rest of the world: He or she has a clear boundary that divides self from other people. Within this bounded self lie the person's unique attributes—his or her abilities, thoughts, feelings, traits, and potentials. The principal goals of the self-contained individual are to develop independence from other people, to attain self-knowledge and realize one's potential, to cultivate and express one's uniqueness, and to become an effective master of one's own destiny. These goals typically invoke Western notions of agency or control. From this perspective, control resides within the person and takes the form of trying to influence or change existing conditions. In addition, morality is asocial; that is, moral principles are independent of social networks and reside in individual consciences, religious principles, or natural phenomena.

This Western type of individuality is easily visible in adages such as "the squeaky wheel gets the grease" and in the popular mass media. Hollywood movie plots often feature rugged heroes (and lately, heroines) who buck the establishment and popular songs proclaim that "I Did It My Way" and "I Gotta

Be Me'' while celebrating ''The Greatest Love of All'' (i.e., to love yourself).

Conceptions of the self-contained individual favor persons over groups. As noted in the first paragraph of this article, the narrower definition of individualism that occurs in English-language dictionaries focuses on the assumption that individuals are prior to groups. In this view, which has a large place in the history of social and economic ideas over the last three centuries, society is an assembly of individuals, each of whom has enlightened self-interest as the primary motive. Social institutions are necessary evils that provide social control and order at the expense of individual freedom and liberty. Table II summarizes the chief advantages and disadvantages of self-contained individualism that proponents and critics have proposed.

TABLE II
Proposed Advantages and Disadvantages of Self-Contained Individualism

Proposed advantages	Proposed disadvantages
Freedom and autonomy; independence; reactance (resisting perceived threats to freedom of action and choice)	Social control via illusion of freedom and autonomy; strong external force needed to ensure social order
Personal responsibility; self-reliance	Lack of social responsibility; undermining of important social bonds and structures
Competitive striving	Failure to cooperate
↓	↓
Personal achievement and success; incentives to innovate	Failure to attain larger social goals
Eudaimonism (self-knowledge, self-actualization)	Selfishness
↓	↓
Potential for high self-esteem	Potential for narcissism
Enlightened self-interest	Mistrust and Machiavellianism
↓	↓
Universal respect for integrity of others and interdependence (democracy and equality)	Isolation/loneliness; alienation/vacuity
Primary control (attempts to maximize reward, minimize punishment by altering existing realities)	Futility; failure to accept, adapt to existing realities, especially those that cannot be changed

III. ENSEMBLED INDIVIDUALISM: INTERDEPENDENT SELVES

Less familiar to members of Western cultures is an individualism that places groups ahead of individuals. The right-hand column of Table I lists the characteristics of ensembled individualism, an indigenous psychology that is arguably a majority view among humans both currently and historically.

The ensembled individual's self–other boundary is fluid: The self does not end at the person's skin but overlaps the selves of individuals in important social groups. Thus, a person's most significant attributes are not private aspects such as thoughts, feelings, or traits, but public roles, statuses, and relationships. In an ensembled culture, the most important goal is to maintain social groups through interdependence and connectedness among single individuals. Thus, it is crucial to fit in with others in important social groups by minimizing conflict and putting the needs of the group of one's personal wants and needs. The ensembled conception of the location of agency or control is broader than its Western counterpart: The individual is but one force in a complex field of forces, so that control resides not only in the individual but also in significant aspects of the social, physical, and supernatural systems in which the individual is embedded. The preferred method of control, which Western psychologists have somewhat ethnocentrically labeled as ''secondary'' control, is to expend effort in accommodating oneself to existing realities. Morality is socially contingent because moral principles are embedded in social networks. Thus, the social effects of an action determine its morality or immorality.

Popular expressions of ensembled individualism often seem odd or incomprehensible to Western observers who take self-contained individualism as a given. For instance, in Japan, ''the nail that sticks out gets pounded down'' and ''to lose is to win'' (i.e., the person who gives way in a dispute ''wins'' by showing tolerance, flexibility, and self-control); disobedient children are locked out of the house rather than sent to their rooms; and auto workers assemble each morning to sing the company song. Another example involves the pre-Glasnost Soviet cinema, which American filmgoers have often derided as ''boy meets tractor'' stories. In a typical Soviet film the rugged individual is the villain and a satisfying plot resolution is the founding of a collective work group and the attainment of a proletarian mass consciousness. Western incomprehension of ensembled individualism has resulted in the labeling of other cultures as "primitive," "antidemocratic," "un-American" and "evil." The presumed advantages and disadvantages of ensembled individualism are listed in Table III.

In reviewing the pros and cons of the two types of individualism, one thing is important to note. Each side sees the "strengths" of the opposite individualism as either contrary or secondary to the virtues of their own position. Some observers of both self-contained and ensembled individualisms have called for a compromise that embraces the best features of both. For instance, David Bakan concludes his book on agency (self-contained individualism) and communion (ensembled individualism), *The Duality of Human Existence* (1966), with the assertion that "the proper way of dying is from fatigue after a life of trying to mitigate agency with communion." Other observers are less optimistic about the possibility of reconciliation: They see the two individualisms as fundamentally incompatible. This position is exemplified by Edward Sampson's statement that "one is not dealing with two opposing tendencies that can balance each other, but two incommensurate systems of belief and understanding."

TABLE III
Proposed Advantages and Disadvantages of Ensembled Individualism

Proposed advantages	Proposed disadvantages
Relationship and connectedness; feeling of belonging, fitting in	Conformity pressures
↓	↓
Mutuality of goals, social exchange, and obligation	Lack of independence, freedom; anti-democracy; xenophobia
Empathy	Erasure of individual differences and uniqueness
Social responsibility; commitment to important social bonds and structures	Absence of personal credit for positive actions; failure as disgrace
Cooperative, collective achievement and fulfillment of larger goals and interests	Lack of incentives to excel and innovate; absence of creativity and originality
Realistic assessment of personal control within the total field of social influences	Lack of personal (primary) control
↓	↓
Interpretive control: finding meaning in things as they are; acceptance	Fatalism Failure to address and solve soluble problems
+	+
Predictive control: ability to accurately anticipate events and conditions; sense of order	Stagnation and boredom
+	+
Vicarious mastery and control: aligning oneself with powerful individuals and groups	Lack of initiative

IV. RELEVANT THEORIES AND ORIENTATIONS

Although they are not identical, a culture's indigenous psychology and the professional psychology practiced by social scientists may show considerable overlap. Science is a human activity and scientific theories are products of human creativity. Where do the concepts and assumptions that are the foundation of science come from? A diverse groups of observers of science that includes practicing scientists such as Stephen Jay Gould and revisionist critics such as Kenneth Gergen all agree that much of scientific creativity is traceable to the ideology of the place and time in which a scientist lives. As a result, we should expect to see that Western psychological science is preoccupied with self-contained individuals. The professional psychology of Eastern cultures, on the other hand, should emphasize the interdependence and secondary control of ensembled individuals.

A. Western Psychology and the Self-Contained Individual

In Western psychology, the indigenous psychology of self-contained individualism is particularly evident in the study of personality. A survey of the ways in which psychologists define "personality" in textbooks reveals three themes that occur almost without exception. The first is the conception of personality as *within* the individual person. All definitions locate personality as something interior to persons, and the authors of these definitions often proceed to make a clear distinction between internal and external determinants of behavior. The second theme in Western definitions of personality is *uniqueness*. Authors emphasize that although psychologists often focus on how people are similar to each other, a good theory of personality has to account for the fact that each person is a unique individual. The final theme in Western definitions of personality is *consistency*. All authors assume that there is a core of stable characteristics that, even if unexpressed, an individual carries with him or her into all situations, no matter what social roles, statuses, or relationships are involved. In summary, the Western definition of personality as a unique set of internal characteristics that produce consistent behavior patterns is basically a reproduction of the self-contained individual that is summarized in Table I.

The self-contained individual is visible in specific personality theories and areas of research. Psychoanalytic theories locate character structure in the dynamic interplay of unconscious forces and structures. Humanistic theories emphasize the pursuit of self-actualization through fidelity to one's own unique experience of the world. Trait theorists believe that behavioral consistency is guided by 5 to 10 neuropsychic structures known as personality traits. Social learning and cognitive theorists focus on the ways in which people learn to subjectively represent the external world and themselves. In addition, there is a vast literature, both professional and popular, that centers on constructs such as self-concept, self-esteem, and self-efficacy. The focus on self-contained individuals in this body of theory and research also generalizes to applications: Most of the psychotherapies that are associated with Western conceptions of personality emphasize the attainment of primary control through insight or behavioral contingency management. It is true that personality theorists and researchers such as Freud, Erikson, Sullivan, Rogers, and Bandura (to name but a few) acknowledge the importance of interpersonal influences, especially parent–child relationships, on the development of personality. However, the personality that develops out of these interactions remains firmly entrenched within the psychic boundaries of self-contained individuals.

The indigenous psychology of self-contained individualism is not limited in its influence to the psychology of personality. Such critics as Seymour Sarason, Edward Sampson, and Kenneth Gergen have pointed out the intrapsychic bias of many subdisciplines of psychology—cognitive, developmental, clinical, and even social psychology—especially as they are practiced in North America. For instance, critics have charged that American social psychological research focuses too heavily on how self-contained individuals perceive themselves and other self-contained individuals rather than on how people mutually influence each others' behavior. One result of this individualistic bias, from the perspective of its opponents, is a psychology that thinks it is discovering universal laws of human behavior but is, in fact, an account of a particular historical period in a particular culture. Another implication is that a psychology that focuses on independent selves is ill equipped to deal with large issues of social change, intergroup cooperation and conflict resolution, and the effective formulation of public policy.

B. Western Approaches Congenial to Ensembled Individualism

Not all Western approaches to professional psychology favor the self-contained form of individualism; some are quite amenable to the interdependent orientation of ensembled individualism. This section will briefly describe two of these Western exceptions.

A major theoretical approach that favors the idea of interdependent selves is *symbolic interactionism*. This point of view is usually most closely associated with George Herbert Mead (*Mind, Self, and Society*, 1934) and a number of other philosophers, sociologists, and psychologists, including C. S. Peirce, James Mark Baldwin, Charles Horton Cooley, William James, John Dewey, and W. I. Thomas. Symbolic interactionists believe that individuals both create and are created by society. Concepts such as "self" and "mind" arise from social interaction that involves the sharing and manipulation of symbolic meanings. For example, a person learns to see himself as others see him and learns to carry an image of himself as reflected in the eyes of significant other people—the concept of the *looking-glass self*. The individual also develops the self-reflective viewpoint of a *generalized other* that represents the society in general. Thus, symbolic interactionists see the individual and the society as part of a mutually defining, never-ending dialectical process. Ironically, this perspective would argue that the self-contained individuals that inhabit Western societies arise from the interdependence of people who are unaware of their ensembled social interactions.

A second example of a Western challenge to self-contained individualism involves feminist contributions to psychology. The school of thought known as *cultural feminism* suggests that women differ from men in very basic psychological and relational ways. As a result, cultural feminists believe that women have not only a distinctively rich self-concept and inner experience but also a special culture that counters the dominant society's sexism through interdependent relationships. A good example is the psychodynamic theory of identity of Nancy Chodorow. This formulation states that in a culture in which women are the primary caretakers of children, the self-concepts of boys and girls are based on different experiences: A girl's identity will be based on perceived similarity to the mother while the boy's identity will emphasize difference. The socialization of girls will center on attachment and bonding with the mother; boys will grow up seeking separation and autonomy. In this way, the patriarchal social structure, with its self-contained indigenous psychology, reproduces itself. Carol Gilligan has added to this picture a theory of moral development in which women's framing of the social world in terms of interconnected relationships leads to a morality based on an ethic of care, whereas the instrumental and rational orientations of men result in an ethic of justice. Thus, women's moral reasoning is characterized by the motive of relieving distress while men's morality is motivated by a need to reinforce rules and boundaries. Thus, both Chodorow and Gilligan describe females' socialization and experience as reflecting ensembled individualism and as contrasting with the male-oriented self-contained individualism of Western society in general. It is important to note that not all feminist analyses focus on ensembled individualism. M. Brinton Lykes has criticized some feminist accounts of women's relational social orientation as involving nothing more than self-contained individuals in interaction. In addition, Rachel Hare-Mustin and Jeanne Maracek point out that some gender theories, including some from a feminist viewpoint, minimize differences between men and women. The implications of this in Western societies would lead to an emphasis on equal access to the options and benefits of self-contained individualism for women and men alike.

Symbolic interactionism and cultural feminism are two examples of Western orientations within professional psychologies that favor ensembled individualism. Other examples, such as Alfred Adler's concept of social interest and systems theories of family interaction and community psychology, could be described. However, it is time to consider non-Western professional psychologies that emphasize interdependent selves.

C. Eastern Professional Psychologies and Ensembled Individualism

This section describes two Japanese systems of psychotherapy, Naikan and Morita therapy. Both therapies are secular enterprises with Buddhist influences; both see the self-involvement and primary control attempts of self-contained individuals as pathological; and both seek to cure troubled people not by removing symptoms but by promoting secondary interpretive control, that is, by guiding sufferers to a new sense of purpose and acceptance of things as they are.

The Naikan method (*nai,* within; *kan,* looking; *naikanho,* method of inner observation) is the creation of Inobu Yashimoto, a former businessman who began to use the method to rehabilitate penitentiary inmates in the 1950s. This approach was later applied to people with mental and physical symptoms and has been widely used by Japanese businesses. The Naikan method is not intended to remove symptoms but to instill a new sense of meaning and purpose in life. More specifically, Lebra states, "through Naikan, . . . resentment and self-pity are expected to be replaced by the realization of one's own egocentric social insensitivity, and insurmountable sense of debt and gratitude to others, and a deep empathetic guilt toward those who have suffered because of one's heartless, ungrateful conduct." The method itself consists of a mixture of isolation and guided meditation. The patient spends the day in a prison cell or in a screened off corner of a room, with no access to conversation or information about the outside world. The therapist or *sensei,* adopting an attitude that combines both deep humility and discipline, instructs the patient to reflect on a series of significant people from the past—the patient's mother and elementary school years are considered to be particularly important—and to meditate on three questions: What care or kindnesses has this person shown to me? What (or how little) have I done to repay that person's kindness? and What troubles and worries did I cause this person? The *sensei* visits the patient hourly to ask about what reflections the patient has had and to give suggestions, advice, and encouragement. According to the Naikan method, the patient will first enter a stage of confusion and resistance, which will eventually give way to a stage of awakening: The patient moves from self-pity to a sense of guilt over past transgressions and confesses to the *sensei.* This stage leads to self-repulsion and depression. Eventually, as the patient comes to give up any of the arrogance of an independent self-concept and realizes the truly ensembled influences on all thoughts and deeds, a sense of tranquillity and hopefulness emerges. The patient is ready to go on with life by making amends for past thoughtlessness and by trying to repay past kindnesses. Thus, Naikan is a tension-producing therapy because it asks patients to reconceptualize themselves as deeply indebted to others; it does this by instilling a sense of shame, thereby building a sense of obligation as a moral constraint.

Morita therapy, on the other hand, is a tension-reducing approach which tries to free patients from overconstraint so that they can live naturally and accept things (including their symptoms) as they are. Unlike Naikan therapists, Morita therapists encourage patients to forget their past and to lose their selves. Morita therapy is a hospital-based treatment named after its founder, Dr. Shoma Morita. The target of treatment is a disorder known as *shinkeishitsu*, which covers a very diverse set of symptoms similar to the Western concept of "neurosis." *Shinkeishitsu*, whatever its specific symptoms, usually includes two common elements: an intense self-consciousness and preoccupation with mental and physical symptoms (real or imagined), and overconcern about the actual, as opposed to the desired, ideal state of mind and body and about the difficulties in overcoming this discrepancy. As an example, one common form of *shinkeishitsu* involves a self-consciousness in interpersonal relationships that is so extreme as to be phobic. The sufferer intensively dwells on the shortcoming—say, a tendency to stare at others or to avoid eye contact—and spends considerable mental and physical effort in a futile attempt to overcome the problem. Morita therapy uses the principle of *arugamama*, that is, accepting things "as they are." The goal is not to remove the troublesome symptoms but to accept them, to rid oneself of an unnatural set of assumptions about the mind and body, and to discard all one's aspirations toward primary control of one's troubles. Patients are encouraged to submit to their symptoms, unite with their symptoms, and encourage the expression of their symptoms—to "let nature take its course." The method involves absolutely isolated bed rest in the hospital or in the therapist's home for a week, followed by 10 days each of light, moderate, and heavy work. The isolation stage usually induces a stark confrontation of the discrepancy between one's actual and ideal state of mind and body. At this point, symptoms and feelings of self-repulsion may intensify. The patient is encouraged to "go ahead and worry" in the expectation that this will help him or her to learn to live with symptoms. In the stage of light work, the patient rediscovers the freshness and charm of the outer world. The moderate work period allows the patient to realize his or her own competence to complete tasks. Finally, in the heavy work stage the patient discovers the capability to complete difficult tasks because they are necessary, regardless of mood, or other impediments. The therapist is very nondirective and allows no questions and answers none. A final component of the therapy is that during their stay, patients enter into an ensembled community that consists of other patients, the therapist, and (if the site of treatment is the therapist's home) his family.

Despite their differing goals and methods, both Naikan and Morita therapies share two common elements: Both discourage self-contained individualism and encourage interdependence, and both seek to instill a sense of interpretive secondary control. Thus, these therapies are clearly reflections of the culture in which they are embedded. As Lebra puts it, both Naikan and Morita therapies seem to be grounded in "the common cultural belief that the individual is not an autonomous, separate entity, and that ideally it should be submerged in nature or the society of which it is only a part."

A number of other professional psychologies could serve to illustrate ensembled cultural notions. For instance, Soviet psychology prior to Glasnost was grounded in the historical and dialectical materialist philosophy of Marx and Engels that was, in part, a rejection of the liberal notion of enlightened self-interest. Marx believed that the essence of humanity resided not in separate individuals, but in "the ensemble of social relations." Soviet psychologists emphasized the social nature of childhood development and the ideal of healthy work in the collective as the hallmark of adulthood. Other examples could be given, and the interested reader is directed to the bibliography at the end of the article and especially to Harry Triandis's review article for further information.

V. PSYCHOLOGICAL RESEARCH ON THE CONSEQUENCES OF INDIVIDUALISM

So far, this article has described self-contained and ensembled individualism. The next step is to ask about consequences. Literature reviews by Hazel

Rose Markus and Shinobu Kitayama and by Harry Triandis are especially helpful in answering the question "What are the implications of individualism for personal and social behaviors?"

Markus and Kitayama proceed from the point of view of schema theory. A schema is a knowledge structure, that is, an organized system or framework of stored information about some stimulus or type of stimulus. Schemata not only serve to organize information in long-term memory, but also they aid in the processing of new information and retrieval of stored knowledge. Thus, for example, if a person has a very elaborate schema for English literature, he or she should be able to more easily (a) learn new information about Charles Dickens and his novels, (b) fill in missing information about Dickens with default knowledge, and (c) retrieve stored information about Dickens from memory, compared to someone whose schema in this area is relatively rudimentary.

Markus and Kitayama point out that there are a number of self-relevant schemata that taken together can be called the *self-system*. As they point out, a large body of research has shown that the self-system is "instrumental in the regulation of intrapersonal processes such as self-relevant information processing, affect regulation, and motivation and in the regulation of interpersonal processes such as person perception, social comparison, and the seeking and shaping of social interaction." Markus and Kitayama believe that "independent versus interdependent construals of the self are among the most general and overarching schemata of the individual's self-system" that "recruit and organize the more specific self-regulatory self-schemata." These authors focus on the implications of individualism for the intrapersonal processes of cognition, emotion, and motivation. Triandis's review adds implications for self-concept and social behavior. Rather than reproduce each article, the following sections give representative research findings.

A. Implications of Individualism for Cognition

Markus and Kitayama point out that when a person searches for meaning in the social world, he or she will be especially attentive to self-relevant stimuli. Independent selves should be most sensitive to information about unique, self-defining attributes while interdependent selves should focus more on information about significant others or about self–other relationships.

One way that this prediction has received support in search is in the area of judgments of similarity between self and others. American students typically judge others to be similar to self but see self as dissimilar to others. That is, when the question about similarity is worded as "Is (self) similar to (other)?" in a group of self-contained individuals, the benchmark of "self" is the more elaborate and distinctive schema and respondents emphasize their own uniqueness and dissimilarity from others. When the question is reversed and the less distinctive schema (other) is the reference point, the tendency to focus on dissimilarity diminishes. A group of ensembled individuals—people who have more elaborate schemata for others—should produce a reversal of the pattern described above. Few researchers have addressed this issue in ensembled cultures, but early findings from students from India tend to support this prediction.

Another cognitive implication of individualism involves the ways in which people describe each other. For instance, a number of studies have compared the descriptions of close acquaintances and accounts of deviant behaviors that students from the United States and India give. Roughly 35 to 50% of Americans' descriptions used trait terms (e.g., selfish, friendly) compared to less than 20% of Indians' responses. The latter groups tended to emphasize behaviors in association with contextual or relational factors (e.g., duties, social roles, and obligations) in their descriptions and accounts. For instance, J. G. Miller (cited in Markus and Kitayama) found that 36% of Indian respondents' accounts of deviant behavior emphasized contextual factors compared to 17% for Americans.

Markus and Kitayama point out that these patterns tend also to hold for self-descriptions. They also note that in the realm of basic cognitive skills (such as reasoning, inferential thinking), different cultures may not differ in actual average performance levels, but different individualisms may influence when and whether skills are used. People with interdependent self-systems may be more selective in using cognitive skills because they attend to cues such as rules of conversation or social roles.

B. Implications of Individualism for Emotion

The emotional implications of individualism center on what Markus and Kitayama call ego-focused versus other-focused emotions. Ego-focused emotions reinforce independent self-systems: They refer to the blocking, satisfaction, or confirmation of an individual's internal attributes. Examples of ego-focused emotions include happiness, anger, pride, sadness, frustration, and so on. Other-focused emotions, such as sympathy, shame, and feelings of fellowship, put interdependence in the spotlight by using other people as the center of attention.

The main prediction about the impact of individualism on emotion is that (a) people will seek positive (and try to avoid negative) emotional states by seeking information that confirms their self-views, and (b) for self-contained individuals, this involves emotional states that confirm or express one's internal attributes, especially those that signify one's autonomy, while for ensembled individuals, the desired states are those that best allow one to be responsive to contextual cues and to succeed in interpersonal relationships. Turning first to ego-focused emotions, a number of studies found divergences when American and Japanese undergraduates judged various aspects of their own and others' emotions such as joy, sadness, anger, guilt, and fear. Compared to the Asian respondents, Americans reported emotions as more intense and longer lasting, and as involving more physical symptoms and a greater need for coping responses. Members of ensembled and self-contained cultures may also disagree about the meaning of certain emotions. For example, Western individuals may see pride as connected to one's own personal accomplishments. Stipek, Weiner, and Li reported that Chinese respondents avoid claims of this type of pride, although pride in a group's achievements would be allowable. Similarly, guilt in the West is most frequently reported as the result of the violation of a law or moral principle, whereas Chinese subjects most frequently saw the origin of guilt as due to harming others psychologically.

Studies of the ego-focused emotion of anger are instructive. Ensembled cultures should find anger to be a threat to interdependence and avoid it. In fact, some anthropologists claim that som ensembled cultures, such as in Tahiti and among Ukta Eskimos, construct reality in such a way that anger is not felt, much less expressed. In Western cultures, there is considerable controversy over whether it is beneficial to express one's anger; in ensembled cultures, there is no controversy—anger should be suppressed. Thus, Chinese conversations are structured to prevent conflict, which seems to Westerners to be excessively indirect and vague. Americans and Western Europeans report feeling anger mostly with close friends and relatives, whereas Japanese informants say that they feel angry only in the presence of strangers.

Kitayama and Markus have done a number of studies comparing ego-focused and other-focused emotions that are indigenous to Japanese culture and language. Many of the emotions had Western counterparts (e.g., pride and anger as ego-focused emotions and guilt and shame as other-focused emotions), but there was a definite trend for other-focused emotions to have no real Western counterparts. These include, for example, *fureai* (feeling of connection with someone), *amae* (hopeful expectation of someone's indulgence and favor), and *oime* (feeling of indebtedness). In one study, Kitayama and Markus had subjects sort 20 Japanese emotions by similarity and used multidimensional scaling to find the dimensions that characterize subjects' similarity judgments. Previous studies using only ego-focused emotions have typically found two dimensions: activation and pleasantness. (For instance, anger is an emotion that is high in activation and low in pleasantness). Kitayama and Markus replicated this finding for ego-focused Japanese emotions, but the inclusion of other-focused emotions caused a third dimension to appear: interpersonal engagement vs disengagement. Ego-focused emotions fell on the interpersonally disengaged end of the dimension, whereas other-focused emotions were at the opposite, engaged pole. (Again, for instance, *amae* and *oime* were both high in interpersonal engagement, but the former was neutral or ambivalent in pleasantness and the latter was the most unpleasant emotion.) These authors also found that respondents who highly endorsed self-contained independence reported experiencing both positive and negative ego-focused emotions more frequently than those who endorsed ensembled interdependence, who said that they experienced positive, negative, and ambivalent other-focused emotions more frequently.

C. Implications of Individualism for Motivation

What moves people to action may differ according to the culture's individualism. Independent self-systems should motivate people to actions that express self-defining inner attributes while interdependent self-systems should move people to actions that favor and encourage relatedness. Among the many areas of motivational research that Markus and Kitayama review, this section gives as examples representative findings in achievement motivation, cognitive dissonance, and self-enhancing biases.

Earlier in this article we saw that achievement motivation is a central advantage claimed for self-contained individualism. Yet many interdependent cultures seem to be very preoccupied with achievement; as Markus and Kitayama point out, Japanese junior high school students adhere to the motto "Pass with four, fail with five," referring to hours of sleep per night. Numerous studies have shown that non-Western achievement motivation is other-oriented—interdependent individuals work hard and achieve in order to fit into, enhance, or meet the expectations of significant groups. Interestingly, interdependent achievement motivation seems less trait-like and more situationally specific than the more autonomous Western variety. When a goal is attained, non-Western achievers seem to lose interest, only to strive again once a new goal is established by a leader who is a symbolic substitute for a family member (e.g., a father-like employer).

A cornerstone of Western social psychological research is the idea that the need for cognitive consistency, or the need to avoid dissonance, is a major motivator of attitude and behavior change. Cognitive dissonance results when a private belief or attitude, especially one that is central to the self-system, is at odds with public behavior. This effect seems to be relevant only for self-contained, independent individuals. For interdependent individuals, core beliefs are secondary to public behaviors; inner feelings are to be restrained in favor of acceptable and expected outward behavior. In other words, in ensembled cultures, public behavior is frequently at odds with private wishes; in such situations, interdependent selves, rather than feeling dissonance, expect that inner feelings will be suppressed in favor of proper behaviors.

A final example of the implications of individualism for motivation occurs in the area of self-enhancing and self-serving biases. Western research has described many ways in which individuals seem motivated to feel good about themselves. A majority of Western adults, and children as young as 4 years old, believe that they are above average on such desirable traits as leadership, intelligence, attractiveness, and friendliness; this is especially true of people with high self-esteem. However, in ensembled cultures, this kind of self-enhancement should be a threat to interdependence. Markus and Kitayama report one of their own studies in which they demonstrated a typical "false uniqueness" effect with American undergraduates: On average, these students assumed that only 30% of other students would be better than themselves on a number of traits and abilities. Japanese students, in contrast and more accurately, estimated that an average of half (50%) of other students would do better. A number of studies report that American undergraduates typically attribute their successes to ability and their failures to task difficulty, a self-serving bias that allows people credit for good outcomes and avoids blame for bad results. Japanese students, on the other hand, attribute their own successes to task ease, luck, and the mental–physical "shape" of the day while at the same time downplaying ability; these students attribute their own failures to lack of effort. Thus, Japanese students show a self-effacing bias in explaining their positive and negative outcomes; related studies have shown an other-enhancing bias in explaining the outcomes of others. [*See* MOTIVATION.]

D. Implications of Individualism for Self-Concept and Social Behaviors

Triandis reviewed theory and research about the effects on self-concept and social behavior of what he called individualistic versus collectivist cultures (i.e., cultures that emphasize self-contained versus ensembled individualism). Turning first to the self-concept, research shows that people in collectivist cultures incorporate more social elements into their self-concepts (i.e., relevant memberships in family ethnic, occupational, institutional, religious, and gender groups) than do members of individualistic cultures. For instance, Triandis did a study using the Twenty Statements Test, which asks respondents to complete the sentence "I am ______" 20 times. Undergraduates from individualistic student bodies at the universities of Illinois, Athens (Greece), and Hong Kong answered the fewest social categories; mean percentages were 19, 15, and 20, respectively. Students at the University of Hawaii are a mix of individualistic people of Northern European descent and more collectivist Asian Americans, and their sentence completions had an average of 29% social categories. The highest average percentage of social categories occurred among university graduates from the Peoples' Republic of China, a very collectivist society: The mean was 52%.

Triandis's discussion of implications of individualism for social behaviors centers on membership in in-groups and out-groups. The self-concept in collectivist cultures (relative to that of individualistic cultures) makes salient to the individual the various elements of relevant collectives, such as roles, statuses, and norms; this in turn should highlight the perception of other people as members of an in-group or out-group, and behavior will be adjusted accordingly. This is evident in a number of different areas of social behavior.

Compared to people from individualistic cultures, those from collectivist cultures emphasize in-group harmony more: They evaluate group partners more positively, choose conflict resolution tactics that minimize bad feelings among group members, give each other more social support, and express greater support of in-group goals. Studies that investigate ratings of actual interactions with in-group and out-group members find that collectivist subjects see interactions with in-group members as more personalized (intimate, deep, and satisfying) and synchronized (effortless and well-coordinated) and less difficult than individualist subjects. There are also larger differences on these rating dimensions reported for in- versus out-group interactions for collectivist subjects. Studies of behavioral intentions show that collectivist selves focus on the survival and benefit of the group while individualistic selves are more attentive to personal concerns. This is illustrated by a study on smoking behavior which found that a collectivist group of Hispanic Americans focused on such concerns as the effects of smoking on the health of others, the setting of a bad example to children, and the annoyance of others with bad smells, whereas an individualist sample of non-Hispanic Americans was mainly worried about the physical symptoms of withdrawal. Another line of research shows that members of collective cultures experience difficulties in meeting and interacting with strangers and members of out-groups. Self-contained individuals, on the other hand, exchange more compliments, meet and cooperate more easily with people they do not know well, and choose to stay in groups that are satisfying and leave those that are not.

There is a large literature that demonstrates that in the distribution of resources, individualistic cultures tend to emphasize equity—the allocation of rewards based on some criterion of merit. Collectivist cultures, on the other hand, distribute resources based on equality or need. Both self-contained and ensembled individualism can foster competition, but the nature of the competition differs. In cultures that emphasize self-contained individualism, competition tends to be interpersonal, that is, between individuals; in ensembled cultures, competition occurs mostly between groups. Similarly, in individualistic cultures, conflict frequently occurs within families whereas in collectivist cultures conflict frequently occurs between families.

VI. CONCLUSION: THE HISTORY AND FUTURE OF THE WESTERN INDIVIDUAL

A. The Origins of Self-Contained Individualism

Roy Baumeister, Philip Cushman, Michel Foucault, and Kenneth Gergen, among others, have traced the history of modern Western conceptions of self and individuality. It is beyond the scope of this article to give a detailed account of the history of self-contained individualism; interested readers should consult the authors listed above, especially Baumeister, whose historical overview informs much of the following presentation.

Until about the 16th century, Western individualism was ensembled: The principle economic and social unit was the family and the universe was viewed as the "Great Chain of Being," a fixed hierarchy stretching from God down to inanimate matter wherein all created things had a place. There was a hierarchy within the "rung" of humanity, so that social standing and status defined self and individuality. A gradual transition to an independent conception of self involved a number of factors, including the disruption of the family and migration to cities of the Industrial Revolution and the Puritan tendency toward introspection in the aid of determining whether one was predestined to Heaven or Hell. Foucault has argued that changes in the politics of power and knowledge in the 17th and 18th centuries led to the invention of the concept of the "individual." More specifically, when the focus of political concern shifted from the nature of the state and the problems of the regent to a wider concern with how to govern and control entire populations, new technologies of discipline flourished in workhouses, hospitals, schools, and prisons. Along with these developments came an interest in scientific classification and, for human populations, "normalization," i.e., statistical measures and judgments about what is normal and what is deviant in human biology and behavior. Government and science thus treated people as objects; the people came in these regimes to see themselves as "subjects" or individuals, usually through the mediation of an authority figure such as a doctor or confessor. Foucault's analysis therefore ties the rise of self-contained individualism, which sees the individual as an opponent of society, to regimes of social discipline and control.

The contribution of late 18th and early 19th century Romanticism to the rise of self-contained individualism is the conception of the self as a passionate core, a soul full of creative potential. In the romantic view, the individual exists prior to and in opposition to society—the individual's duty is to seek his or her own destiny, express a unique personality, and fulfill the self through creativity and passion. The rise of Modernism in the late 19th century brought with it a conception of the self as a rational agent. The characteristics of the core self changed from romantic passion and emotion to cognition and reason. The modernist belief in progress—the march of knowledge toward truth—led to a preoccupation with the pursuit of essence, the thing-in-itself; applied to the individual, this meant a self-concept that is stable, true, and knowable. Cushman has observed that over the course of this century the independent self has changed from a sexually conflicted Victorian self that needed to be controlled and restricted to a post–World War II *empty self* that needs to be filled up. The empty self is an isolated entity that hungers for food, consumer goods, and charismatic leaders; it is the primary means of social control in the debtor economy of modern nations. The beneficiaries of the social construction of the empty self are the industries of advertising and self-improvement. The cost is a society of self-contained individuals who are never satisfied and always disappointed in themselves.

B. The Future of the Western Individual

Kenneth Gergen has argued that the core self of Romanticism and Modernism is giving way to a postmodern *saturated self* that is, in actuality, a multiplicity of selves or no "self" at all. Gergen argues that modern technologies—from the jet plane to TV to electronic telephone and computer networks—have produced social saturation: "Emerging technologies saturate us with the voices of humankind—both harmonious and alien. As we absorb their varied rhymes and reasons, they become part of us and we of them. Social saturation furnishes us with a multiplicity of incoherent and unrelated languages of the self." The saturated self is thus a relational self because a person takes on the values and identities of the many people and situations that he or she encounters, but it is not an ensembled self: There are far too many in-groups to which people can belong in the postmodern era. Nevertheless, the emerging relational reality involves "varying forms of interdependence" that promise the dissolution of our familiar cultural ideology and some uncertainty: "A vast potential looms, but we cannot leap headlong into new vocabularies of being any more than we can speak a foreign language we have never heard." Gergen is optimistic about this "vast potential" of postmodern relational reality to produce "flowering forms of relatedness, a growing consciousness of global interdependence, an organic relationship to our planet, and the withering of lethal conflict."

Another prescription for the demise of the self-contained individual is found in John Canfield's philosophical investigation of the reality of the "self." Canfield surveys philosophical debates about the reality of the self, including both the metaphysical arguments of Descartes, Locke, Hume, Kant, Lichtenberg, Wittgenstein, and Zen Buddhism and the later Wittgenstein's attempt to demolish the metaphysical arguments through an analysis of the uses of "I" in everyday language. On an existential level, people believe that the self, the "I," is a real entity. Canfield disagrees. He believes that "I" denotes something he calls a *persona:* a fantastic, absurd concoction, a member of the unique category of the "quasi-real." Sometimes "I" refers to a real thing, as in "I went to Los Angeles in August of 1985"—eyewitnesses and travel records could demonstrate that a real entity traveled to that place at that time. Sometimes, however, "I" looks real but is not. Just as the "it" of "It can't be 2:30 already!" does not refer to any real entity, Canfield shows in a detailed review of Wittgenstein's analysis of grammar that the subject of the sentence "I believe the self is a knowledge structure" is not a real entity but a grammatical fiction. "I" can also refer to a fictional character, as in "I would have told him where to get off if he'd come to see me"—the only criterion of truth for such a statement is that "I" say it is so, just as an author puts words into the mouth of a fictional character.

Once he has demonstrated that the persona is a quasi-real thing, part fact and part fiction, Canfield describes what it would be like to give up the belief in self as an objective entity in a chapter entitled "No Self." Using the writings of Pascal and the Zen masters Bankei and Huang Po, he describes what is gained and lost "when the fictional self of reverie and thought is laid to rest": What is gained is a world of unified experience, "a new freedom, an ease and a lively and direct contact with the people and things of the world"; what is lost is a lifetime of rumination and reaction centered on the fiction that "is the major factor in our alienation from one another and our life of fear and dread."

The implications of "no self" for the social sciences are enormous. In the first place, "there cannot be a science of our culture's selves, because some of the truths about selves are settled by fiction rules, and science does not incorporate fiction rules. There can, however, be a (mere) anthropology of our self-beliefs. . . ." What Canfield is saying is that a hypothetical science that would go beyond description to try to explain, predict and control the behavior of characters in novels or of the "its" in statements such as "It is snowing" would be absurd and impossible—as is a science of the self.

Canfield's world of "no self" seems as hard to imagine as Gergen's postmodern relational reality. However, Canfield believes that the lives of Zen masters and a number of post-Zen figures demonstrate that no self living is possible. Whether either of these visions of the demise of self-contained individualism is attainable on a wide scale remains in question.

Bibliography

Baumeister, R. F. (1987). How the self became a problem: A psychological review of historical research. *J. Pers. Soc. Psychol.* **52,** 163–176.

Canfield, J. (1990). "The Looking Glass Self: An Examination of Self-Awareness." Praeger, New York.

Cushman, P. (1990). Why the self is empty: Toward a historically situated psychology. *Am. Psychol.* **45,** 599–611.

Foucault, M. (1977). "Discipline and Punish: The Birth of the Prison." Vintage, New York.

Gergen, K. J. (1991). "The Saturated Self: Dilemmas of Identity in Contemporary Life." Basic Books, New York.

Heelas, P., and Lock, A. (1981). "Indigenous Psychologies: The Anthropology of the Self. Academic Press, London.

Lebra, T. S. (1976). "Japanese Patterns of Behavior." University Press of Hawaii, Honolulu.

Markus, H. R., and Kitayama, S. (1991). Culture and the self: Implications for cognition, emotion, and motivation. *Psychol. Rev.* **98,** 224–253.

Sampson, E. E. (1988). The debate on individualism: Indigenous psychologies of the individual and their role in personal and societal functioning. *Am. Psychol.* **43,** 15–22.

Shrauger, J. S., and Schoeneman, T. J. (1979). Symbolic interactionist view of self-concept: Through the looking glass darkly. *Psychol. Bull.* **86,** 549–573.

Triandis, H. C. (1989). The self and social behavior in differing cultural contexts. *Psychol. Rev.* **96,** 506–520.

Weisz, J. R., Rothbaum, F. M., and Blackburn, T. C. (1984). Standing out and standing in: The psychology of control in America and Japan. *Am. Psychol.* **39,** 955–969.

Information Processing and Clinical Psychology

Patrick W. Corrigan and James A. Stephenson
University of Chicago

Glossary

Abnormal behavior Human cognitions and consequent behaviors are unable to assist the individual in coping with the demands of the environment.

Clinical psychology The social science that seeks to evaluate, describe, assess, and treat maladaptive thoughts and behaviors.

Cognitive development As the individual matures, cognitive functions improve commensurate with quantitative changes in corresponding biological structures.

Cognitive rehabilitation The active treatment process in which patients who have suffered acute injuries or chronic disease regain necessary cognitive functions. Cognitive rehabilitation assumes that the central nervous system has a relative plasticity and that specific information processes can be remediated and compensated after being lost to disease or insult.

Cognitive therapy Depressed individuals adopt negative beliefs about the self and world as a method for organizing and acting upon environmental stimuli. Cognitive therapy seeks to alter these beliefs so that the individual can more effectively cope with environmental demands.

Information processing A cognitive model in which macro aspects of sensory input are divided into discrete information bytes and the macro experience of human cognition is divided into composite functions which operate on the discrete bytes.

Serial processing Information is processed in a stepwise fashion one byte at a time.

Social cognition Social schemata act as templates through which social information is encoded and as blueprints that guide interpersonal responses. The most common social cognitive structures focus on situations, persons, and self.

INFORMATION PROCESSING models of human cognition have enabled clinical psychologists to better understand abnormal human behavior, and to better develop treatments for this behavior, by dividing the complex event of cognition into more readily discernible information bytes and processing functions. Specific abnormal behaviors may correspond with deficits in the information processing system which, in turn, may correspond with various deficits in the central nervous system. Interventions designed to compensate for, or circumvent, discrete losses of the information processing system aid clinical psychologists in developing more effective treatment plans for their patients.

I. WHAT IS INFORMATION PROCESSING FOR A CLINICAL PSYCHOLOGIST?

The manner in which humans perceive and comprehend their world has been shown to be one of the principle causes for how individuals act on it. Cognitive science assumes a central role in the psychologists' understanding of how individuals perceive and comprehend, and therefore, of how they behave. Clinical psychologists are particularly interested in

Copyright © 1994 by Academic Press, Inc. All rights of reproduction in any form reserved.

the way in which human behavior has gone awry; i.e., how human cognitions and consequent behaviors no longer serve the individual well. Toward this end, clinical psychology is the social science broadly concerned with three endeavors.

1. Development and evaluation of descriptive and explanatory models of abnormal behavior. Frequently, these endeavors focus on derailed human development and limited social competence.
2. Development of assessment strategies that yield clinically useful descriptions of developmental and social problems.
3. Development of intervention strategies that ameliorate these problems.

Cognitive models in general, and information processing in particular, have been especially powerful paradigms for advancing these goals.

A. What Is Information Processing?

According to this model, the macro aspect of sensory input is divided into discrete information bytes (e.g., visual stimuli can be described in terms of color, contrast, depth, location, and relative size) and the macro experience of human cognition is divided into composite functions (like attention, memory, and response selection) that operate on these bytes and that interact in some meaningful order. Hence, the process of knowing can be understood by studying the various components of the information process individually and together. From a methodological standpoint, breaking down information and cognition into theoretical elements greatly enhances the study of these phenomena.

Information processing models are also appealing because of their apparent correspondence with central nervous system structures and functions. Research in neuropsychology has led to theories about associations between discrete information processes and structures in the central nervous system. For example, ongoing research has shown a significant association between functioning of the hippocampus and consolidation of information from short-term to long-term memory. Associations like these are especially exciting because an epistemological pathway has been identified between what have been parallel and independent sciences: psychology and biology. [*See* HIPPOCAMPAL FORMATION; MEMORY.]

We attempt to show in this article that understanding the endeavors of clinical psychology can be significantly enhanced by adopting an information processing framework. Information processing is not a unitary paradigm, however. Several models have been developed within this branch of cognitive science and are reviewed below.

B. Models of Information Processing

Early information processing theories were considered bottom-up, serial search models of cognition like the one illustrated in Figure 1. Information processing is serial in that it manipulates information in a stepwise fashion one byte at a time. The processing series comprises specific structures (e.g., short-term memory, long-term memory, response selection) and actions that operate on the information (e.g., encoding, consolidation, retrieval) as it moves along the series. These models are bottom-up in that processing is initiated by attention to incoming information rather than by a later stage in information processing.

As presented in Figure 1, the relative infinity of information in the subject's environment is significantly reduced by an attentional filter. Selected information then becomes the figural "shapshot" which is available in iconic memory for a very short time. Most of this information is lost as the icon decays. Remaining information is encoded vis-a-vis

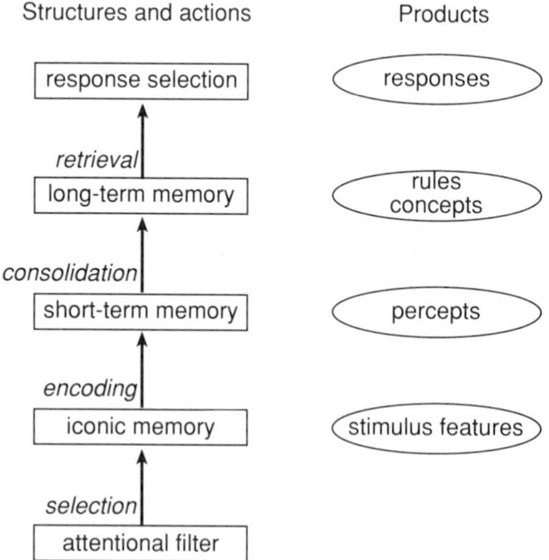

FIGURE 1 A bottom-up model of serial processing that begins with filtering the relative cacophony of stimuli impinging on the individual into a few bytes to be processed. Cognitive processes yield various products as the information bytes progress along the series.

extant memory traces so that information has meaning beyond its stimulus qualities; e.g., that conglomeration of lines and curves, shades and hues is perceived to be the image of a human being.

The amount of information that can be held in short-term or working memory is relatively limited and decays quickly. Depending on the individual's previous experience with the incoming information, his or her mental set, and the environmental conditions, some information in short-term memory will be consolidated into the long-term store. Information in long-term memory may eventually be retrieved. A response may then be elicited in reaction to external stimuli. The generated response may come from several motoric actions arranged hierarchically in the long-term store.

Different stages in the processing series imply different cognitive products (see Fig. 1). Exteroceptive and interoceptive stimuli are the raw data that impinge on the attentional filter. Selective attention results in the person attending to features of impinging stimuli. Comparing sets of stimulus features to previous information yields encoded percepts; "that mass of lines and curves is really my Aunt Lillian." Similarly, sets of percepts produce information categories or concepts. For example, Aunt Lillian, Brother Mike, Father, and Grandmother all make up the category of blood relatives. The relationship between concepts defines rules; "I am more intimate with my blood relatives than my friends."

The cognitive processes in bottom-up models, and their juxtaposition to neighboring processes, readily suggest their utility for clinical psychology. Structures, actions, and products may all serve as the foci of dysfunction. For example, according to Figure 1 cognitive deficits may result from: (1) an overly restrictive attentional filter that results in patients missing key information, (2) inaccurate encoding of incoming information, (3) diminished consolidation to long-term memory, (4) overly inclusive concepts, (5) impoverished set of responses available for selection, and (6) random selection of responses from the response hierarchy. Deficits identified vis-a-vis an information processing model also suggest specific treatment strategies. For example, remediation of attentional deficits may include self-instructional strategies, repeated practice on attentional tasks, and differential reinforcement for attention to targeted stimuli.

Serial processing models, however, provide a cumbersome representation of cognition that does not correspond well with data about the manner in which information is actually processed. For example, given the time constraints of the functioning nervous system, perhaps only a hundred processing steps can be accomplished serially in the half second between perceiving and responding to an environmental stimulus. In actuality, however, this simple cognitive event probably requires hundreds or thousands of steps to complete. Parallel processing models suggest that several processes occur simultaneously during simple tasks.

In parallel distributed processing (PDP) models, cognitive events consist of multiple *interconnected units;* in the general case *all* units are interconnected, receive input from the environment, and send output to the environment. In the simplest models, connections between units are excitatory or inhibitory (on–off switches). In more restricted examples of the general case, some units may receive no input from nor give output to the environment and may be unconnected to other units. This model suggests that multiple processes occur simultaneously thereby surpassing the sluggish mechanism described by a serial processing model.

Transposition of PDP models to clinical psychology has thus far been limited. For example, it has only recently been used to describe the myriad of cognitive deficits found in schizophrenic patients. However, PDP models have an intimate history with neurobiology; investigators from that discipline have described neurological and cognitive events in terms of the network of units and connections. PDP models hold great promise for providing sophisticated neurocognitive formulations of abnormal behavior which may, in turn, lead to more sophisticated treatment prescriptions.

II. PROCESS MODELS OF HUMAN DEVELOPMENT

Clinical psychologists frequently explain adaptive and maladaptive behavior in terms of appropriate behavioral development, especially during childhood. Stage models have been popular for describing human development; individuals progress through significant life stages in which cognitive elements change qualitatively as corresponding biological processes activate. Contrast this view to information processing models of human development where biological structures underlying cognitive functions are believed to be present and functional from birth; development is better described as quantitative changes in these structures and their corresponding cognitive functions. As an example, a process model of memory development is reviewed.

A. The Ontogeny of Human Memory

Adult memory appears to progress through a complex course to maturity. Research has suggested that aspects of human memory are relatively intact from birth. For example, iconic memory operates at similar levels in both younger children and adults; research has shown that children's span of apprehension is quantitatively equal to that of most adults. The size of short-term memory store, however, is much smaller in young children. They recall far fewer items from a word list than older children. Similarly, the size of the long-term store is associated with age; people have more to remember as they add life experiences with age.

Retrieval strategies also differ with age. Older children and adults are more likely to retrieve information from long-term memory quickly. This pattern seems to be specific to recall memory, however. Rates of recognition are actually similar between adults and fairly young children. Strategies that facilitate the original consolidation of information into long-term memory is a significant factor for understanding recall. Research has shown that adults use mnemonic strategies like rehearsal, imagery, and chunking to assimilate information into the long-term store. Children under 5 years old have been shown to have these same strategies at their disposal but rarely use them spontaneously until older.

The process model also yields important descriptors about the elderly end of human development. Overall processing speed seems to diminish as adults pass 60. Therefore, retrieval of information diminishes in speed as people age. Moreover, short-term memory seems to diminish in many older adults, while long-term memory remains relatively intact.

B. The Utility of a Process Model of Cognitive Development

A process model yields several benefits for the clinical psychologist attempting to understand human development. The structure, actions, and products subsumed by an information processing framework suggest specific foci which should change as the child develops. This correspondence is all the more powerful given the relationship between brain function and information processing construct. Future research in neuropsychology should be able to track changes in brain structures and physiology that correlate with the maturation of cognitive structures and actions.

In like fashion, a process model of development yields very specific expectations for guiding educational programs. Very young children lack the attention span and short-term memory to benefit from prolonged instruction. Therefore, class periods should be relatively shorter during the first few grades. Information processing models have also suggested that young children do not readily employ mnemonic strategies like imagery, chunking, and self-direction such that their ability to consolidate information into long-term memory is greatly hampered. Young children experience extreme limits to the breadth of information they can manage and learn as a result. Education during the primary years that includes an intensive focus on *how* to learn will help youngsters increase the amount to be learned.

Process models of development also lead to more specific recommendations for clinical intervention. Traditional cognitive assessment strategies are limited in their correspondence to effective interventions. Clinicians working with patients who are developmentally disabled as indexed by a low IQ score have few ideas about how to improve the person's cognitive functioning in the real world. However, individuals who are developmentally delayed in terms of memory retrieval dysfunction might improve by participating in treatment strategies that target mnemonic strategies. These issues are discussed more fully under Section VII. [*See* COGNITIVE DEVELOPMENT.]

III. UNDERSTANDING ABNORMAL BEHAVIOR COGNITIVELY

The Diagnostic and Statistical Manual (Third Edition Revised: DSM-III-R) of the American Psychiatric Association defines mental disorders as clinically abnormal behaviors that cause significant life distress and/or diminish independent adaptive functioning. Cognitive deficits are the major sequelae of many DSM-III-R mental disorders. For example, schizophrenia has been characterized as a thought disorder and various organic brain syndromes have been described vis-a-vis discrete cognitive deficits. Information processing models have been especially fruitful for elucidating the component aspects of cognitive deficits in each of these psychiatric syndromes. The manner in which the information processing paradigm is useful for describing schizophrenia is described more fully as an example.

A. Schizophrenia Spectrum Disorders and Information Processing

Patients with schizophrenia show deficits in many information processes including selective and sustained attention, recall memory, retrieval, conceptual flexibility, and response selection. The abundance of cognitive deficits common to schizophrenia was a theoretical puzzle for clinical investigators such that early researchers sought to identify the *one* pathological dysfunction in the series of processing stages from which all other information processing deficits might result. Attentional deficits have been thought to be primary such that any subsequent processing dysfunctions result from skewed information entering the system. Conversely, the opposite end of the information process—response selection—has been thought to be the source of the pathognomonic deficit. During normal functioning, responses that surpass a hypothetical response threshold are most likely to be performed with response strength a function of previous experience and current arousal. Schizophrenic patients demonstrate collapsed response hierarchies such that, especially during hyperaroused situations, multiple responses are above threshold and response selection is random.

More recently, the various cognitive deficits of schizophrenia have been explained within the framework of limited information processing capacity. Normal cognition is limited by the amount of information that can be processed simultaneously; for example, most individuals find it difficult to closely attend to a radio show, read the newspaper, and converse with a friend at the same time. The schizophrenic patient's cognitive capacity suffers even greater limits than normals such that their cognitive abilities are easily overwhelmed by demands of many everyday informational tasks. This model has been used to explain the diverse range of cognitive deficits in schizophrenia, including attention, memory, executive functioning, and response selection.

Alternative hypotheses have been offered to explain the schizophrenic patient's limited capacity. On the one hand, schizophrenic patients are thought to have insufficient capacity in steady "reserve," thereby unable to manage normal cognitive tasks.

Conversely, level of capacity is believed to be relatively equal between schizophrenic and normal groups, but less available from the patients. Capacity may be limited by the schizophrenic patient's arousal levels. The relationship between arousal and capacity is described by an inverted U such that during periods of underarousal or overarousal the normal individual experiences diminished capacity. Research suggests that schizophrenic patients demonstrate steady-state hyperarousal or both hypo- and hyperaroused patterns. [*See* SCHIZOPHRENIA.]

B. Traumatic Brain Injury and Information Processing

Traumatic brain injuries are by far the most prevalent form of brain damage for individuals younger than 40. Patients suffering from these injuries show a wide range of information processing deficits depending on the central nervous system locus of the injury. For example, individuals experiencing relatively discrete injuries to the frontal cortex are likely to demonstrate deficits in executive functioning. Therefore, information processing principles provide a neat outline for predicting the effects of specific brain injuries.

The specificity of traumatic insults on the brain depends in part on the type of injury. Closed head injuries tend to result in more global deficits attributed to the brain ricocheting around the skull after impact. Open head injury (perhaps caused by object penetration) tends to localize damage and cause a focal lesion. However, the correspondence between focal lesion and cognitive deficit is not always neat. Deficits in one information process may cascade into a general deficit because of the interrelatedness of the brain and its information processes.

IV. UNDERSTANDING SOCIAL BEHAVIOR COGNITIVELY

Just as long-term memory contains concepts and categories that define the world of objects, so too there exist knowledge structures that describe key interpersonal constructs. Social schemata are the templates by which social information is encoded as well as the blueprints that guide interpersonal responses. Research has focused on several distinct sets of schemata. Two are reviewed here: knowledge structures that represent situations and persons.

A. Situational Schemata

Several features have been identified that comprise schematic descriptions of situations including actions (the component behaviors that comprise an interpersonal event), rules (the expectations that govern behaviors in these situations), affect (emotions that coincide with these actions and rules), and goals (motivations underlying attempted actions). These features are related hierarchically such that definition of certain features restricts the range of subordinates. For example, goals defined by a specific situation narrow the set of rules that define the interaction. The goals implied by driving into a hamburger joint—to get sandwiches fast—preclude rules about social banter between waitress and customer that might be found at a coffee shop.

B. Person Schemata

Personality theorists presume that individuals have enduring traits that explain current functioning as well as predict future behavior across multiple situations. However, personality traits may represent epiphenomena that result from the prototypic manner in which individuals perceive others. Whether or not an individual acts consistently across situations, they are perceived to do so because their actions are understood in terms of various person schema. For example, an extraverted person schema defines individual exemplars as outgoing, chatty, and personable.

Cantor and Mischel have identified several characteristics of person schema including differentiation and concreteness. Differentiation refers to the amount of attributional overlap between two person schemata. A "pleasant person" and an "extravert" share many attributes and therefore have low differentiation. Prototypic opposites like introverts and extroverts have little overlap and high differentiation. Person schema also vary in terms of quality of content or concreteness. Attributes have been divided into four groups: physical appearance or possessions, socioeconomic status, traits (e.g., happy or gloomy), and behavioral attributes (e.g., runs to the train, sloppy).

C. The Value of Social Cognitive Models

Models of social cognition are in many ways more ecologically valid representations of thinking than the more laboratory-based perspectives of information processing discussed above. Rather than describing remote processes like attention and iconic memory, schema theorists describe the manner in which real-world information is understood and stored. Findings from schema theory also provide fruitful heuristics for understanding psychopathology. Qualitative differences between specific schema may account for differential deficits in various neuropsychiatric populations. For example, research suggests that content of situational and person schemata affects the information processing of patients. Depressed populations have been shown to be more sensitive to the negative versus the positive content of schema. Patients with schizophrenia are better able to identify negative facial affect (e.g., angry, depressed, or worried) than more pleasant facial expressions.

In terms of treatment strategies, if the effects of interventions from information processing models generalize, then targeting discrete processing functions like attention, memory, and conceptual flexibility should lead to enhanced functioning in all knowledge domains. However, if rehabilitation strategies based on processing models do not effectively generalize (as the outcome literature suggests), then clinical investigators will need to develop more discrete training strategies specific to social cognitive constructs: e.g., differentially train patients to attend to and encode the features of a situation or the characteristics of a personality. Making social cognition the foundation of rehabilitation and therapy opens entirely new directions in treatment strategy. [*See* SOCIAL COGNITION.]

V. INFORMATION PROCESSING AND ASSESSMENT

Standardized assessment of symptoms, disabilities, and dysfunctions is perhaps the *sine qua non* of the clinical psychologist's profession. In particular, clinical psychologists have developed exquisite strategies for measuring various behavioral, cognitive, and personologic constructs. The high standards required for good psychological assessment assure that tests are administered, scored, and interpreted in similar fashion to all patients. Moreover, good psychometric qualities diminish the confounds that patient and examiner variables may unknowingly wreak on test performance.

Assessment of cognitive abilities has traditionally been dominated by measurement of intelligence. Unfortunately, the intelligence quotient (IQ) is, at best, a generalized and static measure of cognitive functioning with little indication of specific deficits that might account for poor intelligence. Moreover, measurement of IQ yields few useful recommendations regarding strategies for remediating cognitive deficits. The structures and processes of an information processing model yield a broader range of measurement strategies for assessing cognitive deficits. Neuropsychologists, in particular, have been ingenious in developing assessment strategies that putatively represent specific cognitive deficits. These measurements usually take the form of performance tasks in which patients must, for example, recall a series of words from a test list read by the examiner, or recognize test words from the recitation of a paragraph. Performance on these tasks may, in turn, suggest various rehabilitation or therapeutic interventions that remediate the deficit. [*See* INTELLIGENCE.]

Despite the benefits that process-specific measures bring to the assessment enterprise, these strategies have their own set of caveats. Given the serial nature of cognitive structures, no single measure yields a unique description of a corresponding information process. For example, below average scores on the word list not only suggest deficits in verbal recollection, but also poor functioning in sustained attention, verbal encoding, and ability to maintain set. To counter this dilemma, neuropsychologists typically administer a battery of tests and look for dissociations among results to identify deficient information processes. Poor performance on a word list may be attributed to recall memory if the patient performs adequately on other measures in the battery that assess attention, encoding, and maintenance of set.

Like IQ measures, information processing tasks for the most part represent state descriptions of performance: How competent is a patient on a specific information process at the moment of testing? Summaries of cognitive deficits need to be mindful of the dynamic character of processing deficits and account for variables that describe the course of specific information processes. For example, cognitive deficits in schizophrenia are frequently exacerbated by psychotic symptoms. Therefore, description of symptom effects is a necessary component in preparing a treatment plan for these patients.

VI. INFORMATION PROCESSING AND PSYCHOTHERAPY

Psychotherapy is clearly a multifaceted and complex task in which countless patient, therapist, and intervention variables must be accounted for and affected to yield positive outcomes. Cognitive theories have been used to better conceptualize the therapeutic enterprise and improve the efficacy of interventions in the process. In particular, cognitive therapies have been found to be especially effective in the treatment of severe depression.

A. Aaron Beck's Model of Cognitive Therapy

Negative cognitions play a major role in the development and maintenance of depressive symptoms. In particular, individuals who are vulnerable to bouts of depression tend to interpret incoming (and often neutral) information based on their negative self-appraisals; these interpretations tend to be variations of themes about feeling helpless, hopeless, and worthless. In addition, depressed individuals are likely to attribute positive outcomes to external sources and negative outcomes to themselves. [*See* DEPRESSION.]

Distorted cognitions show marked lapses in logical representations of the environment. In general, patients tend to use the information against the self when such reality distortions occur. Some common examples of illogical representations are: arbitrary inference, the drawing of a conclusion from a situation when there is no evidence to support it; selective abstraction, focusing on details taken out of context; and overgeneralization, drawing conclusions about one's ability based on a single incident. Because distorted cognitions are automatic, out of awareness, and highly illogical, the patient has difficulty developing effective strategies for coping. Information processing approaches to the treatment of depression are designed to empower the patient with the knowledge and tools necessary to combat the various elements of distorted cognitions.

The therapeutic intervention developed by Aaron Beck teaches patients a form of hypothesis testing which allows them to challence negative and distorted schemata. First, the therapist assists patients to identify the distorted cognitions and their corresponding effects on emotion. Once the distorted cognitions are identified, the patient subjects his or her beliefs to objective evaluation. It is important to educate the patient to the characteristics of distorted cognitions to facilitate the process of objective evaluation of beliefs. For example, distorted cognitions are automatic and involuntary suggesting that they are not based on logic or truth.

Once patients gain the capacity to question the legitimacy of their cognitions, they learn strategies to logically analyze distorted beliefs. Patients are encouraged to "check" their assumptions about a particular situation against "reality" by surveying others regarding the belief. Cognitions deemed to be invalid or inappropriate are neutralized by stating the reason for inaccuracy and by countering the distortion with a more appropriate belief.

VII. INFORMATION PROCESSING AND REHABILITATION

Rehabilitation defines an active treatment process in which patients who have suffered acute injuries (like a traumatic brain injury due to a car crash) or chronic diseases (like schizophrenia) regain necessary behaviors and cognitive abilities to live independently. Cognitive rehabilitation assumes that the central nervous system has a relative plasticity because specific information processes, and their corresponding central nervous system correlates, can be regained after lost to disease or insult.

A. Natural Recovery of Cognitive Processes

The manner in which rehabilitation strategies ameliorate patients' problems requires understanding of the natural process of recovery of brain function. For example, research has shown that destruction of certain areas of the brain does not result in total loss of the corresponding cognitive function. According to the theory of equipotentiality, other areas of the central nervous system might assume a function lost to a specific lesion. This phenomenon has been shown in language skills where some verbal processing abilities are assumed by the right hemisphere after significant damage to the left hemisphere. An alternate theory to equipotentiality is diaschisis; areas of the brain experience temporary shock, or diaschisis, when they are suddenly deprived of normal stimulation from neighboring, severely damaged regions. Frequently, undamaged tissue receives sufficient stimulation from other undamaged regions such that absent function returns.

Traditionally, it was thought that damaged neurons were irreplaceable. However, research has shown that certain neuronal tracts in the brain may regenerate in a manner similar to patterns of growth that have been demonstrated in the peripheral nervous system, though this regrowth may result in a muted return of cognitive functioning. Some neuronal tracts that lose stimulation from neighboring damaged areas become hypersensitive to the action potential of remaining axons. This hypersensitivity may diminish loss of function related to the damaged area. Interestingly, research has suggested that recovery functions related to denervation hypersensitivity may interact with other restorative processes. For example, research suggests that collateral sprouting may reduce the effects of denervation.

B. Models of Cognitive Rehabilitation

Various models of cognitive rehabilitation have been developed which guide clinical psychologists in developing comprehensive intervention programs specific to the patient's cognitive profile. An integrative model frames behavioral rehabilitation vis-a-vis a combination of relatively disparate professional perspectives: the neurologist's definition of the insult in terms of neuroanatomical foci and physiological sequelae, the neuropsychologist's test description of information processing deficits associated with the injury, and the behaviorist's treatment plans targeting the profile of behavioral problems. This view developed out of a professional consensus regarding the need for blending what had previously been the independent domains of each profession.

Contrast this model to a process model which views deficits as diminutions in specific information processes: e.g., a patient has poor memory because of diminished recall and recognition skills. The model, as presented here for cognitive rehabilitation, includes component processes that address three essential questions:

1. Acquisition. Why have fundamental information processes not developed appropriately? The answer to this question varies depending on the psychopathological category. Developmental disorders like mental retardation and autism imply that certain cognitive capacities are missing at birth or during early developmental periods. Similarly, information processing deficits of most psychiatric disorders may be predetermined as subtle vulnerability, albeit in dormant fashion, since infancy. Conversely, cognitive deficits in organically based patients represent recent loss rather than lack of acquisition. Implicit in the question about acquisition is the belief that some cognitive skills might be acquired that can replace or augment cognitive deficiencies. Of course, there are

biological and behavioral limits to learning certain cognitive skills.

2. Performance. Why are certain cognitive skills that apparently exist in a patient's repertoire not regularly utilized? Could it be that incentive affects the patient's cognition? Patients who are not motivated to recall an event will not remember that situation. Lashley illustrated this point in a poignant example. He bet a patient, who in 900 trials had failed to learn the alphabet, 100 cigarettes that he could not learn the letters. Ten trials later the patient recalled them perfectly. Findings like these suggest that reinforcement strategies are necessary adjuncts to rehabilitation programs.

3. Generalization. Why does improved performance in one treatment milieu not generalize to other situations? All too often little change is observed at home in a patient even though significant improvement is noted in the treatment setting; successful changes accomplished in the treatment setting have not generalized to other environments. Clinicians must include strategies like homework and *in vivo* practice that help patients transfer newly (re)acquired cognitive skills into their world. The Process model is useful for rehabilitation of cognitive deficits because treatment strategies are clearly wedded to the specific, deficient process in question: i.e., to the phenomena that brought about the behavioral excess and deficit, and to the phenomena that maintain these disabilities.

C. Cognitive Rehabilitation and Clinical Practice

Early proponents of cognitive rehabilitation were enamored with the potentials of computer hardware. In the prototypical rehabilitation program, patients were presented test stimuli repeatedly until they demonstrated the appropriate response (Fig. 2). Computers were especially attractive because precise adjustments of test stimuli could be controlled over thousands of iterations. The benefits of computers were frequently augmented by reinforcement strategies, in which patients might receive monetary rewards for correct responses, and by self-instruction, in which patients were taught to speak aloud the goal of the cognitive tasks (e.g., "I am supposed to key press to even numbers only").

Several investigations showed that patients who completed rigorous computer-based cognitive training experienced significant improvements on the variables of interest. Rarely, however, has responding to computer-generated stimuli been shown to generalize to real-world information processing. Clinical investigators have raised questions like what does attending to matrices of test letters have to do with comprehending a request from a cab driver?

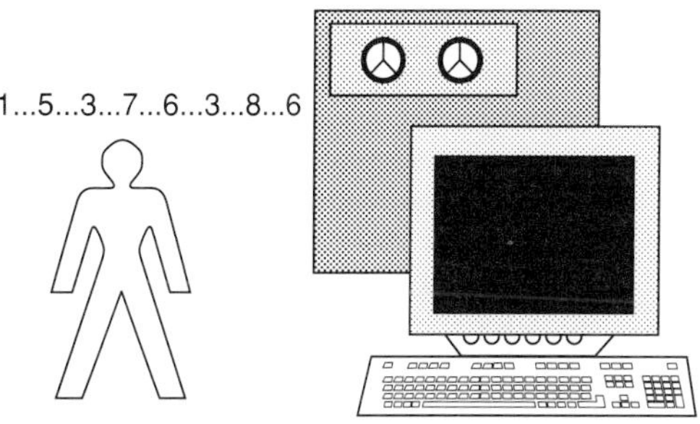

FIGURE 2 A computer-based rehabilitation program in which brain-damaged subjects learn to attend to a series of single-digit numbers. The subject receives a nickel reward for each correct identification.

Investigators have grappled with the ecological validity of cognitive rehabilitation strategies in several ways. Social cognitive models have been used to develop rehabilitation strategies. For example, several studies have shown that the psychiatric patients' ability to learn from social skills training modules (a psychosocial rehabilitation technique in which severely mentally ill patients are taught specific interpersonal and coping skills) is highly associated with level of memory functioning. Therefore, memory enhancement strategies have been incorporated into the social skills training regimen and patients now show a much higher rate of acquiring interpersonal skills.

Alternately, experts in rehabilitation have recommended that environmentally based interventions may provide a useful means for circumventing cognitive deficits in the real world. For example, a straightforward command, "Speak slower," made to family and friends of a severely mentally ill adult will enhance this person's information processing capabilities significantly. Similarly, strategically prepared signs that cue a brain-injured adult when to take his medicine or when she should cook her dinner provide a robust adjunct to short-term memory. Simple environmental changes like these may provide the best prostheses for rehabilitation of information processing deficits.

Bibliography

Abramson, L. Y. (1988). "Social Cognition and Clinical Psychology." Guilford, New York.

Barlow, D. (1988). "Anxiety and Its Disorders." Guilford, New York.

Beck, A. T. (1976). "Cognitive Therapy and the Emotional Disorders." International Universities Press, New York.

Corrigan, P. W., and Yudofsky, S. C. (Eds.) (in press). "Cognitive Rehabilitation and Neuropsychiatric Disorders." American Psychiatric Press, Inc., Washington DC.

Galambos, J. A., Abelson, R. P., and Black, J. B. (1986). "Knowledge Structures." Erlbaum, Hillsdale, NJ.

Ingram, R. E. (Ed.) (1986). "Information Processing Approaches to Clinical Psychology." Academic Press, New York.

Morris, R. G. M. (1989). "Parallel Distributed Processing: Implications for Psychology and Neurobiology." Clarendon Press, Oxford.

Wedding, D., Horton, A. M., and Webster, J. (Eds.) (1986). "The Neuropsychology Handbook: Behavioral and Clinical Perspective." Springer, New York.

INNER SPEECH, COMPOSING, AND THE READING–WRITING CONNECTION

David Yaden
University of Southern California

Dawn Latta
Grand Canyon University

Glossary

Constructivism A group of theories of learning which posit that on the basis of social or cognitive influences, an individual "constructs" concepts as they interact with the world. Learning is not simply a response to environmental stimuli.

First-order symbolization The use of signs, graphic markings, logos, or pictures to represent real-world objects directly.

Ideographic writing The representation of a message or concept through the use of abstract, stylized signs.

Mnemotechnic The use of an array of graphic markings as an aid to memory in recalling the meaning of a message or illustration. These marks do not possess any indigenous sign value.

Pictographic writing The representation of a message through the use of illustrating each of the objects involved in their real-world form.

Second-order symbolization The use of signs to represent other signs. For example, written language symbols represent units of spoken language which, in turn, represent meaning.

Sociohistorical A school of thought in which human learning and development are viewed as a function of internalized social relationships.

Zone of proximal development The difference between the child's actual development without assistance and the level of performance which can be achieved in collaboration with a more mature learner.

THIS ARTICLE focuses on the role of written language in directing and expanding the nature of inner speech development, both during and after the process of interiorization. As outlined by Vygotsky, written speech influences private and inner speech in ways that oral, dialogic speech cannot. Whereas the latter form requires an interlocuter and is carried out, for the most part, at the unconscious level, the structure of written language requires the reader or writer to produce a conscious and "voluntary" attention which forces an analysis of speech forms normally opaque to reflection. Thus, the process of becoming literate and interacting with written forms may allow for the development of further elaborated private and inner speech forms otherwise left dormant by normal oral language interaction.

Of central concern as well in this article is the "reading–writing connection," a linkage which has experienced a recent surge of attention, particularly in literacy education. Although this latter movement has left, for the most part, the explicit language underpinnings of both processes unspecified, the nature of written language development and its relation to the interiorization of private speech forms establishes very clearly (at least theoretically) that the processes of reading and writing are built upon a common substrate of covert language forms.

The purposes of this overview, then, is threefold: To specify the early evolution of written language to its mature form as a second symbol system in children; to outline the characteristics and interac-

Encyclopedia of Human Behavior, Volume 2
Copyright © 1994 by Academic Press, Inc. All rights of reproduction in any form reserved.

tions of three language forms—inner, oral, and written speech; and finally, to discuss the relationship between inner speech, reading, and composing.

I. ORIGINS OF WRITTEN LANGUAGE IN CHILDREN

According to Vygotsky, the origin of written language began as gesture language. From initial gestures, true written forms (defined as second-order symbols) evolve out from three early roots: (a) pictographic writing, (b) scribbling, and (c) children's games. All three of the former begin as direct representations of reality, i.e., as first-order symbols, having meaning *attributed* to them rather than possessing an indigenous sign value (although this develops quickly). In the following discussion, written language's origin through each one will be briefly outlined.

A. Pictographic Writing

In pictographic writing, children draw from memory rather than try to represent the reality of what they see. This practice explains why children's early drawings of people, for instance, often are bizarre, including a head with legs and arms or side profile of a face with both eyes drawn. It is not that children fail to see that these depictions are gross distortions of reality, but rather that their intention (albeit subconscious) is to name and designate, not to represent. Despite the fact that children draw depictions of objects and use a variety of written marks to do so, these are not used symbolically. Drawings of objects initially are meant *to be types of those objects,* not just symbols of them. Eventually, however, as drawing is increasingly accompanied by speech, the child's marking begin to take on a nascent symbolization. This development will be discussed shortly.

B. Scribbling

In experiments, it has been observed that the undifferentiated marks and lines which 3- and 4-year-old children use in drawing pictures are often ancillary and not useful in helping them to remember phrases given to them to recall. However, early on children begin to use these marks as *mnemotechnic* symbols. In other words, for some children the marks function as memory aids to recall each of the phrases as given. Rather than the marks denoting speech, however, they form a kind of topography where each mark is positioned on the page such that the spatial relationship between them facilitates recall of the objects as given. Again, the results of these experiments show that written signs or markings are merely *first-order symbols* at this point, directly denoting objects or actions. *Second-order symbolization* begins to develop when the child discovers that speech itself can be drawn.

C. Children's Games

Children's games and play provide a rich setting for the observation of developing symbolic behavior. Initially, however, the objects of play, in and of themselves, have no meaning, rather the child's own self-motion and gestures assign the functions and meanings the objects are to take on. For example, even though a stick can be used as a horse, the stick itself is not a symbol for a horse, but rather is endowed with meaning as its is placed between the child's legs and can be "ridden." Similarly, experiments have also shown that while 3 and 4 year olds can "read stories in which common objects such as keys or pencils represented characters, for example, these objects functioned only as "points of application" for children's gestures which allowed a story to be made up. However, as an initial root for the development of written language, the ability of children to readily use substitute objects (albeit first order) to designate other objects is a crucial first step in second-order symbolizing. What readily follows this first use of substitute symbols is the ability to abstract certain features of the substitute symbol to refer directly to what is being symbolized. From this latter ability, the representation of spoken words by written words is soon to follow. [*See* PLAY.]

D. First- to Second-Order Symbol Development in Drawing, Scribbling, and Play

Within all of the foregoing precursors to true written language use, shifts from using written marks as first-order depictions to their function as second-order symbols can be noted. In drawing, for instance, children begin to *name* their drawings. With school-age children, this shift can be described as a change from pictographic to ideographic writing, in other words, representing meaning by abstract signs as opposed to illustrating those actions and/or characters. The key element in this shift is the child's use of verbal language to describe what is drawn.

Similarly, the scribbled mnemotechnic marks give way to true second-order symbols when the child realizes that speech "can be drawn." These undifferentiated and topological marks also become increasingly symbolic as children focus upon representing specific content and quantity. In other words, as studies show, as phrases to be remembered become more complex, children tend to differentiate their graphic markings until being invested with speech, the marks themselves carried the primary sign values.

Finally in play, substitute objects initially stand in a complete arbitrary relationship to what is being represented with only children's gestures giving them meaning. However, during the course of play, children begin to abstract certain features of play objects as being representative of some corollary features in environmental objects. This tendency reflects the beginning of a true sign usage since features of the sign itself have an impact on what is represented. Thus, the meaning of the sign becomes more a function of the sign itself and its features rather than simply taking the meaning from the child's gesture.

In all of the situations described above (i.e., children's games, scribbling, and drawing) the evolution of written language development follows a pattern which can be observed as children gradually develop more differentiated and sophisticated sign use in each of these environments. Development in all of these areas sets the stage for the emergence of written languge forms as part of a true second-order symbol system.

E. Second- to First-Order Development

It is important to note, however, that written language, although a second-order symbol system, eventually assumes first-order characteristics in its highest form of development. As the understanding of written language proceeds, spoken language gradually disappears as the intermediary through which meaning is gained. Although written language emanates from spoken language through inner speech, the meanings of this interiorized language are related to the written forms in a highly abstract way and not at all through material sound. These relationships between the highest levels of written and inner language development and dialogic, oral language are discussed in the next section.

II. CHARACTERISTICS OF AND RELATIONSHIPS BETWEEN INNER, ORAL, AND WRITTEN LANGUAGE

A. Inner Speech Form

The differences between inner, oral, and written language in the areas of syntactic, phonological, and lexical structure can clearly be laid out. While inner speech undergoes a complex involution from its origin as social dialogue, in its final interiorized form, it is entirely predicative, fully elliptic, and without any acoustic or auditory representation. In addition to its reduced phonetic forms, inner speech differs in its semantic structure as well. Unlike written language which exists in a full expanded form, inner speech's semantic structure is idiomatic and agglutinative, with a word's "sense" more predominate than its specific meaning. In as much as written language is maximally elaborated, inner speech is the polar opposite, completely telegraphic, with its meanings densely concentrated, yet fluid and dynamic.

B. Written Language Form

Written language, on the other hand as mentioned, is fully expanded in its syntax, phonology, and semantic structure. Whereas inner speech is predicative, written language requires explicit syntactic connections between all grammatical elements. As the former can dispense with any materialized sound, even in mind, written script lays down the phonetic file in its entirety, except intonation and stress, for the most part. Whereas in inner speech, there is a predominance of "sense" over meaning, phrase over word, and context over phrase, written language must be displayed in some spatial sequence with each morpheme (in alphabetic script) represented and needing interpretation. It is not in this latter case that context and prior familiarity do not play a role in the interpretation of an orthography, but rather that the orthography itself must be fully displayed, in its spellings, correct word order, and appropriate referential structure, both internal and exophoric. Finally, the form of written language is abstract, lacking obvious motive and requiring a conscious attention to the structures of language.

C. Oral Language Form

Spoken language shares characteristics with both written and inner speech. While like inner speech, it is spontaneous, involuntary, and for the most part draws upon unconscious and unanalyzed processes, spoken language requires an "interlocuter" and is dialogic, a feature which written langugae shares to some extent, although the social partners (i.e., the audience) are imagined. Oral language must shape itself around a body of shared knowledge among the conversants and is further governed by the interplay of intonation patterns. But its salient characteristic is that it involves "material sound," a feature which is not an ostensible part of either written or inner language. However, despite the differences between these three types of speech, they interact in such a way that each takes on the characteristic features of the other as learning proceeds, with writing, in particular, stimulating the child to a higher level in language development.

D. Relationships between Inner, Oral, and Written Speech

1. Chronological Development

As defined (see Glossary), in a sociohistorical view the higher mental capabilities develop out of interiorized social relationships. And as such, social speech precedes inner speech which, in turn, precedes the development of written language use. What this means is that true written language development (as a second-order symbol system) only follows as social speech completes its final destination as fully internalized inner speech. This "involution," however, happens prior to the child's entry into school. The primary reason why written language development must follow inner speech development is that inner speech serves as an internal rough draft for oral as well as written speech. In other words, "reflection" and "thought" as they are related to the production of written language forms are primarily processes involving verbal thinking (i.e., inner speech forms). Without this internal language, the child's written attempts remain at the level of direct first-order depictions. It is only after the child begins to draw upon his or her internal language that written forms take on true symbolic characteristics as they, in turn, represent the child's thought, first through inner speech and then as expressed through written words.

The interaction of written, oral, and inner speech can be seen in the development of nonspontaneous or scientific concepts. These concepts represent the highest form of conceptual development since they involved volitional, conscious, and analytic processes. On the other hand, for these concepts to become fully functional, they depend upon the processes already developed in spontaneous or "everyday" concepts. Vygotsky further pointed out that the link between the development of these two classes of concepts was the *zone of proximal development,* an area of cognitive interaction whose beginning boundary is defined as what learning the child can accomplish without assistance from adults. For the school child, interaction with adults is the enabling force which effects an increase of conscious and analytic reflection. In addition to this interaction, the learning of certain subjects such as foreign language, grammar, or writing may further facilitate the child's reflective stance.

2. Written Language's Effect upon the Growth of Inner Speech

Given the characteristics of written language as previously discussed, it follows that the teaching of writing has an important place in the curriculum. The teaching of writing directly forces an analytic reflection upon language and encourages the development of second-order symbolization. Given the propensity of young children to begin to symbolize in play, the teaching of writing should be the responsibility of preschool education. In fact, both the sociohistorical and the Montesorri approaches are unique in stressing that young preschool children are optimally ready to learn writing during the preschool period.

Thus, written and inner speech have reciprocal effects upon each other. While inner speech provides the very substance of thought from which interpretation springs, the structure of written language forces an analytic, metalinguistic stance which, in turn, becomes a part of inner speech processing. As the sophisticated, elaborated structures of written language impinge upon the involuntary, spontaneous nature of inner speech, increasing its depth and richness, the interpretation of written structures becomes more facile as this process takes on the automaticity and spontaneous nature characteristic of both inner, monologic and oral dialogic speech forms. Thus, in the final analysis, all types of speech inform one another and provide the child as well as the adult with a multifaceted ability to communicate both intra-psychologically and with peers, both present and absent.

III. A SOCIOHISTORICAL VIEW OF THE READING–WRITING CONNECTION

A. Inner Speech as the Base for Reading and Writing

First of all, it follows that as the development of writing succeeds the development of inner speech, so will the development of reading. In fact, modern researchers have observed the development of writing can be seen long before children attempt to read on their own. However, the empirical dispute as to which comes first, reading or writing, is less important than the fact that oral dialogic and inner speech forms precede them both. What this seems to suggest is that prior to children developing conventional notions of what the written language system represents by way of a second-order symbol system, they need to develop rich, inner speech forms from which to draw when interpreting symbols as well as producing them. The primary connection, then, seems less to be between reading and writing than between inner speech and both forms of communication. Without a well-developed inner language, theoretically at least, neither reading nor writing will have the requisite semantic or syntactic resources needed to drive them both. Finally, since the existence of inner speech itself presupposes a social, external speech, this latter form can as well be seen as a seminal link to successful development of both reading and writing. [*See* READING.]

B. Developing a Metalinguistic Stance

Another link between reading and writing processes has to do with the need for a voluntary attention to the phonological, syntactic, and semantic dimensions of written language forms. Whether one is reading or writing, there is considerable energy expended in attending not only to graphic forms, but also to the syntax of the language as well as contextual and pragmatic aspects which must be fabricated and sustained in the absence of material sound and a specific, situated interlocuter. Given the indigenous abstract nature of written language, it would seem then that a common set of voluntary processes and insights into the structure of these dimensions would exist across both reading and writing and inform them both. One can certainly see in young children the benefits of learning to write in the area of understanding how to conventionally represent sounds with the orthography. Reading researchers as well have made a case that learning to read may be the first time that children are directed to analyzing their oral speech and how it relates to the linear file of letters. What all this points to is that given the necessary conscious awareness which written language demands, both reading and writing as developing abilities should profit simultaneously as a reflective stance is developed in either one.

C. The Role of Inner Speech in Composing

For the last decade or so, researchers in the field of writing have referred to "composing" in at least two ways. Traditionally, composing refers to a writer writing, to the process of putting ideas and words onto paper. Since the advent of reader response approaches to literature and constructivist ways of thinking and knowing, however, composing has also begun to refer to the creation of meaning within the individual. That creation of meaning may be shared orally in a community of readers, writers, and thinkers; it may be written on the page and read from the page; and, it may occur in each person through the private language of that individual. The development of composition research, then, has paralleled much of what Vygotsky has referred to as private or inner speech.

1. Inner Speech and the Creation of Meaning

In writing, the individual writer is expected to perform with language. This facility with language and with expressing ideas in writing is often referred to as written fluency. Earlier research has found that written fluency incorporates aspects of the individual's private language and assumptions about how language functions in meaning-making processes. Traditionally, written fluency involves the speed at which language is produced, the coherence and reasoning evidenced in the writing, the appropriateness of the content of the piece of writing, and the originality and creative uses of language in the piece. Research demonstrates that writers' abilities to tap their inner resources of language greatly influence the quality, richness, and development of writing.

The role of inner speech in writing is thus established in this research.

Other references to writers' reliance on their private and inner speech are abundant in interviews with writers about their own composing processes and in narratives of their reflections on writing. Instructors of writing tell their students to develop a writer's ear and to listen to what they already know and think. Award-winning authors speak of a variety of "dialogues" within themselves, "listening" for an inner voice; in essence, talking to oneself. Indeed, many writers refer to the "voice" of a piece of writing, to capturing a specific voice in the piece, and to developing a writer's sense of voice. These references to voice and to inner speech clearly reflect the centrality of inner speech in literacy and in the development and construction of meaning.

Reflections by authors and instructors of writing support the notion that by relying on inner speech, the thinker–composer becomes his or her own conversational partner, knows exactly what is intended by the ongoing flow of language and thinking, and understands fully the "subtext" of the inner web of meaning. Other writers and researchers in literacy have also referred to composing that occurs first in the mind through inner speech before moving to paper. These writers' strategies show their reliance on their interior speech and on developing a means of moving that inner speech to the page in the form of thoughtful written text.

Discussions of composing and its relation to inner speech are not limited to writers. Psychologists have linked musical intelligence and musical composing to language, and by extension, to writing. As composers report hearing, refining, and reworking musical patterns in their heads, similar is the work of the composer of words, of the writer, to be constantly monitoring, refining, shaping, and representing the words and ideas that are the genesis of written text. Much similarity can be found among the reports of authors on their processes of written composition and those of musical composers, suggesting that inner speech is more meaning-related than word-dependent.

2. Sense versus Meaning Distinctions

One of the most useful applications of the sociohistorical school in theories of composing is the distinction between the "sense" and "meaning" of words. Meaning is only one dimension of sense, the most stable and precise one. Sense, on the other hand, refers to the sum of all the psychological events aroused by a word. A word acquires its sense from the context in which it appears.

Poets have long made such a distinction between the meaning and sense of words. Poets often struggle over the wording of a line or stanza since every word has its own constellations of meaning. The writer must delicately balance the senses of a word and repeated words from one line to the next. For example, T. S. Eliot has noted that the poet's logic centers around a sensitivity to shadings of meaning, and what they imply (or preclude) for neighboring words. He compares the poet's sensitivity to linguistic connotations to the scientist's appreciation for the rules of scientific deduction. This emphasis on semantics, on the meaning and sense of words, again illustrates the ways in which writers rely on their inner speech as a conveyor mechanism to bring thought and language from the realm of inner speech into the visible and more public realm of writing.

3. Types of Inner Speech Rehearsal

References to this use of inner speech in composing are abundant in the research on composing. Many composing researchers and theorists refer to this process as rehearsal or mental planning. Research with high school writers has found that the most fluent writers used at least three forms of rehearsal: (a) oral rehearsal, which is talking out loud about one's plans for what to write and how to express ideas in writing, including the words to be used in the piece of writing and the writer's strategies or techniques that might best convey the writer's sense of inner meaning; (b) written rehearsal, which is the written-down version of oral rehearsal; and (c) mental rehearsal, which is purely interior dialogue about those same factors. Some high school writers have been observed using a combination of oral and mental rehearsal in which talk only to themselves was interspersed with long periods of silence. These writers were clearly combining and interweaving private speech and inner speech in an ongoing clarification of sense and meaning during the acts of composing. Therefore, these findings suggest that those writers who are more able to tap their inner speech, their inner resources of language, use increased imagery, metaphor, syntactic complexity, authority of expression, and personal voice in their writings.

4. Inner Speech and Intuition

The research on writing also suggests connections between intuition, inner speech, and writing. Because of its abbreviated nature, inner speech often occurs as a natural part of the thinker–composer's interior world and beyond his or her conscious awareness. Concepts, ideas, and words may reside in the flow of interior language without surfacing to full attention, thus remaining part of the composer's tacit knowledge. When the opportunity arises to express one's inner dialogue in writing, this tacit knowledge is triggered, intuitions are tapped, and both merge to influence composing and the flow of language from the inside of the writer's head to the outside world.

Contemporary writing researchers refer extensively to inner speech and the tapping of intuition during composing, considering that inner speech is the "wellspring of writing." Composition experts see mature writers as attending to their own inner voices, open to the subtle merging of inner speech and intuition during writing. For example, words emerge on the page without the writer's conscious awareness of exactly what the next word will be until it begins almost to form itself on the page. The time between awareness of a word and its appearance on the page, therefore, is often infinitesimal and submerged in the writer's continuing flow of language. This feature of composing, this rapid merger of conscious and unconscious thoughts into written words, is often referred to as a discovery by writers of what they think and of what they have to say. For these researchers, then, writing is dependent upon, and indeed cannot occur without, inner speech.

A sociohistorical interpretation of inner speech is thus a powerful influence on research in composing. Writing theorists rely on the existence and functioning of inner speech in the formation of meaning and as an integral part of the processes of writing. Further, writers are encouraged to employ inner speech and private speech in their awareness of composing processes. In effect, then, writing—at least that writing that is developed beyond the complexity of a grocery list—cannot occur without inner speech.

As writing is undergirded by inner speech, so is reading. The meaning of words may be conscious, but the "sense" of words is retained in one's inner speech. Reading and writing thus nurture each other through enriching inner speech which, in turn, enables these complex processes.

Bibliography

Latta-Bruton, D. (1985). "Toward Defining Written Fluency: Connecting Product and Process." Unpublished doctoral dissertation. University of Georgia, Athens, Georgia.

Moffett, J. (1985). Liberating inner speech. *College Composition and Communication* **36** (3), 304.

Shanahan, T. (ed.) (1990). "Reading and Writing Together: New Perspectives for the Classroom." Christopher-Gordon Publishers, Norwood, Massachusetts.

Spivey, N. N. (1990). Transforming texts: Constructive processes in reading and writing. *Written Communication* **7** (2), 256.

Tierney, R. J., and Pearson, P. D. (1988). Toward a composing model of reading. In "Perspectives on Literacy" (E. Kintgen, B. Kroll, and M. Rose, eds.). Southern Illinois Press, Carbondale and Edwardsville, Illinois.

Vygotsky, L. (1978). "Mind in Society." Harvard University Press, Cambridge, Massachusetts.

Vygotsky, L. (1987). "The Collected Works" (R. W. Reiber and A. S. Carton, eds.), Vol. I. Plenum Press, New York.

Wertsh, J. V. (1985a). "Culture, Communication, and Cognition: Vygotskian Perspectives." Cambridge University Press, Cambridge, Massachusetts.

Wertsh, J. V. (1985b). "Vygotsky and the Social Formation of Mind." Harvard University Press, Cambridge, Massachusetts.

Yaden, D. B. (1984). Inner speech, oral language and reading: Huey and Vygotsky revisited. *Reading Psychology* **5,** 155.

INTELLIGENCE

Robert J. Sternberg
Yale University

Glossary

Accommodation In Jean Piaget's theory, the modification of mental structures in order to understand new information that does not fit into the old mental structures.

Assimilation In Jean Piaget's theory, the incorporation of new information into already existing mental structures.

Crystallized ability In Raymond Cattell's theory, the ability representing the sum total of all acquired knowledge and skills, as is measured in tests of general knowledge and vocabulary.

Factor analysis A statistical technique for discovering the latent dimensions underlying observable data such as test scores.

Fluid ability In Raymond Cattell's theory, the ability that is used to process novel stimuli, to think flexibly, and to reason rapidly with new data.

General ability The ability alleged by Charles Spearman and others to underlie performance on all tasks requiring intelligence.

Intelligence quotient (IQ) Traditionally, the ratio of mental age to chronological age multiplied by 100 (ratio IQ); in more recent times, a derivative standard score with a mean of 100 and a standard deviation of 15 or 16 (deviation IQ).

Mediated learning experience (MLE) The idea, introduced by Reuven Feuerstein, that children acquire their intelligence when an adult guides them in their understanding of experiences and helps them to interpret and structure these experiences.

Multiple intelligences The idea, introduced by Howard Gardner, that intelligence should not be understood as unitary, but rather as multiple, including linguistic, logical–mathematical, spatial, bodily–kinesthetic, musical, interpersonal, and intrapersonal intelligences.

Percentile The percentage of scores under a given score; for example, a percentile score of 50 (the median) means that 50% of scores are lower than that score.

Primary mental abilities According to Louis Thurstone, the basic abilities of intelligence, including verbal comprehension, verbal fluency, number, inductive reasoning, memory, spatial visualization, and perceptual speed.

Triarchic theory The idea, introduced by Robert Sternberg, that intelligence comprises analytic, synthetic, and practical aspects.

Zone of proximal development The idea, introduced by Lev Vygotsky, of the difference between latent capacity and ability as developed through experience.

INTELLIGENCE, according to *Webster's Ninth New Collegiate Dictionary,* is "(1) the ability to learn or understand or to deal with new or trying situations . . . the skilled use of reason; (2) the ability to apply knowledge to manipulate one's environment or to think abstractly as measured by objective criteria (as tests)." This definition captures well many of our intuitions about the nature of intelligence. But intelligence is more like the abstract concept of beauty than it is like the concrete concept of brain. In the case of brain, everyone agrees that it exists and pretty much agrees as to what it is. In the cases of beauty and of intelligence everyone agrees that they exist, but there is much less agreement as to what they are.

I. DEFINITIONS OF INTELLIGENCE

There are several different approaches one might use to ascertain the definition of intelligence. Two

Copyright © 1994 by Academic Press, Inc. All rights of reproduction in any form reserved.

approaches are extremely simple and convenient, but ultimately inadequate.

One simple approach is to look in a dictionary, as was done above. But few psychologists would rely on a dictionary alone to understand the definition of so complex and variegated a construct as intelligence.

The second of the simple approaches is to define intelligence operationally (in working terms); for example, as "that which intelligence tests measure." This approach circumvents difficult issues of specification of the construct, and also immediately provides a basis for measurements that currently exist. This was the approach taken by Edwin Boring in 1923, in an age in which operational definitions were viewed as more adequate than they are today. There are three rather severe problems with the operational approach. The first is its obvious circularity. The definition justifies the measures, which in turn justify the definition. The second problem is that there are multiple measures of intelligence, not all of which measure precisely the same thing. Do we really want as many definitions as we have measures? The third problem is the vacuousness of the definition. Ultimately, it tells us nothing at all! Clearly, we need approaches that go beyond simple dictionary or operational definitions.

A. Definitions by Experts

What are the experts' opinions regarding the nature of intelligence? The editors of the *Journal of Educational Psychology* sought to answer this question at a 1921 symposium in which 14 experts presented their definitions of intelligence. Sixty-five years later, in 1986, Robert J. Sternberg and Douglas K. Detterman repeated the exercise, seeking definitions of intelligence from 25 experts in the field. (In this same volume, Sternberg and Cynthia A. Berg summarize the results of the two symposia, seeking those elements common to the definitions of large numbers of experts.) Sternberg and Detterman found the following elements of intelligence to be fairly common: (a) adaptation in order to meet the demands of the environment effectively, (b) elementary processes of perception and attention, (c) higher level processes of abstract reasoning, mental representation, problem solving, decision making, (d) ability to learn, and (e) effective behavior in response to problem situations.

In 1981, Sternberg and his colleagues Barbara Conway, Jerry Ketron, and Marty Bernstein mailed questionnaires to a large number of experts in the field. In a first wave of mailings, Sternberg *et al.* asked experts to list behaviors characteristic of intelligence, and in a second wave of mailings, the investigators asked them to rate the importance for intelligence of the various behaviors listed by the participants in the first wave. The investigators then used statistical techniques to determine underlying factors. Three main factors emerged: (a) verbal intelligence (including behaviors such as "is verbally fluent" and "converses easily on a variety of subjects"); (b) problem solving (including behaviors such as "is able to apply knowledge to problems at hand," "makes good decisions," "poses problems in an optimal way," and "plans ahead"); and (c) practical intelligence (including behaviors such as "sizes up situations well," "determines how to achieve goals," "displays awareness of world around him or her," and "displays interest in the world at large").

Four years later, Sternberg asked experts in fields other than psychology how they defined intelligence. What were the differences among fields? Professors of art emphasized knowledge and the ability to use that knowledge in weighing alternative possibilities and in seeing analogies. Unlike art professors, business professors emphasized the ability to think logically, to focus on essential aspects of a problem, and to see where arguments lead. Philosophy professors stressed critical and logical thinking very heavily, especially the ability to follow complex arguments, to find subtle mistakes in these arguments, and to generate counterexamples. The philosophers very clearly emphasized those aspects of logic and rationality essential in analyzing and creating philosophical arguments. The physicists, in contrast, placed more value on precise mathematical thinking, the ability to relate the physical phenomena to the concepts of physics, and to grasp quickly the laws of nature. In other words, the way intelligence is conceived of by experts is in part, but not wholly, domain-specific. The abilities emphasized as important to intelligence by experts within a given discipline depend upon the skills needed within that discipline.

B. Definitions by Laypeople

Another approach to defining intelligence is to examine definitions by laypeople. Why does it matter what laypeople think? It matters because the large majority of judgments about intelligence are made informally in everyday interactions—in social discourse, in job interviews, at work, at school, and so on. In the 1981 study described above, Sternberg and his colleagues found that laypeople emphasize three factors in their conceptions of intelligence: practical problem solving ability, verbal ability, and social competence.

Just how culturally bound are these expert and layperson definitions? Research suggests that there is at least some degree of cultural specificity in definitions of intelligence. For example, Mallory Wober studied two Ugandan tribes. He found that the Baganda tended to associate intelligence with mental order, whereas the Batoro associated it with mental turmoil. Thus, even within a country, differences in conceptions emerged.

Robert Serpell asked Chewa adults in rural eastern Zambia to rate village children on how well they could perform tasks requiring adaptation in the everyday world. He found that ratings did not correlate with children's cognitive test scores, even when the tests that were used were adapted so as to seem culturally appropriate. And Charles Super analyzed concepts of intelligence among the Kokwet of western Kenya. He found intelligence meant a different thing for children versus adults. The word "ngom" was applied to children considered intelligent, and it seemed to carry a connotation of responsibility as well as highly verbal cognitive speed, the quick comprehension of complex matters, and effective management of interpersonal relations. The word "utat" was applied to intelligent adults, and it suggested inventiveness, cleverness, and sometimes wisdom and unselfishness.

In sum, different cultures or even subcultures may have differing conceptions of intelligence, resulting in misunderstandings when members of one group attempt to impose their concept of intelligence on members of another group. (Some of the consequences of such impositions will be discussed below in the section entitled "Cognitive–Contextual Theories of Intelligence.")

II. PSYCHOMETRIC THEORIES OF INTELLIGENCE

Psychometric theories are based on the measurement ("metric") of the psychological ("psycho") construct of intelligence. Psychometric theories generally seek understanding of the structure of intelligence, asking: Is intelligence one thing or many? If it is many, what are the various elements that constitute it? What relation do these elements have to one another—are they all equally important, or are they hierarchically arranged?

Psychometric theorists have in common their use of tests to assess and ultimately to understand the nature of intelligence. The particular tests they use may differ, but the psychometric approach always requires examinees to answer challenging problems of various kinds, usually under some degree of time pressure. For example, examinees might be asked to define a word, such as *Authentic,* or to complete a number series, such as 2, 5, 9, 14, ?, or to complete a verbal analogy, such as *Train : Track :: Airplane : ?*.

Psychometric tests can be scored in many ways; here two of the most common will be discussed. Some scores are expressed in percentile numbers, referring to the percentage of individuals whose scores are below one's own. Thus, the median score is equivalent to the 50th percentile. Another score is the IQ, or intelligence quotient. Originally, such scores were derived by taking a hypothetical mental age (the age at which one is functioning mentally), dividing it by chronological (physical) age, and multiplying by 100. Today, IQs are almost always determined by properties of the normal distribution rather than by the use of mental age. Such IQs are called "deviation IQs," in contrast to the older "ratio IQs," because the former are computed from standard scores based on deviations from the mean of the distribution. In almost all uses of the IQ, the mean score is 100 with a standard deviation of 15 or 16.

A. Two Historical Traditions; Galton and Binet

The psychometric approach has its origins in two great traditions, those of an Englishman, Francis Galton, and of a Frenchman, Alfred Binet.

In 1893, Galton suggested that the basis of intelligence is the capacity for labor and sensitivity to physical stimuli. With regard to the latter, he actually set out to measure basic psychophysical abilities, such as weight discrimination and pitch sensitivity. Galton maintained an anthropometric laboratory at the South Kensington Museum in London for 7 years between 1884 and 1890, where, for a small fee, visitors could have themselves measured on a variety of psychophysical tests.

James McKean Cattell brought many of Galton's ideas to the United States. In 1890, he proposed a series of 50 psychophysical tests, such as dynamometer pressure (greatest possible squeeze of one's hand), rate of arm movement over a distance of 50 cm, the distance on the skin by which two points need to be separated for them to be felt separately, and letter span in memory. But one of Cattell's students, Clark Wissler, collected data showing that the various tests correlated neither with each other nor with grades in college courses. These data seemed to impugn this technique, and left the door wide open for what was to become the more popular approach among those seeking to measure intelligence.

In 1904, the Minister of Public Instruction in Paris named a commission charged with creating tests to ensure that mentally defective children received an adequate education. The commission was especially concerned that children with behavior problems not be classified as mentally retarded. Alfred Binet, working with Theodosius Simon, met the challenge, and formulated a set of tests of higher order thinking and judgmental abilities. Their tests were quite different from those of Galton. They included problems of vocabulary, arithmetic reasoning, spatial visualization, verbal absurdities, and similarities and differences between concepts.

These tests gave rise years later to the Stanford–Binet Intelligence Scales, formulated by Lewis Terman of Stanford University. Items such as those described above formed the basis of the test, which could be used from early childhood through later adulthood. The Standord–Binet scale is still in use, albeit in a different form. Other tests have derived from the approach of Binet as well, the most notable of which are probably the Wechsler scales, which can be used at the preschool level through adulthood.

B. The Factor Theorists

Although Galton and Binet had theoretical ideas about intelligence, neither formulated a full-blown psychological theory. The first of the major psychometric theories was that of British psychologist Charles Spearman, who published his first major article on intelligence in 1904. Spearman noticed that people who performed well on any one of the many mental tests he gave also tended to perform well on other mental tests in his test battery. Spearman devised a statistical technique, "factor analysis," to examine patterns of individual differences in test scores. He argued that factor analysis accounted for the sources of individual differences that underlay the score differences on the various tests he used.

Spearman's factor analyses of test data suggested to him that just two kinds of factors could account for all individual differences in test scores. The first and more important kind of factor Spearman labeled the "general factor," or *g*. Spearman believed that *g* pervaded performance on all tasks requiring intelligence, regardless of their particular form or content. The second kind of factor Spearman labeled as "specific factor," or *s*. Spearman believed that there were many specific factors, but that each was relevant only to a single test. In other words, performance on each test involved some amount of the general factor, which was common to all tests, and some amount of a specific factor, which was unique to that particular test. Spearman and his followers were much more interested in the general factor than in the specific factors. Although Spearman never pinpointed exactly what *g* was, he suggested in 1927 that it might be some form of "mental energy."

The American psychologist Louis Thurstone disagreed not only with Spearman's theory but also with his isolation of a single factor of general intelligence. Thurstone argued that the appearance of a single factor was just an artifact of the way Spearman did his factor analysis, and that if the analysis were done differently and more appropriately, seven factors would appear. These seven factors were Thurstone's "primary mental abilities." The seven primary mental abilities proposed by Thurstone were verbal comprehension (e.g., knowledge of vocabulary, reading), verbal fluency (e.g., producing words and sentences), number (e.g., solving simple numerical problems), spatial visualization (e.g., mentally visualizing and manipulating objects, such as is required to fit objects in the trunk of a car or to find one's way around a city), inductive reasoning (e.g., making predictions about the future from knowledge of the past), memory (e.g., remembering what is learned in school, or remembering people's names), and perceptual speed (e.g., proofreading rapidly for errors).

Other psychologists considered the possibility that there was merit in both points of view, and that perhaps abilities fit into a hierarchical structure, with general ability at the top, and specific abilities at lower levels. Such a hierarchy could accommodate both the Spearmanian and Thurstonian points of view, because it allowed for both the general factor and the primary mental abilities. Philip Vernon and

Raymond Cattell both suggested hierarchial models. Cattell, for example, suggested in 1971 that general ability can be subdivided into two further kinds of abilities, "fluid abilities" and "crystallized abilities." Fluid abilities are the reasoning and problem-solving abilities measured by tests requiring tasks such as completion of a series of numbers, whereas crystallized abilities are a sort of sum-total of one's acquired skills, as might be measured in part, say, by a test of vocabulary.

Most psychologists have agreed that more subdivisions of abilities are needed than were provided by Spearman, but not all have gone to a hierarchical arrangement. Joy Guilford, for example, proposed in 1967 a model allowing for 120 mental abilities. But in Guilford's "structure-of-intellect" model, the abilities are arranged in the form of a cube. The cube was obtained by crossing three dimensions: five different kinds of operations (processes), four different kinds of contents, and six different kinds of products (outcomes). These three facets combine multiplicatively, yielding the 120 ($5 \times 4 \times 6$) different mental abilities. An example of such a mental ability would be cognition (operation) of semantic (content) relations (product), which would be involved in recognizing, say, how the words *Firefighter* and *Police Officer* are similar, and how they are different.

The "golden days" of psychometric theories of intelligence have probably ended. At the least, the number of new psychometric theories proposed in recent years has decreased. Why? First, paradigms tend to shine and fade in an historical progression, and the preeminence of psychometrics lasted quite a long time before it faded. Second, it was difficult to choose among the alternative psychometric theories, because they tended to differ not at base, but primarily in how their proponents treated factor-analytic data. Factor analyses could support one or another theory, depending upon this treatment. Third, the theories generally said relatively little, and in some cases nothing about mental processes. Developmental and cognitive theories, considered below, have had more to say about processes, or how information flows through the mind in intelligent functioning.

III. DEVELOPMENTAL THEORIES OF INTELLIGENCE

A. The Theory of Jean Piaget

Although there have been various developmental theories of intelligence, without question the most influential has been that of Jean Piaget. Piaget first entered the field of cognitive development when, working in Binet's laboratory, he became intrigued with children's wrong answers to Binet's intelligence test items. Through his repeated observation of children's performance and particularly their errors in reasoning, Piaget concluded that there are coherent logical structures underlying children's thought. He also decided, however, that these structures are different from those underlying adult thought.

Piaget, working from the 1920s through the 1970s, believed that there are two interrelated aspects of intelligence: its function and its structure. Piaget, a biologist by training, saw the function of intelligence as no different from the function of other biological activities. He referred to this function as "equilibration": the attainment of equilibrium, or balance, with one's environment. Equilibration is achieved through two different means: "assimilating" the environment to one's preexisting cognitive structures, and "accommodating" new cognitive structures when the stimulation from the environment does not seem to fit any preexisting structures. For example, an American child might assimilate information when she meets a person in Quebec and classifies him as a Frenchman because he speaks French. But after meeting a number of French-speaking individuals in Quebec, she might create a new category through accommodation, the category of "French-Canadian."

Piaget further proposed that the internal organizational structures of intelligence and the manifestations of intelligence in behavior differ with age. He divided intellectual development into a series of four qualitatively discrete periods.

The first period, the sensorimotor period, lasts from approximately birth to 2 years of age. During this period, a child learns how to modify reflexes to make them more adaptive, to coordinate actions, to retrieve hidden objects, and eventually, to begin representing information mentally.

During the second period, called preoperational, which lasts from about 2 to 7 years of age, a child experiences the growth of language and mental imagery. He or she also learns to focus on single perceptual dimensions, such as color and size.

The third period, called concrete-operational, lasts from about 7 to 12 years of age. It is the time during which a child develops an important set of skills referred to as "conservation" skills. For example, suppose that water is poured from a wide, short beaker into a tall and narrow one. A preoperational child, asked which beaker has more water, will say that the second beaker does (the tall, thin one); a concrete-operational child, however, will recognize that the amount of water in the beakers must be the same.

Finally, children emerge into the fourth, formal-operational period, which begins at about age 12 and continues throughout life. The formal-operational child develops thinking skills in all logical combinations and learns to think with abstract concepts. For example, a concrete-operational child asked to determine all possible orderings, or permutations, of four digits such as 3–7–5–8, will have great difficulty doing so. The formal-operational child, however, will adopt a strategy of systematically varying patterns of digits, starting perhaps with the last digit and working toward the first. According to Piaget, this systematic way of thinking is not possible for the normal concrete-operational child.

B. Other Developmental Theories

Other theories of intellectual development, influenced by Piaget, have taken several courses. Many, but not all, have drawn significantly on Piaget.

One course, taken by Pat Arlin, has been to expand on Piaget by suggesting a fifth period of development in adulthood, such as problem finding. Another course, taken by Robbie Case and Kurt Fischer, has been to propose a set of stages related to but different from those of Piaget. Rochel Gelman, Robert Siegler, and David Klahr have proposed cognitive analyses of Piagetian tasks, a point of view consistent with the theories that will be considered in the next section. Micheline Chi, Frank Keil, and Susan Carey, among others, have emphasized the role of knowledge in intellectual development, suggesting that many of the gains that appear to be due to differences in processing are actually due to differences in knowledge structures.

The views of intellectual development described above all emphasize the importance of the organism in intellectual development. But an alternative viewpoint emphasizes the importance of the environmental context and, particularly, the social environment. This view is more related to the cognitive–contextual theories discussed below. Championed originally by Lev Vygotsky, a Soviet psychologist, this viewpoint suggests that intellectual development may be largely influenced by a child's interactions with others. A child sees others thinking and acting in certain ways and then internalizes and imitates what is seen. An Israeli psychologist, Reuven Feuerstein, has elaborated upon this point of view, suggesting that the key to intellectual development is what he calls "mediated learning experience." The parent mediates, or interprets, the environment for the child, and it is largely through this mediation that the child learns to understand and interpret the world.

One other contribution of Vygotsky is worthy of mention here, the concept of a "zone of proximal development." This zone is the difference between a child's latent capacity and his or her developed ability. Feuerstein suggested that the zone can be measured through what is sometimes called dynamic testing. Rather than having a child take a static test, in which the examiner asks questions and merely awaits the child's answer, in dynamic testing, if the child answers incorrectly, the examiner gives the child guided and graded feedback. The examiner infers the child's zone of proximal development by assessing his ability to profit from the feedback. Feuerstein created such a test as early as the 1970s, and in the 1980s, Ann Brown and Joseph Campione devised very sophisticated but somewhat narrower versions of such tests. [*See* COGNITIVE DEVELOPMENT.]

IV. COGNITIVE THEORIES OF INTELLIGENCE

Underlying most cognitive theories of intelligence is the notion that intelligence comprises a set of mental representations (e.g., propositions, images) of information and a set of processes that can operate on these mental representations. A more intelligent person perhaps represents information more effectively or clearly, or processes the information more rapidly or efficaciously.

Cognitive approaches can be subdivided in various ways. We shall discuss here three main approaches, which I will refer to as the "cognitive-correlates," "cognitive-components," and "cognitive-contents" approaches.

A. The Cognitive-Correlates Approach

The cognitive-correlates approach seeks to isolate basic information processes from the tasks studied by cognitive psychologists in their laboratories, and then to correlate these processes to scores on psychometric or other tests of intelligence. Many people trace this approach to the work of Earl Hunt and his colleagues, Nancy Frost, Clifford Lunneborg, and Joe Lewis, who in 1973 and then again in 1975 illustrated how the approach might work. Consider an example. In one task, an experimental subject is shown a pair of letters, such as "A A," "A a," or "A b." The subject must respond as quickly as possible to one of two questions: "Are the two letters the same physically?" or "Are the two letters the same only in name?" (In the first pair, the letters are the same physically, and in the second pair, the letters are the same only in name.)

The psychologists hypothesized that a critical ability underlying intelligence, and especially verbal intelligence, is that of rapidly retrieving lexical information such as letter names from memory. Hence, they were interested in showing that this ability is related to individual differences in performance on verbal-ability tests. They subtracted the reaction time to the question about physical match from the reaction time to the question about name match in order to isolate and set aside the time required for sheer speed of reading letters and pushing buttons on a computer, and more importantly, to isolate the time for additional reflection about the more complex name question. The critical finding was that the score differences seemed to predict psychometric test scores, especially of verbal ability.

Other investigators have used related "cognitive-correlates" techniques. For example, Daniel Keating traced the development of processes such as lexical retrieval over successive ages during childhood. Charles Perfetti showed how these processes applied in more complex tasks, such as reading comprehension. In each of these and other cases, the idea was to show how one could take basic cognitive tasks and then relate parameters of these tasks to scores on standard psychometric measures.

B. The Cognitive-Components Approach

In 1977, Robert Sternberg suggested an alternative approach, sometimes called the "cognitive components" approach, to studying the cognitive processes underlying human intelligence. He argued that Hunt and his colleagues had found only a weak relation between basic cognitive tasks and psychometric test scores because the tasks they were using were at too low a level. Although low-level cognitive processes may be involved in intelligence, they are peripheral rather than central according to Sternberg. He proposed that psychologists should study the tasks on intelligence tests and then determine the mental processes and strategies that people use to perform those tasks.

In his 1977 work and thereafter, Sternberg studied various kinds of reasoning tasks, such as analogies (e.g., *Time : Second :: Distance:* (a) *Hand,* (b) *Foot*), classifications (e.g., *Lion, Cow,* (a) *Goat,* (b) *Blue Jay*), and series problems (e.g., *Infant, Child, Youth, Adolescent,* (a) *Teenager,* (b) *Adult.* Using techniques of mathematical modeling applied to reaction-time data, Sternberg isolated some of the components of information processing. He determined whether each experimental subject did, indeed, use the specified processes, how the processes were combined, how long each process took, and how susceptible each process was to error. Sternberg showed that the same cognitive processes are involved in a variety of intellectual tasks, and he suggested that these and other related processes underlie scores on intelligence tests.

Other investigators have used the cognitive-components approach with considerable success. Roger Shepard, Lynn Cooper, Robert Kail, and James Pellegrino, among others, used these techniques to isolate components of spatial visualization. Marcel Just and Patricia Carpenter showed how the approach could be applied to complex Raven matrix items (which require reasoning with abstract figures moving downward as well as sideways), and they simulated their model via computer. Ronna Dillon, Richard Snow, and others used eye-movement recordings to study components of inductive reasoning. And Lauren Resnick, Guy Groen, and many others formulated componential models of arithmetic computation. A variety of componential types of theories of intelligence were proposed—by John Carroll, Richard Snow, and others—which differed in their detail but had in common their attempt to specify a relatively small number of basic information processes. [*See* REASONING.]

C. The Cognitive-Contents Approach

A third cognitive approach might be called a "cognitive-contents" approach. This approach emphasizes knowledge in intelligent functioning, and particularly in expert functioning (which some feel is analogous to intelligent functioning). The pioneering study using this approach was done by William Chase and Herbert Simon, who followed up some work of Adrian DeGroot by showing that if expert and novice chess players were required to remember positions of pieces on a chess board, experts were superior to novices, but only if the pieces formed a meaningful pattern in the context of the game of chess. This finding was soon replicated in the context of other games, for example, by Judith Reitman for the games of Go and Gomuku.

The underlying principle turned out to be quite general. Other investigators soon showed the importance of knowledge to intelligent functioning in a variety of other domains. For example, Jill Larkin and Herbert Simon showed the importance of knowledge and its organization in the realm of physics, as did Micheline Chi and Robert Glaser.

Chi also showed that whereas adults' memory is almost always better than that of children, children can be shown to have superior memory in domains they know well, such as dinosaurs. Daniel Wagner and others showed that the same holds true cross-culturally. Whereas North Americans show superior performance in familiar domains, people from other cultures (e.g., Moroccans who deal in Oriental rugs) show superior performance in their own more familiar domains (such as the Oriental rugs). This last findings raises questions about cultural generality, to which we will soon turn.

The overall cognitive, or information-processing, approach to intelligence is still being actively pursued by many. But some investigators, including a few who were active in this kind of research, began to feel that something was missing. For example, both Sternberg and Keating suggested independently that these approaches failed sufficiently to take into account the context in which intelligence was operating. What is intelligent in one environment might not be in another environment. Thus, two people with identical cognitive-processing capabilities might be perceived quite differently in two different settings, depending upon the demands of the environments. Cognitive-contextual theories therefore try to take into account context as well as cognition. [*See* VARIABILITY IN BRAIN FUNCTION AND BEHAVIOR.]

V. COGNITIVE–CONTEXTUAL THEORIES OF INTELLIGENCE

Congitive–contextual theories deal with how cognitive processes operate in various environmental contexts. These theories vary widely in their claims.

A. The Roles of Culture and Context

At one extreme, John Berry proposed in 1974 that the idea of psychological universals across cultures should be rejected and that the idea of intelligence must be studied wholly "emically" for each culture (i.e., from within the culture without imposing conceptual systems derived from other cultures). Berry's proposal is called "radical cultural relativism." Berry and his colleague, Sidney Irvine, posited four levels of context that can affect intelligence and the way it is evaluated.

At the highest level is ecological context. This kind of context comprises all of the permanent or almost permanent characteristics that provide the backdrop for human action. It is the natural cultural habitat in which a person lives.

The second kind of context is the experiential context, or the pattern of recurrent experiences within the ecological context that provides a basis for learning and development. When cross-cultural psychologists try to determine independent variables that affect behavior in a particular habitat, they are usually dealing with a level of experiential context.

The third kind of context is the performance context, which is itself nested under the first two kinds. This context comprises the limited set of environmental circumstances that account for particular behaviors at specific points in time.

Finally, nested under these three levels of context is the experimental context. This context comprises environmental characteristics manipulated by psychologists and others to elicit particular responses or test scores. Although this context should be nested within the three described above, it often is not, in which case the experimental context does not represent appropriately the conditions under which a given set of subjects lives.

A less extreme view than that of radical cultural relativism is what might be called "conditional comparativism," a position taken by Michael Cole and his colleagues at the Laboratory of Comparative Human Cognition. Cole and his colleagues asserted in 1982 that the radical cultural-relativists do not take into account that cultures interact. Cole *et al.* assume that learning is context-specific, and that context-specific intellectural achievements are the primary basis for intellectual development. They do not deny the existence of any cross-contextual generality of intelligent behavior, and they state specifically that limited comparisons between cultures are possible—but only if one takes into account how to measure constructs appropriately within the various cultures. Other investigators, such as Patricia Greenfield, Alexander Luria, and William Charlesworth, have taken a similar position.

B. Two Cognitive–Contextual Theories: Gardner and Sternberg

Two rather well-known theories of intelligence that take a less extreme position than complete relativism are those of Howard Gardner and Robert Sternberg.

In a 1983 book, Gardner proposed a theory of what he called "multiple intelligences." Earlier theorists had gone so far as to contend that intelligence comprises multiple abilities. But Gardner went a step further, arguing that there is no single intelligence. In his view, intelligences include, at a minimum, linguistic, logical–mathematical, spatial, musical, bodily–kinesthetic, interpersonal, and intrapersonal abilities.

Some of these intelligences are quite similar to the abilities proposed by psychometric theorists, but others are not. For example, the idea of a musical intelligence is relatively new, as is the idea of a bodily–kinesthetic intelligence, which encompasses the particular faculties of athletes and dancers. Gardner derived his list of intelligences from a variety of sources, including studies of cognitive processing, of brain damage, of exceptional individuals, and of cognition across cultures. Gardner proposed that whereas most concepts of intelligence had been ethnocentric and culturally biased, his was universal, based upon biological and cross-cultural data as well as upon data derived from the cognitive performance of a wide variety of people.

Another theory also taking into account both cognition and context is Sternberg's "triarchic theory" of human intelligence. Sternberg agreed with Gardner that conventional notions of intelligence were too narrow. But in his 1985 book, he disagreed with Gardner as to how psychologists should go beyond traditional conceptions. Sternberg suggested that abilities such as musical and bodily–kinesthetic ones are not intelligences, but talents, in that they are fairly specific and are not required for adaptation in most cultures.

According to Sternberg, intelligence has three aspects. The first aspect consists of the cognitive processes and representations that form the core of all thought, and which form the basis for analytical ability. The second aspect consists of the application of these processes to experience, and especially to novel experience. This involves synthetic ability, or going beyond the information given. The third aspect consists of the application of these processes to experience through the real-world contexts in which the individual lives. According to Sternberg, mental processes serve three functions in these contexts: adaptation to existing environments, the shaping of existing environments to form new ones, and the selection of new environments when old ones prove unsatisfactory.

An intelligent person, in this theory, ultimately is one who capitalizes on whatever strengths he or she has, and who manages simultaneously to compensate for or remedy weaknesses. Thus, a person needs to figure out his or her strengths and weaknesses, and then figure out how to navigate through life, following or changing the "course" as necessary.

VI. BIOLOGICAL THEORIES OF INTELLIGENCE

The theories described above seek to understand intelligence in terms of underlying hypothetical constructs, such as factors or cognitive processes. Some theorists, however, have taken a different approach, seeking to understand intelligence directly in terms of its biological bases. These theorists have used several different approaches, including the study of brain functioning as a whole, as well as studies of hemispheric specialization, brainwaves, bloodflow, and related PET scans, and genetics.

A. The Brain as a Whole

One of the most well-known theories of brain functioning as a whole was proposed by Donald Hebb in 1949. The core of Hebb's theory is the concept of "cell assembly." Hebb proposed that repeated stimulation of specific receptors slowly leads to the formation of an assembly of cells in the association area of the brain. These cells can act briefly as a closed system after stimulation has stopped. Hebb assumed that the occurrence of synaptic activity makes the synapse more readily traversed.

Another general theory that has had wide impact is that of Alexander Luria. Luria suggested in 1973 and again in 1980 that the brain is a highly differentiated system whose parts are responsible for different aspects of a unified whole. In other words, separate cortical regions act together to produce thought and action of various kinds. Luria suggested that the brain comprises three main units. The first, a unit of arousal, includes the brain stem and midbrain structures. Included within this first unit are the medulla, reticular activating system, pons, thalamus, and hypothalamus. The second unit of the brain is a sensori-input unit, which includes the temporal, parietal, and occipital lobes. The third unit includes the frontal cortex, which is involved in organization and planning. It comprises cortical structures anterior to the central sulcus. Two tests of intelligence, one by Alan Kaufman and the other by J. P. Das and Jack Naglieri, are based on this theory of intelligence.

A related "full-brain" approach is to look at the relation between brain size and intelligence. Harry Jerison, for example, concluded in 1982 that brain size relative to weight is highly correlated with intellectual level across but not within species. Recently, it has even been suggested that brain volume within species may distinguish those who are more from less intelligent.

B. Hemispheric Specialization

Studies of hemispheric specialization investigate aspects of intellectual performance as related to the regions of the brain from which they originate. One of the earlier modern theories of this kind was proposed by Roger Sperry. In 1961, Sperry suggested that each hemisphere of the brain behaves in many respects like a separate brain. For example, Sperry and his student, Jerre Levy, asked split-brain patients (individuals who have had the corpus callosum, which connects the two hemispheres of the brain, severed) to match small wooden blocks held in either their left of their right hands (which they did not look at) with corresponding two-dimensional pictures. The researchers found that the left hand did better than the right at this task, but, of more interest, they found that the two hands appeared to use different strategies in solving the problem. Their analysis demonstrated that the right hand found it easier to deal with patterns readily described in words but difficult to discriminate visually. In contrast, the left hand found it easier to deal with patterns requiring visual discrimination. Since the hands are connected contralaterally to the hemispheres of the brain, this result suggested that the left hemisphere was involved in verbal description and the right hemisphere in visual description. [*See* BRAIN.]

Similarly, Franco and Sperry in 1977 tested right-handed split-brain patients and normal control subjects in their ability to match unseen objects by touch with geometric shapes presented visually. They discovered that the patients performed consistently better when using the left hand than when using the right hand, consistent with the notion of right-brain control of the spatial task.

An alternative view has been presented by Michael Gazzaniga, who has argued that the brain is organized modularly into a set of units that work relatively independently and in parallel. In particular, he has suggested that the left hemisphere tries to assign interpretations to the processing of the modules of the right hemisphere of the brain. Thus, the left hemisphere may perceive the individual as operating in a way that does not make any particular sense to it, but its job is to assign meaning to that behavior.

C. Evoked Potentials

Evoked-potential approaches to the study of intelligence measure electrical activity in various portions of the brain to understand intelligence. In one research program, Emanuel Donchin and his colleagues have shown that the P300 wave form (so-called because it is positive and because it occurs roughly 300 ms after stimulation) seems to reflect allocation of cognitive resources to particular tasks. In 1982, Edward Schafer suggested that the tendency to show a large P300 response to surprising stimuli may be an individual-differences variable. Schafer believes that a functionally efficient brain will use fewer neurons to process a stimulus that is familiar and more to process a stimulus that is novel or unfamiliar. [*See* BRAIN ELECTRIC ACTIVITY.]

A similar point of view has been taken by Arthur Jensen and Tony Vernon. They have been engaged in the measurement of actual neuronal conduction velocities, and in 1992 presented data that suggest that more rapid conduction velocities in the arm, for example, are associated with higher levels of intelligence. A somewhat different point of view, taken by Hans Eysenck and various associates, is that it is neuronal accuracy rather than speed that is critical in intelligence. For example, Alan and Elaine Hendrickson have suggested a high correlation between the complexity of the evoked-potential wave and intelligence.

D. Blood Flow and PET Scans

Another relatively new front in brain research has involved the measurement of blood flow in the brain, which is a fairly direct indicator of functional activity in brain tissue. John Horn, for example, reported in 1986 that older adults show decreased blood flow to the brain, and suggested that such decreases are greater in some areas of the brain than in others. In particular, blood flow is decreased to those areas responsible for close concentration, spontaneous alertness, and the encoding of new information.

Richard Haier, a neuroscientist, had volunteers perform various cognitive tasks while doing a PET scan on their brains. In 1991, he found that people with higher IQs seemed to be expending less mental energy in solving tasks than those with lower IQs. In 1992, he found that individuals playing a computer game while still learning it expended more mental energy than those who played it once they knew it well. The suggestion of this research, then, is that greater intelligence is associated with the expenditure of less mental energy in the completion of tasks.

E. Behavior Genetics

Behavior genetic studies seek to understand the genetic transmission of intelligence. To date, they have usually taken the form of studies that investigate intelligence test scores of identical twins reared apart (so as to remove effects of common environments), or the relation of scores between identical versus fraternal twins (the former sharing all their genes in common and the latter only half their genes), or the relation of scores between relatives of various degrees of genetic proximity. These studies have led to varying estimates of the heritability of intelligence. Robert Plomin and Sandra Scarr have estimated that roughly half the variance in intelligence test scores is due to heredity, whereas others, such as Tom Bouchard and Arthur Jensen, have suggested higher estimates in the neighborhood of 80%. [*See* BEHAVIORAL GENETICS.]

It is important to remember that the coefficient of heritability depends upon time, place, population, and range of intelligence test scores. It is not a fixed number. Moreover, higher estimates of genetic influence do not imply that intelligence cannot be increased. Consider an analogy to height. Height has a heritability that is very high—over .9—yet heights have been increasing in the general population over the years. Thus, even an attribute that is heritable is subject to change with improving environmental conditions.

Today there exist a number of programs to improve intelligence, such as those of Reuven Feuerstein and of Richard Herrnstein and his colleagues. These programs seek to teach directly the information-processing skills that underlie intelligent task performance. For example, people are taught how to make better inferences, recognize similarities and differences, apply what they have learned, and so on. We have every reason to believe from the data collected so far that intelligence is, in some degree, teachable and hence modifiable.

Bibliography

Baron, J. (1985). "Rationality and Intelligence." Cambridge University Press, New York.

Case, R. (1985). "Intellectual Development: Birth to Adulthood." Academic Press, New York.

Cattell, R. B. (1971). "Abilities: Their Structure, Growth, and Action." Houghton-Mifflin, Boston.

Ceci, S. J. (1990). "On Intelligence . . . More or Less." Prentice–Hall. Englewood Cliffs, NJ.

Gardner, H. (1983). "Frames of Mind: The Theory of Multiple Intelligences." Basic, New York.

Piaget, J. (1972). "The Psychology of Intelligence." Littlefield Adams, Totowa, NJ.

Sternberg, R. J. (Ed.) (1982). "Handbook of Human Intelligence." Cambridge University Press, New York.

Sternberg, R. J. (1985). "Beyond IQ: A Triarchic Theory of Human Abilities." Cambridge University Press, New York.

Sternberg, R. J. (1990). "Metaphors of Mind: Conceptions of the Nature of Human Intelligence." Cambridge University Press, New York.

Vygotsky, L. S. (1978). "Mind in Society: The Development of Higher Psychological Processes." Harvard University Press, Cambridge, MA.

Intention

Laura E. Stevens and Susan T. Fiske
University of Massachusetts at Amherst

Glossary

Attention Concentration of mental resources or activity.

Hard choice A nondominant or weak alternative.

Intention Mental state inferred when a person has a number of options, chooses to follow one of the available alternatives (especially the nondominant alternative), and focuses attention on that alternative.

Option Cognitively available alternatives.

INTENTION can be defined as a mental state that is attributed to a person when the following three conditions are met. First, the person must have options—a perceived choice among cognitively available alternatives. Second, the person must choose to follow one of the alternatives. Intent is particularly obvious when the person chooses to follow the hard or nondominant alternative. Finally, the person must concentrate attention on the chosen alternative, which facilitates the enactment of the alternative.

I. CONCEPT OF INTENTIONALITY

Intention is an important concept in the field of human behavior. If intention underlies a person's behavior, it can be assumed the person desired to behave in that way. Furthermore, the person had control over the behavior. And, finally, the person can be held responsible for the behavior and the consequences of the behavior.

In fact, the concept of the intentionality historically has been incorporated into a number of psychological theories. Franz Brentano's psychology of acts asserted that mind requires mental activity as well as elements in consciousness. Act psychologists believed that the true nature of mind depends upon the "directedness" of the mental activity. Thus, act psychology advances intentions as the underlying cognitions that provide insight into mental phenomena.

William McDougall's hormic psychology argued that behavior is rooted in instinct. Furthermore, behavior is purposive, guided by efforts, impulses, desires, and volitions. In other words, hormic psychology maintained that all human behavior is guided by intentionality.

Finally, William James included the concept of "will" (intent) in his pragmatic psychology. He posited that all voluntary behavior is rooted in human will. Yet, willing ends with the prevalence of the idea in the mind. Whether the action actually occurs is immaterial. Pragmatic psychology recognizes that intent does not always result in behavior, but, at the same time, all voluntary behavior stems from intent. [*See* FREE WILL.]

It is evident that the concept of intentionality historically has played an important role in the study of human behavior. Yet, very little recent work has been done on the definition of intention. Based on an earlier analysis by Fiske, the following three sections attempt to take the work that has been done and integrate it into the definition of intention presented above: a mental state resulting when a person chooses one of a number of options and focuses attention on that alternative.

II. HAVING OPTIONS

The foundations for many later discussions of intent were laid by James, who defined "volition" (intent)

Copyright © 1994 by Academic Press, Inc. All rights of reproduction in any form reserved.

as a choice between conflicting courses of thought. A individual with two opposing ideas in mind must neutralize one of them. Volition is giving approval to one idea over the other. According to James, the idea of the act precedes giving approval, which paves the way for action. James presented a number of examples of conflicts that are resolved by the exercise of intent, such as staying in a warm bed versus getting out into the cold air.

Edward Tolman's purposive behaviorism elaborated upon James' ideas about intent. However, rather than theorizing about whether a person would get out of bed, Tolman's ideas resulted from analyzing the intentions of rats running through mazes in search of food. Yet, Tolman also believed that intent operated when a task could be performed in more than one way. When changing behavior, an organism displays consciousness and intent because the organism is attempting a new course of action in order to bring about a result. Tolman raised the concept of intent when he became aware of theoretical gaps in associationism while trying to explain rats' seemingly arbitrary choices in a maze.

Kurt Lewin had similar problems trying to explain the choices people make. Lewin and his students argued that behavior is not merely a product of repeated associations. Intent, purpose, and motivation also influence which cognitive structures guide behavior. In Lewin's view, intent prepares a person for a desired behavioral possibility by restructuring the person's cognitions about the behavior. New "valences" are created. These valences represent the relevant behavioral possibilities in the environment. For example, if one has an important letter to mail, the sight of a mailbox takes on a different valence or behavioral pull than it does if one has been warned of a possible letter bomb. In other words, intent motivates valence change, so it influences which of many possible cognitive structures provides the basis for behavior. Once again, intent comes into play when a person is presented with a number of options.

Information-processing theorists also endorsed the idea that cognitive alternatives or options play a major role in intent. George Miller, Eugene Galanter, and Karl Pribram distinguished between an "image," a cognitive structure, and a "plan," a program for action. An image is accumulated, organized knowledge, sometimes called declarative memory. A plan is a hierarchical process that controls the order in which actions occur, sometimes called procedural knowledge. Miller and his colleagues claim that once a plan is chosen, intent is the uncompleted parts of that plan. Again, intent is defined in terms of a choice among cognitively available options.

While each of the presented viewpoints approaches intent somewhat differently, they all agree that intent requires having a number of cognitively available options. These options are not always easily discovered, but their presence is a necessary precondition for intentional behavior.

The necessity of options has been described, but must a person be aware of these options in order to manifest intention? The simplest answer is that options must be potentially cognitively available. Options may not be consciously considered by a person at the moment of decision, but, upon reflection, the person should be able to recognize that there were other possible alternatives. For instance, suppose a white person encounters a middle-aged black woman in an upper-class neighborhood and assumes she is a housekeeper. This inference is probably not considered consciously. However, the perceiver would have to acknowledge that there are other possible ways to think about this person; she may be the mayor. As long as these options are available, even if they are not explicitly considered, intent applies.

Naturally, people sometimes share their active consideration of alternatives with others. However, occasionally a person may not openly acknowledge that options exist, especially when intent would imply responsibility for a harmful act. An observer must concentrate on alternatives that the actor could have had in mind in order to infer intent in these cases. If the person was capable of choosing and enacting any of a number of options, then these options were potentially available and intent applies.

III. MAKING THE HARD CHOICE

When a person has a number of options available, one of those alternatives will most likely be dominant. This alternative may be dominant because, without intervention, it is the thought that would follow by default, because a strong emotion or impulse guides thought that way, or because the association is habitual. In any case, the dominant alternative requires less mental effort than the others. It is the easy choice. For example, most of James' conflicts involve a choice between a strong initial impulse and a more "difficult" but wiser alternative.

Volition is most obvious when the "still, small voice" of a wiser thought actively conflicts with the unacceptable easy alternative. It is the dominant but unwise thought that one is motivated to "neutralize." According to James, if the dominant thought persists despite attempts to neutralize it, the corresponding action will follow. For instance, a typically dominant choice is the thought focusing on the comfort of a warm bed.

A weaker, difficult thought that one is motivated to encourage (e.g., getting out of bed) competes against the dominant thought. This tension between the dominant thoughts and the weaker but preferable thoughts is central to understanding intent. When one chooses the nondominant alternative, making the "hard choice," intent is most obvious. Of course, whenever a person has options, whatever choice the person makes is intentional even if it is the easy choice (the dominant alternative).

Tolman also endorsed the idea that intent is most obvious when someone makes the harder choice. Intent requires making a change, choosing between the previously dominant behavior and a novel nondominant alternative. When the chosen alternative was heretofore weaker but now is the preferable alternative, it requires a more differentiated response and, thus, the operation of intent is most obvious. Like James, Tolman posits that intent is especially clear when a nondominant but preferred course is chosen over a previously dominant course.

Lewin made practically the same point. According to Lewin, intent imposes a new direction on what a person would otherwise do. Intent arises when the situation would lead to actions other than the desired action. In order to engage in the desired action, intent creates valences other than the most usual valences. For example, computers usually have a neutral valence, but the desire to play an entertaining computer game creates a stong pull from a computer. In its most dramatic form, intent interferes with the dominant action in the situation and replaces it with a nondominant alternative.

More recently, information-processing psychologists have been concerned with how people control dominant responses. When instructions (which invoke intentions) override habitual (dominant) responses, the action is considered "controlled"; when instructions do not override habitual responses, the action is considered "automatic." Given the more current discussion of controlled and automatic processes, the concept of intent may no longer seem necessary. However, this information-processing approach cannot adequately replace intention, for several reasons. [*See* Control.]

First, controlled processing is commonly defined as entailing awareness, intent, and interference with other ongoing processes. According to this definition, intent is a criterion for controlled processing. Thus, intent cannot be equated with and must be distinguishable from controlled processing. Otherwise the definition of controlled processing is circular.

Second, the literature on controlled processing does not include any careful examination of intent. Intent has been treated merely as an independent variable that invokes control. The other two criteria for controlled processing, interference and awareness, have been treated as dependent variables that reveal control. Considering the major role intent plays both operationally and conceptually, the research on controlled processing is surprisingly unhelpful.

Third, by definition controlled processing requires awareness or conscious processing. Yet, it is useful to consider unconscious intentions. As already noted, the availability of options is the critical characteristic of intent, not whether the person has consciously considered all of the options.

Finally, intent can provoke either controlled and conscious or uncontrolled and unconscious processes. People choose one alternative over another and the processes associated with the chosen alternative may be controlled or automatic or some combination. In fact, the literature on automatic and controlled processing specifically considers interactions of the two types of processes. The point is that the occurrence of an intent does not determine the nature of the processes that follow. The choice between alternatives is potentially controllable, but the ensuing processes are not necessarily controlled.

The reasons presented above illustrate that intent and controlled processing are not redundant concepts. In the literature on automatic and controlled processes, intent is viewed as an intervening variable that brings about control. Again, in the current information-processing research, intent is particularly obvious when the nondominant alternative is chosen.

IV. PAYING ATTENTION

Thus far, intent has been defined as having options and as especially obvious when one chooses the nondominant alternative. What mechanism do people use to make or to fail to make the "hard choice?" Basically, one makes the hard choice by paying attention to the weaker but preferable alternative. James claimed that sustained attention with effort to a difficult object will lead to volitional action. Thus, the attention must be motivated. For example, in order to resist staying in bed, one must concentrate on getting up in order to actually get out of bed. A failure of attention would lead one to stay in bed.

Lewin claimed that intent creates a tension system. He described intent as a "quasi-need" that creates tension until it is fulfilled. This quasi-need creates valences associated with features of the environment. For instance, a hot fudge sundae could be valenced in terms of its consummatory features (creamy ice cream with thick hot fudge) or in terms of its health implications (540 calories). These valences change to reflect perceived and desired action possibilities. Attention is the way people can override the default valences. With motivated attention, people substitute intentionally imposed valences for ordinary or dominant valences.

The information-processing perspective does not incorporate motivation with intention. Miller and his colleagues embedded behavior in a cybernetic system. The plan (action structure) a person chooses to execute is determined by the values embedded in the image (cognitive structure) of the situation. Values do not operate as valences. Executing a plan usually increases the value of the immediate situation, except when the action is part of a larger plan that is expected to end in a positive value in the long run. Thus, the choice of the plan depends on the value of the expected results.

While Miller and his colleagues did not believe motivation was necessary, they did believe that attention is a determining mechanism for intent. The currently active intent is a plan in working memory, where it can be easily attended to.

Similarly, according to other information-processing psychologists, Timothy Shallice and Donald Norman, the determining mechanism for intent is also attention. Attention helps activate relevant action structures and causes them to become the dominant plan. Except for its abandonment of motivation, this view is close to James' mechanism for intention in which one's attention is focused on the difficult idea, which causes the idea to become dominant.

If attention plays such a large role as a mechanism for intent, does the process have to be conscious? We have already noted that the alternatives need only be potentially, not necessarily consciously, available. The discussion of attention provides additional evidence for unconscious intents.

As noted earlier, intent is only one of three features (intent, awareness, and interference) that distinguish between automatic and controlled processes. Thus, intent must be able to occur without awareness or the criteria are redundant. In fact, some theorists (e.g., Miller) do allow for unconscious intent.

It is important to remember that intent has two forms.The most obvious form of intent is when one makes a hard choice, a conscious decision, by attending to a nondominant course of action, such as getting out of bed in the morning. On the other hand, making the easy choice, unconsciously or semiconsciously choosing to follow a dominant course of action, is also influenced by motivated attention. This form of intent results from a failure of motivated attention. One's attention is distracted away from the difficult but wiser idea and one engages in the dominant behavior, such as staying in bed. Both paying attention to an alternative and avoiding paying attention to an alternative result in intentional actions.

In sum, intent has been defined as occurring when people have options that are potentially available to choose among. This is the only necessary condition for intent. Intent is particularly obvious when a person makes a hard choice to follow a nondominant alternative. Finally, motivated attention appears to mediate intent by allowing the mind to concentrate on and facilitate enacting of the intended alternative.

V. APPLICATIONS

In order fully to understand the concept of intention, it is helpful to illustrate a number of its applications. Intention plays an important role in lay psychology, law, the study of attitudes, and the study of impression formation.

A. Lay Psychology

Ordinary people infer intent all the time. These lay psychologists generally agree with scientific psychologists. Lay people believe intent occurs when people choose among cognitively available alternatives. Furthermore, intent is particularly obvious to lay psychologists when the actions involve rejecting the dominant alternative. Lay perceivers also infer intent when the actor has focused attention on a particular goal. Examining naive psychologists' perspectives on intent helps describe what people view as good evidence for intent, and it points to cues for examining intent.

The ways in which ordinary people infer intent from the behavior of other people was first described by Fritz Heider. According to Heider, people cannot infer true personal causality unless intention ties together cause and effect. The intention, the goal of the action, determines the meaning of the action. The implications of an action will be quite different depending on whether the action is accidental or intentional. It is the difference, Heider illustrates, between a stone accidentally hitting someone and a stone being aimed at someone.

Heider claims ordinary perceivers first analyze whether a person "can" perform an action before they attribute intent. Having options is equivalent to this "can." It requires that a person be able to perform the action or not, and it accounts for the facilitative and inhibitory contingencies of the person's environment. When a person flinches at a hot stove, people do not infer an intentional action. The person did not intend to flinch; rather the environment, the hot stove, caused the reaction. Jones and Davis posit that as long as some desire or volition, which is not a direct result of environmental influence, comes from within the person, intent occurs. Again, intent does not need to be conscious. In sum, perceivers judge how a person's ability combines with the environment in order to decide if the person has the potential to choose among alternatives.

Given alternatives, the choice people make can be informative. Normally, people are expected to opt for the culturally desirable alternative or the alternative that is consistent with their social category or personality. When people choose the socially undesirable alternative or the alternative that is atypical for their social category or personality, they have chosen the nondominant alternative and have made the hard choice. This unexpected behavior is perceived as obviously intentional. To lay perceivers, choosing the otherwise nondominant alternative is viewed as particularly indicative of intent. However, lay psychology is inconsistent about attributing intent to people who follow the dominant alternative (i.e., make the easy choice). Hence, lay psychologists are more variable than scientific psychologists concerning people's choice of the dominant alternative, but agree that following the nondominant alternative is obviously intentional.

In order to infer that a person is intentionally performing an action, perceivers require that the actor be exerting some effort in the direction of the goal. In other words, the person must be "trying" to reach his or her goal. Heider described several different types of evidence that people may use to determine if a person is "trying." Does the person try other behaviors that would have the same effect after the initial behavior has been thwarted? Does the person give up trying once the effect is obtained? Does the person attempt several coordinated behaviors all directed at the same outcome? Each of these pieces of evidence indicates that the person is concentrating attention on the chosen alternative. This evidence may be gathered indirectly, by observing the actor's behavior or by considering the actor's character, or directly, by asking the person. Regardless of how lay psychologists gather the information, they seem to believe attention is a crucial mechanism for intent, as do scientific psychologists.

Overall, naive psychologists tend to agree with scientific psychologists on most of the features of intent. Choice among cognitively available alternatives is determined through consideration of people's abilities and their environment. Choosing a nondominant alternative is also a particularly clear indication of intent to lay psychologists. Finally, naive psychologists search for indications that people have focused attention on an alternative and are "trying" in order to infer intent.

B. Law

As well as giving meaning to everyday actions, intent gives meaning to actions in the law. For instance, *actus non facit reum, nisi mens sit rea* (an act does not render a person guilty, unless the mind is guilty). In fact, intent has many different working definitions in legal settings depending on the context, such as "premeditation" and "fraudulent intent." Many of the principles used by laypeople and some of the principles used by scientific psychologists are used in legal settings to determine perceived intent.

Having options appears to be at the center of legal treatments of intent. According to James Marshall's 1968 book, *Intention in Law and Society*, "In law, intention is assumed to involve the making of choices. . . . Freedom of will is dependent on (1) the capacity of a particular individual to choose his action and (2) the choices which he perceives to be available to him" (pp. 26–27). In order to determine a person's perceived choices, the law considers what a "reasonable person" would know and understand. Furthermore, the individual may not have actually cognitively considered all of the alternatives. The alternatives need only to have been available to a reasonable person.

Legal discussions do not address the conditions under which laypeople are most likely to perceive intent, when the actor makes the hard choice and follows the nondominant alternative. Yet, legal discussions do acknowledge that people's choices are a balance between their inner needs and their need for support from external groups. Interestingly, people who do follow group norms may not view themselves as having made a choice, but the law attributes intent to these people if a reasonable person would have been able to foresee the consequences of the action.

Legal sources concur with scientific and lay psychologists that intent is revealed by what an actor has in mind, the focus of attention. In general, the direction of attention to an alternative (malice aforethought) or away from an alternative (negligence) plays an important role in legal contexts.

In sum, legal writing focuses on having options as a defining feature of intent. However, legal writing does not differentiate making a hard choice, the most obvious instance of intent, from making an easy choice. Finally, the direction of an actor's attention determines intent in legal writing.

C. Attitudes

Intention has also played a major role in attitude research. In particular, Icek Ajzen and Martin Fishbein's theory of reasoned action and Ajzen's theory of planned behavior both posit that behavior is directly determined by people's intentions.

More specifically, behaviors are determined by intentions that directly correspond to the behaviors. For instance, in order to determine if a person is going to take the bus to the museum on Monday, the behavioral intention question should correspond directly to the behavior. In other words, the intention question should ask if the person intends to take the bus to the museum on Monday, not if the person intends to utilize public transportation in the future.

Furthermore, intentions can change over time. A measure of intention taken at some point in time prior to the observation of the behavior may differ from the intention at the time of the observation of the behavior. The longer the period of time between the measurement of intention and the measurement of behavior, the less accurate the prediction of behavior from that intention.

According to Ajzen's theory of planned behavior, intentions themselves are determined by three conceptually independent variables: perceived behavioral control, subjective norms, and attitude toward the behavior. Perceived behavioral control refers to the perceived ease or difficulty of performing the behavior in question. Perceiving one has behavioral control leads to perceiving one has options from which to choose. If a person has control over a behavior, he or she can choose among a number of different courses of action. However, if a person does not have control over a behavior, then no options exist. In this sense, having perceived behavioral control equals having options. Interestingly, research has shown that as perceived behavior control increases, an individual's intention to perform a behavior becomes stronger.

Subjective norms refer to the social pressure that either promotes or inhibits the performance of the behavior. These norms will influence which of the potentially available alternatives a person chooses. Research has demonstrated that when subjective norms promote the performance of a behavior, people are more likely to intend to perform that behavior. On the other hand, if norms inhibit the performance of a behavior, people are less likely to intend to perform that behavior and should be more likely to intend to perform an alternative behavior.

Finally, the attitude toward the behavior refers to the degree to which a person favorably or unfavorably evaluates the behavior. Favorable evaluations are most likely accompanied by increased attention to behavior. Research has indicated that as attitudes become more favorable, intentions to perform the behavior become stronger.

Attitude researchers have been successful predicting people's behavior from their intentions. In addition, they have found that intentions are influenced by perceived behavioral control, subjective norms, and attitude toward the behavior. As described, perceived behavior control leads to options, subjective norms influence people's choice making, and favorable attitudes probably increase attention.

D. Impression Formation

Intention also plays an important role in impression formation and stereotyping. Social perceivers are no longer considered cognitive misers who are mainly concerned with conserving mental resources. In a recent *Annual Review of Psychology* article, "Social Cognition and Social Perception," Fiske pointed out that perceivers now seem to be viewed as motivated tacticians: people who use current goals to choose among a number of possible strategies. In general, recent research in social perception has indicated that some motivations make people more concerned with accuracy, whereas other motivations prompt fast decisions. Inherent in this description of social perceivers is, first, the availability of options (from accuracy to stereotyping and intermediate combinations thereof) and, second, the necessity to choose among these options. Furthermore, in order to process the social information, the perceiver must then devote attention to the chosen processes. [*See* IMPRESSION FORMATION; PREJUDICE AND STEREOTYPES; SOCIAL COGNITION.]

However, prior to the use of these intentional processes, more unconscious and automatic processes of impression formation are engaged. In recent years, these automatic processes have been investigated by researchers. John Bargh has shown that environmental cues can trigger preconscious processes that are dominated by expectancies. Patricia Devine has shown that physical cues (e.g., age, race, and gender) prompt preconscious activation of social stereotypes. While these initial automatic, category-based responses are unintentional, the processes that follow them are intentional. The social perceiver decides whether to use the category-based processing or to use additional accuracy-oriented, attention-demanding, controlled processes.

A good deal of research has investigated motives that drive accuracy-oriented processing. As described, after the initial and unintentional activation of stereotypes, options are available to perceivers. Those who are motivated to do so choose the slower, potentially more accurate processes. These processes are much more conscious than the category-based processes, and perceivers can report using them.

A number of factors can motivate the use of these more accurate processes. Steven Neuberg has shown that having an experimenter simply ask people to be as accurate as possible drives them to gather more information and form more data-driven impressions. Research by Phillip Tetlock has indicated that when people are held accountable and are under pressure to justify their impressions to others, they use a wider range of information and expend more effort. Finally, Fiske and her colleagues have shown that outcome dependency, relying on another person for a desired end (as in teamwork, one-on-one competition, or subordinate status), motivates people to attend to information inconsistent with an initial category and make dispositional inferences about it. In each of the examples presented, the perceiver is somewhat dependent on others and, therefore, has been deprived of some control. This control deprivation motivates social perceivers to process carefully all kinds of information and form more accurate impressions of others.

Overall, perceivers' use of accuracy-oriented processes may seem more intentional than their use of category-oriented processes. Accuracy-oriented processes are the less automatic, nondominant alternative. However, as illustrated above, staying with or failing to go beyond initial automatic processes can also be intentional.

VI. SUMMARY

Intention is a mental state that is attributed to a person when that person has options, chooses to follow one of the alternatives, and concentrates attention on the chosen alternative. Intention is particularly obvious when a person makes a hard choice and decides to follow a nondominant alternative. Lay psychologists attribute intention to social actors on a daily basis. Intention is also an essential part of many legal concepts (e.g., malice aforethought and negligence). Furthermore, research on the attitude–behavior link has indicated that intentions directly affect people's behavior. Finally, intentions drive the processes people use to perceive one another in social interactions.

Bibliography

Eagly, A. H., and Chaiken, S. (1993). The impact of attitudes on behavior. In "The Psychology of Attitudes" (A. H. Eagly and S. Chaiken, Eds.). Harcourt Brace Jovanovich, Fort Worth, TX.

Fiske, S. T. (1989). Examining the role of intent: Toward understanding its role in stereotyping and prejudice. In "Unintended Thought" (J. Uleman and J. Bargh, Eds.). Guilford, New York.

Fiske, S. T. (1993). Social cognition and social perception. In "Annual Review of Psychology." (M. R. Rosenzweig and L. W. Porter, Eds.), Vol. 44. Annual Reviews, Palo Alto, CA.

Uleman, J., and Bargh, J. (Eds.) (1989). "Unintended Thought." Guilford, New York.

Interpersonal Attraction and Personal Relationships

Steve Duck
University of Iowa

Glossary

Attachment The style of approach to relationships that is possibly learned in infancy and which might then affect later adult relationships.

Attraction The initial positive response to another person that indicates a willingness to approach.

Provisions of relationships The resources that are provided by a relationship in terms of psychological and communicative benefits derived from it.

INTERPERSONAL ATTRACTION refers to the degree of liking or attraction felt toward another person by a particular subject and is essentially an individual response to another target person. Attraction may be influenced in form by cultural factors (for example, some cultures find slimness attractive where others find plumpness attractive). By and large, however, the research on interpersonal attraction has focused on the psychological and judgmental responses of one person to another and thus took a one-sided view of the processes of relating.

Personal relationships, by contrast, are long-term, socially structured, organized, and relatively enduring interpersonal phenomena that are founded in each person's liking for the other but are much more than that. Personal relationships involve mutual recognition and mutual influence in ways not necessarily true of feelings of interpersonal attraction. They are also both a reflection of a culture's influences and a reflection of the fact that the individuals in them can create a form of relationship that suits them personally. Thus, two partners may marry (cultural form) but conduct that marriage in a way that contains a number of unique elements and practices.

Historically the field of research into personal relationships was greatly influenced by the field of research in interpersonal attraction and many leaders in the relationships field were also prominent in the field of attraction. However, the linkages are gradually being severed as researchers have become less and less satisfied with the idea that attraction "causes" relationships. Also increasingly rejected is the idea that any form of relationship can be determined by the activities or preferences of one person (as is implicit in the notion that one person's attraction to another is the cause of relationships). Finally the recent emphasis in the personal relationships field on the communicative activity that connects the members of a partnership has caused a move away from an approach to attraction that essentially presumed that (success in) relationships could be predicted on the basis of knowledge of the characteristics of the two partners before they even meet. This latter idea is a favorite of the dating agencies which measure similarities between two people who have not met and then pretend to be able to predict relationship success from there, but it is increasingly regarded as an unsafe and unsatisfactory notion by researchers in relationships.

Encyclopedia of Human Behavior, Volume 2

Copyright © 1994 by Academic Press, Inc. All rights of reproduction in any form reserved.

I. THE STUDY OF ATTRACTION

All relationships have to start somewhere, and all personal relationships between two people of necessity begin as the interactions between two people who do not know each other. Since the relationships that are of interest in most research are voluntary ones, researchers naturally begin by asking themselves how people are drawn into the desire for voluntary interdependence with another person. The first answers were in terms of the features of another person that are attractive and very early work, in the 1920s, attempted to define those physical features and behaviors which were generally regarded as "attractive." This work has a line of continuation in research seeking to explain preferences for certain shapes of silhouettes or physiques but it has been shown that, while ideal types of physique can be specified, the determinants of reactions to such physical characteristics are soundly psychological. Not only do observers review physical characteristics in systematically different ways as a function of personality, but physical attractiveness itself is very often translated into a psychological attractiveness through a belief that "what is beautiful is good." Thus, physically attractive persons have been found to be rated as more intelligent, more interesting, and more socially successful than unattractive persons.

Most psychological work on attraction in general naturally focused on the attractiveness of psychological characteristics rather than physical ones alone. Some of this work focused on the sorts of psychological styles that were universally attractive (for example, extraverts are preferred to introverts), but much of it dealt with the specific psychological similarities between a person and a target other, especially attitudinal similarities, personality complementarity, and role matching. Role matching involves two persons having ideas or "models" about the appropriateness of behaviors in the relationship that have a good fit with one another (for example, when a husband sees the role of a Husband involving the same sorts of behaviors that the wife see a Husband's role as involving). Personality complementarity refers to the match of the general styles of behavior, not just of relational roles. For example if one partner is dominant and the other is submissive then they are complementary in personality style.

On the whole, studies into these latter two possibilities have been unconvincing and it now appears that although the basic ideas are perhaps sound, they deal with too small a piece of the puzzle for their effects not to get swamped in the hurly burly of real life affection-making.

II. ATTITUDINAL SIMILARITY AND ATTRACTION

The idea that attitudinal similarity would cause attraction had many proponents, and many researchers were excited by Ted Newcomb's finding in the early 1950s that persons who lived in the same student house for an extended period of time tended to get on better if they were similar in attitudes and values. The importance of this finding was tempered by the realization that it did not tell us which element caused which (did similarity cause attraction or did attraction cause similarity?). The most important contributor to this issue was therefore Donn Byrne, who developed and enhanced an existing procedure for assessing the influence of attitude similarity upon attraction and thus dealt with the difficult problem of the direction of causality. His approach became known as the Bogus Stranger Paradigm and involved a person filling out an attitude scale and then, after a suitable time interval, being given a scale "from another person, a stranger, in the same study." In fact the second scale had been arranged by Byrne to correspond to a given extent to the subject's own scale responses and the other person did not really exist (hence the name "bogus stranger paradigm"). By arranging for different degrees of correspondence between the subject's own responses and those of the bogus stranger, Byrne was able to conduct a precise test of the effects of certain amounts of similarity of attitudes upon the resulting degree of attraction expressed by the subject toward the stranger.

This approach attracted some ferocious criticism on the basis that it was artificial and overlooked the effects of communication upon the normal conduct of attraction to others. While some of this criticism is certainly misplaced, the paradigm does not adequately represent some of the important processes that do take place in normal relationships, even if it might tell us something about the effects of other processes.

Dissatisfactions with the Bogus Stranger Paradigm created conditions favorable for another approach to be developed and in 1979, Robert Hinde, a distinguished ethologist, proposed that the techniques of ethology could be applied to the study of relationships. He argued that researchers should set out to describe real life behaviors of relating and to tie them to what was known about the nexus of relationships to which persons belonged, especially as they developed over time and over the lifespan. A major contribution of this claim was its insistence on seeing the *behavior* of relating as important and as embedded in a nexus of other influences, one of which was personality and another of which was the effects of society and the range of other relationships to which a person belonged.

III. THE PROVISIONS OF RELATIONSHIPS

Another line of work explored the reasons why people might want, need, or seek relationships with other people in the first place and Robert Weiss proposed that there are seven "provisions" of relationships, that is to say, seven different resources that are provided by relationships and which people find attractive for themselves. These provisions were as follows: (1) *Belonging and a sense of reliable alliance,* that is to say a sense of membership, acceptance, and availability of others to whom one can turn in times of emergency. (2) *Emotional integration and stability,* that is to say a sounding board for our opinions and emotional responses against which we can assess the appropriateness of our own reactions to events and experiences in the world. (3) *Opportunities for communication about ourselves,* that is to say a chance to express our own opinions and values and to "ventilate" about matters that concern us. (4) *Provision of assistance and physical support,* that is to say, relationships offer us social support or help with activities that are too laborious or difficult to be performed alone. (5) *Reassurance of worth and value,* that is to say, evidence that someone cares about and values us for "who we are." (6) *Opportunity to help others,* that is to say, relationships offer people the chance to feel good by doing good to others. (7) *Personality support,* that is to say, relationships offer validation and support for our ways of doing things and our ways of construing and understanding experience: individuals tend to select others who have similar outlooks and which therefore support one another.

Recently researchers have been concerned to discover how a person's approaches to relationships as an adult reflect not only the need for these provisions but also prior experience (usually prior experience in childhood) and the structure of a person's style of personality.

IV. MENTAL MODELS OF RELATIONSHIPS: CHILDHOOD EXPERIENCE AND ADULTHOOD

Since John Bowlby's classic suggestion that maternal deprivation in infancy causes social delinquency in adolescence, developmental psychologists have shown great interest in the parent–child relationship as a seed-bed for later relational predilections. Mary Ainsworth and her colleagues successfully demonstrated the existence of three styles of attachment of a parent (secure, anxious/avoidant, and ambivalent). A *secure* style, where the child feels entirely comfortable in relationships, is apparently derived from a parental sytle where caregiving is readily and freely available to the child and the parent is available, attentive, and responsive to the child's needs. An *anxious/ambivalent* style, where the child is insecure and finds it hard to trust others, is apparently derived from a parental style that is anxious, fussy, out of step with the infant's needs, and so is responsive to the child's needs only unreliably. An *avoidant* style, where the child tends to be active in avoiding relationships, is apparently derived from a parental style that is unresponsive, rejecting, or inattentive.

Some researchers began to speculate that adult romantic attachments would show a similar pattern and might actually be based on infant experience. Cindy Hazan, Phillip Shaver, and their colleagues showed that the three patterns were indeed present in adults as assessed in a variety of situations and by a variety of methods. Large amounts of work have followed. It must be said that virtually none of it conclusively demonstrates continuity between childhood experience and adult preferences, though there is plenty of evidence for parallelism between reports of childhood styles of experience and later adult reports of relational experience. However, the arguments set the stage for consideration of the fact that a person's own styles, backgrounds, and preferences influence and modify the form of relationships in which the people end up, irrespective of general human needs for certain kinds of provisions from relationships.

V. STRATEGIES IN DEVELOPING AND MAINTAINING RELATIONSHIPS

If relationships are not simply caused by the individual characteristics of persons entering them, then they may be affected by the specific behaviors of the participants in particular occasions. Some researchers, especially communication scholars, have asked themselves the broader question of what strategies people use in order to maintain and develop their relationships. William Douglas has explored the ways in which, at the start of relationships, people make tests of one another's interest, for example by asking a particularly difficult favor or by allowing the conversation to lapse in order to see whether the other person is interested enough to pick it up. These tests are direct and calculated ways to establish the other person's interest in continuing a relationship and are strategic actions that are independent of any personal characteristics of the other person.

Leslie Baxter also examined the ways in which people make tests of the commitment of a partner even at the later stages of relating. She found that there were some interesting methods used, most of them to do with the creation of a jealous response in the partner, the extent of which could be used to gauge the partner's interest in the relationship. Another test involved the implicit recognition of the relationship by others (e.g., if a person were invited to visit the inviter's parents and accepted that invitation, then the implication is that the person does not mind that other people know that the relationship exists and characterize it somehow).

Kathryn Dindia and Leslie Baxter also looked at the strategies that partners use to maintain their relationships once they have been formed. The frequent strategies covered in a very large range of options, including general strategies involving openness and honesty or the sharing of feelings, or optimism and being cheerful around one another to help them to feel better. Other strategies included such things as ceremonies (e.g., commemorating the origin of the relationship by special dates or reminiscing about it in ways that celebrated the relationship and special occasions within it), or minor pieces of routine behavior (such as a lunchtime phone call to check the way in which the partner's day was progressing). Another strategy was to ensure that a certain period of time was set aside each week for the partners to be alone together and do whatever they liked, uninterrupted.

It is therefore clear that relationships are often the result of careful management just as much as they may be affected by chance, but are by no means simply created from the matching of attributes of the people entering them. Although this picture is richer than the first researchers into attraction reported, it is not complete until it takes full account of the role of outsiders and of the talk that takes place between people in the everyday interactions of relating.

VI. THE ROLE OF OUTSIDERS IN RELATIONSHIP ACTIVITY

Influences of outsiders on relationships have also been explored. Many younger people meet or become involved with their dating partners through mutual friends or as the result of being members of the same group of friends, for example. However the opportunities provided by go-betweens or mutual acquaintances are not the only influence of outsiders. In some teenage gangs, members are implicitly forbidden to date members of other gangs, and most people are keen to have the approval of their parents for possible marriage partners.

As relationships with a particular partner become more intense and involved, the partners withdraw from their own networks of personal friends in order to spend more time with one another, and the management or juggling of all their relationships as a whole—and the time that they take to conduct—can present quite important difficulties and constraints for the partners. For example, it is a common finding that romantic partners spend almost a third as much time alone with other friends after marriage as they do before marriage. It nevertheless remains true that the inception of a close romantic relationship has consequences on other relationships in which the persons are involved and the management of those issues is likely to have psychological and social consequences. Once again, the issues involved in creating relationships are not reducible to the simple actions of the partners themselves but must be seen in the context of other forces and constraints in life.

VII. ORGANIZATION OF ROLES AND TIME MANAGEMENT

Relationships do not occur in the vacuum that early work on attraction tended to imply. In real life everyday working relationships the partners have various roles and duties to perform, chores to complete, and tasks to undertake, In a relationship such as a marriage there are issues concerning "who does what" and these have to be managed and negotiated between the partners. [This is different from (and not covered by) the discussion of roles above, since the matching of roles implies the matching of ideas about behavior, whereas the present discussion is concerned with the actual behaviors themselves and how the partners feel about them.] Such negotiation and discussions have an impact on the ways in which the relationship itself is experienced by the partners and it affects the development of the relationship.

In a set of studies designed to look at the ways in which partners create a working relationship as their commitment to and emotional involvement with each other increases, Ted Huston and his colleagues have found that there are essentially four pathways by which people move from first meeting to committed relationship and that these pathways are intricately connected with the ways in which the partners distribute their leisure and chore times. In the *accelerated–arrested* track, partners experience a fairly whirlwind type of romance and rapidly fall in love. They quickly develop plans to marry (though they may actually delay the marriage for some long time after they have decided that it will occur). Such couples develop useful strategies for reorganizing their separate lives into one and devolve their duties and chores during the period when they are waiting to marry. By the time that they come to get married the organization of their relational duties is fairly well worked out. The *accelerated* track is characterized by rapid involvement, rapid decision to marry, and rapid execution of the plan (usually all within some 10 months of meeting). These couples tend to devote a little less attention to the working out of the relationship organization and to the creation of complementary roles for the husband and wife. The *intermediate* track is, as the name implies, a relatively slower and less dramatic style of relationship growth that is typically much steadier in many ways than other types. The partners here tend to be the least involved emotionally and to do fewer things as a couple than do people on other relational tracks. They also spend more time alone than with partners or with others. The *prolonged* track is characterized not only by much slower progress toward marriage but also by greater turbulence and greater independence. The partners reported doing fewer leisure activities with each other than the other couples reported.

Related work by Scott Christopher and Rodney Cate has applied the same sorts of analyses to the sexual involvements of teenagers and found that there are also commonly different tracks taken from first meeting to deep sexual involvement. Some couples move from first date to first intercourse within a matter of hours while others do not engage in much sexual activity at all until the relationship is well established. In all these cases there is the possibility of attitudinal and value systems interacting with each other to produce the reported effects, but in any case the studies suggest strongly that the creation of a relationship involves a very large component of the (re)organization of the daily lives of the partners, whether at the level of routine duties or pleasurable restful and relaxing activities.

Thus, relationships are influenced by and in turn influence the ways in which people organize their lives; they are not simply pleasant emotional additives to the partners' lives.

VIII. THE ROLE OF DAILY LIFE AND EVERYDAY TALK

A late addition to the research on relationships has been the recent focus on the conduct of everyday talk. Given that relationships are not merely emotional creations but are also social organizations and role managers, or products of strategic behavior, it is clear that the partners need to conduct their negotiations somehow and that talk is the natural medium for doing this. Second, it is also the case that people just do spend a lot of every day talking to one another and that talk to friends and partners is probably one of the biggest slices out of the total talk that people produce in a day. Third, talk is a means by which attitudes and values are expressed and also a way in which instrumental tasks (like obtaining favors or asking someone out on a date) are accomplished. Talk can also be a very considerable signal of the strength and involvement of a relationship, often being an indicator of the feelings that people have for one another. This happens not only in the obvious ways in which people address explicit emotional messages to one another ("I love you"), but also as a result of some of the other actions that have already been discussed here. For instance, as couples organize the roles and behaviors and duties in their relationship so they also organize the language. Several studies have shown that intimate couples develop private languages or "personal idioms" that enshrine the two partners' nicknames for other people, shorthand terms for parts of the body or sexual activities, and generally playful ways of communicating affection, request, or desires. The extent of development of such personal idioms is a useful measure of the intimacy of a relationship.

The functions of language in the conduct of relationships have been classed as *instrumental* (as above), *indexical* (or indicative of the emotional tone of a relationship), or *essential,* by Steve Duck and Kris Pond. The "essential" role of language is to embody the relationship and make it happen. In a series of studies it was shown that relationship partners report that their most frequent daily conversations with partners had no really important content to them, but were nevertheless relationally important. The very fact that the conversation happened was important to the life of the relationship. This is part of what is meant by the essential function of talk in relationships.

Such work also analyses the role of talk as a presenter of ideas and values to others, such that it presents opportunities to test out the values and attitudes that the other person exposes and test them for validity or for similarity to one's own. The focus on talk thus creates the chance for partners to compare some of the items that have been discussed above, in the conduct of everyday life. However, it goes further than this and proposes that talk is a rhetorical act and serves not only to present ideas but also to persuade others to accept them. It does not necessarily do this in the obvious sense that partners may seek to influence one another directly, but it also does it by presenting "rhetorical visions" (i.e., persuasive images or representations of the world) that the other person may simply adopt or accept without being the subject of strong direct influence. In short, by presenting and exposing the speaker's attitudes to the world, or his or her system of meaning, the conversations of everyday life can create opportunities for others to share the representations that are offered there and to find them relationally persuasive. From such everyday conversations can relationships, liking, and many of the other forceful factors described above be initiated.

Bibliography

Brehm, S. (1992). "Intimate Relationships," 2nd ed. McGraw-Hill, Boston.

Duck, S. W. (1988). "Relating to Others." Brooks/Cole, Monterey, CA.

Duck, S. W. (1991). "Friends, for Life," 2nd ed. Harvester Press, Hemel Hempstead, UK.

Duck, S. W. (in press) "Meaningful Relationships: Talking, Sense and Relating." Sage, Newbury Park, CA.

Hendrick, C., and Hendrick, S. S. (1991). "Liking, Loving and Relating," 2nd ed. Brooks/Cole, Monterey, CA.

O'Connor, P. (1992). "Friendships between Women." Guilford, New York.

Interpersonal Communication

John H. Fleming and Mark Attridge
University of Minnesota

Glossary

Channel The medium used to send a message (voice, gesture, face-to-face, telephone, letter, etc.).

Feedback Information conveyed to the sender by the receiver about the clarity of a message.

Immediacy Nonverbal signals that communicate a person's positive attitude toward another person.

Leakage Nonverbal behaviors that convey (or betray) underlying emotions or intentions that a communicator may be trying to conceal.

Message The content or information to be communicated.

Nonlinguistic behaviors Nonverbal behaviors such as facial expressions, many gestures, and other bodily movements that may co-occur with, but are not linked to, speech.

Nonverbal communication Communicative behavior that takes place through channels other than the verbal channel; includes facial expressions, eye contact, voice quality, bodily posture, position and movement, physical distance, touch, gestures, and appearance. Nonverbal behaviors may be further classified into categories such as signs versus signals, and paralinguistic versus nonlinguistic behaviors.

Overhearer A person for whom a message is not necessarily intended, but who may nonetheless be in a position to receive the message; also referred to as an *eavesdropper*.

Paralinguistic behaviors Nonverbal behaviors such as intonation patterns and some gestures that go along with, and are linked to, speech.

Receiver The person for whom a message is intended. Alternative terms are *decoder, listener, addressee, hearer,* and *message recipient.* These terms differ in the degree to which they imply that the message was necessarily intended for that person.

Sender The person who creates a message and initiates communication. Alternative terms are *speaker, message initiator,* and *encoder.*

Signals Nonverbal behaviors that communicate intentionally (e.g., nodding in agreement).

Signs Nonverbal behaviors that communicate inadvertantly or unintentionally (e.g., blushing from embarrassment). Although some behaviors may qualify as both signals and signs under different circumstances, they differ substantially in terms of the frequencies with which they are used in each of these two ways.

INTERPERSONAL COMMUNICATION encompasses a broad spectrum of behavior, and a wide range of psychological phenomena. Consequently, a concise definition of interpersonal communication is elusive. In essence, the psychology of interpersonal communication concerns the collective processes through which individuals convey information and meaning about themselves, others, and the social world to the various others that make up their social environments, thereby exerting influence over those others. Interpersonal communication is more than verbal behavior and language; it also encompasses nonverbal behavior and a host of other cognitive and motivational processes. Interpersonal communication is more than the transmission of information; it also concerns the negotiation of social reality, the maintenance of social relationships,

Copyright © 1994 by Academic Press, Inc. All rights of reproduction in any form reserved.

and the construction of personal identities and public roles. Consequently, a comprehensive treatment must consider the ways in which communication is used to construct and modify social relationships. Interpersonal communication is the ultimate intersection of the cognitive world and the social world. Social psychology has much to say about interpersonal communication, and it is this body of work that we explore in this article.

I. BASIC APPROACHES TO INTERPERSONAL COMMUNICATION

Imagine for a moment that your social world consisted of an entirely predictable and uniform environment, and a collection of completely trusting, trustworthy, and rational individuals whose motives were never concealed or ulterior, whose meanings and intentions were always unambiguous, and who were unencumbered by concerns about juggling potentially conflicting roles and numerous potential audiences. Imagine, too, that everyone in this world always saw and interpreted everything in the same ways. Sound somewhat strange? If the real world were so ordered, interpersonal communication could not only proceed in a relatively direct and uncomplicated way, but it could also be described and explained on the basis of a relatively small set of rules and maxims. Clearly, however, the real world bears little resemblance to this imaginary place. Everyday interpersonal communication is complicated by a host of factors: People are neither always trustworthy nor trusting; they sometimes deceive and possess ulterior motivations. Human perception and information processing (cognition) are imperfect and not always rational. Situational and contextual factors exert significant influences on the ways in which people interpret other people's actions and the events that surround them. People have needs, motives, plans, and goals. Sometimes these conflict. Finally, people occasionally need help defining situations and self-identities. Frequently they must negotiate sometimes conflicting interpretations of relationships, settings, and behaviors. All of these factors complicate the process of interpersonal communication.

In setting out to describe interpersonal communication, however, many researchers begin by describing how communication should proceed if it were largely organized, rational, and uncomplicated by complex social considerations. These formulations are useful, if not entirely accurate or adequate, stepping stones to more comprehensive treatments and they provide a necessary foundation for understanding the fundamental elements of interpersonal communication. We will treat them briefly in the sections that follow.

A. Basic Information Model (SMCR)

Initially developed by researchers at Bell Laboratories to understand and improve the transmission of information over the telephone, the most general approach to understanding interpersonal communication specifies the elements needed to produce and exchange information. The first element in this model is the *sender*, or the person who wants to communicate with someone else. The sender is also sometimes referred to as the *speaker*, *message initiator*, or *message encoder*. The second element is the *message*, or what it is that the sender wants to communicate. The message must then be sent via a communication *channel*, such as talking over the telephone, speaking in person, writing a letter, using touch or nonverbal gestures, or some combination of these and other channels. The person for whom the message is intended is called the *receiver*. The receiver is also sometimes referred to as the *decoder*, *listener*, *addressee*, *hearer*, or *message recipient*. These terms differ in the degree to which they imply that a particular message was necessarily intended for that person. A person who is not intended to receive a message, but may be in a position to do so is also sometimes called an *overhearer* or an *eavesdropper*. These elements form the Sender-Message-Channel-Receiver (SMCR) model. Although some simple varieties of communication follow this one-way transmission of information from sender to receiver, most communication is bidirectional. People are often simultaneously senders and receivers of multiple messages. The responses that the sender gets from the receiver are collectively called *feedback* and can help the sender to know if the message was received correctly, or if the message must be sent again. An additional and important element in the model is the physical and social environment in which the communication takes place. Noise and other forces that may interfere with or obstruct the communication process are important but often-overlooked features of the environment. Further, both senders and receivers have their own personal characteristics, motivations, and experiences that influence their communication behavior. Although the SMCR model breaks communication into discrete elements, the actual process of communication involves an interplay of the basic elements with each one affecting the others to varying degrees.

Also important is the issue of the intent of the speaker in communicative exchanges. Just as there are messages a speaker intends to send to someone, there are other messages that the speaker does not intend to communicate. For example, a speaker may not wish to communicate (and must therefore conceal) the fact that he or she is nervous about an upcoming speech. Should the speaker's nervousness be communicated, however, it would be done inadvertently or unintentionally. Under slightly different circumstances, consider a man who, while describing how far he has to drive each day for work, mentions that he drives a Mercedes automobile. The intended message focuses on the requirements of his job, yet an unintended message about his social and economic status may be received by the co-worker listening to him.

B. Symbolic Interactionism

In contrast to the basic information approach which focuses on factors that affect how messages are transmitted and received, the symbolic interactionist (SI) approach to communication emphasizes the ways in which information is interpreted. Grounded in sociological theory and the ideas of George Herbert Mead and Erving Goffman, the SI approach considers the meaning of messages to be constructed from the social context and interaction processes in which they are generated. The SI approach contends that it is the symbolic nature of communication that allows for meaning to be negotiated between the individuals involved in the communication, and thus communication evolves to suit the changing needs of the social environment. Further, the purpose of communication is not simply the exchange of information, but the vehicle through which the identity of individuals is created, negotiated, and managed. The messages that people send to one another and how they are interpreted serve to validate (or invalidate) the self-identities of those involved in the communication.

Much of the work on the SI approach to communication grows out of the seminal work of Erving Goffman. Goffman conceptualized human interaction from a *dramaturgical perspective*—he applied a theatrical metaphor to describe how people present themselves to one another. According to Goffman, people are "actors" enacting "roles" for the various "audiences" with whom they come into contact. Actors have a wide variety of resources at their disposal for successful self-presentation. They can exploit areas of the "stage"—front-stage, backstage, behind the scenes, in the wings—to manage their "performances." They can also take advantage of "props" and "costumes" while interacting. Goffman's use of the theatrical metaphor has provided a powerful and wonderfully descriptive way to articulate the complexity of human interaction.

C. Rules Theory and Coordinated Management of Meaning (CMM)

Using the study of language as its basis, the rules theory approach to communication explores the patterns and conditions that guide the production and interpretation of messages. It is proposed that much of communication is governed by rules and that the uncovering and explication of rules allows for both understanding and improving communication. Rules prescribe how people should behave in specific contexts. As rules suggest a course of action but do not determine action, rules can be broken. The consequences of not following a rule are important because they dictate the degree of compliance with the rule; the greater the consequences the greater the compliance. Knowledge of communication rules, and of the consequences of rule noncompliance, is often implicit and assumed to develop from prior instruction and interaction with others. The value of the rules approach is that knowledge of the social world is used as a guide for enacting smooth interactions with others. Given that rules are often applicable only to specific contexts, if communicators properly recognize the context in which they find themselves, they should also know the rules for that context, thus allowing them to communicate effectively. Rules thus remove ambiguity about how to communicate.

Combining the SI and rules theory approaches, the coordinated management of meaning (CMM) approach defines communication as a process in which each person interprets and responds to the acts of another, monitors the sequence, and compares it to his or her desires and expectations. CMM assumes that people are motivated to express themselves in a manner that best allows others to accurately determine their intended meaning. If one receives feedback that his or her message is not being interpreted as it was intended, then he or she should attempt to figure out why and engage in efforts to correct the problem. Such efforts can take the form of message restatements or examination of the interpretive rules appropriate to the social context.

D. Social–Cognitive Perspective

Communication is necessarily a social enterprise. The social–cognitive perspective adds to our understanding of communication through its emphasis on the motives and goals that communicators bring to the communication situation, as well as on the cognitive processes and biases that affect the interpersonal communication endeavor. These processes and biases include people's information processing, attentional, and memorial limitations, inferential shortcuts (or heuristics) that they may use, and the effects of context and other situational variables. The social–cognitive perspective (which has effectively subsumed the Rules and CMM approaches) also takes into account individuals' awareness of and abilities to use and manipulate communication knowledge and rules to form strategies of interpersonal influence. [*See* SOCIAL COGNITION.]

Some researchers have argued that communication is the major way through which social–cognitive processes manifest themselves in everyday life. Consequently, the social–cognitive approach to communication, while incorporating aspects of all of the other major approaches to understanding interpersonal communication, represents a fertile (if not the ultimate) intersection of things cognitive and things social.

In the sections that follow we will describe some of the social–psychological and social–cognitive research and theory that bear directly on interpersonal communication. We begin with a treatment of direct or straightforward communication issues. We then discuss issues related to the more complex arena of nonstraightforward communication, in which the full spectrum of human communication abilities manifest themselves. Finally, we conclude with separate discussions of nonverbal communication, individual differences in communication, and communication in marriage.

II. UNDERSTANDING STRAIGHTFORWARD COMMUNICATION

Although interpersonal communication can be quite complex, it isn't always so. There are times when communication is direct and relatively uncomplicated. At other times communication is indirect, extremely complex, and less than completely straightforward. Rather than arbitrarily labeling communications as either straightforward or nonstraightforward (thus creating an artificial dichotomy), it might be useful to think of communication episodes as falling along a continuum from completely straightforward to completely nonstraightforward. Clearly, most communications fall somewhere between these two extremes. Nonetheless, as a useful organizational tool and to simplify this discussion, we will examine the straightforward and nonstraightforward aspects of communication separately. Keep in mind, however, that this distinction is an arbitrary one. Real-world communications probably contain elements of both and vary along a continuum of "straightforwardness." Some important work has been done to identify the conditions under which communication will proceed in a straightforward manner, and to describe how it ought to proceed. A large proportion of communicative behavior occurs verbally through the use of language. A treatment of psycholinguistics and the psychology of language use is beyond the scope of this article, but interested readers can delve further into this area in one of the books or chapters on the topic cited in the bibliography.

A. Gricean Conversational Maxims

The linguist Grice assumed that the nature of speech is rational and efficient. He proposed that conversation is guided by a general principle of cooperation and the four maxims of quality, quantity, manner, and relevance. The cooperative principle suggests that communicators should make their conversational contributions as is required, when it is needed, and in accordance with the accepted purpose of the conversation. Further, the contribution should be truthful, using only as much information as is needed for the purpose of the exchange, and presented in a clear, brief, and direct manner. All remarks should be relevant to the conversation in which one is participating. There is also the additional concern for politeness that explains the frequent use of indirect statements, this maxim stating that interactants should avoid engaging in acts that threaten the self-esteem and social identities of others in the communication exchange.

Thus, interpersonal exchanges are thought to have a basic foundation of unstated guidelines that promote effective communication in conventional contexts. Failure to follow the conversational guidelines may result in misunderstandings about the intentions of the speaker. For example, to talk at great length about a point that is rather simple, may suggest that the speaker feels his or her audience lacks the ability to easily understand the message (e.g., "talking down" to someone).

B. Axioms of Interpersonal Communication

In the classic book *Pragmatics of Human Communication,* five "truths" about interpersonal communication are described. The first axion is that in an interpersonal setting it is impossible not to communicate. One cannot *not* communicate, as both activity and inactivity have message value and influence the behavior of others. Second, every communication can be understood both at a content level and at a relationship level. At the content level, the message concerns the particular information that is being communicated, but at the relationship level the message can define the nature of the interpersonal relationship between the sender and receiver. For example, the communication relationship can be pleasant or unpleasant, personal or impersonal, leisurely or hurried, and so on. Third, the nature of a relationship is contingent on the interpretation of and memory for the communication exchanges between the communicators. This concerns the identification and "chunking" of specific statements and expressions into larger and more meaningful units. A statement from one person can be viewed both as a response to a previous statement made by the other communicator and as a new action made independently of the other person's prior actions. Differences in interpreting the cause-and-effect sequencing of communication events is inherently problematic when both people are simultaneously senders and receivers of messages. Thus, in a distressed marital couple, the husband may claim "I withdraw because you nag" and the wife may claim "I nag because you withdraw." A fourth axiom is that humans communicate both digitally and analogically. Digital codes are recognized by their arbitrary assigned meaning and their discrete (on–off) usage. The words and sounds of language are good examples of digital codes. For example, the word c-a-t is regarded as meaning a four legged, furry, small animal and the use of c-a-t is reserved only for referring to such. Words are not always good examples of digital codes, though, as the social context can influence how words are interpreted (for example, c-a-t can be interpreted in some circumstances as slang for a person). In contrast, analogic communication codes are not arbitrary and can varying in their appropriateness of application. Most nonverbal expressions are analogic. For example, the meaning of a facial expression of fear is intrinsic—it is part of the experience of fear—and it can vary in intensity of expression. Digital and analogic codes are often used together, with words (digital) conveying the content level of a message and the manner in which the words are spoken (analogic) conveying the relationship level of the message. Lastly, communication exchanges between people will be of either a symmetrical or a complimentary pattern. When two interactants behave similarly, they have a symmetrical relationship. However, when the differences in the interactants' behavior are emphasized, they have a complimentary relationship. For example, when a novice asks a question and an expert provides an answer to the question, it is a complimentary exchange. These axioms of interpersonal communication offer a framework for analyzing the nature of straightforward communication. To make sense of even a brief exchange between two people requires an understanding and mutual acceptance and enactment of basic communication axioms.

C. Sources of Miscommunication and Misunderstanding in Straightforward Communication

The potential sources of miscommunication are many, primarily because immediate and specific feedback are not always provided to communicators by the recipients of their messages. To make matters worse, miscommunications often go undetected. First, in creating a message the sender can fail to take into consideration the personal attributes of the receiver that will affect how the receiver will interpret the message. He or she can make invalid assumptions about the extent of the receiver's knowledge relevant to the communication; these assumptions may render the communication either redundant or uninterpretable. Similarly, the sender can encode the message in language that the receiver does not know (e.g., unfamiliar words, jargon, slang expressions). Second, the choice of the channel used to send the message can be inappropriate or misinterpreted (e.g., a face-to-face visit is too personal, a written letter is too formal, etc.). Next, the physical or social environment also may interfere with or impinge on the communication by being too uncomfortable, noisy, quiet, crowded, or private. A host of cognitive factors may affect the receiver's ability or desire to attend to the content of the message, or these factors may channel the receiver's attention toward irrelevant or distracting aspects of the message or the situation. Finally, the communication rules under which the sender and receiver are operating may not be shared or followed to the same degree for each person.

III. NONSTRAIGHTFORWARD COMMUNICATION

Given the numerous sources of miscommunication and misunderstanding, and the varieties of social needs and goals with which communicators must contend, it is not surprising that a collection of communication dilemmas has been examined and described. It is through an examination of these situations that the full scope of people's interpersonal communication skills, and the variables that enhance or detract from them, can be appreciated.

A. Inconsistent Messages and Sarcasm

Occasionally communications contain mixed or inconsistent elements and sometimes these elements are contradictory. Some researchers have argued that such mixed messages contribute to misunderstandings in interpersonal relationships. For example, a contradictory message is conveyed when a father tells his daughter, "I love you so much" while simultaneously pushing her away from him. Research conducted by Albert Mehrabian and his colleagues suggests that inconsistent messages are more difficult to interpret, less preferred, more likely to generate confusion, and more prone to misunderstanding than are consistent messages. Inconsistent messages can, however, be used tactically to convey meaning in their own right. Sarcasm, for example, involves intentionally mixing inconsistent messages to cancel out or emphasize some aspect of a message's verbal content.

B. Equivocation

In contrast to messages that convey inconsistent or mixed content, some messages contain very little useful content at all. Sometimes communicators wish to skirt or hedge a particular issue. That is, they do not want to provide an unequivocal response to a question, or take an unqualified stand on an issue, even though they are required to provide some kind of statement. In such situations, communicators may resort to a tactic called equivocation. Equivocation is a verbal technique designed to make a communication ambiguous or uninterpretable. Consider the following example. A friend has given you a bizarre gift and you cannot figure out what it is or why it was given. Now you find yourself on the telephone with your friend, who has asked whether you have received the gift. What do you say? According to Janet Bavelas and her colleagues, you may equivocate by saying, "Yes, I received your gift. They say that a person gives what he would like to receive. Hopefully one day I'll be able to return the favor some way or another. Have a nice day." Your response has said very little and you have avoided the sticky issue of identifying the gift and acknowledging your reaction to it.

C. Multiple Audience Problems and Eavesdroppers

Sometimes we find ourselves in communication situations in which our messages will be overheard (received and scrutinized) by some set of persons for whom they are not intended. In other words, people sometimes eavesdrop on communications. Fortunately, people have at their disposal a number of techniques to deal with these problems. The key to dealing with eavesdroppers or other unintended receivers is to obscure the content of the communication so that only those for whom it is intended actually receive it. This can be accomplished in several ways. First, communicators can implement the "special knowledge strategy" by using cryptic or special references to things about which only the intended receivers are likely to know. For example, when describing a location for a friend, a communicator may obscure the location for eavesdroppers by saying, "You know, the place where Tony danced until dawn." Second, communicators can generate complex covert or hidden messages that convey the required information to the appropriate receivers. An employee whose boss arrives in the midst of a personal phone call may begin to converse as though he were speaking to a client, signaling to the friend that he is no longer free to talk openly about personal matters. These kinds of *multiple audience problems* illustrate communicators' abilities to use language tactically to achieve their interpersonal goals.

D. Deception and Lie Detection

No discussion of nonstraightforward communication would be complete without addressing the issue of outright deception. For a variety of practical and ethical reasons, deception or lying is usually not sanctioned by society and the social costs of getting caught lying can be severe. Nonetheless, communicators sometimes try to convey false information or create an untrue impression in a receiver. Because the costs of getting caught are high, however, deceptive communicators are assumed to be nervous and aroused; this nervousness presumably translates into a set of behaviors that may betray the fact that a communicator is being deceptive. For example, the deceiver's hands may tremble and sweat, they may avoid eye contact, their voices may be uneven, or they may fidget nervously. How accurate and useful are these cues? Research has revealed that these behavioral cues are not particularly useful and that liars frequently get away with their lies. Why? Because liars know that they may be scrutinized more closely by suspicious receivers, they pay attention to and try to control those behaviors that may give them away. The end result of this process is essentially a draw, with receivers able to detect deception at rates only slightly better than chance.

IV. NONVERBAL COMMUNICATION

Like its verbal counterpart, nonverbal behavior comprises another channel of interpersonal communication. We have chosen to treat nonverbal communication separately, not because it exists apart from other communication modalities, but because it can be more easily described. In face-to-face interaction, verbal and nonverbal behavior occur simultaneously. [*See* NONVERBAL BEHAVIOR.]

In addition to the words that we use to communicate, a broad spectrum of movements, gestures, and other nonverbal behaviors that accompany our words also communicate a wealth of information to others around us. *Paralinguistic signals* conveyed by our hands and arms add emphasis to our speech; *nonlinguistic signs* communicated via our facial expressions communicate our emotions to others (and some argue, to ourselves). Our movements may suggest our sincerity and enthusiasm (or lack thereof), and our positioning and posture may inadvertently communicate our moods and attitudes. Because it is tied more directly into our central nervous system and because we can exert less conscious control over our nonverbal behaviors than the words that we speak, the nonverbal channel provides a relatively continuous and often useful source of information about both ourselves and others. The nonverbal channel can betray or "leak" information about our attitudes or clues about how we are feeling that we might try to conceal with words. In fact, research suggests that the nonverbal channel actually communicates more diagnostic information than the verbal channel, lending support to the adage that "Actions speak louder than words." This is particularly true when the verbal and nonverbal channels are consistent with one another. For example, a verbal statement of enthusiasm accompanied by a broad smile and emphatic gestures is far more powerful and believable than a similar statement accompanied by a neutral expression and motionless body. When the verbal and nonverbal channels conflict, the nonverbal channel often takes precedence.

Research on nonverbal communication tends to classify nonverbal behaviors into distinct categories based primarily on the body part or activity from which they stem and whether they are emitted intentionally (*signals*) or inadvertently (*signs*). These include facial expressions and eye contact, body posture and positioning, voice quality, the use of physical distance or proximity, dress and personal appearance, and touch. Nonverbal behavior (including what is colloquially referred to as "body language") can communicate dominance or submissiveness, like or dislike, status, apprehension, nervousness, confidence, and a host of other emotions and attitudes. These behaviors also aid in the coordination of conversation and provide feedback that messages are being received properly. Finally, nonverbal paralinguistic behaviors such as gestures can communicate ideas and feelings that are not easily or adequately expressed in words. [*See* GESTURES.]

A. Immediacy

Albert Mehrabian and his colleagues have suggested that a collection of nonverbal behaviors, referred to as immediacy behaviors, can communicate our liking for others. Eye contact, physical proximity, physical contact (touch), and the position of one's body suggest a positive attitude toward another person. Immediacy provides information about a communicator's attitudes that extends well beyond the content of his or her communication. Of course, nonverbal behavior can also be used to communicate dislike for or avoidance of others. An intriguing study conducted by Carl Word and his colleagues demonstrated that white interviewers' nonverbal behaviors not only subtly communicated the interviewers' negative attitudes toward black interviewees, but also accounted for black interviewees' poor performances during the interviews. In that research, the behavior was subtle and unintentional. Nonverbal behavior can also be used intentionally to communicate a lack of interest in social interaction with others we dislike. One of the most effective of such methods is simply to avoid being in physical proximity to those disliked. But what if you find yourself in a situation—the lobby of a building, for example—in which avoidance is impossible. People can send out signals that indicate that they do not wish to engage in conversation. Such barrier signals can include standing far away from others, avoiding eye contact, and displaying closed postures (crossed arms and legs).

B. Distance Zones

Anthropologist Edward Hall has made important contributions to understanding nonverbal communication through his research on variations in the interpersonal distance or personal space between speakers in different social contexts and cultures. Hall has identified four distance zones commonly used in everyday communication by North Americans. *Intimate distance* begins with skin contact and extends out to about 18 in. away from the body. Often only people we trust and feel close to are allowed to enter this intimate distance, usually to communicate about emotions (e.g., romantic kiss, caressing, comforting). Crowded places often make people feel uncomfortable because others are invading their intimate space without invitation. Although infrequent, intimate distance is sometimes violated to express negative emotions and to communicate conflict (e.g., an argument or fight). The second distance zone is *personal distance* and it ranges from 18 in. to 4 ft. away from the body. This "at arm's length" distance is often used for casual conversation where people are just within reach of each other. *Social distance,* the third distance zone, ranges from 4 to about 12 ft. out. Within it are the kinds of communication that often occur in business or formal situations, for example, talking with co-workers or sales people, or sitting in a chair across from the boss in a business meeting. The fourth and farthest distance zone is called *public distance* and it extends from 12 ft. outward to about 25 ft. at its limit. Public distance is often used for communication with a group, such as a teacher addressing a large class or someone delivering a speech to an audience. Determination of what is an "appropriate" interpersonal distance depends on a number of factors, including the nature of the topic being discussed, the relationship between the individuals, the age of the individuals, the attitudes and feelings of the individuals, the physical setting, and so on. Cultural differences in interpersonal distance have also been found such that compared to North Americans, people in Latin America, the Middle East, southern Europe, and parts of Africa have a personal distance zone that is much smaller. Casual conversation between these people often takes place at the outer edges of what most North Americans consider as intimate space. Thus, it is likely that people from different cultures may experience culture shock when trying to communicate with each other due to a reliance on their own culture-specific expectations for what the distance between people signifies. It is critical to recognize that differences between people in the meaning of distance zones can lead to attributional errors concerning the motives and psychological attributes of the other person, attributions which are based simply on how that person is managing their use of interpersonal space. For example, the Iranian who in a face-to-face conversation keeps moving in closer to the American may regard the American as unfriendly and cool, whereas the back-peddling American may think the Iranian is aggressive and pushy.

V. INDIVIDUAL DIFFERENCES

So far, we have described communication processes without discussing the ways in which people can differ with respect to their communication strategies and skills. In this section we first address how all people can use different styles of communicating depending on their goals and the interpersonal context in which they find themselves. We then discuss how different kinds of people communicate as a function of their personality types.

A. Communicator Style

Communicator style refers to the way one interacts to signal how literal meaning should be taken, interpreted, filtered, or understood. An individual does not have one communication style, but rather aspects of many styles that are appropriate to different communication goals and contexts. Three basic communicator style profiles have been identified—open, attentive, and dramatic. Communicating with the open style is the process of transmitting information about the self. It signals that the message is personal, private, unambiguous, and explanatory. Often this involves use of verbal self-disclosure, nonverbal closeness, the expression of emotions, and a receptivity to the others involved in the communication. The open style is often used when one wants to develop a closer relationship with another person. The attentive style of communicating is characterized by giving feedback, active listening, and empathy. It involves the use of open posture, verbal restatement and nondirective responses, and direct eye contact. The attentive style is frequently used when the information the other person has to communicate is considered important, and also when the listener wants to be respectful and encouraging of the speaker. Counselors and therapists frequently use the attentive style. The dramatic style is characterized by the obvious manipulation of messages through exaggerations, fantasies, stories, metaphors, rhythm, and voice to emphasize, downplay,or contradict the literal meaning of the message content. Dramatic style is most often used in humor, educational presentations, gossiping, sarcasm, and insults.

People differ in their orientation toward willingness to communicate. Although willingness to communicate can be affected by situational constraints, trait-like willingness to communicate can influence a wide range of communication activity and is associated with increased frequency and amount of communication. Individuals with a greater willingness to communicate typically experience advantages in school (e.g., positive teacher expectations and high academic achievement), in organizations (e.g., preferred in hiring and promotion decisions, higher work satisfaction), and in social contexts (e.g., have more friends, go on more dates, are seen by others as more socially and physically attractive). In contrast, an unwillingness to communicate, or communication apprehension, is associated with decreased frequency and amount of communication and often results in an individual being a less effective communicator. Communication apprehension can also lead to the formation of negative impressions of the person in the minds of others involved in the communication. Often training in specific interpersonal skills can reduce one's apprehension about communicating with others. Public speaking is one area of communication skills training that has been particularly effective.

B. Personality

Given that people differ from each other in terms of their characteristic ways of thinking, feeling, and acting, it is not surprising that interpersonal communication is also affected by people's personalities. Although there are many ways to examine the interplay of personality and communication, the personality constructs of dogmatism and self-monitoring are two particularly useful constructs that help to identify stable individual differences between people in the interpretation and production of communication behavior. A highly dogmatic person is characterized by mental rigidity and a closed belief system. Highly dogmatic individuals often fail to discriminate between the source and the content of communication messages, treating the message content as one with the source of the message. For dogmatic individuals, the perception of messages is dominated by who the sender is and thus these kinds of individuals are more influenced by authority sources than are those low in dogmatism.

Individuals can also differ in their tendencies to monitor their verbal and nonverbal behaviors and to adapt these behaviors to the requirements of social situations. High self-monitors strive to create a self-image consistent with and appropriate to the contexts in which they find themselves, whereas low self-monitors are more inner directed, using their internal values, beliefs, and attitudes as a guide for their behavior. As the communication of high self-monitors is guided more by social and situational norms of behavior than is that of low self-monitors, high self-monitors tend to be more socially perceptive and competent, to have broader communication response repertoires, to be more verbally and nonverbally expressive, and are more likely to initiate and sustain communication exchanges with others. Due to their greater sensitivity to interpersonal communication cues, high self-monitors are also better at creating deceptive messages and are better at detecting deceit in the messages of others.

VI. CONTEXT-ORIENTED RESEARCH: COMMUNICATION IN MARRIAGE

In recent years, comprehensive research programs conducted by scholars representing a variety of social science disciplines (e.g., communication, family studies, clinical and social psychology) have investigated communication patterns in marital interaction. This body of work indicates that partners in distressed relationships often exhibit ineffective communication behaviors that make it difficult to resolve martial issues. For example, partners in distressed couples often do not share their true feelings with one another, if feelings are expressed the partner does not recognize or respond to them in a constructive manner (e.g., partner complains about something else, changes subject, etc.), partners send messages that are ambiguous or unclear (e.g., mixed messages in verbal and nonverbal channels), specific negative behaviors such as threats, nagging, insults, put-downs, are used in attempts to change the partner's behavior, and the expression of negative feelings leads to a cycle of reciprocal negative statements that escalate the conflict. It is this last behavior pattern that is the hallmark of a troubled relationship and it typically involves distinct male and female roles. The "demand–withdraw" pattern, as it is called, is characterized by demands for attention or communication by the wife which are met with either physical or emotional withdrawal on the part of the husband. This continues in a sequence such that the more the wife demands attention, the more the husband withdraws. An alternative version of this pattern commonly found in distressed marriages, is that (a) the wife expresses negative feelings (in hopes of being comforted by the husband); (b) the husband fails to recognize or acknowledge her feelings (perhaps to avoid an argument or his having to find a solution to the problem); (c) the wife feels neglected and unloved and expresses these feelings; (d) the husband withdraws; (e) the wife tries harder to get husband to talk to her, and so on. [*See* MARITAL DYSFUNCTION.]

That this pattern of communication behavior in distressed relationships has been found so consistently in research studies using different methodologies has led to the conclusion that men and women have different styles of dealing with marital conflict. Suggestions for improving the communication skills of marital partners have centered on training men to express their emotions more clearly and to be more sensitive to the verbal and nonverbal signals of their wives, and on training women to present their concerns in such a way that they are not perceived by the husband as a "problem" that he must fix, but rather as an opportunity for him to empathize with and reciprocate her feelings. Improving marital communication is also linked to the ability of both spouses to develop a greater recognition of the importance of communication in marriage, to know the reasons why couples stop communicating, and to understand the communication process in general. Further, research on the accuracy of communication in the interactions of marital partners with their spouses and with strangers has found that interspouse communication accuracy can be poor yet spouse-to-stranger communication accuracy can be good. This indicates that communication skills may be relationship specific and not easily transferred from one kind of relationship to another. Thus, any communication skills training for spouses should occur in the context of the marital relationship.

A. Nonverbal Communication in Marriage

Psychologist Patricia Noller has been active in a program of research investigating nonverbal communication and marital interaction. Her work has produced some important findings that offer insight into why it is difficult for men and women in relationships to communicate effectively. Detailed analyses of videotaped conversations between spouses have revealed several conclusions: marital partners tend to send many messages with affectively neutral words and to rely on nonverbal channels to make the message positive or negative, women are more expressive than men in that they use more positive and negative messages rather than neutral messages, women tend to be better than men at both sending and interpreting nonverbal messages, and marital satisfaction is more strongly related to the accuracy of sending and receiving of messages for husbands than wives, with low satisfaction husbands tending to make more errors than high satisfaction husbands.

B. Marital Types

A second program of research has demonstrated that not all couples have the same way of approaching marriage and of communicating with each other. Communication scholar Mary Anne Fitzpatrick has generated some interesting findings about individual differences in marital communication. In her research, spouses are classified on the basis of their responses to a self-report scale as having one of three types of marital ideology: traditional, independent, or separate. The three categories of marital ideology are considered to represent cognitive schemata that indicate differing beliefs about and expectations for marriage. Traditionals endorse conventional sex-role orientations and beliefs about marriage; emphasize togetherness, companionship, and sharing; strive for regular patterns of time use and shared use of space; and emphasize stability over satisfaction in the relationship. Independents have liberal sex-role orientations and beliefs about marriage; emphasize both togetherness and autonomy; emphasize relationship satisfaction; and believe in novelty, uncertainty, and change. Separates tend to vacillate between conventional and nonconventional sex-role orientations and beliefs about marriage; are emotionally and psychologically less interdependent with one another than most other couples; keep regular time schedules; and are not very companionable and share little with each other.

Characteristic differences in communication behaviors between the three marital types have been found. Traditionals frequently express positive emotions, self-disclose to one another to a high degree, and tend to avoid conflict except for issues judged as important to the relationship. Traditionals typically monitor what they say to others outside the relationship. Independents report being able to self-disclosure to their partner but do not view the partner as disclosing in return. Independents engage in frequent conflicts with their partner, so much so that they seem to be engaged in a constant struggle about which partner is able to define the relationship. If their demands for compliance from the partner or attempts to exert power-plays to win arguments are ineffective, independents often switch to use of humor or intellectualization as a means to avoid conflict. Independents have open communication with friends and associates. Separates report restricted levels of self-disclosure to their partner and have a complex style of dealing with conflict. While more likely to confront their partner than are other types of couples, separates tend to withdraw when the spouse contests the complaint. They talk less and often resort to blatant types of conflict avoidance, such as denial of disagreement and refusal to discuss the issue. Separates tend to be more expressive with friends than with their spouse. These differences in the communication patterns between marital types provide the basis for greater understanding of marital interaction and also suggest that different approaches are needed for couple counseling or intervention to suit the needs of each type of marriage.

Bibliography

Argyle, M. (1988). "Bodily Communication," 2nd. ed. Methuen & Co., Ltd., London.

Bavelas, J. B., Black, A., Chovil, N., and Mullett, J. (1990). "Equivocal Communication." Sage, Newbury Park, CA.

Clark, H. (1985). Language use and language users. In "Handbook of Social Psychology" (G. Lindzey and E. Aronson, Eds.), 3rd. ed., Vol. II. Random House, New York.

Cody, M. J., and McLaughlin, M. L. (1990). "The Psychology of Tactical Communication." Multilingual Matters, Ltd., Clevendon, England.

Ekman, P. (1985). "Telling Lies: Clues to Deceit in the Marketplace, Politics, and Marriage." Norton, New York.

Ellis, A., and Beattie, G. (1986). "The Psychology of Language and Communication." Guilford, New York.

Goffman, E. (1969). "Strategic Interaction." University of Pennsylvania Press, University Park.

Hall, E. T. (1969). "The Hidden Dimension." Anchor Books, Garden City, NY.

Krauss, R. M., and Fussell, S. R. (1994). Social psychological models of communication. In "Handbook of Personality and Social Psychology" (E. T. Higgins and A. Kruglanski, Eds.). Lawrence Erlbaum, Hillsdale, NJ.

McCroskey, J. C., and Daly, J. A. (Eds.) (1987). "Personality and Interpersonal Communication." Sage, Newbury Park, CA.

Mehrabian, A. (1972). "Nonverbal Communication." Aldine Atherton, Chicago.

Noller, P., and Fitzpatrick, M. A. (Eds.). (1987). "Perspectives on Marital Interaction." Multilingual Matters Ltd., Philadelphia, PA.

Siegman, A. W., and Feldstein, S. (1986). "Nonverbal Behavior and Communication" 2nd. ed. Halstead, New York.

Watzlawick, P., Bavelas, J. B., and Jackson, D. D. (1967). "Pragmatics of Human Communication: A Study of Interactional Patterns, Pathologies, and Paradoxes." Norton, New York.

Interpersonal Perception and Communication

John H. Harvey and Melanie K. Barnes
University of Iowa

Glossary

Attribution The process of inferring causality or responsibility for events observed in the social or physical world.

Communication competence An individual's ability to engage in appropriate and effective interactive behavior in various social settings.

Divergent perspectives hypothesis The prediction that actors and observers will diverge in judging the causes of the actor's behavior; the actor is predicted to emphasize situational determinants of own behavior, while the observer is predicted to stress the actor's dispositional characteristics as determinants.

Expectancy effects Behavior of an individual that is influenced by the expectancy of another individual (similar to self-fulfilling prophecy).

Impression management The selection of certain appearances, behaviors, cues, and messages intended to portray a desired image to others based on role and situational determinants.

Information integration The process of how people combine information about an individual in order to develop a composite personality profile of the individual.

Interpersonal communication The transactional process of dyadic interaction involving both verbal and nonverbal codes and cues.

Interpersonal perception The process of forming an attitude, opinion, or belief about another person through observation of and/or interaction with the person (sometimes used synonymously with social perception or person perception).

Social perception bias A distorted perception of another person that derives from a nonobjective inference process (e.g., viewing victims as always responsible for their distress or difficulty).

INTERPERSONAL PERCEPTION AND COMMUNICATION are concerned with how people form judgments of others and then communicate some aspect of that judgment either verbally or nonverbally to the other person. Research has concentrated on the nature of the social perception process, especially biases inherent in the process. Less research has been done on verbal and nonverbal communication processes that accompany social perception. The full loop from perception of other to communication with other and further steps such as other's reactions are discussed here.

I. PERCEIVER AS INTEGRATOR OF INFORMATION ABOUT OTHER

Almost four decades of research have taught us a great deal about the processes by which perceivers make sense of others' behavior. One of the most basic types of analysis has focused on how a perceiver integrates diverse strands of information about another person in order to form a single impression. Early work suggested that *central traits* imputed to other such as *warm* or *cold* will have an inordinately powerful influence on how other traits are assimilated into a single impression. For exam-

Copyright © 1994 by Academic Press, Inc. All rights of reproduction in any form reserved.

ple, if we hear that a person is *intelligent, skillful, determined, practical, warm,* and *cautious,* we will form a wholistic impression of the person that is more positive than if we hear the person is *intelligent, skillful, determined, practical, cold,* and *cautious.* Because of the presumed centrality of the warm–cold variable, it was posited that an emergent unity (a term taken from *Gestalt* psychology) formed in the perceiver's mind when these traits were included in their respective lists.

This line of research represented one of the first probes of the process of impression formation. Hundreds of studies followed the early work. Other theoretical work on how people integrate varying inputs about others has emphasized the tendency for people to average across different inputs in forming a singular impression. In this model, no conception of emergent unity was necessary. It was assumed that perceivers simply average the favorability of individual traits (treating each one independently) and thereby readily develop a summary impression. [*See* IMPRESSION FORMATION.]

More recent theory and research have advanced beyond the perceiver as integrator metaphor to emphasize general information processing models of social cognition and person memory. One question asked, for example, is how do perceivers assimilate inputs about others based on diverse information, including categorical attributes (e.g., those exhibited by a specific ethnic group) versus based on individual attributes (e.g., an individual's particular personal characteristics)? This emphasis also has involved consideration of attentional and motivational influences in impression formation. As an illustration, a recent finding is that when the costs associated perceiver's judgments are increased, perceivers tend to use more attribute-based processing of others and also exhibit more indecisiveness in making their judgments. As an extension, this body of research has had considerable impact on extant social psychological theories of stereotyping and prejudice. [*See* PREJUDICE AND STEREOTYPES.]

II. PERCEIVER AS PERSONALITY JUDGE AND READER OF EMOTIONS OF OTHER

In our daily interaction with others, we frequently try to assess others' personality characteristics and emotions. Regarding personality traits, an early question concerned whether individuals were "good judges of personality." In the field of work on social perception, this topic produced considerable research in the 1930s and 1940s. This line of work began to die out, however, after it was criticized as not reflecting the multidimensional nature of what would be accurate personality judgments. Essentially, the critique focused on the multidimensional nature of accuracy. An implication of this critique was that if we are trying to evaluate an individual's personality, a premium should be placed on careful analysis of how the individual's various traits deviate from norms in the general population for such traits. It has been shown, for example, that very conservative judges typically are more accurate than are judges who are extreme in their assessments and who are overconfident about the validity of their assessments. From the 1960s to the present, research in this area has focused much less on judgmental accuracy (since it is such a complex topic) than it has on the processes of judging personality.

The act of reading emotions in another person is similar to that of judging other's personality. Early research dating back to the turn of the century involved the procedure of asking perceivers to try to discriminate among different experienced emotions by examining still photographs of the faces of people (sometimes actors who were trying to display particular emotions). Some emotions such as joy and anger could be readily discriminated, whereas others such as anxiety and dejection were much more difficult to differentiate. Research progressed in this area by experimenting with different types of presentation of emotion including that by live actors. As this work continued, it became clear to researchers that the situational context surrounding the expressed emotion is a powerfully informative cue for judging the emotion felt by the individual being observed. More recently, however, researchers again have concentrated on people's judgments of emotion mainly based on facial cues, in photographs and live models. Perceivers appear to be fairly accurate, and across different cultures, in judging emotions from facial displays and without the aid of context. It also has been found, however, that the face is critical in a person's attempts to conceal personal emotional states such as those associated with lying or deception. When perceivers are attempting to determine if an individual is trying to be deceitful, body gestures and vocal quality have been found to be better predictors of accuracy. The study of deception and how perceivers attempt to discern it is a current topic in this area of inquiry, including the dimension of prior relational history between the interactants. [*See* FACIAL EXPRESSIONS OF EMOTION.]

III. PERCEIVER AS ATTRIBUTOR ABOUT OTHER

By far, theory and research on attribution processes have been pursued more comprehensively than any other topic in the domain of interpersonal perception during the last two decades. The overarching question has been, What are the processes involved in a perceiver's inferring of causality or responsibility after observing another person perform some act or be involved in some interpersonal event? This type of question is routine in our lives, for example: "Why did he say such a cruel thing to her?" "Who is responsible for the accident?" "Why and how did their marriage break up?" It is in this area, also, that abundant research has been produced on the many different types of bias and distortion in the social perception process (a topic discussed more fully in the following section). [*See* ATTRIBUTION.]

Generally, attributions of causality and responsibility are viewed as being made either to personal, dispositional qualities of an actor or to situational factors surrounding an actor's behavior. The main basis for attributional activity is thought to be the desire to want order and control in one's understanding of the world. If we do not understand others in our immediate environment and why they behave as they do, and if their behavior may affect us in crucial ways, then we likely will be apprehensive in dealing with them and possibly fearful of what they will do. Thus, presumably as an act of adaptation to their environment, people almost incessantly make attributions and engage in analysis about others and others' lines of action.

An early intriguing line of work concerned differences between actors and observers in judging causality or responsibility for the actor's behavior. According to an influential early hypothesis, the divergent perspectives hypothesis, actors and observers diverge in their attributions of causality because they have greatly different amounts of information about relevant past actions of the actor (the actor having much more than the observer) and because they have quite different perceptual foci; the actor's focus is on the environment, while the observer's focus is on the actor and the actor's behavior. In general, research has corroborated this hypothesis, with certain notable exceptions. One exception is that if an observer is induced to try to see the world from the actor's viewpoint (i.e., be empathic with the actor), such an observer tends to make attributions similar to those of the actor. The actor–observer paradigm has stimulated a great amount of research on attributional processes, and as will be shown, it provides a bridge for linking interpersonal perception and communication phenomena. Also, this paradigm has provided a foundation for exploration of how a perceiver sometimes is motivated to "perceive" another person in various positive or negative lights depending upon the perceiver's set about other (e.g., the perceiver likes other) or the nature of other's acts (e.g., other's acts are especially vivid in nature or consequential in their impact upon others). [*See* ACTOR–OBSERVER DIFFERENCES IN ATTRIBUTION.]

Theoretical work on attributional processes has developed around two major systems of reasoning. The correspondent inference approach emphasizes correspondence in inference between a perceiver's judgments and an actor's personality qualities. In this approach, the perceiver is posited to infer backward from an actor's action and its consequences to qualities of the actor and the circumstances surrounding the action. Given a certain action and outcome (e.g., at a party, a husband makes a sarcastic joke about his wife that she overhears and then shows hurt), presumably the perceiver focuses on relevant dispositional qualities of the actor (e.g., his tendency to be hurtful and ego-centered), his intention or lack thereof to produce a certain consequence, and whether he acted freely in taking the action. The second major approach, the covariation model, emphasizes perceiver's logical deduction of causality based on analysis of whether the actor consistently performs in a certain way (e.g., does the husband regularly tell sarcastic jokes about his wife while attending parties), whether there is consensus among others in the performance (e.g., were other husbands also making sarcastic jokes about their wives), and whether the performance is distinctive (e.g., does the husband tell sarcastic jokes about his wife in all kinds of settings). Given our example, according to the correspondent inference approach, a perceiver would make an attribution of causality for the wife's hurt to the husband's personality—perhaps his cruel tendencies. Using the covariation model, the same kind of attribution would be made if the perceiver judged that the husband typically told such jokes, whether or not he was at a party, and if other husbands were not telling such jokes.

At present, prominent attributional approaches are being wed closely to extant theories in the field of social cognition, a field concerned with processes involved in people's thinking about and memory of others. Several research thrusts now are concerned with how perceivers form biased or unbiased impressions of others depending upon the perceivers' cognitive resources. For example, will perceivers who are expecting to interact with others be overly concerned in preparing to interact and less acute in their observations of those others and then be biased in their impressions? If such sequences occur, they may provide the seed for distorted communications among people. [*See* SOCIAL COGNITION.]

IV. BIASES IN PERCEIVING OTHERS

Actors and observers, or perceivers, diverge on many occasions in their attributions of causality. As discussed in the foregoing section, this divergence is the source of a rich line of research on attributional processes. For example, one such line of work has concerned spouses' divergent perceptions of the causes of conflict in a marriage. The wife may assert that the husband is "emotionally unavailable," while the husband argues that the wife is "sexually uninterested." Who is correct? The question of criteria of accuracy is as prominent in this domain as it is in the area of work on judging personality characteristics. Attribution theorists typically have contended that even if the investigator cannot readily document the validity of the individual's attributions, nonetheless, an individual's *attributional processes and the conditions of when and how attributions are made* can be studied and documented with considerable precision. There is, however, an emerging body of research on when people engage in more rational and informed versus less rational and informed social perception processes—when people are more or less accurate in their judgments. For example, time and accountability pressures and fear of invalidity are factors that tend to influence how fine-tuned and defensibly objective perceivers' attributions about others may be.

In the real world, questions of accuracy in judgment often have major consequences. A therapist working with distressed couples may have to make some judgments about who is more accurate. It is likely that there are grains of truth and falsity in most divergent perceptions, whether entertained by spouses regarding major conflicts or strangers regarding a single event each has observed. Indeed, such processes are exceedingly complex and conducive to bias in many ways. The pervasiveness of interpersonal perceptual bias, or error assuming we can determine a standard of accuracy, continues to be a stimulus for research programs in the attribution area as well as in the realm of interpersonal relationship constructs, such as relational satisfaction and maintenance, management of conflict, and relational termination and longevity.

Another reason why perceptual or attributional bias is such a fertile topic is that biases tend to perseverate. Accordingly, perceivers have a general tendency toward "creeping determinism," to perceive the world selectively as supporting their viewpoints. Hence, even in the face of contradictory information, a perceiver may perseverate in holding a certain view of another. To repudiate that view may lessen the perceiver's confidence in his or her own ability to make sound judgments about others, and more generally it may undermine his or her sense of having a well-conceived view of the world and the way people behave.

One type of powerful bias in interpersonal perception is the tendency to underestimate the importance of base rates. The overlooking of this base rate information is frequently described as a process of selective attention, wherein individuals specifically select what types of stimuli or information to which they will attend and process. An example of this tendency would be to assume that a student visiting a museum for the arts was an arts major. But if it was known that the student was enrolled in a college in which 90% of the students were science majors, it would be more rational to predict that the student was a science major (i.e., there is a 9 to 1 chance that the student is a science major). Perceivers often overlook base rate information because they are so accustomed to making quick inferences about others based on others' appearance or actions; they selectively pay too much attention to highly vivid or salient information and less attention to subtle or abstract information.

An attributional bias known as the false-consensus bias is the assumption that other people have the same reactions to everyday experience that we do. A major reason for this tendency is that when we as perceivers have limited information about an actor, we asume that the actor would respond in the same way to a particular situation as we would. Further, people often select friends who are similar to them. Thus, they may want to believe that others whom they do not know well also will be similar to them and react similarly to the way they react.

Two other attributional biases of note are the tendency not to give enough weight to nonoccurrences and the tendency to stereotype others based on their presumed ethnic, racial, or socioeconomic group. As an illustration of the nonoccurrence situation, if a person chooses not to vote for any candidate in an election, that fact may be as informative about the person as would a particular kind of vote. However, perceivers tend to process as more salient and meaningful the fact of action and its nature than that of nonaction. Regarding stereotyping, this tendency is at the heart of racial or ethnic prejudice. It involves an overlooking of the individuality of each person and a focus on that person's presumed group ties. Studies also have shown that perceivers tend to perceive members of their own groups as being similar to themselves on various dimensions when indeed the members are not similar.

V. LINKING PERCEPTION OF AND COMMUNICATION WITH OTHERS

While one of the primary objectives in forming causal attributions is to attempt to gain order and understanding of one's social world, the process of impression formation is also inherent in the selection of responses to the world and other people. The concept of account-making helps us understand how people form elaborate impressions of others and others' actions in story-like constructions (e.g., "I have an ex-wife who was so neurotic that she couldn't even get dressed in the morning without asking my approval.") and then act in ways associated with these accounts. Work on accounts and account-making suggests that people communicate their stories to others who in turn reciprocate story-telling. This trading of stories may serve informational purposes, but it also influences how the story-tellers feel about one another and even behave toward one another (e.g., "Any man who is as egotistical as this one is in his understanding of his ex-wife has to be watched!"). Essentially, an account is a package of impressions, perceptions, attributions, emotions, description, and other material that is formed in a story-like fashion. Similar to attributions, accounts presumably give the individual a greater sense of control in dealing with the world, and they often are presented to other in order to inform or influence other in some direction.

At a more microscopic level, the catalysts for perception–communication linkages are observed and inferred cues that are informative about other. As individuals attend to certain cues, whether verbal or nonverbal, impressions are formed at four various levels based fundamentally on normative expectancies. Physical characteristics such as height, weight, and facial or physical attributes generally represent the first criteria which are assessed when forming initial impressions. Second, role characteristics are considered, such as teacher–student, buyer–seller, and employer–employee; further, individual mannerisms and actions are considered by the perceiver in terms of appropriateness, efficacy, and consistency. Third, actual interaction patterns are observed and perceptions are created based on how one individual relates to another (e.g., hostile vs friendly; rude vs polite). Finally, impressions are formed at the psychological level and personality attributes such as lazy–motivated, sincere–dishonest, and shy–outgoing are attributed to those who are observed. These perceptions affect not only one's view and interpretation of the world and those within it, but also the verbal and nonverbal responses that are produced in the perceiver.

These linkages establish how perceptions that are formed subsequently influence the messages that are selected and presented to others, as well as how a person's communication style influences observers' perceptions of an interactant's interpersonal attractiveness and effectiveness. These two areas have frequently been studied together under the rubric of a specific line of research known as communication competence. A theoretical link between attribution and interpersonal communication is that people's attributions about others generally guide communication exchanges. As research has shown, for example, if a perceiver believes that a person's performance in school work has been determined mainly by the person's lazy ways and lack of effort, it is likely that the perceiver will be more critical in evaluating the person than if the perceiver's believes that the person's performance has been determined mainly by the person's ability. This attribution–interaction tendency emphasizes the implicit assumption that it is essential, even morally appropriate, for a person to try hard, or exhibit effort, in important areas of life.

Communication competence refers to an individual's ability to engage in appropriate and effective interactive behavior in various social settings. While some researchers consider competence to be a personality trait or an individualized skill, other scholars suggest that competence is situationally located and is a quality of specific interactions. Most contemporary views of communication competence, however, suggest observers' perceptions of one's competence to be as essential in describing a person's actual communication competence as is one's own perception of personal performance or skill. To provide a specific illustration, if an interactant's partner does not find the partner to be normatively competent in certain areas, for example, in being attentive, relaxed, friendly, and precise, then the fact that the individual perceives self to be competent is not as salient when determining social attractiveness, especially in initial interactions. A related concept involves the perceptiveness of various social encounters and attentiveness to sources of information when considering specific interpersonal interactions and communication. This latter concept is known as interaction involvement and involves consideration of the needs and desires both of an actor and of the actor's immediate partner, based on previously established perceptions.

A major theoretical perspective that has generated considerable research in the area of interpersonal communication concerns the roles individuals play in the management of their public face in daily interactions. The presentation of self in everyday life has been an interesting topic for exploration for over four decades. The framework for this analysis involves the proposition that in playing out certain social scenes, people assume different roles—much as do actors on a stage. The image, or face, that is presented to an audience is in fact what that person intends the other to perceive. The process of impression management involves the selection of certain appearances, or public presentations, behaviors, and messages intended to convey a desired image based on role and situational determinants. Individuals are simultaneously interpreting others' actions and forming perceptions, as well as creating images for others to interpret. These processes of impression management and perception formation are intertwined with the process of interpersonal communication. The fact that in any social interaction at least two parties are simultaneously engaged in such processes gives one greater insight into the depth and breadth of human social encounters. To date, social scientists have only begun to probe the recursive features of such encounters and how sequences of perception–behavior unfold between and among interactants over time. [*See* INTERPERSONAL COMMUNICATION.]

In the last two decades, much communication research has focused on an individual's selection and production of messages and on others' responses to those messages. Many of these studies concern initial interaction and have considered both perceptual and communication questions. As an example, physical attractiveness has been noted to affect an observer's perceptions of how interesting and likable a person is believed to be. Additionally, the perception of attitude similarity, whether or not the individuals actually share similar attitudes, is positively linked with how attractive they find one another to be. Research suggests that people are attracted to others whom they think are similar to themselves, or are at least not highly dissimilar along important dimensions such as socio-political attitudes. The knowledge about similarity or dissimilarity of attitudes and beliefs is gained through interpersonal communication, which is the transactional process of dyadic interaction.

One communication theory that considers how individuals deal with novel situations, especially in initial interactions, is uncertainty reduction theory. This theory states that individuals are motivated to gather information in an effort to reduce their uncertainty about new situations or people. Communication is seen as a means of information acquisition in order to test initial interpersonal perceptions. As attributional processes are internalized psychological means of attempting to understand and control one's world, uncertainty reduction is an external means by which individuals acquire various types of information (i.e., physical, cultural, social, and psychological) in order to facilitate understanding and predictability of future events. Once information is acquired, the internalization of that information is what forms an individual's perceptions and attributions.

Based on information that has accrued over time and in a variety of circumstances, a person may be perceived as having certain personality traits such as honesty or trustworthiness. This perception then influences the types of messages that may be shared in future interaction, such as the decision to self-disclose private, potentially embarrassing information. The perceptions that are formed primarily as a result of exchanged information influence subsequent communication interactions. Additionally, subsequent interactions can also affect changes in interpersonal perceptions based upon the receipt of new or conflicting information and thus the communication–perception–attribution is created.

VI. EXPECTANCY EFFECTS

A perceiver's expectations about another person, whether or not based on accurate perceptions or information, can readily influence interaction with the other person. An expectancy confirmation process, which also has been referred to as a "self-fulfilling prophecy," involves perceiver's expectation and related behavior, a target other's reception of the behavior and development of a related self-attribution (e.g., "she thinks I'm crude.") and response that may reinforce the expectation, and then further loops of expectation–behavior–inference about what other thinks—reaction. Some of the earliest and most influential research on expectancy effects was conducted in classroom settings. It was shown that teachers' expectation of improvement in certain children's achievement performance apparently caused an actual improvement. [*See* SELF-FULFILLING PROPHECIES.]

There are many questions that have been investigated regarding expectancy confirmation processes, but still more questions that remain to be explored. Two major questions that have not been investigated fully are: (1) Is it not true that targets of expectancy sometimes know the expectations that are held about them and then act in ways designed to confirm, or disconfirm, the expectations? Apparently, this sequence does occur, but it also is true that people often are unaware of perceiver's expectations; in such cases, the self-fulfilling prophecy seemingly unfolds without much awareness on the part of the target, and maybe even little awareness on the part of the perceiver. The when and how of awareness represent foci for continued research. (2) Is it not true that a perceiver's expectation about an individual will influence that individual's attributions about self and related behavior only if the individual's self-esteem, or other central personality characteristics, is vulnerable to the influences of other's views? Yes, it does appear to be true that some people on some occasions are less susceptible to expectation confirmation sequences. If an individual is quite solid and experienced regarding some personal characteristic and concomitant performance (e.g., that he or she is a fine chef and can almost always cook a good meal), a perceiver's contrary expectations that fly in the face of that self-attribution and knowledge should not have much impact. The topic of when and how self-knowledge and expectancy confirmation go together to influence interaction sequences remains imposing for researchers.

More generally, the area of expectancy effects represents a domain of work that bridges social perception, attribution, and communication. It also makes contact with the rich landscape of self-presentation and impression management. In daily encounters, humans display a symphony of thought, feeling, and behavior that reflects the intricate convergence of these processes.

Bibliography

Berger, C. R. (1979). Beyond initial interaction: Uncertainty, understanding, and the development of interpersonal relationship. In "Language and Social Psychology" (H. Giles and R. St. Clair, Eds.), pp. 122–144. Basil Blackwell, Oxford.

Darley, J. M., and Fazio, R. H. (1980). Expectancy confirmation processes arising in the social interaction sequence. *Am. Psychol.* **35,** 867–881.

Fiske, S. T., and Neuberg, S. L. (1991). A continuium of impression formation from category based to individuating processes: Influences from information and motivation on attention and interpretation. In "Advances in Experimental Social Psychology" (M. P. Zanna, Ed.), Vol. 23, pp. 1–74. Academic Press, New York.

Harvey, J. H., and Weary, G. (1984). Current issues in attribution theory and research. *Annu. Rev. Psychol.* **35,** 427–59.

Harvey, J. H., Weber, A. L., and Orbuch, T. L. (1990). "Interpersonal Accounts: A Social Psychological Perspective." Basil Blackwell, Oxford.

Jones, E. E. (1990). "Interpersonal Perception." Freeman, New York.

Kleinke, C. L. (1986). "Meeting and Understanding People." Freeman, New York.

Kruglanski, A. W. (1989). "Lay Epistemics and Human Knowledge." Plenum, New York.

Spitzberg, B. H., and Cupach, W. R. (1989). "Handbook of Interpersonal Competence Research." Springer-Verlag, New York.

Swann, W. B. (1992). Seeking 'truth,' finding despair: Some unhappy consequences of a negative self-concept. *Curr. Directions Psychol. Sci.* **1,** 15–18.

Swann, W. B. (1984). Quest for accuracy in person perception: A matter of pragmatics. *Psychol. Rev.* **91,** 457–477.